D0705928

International Law

Aspen Casebook Series

International Law

Sixth Edition

Barry E. Carter
Professor of Law
Georgetown University

Allen S. Weiner
Senior Lecturer in Law
Stanford Law School

Published by Wolters Kluwer Law & Business in New York.

Wolters Kluwer Law & Business serves customers worldwide with CCH, Aspen Publishers, and Kluwer Law International products. (www.wolterskluwerlb.com)

To contact Customer Service, e-mail customer.service@wolterskluwer.com, call 1-800-234-1660, fax 1-800-901-9075, or mail correspondence to:

Wolters Kluwer Law & Business
Attn: Order Department
PO Box 990
Frederick, MD 21705

Printed in the United States of America.

1 2 3 4 5 6 7 8 9 0

ISBN 978-0-7355-9810-2

Library of Congress Cataloging-in-Publication Data

Carter, Barry E.
International law / Barry E. Carter, Allen S. Weiner. — 6th ed.
p. cm. — (Aspen casebook series)
Includes index.
ISBN-13: 978-0-7355-9810-2
ISBN-10: 0-7355-9810-X
1. International law—Cases. 2. Casebooks. I. Weiner, Allen S. II. Title.
KZ1242.5.C37 2011
341—dc23

2011025452

SFI label applies to the text stock

About Wolters Kluwer Law & Business

Wolters Kluwer Law & Business is a leading global provider of intelligent information and digital solutions for legal and business professionals in key specialty areas, and respected educational resources for professors and law students. Wolters Kluwer Law & Business connects legal and business professionals as well as those in the education market with timely, specialized authoritative content and information-enabled solutions to support success through productivity, accuracy and mobility.

Serving customers worldwide, Wolters Kluwer Law & Business products include those under the Aspen Publishers, CCH, Kluwer Law International, Loislaw, Best Case, ftwilliam.com and MediRegs family of products.

CCH products have been a trusted resource since 1913, and are highly regarded resources for legal, securities, antitrust and trade regulation, government contracting, banking, pension, payroll, employment and labor, and healthcare reimbursement and compliance professionals.

Aspen Publishers products provide essential information to attorneys, business professionals and law students. Written by preeminent authorities, the product line offers analytical and practical information in a range of specialty practice areas from securities law and intellectual property to mergers and acquisitions and pension/benefits. Aspen's trusted legal education resources provide professors and students with high-quality, up-to-date and effective resources for successful instruction and study in all areas of the law.

Kluwer Law International products provide the global business community with reliable international legal information in English. Legal practitioners, corporate counsel and business executives around the world rely on Kluwer Law journals, looseleafs, books, and electronic products for comprehensive information in many areas of international legal practice.

Loislaw is a comprehensive online legal research product providing legal content to law firm practitioners of various specializations. Loislaw provides attorneys with the ability to quickly and efficiently find the necessary legal information they need, when and where they need it, by facilitating access to primary law as well as state-specific law, records, forms and treatises.

Best Case Solutions is the leading bankruptcy software product to the bankruptcy industry. It provides software and workflow tools to flawlessly streamline petition preparation and the electronic filing process, while timely incorporating ever-changing court requirements.

ftwilliam.com offers employee benefits professionals the highest quality plan documents (retirement, welfare and non-qualified) and government forms (5500/PBGC, 1099 and IRS) software at highly competitive prices.

MediRegs products provide integrated health care compliance content and software solutions for professionals in healthcare, higher education and life sciences, including professionals in accounting, law and consulting.

Wolters Kluwer Law & Business, a division of Wolters Kluwer, is headquartered in New York. Wolters Kluwer is a market-leading global information services company focused on professionals.

To Kathleen, Gregory, and Meghan
—Barry Carter

In Memory of Tim Moy, for whom the chance to teach was learning's reward
—Allen Weiner

Biographies

Barry E. Carter has an extensive background in law, foreign policy, national security, and international business and trade. He is presently a professor of law at Georgetown University Law Center, where he also serves as the Director of its Center on Transnational Business and the Law. In 2006 he received the Law Center's excellence in teaching award. Mr. Carter teaches frequently in other countries about legal issues.

He returned to Georgetown in 1996 after over three years as the Deputy Under Secretary of Commerce for Export Administration. He implemented and enforced a variety of trade and nonproliferation laws. He helped reorganize the 370-person Bureau and manage its $40+ million budget. Mr. Carter also served during that time as the U.S. vice chair to Secretary of Defense William Perry on bilateral committees with Russia, Kazakhstan, Ukraine, and other countries to help eliminate the nuclear weapons in Kazakhstan and Ukraine and to secure nuclear and other dangerous materials in several countries. He was on committees with China. Mr. Carter also assisted countries in converting some of their defense facilities to civilian production, often in joint ventures with U.S. companies.

Before entering the government, Mr. Carter had been a Georgetown professor since 1979 and was Executive Director of the American Society of International Law during 1992-1993. He was a visiting law professor at Stanford in 1990. He served as a senior counsel on the Senate Select Committee on Intelligence Activities in 1975. He was a Fellow at the Institute of Politics at Harvard's Kennedy School of Government and an International Affairs Fellow at the Council on Foreign Relations in 1972. A member of Dr. Henry Kissinger's National Security Council staff from 1970-1972, he worked on nuclear arms negotiations and other national security matters. While an Army officer, he was a program analyst in the Office of the Secretary of Defense. He was a trial and appellate lawyer in private practice for several years in California and Washington, D.C.

Mr. Carter, a native Californian, graduated Phi Beta Kappa from Stanford University, received a master's degree in economics and public policy from Princeton's Woodrow Wilson School of Public and International Affairs, and graduated from Yale Law School, where he was the Projects Editor of the Yale Law Journal.

Professor Carter's book, International Economic Sanctions: Improving The Haphazard U.S. Legal Regime (Cambridge Univ. Press: 1988), received the 1989 annual award from the American Society of International Law (ASIL) for the outstanding new book on international law subjects. He has contributed chapters in books and he has published articles in the California Law Review, Yale Law Journal, Georgetown Law Journal, Daedalus, Scientific American, Washington Post, and other periodicals.

He is a member of the Council on Foreign Relations, the American Law Institute, the American Bar Association, and the ASIL. He is on the U.S. State Department's Advisory Committee on International Economic Policy and chairs its Sanctions Subcommittee. He serves on the advisory council of a political risk insurance company and was on the board of directors of a U.S. international trading company. He has been a member of two binational arbitration panels that reviewed trade matters. He was the chairman of the Advisory Committee of the Defense Budget Project and the vice president of the Arms Control Association.

Allen S. Weiner is a Senior Lecturer in Law and Director of the Program on International and Comparative Law at Stanford Law School. He was initially appointed to the Stanford faculty as the inaugural Warren Christopher Professor of the Practice of International Law and Diplomacy, a chair belonging jointly to Stanford Law School and the Freeman Spogli Institute of International Studies at Stanford University. He teaches in the areas of international law, international security, and international conflict resolution.

Before joining the Stanford faculty in 2003, Mr. Weiner served for 11 years as a practicing international lawyer in the Office of the Legal Adviser of the U.S. Department of State. He has extensive experience in such wide-ranging fields as national security law, the law of war, international dispute resolution, and international criminal law. While based in Washington, he worked on international claims and investment disputes, including litigation before international tribunals and negotiation of a $190 million lump-sum claims settlement agreement with Germany; legal matters arising in the scope of U.S. relations with countries of Latin America and the Caribbean, including the Haitian and Cuban migration crises of 1995 and the interpretation of the Panama Canal Treaties; and the interpretation and application of statutes, treaties, and regimes related to nonproliferation and arms control.

Mr. Weiner later served in the U.S. Embassy in The Hague, first as Legal Attaché and later as Counselor for Legal Affairs, where he was actively engaged in U.S. relations with and litigation before international legal institutions such as the International Court of Justice and the International Criminal Tribunal for the former Yugoslavia. Mr. Weiner also served as the U.S. Agent to the Iran-United States Claims Tribunal and participated in the negotiations leading to the establishment of the Special Scottish Court in the Netherlands before which two Libyans charged with the bombing of Pan Am Flight 103 over Lockerbie, Scotland, were tried.

Mr. Weiner's publications have appeared in the Stanford Law Review, the American Journal of International Law, the Santa Clara Journal of International Law, Lewis & Clark Law Review, and the Los Angeles Times, as well as other periodicals, and as a chapter in an edited volume entitled Intervention, Terrorism, and

Torture: Contemporary Challenges to Just War Theory (Springer: 2007). He is a member of the American Society of International Law, where he serves on the Executive Council, the Council on Foreign Relations, and the Pacific Council on International Policy.

Prior to joining the State Department in 1990, Mr. Weiner clerked for Judge John Steadman on the D.C. Court of Appeals. Mr. Weiner graduated from Stanford Law School as a member of the Order of the Coif in 1989 and magna cum laude from Harvard College in 1985. He was born and raised in Denver, Colorado.

Summary of Contents

Contents

4

International Dispute Resolution 283

6

Foreign Sovereign Immunity and the Act of State Doctrine 535

7

Allocation of Legal Authority Among States 637

8

International Human Rights and Responsibility for Injuries to Aliens 721

9

Law of the Sea 813

12

International Criminal Law 1083

Preface to the Sixth Edition

This casebook is designed for an introductory course in international law. It builds on the traditional theories and concepts of public international law, but it also addresses new institutions and other developments, especially the relationship between international and domestic law and the increasingly blurred line between public and private law. It analyzes as well how public international law frequently affects private activity, both individual and business. It considers how various actors and processes contribute to the development and evolution of international law. This casebook, however, does not cover in detail international trade, investment, or other economic transactions.

This Sixth Edition represents a major updating and revision of the casebook. For example, the Sixth Edition contains materials on:

- the U.N., NATO, and EU military intervention to protect civilians in Libya;
- new developments with respect to Afghanistan, Iran, Iraq, North Korea, and Pakistan;
- new international efforts to address global climate change and other international environmental matters;
- updates to U.S. counter-terrorism policies regarding detention, torture, and rendition, including Boumediene v. Bush;
- other recent Supreme Court decisions in Medellin v. Texas (treaties), Samantar v. Yousef (foreign official immunity), and Morrison v. Nat'l Australia Bank (extraterritorial jurisdiction);
- completely revised European Union sections reflecting passage of the Lisbon Treaty; and
- important decisions by international courts such as Schalk and Kopf v. Austria, the major European Court of Human Rights decision on same-sex marriage.

Every chapter has been updated with new and fascinating issues and materials, and the Notes and Questions have been thoroughly revised throughout the casebook.

Background

The United States and its people increasingly are enmeshed in international transactions and are influenced by developments abroad. The governments of the United States and more than 190 other nations deal daily with a host of issues between one another, with international institutions and organizations (like the United Nations, the World Trade Organization, and the G-20), and with regional organizations (such as the European Union, and the North Atlantic Treaty Organization). The problems range from essential, if mundane, matters (like postal agreements) to those of considerable economic and foreign policy significance (such as financial and other economic sanctions against Iran and Libya). They concern the treatment a state accords its own citizens and prevailing human rights standards. The issues even extend to matters of life and death (e.g., the use of military force and efforts to combat the proliferation of weapons of mass destruction).

Each day public and private entities move across U.S. borders billions of dollars worth of currency and goods, hundreds of thousands of people, and tens of thousands of ships, planes, and other vehicles. They also engage in a tremendous amount of communication to and from the United States, through e-mail messages, telephones, and the Internet.

This international activity usually occurs in carefully structured ways, most often without serious incident. The structure is provided by a complex and evolving mix of international and national law. It is administered and enforced by international and national entities, both public and private.

As a result, U.S. lawyers in all parts of the country are increasingly affected. They need to understand the relevant international law and how it can affect the activities of their clients — whether the client is a government or a private party. For example, can an individual citizen invoke a treaty in domestic litigation? Does a U.S. law against terrorism or against price-fixing extend to activity outside the territory of the United States? How can individuals resort to international tribunals, such as international arbitration?

In addition, lawyers–like all citizens–benefit from understanding how international legal rules may shape and constrain the foreign policy decisions that the United States and other countries make.

Objectives

In introducing students to international law, this casebook has five major objectives:

1. The casebook should make students think about the sources of public international law, its principal theories and concepts, and recent developments in the law. In analyzing sources, particular attention is paid to treaties and customary international law, which students probably have not studied before in depth. Traditional concepts and subjects as they have evolved — such as the various principles for exercising prescriptive jurisdiction, the act of state doctrine, approaches to foreign sovereign immunity, human rights, international environmental law, justifications for the use of military force, and international criminal law — are then addressed in appropriate sections

Historical materials are often used to help define the scope of a principle and to trace its development. Current materials are then extensively drawn upon to note present status, to stimulate students' interest in the issues, and to suggest what the future might hold. Excerpts from the Restatement of the Foreign Relations Law of the United States (Third), including its comments and reporters' notes, are often used because the Restatement generally represents a consensus among a wide range of U.S. international lawyers. Even when the Restatement's views are contested, they can provide a useful starting point for discussion.

2. This casebook also analyzes the supporting institutions that help public international law facilitate the burgeoning international activity. The system is addressed as it has actually developed and as it is likely to develop in the future.

The years immediately after World War II witnessed tremendous creativity and accomplishment in establishing an international system. The United Nations, International Court of Justice (or World Court), World Bank, and International Monetary Fund (IMF) were established. While the International Trade Organization never got off the ground, the General Agreement on Tariffs and Trade (GATT) was signed. This progress stimulated hopes by some observers that a new international order was at hand. Hopes for a new order were also kindled in the 1960s and 1970s as colonialism neared its end and many new countries appeared — usually less developed economically than Europe or North America but strong in their convictions. The end of the Cold War in the 1990s then held out possibilities for greater international cooperation. Throughout these post-World War II years, the growing foreign trade and investment, accompanied by sweeping changes in technology and communications, contributed to a world that has become increasingly interconnected.

The reality of the world today is not, however, a simple structure, but rather a complex mix of international and national law, administered and enforced by a variety of entities. Some of the post-World War II institutions like the World Bank and the IMF have grown and adapted effectively, and a weak GATT has been succeeded by a strong World Trade Organization (WTO). On the other hand, many believe that the United Nations and the International Court of Justice have not lived up to their proponents' expectations. Although the end of the Cold War and the initial U.N. response to the 1990 Iraqi invasion of Kuwait revived hopes for the U.N.'s future, these hopes were since dampened by the legal and diplomatic debate over Iraq in 2002-2003. Some hope that the recent U.N. role in dealing with nonproliferation concerns in Iran and North Korea and humanitarian issues in the Sudan and Libya might mark a resurgence for the United Nations.

At the same time, other formal and informal arrangements have emerged and assumed important roles. These other arrangements include evolving international groups like the G-20 nations, regional organizations such as the European Union and the Association of Southeast Asian Nations (ASEAN), frequent use of international arbitration, the proliferation of international courts and tribunals, including international criminal courts, and a vast array of multilateral and bilateral agreements for various purposes from protection of human rights, to promotion of foreign investment, to the enforcement of arbitral awards.

3. The casebook recognizes and studies the interaction between public international law and national agencies and courts. It is not uncommon for such

entities to look to international law on jurisdictional and interpretive questions, as well as on certain substantive issues such as human rights. The status of international law in the U.S. domestic legal system raises many issues of theoretical and practical importance.

4. Students will also be made aware of how public international law increasingly affects private activity, both individual and business.

For example, a national court might draw in part upon international human rights norms to find multinational corporations or individuals liable for large damage judgments for their activities in foreign countries. Or WTO international trade rules might allow an injured country to impose retaliatory tariffs on imports of hundreds of millions of dollars of goods produced by companies in the country that was found to be violating the rules. On a less dramatic scale, the question of sovereign immunity of foreign governments is not only of interest to governments and their diplomats, but can also be crucial to an American company dealing with a foreign supplier owned by a government.

As a result, the future lawyer should understand how the rapidly increasing body of international law—including multilateral and bilateral agreements—is made, how it can be changed, and how it can affect his or her client's interests. A student should also understand how governments make decisions and how diplomacy operates.

5. Although this casebook focuses on international law, it also aims at educating U.S. lawyers. Consequently, it often considers international law from the American perspective, including substantial sections on the U.S. Constitution and U.S. laws that have international impact. At the same time, because American lawyers must appreciate the different principles and possible strategies under foreign legal systems, materials from other legal systems are included to illustrate contrasting approaches.

Overview of the Structure of the Book

This casebook is designed primarily for an introductory course in international law that involves two to five semester hours. There are sufficient materials to allow professors, within limits, to select their own emphases and to choose among the materials.

Chapter 1 starts with the standard definition of international law, contrasts it with more familiar forms of domestic law, and introduces the ways in which international law is formed and enforced. A section on historical background briefly examines the development of international law and institutions. The third section considers whether and in what ways international law is really law. The fourth section provides some of the various scholarly approaches to international law, including international relations theory, economic analysis, critical legal studies, feminist jurisprudence, and Third World approaches to international law.

The chapter concludes with an updated case study on the terrorist attacks of September 11, 2001, and the U.S. and world reactions to them. This case study illustrates how international law actually works.

Against this background, Chapters 2 and 3 introduce the basic building blocks of international law—treaties and custom—in the international and U.S. domestic context. In Chapter 2 students learn what a "treaty" is and some of the basic rules of treaty law. The chapter also covers the formation of customary international law, including different views about the role of state practice compared to normative statements. There is then an examination of the changing ways in which international law is being made today, including the expanding role played by international organizations, transnational networks of government regulators, and nonstate actors — both multinational corporations and nonprofit groups. Finally, there is a section on the general principles of law of major legal systems as a further source of international law.

Chapter 3 considers the status of treaties and customary international law within the U.S. legal system. It begins by considering the scope of the U.S. treaty power and the circumstances under which treaties are enforceable by private parties in U.S. courts. It then considers the foreign relations powers of the national government more generally, and the constitutional law that governs interactions between Congress and the President in foreign relations. The chapter next discusses the status of customary international law in U.S. courts, with particular emphasis on the use of such law in international human rights litigation. The chapter concludes by examining the role of the individual U.S. states in foreign relations and the circumstances under which their foreign relations activities will be deemed to be preempted.

Chapter 4 examines the major, distinctive means by which international disputes are settled. It starts with the process of international negotiations, turns to the International Court of Justice (ICJ), and then analyzes the development of regional courts (especially the European Union's Court of Justice) and the increasingly important role of international arbitration. As recent examples of international dispute resolution systems, materials are included on the North American Free Trade Agreement (NAFTA) and the WTO. Finally, there is a section on the role of domestic courts and the enforcement of foreign court judgments.

Chapter 5 defines "state" and introduces some of the consequences of statehood, including the issue of recognition by other countries and a new government's obligation to be bound by the past agreements of prior governments. This chapter also considers the key international and regional organizations that appear as actors throughout this book, ranging from the international institutions and organizations (such as the United Nations, IMF, WTO, and G-20) to regional economic or security organizations (such as the European Union and the North Atlantic Treaty Organization).

Chapter 6 considers the immunity that states have from suit in the domestic courts of other states, focusing especially on the immunity provided for in the U.S. Foreign Sovereign Immunities Act. The chapter also considers international and U.S. law relating to the immunity of diplomats and heads of state. Finally, the chapter discusses the "act of state doctrine," a common law doctrine applied by U.S. courts that limits their examination of actions by foreign governments.

Chapter 7 examines the international bases for a state to regulate private conduct within and outside its territory and the evolving international rules limiting extraterritorial application of law. For comparison purposes, the chapter concludes with a section that considers briefly the principles of "private" conflicts of law.

Chapter 8 considers the limitations on the state's treatment of individuals within its territory. It begins with traditional rules protecting aliens and alien property and then explores the expansion of rules that protect the state's own citizens from mistreatment under international human rights law. Among other things, the chapter discusses some of the most important human rights treaties and institutions, looks at the history of U.S. involvement in international human rights law, and examines regional human rights law and institutions.

Chapter 9 deals with the international law of the sea. It briefly considers the centuries-long development of customary international law and the 1958 Geneva Conventions. The focus, though, is on the Law of the Sea Convention, which came into force in 1994 and has been adopted by almost all the major countries of the world, except for the United States, though the United States has accepted many of the Convention's provisions as customary international law.

Chapter 10 introduces the international regimes covering environmental matters. It begins with customary international law principles and "soft law" norms in this field and then describes how these rules are being rapidly supplemented by multilateral treaty regimes. The chapter addresses the international legal response to two challenges in particular: first, the relatively successful international effort to deal with ozone depletion through the Montreal Protocol and other measures, and second, the continuing struggle to respond to climate change with the Kyoto Protocol and other approaches.

Chapter 11 explores international law regarding the use of force. After introductory historical materials, the chapter examines the justifications for the use of force that emerged after World War II, especially the legal norms in the U.N. Charter. The chapter considers norms governing when states may permissibly use force without external authorization. Among the circumstances considered are self-defense (including anticipatory and preemptive or preventive self-defense), the use of force to counter terrorism, and humanitarian intervention. The chapter next addresses peacekeeping and peace enforcement operations authorized by the United Nations, including those following Iraq's invasion of Kuwait in 1990, the 2003 U.S.-led invasion of Iraq, and the 2011 response to abuses against civilians in Libya. (Generally, the chapter draws heavily on examples, such as the conflicts in Vietnam, Kosovo, and Sudan.) A major section on international humanitarian law (the law that deals with the conduct of war) has materials on the Geneva Conventions of 1949 and the 1977 Additional Procotols. Finally, there is a brief section on U.S. domestic law (notably the War Powers Resolution) and a concluding section on international efforts to combat the proliferation of weapons of mass destruction, with a focus on the nuclear proliferation challenges presented by North Korea and Iran.

Chapter 12 on international criminal law begins with a brief look at international cooperation by states to counter transnational crime, including mutual legal assistance treaties, extradition treaties, and irregular rendition practices. It then explores principles of individual responsibility under international law and substantive international offenses including genocide, crimes against humanity, war crimes (grave breaches of the Geneva Conventions), torture, and certain terrorism-related offenses. The final section explores the institutional arrangement for prosecuting international crimes, including domestic courts, international tribunals (e.g., the International Criminal Court), and mixed or "hybrid" courts. The chapter concludes with a brief examination of some alternatives to prosecuting international crimes such as amnesty and truth commissions.

Each chapter contains a broad range of materials to illustrate issues and principles. As suggested by the detailed table of contents, these materials include background information, treaties and other international agreements, domestic laws, and decisions by courts and arbitral panels.

Each chapter also contains frequent questions and short problems for students, often based on recent events or reasonable hypotheticals. These questions and problems are designed to focus students' attention on the major issues and rules, and to challenge students to apply the relevant law from the perspectives of different clients and to explore alternative enforcement strategies.

While the materials in each chapter include key excerpts of important documents, the texts or excerpts of many basic documents are provided in a separate Documentary Supplement. Among the documents there are the U.N. Charter, the ICJ Statute, the New York Convention on the Recognition and Enforcement of Foreign Arbitral Awards, the Treaty on European Union, the Treaty on the Functioning of the European Union (aka The Treaty of Rome), many other multilateral treaties (such as important human rights conventions, the Law of the Sea Convention, and the Montreal Protocol on the Protection of the Ozone Layer), the U.S. Constitution, and key U.S. laws (such as the Foreign Sovereign Immunities Act and the International Emergency Economic Powers Act). There are also many supporting documents — e.g., U.N. resolutions and U.S. congressional resolutions — for the substantial case study on the terrorist attacks of September 11, as well as on Iraq.

Also, to help readers keep abreast of current developments in international law, we have listed many sources (including Web sites) in the casebook and the Documentary Supplement. Further, we direct the reader's attention to the various online and hard copy materials of the American Society of International Law. Its Web site is http://www.asil.org. In addition, there will be a special Web site containing updates to this casebook, at http://www.aspenlawschool.com/books/carterinternationallaw.

In short, our approach is a blend of the traditional and the new. It should provide the basis for a rigorous course in the fascinating subject of international law.

For this Sixth Edition, Professor Carter was primarily responsible for the revisions and updates in Chapters 1A-B, 1E, 3, 4C-F, 5, 6, 7, and 9. Professor Weiner was primarily responsible for changes in Chapters 1C-D, 2, 4A-B, 8, 10, 11, and 12. This edition has also benefited from frequent communication between the two active co-authors, with each making contributions and comments to the other's chapters.

Our efforts on this Sixth Edition were helped considerably by the comments received from many people who have used the earlier editions — faculty, students, and others. As before, we very much welcome your comments on this edition.

Barry E. Carter
Allen S. Weiner

May 2011

Previous Editions

Professor Phillip Trimble and I originally conceived this casebook and co-authored the first three editions. We worked closely and constructively from the beginning of the First Edition. His contributions on the first three editions were and are much appreciated. After Professor Trimble left the academic world in 2001 for other activities, he chose just to comment on the Fourth Edition and did not work on the Fifth or Sixth Edition.

Professor Curtis Bradley was an active co-author for the Fourth Edition. He was primarily responsible for the revisions to about three and one-half chapters. Professors Carter and Bradley also commented on each other's chapters. Professor Allen Weiner became my co-author for the Fifth and now Sixth Editions.

Barry E. Carter

May 2011

Acknowledgments

Many people deserve thanks for the assistance they have given us — from providing the opportunities to learn the intricacies of the subject matter to offering specific advice and comments about this casebook. Although it is impossible to mention everyone who has assisted us, we do want to acknowledge some people who have been particularly helpful.

A number of experts have read all or parts of various drafts of the book and have offered valuable comments. They include Abram Chayes, Rosa Brooks, David Koplow, Robert J. Lieber, John H. McNeill, and David Stewart, plus several anonymous reviewers.

Professor Carter would like to thank several research assistants at Georgetown who especially helped with the research on or drafts of this casebook and the companion documentary supplement. For previous editions these students included Kathryn Bisordi, Benjamin Davidson, Marian Hagler, Megan Logsdon, Nicholas Mitrokostas, Christina Paglia, Gwen Ponder, Ines Radmilovic, and Katherine Schuerman. Particularly helpful on the Sixth Edition were Samantha Clark, Thor Imsdahl, Robert McNamee, and Morgan Mulvenon. Among the supportive Georgetown Law Center staff, Brenda Moore, Sylvia Johnson, and Toni Patterson deserve special mention for helping in many ways.

Professor Weiner would like to thank Stanford Law School students Jessica Rothschild, Jasmine Wahhab, and Eugenio Cárdenas for exemplary research assistance on this edition of the casebook. He also wishes to gratefully acknowledge the invaluable support provided by Paul Lomio, Naheed Zaheer, Rich Porter, Kelly Kuehl, Alba Holgado, and other members of the Robert Crown Law Library at Stanford.

Not to be forgotten are the scores of former students at Georgetown, Stanford, UCLA, and the University of Virginia, who were taught with earlier versions of this material and who helpfully offered suggestions that improved the final product.

Finally, we thank the very supportive people at Wolters Kluwer, including former general manager Steve Errick, Carol McGeehan, Melody Davies, Michael Gregory, John Devins, Katharine Tyler, and Sylvia Rebert.

We gratefully acknowledge the permission granted by the authors, publishers, and organizations to reprint portions of the following copyrighted materials.

Alexander, Lewis. Baseline Delimitation and Maritime Boundaries, 23 Va. J. Intl. L. 503 (1983). Copyright © Virginia Journal of International Law. Reprinted by permission of Virginia Journal of International Law.

American Law Institute. Restatement (3d) Foreign Relations Law of the United States, copyright 1987 by the American Law Institute. Reprinted with permission. All rights reserved.

American Society of International Law. Joint Letter from John B. Bellinger, III, Legal Adviser, U.S. Department of State, and William J. Haynes II, General Counsel, U.S. Department of Defense to Dr. Jakob Kellenberger, President, International Committee of the Red Cross. Copyright © American Society of International Law. Reprinted with permission; permission conveyed through Copyright Clearance Center, Inc.

Anghie, Antony and Chimni, B.S. Third World Approaches to International Law and Individual Responsibility in Internal Conflict: The Methods of International Law (Steven D. Ratner & Anne-Marie Slaughter eds., 2004).

Arms Control Association. ACA Fact Sheet: The Nuclear Nonproliferation Treaty at a Glance, Jan. 2005. Reprinted with permission from the Arms Control Association.

Arms Control Association. Fact Sheet: New START at a Glance (2010). Reprinted with permission from the Arms Control Association.

Aust, Anthony. Modern Treaty Law and Practice (2d ed. 2007). Copyright © Cambridge University Press. Reprinted with the permission of Cambridge University Press.

Bacchus, James. Remarks at the Woodrow Wilson International Center for Scholars (May 1, 2002), Reprinted with permission of author.

Bergen, Peter L. Holy War, Inc. (2001). Copyright © by Peter L. Bergen. Reprinted by permission of the author.

Bermann, George A., et al. Cases and Materials on European Union Law (2nd ed., 2002). Reprinted with permission of Thompson West.

Birnie, Patricia, Alan Boyle & Catherine Redgwell, International Law and the Environment (3rd ed., 2009). Copyright © Oxford University Press. Reprinted by permission of Oxford University Press.

Bodansky, Daniel, The Art and Craft of International Environmental Law (2010). Copyright © American Society of International Law. Reprinted with permission of the American Society of International Law; permission conveyed through Copyright Clearance Center, Inc.

Bodansky, Daniel. The Copenhagen Climate Change Accord, American Society of International Law, ASIL Insights, Vol. 14, Issue 3, (Feb. 12, 2010), http://www.asil.org/insights100212.cfm.

Bodansky, Daniel, Jutta Brunnée & Ellen Hey, International Environmental Law: Mapping the Field, in The Oxford Handbook of International Environmental Law (2007).

Born, Gary B. and Rutledge, Peter B. International Civil Litigation in United States Courts (4th ed. 2007). Reproduced with the kind permission of Aspen Publishers.

Born, Gary B. International Commercial Arbitration in the United States: Commentary and Materials (2001). Reproduced with kind permission of Kluwer Law International.

Born, Gary B. International Commercial Arbitration (2009). Copyright Kluwer Law International. Reprinted with permission.

Boyle, Alan and Christine Chinkin, Making of International Law (2007). Copyright © Oxford University Press. Reprinted by permission of Oxford University Press.

Bradley, Curtis A. Universal Jurisdiction and U.S. Law, 2001 U. Chi. Legal F. 323 (2001). Copyright © 2001 University of Chicago Law School/Student-Edited Publications. Reprinted by permission of University of Chicago Law School/ Student-Edited Publications.

Bradley, Curtis A. and Goldsmith, Jack L. Treaties, Human Rights & Conditional Consent, 149 U. Pa. L. Rev. 399 (2000). Copyright © University of Pennsylvania Law Review. Reproduced with permission of the University of Pennsylvania Law Review; permission conveyed through Copyright Clearance Center, Inc.

Brierly, J.L. The Law of Nations (6th ed., H. Waldock ed. 1963). Copyright © Oxford University Press. Reprinted by permission of Oxford University Press.

Brown, Chester, The Cross-Fertilization of Principles Relating to Procedure and Remedies in the Jurisprudence of International Courts and Tribunals, 30 Loy. L.A. Int'l & Comp. L. Rev. 219 (2008). Reprinted with permission of the Loyola of Los Angeles International and Comparative Law Review.

Brownlie, Ian. International Law and the Use of Force by States (rev. ed. 1991). Copyright © 1991 Oxford University Press. Reprinted with permission of Oxford University Press.

Carter, Barry E. International Economic Sanctions: Improving the Haphazard Regime. Copyright © 1988 Cambridge University Press. Reprinted with the permission of the Cambridge University Press.

Carter, Barry E. Making Progress in International Law and Institutions, Progress in International Institutions (Russell Miller and Rebecca Bratspies eds., 2008). Reprinted with permission from Martinus Nijhoff Press.

Charney, Jonathan I. International Maritime Boundaries (1993). Copyright © Kluwer Academic Publishers. Reprinted by permission of Kluwer Academic Publishers.

Charney, Jonathan I. Universal International Law, 87 Am. J. Intl. L. 529 (1993). Reproduced with permission from 87 AJIL 529 (1993), © The American Society of International Law; permission conveyed through Copyright Clearance Center, Inc.

Christenson, Gordon A. Attributing Conduct to the State: Is Anything New? Remarks on Attribution Issues in State Responsibility, 84 Am. Socy. Intl. L. Proc. 51. Reproduced with permission from 84 ASILP 51, © The American Society of International Law; permission conveyed through Copyright Clearance Center, Inc.

Churchill, Robin R., and Lowe, A. Vaughan. Law of the Sea (3d ed. 1999). Reprinted by permission of the authors and Juris Publishing.

Dellapenna, Joseph. Suing Foreign Governments and Their Corporations (2003). Copyright © 2003 by Brill Publishers. Reprinted with permission.

Dickinson, Laura A. The Promise of Hybrid Courts, 97 Am. J. Intl. L. 295. Reproduced with permission from 97 AJIL 295, © The American Society of International Law; permission conveyed through Copyright Clearance Center, Inc.

Dinstein, Yoram. War, Aggression and Self-Defence (4th ed. 2005). Copyright © 2005 Cambridge University Press. Reprinted with permission of Cambridge University Press.

Driscoll, David. What Is the International Monetary Fund? (1997). Copyright © 1997 by International Monetary Fund. Reproduced with permission of International Monetary Fund in the format Textbook via Copyright Clearance Center.

Edwards, Richard W., Jr. Reservations to Treaties, 10 Mich. J. Intl. L. 362 (1989). Reproduced by permission of Michigan Journal of International Law; permission conveyed through Copyright Clearance Center, Inc.

Engle, Karen. International Human Rights and Feminisms: When Discourses Keep Meeting, in International Law: Modern Feminist Approaches (Doris Buss & Ambreena Manji eds., 2005). Copyright © 2005 by Hart Publishing Limited. Reproduced with permission of Hart Publishing Limited.

Faure, Michael G. and Jergen Lefevere, Compliance with Global Environmental Policy, in The Global Environment: Institutions, Law, and Policy (Regina S. Axelrod, Stacy D. VanDeever & David Leonard Downie eds., 3d ed. 2011). Copyright © 2011 by CQ Press. Reproduced with permission of CQ Press.

Franck, Thomas M. Legitimacy in the International System, 82 Am. J. Intl. L. 705 (1988). Reproduced with permission from 82 AJIL 705 (1988), © The American Society of International Law; permission conveyed through Copyright Clearance Center, Inc.

Franck, Thomas M. Recourse to Force: State Action Against Threats and Armed Attacks (2002). Copyright © 2002 Cambridge University Press. Reprinted with the permission of Cambridge University Press.

Franck, Thomas M. What Happens Now? The United Nations After Iraq, 97 Am. J. Intl. L. 607 (2003). Reproduced with permission from 97 AJIL 607 (2003), © The American Society of International Law; permission conveyed through Copyright Clearance Center, Inc.

GATT Focus. "What Is the WTO?" Published by GATT Information Service, 1994. Reprinted with permission.

Glennon, Michael J. The Fog of Law: Self-Defense, Inherence, and Incoherence in Article 51 of the United Nations Charter, 25 Harv. J.L. & Pub. Poly. 539 (2002). Copyright © Harvard Journal of Law and Public Policy. Reprinted by permission of Harvard Journal of Law and Public Policy; permission conveyed through Copyright Clearance Center, Inc.

Goldsmith, Jack and Posner, Eric A. The New International Law Scholarship, 34 Ga. J. Intl. & Comp. L. 463. Copyright © University of Georgia Law School. Reprinted by permission of Georgia Journal of International and Comparative Law; permission conveyed through Copyright Clearance Center, Inc.

Haberman, Clyde. Japanese Fight Invading Sea for Priceless Speck of Land, N.Y. Times, Jan. 1, 1981, at A1. Copyright © by the New York Times Co. Reprinted with permission.

Hartley, T.C. The Foundations of European Union Law (7th ed., 2010). Reprinted by permission of Oxford University Press.

Hathaway, Oona A., Between Power and Principle: An Integrated Theory of International Law, 72 U. Chi. L. Rev. 469 (2005). Copyright © 2005 University of Chicago Law Review. Reprinted with permission of University of Chicago Law Review; permission conveyed through Copyright Clearance Center, Inc.

Hecker, Siegfried S. Lessons Learned from the North Korean Nuclear Crises, Daedalus (2010). Copyright © 2010 MIT Press Journals. Reprinted with permission.

Henckaerts, Jean-Marie, Customary International Humanitarian Law: A Response to US Comments, 89 Int'l Rev. Red Cross 473 (2007). Copyright © 2007 International Red Cross. Reprinted with permission of International Red Cross.

Henkin, Louis. The Age of Rights (1990). Copyright © Columbia University Press. Reprinted by permission of Columbia University Press; permission conveyed through Copyright Clearance Center, Inc.

Henkin, Louis. How Nations Behave: Law and Foreign Policy (2d ed. 1979). Copyright © Columbia University Press. Reprinted by permission of Columbia University Press; permission conveyed through Copyright Clearance Center, Inc.

Henkin, Louis. U.S. Ratification of Human Rights Conventions: The Ghost of Senator Bricker, 89 Am. J. Intl. L. 341 (1995). Reproduced with permission from 89 AJIL 341 (1995), © The American Society of International Law; permission conveyed through Copyright Clearance Center, Inc.

Henkin, Louis, Right v. Might: International Law and the Use of Force (1991). Copyright © by Council on Foreign Relations Press. Reprinted with permission; permission conveyed through Copyright Clearance Center, Inc.

Horlick, Gary and Debusk, Amanda. Dispute Resolution under NAFTA, Journal of World Trade (1993). Reproduced with the kind permission of Kluwer Law International.

Hufbauer, Gary Clyde and Schott, Jeffrey J. NAFTA: An Assessment (1993). Copyright © 1993 by Peterson Institute for International Economics. Reproduced with permission of Peterson Institute for International Economics in the format Textbook via Copyright Clearance Center.

Hubauer, Gary Clyde and Schott, Jeffrey J. NAFTA Revisited, Pol' Options 83, 83-84 (Oct. 2007).

International Law Association. Statement of Principles, Report of the Sixty-Ninth Conference, London (2000). Reproduced with permission from the International Law Association.

Independent Task Force. Safeguarding Prosperity in a Global Financial System (1999). Copyright © 1999 by the Peterson Institute for International Economics. Reproduced with permission of Peterson Institute for International Economics in the format Textbook via Copyright Clearance Center.

Jackson, John H., Davey, William J., and Sykes, Jr., Alan O. Legal Problems of International Economic Relations: Cases, Materials and Text (5th ed. 2008). Reprinted with permission of Thompson West.

Jennings, Robert and Watts, Arthur, eds. Oppenheim's International Law (9th ed. 1992). Copyright © by Pearson Education, Ltd. Reprinted with permission.

Kalshoven, Frits. Constraints on the Waging of War (1987). Reprinted with permission of Kluwer Academic Publishers; permission conveyed through Copyright Clearance Center, Inc.

Kirgis, Frederic L. North Korea's Withdrawal from the Nuclear Nonproliferation Treaty, ASIL Insights (2003). Reproduced with permission from ASIL Insights. Copyright © by the American Society of International Law.

Kiss, Alexandre and Shelton, Dinah. Guide to International Environmental Law (2007). Copyright © Brill. Reproduced with permission of Brill.

Kiss, Alexandre and Shelton, Dinah. International Environmental Law (3d ed. 2004). Copyright © Brill Publishing. Reprinted with permission.

Koh, Harold Hongju. Why Do Nations Obey International Law? 106 Yale L.J. 2599 (1997). Copyright © Yale Law Journal. Reprinted by permission of The Yale Law Journal Company and William S. Hein Company from The Yale Law Journal, Vol. 106; permission conveyed through Copyright Clearance Center, Inc.

Koskenniemi, Martti. From Apology to Utopia: The Structure of International Legal Argument (2005 rev. ed.). Copyright © Cambridge University Press. Reprinted with the permission of Cambridge University Press.

Levit, Janet Koven. Bottom-Up International Lawmaking: Reflections on the New Haven School of International Law, 32 Yale J. Int'l L. 393 (2007). Copyright © Yale Law Journal. Reprinted by permission of The Yale Law Journal Company and William S. Hein Company from The Yale Law Journal; permission conveyed through Copyright Clearance Center, Inc.

Lodal, Jan. The Price of Dominance: The New Weapons of Mass Destruction and Their Challenge to American Leadership (2001). Copyright © by Council on Foreign Relations Press. Reprinted with permission; permission conveyed through Copyright Clearance Center, Inc.

Lowenfeld, Andreas F. Congress & Cuba: The Helms-Burton Act, 90 Am. J. Intl. L. 419 (1996). Reproduced with permission from 90 AJIL 419 (1996), © The American Society of International Law.

Lowenfeld, Andreas F. Remedies Along with Rights: Institutional Reform of the New GATT, 87 Am. J. Intl. L. 477 (1994). Reproduced with Permission from 87 AJIL 477 (1994), © The American Society of International Law.

Lowenfeld, Andreas F. Trade Controls for Political Ends (1983). Reprinted from International Economic Law with permission. Copyright © 1983 Mathew Bender & Company, Inc., a member of the LexisNexis Group. All rights reserved.

Matthews, Jessica T. Power Shift, Foreign Affairs Jan./Feb. 1997, at 50. Reprinted by permission of FOREIGN AFFAIRS, (1997). Copyright © 1997 by the Council on Foreign Relations, Inc., www.ForeignAffairs.com.

McDonald, Kara C. and Patrick, Stewart M. UN Security Council Enlargement and U.S. Interests, Council on Foreign Relations Special Report (Dec. 2010). Copyright © by Council on Foreign Relations Press.

Menon, P.K. Law of Recognition in International Law: Basic Principles (1994). Copyright © 1994 by Edwin Mellen Press. Reproduced with permission of Edwin Mellen Press in the format Textbook via Copyright Clearance Center.

Merrills, J.G. International Dispute Settlement (4th ed. 2005). Reprinted with the permission of Cambridge University Press. Copyright © 2005 Cambridge University Press

Morris, Madeline. High Crimes and Misconceptions: The ICC and Non-Party States, 64 Law and Contemp. Probs. 13 (2001). Reprinted with permission from Law and Contemporary Problems, a publication of Duke Law School; permission conveyed through Copyright Clearance Center, Inc.

Murphy, John F. The United Nations and the Control of International Violence: A Legal and Political Analysis (1982). Reproduced with permission of Rowman & Littlefield Publishers, Inc.; permission conveyed through Copyright Clearance Center, Inc.

The Netherlands: District Court at the Hague Judgment in *Compagnie Europenne des Pétroles S.A. v. Sensor Nederland B.V.*, 22 I.L.M. 66 (1983). Copyright © by The American Society of International Law. Reproduced with Permission.

Nowak, Manfred. Introduction to the International Human Rights Regime (2003). Copyright © Brill Academic Publishers. Reprinted with permission of Brill Academic Publishers; permission conveyed through Copyright Clearance Center, Inc.

O'Connell, D.P. International Law of the Sea (1982). Copyright © Oxford University Press. Reproduced by permission of Oxford University Press.

O'Connell, Mary Ellen. The UN, NATO, and International Law After Kosovo. Human Rights Quarterly 22:1 (2000). © The Johns Hopkins University Press. Reprinted with permission of The Johns Hopkins University Press; permission conveyed through Copyright Clearance Center, Inc.

Peel, Jacqueline, Environmental Protection in the Twenty-First Century: The Role of International Law, in The Global Environment: Institutions, Law, and Policy (Regina S. Axelrod, Stacy D. VanDeever & David Leonard Downie eds., 3d ed. 2011). Copyright © 2011 by CQ Press. Reproduced with permission of CQ Press.

Posen, Adam. One Fiscal Size Does Not Fit All, Eurointelligence (June 22, 2010).

Ratner, Stephen R., Abrams, Jason S. & James L. Bischoff. Accountability for Human Rights Atrocities in International Law (3d ed. 2009). Copyright © Oxford University Press. Reprinted with permission of Oxford University Press.

Ratner, Steven, R. & Anne-Marie Slaughter, The Methods of International Law (2004). Copyright © American Society of International Law. Reprinted with permission.

Rehman, Javaid. International Human Rights Law (2d ed. 2010). Reprinted with permission of Pearson Education.

Richman, William M. Understanding Conflict of Laws (3rd ed. 2002). Reprinted from Understanding Conflict of Laws, 3d ed, with permission. Copyright 2002 Mathew Bender & Company, Inc., a member of the LexisNexis Group. All rights reserved.

Roberts, Anthea Elizabeth. Traditional and Modern Approaches to Customary International Law: A Reconciliation, 95 Am. J. Intl. L. 757 (2001). Reproduced with permission from 95 AJIL 757, © The American Society of International Law; permission conveyed through Copyright Clearance Center, Inc.

Roth, Kenneth. Human Rights Organizations, in Realizing Human Rights: Moving from Inspiration to Impact (Samantha Power & Graham Allison eds., 2000). Copyright © Palgrave Macmillan. Reproduced with permission of Palgrave Macmillan; permission conveyed through the Copyright Clearance Center, Inc.

Ruggie, John Gerard. Business and Human Rights: The Evolving International Agenda, 101 Am. J. Int'l L. 819 (2007). Copyright © 2007 American Journal of International Law. Reproduced with permission from the American Journal of International Law; permission conveyed through Copyright Clearance Center, Inc.

Sadat, Leila Nadya. Universal Jurisdiction, National Amnesties, and Truth Commissions: Reconciling the Irreconcilable, in Universal Jurisdiction: National Courts and the Prosecution of Serious Crimes Under International Law (Stephen

Macedo ed., 2004). Copyright © 2004 University of Pennsylvania Press. Reproduced with permission from the University of Pennsylvania Press.

Schachter, Oscar. International Law in Theory and Practice (1991). Copyright BRILL. Reprinted by permission of Koninklijke BRILL NV.

Shaw, Malcolm N. International Law (6th ed. 2008). Copyright © M.N. Shaw. Reprinted with the permission of Cambridge University Press.

Shearer, I.A., ed. Starke's International Law (11th ed. 1994). Copyright © by Oxford University Press. Reproduced with permission of Oxford University Press.

Shelton, Dinah. Normative Hierarchy in International Law, 100 Am. J. Intl. L. 291 (2006). Reproduced with permission from 100 AJIL 291 (2006), © The American Society of International Law; permission conveyed through Copyright Clearance Center, Inc.

Simma, Bruno and Alston, Phillip. The Sources of Human Rights Law, 12 Austl Y.B. Intl. L. 82 (1988-1989). Reproduced with permission of the Australian Yearbook of International Law.

Simpson, J.L. and Fox, Hazel. International Arbitration: Law and Practice (Praeger Publishers, an imprint of Greenwood Publishing Group, Inc. Westport, CT 1959). Copyright © 1959 by Frederick A. Praeger, Inc. All rights reserved.

Sinclair, Ian. The Vienna Convention on the Law of Treaties (2d ed. 1984). Reproduced with permission from Sir Ian Sinclair.

Slaughter, Anne-Marie. A New World (2004). Copyright © 2004 Princeton University Press. Reprinted with permission.

Sohn, Louis B. The New International Law Protection of Rights of Individuals Rather Than States, 32 Am. U. L. Rev. 1 (1982). Copyright © American University Law Review. Reprinted by permission of the American University Law Review; permission conveyed through Copyright Clearance Center, Inc.

Sohn, Louis. Peaceful Settlement of Disputes in Ocean Conflicts, 46 L. & Contemp. Probs. 195 (1983). Reprinted by permission.

Solis, Gary D. The ICC and Mad Prosecutors (Remarks at Georgetown University, March 27, 2003). Reprinted by permission of the author.

Solis, Gary D., The Law of Armed Conflict: International Humanitarian Law in War (2010). Copyright © 2010 Cambridge University Press. Reprinted with the permission of the Cambridge University Press.

Stromseth, Jane. Rethinking Humanitarian Intervention: The Case for Incremental Change in Humanitarian Intervention: Ethical, Legal and Political Dilemmas (J.L. Holzgrefe & Robert O. Keohane eds., 2003). Copyright © Cambridge University Press. Reprinted with permission of Cambridge University Press.

Taft, William H., IV and Buchwald, Todd F. Preemption, Iraq, and International Law, 97 Am. J. Intl. L. 557 (2003). Reproduced with permission from 97 AJIL 557 (2003), © The American Society of International Law.

Tams, Christian J. Use of Force Against Terrorist, 20 European J. Inter'l L. 359 (2009). Copyright © Oxford University Press. Reprinted with permission via Copyright Clearance Center.

Theroux, Eugene A. and Peele, Thomas. China and Sovereign Immunity: The Huguang Railway Bonds Case, 2 China Law Reporter 129, 147 (1982-83). Reproduced by permission of the authors.

Tomuschat, Christian. Human Rights: Between Idealism and Realism (2d ed. 2008). Copyright © Oxford University Press. Reprinted with permission from Oxford University Press.

Trachtman, Joel P. The Economic Structure of International Law (2008). Copyright © 2008 Harvard University Press. Reprinted with permission from Harvard University Press via Copyright Clearance Center.

Trimble, Phillip R. Arms Control and International Negotiation Theory, 25 Stan. J. Intl. L. 543 (1989). Copyright © 2002 by the Board of Trustees of the Leland Stanford Junior University; permission conveyed through Copyright Clearance Center, Inc.

Victor, David G., M. Granger Morgan, Jay Apt, John Steinbruner, and Katharine Ricke. The Geoengineering Option: A last Resort Against Global Warming? (2009). Reprinted by permission of FOREIGN AFFAIRS, (March 2009). Copyright © 2009 by the Council on Foreign Relations, Inc., www.ForeignAffairs.com.

Viljoen, Frans. The African Regional Human Rights System in International Protection of Human Rights (Catarina Krause & Martin Scheinin, eds. 2009). Copyright © 2009 Institute for Human Rights. Reprinted with permission.

Von Mehren, Arthur T. From *Vynior's Case* to *Mitsubishi*: The Future of Arbitration and Public Law, 12 Brook. J. Intl. L. 583 (1986). Copyright © 1986 Brooklyn Journal of International Law. Reproduced with permission of Brooklyn Journal of International Law in the format Textbook via Copyright Clearance Center.

Warwick Commission. The Multilateral Trade Regime: Which Way Forward? The Report of the First Warwick Commission, (2007).

Watson, Geoffrey. The Law of State Succession, in Contemporary Practice of Public International Law (Ellen Schaffer & Randall J. Snyder eds., 1997). Copyright © by Oxford University Press, reproduced with permission of Oxford University Press.

Weiner, Allen S. Indirect Expropriations: The Need for a Taxonomy of 'Legitimate' Regulatory Purposes, 5 Intl. L. F. 166 (2003). Reproduced with permission from Kluwer Law International; permission conveyed through Copyright Clearance Center, Inc.

Weiner, Allen S. The Use of Force and Contemporary Security Threats: Old Medicine for New Ills?, 59 Stan. L. Rev. 415 (2006). Reproduced with permission of the Stanford Law Review; permission conveyed through Copyright Clearance Center, Inc.

Editorial Notice

For ease of reading, we are employing a few conventions throughout this casebook:

1. In material excerpted from other sources, additions to the material are indicated by brackets. Ellipses denote the deletion of material.

2. Throughout the book, citations and footnotes are deleted without using an ellipsis, unless an ellipsis serves a pedagogical purpose.

International Law

1

What Is International Law?

A. THE DEFINITION OF "INTERNATIONAL LAW"

We first want you to focus on the different kinds of law that an international lawyer must deal with and on how public international law fits into the picture. You are already familiar with torts, contracts, and possibly some U.S. constitutional law. We assume, however, that you have not been exposed to much international law. Indeed, you may think of it as something entirely different from other kinds of law. You may have some notion that it exists on a higher plane, or you may have heard that international law only concerns governments. You may also be instinctively skeptical as to whether something called "international law" really exists.

In this chapter, we will first introduce you to the definition of international law and provide a series of examples of international and domestic law. Section B consists of materials that sketch the history of international law, which you should read as background for the course. Section C then confronts the skepticism sometimes expressed about international law and raises the following questions: (a) Is international law really "law"? (b) What functions does international law play in the world today? (c) Why is international law binding? (d) What leads states to comply with international law? Section D considers some of the modern theoretical and methodological approaches to international law. Section E presents a case study of the terrorist attacks of September 11, 2001, and the U.S. and world response to them. The case study illustrates international law in action.

Western scholars have often divided the legal universe into two parts or levels—international law and domestic law. International law prescribed rules governing the relations of nation-states (or "states," as they are called in the vocabulary of international law). It encompassed both public and private international law. Domestic law, on the other hand, prescribed rules within a state that governed everything else, mostly the conduct or status of individuals, corporations, domestic governmental units, and other entities.

"Public" international law was distinguished from "private" international law. Public international law primarily governed the activities of governments in relation to other governments. Private international law dealt with the activities of individuals, corporations, and other private entities when they crossed national borders. A large body of private international law consisted of choice-of-law rules (determining, for example, which state's domestic law would apply to transactions, such as an international sales contract, between nationals of two states). Private international law also included substantive terms and conditions that had become customary in certain international practices, such as shipping terms and letters of credit. Recently the scope of private international law has expanded to encompass treaties on many subjects that were traditionally domestic law, such as the U.N. Convention on Contracts for the International Sale of Goods and the Hague Convention on Protection of Children and Cooperation in respect of Intercountry Adoption.

Moreover, norms of public international law increasingly regulate or affect private conduct. For example, states frequently conclude treaties granting rights of trade or investment to nationals of other states, proclaiming individual human rights that are required to be protected, or establishing environmental standards to be followed by industrial plants. Those treaties, which create legally binding obligations under public international law, may also be "incorporated" into domestic law and thereby become domestic legal obligations. Hence, the lines between international law and domestic law, as well as between public law and private law, have thus become blurred and somewhat artificial. Indeed, to some commentators, the intellectual basis for the traditional conceptual structure of the old legal universe seems suspect.

Let's explore briefly the evolving definition of public international law. One of the classic treatises, J.L. Brierly, The Law of Nations (6th ed. 1963), defined international law as

> the body of rules and principles of action which are binding upon civilized states in their relations with one another.

The American Law Institute's Restatement of the Foreign Relations Law of the United States (Third) (1987) (hereinafter referred to as the Restatement) takes a limited step toward recognizing the potential importance of international law for activity traditionally within the domestic or private spheres:

Restatement Section 101

"International law," as used in this Restatement, consists of rules and principles of general application dealing with the conduct of states and of international organizations and with their relations inter se, as well as with some of their relations with persons, whether natural or juridical.

These two definitions focus on the norm or rule of law. Those norms or rules may be created by or found in different instruments or sources.

Article 38 of the Statute of the International Court of Justice, a treaty ratified by the United States and by all other members of the United Nations, contains a traditional statement of those sources. The Restatement offers an alternative exposition of basically the same idea.

Statute of the International Court of Justice

Article 38

The Court, whose function is to decide in accordance with international law such disputes as are submitted to it, shall apply:

(a) international conventions, whether general or particular, establishing rules expressly recognized by the contesting states;

(b) international custom, as evidence of a general practice accepted as law;

(c) the general principles of law recognized by civilized nations;

(d) . . . judicial decisions and the teachings of the most highly qualified publicists of the various nations, as subsidiary means for the determination of rules of law.

Restatement Section 102

(1) A rule of international law is one that has been accepted as such by the international community of states

(a) in the form of customary law;

(b) by international agreement; or

(c) by derivation from general principles common to the major legal systems of the world.

(2) Customary international law results from a general and consistent practice of states followed by them from a sense of legal obligation.

(3) International agreements create law for the states parties thereto and may lead to the creation of customary international law when such agreements are intended for adherence by states generally and are in fact widely accepted.

(4) General principles common to the major legal systems, even if not incorporated or reflected in customary law or international agreements, may be invoked as supplementary rules of international law where appropriate.

Notes and Questions

Problem. As an initial exercise, consider whether the norms or rules established by the legal instruments described below would qualify as international law under either of the two definitions above. You should focus on the norm or rule established by each of the instruments rather than on the instrument itself. (You may assume that a treaty is an agreement between states that is reached by the executive branches of the governments, often with legislative branch support.)

(a) A treaty among several countries prohibiting the use of force except in self-defense.

(b) A treaty between Mexico and the United States establishing the boundary between the two countries.

(c) A treaty between the United States and Japan under which each agrees to permit nationals of the other country to invest freely in its economy and not to expropriate property without payment of just compensation.

(d) An oil concession agreement between the government of Colombia and the Chevron oil company, under which Colombia agrees not to tax Chevron on its income from the concession for ten years. What if the concession agreement contains a clause saying that "this instrument shall have the force of law and shall be interpreted in accordance with generally recognized principles of international law"? Would it make any difference whether the concession agreement provided that disputes would be settled by international arbitration? Or if it provided that disputes would be settled exclusively in Colombian courts?

(e) A provision in the U.S. Constitution that property may not be taken except for public use and on payment of just compensation.

(f) A U.S. statute imposing licensing fees on foreign corporations.

(g) A common law rule announced by the California judiciary imposing strict liability without regard to negligence for damage caused by defective products (including those manufactured by foreign corporations).

(h) A custom long observed by all the countries of the world not to imprison properly accredited diplomats.

1. In the examples above, how was the legal norm formed? Who and/or what institutions were required for its formation?

2. Where would disputes about the validity or meaning of the norm be settled? In connection with this question, see Notes 5 and 6 below.

3. What law would govern the dispute? What difference does it make?

4. What sanctions could be imposed for violation, and who would impose them? It is important to think about sanctions other than some form of judicially imposed remedy. Why might government officials comply with law? Consider how factors such as adverse publicity, habitually following rules and procedures (the usual way a large bureaucracy functions), fear of administrative sanctions, or adverse effects on career development might lead to compliance with international law. A relevant example occurred when two U.S. Border Patrol agents were removed from field duty because they "breached Mexico's sovereignty" by crossing the border in pursuit of two suspects. In a similar incident on the U.S.-Canadian border, the United States protested the Canadian arrest of a person 200 yards inside the United States and demanded to know what steps Canada was taking with respect to the arrested American and with respect to the arresting officer. Canada released the defendant and sought extradition under the extradition treaty between the two countries.

5. Much skepticism about international law is based on the absence of a comprehensive judicial system with compulsory jurisdiction to settle disputes and the absence of a central executive authority to coerce compliance. Nevertheless, as we show in Section C, almost all rules of international law are in fact regularly complied with. Furthermore, as explored in Chapter 4, there is an International Court of Justice (ICJ), which handles some cases, and active regional and specialized international courts. Moreover, there are several means other than court adjudication by which disputes can be settled, including negotiation, mediation, and arbitration pursuant to a general or an ad hoc agreement. Most disputes are settled through negotiation. Consider the description of J. G. Merrills, International Dispute Settlement 2, 8 (4th ed. 2005):

> In fact in practice, negotiation is employed more frequently than all the other methods put together. Often, indeed, negotiation is the only means employed, not just because it is always the first to be tried and is often successful, but also because states may believe its advantages to be so great as to rule out the use of other methods, even in situations

> where the chances of a negotiated settlement are slight. . . . [Negotiations] are reminders of the fact that states are not entities, like individuals, but complex groupings of institutions and interests [such as the various U.S. cabinet departments, like the Departments of Defense, Commerce, Labor, and Agriculture, the legislative branch of the government, and regulatory and law enforcement agencies]. . . . Negotiations between states are usually conducted through 'normal diplomatic channels', that is by the respective foreign offices [i.e., usually the Department of State in the case of the United States], or by diplomatic representatives, who in the case of complex negotiations may lead delegations including representatives of several interested departments of the governments concerned. As an alternative, if the subject matter is appropriate, negotiations may be carried out . . . by representatives of the particular ministry or department responsible for the matter in question—between trade departments in the case of a commercial agreement, for example, or defence ministries in negotiations concerning weapons procurement.

6. Sometimes U.S. courts will look to international law and apply it—for example, by finding it incorporated into U.S. law or by construing statutes to avoid a violation of it. This is especially so when a treaty or other international agreement is involved to which the United States is a party. Article VI of the U.S. Constitution (the so-called Supremacy Clause) expressly makes treaties part of the "supreme Law of the Land." There are, however, questions under U.S. law about whether a treaty is self-executing or whether it needs implementing U.S. legislation. A court might also apply what is called customary international law—that is, the law that results from a general and consistent practice of states that they follow from a sense of legal obligation. One famous example of this is the decision by a U.S. court of appeals in Filartiga v. Pena-Irala (1980). There, the court determined that there was a customary international law norm against official torture, and the court held that an alien could bring suit in a U.S. court for a violation of this norm, pursuant to a U.S. statute that grants the federal courts jurisdiction to hear suits, brought by aliens, for torts "committed in violation of the law of nations. . . ." (These issues, and *Filartiga* and more recent cases, are discussed in Chapter 3.)

B. HISTORY OF PUBLIC INTERNATIONAL LAW AND ALTERNATIVE PERSPECTIVES

1. Introduction

In the preceding section you learned that public international law deals with the activities of nation-states. The contemporary system of international relations is built on the assumption that the nation-state is the primary actor. Nevertheless, the modern nation-state is a relatively recent product of political development in Western Europe. Generally, this is traced to the Renaissance and Reformation, the expansion of trade in the fifteenth and sixteenth centuries, and the European discoveries of the New World. Intellectually, the doctrine of sovereignty and the idea of the secular, territorial state are intimately associated with the creation of the modern system.

Of course, there had been well-organized political units in Europe before this period. And there were great empires for millennia in China, Japan, India, Africa,

Southeast Asia, and the Middle East. Those empires had relations with other peoples, and hence there have been many systems of law that can be seen as predecessors to modern international law. However, even though most states today are non-European, the contemporary system of international law is based on the European model developed over the past four centuries. Some commentators have objected to what they see as a continuation of colonialism and imperialism and have urged abandonment or at least recasting the old Western system.

Throughout this course you should consider the extent to which you believe these objections are justified. As you learn the substantive rules of international law, consider what policies and interests these rules favor (and at whose expense); whether a small developing country would be likely to approve or oppose the rule (and who and what interests within that state would be likely to do so); and whether the legitimation of state authority favors Western or capitalist interests over others. In the following excerpts we introduce you to the basic history of modern international law (Shearer, Shaw, and Carter). Then we present the story of contemporary international law from the perspective of developing countries (Shaw).

I. A. Shearer, Starke's International Law

7-12 (11th ed. 1994)

The modern system of international law is a product, roughly speaking, of only the last four hundred years. It grew to some extent out of the usages and practices of modern European states in their intercourse and communications, while it still bears witness to the influence of writers and jurists of the sixteenth, seventeenth, and eighteenth centuries, who first formulated some of its most fundamental tenets. Moreover, it remains tinged with concepts such as national and territorial sovereignty, and the perfect quality and independence of states, that owe their force to political theories underlying the modern European state system, although, curiously enough, some of these concepts have commanded the support of newly emerged non-European states.

But any historical account of the system must begin with earliest times, for even in the period of antiquity rules of conduct to regulate the relations between independent communities were felt necessary and emerged from the usages observed by these communities in their mutual relations. Treaties, the immunities of ambassadors, and certain laws and usages of war are to be found many centuries before the dawn of Christianity, for example in ancient Egypt and India, while there were historical cases of recourse to arbitration and mediation in ancient China and in the early Islamic world, although it would be wrong to regard these early instances as representing any serious contribution towards the evolution of the modern system of international law.

We find, for example, in the period of the Greek City States, small but independent of one another, evidence of an embryonic, although regionally limited, form of international law which one authority . . . aptly described as "intermunicipal." This "intermunicipal" law was composed of customary rules which had crystallised into law from long-standing usages followed by these cities such as, for instance, the rules as to the inviolability of heralds in battle, the need for a prior declaration of war, and the enslavement of prisoners of war. These rules were applied not only in the relations inter se of these sovereign Greek cities, but as between them and neighbouring states. Underlying the rules there were, however, deep religious influences, characteristic of an era in which the distinctions between law, morality, justice and religion were not sharply drawn.

In the period of Rome's dominance of the ancient world, there also emerged rules governing the relations between Rome and the various nations or peoples with which it had contact. One significant aspect of these rules was their legal character, thus contrasting with the religious nature of the customary rules observed by the Greek City States. But Rome's main contribution to the development of international law was less through these rules than through the indirect influence of Roman law generally, inasmuch as when the study of Roman law was revived at a later stage in Europe, it provided analogies and principles capable of ready adaptation to the regulation of relations between modern states.

Actually, the total direct contribution of the Greeks and Romans to the development of international law was relatively meagre. Conditions favourable to the growth of a modern law of nations did not really come into being until the fifteenth century, when in Europe there began to evolve a number of independent civilised states. Before that time Europe had passed through various stages in which either conditions were so chaotic as to make impossible any ordered rules of conduct between nations, or the political circumstances were such that there was no necessity for a code of international law. Thus in the later period of Roman history with the authority of the Roman Empire extending over the whole civilised world, there were no independent states in any sense, and therefore a law of nations was not called for. During the early medieval era, there were two matters particularly which militated against the evolution of a system of international law:

a. the temporal and spiritual unity of the greater part of Europe under the Holy Roman Empire, although to some extent this unity was notional and belied by numerous instances of conflict and disharmony; and
b. the feudal structure of Western Europe, hinging on a hierarchy of authority which not only clogged the emergence of independent states but also prevented the Powers of the time from acquiring the unitary character and authority of modern sovereign states.

Profound alterations occurred in the fifteenth and sixteenth centuries. The discovery of the New World, the Renaissance of learning, and the Reformation as a religious revolution disrupted the facade of the political and spiritual unity of Europe, and shook the foundations of medieval Christendom. Theories were evolved to meet the new conditions; intellectually, the secular conceptions of a modern sovereign state and of a modern independent Sovereign found expression in the works of Bodin (1530-1596), a Frenchman, Machiavelli (1469-1527), an Italian, and later in the seventeenth century, Hobbes (1588-1679), an Englishman.

With the growth of a number of independent states there was initiated, as in early Greece, the process of formation of customary rules of international law from the usages and practices followed by such states in their mutual relations. So in Italy with its multitude of small independent states, maintaining diplomatic relations with each other and with the outside world, there developed a number of customary rules relating to diplomatic envoys, for example, their appointment, reception and inviolability.[1]

An important fact also was that by the fifteenth and sixteenth centuries jurists had begun to take into account the evolution of a community of independent sovereign states and to think and write about different problems of the law of nations, realising the necessity for some body of rules to regulate certain aspects of the relations between such states. Where there were no established customary rules, these jurists were obliged to devise and fashion working principles by reasoning or analogy. Not only did they draw on the principles of Roman law which had become the subject of revived study in Europe from the end of the eleventh century onwards, but they had recourse also to the precedents of ancient history, to theology, to the canon law, and to the semi-theological concept of the "law of nature," a concept which for centuries exercised a profound influence on the development of international law. Among the early writers who made important contributions to the infant science of the law of nations were . . . Belli (1502-1575), an Italian, Brunus (1491-1563), a German, . . . Suarez (1548-1617), a great Spanish Jesuit, and Gentilis (1552-1608), an Italian who became Professor of Civil Law at Oxford, and who is frequently regarded as the founder of a systematic law of nations. The writings of these early jurists reveal significantly that one major preoccupation of sixteenth century international law was the law of warfare between states, and in this connection it may be noted that by the fifteenth century the European Powers had begun to maintain standing armies, a practice which naturally caused uniform usages and practices of war to evolve.

By general acknowledgment the greatest of the early writers on international law was the Dutch scholar, jurist, and diplomat, Grotius (1583-1645), whose systematic treatise on the subject *De Jure Belli ac Pacis* (The Law of War and Peace) first appeared in 1625. On account of this treatise, Grotius has sometimes been described as the "father of the law of nations," although it is maintained by some that such a description is incorrect on the grounds that his debt to the writings of Gentilis is all too evident and that in point of time he followed writers such as Belli . . . and others mentioned above. Indeed both Gentilis and Grotius owed much to their precursors.

Nor is it exact to affirm that in *De Jure Belli ac Pacis* will be found all the international law that existed in 1625. It cannot, for example, be maintained that Grotius dealt fully with the law and practice of his day as to treaties, or that his coverage of the rules and usages of warfare was entirely comprehensive. Besides, *De Jure Belli ac Pacis* was not primarily or exclusively a treatise on international law, as it embraced numerous topics of legal science, and touched on problems of theological or philosophic interest. Grotius's historical pre-eminence rests rather on his continued inspirational appeal as the creator of the first adequate comprehensive framework of the modern science of international law.

In his book, as befitted a diplomat of practical experience, and a lawyer who had practised, Grotius dealt repeatedly with the actual customs followed by the states of his day. At the same time Grotius was a theorist who espoused certain doctrines.

1. Cf. also the influence of the early codes of mercantile and maritime usage, e.g., the Rhodian Laws formulated between the seventh and the ninth centuries, the Laws or Rolls of Oleron collected in France during the twelfth century, and the Consolato del Mare as to the customs of the sea followed by Mediterranean countries and apparently collected in Spain in the fourteenth century.

One central doctrine in his treatise was the acceptance of the "law of nature" as an independent source of rules of the law of nations, apart from custom and treaties. The Grotian "law of nature" was to some extent a secularised version, being founded primarily on the dictates of reason, on the rational nature of men as social human beings, and in that form it was to become a potent source of inspiration to later jurists.

Grotius has had an abiding influence upon international law and international lawyers, although the extent of this influence has fluctuated at different periods. . . . While it would be wrong to say that his views were always treated as being of compelling authority—frequently they were the object of criticism—nevertheless his principal work, *De Jure Belli ac Pacis*, was continually relied upon as a work of reference and authority in the decisions of courts, and in the textbooks of later writers of standing. Also several Grotian doctrines have left their mark on, and are implicit in the character of modern international law, namely, the distinction between just and unjust war, the recognition of the rights and freedoms of the individual, the doctrine of qualified neutrality, the idea of peace, and the value of periodic conferences between the rulers of states. Nor should it be forgotten that for over three centuries Grotius was regarded as the historic standard-bearer of the doctrine of the freedom of the seas by reason of his authorship of the work, *Mare Liberum*, published in 1609.

The history of the law of nations during the two centuries after Grotius was marked by the final evolution of the modern state-system in Europe, a process greatly influenced by the Treaty of Westphalia of 1648 marking . . . the end of the Thirty Years' War, and by the development from usage and practice of a substantial body of new customary rules. Even relations and intercourse by treaty or otherwise between European and Asian governments or communities contributed to the formation of these rules. Moreover the science of international law was further enriched by the writings and studies of a number of great jurists. Side by side there proceeded naturally a kind of action and reaction between the customary rules and the works of these great writers; not only did their systematic treatment of the subject provide the best evidence of the rules, but they suggested new rules or principles where none had yet emerged from the practice of states. The influence of these great jurists on the development of international law was considerable, as can be seen from their frequent citation by national courts during the nineteenth century and even up to the present time.

. . . In the eighteenth century, there was a growing tendency among jurists to seek the rules of international law mainly in custom and treaties, and to relegate to a minor position the "law of nature," or reason, as a source of principles. . . . There were, however, jurists who at the same time clung to the traditions of the law of nature, either almost wholly, or coupled with a lesser degree of emphasis upon custom and treaties as components of international law. As contrasted with these adherents to the law of nature, writers . . . who attached primary or major weight to customary and treaty rules were known as "positivists."

In the nineteenth century international law further expanded. This was due to a number of factors which fall more properly within the scope of historical studies, for instance, the further rise of powerful new states both within and outside Europe, the expansion of European civilisation overseas, the modernisation of world transport, the greater destructiveness of modern warfare, and the influence of new inventions. All these made it urgent for the international society of states to acquire a system of rules which would regulate in an ordered manner the conduct of international affairs. There was a remarkable development during the century in the law of war and neutrality, and the great increase in adjudications by international arbitral tribunals following the *Alabama Claims Award* of 1872 provided an important new source of rules and principles. Besides, states commenced to acquire the habit of negotiating general treaties in order to regulate affairs of mutual concern. Nor was the nineteenth century without its great writers on international law. . . . The general tendency of these writers was to concentrate on existing practice, and to discard the concept of the "law of nature," although not abandoning recourse to reason and justice where, in the absence of custom or treaty rules, they were called upon to speculate as to what should be the law.

Other important developments have taken place in the twentieth century. The Permanent Court of Arbitration was established by the Hague Conferences of 1899 and 1907. The Permanent Court of International Justice was set up in 1921 as an authoritative international judicial tribunal, and was succeeded in 1946 by the present International Court of Justice.

Malcolm N. Shaw, International Law

30-31 (6th ed. 2008)

The First World War marked the close of a dynamic and optimistic century. European empires ruled the world and European ideologies reigned supreme, but the 1914-18 Great War undermined the foundations of European civilisation. Self-confidence faded, if slowly, the edifice weakened and the universally accepted assumptions of progress were increasingly doubted. Self-questioning was the order of the day and law as well as art reflected this.

The most important legacy of the 1919 Peace Treaty from the point of view of international relations was the creation of the League of Nations. The old anarchic system had failed and it was felt that new institutions to preserve and secure peace were necessary. The League consisted of an Assembly and an executive Council, but was crippled from the start by the absence of the United States and the Soviet Union for most of its life and remained a basically European organisation.

While it did have certain minor successes with regard to the maintenance of international order, it failed when confronted with determined aggressors. Japan invaded China in 1931 and two years later withdrew from the League. Italy attacked Ethiopia, and Germany embarked unhindered upon a series of internal and external aggressions. The Soviet Union, in a final gesture, was expelled from the organisation in 1939 following its invasion of Finland.

Nevertheless much useful groundwork was achieved by the League in its short existence and this helped to consolidate the United Nations later on.

The Permanent Court of International Justice was set up in 1921 at The Hague and was succeeded in 1946 by the International Court of Justice. The International Labour Organisation was established soon after the end of the First World War and still exists today, and many other international institutions were inaugurated or increased their work during this period.

Other ideas of international law that first appeared between the wars included the system of mandates, by which colonies of the defeated powers were administered by the Allies for the benefit of their inhabitants rather than being annexed outright, and the attempt was made to provide a form of minority protection guaranteed by the League. This latter creation was not a great success but it paved the way for later concern to secure human rights.

After the trauma of the Second World War the League was succeeded in 1946 by the United Nations Organisation, which tried to remedy many of the defects of its predecessor. It established its site at New York, reflecting the realities of the shift of power away from Europe, and determined to become a truly universal institution. The advent of decolonisation fulfilled this expectation and the General Assembly of the United Nations currently has 192 member states.

Many of the trends which first came to prominence in the nineteenth century have continued to this day. The vast increase in the number of international agreements and customs, the strengthening of the system of arbitration and the development of international organisations have established the essence of international law as it exists today.

Professor Carter briefly describes the extraordinary developments in international institutions and law that occurred right after World War II and the remarkable evolution that occurred in the last 60 years.

Barry E. Carter, Making Progress in International Law and Institutions*

From Progress in International Institutions (Russell Miller and Rebecca Bratspies eds., 2008) [updated through December 2010]

I. The Creation and Evolution of International Institutions

The vast destruction and searing experience of the Second World War led the victorious Allied leaders to try creatively to build the political and economic structures necessary to avoid further world wars and depressions. The central institution was to be the United Nations. Its primary purpose was to prevent military conflict among its members and to settle international disputes. As a supplement to the U.N., the International Court of Justice (ICJ or World Court) was established as the formal judicial body to resolve legal disputes among nations.

Other key international institutions were designed to deal with economic issues. The International Monetary Fund (IMF) was created to promote international monetary cooperation and stability in foreign exchange. The tremendous economic instability in the period before World War II had been triggered in

*This article draws considerably upon an earlier article by Professor John H. Barton of Stanford and Professor Carter, International Law and Institutions for a New Age, 81 Geo. L.J. (1992). In some parts it is an update of that work.

part by rapid fluctuations in the value of individual nations' currencies and numerous currency restrictions. The International Bank for Reconstruction and Development (or World Bank) was established to help provide funds for the reconstruction of war-ravaged nations and to promote economic development.

An International Trade Organization (ITO) was planned as an institution to provide a structure and enforcement for rules that would regularize and encourage international trade. The worldwide economic problems of the 1930s had also been caused in part by the high tariff barriers adopted by the United States and other countries. U.S. congressional opposition to the ITO, however, meant that the organization never came into existence. A subsidiary agreement, the General Agreement on Tariffs and Trade (GATT), was allowed instead to metamorphose into a skeletal institutional arrangement.

These post-World War II institutions continue to exist today, except for the GATT, which was subsumed into the new World Trade Organization in 1995. Although these institutions have failed to achieve some of their original objectives, they have grown and evolved. The United Nations was confronted with rivalries among the five veto-wielding powers on the Security Council (the United States, Soviet Union, China, England, and France) during the Cold War that developed in the late 1940s and lasted into the early 1990s. During that time, the U.N. shifted from collective security to a new peacekeeping pattern based on the consent of the nations involved. The organization also became active in a number of other areas, such as economic development, human rights, and refugees. The end of the Cold War has seen occasional flashes of new energy in the Security Council, such as its response in 1990-91 to the Iraqi invasion of Kuwait. The organization, however, continues to be hobbled by financial crises, a sluggish bureaucracy, and opposition by some member states to an active role in maintaining peace and security. Although the ICJ's caseload has increased in the past 10-15 years, the ICJ has been much less busy and successful than its creators had hoped, partly because of its slow procedures, the requirement that only states could be parties and that states consent to the court's jurisdiction, and lack of enforcement powers.

The institutional evolution on the economic side has been much more far-reaching. The U.N. has undertaken various activities to promote economic development. Although the IMF was originally designed to support fixed exchange rates, since the 1970s when the United States went off the gold standard and most of the major industrial countries of the world moved toward flexible exchange rates, the IMF has worked to help countries maintain exchange rates within manageable bounds and to assist countries with high debt burdens. In the mid-1990s during the Asian financial crisis and later flare ups in Russia and Latin America, these IMF efforts ran into criticism from some experts that the Fund was being heavy-handed and inflexible in the conditions it demanded from struggling countries. The IMF has since more carefully targeted its activities and the conditions it places on loans.

The World Bank has switched its focus from reconstructing the war-torn countries of Europe to encouraging economic development. With an abundance of competing private capital available in the world for projects that have reasonable expectations of yielding an economic return, the World Bank has increasingly narrowed its efforts to countries that are among the poorest and that are in need of basic infrastructure and services. The IMF and World Bank have also responded constructively to criticism of their environmental and human rights records.

Although the GATT continued to develop through the 1980s and early 1990s, it remained severely limited by the absence of an institutional structure, by its coverage of only trade in goods and not other important matters such as services and intellectual property, and by its weak dispute-settlement process. Recognizing that the GATT was becoming increasingly inadequate as international trade and investment steadily grew, most of the world's nations agreed to create a successor entity, the World Trade Organization (WTO). Coming into existence in 1995, the WTO has an institutional structure, though it still is based on a one-country, one-vote system that requires unanimity on important matters. Reflecting the approximately 2,000 pages of related agreements, the WTO's scope is considerable — the agreements not only include more detailed provisions regarding trade in goods, but also cover trade in services and intellectual property, and have a few measures regulating trade-related investment.

The new WTO dispute resolution system is possibly the most influential international dispute-settlement arrangement in the world. The decisions of a WTO panel or, if appealed, of the Appellate Body, are binding on the disputing parties, except in the highly unlikely situation that all the WTO members (including the winning party in the decision) vote not to accept the report of the panel or the Appellate Body.

While these early international institutions were growing and evolving, a wide range of other international institutions developed. Entities were created to deal with new, often specialized issues, such as the International Atomic Energy Agency (IAEA) in 1957 and the U.N. Environment Programme (UNEP) in 1972. Countries with similar interests have combined in quasi-formal associations, such as the Group of Eight (the United States, Japan, Germany, France, United Kingdom, Italy, Canada, and Russia). The leaders of the Group of Eight countries might discuss a range of issues and immediate crises during one of their annual meetings. The group's record is mixed, with its best successes involving economic issues such as interest rates and exchange rates.

The emergence of regional entities has been at least as dramatic. Starting in the mid-1950s as the European Economic Community, what is now the European Union (EU) has become a vital entity on the world stage, with 27 member states, a combined population of over [490] million, and a combined Gross Domestic Product (GDP) greater than that of the United States. The EU has achieved not only a high level of economic integration, but it has attained a considerable degree of cooperation on immigration and foreign policy.

Other regional arrangements, often focused on trade and sometimes investment, have sprung up or are coming online, including the North American Free Trade Agreement (NAFTA) among Canada, Mexico, and the United States; the Association of Southeast Asian Nations (ASEAN) with 10 member states; the Common Market of the South Cone (Mercosur) with four member states in South America; and Asia-Pacific Economic Cooperation (APEC) with many countries in a loose affiliation. Regional development banks, which substantially supplement the work of the World Bank, exist for Latin America, Asia, Africa, and Eastern Europe.

On the judicial front, the European Court of Justice, one of the EU institutions, and the separate European Court of Human Rights are both active and effective, and the Inter-American Court has recently shown new vigor. Besides regional courts, there has been a growth of specialized international courts. The Law of the Sea Convention led to the creation of the International Tribunal for the Law of the Sea in 1996, and specific conflicts led to the establishment of several special war crimes tribunals, such as the International Criminal Tribunal for Yugoslavia. More recently, the International Criminal Court began operation in 2003.

Beyond such international and regional entities, there are a vast array of new bilateral and multilateral agreements that involve varying degrees of cooperation across a country's borders on a host of issues—ranging from protecting the ozone layer, to combating terrorism, safeguarding diplomatic personnel, establishing free-trade areas, and enforcing arbitral awards.

II. The Changes in International Law

The creation and evolution of various international and regional entities has been paralleled by substantial changes in international law. Most importantly, (1) the individual has become a recognized actor along with states and international organizations; and (2) national, regional, and international tribunals—both judicial and arbitral—have become much more active and effective in enforcing international legal norms.

A. The Individual's Role

The traditional concept of international law was generally one of law between nation states. As late as 1963, a respected English treatise defined public international law as "the body of rules and principles of action which are binding upon civilized states in their relations with one another."

After World War II, the scope of international law expanded from states to include the new international and regional institutions. For example, U.N. organs and agencies were allowed to seek advisory opinions from the ICJ, which was otherwise restricted to disputes among states.

Individuals and, more broadly, persons (a term which also includes corporations and other organizations) have become increasingly accepted as independent actors, subject to and benefiting from international law. This dramatic development had its origins in efforts by states to protect their nationals investing and engaged in business abroad from expropriation or other mistreatment by a host country. Under traditional international law, an investor's home country was considered injured by the host country's mistreatment, and it was up to the home country to seek redress by using diplomatic pressure and sometimes resorting to arbitration. The investor, however, sought independent protection. Many host countries came to recognize the benefits of foreign investment and of resolving disputes with investors. A trend developed toward arbitration between the investor and the host government by a panel that might apply international legal norms.

This trend was part of a much larger development in which the traditional barriers between so-called "public" and "private" international law have eroded and often broken down. Besides the traditional public international law with rules for relations among states, there has long been private international law dealing with the activities of individuals, corporations, and other private entities when their activities crossed national borders. This was particularly true in the "lex mercatoria," or law merchant, which had its origins in the commercial renaissance in

Europe in the eleventh and twelfth centuries, fueled in part by trade with the East. The law merchant developed further in the English common law, and became accepted in the United States for many years.[4] The law merchant still exists as customary international law in, for instance, the often-followed rules for delivery terms (e.g., free-on-board or FOB) and letters of credit published by the International Chamber of Commerce. It has been codified, for example, by U.S. states in the Uniform Commercial Code and accepted in a widely-ratified treaty, the U.N. Convention for Contracts on the International Sale of Goods.[5]

The distinctions between public and private international law have also become increasingly artificial because many states and their instrumentalities have entered the marketplace in a major way—either as traders themselves or to influence industrial policy—and because business and foreign policy have become increasingly intertwined. For example, Iraq's invasion of Kuwait in 1990 and the resulting U.N. economic sanctions involved such traditional issues of public international law as the use of force and sovereignty. However, the implementation of the sanctions significantly affected U.S. and European corporations that did business with Iraq or Kuwait. Other examples of public-private matters include foreign passenger jets crossing national borders and landing at government owned airports and long-term agreements for foreign oil companies to take oil from government-owned coastal areas. Courts, national governments, and international organizations struggle with such issues. Thus, when the European Court of Justice was being developed in the mid-1950s, the countries involved decided that persons, as well as member states, would be allowed standing to challenge Community actions.

The human rights area has occasioned probably the greatest expansion of individual rights and responsibilities under international law. A major step occurred with the response to Nazi Germany's treatment of Jews and other minorities before and during World War II. The Allies adopted the Nuremberg Charter and proceeded after the war with trials of many German Nazis for crimes against not only foreign individuals, but also against German citizens—thus recognizing that the citizens of a state should have some international law protection against even their own government.

Today, there are many widely-ratified treaties, as well as customary international law, that recognize a broad range of human rights, such as the right to be free from official torture.[6] As discussed below, these rights can sometimes even be enforced in a country's domestic courts. In Europe, they can also be enforced before the European Court of Human Rights, which allows individuals to complain against a state that is party to the underlying European Convention for the Protection of

4. In 1842, Justice Story, speaking for a unanimous Supreme Court, wrote in Swift v. Tyson, 41 U.S. (16 Pet.) 1 (1842), "The law respecting negotiable instruments may be truly declared . . . to be in a greater measure, not the law of a single country, but of the commercial world."

5. Harold J. Berman, The Law of International Commercial Transactions (*Lex Mercatoria*), in A Lawyer's Guide to International Business Transactions 1, 5-7 (Walter Sterling Surrey & Don Wallace, Jr., Eds. 1983); *see* Harold Hongju Koh, Dean, Yale Law School, On Law and Globalization, Address at the Annual Meeting of the American Law Institute, May 17, 2006.

6. E.g., International Covenant on Civil and Political Rights, art. 7, Dec. 16, 1966, 999 U.N.T.S. 171 (adopted by over 150 countries, including the United States); Convention Against Torture and Other Cruel, Inhuman, or Degrading Treatment, Dec. 10, 1984, 24 I.L.M. 535 (1985) (over 135 parties to the convention, including the United States); Geneva Convention Relative to the Protection of Civilian Persons in Time of War, art. 3, Aug. 12, 1949, International Committee of the Red Cross (over 190 parties to this and three other Geneva Conventions, including the United States).

Human Rights and Fundamental Freedoms, and the European Court of Justice can address human rights issues in some cases.

B. The Role of International, Regional, and National Tribunals

Equally dramatic as the emergence of the role of the individual in international law is the impressive change and proliferation of mechanisms available to enforce international law.

A traditional, and still important, international enforcement mechanism is reciprocity. For example, a country will often comply with the well-accepted international norms protecting embassies and diplomats because the country realizes that it wants its own embassies and diplomats to be protected by other countries.

The best-known adjudicatory body for international law has been the International Court of Justice (ICJ). It will probably continue to be an important forum for resolving some legal issues between states, including boundary disputes. However, as noted above, the ICJ's caseload has not been heavy, in part because of its slow procedures, the requirement that only states could be parties, and the lack of useful enforcement powers. Although states have complied with the Court's judgments in many cases, there have been some notable exceptions. The U.N. Charter provides that the Security Council may "decide upon measures to be taken to give effect to the [Court's] judgment," but the Security Council has yet to do so.

Although the ICJ has taken steps in recent years to speed up its procedures and be more active, the real growth in formal dispute resolution is occurring in international arbitration, other international and regional courts, and national courts.

1. Arbitration

The rapid growth of cross-border trade and business after World War II led to increased acceptance of international arbitration to settle disputes between a state and a private party (e.g., a foreign investor) or between private parties caught up in, for example, an international trade or investment dispute.

Arbitration has the advantage of flexibility. Parties can choose the place of arbitration and the number, specialization, and even identity of the arbitrators; they can select the procedural rules (including those governing confidentiality and discovery); and they can specify the substantive rules (e.g., an individual country's laws, general principles of international law, and even specially-drafted provisions). This flexibility makes arbitration particularly useful in disputes between countries and investors or between people with economic interests in different nations. Arbitration also involves finality, with the decision of the arbitrator(s) usually not subject to any appellate procedure. Cutting against these advantages is that fact that arbitration, unless carefully managed, can be expensive because the parties compensate the arbitrators and provide the facilities. Also, an arbitrator generally does not have the legal authority to order discovery against persons not parties to the arbitral agreement.

Major impetus for international arbitration was provided by the 1958 New York Convention on the Recognition and Enforcement of Foreign Arbitral Awards (N.Y.

Convention). It has been ratified by over [140] countries, including the United States and all the other major industrialized countries. This treaty provides that, subject to very narrow exceptions, a decision by an international arbitral tribunal sitting in a contracting state will be enforced by the domestic courts of any other contracting country as if the decision were by that domestic court. As a result, a winning party in an international arbitration can usually be assured of collecting against a recalcitrant losing party if the loser has assets — bank accounts, real estate, goods — in any one of the N.Y. Convention countries. It is only necessary to take the arbitral award to the local court for authority to have the assets seized under local law. The U.S. Supreme Court and other nations' courts have generally been strongly supportive of international arbitration in recent years.

Libya's Colonel Qaddafi learned first-hand of this Convention in the 1970s. After he led a military coup over a moderate government, Qaddafi nationalized valuable interests in foreign oil companies operating in Libya. These oil companies had entered into long-term agreements with the prior government, under which the companies were entitled to submit any dispute to arbitration and the principles of international law. Qaddafi claimed that the nationalization decree invalidated these contract provisions and that the companies had to see redress in Libya's domestic courts. The oil companies disagreed and sought arbitration.

The arbitration agreements for three different companies each contained provisions that allowed the appointment of a sole arbitrator even if Libya refused to cooperate. Each of the arbitrators decided that he had jurisdiction over the particular company's dispute and each arbitrator ultimately entered awards against Libya. Qaddafi apparently refused to comply with the decisions, but he eventually agreed to pay tens of millions of dollars. Had Libya tried to resist paying, the successful companies could have moved to enforce their arbitral awards against Libya in, say, Italy, Germany, Switzerland, or any of the other N.Y. Convention countries where Libyan oil, bank accounts, airplanes, or other assets could be found and attached.

As a result of arbitration's flexibility, finality, and enforceability, it has been a growth industry in the last sixty years. For example, [817] requests for international arbitration were filed in [2009] with the International Chamber of Commerce (ICC). Although the ICC is designed to handle commercial disputes, in [10%] of its cases at least one of the parties was a state or parastatal entity, such as government-owned utilities or airlines. Similarly, the American Arbitration Association (AAA) has handled over 600 cases per year.

The World Bank created the International Centre for the Settlement of Investment Disputes (ICSID) to resolve disputes between foreign investors and the host country through conciliation and arbitration. ICSID's own multilateral convention has enforcement provisions similar to those in the N.Y. Convention. Although ICSID began slowly in 1965, its pace of activity has quickened, with 25 new cases in 2005.

Contributing to the renewed acceptance of international arbitration by states has been the success of the Iran-U.S. Claims Tribunal. It was created by the Algiers Accords in January 1981 as part of the arrangement that freed the U.S. hostages seized by Iran and resolved a number of outstanding monetary claims by U.S. and Iranian citizens, as well as their governments, that had arisen from the events during that period. This arbitral tribunal was established in The Hague, Netherlands, with the United States appointing three arbitrators and the Iranians three, and then these six picked three more arbitrators. After initial delays and wrangling among the arbitrators, and against a background of continuing friction and even occasional hostilities between the two countries, the Claims Tribunal ruled on procedural matters, helped settle some claims, and has ruled on the merits on almost all the other claims.

Another example of the preference for arbitration is the choice by Canada, the United States, and Mexico to provide creatively in the North American Free Trade Agreement (NAFTA) for arbitration, with variations, to resolve trade and investment disputes between any two of the countries or between one of the countries and a private party.

The World Trade Organization was similarly creative in adopting its binding dispute resolution system. Disagreements among contracting parties (which, with two exceptions, are countries) are initially addressed and decided by a panel usually composed of three individuals who are accepted by the parties or, if the parties disagree, selected by the WTO Director General. The panel's decision is effectively final unless a party appeals it to the "Appellate Body." The Appellate Body is composed of seven well-recognized experts, with three members sitting on an individual case. The Appellate Body's decision is effectively final.[11] This dispute system is essentially arbitration at the panel level, with the right to appeal to a judicial-like body.

This WTO dispute resolution system now has real teeth. If the losing party does not bring its laws or regulations into conformity with the WTO rules as determined by the panel or Appellate Body, the complaining party may be allowed to retaliate up to an amount equivalent to its injury, until the losing party does comply.[12]

2. *International and Regional Courts*

International law is not just the purview of the ICJ. Although it was essentially the sole international court in 1950, after the war crime trials in the Nuremburg Tribunal and other tribunals had ended, the ICJ now has plenty of company. Specialized international courts and regional courts have come into being, and international law is now more often addressed by domestic courts.

As noted before, the Law of the Sea Convention led to the creation of the International Tribunal for the International Tribunal for the Law of the Sea in 1996. This Tribunal stands as one of the alternatives, besides the ICJ or arbitration, for contracting parties to resolve disputes under the Convention. The International Criminal Court began operation in 2003, designed to exercise jurisdiction over the most serious crimes of international concern, as provided for in the Rome Statute of the International Criminal Court.[13]

11. The decision of the panel or, if appealed, the decision of the Appellate Body is effectively final because the WTO Dispute Settlement Body will not reverse it unless all the contracting parties agree. It is highly unlikely that a winning party will vote against the decision in its favor.

12. Although the WTO dispute system has real teeth, it also has an important escape route for countries that believe their domestic interests are worth protecting in the face of an adverse WTO decision. The losing country can choose to continue to endure the equivalent tariffs against it by the winning country, rather than to change a domestic law or practice that has been found inconsistent with the WTO agreements. . . .

13. http://untreaty.un.org. As of [January 2011], there were [114] parties to the Statute, though the United States is not a party.

However, the new regional courts, especially in Europe, represent the most dramatic increase in international jurisprudential activity. The European Court of Justice had over [560] cases brought to it in [2009]. ECJ decisions can override the domestic law of a member state; these decisions can be based on the Treaty of Rome that established the Community, and can look to the European Convention for the Protection of Human Rights and Fundamental Freedoms.

That Convention, to which [47] European states are parties, is an extensive bill of rights — e.g., prohibiting capital punishment and official torture. The Convention also created the European Court of Human Rights, which saw a staggering [57,100] applications filed in [2009] and reached final judgments on [2,395] applications. All the contracting states have submitted to the compulsory jurisdiction of the court and have agreed to abide by its decisions, which have normally been accepted and implemented. These decisions have covered sensitive areas such as freedom of the press, sexual orientation, and restrictions on government wiretapping. In addition, some of the member states, like France and Italy, have incorporated the European Convention's bill of rights into domestic law.

The success of these European regional courts is, in large part, a result of Europe's overall political moves toward greater integration. The European Union is obviously of vital interest to its member states. The European Court of Human Rights enjoys widespread popular support and prestige in Europe. The courts have focused jurisdiction and relatively easy access, unlike the ICJ. Judicial review, an American invention, has largely taken over in Europe, even in France, which had historically looked to a popularly-elected legislature as a defense against aristocratic judges.

3. Domestic Courts

As international trade, finance, investment, and travel have mushroomed, the domestic courts of most countries have naturally found themselves considering more and more cases that have international ramifications. These courts have sometimes declined to hear such cases because of concerns about the extraterritorial impact of their decisions, and they have developed a variety of doctrines for that purpose, such as the act of state doctrine, political question doctrine, international comity, exhaustion of local remedies, and *forum non conveniens.*

The overall and accelerating trend, however, is to hear more of these cases and effectively develop what amounts to an international common law, or what some call transnational law,[14] that lies between traditional domestic and traditional international law. This common law draws from a country's domestic statutes and court decisions that affect international matters, as well as from international treaties and the other international legal norms generally called customary international law. These doctrines of international common law, or transnational law, are often developed further by international and regional courts and by international arbitrations. Tribunals and scholars in different nations often look to one another's work to develop the harmony needed to make the system work.

14. E.g., Koh, supra note 5; *cf.* Philip C. Jessup, Transnational Law 2 (1956) (employing a broad definition that includes international law as well as all other law "which regulates actions or events that transcend national frontiers").

This international flow of legal ideas is especially important in international economic issues, in human rights issues, and in resolving jurisdictional conflicts. Thus, domestic courts will often entertain claims that foreign corporate conduct violated domestic antitrust law because of the conduct's effects or that a foreign government violated the rights of a domestic business that contracted with it.

This developing role of U.S. domestic courts has been highlighted recently in the United States in the human rights area. In Sosa v. Alvarez-Machain, 542 U.S. 692 (2004), the U.S. Supreme Court addressed the scope of the Alien Tort Statute, which allows suits by an alien for a tort in violation of the "law of nations or a treaty of the United States." Although the Court did not find a violation in the particular facts of the alleged arbitrary arrest, the six Justices in the majority opinion concluded that federal courts could recognize private claims under federal common law for a limited group of violations of international law norms — i.e., ones that had the "definite content and acceptance among civilized nations" that was comparable to the three "historical paradigms familiar when §1350 was enacted" in 1789. One such violation would appear to be official torture.[15]

Also, in Hamdan v. Rumsfeld, 126 S. Ct. 2749, 2793-97 (2006), the five-Justice majority opinion by Justice Stevens held that the military commissions created by President Bush to try al Qaeda detainees did not satisfy the requirements of so-called Common Article 3 of the 1949 Geneva Conventions. Although not deciding whether these Conventions gave rise to judicially enforceable rights for individuals in U.S. courts, *id.* at 2794, the majority struck down these commissions because the Uniform Code of Military Justice, the statutory authority for the President to establish military commissions, is conditioned upon compliance with the laws of war, including the Geneva Conventions, *id.* at 2786. Significantly, the majority found that Common Article 3 of the Geneva Conventions, which the United States had ratified, applied to the conflict against al Qaeda and thus was binding upon the U.S. Government in its treatment of al Qaeda detainees. *Id.* at 2796. . . .

Judgments by domestic courts are, of course, enforceable within their own country, just like any other judgment by the domestic court. As for foreign enforcement, such judgments are usually given considerable respect in other countries, but practices differ among nations and even among the fifty U.S. states and District of Columbia.

Domestic courts also have an influence beyond their specific judgments — their decisions are sometimes cited in other nations' courts and in the regional courts discussed above. This leads to the further development of an international common law or transnational law. It should be noted, though, that the U.S. courts have tended to consider foreign decisions much less than many foreign courts consider U.S. decisions. Recent years, however, have witnessed with some controversy a trend toward more reference to foreign decisions and laws by U.S. courts, including the U.S. Supreme Court.

15. The *Sosa* majority opinion appeared to cite with approval Filartiga v. Pena-Irala, 630 F.2d 876 (2d Cir. 1980) (finding that official torture was actionable under the ATS). 542 U.S. at 731-32.

2. *Developing Countries' Perspective*

Malcolm N. Shaw, International Law

38-41 (6th ed. 2008)

In the evolution of international affairs since the Second World War one of the most decisive events has been the disintegration of the colonial empires and the birth of scores of new states in the so-called Third World. This has thrust onto the scene states which carry with them a legacy of bitterness over their past status as well as a host of problems relating to their social, economic and political development. In such circumstances it was only natural that the structure and doctrines of international law would come under attack. The nineteenth century development of the law of nations founded upon Eurocentrism and imbued with the values of Christian, urbanised and expanding Europe did not, understandably enough, reflect the needs and interests of the newly independent states of the mid- and late twentieth century. It was felt that such rules had encouraged and then reflected their subjugation, and that changes were required.

It is basically those ideas of international law that came to fruition in the last century that have been so clearly rejected, that is, those principles that enshrined the power and domination of the West. The underlying concepts of international law have not been discarded. On the contrary, the new nations have eagerly embraced the ideas of the sovereignty and equality of states and the principles of non-aggression and non-intervention, in their search for security within the bounds of a commonly accepted legal framework.

While this new internationalisation of international law that has occurred in the last fifty years has destroyed its European-based homogenity, it has emphasised its universalist scope. The composition of, for example, both the International Court of Justice and the Security Council of the United Nations mirrors such developments. Article 9 of the Statute of the International Court of Justice points out that the main forms of civilisation and the principal legal systems of the world must be represented within the Court, and there is an arrangement that of the ten non-permanent seats in the Security Council five should go to Afro-Asian states and two to Latin American states (the others going to Europe and other states). The composition of the International Law Commission has also recently been increased and structured upon geographic lines.

The influence of the new states has been felt most of all within the General Assembly, where they constitute a majority of the 192 member states. The content and scope of the various resolutions and declarations emanating from the Assembly are proof of their impact and contain a record of their fears, hopes and concerns.

The Declaration on the Granting of Independence to Colonial Countries and Peoples of 1960, for example, enshrined the right of colonies to obtain their sovereignty with the least possible delay and called for the recognition of the principle of self-determination. This principle . . . is regarded by most authorities as a settled rule of international law although with undetermined borders. Nevertheless, it symbolises the rise of the post-colonial states and the effect they are having upon the development of international law.

Their concern for the recognition of the sovereignty of states is complemented by their support of the United Nations and its Charter and supplemented by their desire for 'economic self-determination' or the right of permanent sovereignty over natural resources. This expansion of international law into the field of economics was a major development of the twentieth century and is evidenced in myriad ways, for example, by the creation of the General Agreement on Tariffs and Trade, the United Nations Conferences on Trade and Development, and the establishment of the International Monetary Fund and World Bank.

The interests of the new states of the Third World are often in conflict with those of the industrialised nations, witness disputes over nationalisations. But it has to be emphasised that, contrary to many fears expressed in the early years of the decolonisation saga, international law has not been discarded nor altered beyond recognition. Its framework has been retained as the new states, too, wish to obtain the benefits of rules such as those governing diplomatic relations and the controlled use of force, while campaigning against rules which run counter to their perceived interests.

While the new countries share a common history of foreign dominance and underdevelopment, compounded by an awakening of national identity, it has to be recognised that they are not a homogenous group. Widely differing cultural, social and economic attitudes and stages of development characterise them, and the rubric of the 'Third World' masks diverse political affiliations. On many issues the interests of the new states conflict with each other and this is reflected in the different positions adopted. The states possessing oil and other valuable natural resources are separated from those with few or none and the states bordering on oceans are to be distinguished from landlocked states. The list of diversity is endless and variety governs the make-up of the southern hemisphere to a far greater degree than in the north.

It is possible that in legal terms tangible differences in approach may emerge in the future as the passions of decolonisation die down and the Western supremacy over international law is further eroded. This trend will also permit a greater understanding of, and greater recourse to, historical traditions and conceptions that pre-date colonisation and an increasing awareness of their validity for the future development of international law.

C. THE NATURE OF INTERNATIONAL LAW AND THE COMPLIANCE CHALLENGE: IS INTERNATIONAL LAW REALLY LAW?

At the beginning of this chapter we anticipated a certain skepticism about the effectiveness of international law. Some believe that international law is a charade: governments comply with it only if it is convenient to do so and disregard it whenever a contrary interest appears. That view seems to be based on an image of global anarchy in which independent "sovereign" states selfishly contend for unilateral advantage. Some of the traditional skepticism about international law may be attributable to the extensive attention given to the highly indeterminate and often unobserved norms against the use of force, a relatively small part of international law. In addition, the most prominent institutions in this century dedicated to advancing the rule of law among states have not lived up to the expectations of their proponents. The League of Nations failed to prevent war, and the United Nations has often proved unable to take decisive action. Some people may also suspect that international law cannot really be law because there is no effective world court or international police force.

In fact, however, the image of global anarchy is not very accurate, as the abundance of international travel, economic interdependence, and transnational cooperation amply demonstrates. And the emphasis on courts and a police force is misleading. Law derives its force from sources other than those two institutions, even in industrialized societies. For example, people often comply with legal norms because of expectations of reciprocal behavior by other members of the society or simply out of a belief that the law is legitimate and therefore ought to be obeyed. Moreover, there can be effective sanctions for breaches of international law, even without centralized adjudication and enforcement agencies, such as through arbitration or unilateral "self-help" retaliatory measures.

Professor Henkin describes the ways in which international law operates and the functions it serves in the world:

Louis Henkin, How Nations Behave: Law and Foreign Policy

13-27, 92-93, 94-95, 98 (2d ed. 1979)

As for international law, much misunderstanding is due to a failure to recognize law where it exists. That failure may be due to a narrow conception of law generally. The layman tends to think of domestic law in terms of the traffic policeman, or judicial trials for the thief or murderer. But law is much more and quite different. . . . [I]n domestic society law includes the scheme and structure of government, and the institutions, forms, and procedures whereby a society carries on its daily activities; the concepts that underlie relations between government and individual and between individuals; the status, rights, responsibilities, and obligations of individuals and incorporated and non-incorporated associations and other groups, the relations into which they enter and the consequences of these relations. Men establish families, employ one another, acquire possessions and trade them, make arrangements, join in groups for ill or good, help or hurt each other, with little thought to law and little awareness that there is law that is relevant. By law, society formalizes these relationships, creates new ones, legitimates some and forbids others, determines the content and consequences of relationships. The individual remains hardly or hazily aware that he is enmeshed and governed by "law"—laws of property, tort, contract, crimes, laws of marriage, divorce, family, inheritance, laws of employment, commerce, association; and that there are procedures and institutions and formalities which are ever there and maintain an order in society, although they may assert themselves only at critical points, when relations are established, or change, or break down.

In relations between nations, too, one tends to think of law as consisting of a few prohibitory rules (for instance, that a government may not arrest another's diplomats) or the law of the U.N. Charter prohibiting war. . . . But international law, too, is much more and quite different. Although there is no international "government," there is an international "society"; law includes the structure of that society, its institutions, forms, and procedures for daily activity, the assumptions on which the society is founded and the concepts which permeate it, the status, rights, responsibilities, obligations of the nations which comprise that society, the various relations between them, and the effects of those relations. Through what we call foreign policy, nations establish, maintain, change, or terminate myriads of relations; law — more or less primitive, more or less sophisticated — has developed to formalize these relationships, to regulate them, to determine their consequences. A major purpose of foreign policy for most nations at most times is to maintain international order so that they can pursue their national interests, foreign and domestic. That order depends on an "infrastructure" of agreed assumptions, practices, commitments, expectations, reliances. These too are international law, and they are reflected in all that governments do.

To move from the abstract, consider some of the "givens" of international relations. First, they are relations between nations (states). The nation is the principal unit. All the forms of intercourse, all the institutions, all the terms even, depend on the existence of "nations." . . . That political society is based on the nation is not commonly seen as involving either policy or law; ordinarily, nationhood is the unspoken assumption of political life. But the nation ("state") is not only a political conception; it is also a fundamental legal construct with important consequences. Statehood — who is and shall be a state — has been one of the major political issues of our day. The legal concept of statehood is crucial, of course, when the character of an entity as a state is itself in issue. . . . It was raised when Palestine was partitioned and Israel created and underlies the recent claims of Palestinians to a state of their own. It was entangled in the question of Chinese representation in the United Nations and still bedevils the future of Taiwan. The "nation" has been in issue in differences over recognition of divided countries and their membership in international organizations — China, Korea, Vietnam, Germany. The legal concept and consequences of nationhood underlie the explosion of "self-determination" which ended Western colonialism and transformed the map of the world, and have troubled even the new nations. . . . It still deeply troubles Cyprus, and also Kashmir. . . . Relations between nations generally begin with "housekeeping arrangements," including recognition and establishment of diplomatic relations. That these involve law (e.g., in regard to recognition, sovereign and diplomatic immunities) is commonly known, but the importance of this law for foreign policy is commonly depreciated. In fact, this law is basic and indispensable, and taken for granted because it rarely breaks down. The newest of nations promptly adopts it and the most radical scrupulously observes it. The occasional exception confirms the obvious, that there would be no relations with a nation that regularly violated embassies and abused diplomats. . . .

The relations of one nation with another, as soon as they begin, are permeated by basic legal concepts: nationality, national territory, property, torts, contracts, the rights and duties and responsibilities of states. These do not commonly figure in major policy doctrines, nor do they commonly occupy the attentions of diplomats. They too are taken for granted because they are rarely in issue. The concept of territory and territorial sovereignty is not prominent in foreign policy; but every foreign policy assumes the integrity and inviolability of the national territory, and any intentional violation would probably lead to major crisis. . . .

Related to territoriality is the concept of internal sovereignty. Except as limited by international law or treaty, a nation is master in its own territory. That principle is fundamental, and commonly observed. Yet it is in issue whenever there is a claim that internal action violates international law. It figures in disputes about nationalization of alien properties and about violations of human rights. . . .

The concepts of property lie deep in international relations. Property rights are taken for granted in all international trade and finance. When a vessel plies the seas, the assumption is that others will observe the international law prohibiting interference with free navigation, recognizing rights of ownership in property, forbidding torts against persons and property. . . .

Law is also essential to foreign policy and to diplomacy in that it provides mechanisms, forms, and procedures by which nations maintain their relations, carry on trade and other forms of intercourse, resolve differences and disputes. There is international law in the establishment and operation of missions and in communications between governments, in the writing of contracts and other commercial paper, in oil concessions, in tariffs and customs practices, in the registry of vessels, the shipment of goods, the forms of payment, in all the intricacies of international trade and finance. . . . For settling disputes, the law provides diplomats with claims commissions, arbitration bodies, mediators and conciliators, even courts.

For foreign policy, perhaps the most important legal mechanism is the international agreement, and the most important principle of international law is *pacta sunt servanda*: agreements shall be observed. This principle makes international relations possible. The mass of a nation's foreign relations involve innumerable agreements of different degrees of formality. The diplomat promotes, develops, negotiates, implements various understandings for various ends, from establishing diplomatic relations to trade, aid, allocation of resources, cultural exchange, common standards of weights and measures, to formal alliances affecting national security, cease-fire and disengagement, arms control, and a regime for outer space. The diplomat hardly thinks of these arrangements and understandings as involving law. He does assume that, if agreement is reached, it will probably be observed; if he did not, he would not bother to seek agreement. No doubt, he thinks that nations generally observe their undertakings because that is "done" in international society and because it is generally in the interest of nations to do so. That is law, the lawyer would say. . . .

. . . Even nations that wish to escape from such arrangements are usually compelled to invoke legal principles of escape — whether by reinterpreting the agreement, by attacking its original validity, or by invoking some principle of law to claim that it permits escape or is no longer valid or binding.

In our times, there flourishes a type of international agreement that has added new dimensions to foreign policy and international law. Much of contemporary international law consists of new arrangements, often among large numbers of nations, to promote cooperation for some common aim. In this category one might place the various intergovernmental organizations and institutions, universal or regional — the United Nations, the World Bank and the Monetary Fund, the FAO, UPU, ITU and the IAEA, OECD, [WTO], the International Coffee Agreement and UNCTAD, NATO and the European Economic Community, the OAS and [AU] . . . — as well as bilateral aid agreements. . . .

Law reflected in the assumptions, concepts, institutions, and procedures of international society is not the kind of international law one commonly thinks about because it does not, on its face, direct governments how to behave. But, in fact, all law is intimately related to national behavior. Even that "submerged" law molds the policies of governments. The concept of the nation determines that the United States has relations with Canada, not with Quebec. The concept of territoriality means that the United States can do largely as it likes within the United States, but is sharply restricted in what it can do outside. There are clear prohibitions in the basic legal concepts, in the rights and duties they imply: territoriality, property, tort imply that the United States cannot, at will, invade or violate the territory or seize the property of another nation. Freedom of the seas means that one nation cannot prevent the vessels of others from going their way. Contracts and agreements are not to be broken. Even organizations for cooperative welfare, though commonly distinguished from traditional law of "abstention," impose obligations on members which they must "abstain" from violating: they may not interfere with the international mails; they must pay budget assessments to the FAO. . . .

The student of foreign affairs may grant, if the lawyer insists, that the law implied in international society gives some direction to national policies and places some limitations on how nations behave. But he remains skeptical of the influence of law as it is commonly and more narrowly conceived, of that law which seeks to control the conduct of nations within the framework of the society of nations. In particular, he questions whether nations really observe the important prohibitory norms of international law or really keep their important agreements. Governments may sometimes act consistently with norms or obligations, but, he insists, only when it is in their interest to do so; and it is their interest, not the law, which governs their behavior. Such skepticism in the diplomat and the policy-maker is sometimes reflected in the foreign policies they promulgate and carry out.

The tendency to dismiss international law reflects impressions sometimes summed up in the conclusion that it is not really law because international society is not really a society: the world of nations is a collection of sovereign states, not an effective body politic which can support effective law. In this judgment are subsumed a number of alleged weaknesses and inadequacies.

The society of nations has no effective law-making body or process. General law depends on consensus: in principle, new law, at least, cannot be imposed on any state; even old law cannot survive if enough states, or a few powerful and influential ones, reject it. New universal law, then, can come about only through long, gradual, uncertain "accretion" by practice and acquiescence, or through multilateral treaties difficult to negotiate and more difficult to get accepted. Law is also slow and difficult to clarify, or amend, or repeal. The law is therefore haphazard and static. As concerns customary law in particular, there is often uncertainty and little confidence as to what it is. The law is also inadequate, for many important actions and relations remain unregulated. There are important disorders—for example, the arms race or the oil embargo—which are not subject to law. In the absence of special undertakings, nations may engage in economic warfare, may boycott, even starve each other. And law has not achieved a welfare society: there is no law requiring social and economic assistance by the very rich to the very poor, or providing community relief even to the starving.

Also lacking is an effective judiciary to clarify and develop the law, to resolve disputes impartially, and to impel nations to observe the law. The International Court of Justice does not satisfy these needs. Its jurisdiction and procedures are starkly insufficient: jurisdiction requires the consent of the parties, and few consent to it; only a minority of nations have accepted the Court's compulsory jurisdiction, some of these with important reservations. . . . The Court's justice is slow, expensive, uncertain: even nations which can invoke the Court's compulsory jurisdiction are reluctant to do so. Nations still prefer the flexibility of diplomacy to the risks of third-party judgment. In the result, few issues of substantial significance to international order ever get to the Court. No one would claim that the Court has a major influence in international affairs.

The greatest deficiency, as many see it, is that international society lacks an executive authority with power to enforce the law. There is no police system whose pervasive presence might deter violation. The society does not consider violations to be crimes or violators criminals, and attaches no stigma which might itself discourage violation. Since nations cannot be made to observe rules and keep promises, they will not do so when they deem it in their interest not to do so. . . .

In sum, to many an observer, governments seem largely free to decide whether to agree to new law, whether to accept another nation's view of existing law, whether to comply with agreed law. International law, then, is voluntary and only hortatory. It must always yield to national interest. Surely, no nation will submit to law any questions involving its security or independence, even its power, prestige, influence. Inevitably, a diplomat holding these views will be reluctant to build policy on law he deems ineffective. He will think it unrealistic and dangerous to enact laws which will not be observed, to build institutions which will not be used, to base his government's policy on the expectation that other governments will observe law or agreement. Since other nations do not attend to law except when it is in their interest, the diplomat might not see why his government should do so at the sacrifice of important interests. He might be impatient with his lawyers who tell him that the government may not do what he would like to see done.

These depreciations of international law challenge much of what the international lawyer does. Indeed, some lawyers seem to despair for international law until there is world government or at least effective international organization. But most international lawyers are not dismayed. Unable to deny the limitations of international law, they insist that these are not critical, and they deny many of the alleged implications of these limitations. If they must admit that the cup of law is half-empty, they stress that it is half-full. . . . They insist that despite inadequacies in legislative method, international law has grown and developed and changed. If international law is difficult to make, yet it is made; if its growth is slow, yet it grows. If there is no judiciary as effective as in some developed national systems, there is an International Court of Justice whose judgments and opinions, while few, are respected. The inadequacies of the judicial system are in some measure supplied by other bodies: international disputes are resolved and law is developed through a network of arbitrations by continuing or ad hoc tribunals. National courts help importantly to determine, clarify, develop international law. Political bodies like the Security Council and the General Assembly of the United Nations also apply law, their actions and resolutions interpret and develop the law, their judgments help to deter violations in some measure. If there is no international executive to enforce international law, the United Nations has some enforcement powers and there is "horizontal enforcement" in the reactions of other nations. The gaps in substantive law are real and many and require continuing effort to fill them, but they do not vitiate the force and effect of the law that exists, in the international society that is.

Above all, the lawyer will insist, critics of international law ask and answer the wrong questions. What matters is not whether the international system has legislative, judicial, or executive branches, corresponding to those we have become accustomed to seek in a domestic society; what matters is whether international law is reflected in the policies of nations and in relations between nations. The question is not whether there is an effective legislature; it is whether there is law that responds and corresponds to the changing needs of a changing society. The question is not whether there is an effective judiciary, but whether disputes are resolved in an orderly fashion in accordance with international law. Most important, the question is not whether law is enforceable or even effectively enforced; rather, whether law is observed, whether it governs or influences behavior, whether international behavior reflects stability and order. The fact is, lawyers insist, that nations have accepted important limitations on their sovereignty, that they have observed these norms and undertakings, that the result has been substantial order in international relations.

In the end, the issues do not turn on theoretical answers to theoretical questions, or on unexamined impressions or assertions about the fate and influence of law in the chancelleries of nations. We must examine as well as we can the role that law, in fact, plays in daily diplomacy, the extent to which law, in fact, affects the behavior of nations, the contribution which law, in fact, makes to order and welfare. . . .

Too much is made of the fact that nations act not out of "respect for law" but from fear of the consequences of breaking it. And too much is made of the fact that the consequences are not "punishment" by "superior," legally constituted authority, but are the response of the victim and his friends and the unhappy results for friendly relations, prestige, credit, international stability, and other interests which in domestic society would be considered "extra-legal." The fact is that, in domestic society, individuals observe law principally from fear of consequences, and there are "extra-legal" consequences that are often enough to deter violation, even were official punishment lacking. . . . In the mainstreams of domestic society an illegal action tends to bring social opprobrium and other extra-legal "costs" of violation. This merely emphasizes that law often coincides so clearly with the interests of the society that its members react to antisocial behavior in ways additional to those prescribed by law. In international society, law observance must depend more heavily on these extra-legal sanctions, which means that law observance will depend more closely on the law's current acceptability and on the community's — especially the victim's — current interest in vindicating it. It does not mean that law is not law, or that its observance is less law observance. . . .

In large part, . . . the argument that nations do pursuant to law only what they would do anyhow is plain error. The fact that particular behavior is required by law brings to play those ultimate advantages in law observance that suppress temptations and override the apparent immediate advantages from acting otherwise. . . . In regard to treaties, surely, it is not the case that nations act pursuant to agreement as they would have acted if there were none, or if it were not established that agreements should be observed. Nations do not give tariff concessions, or extradite persons, or give relief from double taxation, except for some *quid pro quo* pursuant to an agreement which they expect to be kept. Nations may do some things on the basis of tacit understanding or on a conditional reciprocal basis: If you admit my goods, I will admit yours. But that too is a kind of agreement, and usually nations insist on the confidence and stability that come with an express undertaking. . . .

Whether, in the total, there is an effective "international order" is a question of perspective and definition. Order is not measurable, and no purpose is served by attempts to "grade" it in a rough impressionistic way. How much of that order is attributable to law is a question that cannot be answered in theory or in general, only in time and context. Law is one force — an important one among the forces that govern international relations at any time; the deficiencies of international society make law more dependent on other forces to render the advantages of observance high, the costs of violation prohibitive.

Notes and Questions

1. Summarize Henkin's main points. Has he convinced you that international law is "law"? In a now famous statement, Henkin declared that "almost all nations observe almost all principles of international law and almost all of their obligations almost all of the time." Henkin, How Nations Behave: Law and Foreign Policy 47 (2d ed. 1979). Do you agree that international law has a significant effect on national behavior?

2. Is it accurate to describe compliance with international law as "voluntary"? Why is there compliance with law in domestic systems? Are the reasons for compliance in the international system different? What sanctions can be imposed for violations of international law?

3. What differences are there between the legal institutions in the international community and those in domestic systems, such as in the United States? What are the similarities? Is a centralized legislature necessary in order for there to be law? How about a court with general, compulsory jurisdiction? An executive agency with enforcement powers?

4. It is easy to think of examples, of course, in which states have acted in violation of international law. Does this show that international law is not really "law"? Is it easy to think of examples of violations of domestic law?

5. Henkin argues that nations accept legal restraints on their behavior in order to secure the "ultimate advantages" of law observance. Does the fact that states may comply with an international rule to gain the benefits of reciprocal performance of that rule by other states affect your view of whether international law is law? When might a state be tempted to violate even such a reciprocal international legal norm — governing, for example, protection of diplomats, rights over the sea, or nonuse of force? Under what circumstances do the short-term benefits of violating a legal rule outweigh the "ultimate advantages" of a stable system in which all nations benefit from compliance with the rules? If a state violates the law, is it less likely to gain the benefits of the restraints international law imposes on other nations?

6. Much of the debate about whether international law is law assumes a clear dichotomy between what is "law" and "not law." Some international relations theorists, in comparison, offer a more nuanced approach that focuses on the degree to which a rule or norm is "legalized." The degree of legalization of a norm depends on three variables: (1) "obligation," or the binding character of a rule or commitment; (2) "precision," or the specificity of the rule of commitment; and (3) "delegation," or the degree to which third parties have been granted authority to implement, interpret, and apply the rule, to resolve disputes about it, and to make further rules related to it. See Kenneth W. Abbott, Robert O. Keohane,

Andrew Moravcsik, Anne-Marie Slaughter & Duncan Snidal, The Concept of Legalization, 54 Int'l Org. 401 (2000). To what extent are different rules of international law "legalized" under this kind of framework?

Most international law is found either in international agreements or in rules based on custom. That much is not controversial. A central question that has vexed international law advocates, and that has fueled the skepticism about international law, is how it can bind "sovereign" states. This debate has often been couched in terms of the legal theories (summarized below) known as "positivism" and "natural law."

Of course, if a "sovereign state" is defined as one that is not subject to law, the definition answers the question. Some commentators (the positivists) have tried to accept that definition and then to create a theory of why sovereign states are still bound by international law based on the proposition that such states *consent* to be bound by international law. Restatement section 102, quoted above, seems to follow this path. The theory is obviously incomplete, to say the least, because it does not explain why consent is binding or why it cannot be revoked.

Other commentators have sought to base the validity of international law on some fundamental principle, like earlier natural law scholastics who appealed to the commands of God, or those who rested their arguments on right, reason, and a secular law of nature. Professor Brierly summarizes the traditional debate:

J. L. Brierly, The Law of Nations

49-56 (Humphrey Waldock ed., 6th ed. 1963)

Traditionally there are two rival doctrines which attempt to answer the question why states should be bound to observe the rules of international law.

The doctrine of "fundamental rights" is a corollary of the doctrine of the "state of nature," in which men are supposed to have lived before they formed themselves into political communities or states; for states, not having formed themselves into a super-state, are still supposed by the adherents of this doctrine to be living in such a condition. It teaches that the principles of international law, or the primary principles upon which the others rest, can be deduced from the essential nature of the state. Every state, by the very fact that it is a state, is endowed with certain fundamental, or inherent, or natural, rights. Writers differ in enumerating what these rights are, but generally five rights are claimed, namely self-preservation, independence, equality, respect, and intercourse. It is obvious that the doctrine of fundamental rights is merely the old doctrine of the natural rights of man transferred to states. . . .

[Brierly then criticizes the idea of "natural" rights on the grounds that rights can only exist as part of a legal system. Moreover, the natural rights doctrine emphasizes individual rights at the expense of equally important social bonds and ignores the historical processes leading to the contemporary character of the state. He argues that the doctrine of natural rights also could inappropriately serve to inhibit movement toward the closer interdependence of states and therefore away from a global structure that the natural rights doctrine would stabilize "as though it were part of the fixed order of nature."]

The doctrine of positivism, on the other hand, teaches that international law is the sum of the rules by which states have *consented to* be bound, and that nothing can be law to which they have not consented. This consent may be given expressly, as in a treaty, or it may be implied by a state acquiescing in a customary rule. But the assumption that international law consists of nothing save what states have consented to is an inadequate account of the system as it can be seen in actual operation, and even if it were a complete account of the contents of the law, it would fail to explain why the law is binding. . . . [A] customary rule is observed, not because it has been consented to, but because it is believed to be binding, and whatever may be the explanation or the justification for that belief, its binding force does not depend, and is not felt by those who follow it to depend, on the approval of the individual or the state to which it is addressed. Further, in the practical administration of international law, states are continually treated as bound by principles which they cannot, except by the most strained construction of the facts, be said to have consented to, and it is unreasonable, when we are seeking the true nature of international rules, to force the facts into a preconceived theory instead of finding a theory which will explain the facts as we have them. For example, a state which has newly come into existence does not in any intelligible sense *consent* to accept international law; it does not regard itself, and it is not regarded by others, as having any option in the matter. The truth is that states do not regard their international legal relations as resulting from consent, except when the consent is express, and that the theory of implied consent is a fiction invented by the theorist; . . . even if the theory did not involve a distortion of the facts, it would fail as an explanation. For consent cannot of itself create an obligation; it can do so only within a system of law which declares that consent duly given, as in a treaty or a contract, shall be binding on the party consenting. To say that the rule *pacta servanda sunt* is itself founded on consent is to argue in a circle. A consistently consensual theory again would have to admit that if consent is withdrawn, the obligation created by it comes to an end. . . .

There need be no mystery about the source of the obligation to obey international law. The same problem arises in any system of law and it can never be solved by a merely *juridical* explanation. The answer must be sought outside the law, and it is for legal philosophy to provide it. The notion that the validity of international law raises some peculiar problem arises from the confusion which the doctrine of sovereignty has introduced into international legal theory. Even when we do not believe in the absoluteness of state sovereignty we have allowed ourselves to be persuaded that the fact of their sovereignty makes it necessary to look for some specific quality, not to be found in other kinds of law, in the law to which states are subject. We have accepted a false idea of the state as a personality with a life and a will of its own, still living in a "state of nature," and we contrast this with the "political" state in which individual men have come to live. But this assumed condition of states is the very negation of law, and no ingenuity can explain how the two can exist together. It is a notion as false analytically as it admittedly is historically. The truth is that states are not persons, however convenient it may often be to personify them; they are merely *institutions*, that is to say, organizations which men establish among themselves for securing certain objects, of which the most fundamental is a system of order within which the activities of their common life can be carried on. They have no wills except the wills of the individual human beings who direct their affairs; and they exist not in a political vacuum but in continuous political relations with one another. Their subjection to law is as yet imperfect, though it is real as far as it goes; the problem of extending it is one of great practical difficulty, but it is not one of intrinsic impossibility. There are important differences between international law and the law under which individuals live in a state, but those differences do not lie in metaphysics or in any mystical qualities of the entity called state sovereignty.

The international lawyer then is under no special obligation to explain why the law with which he is concerned should be binding upon its subjects. If it were true that the essence of all law is a command, and that what makes the law of the state binding is that for some reason, for which no satisfactory explanation can ever be given, the will of the person issuing a command is superior to that of the person receiving it, then indeed it would be necessary to look for some special explanation of the binding force of international law. But that view of the nature of law has been long discredited. If we are to explain why any kind of law is binding, we cannot avoid some such assumption as that which the Middle Ages made, and which Greece and Rome had made before them, when they spoke of natural law. The ultimate explanation of the binding force of all law is that man, whether he is a single individual or whether he is associated with other men in a state, is constrained, in so far as he is a reasonable being, to believe that order and not chaos is the governing principle of the world in which he has to live.

The positivist, or voluntarist, view of international law stresses that because sovereign states are one another's legal equals, no nation can impose legal restraints on another. States consequently are bound only by the particular legal restrictions to which they have consented. The Permanent Court of International Justice, predecessor to today's International Court of Justice, articulated a classic formulation of the positivist view of international law in the *Lotus* Case.

The Case of the S.S. "Lotus" (France v. Turkey)

1927 P.C.I.J. (ser. A) No. 10

[The case arose after the French steamer *Lotus* and the Turkish steamer *Boz-Kourt* collided on the high seas, resulting in the death of eight sailors and passengers aboard the *Boz-Kourt.* When the *Lotus* arrived in Constantinople, Turkish authorities initiated criminal proceedings against Lieutenant Demons, the French watch officer aboard the *Lotus.* By agreement of the parties, the Court was asked to decide whether Turkey had "acted in conflict with the principles of international law" by asserting criminal jurisdiction over a non-Turkish national for an offense occurring outside Turkish territory.]

The Court, having to consider whether there are any rules of international law which may have been violated by the prosecution in pursuance of Turkish law of Lieutenant Demons, is confronted . . . by a question of principle which . . . has proved to be a fundamental one. The French Government contends that the Turkish Courts, in order to have jurisdiction, should be able to point to some title to jurisdiction recognized by international law in favour of Turkey. On the other hand, the Turkish Government takes the view that [the exercise of Turkish jurisdiction is permissible] whenever such jurisdiction does not come into conflict with a principle of international law. . . .

[The latter view is] dictated by the very nature and existing conditions of international law.

International law governs relations between independent States. The rules of law binding upon States therefore emanate from their own free will as expressed in conventions or by usages generally accepted as expressing principles of law and established in order to regulate the relations between these co-existing independent communities or with a view to the achievement of common aims. Restrictions upon the independence of States cannot therefore be presumed.

Now the first and foremost restriction imposed by international law upon a State is that — failing the existence of a permissive rule to the contrary — it may not exercise its power in any form in the territory of another State. In this sense jurisdiction is certainly territorial; it cannot be exercised by a State outside its territory except by virtue of a permissive rule derived from international custom or from a convention.

It does not, however, follow that international law prohibits a State from exercising jurisdiction in its own territory, in respect of any case which relates to acts which have taken place abroad, and in which it cannot rely on some permissive rule of international law. Such a view would only be tenable if international law contained a general prohibition to States to extend the application of their laws and the jurisdiction of their courts to persons, property and acts outside their territory, and if, as an exception to this general prohibition, it allowed States to do so in certain specific cases. But this is certainly not the case under international law as it stands at present. . . .

In these circumstances, all that can be required of a State is that it should not overstep the limits which international law places upon its jurisdiction; within these limits, its title to exercise jurisdiction rests in its sovereignty.

It follows from the foregoing that the contention of the French Government to the effect that Turkey must in each case be able to cite a rule of international law authorizing her to exercise jurisdiction, is opposed to the generally accepted international law. . . .

Notes and Questions

1. Why is domestic law binding? What are the sources of domestic criminal law, contract law, and constitutional law? Why are those bodies of law generally followed and considered binding? Doesn't the validity of any legal norm ultimately rest on some form of fiction or partial fiction — for example, that a legislature reflects the will of the people or that a court applies neutral principles of law or legislative intent? Is international law any different? Is the role of sanctions significantly different in the case of international law?

2. Isn't consent an appealing fiction to explain the binding nature of international law? It is used to explain the value of personal choice and the basis of contract and is not limited to Western civilization. What are the problems with maintaining that the consent of a state binds it and its people?

3. Why is international law binding under a natural law approach? If the basis of authority is religion or "reason" or "nature," how do we determine the relevant rules? Does it follow that international law is based on Western cultural values and is therefore illegitimate with respect to the rest of the world?

4. Consider the following argument by Professor Jonathan Charney, particularly in light of the voluntarist approach to international law reflected in the *Lotus* case:

> The international community [today] faces an expanding need to develop universal norms to address global concerns. Perhaps one of most salient of these concerns is to protect the earth's environment. While many environmentally harmful activities result only in local damage, others have an impact far beyond the boundaries of the states in which they take place and may cause damage to the earth's environment as a whole. For example, the discharge of some substances into the atmosphere may adversely affect the global climate or the ozone layer. Discharges that pollute the common spaces of the oceans may also have a global impact and thus raise similar concerns. Current threats to the environment highlight the importance of establishing norms to control activities that endanger all nations and peoples, regardless of where the activities take place. Acts of international terrorism, the commission of international crimes (such as genocide and war crimes), and the use of nuclear weapons pose similar global problems and have been on the international agenda for some time.
>
> To resolve such problems, it may be necessary to establish new rules that are binding on all subjects of international law regardless of the attitude of any particular state. For unless all states are bound, an exempted recalcitrant state could act as a spoiler for the entire international community. Thus, states that are not bound by international laws designed to combat universal environmental threats could become havens for the harmful activities concerned. Such states might have an economic advantage over states that are bound because they would not have to bear the costs of the requisite environmental protection. They would be free riders on the system and would benefit from the environmentally protective measures introduced by others at some cost. Furthermore, the example of such free riders might undermine the system by encouraging other states not to participate, and could thus derail the entire effort. Similarly, in the case of international terrorism, one state that serves as a safe haven for terrorists can threaten all. War crimes, apartheid, or genocide committed in one state might threaten international peace and security worldwide. Consequently, for certain circumstances it may be incumbent on the international community to establish international law that is binding on all states regardless of any one state's disposition. [Jonathan I. Charney, Universal International Law, 87 Am. J. Int'l L. 529, 529-530 (1993)]

Do you agree with Professor Charney's assessment? How can the international community go about creating this sort of universal international law? How would this law be enforced? When such law is invoked against them, will nations regard it as legitimate? For a discussion of the rise of new forms of "nonconsensual international lawmaking," see Laurence R. Helfer, Nonconsensual International Lawmaking, 2008 U. Ill. L. Rev. 71 (2008).

Closely related to questions about whether international law is "law" and what makes international law binding are questions about the extent to which states comply with the requirements of international law and why they do so. Professor Franck offers an explanation of the power of international law and its basis in legitimacy:

Thomas M. Franck, Legitimacy in the International System

82 Am. J. Int'l L. 705, 705, 707-709, 712-716, 725-726, 735-736, 740-741, 751-752, 759 (1988)

The surprising thing about international law is that nations ever obey its strictures or carry out its mandates. . . .

Why should rules, unsupported by an effective structure of coercion comparable to a national police force, nevertheless elicit so much compliance, even against perceived self-interest, on the part of sovereign states? Perhaps finding an answer to this question can help us to find a key to a better, yet realistic, world order. The answer, if there is one, may also incidentally prove useful in designing more widely obeyed, less coerced, laws for ordering the lives of our cities and states. . . .

[Professor Franck recounts a 1988 episode in which the United States became aware of a ship bound for Iran with a load of Chinese-made Silkworm missiles. Even though the Department of Defense believed the successful delivery of the weapons would increase materially the danger to U.S. vessels and interests in the region, the United States did not intercept the delivery because doing so would have violated "universally recognized rules of war and neutrality" and would have constituted an "aggressive blockade, an act tantamount to a declaration of war against Iran."]

. . . Washington voluntarily chose to obey a rule in the Persian Gulf conflict. Yet it does not always obey all international rules. Some rules are harder to disobey — more persuasive in their pull to compliance — than others. This is known intuitively by the legions of Americans who deliberately underreport the dutiable price of goods purchased abroad, and by the aficionados who smuggle Cuban cigars into the country behind pocket handkerchiefs, but would not otherwise commit criminal fraud. That some rules *in themselves* seem to exert more pull to compliance than others is the starting point in the search for a theory of legitimacy. . . .

[M]ost students of law, power and structure in society have sought to identify other characteristics [besides power] that conduce to the rule of law. . . .

Four elements — the indicators of rule legitimacy in the community of states — are identified and studied in this essay. They are *determinacy, symbolic validation, coherence* and *adherence* (to a normative hierarchy). To the extent rules exhibit these properties, they appear to exert a strong pull on states to comply with their commands. To the extent these elements are not present, rules seem to be easier to avoid by a state tempted to pursue its short-term self-interest. This is not to say that the legitimacy of a rule can be deduced solely by counting how often it is obeyed or disobeyed. While its legitimacy may exert a powerful pull on state conduct, yet other pulls may be stronger in a particular circumstance. The chance to take a quick, decisive advantage may overcome the counterpull of even a highly legitimate rule. In such circumstances, legitimacy is indicated not by obedience, but by the discomfort disobedience induces in the violator. . . . The variable to watch is not compliance but the strength of the compliance pull, whether or not the rule achieves actual compliance in any one case.

Each rule has an inherent pull power that is independent of the circumstances in which it is exerted, and that varies from rule to rule. This pull power is its index of legitimacy. For example, the rule that makes it improper for one state to infiltrate spies into another state in the guise of diplomats is formally acknowledged by almost every state, yet it enjoys so low a degree of legitimacy as to exert virtually no pull towards compliance. As Schachter observes, "some 'laws,' though enacted properly, have so low a degree of probable compliance that they are treated as 'dead letters' and . . . some treaties, while properly concluded, are considered 'scraps of paper.' " By way of contrast, we have noted, the rules pertaining to belligerency and neutrality actually exerted a very high level of pull on Washington in connection with the Silkworm missile shipment in the Persian Gulf. . . .

Perhaps the most self-evident of all characteristics making for legitimacy is textual *determinacy.* What is meant by this is the ability of the text to convey a clear message, to appear transparent in the sense that one can see through the language to the meaning. Obviously, rules with a readily ascertainable meaning have a better chance than those that do not to regulate the conduct of those to whom the rule is addressed or exert a compliance pull on their policymaking process. Those addressed will know precisely what is expected of them, which is a necessary first step towards compliance. . . .

Indeterminacy . . . has costs. Indeterminate normative standards not only make it harder to know what conformity is expected, but also make it easier to justify noncompliance. Put conversely, the more determinate the standard, the more difficult it is to resist the pull of the rule to compliance and to justify noncompliance. Since few persons or states wish to be perceived as acting in obvious violation of a generally recognized rule of conduct, they may try to resolve the conflicts between the demands of a rule and their desire not to be fettered, by "interpreting" the rule permissively. A determinate rule is less elastic and thus less amenable to such evasive strategy than an indeterminate one. . . .

There is another sense in which determinacy increases the legitimacy of a rule text. A rule of conduct that is highly transparent—its normative content exhibiting great clarity—actually *encourages* gratification deferral and rule compliance. States, in their relations with one another, frequently find themselves tempted to violate a rule of conduct in order to take advantage of a sudden opportunity. If they do not do so, but choose, instead, to obey the rule and forgo that gratification, it is likely to be because of their longer term interests in seeing a potentially useful rule reinforced. They can visualize future situations in which it will operate to their advantage. But they will only defer the attainable short-term gain if the rule is sufficiently specific to support reasonable expectations that benefit can be derived in a contingent future by strengthening the rule in the present instance. . . .

As determinacy is the linguistic or literary-structural component of legitimacy, so *symbolic validation, ritual* and *pedigree* provide its cultural and anthropological dimension. As with determinacy, so here, the legitimacy of the rule—its ability to exert pull to compliance and to command voluntary obedience—is to be examined in the light of its ability to communicate. In this instance, however, what is to be communicated is not so much content as *authority*: the authority of a rule, the authority of the originator of a validating communication and, at times, the authority bestowed on the recipient of the communication. The communication of authority, moreover, is symbolic rather than literal. We shall refer to these symbolically validating communications as cues. . . .

Symbolic validation, like determinacy, serves to legitimize rules. But like determinacy, symbolic validation is not quite as simple a notion as it may initially appear. For example, . . . a pedigree [—a subset of cues that seek to enhance the compliance pull of rules or rule-making institutions by emphasizing their historical origins, their cultural or anthropological deep-rootedness—] only confers actual rights and duties when the standards for pedigreeing are applied *coherently*. When, on the contrary, symbols, ritual and pedigree are dispensed capriciously, the desired effect of legitimization may not accrue. . . .

[Ronald] Dworkin has pointed out that coherence . . . is a key factor in explaining why rules compel. He observes that a rule is coherent when like cases are treated alike in application of the rule and when the rule relates in a principled fashion to other rules of the same system. Consistency requires that a rule . . . , whatever its content, be applied uniformly in every "similar" or "applicable" instance. . . .

[Coherence also] encompasses the further notion that a rule, standard or validating ritual gathers force if it is seen to be connected to a network of other rules by an underlying general principle. . . .

By focusing on the connections between specific rules and general underlying principles, we have emphasized the horizontal aspect of our central notion of a community of legitimate rules. However, there are vertical aspects of this community that have even more significant impact on the legitimacy of rules. . . .

Adherence . . . is used here to mean the vertical nexus between a single *primary rule of obligation* ("cross on the green; stop on the red") and a pyramid of secondary rules about how rules are made, interpreted and applied: rules, in other words, about rules. These may be labeled *secondary rules of process*. Primary rules of obligation that lack adherence to a system of secondary rules of process are mere ad hoc reciprocal arrangements. . . . A rule, in summary, is more likely to obligate if it is made within the procedural and institutional framework of an organized community than if it is strictly an ad hoc agreement between parties in the state of nature. . . .

According to Dworkin, a true community, as distinguished from a mere rabble, or even a system of random primary rules of obligation, is one in which the members

> accept that they are governed by common principles, not just by rules hammered out in political compromise. . . . Members of a society of principle accept that their political rights and duties are not exhausted by the particular decisions their political institutions have reached, but depend, more generally, on the scheme of principles those decisions presuppose and endorse. So each member accepts that others have rights and that he has duties flowing from that scheme. . . .

Nor are these rights and duties "conditional on his wholehearted approval of that scheme; these obligations arise from the historical fact that his community has adopted that scheme, . . . not the assumption that he would have chosen it were the choice entirely his." . . .

. . . What a rule community, a community of principle, does is to validate behavior in accordance with rules and applications of rules that confirm principled coherence and adherence, rather than acknowledging only the power of power. A rule community operates in conformity not only with primary rules but also with secondary ones — rules about rules — which are generated by valid legislative and adjudicative institutions. Finally, a community accepts its ultimate secondary rules of recognition not consensually, but as an inherent concomitant of membership status.

In the world of nations, each of these described conditions of a sophisticated community is observable today, even though imperfectly. This does not mean that its rules will never be disobeyed. It does mean, however, that it is usually possible to distinguish rule compliance from rule violation, and a valid rule or ruling from an invalid one. It also means that it is not necessary to await the millennium of Austinian-type world government to proceed with constructing — perfecting — a system of rules and institutions that will exhibit a powerful pull to compliance and a self-enforcing degree of legitimacy.

Professors Goldsmith and Posner express skepticism about whether the force of international law is based on the concepts of legality or morality. They provide an interest-based, or instrumental, account of the way in which international law operates:

Jack Goldsmith & Eric A. Posner, The New International Law Scholarship

34 Ga. J. Int'l & Comp. L. 463, 464, 466-468 (2006)

The primary intellectual target of [our book *The Limits of International Law*] is the claim — widespread in earlier generations of international law scholarship, and still dominant today — that nations comply with international law for non-instrumental reasons. Non-instrumental explanations for compliance can include a sense of obligation to comply (*opinio juris*), or international law's normative pull, or the absorption of international law into a nation's value set. . . .

Our essential claims are as follows. International law provides a focal point for coordination, and establishes what counts as cooperation in a prisoner's dilemma.* Such patterns of behavior can arise in a decentralized fashion, in which case they are identified as rules of customary international law (CIL). But CIL rules tend to be relatively unclear, making cooperation and coordination by custom relatively

*[In the classic "prisoner's dilemma," the police arrest two suspects, Anne and Bill, on suspicion of bank robbery. Without a confession, the police have insufficient evidence for a bank robbery conviction. As a result, the police separate Anne and Bill and make the same offer to each: if one testifies for the prosecution against the other and the other remains silent, the betrayer goes free and the silent accomplice will receive a ten-year sentence. If both confess, each will be convicted of bank robbery, but each will receive only a five-year sentence as a reward for cooperating. If both prisoners stay silent, they can be convicted only of a minor weapons possession charge for which the maximum sentence is one year. Each prisoner must make the choice of whether to betray the other or to remain silent.

In the absence of cooperation, each prisoner is better off confessing than remaining silent. If Bill confesses, Anne knows she will get a ten-year sentence if she stays silent, but only a five-year sentence if she confesses, which gives her incentive to confess. On the other hand, Anne knows that if Bill remains silent, she will get a one-year sentence if she stays silent and will go free if she confesses. Again, she has incentive to confess.

The "dilemma" is that the outcome obtained when each prisoner pursues the self-interested strategy of confessing is worse for each than the outcome they would have obtained had both remained silent. The prisoner's dilemma highlights the possibility of conflict between individual and group rationality. If agreements to secure cooperation can be reached and enforced, members of a group can maximize their welfare by acting contrary to their individual self-interest. — Eds.]

fragile. Through communication, negotiation, and drafting common documents, nations can clarify their expectations about the opportunities for the joint gains that can be achieved by coordination and cooperation. In a repeated prisoner's dilemma, a clear rule of cooperation can reduce both opportunism and unintended defections from the cooperative game. In a coordination situation, a clear rule reduces the likelihood of an unintended failure of coordination.

Once the rule of cooperation or focal point for coordination is established by custom or treaty, nations comply for one of three general (and not mutually exclusive) reasons. The first is fear of retaliation in a prisoner's dilemma. Each state complies with the rule because it fears retaliation, and a loss of the cooperative surplus, if it does not. The second is fear of a failure of coordination. A CIL rule or treaty works by aligning the relevant expectations and helping parties to avoid the costs of failing to coordinate. A third and quite different reason is fear of reputational loss from failing to comply with the rule.

Under this theory, international law does not pull states toward compliance contrary to their interests. International law emerges from states pursuing their interests to achieve mutually beneficial outcomes, and it is sustained to the degree to which it continues to serve those interests. When international law changes, as it often does, it does so because state interests (again, state preferences over international relations outcomes) change due (for example) to changes in technology, or in relative wealth, or in domestic government. The transition from the old to new rule of international law is not always smooth, for the world lacks stable international institutions — legislatures, regulatory agencies, effective courts — to facilitate the change. Instead, we often see violation, rhetorical clashes, retaliation, and sometimes war as the international order shifts from an old to a new equilibrium.

With this background, it should be clear that we do not . . . think international law is irrelevant or unimportant. It is very important, and indeed often crucial, in helping nations to reap gains from (and avoid losses from) interaction. Nor do we think that international law is inconsequential. The terms of a treaty matter to the gains that each state receives from the treaty through cooperation or coordination. That is why states negotiate so intensely over treaty terms. We even accept that international law "constrains" states, as long as one is careful to understand "constraint" to mean that when international law establishes a focal point for coordination or the cooperative solution in a prisoner's dilemma, nations wanting to reap the benefits of coordination or cooperation will be constrained to abide by the coordinating or cooperating solution.

We do, however, think that it is generally wrong and theoretically unhelpful to view international law as an exogenous force on state behavior. . . .

It is true that our book emphasizes the "*Limits*" of international law, and that we are more skeptical than most scholars about what international law might accomplish. But it is important to understand why, in our view, international law is so limited. International law is limited because it is a product of, and is bounded by, state interests and the distribution of power. Given the multiple conflicted interests of states on various issues, and the particular distribution of state power with respect to those issues, many global problems are unsolvable. To recognize this point is not to reject international law.

Professor Koh offers an account of why states comply with international law (going beyond self-interest and the force of legitimacy) that focuses in part on the role of substate transnational actors.

Harold Hongju Koh, Why Do Nations Obey International Law?

106 Yale L.J. 2599, 2624, 2630-2634, 2646-2649 (1997)

By the 1970s and '80s, the legal landscape had altered significantly. The growth of international regimes and institutions, the proliferation of nonstate actors, and the increasing interpenetration of domestic and international systems inaugurated the era of "transnational relations," defined by one scholar as "regular interactions across national boundaries ari[sing] when at least one actor is a non-state agent or does not operate on behalf of a national government or an intergovernmental organization." Multinational enterprises, nongovernmental organizations, and private individuals reemerged as significant actors on the transnational stage. . . . Instead of focusing narrowly on nation-states as global actors, scholars began to look as well at transnational networks among nonstate actors, international institutions, and domestic political structures as important mediating forces in international society. . . .

In the last five years, these developments have returned the compliance question to center stage in the journals of international theory. . . .

The compliance literature has followed three distinct explanatory pathways. . . . The first, not surprisingly, is a rationalistic instrumentalist strand that views international rules as instruments whereby states seek to attain their interests in wealth, power, and the like . . . [and employs] sophisticated techniques of rational choice theory to argue that nation-states obey international law when it serves their short or long term self-interest to do so. . . .

A second explanatory pathway follows a Kantian, liberal vein. The Kantian thread divides into two identifiable strands: one based on Franck's notion of rule-legitimacy, and another that makes more expansive claims for the causal role of national identity. . . . [T]he determinative factor for whether nations obey can be found, not at a systemic level, but at the level of domestic structure. Under this view, compliance depends significantly on whether or not the state can be characterized as "liberal" in identity, that is, having a form of representative government, guarantees of civil and political rights, and a judicial system dedicated to the rule of law. Flipping the now-familiar Kantian maxim that "democracies don't fight one another," these theorists posit that liberal democracies are more likely to "do law" with one another, while relations between liberal and illiberal states will more likely transpire in a zone of politics.

The third strand is a "constructivist" strand, based broadly on notions of both identity-formation and international society. Unlike interest theorists, who tend to treat state interests as given, "constructivists" have long argued that states and their interests are socially constructed by "commonly held philosophic principles, identities, norms of behavior, or shared terms of discourse." Rather than arguing that state actors and interests create rules and norms, constructivists argue that "[r]ules and norms *constitute* the international game by determining who the actors are, what rules they must follow if they wish to ensure that particular consequences follow from specific acts, and how titles to possessions can be established and transferred." Thus constructivists see norms as playing a critical role in the formation of national identities. . . .

[Under this view,] the norms, values, and social structure of international society . . . help . . . form the identity of actors who operate within it. Nations thus obey international rules not just because of sophisticated calculations about how compliance or non-compliance will affect their interests, but because a repeated habit of obedience remakes their interests so that they come to value rule compliance. . . . [S]tates follow specific rules, even when inconvenient, because they have a longer-term interest in the maintenance of law-impregnated international community.

Each of these explanatory threads has significant persuasive power, and strongly complements the others. Yet . . . none of these approaches provides a sufficiently "thick" theory of the role of international law in promoting compliance with shared global norms. The short answer to the question, "Why do nations obey international law?" is not simply: "interest"; "identity"; "identity-formation"; and/or "international society." A complete answer must also account for the importance of *interaction* within the transnational legal process, *interpretation* of international norms, and domestic *internalization* of those norms as determinants of why nations obey. What is missing, in brief, is a modern version of the fourth historical strand of compliance theory—the strand based on *transnational legal process*. . . .

[S]uch a process can be viewed as having three phases. One or more transnational actors provokes an *interaction* (or series of interactions) with another, which forces an *interpretation* or enunciation of the global norm applicable to the situation. By so doing, the moving party seeks not simply to coerce the other party, but to *internalize* the new interpretation of the international norm into the other party's internal normative system. The aim is to "bind" that other party to obey the interpretation as part of its internal value set. Such a transnational legal process is normative, dynamic, and constitutive. The transaction generates a legal rule which will guide future transnational interactions between the parties; future transactions will further internalize those norms; and eventually, repeated participation in the process will help to reconstitute the interests and even the identities of the participants in the process.

The Anti-Ballistic Missile Treaty Reinterpretation Debate represents one recent example of this phenomenon from United States foreign policy. To simplify a complex story, in 1972, the United States and the U.S.S.R. signed the bilateral Anti-Ballistic Missile Treaty (ABM Treaty), which expressly banned the development of space-based systems for the territorial defense of our country. Thirteen years later, in October 1985, the Reagan Administration proposed the Strategic Defense Initiative (SDI), popularly called "Star Wars," which amounted to a space-based antiballistic missile system for American territorial defense. To skirt the plain language of the ABM Treaty, the Reagan Administration proposed to "reinterpret" it to permit SDI, essentially amending the treaty without the consent of either the Senate or the Soviet Union. That decision triggered an eight-year battle in which numerous present and former government officials, including six former Secretaries of Defense and numerous key Senators (principally Sam Nunn, Chairman of the Senate Armed Services Committee), rallied in support of the original treaty interpretation. One key player in the fight against the ABM treaty reinterpretation was Gerard C. Smith, the chief

American negotiator at SALT I and principal negotiator of the ABM Treaty, who chaired the boards of two influential nongovernmental organizations, the Arms Control Association and the National Committee to Save the ABM Treaty.

The ABM controversy raged in many fora: Senate hearings, debates over other arms control treaties, journal articles, and op-ed columns. In the end, Congress withheld appropriations from SDI tests that did not conform with the treaty; the Senate reported the ABM Treaty Interpretation Resolution, which reaffirmed its original understanding of the treaty; and in 1988 the Senate attached a condition to the Intermediate-Range Missile Treaty, which specified that the United States would interpret the treaty in accordance with the understanding shared by the President and the Senate at the time of advice and consent. In response, the Reagan and Bush Administrations maintained that their broad reinterpretation was "legally correct," but announced that they would comply with the original understanding as a matter of "policy." In 1993, the episode ended, when President Clinton repudiated the unilateral Reagan reinterpretation and announced that his administration would abide by the original ABM treaty interpretation.

None of this legal dispute reached any court. Indeed, had one stopped tracing the process of the dispute in 1987, one might have concluded that the United States had violated the treaty and gotten away with it. But in the end, the ABM Treaty Reinterpretation Debate demonstrates how the world's most powerful nation, the United States, returned to compliance with international law.

Standing alone, neither interest, identity, or international society provides sufficient explanation for why the United States government obeyed the original ABM Treaty interpretation. Presumably, the U.S. national interest in deploying SDI remained roughly the same under either legal interpretation, as did the liberal identity of the American polity. If the response of international society, in the form of allies' and treaty partners' resistance to the reinterpretation, was not enough to block the reinterpretation in 1985, it is unclear why that resistance should have become overwhelming by 1993.

In my view, a transnational legal process explanation provides the missing link. Transnational actors such as a U.S. Senator (Sam Nunn), a private "norm entrepreneur" (Gerard Smith), and several nongovernmental organizations (the Arms Control Association and the National Committee to Save the ABM Treaty) formed an "epistemic community" to address the legal issue. That community mobilized elite and popular constituencies and provoked a series of interactions with the U.S. government in a variety of fora. They challenged the Administration's broad reinterpretation of the treaty norm with the original narrow interpretation in both public and private settings, and succeeded in internalizing the narrow interpretation into several legislative products. In the end, the executive branch responded by internalizing that interpretation into its own official policy statement. Thus, the episode proved normative . . . and constitutive of U.S. national interests supporting the original ABM treaty interpretation. In this dynamic process, the episode established a precedent for the next debate over the antiballistic missile issue. . . .

This example reveals that the various theoretical explanations offered for compliance are complementary, not mutually exclusive. In his classic statement of neorealism, *Man, the State and War*, Kenneth Waltz posited three levels of analysis, or "images," at which international relations could be explained: the international system (systemic); the state (domestic politics); and the individuals and groups who make up the state (psychological/bureaucratic). These images are not mutually exclusive, but sit atop one another like a layer cake; thus, interest and international society theorists seek to explain compliance primarily at the level of the international system, while identity theorists seek to explain it at the level of domestic political structure. Transnational legal process analysts, by contrast, seek to supplement these explanations with reasons for compliance that are found at a *transactional* level: *interaction, interpretation,* and *internalization* of international norms into domestic legal structures. While the interest, identity, and international society approaches all provide useful insights, none, jointly or severally, provides a sufficiently thick explanation of compliance with international obligations.

Notes and Questions

1. Do you agree with Professor Franck concerning the factors that make legal rules legitimate? Based on the factors identified by Professor Franck, how can international law's legitimacy be enhanced?

2. Professors Goldsmith and Posner expressly reject the notion that compliance with international law can be based on appeals to legality or morality and argue that international law reflects the pursuit by states of self-interest. Professor Henkin, in contrast, characterizes as "plain error" the argument that nations only do pursuant to law what they would do anyhow. In what ways does Professor Henkin's description of the influence of international law differ from that of Professors Goldsmith and Posner? Aren't there also important similarities between the two approaches?

3. How persuasive is Professor Koh's "transnational legal process" explanation for national compliance with international law? Professor Koh uses the debate about the reinterpretation of the ABM treaty—from which the United States withdrew in 2002—as an example. Can you think of recent examples of the "transnational legal process" operating to produce compliance with international law?

4. In 2010 remarks to the American Society of International Law, State Department Legal Adviser Harold Koh made the following comments:

> [This Administration has] a commitment to living our values by respecting the rule of law. . . . [B]oth the President and Secretary [of State] Clinton are outstanding lawyers, and they understand that by imposing constraints on government action, law legitimates and gives credibility to governmental action. As the President [has] emphasized . . . , the American political system was founded on a vision of common humanity, universal rights and rule of law. "Fidelity to [these] values" makes us stronger and safer. This also means following universal standards, not double standards. In his Nobel lecture at Oslo, President Obama affirmed that "[a]dhering to standards, international standards, strengthens those who do, and isolates those who don't." And . . . Secretary Clinton [has] reiterated that "a commitment to human rights starts with universal standards and with holding everyone accountable to those standards, including ourselves." [Harold Hongju Koh, The Obama Administration and International Law, Remarks at Annual Meeting of the American Society of

International Law (March 25, 2010), available at http://www.state.gov/s/l/releases/remarks/139119.htm.]

Reflecting the views of other states, a Canadian representative to the United Nations, speaking on behalf of Canada, Australia, and New Zealand, offered the following views:

> The significance of the rule of law at the international level cannot be overstated. We live in a truly interdependent world. Today, we face global challenges which no one country can resolve on its own, such as climate change, the global financial crisis, nuclear non-proliferation and disarmament, terrorism, and gross violations of human rights. To meet these challenges, it is imperative that states adhere to rule of law at the international level to promote peaceful coexistence and cooperation among states. The past several years have witnessed an increase in the use by states of treaty-based mechanisms and global institutions to address international disputes and alleged violations of international law. . . .
>
> Importantly, efforts to promote the rule of law at the international level work to bolster the rule of law at the national level. The common principles identified by states, in tandem with an agreement to abide by them, become the basis on which much national legislation is written — for example, in the areas of children's rights, trade law, access to information, and access to justice in environmental matters. [Keith Morrill, Representative of Canada, The Rule of Law at an International Level, Statement to the United Nations at the Sixth Committee on behalf of Australia, New Zealand and Canada (Oct. 14, 2009), available at http://www.canadainternational.gc.ca/prmny-mponu/canada_un-canada_onu/statements-declarations/international_rights-droit_international/20091014_Morrill_RoL-EdD.aspx.]

How, if at all, do these views comport with the theoretical accounts of compliance with international law advanced by Professors Henkin, Goldsmith and Posner, Franck, and Koh?

5. Do you think that international law influences government decision makers? In what ways do states treat international law as law, and why do they do so? Do they act out of a respect for law? Or just fear of sanctions? Out of self-interest? Or beliefs about what is morally right? Can you separate these factors?

6. For an additional discussion of the reasons that states comply with international law, see Abram Chayes & Antonia Handler Chayes, The New Sovereignty: Compliance with International Regulatory Agreements (1995); and Andrew T. Guzman, How International Law Works: A Rational Choice Theory (2008).

D. INTERNATIONAL LAW THEORY AND METHODOLOGY

This section provides an overview of some of the modern theoretical and methodological approaches to international law. It is not expected that students will master these approaches in the basic international law course, especially at the beginning of the course. Students may find it useful, however, to have a sense of different ways of thinking about international law before evaluating the substantive international law topics in subsequent chapters.

1. *Overview*

Excerpted below is a brief description of some of the modern approaches to international law. This excerpt is followed by more in-depth materials discussing some of the specific approaches.

Steven R. Ratner & Anne-Marie Slaughter, Appraising the Methods of International Law: A Prospectus for Readers

The Methods of International Law 1, 5-8 (Steven R. Ratner & Anne-Marie Slaughter eds., 2004)

Positivism. Positivism summarizes a range of theories that focus upon describing the law as it is, backed up by effective sanctions, with reference to formal criteria, independently of moral or ethical considerations. For positivists, international law is no more or less than the rules to which states have agreed through treaties, custom, and perhaps other forms of consent. In the absence of such evidence of the will of states, positivists will assume that states remain at liberty to undertake whatever actions they please. Positivism also tends to view states as the only subjects of international law, thereby discounting the role of nonstate actors. It remains the lingua franca of most international lawyers, especially in continental Europe.

New Haven School (policy-oriented jurisprudence). Established by Harold Lasswell and Myres McDougal of Yale Law School beginning in the mid-1940s, the New Haven School eschews positivism's formal method of searching for rules as well as the concept of law as based on rules alone. It describes itself as a policy-oriented perspective, viewing international law as a process of decision making by which various actors in the world community clarify and implement their common interests in accordance with their expectations of appropriate processes and of effectiveness in controlling behavior. Perhaps the New Haven School's greatest contribution has been its emphasis on both what actors say and what they do.

International legal process. International legal process (ILP) refers to the approach first developed by Abram Chayes, Thomas Ehrlich, and Andreas Lowenfeld at Harvard Law School in the 1960s. Building on the American legal process school, it has seen the key locus of inquiry of international law as the role of law in constraining decision makers and affecting the course of international affairs. Legal process theory has recently enjoyed a domestic revival, which seeks to underpin precepts about process with a set of normative values. Some ILP scholars are following suit.

Critical legal studies. Critical legal studies (CLS) scholars have sought to move beyond what constitutes law, or the relevance of law to policy, to focus on the contradictions, hypocrisies, and failings of international legal discourse. The diverse group of scholars who often identify themselves as part of the "New Stream" have emphasized the importance of culture to legal development and offered a critical view of the progress of the law in its confrontations with state sovereignty. Like the deconstruction movement, which is the intellectual font of many of its ideas, critical legal studies has focused on the importance of language.

International law and international relations. IR/IL is a purposefully interdisciplinary approach that seeks to incorporate into international law the insights of international relations theory regarding the behavior of international actors. The most recent round of IR/IL scholarship seeks to draw on contemporary developments and strands in international relations theory, which is itself a relatively young discipline. The results are diverse, ranging from studies of compliance, to analyses of the stability and effectiveness of international institutions, to the ways that models of state conduct affect the content and subject of international rules.

Feminist jurisprudence. Feminist scholars of international law seek to examine how both legal norms and processes reflect the domination of men, and to reexamine and reform these norms and processes so as to take account of women. Feminist jurisprudence has devoted particular attention to the shortcomings in the international protection of women's rights, but it has also asserted deeper structural challenges to international law, criticizing the way law is made and applied as insufficiently attentive to the role of women. Feminist jurisprudence has also taken an active advocacy role.

Third world approaches to international law. TWAIL is an overtly postcolonial set of perspectives on international law. A first generation of TWAIL scholars sought to work within an essentially positivist view of international law to benefit newly independent states after World War II; more recent scholars view colonialism as a permanently embedded concept in both international norms and the processes used for prescribing and applying them. TWAIL scholars have thus examined the dependency of many states and societies on Western conceptions of international law and have sought to challenge them, both within existing structures and in alternative fora.

Law and economics. In its domestic incarnation, which has proved highly significant and enduring, law and economics has both a descriptive component that seeks to explain existing rules as reflecting the most economically efficient outcome, and a normative component that evaluates proposed changes in the law and urges adoption of those that maximize wealth. Game theory and public choice theory are often considered part of law and economics. In the international area, it has begun to address commercial and environmental issues.

2. *International Relations Theory*

Oona A. Hathaway, Between Power and Principle: An Integrated Theory of International Law

72 U. Chi. L. Rev. 469, 476-479, 481-485 (2005)

[O]ver the past decade, two broad theoretical approaches regarding the role of international law in state behavior have started to cut across the [longstanding] disciplinary divide between political science and international legal scholarship. The first, which I term the interest-based approach, argues that states create and comply with international law only when there is some clear objective reward for doing so; in other words, states follow consequentialist reasoning. . . . The second, which I label the norm-based approach, argues that governments create and comply with treaties not only because they expect a reward for doing so, but also because of their commitment (or the commitment of transnational actors that influence them) to the norms or ideas embodied in the treaties. . . . Moreover, nonstate and substate actors are the focus of much more attention in the norm-centered account than in the interest-centered one, for they play an important role in constructing state preferences. . . .

A. Interest-Based Models

The interest-based approach has its roots in the realist view of international cooperation, which became dominant in American political science scholarship in the wake of World War II. In this view, states are rational, unitary actors in pursuit of self-interest. Early realist accounts used this vision of state action to argue that international agreements exist and are enforced only when they serve the interests of the most powerful states. More recent scholarship, by contrast, argues that regimes—including legal regimes—can influence the behavior of international actors. States create and comply with the requirements of international regimes, these scholars claim, because the regimes allow states to engage in cooperative activity that would otherwise be impossible. By allowing states to restrain themselves and others from pursuing short-term interests at the expense of shared long-term goals, regimes make it possible for states to obtain benefits that exceed the costs of membership. Yet as different as the many variants of this approach are, they share at least two key assumptions: States engage in consequentialist means-end calculations, and state interests can be deduced from the state's material characteristics and the objective conditions it faces. Moreover, these models traditionally focused exclusively on state-level interactions, with scholars largely ignoring substate dynamics. . . .

B. Norm-Based Models

Norm-based models of international law reject rationalist scholars' contention that the consequentialist pursuit of self-interest alone can explain state behavior. While acknowledging that state behavior is often motivated by self-interest, normative scholars contend that it is also motivated by the power of principled ideas—ideas that are not given by nature but are themselves constructed through interaction among individuals, groups, and states.

There is a rich normative scholarship in both political science and law. In political science, the norm-based scholarship is built on the insights of "constructivist" theory. In this view, interest-based scholars are wrong to assume that states engage only in consequentialist pursuit of objective self-interest. Rather, states internalize norms and act in accordance with them because they understand them to be correct or appropriate. Moreover, in contrast with the rationalist approach, the normative approach argues that transnational actors and their interests are not fully formed or unchanging. Rather, they are constituted or "constructed" by and through interaction with one another. In other words, "[t]he international system can change what states want." International law can change state action, in this view, "not by constraining states with a given set of preferences from acting, but by changing their preferences."

The legal norm-based scholarship starts with the assumption that nations obey international law "almost all of the time." It also takes international law as a given, for the most part assuming that treaties exist and states join them without seeking to explain why or when they do so. Hence these theories focus almost exclusively on the question of compliance: Why, they ask, do states obey international law most of the time?

In legal scholarship, two separate variants of normative theory have gained widespread attention—fairness theory and legal process theory. The fairness model primarily associated with Thomas Franck focuses on the perceived fairness of the legal obligations at issue: A "fair" legal obligation exerts a "compliance pull" that leads states to comply with it. A second legal normative account instead focuses on legal process, with separate branches of the theory focusing on horizontal and vertical interactions among countries. Abram and Antonia Chayes offer a model of *horizontal* legal process, which they entitle "managerial legal process." In this view, states obey international law not because of sanctions, but because their prior agreement to do so creates an "obligation of obedience." Harold Koh's related "transnational legal process theory" focuses less on horizontal ties across states and more on *vertical* interactions within states and between the international and domestic arenas. In his view, state behavior is influenced by international law through a process of "interaction, interpretation, internalization, and obedience," by virtue of the efforts of various agents of internalization, including transnational norm entrepreneurs. A central step in this process is legal internalization—"when an international norm is incorporated into the domestic legal system through executive action, judicial interpretation, legislative action, or some combination of the three." When that internalization is complete, Koh argues, states comply.

Norm-based scholarship offers an important corrective to rationalist theories by focusing attention on the powerful role of ideas in international law. Many norm-based accounts also encourage attention to the role and influence of nonstate actors that are often ignored in traditional interest-based accounts. . . .

C. A Promising Convergence

A more recent strand of scholarship in the rationalist vein offers the promise of finding some common ground between interest-based and norm-based approaches. This model [is] termed the "liberal institutionalist" perspective by its proponents (sometimes also referred to as "institutional liberalism"). . . . The theory, which has been developed and applied by both legal and political science scholars, opens the black box of domestic politics that is largely unexamined by other interest-based scholars, and looks to the political institutions, interest groups, and state actors that shape state preferences to explain state behavior in the international arena. In this view, states pursue the aims preferred by "powerful domestic interest groups enfranchised by representative institutions and practices." Hence, state behavior is the result of complex interactions between political players at the domestic level, and cannot be explained as simply resulting from power-maximizing behavior or strategic calculation by a unitary actor.

This strand of interest-focused thought, like most norm-based explanations of state decisions to join treaties, calls for us to peer inside the state, looking for the individuals and groups that influence governments through political institutions and social practices. The two approaches differ primarily in the assumptions made about the motivations of these actors and the source of their interests. Whereas liberal theory assumes that the relevant actors are motivated by objective self-interest, normative theory focuses attention on actors presumably motivated primarily by ideas—ideas that are constructed through interactions between and among states and nonstate actors. Norm-based theory also places greater emphasis than liberal theory on horizontal connections across states and less emphasis on domestic regime type.

For an overview of the literature exploring the relationship between international relations theory and international law, see Robert J. Beck, International Law and International Relations Scholarship, in Routledge Handbook of International Law (David Armstrong ed., 2009). Collections of additional writings on these subjects include Oona A. Hathaway & Harold Hongju Koh, Foundations of International Law and Politics (2005); and International Law and International Relations (Beth A. Simmons & Richard H. Steinberg eds., 2006).

3. *Economic Analysis of International Law*

Joel P. Trachtman, The Economic Structure of International Law

2, 4-7, 10-11, 15-16 (2008)

Economic analysis holds great promise for international law. This promise lies in the ability of economic analysis to suggest useful methods for analyzing the actual or potential consequences of particular legal rules. . . .

Economic models begin with price theory, which assumes that, all things being equal, people prefer cheaper goods and services, as well as more efficient means of achieving their nonconsumption goals. . . .

An additional level of complexity is added by transaction costs analysis, which simply recognizes, within price theory, that there are costs to engaging in transactions, and that these costs may prevent otherwise efficient transactions or may account for institutional structures.

A third level of complexity is added by game theory, which recognizes that the strategic position of states may prevent or add costs to otherwise efficient agreements. . . .

I will now provide some examples of the application of price theory, transaction costs analysis, [and] game theory . . . in international law. . . .

Price theory is the basis for cost-benefit analysis: in seeking to achieve our preferences, we seek to maximize benefits and minimize costs (benefits and costs are measured in terms of the achievement of our preferences, which are not necessarily monetized or monetizable). Therefore, if my preferences include engagement in ethnic cleansing, I would examine the costs of weapons, of retaliation by my target, or of my reputation. If there exists an international legal rule against ethnic cleansing that is enforced and could result in my punishment, I would examine the discounted costs of punishment. The discount factor would relate to the likelihood of my apprehension and punishment, and the delay until my apprehension and punishment. Therefore, based on the price theory model, we would hypothesize that, mutatis mutandis, a reliably enforceable legal rule with substantial punishment would reduce the likelihood of ethnic cleansing. . . .

Transaction cost economics addresses the difficulty of identifying partners for the exchanges of goods, service, or promises; negotiating exchange; and enforcing terms of exchange. In international law, we might consider the difficulty of establishing treaties dealing with specific (as opposed to more general) environmental problems. Thus, there may be a smelter in Canada that causes air pollution that, due to prevailing winds, travels to the United States. While it may be useful to deal with some larger environmental issues between the United States and Canada, this particular issue may be too small to merit the devotion of diplomatic energy. Absent transaction costs, this cross-border issue might be resolved, but given transaction costs it goes unresolved. In this case, the cost of the injury would remain with the injured person in the United States. This may be efficient: transaction costs are real costs. However, there may be ways to reduce transaction costs to establish a rule of liability, such as *sic utere tuo*, to the effect that the polluter is responsible for damage to others. Given a rule such as *sic utere tuo*, it may be easier for the parties to negotiate a solution that minimizes the joint costs.

Game theory can help us to understand possible solutions to problems of international cooperation. . . . The prisoner's exchange dilemma . . . provides a way of understanding the problem of cooperation in circumstances where each individual can do better by violating a customary international law rule or treaty, but both states will do worse if both violate the rule or treaty. The bilateral prisoner's dilemma, resulting in inefficient violation by both sides, may be escaped by repetition. If you violate the first time, I can retaliate later. If you understand this and value the future sufficiently (i.e., are sufficiently patient), you may determine not to violate the first time. The shadow of the future provides incentives for cooperation. The development of customary international law may be understood in this way. . . .

[A]ccording to the economic perspective, the international system, like economic markets, is formed by the interaction of self-regarding units — largely, but not exclusively, states. These utilitarian states interact to "overcome the deficiencies that make it impossible to consummate . . . mutually beneficial agreements. Actors in each system are willing — to some extent — to relinquish autonomy in order to obtain certain benefits. . . . [States enter the market of international relations in order to obtain gains from exchange.]"

The assets traded in this international "market" are not goods or services per se, but assets peculiar to states: components of power, or jurisdiction. "Jurisdiction" is the word that lawyers use for allocation of authority: the institutionalized exercise of power. In a legal context, power is effective jurisdiction, including jurisdiction to prescribe, jurisdiction to adjudicate, and jurisdiction to enforce. In international society, the equivalent of the market is simply the place where states interact to cooperate on particular issues — to trade in power — in order to maximize their baskets of preferences. Thus, the transaction in jurisdiction is the fundamental unit of analysis. . . . [T]he model . . . looks to *public* welfare maximization, in the sense [of] maximization of the achievement of the regulatory concerns of states.

The central theory suggested by the economic approach to international law is that states use and design international transactions (including all rules of international law) or institutions to maximize the participants' net gains, which equal the excess of transaction gains from engaging in intergovernmental transactions, over the sum of transaction losses from engaging in intergovernmental transactions and transaction costs of intergovernmental transactions (including transaction costs of international agreement or of creating and running institutions). Most, if not all, international law may be characterized as involving transactions in jurisdiction, either horizontal or vertical, with this purpose in mind. . . .

It may be useful to have in mind a couple of examples. An international legal rule prohibiting the acquisition of territory by use of force may be seen as maximizing net benefits by virtue of the greater security that states enjoy, allowing individual states to spend less on self-defense. They may spend less on self-defense because the threat of aggression is reduced by virtue of the fact that the rewards of aggression are reduced insofar as aggression cannot be the basis for the acquisition of territory. Absent this legal prohibition, each state has the authority to acquire territory by force, but by entering into this rule, each transfers this authority away. It is a transaction in authority.

Similarly, international human rights treaties may be understood as transactions in authority. Although it is sometimes difficult to see the externality when one state abuses the human rights of its own citizens, these externalities may arise in the form of instability, refugees, competitive externalities, or simply feelings of concern. When states enter into these treaties, they are implicitly bartering autonomy to commit human rights abuses. This is also a transaction in authority. Of course, it may be necessary to provide other inducement or side payments in particular cases. But the main point is that we can understand these transactions as transactions in authority. Another word for authority in our context is jurisdiction.

For additional discussion of law and economics approaches to international law, see Alan O. Sykes, International Law, in Handbook of Law and Economics 757 (2007); Kyle Bagwell, Remedies in the WTO: An Economic Perspective, in The WTO: Governance, Dispute Settlement & Developing Countries (Merit E. Janow, Victoria Donaldson & Alan Yanovich eds., 2008); and the essays in connection with the University of Illinois Symposium on Public International Law and Economics, 2008 U. Illinois L. Rev. 1 (2008).

4. *Critical Legal Studies*

Martti Koskenniemi, From Apology to Utopia: The Structure of International Legal Argument

1, 3-4, 6, 11-13 (rev. 2005)

This is not only a book in international law. It is also an exercise in social theory and social philosophy. One of the principal theses of the book is that it is neither useful nor ultimately possible to work with international law in abstraction from descriptive theories about the character of social life among States and normative views about the principles of justice which should govern international conduct. . . .

The modern international lawyer has assumed that frustration about theory can be overcome by becoming doctrinal, or technical. But it is doubtful whether this strategy has ever worked out very well. For the lawyer is constantly faced with two disappointing experiences. In the first place, the doctrinal outcomes often seem irrelevant. In the practice of States and international organizations these are every day overridden by informal, political practices, agreements and understandings.

If they are not overridden, this seems to be more a matter of compliance being politically useful than a result of the "legal" character of the outcomes or the methods whereby they were received. To explain that despite this experience, international law is in some sense "relevant" will, however, demand a "theoretical" discussion about how to disentangle law from other aspects of social life among States. And this would seem to involve precisely the sort of conceptual analysis from which will emerge the indeterminate classic controversies about the "nature" of law. In the second place, most doctrinal outcomes remain controversial. Anyone with some experience in doctrinal argument will soon develop a feeling of *déjá-vu* towards that argument. In crucial doctrinal areas, treaties, customary law, general principles, *jus cogens* and so on conflicting views are constantly presented as "correct" normative outcomes. Each general principle seems capable of being opposed with an equally valid counter-principle. Moreover, these conflicting views and principles are very familiar and attempts to overcome the conflicts they entail seem to require returning to "theory" which, however, merely reproduces the conflicts at a higher level of abstraction. There is this dilemma: In order to avoid the problems of theory, the lawyer has retreated into doctrine. But doctrine constantly reproduces problems which seem capable of resolution only if one takes a theoretical position. . . .

Now, when one starts to deal with an international legal problem, say a dispute about the rights of States, one very soon enters certain controlling assumptions which seem to demand solution before the problem can even be approached in some determinate way and a legal solution be suggested. Do these rights exist simply by virtue of statehood? Do they emerge from some higher normative code? Or are they merely legislative constructions? . . . One needs to explicate the assumptions about the present character of social life among States and on the desirable forms of such life which make it seem that one's doctrinal outcomes are justified even as they remain controversial. . . .

The approach followed here is one of "regressive analysis." I shall attempt to investigate discourse about international law by arguing back to the existence of certain conditions without which this discourse could not possess the kind of self-evidence for professional lawyers which it has. In other words, I shall argue, as it were, "backwards" from explicit arguments to their "deep-structure," the assumptions within which the problems which modern lawyers face, either in theory or in doctrine, are constituted.

The approach could also be labelled "deconstructive." By this contentious term I intend to refer less to certain metaphysical doctrines than a method, a general outlook towards analyzing intellectual operations through which the social world appears to us the way it does. . . .

. . . I shall argue that express arguments and doctrines about international law are only a contingent surface of a socially shared manner of envisaging international relations. A deconstruction of international legal argument will then inevitably relate that argument to that historically conditioned "code"—or "conceptual scheme." As it makes explicit that hidden code it bears a *critical potential.* For it is clear that this cannot be a code which is somehow "inherent" in the contexts in which we use it. It has neither descended from heaven to determine what we can see in international life, nor emerged as an aprioristic construction of an autonomous individual. Men, as Max Horkheimer points out, are the product of history and "the way they see and hear is inseparable from the social life-process."

... [T]he point is that the concepts and categories with which we orient ourselves in the world are internalized in a process of *socialization.* We don't choose to use the concepts of international law when we enter into international legal discourse. Rather, we must take a pre-existing language, a pre-existing system of interpreting the world and move within it if we wish to be heard and understood. In this sense, language precedes thought: We do not say that peoples have a right of self-determination because we think so. Rather, we come to think so because that is what we say. ...

[International law] conveys to us a certain interpretation of the social reality to which it is addressed, under the veil of objectivity, or naturalness. Deconstruction seeks to bring out the conventional character of this interpretation and its dependence on certain contestable assumptions. It becomes critical as it shows that legal argument cannot produce the kinds of objective resolutions it claims to produce — indeed, the production of which it assumes for its principal justification. Thus it opens up a possibility for alternative descriptive — and simultaneously normative — characterizations of the world in which States live.

By providing an "insider's view" to legal discourse, such an approach might produce a therapeutic effect on lawyers frustrated with their inability to cope with the indeterminacy of theory and the irrelevance of doctrine. It will indicate that legal discourse cannot permanently solve the lawyer's problems for him. The line drawn in the midst of the universe of normative statements which has separated "subjective" politics from "objective" law will appear without foundation. By thus "politicizing" law (but equally "legalizing" politics) an analysis of its structure might point a way towards an alternative way of understanding the relationship between law and its neighboring discourses, social description and political prescription.

For additional discussion of critical legal studies as applied to international law, see Anthony Carty, Philosophy of International Law (2007); International Law and its Others (Anne Orford ed., 2006); David Kennedy, A New Stream of International Law Scholarship, 7 Wisc. Int'l L.J. 1 (1988); and Phillip R. Trimble, International Law, World Order and Critical Legal Studies, 42 Stan. L. Rev. 811 (1990).

5. *Feminist Jurisprudence*

Professor Karen Engle recounts key developments in the evolution of feminist approaches to international law in recent decades, with a particular focus on human rights concerns:

Karen Engle, International Human Rights and Feminisms: When Discourses Keep Meeting

International Law: Modern Feminist Approaches 47, 51-54, 60-62
(Doris Buss & Ambreena Manji eds., 2005)

Liberal Inclusion: 1985-1990

Liberal inclusionists argued that women should *and could* be included in international human rights and humanitarian law. Women were as much subjects of international law as were men and thus, if properly applied, international legal doctrine could assimilate women's concerns.

Much of the scholarship during this era argued for doctrinal inclusion and institutional expansion. Liberal inclusionists argued that women were, in principle, protected from rape in armed conflict by humanitarian law of war, protected from domestic violence and cliteridectomy by international human rights law, and guaranteed economic and social rights such as the right to health. . . . [T]he necessary international legal doctrine existed to assimilate women into existing international human rights law and institutions. If the doctrine was not being used to protect women's rights, it was due to a lack of enforcement, not a lack of law.

Some liberal inclusionists focused on enforcement. Much work was spent analyzing international institutions to see why mainstream institutions failed to address women's issues. While some argued that increasing the number of women in these organizations might lead to greater attention to women's needs, others aimed to have the institutions recognize that, because institutional legal doctrine covered women, the mandates of the institutions must follow suit. . . .

Structural Bias Critique: 1987-1995

For structural bias critics, simple inclusion of women into international law was impossible. International law was seen as male and therefore structurally biased against women. Implicit in the structural bias approach, then, was a critique of liberal inclusion. The structure of international law prevented women's assimilation; the regime must be changed to accommodate women.

Structural bias feminists address many of the same issues as liberal inclusion feminists. They too were concerned about the laws of war, domestic violence and clitoridectomy. To the extent that international legal doctrine offered protection to women in these areas, it did so for the wrong reasons or with the wrong emphasis. Hilary Charlesworth argued, for example, that even though rape during armed conflict clearly violated international law, international law was concerned about women's honour (and therefore about the men who were harmed by the attack on this honour) or about genocide, not about women — *qua women* — as subjects of international law. Most structural bias critics agreed with liberal inclusionists that international legal institutions failed to address women's issues. For structural bias critics, however, some major reordering of international legal doctrine and institutions would be required to accommodate women. As Dorothy Thomas put it: "The fundamental challenge for the movement for women's human rights is that it not become a reformist project; its recipe should not read, 'Add women and stir,' but 'Add women and alter.' " . . .

Structural bias critics identified a series of dichotomies in public international law that perpetuated the inability of international human rights law to attend to women. The most commonly discussed dichotomy was the public/private distinction. For some critics, the distinction actually existed; international law only applied to the public sphere. Torture, for example, might well lie outside international law to the extent that it involved private individuals. And while state *action* might bring torture within the scope of human rights law, state *inaction* with regard to violence against women was likely to leave women outside international law's scope. Thus, a radical reordering of the international legal order was called for. In particular, human rights law needed to apply to non-state actors.

Other critics of the public/private distinction tended not to see that distinction as embedded in the doctrine of international law. Rather, the public/private distinction was more a problem of ideology that doctrine. These critics argued that the pubic/private distinction was broken down in international law all the time (the prohibition on slavery was commonly given as an example of international law's intervention in the private realm), but not when doing so would offer protection to women. This bias was considered structural, but not as intransigent as the first view suggested. . . .

By focusing on women's "private" lives, structural bias feminists treated the private as the locus of women's oppression. Women were more directly oppressed by their families than by their governments, although government inaction facilitated the perpetuation of that oppression. Thus, culture was seen as responsible for the bulk of women's problems. It is therefore not surprising that structural bias feminists tended to focus on female genital mutilation, domestic violence, and even food taboos that kept women undernourished.

The public/private distinction might be the most discussed example of structural gender bias in international law, but the literature is filled with a number of others. International law's priority of the state over civil society and of civil and political rights over economic and social rights, for example, were also seen both to represent and constitute structural bias against women. . . .

[The critiques of structural bias critics] center around an understanding of international law as male or as reflecting male bias. . . .

[S]tructural bias feminists aim to analyze international law for its deployment of literal or metaphorical distinctions between male and female. . . .

Third World Feminists Critiques: Since 1992

. . . Third world feminist critiques of international law implicitly challenge liberal and structural bias feminism by suggesting that the effects of international law on women must be examined in light of class, culture and race. Third world feminist approaches to structural bias feminism make these critiques explicit. Again, there is both a liberal inclusion and a structural bias form of the critique.

The liberal inclusion form argues that structural bias feminists fail to include third world women in their analysis. The position tends to assume that third world women *could* be assimilated to the structural bias critique without disrupting the analysis; they would simply need to be included. . . .

The structural bias form of the third world feminist critique refuses the gesture to add third world women and stir. In effect, it suggested that attending to third world women would require a radical restructuring of the structural bias critique. A number of third world feminist critiques have been aimed at structural bias feminism. . . . First, through an overt (re)assertion of the distinction between the first and third worlds, those who approach structural bias feminism from this third world perspective often argue that Western feminism has misrepresented women through its near exclusive focus on culture. Second, they suggested that this focus displaces those issues that have the greatest importance to women in the third world. Third, they argue that first world feminists are complicit in the perpetuation of colonial or neocolonial agendas. . . .

Third world feminist approaches have challenged the representations about non-Western women they argue are made by both liberal inclusionist and structural bias approaches to women's human rights. In particular, they critique the conflation of the interests of women in the first and third worlds, and argue for the need to attend to cultural differences. Aihwa Ong asserts, for example, that "North-South conflict erupts when liberal feminists disregard alternative political moralities that shape the ways women in other societies make moral judgments about their interests and goals in life, and use other cultural criteria about what it means to be female and human." Much of the early . . . third world feminist [writing] calls attention to cultural differences that authors believe are ignored by liberal and structural bias feminists, as well as to the failure of first world feminists to see similar types of oppression in their own cultures. . . .

In addition to questioning first world feminist understandings of culture, third world feminist critics also challenge the structural bias focus on culture at the principle site of women's oppression. As [Leslye] Obiora puts it: "The truth of the matter is that, despite popular feminist discourses, culture may not be the dispositive influence on the responses of women." For many third world critics, the focus on culture or "private" sphere rights detracts from issues and concerns of greater importance to women in the third world. As Obiora explains, "[c]ampaigns for sexual rights and freedoms [have been] disparaged as the trite obsession of privileged Western feminists by some [third world] feminists who preferred to emphasize economic concerns." Even when Western feminists attempt to address economic issues, such as the rights of female workers in the third world, third world critics argue that they sometimes miss the source of the problems by analyzing them through the structural bias lens. Ong notes, for example, that it is not only "local patriarchal norms" that are responsible for mistreatment of female workers, and that if Western feminists really want to address the problems of women's inequalities, they will need "to confront not only cultural practices in Third World countries, but also metropolitan capitalist enterprises that are driven by profits to seek cheap female labor in the South."

For additional discussion of feminist perspectives on international law beyond the excellent collection of essays in International Law: Modern Feminist Approaches (Doris Buss & Ambreena Manji eds., 2005), see Hilary Charlesworth & Christine Chinkin, The Boundaries of International Law: A Feminist Analysis (2000); Catherine A. MacKinnon, Are Women Human?: And Other International Dialogues (2006); Fionnuala Ni Aolain & Michael Hamilton, Gender and the Rule of Law in Transitional Societies, 18 Minn. J. Int'l L 380 (2009); and Dianne Otto, The Exile of Inclusion: Reflections on Gender Issues in International Law Over the Last Decade, 10 Melb. J. Int'l L. 11 (2009).

6. *Third World Approaches to International Law*

Antony Anghie & B.S. Chimni, Third World Approaches to International Law and Individual Responsibility in Internal Conflict

The Methods of International Law 185, 186-190, 192-194
(Steven D. Ratner & Anne-Marie Slaughter eds., 2004)

For [Third World Approaches to International Law (TWAIL)] scholars, international law makes sense only in the context of the lived history of the peoples of the Third World. Two important characteristics of TWAIL thinking emerge from this. First, the experience of colonialism and neo-colonialism has made Third World peoples acutely sensitive to power relations among states and to the way in which any proposed international rule or institution will actually affect the distribution of power between states and peoples. Second, it is the actualized experience of these peoples, and not merely that of the States that represent them in international fora, that is the interpretive prism through which the rules of international law are to be evaluated. This is because . . . Third World states often act against the interests of their peoples. For us, then, Third World peoples' resistance to, or acceptance of, international rules and practices that affect their lives offers strong evidence of the justice or injustice of those rules and practices. By evaluating positivist rules through the lens of the lived experience of Third World peoples, TWAIL scholars seek to transform international law from a language of oppression to a language of emancipation — a body of rules and practices that reflect and embody the struggles and aspirations of Third World peoples and that, thereby, promote truly global justice. . . .

[The first generation of post-colonial international TWAIL scholarship (TWAIL I)] indicted colonial international law for legitimizing the subjugation and oppression of Third World peoples. Nineteenth century international law, for instance, excluded non-European states from the realm of sovereignty, upheld the legality of unequal treaties between European powers and non-European powers, and ruled that it was completely legal to acquire sovereignty over non-European societies by conquest. . . .

[Nevertheless,] TWAIL I adopted a non-rejectionist stance toward modern international law [and] . . . believed that . . . the UN [could] bring about the changes necessary to usher in a just world order. . . .

In the last decade or so, what might be termed TWAIL II scholarship has attempted to reassess both the relationship between international law and the Third World, and the approaches taken by TWAIL I. . . .

Critiquing the Post-Colonial State

. . . [Although TWAIL II scholars, like their TWAIL I predecessors,] recogniz[e] the fundamental importance of the doctrine of sovereignty for advancing Third World interests and protection and preserving Third World states against various forms of intervention, [they] have developed powerful critiques of the Third World nation-state, or the processes of this formation and its resort to violence and authoritarianism. Corresponding with this is a concern to identify and give voice to the people within Third World states—women, peasants, workers, minorities—who have been generally excluded from TWAIL I scholarship. . . .

The Structure of Colonialism: The Civilizing Mission

We have said that international law has historically suppressed Third World peoples. How does this suppression take place, what are the techniques and technologies by which it is effected? . . . [S]uch inquiries use an analytic framework derived from the concept of the "civilizing mission." This concept justified the continuous intervention by the West in the affairs of Third World societies and provided the moral basis for the economic exploitation of the Third World that has been an essential part of colonialism.

The "civilizing mission" operates by characterizing non-European peoples as the "other"—the barbaric, the backward, the violent—who must be civilized, redeemed, developed, pacified. Race has played a crucially important role in constructing and defining the other. . . .

These ideas of the backward and primitive, we argue, exercise a powerful and unstated influence on international law. More particularly, in the context of the ongoing violence of the international system, it is significant that since the beginning of international law, it is frequently the "other," the non-European tribes, infidels, barbarians, who are identified as the source of all violence, and who must therefore be suppressed by an even more intense violence. However, this violence, when administered by the colonial power, is legitimate because it is inflicted in self-defense, or because it is humanitarian in character and indeed seeks to save the non-European people from themselves.

What is remarkable is the way in which the project of the civilizing mission has endured over time, and how essential its structure is preserved in certain versions of contemporary initiatives, for example, of "development," democratization, human rights, and "good governance," which posit a Third World that is lacking and deficient and in need of international intervention for its salvation. . . .

TWAIL and the Politics of Knowledge

. . . [With regard to the] question of how knowledge about international law is produced . . . a powerful division of intellectual labor prevails: Northern scholars and Northern institutions set these important standards. . . . [S]cholarship cannot be separated from the institutional resources—law schools, journals, publishers—that enable its production.

TWAIL has thus found it difficult to assert itself in an institutional setting that, when it is not generally uncomprehending of TWAIL's history and aims, seeks to incorporate TWAIL into a familiar geography of alliances and rivalries.

For additional writing reflecting Third World approaches to international law, see International Law and the Third World: Reshaping Justice (Richard Falk, Balakrishnan Rajagopal & Jacqueline Stevens eds., 2008); Makau Mutua, Human Rights: A Political and Cultural Critique (2002); Upendra Baxi, What May the "Third World" Expect from International Law?, 27 Third World Quarterly 713 (2006); and James Gathii, Alternative and Critical: The Contribution of Research and Scholarship on Developing Countries to International Legal Theory," 41 Harv. Int'l L. J. 263 (2000).

Bibliography

Standard texts on international law include Ian Brownlie, Principles of Public International Law (7th ed. 2008); Oppenheim's International Law (Robert Jennings & Arthur Watts eds., 9th ed. 1992); Peter Malanczuk, Akehurst's Modern Introduction to International Law (7th ed. 1997); Malcolm N. Shaw, International Law (6th ed. 2008); and I.A. Shearer, Starke's International Law (11th ed. 1994). More summary treatments can be found in Sean D. Murphy, Principles of International Law (2006); and David J. Bederman, International Law Frameworks (3rd ed. 2010).

E. INTERNATIONAL LAW IN ACTION: THE U.S. AND INTERNATIONAL RESPONSE TO THE ATTACKS OF SEPTEMBER 11, 2001

In this section we recount the events surrounding the terrorist attacks of September 11, and the U.S. and international response to them through about 2004.* These events fundamentally altered the existing relations among many states and other entities and have had a major impact on international law. This case study, designed to stimulate your thinking about the role of international law, includes many accompanying questions, questions that you will be able to answer much more knowledgeably later in the course. In later chapters we also use the collective reaction to the attacks for occasional questions.

1. *Introduction*

September 11, 2001, started as a relatively peaceful day in the world. However, as people began arriving at work on the U.S. east coast, the calm of a crisp, clear day was shattered. American Airlines Flight 11, out of Boston and destined for San Francisco, was hijacked in mid-air by Mohammed Atta and four accomplices. Atta then diverted the large Boeing 767 and crashed it at high speed and full of fuel into the North Tower of New York City's World Trade Center at 8:46 a.m.

As fire and police forces converged on the building and sketchy initial media reports circulated widely, a second large passenger jet, United Airlines Flight 175, slammed into the South Tower at 9:03 a.m., making clear that the events were no accident. About 30 minutes later, American Airlines Flight 77, originating at Dulles Airport near Washington, D.C., and destined for Los Angeles, flew low along the Potomac River and initially appeared headed toward the White House. Possibly because the hijacker pilot had trouble picking out the White House, the plane veered and found a target about two miles away, hitting the highly visible Pentagon at ground level. A fourth hijacked plane, United Airlines Flight 93, plummeted into an empty field in western Pennsylvania about 20 minutes later. Some of its passengers, who had learned of the first attacks from family and friends over cellular phones, had valiantly decided to rush the cockpit and to try to retake control of the plane, rather than let it serve as another flying bomb. In the ensuing struggle

*More recent information is sometimes provided in the text or footnotes.

between the four trained hijackers, who were armed with box cutters (which contain razor blades), and the passengers, who might have commandeered the food cart and tableware, the plane crashed far from its apparent target of the U.S. Capitol or the White House.

Nearly 3,000 innocent people were killed at the World Trade Center site, the Pentagon, and aboard the four aircraft, in addition to the 19 hijackers. The victims include 343 firefighters who had rushed without hesitation to the aid of people at the World Trade Center and 72 law enforcement officers. More Americans died in the attacks on September 11 than on any other single day in U.S. history, except during the Civil War battles at Antietam and Gettysburg. The Japanese attack on Pearl Harbor, another highly destructive sneak attack, killed about 2,400 people, mostly sailors and other military personnel. But Pearl Harbor was an attack on a military target for a military purpose — to weaken or cripple the ability of the United States to fight a naval war in the Pacific — and Gettysburg and Antietam were full-fledged military battles. By contrast, the terrorists on September 11 intentionally targeted civilians as part of their attempt to inflict symbolic and physical damage. The World Trade Center had been the target of a terrorist bombing in February 1993 and stood as a visible symbol of the United States and its economic power, and the Pentagon was a symbol of the U.S. government and its military. Nationals of more than 80 countries were murdered in the attacks, including many Muslims. Great Britain alone lost at least 67 citizens, making September 11 the deadliest terrorist attack in its history as well.

2. *Historical Background*

The attacks were deliberate and carefully planned. The United States quickly established that Osama bin Laden and his Al Qaeda organization were behind them. The following excerpts provide some historical background.

Bin Laden and Al Qaeda

Osama bin Laden's *jihadi* career began in the 1980s, fighting the Soviets in Afghanistan.

Peter L. Bergen, Jr., Holy War, Inc.: Inside the Secret World of Osama bin Laden

53-54, 62, 80-81, 88, 98-99 (2002)

Within weeks of the Soviet invasion [in December 1979, Osama] bin Laden, then twenty-two, voted with his feet and his wallet, heading to Pakistan to meet with Afghan [opposition] leaders. . . . He then returned to Saudi Arabia and started lobbying his family and friends to provide money to support the Afghan guerrillas and continued making short trips to Pakistan for his fund-raising work.

In the early 1980s bin Laden, already an expert in demolition from time spent working in his family's construction business, made his first trips into Afghanistan, bringing with him hundreds of tons of construction machinery, bulldozers, loaders, dump trucks, and equipment for building trenches, which he put at the disposal of the *mujahideen.* The machinery would be used to build rough roads, dig tunnels into the mountains for shelter, and construct rudimentary hospitals. Bin Laden's followers also set up mine-sweeping operations in the Afghan countryside.

Despite the fact that the United States was also supporting the mujahideen, bin Laden was already voicing anti-American sentiments during the early eighties. . . .

In 1984 bin Laden set up a guesthouse in Peshawar[, Pakistan] for Muslims drawn to the jihad. It was called *Beit al-Ansar,* or House of the Supporters, an allusion to the Prophet Muhammad's followers who helped him when he had to flee his native Mecca for Medina. Initially the house was simply a way station for those who would be sent for training with one of the Afghan factions. Later, bin Laden would form his own military operation. . . .

The Afghan war did not only move men like bin Laden spiritually; it also enabled them to meet key figures in terrorist organizations in the Arab world. In 1987 bin Laden was introduced to members of Egypt's Jihad group, the organization behind the 1981 assassination of Egyptian President Anwar Sadat. A leader of the group, Ayman al-Zawahiri, had settled in Peshawar and was putting his skills as a physician to work at a hospital for Afghan refugees. In 1989, bin Laden founded al-Qaeda, the "base" in Arabic, an organization that would eventually merge with al-Zawahiri's Jihad group. . . .

[When the Soviets finally withdrew from Afghanistan in 1989, bin Laden left as well, returning to his native Saudi Arabia at the age of 32. Bin Laden's anti-Americanism found a target in 1990, when the Persian Gulf War brought hundreds of thousands of U.S. troops to Saudi Arabia, in violation of what bin Laden saw as the prophet's command to "let there be no two religions in Arabia."]

. . . [B]in Laden had been denouncing Americans well before he was forced to put up with them in the flesh. On his return from the Afghan war . . . , he was quickly in demand as a speaker in mosques and homes, and one of his principal themes was a call for a boycott of American goods because of that country's support for Israel. Hundreds of thousands of recordings of his speeches circulated in the Saudi kingdom.

Ironically, bin Laden was sympathetic to the underlying cause of the U.S. presences in Saudi Arabia: the war against Saddam Hussein. . . .

After Hussein's forces did invade the small, oil-rich state [of Kuwait] on August 1, 1990, and threaten the security of Saudi Arabia, bin Laden immediately volunteered his services and those of his holy warriors. The Saudi army and his own men would be enough to defend the Kingdom, he reasoned; after all, hadn't his own troops been instrumental in driving the Russians from Afghanistan?

The Saudis did not take the offer seriously. Despite the tens of billions of dollars they had spent on their own army, they turned instead for help to the U.S. government and then-President Bush. . . .

Bin Laden's opposition to the presence of American troops was echoed by two prominent religious scholars, Sarar al-Hawali and Salman al-'Auda, who were subsequently jailed by the Saudis. Bin Laden, whose credentials as a religious scholar are nonexistent, often cites al-Hawali and al-'Auda to justify his own pronouncements against the United States. . . .

[By 1991 the Saudi regime was fed up with bin Laden's anti-government critiques and effectively put him under house arrest. But bin Laden was able to use his family connections to leave the kingdom, and he moved his base of operations to Sudan, then under the de facto rule of an Islamist cleric.

[From his base in Sudan, bin Laden simultaneously ran both a legitimate business operation and a terrorist organization. He plausibly claims responsibility for the deaths of 18 American soldiers in Mogadishu in 1993, which helped lead the United States to withdraw from Somalia. The 1993 bombing of the World Trade Center was carried out by a group of terrorists connected to the Al Qaeda network. For example, the bomber was apparently trained in explosives by Al Qaeda instructors in Afghanistan.]

In 1995 the de facto ruler of Sudan . . . organized an Islamic People's Congress, during which bin Laden was able to meet with leaders of militant groups from Pakistan, Algeria, and Tunisia as well as the Palestinian Islamic Jihad and Hamas. At the same time, al-Qaeda sought to forge alliances with the Iranian-backed Hezbollah, based in southern Lebanon. Despite their disputes over religious doctrine — Hezbollah is Shia, while bin Laden espouses a conservative Sunni Islam — the two groups buried their differences to make war against their common enemy, the United States. Al-Qaeda members traveled to Lebanon, where the group maintained a guesthouse, and, with Hezbollah, learned how to bomb large buildings. Bin Laden, meanwhile, met with Imad Mughniyeh, the secretive, Iran-based head of Hezbollah's security service. This was an important meeting. It was Mughniyeh who masterminded the suicide truck bombing of the Marine barracks in Beirut in 1983, which killed 241 American servicemen and precipitated a U.S. pull-out from Lebanon within a few months.

. . . [T]he Beirut model was one bin Laden hoped to follow. . . .

[Finally, under intense U.S. pressure, Sudan expelled bin Laden in 1996. Sudan offered to send him to Saudi Arabia or the United States for detention. However, the Saudis, who had taken the unusually severe step of stripping bin Laden of his citizenship in 1994, refused to accept him. The United States determined it could not make a case against him. He went instead to Afghanistan.]

[The Taliban regime treated bin Laden as an honored guest. In return, he provided money and warriors to the cash-strapped Taliban to help them in the civil war.]

On February 22, 1998, bin Laden upped the ante considerably when he announced the formation of the World Islamic Front for Jihad against the Jews and the Crusaders. Cosignatories of the agreement included Ayman al-Zawahiri of Egypt's Jihad Group, bin Laden's most trusted lieutenant; Rifia Ahmed Taha of Egypt's Islamic Group; and the leaders of Pakistani and Bangladeshi militant organizations. All were brought together under one umbrella for the first time.

Because the announcement inaugurating the World Islamic Front is the key text that set the stage for al-Qaeda's terrorist attacks, it is worth quoting at some length.

> Since Allah spread out the Arabian Peninsula, created its desert, and drew its seas, no such disaster has ever struck as when those Christian legions spread like pest, crowded its land, ate its resources, eradicated its nature, and humiliated its leaders. . . . No one argues today over three facts repeated by witnesses and agreed upon by those who are fair. . . . They are: Since about seven years ago, America has been occupying the most sacred lands of Islam: the Arabian Peninsula. It has been stealing its resources, dictating to its leaders, humiliating its people, and frightening its neighbors. It is using its rule in

> the Peninsula as a weapon to fight the neighboring peoples of Islam. . . . The most evident proof is when the Americans went too far in their aggression against the people of Iraq. . . . Despite major destruction to the Iraqi people at the hand of the Christian alliance and the great number of victims exceeding one million, Americans are trying once again to repeat these horrifying massacres as if they are not satisfied with the long blockade or the destruction. Here they come today to eradicate the rest of these people and to humiliate its Muslim neighbors. Although the Americans' objectives of these wars are religious and economic, they are also to serve the Jewish state and distract from its occupation of the Holy Land and its killing of Muslims therein. The most evident proof thereof is their persistence to destroy Iraq, the most powerful neighboring Arab state. . . . All those crimes and calamities are an explicit declaration by the Americans of war on Allah, His Prophet, and Muslims. . . . Based upon this and in order to obey the Almighty, we hereby give all Muslims the following judgment: The judgment to kill and fight Americans and their allies, whether civilians or military, is an obligation for every Muslim who is able to do so in any country. . . . In the name of Allah, we call upon every Muslim, who believes in Allah and asks for forgiveness, to abide by Allah's order by killing Americans and stealing their money anywhere, anytime, and whenever possible. We also call upon Muslim scholars, their faithful leaders, young believers, and soldiers to launch a raid on the American soldiers of Satan and their allies of the Devil.

A CIA analysis point out: "These *fatwas* are the first from these groups that explicitly justify attacks on American civilians anywhere in the world." . . .

On August 7, 1998, Al Qaeda operatives bombed the U.S. embassies in Nairobi, Kenya, and Dar-es-Salaam, Tanzania, killing 224 people, mostly Africans. For much of the West, this was the first time the name Osama bin Laden made headlines. The United States responded with cruise missile attacks against Al Qaeda training installations in Afghanistan and an attack against a chemical plant in Sudan that it later appeared was not connected with Al Qaeda. A U.S. grand jury subsequently indicted bin Laden in absentia for the bombing of the U.S. embassies.

On October 12, 2000, two suicide bombers exploded a bomb aboard a small boat alongside the U.S.S. Cole, which was refueling in a Yemenese port, severely damaging the destroyer and killing 17 people. This attack, which was apparently planned by Al Qaeda, drew virtually no retaliatory response from the United States. It was Al Qaeda's last attack before September 11 and might well have encouraged bin Laden to believe that the United States would not respond in any significant military way to an attack.

Bin Laden's Beliefs

Bin Laden professes a sect of Sunni Islam called Wahhabi. Professor Karen Armstrong describes the origins of this sect.

Karen Armstrong, The Battle for God

44 (2000)

On the margins of the [Ottoman] empire, where Ottoman decline was most acutely felt, people responded to the change and unrest as they had always done — in religious terms. In the Arabian Peninsula, Muhammad ibn Abd al-Wahhab (1703-92) managed to break away from Istanbul and create a state of his own in central Arabia and the Persian Gulf region. Abd al-Wahhab was a typical Islamic reformer. He met the current crisis by returning to the Koran and the Sunnah, and by vehemently rejecting medieval jurisprudence, mysticism, and philosophy. Because they diverged from this pristine Islam, as he envisaged it, Abd al-Wahhab declared the Ottoman sultans to be apostates, unworthy of the obedience of the faithful and deserving of death. Their Shariah state was inauthentic. Instead, Abd al-Wahhab tried to create an enclave of pure faith, based on the practice of the first Muslim community in the seventh century. It was an aggressive movement, which imposed itself on the people by force.

Wahhabi Islam remains the official religion of the house of Saud today, and it remains very conservative. Reinterpretation of issues decided by the Qu'ran, *hadith*, or early jurists is forbidden, although some flexibility is permitted when new issues arise. Strict conformity with its precepts is enforced by the *mutawwiin*, who are authorized to supervise dress, public behavior, and public prayer. In recent years, the Saudi regime has taken to discouraging and even banning non-Muslim worship in the kingdom.

For bin Laden, however, his particular sect takes second place to his agenda. Not only was he closely allied with the Taliban, whose own reactionary, puritanical breed of Islam, known as Deobandi, differs in a number of ways from Wahhabi, but he has made alliances with Islamist groups from Yemen, Egypt, and various other African and Middle Eastern countries. In these countries, and especially in Egypt, the homeland of many of the top Al Qaeda leaders, Wahhabi had little influence. Bin Laden's alliance with the *shi'ite* Hezbollah organization is even more telling. Bin Laden was willing to bury a millennium of religious difference for the knowledge to make Al Qaeda more effective.

Bin Laden's ultimate goal is far grander than the mere expulsion of the infidel from Saudi Arabia. As Peter Bergen explains:

> In all the tens of thousands of words that bin Laden has uttered on the public record there are some significant omissions: he does not rail against the pernicious effects of Hollywood movies, or against Madonna's midriff, or against the pornography protected by the U.S. Constitution. Nor does he inveigh against the drug and alcohol culture of the West, or its tolerance for homosexuality. . . .
>
> Judging by his silence, bin Laden cares little about such cultural issues. What he condemns the United States for is simple: its policies in the Middle East. Those are, to recap briefly: the continued American military presence in Arabia, U.S. support for Israel, its continued campaign against Iraq, and its support for regimes such as Egypt and Saudi Arabia that bin Laden regards as apostates from Islam.
>
> Bin Laden is at war with the United States, but his is a political war, justified by his own understanding of Islam, and directed at the symbols and institutions of American power. . . .
>
> Bin Laden envisaged his own counterpoint to the mark of globalization—the restoration of the *Khalifa*, or caliphate, which would begin from Afghanistan. Not since the final demise of the Ottoman Empire after the end of World War I had there been a Muslim entity that more or less united the *umma*, the community of Muslim believers, under the green flag of Islam. In this view, the treaties that followed World War I had carved up the Ottoman Empire, "the Sick Man of Europe," into ersatz

entities like Iraq and Syria. Bin Laden aimed to create the conditions for the rebirth of the *Khalifa*, where the *umma* would live under the rule of the Prophet Muhammad in a continuous swath of green from Tunisia to Indonesia, much as the red of the British empire colored maps from Egypt to Burma before World War II. As a practical matter, the restoration of the *Khalifa* had about as much chance as the Holy Roman Empire suddenly reappearing in Europe, but as a rhetorical device the call for its return exercised a powerful grip on bin Laden and his followers. (Bergen, 226-227, 20-21.)

The Taliban

It is also helpful to understand the Taliban, who provided bin Laden and Al Qaeda an important sanctuary in Afghanistan.

After the Soviet withdrawal from Afghanistan in 1989, various Afghan factions and warlords embroiled the country in a fierce power struggle. In reaction to the prevalent anarchy and warlordism, a new movement of former *mujahideen* (freedom fighters) began. This new movement, called the Taliban, took its name from the word *talib*, which means pupil. With substantial support from Pakistan, the Taliban successfully dedicated itself to removing warlords, sustaining order, and imposing an extreme interpretation of Islam on Afghanistan.

By 1994, the Taliban had captured the southern city of Kandahar, and by the fall of 1996, the regime extended its control over the capital city of Kabul and other strategic regions.

The ultra-purist version of Islam espoused by the Taliban was based in part on the rural Pashtun tradition. However, in the process of imposing this extreme interpretation of Islam, the Taliban committed grave human rights violations against the Afghan people.

Some of the Taliban's most shocking policies were directed against Afghan women. Women were forced to wear a traditional body garment called a burqa, and they could not leave home without an accompanying male relative. The Taliban forbade girls from obtaining an education and prohibited women from working outside the home. Moreover, women's access to health care was restricted, and women did not have the right to vote.

The Taliban also systematically opposed religious freedom. In early 2001, Taliban leader Mullah Omar ordered the destruction of all Buddhist statues in Afghanistan on the grounds that religious representations were un-Islamic. As a result, thousands of Buddhist statues were demolished, including some dating back to the third and fifth centuries. The Taliban's massive human rights violations also extended to their mistreatment of ethnic minorities.

Not only were the Taliban's social and religious policies objectionable, but their economic activities also stirred international concern. After the disintegration of central authority following the Soviet withdrawal, opium became the sole cash crop for many Afghans. Opium-derived revenues soon became a major source of funding for the Taliban, including nearly $40 million per year in opium taxes alone.

In part because of its human rights violations and reliance on opium exports, the Taliban were not accepted by the international community. Even though the Taliban controlled roughly 90 percent of Afghanistan from about 1998 onward, only three countries (Pakistan, Saudi Arabia, and United Arab Emirates) had formally recognized the Taliban as Afghanistan's legitimate government by September 2001. Afghanistan's seat in the U.N. General Assembly continued to be held by the Taliban's opposition, known as the Northern Alliance, even though its control over Afghan territory had dwindled.

3. Initial Reactions to the September 11 Attacks

United States

Despite the tremendous shock, confusion, and mourning on September 11 and the days immediately after, the United States responded rapidly. First to react were the brave firefighters, police officers, and other emergency personnel who rushed to the scene at the World Trade Center and the Pentagon. U.S. Air National Guard interceptors were soon scrambled, though minutes too late to prevent the attack on the Pentagon. Then the actions of the heroic passengers on the flight over Pennsylvania stopped that hijacked plane from possibly crashing into the U.S. Capitol or White House.

At 9:25 a.m. on September 11, the Federal Aviation Administration suspended flight takeoffs across the country and ordered all civilian planes to land at the nearest airport. Military forces were alerted and mobilized. By early afternoon, the Navy dispatched two aircraft carriers to New York harbor and scrambled five warships along the eastern seaboard, and fighter planes were ordered to patrol over major cities.

The investigation of the attacks was underway almost immediately. Within a few days, the 19 hijackers had been identified, and attention focused on Osama bin Laden.

President George W. Bush addressed the nation the night of September 11 and ordered a number of measures that day and in the days following. Among them, on September 14, President Bush declared a national emergency under the National Emergencies Act (50 U.S.C. §1621) and called up 50,000 reservists for the purpose of "homeland defense." At the same time, both houses of Congress passed by large margins the Authorization for Use of Military Force Resolution (AUMF), and President Bush signed it into law on September 18. The AUMF provided in pertinent part:

> That the President is authorized to use all necessary and appropriate force against those nations, organizations, or persons he determines planned, authorized, committed, or aided the terrorist attacks that occurred on September 11, 2001, or harbored such organizations or persons, in order to prevent any future acts of international terrorism against the United States by such nations, organizations or persons. (P.L. 107-40)*

On September 23, President Bush invoked the International Emergency Economic Powers Act (IEEPA). IEEPA provides the President with sweeping emergency powers in the international arena. It is designed to deal "with any unusual or extraordinary threat, which has its source in whole or substantial part outside the

*The Joint Resolution also specifically indicated that it was intended to constitute specific statutory authorization within the meaning of section 5(b) of the War Powers Resolution of 1973. (The War Powers Resolution is discussed in Chapter 11.)

United States, to the [U.S.] national security, foreign policy, or economy." If the President determines that such a threat exists, he can declare a national emergency as Bush did on September 14 under the National Emergencies Act (NEA). IEEPA then authorizes him to employ a wide range of economic powers, such as cutting off exports or imports with a particular country, or (especially relevant here) restricting public and private financial transactions with a particular country or particular foreign individuals or entities. (IEEPA is discussed further in Chapter 3.) The following is an excerpt of President Bush's Executive Order freezing the assets of terrorist groups.

President Bush, Blocking Property and Prohibiting Transactions With Persons Who Commit, Threaten to Commit, or Support Terrorism

Exec. Order 13,224 (Sept. 23, 2001), 66 Fed. Reg. 49,079

By the authority vested in me as President by the Constitution and the laws of the United States of America, including the International Emergency Economic Powers Act (50 U.S.C. 1701 et seq.) (IEEPA), the National Emergencies Act (50 U.S.C. 1601 et seq.), section 5 of the United Nations Participation Act of 1945, as amended (22 U.S.C. 287c) (UNPA) . . . and in view of United Nations Security Council Resolution[s] . . .

I, GEORGE W. BUSH, President of the United States of America, find that grave acts of terrorism . . . by foreign terrorists, including the terrorist attacks in New York, Pennsylvania, and the Pentagon committed on September 11, 2001, acts recognized and condemned in UNSCR [U.N. Security Council Resolution] 1368 of September 12, 2001, and UNSCR 1269 of October 19, 1999, and the continuing and immediate threat of further attacks on United States nationals or the United States constitute an unusual and extraordinary threat to the national security, foreign policy, and economy of the United States, and . . . hereby declare a national emergency to deal with that threat. I also find that because of the pervasiveness and expansiveness of the financial foundation of foreign terrorists, financial sanctions may be appropriate for those foreign persons that support or otherwise associate with these foreign terrorists. . . .

I hereby order:

Section 1. Except to the extent required by section 203 (b) of IEEPA (50 U.S.C. 1702(b)), or provided in regulations, orders, directives, or licenses that may be issued pursuant to this order, and notwithstanding any contract entered into or any license or permit granted prior to the effective date of this order, all property and interests in property of the following persons that are in the United States or that hereafter come within the United States, or that hereafter come within the possession or control of United States persons are blocked:

(a) foreign persons listed in the Annex to this order;

(b) foreign persons determined by the Secretary of State, in consultation with the Secretary of the Treasury and the Attorney General, to have committed, or to pose a significant risk of committing, acts of terrorism that threaten the security of U.S. nationals or the national security, foreign policy, or economy of the United States;

(c) persons determined by the Secretary of the Treasury, in consultation with the Secretary of State and the Attorney General, to be owned or controlled by, or to act for or on behalf of those persons listed in the Annex to this order or those persons determined to be subject to subsection 1(b), 1(c), or 1(d)(i) of this order; . . .

Sec. 2. Except to the extent required by section 203(b) of IEEPA (50 U.S.C. 1702(b)), or provided in regulations, orders, directives, or licenses that may be issued pursuant to this order, and notwithstanding any contract entered into or any license or permit granted prior to the effective date:

(a) any transaction or dealing by United States persons or within the United States in property or interests in property blocked pursuant to this order is prohibited, including but not limited to the making or receiving of any contribution of funds, goods, or services to or for the benefit of those persons listed in the Annex to this order or determined to be subject to this order;

(b) any transaction by any United States person or within the United States that evades or avoids, or has the purpose of evading or avoiding, or attempts to violate, any of the prohibitions set forth in this order is prohibited. . . .

Sec. 3. For purposes of this order: . . .

(c) the term "United States person" means any United States citizen, permanent resident alien, entity organized under the laws of the United States (including foreign branches), or any person in the United States; and

(d) the term "terrorism" means an activity that—

(i) involves a violent act or an act dangerous to human life, property, or infrastructure; and

(ii) appears to be intended—

(A) to intimidate or coerce a civilian population;

(B) to influence the policy of a government by intimidation or coercion; or

(C) to affect the conduct of a government by mass destruction, assassination, kidnapping, or hostage-taking. . . .

Sec. 6. The Secretary of State, the Secretary of the Treasury, and other appropriate agencies shall make all relevant efforts to cooperate and coordinate with other countries . . . to achieve the objectives of this order, including the prevention and suppression of acts of terrorism, the denial of financing and financial services to terrorists and terrorist organizations, and the sharing of intelligence about funding activities in support of terrorism. . . .

GEORGE W. BUSH, THE WHITE HOUSE, September 23, 2001.

This new order froze all the assets in the United States or in possession of U.S. entities of 27 terrorists, terrorist organizations, and charitable organizations believed to fund terrorist organizations. Included in the annex to the order were bin Laden, Al Qaeda, and several allied terrorist groups and individual members of Al Qaeda. The assets of the Taliban, amounting to $265 million within the United States, had already been frozen in 1999 as part of the response to the embassy bombings in Kenya and Tanzania. The U.S. government added an additional 39 individuals and entities to its list on October 12, 2001, and continued to add to it as new information arose. As of January 2003, there were over 200 individuals and entities on Bush's freeze list, including terrorist groups as wide-ranging as Palestinian Hamas, Kashmiri Lashkar-e-Tayyiba, and Basque ETA.*

Most of Al Qaeda's funds are located outside the United States, so international support for the freezing of terrorist assets has been important to the effectiveness of the program. To help this process, the U.N. Security Council had decided in Resolution 1373 of September 28, 2001, that all member states should "[f]reeze without delay funds and other financial assets or economic resources of persons who commit, or attempt to commit, terrorist acts or participate in or facilitate the commission of terrorist acts."

As of January 2003, the U.S. government reported that 161 other countries had issued their own blocking statutes. Overall, $123 million in terrorist assets had been frozen worldwide, $36 million of that had been blocked domestically in the United States, and the remaining $87 million had been blocked by other countries.

NATO

On September 12, the North Atlantic Treaty Organization (NATO) expressed its willingness to invoke Article 5 of its founding treaty for the first time in its history if it were determined that the September 11 attacks were indeed directed from abroad. Article 5 states:

> The Parties agree that an armed attack against one or more of them in Europe or North America shall be considered an attack against them all and consequently they agree that, if such an armed attack occurs, each of them, in exercise of the right of individual or collective self-defence recognized by Article 51 of the Charter of the United Nations, will assist the Party or Parties so attacked by taking forthwith, individually and in concert with the other Parties, such action as it deems necessary, including the use of armed force, to restore and maintain the security of the North Atlantic area.
>
> Any such armed attack and all measures taken as a result thereof shall immediately be reported to the Security Council. Such measures shall be terminated when the Security Council has taken the measures necessary to restore and maintain international peace and security.

On October 2, the NATO Secretary General stated that NATO had determined that Al Qaeda was involved in the September 11 attacks. Accordingly, "it has now been determined that the attack against the United States on 11 September was directed from abroad and shall therefore be regarded as an action covered by Article 5." Despite this rapid and heartening show of support, the role of the NATO Alliance in the ensuing military response was limited. Although some NATO members provided forces to the U.S.-led campaign in Afghanistan (namely, Britain, Canada, and France), most members limited themselves to opening their airspace to American military flights and providing some logistical support. In part, this was because the United States did not ask some of these countries to do more. Possibly the most important role played by the Alliance as an entity was to authorize the dispatch of NATO early-warning aircraft to patrol U.S. airspace, freeing American aircraft for an offensive role in Afghanistan.

*By January 2010, there were over 535 individuals and entities on the list.

The United Nations

The United Nations had been actively involved in the struggle against terrorism and quickly reacted to the attacks of September 11. Essentially all the countries of the world are members of the United Nations, with 192 member states as of March 2007.* The basic document for the United Nations is its Charter (which is a treaty), and a fundamental provision of the Charter is Article 2(4). It provides: "All Members shall refrain in their international relations from the threat or use of force against the territorial integrity or political independence of any state. . . ." The only explicit exception in the Charter for a country to use force is found in Article 51:

> Nothing in the present Charter shall impair the inherent right of individual or collective self-defense if an armed attack occurs against a Member of the United Nations, until the Security Council has taken the measures necessary to maintain international peace and security. Measures taken by Members in the exercise of this right of sell-defense shall be immediately reported to the Security Council and shall not in any way affect the authority and responsibility of the Security Council under the present Charter to take at any time such action as it deems necessary in order to maintain or restore international peace and security.

In response to a breach of peace or threat of aggression, the Security Council has the power under Chapter VII of the U.N. Charter, especially Articles 39-42, to decide on a wide range of economic and military measures and to call on all U.N. member states to apply these measures. (The U.N. Charter is in the Documentary Supplement.)

The Security Council has 15 members, with five permanent, veto-wielding members (China, France, Russia, the United Kingdom, and the United States). During the Cold War, the Security Council was often hamstrung by the veto, or the threat of veto, by one or more of the five permanent members. However, with the thawing of the Cold War, the Security Council has begun cooperating in an unprecedented way. The Security Council reacted quickly and strongly to the Iraqi invasion of Kuwait in 1990, and it played a major role in the conflict in the former Yugoslavia during the late 1990s, though it was NATO that finally took the lead in using military force against Serbia over Kosovo.

Before September 11

Prior to the terrorist attacks, the U.N. Security Council passed several resolutions condemning the Taliban for harboring terrorists and protecting terrorist training camps. After the bombings of the U.S. embassies in Kenya and Tanzania in 1999, the Security Council passed Resolution 1267, which demanded that the Taliban turn over Osama bin Laden to appropriate authorities in a country where he would be arrested. Additionally, Resolution 1267 called upon all states to prevent any Taliban-operated aircraft from taking off or landing in their territory. The

*As noted earlier, Afghanistan was a U.N. member, but in September 2001 the Northern Alliance was the recognized government, not the Taliban regime. The government of Hamid Karzai gained the seat in December 2001.

resolution further required states to freeze all assets derived from property owned or controlled by the Taliban.

In December 2000, the Security Council passed Resolution 1333 condemning the Taliban for its support of terrorist activity. The resolution demanded the Taliban's compliance with Resolution 1267. It also mandated additional actions against the Taliban by member states, such as preventing the supply of arms, military equipment, and certain chemicals to the Taliban. At the same time, the resolution contained provisions designed to maintain some humanitarian aid to the Afghan people.

It was clear even before September 11 that the Taliban failed to comply with the anti-terrorism provisions of these and other resolutions.

After September 11

The day after the September 11 attacks, the Security Council, operating from U.N. headquarters that are only a few miles away from the World Trade Center, swiftly and unanimously passed Resolution 1368. The resolution both condemned the terrorist attacks and reaffirmed the United States' right of self-defense.

U.N. Security Council Resolution 1368

(Sept. 12, 2001)

The Security Council,

Reaffirming the principles and purposes of the Charter of the United Nations,

Determined to combat by all means threats to international peace and security caused by terrorist acts,

Recognizing the inherent right of individual or collective self-defence in accordance with the Charter,

1. *Unequivocally condemns* in the strongest terms the horrifying terrorist attacks which took place on 11 September 2001 . . . and regards such acts, like any act of international terrorism, as a threat to international peace and security;

2. *Expresses* its deepest sympathy and condolences to the victims and their families and to the people and Government of the United States of America;

3. *Calls* on all States to work together urgently to bring to justice the perpetrators, organizers and sponsors of these terrorist attacks and *stresses* that those responsible for aiding, supporting or harbouring the perpetrators, organizers and sponsors of these acts will be held accountable;

4. *Calls also* on the international community to redouble their efforts to prevent and suppress terrorist acts including by increased cooperation and full implementation of the relevant international anti-terrorist conventions and Security Council resolutions, in particular resolution 1269 (1999) of 19 October 1999;

5. *Expresses* its readiness to take all necessary steps to respond to the terrorist attacks of 11 September 2001, and to combat all forms of terrorism, in accordance with its responsibilities under the Charter of the United Nations;

6. *Decides* to remain seized of the matter.

Although Resolution 1368 was a quickly drafted response to the attacks on September 11, its language had important legal consequences. First, Resolution 1368 described the terrorist attacks as a "threat to international peace and security," thus bringing them within the scope of Chapter VII of the U.N. Charter, which raised the possibility of U.N. enforcement actions. Second, Resolution 1368 recognized the legal right of individual or collective self-defense in accordance with the Charter. Many observers have interpreted this language to mean that the Security Council implicitly recognized that a state could respond militarily against those responsible for the attacks, even though the terrorists were not state actors. Prior to September 11, the Security Council had failed to reach a unanimous position on unilateral retaliation for terrorist attacks. Moreover, when the General Assembly spoke on the issue, it often condemned such unilateral military responses.

Although the Council's resolution suggests that a nation has a right of self-defense in response to international terrorism, according to Article 51 of the Charter, the right to individual or collective self-defense is only an interim right — "until the Security Council has taken measures necessary to maintain international peace and security." Hence, the Security Council could try to take charge in the future, but a permanent member could use its veto power to block the Security Council.

On September 28, the Security Council followed up Resolution 1368 with an even stronger anti-terrorism declaration in Resolution 1373. Specifically, it stated that member states should implement domestic legislation that would fight the "international threat to peace and security" that terrorism had become and that all states shall take a number of other steps.

U.N. Security Council Resolution 1373

(Sept. 28, 2001)

The Security Council . . .

2. *Decides also* that all States shall:

(a) Refrain from providing any form of support, active or passive, to entities or persons involved in terrorist acts, including by suppressing recruitment of members of terrorist groups and eliminating the supply of weapons to terrorists;

(b) Take the necessary steps to prevent the commission of terrorist acts, including by provision of early warning to other States by exchange of information;

(c) Deny safe haven to those who finance, plan, support, or commit terrorist acts, or provide safe havens;

(d) Prevent those who finance, plan, facilitate or commit terrorist acts from using their respective territories for those purposes against other States or their citizens;

(e) Ensure that any person who participates in the financing, planning, preparation or perpetration of terrorist acts or in supporting terrorist acts is brought to justice and ensure that, in addition to any other measures against them, such terrorist acts are established as serious criminal offences in domestic laws and regulations and that the punishment duly reflects the seriousness of such terrorist acts;

(f) Afford one another the greatest measure of assistance in connection with criminal investigations or criminal proceedings relating to the financing or support of terrorist acts, including assistance in obtaining evidence in their possession necessary for the proceedings;

(g) Prevent the movement of terrorists or terrorist groups by effective border controls and controls on issuance of identity papers and travel documents, and through measures for preventing counterfeiting, forgery or fraudulent use of identity papers and travel documents;

3. *Calls* upon all States to:

(a) Find ways of intensifying and accelerating the exchange of operational information, especially regarding actions or movements of terrorist persons or networks; forged or falsified travel documents; traffic in arms, explosives or sensitive materials; use of communications technologies by terrorist groups; and the threat posed by the possession of weapons of mass destruction by terrorist groups; . . .

(c) Cooperate, particularly through bilateral and multilateral arrangements and agreements, to prevent and suppress terrorist attacks and take action against perpetrators of such acts;

(d) Become parties as soon as possible to the relevant international conventions and protocols relating to terrorism, including the International Convention for the Suppression of the Financing of Terrorism of 9 December 1999;

(e) Increase cooperation and fully implement the relevant international conventions and protocols relating to terrorism and Security Council resolutions 1269 (1999) and 1368 (2001);

(f) Take appropriate measures in conformity with the relevant provisions of national and international law, including international standards of human rights, before granting refugee status, for the purpose of ensuring that the asylum-seeker has not planned, facilitated or participated in the commission of terrorist acts;

(g) Ensure, in conformity with international law, that refugee status is not abused by the perpetrators, organizers or facilitators of terrorist acts, and that claims of political motivation are not recognized as grounds for refusing requests for the extradition of alleged terrorists.

The U.N. General Assembly also addressed the issue of international terrorism after the September 11 attacks. Each country's U.N. permanent representative spoke in a week-long debate on the question of terrorism. Perhaps the most controversial aspect of the discussions centered on whether the U.N. should set a specific definition as to what constitutes terrorism. Both the need for such a definition and the content of such a definition produced considerable debate and disagreement. Despite the General Assembly's efforts, no general consensus on the definition of terrorism was reached.

Notes and Questions

1. As noted above, the AUMF Resolution authorized the President to "use all necessary and appropriate force" against countries that had "aided the terrorist attacks that occurred on September 11, 2001." Do you think that President Bush could have proceeded to conduct the major U.S. operations against the Taliban in Afghanistan that began in October 2001, even if Congress had not passed this or any similar resolution? What about Article I, Section 8, clause 11 of the U.S. Constitution, which gives Congress the power "[t]o declare War"? Given the broadly phrased AUMF resolution, did Congress cede all responsibilities and authority for

conducting military operations in Afghanistan? If Congress later thought that the Bush Administration and the military might be failing to take sufficient precautions to protect innocent Afghan civilians, what steps were available to Congress?

2. Did the AUMF also give the President the authority to launch a major military attack on a third country, such as Iraq or Iran, if the President determined that there was sufficient evidence to demonstrate that one of those countries had provided material support to the hijackers?

3. The scope of the AUMF has been widely debated. Bush Administration officials claimed the AUMF constituted broad congressional authorization for the President to conduct the war on terrorism and sought to justify many executive actions under it. This included the creation of special military commissions to try detainees held at Guantanamo Bay, Cuba (which is discussed below in this chapter and in Chapters 3 and 12), as well as the National Security Agency's (NSA) intercepting and listening to some telephone calls between U.S. citizens in the United States and individuals abroad, without seeking warrants from a U.S. federal court. (Chapter 3 contains a general analysis of the President's powers in foreign relations.)

4. As noted above, President Bush issued an Executive Order on September 23, 2001, invoking a broad U.S. law, IEEPA, to block (or freeze) the assets of Al Qaeda and other terrorist groups and individuals when the assets are in the United States or under the control of "U.S. persons." This phrase was defined to include, among others, U.S. individual citizens and U.S. corporations, even if they were abroad. What authority does a U.S. President have to regulate assets in other countries, such as Saudi Arabia, even if they are held by a "U.S. person"? Does it matter that most other countries agreed to cooperate with the U.S. order? What if Saudi Arabia disagreed with some of the Executive Order's designations of terrorist groups and individuals and directed that a U.S. company in Saudi Arabia should not freeze the assets of those disputed entities? Whose law controls?

5. Assume that the scope of the Executive Order, issued pursuant to IEEPA, was extended to include, besides U.S. individual citizens and U.S. corporations, "any corporation, wherever organized or doing business, that is owned or controlled by a U.S. corporation" — that is, foreign subsidiaries of a U.S. corporation. Does the U.S. President have the power to order an Italian subsidiary of a U.S. corporation to freeze assets that it might have in its possession in Italy from Al Qaeda or the Taliban (e.g., a bank deposit, or advances for goods that have yet to be delivered)? Should the President have this power? What are the rights of the government of Italy? (We will return to these questions in Chapter 7.)

6. NATO was created in 1949 to provide a counterweight to the Soviet Union and its satellite states in Eastern Europe. Its primary purpose was to discourage a Soviet attack on Western European democracies. With the end of the Cold War, its mission has been redefined. It has expanded in recent years to include some of its former adversaries in Eastern Europe and has even created a system by which Russia can have a nearly equal say in its deliberations. NATO forces fought the war against Milosevic in the former Yugoslavia and then provided peacekeepers in Kosovo afterwards.

When NATO invoked Article 5 against Al Qaeda on October 2, 2001, what were the obligations of the 19 countries then in NATO? Does Article 5 require each country to assist the United States?

After invoking Article 5 for the first time in its history, NATO's most important action was to contribute five early warning aircraft to the defense of United States skies. Why did the United States and just a few allies, and not NATO, take the lead in operations against Al Qaeda and the Taliban?

7. As noted earlier, from 1998 to 2001, the Taliban controlled about 90 percent of Afghanistan, but only three countries recognized the Taliban as the legitimate government of Afghanistan, with most of the remaining countries recognizing the rival Northern Alliance. Moreover, while Afghanistan is a member state of the United Nations and has signed the U.N. Charter, the United Nations continued to recognize the Northern Alliance as that state's government. What does recognition mean when a group (such as the Northern Alliance) cannot exercise effective control over its own territory? What effect does non-recognition have on a regime that is the de facto government of a state? (We return to these questions in Chapter 5.)

8. Security Council Resolution 1368 declared terrorism a threat to international peace and security. This finding is a precondition to any use by the Security Council of its Chapter VII powers under the U.N. Charter—including the authority to direct member states to take certain actions. Resolution 1373 exercised these powers for the first time after September 11, obligating member states to deny terrorists safe haven in their territories, to refrain from supporting terrorists, and to bring terrorists and their supporters to justice. Was the Taliban bound by Resolution 1373?

Of course, the Taliban did not abide by Resolution 1373. Were states other than Afghanistan authorized to use force to ensure compliance by the Taliban? Were they obligated to do so? If Resolution 1373 was not sufficient authority for a state to take action against the Taliban, could the Security Council have specifically authorized or required the use of force against the Taliban?

9. Resolution 1368 recognized the inherent right of individual and collective self-defense acknowledged in Article 51 of the U.N. Charter and called on member states to ensure that the perpetrators of the September 11 attacks are held accountable. Did this authorize the use of force by the United States? By Great Britain? Whatever your answer about Resolution 1368, does international law require that the United States obtain U.N. Security Council authorization to use force against those who supported the September 11 terrorists? Did Great Britain need authorization? Does "collective self-defense" include only recognized regional groups, such as NATO, or can informal coalitions be developed? See also U.N. Charter Article 52.

4. Building a Coalition

In his September 20, 2001, address to a joint session of Congress, President Bush issued an ultimatum to the Taliban:

> Deliver to United States authorities all the leaders of Al Qaida who hide in your land. Release all foreign nationals, including American citizens, you have unjustly imprisoned. Protect foreign journalists, diplomats, and aid workers in your country. Close immediately and permanently every terrorist training camp in Afghanistan, and hand over every terrorist and every person in their support structure to appropriate authorities. Give the United States full access to terrorist training camps, so we can

> make sure they are no longer operating. These demands are not open to negotiation or discussion. The Taliban must act and act immediately. They will hand over the terrorists, or they will share in their fate.

The Taliban attempted to negotiate turning over bin Laden in the days after September 20, but the Taliban sought to impose conditions that President Bush had already said were unacceptable. In the meantime, the Taliban was losing what little international support it might have had. Both Saudi Arabia and the United Arab Emirates severed their diplomatic ties with the Taliban, leaving Pakistan as the only country that recognized the Taliban, and this was primarily to keep open a channel for negotiations.

Even before President Bush's September 20 speech, the United States had initiated far-ranging diplomatic negotiations with many countries to seek their understanding and possible cooperation for a military response. General Pervez Musharraf of Pakistan was crucial to this emerging coalition. Although Pakistan's intelligence services had supported the Taliban in its rise to power and Islamic groups protested cooperation with the United States, Musharraf promptly condemned the attacks and the Taliban for harboring bin Laden, and agreed to allow the United States and its coalition to use Pakistani airspace and eventually airbases. With these steps, Musharraf reversed what had been an increasingly chilled U.S.-Pakistani relationship.

Also important was the agreement of the former Soviet republics of Uzbekistan, Kyrgyzstan, and Tajikistan, which faced internal threats from Al Qaeda-linked Islamist movements, to permit U.S. forces to operate from bases in their territory in exchange for increased U.S. aid and closer political and security ties. Similarly, Kuwait and Qatar, two Muslim countries in the Middle East, allowed the use of existing airbases for U.S. air strikes in Afghanistan.

Although several European countries offered military support as well, the United States chose to use primarily its own forces and those of the Northern Alliance and other indigenous Afghan forces, with limited military assistance from British troops (as well as Australian and Canadian forces). Other European countries were asked to provide humanitarian aid and sometimes overflight permission for U.S. military aircraft. Turkey allowed the use of important airbases there.

President Vladimir Putin of Russia agreed to provide more Soviet-era arms and munitions to the Northern Alliance, with which it already had ties. Russia also let the U.S. military operate freely in the former Soviet republics that Russia still considered to be in the Russian sphere of influence. Putin's price for this cooperation was not completely clear to observers, but aside from closer ties generally with the West, one benefit has been a freer hand in dealing with the separatist Chechens, some of whom have links to Al Qaeda.

China's support publicly and in the United Nations had considerable political value for the United States, though China also used the rhetoric of the "war on terrorism" to justify its crackdown on its own Islamic separatist minority, the Uighurs in Xinjiang province. Finally, while most of the Muslim states of the Middle East were not forthcoming with material support, several provided intelligence and law enforcement assistance in disrupting Al Qaeda networks outside of Afghanistan.

5. *The Military Campaign*

With the coalition assembled and with U.S. air, ground, and naval units moved thousands of miles into forward positions, President Bush gave the order on October 7, 2001, to begin the campaign against Afghanistan, code-named Operation Enduring Freedom. Nighttime airstrikes began on October 7 and continued for three nights, after which the United States declared that it had established air supremacy and could now bomb in daylight and, when appropriate, send in ground forces. The strikes, which targeted Taliban tanks, artillery, weapons and fuel depots, and command centers, as well as Al Qaeda training camps, were carried out by ship-launched cruise missiles and bombers. Meanwhile, the allies dropped food rations, trying to minimize the bombing campaign's impact on civilians. By October 19, American Special Forces were able to land and to carry out raids and other missions near Taliban strongholds.

The ground war began in earnest in the closing days of October. The U.S. air campaign shifted its emphasis to supporting the ground forces of the Northern Alliance, a group of mostly Tajik and Uzbek warlords who were at that time the only effective anti-Taliban rebels. Their charismatic leader, Ahmad Shah Massood, had been assassinated just two days before the September 11 attacks, almost certainly by Al Qaeda. However, his faction still controlled significant amounts of territory when Operation Enduring Freedom began. The United States began targeting Taliban troop concentrations in the north and, in particular, those forces opposing Northern Alliance fighters.

The first major successes of this coordinated campaign came in mid-November. On November 9, the northern stronghold of Mazar-e-Sharif fell to the Northern Alliance, operating in coordination with U.S. forces. After that initial victory, the rest of the country fell relatively quickly. Northern Alliance forces took the capital, Kabul, from retreating Taliban forces on November 12, and the cities of Herat, Jalalabad, and Konduz fell within weeks. U.S. forces were able to occupy Bagram Air Force Base, about 27 miles north of Kabul, and use it as a staging area for other operations. The success of the Northern Alliance and the promise of American air support encouraged rebel groups in other parts of Afghanistan to rise up against the Taliban. One of these groups, under the leadership of Hamid Karzai, accepted the surrender of the Taliban capital of Kandahar on December 6. (As discussed below, Karzai had been chosen to lead an interim post-Taliban government days earlier.)

Remnants of the Taliban and Al Qaeda retreated to tunnel complexes built to house *mujahideen* fighting against the Soviets, such as Tora Bora, near the Pakistani border. Tora Bora fell on December 16 to a combination of American precision bombs and local forces the Americans called the "Eastern Alliance." However, the Eastern Alliance failed to follow up its victory, and there were insufficient U.S. forces on the ground to prevent hundreds of Al Qaeda members, apparently including bin Laden, from escaping into the relatively lawless tribal regions of Pakistan. Another attack on an Al Qaeda cave complex in February and March 2002 was more successful. Over 1,000 U.S. infantrymen led the attack, called Operation Anaconda, against regrouping Al Qaeda in the Shah-i-kot valley, and they were able to prevent most of the fighters from escaping.

After Operation Anaconda, the remnants of Al Qaeda mostly scattered to tribal areas of Pakistan and Afghanistan. Cooperative operations between U.S. and allied forces and some local warlords against pockets of fighters continued, but nothing on the scale of Anaconda or Tora Bora.

Notes and Questions

1. Mostly through Pakistani intermediaries, the United States apparently communicated with Taliban representatives in an attempt to capture bin Laden and his accomplices without war. How could the United States negotiate with the Taliban without recognizing them?

2. On August 2, 1990, an Iraqi army invaded and occupied Kuwait. The reaction around the world was all but instantaneous and, with very few exceptions, entirely negative. The United Nations and the governments of most nation-states condemned the invasion as a violation of international law. Yet the U.S. attack on the Taliban was criticized only by a small minority of Muslim states, most of which dropped their objections when the invasion succeeded beyond expectations. Why did the world community condemn the Iraqi invasion, but not the U.S. attacks? Were the U.S. attacks consistent with international law? If so, what principles provided the justification for them? Besides the fact that the United States was responding to the September 11 attacks on its territory that were organized by Al Qaeda, does it help that the United States was also operating in conjunction with the Northern Alliance?

3. Given that most countries and the United Nations recognized the Northern Alliance as the government of Afghanistan, were the U.S. attacks in Afghanistan an "invasion" of Afghanistan? Did the United States "declare war" or "go to war" against Afghanistan? How would you characterize the U.S. operations against the Taliban and Al Qaeda? Was the United States intervening in a civil war?

4. Review Note 9 in the last set of Notes and Questions. If you think that the United States might have been justified in attacking the Taliban and Al Qaeda under Article 51 of the U.N. Charter and/or pursuant to U.N. Security Council Resolutions 1368 and 1373, did the attack have to be proportional? The United States made the overthrow of the Taliban one of its explicit objectives when the U.S. offensive began. If it could have uprooted Al Qaeda without bringing down the Taliban, should it have had to?

5. One notable aspect of the conflict in Afghanistan was the increased use of high-technology warfare. Perhaps the most important innovation was the widespread use of "smart bombs," guided by Global Positioning System (GPS) satellites. As many as 70 percent of the bombs used in Afghanistan were smart bombs (versus about 9 percent in the 1991 Persian Gulf War). Most were ordinary bombs equipped with a JDAM (for Joint Direct Attack Munitions), a kit that costs about one-fifth what a Gulf War laser-guided bomb did. The kit allows a bomb to guide itself to within three feet of a target. Other high-tech American advances that transformed this war include infantry equipment such as night-vision goggles, as well as the "Predator" unmanned aircraft, which were used to take images and, later in the campaign, to fire missiles.

This high technology was often combined with old-fashioned low-tech warfare. There were situations when an American soldier, traveling on horseback and accompanied by Afghan forces using World War I-era rifles, would enter target coordinates into a state-of-the-art laptop computer. Within minutes, the command center in

Saudi Arabia would relay the coordinates to a 1970s-era bomber, which would drop a GPS-guided bomb on Taliban or Al Qaeda troop concentrations or installations.

The use by American forces of high-tech weaponry kept both U.S. and civilian casualties relatively low. One result was that far fewer civilian targets were hit by stray bombs, although some mistakes still occurred, largely as a result of human error and equipment failure.

Despite a low ratio of civilian casualties compared to past military actions, even ones as recent as the Kosovo air campaign, the U.S. military was criticized for some operations that resulted in civilian casualties. Is the United States or its soldiers responsible when a bomb goes astray in an area of conflict? What if human error is the cause and the bomb is mistakenly programmed with the coordinates of a hospital, or a U.S. gunship fires on a wedding party? In at least one such case, the United Nations faced pressure to perform an independent investigation. What limits should international law place on warfare? With the recent creation of an International Criminal Court, do U.S. soldiers have to worry about being criminally charged for decisions made under fire? (These questions are discussed more fully in Chapters 11 and 12.)

6. *Transition and Peacekeeping*

The Bonn Compromise

As the United States and Britain launched their military operations in Afghanistan, President Bush called on the United Nations to help rebuild a post-war Afghanistan. However, after the very troubled experience of peacekeeping operations in Somalia, U.N. officials were wary of taking on the nation-building role in Afghanistan. Nevertheless, U.N. Secretary-General Kofi Annan appointed a former Algerian foreign minister, Lakhdar Brahimi, as U.N. envoy for the Afghan peace settlement. As discussed below, backed by the United States and other countries, Brahimi successfully negotiated an agreement in Bonn, Germany, that set up an interim Afghan administration. In addition, Brahimi and a number of countries shaped the U.N. aid programs that sustained much of Afghanistan's population.

The Bonn conference brought together the leaders of the four primary Afghan factions: the Northern Alliance, representing the Uzbek and Tajik minorities, and the Rome, Peshawar, and Cyprus groups, representing Pashtuns connected to former King Mohammed Zahir Shah, to Pakistan, and to Iran, respectively. The conference met from November 27 through December 5, 2001, and created an interim government under the leadership of Hamid Karzai, who was absent from the meeting because he was commanding the assault on Kandahar. The meeting also provided for a *loya jirga,* or "grand council," to establish a transitional government that would lead for up to two years, followed by elections and ratification of a new constitution in 2004.

Peacekeeping Efforts

In December 2001, after the negotiation of the Bonn agreement, the U.N. Security Council passed Resolution 1386, which established an International

Security Assistance Force (ISAF) to aid in maintaining peace and security in Kabul. Resolution 1386 authorized the ISAF to take "all necessary measures" to fulfill the peacekeeping mission. Everyone recognized that this might include the use of force.

U.N. Security Council Resolution 1386

(Dec. 20, 2001)

The Security Council . . .

1. *Authorizes*, as envisaged in Annex 1 to the Bonn Agreement, the establishment for 6 months of an International Security Assistance Force to assist the Afghan Interim Authority in the maintenance of security in Kabul and its surrounding areas, so that the Afghan Interim Authority as well as the personnel of the United Nations can operate in a secure environment;

2. *Calls upon* member states to contribute personnel, equipment and other resources to the International Security Assistance Force, and invites those member states to inform the leadership of the Force and the Secretary-General;

3. *Authorizes* the member states participating in the International Security Assistance Force to take all necessary measures to fulfil its mandate;

4. *Calls upon* the International Security Assistance Force to work in close consultation with the Afghan Interim Authority in the implementation of the force mandate, as well as with the Special Representative of the Secretary-General;

5. *Calls upon* all Afghans to cooperate with the International Security Assistance Force and relevant international governmental and non-governmental organizations, and welcomes the commitment of the parties to the Bonn Agreement to do all within their means and influence to ensure security . . . ;

6. *Takes note* of the pledge made by the Afghan parties to the Bonn Agreement in Annex 1 to that Agreement to withdraw all military units from Kabul . . . ;

7. *Encourages* neighbouring States and other member states to provide to the International Security Assistance Force such necessary assistance as may be requested, including the provision of overflight clearances and transit;

8. *Stresses* that the expenses of the International Security Assistance Force will be borne by the participating member states concerned, *requests* the Secretary-General to establish a trust fund through which contributions could be channelled to the member states or operations concerned, and encourages member states to contribute to such a fund; . . .

10. *Calls on* member states participating in the International Security Assistance Force to provide assistance to help the Afghan Interim Authority in the establishment and training of new Afghan security and armed forces;

11. *Decides* to remain actively seized of the matter.

Participation in the ISAF originally totaled roughly 4,600 troops from 122 different countries. The leadership of the ISAF initially rotated among Western countries, but NATO took over leadership of the ISAF in August 2003. This was NATO's first mission outside the Euro-Atlantic area in its history. Primarily, the ISAF aimed to assist in maintaining security, develop Afghan national security structures, assist the nation's reconstruction, and aid the training of Afghan security forces.

The ISAF was initially limited to Kabul, but its area of responsibility expanded to include about 50 percent of the country by 2006.*

Substantial numbers of separate U.S. forces remained in Afghanistan to track down Taliban and Al Qaeda remnants. The United States helped coordinate the peacekeeping operations and provided intelligence assistance to the peacekeeping troops. In addition, the United States supplied equipment and training to Afghan security forces.

In addition to establishing the ISAF, the U.N. Security Council passed Resolution 1401 in March 2002, which approved the establishment of the United Nations Assistance Mission in Afghanistan (UNAMA) a small-scale peacekeeping project. The UNAMA coordinates relief and reconstruction efforts, narcotics control, and other U.N. activities in Afghanistan. The UNAMA led efforts to organize the 2004 presidential elections and 2005 National Assembly elections.

Government

The *loya jirga* called for in the Bonn Agreement met practically on schedule in June 2002 and elected Hamid Karzai as the president of the transitional government. Many participants were disappointed with the outcome, however, because decisions appeared to have been made before the council met. Karzai was elected with 80 percent of the vote, but only after Burhanuddin Rabbani, the Tajik former president and a leader of the Northern Alliance, and the popular ex-king Mohammed Zahir Shah declared that they would not stand for election. These withdrawals were perceived by many Afghans to have been engineered by the U.S. government, which supported Karzai. Zahir Shah was given the formal title "Father of the Nation" and a series of ceremonial responsibilities, but no political role. The *loya jirga* disbanded without an agreement on the makeup or powers of a national parliament. On June 24, Karzai and his cabinet were sworn into office.

The transitional government drafted a constitution, which was ratified by a Constitutional *Loya Jirga* on January 4, 2004. Under this new constitution, Afghanistan's first national democratic presidential election was conducted on October 9, 2004. Hamid Karzai was elected President with about 55 percent of the vote, and he was inaugurated in December 2004. Elections for the lower house of the National Assembly were conducted in September 2005. Members of the upper house of the National Assembly are indirectly elected by the provincial councils and by reserved presidential appointments.

As of 2005, the Karzai government still faced serious opposition to its effective governance over Afghanistan. First, the problems of poverty, illiteracy, disease, and repression of women were still widespread. Second, many Afghans perceived the Karzai government as corrupt, and many resented the U.S. and other foreign troops, who were seen as supporting the Karzai government. Third, the Taliban, allied with drug lords and other groups who were unhappy with the Karzai government, had regrouped. The Taliban extended their control over some areas and were engaged in hostilities with U.S., NATO, and Afghan forces.

*After August 2006, the ISAF further expanded its role to take over the lead military role from U.S. troops in southern Afghanistan, where Taliban holdouts have a significant presence. By December 2010, NATO was leading some 132,000 troops from 48 countries.

Notes and Questions

1. As outrageous as the Taliban were and as justified as the U.S. invasion might have been, did the United States and its allies have the right or responsibility to influence the regime change by toppling the Taliban and pushing for the installation of Hamid Karzai? Should international law have anything to say about the concept of nation building?

2. U.N. peacekeeping forces were sent to Kabul at the request of the Bonn meeting to prevent anarchy or warlordism from filling the void left by the Taliban's totalitarian rule. The United Nations authorized peacekeeping missions dozens of times in the 1990s, and there have been both notable successes and failures. (See Chapter 11.) What is the obligation of the United Nations to maintain order in a country like Afghanistan, which has not known peace since 1979? What is the obligation of the United States to see through a regime change that it helped initiate, until there is stability?

7. *Rights of Detainees*

In the course of the armed conflict in Afghanistan, the U.S. forces captured and detained, or had handed over to them by its allies, hundreds of persons associated with either the former Taliban regime or Al Qaeda. These persons were initially detained in Afghanistan and on U.S. naval vessels in the region. Beginning in January 2002, many detainees were transported to the U.S. naval base at Guantanamo Bay, Cuba. The number of detainees at the facility peaked at 680 in May 2003.*

The U.S. detention of the Taliban and Al Qaeda led to questions about their status under the Geneva Conventions of 1949. These are four treaties concluded at the end of World War II that were intended to reduce the human suffering caused by war. The treaties provide for the amelioration of the conditions of the wounded and sick in armed forces in the field (First Geneva Convention); amelioration of the conditions of the wounded, sick, and shipwrecked members of armed forces at sea (Second Geneva Convention); humane treatment of prisoners of war (Third Geneva Convention); and the protection of the civilian persons in time of war (Fourth Geneva Convention). As of January 2003, there were 190 parties to the Geneva Conventions, including the United States and Afghanistan.

The Geneva Conventions generally apply in the case of armed conflict between states that are parties to the Conventions. In addition, the four Conventions contain an identical Article 3, which applies to "armed conflict not of an international character occurring in the territory of one of the" parties to the Conventions. It provides that the people taking no part in hostilities, including detained members of the armed forces, "shall in all circumstances be treated humanely." It prohibits, among other acts: "violence to life and person, in particular . . . cruel treatment and torture"; "outrages upon personal dignity, in particular, humiliating and degrading treatment"; and "the passing of sentences . . . without previous judgment pronounced by a regularly constitute court affording all the judicial guarantees which are recognized as indispensable by civilized peoples." (Common Article 3

*Although the United States began releasing some prisoners and the process accelerated with the Obama administration, about 173 detainees still remained at Guantanamo Bay in January 2011.

and other excerpts of the Third Geneva Convention are in the Documentary Supplement.)

Initially, "U.S. officials referred to the detainees as 'unlawful combatants,' whom the United States regarded as falling outside the protections of the Third Geneva Convention, but who would nevertheless be treated humanely. . . . [Thus,] on January 18, [2002,] President Bush initially decided (without making any public announcement) that the Third Geneva Convention did not apply to any of the detainees."*

The U.S. government's position quickly changed, however, in part because of considerable criticism from other Western countries and legal scholars. Hence, on February 7, 2002, the Bush Administration announced the U.S. government's new stance. In an official fact sheet on the status of detainees at Guantanamo the White House outlined that U.S. policy was "to treat all of the individuals detained at Guantanamo humanely and, to the extent appropriate and consistent with military necessity, in a manner consistent with principles of the Third Geneva Convention of 1949." However, "the President has determined that the Geneva Convention applies to the Taliban detainees, but *not* to the al-Qaida detainees." Al Qaeda members were not given prisoner-of-war (POW) status under the Third Geneva Convention because Al Qaeda was not "a state party to the Geneva Convention" but rather "a foreign terrorist group." As for the Taliban detainees, the President determined that, although the terms of the Geneva Convention do not grant them POW status, many POW privileges would nevertheless be provided them as a matter of policy.

Although the government's policy was to treat the detainees humanely, reports of aggressive and abusive interrogative techniques at the Guantanamo facility surfaced in later months. Some believe that the Bush Administration's disregard for the Geneva Conventions fostered confusion about rules regarding treatment and helped lead to a culture of abuse at Guantanamo, Abu Ghraib, and possibly other locations.

On November 13, 2001, President Bush issued a broad Order titled "Detention, Treatment, and Trial of Certain Non-Citizens in the War Against Terrorism" that called for the creation of military tribunals with exclusive jurisdiction, targeted at trying members of Al Qaeda, persons involved in acts of international terrorism against the United States, and those who knowingly harbored such terrorists. At a later interview, President Bush commented that the United States will "be using the tribunals if in the course of bringing someone to justice it may jeopardize or compromise the national security interests." The President's order directed the Secretary of Defense, Donald Rumsfeld, to issue other orders and regulations required for the operation of military tribunals. On March 21, 2002, the Department of Defense (DoD) issued "Military Commission Order No. 1" that outlined "procedures for trials by military commission of certain non-United States citizens in the war against terrorism."

Several groups in the United States tried to litigate the issue of detention in U.S. courts. Their efforts were initially unsuccessful, however, as U.S. federal courts held that they lacked jurisdiction because the detainees were not within the territorial jurisdiction of the courts. See, e.g., Odah v. United States, 321 F.3d 1134 (D.C. Cir

*Sean D. Murphy, Decision Not to Regard Persons Detained in Afghanistan as POWs, 96 Am. J. Int'l L. 475, 476-477 (2002).

2003). However, the Supreme Court ruled that the Guantanamo Bay detainees could bring habeas corpus petitions challenging the basis for their detention in federal courts in Rasul v. Bush, 542 U.S. 466, 483 (2004).*

Bibliography

There is extensive literature on the September 11 attacks and the U.S. and world response. A few examples are: National Commission on Terrorist Attacks upon the United States, The 9/11 Commission Report: Final Report of the National Commission on Terrorist Attacks upon the United States (2004) (a thoroughly researched, well-written, and thoughtful report and analysis); Bob Woodward, Bush at War (2002).

Up-to-date information on all U.N. activities regarding the September 11 attacks, Afghanistan, and Iraq can be found on the excellent U.N. Web site at http://www.un.org. Information about NATO's response to the September 11 attacks and presence in Afghanistan can be found on the NATO Web site at http://www.nato.int.

*In a case involving an American citizen who took up arms with the Taliban, Hamdi v. Rumsfeld, 542 U.S. 507, 520-521 (2004), a plurality of the U.S. Supreme Court, while recognizing the unconventional nature of the war on terror, found that the United States can detain enemy combatants, including American citizens, indefinitely until hostilities are over.

Later, Salim Ahmed Hamdan, a Yemeni national who was once Osama bin Laden's driver, brought a habeas corpus challenge, claiming that the military commission that had charged him lacked authority to try him under domestic and international law. In Hamdan v. Rumsfeld, 548 U.S. 557 (2006), the U.S. Supreme Court held that the military commissions created under "Military Commission Order No. 1" violated U.S. law and Common Article 3 of the Geneva Conventions. The opinion by Justice Stevens for the five-Justice majority explicitly rejected the government's argument that Common Article 3 of the Geneva Conventions does not apply to detainees captured in the war against Al Qaeda.

Soon after the *Hamdan* decision, the Bush Administration acknowledged that Common Article 3 applied to the activities of all U.S. government agencies, including the Defense Department and CIA. In September 2006, Congress passed the Military Commissions Act of 2006, Pub. L. No. 109-366, 120 Stat. 2600. Among its many provisions, The Act provided congressional approval for the creation of military commissions that provided more due process protections than the commissions created by President Bush's Order. The new commissions, however, did not provide all the protections of a military court-martial or a criminal trial. (For further discussion, see Chapter 3.B.4.)

2

The Creation of International Norms — Treaties, Customary Law, International Organizations, and Private Norm-Creation

In this chapter, we first take up two traditional components, or "sources," of public international law, treaties and customary international law, as well as the phenomenon of "soft law." We then examine the increasingly important law-generating work of international organizations and transnational networks of government regulators, as well as the activities of "nongovernmental organizations" (NGOs) and multinational (or "transnational") corporations,* which are growing more influential in international law-making processes. Finally, we address the third traditional component of public international law, the general principles of law common to the major legal systems of the world.

A. TREATIES

Treaties have become the most important source of international law and are the means by which international organizations are created. The database of treaties registered or filed and recorded with the United Nations since 1946 contains over 158,000 treaties and related subsequent actions. The United States is a party to literally thousands of international agreements that are categorized as "treaties" under international law. These agreements can be bilateral (i.e., between two countries) or multilateral. They can be labeled in a variety of ways, such as treaty, convention (often used for multilateral agreements), agreement, covenant, charter, statute, and protocol. These agreements cover a broad range of subjects, reflecting the growing complexity of international life. Bilateral agreements might deal with extradition, visas, aircraft landing rights, taxation, and investment. Multilateral agreements range from the United Nations Charter, the Agreement Establishing

*The terms "multinational corporation" and "transnational corporation" are essentially interchangeable.

the World Trade Organization, the International Covenant on Civil and Political Rights, and the Law of the Sea Convention.

Whether an instrument is a treaty or not carries a number of significant legal consequences. Under international law a treaty creates international legal obligations, with corresponding duties of compliance and entitlement to remedies, including rights of retaliation, in the event of a breach. A treaty may also create domestic legal obligations.

The U.S. domestic law relating to treaties is rather complicated and will be more fully explored in the next chapter. For present purposes it is important to recognize the differences in terminology used in international law and U.S. domestic law. In international parlance all written international agreements are referred to as "treaties." In U.S. law only some international agreements are called "treaties," *viz.*, those agreements concluded by the President with the advice and consent, or approval, of two-thirds of the Senate. The President may also conclude other international agreements on the basis of an authorization by the Congress as a whole or on the basis of his independent constitutional authority (such as his commander-in-chief power). Those other international agreements concluded by the President are sometimes called "executive agreements," even though they are still called "treaties" for purposes of international law.

Domestically, treaties approved by two-thirds of the Senate are the "law of the land" under the Constitution and may be directly enforceable in the courts. Executive agreements may also have legal status in the United States. This domestic incorporation of treaties into U.S. law is explored in Chapter 3. Sometimes domestic law will also simply refer to "international law" or will use a concept of international law for domestic purposes. For example, the Alien Tort Statute (or Alien Tort Claims Act) confers federal court jurisdiction over certain cases involving violations of "the law of nations or a treaty of the United States." (See Chapter 3.) The federal criminal code punishes "piracy as defined by the law of nations."

1. *The Formation of Treaties*

a. What Is a "Treaty"?

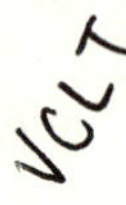

The Vienna Convention on the Law of Treaties sets forth a comprehensive set of rules governing the formation, interpretation, and termination of treaties concluded after the Vienna Convention's entry into force in 1980. As noted by a British legal expert:

> The UN General Assembly established the International Law Commission in 1947 with the object of promoting the progressive development of international law and its codification. The law of treaties was one of the topics selected by the Commission at its first session in 1949 as being suitable for codification. A series of eminent British international legal scholars (James Brierly, Hersch Lauterpacht, Gerald Fitzmaurice and Humphrey Waldock) were appointed as Special Rapporteurs. Their task was to draw up a coherent account of the already well-developed customary international law on treaties. The Commission adopted a final set of draft articles in 1966. They were considered by the United Nations Conference on the Law of Treaties in Vienna in 1968 and 1969. The Convention was adopted on 22 May 1969 and entered into force on 27 January 1980. [Anthony Aust, Modern Treaty Law and Practice 6 (2d ed. 2007).]

As of February 2011, 111 states were parties to the Convention. (The Convention is in the Documentary Supplement.) The United States, however, has signed but not ratified the Convention, so the United States is not a party to the Convention and not formally covered by it. Nevertheless, U.S. officials have consistently stated that at least most of the Convention's provisions represent customary international law, and U.S. courts have frequently relied on its terms. In his 1971 letter transmitting the Vienna Convention to the President, Secretary of State William P. Rogers called it "a generally agreed body of rules to govern all aspects of treaty making and treaty observance." See also Restatement (Third) of Foreign Relations Law pt. III, introductory note (1987) (documenting U.S. acceptance of the terms of the Convention).

Consequently, the rules set forth in the Vienna Convention are relevant to the work of private lawyers, as well as government officials, who must consider the impact of a treaty on a proposed course of conduct. The following provisions of the Convention define what treaties are and how they are made.

Vienna Convention on the Law of Treaties

Article 2. Use of Terms

For the purposes of the present Convention . . . "treaty" means an international agreement concluded between States in written form and governed by international law, whether embodied in a single instrument or in two or more related instruments and whatever its particular designation . . . [and a "party" to a treaty] means a State which has consented to be bound by the treaty. . . .

Article 11. Means of Expressing Consent to Be Bound by a Treaty

The consent of a State to be bound by a treaty may be expressed by signature, exchange of instruments constituting a treaty, ratification, acceptance, approval or accession, or by any other means if so agreed.

Article 2 of the Convention does not tell us much about the characteristics required of these instruments because it leaves unanswered the question of the definition of "international agreement." It does, however, limit the field to some extent in that *states* must be parties, the agreement must be governed by *international law*, and it must be in *writing*. The Restatement offers some additional detail about the nature of international agreements:

Restatement Section 301

Comment

. . . The terminology used for international agreements is varied. Among the terms used are: treaty, convention, agreement, protocol, covenant, charter, statute, act, declaration, *concordat*, exchange of notes, agreed minute, memorandum of agreement, memorandum of understanding, and *modus vivendi*. Whatever their designation, all agreements have the same legal status, except as their provisions or the circumstances of their conclusion indicate otherwise. . . .

. . . Since an international agreement does not require consideration . . . its obligations may be wholly unilateral, flowing from one party only, as in a peace treaty following unconditional surrender. . . .

. . . An international agreement, as defined, does not include a contract by a state, even with another state, that is essentially commercial in character and is intended to be governed by some national or other body of contract law. Examples include a loan agreement, a lease of a building, or a sale of goods.

[A] n international agreement is one intended to be legally binding and to have legal consequences. . . .

Notes and Questions

1. Recall that, according to the Restatement, "an international agreement is one intended to be legally binding" and the Vienna Convention refers to "consent." If the principal test is whether the parties intended to be bound, how do you know? Besides the text, what other places could you look to discern the intent of a party to an agreement?

2. Suppose the United States and India made an agreement for the sale of aircraft and provided that it would be governed by the law of New York. Would that agreement be a "treaty"? Would it be legally binding and enforceable in accordance with its terms?

3. The definition of a "treaty" in Article 2 of the Vienna Convention is limited to agreements "in written form." That does not mean, however, that states may not conclude valid and legally binding oral agreements. The Convention specifically notes that the fact that it does not apply to "international agreements not in written form" does not affect "the legal force of such agreements." The Comment to section 301 of the Restatement notes:

> . . . While most international agreements are in writing, written form is not essential to their binding character. The Vienna Convention specifies (Article 2(1)(a)) that it applies only to written agreements, but under customary international law oral agreements are no less binding although their terms may not be readily susceptible of proof.

In the *Legal Status of Eastern Greenland* case (Denmark v. Norway), the Permanent Court of International Justice had to determine the legal character of an oral statement by the Norwegian foreign minister to his Danish counterpart in the context of discussions about Danish claims to sovereignty over Greenland. These talks also concerned Norway's claims to sovereignty over the island of Spitzbergen. During the discussions (which the Norwegian Foreign Minister recorded in writing), the Danish minister outlined Denmark's efforts to secure international recognition of its territorial claims over Greenland and stated that Denmark was confident that Norway "will not make any difficulties in the settlement of this question." The Norwegian minister, in a subsequent meeting, replied that "the Norwegian Government would not make any difficulties in the settlement of this question." The Court concluded that the Norwegian Minister's oral declaration was binding.

> The Court considers it beyond all dispute that a reply of this nature given by the Minister for Foreign Affairs on behalf of his Government in response to the request by the diplomatic representative of a foreign Power, in regard to a question falling within his province, is binding upon the country to which the Minister belongs. [1933 P.C.I.J. (ser. A/B), No. 53, at 53 (Apr. 5).]

4. The Vienna Convention defines a treaty as an agreement concluded "between States." But a state can, in some circumstances, also assume binding legal obligations through unilateral acts or statements. Such unilateral acts or statements do not amount to a treaty, but can be another manner in which a state assumes obligations under international law. As the Restatement notes:

> A unilateral statement is not an agreement, but may have legal consequences and may become a source of rights and obligations on principles analogous to estoppel. It may also contribute to customary law. [Restatement Section 301 comment.]

In the *Nuclear Tests* cases (Australia v. France; New Zealand v. France), Australia and New Zealand initiated litigation in the ICJ challenging the legality of atmospheric nuclear weapons tests conducted by France in the Pacific Ocean. After the cases were filed, French officials, including the French President, announced that France had completed the course of its atmospheric nuclear tests. In deciding whether to address the merits of the case, the Court considered the legal effect of these statements. The Court concluded that a unilateral declaration, "given publicly, and with an intent to be bound, even though not made within the context of international negotiations, is binding." The Court noted that although "not all unilateral acts imply obligation," the French President had made a public statement addressed "to the international community as a whole"; the Court concluded that this statement constituted "an undertaking possessing legal effect." Nuclear Tests (Australia v. France), 1974 I.C.J. 253, 267, 269.

In 2006, the International Law Commission (ILC) adopted a set of principles entitled "Guiding Principles Applicable to Unilateral Declarations of States Capable of Creating Legal Obligations" and accompanying commentaries. Report of the International Law Commission to the General Assembly, U.N. GAOR Supp. 10, U.N. Doc. A/61/10, at 362 (2006). The principles, which stipulate that they apply "only to unilateral acts *stricto sensu*, i.e. those taking the form of formal declarations formulated by a State with the intent to produce obligations under international law," affirm that "[d]eclarations publicly made and manifesting the will to be bound may have the effect of creating legal obligations." Id. at 368. According to these principles, "[a] unilateral declaration that has created legal obligations for the State making the declaration cannot be revoked arbitrarily." Id. at 369. One commentator, who was member of the ILC at the time, has emphasized the limited scope of these principles, noting that they "do not apply to policy statements or even formal declarations that were not specifically intended to create legal results, even if other states might have relied upon them or asserted that they were legally binding." Michael J. Matheson, The Fifty-Eighth Session of the International Law Commission, 101 Am. J. Int'l L. 407, 421-422 (2007).

5. Although the 1969 Vienna Convention on the Law of Treaties defines a treaty as an agreement concluded "between States," states can also conclude "treaties"

with international organizations, and international organizations can conclude "treaties" with other international organizations. The United States and the United Nations, for instance, are parties to the Agreement Between the United Nations and the United States Regarding the Headquarters of the United Nations, more commonly known as the U.N. Headquarters Agreement. The Vienna Convention on the Law of Treaties Between States and International Organizations or Between International Organizations, which contains provisions similar to the 1969 Vienna Convention on the Law of Treaties, applies to treaties entered into by international organizations. It was concluded in 1986 but has yet to enter into force.

b. Distinguishing Treaties from Political Commitments

Not every document that states negotiate and conclude in the course of their international relations constitutes a treaty or is meant to be binding under international law. As the Reporters' Notes to Section 301 of the Restatement observe:

> . . . An example of a nonbinding agreement is the Final Act of the Conference on Security and Cooperation in Europe signed at Helsinki on August 1, 1975, which avoids words of legal undertaking, is designated as "not eligible for registration under Article 102 of the [U.N.] Charter," and was clearly intended not to be legally binding. Other examples include the various codes of conduct for multinational enterprises, which are characterized as voluntary and not legally binding, with respect to both the enterprises and to the states involved.
>
> Parties sometimes prefer a non-binding agreement in order to avoid legal remedies. Nevertheless, the political inducements to comply with such agreements may be strong and the consequences of noncompliance may sometimes be serious. . . . A non-binding agreement is sometimes used in order to avoid processes required by a national constitutional system for making legally-binding agreements. . . .

Even if a commitment is not legally binding, it may still carry force as a "political commitment." Governments may develop expectations of compliance with political commitments, invoke them in public debate to marshal support, and even impose sanctions for their violation. Given the absence of a general dispute settlement and enforcement mechanism for violations of legally binding commitments, the practical significance of the distinction between legal and political commitments may be blurred in particular cases.

As Professor Oscar Schachter observed, such political commitments

> take many forms and are designated by various names. Many are informal: communiqués, statements by high officials, correspondence, unwritten understandings as to future conduct. Others are more formal: proclamations by Heads of State, "final acts" of conferences, written agreements signed by the highest officials. . . . [N]either the form nor name of a document is decisive of its legal or non-legal character. . . . [Oscar Schachter, International Law in Theory and Practice 95 (1991).]

Against this background we now consider three instruments concluded by states addressing important international issues. Are they "treaties" within the meaning of the Vienna Convention?

(1) *United States-Japan FCN Treaty*

Since the eighteenth century a significant component of U.S. foreign economic policy has been the conclusion of treaties of Friendship, Commerce, and Navigation (FCN Treaties). Those treaties established favorable terms for mutual travel, trade shipping, and investment with other countries. Article VII of the 1953 United States-Japan FCN Treaty is a typical provision:

Article VII

1. Nationals and companies of either Party shall be . . . permitted . . . : (a) to establish and maintain branches, agencies, offices, factories and other establishments appropriate to the conduct of their business; (b) to organize companies under the general company laws of such other Party, and to acquire majority interests in companies of such other Party; and (c) to control and manage enterprises which they have established or acquired.

(2) *Brazil-Turkey-Iran Joint Declaration*

In May 2010, officials from Brazil and Turkey traveled to Tehran to meet with Iranian officials in an attempt to find a solution to the crisis related to Iran's efforts to develop a nuclear energy program, which the United States and many other countries believe is aimed at developing nuclear weapons. This diplomatic initiative was meant to be an alternative to the ultimately unsuccessful negotiations in which Iran had participated in 2009 with the "Vienna group"—officials from Russia, France, the United States, and the International Atomic Energy Agency. At the conclusion of the May 2010 meeting, the foreign ministers of Brazil, Turkey, and Iran produced and signed a document called a "Joint Declaration" memorializing the results of the negotiations. Here is key language from the Joint Declaration:

Having met in Tehran, . . . the undersigned have agreed on the following Declaration:

5. . . . [I]n order to facilitate . . . nuclear co-operation . . . , the Islamic Republic of Iran agrees to deposit 1,200 kg (2,600 lb) LEU [low-enriched uranium] in Turkey. While in Turkey, this LEU will continue to be the property of Iran. Iran and the IAEA [International Atomic Energy Agency] may station observers to monitor the safekeeping of the LEU in Turkey. . . .
6. Iran will notify the IAEA in writing through official channels of its agreement with the above within seven days following the date of this declaration. Upon the positive response of the Vienna Group (US, Russia, France and the IAEA), further details of the exchange will be elaborated through a written agreement and proper arrangement between Iran and the Vienna Group that specifically committed themselves to deliver 120 kg of fuel needed for the Tehran Research Reactor (TRR).
7. When the Vienna Group declares its commitment to this provision, then both parties would commit themselves to the implementation of the agreement mentioned in item 6.

   Islamic Republic of Iran expressed its readiness to deposit its LEU (1,200 kg) within one month. On the basis of the same agreement, the Vienna Group should deliver 120 kg fuel required for TRR in no later than one year.

8. In case the provisions of this declaration are not respected, Turkey, upon the request of Iran, will return swiftly and unconditionally Iran's LEU to Iran.*

(3) 2010 G-8 Declaration

The Group of Eight is composed of certain major countries that share common interests and sometimes take coordinated actions. The Heads of State meet for a private session on an annual basis, and ministers might meet on other occasions. (The present membership is the United States, Canada, England, France, Germany, Italy, Japan, and Russia. See discussion in Chapter 5.)

At the 2010 G-8 summit in Muskoka, Canada, the heads of government issued a lengthy Declaration entitled "Recovery and New Beginnings." The subsection on environmental issues included the following language regarding efforts to reduce greenhouse gas emissions:

Environmental Sustainability and Green Recovery

21. Among environmental issues, climate change remains top of mind. . . . [W]e recognize the scientific view that the increase in global temperature should not exceed 2 degrees Celsius compared to pre-industrial levels. Achieving this goal requires deep cuts in global emissions. Because this global challenge can only be met by a global response, we reiterate our willingness to share with all countries the goal of achieving at least a 50% reduction of global emissions by 2050, recognizing that this implies that global emissions need to peak as soon as possible and decline thereafter. We will cooperate to that end. As part of this effort, we also support a goal of developed countries reducing emissions of greenhouse gases in aggregate by 80% or more by 2050, compared to 1990 or more recent years. Consistent with this ambitious long-term objective, we will undertake robust aggregate and individual mid-term reductions, taking into account that baselines may vary and that efforts need to be comparable. Similarly, major emerging economies need to undertake quantifiable actions to reduce emissions significantly below business-as-usual by a specified year.

Notes and Questions

1. Are all the commitments quoted in subsections (1), (2), and (3) above legally binding agreements? In addition to analysis of the text, what else would you like to know in answering this question?

2. Is it possible for some portions of an instrument to be legally binding and others not? If so, how do you distinguish the binding from the nonbinding provisions? Would a document of this type be a treaty?

3. Why would a state (or a negotiator) want to make an instrument sound binding but not actually be binding?

*[The Vienna Group did not agree to the arrangement proposed in the document, and Iran did not deposit 1,200 kg of LEU in Turkey. — Eds.]

4. What force do political commitments have? If an instrument is not legally binding, will states have any reason to fulfill the commitments in it? Consider Professor Schachter's analysis of the force of political commitments:

> . . . States entering into a non-legal commitment generally view it as a political (or moral) obligation and intend to carry it out in good faith. Other parties and other States concerned have reason to expect such compliance and to rely on it. What we must deduce from this, I submit, is that the political texts which express commitments and positions of one kind or another are governed by the general principle of good faith. . . .
>
> It is also worth noting that the violation of a political [commitment] justifies the victim of that violation in using all the means permissible under international law to bring about a cessation of that violation and to obtain reparation. . . .
>
> These juridical effects of a political engagement are limited. They do not extend so far as to impose on the States concerned a legal responsibility to provide reparation for a breach nor do they furnish ground for judicial action on the basis of international law. Moreover they do not limit the right of the parties to terminate the non-legal undertaking when political circumstances are deemed by that State to warrant termination.
>
> The fact that non-binding [commitments] may be terminated easily does not mean that they are illusory. . . . As long as they do last, even non-binding agreements can be authoritative and controlling for the parties. It would seem sensible to recognize that non-binding agreements may be attainable when binding treaties are not and to seek to reinforce their moral and political commitments when they serve ends we value. [Oscar Schachter, International Law in Theory and Practice 100-101 (1991).]

5. How could states have "reason to expect," in Professor Schachter's words, another state to comply with a commitment that intentionally was made nonbinding? And what is the significance, in terms of compliance, that political commitments may not be subjected to the same domestic political process in their formation? An Executive Branch official may make what other states consider to be a political commitment. But under the U.S. Constitution, at least some forms of legally binding international agreements require the participation of the Congress or the Senate. See Chapter 3. The making of a political commitment has not been subjected to the same process of publicity, consensus building, and support normally accompanying congressional approval of such agreements. In light of this, shouldn't a state rely on a political commitment at its peril?

6. Although political commitments may not be legally binding, they can contribute to the formulation of what is referred to as "soft law," which is discussed below in Section B.

c. Obligation Not to Defeat the Object and Purpose

When states do decide to enter into a legally binding treaty, it is not uncommon at the successful conclusion of the negotiation process for executive branch negotiators to sign the treaty, subject to the understanding that it must be approved by each state's legislature before it has the force of law. Article 18 of the Vienna Convention imposes limited obligations on a state that has signed a treaty, but has not yet brought it into force.

Article 18. Obligation Not to Defeat the Object and Purpose of a Treaty Prior to Its Entry into Force

A State is obliged to refrain from acts which would defeat the object and purpose of a treaty when:

(a) it has signed the treaty or has exchanged instruments constituting the treaty subject to ratification, acceptance or approval, until it shall have made its intention clear not to become a party to the treaty; or

(b) it has expressed its consent to be bound by the treaty, pending the entry into force of the treaty and provided that such entry into force is not unduly delayed.

On December 31, 2000, shortly before President Bill Clinton left office, the United States signed the Rome Statute of the International Criminal Court. (See Chapter 12.) At the time, President Clinton noted "our concerns about the significant flaws in the treaty," but hoped that the U.S. signature might provide influence to obtain some changes in the ICC. The Clinton Administration never transmitted the Rome Statute to the U.S. Senate for its advice and consent, which is required before the United States can ratify a treaty. When the Bush Administration took office on January 20, 2001, it expressed more fundamental objections to the Rome Statute and concluded that the ICC's flaws could not be addressed.

In light of this determination that the Rome Statute could not be fixed, the United States sent a brief letter to the Secretary-General of the United Nations, stating that "the United States does not intend to become a party to the treaty. . . . Accordingly, the United States has no legal obligations arising from its signature on December 31, 2000." Some newspapers headlined that the United States had "unsigned" the treaty, but this was not technically accurate. The United States did not physically remove its original signature, but rather signified that since it no longer intended to become a party to the treaty, it was not obliged under Article 18 of the Vienna Convention "to refrain from acts which would defeat the object and purpose" of the Rome Statute.

How necessary was this step? What is the "object and purpose" of the Rome Statute that created and regulated a new international entity? Did President Clinton's announced concerns at the signing provide a basis for saying the United States, even at the moment of signature, did not intend to become bound by the Rome Statute? Or, how long does this obligation last after a state has signed the treaty? Could a long delay in ratifying the treaty be interpreted as signaling a clear intent not to become a party to the treaty?

Similar questions might arise with other treaties that the United States has signed, but not ratified. For example, in July 1994, the United States signed the 1982 Convention on the Law of the Sea. President Clinton transmitted the multilateral Convention and a companion 1994 agreement to the U.S. Senate for its advice and consent in October 1994. The Convention actually came into force a month later and the agreement two years later. Although the Senate Foreign Relations Committee has voted to approve ratification of the Convention, the full Senate has not, as of February 2011, voted to give its advice and consent. Is the United States still obliged to refrain from acts that would defeat the object and purpose of that

Convention and the companion agreement? (See Chapter 9 for a discussion of the Law of the Sea Convention, especially Section I.)

Notes and Questions

1. The obligation not to defeat the object and purpose of a treaty does not mean that a state must comply with all provisions of the treaty. If it did, there would be no difference between merely signing a treaty and becoming a party to it. What standard should we use to assess whether an act would defeat the object and purpose of a treaty? If a state signed but had not yet ratified a treaty prohibiting the death penalty, would the execution of a convicted criminal defeat the object and purpose? The United States has signed, but not ratified, the Comprehensive Nuclear Test Ban Treaty, which prohibits all nuclear testing. Would the United States violate its obligation not to defeat the object and purpose of the treaty by carrying out an underground test of a new nuclear warhead? One commentator, basing his argument in part on the drafting history of Article 18, suggests that the obligation not to defeat the object and purpose of a treaty "is best construed as precluding only actions that would substantially undermine the ability of the parties to comply with, or benefit from, the treaty after ratification." Curtis Bradley, Unratified Treaties, Domestic Politics, and the U.S. Constitution, 48 Harv. Int'l L.J. 307, 308 (2007).

2. Is the United States under an obligation not to defeat the object and purpose of the Vienna Convention on the Law of Treaties itself, which came into force in 1980? The United States signed the Convention in 1970 and President Nixon transmitted it to the U.S. Senate in 1971, but the Senate has yet to give its advice and consent.

3. Does the Bush administration's letter regarding the Rome Statute provide evidence that the United States accepts the rule in Article 18 of the Vienna Convention as constituting customary international law? Senior U.S. officials have previously characterized the obligation not to defeat the object and purpose of a treaty as "widely recognized in customary international law." Robert E. Dalton, The Vienna Convention on the Law of Treaties: Consequences for the United States, 78 Am. Soc'y Int'l L. Proc. 276, 278 (1984) (quoting Secretary of State William P. Rogers).

2. *Observance and Interpretation of Treaties*

Article 26 of the Vienna Convention expresses the fundamental and widely accepted rule of *pacta sunt servanda:* "Every treaty in force is binding upon the parties to it and must be performed by them in good faith." As a Comment to the Restatement notes, this rule "lies at the core of the law of international agreements and is perhaps the most important principle of international law." A corollary of the rule, reflected in Article 27 of the Vienna Convention, is that a state "may not invoke the provisions of its internal law as justification for its failure to perform a treaty." This reflects a broader international rule that a state "cannot use [its] internal law as a means of escaping international responsibility." Draft Articles on the Responsibility of States for Internationally Wrongful Acts, in Report of the International Law Commission on the Work of Its Fifty-third Session, U.N. Doc. A/56/10, at 38 (2001). The *pacta sunt servanda* rule is subject, however, to the rules concerning the validity and termination of treaties discussed below.

Other frequently cited provisions of the Vienna Convention are those dealing with treaty interpretation (Articles 31 and 32). They provide:

Article 31. General Rule of Interpretation

1. A treaty shall be interpreted in good faith in accordance with the ordinary meaning to be given to the terms of the treaty in their context and in light of its object and purpose.

2. The context for the purpose of the interpretation of a treaty shall comprise, in addition to the text, including its preamble and annexes:

(a) any agreement relating to the treaty which was made between all the parties in connection with the conclusion of the treaty;
(b) any instrument which was made by one or more parties in connection with the conclusion of the treaty and accepted by the other parties as an instrument related to the treaty.

3. There shall be taken into account, together with the context:

(a) any subsequent agreement between the parties regarding the interpretation of the treaty or the application of its provisions;
(b) any subsequent practice in the application of the treaty which establishes the agreement of the parties regarding its interpretation;
(c) any relevant rules of international law applicable in the relations between the parties.

4. A special meaning shall be given to a term if it is established that the parties so intended.

Article 32. Supplementary Means of Interpretation

Recourse may be had to supplementary means of interpretation, including the preparatory work of the treaty and the circumstances of its conclusion, in order to confirm the meaning resulting from the application of Article 31, or to determine the meaning when the interpretation according to Article 31:

(a) leaves the meaning ambiguous or obscure; or
(b) leads to a result which is manifestly absurd or unreasonable.

The rules of interpretation contained in the Vienna Convention are somewhat different from the rules that a U.S. court would apply to interpret a contract or a statute. The Restatement contrasts the approach likely to be taken by U.S. courts (and presumably by other U.S. authorities, such as the Departments of State, Defense, Treasury, or Commerce, or by the Congress).

Restatement Section 325

Comment

. . . The Vienna Convention, in Article 32, requires the interpreting body to conclude that the "ordinary meaning" of the text is either obscure or unreasonable before it can look to "supplementary means." . . . Article 32 of the Vienna Convention reflects reluctance to permit the use of materials constituting the development and negotiation of an agreement (*travaux preparatoires*) as a guide to the interpretation of an agreement. The Convention's inhospitality to *travaux* is not wholly consistent with the attitude of the International Court of Justice and not at all with that of United States courts. . . .

. . . Courts in the United States are generally more willing than those of other states to look outside the instrument to determine its meaning. In most cases, the United States approach would lead to the same result, but an international tribunal using the approach called for by this section might find the United States interpretation erroneous and United States action pursuant to that interpretation a violation of the agreement.

Reporters' Notes

1. . . . Some states at the Vienna Conference objected to resort to *travaux* as contrary to their traditions, in which resort to legislative history to interpret domestic statutory questions is impermissible, or at least uncommon. Some were concerned that if resort to *travaux* were accepted, a state might be deterred from acceding to a multilateral convention negotiated at a conference that it had not attended. Others feared that resort to *travaux* would favor nations with long-maintained and well-indexed archives. . . .

Notes and Questions

1. The Convention's rules regarding interpretation have been widely applied, or at least cited, by U.S. domestic courts (including the Supreme Court), congressional committees, bilateral trade dispute-settlement panels, the WTO Appellate Body, arbitral bodies, and the International Court of Justice.

2. What is the purpose of treaty interpretation — to ascertain the meaning of the text or the intent of the parties? Or is it to determine how to apply treaty language to situations that may not have been contemplated when the treaty was concluded? Are these different? What practical difference would it make? If the objective is to ascertain the meaning of the text (as opposed to the intent of the parties), would the negotiation history *(travaux)* be relevant? How does the Vienna Convention resolve this issue? In any given dispute, is it likely that the meaning of the text will prove to be unambiguous? If not, is the *travaux* likely to be any less ambiguous? Will interpreting a treaty "in light of its object and purpose" assist in determining how to apply the treaty to unforeseen circumstances?

3. Do "supplementary" means of interpretation used in Article 32 mean "subordinate"? Is there any case where the use of *travaux*, or negotiating history, would be excluded? Professor Frankowska writes:

> Obviously, article 32 is depicted inaccurately [in the Restatement comment quoted above]. No mention is made of the fact that article 32 permits recourse to the *travaux*

> to confirm the meaning of the terms of the treaty, a clause which changes the whole tenor of the article. In spite of what the Restatement suggests, it is possible for the courts to look to the authority of the Vienna Convention while using the *travaux* in accordance with the American judicial tradition. [Maria Frankowska, The Vienna Convention on the Law of Treaties Before United States Courts, 28 Va. J. Int'l L. 281, 335 (1988).]

Do you agree?

4. The "ordinary meaning" of a word in English can be different from its "ordinary meaning" in German or another language. If the texts of the treaties in those languages are equally authentic, as is the common practice, the interpreter must resort to context and external sources to determine *the*—or *a*—proper interpretation. Do you think that there is always a single correct interpretation? Consider how the Vienna Convention addresses situations in which different languages used in a treaty produce different meanings in Article 33.

5. Why is the definition of "context" in Article 31 of the Convention so narrow? Should declarations and resolutions adopted at a diplomatic conference recommending a treaty, or authoritative explanations or reports prepared by drafters, be regarded as part of the "context"?

6. Why should the *travaux* not be accorded equal weight with the text and subsequent practice of the parties? What about domestic legislative history, such as the report of the delegation, a letter of transmittal of the treaty by the President, Senate or Congressional hearings and committee reports, or statements by delegates? For example, if one party believes that a specific treaty provision prohibits a particular practice, but the other party believes that the practice is not prohibited, should the dispute be resolved with reference to unilateral statements made by one party to its legislature? In another situation, would the unilateral behavior or practice of a party to a treaty, which was known to and acquiesced in by the other party, amount to an "agreement" of the parties that would appropriately be treated as part of the treaty's context under the Vienna Convention?

3. Invalidity of Treaties

Articles 46-52 of the Convention are provisions dealing with the possible invalidity of a treaty. They cover a state or its representative's competence to conclude a treaty, error, fraud, corruption, and duress. (See the Documentary Supplement for their texts.) In many ways, these provisions are analogous to the contract rules found in many nations. However, Article 52 on "Coercion of a State by the Threat or Use of Force" evoked considerable debate during the drafting process. Professor Sinclair describes the background:

> Article 52 of the Convention deals with coercion of the State itself and again lays down a rule of absolute nullity. The Commission, after reviewing the history of the matter and taking into account the clear-cut prohibition of the threat or use of force in Article 2(4) of the United Nations Charter, considered that these developments "justify the conclusion that the invalidity of a treaty procured by the illegal threat or use of force is a

principle which is *lex lata* in the international law of today." Discussion at the Conference on this article tended to concentrate on two issues:

(a) Whether the expression "threat or use of force" could, or should, be interpreted as covering economic and political pressure.
(b) The temporal application of the rule — that is to say, the date from which the rule invalidating a treaty procured by the threat or use of force in violation of the principles of international law embodied in the Charter may be said to operate.

The records of the Conference reveal strongly conflicting views on both these points. That the rule now embodied in Article 52 of the Convention represents the modern law on this topic is beyond serious dispute; but there are clearly uncertainties about the scope of the rule and its temporal application. . . . From this, it may be concluded that Article 52 may savour more of codification than of progressive development, at least insofar as the expression "threat or use of force" is confined to physical or armed force and no question arises as to the temporal application of the rule. . . . [Ian Sinclair, The Vienna Convention on the Law of Treaties 16-17 (2d ed. 1984).]

As Professor Sinclair notes, there could be uncertainties about Article 52's scope. For example, in early 2010 fears about Greece's indebtedness created a financial crisis that brought the Greek economy to the verge of collapse. The International Monetary Fund offered a critical loan of nearly $40 billion loan to Greece, but imposed strict conditions on Greek economic policies, including a combination of spending cuts and revenue increases. Could Greece validly argue later that the IMF-Greek agreement was void?

What about the agreements that come in the midst of a crisis, or even after hostilities end, where one or more countries might have gained the upper hand over another country? For example, in early 1999, key international states known as the Contact Group (the United States, Britain, France, Italy, Germany, and Russia) sought to broker a peaceful resolution to the Kosovo crisis (discussed in Chapter 11), and organized peace talks at Rambouillet, France. Leaders of NATO states threatened to use force against the Federal Republic of Yugoslavia if it did not agree to the terms that had been proposed by the Contact Group at the Rambouillet conference. Had Yugoslavia accepted those terms, would the agreement have been valid? What about the agreement Yugoslavia did sign in June 1999, after the NATO bombing campaign against it, accepting the withdrawal of its forces from Kosovo? Or what about the Algiers Accords, the agreement that ended the 1979-1981 Iranian hostage crisis by, among other things, bringing about the release of U.S. embassy personnel who had been held as hostages by Iran for over one year? The agreement required the United States, in exchange, to return to Iran certain funds and properties that had been blocked by the U.S. government in response to the hostage-taking. Could the United States later claim that the agreement was invalid? (See discussion of Dames & Moore in Chapter 3.)

4. *Reservations*

Sometimes a party to a treaty may wish to accept most of its obligations, but not all of them. There are many possible reasons for this. Sometimes the country might not agree with a particular provision, or it might not wish to accept a dispute settlement provision (such as reference of disputes to the ICJ), or it might not have the constitutional power to accept a particular provision (e.g., a federal state may not be able to bind its constituent states or provinces).

In such a case the party may seek to enter a "reservation" to the treaty. The Vienna Convention defines a "reservation" in Article 2(1)(d) as "a unilateral statement, however phrased or named, made by a State, when signing, ratifying, accepting, approving or acceding to a treaty, whereby it purports to exclude or modify the legal effect of certain provisions of the treaty in their application to that State."

Professor Edwards provides more background about the possible reasons for reservations.

Richard W. Edwards, Jr., Reservations to Treaties

10 Mich. J. Int'l L. 362, 362-364 (1989)

The subject matter of multilateral treaties has an immensely wide range, including, inter alia, rights respecting international waterways, trade and finance, alliances and military affairs, settlement of disputes, and creation of both general and highly specialized international and regional organizations. Multilateral treaties have also led to the creation and codification of legal regimes applicable to such diverse concerns as arms control, the conduct of military hostilities, educational and cultural exchanges, diplomatic and consular relations, international trade, intellectual property, the law of the sea, the use of the radio spectrum, and the protection of human rights. The number of nation States participating in treaties has greatly expanded in the period since World War II. . . .

The difficulty of fashioning agreed rules applicable to all parties to an international agreement has inspired the use of reservations. . . . [A] reservation can be roughly defined as a unilateral statement made by a State or international organization, when signing, ratifying, acceding, or otherwise expressing its consent to be bound by an international agreement, whereby it purports to exclude or to modify the legal effect of certain provisions of the international agreement in their application to that State or organization. Reasons for reservations include:

1. A State or international organization may wish to be a party to an international agreement while at the same time not yielding on certain substantive points believed to be against its interests.
2. A State or international organization may wish to be a party to an international agreement while at the same time not binding itself to certain procedural obligations, such as compulsory settlement of disputes in the form specified in a compromissory clause.
3. A State may wish to assure that its treaty obligations are compatible with peculiarities of its local law.
4. A State may want to preclude a treaty's application to subordinate political entities in a federal system or to foreign territories for which the State would otherwise have international responsibility.

These reasons could motivate any State, regardless of its form of government, to interpose a reservation when it expresses its consent to be bound by a treaty.

Let's now consider the process for making reservations, and their implications, as provided for in Articles 19-23 on the Vienna Convention on the Law of Treaties. These Articles are excerpted below.

Vienna Convention

Article 19. Formulation of Reservations

A State may, when signing, ratifying, accepting, approving or acceding to a treaty, formulate a reservation unless:

(a) the reservation is prohibited by the treaty;

(b) the treaty provides that only specified reservations, which do not include the reservation in question, may be made; or

(c) in cases not falling under sub-paragraphs (a) and (b), the reservation is incompatible with the object and purpose of the treaty.

Article 20. Acceptance of and Objection to Reservations

1. A reservation expressly authorized by a treaty does not require any subsequent acceptance by the other contracting States unless the treaty so provides.

2. When it appears from the limited number of the negotiating States and the object and purpose of a treaty that the application of the treaty in its entirety between all the parties is an essential condition of the consent of each one to be bound by the treaty, a reservation requires acceptance by all the parties.

3. When a treaty is a constituent instrument of an international organization and unless it otherwise provides, a reservation requires the acceptance of the competent organ of that organization.

4. In cases not falling under the preceding paragraphs and unless the treaty otherwise provides:

(a) acceptance by another contracting State of a reservation constitutes the reserving State a party to the treaty in relation to that other State if or when the treaty is in force for those States;

(b) an objection by another contracting State to a reservation does not preclude the entry into force of the treaty as between the objecting and reserving States unless a contrary intention is definitely expressed by the objecting State;

(c) an act expressing a State's consent to be bound by the treaty and containing a reservation is effective as soon as at least one other contracting State has accepted the reservation.

5. For the purposes of paragraphs 2 and 4 and unless the treaty otherwise provides, a reservation is considered to have been accepted by a State if it shall have raised no objection to the reservation by the end of a period of twelve months after it was notified of the reservation or by the date on which it expressed its consent to be bound by the treaty, whichever is later.

Article 21. Legal Effects of Reservations and of Objections to Reservations

1. A reservation established with regard to another party in accordance with articles 19, 20 and 23:

(a) modifies for the reserving State in its relations with that other party the provisions of the treaty to which the reservation relates to the extent of the reservation; and

(b) modifies those provisions to the same extent for that other party in its relations with the reserving State.

2. The reservation does not modify the provisions of the treaty for the other parties to the treaty *inter se.*

3. When a State objecting to a reservation has not opposed the entry into force of the treaty between itself and the reserving State, the provisions to which the reservation relates do not apply as between the two States to the extent of the reservation. . . .

Article 23. Procedure Regarding Reservations

1. A reservation, an express acceptance of a reservation and an objection to a reservation must be formulated in writing and communicated to the contracting States and other States entitled to become parties to the treaty. . . .

When the United States became a party to the multilateral Convention on the Prevention and Punishment of the Crime of Genocide in 1988, one of the reservations it formulated concerned Article IX, which vested the International Court of Justice with jurisdiction over any dispute concerning the interpretation or application of the treaty. The United States reservation provided that "before any dispute to which the United States is a party may be submitted to the jurisdiction of the International Court of Justice . . . , the specific consent of the United States is required in each case."

Consider the responses by the Netherlands and the United Kingdom to the United States reservation:

Declaration of the Netherlands

27 December 1989

. . . [T]he Government of the Kingdom of the Netherlands recalls its declaration, made on 20 June 1966 on the occasion of the accession of the Kingdom of the Netherlands to the Convention . . . stating that in its opinion the reservations in respect of article IX of the Convention, . . . were incompatible with the object and purpose of the Convention, and that the Government of the Kingdom of the Netherlands did not consider states making such reservations parties to the Convention. Accordingly, the Government of the Kingdom of the Netherlands does not consider the United States of America a party to the Convention. . . .

Declaration of the United Kingdom of Great Britain and Northern Ireland

22 December 1989

The Government of the United Kingdom have consistently stated that they are unable to accept reservations to article IX. Accordingly, in conformity with the attitude adopted by them in previous cases, the Government of the United Kingdom do not accept the first reservation entered by the United States of America.

Notes and Questions

1. If a state formulates a reservation that is expressly prohibited by a treaty or is incompatible with its object and purpose, what is the effect of the reservation? Should we treat the state as a party to the treaty and give no legal effect to, or "sever," the impermissible reservation? Or does such a reservation mean that the state has not in fact consented to be bound by, and consequently is not a party to, the treaty?

2. What is the effect of the U.S. reservation to Article IX of the Genocide Convention on the legal obligations between the United States and other parties to the treaty that raised no objection to the reservation? What is the effect on the legal obligations between the United States and the Netherlands? Between the United States and the United Kingdom? What if a state objects to a reservation but does not state its reasons or express a position on whether the reservation precludes entry into force of the whole treaty between the two countries?

3. Are Articles 19 through 23 essentially applicable only to multilateral treaties and not bilateral ones? If the treaty is a bilateral treaty, can one of the two state parties make a reservation (as defined in Article 2(1)(d) of the Vienna Convention)? The Restatement suggests that "if a reservation is attached at ratification, it constitutes in effect a rejection of the original tentative agreement and a counter-offer of a new agreement." Restatement, §313 comment f. What might be the alternative to seeking to make a reservation for a state that, after initially negotiating and signing the bilateral treaty, discovers a problem with a substantive provision of the treaty or decides that a provision is ambiguous? Can this be a request for a modification in the treaty? This situation might arise during the domestic process of obtaining the advice and consent of a legislative body.

4. Should a unilateral interpretation, also sometimes referred to as an interpretative declaration, of an ambiguous provision of a treaty be treated as a reservation? In principle, is there anything wrong with treating it as a reservation? If the unilateral interpretation is made during the negotiating process on the treaty, might it also become an element in the interpretation of the treaty under Articles 31 and 32?

5. The flexible approach for reservations to multilateral conventions embodied in the Vienna Convention, especially Article 20(4), reflects the view adopted in the

International Court of Justice's Advisory Opinion on Reservations to the Genocide Convention, 1951 I.C.J. 15 (May 28). As the Court observed:

> [On one hand,] [i]t is well established that in its treaty relations a State cannot be bound without its consent, and that consequently no reservation can be effective against any State without its agreement thereto. It is also a generally recognized principle that a multilateral convention is the result of an agreement freely concluded upon its clauses and that consequently none of the contracting parties is entitled to frustrate or impair, by means of unilateral decisions or particular agreements, the purpose and *raison d'etre of* the convention. To this principle was linked the notion of the integrity of the convention as adopted, a notion which in its traditional concept involved the proposition that no reservation was valid unless it was accepted by all the contracting parties without exception, as would have been the case if it had been stated during the negotiations.
>
> This concept, which is directly inspired by the notion of contract, is of undisputed value as a principle. However, as regards the Genocide Convention, it is proper to refer to a variety of circumstances which would lead to a more flexible application of this principle. Among these circumstances may be noted the clearly universal character of the United Nations under whose auspices the Convention was concluded, and the very wide degree of participation envisaged by Article XI of the Convention. Extensive participation in conventions of this type has already given rise to greater flexibility in the international practice concerning multilateral conventions. More general resort to reservations, very great allowance made for tacit assent to reservations, the existence of practices which go so far as to admit that the author of reservations which have been rejected by certain contracting parties is nevertheless to be regarded as a party to the convention in relation to those contracting parties that have accepted the reservations — all these factors are manifestations of a new need for flexibility in the operation of multilateral conventions. . . .
>
> It has [on the other hand] . . . been argued that any State entitled to become a party to the Genocide Convention may do so while making any reservation it chooses by virtue of its sovereignty. The Court cannot share this view. It is obvious that so extreme an application of the idea of State sovereignty would lead to a complete disregard of the object and purpose of the Convention.

6. Some multilateral treaties prohibit reservations. What are the reasons why a treaty, say, establishing a new institution or a new regime of laws should prohibit reservations? For example, the Rome Statute of the International Criminal Court, which came into force in 2002, prohibits reservations (Article 120).

7. The 1982 Law of the Sea Convention also prohibited reservations (Article 309). However, the problems that the United States and several other countries had with the deep seabed mining provisions of the 1982 Convention led to the imaginative solution where a later companion agreement was negotiated in 1994 that has the effect of amending the objectionable provisions in the 1982 Convention. (See Chapter 9.)

8. It appears that most multilateral conventions do not have reservations, whether because they are prohibited or because countries choose not to make reservations. Reservations are particularly rare when the conventions are limited to a few states. For example, see John King Gamble, Reservations to Multilateral Treaties: A Macroscopic View of State Practice, 74 Am. J. Int'l L. 372 (1980). For some accounts of why reservations are relatively rare, see Vincy Fon & Francesco

Parisi, The Economics of Treaty Ratification, 5 J. L. Econ. & Pol'y 209 (2009); and Francesco Parisi & Catherine Sevcenko, Treaty Reservations and the Economics of Article 21(1) of the Vienna Convention, 21 Berkeley J. Int'l L. 1 (2003).

9. Reservations are nevertheless often made by the United States and other countries in conventions on human rights. Indeed, the frequency of these reservations led the U.N. Human Rights Committee and the International Law Commission to study these reservations. In its General Comment No. 24, the U.N. Human Rights Committee took the position in 1994 that it had the authority "to determine whether a specific reservation is compatible with the object and purpose" of the International Covenant on Civil and Political Rights. It also took the view that a reservation incompatible with the object and purpose of a treaty "will generally be severable, in the sense that the [treaty] will be operative for the reserving party without the benefit of the reservation." The United States and the United Kingdom objected to the Committee's claim of authority. (See Chapter 3 for a discussion of U.S. practice and the possible reasons for the U.S. use of reservations. See also Chapter 8.)

10. Do you think a reservation that, say, rejects a prohibition on capital punishment in a human rights treaty should be regarded as incompatible with the object and purpose of the agreement for purposes of Article 19 of the Vienna Convention? Who is entitled to make that judgment?

5. Termination and the Suspension of the Operation of Treaties

In the event of a material breach of a treaty, it has long been recognized and generally accepted that the affected party may unilaterally terminate the treaty or suspend the performance of its own obligations. The Vienna Convention provides:

Vienna Convention

Article 60. Termination or Suspension of the Operation of a Treaty as a Consequence of Its Breach

1. A material breach of a bilateral treaty by one of the parties entitles the other to invoke the breach as a ground for terminating the treaty or suspending its operation in whole or in part.

2. A material breach of a multilateral treaty by one of the parties entitles:

(a) the other parties by unanimous agreement to suspend the operation of the treaty in whole or in part or to terminate it either:

(i) in the relations between themselves and the defaulting State, or

(ii) as between all the parties;

(b) a party specially affected by the breach to invoke it as a ground for suspending the operation of the treaty in whole or in part in the relations between itself and the defaulting State;

(c) any party other than the defaulting State to invoke the breach as a ground for suspending the operation of the treaty in whole or in part with respect to itself if the treaty is of such a character that a material breach of its provisions by one party radically changes the position of every party with respect to the further performance of its obligations under the treaty.

3. A material breach of a treaty, for the purposes of this article, consists in:

(a) a repudiation of the treaty not sanctioned by the present Convention; or

(b) the violation of a provision essential to the accomplishment of the object or purpose of the treaty.

4. The foregoing paragraphs are without prejudice to any provision in the treaty applicable in the event of a breach.

5. Paragraphs 1 to 3 do not apply to provisions relating to the protection of the human person contained in treaties of a humanitarian character, in particular to provisions prohibiting any form of reprisals against persons protected by such treaties.

Notes and Questions

1. Summarize in a sentence or two the standard that must be met under Article 60 for a state to be justified in not performing a treaty obligation.

2. What can a state do in the event of a "material breach"? For example, if Chile violated a bilateral trade agreement with the United States providing for free trade in all products by restricting trade in American exports of designer blouses (but not computers, aircraft, and grain), what remedy would be available to the United States? Could the United States terminate the entire agreement? Would your answer change if the volume of trade in designer blouses amounted to less than $5 million out of a total of $5 billion in annual trade?

3. How do the remedies under the Vienna Convention differ from those available for breach of contract under the domestic law? What are the purposes and advantages or disadvantages of the different remedies that may be available?

4. Does Article 60 provide rules on when a state may, in response to a material breach, suspend operation of a treaty only in part, rather than in whole? Is there a requirement that the response to a material breach of a treaty be proportionate? During negotiations on the Vienna Convention, the U.S. negotiators sought to introduce "an element of proportionality" into Article 60. They proposed adding, at the end of paragraph 1 of Article 60, the following language: "as may be appropriate considering the nature and extent of the breach and the extent to which the treaty obligations have been performed." The amendment did not enjoy support, and the U.S. delegation withdrew it. See Richard D. Kearney & Robert E. Dalton, The Treaty on Treaties, 64 Am. J. Int'l L. 495, 540 (1970).

5. Who determines whether there has been a material breach? Whether the remedy should be suspension of part of or all of the treaty? Or some other remedy?

6. Articles 65 and 66 of the Vienna Convention provide for compulsory but nonbinding conciliation of disputes over the validity or interpretation of a treaty. There is a strong case that these provisions do not amount to customary international law, especially the specific provisions of the Annex regarding the establishment of a Conciliation Commission. If a state declared a material breach of a treaty (in effect relying on the terms of Article 60), do you think that it would be obligated to give formal notice and make some attempt with the offending treaty partner to settle the dispute? Or must it use some form of third-party dispute settlement? Should states like the United States that are not parties to the Vienna

Convention respect all, or some, of the dispute settlement provisions of Articles 65 and 66? Why or why not?

Besides Article 60 on material breach, the Vienna Convention contains other provisions allowing for termination or suspension of the operation of a treaty. Article 61 deals with impossibility of performance as a basis for terminating or withdrawing from a treaty. Article 62 deals with the permissibility of terminating a treaty because of a "fundamental change in circumstances" (the doctrine of *rebus sic stantibus*). (Both articles are in the Documentary Supplement.) Sinclair traces the formulation of Article 62:

> . . . The concept that . . . a treaty may become inapplicable by reason of a fundamental change in circumstances obviously presents serious dangers to the security of treaties. Nevertheless, the doctrine that a fundamental change of circumstances may operate to bring about the termination of a treaty is of ancient origin. . . .
>
> . . . [D]iplomatic practice in the nineteenth century—and, particularly, the invocation by Russia of the *rebus* doctrine to justify her assertion in 1870 that the provisions of the 1856 Treaty regarding the neutralization of the Black Sea were no longer binding upon her . . . began to demonstrate some of the dangers inherent in the notion of the clause; and indeed the *rebus* doctrine fell into serious disrepute during the inter-war period, largely as a result of its indiscriminate invocation by States in the period immediately preceding 1914 to escape from inconvenient treaty obligations. . . .
>
> Against this background, the Commission approached the formulation of a text on *rebus sic stantibus* with considerable caution. After extensive debate, they decided to formulate it in negative terms, declaring that a fundamental change of circumstances which had occurred with regard to those existing at the time of the conclusion of a treaty might not be invoked as a ground for terminating or withdrawing from the treaty unless two conditions were met:
>
> (a) the existence of those circumstances constituted an essential basis of the consent of the parties to be bound by the treaty; *and*
> (b) the effect of the change was radically to transform the scope of obligations still to be performed under the treaty.
>
> To this the Commission proposed two exceptions:
>
> (a) a fundamental change of circumstances could not be invoked as a ground for terminating or withdrawing from a treaty establishing a boundary;
> (b) a fundamental change of circumstances could not be invoked if it was the result of a breach by the invoking party either of the treaty or of a different international obligation owed to the other parties to the treaty. . . .
>
> Some interesting points were made in the course of the debate. In the first place, it was suggested, and not denied, that a State would not be entitled to invoke its own acts or omissions as amounting to a fundamental change of circumstances giving rise to the operation of Article 62. Attention was also directed to the view expressed by some members of the Commission, and recorded in the commentary to the Commission's proposal, that "a subjective change in the attitude or policy of a Government could never be invoked as a ground for terminating, withdrawing from or suspending the operation of a treaty." . . . [Ian Sinclair, The Vienna Convention on the Law of Treaties 192-195 (2d ed. 1984).]

Case Concerning the Gabcikovo-Nagymaros Project (Hungary v. Slovakia)

Int'l Court of Justice
1997 I.C.J. 7 (Sept. 25)

[In this case, Slovakia asked the International Court of Justice (ICJ) to rule on, among other issues, the validity of Hungary's termination of a 1977 Treaty with Slovakia's predecessor state (Czechoslovakia). The 1977 Treaty concerned the construction and operation of an elaborate system of locks on the Danube River, which formed part of the border between the two countries. The joint project, devised when Hungary and Czechoslovakia were communist command economies, was aimed at the production of hydroelectricity, the improvement of navigation on the relevant section of the Danube, and the protection of the areas along the banks against flooding. After the fall of communist regimes in both countries, questions arose on both sides of the Danube, but especially in Hungary, about the economic viability of the Gabcikovo-Nagymaros project and its potentially harmful environmental impact. In 1989, Hungary suspended and later abandoned its participation in the project. In 1992, it purported to terminate the 1977 Treaty.

In arriving at its decision, the ICJ relied heavily on the 1969 Vienna Convention on the Law of Treaties. Even though the countries had not ratified the Vienna Convention at the time of their 1977 Treaty, the ICJ concluded that Articles 60 to 62 of the Vienna Convention were "declaratory of customary law." The ICJ then applied these articles to Hungary's arguments that it should be allowed to terminate the 1977 Treaty.]

94. Hungary's [impossibility of performance] argument . . . [was predicated on its view] that it could not be "obliged to fulfil a practically impossible task, namely to construct a barrage system on its own territory that would cause irreparable environmental damage". [Hungary] concluded that

> "By May 1992 the essential object of the Treaty—an economic joint investment which was consistent with environmental protection and which was operated by the two parties jointly—had permanently disappeared, and the Treaty had thus become impossible to perform." . . .

102. Hungary . . . relied on the principle of the impossibility of performance as reflected in Article 61 of the Vienna Convention on the Law of Treaties. Hungary's interpretation of the wording of Article 61 is, however, not in conformity with the terms of that Article. . . .

103. Hungary contended that the essential object of the Treaty—an economic joint investment which was consistent with environmental protection and which was operated by the two contracting parties jointly—had permanently disappeared and that the Treaty has thus become impossible to perform. . . . [I]f the joint exploitation of the investment was no longer possible, this was originally because Hungary did not carry out most of the works for which it was responsible under the 1977 Treaty; Article 61, paragraph 2, of the Vienna Convention expressly provides that impossibility of performance may not be invoked for the termination of a treaty by a party to that treaty when it results from that party's own breach of an obligation flowing from the treaty.

104. Hungary further argued that it was entitled to invoke a number of events which, cumulatively, would have constituted a fundamental change of circumstances. In this respect it specified profound changes of a political nature, the Project's diminishing economic viability, the progress of environmental knowledge and the development of new norms and prescriptions of international environmental law. . . .

The prevailing political situation was certainly relevant for the conclusion of the 1977 Treaty. But the Court will recall that the Treaty provided for a joint investment programme for the production of energy, the control of floods and the improvement of navigation on the Danube. In the Court's view, the prevalent political conditions were thus not so closely linked to the object and purpose of the Treaty that they constituted an essential basis of the consent of the parties and, in changing, radically altered the extent of the obligations still to be performed. The same holds good for the economic system in force at the time of the conclusion of the 1977 Treaty. Besides, even though the estimated profitability of the Project might have appeared less in 1992 than in 1977, it does not appear from the record before the Court that it was bound to diminish to such an extent that the treaty obligations of the parties would have been radically transformed as a result.

The Court does not consider that new developments in the state of environmental knowledge and of environmental law can be said to have been completely unforeseen. . . .

The changed circumstances advanced by Hungary are, in the Court's view, not of such a nature, either individually or collectively, that their effect would radically transform the extent of the obligations still to be performed in order to accomplish the Project. A fundamental change of circumstances must have been unforeseen; the existence of the circumstances at the time of the Treaty's conclusion must have constituted an essential basis of the consent of the parties to be bound by the Treaty. The negative and conditional wording of Article 62 of the Vienna Convention . . . is a clear indication moreover that the stability of treaty relations requires that the plea of fundamental change of circumstances be applied only in exceptional cases.

Questions

1. In the *Gabcikovo* decision excerpted above, is the Court correct that "the stability of treaty relations requires that the plea of fundamental change of circumstances be applied only in exceptional cases"?

2. Why did the drafters of the Vienna Convention decide on narrow exceptions, such as Articles 61 and 62? What is the value of, and whose interests are most protected by, the approach adopted by the Convention in this respect?

3. Does the Vienna Convention seem to protect continuation of agreements and therefore the status quo? If so, does that mean that treaty regimes are inherently conservative and difficult to change?

6. *Withdrawal from or Denunciation of a Treaty*

Most recent treaties contain clauses providing the bases for withdrawal from, or denunciation of, the treaty. The treaties usually specify the duration or date of termination of the treaty, and/or the conditions or events that allow for termination or the right to withdraw or denounce the treaty. For example, the 1994 Agreement Establishing the World Trade Organization provides in Article XV that "Any Member may withdraw from this Agreement. Such withdrawal . . . shall take effect upon the expiration of six months from the date on which written notice of withdrawal is received by the Director-general of the WTO."

The Vienna Convention recognizes the right, and the now common practice, of states to include withdrawal clauses in treaties. Article 54 provides that the termination of a treaty or a party's withdrawal may take place "in conformity with the provisions of the treaty" or "at any time by consent of all the parties. . . ."

If, however, the treaty contains no such provisions regarding termination, withdrawal, or denunciation, then Article 56 of the Vienna Convention provides that the treaty "is not subject to denunciation or withdrawal" unless:

> (a) it is established that the parties intended to admit the possibility of denunciation or withdrawal; or
>
> (b) a right to denunciation or withdrawal may be implied by the nature of the treaty.

The International Court of Justice addressed this situation, where a treaty failed to include provisions for termination, denunciation, or withdrawal, in the Case Concerning the Gabcikovo-Nagymaros Project (Hungary v. Slovakia), 1997 I.C.J. 7 (Sept. 25). In that case, which is also discussed in section 5 above, Hungary attempted to terminate a 1977 bilateral treaty without the other party's consent. After several years of difficult negotiations between Hungary and Czechoslovakia (the predecessor of Slovakia), the Hungarian Government notified Czechoslovakia that it was considering the treaty terminated, effective six days later. The ICJ held that Hungary could not terminate the treaty in this manner. In its judgment, the ICJ said:

> 100. The 1977 Treaty does not contain any provision regarding its termination. Nor is there any indication that the parties intended to admit the possibility of denunciation or withdrawal. On the contrary, the Treaty establishes a long-standing and durable regime of joint investment and joint operation. Consequently, the parties not having agreed otherwise, the Treaty could be terminated only on the limited grounds enumerated in the Vienna Convention. . . .
>
> 109. . . . [I]t should be noted that, according to Hungary's Declaration of 19 May 1992, the termination of the 1977 Treaty was to take effect as from 25 May 1992, that is only six days later. Both parties agree that Articles 65 to 67 of the Vienna Convention . . . , if not codifying customary law, at least generally reflect customary international law and contain certain procedural principles which are based on an obligation to act in good faith. . . .
>
> The termination of the Treaty by Hungary was to take effect six days after its notification. On neither of these dates had Hungary suffered injury resulting from acts of Czechoslovakia. The Court must therefore confirm its conclusion that Hungary's termination of the Treaty was premature.

Notes and Questions

1. Should it be difficult to withdraw from treaties? If it is difficult, what effect, if any, will this have on the ratification of treaties? Is it better to have a regime under

which a country that is unhappy with a treaty can withdraw from it, rather than a regime under which the country feels compelled to breach that treaty?

2. In January 2003, as tensions between the North Korea and the United States and other states over North Korea's suspected nuclear weapons program grew, North Korea announced that it was withdrawing from the Nuclear Nonproliferation Treaty (NPT). Article X(1) is the NPT's withdrawal clause; it provides:

> Each Party shall in exercising its national sovereignty have the right to withdraw from the Treaty if it decides that extraordinary events, related to the subject matter of this Treaty, have jeopardized the supreme interests of its country. It shall give notice of such withdrawal to all other Parties to the Treaty and to the United Nations Security Council three months in advance. Such notice shall include a statement of the extraordinary events it regards as having jeopardized its supreme interests.

In announcing its withdrawal from the NPT, North Korea declared that "[a] dangerous situation where our nation's sovereignty and our state's security are being seriously violated is prevailing on the Korean peninsula due to the US vicious hostile policy towards [North Korea]." North Korea's statement included President Bush's characterization of North Korea as a member of states comprising an "axis of evil" and U.S. efforts to pursue resolutions condemning North Korea's noncompliance with the NPT as a basis for its "self-defensive" withdrawal from the treaty.

Is it for North Korea, or for other states, to decide whether North Korea's stated reasons for withdrawing from the NPT satisfy Article X(1) of the treaty? Or should an international organization decide? Did North Korea's withdrawal from the NPT violate the treaty? Was it consistent with the Vienna Convention on the Law of Treaties?

3. Reflecting the development of new defensive missile technologies and the emergence of new threats from rogue states, the administration of President George W. Bush decided that it was in the U.S. interest to build a limited missile defense system. The United States accordingly gave formal notice to Russia in December 2001 that it would withdraw from the nearly 30-year old Treaty on the Limitation of Anti-Ballistic Missile Systems (the ABM Treaty), effective June 2002. Article XV(2) of the treaty provides that: "Each Party shall, in exercising its national sovereignty, have the right to withdraw from this Treaty if it decides that extraordinary events related to the subject matter of this Treaty have jeopardized its supreme interests. It shall give notice of its decision prior to the withdrawal from the Treaty. . . ."

Is it for the United States, or for other states, to decide whether the emergence of new threats to the United States and the development of new technologies constituted "extraordinary events" that "jeopardized [U.S.] supreme interests"? Was the U.S. withdrawal a breach of the ABM Treaty? Was it consistent with the Vienna Convention on the Law of Treaties?

4. The International Covenant on Civil and Political Rights (ICCPR), an important human rights treaty that has been ratified by over 165 states, does not contain a withdrawal clause. In 1998, the Human Rights Committee established by the ICCPR concluded that countries are not allowed to withdraw from this treaty. The Committee reasoned that the rights under the ICCPR "belong to the people living in the territory of the State party" and that "once the people are accorded the protection of the rights under the Covenant, such protection devolves with territory and continues to belong to them, notwithstanding change in Government of the State party,

including . . . any subsequent action of the State party designed to divest them of the rights guaranteed by the Covenant." Are you persuaded? (See discussion of the ICCPR in Chapter 8.)

5. In 1997, North Korea, formally known as the Democratic People's Republic of Korea (DPRK), notified the U.N. Secretary General of its withdrawal from the ICCPR. In response, the Secretariat noted that the Covenant does not contain a withdrawal provision and expressed the view that the DPRK's withdrawal from the Covenant "would appear impossible without the consent of all State parties" to the Covenant. See U.N. Secretary-General, Depository Notification of the Democratic Republic of North Korea, U.N. Doc. C.N.467.1997-TREATIES-10 (Nov. 12, 1997). Are you persuaded? How does the Secretary-General's analysis differ from that of the Human Rights Committee described in the preceding note?

7. *Jus Cogens*

Growing attention has been paid in recent years to the concept of "peremptory," or *jus cogens,* norms. Peremptory norms are not an independent "source" of international law. Rather, they are rules—whatever their source—that possess a different normative character from "ordinary" international law rules. *Jus cogens* norms are said to be so fundamental that they bind all states, and no nation may derogate from or agree to contravene them. Although the notion had previously received attention from academic commentators, it was initially recognized by states in Articles 53 and 64 of the Vienna Convention on the Law of Treaties. Professor Aust explains the background:

Anthony Aust, Modern Treaty Law and Practice

319-320 (2d ed. 2007)

The concept of *jus cogens* (peremptory norm of general international law) was controversial at the time of the Vienna Conference. Now it is more the scope and applicability of the concept which is debated. *Jus cogens* is defined in Article 53 for the purposes of the Convention as:

> a norm accepted and recognized by the international community of States as a whole as a norm from which no derogation is permitted and which can be modified only by a subsequent norm of general international law having the same character.

There is no agreement on the criteria for identifying which norms of general international law have a peremptory character. Whether a norm of general international law has it depends on the particular nature of the subject matter. Perhaps the only generally accepted example is the prohibition on the use of force as laid down in the UN Charter. The prohibitions on genocide, slavery and torture may also be said to be *jus cogens.* This is so even where such acts are prohibited by treaties which parties to them can denounce. But it would be rash to assume that all prohibitions contained in human rights treaties are *jus cogens,* or even part of customary international law. Some rights, such as the freedom of association, are far from being generally accepted as customary law; and a state can usually derogate from others (e.g., due process) in time of public emergency. Article 53 does not therefore attempt to list examples of *jus cogens*, leaving that to be worked out by state practice and in the jurisprudence of international tribunals. . . .

The vast majority of rules do not of course have the character of *jus cogens*, and states are therefore free to contract out of them; and a treaty which conflicts with general international law is not necessarily void. Similarly, if a treaty provides that no derogation from it is permitted, but later a party concludes a treaty which conflicts with it, the latter treaty is not void although the party may be liable for breach of the earlier treaty.

The consequences of the invalidity of a treaty that conflicts with *jus cogens* under Article 53 or Article 64 are dealt with in Article 71. Unfortunately, there are no reported instances of Articles 53 or 64, as such, being invoked.

Professor Shelton addresses the source and content of *jus cogens* and considers the practical impact of identifying such a category of rules:

Dinah Shelton, Normative Hierarchy in International Law

100 Am. J. Int'l L. 291, 297, 299-300, 302-304 (2006)

In Theory

The theory of *jus cogens* or peremptory norms posits the existence of rules of international law that admit of no derogation and that can be amended only by a new general norm of international law of the same value. It is a concept that lacks both an agreed content and consensus in state practice. . . .

Sources of peremptory norms. . . . A strictly voluntarist view of international law rejects the notion that a state may be bound by an international legal rule without its consent and thus does not recognize a collective interest that is capable of overriding the will of an individual member of the society. . . .

The provisions . . . adopted [in the Vienna Convention on the Law of Treaties] limited the ability of states to escape fundamental norms, but they also established state consent as the foundation for such rules. . . . Article 53 demands that there first be established a norm of general international law and, second, that the *international community of states as a whole* agree that it is a norm from which no derogation is possible. While this definition precludes an individual state from vetoing the emergence of a peremptory norm, it sets a high threshold for identifying such a norm and bases the identification squarely in state consent. . . .

Many scholars have long objected that the source of international obligation cannot lie in consent, but must be based on a prior, fundamental norm that imposes a duty to comply with obligations freely accepted. . . . Some scholars object that positivism does not adequately describe the reality of the current international order. . . . The [international] community consists of states that live within a legal framework of a few basic rules that nonetheless allow them considerable freedom of action. Out of the community come common values and fundamental principles that bind the entire society.

It is certainly rational to accept that such a framework has become necessary in the light of global problems threatening human survival in an unprecedented fashion. The emergence of global resource crises, such as the widespread depletion of commercial fish stocks, the destruction of the stratospheric ozone layer, and anthropogenic climate change, has produced growing concern about the "free rider," the holdout state that benefits from legal regulation accepted by others while enhancing its own profits through continued utilization of the resource or ongoing production and sale of banned substances. Recalcitrant states not only profit by rejecting regulatory regimes adopted by the overwhelming majority of states, they threaten the effectiveness of such regimes and pose risks to all humanity. The traditional consent-based international legal regime lacks a legislature to override the will of dissenting states, but efforts to affect their behavior are being made [in part] through the doctrine of peremptory norms or universal law applicable to all states, ...

In sum, the source of peremptory norms has been variously attributed to state consent, natural law, necessity, international public order, and the development of constitutional principles. The different theories lead to considerably different content for *jus cogens* norms and consequences for their breach. . . .

The content of jus cogens. Neither the International Law Commission nor the Vienna Convention on the Law of Treaties developed an accepted list of peremptory norms, although both made reference in commentaries and discussion to the norms against genocide, slave trading, and the use of force other than in self-defense. . . .

Since the adoption of the Vienna Convention, the literature has abounded in claims that additional international norms constitute *jus cogens*. Proponents have argued for the inclusion of all human rights, all humanitarian norms (human rights and the laws of war), or singly, the duty not to cause transboundary environmental harm, freedom from torture, the duty to assassinate dictators, the right to life of animals, self-determination, the right to development, free trade, and territorial sovereignty (despite legions of treaties transferring territory from one state to another). During the Cold War, Soviet writers asserted the invalidity of treaties that conflicted with the "basic principles and concepts" of international law, defined to include universal peace and security of nations; respect for sovereignty and territorial integrity; noninterference in internal affairs; equality and mutual benefit between nations; and *pacta sunt servanda*. Examples of invalid agreements included the NATO pact, the peace treaty between the United States and Japan, the SEATO agreement, and the U.S.-UK agreement on establishing air bases. In most instances, little evidence has been presented to demonstrate how and why the preferred norm has become *jus cogens*. Wladyslaw Czaplinksi correctly comments that "the trend to abuse the notion of *jus cogens* is always present among international lawyers." . . .

Notes and Questions

1. The definition of *jus cogens* in the Vienna Convention on the Law of Treaties as a norm "accepted and recognized by the international community of States as a whole" suggests that norms acquire a peremptory character through a process similar to the way state practice attains customary international law status. In determining whether a norm is peremptory, what qualifies as "the international

community of States as a whole"? Does that mean all states? If unanimity is not required, how many "dissenters" can there be before a norm is no longer accepted by the international community as a whole? One? Two? Five? Do the views of all states count equally in making this determination?

2. The characterization of a legal norm as peremptory seems to require not only a universal, or nearly universal, belief by states that the norm is binding, but also a belief that the norm is so fundamental that other states may not derogate from it. How do we ascertain whether states believe not only that they are legally bound by a rule, but additionally that the rule is so fundamental that all states are bound by it?

3. Does the doctrine of *jus cogens* merely enable diplomats, judges, and lawyers to justify preferred policy results? If you think that judges (or scholars) do not make decisions that way, how do you think they would go about a disinterested search for the norms of *jus cogens?*

4. A report produced by a Study Group of the International Law Commission commented that "[t]he problem of how to identify *jus cogens* is not easy to resolve *in abstracto*," but nevertheless suggested that "the most frequently cited candidates for the status of *jus cogens* include: (a) the prohibition of aggressive use of force; (b) the right to self-defence; (c) the prohibition of genocide; (d) the prohibition of torture; (e) crimes against humanity; (f) the prohibition of slavery and slave trade; (g) the prohibition of piracy; (h) the prohibition of racial discrimination and apartheid, and (i) the prohibition of hostilities directed at civilian population ('basic rules of international humanitarian law')." Report of the Study Group of International Law Commission, Fragmentation of International Law: Difficulties Arising from the Diversification and Expansion of International Law, U.N. Doc. A/CN.4/L.682, at 189 (2006).

5. Can you think of examples of agreements between states that would violate a *jus cogens* norm, and that would accordingly be void under Article 53 of the Vienna Convention on the Law of Treaties? Are states likely to enter into agreements to enslave the population of another country? To deny the right of self-determination, to violate the law of peaceful co-existence, to commit the international crime of apartheid, or to engage in torture, state terrorism, or the capital punishment of juveniles?

6. The practical impact of *jus cogens* has been limited. It has not, for instance, been invoked to void a treaty. The concept has, however, appeared in discussions of what constitutes customary international law and whether certain norms have greater weight. We turn to customary international law in Section B.

7. For additional perspectives on *jus cogens* norms, see Evan J. Criddle & Evan Fox-Decent, A Fiduciary Theory of *Jus Cogens*, 34 Yale J. Int'l L. 331 (2009); and Alexadner Orakhelashvili, Peremptory Norms in International Law (2006).

B. CUSTOMARY INTERNATIONAL LAW

1. *Formation of Customary International Law*

Until recently, international law for the most part consisted of customary law. In the last decades, treaties have increasingly become the means by which law is made in the international system. Yet many important legal rules continue to arise principally from customary international law. In addition, many rules otherwise covered by major multilateral treaties, such as the Vienna Convention on Diplomatic Relations, the Law of the Sea Convention, and the 1977 Protocols to the Geneva Conventions on the laws of war, are said either to have codified settled customary international law or to have "crystallized" emerging customary international law. In such cases, the customary rules retain independent force and bind even those states that are not parties to the treaty.

a. Elements of Customary International Law

The traditional definition of customary international law includes both an objective element (state practice) and a subjective element *(opinio juris)*. The 1987 Restatement defines customary international law and explains these elements as follows:

Restatement Section 102

(2) Customary international law results from a general and consistent practice of states followed by them from a sense of legal obligation. . . .

Comment

. . . *b. Practice as customary law.* "Practice of states," . . . includes diplomatic acts and instructions as well as public measures and other governmental acts and official statements of policy, . . . Inaction may constitute state practice, as when a state acquiesces in acts of another state that affect its legal rights. The practice necessary to create customary law might be of comparatively short duration, but under Subsection (2) it must be "general and consistent." A practice can be general even if it is not universally followed; there is no precise formula to indicate how widespread a practice must be, but it should reflect wide acceptance among the states particularly involved in the relevant activity. . . . A principle of customary law is not binding on a state that declares its dissent from the principle during its development.

c. Opinio juris. For a practice of states to become a rule of customary international law it must appear that the states follow the practice from a sense of legal obligation *(opinio juris sive necessitates);* a practice that is generally followed but which states feel legally free to disregard does not contribute to customary international law. A practice initially followed by states as a matter of courtesy or habit may become law when states generally come to believe that they are under a legal obligation to comply with it. It is often difficult to determine when that transformation into law has taken place. Explicit evidence of a sense of legal obligation (e.g., by official statements) is not necessary; *opinio juris* may be inferred from acts or omissions.

An unsettled issue regarding the formation of customary international law is precisely what qualifies as "state practice." Professor Shearer has written that "both conduct and statements (written and oral) are on the same footing" in the formulation of customary international law. I.A. Shearer, Starke's International Law 32

(11th ed. 1994). Others treat statements by government actors not as practice, but rather as evidence of *opinio juris*.

Anthea Roberts posits the existence of two different types of customary international law—"traditional custom" and "modern custom"—that display varying mixtures of the elements of practice and subjective belief:

> What I have termed traditional custom results from general and consistent practice followed by states from a sense of legal obligation. It focuses primarily on state practice in the form of interstate interaction and acquiescence. *Opinio juris* is a secondary consideration invoked to distinguish between legal and nonlegal obligations. Traditional custom is evolutionary and is identified through an *inductive* process in which a general custom is derived from specific instances of state practice. This approach is evident in *S.S. Lotus*, where the Permanent Court of International Justice inferred a general custom about objective territorial jurisdiction over ships on the high seas from previous instances of state action and acquiescence.
>
> By contrast, modern custom is derived by a *deductive* process that begins with general statements of rules rather than particular instances of practice. This approach emphasizes *opinio juris* rather than state practice because it relies primarily on statements rather than actions. Modern custom can develop quickly because it is deduced from multilateral treaties and declarations by international fora such as the General Assembly, which can declare existing customs, crystallize emerging norms, and generate new customs. . . . A good example of the deductive approach is the Merits decision [of the International Court of Justice] in *Military and Paramilitary Activities in and Against Nicaragua*. The Court paid lip service to the traditional test for custom but derived customs of non-use of force and nonintervention from statements such as General Assembly resolutions. The Court did not make a serious inquiry into state practice, . . .
>
> Frederic Kirgis rationalizes the divergence in custom by analyzing the requirements of state practice and *opinio juris* on a sliding scale. At one end, highly consistent state practice can establish a customary rule without requiring *opinio juris*. However, as the frequency and consistency of state practice decline, a stronger showing of *opinio juris* will be required. Kirgis argues that the exact trade-off between state practice and *opinio juris* will depend on the importance of the activity in question and the reasonableness of the rule involved. [Anthea Elizabeth Roberts, Traditional and Modern Approaches to Customary International Law: A Reconciliation, 95 Am. J. Int'l L. 757, 758-760 (2001).]

Disagreement about what behavior contributes to the formation of customary international law arose following the 2005 publication by the International Committee for the Red Cross (ICRC) of a major study purporting to summarize the customary rules of the law of armed conflict, or "international humanitarian law." Jean-Marie Henckaerts & Louise Doswald-Beck, Customary International Humanitarian Law (2005). The ICRC is a Swiss-based humanitarian organization that promotes the development of international humanitarian law and monitors its implementation. (International humanitarian law is discussed in more detail in Chapter 11.) The principal lawyers at the U.S. State and Defense Departments wrote to the ICRC to express concerns about the methods the ICRC had used to determine the existence of rules of customary international law. On the issue of what constitutes state practice, the U.S. officials wrote:

> [W]e are troubled by the type of practice on which the [ICRC] Study has, in too many places, relied. . . . [T]he study places too much emphasizes on written materials, such

> as military manuals and other guidelines published by States, as opposed to actual operational practice by States during armed conflict. Although manuals may provide important indications of State behavior and *opinio juris,* they cannot be a replacement for meaningful assessment of operational State practice in connection with actual military operations. We are also troubled by the extent to which the Study relies on non-binding resolutions of the General Assembly, given that States may lend their support to a particular resolution, for reasons having nothing to do with a belief that the propositions in it reflect customary international law. [Joint Letter from John B. Bellinger, III, Legal Adviser, U.S. Department of State, and William J. Haynes II, General Counsel, U.S. Department of Defense, to Dr. Jakob Kellenberger, President, International Committee of the Red Cross, Nov. 3, 2006, *reprinted in* 46 ILM 514, 515 (2007).]

In a response to the U.S. comments, one of the authors of the ICRC study observed:

> A study on customary international law has to look at the combined effect of what states say and what they actually do. As a result, "operational State practice in connection with actual military operations" was collected and analysed. To the extent that they were available, the Study considered official reports and statements on the conduct of actual military operations. . . . But an examination of operational practice alone is not enough. In order to arrive at an accurate assessment of customary international law one has to look beyond a mere description of actual military operations and examine the legal assessment of such operations. This requires an analysis of official positions taken by the parties involved, as well as other states. When a given operational practice is generally accepted— for example military installations are targeted—this supports the proposition underlying that practice, namely that military installations constitute lawful military targets. But when an operational practice is generally considered to be a violation of existing rules—for example civilian installations are targeted—that is all it is, a violation. . . . The conclusion that these acts are considered to be violations of existing rules can be derived only from the way they are received by the international community through verbal acts, such as military manuals, national legislation, national and international case-law, resolutions of international organizations and official statements. These verbal acts provide the lens through which to look at operational practice. . . .
>
> As a result of the above considerations, the Study had to take into account resolutions adopted by states in the framework of international organizations, in particular the United Nations and regional organizations. As indicated, the Study is premised on the recognition that "resolutions are normally not binding in themselves and therefore the value accorded to any particular resolution depends on its content, its degree of acceptance and the consistency of State practice outside it." A list containing the voting record of all cited General Assembly resolutions was therefore included in the Study and used during the assessment. Most importantly, resolutions were always assessed together with other state practice and were not used to tip the balance in favour of a rule being customary. [Jean-Marie Henckaerts, Customary International Humanitarian Law: A Response to US Comments, 89 Int'l Rev. Red Cross 473, 477-78 (2007).]

Notes and Questions

1. The practice of calling an ambassador "Your Excellency" has been followed for centuries. Why is it not legally binding?

2. How would you decide whether customary international law prohibited customs searches of diplomats in transit? If you could show many statements of

diplomats asserting their immunity, a U.N. conference producing a draft treaty codifying that immunity, and copies of administrative directions for customs officials issued by governments of a large number of states not to search or arrest diplomats in transit (which were almost always followed), would that be enough? Does your answer depend on whether you are a diplomat or a law enforcement official concerned about drug smuggling and terrorism? What if you could only show the first two mentioned types of evidence?

3. One of the challenges in determining the content of customary international law is collecting evidence of the relevant state practice. Historically, in order to ascertain the content of what Roberts calls "traditional" customary law,

> it was necessary to examine in full detail the practice and related legal convictions *(opinio juris)* of States. Most of the major treatises in international law [in the nineteenth and early twentieth centuries] purported to follow this methodology though they varied considerably in their fidelity to the ideal of positivist doctrine. The favoured instruments of the positivist methodology were the national digests of State practice prepared by, or in close association with, the government of the State concerned. These digests were widely lauded and strongly encouraged by the profession. They were considered to provide the hard facts of law necessary for an inductive approach. They were mainly systematic collections of legal conclusions and facts expressed in diplomatic correspondence and in governmental officials' legal opinions. Since only a few countries produced such digests, the data in the digests fell far short of representing State practice in general. But as it was very hard to obtain evidence of practice in the absence of the digests, those that were produced were much relied upon and often treated as highly persuasive evidence of customary law. Many legal opinions as well as arguments before courts and international commissions used those digests as a primary source of authoritative law. [Oscar Schachter, International Law in Theory and Practice 36 (1991).]

4. In the Paquete Habana, 175 U.S. 677 (discussed in Chapter 3), the U.S. Supreme Court engaged in an extensive examination of the practice of a number of different states over several hundred years in determining that customary international law prohibited the capture as war prizes of private coastal fishing vessels belonging to the enemy nation.

5. Is it plausible to accord statements and conduct the same weight as forms of state practice, as Professor Shearer suggests? Are diplomatic protests and other communications of the kind canvassed in old international law digests statements or conduct? Does it matter whether the statements in question are genuinely held beliefs or merely made for purposes of political expedience? What value as evidence of practice should be accorded to a statement of the Saudi government that women are entitled to equal treatment within the law?

6. The legitimacy of "modern" or "new" customary international law based largely on normative declarations by states has been emphatically challenged. According to one scholar, "new" customary international law

> is simply not based on the inductive method and cannot be justified as a social fact. . . .
>
> [Moreover], international resolutions and declarations neither constitute *opinio juris*, nor evidence that states actually accept these norms as obligatory. . . .
>
> Aspirational or recommendary instruments, enacted while states remain unwilling to sign concrete treaties, provide compelling evidence that states lack the normative

conviction necessary to create customary obligations, rather than evidence that states believe these norms are binding. . . .

"New [customary international law]" analysis has a bootstrap quality. It purports to create a legal obligation for all without the acceptance of these norms as binding by the multitude of states. This impressionistic disarray allows the scholar, advocate, or judge in the few cases that are adjudicated to subjectively arrive at a conclusion affected by normative predilection. The [customary international law] of human rights is a product of the normative perspective of academics and advocates practicing human rights law, not the social fact of states accepting legal norms.

There is much to commend in these creative and romantic approaches to the normative by environmental and human rights advocates, but the legal obligation of states must be grounded in state acceptance, not in the preferences of advocates and judges. [J. Patrick Kelly, The Twilight of Customary International Law, 40 Va. J. Int'l L. 449, 485-487, 492 (2000).]

7. What position along the spectrum from "traditional" to "modern" customary international law does the United States take regarding the ICRC's study on customary international humanitarian law? What about the ICRC? Does the co-author of the ICRC study suggest that statements themselves give rise to customary international law obligations?

8. The role of General Assembly resolutions in the development of customary international law has given rise to considerable discussion. Although that discourse could be seen as simply another manifestation of the "acts versus statements" debate addressed above, the prominence of the General Assembly as the United Nations deliberative body in which all states participate raises additional complexities. These issues are particularly acute in the case of General Assembly resolutions that express principles and rules of law. One distinguished commentator observed:

. . . [S]uch resolutions are not a formal source of law within the explicit categories of Article 38(1) of the Statute of the International Court of Justice. It is also clear that under the United Nations Charter the General Assembly does not have the legal power to make law or to adopt binding decisions except for certain organizational matters (such as procedural rules, regulations for the Secretariat and subsidiary bodies and financial decisions). Yet few would deny that General Assembly resolutions have had a formative influence in the development of international law in matters of considerable importance to national States. . . .

[Where a resolution expressing principles and rules of law is unanimously adopted, let us take a closer look at the assumption that this] is enough to constitute conclusive evidence that the declared rule or principle is law. Are there good reasons to question that assumption? One plausible reason is that a vote for a resolution may not be intended to signify agreement on the legal validity of the asserted norm. There is evidence that governments do not always have that intent when they vote for a resolution or fail to object to it. They may assume that since resolutions generally have no more than recommendatory effect, their vote should mean no more than that. They may cast their vote solely on political grounds. . . .

It still remains important to clarify the legal force of the declaration and determinations of law. . . . [It seems most appropriate to treat] law-declaring resolutions as evidence for the asserted proposition of law. This would be compatible with the basic principle that such resolutions are not binding in the sense that treaties or judicial judgments are legally binding on the parties. However, it recognizes that

> interpretations and declarations of law by the Assembly are official expressions of the governments concerned and consequently are relevant and entitled to be given weight in determinations of the law in question. By characterizing them as "evidentiary" we invite an assessment of the pertinent data. We would assess the degree and character of support received in the United Nations and the relation if any of the asserted rule to an underlying Charter or customary law principle. Moreover, relevant State practice and *opinio juris* manifested outside of the United Nations would be considered. . . . [Oscar Schachter, International Law in Theory and Practice 85, 88-89 (1991).]

Does this view seem persuasive to you? If so, what would be the legal effect of a "law-declaring resolution" that is adopted by a very wide margin, but not unanimously? Would the nonconcurring states be bound?

9. More generally, if a General Assembly resolution does not make law, but simply reflects evidence of a rule of customary law, why shouldn't a person who wants to establish the existence of that rule be required to show the underlying state practice independently of the General Assembly resolution? Do you think that the mere existence of a General Assembly debate (or the convening of an international conference) can stimulate the development of, or a change in, state practice? Even if this is so, shouldn't the burden be on the proponent of a new rule to show the underlying state practice? Do you think states might be more willing to vote for a General Assembly resolution declaring a rule of customary international law than they would be to become parties to a treaty embodying that rule? If so, why?

10. What effect does the violation of a purported rule of customary international law have on the existence of such a rule? For example, can we find a customary rule prohibiting torture if states say they condemn torture, but if in fact some of them tolerate it? The International Court of Justice attempted to address this question in explaining why instances of the use of force by states against one another in practice do not invalidate the customary international law prohibition on such use of force:

> 184. Bound as it is by Article 38 of its Statute to apply, *inter alia*, international custom "as evidence of a general practice accepted as law", the Court may not disregard the essential role played by general practice. . . . [I]n the field of customary international law, the shared view of the Parties as to the content of what they regard as the rule is not enough. The Court must also satisfy itself that the existence of the rule in the *opinio juris* of States is confirmed by practice. . . .
>
> 186. It is not to be expected that in the practice of States the application of the rules in question should have been perfect, in the sense that States should have refrained, with complete consistency, from the use of force or from intervention in each other's internal affairs. The Court does not consider that, for a rule to be established as customary, the corresponding practice must be in absolutely rigorous conformity with the rule. In order to deduce the existence of customary rules, the Court deems it sufficient that the conduct of States should, in general, be consistent with such rules, and that instances of State conduct inconsistent with a given rule should generally have been treated as breaches of that rule, not as indications of the recognition of a new rule. If a State acts in a way prima facie incompatible with a recognized rule, but defends its conduct by appealing to exceptions or justifications contained within the rule itself, then whether or not the State's conduct is in fact justifiable on that basis, the significance of that attitude is to confirm rather than to weaken the rule.

[Military and Paramilitary Activities in and Against Nicaragua (Nicaragua v. United States of America), 1986 I.C.J. 14, 97-98 (June 27).]

The International Law Association (ILA) in 2000 adopted a Statement of Principles regarding customary international law that had been prepared by a distinguished committee, mainly composed of international law professors from outside the United States. These efforts resulted in the working definition of customary international law that follows. Consider the ways in which this definition is similar to, and differs from, the Restatement formulation.

International Law Association, Statement of Principles Applicable to the Formation of General Customary International Law

Report of the Sixty-Ninth Conference, London, 712, 719-721, 738 (2000)

1. Working definition

(i) Subject to the Sections which follow, a rule of customary international law is one which is created and sustained by the constant and uniform practice of States and other subjects of international law in or impinging upon their international legal relations, in circumstances which give rise to a legitimate expectation of similar conduct in the future.

(ii) If a sufficiently extensive and representative number of States participate in such a practice in a consistent manner, the resulting rule is one of "general customary international law." Subject to Section 15, such a rule is binding on all States.

(iii) Where a rule of general customary international law exists, for any particular State to be bound by that rule it is not necessary to prove either that State's consent to it or its belief in the rule's obligatory or (as the case may be) permissive character.

Commentary. . . .

[b] (4) The definition in (i) and (ii) does not *expressly* say anything about the so-called subjective element in customary law — the element of belief or consent — though there is an indirect allusion to this in the words "in circumstances which give rise to a legitimate expectation of similar conduct in the future." Although traditional formulations often describe customary international law as a combination of the "objective" (or "material") element — State practice — and the "subjective" element *(opinio juris sive necessitatis),* it will be seen later that, in the opinion of the Committee, this would be an over-simplification. . . . [I]t is not *usually* necessary to demonstrate the existence of the subjective element before a customary rule can be said to have come into being. There are, however, circumstances where it is necessary, and the Committee also took the view that assent to a rule can create a binding obligation. But these circumstances are so varied that they need to be dealt with specifically, rather than in a working definition. . . .

15. If whilst a practice is developing into a rule of general law, a State persistently and openly dissents from the rule, it will not be bound by it.

The International Court of Justice, in its Advisory Opinion on the Legality of the Threat or Use of Nuclear Weapons, was required to assess the role of *opinio juris* in addressing the U.N. General Assembly's request for an opinion on the question of whether "the threat or use of nuclear weapons [is] in any circumstances permitted under international law." Consider the ICJ's discussion of *opinio juris* and whether a rule of customary international law prohibiting the use of nuclear weapons exists:

> 64. The Court will now turn to an examination of customary international law to determine whether a prohibition of the threat or use of nuclear weapons as such flows from that source of law. As the Court has stated, the substance of that law must be "looked for primarily in the actual practice and *opinio juris* of States."
>
> 65. States which hold the view that the use of nuclear weapons is illegal have endeavoured to demonstrate the existence of a customary rule prohibiting this use. They refer to a consistent practice of non-utilization of nuclear weapons by States since 1945 and they would see in that practice the expression of an *opinio juris* on the part of those who possess such weapons.
>
> 66. Some other States, which assert the legality of the threat and use of nuclear weapons in certain circumstances, invoked the doctrine and practice of deterrence in support of their argument. They recall that they have always, in concert with certain other States, reserved the right to use those weapons in the exercise of the right to self-defence against an armed attack threatening their vital security interests. In their view, if nuclear weapons have not been used since 1945, it is not on account of an existing or nascent custom but merely because circumstances that might justify their use have fortunately not arisen.
>
> 67. The Court does not intend to pronounce here upon the practice known as the "policy of deterrence." It notes that it is a fact that a number of States adhered to that practice during the greater part of the Cold War and continue to adhere to it. Furthermore, the members of the international community are profoundly divided on the matter of whether non-recourse to nuclear weapons over the past 50 years constitutes the expression of an *opinio juris.* Under these circumstances the Court does not consider itself able to find that there is such an *opinio juris.* [Legality of the Threat or Use of Nuclear Weapons (Advisory Opinion), 1996 I.C.J. 226, 253-254 (July 8).]

Notes and Questions

1. The International Law Association's Statement of Principles appears to downplay the significance of the subjective element of customary international law, stating: "It is not *usually* necessary to demonstrate the existence of the subjective element before a customary rule can be said to come into being." Why do you think that the ILA took a position discounting the importance of *opinio juris*? Might this, in part, reflect the problems of establishing the subjective belief of states? Should widespread practice be enough to establish the existence of a binding rule of international law? What is the relationship between state's "subjective" motivations and what seems to be the ILA's reliance-based notion that practice can give rise to an

expectation on the part of other states of continued performance? What are the advantages and disadvantages of the approach in the ILA's Principles? For an article questioning how much of a change was really being proposed by the Association, see Sienho Yee, The News that Opinio Juris "Is Not a Necessary Element of Customary [International] Law" Is Greatly Exaggerated, 43 German Y.B. of Int'l L. 227 (2000).

2. In the exchange of comments over the ICRC's study on the customary rules of international humanitarian law, the U.S. expressed concern about the ICRC's treatment of *opinio juris*:

> [T]he Study tends to merge the practice and *opinio juris* requirements into a single test. In the Study's own words,
>
> > "it proved very difficult and largely theoretical to strictly separate elements of practice and legal conviction. More often than not, one and the same act reflects both practice and legal conviction. . . . When there is sufficiently dense practice, an *opinio juris* is generally contained within that practice and, as a result, it is not usually necessary to demonstrate separately the existence of an *opinio juris*."
>
> The United States does not believe that this is an appropriate methodological approach. Although the same action may serve as evidence both of State practice and *opinio juris*, the United States does not agree that *opinio juris* simply can be inferred from practice. Both elements instead must be assessed separately in order to determine the presence of a norm of customary international law. For example, Additional Protocols I and II to the Geneva Conventions contain far-reaching provisions, but States did not at the time of their adoption believe that all of those instruments' provisions reflected rules that already had crystallized into customary international law; indeed, many provisions were considered ground-breaking and gap-filling at the time. One therefore must be cautious in drawing conclusions as to *opinio juris* from the practice of States that are parties to conventions, since their actions often are taken pursuant to their treaty obligations, particularly *inter se*, and not in contemplation of independently binding customary international law norms. . . .
>
> The United States is troubled by the Study's heavy reliance on military manuals. The United States does not agree that *opinio juris* has been established when the evidence of a State's sense of legal obligation consists predominately of military manuals. Rather than indicating a position expressed out of a sense of a customary legal obligation, in the sense pertinent to customary international law, a State's military manual often (properly) will recite requirements applicable to that State under treaties to which it is a party. Reliance on provisions of military manuals designed to implement treaty rules provides only weak evidence that those treaty rules apply as a matter of customary international law in non-treaty contexts. Moreover, States often include guidance in their military manuals for policy, rather than legal, reasons. For example, the United States long has stated that it will apply the rules in its manuals whether the conflict is characterized as international or non-international, but this clearly is not intended to indicate that it is bound to do so as a matter of law in non-international conflicts. . . .
>
> A more rigorous approach to establishing *opinio juris* is required. It is critical to establish by positive evidence, beyond mere recitations of existing treaty obligations or statements that as easily may reflect policy considerations as legal considerations, that States consider themselves legally obligated to follow the courses of action reflected in the rules. [Joint Letter from John B. Bellinger, III, and William J. Haynes II to Dr. Jakob Kellenberger, supra, 46 ILM at 515-516 (2007).]

One of the ICRC study's authors responded that the study "did not simply infer *opinio juris* from practice," but was based on a separate analysis of whether, for each rule, "the practice [that] attested to the existence of a rule of law was inspired merely by non-legal considerations of convenience, comity or policy." Jean-Marie Henckaerts, Customary International Humanitarian Law: A Response to US Comments, supra, 89 Int'l Rev. Red Cross at 482.

3. Based on your still growing knowledge of what might constitute customary international law, do you think that any or all of the following activities are a violation of a norm of customary international law: genocide or the killing of all or part of a national, ethnic, racial, or religious group; torturing enemy soldiers or terrorists after catching them to obtain important information; substantial pollution of a major river that flows into the ocean; engaging in racial and/or sex discrimination in the workplace; and failing to obtain informed consent from a group of adults in a developing country before testing a not yet fully approved medicine on them?

4. Is it likely that some, or all, of the activities listed in the previous paragraphs would be illegal under the laws of the country where the practices are occurring? Is it likely that some of these practices are covered under multilateral treaties? How would your answer to either of these questions affect your answer to whether the particular activity is a violation of a norm of customary international law?

5. Let's assume that customary international law prohibits customs searches of diplomats in transit and that there are no relevant treaties. In light of recent acts of terrorism, could the United Kingdom start such searches? If not, how can customary law ever change? What would be the consequence if the United Kingdom violated this customary international law?

Professor Michael Reisman characterizes the process in the following way:

> International law is still largely a decentralized process, in which much law making (particularly for the most innovative matters) is initiated by unilateral claim, whether explicit or behavioral. Claims to change inherited security arrangements, or any other part of the law, ignite a process of counterclaims, responses, replies, and rejoinders until stable expectations or right behavior emerge. Since every legal regime perforce benefits some actors more than others, no sooner does a new normative arrangement stabilize that it, too, comes under stress from new claims for change, in an ongoing bargaining process between sometimes rapidly shifting coalitions. Hence the ceaseless dialectic of international law: Whether by diplomatic communication or state behavior, one state claims from other acquiescence in a new practice. Insofar as that new practice is accepted in whole or in part, the practice becomes part of the law. [W. Michael Reisman, Assessing Claims to Revise the Laws of War, 97 Am. J. Int'l L. 82, 82 (2003).]

6. As discussed in Chapter 1.C, Professors Jack Goldsmith and Eric Posner, in their book The Limits of International Law (2005), take issue with the notion that states comply with international law rules—including customary international law—due to any sense of legal or moral obligation. They ground the formulation of rules of international law, as well as compliance with them, in efforts by states to coordinate and cooperate with others in the pursuit of their self-interest in international affairs. If a state decides to act in compliance with a rule of customary international law, even though it will give up some short-term benefit by doing so, does it matter whether the state acts because it seeks the long-term advantages of

participation in a mutually beneficial cooperative arrangement with other states, rather than acting from a sense of legal obligation?

For some of the academic debate on The Limits of International Law, see the symposium issue on the book published by the Georgia Journal of International and Comparative Law, 34 Ga. J. Int'l & Comp. L. 253 et seq. (2006). For discussion of the debate about the formation of customary international law, see Andrew T. Guzman, Saving Customary International Law, 27 Mich. J. Int'l L. 115 (2005); George Norman & Joel P. Trachtman, The Customary International Law Game, 99 Am. J. Int'l L. 541 (2005).

b. Whose Practice? Who Is Bound?

The ILA working definition of customary international law excerpted above notes explicitly that if state practice giving rise to a customary international law rule is "sufficiently extensive and representative," the resulting rule is binding on *all* states. The Restatement Comment also states that practice can be sufficiently "general" to give rise to a rule of customary international law "even if it is not universally followed."

At the same time, the Restatement Comment notes that the relevant practice must include states "particularly involved in the relevant activity." To like effect, the ILA Commentary to the ILA Principles states that "if important actors [in an area of activity] do *not* accept the practice, it cannot mature into a rule of general customary law." International Law Association, Statement of Principles Applicable to the Formation of General Customary International Law, Report of the Sixty-Ninth Conference, supra, at 737 (Commentary to Section 14). These comments highlight the role of *specially affected states* in the formation of customary international law. In the North Sea Continental Shelf Cases (Federal Republic of Germany v. Denmark; Federal Republic of Germany v. Netherlands), the ICJ examined whether a rule concerning the delimitation of continental shelf boundaries contained in a multilateral convention had generated a rule of customary international law that was binding even for states that were not parties to the treaty. The Court noted:

> 73. With respect to the other elements usually regarded as necessary before a conventional rule can be considered to have become a general [customary] rule of international law, it might be that, even without the passage of any considerable period of time, a very widespread and representative participation in the convention might suffice of itself, provided it included that of States whose interests were specially affected. . . . [1969 I.C.J. 4, 43 (Feb. 20).]

A further consideration to take into account in analyzing when a customary international law rule has come into existence, and which states are bound by the rule, is the status of *persistent objectors.* As Section 15 of the ILA's Principles notes, a state that "persistently and openly dissents from" from a purported rule while practice is developing into a rule of general law will not be bound by the rule. The Restatement recognizes the same principle, stating: "[A] state that indicates its dissent from a practice while the law is still in the process of development is not bound by that rule even after it matures." Restatement §102 comment d. The Commentary to the ILA Statement of Principles elaborates:

> . . . There is fairly widespread agreement that, even if there is a persistent objector rule in international law, it applies only when the customary rule is in the process of emerging. It does not, therefore, benefit States which came into existence only after the rule matured, or which became involved in the activity in question only at a later stage. Still less can it be invoked by those who existed at the time and were already engaged in the activity which is the subject of the rule, but failed to object at that stage. In other words, there is no "subsequent objector" rule. . . .
>
> . . . Although some authors question the existence of this rule, most accept it as part of current international law. . . . As a matter of policy, the persistent objector rule could be regarded as a useful compromise. It respects States' sovereignty and protects them from new law imposed on them against their will by a majority; but at the same time, if the support for the new rule is sufficiently widespread, the convoy of the law's progressive development can move forward without having to wait for the slowest vessel. [International Law Association, Statement of Principles Applicable to the Formation of General Customary International Law, Report of the Sixty-Ninth Conference, supra, at 738-739 (Commentary to Section 15).]

Notes and Questions

1. How consensual is customary international law? Does the general and widespread practice of states that creates a customary law rule serve as evidence of consent, even for those states that are silent and do not actively participate in the practice while the rule is emerging? Should customary international law bind a newly emerging state, like the many states established after the end of the colonial era, that had no opportunity to object to emerging customary rules? Should such a state be bound even if it attempts to reject the rule when it attains independence—for example, by passing a domestic law contrary to the rule or by making a statement in the U.N. General Assembly?

2. Is there a customary international law prohibition on the death penalty? As of 2009, according to Amnesty International, 139 countries have abolished the death penalty, either in law or in practice (by not carrying out any executions during the past ten years). In comparison, 58 states retain the death penalty, although most did not use it in 2009. Amnesty International, Abolitionist and Retentionist Countries, http://www.amnesty.org/en/death-penalty/abolitionist-and-retentionist-countries. Is that practice sufficiently "general and consistent," in the Restatement formulation, or sufficiently "extensive and representative," in the ILA formulation, to generate a customary international law rule? Does the number of states that retain the death penalty mean that there is no customary international law prohibition? Or does it mean that a customary international law prohibition has come into effect but that the retentionist states are persistent objectors that are not bound by the rule? In assessing whether there is a customary international law prohibition, would any states be considered "specially affected"?

3. Although a state may object to the application to it of an emerging "ordinary" customary international law rule, consent is generally said not to be required for *jus cogens* norms (such as rules against genocide, slavery, and official

torture). See Michael Byers, Custom, Power, and the Power of Rules 194-195 (1999); Louis Henkin, International Law: Politics, Values and Functions, 216 Recueil des Cours 9, 60 (1989). *Jus cogens*, or "peremptory," norms are discussed in Section A above. Would it be possible for a state to be a "persistent objector" to the claim that a norm has the status of *jus cogens*? The prohibition on apartheid, for example, is often identified as a *jus cogens* norm. Could South Africa, when it practiced apartheid, argue that it was not bound by the prohibition on apartheid because its longstanding practice of official racial discrimination constituted persistent objection to that prohibition? If a state can object to the characterization of a norm as peremptory, is it nonderogable? If the state cannot object, on what basis can *jus cogens* norms be imposed on states that don't accept them?

4. Historically, cases in which states persistently object to an emerging rules and claim "consequent exemption from a principle that became generally customary law [have] been rare." Restatement §102 comment d.

5. In a 1950 judgment in the Asylum Case (Colombia v. Peru), the International Court of Justice entertained the possibility of recognizing a "regional or local custom peculiar to" a particular group of states — in that case, Latin American states. The Court stated:

> The Party which relies on a custom of this kind must prove that this custom is established in such a manner that it has become binding on the other Party. [It] must prove that the rule invoked by it is in accordance with a constant and uniform usage practised by the States in question, and that this usage is the expression of [an acceptance of legal rights and duties.] [1950 I.C.J. 266, 276 (Nov. 20).]

Although claims for the existence of a regional customary norm are not common, might there be instances where arguments for a regional customary norm could have force? Consider the question of democratic governance in the Inter-American region. The Organization of American States (OAS), in the Protocol of Washington signed in 1992, agreed on a mechanism providing for the suspension from the OAS of any "democratically constituted [OAS member] government [that] has been overthrown by force." Protocol of Amendments to the Charter of the Organization of American States (A-56) art. 1, Dec. 14, 1992, OEA/Ser.A/2 Add. 3. Relying on this mechanism, the OAS General Assembly in July 2009 voted to suspend Honduras from participation in the OAS following a "coup d'état against the constitutional government of President José Manuel Zelaya Rosales, as well as his arbitrary detention and expulsion from the country, which produced an unconstitutional alteration of the democratic order." OEA/Ser.P, AG/RES. 2 (XXXVII-E/09) (July 4, 2009). The OAS not only suspended Honduras but also encouraged OAS member states "to review their relations with the Republic of Honduras during the period of the diplomatic initiatives for the restoration of democracy and the rule of law in the Republic of Honduras and the reinstatement of President José Manuel Zelaya Rosales." As you will see in Chapter 5, there are different views about the requirement under customary international law for states to recognize the government of another state. Could the OAS's call for states to seek the reinstatement of the Zelaya government reflect the emergence of a regional customary norm in the Inter-American system against recognizing governments that come to power through extraconstitutional means?

2. *The Effect of Treaties on Customary International Law*

Not only do treaties serve as a primary source of international law (as discussed in Section A of this chapter), but treaties can also play a significant role in the development of customary international law.

It is useful to think of three ways in which treaties and customary international law may be related. First, a treaty may simply attempt to codify existing customary international law rules. One of the functions of the International Law Commission, a U.N. body comprising 34 international law experts elected by the General Assembly, is to draft multilateral treaties for adoption by states that codify international law "in fields where there already has been extensive State practice, precedent and doctrine." Art. 15, Statute of the International Law Commission. The ILC has adopted a number of significant codification treaties, including the Vienna Convention on the Law of Treaties and the Vienna Convention on Diplomatic Relations.

Second, a treaty may "crystallize" customary practice that is in the process of forming. In the North Sea Continental Shelf cases before the ICJ, which involved a dispute over the delimitation of the continental shelf appurtenant to Germany, Denmark, and the Netherlands in the North Sea, Denmark and the Netherlands argued that the continental shelf should be delimited in accordance with the principle of "equidistance" established in Article 6 of the 1958 Geneva Convention on the Continental Shelf. Although Germany was not a party to the Convention, Denmark and the Netherlands claimed that the equidistance principle for delimiting the continental shelf had developed into a rule customary international law. As the Court explained:

> Their contention was, . . . that although prior to the Conference, continental shelf law was only in the formative stage, and State practice lacked uniformity, . . . "the process of the definition and consolidation of the emerging customary law took place through the work of the International Law Commission, the reaction of governments to that work and the proceedings of the Geneva Conference"; and this emerging customary law became "crystallized in the adoption of the Continental Shelf Convention by the Conference".
>
> . . . [T]he Court cannot accept [this contention] as regards the delimitation provision (Article 6). . . . [T]he principle of equidistance . . . was proposed by the Commission with considerable hesitation, somewhat on an experimental basis, at most *de lege ferenda* [what the law ought to be] and not at all *de lege lata* [what the law is] or as an emerging rule of customary international law. This is clearly not the sort of foundation on which Article 6 of the Convention could be said to have reflected or crystallized such a rule. [North Sea Continental Shelf cases (Federal Republic of Germany v. Denmark; Federal Republic of Germany v. Netherlands), 1969 I.C.J. 3, 39 (Feb. 20).]

Third, a treaty may announce a new rule or create a new norm that gives rise to practice, even among nonparties, that produces a rule of customary international law. In the North Sea Continental Shelf case, Denmark and the Netherlands argued that even if the delimitation principle in Article 6 of the 1958 Geneva Convention on the Continental Shelf had not yet crystallized existing practice, it was instead a "norm-creating provision" that had been recognized as a customary international norm and was accordingly binding even for countries that were not a party to the Convention. The Court held open the possibility that a rule in a treaty could generate a new customary international norm, but cautioned that "this result is not lightly to be regarded as having been attained." Id. at 42. Particularly where only a short period of time has elapsed since the adoption of the convention in question, the Court noted,

> an indispensable requirement would be that within the period in question, . . . State practice, including that of States whose interests are specially affected, should have been both extensive and virtually uniform in the sense of the provision invoked; and should moreover have occurred in such a way as to show a general recognition that a rule of law or legal obligation is involved. [Id. at 44.]

The Restatement addresses the relationship between treaties and customary international law, including the possibility of conflict between these two sources of international law.

Restatement Section 102

Comment

f. *International agreement as source of law.* An international agreement creates obligations binding between the parties under international law. Ordinarily, an agreement between states is a source of law only in the sense that a private contract may be said to make law for the parties under the domestic law of contracts. Multilateral agreements open to all states, however, are increasingly used for general legislation, whether to make new law, as in human rights, or for codifying and developing customary law, as in the Vienna Convention on the Law of Treaties. . . .

j. *Conflict between international agreement and customary law.* Customary law and law made by international agreement have equal authority as international law. Unless the parties evince a contrary intention, a rule established by agreement supersedes for them a prior inconsistent rule of customary international law. . . . A new rule of customary law will supersede inconsistent obligations created by earlier agreement if the parties so intend and the intention is clearly manifested.

Notes and Questions

1. How does widespread ratification of a treaty contribute to the development of customary international law? Does ratification of a treaty by itself suggest that the ratifying nations believe the norms in the treaty are legally binding in the absence of a treaty? If treaties can create customary international law that is binding on non-ratifying states, does this diminish the importance of the act of ratification of treaties?

2. Should there be a negative implication drawn from the failure of a state to ratify a treaty? If most (say, 80 percent) of the countries of the world were to ratify a treaty that a particular state strongly opposes, could that state ever be bound by some of the provisions of that treaty as norms of customary international law? For example, in 1999, the Ottawa Convention Banning Anti-Personnel Landmines entered into force. As of February 2011, 156 states had become parties to Convention, but the United States, which insists on the right to retain the right to use certain types of anti-personnel landmines in certain military scenarios, has not. Could other

states argue that the United States is now prohibited, as a matter of customary international law, from using anti-personnel landmines covered by the treaty?

3. In terms of the impact of a treaty on the development of customary international law, does it matter whether the countries that have ratified a treaty fully comply with it? For example, as discussed in Chapter 8, almost all countries except for the United States have ratified the Convention on the Rights of the Child, yet many of the ratifying countries probably do not accord children all the rights specified in the Convention.

4. Doesn't the doctrine expressed in the Restatement, by which a subsequent custom supersedes a treaty, introduce great uncertainty about the continuing validity of treaties? Is that desirable? Can a custom be used to interpret a treaty under Articles 31 and 32 of the Vienna Convention?

5. Which form of law making, treaty or custom, is more likely to be able to adapt to new circumstances? Which is easier to change? Which is more likely to be responsive to the interests of a developing state? To the United States?

3. "Soft Law"

In coordinating their international activities, states have increasingly come to rely on the use of what is known as "soft law." Soft law is not an independent source of law, but rather an expression of commitments that are not themselves legally binding. One scholar has defined soft law as "international law-making that is designed, in whole or part, not to be enforceable." See W. Michael Reisman, The Supervisory Jurisdiction of the International Court of Justice, 258 Rec. des Cours 180 (1996). Other writers characterize soft law as "nonbinding rules or instruments that interpret or inform our understanding of binding legal rules or represent promises that in turn create expectations about future conduct." Andrew T. Guzman & Timothy L. Meyer, International Soft Law, 2 J. Legal Anal. 171, 174 (2010). Soft law can include such diverse quasi-legal instruments as formal statements from international organizations or multilateral meetings to codes of conduct from interest groups. See Commitment and Compliance: The Role of Non-Binding Norms in the International Legal System (Dinah Shelton ed., 2000).

There are many examples of soft law norms, and states use a variety of forms to establish them. Their shared characteristic is that states, at least at the moment they create these norms, do not wish to assumed binding legal obligations:

> Soft law often takes the form of an international instrument that has some of the features of a formal treaty, but falls short of the requirements to be one. In general, this means that the states involved do not intend to be bound by international law. Examples of this type of soft law abound. The Universal Declaration of Human Rights, for example, lays out a set of human rights obligations for states, but is explicitly not "binding" on states. The Basle Accords seek to improve banking regulatory practices and are also soft law. The Nuclear Suppliers Group Guidelines are a set of export control guidelines governing the transfer of nuclear materials between states promulgated by the 45-member Nuclear Suppliers Group, or London Club. The Guidelines are not legally binding, but provide content to the legally binding — but vague — export control obligation established by the Nuclear Nonproliferation Treaty. . . . [Guzman & Meyer, International Soft Law, supra, 2 J. Legal Anal. at 187-188.]

Although soft law is nonbinding, it may lead to some compliance with its standards. It can also generate state practice that gives rise to new customary international law rules. In addition, it can serve as an interim stage in the development of international law and can later be codified in the form of treaties. Much of today's international environmental law (discussed in Chapter 10) is, or has grown out of, soft law.

Notes and Questions

1. What reasons might explain why states would favor the use of soft law over hard law? In the United States, might the executive branch be concerned about the difficulty in obtaining Senate ratification of an instrument adopted as a treaty, as opposed to a soft-law declaration?

2. Professor Chinkin has noted that the use of soft law instruments sometimes reflects a "compromise between those States which did not favour any regulatory instrument and those which would have preferred the conclusion of a treaty." Christine M. Chinkin, The Challenge of Soft Law: Development and Challenge in International Law, 38 Int'l & Comp. L. Q. 850, 861 (1989). She also observes that soft law instruments "allow for the incorporation of conflicting standards and goals and provide States with the room to manoeuvre in the making of claims and counterclaims." Id. at 866.

3. The evolution of international rules aimed at prohibiting the participation of transnational corporations in bribery illustrates the operation of soft law. In 1977, the U.S. Congress passed the Foreign Corrupt Practices Act (FCPA), which provided criminal penalties for defined corrupt practices, such as bribery of foreign officials by American nationals, American corporations, or their subsidiaries in order to get business. American companies expressed concern that the legislation would put them at a competitive disadvantage vis-à-vis European or Asian corporate competitors.

In 1994, the Organisation for Economic Cooperation and Development (OECD), an international organization comprising the world's leading industrial states, produced its nonbinding Recommendation on Bribery in International Business Transactions, which called on OECD member states to take effective measures to deter, prevent, and combat bribery of foreign public officials. In 1996, in response to a United States initiative, the U.N. General Assembly adopted the "Declaration on Corruption and Bribery in Transnational Commercial Activities." The Declaration called states to criminalize both domestic and international bribery and to prohibit the tax deductibility of bribes. For its part, the OECD continued to work on the problem of bribery and in 1997 adopted the OECD Convention on Combating Bribery of Foreign Public Officials in International Business Transactions. Unlike the earlier nonbinding instruments, the Convention obligates the states that are parties to criminalize bribery of foreign public officials in the conduct of international business. As of February 2011, 38 countries have ratified the Convention and enacted the required implementing legislation making bribery of foreign public officials a crime. Besides the United States, they include other major industrial countries such as Japan, most European Union members, and Brazil.

Efforts to adopt binding instruments to combat corruption have since moved beyond the context of the OECD. In 2003, the U.N. General Assembly adopted a

United Nations Convention Against Corruption. The Convention encourages the adoption of policies to prevent corruption, requires parties to criminalize a wide range of acts of corruption, and includes innovative provisions for the recovery of assets plundered through corruption. The Convention entered into force in December 2005. As of February 2011, 148 countries, including the United States, had ratified or acceded to the Convention.

In addition to governments and corporation, nongovernmental organizations played an active role in the effort to combat corruption in international business transactions. As Professor Deming explains:

> In May 1993, an international, nonprofit NGO known as Transparency International (TI) was established to curb corruption in international business transactions. TI is headquartered in Germany and has chapters in almost fifty countries. TI has taken a prominent role in pressing governments and international organizations to adopt measures designed to deter corruption in the conduct of international business. Other organizations like the American Bar Association (ABA) and more recently the International Bar Association (IBA) have taken official positions to support and endorse efforts by the international community, by national governments, and by non-governmental organizations to encourage the adoption of effective legal measures, which are actively implemented and enforced, to deter corrupt practices in the conduct of international business. . . . [See Stuart H. Deming, Foreign Corrupt Practices, 31 Int'l Law. 695, 698 (1997).]

After more than 20 years, what began as set of soft law recommendations had developed into a broad set of binding international law rules. Nongovernmental entities were important actors in this process. In the next section, we consider the role of entities other than states in creating international law.

C. INTERNATIONAL ORGANIZATIONS AND NONGOVERNMENTAL ORGANIZATIONS (NGOs) AS CREATORS OF LAW

International law has traditionally been made by governments, normally through the conclusion of treaties or through state practice amounting to customary law. Treaties have been especially prominent since World War II. Now, however, international law is increasingly being made by international organizations, networks of governmental regulators, and nonstate actors. In a few cases, states have delegated authority to international organizations to create binding rules. More typically, international organizations develop norms and standards that are not legally binding as a formal matter. These norms may nevertheless have a significant impact on governments, multinational corporations, and people throughout the world. Private actors, especially a dramatically expanding array of private, non-governmental organizations (NGOs) and multinational corporations, are also playing a growing and important role in creating international norms.

In this section, we look first at the scope, organization, and law-making authority of international organizations. Next, we look at some of the newer "bottom-up" approaches to creating international law. We consider the way networks of governmental officials increasingly coordinate their efforts and harmonize legal rules in order to regulate transnational activities. We next explore the growing impact of NGOs on law making and the creation of norms by governments and international organizations. We conclude by looking at transnational corporations, not only as actors that independently engage in international standard setting and other conduct traditionally associated with governmental regulations but also as subjects of efforts to develop international rules and frameworks to regulate their conduct.

1. *International Organizations*

States create intergovernmental organizations for the purpose of accomplishing generally shared social or economic objectives. For example, the World Health Organization was created to assist in the reduction of disease. The World Bank raises money in international capital markets and makes loans for economic development projects. The International Atomic Energy Agency (IAEA) promotes the safe and peaceful use of nuclear energy. And the International Civil Aviation Organization (ICAO) promotes civil aviation. See Chapter 1.B for an overall history of international institutions after World War II.

These organizations serve as a forum for the exchange of information and views. They may also carry out research and other projects directly. They also play a very significant role in creating new international legal norms. In the words of Professor Alvarez:

> Although some may prefer to describe [international organizations (IOs)] as merely "arenas" for lawmaking action, IOs—whether traditional or not—are for all practical purposes a new kind of lawmaking actor, to some degree autonomous from the states that establish them. IOs can now be seen not only as capable of concluding treaties with other international legal persons (other IOs or states) but as vehicles for the forms of regulation associated with the executive branches of government or national administrative agencies—and not just in technocratic fields of the law such as civil aviation and telecommunications; this aspect also bears on issues of "high politics," as through the fertile acts of improvisation that have transformed Chapters VI and VII of the UN Charter to permit the contracting out of the use of force, diverse types of multilateral sanctions, and peacekeeping/peace enforcement actions or determinations by the International Atomic Energy Agency (IAEA) with respect to arms control. . . . [IO] organs and the individuals working within them (from secretaries general to IO-designated experts) are having an independent impact on international law. [José E. Alvarez, Centennial Essay: In Honor of the 100th Anniversary of the AJIL and the ASIL: International Organizations: Then and Now, 100 Am. J. Int'l L. 324, 334 (2006).]

International organizations are created by treaty, and their areas of competence are quite diverse. Their work ranges from controversial political issues (as in the United Nations) to mostly uncontroversial matters (as in the Universal Postal Union). For example, the U.N. Security Council has authority to impose legally binding economic sanctions as it has done against North Korea and Iran and against individuals associated with Al Qaeda and persons interfering with the peace process in Somalia. The IAEA conducts on-site inspections to ensure that nuclear energy projects are not converted to military purposes. The ICAO Council has authority to impose safety regulations for aircraft and air navigation. The International Maritime

Organization (IMO) establishes shipping rules, and the World Health Organization (WHO) adopts health regulations. The International Whaling Commission (IWC) establishes limits on whaling. The actions of these international organizations may be automatically legally binding on all parties (as with some Security Council decisions), or their actions can be binding on a party if it does not "opt out" of the obligation (as in the WHO, IWC, and ICAO). Other organizations—such as Organization for Economic Cooperation and Development (OECD) and the International Labor Organization (ILO)—propose standards, rules, or regulations to member states for them to consider adopting. Professor Shaw describes how many of the United Nation's specialized agencies, which are "established by inter-governmental agreement [that have] wide international responsibilities in economic, social, cultural and other fields that have been brought into relationship with the United Nations," can bring practical political pressures on states to accept their law-making output.

> Most of the specialised agencies have devised means whereby the decisions of the particular organisation can be rendered virtually binding upon members. This is especially so with regard to the International Labour Organisation (established in 1919 to protect and extend the rights of workers), UNESCO (the UN Educational, Scientific and Cultural Organisation established to further the increase and diffusion of knowledge by various activities, including technical assistance and co-operative ventures with national governments) and the World Health Organisation (established in 1946 with the aim of unifying the standards of health care). Although such institutions are not able to legislate in the usual sense, they are able to apply pressures quite effectively to discourage noncompliance with recommendations or conventions. [Malcolm N. Shaw, International Law 1285 (6th ed. 2008.)]

Notes and Questions

1. How and why do the pressures to accept international recommendations that Shaw refers to actually work? Do these pressures operate at the domestic level, the international level, or both? Which type of pressure would be more effective?

2. Voting procedures for the adoption of decisions vary considerably from international organization to international organization. Some organizations take decisions only by consensus. For others, decisions can be taken by majority vote; in still others, a super-majority may be required. In addition, although many organizations apply a one-state, one-vote principle, other organizations weigh the votes of members according to some formula meant to capture their real interest. In considering these voting schemes, however, it is important to recall that

> only a small number of existing international organisations are endowed with the power to take decisions—or, in broader terms, institutional acts—which are binding *per se* on their members or on other addressees in the "external sphere" (i.e. not regarding matters relating to the functioning of the organisation itself). [Philippe Sands & Pierre Klein, Bowett's Law of International Institutions 267 (6th ed. 2009).]

3. Perhaps the most prominent example of delegation by states of law-making authority is the power of the 15-member U.N. Security Council to decide on

measures to address threats to international peace and security, breaches of the peace, or acts of aggression. These decisions bind all U.N. member states. Another example of delegation of law-making power that reaches deeply into matters traditionally of domestic concern is found in the European Union (EU), with its 27 member states and a population greater than the United States. Starting with the Treaty of Rome that established the European Economic Community, there have been amendments to the treaty and new treaties. In the present EU, the EU Council has the power to adopt, for example, regulations and directives based on proposals from the EU Commission and passed through the Parliament. Regulations can be directly binding on member states and persons within member states. Most Council regulations require approval by only a "qualified majority" of member states, which means the Council can enact regulations that bind states that have voted against them. Council regulations can even preempt a member state's laws. (See the sections in Chapters 4 and 5 on the European Union.)

4. See generally José E. Alvarez, International Organizations as Law-makers (2005); Ian Johnstone, Law-Making through the Operational Activities of International Organization, 40 Geo. Wash. Int'l L. Rev. 87 (2008); Philippe Sands & Pierre Klein, Bowett's Law of International Institutions (6th ed. 2009).

2. *Intergovernmental Networks*

Traditionally, states have acted in a highly centralized manner in creating international legal rules, especially when they negotiate treaties. Such negotiations are typically led by officials from each state's foreign ministry, and each state's negotiating positions are carefully coordinated in advance with other concerned government agencies. Anne-Marie Slaughter has identified a more decentralized process of intergovernmental regulation carried out through transnational government networks:

Anne-Marie Slaughter, A New World Order

1-7 (2004)

[Governments] operate through global networks. . . . Networks of government officials—police investigators, financial regulators, even judges and legislators—increasingly exchange information and coordinate activity to combat global crime and address common problems on a global scale. . . .

[After September 11], networks of financial regulators working to identify and freeze terrorist assets, of law enforcement officials sharing vital information on terrorist suspects, and of intelligence operatives working to preempt the next attack have been . . . important. . . .

[N]etworks of finance ministers and central bankers have been critical players in responding to national and regional financial crises. . . .

Beyond national security and the global economy, networks of national officials are working to improve environmental policy across borders. . . .

[These networks] expand regulatory reach, allowing national government officials to keep up with corporations, civic organizations, and criminals. They build trust and establish relationships among their participants that then create incentives to establish a good reputation and avoid a bad one. These are the conditions essential for long-term cooperation. They exchange regular information about their own activities and develop databases of best practices, or, in the judicial case, different approaches to common legal issues. They offer technical assistance and professional socialization to members from less developed nations, whether regulators, judges, or legislators. . . .

[T]o see these networks as they exist, much less to imagine what they could become, requires a . . . conceptual shift. Stop imagining the international system as a system of states — unitary entities like billiard balls or black boxes — subject to rules created by international institutions that are apart from, "above" these states. Start thinking about a world of governments, with all the different institutions that perform the basic function of governments — legislation, adjudication, implementation — interacting both with each other domestically and also with their foreign and supranational counterparts. States still exist in this world; indeed, they are crucial actors. But they are "disaggregated." They relate to each other not only through the Foreign Office, but also through regulatory, judicial, and legislative channels. . . .

[Viewing the world this way makes] it possible to imagine a genuinely new set of possibilities for a future world order. The building blocks of this order would not be states but parts of states: courts, regulatory agencies, ministries, legislatures. The government officials within these various institutions would participate in many different types of networks, creating links across national borders and between national and supranational institutions. . . .

Question

What are the advantages of international law making through the transnational networks Professor Slaughter describes? The disadvantages?

3. Nongovernmental Organizations (NGOs)

In the past 25 years or so, one of the most striking developments in international affairs has been the increased prominence of NGOs. According to the U.N. secretary-general, the number of international NGOs "grew forty-fold over the course of the twentieth century to more than 37,000 in 2000." Report of the Secretary-General, Strengthening the United Nations: An Agenda for Further Change, U.N. Doc. 1/57/387, at §134 (2002). Dr. Jessica Mathews suggests that published figures on the number of NGOs are "badly misleading" and that the "true number is certainly in the millions, from the tiniest village association to influential but modestly funded international groups like Amnesty International to larger global activist organizations like Greenpeace and giant service providers like CARE, which has an annual budget of nearly $400 million." Jessica T. Mathews, Power Shift, Foreign Aff., Jan./Feb. 1997, at 50, 52-53. NGOs have drafted treaties, lobbied governments, helped develop and implement soft law, and played a critical role in forming the coalitions that contribute to international norm formation, interpretation, and implementation. The discussion above about Transparency International's anticorruption efforts is one example.

One way NGOs shape the development of international law is through their transnational efforts to shape the agendas of the traditional creators of international law.

> Individuals can act as trans-sovereign entrepreneurs by playing a key and persistent role in pushing for normative change. Domestic and international groups can mobilize around major issues of concern and put pressure on state and international bodies to adopt and enforce norms. For example, by investigating, publicizing, and naming human rights norms, human rights NGOs can influence domestic and international agendas on such matters as the environment, landmines, women's human rights, and recognition of human rights in general. Indeed, increasingly, it is "from the NGOs that new ideas, approaches, and solutions are springing forth" at the local, national, regional, and international levels. Beyond influencing the official state and international agendas, these nonstate actors can help shape their communities, creating a sensibility to norms that "infiltrate deliberations at the individual, organizational, corporate, governmental, and interstate level to shape world collective life." [Julie Mertus, Considering Nonstate Actors in the New Millennium: Toward Expanded Participation in Norm Generation and Norm Application, 32 N.Y.U. J. Int'l L. & Pol. 537, 554-555 (2000).]

NGOs can also play a more direct role in shaping the development—or preventing the adoption of—international instruments. In the first excerpt below, Dr. Mathews shows how NGOs contributed to the conclusion of the U.N. Framework Convention on Climate Change in Rio de Janeiro. The second excerpt recounts how NGOs succeeded in opposing a multilateral government attempt to negotiate a treaty on the protection of international investments.

Jessica T. Mathews, Power Shift

Foreign Aff., Jan./Feb. 1997, at 50, 55-56

In international organizations, as with governments at home, NGOs were once largely relegated to the hallways. Even when they were able to shape governments' agendas, as the Helsinki Watch human rights groups did in the Conference on Security and Cooperation in Europe in the 1980s, their influence was largely determined by how receptive their own government's delegation happened to be. Their only option was to work through governments.

All that changed with the negotiation of the global climate treaty, culminating at the Earth Summit in Rio de Janeiro in 1992. With the broader independent base of public support that environmental groups command, NGOs set the original goal of negotiating an agreement to control greenhouse gases long before governments were ready to do so, proposed most of its structure and content, and lobbied and mobilized public pressure to force through a pact that virtually no one else thought possible when the talks began.

More members of NGOs served on government delegations than ever before, and they penetrated deeply into official decision-making. They were allowed to attend the small working group meetings where the real decisions in international negotiations are made. The tiny nation of Vanuatu turned its delegation over to an NGO with expertise in international law (a group based in London and funded by an American foundation), thereby making itself and the other sea-level island states major players in the fight to control global warming. ECO, an NGO-published daily newspaper, was negotiators' best source of information on the progress of the official talks and became the forum where governments tested ideas for breaking deadlocks.

Whether from developing or developed countries, NGOs were tightly organized in a global and half a dozen regional Climate Action Networks, which were able to bridge North-South differences among governments that many had expected would prevent an agreement. United in their passionate pursuit of a treaty, NGOs would fight out contentious issues among themselves, then take an agreed position to their respective delegations. When they could not agree, NGOs served as invaluable back channels, letting both sides know where the other's problems lay or where a compromise might be found.

As a result, delegates completed the framework of a global climate accord in the blink of a diplomat's eye — 16 months — over the opposition of the three energy superpowers, the United States, Russia, and Saudi Arabia. The treaty entered into force in record time just two years later. Although only a framework accord whose binding requirements are still to be negotiated, the treaty could force sweeping changes in energy use, with potentially enormous implications for every economy. . . .

Alan Boyle & Christine Chinkin, The Making of International Law

76-77 (2007)

NGOs have also prevented treaty-making. A notorious example is that of the [Multilateral Agreement on Investment (MAI)] that was being negotiated within the Organisation for Economic Cooperation and Development (OECD) in the mid-1990s. Concern was expressed about the proposed treaty when it was leaked in 1997. A coalition of NGOs and consumer groups reacted strongly to what they saw as secret negotiations over a treaty to protect the rights of foreign investors and restrict the ability of governments to legislate in the public interest, for example with respect to the environment and labour rights. The MAI became the focus of anti-globalisation and anti-multinational corporate activity. A global campaign was waged against it, primarily through the internet. Different reasons have been put forward for the success of NGOs in their confrontation with the business community and with the OECD negotiators. First, the OECD discounted likely NGO opinion and omitted to put an appropriate "NGO strategy" in place. . . . Second, was the influence of committed individuals who took it upon themselves to provide information, offer analysis and forceful explanations. Third, was the crucial role of the internet in coordinating global activities. . . . [T]here was no formal NGO secretariat but instead the formation of ever-growing networks through e-mail distribution lists between known activists and others. NGOs directed their campaigns at citizens (raising awareness, education on the issues and framing arguments) and at governments (through similar strategies). NGO activity has been described as follows:

> Hundreds of advocacy groups, attempting to galvanize opposition to the MAI, used terms and examples that brought their message home to the public. Their sites on the

World Wide Web were colorful and easy to use, offering primers on the MAI that anyone could understand.

By the time the OECD negotiators accepted the need for consultation with NGOs the atmosphere had become too confrontational for cooperation. Eventually the negotiations were abandoned in December 1998. . . . The failure of the MAI is seen as a success for concerted NGO action against the power of organized business. "This experience represents one of the fastest, most resounding defeats for a treaty—a defeat attributable to the efforts of NGOs. . . ."

Notes and Questions

1. In addition to their prominent role in global climate change talks, NGOs were key players in the negotiation of the Ottawa Landmines Ban Convention. See To Walk Without Fear: The Global Movement to Ban Landmines (Maxwell A. Cameron, Robert J. Lawson & Brian W. Tomlin eds., 1998). The International Campaign to Ban Landmines and activist Jody Williams won the Nobel Peace Prize in 1997 for their efforts to secure a global ban on landmines. NGOs also participated actively in the negotiations leading to the adoption of the Kyoto Protocol to the United Nations Framework Convention on Climate Change and the Rome Statute of the International Criminal Court (ICC). See Anna-Karin Lindblom, Non-Governmental Organisations in International Law (2005).

2. Is the expanding influence of NGOs on the development of international law a positive or negative development? Professors Boyle and Chinkin summarize some of the arguments:

> [I]t has been suggested that NGO participation constitutes a "sea-change" in international law-making by democratising it and thus legitimising the essentially non-democratic processes of international law. It strips away the myth of the monolithic state and allows disagreement with the official state view to be voiced at the international level. The expression of a cosmopolitan, popular will through the NGO voice—the "conscience of the world"—is itself seen by some as a basis of legitimacy. . . .
>
> [On the other hand,] NGOs are often non-democratic, self-appointed, may consist of only a handful of people and determine their own agendas with an evangelical or elitist zeal. There is no guarantee that the views expressed by even high-profile NGOs are representative, either generally, or even with respect to their claimed constituencies. Their internal decision-making processes may not be transparent. . . . The need for many NGOs to account to donors for their expenditures gives rise to the questions about the latter's influence on setting priorities. [Boyle & Chinkin, The Making of International Law, supra, at 58.]

3. Some countries have begun pursuing aggressive legal strategies to check the growing power of international NGOs. The U.S. State Department reports that China, for example, has pursued aggressive efforts to monitor Internet use, control content, restrict information, block access to foreign and domestic Web sites, encourage self-censorship, and punish those who violated regulations. The Chinese government employed thousands of persons at the national, provincial, and local levels to monitor electronic communications. In 2006, Russia adopted a law

requiring NGOs to register with the Russian government. The law requires NGOs to notify the government about their external funding sources and how funds are spent. The government is also empowered to conduct checkups of NGO activities to assess whether they are acting in accordance with the objectives stated in their founding documents. See International Center for Not-for-Profit Law, Analysis of Law #18-FZ on Introducing Amendments to Certain Legislative Acts of the Russian Federation (Feb. 17, 2006). NGOs have expressed concern that the legislation gives Russia tools to control NGOs that are critical of the government. Russia and China are not alone in this regard. According to the 2009 U.S. State Department Country Reports on Human Rights Practices published in March 2010, "no fewer than 25 governments have [since 2008] imposed new restrictions on the ability of [NGOs] to register, to operate freely, or to receive foreign funding, adversely impacting freedom of association."

4. For additional reading on the role of NGOs, see Non-State Actors and Human Rights (Philip Alston ed., 2005); Steve Charnovitz, Nongovernmental Organizations and International Law, 100 Am. J. Int'l L. 348 (2006); and Peter J. Spiro, The Democratic Accountability of Non-Governmental Organizations, 3 Chi. J. Int'l L. 161 (2002), and the sources cited there.

4. *Multinational Corporations*

In recent decades, multinational corporations (MNCs)* have grown in number, size, and influence. One observer notes that "[a]ccording to the most recent figures, seventy-seven thousand transnational firms span the global economy today, with some 770,000 subsidiaries and millions of suppliers — Wal-Mart alone is reported to have more than sixty thousand suppliers. Transnationals operate in more countries than ever before. . . ." John Gerard Ruggie, Business and Human Rights: The Evolving International Agenda, 101 Am J. Int'l L. 819, 823-824 (2007).

The growth of multinational corporations poses implications for global governance. Transnational corporations engage in activities, and participate in the development of regulatory structures, in spheres that in the past were the exclusive responsibility of governments.

> . . . [M]ultinationals navigate in increasingly complex and unstable global environments and have started to play a more active role in the transnational attempt to define and enforce governance policies, institutions and processes. Anecdotal evidence shows that some corporations have already assumed responsibilities that were once regarded as belonging to government. They engage in public health projects, education and protection of human rights while operating in countries with repressive regimes. They address social ills such as AIDS, malnutrition, homelessness and literacy. They engage in self-regulation to fill gaps in legal regulations and to promote society peace and stability. Therefore, some corporations are not simply complying with social standards set in legal and moral terms; they are engaging in discourses that aim to redefine those standards in a changing, globalized world.

*"Multinational corporations" are also referred to as "transnational corporations," or TNCs. The terms are essentially interchangeable.

> In a globalized world, global governance, referring to rule making and enforcement on a global scale, is no longer the purview of governments alone. Today, MNCs as well as civil society groups participate in the formulation and implementation of regulations in policy areas that were once regarded as sole responsibility of state agencies. [Andreas Georg Scherer & Guido Palazzo, Introduction: Corporate Citizenship in a Globalized World, in Handbook of Research on Global Corporate Citizenship 1, 2-3 (Andreas Georg Scherer & Guido Palazzo eds., 2008).]

Professor Janet Koven Levit provides the following illustration of how transnational corporations engage in activities that are tantamount to international law creation in one particular sphere, namely, the field of export credit insurance.

Janet Koven Levit, Bottom-Up International Lawmaking: Reflections on the New Haven School of International Law

32 Yale J. Int'l L. 393, 400-401 (2007)

Export credit insurance, one form of officially supported export credit, functions like automobile insurance, except that the asset the insurance company protects is not a car but rather a trade receivable. Private insurance companies, such as Chubb, American International Group, Inc., and FCIA Management Company, Inc., as well as ECAs [export credit agencies], such as the Export-Import Bank of the United States (the U.S. ECA), issue export credit insurance policies. ECA participation in the export credit insurance industry marks it as a potential breeding ground for subsidies and thus a potential target for transnational coordination and regulation.

Indeed, that is what happened, although it did not start with some ministerial or founding of a large institution, WTO-style. Instead, it started in 1934 in Berne, Switzerland, between friends over drinks, when a small group of European export credit insurers decided to pool experiential data regarding claims and recovery experiences in the name of sound insurance practices. This informal gather gave birth to the Berne Union. Following World War II, when government ECAs began using export credit insurance as an aggressive backdoor to export subsidies, the Berne Union members — private insurers and government technocrats — decided to transform the Berne Union from a mere trade association into a regular to target abusive and aggressive subsidy practices.

Thus, over the years, the members have used the semi-annual Berne Union get-togethers as a focal point to collect and share their practices and approaches to a variety of regulatory questions, and they have codified these in a living document called the "General Understanding." The General Understanding essentially divides the universe of insurable goods and services into seven baskets. Within each category, the General Understanding prescribes specific, technical, and at times cumbersome rules to standardize the type of insurance products that members may offer and circumscribe the terms that such policies may contain. Thus, the General Understanding is a regulatory matrix for the export credit insurance industry, essentially translating insurers' on-the-ground experiences into a set of technical rules designed to calibrate transactions, discipline ensuing practice, and thereby prevent an export insurance policy from masking a predatory export subsidy.

While the General Understanding is technically not international law, these rules nevertheless function as law should—they are authoritative and effectively binding.

Transnational corporations additionally play a major role in setting the technical and legal standards that regulate activity in their fields, often acting through institutions like the International Organization for Standardization (ISO) that are "relatively hidden from public view but which have a real impact on everyday life." Thomas G. Weiss, Foreword to Craig N. Murphy & Joanne Yates, the International Organization for Standardization xii (2009). The ISO is a network of the national standards institutes of 159 countries.

> The ISO is a non-governmental institution (albeit one that was established under the aegis of the UN) bridging public and private sectors and is the self-proclaimed international standard setter for "business, government and society" through its pursuit of voluntary standards. The organization boasts having developed more than 17,000 international standards in its 60-year history and claims that it is engaged in producing an additional 1,100 standards each year. These standards range from those dealing with size, clarity, and weights of jewelry through clothing measures to systems businesses ought to put in place to enhance consumer satisfaction. Id. at xiii.

Transnational corporations play a major role in the international standard-setting process. Although many of the ISO's member institutes are part of the governmental structure of their countries or are mandated by their government, others have their roots uniquely in the private sector, having been set up by national partnerships of industry associations. In addition, according to Professors Murphy and Yates, much of the work of the ISO is done through the work of "technical committees" comprised of volunteers employed by "companies that a proposed standard will affect." Id. at 32. Studies of the work of the ISO suggest that its process of drafting standards is "dominated by officials from transnational industrial producers, industry associations, and industry consultants." Naomi Roht-Arriaza, "Soft Law" in a "Hybrid" Organization: The International Organization for Standardization, in Commitment and Compliance: The Role of Non-Binding Norms in the International Legal System 263, 266 (Dinah Shelton ed., 2000).

Transnational corporations pose significant international issues not only as participants in the law-making process but also as potential subjects of international regulation. Unlike purely domestic corporations, such corporations may be difficult to regulate under a single state's domestic law, a challenge compounded by the size and influence of some of the largest transnational corporations. In some cases, according to one observer, "the government of a state [where a corporation does business] is less economically powerful than the corporation." Robert McCorquodale, 87 J. Bus. Ethics 385, 387 (2009). Professor John Ruggie, who serves as the Special Representative of the Secretary-General on the issue of human rights and transnational corporations and other business enterprises, explains:

> Transnational corporate networks pose a regulatory challenge to the international legal system. To begin with, in legal terms purchasing goods and services from

> unrelated suppliers generally is considered an arm's-length market exchange, not an intrafirm transaction. Among related parties, a parent company and its subsidiaries are distinct legal entities, and even large-scale projects may be incorporated separately. Any one of them may be engaged in joint ventures with other firms or governments. Owing to the doctrine of limited liability, a parent company generally is not legally liable for wrongs committed by a subsidiary even where it is the sole shareholder, unless the subsidiary is under such close operational control by the parent that it can be seen as the parent's mere agent. Each legally distinct entity is subject to the laws of the countries in which it operates, but the transnational corporate group or network as a whole is not governed directly by international law. [John Gerard Ruggie, Business and Human Rights: The Evolving International Agenda, 101 Am J. Int'l L. 819, 824 (2007).]

Beginning in the 1970s, some states pursued efforts through the United Nations to develop a Code of Conduct to make transnational corporations more accountable to the states in which they operated, particularly with respect to such issues as labor standards, human rights, development, and technology transfers. In part due to the threat of a U.N.-based code of conduct, the leading industrialized states, acting through the Organisation for Economic Cooperation and Development (OECD), adopted a nonbinding Declaration on International Investment and Multinational Enterprises. The OECD has since followed up on the Declaration with the OECD Guidelines for Multinational Enterprises, a set of recommendations addressed by governments to multinational enterprises operating in or from adhering countries. The Guidelines provide voluntary principles and standards for responsible business conduct in areas such as employment and industrial relations, human rights, environment, information disclosure, combating bribery, consumer interests, science and technology, competition, and taxation.

Yet another approach to dealing with the activities of transnational corporations involves the collective participation of governments, international organizations, corporations, and NGOs; it reflects what Janet Koven Levit has called "bottom-up international law making." Professor Ruggie elaborates:

> Beyond the intergovernmental system, a third type of initiative is emerging having the force of soft law and/or involves partial legalization; it is a multistakeholder form that engages corporations directly, along with states and civil society organizations, in addressing sources of corporate-related human rights abuses. Most prominent among them are the Voluntary Principles on Security and Human Rights, to promote corporate human rights risk assessments and the training of security providers in the extractive sector; the Kimberley Process Certification Scheme, to stem the flow of "conflict diamonds"; and the Extractive Industries Transparency Initiative, to establish a degree of revenue transparency in the sums companies pay to host governments. Each seeks to enhance the responsibility and accountability of states and corporations alike by means of operational standards and procedures for firms, often together with regulatory action by governments, both supported by transparency mechanisms.
>
> Kimberley, for instance, involves a global certification scheme implemented through domestic law, whereby states seek to ensure that the diamonds they trade are from Kimberley-compliant countries by requiring detailed packaging protocols and certification, coupled with chain-of-custody warranties by companies. The Voluntary Principles have been incorporated in legal agreements between companies and host governments in several countries. And while the Extractive Industries

Transparency Initiative is voluntary for governments, once they sign up, companies are legally required to make their government payments public. Although each has weaknesses that require improvement, the relative ease and speed with which such arrangements can be established, and the flexibility with which they can operate, make them an important complement to the traditional state-based treaty-making and soft law standard-setting processes. [Ruggie, Business and Human Rights: The Evolving International Agenda, supra, 101 Am J. Int'l L. at 835.]

Notes and Questions

1. The OECD Guidelines for Multinational Enterprises are nonbinding. What difference would it make whether a code is legally binding or not? How could such an instrument be used and by whom?

2. The Voluntary Principles on Security and Human Rights referred to in the Ruggie excerpt emerged from an initiative launched by the United States and the United Kingdom, along with companies in the extractive and energy sectors and NGOs, to adopt a set of voluntary principles to guide companies in carrying out their operations in a manner that ensures respect for human rights and fundamental freedoms.

3. In January 1998, U.N. Secretary-General "proposed a 'Global Compact' of shared values and principles. The original Global Compact asked businesses to voluntarily support and adopt nine . . . core principles, which are divided into categories dealing with general human rights obligations, standards of labor, and standards of environmental protection. In 2004 the Global Compact added a tenth core principle on corruption." David Weissbrodt, International Standard-Setting on the Human Rights Responsibilities of Business, 26 Berkeley J. Int'l L. 373, 379 (2008). As of 2008, some 3,700 companies had joined the Global Compact, "but there remain about 67,000 other transnational corporations which have not yet joined." Id. at 381.

4. Corporations have sometimes adopted their own codes — either independently or together with other firms — for dealing with such issues as labor conditions. In the mid-1970s, for example, many foreign firms doing business in South Africa adopted the "Sullivan Principles," which established minimum and nondiscriminatory working conditions. More recent efforts are described by Professor Ruggie:

> [A]n expanding universe of self-regulation in the business and human rights domain can be seen in individual company practices, industry initiatives, and multi-stakeholder efforts. . . .
>
> . . . [V]oluntary initiatives have expanded rapidly in recent years. [A survey I conducted of the Fortune Global 500 firms (FG500)] suggests that substantial policy diffusion is going on: almost all respondents report having some human rights policies or management practices in place. . . . Uptake is concentrated among European, North American, and, to a lesser extent, Japanese firms. . . .
>
> Leading firms, collective initiatives, and socially responsible investment indices recognize a broad array of human rights. . . . Labor rights are the most widely recognized across all regions and sectors, topped by nondiscrimination. Recognition of other rights broadly tracks industry sectors. The extractive industry, for example, ranks community rights and the security of the person more highly than other sectors, while

> financial services stress privacy rights. In formulating their human rights policies, companies typically draw on international instruments or initiatives. [Ruggie, Business and Human Rights: The Evolving International Agenda, supra, 101 Am J. Int'l L. at 835-836.]

What are the corporate motivations for such codes? Can you think of strategies to expand their acceptance by the corporate community?

5. Professor Ruggie also notes some of the limits of voluntary corporate codes of social responsibility:

> The Achilles heel of self-regulatory arrangements to date is their underdeveloped accountability mechanisms. Company initiatives increasingly include rudimentary forms of internal and external reporting, as well as some form of supply-chain monitoring. But no universally—or even widely—accepted standards yet exist for these practices. . . . Experience to date has shown that supply-chain monitoring by itself produces only limited behavioral changes at the factory level. . . . Relatively few companies that engage in large-footprint projects seem ever to have conducted a full-fledged human rights impact assessment, although a larger number includes selected human rights criteria in broader social/environmental assessments. And only a few such projects provide for community complaints procedures or remedies. [Ruggie, Business and Human Rights: The Evolving International Agenda, supra, 101 Am J. Int'l L. at 836-837.]

D. GENERAL PRINCIPLES OF LAW

Article 38 of the Statute of the International Court of Justice (ICJ) lists the formal sources of international law to be applied by the Court. (See Chapter 1.) In addition to treaties and customary international law, it includes "the general principles of law recognized by civilized nations." (Recall that the Restatement definition also refers to "general principles common to the major legal systems of the world.") Professor Shaw explains:

Malcolm N. Shaw, International Law

98-102, 105 (6th ed. 2008)

General Principles of Law

In any system of law, a situation may very well arise where the court in considering a case before it realises that there is no law covering exactly that point, neither parliamentary statute nor judicial precedent. In such instances the judge will proceed to deduce a rule that will be relevant, by analogy from already existing rules or directly from the general principles that guide the legal system, whether they be referred to as emanating from justice, equity or considerations of public policy. Such a situation is perhaps even more likely to arise in international law because of the relative underdevelopment of the system in relation to the needs with which it is faced.

There are fewer decided cases in international law than in a municipal system and no method of legislating to provide rules to govern new situations. It is for such a reason that the provision of "the general principles of law recognised by civilised nations" was inserted into article 38 as a source of law, to close the gap that might be uncovered in international law and solve this problem which is known legally as *non-liquet*. . . .

. . . [M]ost writers are prepared to accept that the general principles do constitute a separate source of law but of fairly limited scope, and this is reflected in the decisions of the Permanent Court of International Justice and the International Court of Justice. It is not clear, however, in all cases, whether what is involved is a general principle of law appearing in municipal systems or a general principle of international law. But perhaps this is not a terribly serious problem since both municipal legal concepts and those derived from existing international practice can be defined as falling within the recognised catchment area.

While the reservoir from which one can draw contains the legal operations of 190 or so states, it does not follow that judges have to be experts in every legal system. There are certain common themes that run through the many different orders. Anglo-American Common Law has influenced a number of states throughout the world, as have the French and Germanic systems. There are many common elements in the law in Latin America, and most Afro-Asian states have borrowed heavily from the European experience in their efforts to modernise the structure administering the state and westernise economic and other enterprises.

Reference will now be made to some of the leading cases in this field to illustrate how this is working out in practice.

In the *Chorzow Factory* case in 1928, which followed the seizure of a nitrate factory in Upper Silesia by Poland, the Permanent Court of International Justice declared, "it is a general conception of law that every violation of an engagement involves an obligation to make reparation." The Court also regarded it as:

> a principle of international law that the reparation of a wrong may consist in an indemnity corresponding to the damage which the nationals of the injured state have suffered as a result of the act which is contrary to international law.

The most fertile fields, however, for the implementation of municipal law analogies have been those of procedure, evidence and the machinery of the judicial process. . . . The International Court of Justice in the *Corfu Channel* case, when referring to circumstantial evidence, pointed out that "this indirect evidence is admitted in all systems of law and its use is recognised by international decisions." International judicial reference has also been made to the concept of *res judicata*, that is that the decision in the circumstances is final, binding and without appeal.

In the *Administrative Tribunal* case the Court dealt with the problem of the dismissal of members of the United Nations Secretariat staff and whether the General Assembly had the right to refuse to give effect to awards to them made by the relevant Tribunal. In giving its negative reply, the Court emphasised that:

> according to a well-established and generally recognised principle of law, a judgment rendered by a judicial body is res judicata and has binding force between the parties to the dispute. . . .

The Court has also considered the principle of estoppel which provides that a party that has acquiesced in a particular situation cannot then proceed to challenge it. In the *Temple* case the International Court of Justice applied the doctrine, but in the *Serbian Loans* case in 1929, in which French bondholders were demanding payment in gold francs as against paper money upon a series of Serbian loans, the Court declared the principle inapplicable. . . .

Thus, it follows, that it is the Court which has the discretion as to which principles of law to apply in the circumstances of the particular case under consideration, and it will do this upon the basis of the inability of customary and treaty law to provide the required solution. In this context, one must consider the *Barcelona Traction* case between Belgium and Spain. The International Court of Justice relied heavily upon the municipal law concept of the limited liability company and emphasised that if the Court were to decide the case in disregard of the relevant institutions of municipal law it would, without justification, invite serious legal difficulties. It would lose touch with reality, for there are no corresponding institutions of international law to which the Court could resort.

However, international law did not refer to the municipal law of a particular state, but rather to the rules generally accepted by municipal legal systems, which, in this case, recognise the idea of the limited company.

The Iran-United States Claims Tribunal, which decided hundreds of disputes between private American and Iranian governmental entities, relied extensively on general principles of law, particularly general principles of commercial law. According to one tribunal judge and his co-author, where disputes could not be resolved on the basis of the underlying contracts due to gaps or ambiguities,

> [T]he Tribunal's marked preference has been to interpret contracts by applying general principles of law and *lex mercatoria* (without referring to it by name). Unjust enrichment and *force majeure* are two areas in which general principles of commercial law have played a particularly significant rule. The Tribunal has applied such principles to reach the following conclusions:
>
> (i) "when a promissory note is given for an obligation, the obligation is, unless otherwise agreed, at least suspended until the note matures";
> (ii) "generally a subcontractor has no direct rights as against the party with whom the contractor has a contract";
> (iii) "limitation-of-liability clauses in general will not be given effect for a specific default when that default arose through an intentional wrong or gross negligence on the part of the one invoking the limitation"; and
> (iv) "no one should be allowed to reap advantages from their own wrong, *Nulles Commodum Capere De Sua Injuria Propria.*" [Charles N. Brower & Jason D. Brueschke, The Iran-United States Claims Tribunal 637-638 (1998).]

A prominent example of judges seeking to derive general principles of law is found in the 1997 opinion by two judges on the International Criminal Tribunal for the former Yugoslavia (ICTY) in Prosecutor v. Drazen Erdemović, Case No. IT-96-22-A, Judgment (Oct. 7, 1997) (Joint Separate Opinion of Judges McDonald and Vohrah), reprinted in 111 I.L.R. 298. There, the defendant had been convicted of participating in mass executions of unarmed Bosnian Muslims. He pleaded guilty, but stated the following at his sentencing hearing:

> Your Honour, I had to do this. If I had refused, I would have been killed together with the victims. When I refused, they told me: "If you are sorry for them, stand up, line up with them and we will kill you too". I am not sorry for myself but for my family, my wife and son who then had nine months, and I could not refuse because then they would have killed me. . . .

In trying to determine whether duress (in the sense of "imminent threats to the life of the accused if he refuses to commit a crime") was a complete defense for the defendant, two of the five appellate judges referred to Article 38 of the ICJ and many of the cases cited in the Shaw excerpt above to indicate that it was appropriate to look for a general principle of law recognized by civilized nations. The judges then carefully reviewed the penal codes of 15 countries with civil law systems and the case law of 8 countries with common law traditions, as well as the criminal laws of some other states. Based on that survey, the judges concluded that:

> 66. . . . [I]t is, in our view, a general principle of law recognised by civilised nations that an accused person is less blameworthy and less deserving of the full punishment when he performs a certain prohibited act under duress. . . .
> 67. The rules of the various legal systems of the world are, however, largely inconsistent regarding the specific question whether duress affords a complete defence to a combatant charged with a war crime or a crime against humanity involving the killing of innocent persons. [Id. ¶¶66 & 67.]

Given the factual situation in the case, the judges voted as part of the majority to rule that duress did not afford a complete defense for a soldier who was charged with a crime against humanity and/or a war crime involving the killing of innocent human beings. For additional discussion of this decision, see Rosa Ehrenreich Brooks, Law in the Heart of Darkness: Atrocity & Duress, 43 Va. J. Int'l L. 861 (2003).

Notes and Questions

1. As the Shaw excerpt indicates, the most fertile fields for the use of general principles of law of the major legal systems are in the realms of "procedure, evidence, and machinery of due process." Besides the possible principles of res judiciata, estoppel, and the use of circumstantial evidence discussed there, what other procedural, evidentiary, and due process rules that you are familiar with from the U.S. legal system might be useful? What about statutes of limitations? Laches? Ex post facto? Burdens of proof and of the production of evidence?

2. How are general principles different than customary international law? Although general principles of law are a separate source in the ICJ Statute and the Restatement for determining international law, might there be some overlap with customary international law? For example, in looking to state practices for determining customary international law, can the civil laws and case law of states

be considered relevant practices? (See the discussion of customary international law in Chapter 3, including the *Filartiga* case.)

At this point you should have a sense of the major sources of traditional public international law. You should be aware of the changing environment in which international norms are formed and the range of views about how those norms develop. This complements your familiarity with the various categories of domestic law, such as constitutional law, statutes, administrative regulation, and common law that affect transnational activity. Of course, there is enormous variety of domestic law around the world. The United Kingdom does not have a written constitution. Civil law countries are often said to more generally rest law-making power in the legislature, not the courts. In Japan, the right of judicial review is guaranteed by law, but Japanese companies may be less inclined to resort to law suits if they have a disagreement with the government. In many other countries litigation is also relatively uncommon.

It is important that you as a lawyer be aware of the potential significance of these differences. Provisions of a bilateral treaty may well mean different things in the two countries because of differences in the way in which treaties are authorized, in the way public international law is implemented, and in the roles of courts, the bureaucracy, local governments, trade associations, and individual persons whose conduct is supposed to be affected by the treaty. You may know what the treaty requires and how it should be interpreted, but until you understand the domestic thicket in which it operates you cannot advise a client about the legal implications of a course of conduct. Thus, if your client (or government) proposes a transaction involving Japan, you may raise questions and try to anticipate problems about Japanese law, but in the end you will need to call on specialized help (and may indeed be required by law to do so).

As a student trained at an American law school, your likely role as a lawyer will be, at least primarily, to give advice on U.S. law or international law from a U.S. perspective. This will be true whether you are in private practice, work for a corporation or a private voluntary organization, or serve as counsel to a government agency. A thorough understanding of the U.S. constitutional framework is indispensable. In the next chapter we will look at how the United States participates in the conclusion of international agreements and the creation of customary international law, and how those types of traditional public international law can affect private conduct.

Bibliography

Introduction. There are extensive sources of international law. Several helpful guides for doing research in various international law fields can be found on the Georgetown University Law Center's library Web page at http://www.ll.georgetown.edu/research. For a tutorial on treaty research, see http://www.ll.georgetown.edu/tutorials/intl/index.html. Some of the basic sources for doing international law research include Edmund Jan Osmanczyk, The Encyclopedia of the United Nations and International Agreements (3d ed. 2003); Parry & Grant Encyclopaedic Dictionary of International Law (John P. Grant & Craig Barker eds., 2004); Encyclopedia of

Public International Law (1981-1990) and the new edition (2000); and Restatement (Third) of Foreign Relations Law of the United States (1987).

1. *Compilations of treaties.* All treaties registered with the United Nations are compiled in the U.N. Treaty Series. A subscription database located at http://treaties.un.org contains most of them. There is also a League of Nations Treaty Series. United States treaties are published in the Treaties and Other International Acts Series (TIAS) and in turn compiled in the U.S. Treaties and Other International Agreements (UST) volumes. The British Treaty Series covers the period from 1892. A historical compilation was done by Clive Parry, The Consolidated Treaty Series, 1648-1919 (1969).

The State Department's annual Treaties in Force (located at http://www.state.gov/s/l/treaty/treaties/) lists each treaty and other international agreements to which the United States is a party, gives citations, and lists other parties to the agreements.

2. *Diplomatic and other practice.* There is a Digest of U.S. Practice in International Law, which used to be published by the Department of State, but is now being published by the International Law Institute. The predecessor compilations are Marjorie M. Whiteman, Digest of International Law (1963-1973); Green Haywood Hackworth, Digest of International Law (1973); and John Basset Moore, Digest of International Law (1906). These volumes contain diplomatic notes, briefs and memoranda, policy statements, judicial decisions, and other documents that may be useful in learning about events and in determining customary international law.

3. *Judicial and arbitral decisions.* Judicial decisions from all countries are collected in International Law Reports, including its predecessors, the Annual Digest of Public International Law Cases and the Annual Digest and Reports of Public International Law Cases. British and Commonwealth decisions are found in Commonwealth International Law Cases (Clive Parry & J. A. Hopkins eds., 1974-present).

The International Court of Justice (located at http://www.icj-cij.org) and its predecessor, the Permanent Court of International Justice, publish official reports of decisions. See also the Yearbook of the International Court of Justice. (The ICJ is discussed further in Chapter 4.)

Some arbitral decisions are collected in United Nations Reports of Arbitral Awards. See also the Iran-U.S. Claims Tribunal Reports (1981-present).

The European Union's Court of Justice (whose Web site is at http://curia.europa.eu/jcms/jcms/j_6/) publishes official Reports of Cases before the Court. See Chapters 4 and 8 for additional citations. Both the European Court of Human Rights (located at http://www.echr.coe.int/echr/Homepage_EN) and the Inter-American Court of Human Rights (located at http://www.corteidh.or.cr) publish two series, one covering judgments, decisions, and opinions, and the other covering pleadings, oral arguments, and documents.

4. *Yearbooks.* Many yearbooks and other similar periodicals contain current judicial decisions and state practice as well as scholarly articles. They include the American Journal of International Law, the British Yearbook of International Law, the Japanese Annual of International Law, the Chinese Yearbook of International Law, the Chinese Yearbook of International Law and Affairs (Taiwan), the Indian Journal of International Law, the Canadian Yearbook of International Law, the

Australian Yearbook of International Law, Annuaire Francais de Droit International, and the German Yearbook of International Law.

For other current compilations of important documents, see the American Society of International Law's International Legal Materials (located on the Web at http://www.asil.org/ilm/ilmindx.htm) and International Law in Brief (located at http://www.asil.org/ilibmenu.cfm).

5. *Standard treatises on treaties.* These include Anthony Aust, Modern Treaty Law and Practice (2d ed. 2007); and Arnold Duncan McNair, The Law of Treaties (1986). More works focusing on the Vienna Convention include Ian Sinclair, The Vienna Convention on the Law of Treaties (2d ed. 1984); and Shabtai Rosenne, The Law of Treaties — A Guide to the Legislative History of the Vienna Convention (1970).

3

International Law in the United States

In this chapter, we examine traditional public international law (treaties and customary law) in the U.S. context. The focus is on the U.S. constitutional structure and how it affects U.S. participation in treaty and customary international law making, and how in turn that law making can affect rights and duties under U.S. domestic law.

In Section A we examine the scope of the Article II treaty power, the limitations on that power, and the status of those treaties as U.S. domestic law. In Section B we take up the other sources of presidential power to conclude international agreements on behalf of the United States, and we also examine the scope of presidential power to conduct foreign affairs generally. In Section C we deal with the formation of customary international law and its status in the U.S. domestic legal system. Finally, in Section D we examine the constitutional limitations on the 50 states in matters touching foreign affairs.

A. ARTICLE II TREATIES

As noted in Chapter 2, the Vienna Convention uses the term "treaty" in a broader sense than does the U.S. Constitution. In U.S. practice a "treaty" is only one of four types of international agreement. Articles II and VI of the Constitution provide:

U.S. Constitution

Article II

Section 2. [2] He [the President] shall have Power, by and with the advice and consent of the Senate to make Treaties, provided two thirds of the Senators present concur. . . .

Article VI

[2] This Constitution and the Laws of the United States which shall be made in Pursuance thereof; and all Treaties made, under the Authority of the United States, shall be the supreme Law of the Land; and the Judges in every State shall be bound

thereby, any Thing in the Constitution or Laws of any State to the Contrary notwithstanding.

In addition to Article II treaties, it is generally accepted that the President may conclude international agreements on behalf of the United States on the basis of congressional authorization, on the basis of the President's independent constitutional authority to conduct foreign relations, or on the basis of authorization contained in an earlier Article II treaty. We will discuss these other international agreements in Section B below. Here we will outline the scope of the Article II treaty power and the limitations on that power.

1. *Scope of the Treaty Power and Limitations Thereon*

Although the term "treaty" is not defined in the Constitution, by practice it has come to include any international agreement, regardless of subject matter, that has been approved by a two-thirds vote of the Senate.

Today there is not much controversy over the scope of the treaty power. Some commentators have suggested that a treaty must deal with matters of "international concern." Now, however, matters of international concern would seem to include almost anything a government might want to conclude an agreement about, particularly given the substantial expansion of attentiveness to human rights and the increase in the acceptance of general economic, social, and environmental regulation. There is also Supreme Court dicta describing the treaty power in broad (although not necessarily unlimited) terms. For example, in Asakura v. City of Seattle, the Court stated: "The treaty-making power of the United States is not limited by any express provision of the Constitution, and though it does not extend 'so far as to authorize what the Constitution forbids,' it does extend to all proper subjects of negotiation between our government and other nations." 265 U.S. 332, 341 (1924) (quoting Geofroy v. Riggs, 133 U.S. 258, 267 (1890)).

Even if the treaty power is not limited by subject matter, it is possible that it is limited by principles of U.S. federalism. The Constitution makes clear that treaties are the supreme law of the land and therefore preempt inconsistent state law. But this is also true of federal statutes, and the power to make federal statutory law has (at least sometimes) been thought to be constrained by principles of federalism. The Supreme Court addressed the relationship between the treaty power and U.S. federalism in the Missouri v. Holland decision below.

In that case, to counteract an alarming decline in migrating ducks and geese, Congress had passed a law in 1913 to regulate hunting of migratory birds. However, the law was vigorously attacked by conservatives on the grounds that it invaded states' rights protected by the Tenth Amendment to the Constitution, and at least one U.S. district court had held it unconstitutional. The federal government then concluded a treaty in 1916 with the United Kingdom (which was handling Canada's external relations at the time), and Congress passed legislation in 1918 to implement the treaty obligations.

Missouri v. Holland

U.S. Supreme Court
252 U.S. 416 (1920)

Mr. Justice HOLMES delivered the opinion of the Court.

This is a bill in equity brought by the State of Missouri to prevent a game warden of the United States from attempting to enforce the Migratory Bird Treaty Act of July 3, 1918, and the regulations made by the Secretary of Agriculture in pursuance of the same. The ground of the bill is that the statute is an unconstitutional interference with the rights reserved to the States by the Tenth Amendment, and that the acts of the defendant done and threatened under that authority invade the sovereign right of the State and contravene its will manifested in statutes. . . . A motion to dismiss was sustained by the District Court on the ground that the act of Congress is constitutional. . . .

The State appeals.

On December 8, 1916, a treaty between the United States and Great Britain was proclaimed by the President. It recited that many species of birds in their annual migrations traversed certain parts of the United States and of Canada, that they were of great value as a source of food and in destroying insects injurious to vegetation, but were in danger of extermination through lack of adequate protection. It therefore provided for specified close seasons and protection in other forms, and agreed that the two powers would take or propose to their law-making bodies the necessary measures for carrying the treaty out. The above mentioned Act of July 3, 1918, entitled an act to give effect to the convention, prohibited the killing, capturing or selling any of the migratory birds included in the terms of the treaty except as permitted by regulations compatible with those terms, to be made by the Secretary of Agriculture. Regulations were proclaimed on July 31, and October 25, 1918. It is unnecessary to go into any details, because, as we have said, the question raised is the general one whether the treaty and statute are void as an interference with the rights reserved to the States.

To answer this question it is not enough to refer to the Tenth Amendment, reserving the powers not delegated to the United States, because by Article II, §2, the power to make treaties is delegated expressly, and by Article VI treaties made under the authority of the United States, along with the Constitution and laws of the United States made in pursuance thereof, are declared the supreme law of the land. If the treaty is valid there can be no dispute about the validity of the statute under Article I, §8, as a necessary and proper means to execute the powers of the Government. The language of the Constitution as to the supremacy of treaties being general, the question before us is narrowed to an inquiry into the ground upon which the present supposed exception is placed.

It is said that a treaty cannot be valid if it infringes the Constitution, that there are limits, therefore, to the treaty-making power, and that one such limit is that what an act of Congress could not do unaided, in derogation of the powers reserved to the States, a treaty cannot do. An earlier act of Congress that attempted by itself and not in pursuance of a treaty to regulate the killing of migratory birds within the States had been held bad in the District Court. United States v. Shauver, 214 Fed. Rep. 154. United States v. McCullagh, 221 Fed. Rep. 288. Those decisions were supported by arguments that migratory birds were owned by the States in their sovereign capacity for the benefit of their people, and that under cases like Geer v. Connecticut, 161 U.S. 519, this control was one that Congress had no power to displace. The same argument is supposed to apply now with equal force.

Whether the two cases cited were decided rightly or not they cannot be accepted as a test of the treaty power. Acts of Congress are the supreme law of the land only when made in pursuance of the Constitution, while treaties are declared to be so when made under the authority of the United States. It is open to question whether the authority of the United States means more than the formal acts prescribed to make the convention. We do not mean to imply that there are no qualifications to the treaty-making power; but they must be ascertained in a different way. It is obvious that there may be matters of the sharpest exigency for the national well being that an act of Congress could not deal with but that a treaty followed by such an act could, and it is not lightly to be assumed that, in matters requiring national action, "a power which must belong to and somewhere reside in every civilized government" is not to be found. Andrews v. Andrews, 188 U.S. 14, 33. What was said in that case with regard to the powers of the States applies with equal force to the powers of the nation in cases where the States individually are incompetent to act. We are not yet discussing the particular case before us but only are considering the validity of the test proposed. With regard to that we may add that when we are dealing with words that also are a constituent act, like the Constitution of the United States, we must realize that they have called into life a being the development of which could not have been foreseen completely by the most gifted of its begetters. It was enough for them to realize or to hope that they had created an organism; it has taken a century and has cost their successors much sweat and blood to prove that they created a nation. The case before us must be considered in the light of our whole experience and not merely in that of what was said a hundred years ago. The treaty in question does not contravene any prohibitory words to be found in the Constitution. The only question is whether it is forbidden by some invisible radiation from the general terms of the Tenth Amendment. We must consider what this country has become in deciding what that Amendment has reserved.

The State as we have intimated founds its claim of exclusive authority upon an assertion of title to migratory birds, an assertion that is embodied in statute. No doubt it is true that as between a State and its inhabitants the State may regulate the killing and sale of such birds, but it does not follow that its authority is exclusive of paramount powers. To put the claim of the State upon title is to lean upon a slender reed. Wild birds are not in the possession of anyone; and possession is the beginning of ownership. The whole foundation of the State's rights is the presence within their jurisdiction of birds that yesterday had not arrived, tomorrow may be in another State and in a week a thousand miles away. If we are to be accurate we cannot put the case of the State upon higher ground than that the treaty deals with creatures that for the moment are within the state borders, that it must be carried out by officers of the United States within the same territory, and that but for the treaty the State would be free to regulate this subject itself.

As most of the laws of the United States are carried out within the States and as many of them deal with matters which in the silence of such laws the State might regulate, such general grounds are not enough to support Missouri's claim. Valid treaties of course "are as binding within the territorial limits of the States as they are elsewhere throughout the dominion of the United States." Baldwin v. Franks, 120 U.S. 678, 683. No doubt the great body of private relations usually fall within the control of the State, but a treaty may override its power. . . .

Here a national interest of very nearly the first magnitude is involved. It can be protected only by national action in concert with that of another power. The subject-matter is only transitorily within the State and has no permanent habitat therein. But for the treaty and the statute there soon might be no birds for any powers to deal with. We see nothing in the Constitution that compels the Government to sit by while a food supply is cut off and the protectors of our forests and our crops are destroyed. It is not sufficient to rely upon the States. The reliance is vain, and were it otherwise, the question is whether the United States is forbidden to act. We are of opinion that the treaty and statute must be upheld.

As the Court noted in Missouri v. Holland, Article VI of the Constitution states that federal statutes must be "made in Pursuance" of the Constitution, whereas it states that treaties must be made "under the Authority of the United States." This difference in wording (and some of the Court's statements in Missouri v Holland) might suggest that the treaty makers have the power to disregard even the individual rights protections in the Constitution. The Supreme Court addressed this issue in the decision below.

Reid v. Covert

U.S. Supreme Court
354 U.S. 1 (1957)

[Defendants were the civilian spouses of U.S. servicemen who murdered their husbands on the overseas bases where they were stationed. Defendants were tried by court-martial under the Uniform Code of Military Justice (UCMJ), which permitted military trials of such civilian dependants. They were sentenced to death. Under the UCMJ, defendants were not entitled to a grand jury or a jury trial. An international agreement between the United States and United Kingdom conferred exclusive criminal jurisdiction on the United States over such crimes by civilian dependents, and the government argued that the UCMJ in this situation was legislation necessary and proper to carry out an international agreement of the United States.]

Mr. Justice Black announced the judgment of the Court and delivered an opinion, in which the Chief Justice, Mr. Justice Douglas, and Mr. Justice Brennan join. . . .

At the beginning we reject the idea that when the United States acts against citizens abroad it can do so free of the Bill of Rights. The United States is entirely a creature of the Constitution. Its power and authority have no other source. It can only act in accordance with all the limitations imposed by the Constitution. When the Government reaches out to punish a citizen who is abroad, the shield which the Bill of Rights and other parts of the Constitution provide to protect his life and liberty should not be stripped away just because he happens to be in another land. This is not a novel concept. To the contrary, it is as old as government. It was recognized long before Paul successfully invoked his right as a Roman citizen to be tried in strict accordance with Roman law. . . . The rights and liberties which citizens of our country enjoy are not protected by custom and tradition alone, they have been jealously preserved from the encroachments of Government by express provisions of our written Constitution.

Among those provisions, Art. III, §2 and the Fifth and Sixth Amendments are directly relevant to these cases. Article III, §2 lays down the rule that:

> The Trial of all Crimes, except in Cases of Impeachment, shall be by Jury; and such Trial shall be held in the State where the said Crimes shall have been committed; but when not committed within any State, the Trial shall be at such Place or Places as the Congress may by Law have directed.

The Fifth Amendment declares:

> No person shall be held to answer for a capital, or otherwise infamous crime, unless on a presentment or indictment of a Grand Jury, except in cases arising in the land or naval forces, or in the Militia, when in actual service in time of War or public danger. . . .

And the Sixth Amendment provides:

> In all criminal prosecutions, the accused shall enjoy the right to a speedy and public trial, by an impartial jury of the State and district wherein the crime shall have been committed. . . .

The language of Art. III, §2 manifests that constitutional protections for the individual were designed to restrict the United States Government when it acts outside of this country, as well as here at home. After declaring that all criminal trials must be by jury, the section states that when a crime is "not committed within any State, the Trial shall be at such Place or Places as the Congress may by Law have directed." If this language is permitted to have its obvious meaning, §2 is applicable to criminal trials outside of the States as a group without regard to where the offense is committed or the trial held. From the very first Congress, federal statutes have implemented the provisions of §2 by providing for trial of murder and other crimes committed outside the jurisdiction of any State "in the district where the offender is apprehended, or into which he may first be brought." The Fifth and Sixth Amendments, like Art. III, §2, are also all inclusive with their sweeping references to "no person" and to "all criminal prosecutions." . . .

. . . While it has been suggested that only those constitutional rights which are "fundamental" protect Americans abroad, we can find no warrant, in logic or otherwise, for picking and choosing among the remarkable collection of "Thou shall nots" which were explicitly fastened on all departments and agencies of the Federal Government by the Constitution and its Amendments. Moreover, in view of our heritage and the history of the adoption of the Constitution and the Bill of Rights, it seems peculiarly anomalous to say that trial before a civilian judge and by an independent jury picked from the common citizenry is not a fundamental right. As Blackstone wrote in his Commentaries:

> . . . the trial by jury ever has been, and I trust ever will be, looked upon as the glory of the English law. And if it has so great an advantage over others in regulating civil property, how much must that advantage be heightened when it is applied to criminal cases! . . . [I]t is the most transcendent privilege which any subject can enjoy, or wish for. . . .

II

At the time of Mrs. Covert's alleged offense, an executive agreement was in effect between the United States and Great Britain which permitted United States' military courts to exercise exclusive jurisdiction over offenses committed in Great Britain by American servicemen or their dependents. For its part, the United States agreed that these military courts would be willing and able to try and to punish all offenses against the laws of Great Britain by such persons. [This executive agreement was concluded by the President on the basis of implied authorization from a prior Article II treaty approved by the Senate. Consequently, the Court treated the executive agreement as if it had the same legal effect as an Article II treaty.]

. . . Even though a court-martial does not give an accused trial by jury and other Bill of Rights protections, the Government contends that Art. 2(11) of the UCMJ, insofar as it provides for the military trial of dependents accompanying the armed forces in Great Britain . . . can be sustained as legislation which is necessary and proper to carry out the United States' obligations under the international agreements made with those countries. The obvious and decisive answer to this, of course, is that no agreement with a foreign nation can confer power on the Congress, or on any other branch of Government, which is free from the restraints of the Constitution.

Article VI, the Supremacy Clause of the Constitution, declares:

> This Constitution, and the Laws of the United States which shall be made in Pursuance thereof; and all Treaties made, or which shall be made, under the Authority of the United States, shall be the supreme Law of the Land. . . .

There is nothing in this language which intimates that treaties and laws enacted pursuant to them do not have to comply with the provisions of the Constitution. Nor is there anything in the debates which accompanied the drafting and ratification of the Constitution which even suggests such a result. These debates as well as the history that surrounds the adoption of the treaty provision in Article VI make it clear that the reason treaties were not limited to those made in "pursuance" of the Constitution was so that agreements made by the United States under the Articles of Confederation, including the important peace treaties which concluded the Revolutionary War, would remain in effect. It would be manifestly contrary to the objectives of those who created the Constitution, as well as those who were responsible for the Bill of Rights — let alone alien to our entire constitutional history and tradition — to construe Article VI as permitting the United States to exercise power under an international agreement without observing constitutional prohibitions.

In effect, such construction would permit amendment of that document in a manner not sanctioned by Article V. The prohibitions of the Constitution were designed to apply to all branches of the National Government and they cannot be nullified by the Executive or by the Executive and the Senate combined. . . .

This Court has also repeatedly taken the position that an Act of Congress, which must comply with the Constitution, is on a full parity with a treaty, and that when a statute which is subsequent in time is inconsistent with a treaty, the statute to the extent of conflict renders the treaty null. It would be completely anomalous to say that a treaty need not comply with the Constitution when such an agreement can be overridden by a statute that must conform to that instrument.

There is nothing in Missouri v. Holland, 252 U.S. 416, which is contrary to the position taken here. There the Court carefully noted that the treaty involved was not inconsistent with any specific provision of the Constitution. The Court was concerned with the Tenth Amendment which reserves to the States or the people all power not delegated to the National Government. To the extent that the United States can validly make treaties, the people and the States have delegated their power to the National Government and the Tenth Amendment is no barrier. . . .

Harlan, J., concurring. . . .

. . . I do not think that it can be said that these safeguards of the Constitution are never operative without the United States, regardless of the particular circumstances. On the other hand, I cannot agree with the suggestion that every provision of the Constitution must always be deemed automatically applicable to American citizens in every part of the world. For *Ross* and the *Insular Cases* do stand for an important proposition, one which seems to me a wise and necessary gloss on our Constitution. The proposition is, of course, not that the Constitution "does not apply" overseas, but that there are provisions in the Constitution which do not *necessarily* apply in all circumstances in every foreign place. In other words, it seems to me that the basic teaching of *Ross* and the *Insular Cases* is that there is no rigid and abstract rule that Congress, as a condition precedent to exercising power over Americans overseas, must exercise it subject to all the guarantees of the Constitution, no matter what the conditions and considerations are that would make adherence to a specific guarantee altogether impracticable and anomalous. . . .

I think the above thought is crucial in approaching the cases before us. Decision is easy if one adopts the constricting view that these constitutional guarantees as a totality do or do not "apply" overseas. But, for me, the question is *which* guarantees of the Constitution *should* apply in view of the particular circumstances, the practical necessities, and the possible alternatives which Congress had before it. The question is one of judgment, not of compulsion. And so I agree with my brother Frankfurter that, in view of *Ross* and the *Insular* Cases, we have before us a question analogous, ultimately, to issues of due process; one can say, in fact, that the question of which specific safeguards of the Constitution are appropriately to be applied in a particular context overseas can be reduced to the issue of what process is "due" a defendant in the particular circumstances of a particular case.

On this basis, I cannot agree with the sweeping proposition that a full Article III trial, with indictment and trial by jury, is required in every case for the trial of a civilian dependent of a serviceman overseas. The Government, it seems to me, has made an impressive showing that at least for the run-of-the-mill offenses committed by dependents overseas, such a requirement would be as impractical and anomalous as it would have been to require jury trial for Balzac in *Porto Rico.*[12] Again, I need not go into details, beyond stating that except for capital offenses, such as we have here, to which, in my opinion, special considerations apply, I am by no means ready to say that Congress' power to provide for trial by court-martial of civilian dependents overseas is limited by Article III and the Fifth and Sixth Amendments. Where, if at all, the dividing line should be drawn among cases not capital, need not now be decided. We are confronted here with capital offenses alone; and it seems to me particularly unwise now to decide more than we have to. Our far-flung foreign military establishments are a new phenomenon in our national life, and I think it would be unfortunate were we unnecessarily to foreclose, as my four brothers would do, our future consideration of the broad questions involved in maintaining the effectiveness of these national outposts, in the light of continuing experience with these problems.

[Concurring opinion of Justice FRANKFURTER and dissenting opinions of Justices CLARK and BURTON omitted.]

Notes and Questions

1. Does Missouri v. Holland mean that a treaty under Article II of the Constitution can be used to regulate matters beyond the scope of Congress's Article I legislative powers, at least if no individual liberty protected by the Bill of Rights is involved?

2. In Reid v. Covert, does Justice Black persuasively distinguish *Holland*? Or does Reid v. Covert completely overturn *Holland*? Or just to the extent that the liberty is specifically mentioned (like the right to a jury trial) in the Bill of Rights? In Boos v. Barry, 485 U.S. 312 (1988), the Court confirmed that the treaty power is subject to individual rights limitations. There, the Court held that legislation prohibiting the display of any sign within 500 feet of a foreign embassy if that sign tends to bring that foreign government into "public odium" or "public disrepute" violated the First Amendment. The Court held this even though the legislation was designed to

12. The practical circumstances requiring some sort of disciplinary jurisdiction have already been adverted to. These circumstances take on weight when viewed in light of the alternatives available to Congress—certainly a crucial question in weighing the need for dispensing with particular constitutional guarantees abroad. What are these alternatives? (1) One is to try all offenses committed by civilian dependents abroad in the United States. But the practical problems in the way of such a choice are obvious and overwhelming. To require the transportation home for trial of every petty black marketeer or violator of security regulations would be a ridiculous burden on the Government, quite aside from the problems of persuading foreign witnesses to make the trip and of preserving evidence. . . . (2) Civilian trial overseas by the United States also presents considerable difficulties. If juries are required, the problem of jury recruitment would be difficult. Furthermore, it is indeed doubtful whether some foreign governments would accede to the creation of extraterritorial United States civil courts within their territories—courts which by implication would reflect on the fairness of their own tribunals and which would smack unpleasantly of consular courts set up under colonial "capitulations." (3) The alternative of trial in foreign courts, in at least some instances, is no more palatable. Quite aside from the fact that in some countries where we station troops the protections granted to criminal defendants compare unfavorably with our own minimum standards, the fact would remain that many of the crimes involved—particularly breaches of security—are not offenses under foreign law at all, and thus would go completely unpunished. Add to this the undesirability of foreign police carrying out investigations in our military installations abroad, and it seems to me clear that this alternative does not commend itself.

implement the Vienna Convention on Diplomatic Relations. Quoting the *Reid* plurality opinion, the Court stated that "it is well established that 'no agreement with a foreign nation can confer power on the Congress, or on any other branch of Government, which is free from the restraints of the Constitution.' " Id. at 324.

3. The Tenth Amendment provides that: "The powers not delegated to the United States by the Constitution, nor prohibited by it to the States, are reserved to the States respectively, or to the people." Article I, Section 10 proscribes individual states from treaty making, and Article II gives the President the power, with the advice and consent of the Senate, to make treaties. Although this Constitutional arrangement indicates that the federal power to make treaties is exclusive, does it necessarily suggest an unlimited treaty power?

4. In the 1990s, the Rehnquist Court renewed focus on federalism and the limits of Congressional power. The Court struck down statutes that it thought impinged on states' rights. See, e.g., United States v. Lopez, 514 U.S. 549 (1995) (limiting the scope of Congress's commerce power); New York v. United States, 505 U.S. 144 (1992) (invalidating legislation that "commandeers" state legislatures); Printz v. United States, 521 U.S. 898 (1997) (invalidating legislation that "commandeers" state executive officials). For example, in *Printz* Congress passed the Brady Act, which required a jurisdiction's chief law enforcement officer, a state executive official, to perform background checks of prospective gun buyers. Under an "anti-commandeering" doctrine, the Supreme Court invalidated the Act because the Constitution does not allow the "Federal Government [to] compel the States to implement, by legislation or executive action, federal regulatory programs." *Printz*, 521 U.S. at 925.

5. Assume that the Tenth Amendment protects the right of a U.S. state government to determine how to invest the funds in its state treasury. Could the United States conclude a treaty under which the parties agreed that no government funds (including those of state and local governments) could be invested in securities issued by the government of Iran or by entities incorporated in Iran? Would such a treaty be effective as U.S. law—for example, could the U.S. Attorney General enforce divestment by a recalcitrant state treasurer through the federal courts? (Federalism issues are discussed further in Section D, below.)

6. As we discuss in Chapter 8, one of the most important developments in international law has been the rise of international human rights law. Prior to World War II, international law did not typically regulate the relationship between nations and their citizens. Soon after the war, with the experience of the Holocaust and other atrocities fresh in mind, the international community began to develop a comprehensive body of international human rights law. Today, there are numerous multilateral human rights treaties. One of the most important of these treaties is the International Covenant on Civil and Political Rights, which the United States ratified in 1992. The Covenant, which is reprinted in the Documentary Supplement, contains a long list of rights relating to, among other things, discrimination, criminal procedure, religious freedom, freedom of association, and marriage. Do all of these human rights protections fall within the subject matter scope of the U.S. treaty power? Is there any subject that could not be regulated by treaty?

7. The Second Optional Protocol to the ICCPR, which has been ratified by over 110 countries (but not by the United States), prohibits the use of the death penalty. Could the President and Senate validly ratify this treaty and thereby preempt

U.S. states from utilizing the death penalty? In answering this question, does it matter whether Congress has the constitutional power to preempt the death penalty under state law by a federal statute and without a treaty?

8. Another issue in Reid v. Covert was whether the constitutional rights at issue applied to prosecutions conducted outside of U.S. territory. Justice Black's plurality opinion reasons that the United States "is entirely a creature of the Constitution" and thus must act, even outside U.S. territory, in "accordance with all the limitations imposed by the Constitution." In his concurring opinion, Justice Harlan disagreed for the reasons excerpted above. He nevertheless concurred because the case involved capital offenses. Several years later, however, a majority of the Court extended the holding in Reid to noncapital offenses. See Kinsella v. United States ex rel. Singleton, 361 U.S. 234 (1960).

Later, in United States v. Verdugo-Urquidez, 494 U.S. 259 (1990), the Supreme Court held that the Fourth Amendment did not apply to the search and seizure by U.S. agents of property owned by a nonresident alien and located abroad. The U.S. agents sought and received the cooperation of Mexican authorities in the search of the defendant's residence in Mexico. The Court distinguished the Fourth Amendment, which refers to rights of "the people," from the Fifth and Sixth Amendments, which refer to the rights of a "person" and the "accused." The phrase "the people," the Court reasoned, "refers to a class of persons who are part of a national community or who have otherwise developed sufficient connection with this country to be considered part of that community." Id. at 265. The Court rejected the broad reasoning of Justice Black's plurality opinion in Reid, noting that the actual holding in Reid was simply "that United States citizens stationed abroad could invoke the protection of the Fifth and Sixth Amendments." Id. at 270.

Then, in Boumediene v. Bush, 553 U.S. 73 (2008), the U.S. Supreme Court noted that the Court had never before held that noncitizens detained by the U.S. government in territory over which another country maintained *de jure* sovereignty had any rights under the U.S. Constitution. However, the Court concluded in *Boumediene* that the noncitizen detainees at Guantanamo Bay, Cuba, have the constitutional privilege of habeas corpus and were not barred from invoking the Suspension Clause's protections. The Court found that the United States exercises complete and total control over Guantanamo Bay, even though Cuba retains "ultimate sovereignty" over the territory.

We further consider the extraterritorial application of the U.S. Constitution, and other U.S. domestic law, in the discussions of the *Boumediene* case in section B.4 in this chapter and in Chapter 7.

9. It might be useful to highlight the process involved in the U.S. ratification of a treaty. After successful negotiations between U.S. executive branch representatives and representatives from another country (or countries), the U.S. President or (more likely) his designee signs for the United States. Once signed, the treaty is transmitted to the U.S. Senate, typically with accompanying transmittal documents that might explain the contents and effect of the treaty. The Senate Foreign Relations Committee then needs to conduct a hearing and vote whether to send the treaty to the whole Senate for its advice and consent. Once before the full Senate, the Constitution requires in Article I(2)II that "two-thirds of the Senators present concur." As discussed below, the Senate might add reservations, understandings, and declarations (RUDs) limiting or clarifying the U.S. obligations under the

treaties, including whether a treaty is "self-executing" or not. After the Senate has advised and consented, the President can then ratify the treaty according to the procedures established in the treaty, usually by depositing the required instrument of ratification with the designated depository for the treaty.

2. *The Effect of Article II Treaties as Domestic Law*

a. Self-Executing and Non-Self-Executing Treaties

Article VI of the Constitution provides that: "This Constitution and the Laws of the United States which shall be made in Pursuance thereof, and all Treaties made, or which shall be made, under the Authority of the United States, shall be the supreme Law of the Land, and the Judges in every State shall be bound thereby, any Thing in the Constitution or Laws of any State to the Contrary notwithstanding." Hence, an Article II treaty has status as U.S. domestic law, in addition to creating an obligation for the United States under international law (under the traditional division of the legal universe into international and domestic spheres). Moreover, the Article VI Supremacy Clause places treaties higher than state constitutions and laws in the hierarchy of domestic law, and it confers equal status to federal laws and treaties.

The Supreme Court, however, has long recognized a distinction between self-executing treaties, which become domestically enforceable federal law upon ratification, and non-self-executing treaties, which only become domestically enforceable through implementing legislation passed by Congress.

Although it is often clear whether a treaty is self-executing or not, the issue arises sometimes and can cause difficulties. The Restatement provides some guidance.

Restatement

§111. International Law and Agreements as Law of the United States

(4) An international agreement of the United States is "non-self-executing"

(a) if the agreement manifests an intention that it shall not become effective as domestic law without the enactment of implementing legislation,

(b) if the Senate in giving consent to a treaty, or Congress by resolution, requires implementing legislation, or

(c) if implementing legislation is constitutionally required.

Comment

h. Self-executing and non-self-executing international agreements. In the absence of special agreement, it is ordinarily for the United States to decide how it will carry out its international obligations. Accordingly, the intention of the United States determines whether an agreement is to be self-executing in the United States or should await implementation by legislation or appropriate executive or administrative action. If the international agreement is silent as to its self-executing character and the intention of the United States is unclear, account must be taken of any statement by the President in concluding the agreement or in submitting it to the Senate for consent or to the Congress as a whole for approval, and of any expression by the Senate or by the Congress in dealing with the agreement. . . . After the agreement is concluded, often the President must decide in the first instance whether the agreement is self-executing, i.e., whether existing law is adequate to enable the United States to carry out its obligations, or whether further legislation is required. Congress may also consider whether new legislation is necessary and, if so, what it should provide. Whether an agreement is to be given effect without further legislation is an issue that a court must decide when a party seeks to invoke the agreement as law. . . .

i. . . . An international agreement cannot take effect as domestic law without implementation by Congress if the agreement would achieve what lies within the exclusive law-making power of Congress under the Constitution. Thus, an international agreement providing for the payment of money by the United States requires an appropriation of funds by Congress in order to effect the payment required by the agreement. It has been commonly assumed that an international agreement cannot itself bring the United States into a state of war. Similarly, it has been assumed that an international agreement creating an international crime (e.g., genocide) or requiring states parties to punish certain actions (e.g., hijacking) could not itself become part of the criminal law of the United States, but would require Congress to enact an appropriate statute before an individual could be tried or punished for the offense. It has also been suggested that a treaty cannot "raise revenue" by itself imposing a new tax or new tariff, in view of the provision in Article I, Section 7: "All Bills for raising Revenue shall originate in the House of Representatives." Treaties of friendship, commerce and navigation, however, frequently affect tariffs and trade by "most-favored-nation," "national treatment," and analogous clauses. . . .

The two decisions below illustrate this distinction between self-executing and non-self-executing treaties. The second case, *Medellin,* is now the leading case on the subject.

Asakura v. City of Seattle

U.S. Supreme Court
265 U.S. 332 (1924)

Mr. Justice BUTLER delivered the opinion of the Court.

Plaintiff in error is a subject of the Emperor of Japan, and, since 1904, has resided in Seattle, Washington. Since July, 1915, he has been engaged in business there as a pawnbroker. The city passed an ordinance, which took effect July 2, 1921, regulating the business of pawnbroker and repealing former ordinances on the same subject. It makes it unlawful for any person to engage in the business unless he shall have a license, and the ordinance provides "that no such license shall be granted unless the applicant be a citizen of the United States." Violations of the ordinance are punishable by fine or imprisonment or both. Plaintiff in error brought this suit in the Superior Court of King County, Washington, against the city, its Comptroller and its Chief of Police to restrain them from enforcing the ordinance against him. He attacked the ordinance on the ground that it violates the treaty between the United States and the Empire of Japan, proclaimed April 5, 1911, 37 Stat. 1504. . . . It was shown that he had about $5,000 invested in his business, which would be broken up and destroyed by the enforcement of the ordinance. The Superior Court granted the relief prayed. On appeal, the Supreme Court of the State held the ordinance valid and reversed the decree. . . .

Does the ordinance violate the treaty? Plaintiff in error invokes and relies upon the following provisions: "The citizens or subjects of each of the High Contracting Parties shall have liberty to enter, travel and reside in the territories of the other to carry on trade, wholesale and retail, to own or lease and occupy houses, manufactories, warehouses and shops, to employ agents of their choice, to lease land for residential and commercial purposes, and generally to do anything incident to or necessary for trade upon the same terms as native citizens or subjects, submitting themselves to the laws and regulations there established. . . . The citizens or subjects of each . . . shall receive, in the territories of the other, the most constant protection, and security for their persons and property. . . ."

A treaty made under the authority of the United States "shall be the supreme law of the land; and the judges in every State shall be bound thereby, any thing in the constitution or laws of any State to the contrary notwithstanding." Constitution, Art. VI, §2.

The treaty-making power of the United States is not limited by any express provision of the Constitution, and, though it does not extend "so far as to authorize what the Constitution forbids," it does extend to all proper subjects of negotiation between our government and other nations.

. . . The treaty was made to strengthen friendly relations between the two nations. As to the things covered by it, the provision quoted establishes the rule of equality between Japanese subjects while in this country and native citizens. Treaties for the protection of citizens of one country residing in the territory of another are numerous, and make for good understanding between nations. The treaty is binding within the State of Washington. . . . The rule of equality established by it cannot be rendered nugatory in any part of the United States by municipal ordinances or state laws. It stands on the same footing of supremacy as do the provisions of the Constitution and laws of the United States. It operates of itself without the aid of any legislation, state or national; and it will be applied and given authoritative effect by the courts. . . .

The purpose of the ordinance complained of is to regulate, not to prohibit, the business of pawnbroker. But it makes it impossible for aliens to carry on the business. It need not be considered whether the State, if it sees fit, may forbid and destroy the business generally. Such a law would apply equally to aliens and citizens, and no question of conflict with the treaty would arise. The grievance here alleged is that plaintiff in error, in violation of the treaty, is denied equal opportunity. . . .

Decree reversed.

Medellin v. Texas

U.S. Supreme Court
552 U.S. 491 (2008)

Chief Justice ROBERTS delivered the opinion of the Court[, in which Justices SCALIA, KENNEDY, THOMAS, and ALITO joined].

The International Court of Justice (ICJ), located in the Hague, is a tribunal established pursuant to the United Nations Charter to adjudicate disputes between member states. In the *Case Concerning Avena and Other Mexican Nationals* (*Mex.* v. *U.S.*), 2004 I. C. J. 12 (Judgment of Mar. 31) (*Avena*), that tribunal considered a claim brought by Mexico against the United States. The ICJ held that, based on violations of the Vienna Convention, 51 named Mexican nationals were entitled to review and reconsideration of their state-court convictions and sentences in the United States. This was so regardless of any forfeiture of the right to raise Vienna Convention claims because of a failure to comply with generally applicable state rules governing challenges to criminal convictions.

. . . . After the *Avena* decision, President George W. Bush determined, through a Memorandum for the Attorney General (Feb. 28, 2005) (Memorandum or President's Memorandum), that the United States would "discharge its international obligations" under *Avena* "by having State courts give effect to the decision."

Petitioner Jose Ernesto Medellin, who had been convicted and sentenced in Texas state court for murder, is one of the 51 Mexican nationals named in the *Avena* decision. Relying on the ICJ's decision and the President's Memorandum, Medellin filed an application for a writ of habeas corpus in state court. The Texas Court of Criminal Appeals dismissed Medellin's application as an abuse of the writ under state law, given Medellin's failure to raise his Vienna Convention claim in a timely manner under state law. We granted certiorari to decide two questions. *First*, is the ICJ's judgment in *Avena* directly enforceable as domestic law in a state court in the United States? *Second*, does the President's Memorandum independently require the States to provide review and reconsideration of the claims of the 51 Mexican nationals named in *Avena* without regard to state procedural default rules? We conclude that neither *Avena* nor the President's Memorandum constitutes directly enforceable federal law that pre-empts state limitations on the filing of successive habeas petitions. We therefore affirm the decision below.

I. . . .

In 1969, the United States . . . ratified the Vienna Convention on Consular Relations (Vienna Convention or Convention) and the Optional Protocol Concerning the Compulsory Settlement of Disputes to the Vienna Convention (Optional Protocol or Protocol). . . . [The Convention] provides that if a person detained by a foreign country "so requests, the competent authorities of the receiving State shall, without delay, inform the consular post of the sending State" of such detention, and "inform the [detainee] of his righ[t]" to request assistance from the consul of his own state. Art. 36(1)(b), *id.*, at 101.

The Optional Protocol provides a venue for the resolution of disputes arising out of the interpretation or application of the Vienna Convention. Under the

Protocol, such disputes "shall lie within the compulsory jurisdiction of the International Court of Justice" and "may accordingly be brought before the [ICJ] . . . by any party to the dispute being a Party to the present Protocol." . . .

The ICJ is "the principal judicial organ of the United Nations." United Nations Charter, Art. 92 (1945). . . .

Under Article 94(1) of the U. N. Charter, "[e]ach Member of the United Nations undertakes to comply with the decision of the [ICJ] in any case to which it is a party." The ICJ's jurisdiction in any particular case, however, is dependent upon the consent of the parties. . . . By ratifying the Optional Protocol to the Vienna Convention, the United States consented to the specific jurisdiction of the ICJ with respect to claims arising out of the Vienna Convention. On March 7, 2005, subsequent to the ICJ's judgment in *Avena,* the United States gave notice of withdrawal from the Optional Protocol. . . .

Petitioner Jose Ernesto Medellin, a Mexican national, has lived in the United States since preschool. A member of the "Black and Whites" gang, Medellin was convicted of capital murder and sentenced to death in Texas for the gang rape and brutal murders of two Houston teenagers. . . .

Medellin then filed a habeas petition in Federal District Court. [He claimed that local Texas law enforcement officials did not inform him after his arrest of his Vienna Convention right to have the Mexican consulate notified of his detention.] The District Court denied relief, holding that Medellin's Vienna Convention claim was procedurally defaulted [because he had not raised it in a timely manner] and that Medellin had failed to show prejudice arising from the Vienna Convention violation. While Medellin's application for a certificate of appealability was pending in the Fifth Circuit, the ICJ issued its decision in *Avena.* . . . In the ICJ's determination, the United States was obligated "to provide, by means of its own choosing, review and reconsideration of the convictions and sentences of the [affected] Mexican nationals." . . .

This Court granted certiorari. Before we heard oral argument, however, President George W. Bush issued his Memorandum for the United States Attorney General, providing:

> "I have determined, pursuant to the authority vested in me as President by the Constitution and the laws of the United States of America, that the United States will discharge its international obligations under the decision of the International Court of Justice in [*Avena*], by having State courts give effect to the decision in accordance with general principles of comity in cases filed by the 51 Mexican nationals addressed in that decision." . . .

II

Medellin first contends that the ICJ's judgment in *Avena* constitutes a "binding" obligation on the state and federal courts of the United States. He argues that "by virtue of the Supremacy Clause, the treaties requiring compliance with the *Avena* judgment are *already* the 'Law of the Land' by which all state and federal courts in this country are 'bound.' " Accordingly, Medellin argues, *Avena* is a binding federal rule of decision that pre-empts contrary state limitations on successive habeas petitions.

No one disputes that the *Avena* decision — a decision that flows from the treaties through which the United States submitted to ICJ jurisdiction with respect to Vienna Convention disputes—constitutes an *international* law obligation on the part of the United States. But not all international law obligations automatically constitute binding federal law enforceable in United States courts. The question we confront here is whether the *Avena* judgment has automatic *domestic* legal effect such that the judgment of its own force applies in state and federal courts.

This Court has long recognized the distinction between treaties that automatically have effect as domestic law, and those that—while they constitute international law commitments—do not by themselves function as binding federal law. The distinction was well explained by Chief Justice Marshall's opinion in *Foster v. Neilson,* 27 U.S. 253, which held that a treaty is "equivalent to an act of the legislature," and hence self-executing, when it "operates of itself without the aid of any legislative provision." When, in contrast, "[treaty] stipulations are not self-executing they can only be enforced pursuant to legislation to carry them into effect." *Whitney v. Robertson,* 124 U.S. 190, 194 (1888). . . .[2]

A treaty is, of course, "primarily a compact between independent nations." *Head Money Cases,* 112 U.S. 580, 598 (1884). It ordinarily "depends for the enforcement of its provisions on the interest and the honor of the governments which are parties to it." *Ibid.* . . . "If these [interests] fail, its infraction becomes the subject of international negotiations and reclamations. . . . It is obvious that with all this the judicial courts have nothing to do and can give no redress." *Head Money Cases, supra.* Only "[i]f the treaty contains stipulations which are self-executing, that is, require no legislation to make them operative, [will] they have the force and effect of a legislative enactment." *Whitney, supra.* . . .[3]

Medellin . . . nonetheless contend[s] that the Optional Protocol, United Nations Charter, and ICJ Statute supply the "relevant obligation" to give the *Avena* judgment binding effect in the domestic courts of the United States. Because none of these treaty sources creates binding federal law in the absence of implementing legislation, and because it is uncontested that no such legislation exists, we conclude that the *Avena* judgment is not automatically binding domestic law.

A

The interpretation of a treaty, like the interpretation of a statute, begins with its text. *Air France v. Saks,* 470 U.S. 392, 396-397(1985). Because a treaty ratified by the United States is "an agreement among sovereign powers," we have also considered as "aids to its interpretation" the negotiation and drafting history of the treaty as well as "the postratification understanding" of signatory nations. *Zicherman v. Korean Air Lines Co.*, 516 U.S. 217, 226 (1996). . . .

The most natural reading of the Optional Protocol is as a bare grant of jurisdiction. It provides only that "[d]isputes arising out of the interpretation or

2. The label "self-executing" has on occasion been used to convey different meanings. What we mean by "self-executing" is that the treaty has automatic domestic effect as federal law upon ratification. Conversely, a "non-self-executing" treaty does not by itself give rise to domestically enforceable federal law. Whether such a treaty has domestic effect depends upon implementing legislation passed by Congress.

3. Even when treaties are self-executing in the sense that they create federal law, the background presumption is that "[i]nternational agreements, even those directly benefiting private persons, generally do not create private rights or provide for a private cause of action in domestic courts." 2 Restatement (Third) of Foreign Relations Law of the United States §907, Comment *a,* p. 396 (1986).

application of the [Vienna] Convention shall lie within the compulsory jurisdiction of the International Court of Justice" and "may accordingly be brought before the [ICJ] . . . by any party to the dispute being a Party to the present Protocol." Art. I. The Protocol says nothing about the effect of an ICJ decision and does not itself commit signatories to comply with an ICJ judgment. The Protocol is similarly silent as to any enforcement mechanism.

The obligation on the part of signatory nations to comply with ICJ judgments derives not from the Optional Protocol, but rather from Article 94 of the United Nations Charter—the provision that specifically addresses the effect of ICJ decisions. Article 94(1) provides that "[e]ach Member of the United Nations *undertakes to comply* with the decision of the [ICJ] in any case to which it is a party." The Executive Branch contends that the phrase "undertakes to comply" is not "an acknowledgement that an ICJ decision will have immediate legal effect in the courts of U. N. members," but rather "a *commitment* on the part of U. N. members to take *future* action through their political branches to comply with an ICJ decision."

We agree with this construction of Article 94. The Article is not a directive to domestic courts. It does not provide that the United States "shall" or "must" comply with an ICJ decision, nor indicate that the Senate that ratified the U. N. Charter intended to vest ICJ decisions with immediate legal effect in domestic courts. Instead, "[t]he words of Article 94 . . . call upon governments to take certain action.". . . . In other words, the U. N. Charter reads like "a compact between independent nations" that "depends for the enforcement of its provisions on the interest and the honor of the governments which are parties to it."

The remainder of Article 94 confirms that the U. N. Charter does not contemplate the automatic enforceability of ICJ decisions in domestic courts. Article 94(2)—the enforcement provision—provides the sole remedy for noncompliance: referral to the United Nations Security Council by an aggrieved state.

The U. N. Charter's provision of an express diplomatic—that is, nonjudicial—remedy is itself evidence that ICJ judgments were not meant to be enforceable in domestic courts. First, the Security Council must "dee[m] necessary" the issuance of a recommendation or measure to effectuate the judgment. Second, as the President and Senate were undoubtedly aware in subscribing to the U. N. Charter and Optional Protocol, the United States retained the unqualified right to exercise its veto of any Security Council resolution. . . .

. . . [Medellin's] construction would eliminate the option of noncompliance contemplated by Article 94(2), undermining the ability of the political branches to determine whether and how to comply with an ICJ judgment. Those sensitive foreign policy decisions would instead be transferred to state and federal courts charged with applying an ICJ judgment directly as domestic law. . . . This result would be particularly anomalous in light of the principle that "[t]he conduct of the foreign relations of our Government is committed by the Constitution to the Executive and Legislative—'the political'—Departments." . . .

B. . . .

The interpretive approach employed by the Court today—resorting to the text—is hardly novel. . . .

As against this time-honored textual approach, the dissent proposes a multifactor, judgment-by-judgment analysis that would "jettiso[n] relative predictability for the open-ended rough-and-tumble of factors." The dissent's novel approach to deciding which (or, more accurately, when) treaties give rise to directly enforceable federal law is arrestingly indeterminate. Treaty language is barely probative. Determining whether treaties themselves create federal law is sometimes committed to the political branches and sometimes to the judiciary. Of those committed to the judiciary, the courts pick and choose which shall be binding United States law—trumping not only state but other federal law as well—and which shall not. They do this on the basis of a multifactor, "context-specific" inquiry. Even then, the same treaty sometimes gives rise to United States law and sometimes does not, again depending on an ad hoc judicial assessment.

Our Framers established a careful set of procedures that must be followed before federal law can be created under the Constitution—vesting that decision in the political branches, subject to checks and balances. U.S. Const., Art. I, §7. They also recognized that treaties could create federal law, but again through the political branches, with the President making the treaty and the Senate approving it. . . .

The dissent's approach risks the United States' involvement in international agreements. It is hard to believe that the United States would enter into treaties that are sometimes enforceable and sometimes not. Such a treaty would be the equivalent of writing a blank check to the judiciary. Senators could never be quite sure what the treaties on which they were voting meant. . . .

In this case, the dissent—for a grab bag of no less than seven reasons—would tell us that this *particular* ICJ judgment is federal law.

Nor is it any answer to say that the federal courts will diligently police international agreements and enforce the decisions of international tribunals only when they *should be* enforced. . . . The dissent's . . . approach would assign to the courts—not the political branches—the primary role in deciding when and how international agreements will be enforced. . . . [This] is tantamount to vesting with the judiciary the power not only to interpret but also to create the law.

C

Our conclusion that *Avena* does not by itself constitute binding federal law is confirmed by the "postratification understanding" of signatory nations. There are currently 47 nations that are parties to the Optional Protocol and 171 nations that are parties to the Vienna Convention. Yet neither Medellin nor his *amici* have identified a single nation that treats ICJ judgments as binding in domestic courts. . . .

Our conclusion is further supported by general principles of interpretation. To begin with, we reiterated in *Sanchez-Llamas* what we heard in *Breard,* that "absent a clear and express statement to the contrary, the procedural rules of the forum State govern the implementation of the treaty in that State." 548 U.S. at 351. . . .

Our prior decisions identified by the dissent as holding a number of treaties to be self-executing, see . . . Appendix A, stand only for the unremarkable proposition that some international agreements are self-executing and others are not. It is well settled that the "[i]nterpretation of [a treaty] . . . must, of course, begin with the language of the Treaty itself." *Sumitomo Shoji America, Inc.*, 457 U.S., at 180. As a result, we have held treaties to be self-executing when the textual provisions indicate that the President and Senate intended for the agreement to have domestic effect.

. . . And whether the treaties underlying a judgment are self-executing so that the judgment is directly enforceable as domestic law in our courts is, of course, a matter for this Court to decide. See *Sanchez-Llamas, supra*. . . .

The dissent worries that our decision casts doubt on some 70-odd treaties under which the United States has agreed to submit disputes to the ICJ according to "roughly similar" provisions. . . .

. . . Contrary to the dissent's suggestion, neither our approach nor our cases require that a treaty provide for self-execution in so many talismanic words; that is a caricature of the Court's opinion. Our cases simply require courts to decide whether a treaty's terms reflect a determination by the President who negotiated it and the Senate that confirmed it that the treaty has domestic effect. . . .

III

Medellin next argues that the ICJ's judgment in *Avena* is binding on state courts by virtue of the President's February 28, 2005 Memorandum. The United States contends that while the *Avena* judgment does not of its own force require domestic courts to set aside ordinary rules of procedural default, that judgment became the law of the land with precisely that effect pursuant to the President's Memorandum and his power "to establish binding rules of decision that preempt contrary state law." Accordingly, we must decide whether the President's declaration alters our conclusion that the *Avena* judgment is not a rule of domestic law binding in state and federal courts. . . .

The United States maintains that the President's constitutional role "uniquely qualifies" him to resolve the sensitive foreign policy decisions that bear on compliance with an ICJ decision and "to do so expeditiously." We do not question these propositions. . . . In this case, the President seeks to vindicate United States' interests in ensuring the reciprocal observance of the Vienna Convention, protecting relations with foreign governments, and demonstrating commitment to the role of international law. These interests are plainly compelling.

Such considerations, however, do not allow us to set aside first principles. The President's authority to act, as with the exercise of any governmental power, "must stem either from an act of Congress or from the Constitution itself." *Youngstown, supra*, at 585; *Dames & Moore v. Regan*, 453 U.S. 654, 668 (1981). . . .

. . . The President has an array of political and diplomatic means available to enforce international obligations, but unilaterally converting a non-self-executing treaty into a self-executing one is not among them. The responsibility for transforming an international obligation arising from a non-self-executing treaty into domestic law falls to Congress. As this Court has explained, when treaty stipulations are "not self-executing they can only be enforced pursuant to legislation to carry them into effect." *Whitney, supra*, at 194. . . .

The judgment of the Texas Court of Criminal Appeals is affirmed.

It is so ordered.

Justice STEVENS, concurring in the judgment.

There is a great deal of wisdom in Justice Breyer's dissent. I agree that the text and history of the Supremacy Clause, as well as this Court's treaty-related cases, do not support a presumption against self-execution. I also endorse the proposition that the Vienna Convention . . . "is itself self-executing and judicially enforceable." . . . In the end, however, I am persuaded that the relevant treaties do not authorize this Court to enforce the judgment of the International Court of Justice (ICJ) in [*Avena*]. . . .

. . . In my view, the words "undertakes to comply" — while not the model of either a self-executing or a non-self-executing commitment — are most naturally read as a promise to take additional steps to enforce ICJ judgments. . . .

Even though the ICJ's judgment in *Avena* is not "the supreme Law of the Land," no one disputes that it constitutes an international law obligation on the part of the United States. By issuing a memorandum declaring that state courts should give effect to the judgment in *Avena*, the President made a commendable attempt to induce the States to discharge the Nation's obligation. I agree with the Texas judges and the majority of this Court that the President's memorandum is not binding law. Nonetheless, the fact that the President cannot legislate unilaterally does not absolve the United States from its promise to take action necessary to comply with the ICJ's judgment. . . .

Justice BREYER, with whom Justice SOUTER and Justice GINSBURG join, dissenting. . . .

The critical question here is whether the Supremacy Clause requires Texas to follow, *i.e.*, to enforce, this ICJ judgment. The Court says "no." And it reaches its negative answer by interpreting the labyrinth of treaty provisions as creating a legal obligation that binds the United States internationally, but which, for Supremacy Clause purposes, is not automatically enforceable as domestic law. In the majority's view, the Optional Protocol simply sends the dispute to the ICJ; the ICJ Statute says that the ICJ will subsequently reach a judgment; and the U. N. Charter contains no more than a promise to " 'undertak[e] to comply' " with that judgment. Such a promise, the majority says, does not as a domestic law matter (in Chief Justice Marshall's words) "operat[e] of itself without the aid of any legislative provision." *Foster* . . .

In my view, the President has correctly determined that Congress need not enact additional legislation. The majority places too much weight upon treaty language that says little about the matter. The words " 'undertak[e] to comply,' " for example, do not tell us whether an ICJ judgment rendered pursuant to the parties' consent to compulsory ICJ jurisdiction does, or does not, automatically become part of our domestic law. To answer that question we must look instead to our own domestic law, in particular, to the many treaty-related cases interpreting the Supremacy Clause. Those cases, including some written by Justices well aware of the Founders' original intent, lead to the conclusion that the ICJ judgment before us is enforceable as a matter of domestic law without further legislation.

A

Supreme Court case law stretching back more than 200 years helps explain what, for present purposes, the Founders meant when they wrote that "all Treaties . . . shall be the supreme Law of the Land." Art. VI, cl. 2. . . .

[T]his Court has frequently held or assumed that particular treaty provisions are self-executing, automatically binding the States without more. See Appendix A, *infra* (listing, as examples, 29 such cases, including 12 concluding that the treaty provision invalidates state or territorial law or policy as a consequence). As far as I can tell, the Court has held to the contrary only in two cases: *Foster, supra,* which was later reversed, and *Cameron Septic Tank Co. v. Knoxville, 227 U.S. 39 (1913),* where specific congressional actions indicated that Congress thought further legislation necessary. The Court has found "self-executing" provisions in multilateral treaties as well as bilateral treaties. And the subject matter of such provisions has varied widely. . . .

All of these cases make clear that self-executing treaty provisions are not uncommon or peculiar creatures of our domestic law; that they cover a wide range of subjects; that the Supremacy Clause itself answers the self-execution question by applying many, but not all, treaty provisions directly to the States; and that the Clause answers the self-execution question differently than does the law in many other nations. The cases also provide criteria that help determine *which* provisions automatically so apply—a matter to which I now turn.

B

The case law provides no simple magic answer to the question whether a particular treaty provision is self-executing. But the case law does make clear that, insofar as today's majority looks for language about "self-execution" in the treaty itself and insofar as it erects "clear statement" presumptions designed to help find an answer, it is misguided.

The many treaty provisions that this Court has found self-executing contain no textual language on the point (see Appendix A, *infra).* Few, if any, of these provisions are clear. Those that displace state law in respect to such quintessential state matters as, say, property, inheritance, or debt repayment, lack the "clea[r] state[ment]" that the Court today apparently requires. . . . These many Supreme Court cases finding treaty provisions to be self-executing cannot be reconciled with the majority's demand for textual clarity.

Indeed, the majority does not point to a single ratified United States treaty that contains the kind of "clea[r]" or "plai[n]" textual indication for which the majority searches. . . . [T]he issue whether further legislative action is required before a treaty provision takes domestic effect in a signatory nation is often a matter of how that nation's domestic law regards the provision's legal status. And that domestic status-determining law differs markedly from one nation to another. As Justice Iredell pointed out 200 years ago, Britain, for example, taking the view that the British Crown makes treaties but Parliament makes domestic law, virtually always requires parliamentary legislation. On the other hand, the United States, with its Supremacy Clause, does not take Britain's view. And the law of other nations, the Netherlands for example, directly incorporates many treaties concluded by the executive into its domestic law even without explicit parliamentary approval of the treaty.

The majority correctly notes that the treaties do not explicitly state that the relevant obligations are self-executing. But given the differences among nations, why would drafters write treaty language stating that a provision about, say, alien property inheritance, is self-executing? How could those drafters achieve agreement when one signatory nation follows one tradition and a second follows another? . . .

In a word, for present purposes, the absence or presence of language in a treaty about a provision's self-execution proves nothing at all. At best the Court is hunting the snark. At worst it erects legalistic hurdles that can threaten the application of provisions in many existing commercial and other treaties and make it more difficult to negotiate new ones.

The case law also suggests practical, context-specific criteria that this Court has previously used to help determine whether, for Supremacy Clause purposes, a treaty provision is self-executing. The provision's text matters very much. But that is not because it contains language that explicitly refers to self-execution. For reasons I have already explained, one should not expect *that* kind of textual statement. Drafting history is also relevant. But, again, that is not because it will explicitly address the relevant question. Instead text and history, along with subject matter and related characteristics will help our courts determine whether, as Chief Justice Marshall put it, the treaty provision "addresses itself to the political . . . department[s]" for further action or to "the judicial department" for direct enforcement.

In making this determination, this Court has found the provision's subject matter of particular importance. Does the treaty provision declare peace? Does it promise not to engage in hostilities? If so, it addresses itself to the political branches. Alternatively, does it concern the adjudication of traditional private legal rights such as rights to own property, to conduct a business, or to obtain civil tort recovery? If so, it may well address itself to the Judiciary. Enforcing such rights and setting their boundaries is the bread-and-butter work of the courts. See, *e.g.*, *Clark v. Allen*, 331 U.S. 503 (1947) (treating provision with such subject matter as self-executing); *Asakura v. Seattle*, 265 U.S. 332 (1924) (same).

One might also ask whether the treaty provision confers specific, detailed individual legal rights. Does it set forth definite standards that judges can readily enforce? Other things being equal, where rights are specific and readily enforceable, the treaty provision more likely "addresses" the judiciary.

Alternatively, would direct enforcement require the courts to create a new cause of action? Would such enforcement engender constitutional controversy? Would it create constitutionally undesirable conflict with the other branches? In such circumstances, it is not likely that the provision contemplates direct judicial enforcement.

Such questions, drawn from case law stretching back 200 years, do not create a simple test, let alone a magic formula. But they do help to constitute a practical, context-specific judicial approach, seeking to separate run-of-the-mill judicial matters from other matters, sometimes more politically charged, sometimes more clearly the responsibility of other branches, sometimes lacking those attributes that would permit courts to act on their own without more ado. And such an approach is all that we need to find an answer to the legal question now before us.

C

Applying the approach just described, I would find the relevant treaty provisions self-executing as applied to the ICJ judgment before us (giving that judgment domestic legal effect) for the following reasons, taken together.

First, the language of the relevant treaties strongly supports direct judicial enforceability, at least of judgments of the kind at issue here. The Optional Protocol bears the title "Compulsory Settlement of Disputes," thereby emphasizing the mandatory and binding nature of the procedures it sets forth. The body of the Protocol says specifically that "any party" that has consented to the ICJ's "compulsory jurisdiction" may bring a "dispute" before the court against any other such party. And the Protocol contrasts proceedings of the compulsory kind with an alternative "conciliation procedure," the recommendations of which a party may decide "not" to "accep[t]." Thus, the Optional Protocol's basic objective is not just to provide a forum for *settlement* but to provide a forum for *compulsory* settlement.

Moreover, in accepting Article 94(1) of the Charter, "[e]ach Member . . . undertakes to comply with the decision" of the ICJ "in any case to which it is a party." And the ICJ Statute (part of the U. N. Charter) makes clear that, a decision of the ICJ between parties that have consented to the ICJ's compulsory jurisdiction has "*binding force* . . . between the parties and in respect of that particular case." Enforcement of a court's judgment that has "binding force" involves quintessential judicial activity.

True, neither the Protocol nor the Charter explicitly states that the obligation to comply with an ICJ judgment automatically binds a party *as a matter of domestic law* without further domestic legislation. *But how could the language of those documents do otherwise?* The treaties are multilateral. And, as I have explained, some signatories follow British further-legislation-always-needed principles, others follow United States Supremacy Clause principles, and still others, *e.g.*, the Netherlands, can directly incorporate treaty provisions into their domestic law in particular circumstances. Why, given national differences, would drafters, seeking as strong a legal obligation as is practically attainable, use treaty language that *requires* all signatories to adopt uniform domestic-law treatment in this respect? . . .

The absence of that likely unobtainable language can make no difference. We are considering the language for purposes of applying the Supremacy Clause. And for that purpose, this Court has found to be self-executing multilateral treaty language that is far less direct or forceful (on the relevant point) than the language set forth in the present treaties. The language here in effect tells signatory nations to make an ICJ compulsory jurisdiction judgment "as binding as you can." Thus, assuming other factors favor self-execution, the language *adds,* rather than *subtracts,* support.

[T]he United States has ratified approximately 70 treaties with ICJ dispute resolution provisions roughly similar to those contained in the Optional Protocol; many of those treaties contemplate ICJ adjudication of the sort of substantive matters (property, commercial dealings, and the like) that the Court has found self-executing, or otherwise appear addressed to the judicial branch. See Appendix B, *infra.* None of the ICJ provisions in these treaties contains stronger language about self-execution than the language at issue here. . . . In signing these treaties (in respect to, say, alien land ownership provisions) was the United States engaging in a near useless act? . . .

Second, the Optional Protocol here applies to a dispute about the meaning of a Vienna Convention provision that is itself self-executing and judicially enforceable. The Convention provision is about an individual's "rights," namely, his right upon being arrested to be informed of his separate right to contact his nation's consul.

The dispute arises at the intersection of an individual right with ordinary rules of criminal procedure; it consequently concerns the kind of matter with which judges are familiar. The provisions contain judicially enforceable standards. . . . And the judgment itself requires a further hearing of a sort that is typically judicial.

This Court has found similar treaty provisions self-executing. . . . It is consequently not surprising that, when Congress ratified the Convention, the State Department reported that the "Convention is considered entirely self-executive and does not require any implementing or complementing legislation." . . .

Third, logic suggests that a treaty provision providing for "final" and "binding" judgments that "settl[e]" treaty-based disputes is self-executing insofar as the judgment in question concerns the meaning of an underlying treaty provision that is itself self-executing. . . .

Fourth, the majority's very different approach has seriously negative practical implications. The United States has entered into at least 70 treaties that contain provisions for ICJ dispute settlement similar to the Protocol before us. Many of these treaties contain provisions similar to those this Court has previously found self-executing — provisions that involve, for example, property rights, contract and commercial rights, trademarks, civil liability for personal injury, rights of foreign diplomats, taxation, domestic-court jurisdiction, and so forth. . . . If the Optional Protocol here, taken together with the U. N. Charter and its annexed ICJ Statute, is insufficient to warrant enforcement of the ICJ judgment before us, it is difficult to see how one could reach a different conclusion in any of these other instances. . . .

Fifth, other factors, related to the particular judgment here at issue, make that judgment well suited to direct judicial enforcement. The specific issue before the ICJ concerned " 'review and reconsideration' " of the "possible prejudice" caused in each of the 51 affected cases by an arresting State's failure to provide the defendant with rights guaranteed by the Vienna Convention. This review will call for an understanding of how criminal procedure works, including whether, and how, a notification failure may work prejudice. As the ICJ itself recognized, "it is the judicial process that is suited to this task." Courts frequently work with criminal procedure and related prejudice. Legislatures do not. Judicial standards are readily available for working in this technical area. Legislative standards are not readily available. Judges typically determine such matters, deciding, for example, whether further hearings are necessary, after reviewing a record in an individual case. Congress does not normally legislate in respect to individual cases. . . .

Sixth, to find the United States' treaty obligations self-executing as applied to the ICJ judgment (and consequently to find that judgment enforceable) does not threaten constitutional conflict with other branches; it does not require us to engage in nonjudicial activity; and it does not require us to create a new cause of action. The only question before us concerns the application of the ICJ judgment as binding law applicable to the parties in a particular criminal proceeding that Texas law creates independently of the treaty. I repeat that the question before us does not involve the creation of a private right of action. . . .

Seventh, neither the President nor Congress has expressed concern about direct judicial enforcement of the ICJ decision. To the contrary, the President favors enforcement of this judgment. Thus, insofar as foreign policy impact, the interrelation of treaty provisions, or any other matter within the President's special treaty, military, and foreign affairs responsibilities might prove relevant, such factors *favor*, rather than militate against, enforcement of the judgment before us.

For these seven reasons, I would find that the United States' treaty obligation to comply with the ICJ judgment in *Avena* is enforceable in court in this case without further congressional action. . . . The majority reaches a different conclusion because it looks for the wrong thing (explicit textual expression about self-execution) using the wrong standard (clarity) in the wrong place (the treaty language). Hunting for what the text cannot contain, it takes a wrong turn. It threatens to deprive individuals, including businesses, property owners, testamentary beneficiaries, consular officials, and others, of the workable dispute resolution procedures that many treaties, including commercially oriented treaties, provide. In a world where commerce, trade, and travel have become ever more international, that is a step in the wrong direction. . . .

III

Because the majority concludes that the Nation's international legal obligation to enforce the ICJ's decision is not automatically a domestic legal obligation, it must then determine whether the President has the constitutional authority to enforce it. And the majority find that he does not. . . .

Given my view of this case, I need not answer the questions. And I should not try to do so. That silence, however, cannot be taken as agreement with the majority's Part III conclusion. . . .

IV

. . . [A] strong line of precedent, likely reflecting the views of the Founders, indicates that the treaty provisions before us and the judgment of the International Court of Justice address themselves to the Judicial Branch and consequently are self-executing. In reaching a contrary conclusion, the Court has failed to take proper account of that precedent and, as a result, the Nation may well break its word even though the President seeks to live up to that word and Congress has done nothing to suggest the contrary.

For the reasons set forth, I respectfully dissent.

APPENDIXES TO OPINION OF BREYER, J.

A. Examples of Supreme Court decisions considering a treaty provision to be self-executing. . . . [The Appendix lists 29 treaties.]

B. United States treaties in force containing provisions for the submission of treaty-based disputes to the International Court of Justice. . . . [This Appendix lists 45 treaties.]

Notes and Questions

1. Why did the Court in *Asakura* find the treaty provision there to be judicially enforceable (even though it did not use the term "self-executing")? How could one redraft the treaty language in *Asakura* to make it non-self-executing? What other

remedies, besides possible treaty enforcement in U.S. courts, might be available to the Japanese national in *Asakura?*

2. The majority opinion in *Medellin* assumed, without deciding, that the Vienna Convention was self-executing and that Article 36 grants foreign nationals, like Medellin, "an individually enforceable right to request that their consular officers be notified of their detention, and an accompanying right to be informed by authorities of the availability of consular notification." The majority noted, however, that it considered the question to be whether the ICJ's judgment in *Avena* "has binding effect in domestic courts under the Optional Protocol, ICJ Statute, and U.N. Charter." What was the Court's holding in *Medellin*? Why?

3. What did the majority in *Medellin* assume was the starting presumption, whether a treaty that the United States ratified was self-executing or not, if there was not a clear indication in the treaty text?

4. Why did the dissenting opinion by Justice Breyer argue that the ICJ judgment was enforceable as a matter of domestic law without further legislation? Review Justice Breyer's reasons and the reasoning of the majority. Does the dissenting opinion call for a starting presumption that a treaty that the United States has ratified is self-executing? Which opinion do you find more persuasive?

5. Many observers consider that the majority opinion in *Medellin* was a departure from the past approach of the U.S. Supreme Court regarding whether a treaty was self-executing or not. For example, Professor Carlos Vazquez has argued that the language of the Supremacy Clause and past case law should lead to a presumption that treaties are self-executing absent a clear indication to the contrary. Carlos Manuel Vazquez, Treaties as Law of the Land; The Supremacy Clause and the Judicial Enforcement of Treaties, 122 Harv. L. Rev. 599, 612-623 (2008). By contrast, others have argued that a new presumption in favor of non-self-execution is an acceptable application of the separation of powers doctrine and is not barred by the text and history of the Supremacy Clause. See David H. Moore, Law(makers) of the Land: The Doctrine of Treaty Non-Self-Execution, 122 Harv. L. Rev. F. 32, 43-47 (2009).

6. Why might it be unconstitutional to conclude a self-executing treaty that appropriates U.S. government funds, or imposes a tax, as opposed to a treaty that changes state commercial law?

7. What are the advantages and disadvantages of making treaties self-executing? Wouldn't making all treaties self-executing ease foreign relations problems for the President? It might allow the President to act quickly in the face of rapidly moving developments. It could also avoid possible disagreements with other state parties that a non-self-executing treaty might create over whether the United States implementing legislation was consistent with the treaty. On the other hand, if you were a Senator concerned about the possible breadth of provisions in, say, an international human rights treaty, would you prefer to advise and consent to the treaty as a self-executing treaty, or as a non-self-executing one that would involve the opportunity to influence implementing legislation?

8. Among the branches of the U.S. government, which branch's interpretation of a treaty is controlling? The Supreme Court has stated that "while courts interpret treaties for themselves, the meaning given them by the departments of government particularly charged with their negotiation and enforcement is given great weight." Sanchez-Llamas v. Oregon, 548 U.S. 331, 355(2006) (quoting Kolovrat v. Oregon,

366 U.S. 187, 194 (1961)); see, e.g., United States v. Stuart, 489 U.S. 353, 369 (1989); Sumitomo Shoji America, Inc. v. Avagliano 457 U.S. 176, 184-185 (1982). However, the Court has declined in some instances to accept the executive branch's treaty interpretation. See, e.g., Reid v. Covert, 354 U.S. 1, 16 (1957) (concluding that the executive branch's interpretation violated the Constitution); Perkins v. Elg, 307 U.S. 325, 347-349 (1939) (declining to adopt an executive interpretation that conflicted with previous executive branch practice). Do you agree with this general approach of the U.S. courts?

9. After the Supreme Court's decision in *Medellin* in March 2008, the state of Texas made plans to go ahead with Medellin's execution on August 5, 2008. Although there was considerable further litigation in the ICJ and U.S. Supreme Court, Texas proceeded with the execution by lethal injection on August 5. As the Court noted above in *Medellin,* however, "No one disputes that the *Avena* decision," in which the ICJ held that Medellin and the other Mexican nationals were entitled to a review and reconsideration of their state-court convictions and sentences, "constitutes an *international law* obligation on the part of the United States." What recourse, if any, might Mexico have had in response to a breach of that obligation?

10. Also after *Medellin,* the U.S. Senate's Foreign Relations Committee examined the Senate's practice in dealing with the questions of self-execution or not and judicial enforceability of self-executing treaties. Starting in 2008, more care was taken to make explicit statements about these issues when the committee and the Senate voted. For example, in considering a new extradition treaty with the United Kingdom in 2010, the U.S. Senate included an express declaration that the treaty is self-executing. See John Crook, Contemporary Practice of the United States Relating to International Law: General International Law and U.S. Foreign Relations Law: Senate Foreign Relations Committee Documents Self-Executing Character of New Extradition Treaties, 104 A.J.I.L. 100, 100-01 (2010).

11. In a post-*Medellin* decision, Brzak v. United Nations, 597 F.3d 107 (2d Cir. 2010), a Second Circuit Court of Appeals decided that the Convention on Privileges and Immunities of the United Nations (CPIUN), 21 U.S.T. 1418, was self-executing. The text of the Convention stated that when a party deposited its instrument of accession it would "be in a position under its own law to give effect to the terms of this convention." Applying *Medellin,* the Second Circuit concluded that, based on the treaty's text, as well as statements from the Senate and the executive branch, the court had "little difficulty concluding that the CPIUN is self-executing." Id. at 111.

b. Reservations

As indicated in Chapter 2, a state may under some circumstances enter a "reservation" to its full adherence to a treaty. In U.S. practice the President would communicate any U.S. reservation to the other treaty partners when he ratifies the treaty (i.e., when he takes the formal act required to indicate U.S. adherence to the treaty). Accordingly, the President may initially decide what reservations are appropriate, and he would normally indicate those views when he sends a treaty to the Senate for its advice and consent to ratification. In addition, especially in recent years, the Senate has initiated or required the entry of substantive reservations to treaties as part of its "advice and consent" role.

In addition to reservations, which constitute qualifications to particular treaty terms, the President and Senate also sometimes attach "understandings" and "declarations" to the U.S. ratification of treaties. Understandings are interpretive statements that clarify or elaborate on, rather than change, the provisions of the treaty. Similarly, declarations are statements of policy relating to the treaty that do not alter or limit its substantive provisions. Collectively, reservations, understandings, and declarations are sometimes referred to as "RUDs."

The President and Senate have often attached RUDs to the U.S. ratification of human rights treaties. For example, they attached the following RUDs to U.S. ratification in 1992 of the International Covenant on Civil and Political Rights:

> I. The Senate's advice and consent is subject to the following reservations:
>
> (1) That Article 20 does not authorize or require legislation or other action by the United States that would restrict the right of free speech and association protected by the Constitution and laws of the United States.
>
> (2) That the United States reserves the right, subject to its Constitutional constraints, to impose capital punishment on any person (other than a pregnant woman) duly convicted under existing or future laws permitting the imposition of capital punishment, including such punishment for crimes committed by persons below eighteen years of age.
>
> (3) That the United States considers itself bound by Article 7 to the extent that "cruel, inhuman or degrading treatment or punishment" means the cruel and unusual treatment or punishment prohibited by the Fifth, Eighth and/or Fourteenth Amendments to the Constitution of; the United States, . . .
>
> II. The Senate's advice and consent is subject to the following understandings, which shall apply to the obligations of the United States under this Covenant:
>
> (1) That the Constitution and laws of the United States guarantee all persons equal protection of the law and provide extensive protections against discrimination. The United States understands distinctions based upon race, color, sex, language, religion, political or other opinion, national or social origin, property, birth or any other status — as those terms are used in Article 2, paragraph 1 and Article 26 — to be permitted when such distinctions are, at minimum, rationally related to a legitimate governmental objective. The United States further understands the prohibition in paragraph 1 of Article 4 upon discrimination, in time of public emergency, based "solely" on the status of race, color, sex, language, religion or social origin not to bar distinctions that may have a disproportionate effect upon persons of a particular status. . . .
>
> (5) That the United States understands that this Covenant shall be implemented by the Federal Government to the extent that it exercises legislative and judicial jurisdiction over the matters covered therein, and otherwise by the state and local governments; to the extent that state and local governments exercise jurisdiction over such matters, the Federal Government shall take measures appropriate to the Federal system to the end that the competent authorities of the state or local governments may take appropriate measures for the fulfillment of the Covenant.
>
> III. The Senate's advice and consent is subject to the following declarations:
>
> (1) That the United States declares that the provisions of Articles 1 through 27 of the Covenant are not self-executing. . . .
>
> IV. The Senate's advice and consent is subject to the following proviso, which shall not be included in the instrument of ratification to be deposited by the President:
>
> Nothing in this Covenant requires or authorizes legislation, or other action, by the United States of America prohibited by the Constitution of the United States as interpreted by the United States.

Notes and Questions

1. Since the 1980s the use of RUDs, especially for human rights treaties, has become common. The RUDs above for the ICCPR are a good example. Other examples include the RUDs for the Convention on the Prevention and Punishment of the Crime of Genocide (Genocide Convention) and the Convention Against Torture and Other Cruel, Inhuman, or Degrading Treatment or Punishment (Torture Convention). (These conventions, and some of the RUDs, are found in the Documentary Supplement.) RUDs are added for several reasons, including concerns by some that the provisions of a treaty might conflict with the Constitution or U.S. policies or that they are vaguely worded or that they might affect the balance of power between the federal and state governments.

The RUDs for the ICCPR provide examples of reservations that seek to limit or alter the substantive terms of the treaty because of a desire to avoid constitutional conflicts or policy disagreements. For example, although the ICCPR prohibits juvenile execution, when giving its advice and consent, the Senate reserved the right to execute anyone with the exception of pregnant women. Note that this reservation has since been effectively rendered moot by the Supreme Court's interpretation of the Eighth Amendment's Cruel and Unusual Punishment Clause to prohibit juvenile execution in Roper v. Simmons, 543 U.S. 551 (2005).

As for dealing with vague wording in the treaty's provisions, the ICCPR RUDs followed a frequent approach of declaring that substantive provisions of the treaty were non-self-executing and, hence, were not domestically enforceable in U.S. courts. To date, Congress has not passed implementing legislation. See Serra v. Lappin, 600 F.3d 1191, 1197 (9th Cir. 2010), holding that inmates of a federal prison do not have standing based on the ICCPR to challenge the wage rates paid them for work performed during their sentences.

The ICCPR RUDs also provide more precise definitions of vague or ambiguous treaty terms—for example, clarifying that the anti-discrimination sections of the ICCPR permitted "distinctions [that] are, at minimum, rationally related to a legitimate governmental interest." These approaches help avoid the possibility that a court might say that a treaty provision supersedes state law or an earlier inconsistent federal statute.

2. The U.S. practice of attaching RUDs to human rights treaties has its detractors. They argue that U.S. RUDs emasculate the obligations that U.S. treaty makers purported to undertake when negotiating and signing human rights treaties. For example, the United States attached a reservation to the Torture Convention that limited the definition of "cruel, inhuman or degrading treatment" to that conduct prohibited by the Fifth, Eighth, and Fourteenth Amendments of the Constitution. Professor Henkin, an opponent of these types of pervasive RUDs, suggests that "reservations designed to reject any obligation to rise above existing [U.S.] law and practice are of dubious propriety: if states generally entered such reservations, the convention would be futile." Louis Henkin, U.S. Ratification of Human Rights Conventions: The Ghost of Senator Bricker, 89 Am. J. Int'l L. 341, 343 (1995).

Proponents of RUDs note that their use has garnered bipartisan support in Congress and was instrumental in ending in the 1980s a deadlock that had blocked for years the U.S. ratification of major human rights treaties. Supporters also point out that, even with reservations making all or most of a treaty non-self-executing, the

United States is binding itself internationally to these treaties. And the United States has actually passed federal laws to implement the Genocide and Torture Conventions. Moreover, when reservations go only to particular provisions of a treaty, the rest of the treaty continues to apply. See Curtis A. Bradley & Jack L. Goldsmith, Treaties, Human Rights, and Conditional Consent, 149 U. Pa. L. Rev. 399, 456-468 (2000).

Do you believe that RUDs should be employed frequently, sparingly, or not at all? When are RUDs most appropriate? Not appropriate?

3. Does the Constitutional process for consenting to and ratifying treaties mean that the U.S. Senate can consent to treaties that, when ratified, have the force of federal law under the Supremacy Clause without the involvement of the U.S. House of Representatives?

4. Do RUDs give the Senate a unilateral power to change signed, but not yet ratified, treaties? Is it relevant that the President still has the choice of whether or not to ratify the treaty by depositing the instruments of ratification?

c. Last-in-Time Rule

The Constitution provides that both treaties and federal statutes are part of the supreme law of the land and thus preempt inconsistent state law. The Constitution does not specify, however, the relationship between treaties and statutes. The Supreme Court nevertheless has long held that self-executing treaties and federal statutes have essentially equal status under U.S. law, such that the later in time will prevail under U.S. law in the event of a conflict.

The Court applied this "last-in-time rule" in the decision below.

Breard v. Greene

U.S. Supreme Court
523 U.S. 371 (1998)

Per Curiam.

Angel Francisco Breard is scheduled to be executed by the Commonwealth of Virginia this evening at 9:00 p.m. Breard, a citizen of Paraguay, came to the United States in 1986, at the age of 20. In 1992, Breard was charged with the attempted rape and capital murder of Ruth Dickie. . . . Following a jury trial in . . . Arlington County, Virginia, Breard was convicted of both charges and sentenced to death. On appeal, the Virginia Supreme Court affirmed Breard's convictions and sentences, and we denied certiorari. . . .

Breard then filed a motion for habeas relief under 28 U.S.C. §2254 in Federal District Court on August 20, 1996. In that motion, Breard argued for the first time that his conviction and sentence should be overturned because of alleged violations of the Vienna Convention on Consular Relations (Vienna Convention), at the time of his arrest. Specifically, Breard alleged that the Vienna Convention was violated when the arresting authorities failed to inform him that, as a foreign national, he had the right to contact the Paraguayan Consulate. The District Court rejected this claim, concluding that Breard procedurally defaulted the claim when he failed to raise it in state court and that Breard could not demonstrate cause and prejudice for this default. The Fourth Circuit affirmed. Breard has petitioned this Court for a writ of certiorari. . . .

On April 3, 1998, nearly five years after Breard's conviction became final, the Republic of Paraguay instituted proceedings against the United States in the International Court of Justice (ICJ), alleging that the United States violated the Vienna Convention at the time of Breard's arrest. On April 9, the ICJ noted jurisdiction and issued an order requesting that the United States "take all measures at its disposal to ensure that Angel Francisco Breard is not executed pending the final decision in these proceedings. . . ." The ICJ set a briefing schedule for this matter, with oral argument likely to be held this November. Breard then filed a petition for an original writ of habeas corpus and a stay application in this Court in order to "enforce" the ICJ's order. Paraguay filed a motion for leave to file a bill of complaint in this Court, citing this Court's original jurisdiction over cases "affecting Ambassadors . . . and Consuls." U.S. Const., Art. Ill, §2.

It is clear that Breard procedurally defaulted his claim, if any, under the Vienna Convention by failing to raise that claim in the state courts. Nevertheless, in their petitions for certiorari, both Breard and Paraguay contend that Breard's Vienna Convention claim may be heard in federal court because the Convention is the "supreme law of the land" and thus trumps the procedural default doctrine. This argument is plainly incorrect for two reasons.

First, while we should give respectful consideration to the interpretation of an international treaty rendered by an international court with jurisdiction to interpret such, it has been recognized in international law that, absent a clear and express statement to the contrary, the procedural rules of the forum State govern the implementation of the treaty in that State. This proposition is embodied in the Vienna Convention itself, which provides that the rights expressed in the Convention "shall be exercised in conformity with the laws and regulations of the receiving State," provided that "said laws and regulations must enable full effect to be given to the purposes for which the rights accorded under this Article are intended." Article 36(2), [1970]. It is the rule in this country that assertions of error in criminal proceedings must first be raised in state court in order to form the basis for relief in habeas. Claims not so raised are considered defaulted. By not asserting his Vienna Convention claim in state court, Breard failed to exercise his rights under the Vienna Convention in conformity with the laws of the United States and the Commonwealth of Virginia. Having failed to do so, he cannot raise a claim of violation of those rights now on federal habeas review.

Second, although treaties are recognized by our Constitution as the supreme law of the land, that status is no less true of provisions of the Constitution itself, to which rules of procedural default apply. We have held "that an Act of Congress . . . is on a full parity with a treaty, and that when a statute which is subsequent in time is inconsistent with a treaty, the statute to the extent of conflict renders the treaty null." Reid v. Covert, 354 U.S. 1, 18 (1957) (plurality opinion); see also Whitney v. Robertson, 124 U.S. 190, 194 (1888) (holding that if a treaty and a federal statute conflict, "the one last in date will control the other"). The Vienna Convention — which arguably confers on an individual the right to consular assistance following arrest — has continuously been in effect since 1969. But in 1996, before Breard filed his habeas petition raising claims under the Vienna Convention,

Congress enacted the Antiterrorism and Effective Death Penalty Act (AEDPA), which provides that a habeas petitioner alleging that he is held in violation of "treaties of the United States" will, as a general rule, not be afforded an evidentiary hearing if he "has failed to develop the factual basis of [the] claim in State court proceedings." 28 U.S.C.A. §§2254(a), (e) (2) (Supp. 1998). Breard's ability to obtain relief based on violations of the Vienna Convention is subject to this subsequently-enacted rule, just as any claim arising under the United States Constitution would be. This rule prevents Breard from establishing that the violation of his Vienna Convention rights prejudiced him. Without a hearing, Breard cannot establish how the Consul would have advised him, how the advice of his attorneys differed from the advice the Consul could have provided, and what factors he considered in electing to reject the plea bargain that the State offered him.

Notes and Questions

1. Does *Breard* conclude that the Vienna Convention on Consular Relations is inconsistent with the above quoted language of the federal Antiterrorism and Effective Death Penalty Act (AEDPA)? If not, why did the Court include a discussion of the last-in-time rule?

2. In Whitney v. Robertson, 124 U.S. 190, 194 (1888), the Supreme Court addressed the relationship between treaties ratified by the United States and federal laws:

> By the Constitution a treaty is placed upon the same footing, and made of like obligation, with an act of legislation. Both are declared by that instrument to be the supreme law of the land, and no superior efficacy is given to either over the other. When the two relate to the same subject, the courts will always endeavor to construe them so as to give effect to both, if that can be done without violating the language of either; but if the two are inconsistent, the one last in date will control the other.

See also Chae Chan Ping v. United States (Chinese Exclusion Case), 130 U.S. 581 (1889); Edye v. Robertson (Head Money Cases), 112 U.S. 580 (1884).

3. This long-established doctrine of later in time has rarely been applied in practice. There is apparently only one case where the treaty makers have overridden a prior act of Congress. Cook v. United States, 288 U.S. 102 (1933); see Phillip R. Trimble, International Law: United States Foreign Relations Law 160 (2002). In the possible reverse situation of a federal statute overriding a treaty provision, the courts try to avoid this situation. The courts require a clear expression of congressional intent, in some cases almost an explicit declaration. See, e.g., Trans World Airlines, Inc. v. Franklin Mint Corp., 466 U.S. 243, 252 (1984) ("There is, first, a firm and obviously sound canon of construction against finding implicit repeal of a treaty in ambiguous congressional action."). Indeed, as discussed below at Chapter 3.C.2, it is a hallowed and frequently invoked canon of statutory interpretation that a court will not construe an act of Congress to be inconsistent with international law if another construction is possible. This maxim dates at least to an opinion of Chief Justice Marshall in The Charming Betsy, 6 U.S. (2 Cranch) 64 (1804), and continues to be invoked and generally followed.

4. Invalidating a treaty by passing an inconsistent federal statute does not terminate the United States' international obligations to its treaty partners. The United

States' obligations remain intact. (As discussed in Chapter 2 and below, however, the United States can free itself from its obligations under a treaty by withdrawing from it according to the treaty's provisions.)

5. Are there any good arguments for never overriding a treaty obligation, even by subsequent act of Congress? As just noted above, the United States is still bound internationally, even if not domestically. Some countries regard treaties as always superior to domestic legislation. Wouldn't that approach foster greater stability in international relations? Isn't that increasingly important in the world? Would that approach be consistent with Article VI of the U.S. Constitution?

d. Treaty Termination, Reinterpretation, and the Political Question Doctrine

Termination. As discussed in Chapter 2, most recent treaties contain clauses providing the bases for withdrawal from the treaty. The treaties usually specify their duration or date of termination, and/or the conditions or events that allow for termination or the right to withdraw. Article 54 of the Vienna Convention on Treaties also addresses the matter.

In the United States, although Article II provides for the ratification of treaties by the President with the advice and consent of the Senate, the Constitution is silent on the procedural requirements of treaty termination. As discussed above, Congress can pass later federal legislation that overrides a treaty under domestic law, but this does not relieve the United States of its international obligations to its treaty partners.

The omission from the Constitution of the domestic procedures for treaty termination gives rise to separation of powers issues. Once a treaty formally enters into force, does the fact that treaty making requires a two-thirds concurrence by the Senate provide an argument that termination should also require its approval? Is unilateral treaty termination part of the President's foreign affairs powers? Does the placement of the treaty power in Article II, rather than in Article I with Congress's enumerated powers, provide a textual argument the president can unilaterally terminate treaties?

The Constitution's framers apparently sought to avoid making it too easy to conclude treaties with other countries by requiring the advice and consent of a super-majority of the Senate. Allowing the President unilateral power to terminate treaties, however, would facilitate extricating the U.S. from agreements and obligations with foreign countries. Is termination by the President alone preferable to requiring the involvement of the Senate? Is it better that terminating treaties is easier than concluding them?

The Supreme Court encountered the question of the constitutionality of the President's unilateral termination of a treaty in Goldwater v. Carter, 444 U.S. 996 (1979). In 1978, President Jimmy Carter extended President Richard Nixon's diplomatic initiative with the People's Republic of China (PRC) by unilaterally withdrawing from a mutual defense treaty with the Taiwan-based Republic of China (ROC), invoking the treaty's provision allowing termination upon one year's notice. Several members of Congress, including Senator Barry Goldwater, filed suit in federal court challenging the President's authority to terminate the treaty.

The plaintiffs argued that treaty termination required a two-thirds concurrence of the Senate or an endorsement by majority vote of both Houses.

The district court held treaty termination required concurrence of two-thirds of the Senate or approval by Congress. See Goldwater v. Carter, 481 F. Supp. 949 (D.D.C. 1979). The court of appeals, reaching the merits, reversed the district court and held that the Constitution permitted unilateral termination by the President without any action by either house of Congress. See 617 F.2d 697 (D.C. Cir. 1979). The Supreme Court granted certiorari, summarily vacated the court of appeals, and remanded the case for dismissal. An opinion by then-Justice Rehnquist, joined by three other Justices, found that the constitutionality of President Carter's termination of the mutual defense treaty was a non-justiciable "political question." Justice Powell believed that because Congress had not yet acted to prevent President Carter's termination of the treaty the dispute was not yet ripe for adjudication. Justices White and Blackmun believed that the issue should have been more fully considered before the Court rendered any decision. Justice Brennan opined that the President had the requisite authority because he had the authority to recognize foreign governments. Justice Marshall concurred in the result. See 444 U.S. 997 (1979).

Controversy over a president's unilateral termination of a treaty arose again when President George W. Bush terminated the bilateral Anti-Ballistic Missile (ABM) Treaty, which entered into force between the United States and the Soviet Union in 1972. Intended to facilitate the Cold War policy of "mutually assured destruction," the treaty permitted only a limited number of anti-ballistic missile interceptors and deployment sites, and it placed limits on the development and testing of new ABM systems. In December of 2001, without seeking the approval of the Congress, President Bush informed the Russian government that the United States intended to withdraw from the treaty pursuant to the treaty provision that permitted termination if a party "decides that extraordinary events related to the subject matter of this Treaty have jeopardized its supreme interests." The Bush administration rationalized its termination of the treaty on the basis of plans to develop and deploy an ABM system, with interceptors located in Alaska, to defend against rogue states (e.g., North Korea) or accidental launches, as well as the United States' improving relationship with Russia. In 2002, several members of Congress, led by Dennis Kucinich, a Representative from Ohio, filed suit against President Bush to prevent termination of the ABM Treaty. See Kucinich v. Bush, 236 F. Supp. 2d 1 (D.D.C. 2002). Although Justice Rehnquist's opinion in *Goldwater* only garnered a plurality, the District Court for the District of Columbia found, among other reasons, that his conclusion that treaty termination was a non-justiciable political question was "instructive and compelling."

Reinterpretation. President Bush's termination of the ABM Treaty is not the only time that treaty has raised constitutional questions. It also led to questions whether a President can reinterpret a treaty in a way that differs from the meaning given it by the President and Senate at the time of ratification. In 1983 President Reagan delivered a speech announcing the launch of the Strategic Defense Initiative (SDI), a program whose goal was to produce a space-based missile defense system. Even though Article V (1) of the ABM Treaty had been read by many in the past to prohibit such systems, the Reagan administration advocated a broad reading of the treaty to permit the United States to develop technologies not in existence in 1972 when the treaty entered into force. Many people who had been involved in the initial negotiations and ratification of the treaty, including several Senators, reacted negatively, arguing that the administration's new interpretation was based upon a disingenuous reading of the treaty's negotiating records.

The Reagan Administration eventually acquiesced in the original understanding backed by the Senate, though it continued to assert that the President possessed the constitutional authority to unilaterally reinterpret treaties. During this period, Congress conditioned the appropriation of funds to the Defense Department on their use for purposes consistent with the original understanding. Also, in an effort to preempt future administration attempts to reinterpret treaties, the Senate included a reservation to the subsequent Intermediate Nuclear Forces (INF) Treaty with the Soviet Union that restricted that treaty's interpretation to the shared understanding actually held by the President and the Senate at the time of ratification and required that the Senate consent to any future reinterpretation. The Reagan Administration argued against this condition, but went ahead with ratification of the treaty with that condition.

Does the President have the constitutional authority to interpret a treaty in a way that conflicts with the interpretation given its terms at the time of ratification? Does the Senate's successful rebuff of President Reagan's reinterpretation provide an argument that the constitutional issues at stake were more amenable to political, rather than judicial, resolution? Does the issue of unilateral Presidential reinterpretation of treaties raise the same sort of constitutional questions as unilateral Presidential withdrawal from treaties? If so, is then-Justice Rehnquist's opinion in *Goldwater* also applicable to the reinterpretation debate?

For an argument in support of the broad reading of the ABM Treaty written by its principle architect in the Reagan administration, see Abraham D. Sofaer, The ABM Treaty and the Strategic Defense Initiative, 99 Harv. L. Rev. 1972 (1986). For the opposing view, see David A. Koplow, Constitutional Bait and Switch: Executive Reinterpretation of Arms Control Treaties, 137 U. Pa. L. Rev. 1353 (1989).

Political Question Doctrine. The judiciary has crafted several non-justiciability doctrines that limit the courts' ability to hear certain foreign affairs cases, including those involving treaty termination and treaty reinterpretation issues. As illustrated in the *Goldwater* case, one of these doctrines is the political question doctrine.*

Chief Justice Marshall recognized long ago in Marbury v. Madison that "questions, in their very nature political, or which are, by the Constitution and laws, submitted to the executive," are not amenable to adjudication in the courts. 5 U.S. (Cranch 1) 137, 170 (1803). The rationale underlying the political question doctrine is that some constitutional issues are non-justiciable because their resolution is better suited for the political process or because the Constitution itself delegates the particular constitutional powers in dispute to the President or Congress.

*For other limiting doctrines, see the discussion below in Chapter 3.B.4 about state secrets and in Chapter 7.B.2 about comity, *forum non conveniens*, and exhaustion of local remedies.

In Baker v. Carr, 369 U.S. 186, 217 (1962), the Court formulated a list of situations where the political question doctrine might be invoked:

> Prominent on the surface of any case held to involve a political question is found a textually demonstrable constitutional commitment of the issue to a coordinate political department; or a lack of judicially discoverable and manageable standards for resolving it; or the impossibility of deciding without an initial policy determination of a kind clearly for nonjudicial discretion; or the impossibility of a court's undertaking independent resolution without expressing lack of the respect due coordinate branches of government; or an unusual need for unquestioning adherence to a political decision already made; or the potentiality of embarrassment from multifarious pronouncements by various departments on one question.

Writing for the plurality in *Goldwater* in 1979, then-Justice Rehnquist concluded that "[i]n light of the absence of any constitutional provision governing the termination of a treaty, and the fact that different termination procedures may be appropriate for different treaties the instant case in my view also must surely be controlled by political standards." *Goldwater*, 444 U.S. at 1003 (internal citations omitted). The nature of the constitutional powers at issue contributed heavily to his analysis: "this action . . . [was] entirely external to the United States and [falls] within the category of foreign affairs." Justice Brennan responded:

> In stating that this case presents a nonjusticiable "political question," Mr. Justice Rehnquist, in my view, profoundly misapprehends the political-question principle as it applies to matters of foreign relations. Properly understood, the political-question doctrine restrains courts from reviewing an exercise of foreign policy judgment by the coordinate political branch to which authority to make that judgment has been "constitutionally committed." But the doctrine does not pertain when a court is faced with the *antecedent* question whether a particular branch has been constitutionally designated as the repository of political decisionmaking power. The issue of decisionmaking authority must be resolved as a matter of constitutional law, not political discretion; accordingly, it falls within the competence of the courts.

Id. at 1006-07 (internal quotations omitted).

Is Justice Rehnquist's or Justice Brennan's view more persuasive? Although eschewing the political question doctrine, Justice Brennan ultimately concluded that because the power to officially recognize foreign governments resided in the Executive Branch, President Carter's termination of the treaty without the consent of either branch of Congress was constitutional. Does the political question doctrine mean in many cases that the political branch (the President or Congress) that acted will not be blocked by the courts?

The D.C. Circuit recently considered the political question doctrine in El-Shifa v. United States, 607 F.3d 836 (D.C. Cir. 2010) (en banc). There, a Sudanese pharmaceutical company sued the United States for actions ordered by President Clinton in 1988 against its plant in Sudan after Al Qaeda successfully attacked two U.S. embassies in Kenya and Tanzania. The plaintiffs alleged that the U.S. actions violated international law norms requiring compensation for "unjustified" destruction of its plant by a U.S. cruise missile strike and that statements by the President and other executive officials describing El-Shifa as having connections to Osama bin

Laden constituted defamation. (There was some evidence in the press after the attack that the company and the plant were not related to Al Qaeda.) The D.C. Circuit noted that "courts are not a forum for reconsidering the wisdom of discretionary decisions made by the political branches in the realm of foreign policy or national security." The court concluded that both claims involved discretionary decisions constitutionally committed to the political branches and also that there were not judicially manageable standards for evaluating whether the missile strike was "unjustified." Hence, the claims were barred by the political question doctrine.

Given that the Constitution allocates the various powers for conducting foreign affairs to the President and Congress (as discussed more fully in the next section), what role, if any, should courts play in adjudicating disputes arising out of that context? Does the courts' understanding, or lack thereof, about foreign affairs issues make it more likely that erroneous or uninformed decisions will result? Are standard methods of constitutional interpretation ineffective when adjudicating foreign affairs issues? Are there prudential reasons, such as the need to speak with one voice internationally, why the courts should avoid issues better suited for resolution through the political process? Does the political question doctrine conflict with Chief Justice Marshall's imperative in *Marbury* that "[i]t is emphatically the province and duty of the judicial department to say what the law is"? 5 U.S. (1 Cranch) at 177.

For notable foreign affairs cases where the Court did not invoke the political question doctrine even though separation of powers issues were at stake, see, for example, Dames & Moore v. Regan, 453 U.S. 654 (1981), and Youngstown Sheet and Tube Co. v. Sawyer, 343 U.S. 579 (1952). (Both cases are excerpted below.)

B. PRESIDENTIAL POWER AND OTHER INTERNATIONAL AGREEMENTS

In addition to the power conferred by Article II of the Constitution, the President has three other sources of authority to conclude international agreements on behalf of the United States: (1) authority based on a prior Article II treaty, (2) authority from the Congress, and (3) independent authority conferred directly by the Constitution. Within the third category, the President has express constitutional authority (like the commander-in-chief-power) and implied constitutional authority (to conduct foreign relations). In this section we will focus on the last two categories of executive agreement (the first category is simply an extension of the basic Article II doctrine). But first we begin with a general discussion of presidential power.

As background for both the discussion of presidential power and the discussion of executive agreements, review the following constitutional grants of power to Congress and the President.

U.S. Constitution

Article I

Section 1. All legislative Powers herein granted shall be vested in a Congress of the United States, which shall consist of a Senate and House of Representatives. . . .

Section 7. [1] All Bills for raising Revenue shall originate in the House of Representatives; but the Senate may propose or concur with Amendments as on other Bills. . . .

Section 8. [1] The Congress shall have Power To lay and collect Taxes, Duties, Imposts and Excises, to pay the Debts and provide for the common Defence and general Welfare of the United States; but all Duties, Imposts and Excises shall be uniform throughout the United States;

[2] To borrow money on the credit of the United States;

[3] To regulate Commerce with foreign Nations, and among the several States, and with the Indian Tribes;

[4] To establish an uniform Rule of Naturalization, and uniform Laws on the subject of Bankruptcies throughout the United States;

[5] To coin Money, regulate the Value thereof, and of foreign Coin, and fix the Standard of Weights and Measures;

[6] To provide for the Punishment of counterfeiting the Securities and current Coin of the United States; . . .

[10] To define and punish Piracies and Felonies committed on the high Seas, and Offenses against the Law of Nations;

[11] To declare War, grant Letters of Marque and Reprisal, and make Rules concerning Captures on Land and Water;

[12] To raise and support Armies, but no Appropriation of Money to that Use shall be for a longer Term than two Years;

[13] To provide and maintain a Navy;

[14] To make Rules for the Government and Regulation of the land and naval Forces;

[15] To provide for calling forth the Militia to execute the Laws of the Union, suppress Insurrections and repel Invasions;

[16] To provide for organizing, arming, and disciplining, the Militia, and for governing such Part of them as maybe employed in the Service of the United States, reserving to the States respectively, the Appointment of the Officers, and the Authority of training the Militia according to the discipline prescribed by Congress; . . .

[18] To make all Laws which shall be necessary and proper for carrying into Execution the foregoing Powers, and all other Powers vested by this Constitution in the Government of the United States, or in any Department or Officer thereof.

Section 9. . . . [7] No money shall be drawn from the Treasury, but in Consequence of Appropriations made by Law; and a regular Statement and Account of the Receipts and Expenditures of all public Money shall be published from time to time.

Article II

Section 1. [1] The executive Power shall be vested in a President of the United States of America. . . .

Section 2. [1] The President shall be Commander in Chief of the Army and Navy of the United States, . . .

[2] He shall have Power, by and with the Advice and Consent of the Senate to make Treaties, provided two thirds of the Senators present concur; and he shall

nominate, and by and with the Advice and Consent of the Senate, shall appoint Ambassadors, other public Ministers and Consuls, . . .

Section 3. [1] . . . He shall receive Ambassadors and other public Ministers. . . .

1. Presidential Foreign Relations Power

Unlike the long list of congressional foreign affairs powers in Article I of the Constitution, there are only a few presidential foreign relations powers enumerated in Article II, and even some of those powers (such as treaty making) require senatorial consent. Nevertheless, the President has always exercised substantial foreign relations power. Indeed, the President is often described as having the dominant role in the conduct of U.S. foreign relations. The two decisions below consider the sources and scope of presidential foreign relations authority.

United States v. Curtiss-Wright Corp.

U.S. Supreme Court
299 U.S. 304 (1936)

Mr. Justice SUTHERLAND delivered the opinion of the Court.

On January 27, 1936, an indictment was returned in the court below, the first count of which charges that appellees, beginning with the 29th day of May, 1934, conspired to sell in the United States certain arms of war, namely fifteen machine guns, to Bolivia, a country then engaged in armed conflict in the Chaco, in violation of the Joint Resolution of Congress approved May 28, 1934, and the provisions of a proclamation issued on the same day by the President of the United States pursuant to authority conferred by §1 of the resolution. In pursuance of the conspiracy, the commission of certain overt acts was alleged, details of which need not be stated. The Joint Resolution (c.365, 48 Stat. 811) follows:

> *Resolved by the Senate and House of Representatives of the United States of America in Congress assembled,* That if the President finds that the prohibition of the sale of arms and munitions of war in the United States to those countries now engaged in armed conflict in the Chaco may contribute to the reestablishment of peace between those countries, and if after consultation with the governments of other American Republics and with their cooperation as well as that of such other governments as he may deem necessary, he makes proclamation to that effect, it shall be unlawful to sell, except under such limitations and exceptions as the President prescribes, any arms or munitions of war in any place in the United States to the countries now engaged in that armed conflict, or to any person, company, or association acting in the interest of either country, until otherwise ordered by the President or by Congress. . . .

. . . [A]ppellees urge that Congress abdicated its essential functions and delegated them to the Executive.

Whether, if the Joint Resolution had related solely to internal affairs it would be open to the challenge that it constituted an unlawful delegation of legislative power to the Executive, we find it unnecessary to determine. The whole aim of the resolution is to affect a situation entirely external to the United States, and falling within the category of foreign affairs. The determination which we are called to make, therefore, is whether the Joint Resolution, as applied to that situation, is vulnerable to attack under the rule that forbids a delegation of the law-making power. In other words, assuming (but not deciding) that the challenged delegation, if it were confined to internal affairs, would be invalid, may it nevertheless be sustained on the ground that its exclusive aim is to afford a remedy for a hurtful condition within foreign territory?

It will contribute to the elucidation of the question if we first consider the differences between the powers of the federal government in respect of foreign or external affairs and those in respect of domestic or internal affairs. That there are differences between them, and that these differences are fundamental, may not be doubted.

The two classes of powers are different, both in respect of their origin and their nature. The broad statement that the federal government can exercise no powers except those specifically enumerated in the Constitution, and such implied powers as are necessary and proper to carry into effect the enumerated powers, is categorically true only in respect of our internal affairs. In that field, the primary purpose of the Constitution was to carve from the general mass of legislative powers *then possessed by the states* such portions as it was thought desirable to vest in the federal government, leaving those not included in the enumeration still in the states. Carter v. Carter Coal Co., 298 U.S. 238, 294. That this doctrine applies only to powers which the states had, is self evident. And since the states severally never possessed international powers, such powers could not have been carved from the mass of state powers but obviously were transmitted to the United States from some other source. During the colonial period, those powers were possessed exclusively by and were entirely under the control of the Crown. By the Declaration of Independence, "the Representatives of the United States of America" declared the United [not the several] Colonies to be free and independent states, and as such to have "full Power to levy War, conclude Peace, contract Alliances, establish Commerce and to do all other Acts and Things which Independent States may of right do."

As a result of the separation from Great Britain by the colonies acting as a unit, the powers of external sovereignty passed from the Crown not to the colonies severally, but to the colonies in their collective and corporate capacity as the United States of America. Even before the Declaration, the colonies were a unit in foreign affairs, acting through a common agency—namely the Continental Congress, composed of delegates from the thirteen colonies. That agency exercised the powers of war and peace, raised an army, created a navy, and finally adopted the Declaration of Independence. Rulers come and go; governments end and forms of government change; but sovereignty survives. A political society cannot endure without a supreme will somewhere. Sovereignty is never held in suspense. When, therefore, the external sovereignty of Great Britain in respect of the colonies ceased, it immediately passed to the Union. . . .

It results that the investment of the federal government with the powers of external sovereignty did not depend upon the affirmative grants of the Constitution. The powers to declare and wage war, to conclude peace, to make treaties, to maintain diplomatic relations with other sovereignties, if they had never been mentioned in the Constitution, would have vested in the federal government as necessary concomitants of nationality. Neither the Constitution nor the laws passed in pursuance of it have any force in foreign territory unless in respect of our own citizens (see American Banana Co. v. United Fruit Co., 213 U.S. 347, 356); and operations of the nation in such territory must be governed by treaties, international understandings and compacts, and the principles of international law. As a member of the family of nations, the right and power of the United States in that field are equal to the right and power of the other members of the international family. Otherwise, the United States is not completely sovereign. The power to acquire territory by discovery and occupation, the power to expel undesirable aliens, the power to make such international agreements as do not constitute treaties in the constitutional sense (Altman & Co. v. United States, 224 U.S. 383, 600-601), none of which is expressly affirmed by the Constitution, nevertheless exist as inherently inseparable from the conception of nationality. This the court recognized, and in each of the cases cited found the warrant for its conclusions not in the provisions of the Constitution, but in the law of nations. . . .

Not only, as we have shown, is the federal power over external affairs in origin and essential character different from that over internal affairs, but participation in the exercise of the power is significantly limited. In this vast external realm, with its important, complicated, delicate and manifold problems, the President alone has the power to speak or listen as a representative of the nation. He makes treaties with the advice and consent of the Senate; but he alone negotiates. Into the field of negotiation the Senate cannot intrude; and Congress itself is powerless to invade it. As Marshall said in his great argument of March 7, 1800, in the House of Representatives, "The President is the sole organ of the nation in its external relations, and its sole representative with foreign nations." . . .

It is important to bear in mind that we are here dealing not alone with an authority vested in the President by an exertion of legislative power, but with such an authority plus the very delicate, plenary and exclusive power of the President as the sole organ of the federal government in the field of international relations — a power which does not require as a basis for its exercise an act of Congress, but which, of course, like every other governmental power, must be exercised in subordination to the applicable provisions of the Constitution. It is quite apparent that if, in the maintenance of our international relations, embarrassment — perhaps serious embarrassment — is to be avoided and success for our aims achieved, congressional legislation which is to be made effective through negotiation and inquiry within the international field must often accord to the President a degree of discretion and freedom from statutory restriction which would not be admissible were domestic affairs alone involved. Moreover, he, not Congress, has the better opportunity of knowing the conditions which prevail in foreign countries, and especially is this true in time of war. He has his confidential sources of information. He has his agents in the form of diplomatic, consular and other officials. Secrecy in respect of information gathered by them may be highly necessary, and the premature disclosure of it productive of harmful results. Indeed, so clearly is this true that the first President refused to accede to a request to lay before the House of Representatives the instructions, correspondence and documents relating to the negotiation of the Jay Treaty — a refusal the wisdom of which was recognized by the House itself and has never since been doubted.

Youngstown Sheet & Tube Co. v. Sawyer

U.S. Supreme Court
343 U.S. 579 (1952)

Mr. Justice BLACK delivered the opinion of the Court.

We are asked to decide whether the President was acting within his constitutional power when he issued an order directing the Secretary of Commerce to take possession of and operate most of the Nation's steel mills. The mill owners argue that the President's order amounts to law-making, a legislative function which the Constitution has expressly confided to the Congress and not to the President. The Government's position is that the order was made on findings of the President that his action was necessary to avert a national catastrophe which would inevitably result from a stoppage of steel production, and that in meeting this grave emergency the President was acting within the aggregate of his constitutional powers as the Nation's Chief Executive and the Commander in Chief of the Armed Forces of the United States. The issue emerges here from the following series of events:

In the latter part of 1951, a dispute arose between the steel companies and their employees over terms and conditions that should be included in new collective bargaining agreements. Long-continued conferences failed to resolve the dispute. On December 18, 1951, the employees' representatives, United Steelworkers of America, C.I.O., gave notice of an intention to strike when the existing bargaining agreements expired on December 31. The Federal Mediation and Conciliation Service then intervened in an effort to get labor and management to agree. This failing, the President on December 22, 1951, referred the dispute to the Federal Wage Stabilization Board to investigate and make recommendations for fair and equitable terms of settlement. This Board's report resulted in no settlement. On April 4, 1952, the Union gave notice of a nation-wide strike called to begin at 12:01 a.m. April 9. The indispensability of steel as a component of substantially all weapons and other war materials led the President to believe that the proposed work stoppage would immediately jeopardize our national defense and that governmental seizure of the steel mills was necessary in order to assure the continued availability of steel. Reciting these considerations for his action, the President, a few hours before the strike was to begin, issued Executive Order 10340. . . . The order directed the Secretary of Commerce to take possession of most of the steel mills and keep them running. The Secretary immediately issued his own possessory orders, calling upon the presidents of the various seized companies to serve as operating managers for the United States. They were directed to carry on their activities in accordance with regulations and directions of the Secretary. The next morning the President sent a message to Congress reporting his action. Twelve days later he sent a second message. Congress has taken no action. . . .

The President's power, if any, to issue the order must stem either from an act of Congress or from the Constitution itself. There is no statute that expressly authorizes the President to take possession of property as he did here. Nor is there any act of Congress to which our attention has been directed from which such a power can fairly be implied. Indeed, we do not understand the Government to rely on statutory authorization for this seizure. There are two statutes which do authorize the President to take both personal and real property under certain conditions. However, the Government admits that these conditions were not met and that the President's order was not rooted in either of the statutes. The Government refers to the seizure provisions of one of these statutes (§201 (b) of the Defense Production Act) as "much too cumbersome, involved, and time-consuming for the crisis which was at hand."

Moreover, the use of the seizure technique to solve labor disputes in order to prevent work stoppages was not only unauthorized by any congressional enactment; prior to this controversy, Congress had refused to adopt that method of settling labor disputes. When the Taft-Hartley Act was under consideration in 1947, Congress rejected an amendment which would have authorized such governmental seizures in cases of emergency. Apparently it was thought that the technique of seizure, like that of compulsory arbitration, would interfere with the process of collective bargaining. Consequently, the plan Congress adopted in that Act did not provide for seizure under any circumstances. Instead, the plan sought to bring about settlements by use of the customary devices of mediation, conciliation, investigation by boards of inquiry, and public reports. In some instances temporary injunctions were authorized to provide cooling-off periods. All this failing, unions were left free to strike after a secret vote by employees as to whether they wished to accept their employers' final settlement offer.

It is clear that if the President had authority to issue the order he did, it must be found in some provision of the Constitution. And it is not claimed that express constitutional language grants this power to the President. The contention is that presidential power should be implied from the aggregate of his powers under the Constitution. Particular reliance is placed on provisions in Article II which say that "The executive Power shall be vested in a President . . ."; that "he shall take Care that the Laws be faithfully executed"; and that he "shall be Commander in Chief of the Army and Navy of the United States."

The order cannot properly be sustained as an exercise of the President's military power as Commander in Chief of the Armed Forces. The Government attempts to do so by citing a number of cases upholding broad powers in military commanders engaged in day-to-day fighting in a theater of war. Such cases need not concern us here. Even though "theater of war" be an expanding concept, we cannot with faithfulness to our constitutional system hold that the Commander in Chief of the Armed Forces has the ultimate power as such to take possession of private property in order to keep labor disputes from stopping production. This is a job for the Nation's lawmakers, not for its military authorities.

Nor can the seizure order be sustained because of the several constitutional provisions that grant executive power to the President. In the framework of our Constitution, the President's power to see that the laws are faithfully executed refutes the idea that he is to be a lawmaker. The Constitution limits his functions in the lawmaking process to the recommending of laws he thinks wise and the vetoing of laws he thinks bad. And the Constitution is neither silent nor equivocal about who shall make laws which the President is to execute. The first section of the first article says that "All legislative Powers herein granted shall be vested in a Congress of the United States. . . ." After granting many powers to the Congress, Article I goes on to provide that Congress may "make all Laws which shall be necessary and proper for carrying into Execution the foregoing Powers, and all other Powers vested by this Constitution in the Government of the United States, or in any Department or Officer thereof."

The President's order does not direct that a congressional policy be executed in a manner prescribed by Congress — it directs that a presidential policy be executed in a manner prescribed by the President. The preamble of the order itself, like that of many statutes, sets out reasons why the President believes certain policies should be adopted, proclaims these policies as rules of conduct to be followed, and again, like a statute, authorizes a government official to promulgate additional rules and regulations consistent with the policy proclaimed and needed to carry that policy into execution. The power of Congress to adopt such public policies as those proclaimed by the order is beyond question. It can authorize the taking of private property for public use. It can make laws regulating the relationships between employers and employees, prescribing rules designed to settle labor disputes, and fixing wages and working conditions in certain fields of our economy. The Constitution does not subject this lawmaking power of Congress to presidential or military supervision or control. . . .

Mr. Justice JACKSON, concurring in the judgment and opinion of the Court.

. . . A judge, like an executive adviser, may be surprised at the poverty of really useful and unambiguous authority applicable to concrete problems of executive power as they actually present themselves. Just what our forefathers did envision, or would have envisioned had they foreseen modern conditions, must be divined from materials almost as enigmatic as the dreams Joseph was called upon to interpret for Pharaoh. A century and a half of partisan debate and scholarly speculation yields no net result but only supplies more or less apt quotations from respected sources on each side of any question. They largely cancel each other. And court decisions are indecisive because of the judicial practice of dealing with the largest questions in the most narrow way.

The actual art of governing under our Constitution does not and cannot conform to judicial definitions of the power of any of its branches based on isolated clauses or even single Articles torn from context. While the Constitution diffuses power the better to secure liberty, it also contemplates that practice will integrate the dispersed powers into a workable government. It enjoins upon its branches separateness but interdependence, autonomy but reciprocity. Presidential powers are not fixed but fluctuate, depending upon their disjunction or conjunction with those of Congress. We may well begin by a somewhat over-simplified grouping of practical situations in which a President may doubt, or others may challenge, his powers, and by distinguishing roughly the legal consequences of this factor of relativity.

1. When the President acts pursuant to an express or implied authorization of Congress, his authority is at its maximum, for it includes all that he possesses in his own right plus all that Congress can delegate.[2] In these circumstances, and in these only, may he be said (for what it may be worth) to personify the federal sovereignty.

2. It is in this class of cases that we find the broadest recent statements of presidential power, including those relied on here, United States v. Curtiss-Wright Corp., 299 U.S. 304, involved, not the question of the President's power to act without congressional authority, but the question of his right to act under and in accord with an Act of Congress. . . .

That case does not solve the present controversy. It recognized internal and external affairs as being in separate categories, and held that the strict limitation upon congressional delegations of power to the

If his act is held unconstitutional under these circumstances, it usually means that the Federal Government as an undivided whole lacks power. A seizure executed by the President pursuant to an Act of Congress would be supported by the strongest of presumptions and the widest latitude of judicial interpretation, and the burden of persuasion would rest heavily upon any who might attack it.

2. When the President acts in absence of either a congressional grant or denial of authority, he can only rely upon his own independent powers, but there is a zone of twilight in which he and Congress may have concurrent authority, or in which its distribution is uncertain. Therefore, congressional inertia, indifference or quiescence may sometimes, at least as a practical matter, enable, if not invite, measures on independent presidential responsibility. In this area, any actual test of power is likely to depend on the imperatives of events and contemporary imponderables rather than on abstract theories of law.

3. When the President takes measures incompatible with the expressed or implied will of Congress, his power is at its lowest ebb, for then he can rely only upon his own constitutional powers minus any constitutional powers of Congress over the matter. Courts can sustain exclusive presidential control in such a case only by disabling the Congress from acting upon the subject. Presidential claim to a power at once so conclusive and preclusive must be scrutinized with caution, for what is at stake is the equilibrium established by our constitutional system.

Into which of these classifications does this executive seizure of the steel industry fit? It is eliminated from the first by admission, for it is conceded that no congressional authorization exists for this seizure. . . .

Can it then be defended under flexible tests available to the second category? It seems clearly eliminated from that class because Congress has not left seizure of private property an open field but has covered it by three statutory policies inconsistent with this seizure. In cases where the purpose is to supply needs of the Government itself, two courses are provided: one, seizure of a plant which fails to comply with obligatory orders placed by the Government; another, condemnation of facilities, including temporary use under the power of eminent domain. The third is applicable where it is the general economy of the country that is to be protected rather than exclusive governmental interests. None of these were invoked. In choosing a different and inconsistent way of his own, the President cannot claim that it is necessitated or invited by failure of Congress to legislate upon the occasions, grounds and methods for seizure of industrial properties.

This leaves the current seizure to be justified only by the severe tests under the third grouping, where it can be supported only by any remainder of executive power after subtraction of such powers as Congress may have over the subject. In short, we can sustain the President only by holding that seizure of such strike-bound industries is within his domain and beyond control by Congress. Thus, this Court's first review of such seizures occurs under circumstances which leave presidential power most vulnerable to attack and in the least favorable of possible constitutional postures.

President over internal affairs does not apply with respect to delegations of power in external affairs. It was intimated that the President might act in external affairs without congressional authority, but not that he might act contrary to an Act of Congress . . .

I did not suppose, and I am not persuaded, that history leaves it open to question, at least in the courts, that the executive branch, like the Federal Government as a whole, possesses only delegated powers. The purpose of the Constitution was not only to grant power, but to keep it from getting out of hand. However, because the President does not enjoy unmentioned powers does not mean that the mentioned ones should be narrowed by a niggardly construction. Some clauses could be made almost unworkable, as well as immutable, by refusal to indulge some latitude of interpretation for changing times. I have heretofore, and do now, give to the enumerated powers the scope and elasticity afforded by what seem to be reasonable, practical implications instead of the rigidity dictated by a doctrinaire textualism.

The Solicitor General seeks the power of seizure in three clauses of the Executive Article, the first reading, "The executive Power shall be vested in a President of the United States of America." Lest I be thought to exaggerate, I quote the interpretation which his brief puts upon it: "In our view, this clause constitutes a grant of all the executive powers of which the Government is capable." If that be true, it is difficult to see why the forefathers bothered to add several specific items, including some trifling ones.[9]

The example of such unlimited executive power that must have most impressed the forefathers was the prerogative exercised by George III, and the description of its evils in the Declaration of Independence leads me to doubt that they were creating their new Executive in his image. . . . And if we seek instruction from our own times, we can match it only from the executive powers in those governments we disparagingly describe as totalitarian. I cannot accept the view that this clause is a grant in bulk of all conceivable executive power but regard it as an allocation to the presidential office of the generic powers thereafter stated.

The clause on which the Government next relies is that "The President shall be Commander in Chief of the Army and Navy of the United States. . . ." These cryptic words have given rise to some of the most persistent controversies in our constitutional history. Of course, they imply something more than an empty title. But just what authority goes with the name has plagued presidential advisers who would not waive or narrow it by nonassertion yet cannot say where it begins or ends. It undoubtedly puts the Nation's armed forces under presidential command. Hence, this loose appellation is sometimes advanced as support for any presidential action, internal or external, involving use of force, the idea being that it vests power to do anything, anywhere, that can be done with an army or navy.

That seems to be the logic of an argument tendered at our bar — that the President having, on his own responsibility, sent American troops abroad derives from that act "affirmative power" to seize the means of producing a supply of steel for them. To quote, "Perhaps the most forceful illustration of the scope of Presidential power in this connection is the fact that American troops in Korea, whose safety and effectiveness are so directly involved here, were sent to the field by an exercise of the President's constitutional powers." Thus, it is said, he has invested himself with "war powers."

9. ". . . he may require the Opinion, in writing, of the principal Officer in each of the executive Departments, upon any Subject relating to the Duties of their respective Offices. . . ." U.S. Const., Art. II, §2. He ". . . shall Commission all the Officers of the United States." U.S. Const., Art. II, §3. Matters such as those would seem to be inherent in the Executive if anything is.

I cannot foresee all that it might entail if the Court should indorse this argument. Nothing in our Constitution is plainer than that declaration of a war is entrusted only to Congress. Of course, a state of war may in fact exist without a formal declaration. But no doctrine that the Court could promulgate would seem to me more sinister and alarming than that a President whose conduct of foreign affairs is so largely uncontrolled, and often even is unknown, can vastly enlarge his mastery over the internal affairs of the country by his own commitment of the Nation's armed forces to some foreign venture. . . .

. . . [T]he Constitution did not contemplate that the title Commander in Chief *of the Army and Navy* will constitute him also Commander in Chief of the country, its industries and its inhabitants. . . .

We should not use this occasion to circumscribe, much less to contract, the lawful role of the President as Commander in Chief. I should indulge the widest latitude of interpretation to sustain his exclusive function to command the instruments of national force, at least when turned against the outside world for the security of our society. But, when it is turned inward not because of rebellion, but because of a lawful economic struggle between industry and labor, it should have no such indulgence. His command power is not such an absolute as might be implied from that office in a militaristic system, but is subject to limitations consistent with a constitutional Republic whose law and policymaking branch is a representative Congress. The purpose of lodging dual titles in one man was to insure that the civilian would control the military, not to enable the military to subordinate the presidential office. No penance would ever expiate the sin against free government of holding that a President can escape control of executive powers by law through assuming his military role. What the power of command may include I do not try to envision, but I think it is not a military prerogative, without support of law, to seize persons or property because they are important or even essential for the military and naval establishment.

The Solicitor General lastly grounds support of the seizure upon nebulous, inherent powers never expressly granted but said to have accrued to the office from the customs and claims of preceding administrations. The plea is for a resulting power to deal with a crisis or an emergency according to the necessities of the case, the unarticulated assumption being that necessity knows no law.

Loose and irresponsible use of adjectives colors all non-legal and much legal discussion of presidential powers. "Inherent" powers, "implied" powers, "incidental" powers, "plenary" powers, "war" powers and "emergency" powers are used, often interchangeably and without fixed or ascertainable meanings.

The vagueness and generality of the clauses that set forth presidential powers afford a plausible basis for pressures within and without an administration for presidential action beyond that supported by those whose responsibility it is to defend his actions in court. The claim of inherent and unrestricted presidential powers has long been a persuasive dialectical weapon in political controversy. . . . [A] judge cannot accept self-serving press statements of the attorney for one of the interested parties as authority in answering a constitutional question. . . .

The Solicitor General, acknowledging that Congress has never authorized the seizure here, says practice of prior Presidents has authorized it. He seeks color of legality from claimed executive precedents. . . .

The appeal, however, that we declare the existence of inherent powers *ex necessitate* to meet an emergency asks us to do what many think would be wise, although it is something the forefathers omitted. They knew what emergencies were, knew the pressures they engender for authoritative action, knew, too, how they afford a ready pretext for usurpation. We may also suspect that they suspected that emergency powers would tend to kindle emergencies. Aside from suspension of the privilege of the writ of habeas corpus in time of rebellion or invasion, when the public safety may require it, they made no express provision for exercise of extraordinary authority because of a crisis. . . .

The Executive, except for recommendation and veto, has no legislative power. The executive action we have here originates in the individual will of the President and represents an exercise of authority without law. No one, perhaps not even the President, knows the limits of the power he may seek to exert in this instance and the parties affected cannot learn the limit of their rights. We do not know today what powers over labor or property would be claimed to flow from Government possession if we should legalize it, what rights to compensation would be claimed or recognized, or on what contingency it would end. With all its defects, delays and inconveniences, men have discovered no technique for long preserving free government except that the Executive be under the law, and that the law be made by parliamentary deliberations.

Such institutions may be destined to pass away. But it is the duty of the Court to be last, not first, to give them up.

[Concurring opinions of Justices FRANKFURTER, DOUGLAS, BURTON, and CLARK, and dissenting opinions of Chief Justice VINSON and Justices REED and MINTON omitted.]

Notes and Questions

1. What was actually decided in *Curtiss-Wright*? Is the Court's effusive language on the subject of presidential power necessary to the decision? Was this a case of congressional delegation of power rather than independent presidential power?

2. Does the Court's distinction in *Curtiss-Wright* between constitutional powers in the domestic and external realms make sense? How can courts tell whether a case raises an issue of domestic or external power? Couldn't *Curtiss-Wright* itself be characterized as a domestic case because it involved attempted sales by an American company and the company's U.S. citizen officers? In our increasingly globalized world, is the domestic/foreign distinction a tenable basis for such important differences in constitutional doctrine?

3. How tenable is the Court's claim in *Curtiss-Wright* that the foreign relations powers of the federal government are derived from a source other than the U.S. Constitution? Is this claim consistent with the idea of a limited national government regulated by a written constitution? With the actual allocation of foreign relations powers in the Constitution itself? If the national government does have extra-constitutional foreign relations powers, what are they?

4. What are the implications of the Court's suggestion in *Curtiss-Wright* that international law notions of sovereignty are the source of the U.S. foreign relations power? International law might dictate that nationhood requires, for example, the ability to engage in international relations and make treaties. But does it also specify

the particular allocation of foreign relations power *within* a sovereign—for example, between political branches, or between national and sub-national governments?

5. The steel seizure at issue in *Youngstown* took place in the midst of, and indeed in alleged furtherance of, the Korean War. Under the analysis in *Curtiss-Wright*, isn't the Korean War an "external affair" regarding which the President has plenary power? Why does the Court take such a different approach to constitutional limits in *Youngstown*, where the majority opinion does not even cite *Curtiss-Wright*? Are the holdings in *Curtiss-Wright* and *Youngstown* reconcilable, as Justice Jackson suggests in note 2 of his concurrence?

6. What was the critical fact in *Youngstown*? Would or should the decision have been the same if Congress had never considered the Taft-Hartley Act? Is it clear that President Truman's actions in *Youngstown* fell within Justice Jackson's third category, as Jackson argues?

7. Justice Jackson's concurrence in *Youngstown*, especially its articulation of three categories of presidential power, has been very influential. Indeed, courts and commentators often give more weight to Jackson's concurrence than to the majority opinion. Why do you think this is so? How much guidance does Jackson's framework provide in ascertaining the scope of presidential power?

2. *Executive Agreement*

International agreements concluded by the United States other than Article II treaties are generally referred to as "executive agreements." Those executive agreements that are based on congressionally delegated or statutory authority are often referred to as "congressional-executive agreements." Those executive agreements that are based on independent presidential constitutional authority are sometimes called "presidential executive agreements" or "sole executive agreements." The State Department has promulgated an internal regulation that describes the different kinds of executive agreement and the factors taken into account in choosing among them.

Department of State Circular 175[1]

. . . There are three constitutional bases for international agreements other than treaties as set forth below. An international agreement may be concluded pursuant to one or more of these constitutional bases:

(1) Agreements Pursuant to Treaty

The President may conclude an international agreement pursuant to a treaty brought into force with the advice and consent of the Senate, whose provisions constitute authorization for the agreement by the Executive without subsequent action by the Congress;

1. This circular is part of the Federal Regulations at 22 C.F.R. §181.4 and at 11 U.S. Dep't of State, Foreign Affairs Manual §720 (2006). It is still referred to as the "Circular 175" procedure.

(2) Agreements Pursuant to Legislation

The President may conclude an international agreement on the basis of existing legislation or subject to legislation to be enacted by the Congress; and

(3) Agreements Pursuant to the Constitutional Authority of the President

The President may conclude an international agreement on any subject within his constitutional authority so long as the agreement is not inconsistent with legislation enacted by the Congress in the exercise of its constitutional authority. The constitutional authority for the President to conclude international agreements include:

(a) The President's authority as Chief Executive to represent the nation in foreign affairs;

(b) The President's authority to receive ambassadors and other public ministers;

(c) The President's authority as "Commander-in-Chief"; and

(d) The President's authority to "take care that the laws be faithfully executed."

721.3 Considerations for Selecting Among Constitutionally Authorized Procedures

In determining a question as to the procedure which should be followed for any particular international agreement, due consideration is given to the following factors . . . :

a. The extent to which the agreement involves commitments or risks affecting the nation as a whole;

b. Whether the agreement is intended to affect State laws;

c. Whether the agreement can be given effect without the enactment of subsequent legislation by the Congress;

d. Past United States practice with respect to similar agreements;

e. The preference of the Congress with respect to a particular type of agreement;

f. The degree of formality desired for an agreement;

g. The proposed duration of the agreement, the need for prompt conclusion of an agreement, and the desirability of concluding a routine or short-term agreement; and

h. The general international practice with respect to similar agreements.

Notes and Questions

1. Restatement Section 111, Comment d, notes that: "International agreements of the United States other than treaties, . . . while not mentioned specifically in the Supremacy Clause, are also federal law and as such as supreme over State law."

2. How useful do you think the factors listed in Circular 175 are in actual situations for selecting among the types of international agreement to use? Can you prepare a more precise set of criteria or specify how the various factors should be balanced in particular cases?

3. In 1972, Congress enacted the Case Act, which requires the Secretary of the State to transmit to Congress a copy of all international agreements concluded by

the United States (except, of course, treaties approved by the Senate). Passed near the end of the U.S. involvement in hostilities in Vietnam, the Act was part of the congressional effort to control presidential power in foreign affairs. The perception was that in the absence of such reporting requirements, the President could make secret commitments, leading to unfortunate consequences suffered by the nation as a whole, without the benefit of advice or review by the Senate or Congress. Consequently, by forcing disclosure, Congress might introduce a cautionary influence on presidential behavior.

A study by the Senate found that the Act "has been helpful in apprising Congress of executive agreements," and that the Act "has contributed to improved relations between Congress and the executive branch in the area of executive agreements." See Congressional Research Service, Treaties and Other International Agreements: The Role of the United States Senate, S. Prt. 106-71,106th Cong., 2d Sess., at 225 (2001). Between 1978 and 1999, more than 7,000 agreements were transmitted to Congress pursuant to the Act. See id. at 226-227.

Case Act

1 U.S.C. §112b (as amended)

(a) The Secretary of State shall transmit to the Congress the text of any international agreement (including the text of any oral international agreement, which agreement shall be reduced to writing), other than a treaty, to which the United States is a party as soon as practicable after such agreement has entered into force with respect to the United States but in no event later than sixty days thereafter. . . .

The criteria for determining which agreements should or must be submitted to the Senate for advice and consent to ratification sometimes seem to be more political, depending on a calculation of the votes in Congress and the Senate, than legal or principled. On the other hand, precedent plays a highly significant role. The determining criteria in many cases seem to be historical: traditionally most agreements dealing with human rights, extradition, diplomatic and consular privileges, military alliances, war and peace, arms control, boundaries, immigration, intellectual property, taxation, and the environment have been submitted to the Senate as Article II treaties. Most, but not all, agreements to join international organizations have also been concluded under Article II. However, international agreements dealing with trade, finance, energy, fisheries, postal matters, and bilateral aviation relations have regularly been concluded as congressional-executive agreements. Senators have occasionally asserted that "major" agreements or "major military" agreements must be submitted to the Senate under Article II.

a. Congressional-Executive Agreements

Congressional-executive agreements are international agreements authorized in advance, or approved after the fact, by a majority of both houses of Congress. A simple example of a congressional-executive agreement is one specifically authorized by statute or joint resolution of Congress.* For example, there is the joint resolution authorizing U.S. participation in the International Monetary Fund and the World Bank:

> The President is hereby authorized to accept membership for the United States in the International Monetary Fund [and in the World Bank] provided for by the Articles of Agreement of the Fund and the Articles of Agreement of the Bank as set forth in the Final Act of the United Nations Monetary and Financial Conference and dated July 23, 1944, and deposited in the archives of the Department of State.

Sometimes the congressional backing is not as direct or clear. For example, authority to implement aviation agreements granting landing rights to foreign air carriers has been inferred from statutory provisions that merely refer to such agreements. The rationale is that Congress must have approved the idea of executive conclusion of such agreements or it would not have mentioned them.

Notes and Questions

1. There are two types of congressional-executive agreements: *ex ante* delegations of authority to the President to conduct agreements and *ex post* approval of agreements the President has concluded. The North American Free Trade and the World Trade Organization agreements approved by Congress in 1993 and 1994, respectively, are examples of congressional-executive agreements approved *ex post.* A recent careful study found that much more common are executive agreements negotiated by the President using authority delegated in advance by Congress. Indeed, considering treaties and all types of executive agreements together, the study concludes that the *ex ante* congressional-executive agreements "make up the vast majority of international agreements in force for the United States today." Oona A. Hathaway, Presidential Power over International Law: Restoring the Balance, 119 Y.L.J. 140, 149 (2009).

2. Both the number of non-treaty international agreements (including congressional-executive agreements and presidential executive agreements) and the ratio of non-treaty international agreements to treaties have increased during the history of the United States. From 1789 to 1839, the United States only entered into 27 non-treaty international agreements and 60 treaties, or a ratio 0.45:1. From 1939 to 2009, it is estimated that the United States entered into about 16,500 non-treaty international agreements and 1,100 treaties, or a ratio of 15:1. See Michael John Garcia, Congressional Research Service, International Law and Agreements: Their Effect Upon U.S. Law 3. A large percentage of those non-treaty international agreements were congressional-executive agreements. Another study found that over 85 percent of the non-treaty agreements between 1946 and 1972 were congressional-executive agreements. Congressional Research Service, Treaties and Other International Agreements 39 (2001); see also the study cited in Note 1 above. What might explain the dramatic growth in the number and proportion of

*A "joint resolution" is passed by both Houses and is signed by the President. It has the same legal effect as a statute. A concurrent resolution, on the other hand, is passed by both Houses but is not presented to the President and has no legal effect. A "sense of the Senate" or "sense of the House" resolution is passed by only one House and also has no legal effect.

non-treaty international agreements, especially congressional-executive agreements, in the twentieth century? Might the difficulty of obtaining a two-thirds vote of the Senate explain the trend toward executive agreements versus treaties? And, might frictions between the Executive Branch and Congress be minimized by involving Congress into international agreements, rather than the Executive Branch trying to go it alone?

3. The U.S. Supreme Court has appeared to assume the constitutionality of congressional-executive agreements in several decisions. For example, in Weinberger v. Rossi, 456 U.S. 25 (1982), the Court interpreted the word "treaty" in an employment discrimination law case to include congressional-executive agreements as well as Article II treaties. See also B. Altman & Co. v. United States, 224 U.S. 583, 600-601 (1912) ("treaty" in a jurisdictional law interpreted to include congressional-executive agreements).

4. The Restatement (Section 303, comment e) and most observers believe that congressional-executive agreements are interchangeable with Article II treaties in every instance. If so, what does this mean for the President's calculations about whether to submit a particular international agreement as a treaty? Can the President resubmit an international agreement as a congressional-executive agreement for a majority vote in both houses if the agreement was submitted as a treaty but failed to receive a two-thirds vote of consent in the Senate, or vice versa? What might congressional leaders think of the second attempt on a particular agreement?

5. Scholars have engaged in a lively debate about the legitimacy of congressional-executive agreements in some circumstances. Compare, for example, Bruce Ackerman & David Golove, Is NAFTA Constitutional?, 108 Harv. L. Rev. 799 (1995), and David Golove, Against Free-Form Formalism, 73 N.Y.U. L. Rev. 1791 (1998), with Laurence H. Tribe, Taking Text and Structure Seriously: Reflections on the Free-Form Method in Constitutional Interpretation, 108 Harv. L. Rev. 1221 (1995).

b. Presidential Executive Agreements

Some of the most contentious foreign affairs cases have involved presidential executive agreements. In these situations the President has chosen not to use the procedure established in Article II of the Constitution for treaties and does not have a delegation of authority or other expression of support from Congress. Presidential executive agreements have been used infrequently (accounting for less than 10 percent of all U.S. international agreements). Usually they have been employed for technical or minor "housekeeping" matters, such as postal agreements, that did not seem to require the attention of, or support from, Congress. However, on occasion, they have been used to address major diplomatic issues (such as the Iran hostage crisis) where the President felt that congressional support was not necessary or could not be obtained (if at all) in a timely fashion.

To date Congress has not attempted to limit this presidential power, although Congress passed the Case Act, discussed above, to require that presidential executive agreements be reported to it after the fact.

In United States v. Belmont, 301 U.S. 324 (1937) and United States v. Pink, 315 U.S. 203 (1942), the Supreme Court upheld the validity of presidential executive agreements against the claim that Article II required the participation of the Senate for the conclusion of such agreements. Moreover, in *Belmont* and in *Pink* (which is excerpted below), the Court held that the executive agreement in question superseded the otherwise applicable state law.

United States v. Pink

U.S. Supreme Court
315 U.S. 203 (1942)

[Throughout the twentieth century revolutionary governments frequently nationalized property, including American property in the nationalizing State and property of citizens and corporations of the nationalizing State in the United States. Under the U.S. view of international law, the nationalizing State is under a duty to pay compensation to the United States to recompense the injuries done to U.S. nationals. The United States has typically reacted to confiscatory nationalizations by revolutionary governments by freezing the assets of those governments and their nationals in the United States. The United States and the revolutionary government then have frequently settled the outstanding international claims and other issues through a "lump sum claims agreement" under which, *inter alia*, the revolutionary government agrees to pay compensation to the United States in respect of the nationalized property of U.S. citizens. The amount paid has often been the same as the amount of frozen assets held in the United States.

[After the 1917 Revolution, the Soviet government nationalized private property, including the First Russian Insurance Co., which had a branch in New York. Under New York law the Soviet nationalization decree arguably would not be recognized by New York State courts because it would violate New York State public policy. Therefore the Soviet government's ownership claim would not be enforced in the New York courts. In 1933 the United States agreed to grant diplomatic recognition to the Soviet government, and the Soviets assigned to the U.S. government its claims to certain nationalized assets in the United States, including the assets of the nationalized First Russian Insurance Co. The U.S. government in turn planned to use those assets to pay American nationals whose property in Russia had been seized by the Soviets. The agreement was called the Litvinov Assignment, and it was a presidential executive agreement.

[In this case the U.S. government, as successor to the Soviet government, sued the insurance commissioner of New York to claim the New York assets of the First Russian Insurance Co. (even though the Soviet government presumably could not have successfully maintained such an action under New York law). The other claimants to the assets were foreign creditors of the company.]

Mr. Justice Douglas delivered the opinion of the Court. . . .

At the outset, it should be noted that, so far as appears, all creditors whose claims arose out of dealings with the New York branch have been paid. . . . The contest here is between the United States and creditors of the Russian corporation who, we assume, are not citizens of this country and whose claims did not arise out of transactions with the New York branch. The United States is seeking to protect not only claims which it holds but also claims of its nationals [against the Soviet Union in respect of their nationalized property]. Such claims did not arise out of transactions with this Russian corporation; they are, however, claims against Russia or its nationals. The existence of such claims and their non-payment had for years been one of the barriers to recognition of the Soviet regime by the Executive Department. The purpose of the discussions leading to the policy of recognition was to resolve "all questions outstanding" between the two nations. Settlement of all American claims against Russia was one method of removing some of the prior objections to recognition based on the Soviet policy of nationalization. The Litvinov Assignment was not only part and parcel of the new policy of recognition, it was also the method adopted by the Executive Department for alleviating in this country the rigors of nationalization. Congress tacitly recognized that policy. Acting in anticipation of the realization of funds under the Litvinov Assignment, it authorized the appointment of a Commissioner to determine the claims of American nationals against the Soviet Government. Joint Resolution of August 4, 1939, 53 Stat. 1199 [under which Congress provided a statutory procedure for determining the value of those claims and for paying those claims out of the Soviet assets transferred to the United States government under the Litvinov Assignment]. . . .

If the priority had been accorded American claims by treaty with Russia, there would be no doubt as to its validity. The same result obtains here. The powers of the President in the conduct of foreign relations included the power, without consent of the Senate, to determine the public policy of the United States with respect to the Russian nationalization decrees. "What government is to be regarded here as representative of a foreign sovereign state is a political rather than a judicial question, and is to be determined by the political department of the government." Guaranty Trust Co. v. United States, [304 U.S. 126, 137 (1938)]. That authority is not limited to a determination of the government to be recognized. It includes the power to determine the policy which is to govern the question of recognition. Objections to the underlying policy as well as objections to recognition are to be addressed to the political department and not to the courts. As we have noted, this Court in the *Belmont* case recognized that the Litvinov Assignment was an international compact which did not require the participation of the Senate. It stated: "There are many such compacts, of which a protocol, a modus vivendi, a postal convention, and agreements like that now under consideration are illustrations." Recognition is not always absolute; it is sometimes conditional. Power to remove such obstacles to full recognition as settlement of claims of our nationals certainly is a modest implied power of the President who is the "sole organ of the federal government in the field of international relations." United States v. Curtiss-Wright Corp. Effectiveness in handling the delicate problems of foreign relations requires no less. Unless such a power exists, the power of recognition might be thwarted or seriously diluted. No such obstacle can be placed in the way of rehabilitation of relations between this country and another nation, unless the historic conception of the powers and responsibilities of the President in the conduct of foreign affairs is to be drastically revised. It was the judgment of the political department that full recognition of the Soviet Government required the settlement of all outstanding problems including the claims of our nationals. Recognition and the Litvinov Assignment were interdependent. We would usurp the executive function if we held that that decision was not final and conclusive in the courts.

"All constitutional acts of power, whether in the executive or in the judicial department, have as much legal validity and obligation as if they proceeded from the legislature, . . ." The Federalist, No. 64. A treaty is a "Law of the Land" under the supremacy clause (Art. VI, Cl. 2) of the Constitution. Such international compacts and agreements as the Litvinov Assignment have a similar dignity. . . .

[Concurring opinion of Justice FRANKFURTER and dissenting opinion of Chief Justice STONE and Justice ROBERT omitted.]

The legal authority of presidential executive agreements was bolstered in the following case, which grew out of the 1979 Iranian revolution.

Dames & Moore v. Regan

U.S. Supreme Court
453 U.S. 654 (1981)

[Iranian militants occupied the U.S. embassy in Tehran and began holding as hostages the American diplomatic personnel there on November 4, 1979. The Iranian revolutionary government soon sided with the hostage-taking and took over the negotiations with the U.S. government about the possible release of 53 hostages. The Iranian government was also repudiating its predecessor's contracts with U.S. companies. During this turmoil, U.S. intelligence agencies learned that the Iranian government was about to withdraw its billions of dollars on deposit in U.S. banks. On November 14, President Jimmy Carter declared a national emergency and, pursuant to the International Emergency Economic Powers Act (IEEPA), he blocked the transfer of all assets of the Iranian government, including its controlled entities and the Central Bank of Iran, that were within U.S. jurisdiction. This order froze about $12 billion of Iranian funds in U.S. banks or in the possession of U.S. corporations, whether located in the United States or abroad.

[President Carter later authorized the initiation of judicial proceedings against Iran in U.S. courts and the entry of pre-judgment attachments, but his orders did not allow the entry of any final judgment. In December 1979, Dames & Moore filed suit in a U.S. district court in California against the Iranian government, the Atomic Energy Organization of Iran, and a number of Iranian banks. Dames & Moore sought to recover over $3 million allegedly owed to its subsidiary for work performed under a contract with the energy organization. To secure any judgment that might be entered against certain Iranian banks, the U.S. district court issued pre-judgment attachments against their property.

[On January 20, 1981, Iran released the U.S. hostages pursuant to the Algiers Accords, a presidential executive agreement, that had been entered into the day before. Under the Accords, the United States agreed "to terminate all legal proceedings in United States courts involving claims of United States persons and institutions against Iran and its state enterprises, to nullify all attachments and judgments obtained therein, to prohibit all further litigation based on such claims, and to bring about the termination of such claims through binding arbitration [before a special Claims Tribunal to be established in The Hague, Netherlands]."

President Carter immediately issued executive orders implementing the provisions of the Accords just before leaving office.

[In February 1981, President Ronald Reagan issued an executive order in which he "ratified" President Carter's executive orders implementing the Accords. Moreover, he "suspended" all "claims which may be presented to the . . . [Claims] Tribunal" and provided that such claims "shall have no legal effect in any action now pending in any" U.S. court. The suspension of any particular claim would be terminated if the Claims Tribunal determined that it had no jurisdiction over that claim. Claims would be discharged for all purposes when the Claims Tribunal either awarded some recovery and that amount is paid, or determines that no recovery is due.

[Dames & Moore challenged President Carter's and President Reagan's implementing orders.]

Justice REHNQUIST delivered the opinion of the Court. . . .

The parties and the lower courts, confronted with the instant questions, have all agreed that much relevant analysis is contained in Youngstown Sheet & Tube Co. v. Sawyer, 343 U.S. 579 (1952). . . .

Although we have in the past found and do today find Justice Jackson's classification of executive actions into three general categories analytically useful, we should be mindful of Justice Holmes' admonition, quoted by Justice Frankfurter in *Youngstown*, that "[t]he great ordinances of the Constitution do not establish and divide fields of black and white." Justice Jackson himself recognized that his three categories represented "a somewhat oversimplified grouping," and it is doubtless the case that executive action in any particular instance falls, not neatly in one of three pigeonholes, but rather at some point along a spectrum running from explicit congressional authorization to explicit congressional prohibition. This is particularly true as respects cases such as the one before us, involving responses to international crises the nature of which Congress can hardly have been expected to anticipate in any detail. . . .

IV

Although we have concluded that the IEEPA [International Emergency Economic Powers Act] constitutes specific congressional authorization to the President to nullify the attachments and order the transfer of Iranian assets, there remains the question of the President's authority to suspend claims pending in American courts. Such claims have, of course, an existence apart from the attachments which accompanied them. In terminating these claims through Executive Order No. 12294, the President purported to act under authority of both the IEEPA and 22 U.S.C. §1732, the so-called "Hostage Act."[7]

We conclude that although the IEEPA authorized the nullification of the attachments, it cannot be read to authorize the suspension of the claims. The claims

7. Judge Mikva, in his separate opinion in American Int'l Group, Inc. v. Islamic Republic of Iran, 657 F.2d 430, 452 (1981), argued that the moniker "Hostage Act" was newly coined for purposes of this litigation. Suffice it to say that we focus on the language of 22 U.S.C. §1732, not any shorthand description of it. See W. Shakespeare, Romeo and Juliet, Act II, scene 2, line 43 ("What's in a name?").

of American citizens against Iran are not in themselves transactions involving Iranian property or efforts to exercise any rights with respect to such property. An in personam lawsuit, although it might eventually be reduced to judgment and that judgment might be executed upon, is an effort to establish liability and fix damages and does not focus on any particular property within the jurisdiction. The terms of the IEEPA therefore do not authorize the President to suspend claims in American courts. This is the view of all the courts which have considered the question.

The Hostage Act, passed in 1868, provides:

> Whenever it is made known to the President that any citizen of the United States has been unjustly deprived of his liberty by or under the authority of any foreign government, . . . the President shall use such means, not amounting to acts of war, as he may think necessary and proper to obtain or effectuate [their] release. . . .

We are reluctant to conclude that this provision constitutes specific authorization to the President to suspend claims in American courts. Although the broad language of the Hostage Act suggests it may cover this case, there are several difficulties with such a view. The legislative history indicates that the Act was passed in response to a situation unlike the recent Iranian crisis. Congress in 1868 was concerned with the activity of certain countries refusing to recognize the citizenship of naturalized Americans traveling abroad, and repatriating such citizens against their will. These countries were not interested in returning the citizens in exchange for any sort of ransom. . . . The legislative history is also somewhat ambiguous on the question whether Congress contemplated Presidential action such as that involved here or rather simply reprisals directed against the offending foreign country and *its* citizens.

Concluding that neither the IEEPA nor the Hostage Act constitutes specific authorization of the President's action suspending claims, however, is not to say that these statutory provisions are entirely irrelevant to the question of the validity of the President's action. We think both statutes highly relevant in the looser sense of indicating congressional acceptance of a broad scope for executive action in circumstances such as those presented in this case. . . . The IEEPA delegates broad authority to the President to act in times of national emergency with respect to property of a foreign country. The Hostage Act similarly indicates congressional willingness that the President have broad discretion when responding to the hostile acts of foreign sovereigns. . . .

. . . [W]e cannot ignore the general tenor of Congress's legislation in this area in trying to determine whether the President is acting alone or at least with the acceptance of Congress. As we have noted, Congress cannot anticipate and legislate with regard to every possible action the President may find it necessary to take or every possible situation in which he might act. Such failure of Congress specifically to delegate authority does not, "especially . . . in the areas of foreign policy and national security," imply "congressional disapproval" of action taken by the Executive. Haig v. Agee, [453 U.S. 280, 291 (1981)]. On the contrary, the enactment of legislation closely related to the question of the President's authority in a particular case which evinces legislative intent to accord the President broad discretion may be considered to "invite" "measures on independent presidential responsibility," *Youngstown*, 343 U.S., at 637 (Jackson, J., concurring). At least this is so where there is no contrary indication of legislative intent and when, as here, there is a history of congressional acquiescence in conduct of the sort engaged in by the President. It is to that history which we now turn.

Not infrequently in affairs between nations, outstanding claims by nationals of one country against the government of another country are "sources of friction" between the two sovereigns. United States v. Pink, 315 U.S. 203, 225 (1942). To resolve these difficulties, nations have often entered into agreements settling the claims of their respective nationals. As one treatise writer puts it, international agreements settling claims by nationals of one state against the government of another "are established international practice reflecting traditional international theory." L. Henkin, Foreign Affairs and the Constitution 262 (1972). Consistent with that principle, the United States has repeatedly exercised its sovereign authority to settle the claims of its nationals against foreign countries. Though those settlements have sometimes been made by treaty, there has also been a longstanding practice of settling such claims by executive agreement without the advice and consent of the Senate. Under such agreements, the President has agreed to renounce or extinguish claims of United States nationals against foreign governments in return for lump-sum payments or the establishment of arbitration procedures. To be sure, many of these settlements were encouraged by the United States claimants themselves, since a claimant's only hope of obtaining any payment at all might lie in having his Government negotiate a diplomatic settlement on his behalf. But it is also undisputed that the "United States has sometimes disposed of the claims of its citizens without their consent, or even without consultation with them, usually without exclusive regard for their interests, as distinguished from those of the nation as a whole." It is clear that the practice of settling claims continues today. Since 1952, the President has entered into at least 10 binding settlements with foreign nations, including an $80 million settlement with the People's Republic of China.

Crucial to our decision today is the conclusion that Congress has implicitly approved the practice of claim settlement by executive agreement. This is best demonstrated by Congress's enactment of the International Claims Settlement Act of 1949, 64 Stat. 13, as amended, 22 U.S.C. §1621 et seq. The Act had two purposes: (1) to allocate to United States nationals funds received in the course of an executive claims settlement with Yugoslavia, and (2) to provide a procedure whereby funds resulting from future settlements could be distributed. To achieve these ends Congress created the International Claims Commission, now the Foreign Claims Settlement Commission, and gave it jurisdiction to make final and binding decisions with respect to claims by United States nationals against settlement funds. 22 U.S.C. §1623(a). By creating a procedure to implement future settlement agreements, Congress placed its stamp of approval on such agreements. . . .

Over the years Congress has frequently amended the International Claims Settlement Act to provide for particular problems arising out of settlement agreements, thus demonstrating Congress' continuing acceptance of the President's claim settlement authority. . . .

Finally, the legislative history of the IEEPA further reveals that Congress has accepted the authority of the Executive to enter into settlement agreements. Though the IEEPA was enacted to provide for some limitation on the President's emergency powers, Congress stressed that "[n]othing in this act is intended . . . to interfere with the authority of the President to [block assets], or to impede the settlement of claims of U.S. citizens against foreign countries." . . .

Petitioner raises two arguments in opposition to the proposition that Congress has acquiesced in this longstanding practice of claims settlement by executive agreement. . . .

Petitioner . . . asserts that Congress divested the President of the authority to settle claims when it enacted the Foreign Sovereign Immunities Act of 1976 (hereinafter FSIA), 28 U.S.C. §§1330, 1602 et seq. . . . According to petitioner, the principal purpose of the FSIA was to depoliticize . . . commercial lawsuits by taking them out of the arena of foreign affairs . . . and by placing them within the exclusive jurisdiction of the courts. . . .

. . . [W]e do not believe that the President has attempted to divest the federal courts of jurisdiction. Executive Order No. 12294 purports only to "suspend" the claims, not divest the federal court of "jurisdiction." As we read the Executive Order, those claims not within the jurisdiction of the Claims Tribunal will "revive" and become judicially enforceable in United States courts. This case, in short, illustrates the difference between modifying federal-court jurisdiction and directing the courts to apply a different rule of law. The President has . . . simply effected a change in the substantive law governing the lawsuit.

In light of all of the foregoing — the inferences to be drawn from the character of the legislation Congress has enacted in the area, such as the IEEPA and the Hostage Act, and from the history of acquiescence in executive claims settlement — we conclude that the President was authorized to suspend pending claims pursuant to Executive Order No. 12294. As Justice Frankfurter pointed out in *Youngstown*, 343 U.S., at 610-611, "a systematic, unbroken, executive practice, long pursued to the knowledge of the Congress and never before questioned . . . may be treated as a gloss on 'Executive Power' vested in the President by §1 of Art. II." Past practice does not, by itself, create power, but "long-continued practice, known to and acquiesced in by Congress, would raise a presumption that the [action] had been [taken] in pursuance of its consent. . . ." United States v. Midwest Oil Co., 236 U.S. 459,474 (1915). Such practice is present here and such a presumption is also appropriate. In light of the fact that Congress may be considered to have consented to the President's action in suspending claims, we cannot say that action exceeded the President's powers.

Our conclusion is buttressed by the fact that the means chosen by the President to settle the claims of American nationals provided an alternative forum, the Claims Tribunal, which is capable of providing meaningful relief. The Solicitor General also suggests that the provision of the Claims Tribunal will actually *enhance* the opportunity for claimants to recover their claims, in that the Agreement removes a number of jurisdictional and procedural impediments faced by claimants in United States courts.* Although being overly sanguine about the chances of United States claimants before the Claims Tribunal would require a degree of naiveté which should not be demanded even of judges, the Solicitor General's point cannot be discounted. Moreover, it is important to remember that we have already held that

*[In its contract Dames & Moore agreed to submit disputes to the courts of Iran. In such a case it was unclear whether it could take advantage of the arbitration in the Hague Tribunal. Dames & Moore argued that the contract, including the forum selection, was void.–Eds.]

the President has the *statutory* authority to nullify attachments and to transfer the assets out of the country. The President's power to do so does not depend on his provision of a forum whereby claimants can recover on those claims. The fact that the President has provided such a forum here means that the claimants are receiving something in return for the suspension of their claims, namely, access to an international tribunal before which they may well recover something on their claims. Because there does appear to be a real "settlement" here, this case is more easily analogized to the more traditional claim settlement cases of the past.

Just as importantly, Congress has not disapproved of the action taken here. Though Congress has held hearings on the Iranian Agreement itself, Congress has not enacted legislation, or even passed a resolution, indicating its displeasure with the Agreement. Quite the contrary, the relevant Senate Committee has stated that the establishment of the Tribunal is "of vital importance to the United States." S. Rep. No. 97-71, p.5 (1981). We are thus clearly not confronted with a situation in which Congress has in some way resisted the exercise of Presidential authority.

Finally, we re-emphasize the narrowness of our decision. We do not decide that the President possesses plenary power to settle claims, even as against foreign governmental entities. As the Court of Appeals for the First Circuit stressed, "[t]he sheer magnitude of such a power, considered against the background of the diversity and complexity of modern international trade, cautions against any broader construction of authority than is necessary." Chas. T. Main Int'l, Inc. v. Khuzestan Water & Power Authority, 651 F.2d, at 814. But where, as here, the settlement of claims has been determined to be a necessary incident to the resolution of a major foreign policy dispute between our country and another, and where, as here, we can conclude that Congress acquiesced in the President's action, we are not prepared to say that the President lacks the power to settle such claims.

V

We do not think it appropriate at the present time to address petitioner's contention that the suspension of claims, if authorized, would constitute a taking of property in violation of the Fifth Amendment to the United States Constitution in the absence of just compensation. Both petitioner and the Government concede that the question whether the suspension of the claims constitutes a taking is not ripe for review. . . .

. . . [T]o the extent petitioner believes it has suffered an unconstitutional taking by the suspension of the claims, we see no jurisdictional obstacle to an appropriate action in the United States Court of Claims under the Tucker Act.

The judgment of the District Court is accordingly affirmed, and the mandate shall issue forthwith.

[Concurring opinion of Justice Stevens and concurring and dissenting opinion of Justice Powell omitted.]

Notes and Questions

1. As noted earlier, presidential executive agreements generally deal with minor issues like postal agreements. However, presidential executive agreements can also deal with important international issues. As noted by the Supreme Court,

"[t]he Yalta and Potsdam Agreements envisioning dismantling of Germany's industrial assets, public and private, and the follow-up Paris Agreement aspiring to settle the claims of western nationals against the German Government and private agencies were made as executive agreements." Am. Ins. Assn. v. Garamendi, 539 U.S. 396, 416, n. 8 (2003).

2. What is the constitutional basis for the President to conclude presidential executive agreements? Does this power derive from the President's power to receive ambassadors? Or from the President's role as the head of the Executive Branch? Or from some other power? In *Pink*, the Court traced the President's authority to enter into the Litinov Assigment to his power in Article II of the Constitution to "receive Ambassadors and other public Ministers." Note at the end of the *Pink* excerpt that the Court observes: "A treaty is a 'Law of the Land' under the supremacy clause (Art. VI. Cl. 2) of the Constitution. Such international compacts and agreements as the Litvinov Assignment have a similar dignity."

3. Do you draw the same inference from the IEEPA and Hostage Act as the Court? Isn't the opposite inference equally possible? Is the Court's reliance on congressional acquiescence persuasive? In what did Congress acquiesce?

4. In which category of Jackson's concurrence in *Youngstown* do you place the *Dames & Moore* case? Do you agree with then-Professor Harold Hongju Koh that the approach in *Dames & Moore* "elevat[es] the president's power from the twilight zone—Jackson's category two—to its height in Jackson's category one" and "effectively follow[s] the dissenting view in *Youngstown*, which had converted legislative silence into consent, thereby delegating to the President authority that Congress itself had arguably withheld"? Koh, The National Security Constitution: Sharing Power After the Iran-Contra Affair 139 (1990).

5. Can a presidential executive agreement override prior federal legislation? Cf. United States v. Guy W. Capps, Inc., 204 F.2d 655, 659-660 (4th Cir. 1953) ("We think that whatever the power of the executive with respect to making executive trade agreements regulating foreign commerce in the absence of action by Congress, it is clear that the executive may not through entering into such an agreement avoid complying with a regulation prescribed by Congress."), aff'd on other grounds, 348 U.S. 296 (1955). As noted above, in *Belmont* and *Pink*, the U.S. Supreme Court concluded that a presidential executive agreement should override state law.

6. In what sense was the claim in *Dames & Moore* suspended? The Algiers Accords provided that "[t]he United States agrees to terminate all legal proceedings in United States courts involving claims of United States persons and institutions against Iran and its state enterprises." However, as the Court notes in *Dames & Moore*, the executive order implementing the Algiers Accords used the verb "suspend." Why the different language? Is the Supreme Court's explanation persuasive? After the Algiers Accords, was Dames & Moore's claim subject to a different rule of law, or simply a different tribunal, or both?

7. *Postscript.* Dames & Moore took its case to the Iran-United States Claims Tribunal, as required by the Algiers Accords. The Tribunal awarded Dames & Moore (a) $100,000, plus interest, against the Islamic Republic of Iran; and (b) $108,435, plus interest, against the National Iranian Gas Company. See Award No. 97-54-3. 4 Iran-US. C.T.R. 212 (1983).

8. Given your understanding now of the status under U.S. law of treaties and other international agreements, when should the President use the Article II treaty

form, as opposed to a congressional-executive agreement or a presidential executive agreement? Do you now believe that the factors in Circular 175 are helpful? For example, assume the President is about to sign a major agreement with Japan, the United Kingdom, Germany, France, Italy, and Canada regarding measures to stop North Korea and Iran from selling nuclear weapons materials to non-nuclear states. The agreement would include new intelligence sharing and proactive measures such as boarding freighters on the high seas and diverting aircraft of other countries. What type of international agreement should the President use under U.S. law? Would your answer to this question be different if the agreement were controversial? If the preventive measures might conflict with existing treaty obligations regarding aviation or the law of the sea? If quick implementation were important? If you were the White House counsel to the President rather than a senator from New York, or a congresswoman from California?

3. National Emergency Legislation

In the Iran hostage crisis the President attached or froze Iranian assets pursuant to a delegation of congressional authority under the International Emergency Economic Powers Act (IEEPA). The *Dames & Moore* opinion upheld the authority of the President to nullify previously issued attachments and to transfer the Iranian property back to Iran. Presidential authority under IEEPA can be vitally important to private entities that get caught up in the larger foreign policy picture.

Congress has legislated extensive powers to the President for use in a national emergency. Since 1976, the National Emergencies Act (NEA) has provided the procedures for declaring, conducting, and terminating emergencies. However, it provides no new authority to the President but leaves that to other legislation. In the international area, IEEPA is usually the statutory vehicle (in addition to the President's existing non-emergency powers) for major economic steps by the President during a declared national emergency. (The texts of the NEA and IEEPA are in the Documentary Supplement.)

IEEPA is designed to deal with "any unusual or extraordinary threat, which has its source in whole or substantial part outside the United States, to the [U.S.] national security, foreign policy, or economy." 50 U.S.C. §1701(e). If the President determines that such a threat exists, he can declare a national emergency under the NEA. IEEPA then authorizes him, pursuant to sweeping language in section 1702(a), to employ a very wide range of economic sanctions, such as cutting off exports or imports, or restricting private financial transactions. (Control over financial transactions was used to effectively restrict travel to or in another country until IEEPA was amended in 1994 to exempt financial transactions ordinarily incident to travel. There are a few other exceptions at section 1702(b).)

Before exercising these authorities, the President is directed "in every possible instance" to consult with Congress. Moreover, if he does use IEEPA, he must immediately make a report to Congress explaining his actions. Id. at §1703(a) and (b). The President can continue IEEPA sanctions until he terminates the emergency or unless Congress acts to terminate it by joint resolution. Alternatively, the emergency automatically lapses after one year if the President does not renew it.

The Past and Present Uses of IEEPA

Except for some restrictions against Cuba, which are based on the Trading with the Enemy Act (a statute which IEEPA replaced), IEEPA now provides the usual statutory basis for employing many economic tools during a declared national emergency. Presidents have increasingly resorted to the law.

Passed in 1977, IEEPA was not used until the 1979-1981 Iranian hostage crisis, discussed in *Dames & Moore* above. Receiving reports that the government of Iran was about to withdraw its billions of dollars on deposit in U.S. banks, President Carter declared a national emergency in November 1979 and, pursuant to IEEPA, blocked the transfer of all property of the Iranian government. The order froze about $12 billion of Iranian funds in U.S. banks or in the possession of U.S. corporations, whether located in the United States or abroad. IEEPA controls were later expanded to cut off almost all trade with Iran.

In 1981 President Carter and then President Reagan took a number of steps to implement the so-called Algiers Accords, which resulted in the release of the hostages and the termination of the U.S. sanctions. These included ordering the transfer of billions of dollars back to Iran or to trust funds and suspending claims against Iran that were pending in U.S. courts. All the Iranian sanctions and the actions to end them were upheld by U.S. courts under IEEPA, except that the Supreme Court in Dames & Moore v. Regan looked to additional authority to uphold the suspension of the claims then pending in U.S. courts.

On May 1, 1985, President Reagan declared a national emergency and ordered a number of actions against Nicaragua. These included a ban on the import of Nicaraguan goods; a ban on the export of all goods to Nicaragua not destined for the U.S.-backed Contras; and prohibitions on Nicaraguan vessels and air carriers entering the United States. President George H. W. Bush ended the IEEPA sanctions after the Sandinistas were defeated in elections in Nicaragua in March 1990.

President Reagan later imposed IEEPA sanctions against South Africa, Libya, and Panama. Presidents Bush and Clinton declared national emergencies in response to the Iraqi invasion of Kuwait and troubles in the former Yugoslavia, Haiti, and Angola. President Clinton also declared a national emergency and imposed sanctions with regard to Rwanda. And Presidents Reagan, Bush, and Clinton used IEEPA to continue U.S. export controls on dual-use items (i.e., items that could be used for both commercial and military purposes, such as high-powered computers and transport aircraft) when there were delays in Congress renewing the Export Administration Act.

President Clinton also started to use the IEEPA powers frequently to combat terrorism, international drug traffic, and the proliferation of weapons of mass destruction — sometimes in very focused ways against individuals and non-state entities. For example, in January 1995, he froze any assets in the United States, or in the control of U.S. persons, of designated terrorist organizations and prohibited any transaction or dealing by U.S. persons or within the United States of any interests in property with these groups. In October 1995, President Clinton applied similar restrictions against four foreign individuals designated as significant narcotics traffickers, and later added more individuals. In July 1998, he imposed a variety of economic sanctions against any foreign person whom the Secretary of State might designate as having materially contributed, or attempted to contribute, to the efforts of any foreign country or entity to develop weapons of mass destruction or missiles capable of delivering such weapons.

President George W. Bush continued the IEEPA sanctions existing at the start of his Administration — for example, against Iran, Iraq and Libya, as well as against designated terrorists, narcotics traffickers, and proliferators. Like his predecessors, he also used IEEPA to continue export controls when a congressionally passed export law lapsed in 2001. As discussed in Chapter 1.E., President Bush declared a new national emergency after the attacks of September 11 and froze the assets of, and imposed other financial sanctions, against Osama bin Laden, Al Qaeda, and other terrorists and terrorist organizations. The administration's expanding list of targeted individuals and other non-state entities reflected the increased use of selective sanctions.

In March 2003, President Bush also invoked a new IEEPA provision added after the attacks of September 11, 2001. Going beyond IEEPA's existing authorization to, among other steps, freeze foreign assets, the new provision authorizes the President to "confiscate any property" of any foreign person, entity, or country that has attacked the United States or that is engaged in armed hostilities with the United States. (Section 1702(a) (1) (C).) The provision also gives the President discretion on how to use the assets. After the United States and its coalition partners began hostilities against Iraq in March 2003, President Bush directed the confiscation of the approximately $1.7 billion in Iraqi assets that had been frozen before under IEEPA, mostly from the time of Iraq's invasion of Kuwait in 1990. Over the objections of some American plaintiffs who had obtained U.S. court judgments against Iraq but had not yet been able to collect, the Bush Administration transferred the confiscated assets to the Coalition Provisional Authority in Iraq to be used in the reconstruction and development of Iraq.

President Barak Obama has generally continued the existing national emergencies and IEEPA sanctions against specific countries and various individuals and groups such as terrorists. He has also declared new emergencies and imposed sanctions. For example, he declared a national emergency with regard to Somalia in April 2010 after the number of pirate attacks launched from the Somali coast quadrupled between 2007 and 2009. Also, guerrilla fighters in Somalia were openly receiving aid from Al Qaeda.

Notes and Questions

1. Are the IEEPA requirements of consulting with and reporting to Congress likely to have any effect on the President's decision making? How much consultation is required?

2. Have Presidents declared too many "national emergencies"? Are there any significant differences among the emergencies that have been declared?

3. Do you think a litigant could successfully challenge a President's determination that an "unusual and extraordinary threat" exists?

4. Should the President be required to obtain specific legislative approval, rather than be allowed to resort to IEEPA in specific emergencies? If so, how could one define them? If not, what are the effective limits on a President's use of IEEPA? For example, should the sanctions against Nicaragua in 1985 have required specific congressional approval? What about the 1995 sanctions against four foreign individuals designated as significant narcotics traffickers?

5. Are the termination provisions for national emergencies and IEEPA adequate? As noted above, the President can terminate the national emergency. Alternatively, it will automatically terminate in one year unless the President renews it, but renewal is a simple matter of publishing a brief notice in the Federal Register.

The National Emergency Act as passed had a third termination provision — by a concurrent resolution of Congress (which cannot be vetoed). This was effectively invalidated by the decisions of the U.S. Supreme Court striking down "legislative vetoes" such as this. See Immigration and Naturalization Service v. Chadha, 462 U.S. 919 (1983). Congress then amended the provision to provide instead for termination by a joint resolution. See 50 U.S.C. §1622 (Supp. III 1985). Since the President can veto a joint resolution, however, the practical effect of this amendment is that a declared national emergency can probably continue at the President's pleasure. (Congress would be unlikely to muster the two-thirds vote of both houses necessary to override the veto.)

Would it be a good idea to provide for automatic termination of a declared national emergency after, say, six months or a year? In other words, should the President be required to obtain the legislative support of Congress for continuing international economic measures initially imposed pursuant to IEEPA? Would this require the President to pursue policies that have public support? Would it unnecessarily bind the President's hands?

6. For additional discussion of U.S. laws concerning economic sanctions, particularly to advance international human rights objectives, see the materials and sources in Chapter 8.B.8.b. A list of all national emergencies declared between 1976 and 2007 appears in a periodically updated congressional report. Congressional Research Service, National Emergency Powers, 15-17 (August 2007). Additional and more recent information can be found on the Web site of the Department of Treasury, http://www.treasury.gov, under the listing for Treasury's Office of Foreign Asset Controls (OFAC), which administers the TWEA and IEEPA sanctions.

4. *Presidential Powers and the Global Struggle Against Terrorism*

After the terrorist attacks of September 11, 2001, besides invoking IEEPA, President George W. Bush actively asserted broad executive powers in several areas. As mentioned in the case study in Chapter 1, three days after the attacks, Congress passed the Authorization for Use of Military Force (AUMF) resolution, authorizing the President

> . . . [T]o use all necessary and appropriate force against those nations, organizations, or persons he determines planned, authorized, committed, or aided the terrorist attacks that occurred on September 11, 2001, or harbored such organizations or persons, in order to prevent any future acts of international terrorism against the United States by such nations, organizations or persons. (P.L. 107-40, 115 Stat 224)

President Bush signed the AUMF on September 18, 2001.

In October 2001, major military operations in Afghanistan began against Al Qaeda and the Taliban government that harbored and supported Al Qaeda. During the armed conflict, hundreds of people associated with the Taliban or Al Qaeda were detained. Many of these detainees were held at a prison facility at the U.S. naval base in Guantanamo Bay beginning in January 2002. The two cases that follow, Hamdi v. Rumsfeld and Hamdan v. Rumsfeld, arose out of detentions of Taliban and Al Qaeda detainees, respectively.

In *Hamdi,* Justice O'Connor (joined by Chief Justice Rehnquist, Justice Kennedy, and Justice Breyer) concluded that Congress authorized the detention of combatants in the narrow circumstances alleged in the case. Due process, however, required that a U.S. citizen held in the United States as an enemy combatant should be given a meaningful opportunity to contest the factual basis for that detention before a neutral decision maker. Justice Souter (joined by Justice Ginsburg) believed that the detention of this U.S. citizen (Yaser Esam Hamdi) was unauthorized, but they joined with the plurality to conclude that on remand Hamdi should have a meaningful opportunity to offer evidence that he is not an enemy combatant. Justice Scalia (joined by Justice Stevens) dissented, saying that only a suspension of the writ of habeas corpus, which had not occurred, could justify the indefinite detention of a citizen without charge. Justice Thomas also dissented, but for different reasons. He concluded that Congress had authorized the President in the AUMF to detain enemy combatants and that the President's determination that Hamdi was an enemy combatant was not subject to judicial review.

The discussion in the case specifically included an analysis of the AUMF and the allocation of powers among the President, Congress, and the courts.

Hamdi v. Rumsfeld

U.S. Supreme Court
542 U.S. 507 (2004)

Justice O'CONNOR announced the judgment of the Court and delivered an opinion, in which Chief Justice [REHNQUIST], Justice KENNEDY, and Justice BREYER join.

At this difficult time in our Nation's history, we are called upon to consider the legality of the Government's detention of a United States citizen on United States soil as an "enemy combatant" and to address the process that is constitutionally owed to one who seeks to challenge his classification as such. . . .

I

. . . This case arises out of the detention of a man whom the Government alleges took up arms with the Taliban during this conflict. His name is Yaser Esam Hamdi. Born an American citizen in Louisiana in 1980, Hamdi moved with his family to Saudi Arabia as a child. By 2001, the parties agree, he resided in Afghanistan. At some point that year, he was seized by members of the Northern Alliance, a coalition of military groups opposed to the Taliban government, and eventually was turned over to the United States military. The Government asserts that it initially detained and interrogated Hamdi in Afghanistan before transferring him to the United States Naval Base in Guantanamo Bay in January 2002. In April 2002, upon learning that Hamdi is an American citizen, authorities transferred him to a naval brig in Norfolk, Virginia, where he remained until a recent transfer to a brig in Charleston, South Carolina. The Government contends that Hamdi is an "enemy combatant," and that this status justifies holding him in the United States indefinitely—without formal charges or proceedings. . . .

[Hamdi's father brought a habeas corpus petition. A Defense Department official, Michael Mobbs, sent a declaration (the Mobbs Declaration) alleging various details regarding Hamdi's associations with the Taliban in Afghanistan and his surrendering of an assault rifle to the Northern Alliance. The District Court found the declaration, standing alone, did not support Hamdi's detention and ordered the Government to provide various materials for an *in camera* review. The U.S. Court of Appeals for the Fourth Circuit reversed the District Court's order, stressing that, because Hamdi was captured in an active combat zone, no factual inquiry was necessary. The appeals court ordered the habeas petition dismissed.]

II

The threshold question before us is whether the Executive has the authority to detain citizens who qualify as "enemy combatants." . . . [F]or purposes of this case, the "enemy combatant" that [the Government] is seeking to detain is an individual who, it alleges, was " 'part of or supporting forces hostile to the United States or coalition partners' " in Afghanistan and who " 'engaged in an armed conflict against the United States' " there. We therefore answer only the narrow question before us: whether the detention of citizens falling within that definition is authorized.

The Government maintains that no explicit congressional authorization is required, because the Executive possesses plenary authority to detain pursuant to Article II of the Constitution. We do not reach the question whether Article II provides such authority, however, because we agree with the Government's alternative position, that Congress has in fact authorized Hamdi's detention, through the AUMF.

Our analysis on that point . . . substantially overlaps with our analysis of Hamdi's principal argument for the illegality of his detention. He posits that his detention is forbidden by 18 U.S.C. §4001(a). Section 4001(a) states that "[n]o citizen shall be imprisoned or otherwise detained by the United States except pursuant to an Act of Congress." Congress passed §4001(a) in 1971 as part of a bill to repeal the Emergency Detention Act of 1950, which provided procedures for executive detention. . . . Congress was particularly concerned about the possibility that the [1950] Act could be used to reprise the Japanese internment camps of World War II.

The Government . . . maintains that §4001(a) is satisfied, because Hamdi is being detained "pursuant to an Act of Congress"—the AUMF. . . . [F]or the reasons that follow, we conclude that the AUMF is explicit congressional authorization for the detention of individuals in the narrow category we describe (assuming, without deciding, that such authorization is required), and that the AUMF satisfied §4001(a)'s requirement that a detention be "pursuant to an Act of Congress" (assuming, without deciding, that §4001(a) applies to military detentions).

The AUMF authorizes the President to use "all necessary and appropriate force" against "nations, organizations, or persons" associated with the September 11, 2001, terrorist attacks. There can be no doubt that individuals who fought against the United States in Afghanistan as part of the Taliban, an organization known to have supported the al Qaeda terrorist network responsible for those attacks, are individuals Congress sought to target in passing the AUMF. We conclude that detention of individuals falling into the limited category we are considering, for the duration of the particular conflict in which they were captured, is so fundamental and accepted an incident to war as to be an exercise of the "necessary and appropriate force" Congress has authorized the President to use.

The capture and detention of lawful combatants and the capture, detention, and trial of unlawful combatants, by "universal agreement and practice," are "important incident[s] of war." Ex parte Quirin, [317 U.S. 1, 28 (1947)]. The purpose of detention is to prevent captured individuals from returning to the field of battle and taking up arms once again.

There is no bar to this Nation's holding one of its own citizens as an enemy combatant. In *Quirin*, one of the detainees, Haupt, alleged that he was a naturalized United States citizen. We held that "[c]itizens who associate themselves with the military arm of the enemy government, and with its aid, guidance and direction enter this country bent on hostile acts, are enemy belligerents within the meaning of . . . the law of war." . . . A citizen, no less than an alien, can be "part of or supporting forces hostile to the United States or coalition partners" and "engaged in an armed conflict against the United States;" such a citizen, if released, would pose the same threat of returning to the front during the ongoing conflict.

In light of these principles, it is of no moment that the AUMF does not use specific language of detention. Because detention to prevent a combatant's return to the battlefield is a fundamental incident of waging war, in permitting the use of "necessary and appropriate force," Congress has clearly and unmistakably authorized detention in the narrow circumstances considered here.

Hamdi objects, nevertheless, that Congress has not authorized the *indefinite* detention to which he is now subject. . . . We recognize that the national security underpinnings of the "war on terror," although crucially important, are broad and malleable. As the Government concedes, "given its unconventional nature, the current conflict is unlikely to end with a formal cease-fire agreement." The prospect Hamdi raises is therefore not far-fetched. If the Government does not consider this unconventional war won for two generations, and if it maintains during that time that Hamdi might, if released, rejoin forces fighting against the United States, then the position it has taken throughout the litigation of this case suggests that Hamdi's detention could last for the rest of his life.

It is a clearly established principle of the law of war that detention may last no longer than active hostilities. See Article 118 of the Geneva Convention (III) Relative to the Treatment of Prisoners of War, Aug. 12, 1949. See also . . . Hague Convention (IV), *supra*, Oct. 18, 1907, 36 Stat 2301 ("conclusion of peace" (Art. 20)); Geneva Convention, *supra*, July 27, 1929, 47 Stat 2055 (repatriation should be accomplished with the least possible delay after conclusion of peace (Art. 75)).

Hamdi contends that the AUMF does not authorize indefinite or perpetual detention. Certainly, we agree that indefinite detention for the purpose of interrogation is not authorized. Further, we understand Congress' grant of authority for the use of "necessary and appropriate force" to include the authority to detain for the duration of the relevant conflict, and our understanding is based on longstanding law-of-war principles. If the practical circumstances of a given conflict are entirely unlike those of the conflicts that informed the development of the law of war, that understanding may unravel. But that is not the situation we face as of this date. Active combat operations against Taliban fighters apparently are ongoing in Afghanistan. The United States may detain, for the duration of these hostilities, individuals legitimately determined to be Taliban combatants who "engaged in an armed conflict against the United States." If the record establishes that United States troops are still involved in active combat in Afghanistan, those detentions are part of the exercise of "necessary and appropriate force," and therefore are authorized by the AUMF. . . .

III . . .

[The Government argues] that further factual exploration [about Hamdi's detention] is unwarranted and inappropriate in light of the extraordinary constitutional interests at stake. . . . At most, the Government argues, courts should review its determination that a citizen is an enemy combatant under a very deferential "some evidence" standard. Under this review, a court would assume the accuracy of the Government's articulated basis for Hamdi's detention, as set forth in the Mobbs Declaration, and assess only whether that articulated basis was a legitimate one.

In response, Hamdi emphasizes that this Court consistently has recognized that an individual challenging his detention may not be held at the will of the Executive without recourse to some proceeding before a neutral tribunal to determine whether the Executive's asserted justifications for that detention have basis in fact and warrant in law. . . .

[After applying a balancing test between Hamdi's interests and the Government's interests, the plurality concluded that Hamdi, as an American citizen, was entitled to "receive notice of the factual basis for his classification, and a fair opportunity to rebut the Government's factual assertions before a neutral decisionmaker."]

In so holding, we necessarily reject the Government's assertion that separation of powers principles mandate a heavily circumscribed role for the courts in such circumstances. Indeed, the position that the courts must forgo any examination of the individual case and focus exclusively on the legality of the broader detention scheme cannot be mandated by any reasonable view of separation of powers, as this approach serves only to *condense* power into a single branch of government. We have long since made clear that a state of war is not a blank check for the President when it comes to the rights of the Nation's citizens. *Youngstown Sheet & Tube,* 343 U.S., at 587. Whatever power the United States Constitution envisions for the Executive in its exchanges with other nations or with enemy organizations in times of conflict, it most assuredly envisions a role for all three branches when individual liberties are at stake. . . .

The judgment of the United States Court of Appeals for the Fourth Circuit is vacated, and the case is remanded for further proceedings. . . .

Justice SOUTER, with whom Justice GINSBURG joins, concurring in part, dissenting in part, and concurring in the judgment.

. . . The plurality . . . accept[s] the Government's position that if Hamdi's designation as an enemy combatant is correct, his detention (at least as to some period) is authorized by an Act of Congress as required by §4001(a), that is, by the Authorization for Use of Military Force (hereinafter Force Resolution). . . . I disagree and respectfully dissent. The Government has failed to demonstrate that the Force Resolution authorizes the detention complained of here even on the facts the Government claims. If the Government raises nothing further than the record now shows, the Non-Detention Act entitles Hamdi to be released. . . .

[Justice Souter begins with the premise that an explicit congressional authorization to detain should be required to override §4001(a).]

III

Under this principle of reading §4001(a) robustly to require a clear statement of authorization to detain, none of the Government's arguments suffices to justify Hamdi's detention. . . .

. . . Since the Force Resolution was adopted one week after the attacks of September 11, 2001, it naturally speaks with some generality, but its focus is clear, and that is on the use of military power. It is fairly read to authorize the use of armies and weapons, whether against other armies or individual terrorists. But . . . it never so much as uses the word detention, and there is no reason to think Congress might have perceived any need to augment Executive power to deal with dangerous citizens within the United States, given the well-stocked statutory arsenal of defined criminal offenses covering the gamut of actions that a citizen sympathetic to terrorists might commit. . . .

. . . [I]t is instructive to recall Justice Jackson's observation that the President is not Commander in Chief of the country, only of the military. Youngstown Sheet & Tube Co. v. Sawyer, 343 U.S. 579, 643-644 (1952) (concurring opinion); see also id., at 637-638 (Presidential authority is "at its lowest ebb" where the President acts contrary to congressional will). . . .

[Justice Scalia, joined by Justice Stevens, dissented, essentially stating that only a suspension of the writ of habeas corpus, which had not occurred, could justify the indefinite detention of a citizen without being charged.]

Justice Thomas, dissenting.

The Executive Branch, acting pursuant to the powers vested in the President by the Constitution and with explicit congressional approval, has determined that Yaser Hamdi is an enemy combatant and should be detained. This detention falls squarely within the Federal Government's war powers, and we lack the expertise and capacity to second-guess that decision. . . .

Although the President very well may have inherent authority to detain those arrayed against our troops, I agree with the plurality that we need not decide that question because Congress has authorized the President to do so. [He specifically cited and discussed the AUMF.]

Accordingly, the President's action here is "supported by the strongest of presumptions and the widest latitude of judicial interpretation." *Dames & Moore*, 453 U.S., at 668 (internal quotation marks omitted). . . .

In *Hamdan* below, the U.S. Supreme Court decided, by a 5-3 vote (with Chief Justice Roberts not participating), that the military commissions established by President George W. Bush were not expressly authorized by any congressional Act. The opinions include considerable discussion of the AUMF, the Geneva Conventions, and the allocation of powers among the three U.S. branches of government.

Hamdan v. Rumsfeld

U.S. Supreme Court
548 U.S. 557 (2006)

Justice STEVENS announced the judgment of the Court and delivered the opinion of the Court with respect to Parts I through IV, Parts VI through VI-D-iii, Part VI-D-v, and Part VII, and an opinion with respect to Parts V and VI-D-iv, in which Justice SOUTER, Justice GINSBURG, and Justice BREYER join.

Petitioner Salim Ahmed Hamdan, a Yemeni national, is in custody at an American prison in Guantanamo Bay, Cuba. In November 2001, during hostilities between the United States and the Taliban (which then governed Afghanistan), Hamdan was captured by militia forces and turned over to the U.S. military. In June 2002, he was transported to Guantanamo Bay. Over a year later, the President deemed him eligible for trial by military commission for then-unspecified crimes. After another year had passed, Hamdan was charged with one count of conspiracy "to commit . . . offenses triable by military commission."

Hamdan filed petitions for writs of habeas corpus and mandamus to challenge the Executive Branch's intended means of prosecuting this charge. He concedes that a court-martial constituted in accordance with the Uniform Code of Military Justice (UCMJ), 10 U.S.C. §801 et seq., would have authority to try him. His objection is that the military commission the President has convened lacks such authority . . .

I . . .

On November 13, 2001, . . . the President issued a comprehensive military order intended to govern the "Detention, Treatment, and Trial of Certain Non-Citizens in the War Against Terrorism" (hereinafter November 13 Order or Order). Those subject to the November 13 Order include any noncitizen for whom the President determines "there is reason to believe" that he or she (1) "is or was" a member of al Qaeda or (2) has engaged or participated in terrorist activities aimed at or harmful to the United States. Any such individual "shall, when tried, be tried by military commission for any and all offenses triable by military commission that such individual is alleged to have committed, and may be punished in accordance with the penalties provided under applicable law, including imprisonment or death." . . .

On July 3, 2003, the President announced his determination that Hamdan and five other detainees at Guantanamo Bay were subject to the November 13 Order and thus triable by military commission. [Hamdan was charged with conspiring with

Al Qaeda members to commit offenses triable by military commission. "Overt acts" that Hamdan allegedly committed as part of this conspiracy included serving as Osama bin Laden's "bodyguard and personal driver" and transporting Al Qaeda weapons.]

IV . . .

The Constitution makes the President the "Commander in Chief" of the Armed Forces, Art. II, §2, cl. 1, but vests in Congress the powers to "declare War . . . and make Rules concerning Captures on Land and Water," Art. I, §8, cl. 11, to "raise and support Armies," id., cl. 12, to "define and punish . . . Offences against the Law of Nations," id., cl. 10, and "To make Rules for the Government and Regulation of the land and naval Forces," id., cl. 14. The interplay between these powers was described by Chief Justice Chase in the seminal case of Ex parte Milligan:

> "The power to make the necessary laws is in Congress; the power to execute in the President. Both powers imply many subordinate and auxiliary powers. Each includes all authorities essential to its due exercise. But neither can the President, in war more than in peace, intrude upon the proper authority of Congress, nor Congress upon the proper authority of the President. . . . Congress cannot direct the conduct of campaigns, nor can the President, or any commander under him, without the sanction of Congress, institute tribunals for the trial and punishment of offences, either of soldiers or civilians, unless in cases of a controlling necessity, which justifies what it compels, or at least insures acts of indemnity from the justice of the legislature." 71 U.S. 2, 139-140.

Whether Chief Justice Chase was correct in suggesting that the President may constitutionally convene military commissions "without the sanction of Congress" in cases of "controlling necessity" is a question this Court has not answered definitively, and need not answer today. For we held in *Quirin* that Congress had, through Article of War 15,* sanctioned the use of military commissions in such circumstances. 317 U.S., at 28. Article 21 of the UCMJ [Uniform Code of Military Justice, which was enacted by Congress], the language of which is substantially identical to the old Article 15 . . . reads as follows:

> "Jurisdiction of courts-martial not exclusive.
>
> "The provisions of this code conferring jurisdiction upon courts-martial shall not be construed as depriving military commissions, provost courts, or other military tribunals of concurrent jurisdiction in respect of offenders or offenses that by statute or by the law of war may be tried by such military commissions, provost courts, or other military tribunals."

. . . Contrary to the Government's assertion, . . . even *Quirin* did not view the authorization as a sweeping mandate for the President to "invoke military commissions when he deems them necessary." Rather, the *Quirin* Court recognized that Congress had simply preserved what power, under the Constitution and the

*[The Articles of War were a legislative code defining crimes applicable to the U.S. armed forces. They were the forerunner to the Uniform Code of Military Justice (UCMJ).–Eds.]

common law of war, the President had had before 1916 to convene military commissions—with the express condition that the President and those under his command comply with the law of war.[23] . . .

The Government would have us . . . find in either the AUMF or the [2005 Detainee Treatment Act (DTA), which vests exclusive jurisdiction to determine the validity of final decisions of the military commissions in the U. S. Court of Appeals for the District of Columbia Circuit,] specific, overriding authorization for the very commission that has been convened to try Hamdan. Neither of these congressional Acts, however, expands the President's authority to convene military commissions. First, while we assume that the AUMF activated the President's war powers, see Hamdi v. Rumsfeld, 542 U.S. 507 (2004) (plurality opinion), and that those powers include the authority to convene military commissions in appropriate circumstances, there is nothing in the text or legislative history of the AUMF even hinting that Congress intended to expand or alter the authorization set forth in Article 21 of the UCMJ.

Likewise, the DTA cannot be read to authorize this commission. Although the DTA, unlike either Article 21 or the AUMF, was enacted after the President had convened Hamdan's commission, it contains no language authorizing that tribunal or any other at Guantanamo Bay. The DTA obviously "recognizes" the existence of the Guantanamo Bay commissions in the weakest sense, because it references some of the military orders governing them and creates limited judicial review of their "final decisions." But the statute also pointedly reserves judgment on whether "the Constitution and laws of the United States are applicable" in reviewing such decisions and whether, if they are, the "standards and procedures" used to try Hamdan and other detainees actually violate the "Constitution and laws."

Together, the UCMJ, the AUMF, and the DTA at most acknowledge a general Presidential authority to convene military commissions in circumstances where justified under the "Constitution and laws," including the law of war. Absent a more specific congressional authorization, the task of this Court is . . . to decide whether Hamdan's military commission is so justified. It is to that inquiry we now turn.

V

[A plurality of the Court concluded that the charge against Hamdan of conspiracy "to commit . . . offenses triable by military commission" was not itself a violation of the common law of war and hence was not triable by a military commission.]

VI

Whether or not the Government has charged Hamdan with an offense against the law of war cognizable by military commission, the commission lacks power to proceed. The UCMJ conditions the President's use of military commissions on compliance not only with the American common law of war, but also with the rest of the

23. Whether or not the President has independent power, absent congressional authorization, to convene military commissions, he may not disregard limitations that Congress has, in proper exercise of its own war powers, placed on his powers. See Youngstown Sheet & Tube Co. v. Sawyer, 343 U.S. 579, 637 (1952) (Jackson, J., concurring). The Government does not argue otherwise.

UCMJ itself, insofar as applicable, and with the "rules and precepts of the law of nations," — including, *inter alia*, the four Geneva Conventions signed in 1949. The procedures that the Government has decreed will govern Hamdan's trial by commission violate these laws. . . .

[Under the commission procedures, the defendant and his civilian counsel may be excluded from closed sessions of the trial, and *any* evidence could be admitted if the presiding officer concluded that the evidence would have probative value to a reasonable person, including hearsay evidence, evidence obtained by coercion, and unsworn testimony. The UCMJ §836 provides that the procedures of military commissions may only deviate from the uniform procedures for courts-martial if it is impracticable to apply the rules for courts-martial. The Court held that "[n]othing in the record before us demonstrates that it would be impracticable to apply court-martial rules in this case," including the right of the defendant to be present. Thus, the military commission's procedures did not satisfy the requirements for deviation from the uniform procedures.]

D

The procedures adopted to try Hamdan also violate the Geneva Conventions. . . .

i

[The opinion assumes that the 1949 Geneva Conventions were non-self-executing and, "absent some other provision of law, preclude[d] Hamdan's invocation" of the Conventions' provisions] as an independent source of law binding the Government's actions and furnishing petitioner with any enforceable right. [However, the opinion notes that the Conventions' provisions are] part of the law of war. And compliance with the law of war is the condition upon which the authority set forth in Article 21 is granted.

ii

. . . [T]here is at least one provision of the Geneva Conventions that applies here even if the relevant conflict is not one between signatories. Article 3, often referred to as Common Article 3 because . . . it appears in all four Geneva Conventions, provides that in a "conflict not of an international character occurring in the territory of one of the High Contracting Parties, each Party to the conflict shall be bound to apply, as a minimum," certain provisions protecting "persons taking no active part in the hostilities, including members of armed forces who have laid down their arms and those placed *hors de combat* by . . . detention." One such provision prohibits "the passing of sentences and the carrying out of executions without previous judgment pronounced by a regularly constitute court affording all the judicial guarantees which are recognized as indispensable by civilized peoples." . . .

iii

Common Article 3 . . . requires that Hamdan be tried by a "regularly constituted court affording all the judicial guarantees, which are recognized as indispensable by civilized peoples." . . .

. . . At a minimum, a military commission "can be 'regularly constituted' by the standards of our military justice system only if some practical need explains deviations from court-martial practice." As we have explained, see Part VI-C, *supra*, no such need has been demonstrated here.

iv [representing the views of four Justices and not concurred in by Justice KENNEDY]

Inextricably intertwined with the question of regular constitution is the evaluation of the procedures governing the tribunal and whether they afford "all the judicial guarantees which are recognized as indispensable by civilized peoples [within the meaning of Common Article 3 of the Geneva Conventions]." . . .

We agree with Justice Kennedy that the procedures adopted to try Hamdan deviated from those governing courts-martial in ways not justified by any "evident practical need," and for that reason, at least, fail to afford the requisite guarantees [under the Uniform Code of Military Justice]. We add only that, as noted in Part VI-A, *supra*, various provisions of Commission Order No. 1 dispense with the principles, articulated in Article 75 [of Protocol I Additional to the Conventions of 1949] and indisputably part of the customary international law, that an accused must, absent disruptive conduct or consent, be present for his trial and must be privy to the evidence against him. That the Government has a compelling interest in denying Hamdan access to certain sensitive information is not doubted. But, at least absent express statutory provision to the contrary, information used to convict a person of a crime must be disclosed to him.

v

Common Article 3 obviously tolerates a great degree of flexibility in trying individuals captured during an armed conflict; its requirements are general ones, crafted to accommodate a wide variety of legal systems. But *requirements* they are nonetheless. The commission that the President has convened to try Hamdan does not meet those requirements.

VII

We have assumed, as we must, that the allegations made in the Government's charge against Hamdan are true. We have assume, moreover, that the truth of the message implicit in that charge–viz., that Hamdan is a dangerous individual whose beliefs, if acted upon, would cause great harm and even death to innocent civilians, and who would act upon those beliefs if given the opportunity. It bears emphasizing that Hamdan does not challenge, and we do not today address, the Government's power to detain him for the duration of active hostilities in order to prevent such harm. But in undertaking to try Hamdan and subject him to criminal punishment, the Executive is bound to comply with the Rule of Law that prevails in this jurisdiction.

The judgment of the Court of Appeals is reversed, and the case is remanded for further proceedings. . . .

THE CHIEF JUSTICE took no part in the consideration or decision of this case.

Justice BREYER, with whom Justice KENNEDY, Justice SOUTER, and Justice GINSBURG join, concurring.

. . . The Court's conclusion ultimately rests upon a single ground: Congress has not issued the Executive a "blank check." Cf. Hamdi v. Rumsfeld, 542 U.S. 507, 536 (2004) (plurality opinion). Indeed, Congress has denied the President the legislative authority to create military commissions of the kind at issue here. Nothing prevents the President from returning to Congress to seek the authority he believes necessary. . . .

Justice KENNEDY, with whom Justice SOUTER, Justice GINSBURG, and Justice BREYER join as to Parts I and II, concurring in part.

[The President's Order No. 1] exceeds limits that certain statutes, duly enacted by Congress, have placed on the President's authority to convene military courts. This is not a case, then, where the Executive can assert some unilateral authority to fill a void left by congressional inaction. . . .

I

Trial by military commission raises separation-of-powers concerns of the highest order. Located with a single branch, these courts carry the risk that offenses will be defined, prosecuted, and adjudicated by executive officials without independent review. Concentration of power puts personal liberty in peril of arbitrary action by officials, an incursion the Constitution's three-part system is designed to avoid. . . .

The proper framework for assessing whether Executive actions are authorized is the three-part scheme used by Justice Jackson in his opinion in Youngstown Sheet & Tube Co. v. Sawyer, 343 U.S. 579 (1952). "When the President acts pursuant to an express or implied authorization of Congress, his authority is at its maximum, for it includes all that he possesses in his own right plus all that Congress can delegate." Id., at 635. "When the President acts in absence of either a congressional grant or denial of authority, he can only rely upon his own independent powers, but there is a zone of twilight in which he and Congress may have concurrent authority, or in which its distribution is uncertain." Id., at 637. And "when the President takes measures incompatible with the expressed or implied will of Congress, his power is at its lowest ebb." Ibid.

In this case, . . . the President has acted in a field with a history of congressional participation and regulation. In the Uniform Code of Military Justice . . . , Congress has set forth governing principles for military courts. The UCMJ as a whole establishes an intricate system of military justice. It authorizes courts-martial in various forms. . . . While these laws provide authority for certain forms of military courts, they also impose limitations, at least two of which control this case. If the President has exceeded these limits, this becomes a case of conflict between Presidential and congressional action — a case within Justice Jackson's third category, not the second or first.

One limit on the President's authority is contained in §836 of the UCMJ. . . . [That section includes the requirement that] "insofar as practicable" all rules . . . must be the same for military commissions as for courts-martial unless such uniformity is impracticable. . . .

[Another limit appears in Article 21 (10 U.S.C. §821), which] . . . extends only to "offenders or offenses" that "by statute or by law of war may be tried by" such military commissions. The Government does not claim to base the charges against Hamdan on a statute; instead it invokes the law of war. That law, as the Court explained in *Ex parte* Quirin, derives from "rules and precepts of the law of nations"; it is the body of international law governing armed conflict. If the military commission at issue is illegal under the law of war, then an offender cannot be tried "by the law of war" before that commission.

The Court is correct to concentrate on one provision of the law of war that is applicable to our Nation's armed conflict with al Qaeda in Afghanistan and, as a result, to the use of a military commission to try Hamdan. That provision is Common Article 3. . . . By Act of Congress, moreover, violations of Common Article 3 are considered "war crimes," punishable as federal offenses, when committed by or against United States nationals and military personnel. See 18 U.S.C. §2441.[1]

There should be no doubt, then, that Common Article 3 is part of the law of war as that term is used in §821. . . .

Assuming the President has authority to establish a special military commission to try Hamdan, the commission must satisfy Common Article 3's requirement of a "regularly constituted court affording all the judicial guarantees which are recognized as indispensable by civilized peoples." . . . The Court correctly concludes that the military commission here does not comply with this provision. . . .

II . . .

[Because of its structure,] Hamdan's military commission exceeds the bounds Congress has placed on the President's authority in §§836 and 821 of the UCMJ. Because Congress has prescribed these limits, Congress can change them, requiring a new analysis consistent with the Constitution and other governing laws. At this time, however, we must apply the standards Congress has provided. By those standards the military commission is deficient. . . .

[Justice SCALIA, joined by Justice THOMAS and Justice ALITO, dissented on the grounds that the Court should not have jurisdiction over the case because of the Detainee Treatment Act (DTA).]

Justice THOMAS, with whom Justice SCALIA joins, and with whom Justice ALITO joins in all but Parts I, II-C-1, and III-B-2, dissenting. . . .

. . . [T]he President's decision to try Hamdan before a military commission for his involvement with al Qaeda is entitled to a heavy measure of deference. In the present conflict, Congress has authorized the President "to use all necessary and appropriate force against those nations, organizations, or persons *he determines* planned, authorized, committed, or aided the terrorist attacks that occurred on September 11, 2001 . . . in order to prevent any future acts of international terrorism against the United States by such nations, organizations or persons."[AUMF]

1. [Section 2441 provided at this time, in relevant part:

§2441. War crimes

(a) Offense. Whoever, whether inside or outside the United States, commits a war crime, in any of the circumstances described in subsection (b), shall be fined under this title or imprisoned for life or any terms of years, or both, and if death results to the victim, shall also be subject to the penalty of death.

(b) Circumstances. The circumstances referred to in subsection (a) are that the person committing such war crime or the victims of such war crime is a member of the Armed Forces of the United States or a national of the United States. . . .

(c) Definition. As used in this section the term "war crime" means any conduct— . . .

(3) which constitutes a violation of common Article 3 of the international conventions signed at Geneva, 12 August 1949 . . . –EDS.]

(emphasis added). As a plurality of the Court observed in *Hamdi*, the "capture, detention, and *trial* of unlawful combatants, by 'universal agreement and practice,' are 'important incidents of war,'" *Hamdi*, 542 U.S., at 518 (quoting *Quirin*, supra, at 28, 30; emphasis added), and are therefore "an exercise of the 'necessary and appropriate force' Congress has authorized the President to use." *Hamdi*, 542 U.S., at 518; id., at 587 (THOMAS, J., dissenting). . . .

Although the Court concedes the legitimacy of the President's use of military commissions in certain circumstances, it suggests that the AUMF has no bearing on the scope of the President's power to utilize military commissions in the present conflict. Instead, the Court determines the scope of this power based exclusively on Article 21 of the Uniform Code of Military Justice. . . . Nothing in the language of Article 21, however, suggests that it outlines the entire reach of congressional authorization of military commissions in all conflicts. . . . Indeed, consistent with *Hamdi*'s conclusion that the AUMF itself authorizes the trial of unlawful combatants, the original sanction for military commissions historically derived from congressional authorization of "the initiation of war" with its attendant authorization of "the employment of all necessary and proper agencies for its due prosecution." Accordingly, congressional authorization for military commissions pertaining to the instant conflict derives not only from Article 21 of the UCMJ, but also from the more recent, and broader, authorization contained in the AUMF.[2]

I note the Court's error respecting the AUMF . . . to emphasize the complete congressional sanction of the President's exercise of his commander-in-chief authority to conduct the present war. In such circumstances, . . . our duty to defer to the Executive's military and foreign policy judgment is at its zenith. . . .

[Justice ALITO, joined in part by Justices SCALIA and THOMAS, dissented on the grounds that the military commission was "a regularly constituted court" satisfying the requirements of Common Article 3, interpreting the term to mean "a court that has been appointed, set up, or established in accordance with the domestic law of the appointing country." Unlike the majority, Justice Alito did not regard compliance with the procedures of the UCMJ as requisite for a "regularly constituted court" and regarded the military commission's procedures as adequate to guarantee against summary justice.]

Notes and Questions

1. Did the U.S. Supreme Court treat the AUMF differently in *Hamdi* and *Hamdan*? Compare these opinions with the three categories of presidential action identified in Justice Jackson's concurrence in *Youngstown* and reiterated in Justice Kennedy's concurrence in *Hamdan*. In both cases, the President's actions may run counter to a preexisting statute: the President's detention of Hamdi appears contrary to section 4001(a), and the President's creation of the military commission to try Hamdan did not satisfy the standards set forth in the UCMJ. However, the four-Justice *Hamdi* plurality, plus Justice Thomas in his dissenting opinion, found that

2. Although the President very well may have inherent authority to try unlawful combatants for violations of the law of war before military commissions, we need not decide that question because Congress has authorized the President to do so.

the AUMF authorized Hamdi's detention, thus placing the President's actions in Justice Jackson's first category, whereas the *Hamdan* majority found that the AUMF did not authorize military commissions, thus placing the President's action in Justice Jackson's third category. What does this different treatment suggest about the scope of the AUMF?

2. *The independent constitutional authority of the President.* Both *Hamdi* and *Hamdan* avoid deciding the issue of whether the President could conduct the actions at issue on the basis of his independent, or plenary, constitutional authority under Article II. Recall the provisions of Article II listed previously in this chapter. Are some (or all) of these presidential powers implicated in the struggle against terrorism? If so, how? How does the Commander-in-Chief power relate to the AUMF? What does footnote 23 of the Court's opinion in *Hamdan* (which represented the views of five Justices in that section) suggest about the limits of these independent constitutional powers and, more generally, about the Court's attitude toward the assertion of broad executive power in the global war on terror?

3. *Geneva Conventions.* In *Hamdan,* does the Court's opinion decide whether or not the Geneva Conventions, or any part of them, are self-executing and provide an individual with enforceable rights in the U.S. courts? (See, for example, the Court's opinion at VI.D.i.) Is Common Article 3 made a part of U.S. law by virtue of the provisions of other U.S. laws (e.g., UCMJ Article 21 and 18 U.S.C. §2441)?

4. *Postscript for Hamdi.* Yaser Hamdi never received his hearing. Instead, he was released in October 2004 and deported to Saudi Arabia, on the condition that he renounce his U.S. citizenship; never travel to Afghanistan, Iraq, Israel, Pakistan, Syria, the West Bank, or Gaza; and report any intent to travel outside Saudi Arabia for the next 15 years.

5. *Postscript for the military commissions (2006-2008).* Soon after the *Hamdan* decision, the Bush Administration acknowledged the Court's holding that Common Article 3's requirements applied to the Guantanamo detainees, as well as people detained and interrogated in CIA custody. The Bush Administration also called for legislation to allow the military commissions to proceed. In September 2006, with mid-term elections approaching, Congress passed the Military Commissions Act of 2006 (MCA), Pub. L. No. 109-366, 120 Stat. 2600. The Act provided congressional approval for the creation of military commissions that provided more due process protections than the commissions created earlier by President Bush's Executive Order. The new commissions, however, would not provide all the protections of a military court-martial under the Uniform Code of Military Justice or a criminal trial in a U.S. district court. The Act also clarified the interrogation techniques that may be used on terrorism suspects considered "unlawful enemy combatants," who are granted fewer protections than are prisoners of war. Further, the Act specified that, "[a]s provided by the Constitution and by this section [Section 6], the President has the authority for the United States to interpret the meaning and application of the Geneva Conventions and to promulgate higher standards and administrative regulations for violations of treaty obligations. . . ."

Critics of the MCA raised a number of objections that quickly were reflected in litigation. Especially serious constitutional questions were raised about Section 7(a) of the MCA which provided, in part, that: "No court, justice, or judge shall have jurisdiction to hear or consider an application for a writ of habeas corpus filed by or on behalf of an alien detained by the United States who has been determined by the United States to have been properly detained as an enemy combatant or is awaiting such determination." Article I, Section 9 (2) of the Constitution provides, however, that: "The privilege of the Writ of Habeas Corpus shall not be suspended, unless when in Cases of Rebellion or Invasion the pubic Safety may require it."

6. *Boumediene v. Bush, 553 U.S. 73 (2008) and beyond.* In this case, the U.S. Supreme Court in a strongly divided 5-4 decision ruled that Section 7 of the MCA operated as an unconstitutional suspension of the writ of habeas corpus against petitioners who had been designated as enemy combatants and were located at Guantanamo Bay. The Court's majority (in an opinion by Justice Kennedy) found that the Detainee Treatment Act's procedures for reviewing detainees' status were not an adequate and effective substitute for the habeas writ.

To come to this conclusion, the Court needed to address the threshold question whether petitioners were barred from seeking the writ or invoking the protection of the U.S. Constitution's Suspension Clause because of their physical location at Guantanamo Bay. The Court recognized that Guantanamo Bay was not formally part of the United States. Although Cuba retained "ultimate sovereignty," the United States exercised "complete jurisdiction and control." The Court considered that:

> [A]t least three factors are relevant in determining the reach of the Suspension Clause: (1) the citizenship and status of the detainee and the adequacy of the process through which that status determination was made; (2) the nature of the sites where apprehension and then detention took place; and (3) the practical obstacles inherent in resolving the prisoner's entitlement to the writ." Id. at 766.

Applying those factors, the Court concluded that the Suspension Clause had full effect at Guantanamo Bay.

In 2009, Congress enacted a new version of the MCA. Among other provisions, it included a new definition that authorized the trial of "unprivileged enemy belligerents." These were persons who "purposefully and materially supported hostilities against the United States or its coalition partners."

In 2010 a Guantanamo detainee's habeas petition that a U.S. district court had promptly revived after *Boumediene* reached the D.C. Circuit of Appeals. The district court had created several procedures to handle the difficult nature of a trial before a military commission, and it had ultimately upheld the detention of Ghaleb Nassar Al-Bihani. Al-Bihani challenged the sufficiency of these procedures. The D.C. Circuit affirmed the lower court's decision and in doing so clarified the definition of certain terms in the AUMF and MCA (as amended in 2009). Al-Bihani v. Obama, 590 F.3d 866, 871 (D.C. Cir. 2010).

Also, in 2010, the D.C. Circuit considered the habeas corpus petitions of three military detainees held by the United States at Bagram Air Force Base in Afghanistan. Applying the factors listed in *Boumediene,* the court in Al Maqaleh v. Gates held that the jurisdiction of the courts to afford habeas corpus relief or the protection of the Suspension Clause did not extend to aliens detained in the Bagram facility in the Afghan theater of war. Although the citizenship of the detainees, who were Yemeni and Tunisian nationals, weighed in favor of finding jurisdiction over the petitioners' claims, the court held that the site of the military base and the practical obstacles to extending habeas review to a theater of war weighed "overwhelmingly" in favor of dismissing the claims. 605 F.3d 84. 97 (D.C. Cir. 2010).

7. *The 2002 "torture memo."* An August 1, 2002 memorandum from former U.S. Assistant Attorney General Jay S. Bybee to former Counsel to the President Alberto R. Gonzales examined the standards for interrogation under the statute implementing the Convention Against Torture and Other Cruel, Inhuman and Degrading Treatment or Punishment, which the United States had ratified. The memorandum interpreted 18 U.S.C. §2340 to mean that, for an act to constitute torture,

> it must inflict pain that is difficult to endure. . . . Where the pain is physical, it must be of an intensity akin to that which accompanies serious physical injury, such as death or organ failure. Severe mental pain requires suffering not just at the moment of infliction but it also requires lasting psychological harm, such as seen in mental disorders like posttraumatic stress disorder. (Memorandum, at pages 1 and 46, reprinted in the The Torture Papers: The Road to Abu Ghraib at 172 (Karen J. Greenberg & Joshua L. Dratel eds., 2005) (Torture Papers).)

The memorandum went on to conclude that:

> Any effort by Congress to regulate the interrogation of battlefield combatants would violate the Constitution's sole vesting of the Commander-in-Chief authority in the President. . . . We have . . . demonstrated that Section 2340A, as applied to interrogations of enemy combatants ordered by the President pursuant to his Commander-in-Chief power would be unconstitutional. (Page 39.)

Because the Office of Legal Counsel in the Department of Justice, which Bybee then headed, provides authoritative legal opinions for the Executive Branch, this memorandum was one of the major Bush Administration documents providing guidance for the activities of the Department of Defense and CIA during 2002-2004.

The 48-page memorandum, which was apparently authored in large part by John Yoo, Bybee's deputy, cited many U.S. court cases and other precedents in its extensive discussion of the powers of the President to suspend treaties and its claim that certain laws might be unconstitutional as infringing on the President's powers. However, the memorandum did not even cite *Youngstown Sheet & Tube* or *Dames & Moore.* Do you think that *Youngstown* should at least have been considered, both as an important Supreme Court precedent and because of its analytical approach?

The memorandum was classified secret at the time and the working drafts were reportedly not widely circulated even within the Executive Branch. Do you think that a U.S. government lawyer drafting an important policy memorandum that affects lives has a responsibility to ensure that such a memorandum is carefully researched and balanced, especially if there will be little opportunity for others to analyze and discuss its conclusions? See Richard B. Bilder and Detlev F. Vagts, Speaking Law to Power: Lawyers and Torture, 98 Am. J. Int'l L. 689 (2004).*

*"[G]overnment attorneys . . . have responsibilities and obligations that go beyond those of private attorneys. Thus, the government lawyer's 'client' is not simply his or her administrative superior, but also the government agency or military service for which he or she works, the U.S. government as a whole, and indeed the American public and its collective interests and values. Moreover, government attorneys have a

The memorandum was widely criticized when it became public in spring 2004. The Bush Administration took the unusual step of "withdrawing" the 2002 memorandum in June 2004 and asking for a "replacement memorandum." The resulting memorandum of December 30, 2004, explicitly disagreed with the 2002 memorandum's definition of torture. Regarding the 2002 memorandum's position that Congress could not, by criminal statute, regulate the conduct of interrogations authorized under the President's constitutional war-time authorities, the 2004 memorandum stated that "[b]ecause the discussion in that memorandum concerning the President's Commander-in-Chief power . . . was — and remains — unnecessary, it has been eliminated from the analysis that follows." Memorandum from Acting Assistant Attorney General Daniel Levin to Deputy Attorney General James B. Comfrey (Dec. 30, 2004) (Re: Legal Standards Applicable under 18 U.S.C. §§2340-2340A) http://www.usdoj.gov/olc/dagmemo.pdf.

In 2009, the Department of Justice's Office of Professional Responsibility (OPR) concluded a four-year investigation of the 2002 torture memo along with related memos signed by Bybee and Yoo. The OPR report concluded that Bybee and Yoo had committed professional misconduct in their preparation of the memos. However, a later memo from the Office of the Deputy Attorney General disagreed with the report's findings and decided that the Justice Department would not pursue any professional sanctions against the former OLC attorneys.

On his second full day in office, President Barak Obama issued Executive Order 13,491 (Jan. 22, 2009), 74 Fed. Reg. 4893, in which he expressly set Common Article 3 of the Geneva Conventions as a minimum baseline for the treatment and interrogation of individuals detained in any armed conflict and provided that such persons shall be treated humanely and consistent with the provisions of the U.S. Arm Field Manual, various U.S. statutes, and the Convention on Torture.

President Obama also issued another Executive Order the same day that called for a prompt review of the factual and legal bases for the continued detention of all individuals currently detained at Guantanamo Bay and directed that the detention facilities at Guantanamo should be closed within one year. A variety of circumstances, including new attempted terrorist attacks in the United States and political opposition in Congress and elsewhere, led to the Guantanamo facilities remaining open, although the Administration substantially reduced the number of detainees held there. In March 2001, the Administration announced that military commission trials at Guantanamo would resume.

There is an extensive literature on the August 2002 "torture" memorandum and its aftermath. See, for example, Jens David Ohlin, The Torture Lawyers, 51 Harv. Int'l L.J. 193 (2010).

8. *Extraordinary rendition.* Another controversial policy of the Bush Administration was extraordinary rendition — transferring detainees from occupied Iraq, from the United States, or from other countries to third countries for detention and interrogation. The renditions were often accompanied by allegations of prisoner mistreatment in the countries to which the detainees were moved. These renditions

---

particular obligation to act responsibly in formulating advice or arguments regarding constitutional or international legal questions. For this opinions on such matters may often not be subject to definitive judicial or other impartial review. . . ." Id. at 693.

were, again, apparently supported by legal memos from the Office of Legal Counsel. For example, Memorandum from Jack Goldsmith, Assistant Attorney, to William H. Taft, IV, General Counsel, U.S. Dept. of State, et al., Memorandum for Alberto R. Gonzales, Counsel to the President, Permissibility of Relocating Certain "Protected Persons" from Occupied Iraq (Mar. 19, 2004), *reprinted in* Torture Papers at 366. Although the Goldsmith memo was stamped "Draft," it was circulated to the general counsels at the CIA, the National Security Council, and the State and Defense departments. There are reports that it provided a "green light" for transferring detainees out of Iraq to other locations. E.g., Dana Priest, Memo Lets CIA Take Detainees Out of Iraq, Wash. Post, Oct. 24, 2004, at A1.

When these rendition practices leaked to the media in 2004, there was an outcry from foreign countries that might have unwittingly served as a place where people were initially seized or as transit points for the renditions. For example, in 2006, Italian prosecutors issued arrest warrants alleging that 25 operatives apparently from the U.S. Central Intelligence Agency (CIA) and a U.S. Air Force officer were involved in the 2003 abduction of a militant Egyptian cleric who was grabbed off the streets of Milan, Italy, and then handed over to Egyptian security services that tortured him. In January 2007, German prosecutors issued arrest warrants for 13 people it named as CIA operatives who were allegedly involved in seizing Khaled el-Masri, a German citizen, in Macedonia and transporting him to Afghanistan where he said he was shackled, beaten, and interrogated before being released without charges.

Criticism of the rendition practices also grew in the United States. See, e.g., Jane Mayer, Outsourcing Torture: The Secret History of America's 'Extraordinary Rendition' Program, New Yorker, Feb. 14, 2005.

A careful legal analysis of these extraordinary rendition practices concluded that the practices were not permissible under existing, well-established norms of international law. See Leila Nadya Sadat, Ghost Prisoners and Black Sites: Extraordinary Rendition Under International Law, 37 Case Western Res. J. Int'l L. 309 (2006), especially pages 324-342 regarding the Goldsmith memo.

In one of his January 22, 2009, Executive Orders, President Obama directed the CIA to "close as expeditiously as possible any detention facilities that it currently operates." Exec. Order No. 13,491, supra at 4894. The same executive order established a Special Task Force to review and make recommendations for updating U.S. policies regarding interrogation and the transfer of detainees.

The controversial case of Mahar Arar illustrates the ongoing tensions regarding U.S. rendition practices. In 2002, the Canadian government suspected Maher Arar, a dual citizen of Canada and Syria, of having terrorist ties. U.S. officials arrested Arar at John F. Kennedy Airport and transported him to Syria, where he was held for one year and released without charges. Arar alleged that while he was in Syria he was beaten and held in a small underground cell.

In 2007, the Canadian government apologized to Arar for sending mistaken information to the United States, cleared Arar of suspicion, and later paid him compensation. No similar apology came from the U.S. government. After Arar sued the U.S. government, the United States urged the court to dismiss the case on the grounds that the subject matter of the case was a state secret. Without reaching the state secrets issue, the Second Circuit concluded that Congress had not created a private damages remedy for violations of the 5th Amendment and dismissed the case. Arar v. Ashcroft, 585 F.3d 559, 571-82 (2d Cir. 2009), cert. denied, 78 U.S.L.W. 3730 (U.S. June 14, 2010).

9. *The National Security Agency's Warrantless Surveillance Program.* In 2005, the New York Times reported that, soon after the September 11 attacks, President Bush authorized the National Security Agency (NSA) to conduct electronic surveillance (wiretapping) within the United States without seeking warrants. The NSA program, called the Terrorist Surveillance Program, involved monitoring of international calls and e-mails where, in theory, at least one party is suspected of having links to Al Qaeda or an affiliated terrorist organization in order to create an early warning system for terrorist attacks. There were questions raised about how carefully the intercept criteria were being applied and whether many people with no ties to terrorist groups might have been overheard. Answers to these questions were hampered because the details of the program were still classified.

As in *Hamdi* and *Hamdan*, a statute was implicated in the controversy. The Foreign Intelligence Surveillance Act of 1978 (FISA), 50 U.S.C. §§1801 et seq., provided a comprehensive procedure for obtaining warrants for electronic surveillance from a special federal court. FISA also allowed the Attorney General to authorize electronic surveillance in an emergency situation for 72 hours without a warrant. The statute also allowed for warrantless surveillance "for a period not to exceed fifteen calendar days following a declaration of war by Congress." Congress provided that FISA, and other specific statutory provisions, were "the exclusive means by which electronic surveillance . . . may be conducted." Electronic surveillance "not authorized by statute" was a criminal offense.

The Bush Administration presented several justifications for the program in 2005-2006. Based on the *Hamdi* decision, the Bush Administration claimed the AUMF was an implicit statutory authorization to gain intelligence in this manner to conduct the war on terrorism. The Bush Administration argued that following the procedures in FISA, including the review process for emergency authorizations, would cause undue delay, particularly when intelligence officers may need immediate access to information about imminent terrorist attacks. The Bush Administration further characterized the program as an exercise of the President's independent constitutional authority as Commander-in-Chief to gain intelligence about the enemy.

Critics of the program presented several rebuttals. They claimed that 50 U.S.C. §2511(2)(f) and the *Hamdan* decision foreclosed the Bush Administration's argument that the AUMF has implicitly authorized the program. Critics also believed the FISA procedures provide an appropriate balance between protection of civil liberties and the need to gain intelligence for national security purposes. Looking to footnote 23 in *Hamdan*, they argued that the President, even when exercising his Commander-in-Chief power, cannot ignore the limitations Congress has set forth in FISA.

Who had the better of these legal arguments? Considering the interpretations of the AUMF in *Hamdi* and *Hamdan*, was the NSA program authorized by the AUMF? Was the NSA program a lawful exercise of the President's powers as Commander-in-Chief?

Congress responded by passing the FISA Amendments Act of 2008. P.L. 110-261, 122 Stat. 2436 (2008). The amendments had two major effects. First, they updated the statutory authorization for electronic surveillance. Second, they provided immunity from liability for private telecommunications companies that had cooperated with the U.S. government to carry out the warrantless surveillance program between 2001 and 2007. See 50 U.S.C. §1885.

The immunity provision was the most controversial aspect of the amendments. Members of Congress and legal scholars raised concerns that immunity would prevent courts from ever litigating the constitutionality or legality of the Bush Administration surveillance program. However, courts have not avoided the issue. In 2010, the district court for the Northern District of California, in consolidated litigation concerning four suits filed against the U.S. government, held that the warrantless electronic surveillance program was illegal as a violation of FISA. In re: NSA Telecomm. Records Litig., 700 F. Supp.2d 1182 (N.D. Cal 2010). Much of the litigation leading up to the 2010 decision revolved around the government's assertion of the state secrets privilege (see discussion below). However, the U.S. district court utilized provisions of the updated FISA statute, such as section 1806(f) allowing for in camera review of privileged evidence, to allow the litigation to go forward. See id. at 1194.

10. *State secrets privilege.* This privilege is an evidentiary rule that permits the Executive Branch to avoid providing information about military, security, or diplomatic secrets during discovery in civil trials. United States v. Reynolds, 345 U.S. 1 (1953), established that such sensitive information was privileged and thus immunized from production during discovery under Federal Rule of Civil Procedure 26, which states that "parties may obtain discovery of any matter, not privileged," that is relevant to the suit.

To establish a claim for privilege as a state secret, the government must (1) make a formal claim of privilege (2) invoked by the head of a department (3) who has personally considered the matter. *Reynolds,* 345 U.S. at 7-8. The court must then determine whether invocation of privilege is appropriate "without forcing the disclosure of the very thing the privilege is designed to protect." Id. at 8. The court's inquiry should focus on whether there is a "reasonable danger" military secrets will be divulged by requiring production of certain documents or witnesses. *Reynolds,* 345 U.S. at 10. Judicial deference in this area is high; the courts often rely solely on affidavits filed by Executive Branch officials.

Because the state secrets privilege is absolute, successful assertion of the privilege usually spells defeat for a plaintiff's case. First, a court can dismiss a case where "the very subject of the litigation is itself a state secret [such that] the case [cannot] be tried without compromising sensitive . . . secrets." Sterling v. Tenet, 416 F.3d 338, 348-349 (4th Cir. 2005); see also Kasza v. Browner, 133 F.3d 1159, 1166 (9th Cir. 1998). Second, "if the privilege deprives the *defendant* of information that would otherwise give the defendant a valid defense to the claim, then the court may grant summary judgment to the defendant." Hepting v. AT&T Corp., 439 F. Supp. 974 (N.D. Cal. 2006) (quoting *Kasza,* 133 F.3d at 1166) (emphasis in original). Third, a court can dismiss a claim if a plaintiff cannot obtain the evidence necessary to establish a *prima facie* case because the evidence is protected from discovery by the state secrets privilege. See *Kasza,* 133 F.3d at 1166. If, however, the plaintiff's claim can be litigated without requiring reference to state secrets, courts might try to determine if special procedural mechanisms may be adequate to prevent disclosure of the state secrets in the course of the litigation.

A recent example of a whole case being dismissed is Mohamed v. Jeppesen Dataplan, Inc., 614 F.3d 1070 (9th Cir. 2010)(en banc). Binyam Mohamed, one of the five plaintiffs and an Ethiopian citizen, alleged that he had been arrested in Pakistan, flown by U.S. agents, and delivered to Moroccan agents in Morocco, where he was tortured over an 18-month period. He was then allegedly returned by U.S. agents to a CIA "dark site" in Afghanistan and then sent to Guantanamo Bay, where he remained for nearly five years before being released and returned to the United Kingdom. The defendant private company was alleged to have provided flight planning and logistical support to the aircraft and crew on the flights in violation of the Alien Tort Statute. The U.S. government intervened, moving for dismissal under the state secrets privilege. In a 6-5 en banc decision, the Ninth Circuit Court of Appeals held that the U.S. government's valid assertion of the state secrets privilege warranted dismissal of the litigation. See also El-Masri v. Tenet, 479 F.3d 296 (4th Cir.), cert. denied, 2007 U.S. Lexis 11351 (Oct. 9, 2007) (another rendition case under the ATS and also the U.S. Constitution dismissed on grounds of the state secrets privilege).

In 2009, civil liberties lawyers and others criticized the Obama Administration for initially continuing the aggressive use of the state secrets privilege in the *Jeppesen Dataplan* proceedings and in at least one other case. In any event, after a review, Attorney General Eric Holder announced on September 23, 2009, new policies and procedures governing invocation of the privilege that were designed to "provide greater accountability and reliability in the invocation of the state secrets privilege in litigation." How these new policies and procedures will actually impact the use of the privilege was yet to be clear as of January 2011.

For a thorough historical analysis of the privilege, see Laura K. Donohue, The Shadow of State Secrets, 159 U. Pa. L. Rev. 77 (2010).

As the *Hamdi* plurality notes, the struggle against terrorism is an unconventional conflict and is unlikely to end in a formal cease fire, unlike many (but not all) more traditional wars between states. Some doubt whether the struggle against terrorism will ever truly end. Furthermore, because of the nature of terrorist networks and terrorist attacks, the conflict takes place domestically and abroad. What, then, are the limits of the President's powers pursuant to the AUMF and the President's independent constitutional authority, especially the Commander-in-Chief power, in this situation? Does international law help define those limits? How should it?

C. CUSTOMARY INTERNATIONAL LAW

As compared with treaties, the Constitution is relatively silent about the formation and domestic status of customary international law. Indeed, the only mention in the Constitution to customary international law, which was referred to at the time of the Founding as part of the "law of nations," is a grant of power to Congress to "define and punish . . . Offenses against the Law of Nations." Art. I, §8, cl. 10. Moreover, as we learned in Chapter 2, customary international law is more diffuse than treaty law. It consists of obligations inferred from the general and consistent practice of states followed out of a sense of legal obligation (*opinio juris*). That practice may be found in state conduct, diplomatic correspondence, official statements, military and administrative practice, treaties, and judicial decisions, as well as national legislation. Consequently, all the law-making powers reflected in the Constitution—ranging from presidential foreign affairs authority, delegated legislative authority, the treaty power, the entire Article I legislative power, and Article III—are involved in the making of customary international law by the United States.

Some controversy surrounds the domestic legal status of customary international law. Recall that Article VI of the Constitution provides that treaties are the supreme law of the land. As a result, treaties (at least if they are self-executing) preempt inconsistent state law. In addition, under the last-in-time rule, treaties can, at least in theory, override earlier inconsistent statutes. Customary international law, however, is not mentioned in Article VI. The U.S. Supreme Court recently addressed the role of customary international law in an extensive opinion in Alvarez-Machain v. Sosa, 542 U.S. 692 (2004), which is excerpted below. However, some questions still remain about the relationships between customary international law and state law, federal statutes, and Executive Branch action.

1. Part of Our Law

In several decisions, the Supreme Court has referred to customary international law as "part of our law" or part of the "law of the land." The most famous of these decisions is The Paquete Habana. It was a case in the federal courts on the basis of federal admiralty jurisdiction. In admiralty cases the courts apply admiralty or maritime law, a separate body of law that historically was part of the "law of nations" and was considered to be applicable—uniformly—throughout the seafaring world. One part of this law was prize law, dealing with the rights of persons to capture enemy vessels and cargoes during wartime.

The Paquete Habana

U.S. Supreme Court
175 U.S. 677 (1900)

Mr. Justice Gray delivered the opinion of the court.

These are two appeals from decrees of the District Court of the United States for the Southern District of Florida, condemning two fishing vessels and their cargoes as prize of war.

Each vessel was a fishing smack, running in and out of Havana, and regularly engaged in fishing on the coast of Cuba; sailed under the Spanish flag; was owned by a Spanish subject of Cuban birth, living in the city of Havana; was commanded by a subject of Spain also residing in Havana; and her master and crew had no interest in the vessel, but were entitled to shares, amounting in all to two thirds, of her catch, the other third belonging to her owner. Her cargo consisted of fresh fish, caught by her crew from the sea, put on board as they were caught, and kept and sold alive. Until stopped by the blockading squadron, she had no knowledge of the existence of the war, or of any blockade. She had no arms or ammunition on board, and made no attempt to run the blockade after she knew of its existence, nor any resistance at the time of the capture. . . .

Both the fishing vessels were brought by their captors into Key West. A libel for the condemnation of each vessel and her cargo as prize of war was there filed in April 27, 1898; a claim was interposed by her master, on behalf of himself and the other members of the crew, and of her owner: evidence was taken, showing the facts above stated; and on May 30,1898, a final decree of condemnation and sale was entered, "the court not being satisfied that as a matter of law, without any ordinance, treaty or proclamation, fishing vessels of this class are exempt from seizure."

Each vessel was thereupon sold by auction; the Paquete Habana for the sum of $490; and the Lola for the sum of $800. . . .

We are then brought to the consideration of the question whether, upon the facts appearing in these records, the fishing smacks were subject to capture by the armed vessels of the United States during the recent war with Spain.

By an ancient usage among civilized nations, beginning centuries ago, and gradually ripening into a rule of international law, coast fishing vessels, pursuing their vocation of catching and bringing in fresh fish, have been recognized as exempt, with their cargoes and crews, from capture as prize of war.

This doctrine, however, has been earnestly contested at the bar; and no complete collection of the instances illustrating it is to be found, so far as we are aware, in a single published work, although many are referred to and discussed by the writers on international law. . . . It is therefore worth the while to trace the history of the rule, from the earliest accessible sources, through the increasing recognition of it, with occasional setbacks, to what we may now justly consider as its final establishment in our own country and generally throughout the civilized world.

[The Court then proceeds to trace the history of the rule through an extensive examination of state practice, beginning with the issuance of orders by Henry IV to his admirals in 1403 and 1406.]

Since the English orders in council of 1806 and 1810 in favor of fishing vessels employed in catching and bringing to market fresh fish, no instance has been found in which the exemption from capture of private coast fishing vessels, honestly pursuing their peaceful industry, has been denied by England, or by any other nation. And the Empire of Japan (the last State admitted into the rank of civilized nations), by an ordinance promulgated at the beginning of its war with China in August, 1894, established prize courts, and ordained that "the following enemy's vessels are exempt from detention"—including in the exemption "boats engaged in coast fisheries," as well as "ships engaged exclusively on a voyage of scientific discovery, philanthropy or religious mission." Takahashi, International Law, 11, 178.

International law is part of our law, and must be ascertained and administered by the courts of justice of appropriate jurisdiction, as often as questions of right depending upon it are duly presented for their determination. For this purpose, where there is no treaty, and no controlling executive or legislative act or judicial decision, resort must be had to the customs and usages of civilized nations; and, as evidence of these, to the works of jurists and commentators, who by years of labor, research and experience, have made themselves peculiarly well acquainted with the subjects of which they treat. Such works are resorted to by judicial tribunals, not for the speculations of their authors concerning what the law ought to be, but for trustworthy evidence of what the law really is. Hilton v. Guyot, 159 U.S. 113, 163, 164, 214, 215. . . .

This review of the precedents and authorities on the subject appears to us abundantly to demonstrate that at the present day, by the general consent of the civilized nations of the world, and independently of any express treaty or other public act, it is an established rule of international law, founded on considerations of humanity to a poor and industrious order of men, and of the mutual convenience of belligerent States, that coast fishing vessels, with their implements and supplies, cargoes and crews, unarmed, and honestly pursuing their peaceful calling of catching and bringing in fresh fish, are exempt from capture as prize of war.

The exemption, of course, does not apply to coast fishermen or their vessels, if employed for a warlike purpose, or in such a way as to give aid or information to the enemy; nor when military or naval operations create a necessity to which all private interests must give way. . . .

This rule of international law is one which prize courts, administering the law of nations, are bound to take judicial notice of, and to give effect to, in the absence of any treaty or other public act of their own government in relation to the matter. . . .

The position taken by the United States during the recent war with Spain was quite in accord with the rule of international law, now generally recognized by civilized nations, in regard to coast fishing vessels.

On April 21, 1898, the Secretary of the Navy gave instructions to Admiral Sampson commanding the North Atlantic Squadron, to "immediately institute a blockade of the north coast of Cuba, extending from Cardenas on the east to Bahia Honda on the west." The blockade was immediately instituted accordingly. On April 22, the President issued a proclamation, declaring that the United States had instituted and would maintain that blockade, "in pursuance of the laws of the United States, and the law of nations applicable to such cases." 30 Stat. 1769. And by the act of Congress of April 25, 1898, c.189, it was declared that the war between the United States and Spain existed on that day, and had existed since and including April 21. 30 Stat. 364.

On April 26, 1898, the President issued another proclamation, which, after reciting the existence of the war, as declared by Congress, contained this further recital: "It being desirable that such war should be conducted upon principles in harmony with the present views of nations and sanctioned by their recent practice." This recital was followed by specific declarations of certain rules for the conduct of the war by sea, making no mention of fishing vessels. 30 Stat. 1770. But the proclamation clearly manifests the general policy of the Government to conduct the war in accordance with the principles of international law sanctioned by the recent practice of nations. . . .

Upon the facts proved in either case, it is the duty of this court, sitting as the highest prize court of the United States, and administering the law of nations, to declare and adjudge that the capture was unlawful, and without probable cause; and it is therefore, in each case,

Ordered, that the decree of the District Court be reversed, and the proceeds of the sale of the vessel, together with the proceeds of any sale of her cargo, be restored to the claimant, with damages and costs.

[Dissenting opinion of Mr. Chief Justice FULLER, with whom concurred Mr. Justice HARLAN and Mr. Justice McKENNA, omitted.]

Customary international law has been prominently involved in the human rights area. Consider the following materials:

Filartiga v. Pena-Irala

U.S. Court of Appeals
630 F.2d 876 (2d Cir. 1980)

KAUFMAN, Circuit Judge:

Upon ratification of the Constitution, the thirteen former colonies were fused into a single nation, one which, in its relations with foreign states, is bound both to observe and construe the accepted norms of international law, formerly known as the law of nations. . . .

Implementing the constitutional mandate for national control over foreign relations, the First Congress established original district court jurisdiction over "all causes where an alien sues for a tort only [committed] in violation of the law of nations." Judiciary Act of 1789, ch. 20, §9(b) (1789), codified at 28 U.S.C. §1350. Construing this rarely-invoked provision, we hold that deliberate torture perpetrated under color of official authority violates universally accepted norms of the international law of human rights, regardless of the nationality of the parties. Thus, whenever an alleged torturer is found and served with process by an alien within our borders, §1350 provides federal jurisdiction. Accordingly, we reverse the judgment of the district court dismissing the complaint for want of federal jurisdiction.

I

The appellants, plaintiffs below, are citizens of the Republic of Paraguay. Dr. Joel Filartiga, a physician, describes himself as a longstanding opponent of the government of President Alfredo Stroessner, which has held power in Paraguay since 1954. His daughter, Dolly Filartiga, arrived in the United States in 1978 under a visitor's visa, and has since applied for permanent political asylum. The Filartigas brought this action in the Eastern District of New York against Americo Norberto Pena-Irala (Pena), also a citizen of Paraguay, for wrongfully causing the death of Dr. Filartiga's seventeen-year-old son, Joelito. Because the district court dismissed the action for want of subject matter jurisdiction, we must accept as true the allegations contained in the Filartigas' complaint and affidavits for purposes of this appeal.

The appellants contend that on March 29, 1976, Joelito Filartiga was kidnapped and tortured to death by Pena, who was then Inspector General of Police in Asuncion, Paraguay. Later that day, the police brought Dolly Filartiga to Pena's home where she was confronted with the body of her brother, which evidenced marks of severe torture. As she fled, horrified, from the house, Pena followed after her shouting, "Here you have what you have been looking for for so long and what you deserve. Now shut up." The Filartigas claim that Joelito was tortured and killed in retaliation for his father's political activities and beliefs.

Shortly thereafter, Dr. Filartiga commenced a criminal action in the Paraguayan courts against Pena and the police for the murder of his son. As a result, Dr. Filartiga's attorney was arrested and brought to police headquarters where, shackled to a wall, Pena threatened him with death. This attorney, it is alleged, has since been disbarred without just cause. . . .

In July of 1978, Pena sold his house in Paraguay and entered the United States under a visitor's visa. He was accompanied by Juana Bautista Fernandez Villalba, who had lived with him in Paraguay. The couple remained in the United States beyond the term of their visas, and were living in Brooklyn, New York, when Dolly Filartiga, who was then living in Washington, D.C., learned of their presence. Acting on information provided by Dolly the Immigration and Naturalization Service arrested Pena and his companion, both of whom were subsequently ordered deported on April 5, 1979 following a hearing. They had then resided in the United States for more than nine months.

Almost immediately, Dolly caused Pena to be served with a summons and civil complaint at the Brooklyn Navy Yard, where he was being held pending deportation. The complaint alleged that Pena had wrongfully caused Joelito's death by torture and sought compensatory and punitive damages of $10,000,000. . . . The cause of action is stated as arising under "wrongful death statutes; the U.N. Charter; the Universal Declaration on Human Rights; the U.N. Declaration Against Torture; the American Declaration of the Rights and Duties of Man; and other pertinent declarations, documents and practices constituting the customary international law of human rights and the law of nations," as well as 28 U.S.C. §1350. . . .

II

Appellants rest their principal argument in support of federal jurisdiction upon the Alien Tort Statute, 28 U.S.C. §1350, which provides: "The district courts shall have original jurisdiction of any civil action by an alien for a tort only, committed in violation of the law of nations or a treaty of the United States." Since appellants do not contend that their action arises directly under a treaty of the United States, a threshold question on the jurisdictional issue is whether the conduct alleged violates the law of nations. In light of the universal condemnation of torture in numerous international agreements, and the renunciation of torture as an instrument of official policy by virtually all of the nations of the world (in principle if not in practice), we find that an act of torture committed by a state official against one held in detention violates established norms of the international law of human rights, and hence the law of nations.

The Supreme Court has enumerated the appropriate sources of international law. The law of nations "may be ascertained by consulting the works of jurists, writing professedly on public law; or by the general usage and practice of nations; or by judicial decisions recognizing and enforcing that law." . . .

The Paquete Habana, 175 U.S. 677 (1900), reaffirmed that

> where there is no treaty, and no controlling executive or legislative act or judicial decision, resort must be had to the customs and usages of civilized nations; and, as evidence of these, to the works of jurists and commentators, who by years of labor, research and experience, have made themselves peculiarly well acquainted with the subjects of which they treat. Such works are resorted to by judicial tribunals, not for the speculations of their authors concerning what the law ought to be, but for trustworthy evidence of what the law really is.

. . . *Habana* is particularly instructive for present purposes, for it held that the traditional prohibition against seizure of an enemy's coastal fishing vessels during wartime, a standard that began as one of comity only, had ripened over the preceding century into "a settled rule of international law" by "the general assent of civilized nations." Thus it is clear that courts must interpret international law not as it was in 1789, but as it has evolved and exists among the nations of the world today.

The requirement that a rule command the "general assent of civilized nations" to become binding upon them all is a stringent one. Were this not so, the courts of one nation might feel free to impose idiosyncratic legal rules upon others, in the name of applying international law. Thus, in Banco Nacional de Cuba v. Sabbatino, 376 U.S. 398 (1964), the Court declined to pass on the validity of the Cuban government's expropriation of a foreign-owned corporation's assets, noting the sharply conflicting views on the issue propounded by the capital-exporting, capital-importing, socialist and capitalist nations.

The case at bar presents us with a situation diametrically opposed to the conflicted state of law that confronted the *Sabbatino* Court. Indeed, . . . there are few, if any, issues in international law today on which opinion seems to be so united as the limitations on a state's power to torture persons held in its custody.

The United Nations Charter (a treaty of the United States, see 59 Stat. 1033 (1945)) makes it clear that in this modern age a state's treatment of its own citizens is a matter of international concern. It provides:

> With a view to the creation of conditions of stability and well-being which are necessary for peaceful and friendly relations among nations . . . the United Nations shall promote . . . universal respect for, and observance of, human rights and fundamental freedoms for all without distinctions as to race, sex, language or religion.

Id. Art. 55. And further:

> All members pledge themselves to take joint and separate action in cooperation with the Organization for the achievement of the purposes set forth in Article 55.

Id. Art. 56.

While this broad mandate has been held not to be wholly self-executing, this observation alone does not end our inquiry. For although there is no universal agreement as to the precise extent of the "human rights and fundamental freedoms" guaranteed to all by the Charter, there is at present no dissent from the view that the guaranties include, at a bare minimum, the right to be free from torture. This prohibition has become part of customary international law, as evidenced and defined by the Universal Declaration of Human Rights, General Assembly Resolution 217 (III) (A) (Dec. 10, 1948) which states, in the plainest of terms, "no one shall be subjected to torture."[10] The General Assembly has declared that the Charter precepts embodied in this Universal Declaration "constitute basic principles of international law." G.A. Res. 2625 (XXV) (Oct. 24, 1970).

10. Eighteen nations have incorporated the Universal Declaration into their own constitutions. 48 Revue Internationale de Droit Penal Nos. 3 & 4, at 211 (1977).

Particularly relevant is the Declaration on the Protection of All Persons from Being Subjected to Torture, General Assembly Resolution 3452 (1975), which is set out in full in the margin. The Declaration expressly prohibits any state from permitting the dastardly and totally inhuman act of torture. Torture, in turn, is defined as "any act by which severe pain and suffering, whether physical or mental, is intentionally inflicted by or at the instigation of a public official on a person for such purposes as . . . intimidating him or other persons." . . . This Declaration, like the Declaration of Human Rights before it, was adopted without dissent by the General Assembly.

These U.N. declarations are significant because they specify with great precision the obligations of member nations under the Charter. Since their adoption, "[m]embers can no longer contend that they do not know what human rights they promised in the Charter to promote." Sohn, "A Short History of United Nations Documents on Human Rights," [1968] . . . Moreover, a U.N. Declaration is, according to one authoritative definition, "a formal and solemn instrument, suitable for rare occasions when principles of great and lasting importance are being enunciated." 34 U.N. ESCOR, Supp. (No. 8) 15 (1962) (memorandum of Office of Legal Affairs, U.N. Secretariat). Accordingly, it has been observed that the Universal Declaration of Human Rights "no longer fits into the dichotomy of 'binding treaty' against 'non-binding pronouncement,' but is rather an authoritative statement of the international community." . . . Thus, a Declaration creates an expectation of adherence, and "insofar as the expectation is gradually justified by State practice, a declaration may by custom become recognized as laying down rules binding upon the States." 34 U.N. ESCOR, supra. Indeed, several commentators have concluded that the Universal Declaration has become, *in toto*, a part of binding, customary international law. . . .

Turning to the act of torture, we have little difficulty discerning its universal renunciation in the modern usage and practice of nations. The international consensus surrounding torture has found expression in numerous international treaties and accords. E.g., American Convention on Human Rights, Art. 5 ("No one shall be subjected to torture or to cruel, inhuman or degrading punishment or treatment"); International Covenant on Civil and Political Rights, U.N. General Assembly Res. 2200 (Dec. 16,1966) (identical language); European Convention for the Protection of Human Rights and Fundamental Freedoms, Art. 3. The substance of these international agreements is reflected in modern municipal—i.e. national—law as well. Although torture was once a routine concomitant of criminal interrogations in many nations, during the modern and hopefully more enlightened era it has been universally renounced. According to one survey, torture is prohibited, expressly or implicitly, by the constitutions of over fifty-five nations, including both the United States and Paraguay. Our State Department reports a general recognition of this principle:

> There now exists an international consensus that recognizes basic human rights and obligations owed by all governments to their citizens. . . . There is no doubt that these rights are often violated; but virtually all governments acknowledge their validity.

Department of State, Country Reports on Human Rights for 1979. . . . We have been directed to no assertion by any contemporary state of a right to torture its own or another nation's citizens. Indeed, United States diplomatic contacts confirm the universal abhorrence with which torture is viewed:

> In exchanges between United States embassies and all foreign states with which the United States maintains relations, it has been the Department of State's general experience that no government has asserted a right to torture its own nationals. Where reports of torture elicit some credence, a state usually responds by denial or, less frequently, by asserting that the conduct was unauthorized or constituted rough treatment short of torture.[15]

Memorandum of the United States as Amicus Curiae at 16 n.34.

Having examined the sources from which customary international law is derived — the usage of nations, judicial opinions and the works of jurists — we conclude that official torture is now prohibited by the law of nations. The prohibition is clear and unambiguous, and admits of no distinction between treatment of aliens and citizens. . . . The treaties and accords cited above, as well as the express foreign policy of our own government, all make it clear that international law confers fundamental rights upon all people vis-à-vis their own governments. While the ultimate scope of those rights will be a subject for continuing refinement and elaboration, we hold that the right to be free from torture is now among them. We therefore turn to the question whether the other requirements for jurisdiction are met.

III

Appellee submits that even if the tort alleged is a violation of modern international law, federal jurisdiction may not be exercised consistent with the dictates of Article III of the Constitution. The claim is without merit. Common law courts of general jurisdiction regularly adjudicate transitory tort claims between individuals over whom they exercise personal jurisdiction, wherever the tort occurred. Moreover, as part of an articulated scheme of federal control over external affairs, Congress provided, in the first Judiciary Act, §9(b), 1 Stat. 73, 77 (1789), for federal jurisdiction over suits by aliens where principles of international law are in issue. The constitutional basis for the Alien Tort Statute is the law of nations, which has always been part of the federal common law.

It is not extraordinary for a court to adjudicate a tort claim arising outside of its territorial jurisdiction. A state or nation has a legitimate interest in the orderly resolution of disputes among those within its borders, and where the lex loci delicti commissi is applied, it is an expression of comity to give effect to the laws of the state where the wrong occurred. . . .

In the twentieth century the international community has come to recognize the common danger posed by the flagrant disregard of basic human rights and particularly the right to be free of torture. Spurred first by the Great War, and

15. The fact that the prohibition of torture is often honored in the breach does not diminish its binding effect as a norm of international law. As one commentator has put it, "The best evidence for the existence of international law is that every actual State recognizes that it does exist and that it is itself under an obligation to observe it. States often violate international law, just as individuals often violate municipal law; but no more than individuals do States defend their violations by claiming that they are above the law." J. Brierly, The Outlook for International Law 4-5 (Oxford 1944).

then the Second, civilized nations have banded together to prescribe acceptable norms of international behavior. From the ashes of the Second World War arose the United Nations Organization, amid hopes that an era of peace and cooperation had at last begun. Though many of these aspirations have remained elusive goals, that circumstance cannot diminish the true progress that has been made. In the modern age, humanitarian and practical considerations have combined to lead the nations of the world to recognize that respect for fundamental human rights is in their individual and collective interest. Among the rights universally proclaimed by all nations, as we have noted, is the right to be free of physical torture. Indeed, for purposes of civil liability, the torturer has become like the pirate and slave trader before him hostis humani generis, an enemy of all mankind. Our holding today, giving effect to a jurisdictional provision enacted by our First Congress, is a small but important step in the fulfillment of the ageless dream to free all people from brutal violence.

Notes and Questions

1. What is the holding of *The Paquete Habana* case? What is the meaning of the Court's statement that "international law is part of our law"? What is the significance of the Court's statements that customary international law applies "where there is no treaty, and no controlling executive or legislative act," and that courts must "give effect to" customary international law "in the absence of any treaty or other public act of [the] government in relation to the matter"? What would the court have held if there had been no reference to the "law of nations" in the presidential proclamation? What if Congress had provided in the declaration of war that all Spanish vessels were subject to capture?

2. As we will discuss in Chapter 8, only after World War II did a state's treatment of its own nationals become a subject of international law. Partly for this reason, the Alien Tort Statute (ATS), also referred to as the Alien Tort Claims Act (ATCA), was rarely successfully invoked before the *Filartiga* ruling. In fact, only two courts had upheld jurisdiction under the ATS. See Adra v. Clift, 195 F. Supp. 857 (D. Md. 1961); Bolchos v. Darrell, 3 F. Cas. 810 (D.S.C. 1795) (No. 1607).

3. In *Filartiga,* what was the rule of international law involved? What evidence did the court cite in support of that rule? What role did state practice play in the court's analysis? What is the significance of footnote 15 of the court's opinion? How does the Supreme Court's use of international law in *The Paquete Habana* compare with the Second Circuit's use of international law in *Filartiga*?

4. *Filartiga* held that customary international law is "part of the federal common law." Does this mean that customary international law norms have the same force of law as self-executing treaties or statutes in the U.S. domestic legal system? If so, does customary international law preempt state law when there is a conflict between the two? Should it? Must the President comply with customary international law pursuant to his duty to "take Care that the Laws be faithfully executed" under Article II, section 3 of the Constitution, or can the President and other Executive Branch officials violate customary international law?

5. In Garcia-Mir v. Meese, 788 F.2d 1446 (11th Cir. 1986), the court rejected the argument that customary international law is judicially enforceable against actions by the President or high-level Executive Branch officials. In that case, the

U.S. Attorney General had, without specific statutory authority, decided to incarcerate indefinitely a group of Cuban refugees, pending efforts to deport them. They had been granted a special immigration parole status, but their parole was later revoked. In response to the refugees' argument that this incarceration violated customary international law, the court cited the language from *The Paquete Habana* that public international law is controlling only "where there is no treaty and no controlling executive or legislative act or judicial decision." The court found that the Attorney General's determination constituted a "controlling executive act" that justified "disregard[ing] [customary] international law in service of domestic needs." Some other courts have similarly rejected the argument that customary international law can bind the President or other high-level Executive Branch officials. See, e.g., Barrera-Echavarria v. Rison, 44 F.3d 1441, 1451 (9th Cir. 1995); Gisbert v. United States Attorney General, 988 F.2d 1437, 1448 (5th Cir. 1993).

6. Although courts have recognized that customary international law is part of federal common law, most lower courts have held that Congress can pass legislation that violates a preexisting rule of customary international law. See, e.g., Guaylupo-Moya v. Gonzales, 423 F.3d 121 (2nd Cir. 2005); *Garcia-Mir*, supra; United States v. Yunis, 924 F.2d 1086, 1091 (D.C. Cir. 1991).

7. As discussed earlier in Section A.2.c., passing an inconsistent federal statute does not terminate the international obligations of the United States to its treaty partners. Now, if Congress passes a federal law that is inconsistent with a preexisting rule of customary international law, is the United States somehow still bound by the customary international law rule? If so, what countries or other entities might claim some rights to enforce the U.S. obligation, and how might they try to do this? At what point might the U.S. law change the content of the customary international law rule?

In 1992, Congress enacted a statute that gives both foreign and U.S. victims of torture and "extrajudicial killing" the right to sue for damages in U.S. courts.

Torture Victim Protection Act

Act March 12, 1992, P.L. 102-256, 106 Stat. 73

Sec. 1. Short Title

This Act may be cited as the "Torture Victim Protection Act of 1991."

Sec. 2. Establishment of Civil Action

(a) Liability. An individual who, under actual or apparent authority, or color of law, of any foreign nation—

(1) subjects an individual to torture shall, in a civil action, be liable for damages to that individual; or

(2) subjects an individual to extrajudicial killing shall, in a civil action, be liable for damages to the individual's legal representative, or to any person who may be a claimant in an action for wrongful death.

(b) Exhaustion of remedies. A court shall decline to hear a claim under this section if the claimant has not exhausted adequate and available remedies in the place in which the conduct giving rise to the claim occurred.

(c) Statute of limitations. No action shall be maintained under this section unless it is commenced within 10 years after the cause of action arose.

Sec. 3. Definitions

(a) Extrajudicial killing. For the purposes of this Act, the term "extrajudicial killing" means a deliberated killing not authorized by a previous judgment pronounced by a regularly constituted court affording all the judicial guarantees which are recognized as indispensable by civilized peoples. Such term, however, does not include any such killing that, under international law, is lawfully carried out under the authority of a foreign nation.

(b) Torture. For the purposes of this Act—

(1) the term "torture" means any act, directed against an individual in the offender's custody or physical control, by which severe pain or suffering (other than pain or suffering arising only from or inherent in, or incidental to, lawful sanctions), whether physical or mental, is intentionally inflicted on that individual for such purposes as obtaining from that individual or a third person information or a confession, punishing that individual for an act that individual or a third person has committed or is suspected of having committed, intimidating or coercing that individual or a third person, or for any reason based on discrimination of any kind; and

(2) mental pain or suffering refers to prolonged mental harm caused by or resulting from—

(A) the intentional infliction or threatened infliction of severe physical pain or suffering;

(B) the administration or application, or threatened administration or application, of mind altering substances or other procedures calculated to disrupt profoundly the senses or the personality;

(C) the threat of imminent death; or

(D) the threat that another individual will imminently be subjected to death, severe physical pain or suffering, or the administration or application of mind altering substances or other procedures calculated to disrupt profoundly the senses or personality.

Notes and Questions

1. The 1991 legislative history of the Torture Victim Protection Act (TVPA) expresses support for the *Filartiga* approach to human rights litigation under the Alien Tort Statute.

> The TVPA would establish an unambiguous basis for a cause of action that has been successfully maintained under an existing law, section 1350. . . . Section 1350 has other important uses and should not be repealed. . . . At least one Federal judge, however, has questioned whether section 1350 can be used by victims of torture committed in foreign nations absent an explicit grant of a cause of action by Congress. . . . The TVPA would provide such a grant, and would also enhance the remedy already available under Section 1350 in an important respect: while the [ATS] provides a remedy to aliens only, the TVPA would extend a civil remedy also to U.S. citizens who may have been tortured abroad. . . . At the same time, claims based

> on torture or summary executions do not exhaust the list of actions that may appropriately be covered by Section 1350. Consequently, that statute should remain intact. [Torture Victim Protection Act of 1991, S. Rep. 102-249, 102d Cong. (Nov. 19, 1991).]

2. Besides extending the remedy to U.S. citizen-plaintiffs, the TVPA included limitations that do not appear in the ATS. Compare the ATS and TVPA. What limitations do you find?

3. Should some of the TVPA limitations be read into the ATS? Several U.S. courts of appeals have borrowed the TVPA's ten-year statute of limitations for the ATS. See, e.g., Chavez v. Carranza, 559 F.3d 486, 492 (6th Cir. 2009); Pappa v. United States, 281 F.3d 1004 (9th Cir. 2002). But cf. Jean v. Dorelian, 431 F.3d 776 (11th Cir. 2005) (the statutes of limitations under TVPA and implicitly under ATS can be tolled until the defendant enters the United States). The TVPA's requirement for exhaustion of remedies has not been read into the ATS. However, at least one court has determined that there should be a judge-made prudential exhaustion requirement for certain kinds of claims arising under the ATS, specifically claims arising from customary international law norms that are not yet considered matters of "universal concern." Sarei v. Rio Tinto, 650 F. Supp. 2d 1004, 1024-32 (C.D. Cal. 2009), on appeal at 2010 U.S. App. LEXIS 22001 (9th Cir. Cal., Octr. 26, 2010).

4. In Kadic v. Karadzic, 70 F.3d 232, 239 (2d Cir. 1995), the Second Circuit Court of Appeals significantly extended the scope of Alien Tort Statute (ATS) litigation by holding "that certain forms of conduct violate the law of nations whether undertaken by those acting under the auspices of a state or only as private individuals." In *Kadic*, Bosnian Croats and Muslims sued Radovan Karadzic, the President of a self-proclaimed Bosnian-Serb republic within Bosnia-Herzegovina and the leader of the Bosnian-Serb military forces, under the ATS and TVPA, for claims involving genocide, war crimes, and the infliction of death, torture, and degrading treatment by the Bosnian-Serb forces during the Bosnian civil war. Such alleged atrocities included rape, forced prostitution, forced impregnation, torture, and summary execution.

After noting that the law of nations had long applied to acts of individuals like piracy and later the slave trade and war crimes, the *Kadic* court held that private individuals, as well as individuals acting under color of law, could be liable under international law and thus under the ATS for genocide and war crimes and other violations of international humanitarian law. The Court held that non-state actors could not be liable for torture and summary execution under the ATS, however, because "torture and summary execution — when not perpetrated in the course of genocide or war crimes — are proscribed by international law only when committed by state officials or under color of law." Id. at 243. The court additionally held that a private individual could be considered a state actor, and thus liable for claims like torture and summary execution that require state action, if the individual acted in concert with state officials or with significant state aid.

5. The *Kadic* decision facilitated a wave of ATS cases against private corporations, from the United States and abroad, with respect to alleged human rights and environmental abuses committed in foreign countries. See, e.g., Doe v. Unocal Corp., 110 F. Supp. 2d 1294 (C.D. Cal. 2000) (settled while on appeal and after the decision in *Sosa* below) (suit by Myanmar, or Burmese, citizens against U.S. corporations and their executives for alleged human rights abuses committed, in

least in part by the Myanmar government, in connection with construction of a oil pipeline in Myanmar); Flores v. Southern Peru Copper Corp., 414 F.3d 233 (2d Cir. 2003) (suit by Peruvian plaintiffs against a U.S. mining company for infringing upon their "right to health" and "right to sustainable development.")

See Chapter 10 for additional cases alleging environmental abuses. Chapter 8.B.8.d. notes other human rights cases. Also, as noted there, an important split has recently developed among the lower federal courts over whether corporations, as distinct from private individuals, can be sued under the ATS (e.g., Kiobel v. Royal Dutch Petroleum 621 F.3d 111 [2d Cir. 2010]).

6. When private individuals or corporations are sued under the ATS, depending on the allegations, the court may have to consider the extent to which state action is required for violations, the circumstances when state action might be imputed to private actors, and whether liability can be grounded on the concept of "aiding and abetting" or some other accomplice theory. See further discussion in Chapter 8.B.8.d.

7. By its terms, the ATS can be invoked only by alien plaintiffs. Although the TVPA can be invoked by U.S. citizens, it applies only when the defendant has acted "under actual or apparent authority, or color of law, of any foreign nation." Thus, U.S. citizens who sue domestic defendants for violations of customary international law cannot invoke either the ATS or the TVPA. In this context, a number of courts have held that the plaintiffs lack a private right of action.

Prior to the Supreme Court's 2004 opinion in *Sosa*, excerpted below, there was a growing debate over whether the ATS provided only a basis for subject matter jurisdiction or whether it also provided a statutory basis for a cause of action. A related question was, if the ATS provided a statutory basis for a cause of action, which causes of action were allowed?

Sosa v. Alvarez-Machain

U.S. Supreme Court
542 U.S. 692 (2004)

SOUTER, J., delivered the opinion of the Court, Parts I and III of which were unanimous, Part II of which was joined by REHNQUIST, C. J., and STEVENS, O'CONNOR, SCALIA, KENNEDY, and THOMAS, JJ., and Part IV of which was joined by STEVENS, O'CONNOR, KENNEDY, GINSBURG, and BREYER, JJ. SCALIA, J., filed an opinion concurring in part and concurring in the judgment, in which REHNQUIST, C. J., and THOMAS, J., joined. GINSBURG, J., filed an opinion concurring in part and concurring in the judgment, in which BREYER, J., joined. BREYER, J., filed an opinion concurring in part and concurring in the judgment.

Justice SOUTER delivered the opinion of the Court.

The two issues are whether respondent Alvarez-Machain's allegation that the Drug Enforcement Administration instigated his abduction from Mexico for criminal trial in the United States supports a claim against the Government under the Federal Tort Claims Act (FTCA or Act), 28 U.S.C. §1346(b)(1),

§§2671-2680, and whether he may recover under the Alien Tort Statute (ATS), 28 U.S.C. §1350. We hold that he is not entitled to a remedy under either statute.

I [Unanimous]

We have considered the underlying facts before, *United States* v. *Alvarez-Machain*, 504 U.S. 655 (1992). In 1985, an agent of the Drug Enforcement Administration (DEA), Enrique Camarena-Salazar, was captured on assignment in Mexico and taken to a house in Guadalajara, where he was tortured over the course of a 2-day interrogation, then murdered. Based in part on eyewitness testimony, DEA officials in the United States came to believe that respondent Humberto Alvarez-Machain (Alvarez), a Mexican physician, was present at the house and acted to prolong the agent's life in order to extend the interrogation and torture.

In 1990, a federal grand jury indicted Alvarez for the torture and murder of Camarena-Salazar, and the United States District Court . . . issued a warrant for his arrest. The DEA asked the Mexican Government for help in getting Alvarez into the United States, but when the requests and negotiations proved fruitless, the DEA approved a plan to hire Mexican nationals to seize Alvarez and bring him to the United States for trial. As so planned, a group of Mexicans, including petitioner Jose Francisco Sosa, abducted Alvarez from his house, held him overnight in a motel, and brought him by private plane to El Paso, Texas, where he was arrested by federal officers.

Once in American custody, Alvarez moved to dismiss the indictment on the ground that his seizure was "outrageous governmental conduct," and violated the extradition treaty between the United States and Mexico. The District Court agreed, the Ninth Circuit affirmed, and we reversed, holding that the fact of Alvarez's forcible seizure did not affect the jurisdiction of a federal court. The case was tried in 1992, and ended at the close of the Government's case, when the District Court granted Alvarez's motion for a judgment of acquittal.

In 1993, after returning to Mexico, Alvarez began the civil action before us here. He sued Sosa, Mexican citizen and DEA operative Antonio Garate-Bustamante, five unnamed Mexican civilians, the United States, and four DEA agents. So far as it matters here, Alvarez sought damages from the United States under the FTCA, alleging false arrest, and from Sosa under the ATS, for a violation of the law of nations. . . .

The District Court granted the Government's motion to dismiss the FTCA claim, but awarded summary judgment and $25,000 in damages to Alvarez on the ATS claim. A three-judge panel of the Ninth Circuit then affirmed the ATS judgment, but reversed the dismissal of the FTCA claim.

A divided en banc court came to the same conclusion. 331 F.3d, at 641. As for the ATS claim, the court called on its own precedent, "that [the ATS] not only provides federal courts with subject matter jurisdiction, but also creates a cause of action for an alleged violation of the law of nations." The Circuit then relied upon what it called the "clear and universally recognized norm prohibiting arbitrary arrest and detention," to support the conclusion that Alvarez's arrest amounted to a tort in violation of international law. . . . We granted certiorari in these companion cases to clarify the scope of both the FTCA and the ATS. We now reverse in each.

II [Seven Justices]

[This discussion of the FTCA claims is omitted. Briefly, the FTCA waives sovereign immunity for the United States in suits "for . . . personal injury . . . caused by the negligent or wrongful act or omission of any [U.S. Government] employee while acting within the scope of his office or employment." 28 U.S.C. §1346(b)(1), However, the FTCA has an exception to the waiver of immunity for claims "arising in a foreign country," which the Court held barred Alvarez's claim because it was based on an injury suffered in Mexico.]

III [Unanimous]

Alvarez has also brought an action under the ATS against petitioner, Sosa, who argues (as does the United States supporting him) that there is no relief under the ATS because the statute does no more than vest federal courts with jurisdiction, neither creating nor authorizing the courts to recognize any particular right of action without further congressional action. Although we agree the statute is in terms only jurisdictional, we think that at the time of enactment the jurisdiction enabled federal courts to hear claims in a very limited category defined by the law of nations and recognized at common law. We do not believe, however, that the limited, implicit sanction to entertain the handful of international law *cum* common law claims understood in 1789 should be taken as authority to recognize the right of action asserted by Alvarez here.

A

Judge Friendly called the ATS a "legal Lohengrin," *IIT* v. *Vencap, Ltd.*, 519 F.2d 1001, 1015 (CA2 1975); "no one seems to know whence it came," *ibid.*, and for over 170 years after its enactment it provided jurisdiction in only one case. The first Congress passed it as part of the Judiciary Act of 1789, in providing that the new federal district courts "shall also have cognizance, concurrent with the courts of the several States, or the circuit courts, as the case may be, of all causes where an alien sues for a tort only in violation of the law of nations or a treaty of the United States."[10]

The parties and *amici* here advance radically different historical interpretations of this terse provision. Alvarez says that the ATS was intended not simply as a jurisdictional grant, but as authority for the creation of a new cause of action for torts in violation of international law. We think that reading is implausible. As enacted in 1789, the ATS gave the district courts "cognizance" of certain causes of action, and the term bespoke a grant of jurisdiction, not power to mold substantive law. See, *e.g.*, The Federalist No. 81, pp 447, 451 (J. Cooke ed. 1961) (A. Hamilton) (using "jurisdiction" interchangeably with "cognizance"). The fact that the ATS was placed in §9 of the Judiciary Act, a statute otherwise exclusively concerned with federal-court jurisdiction, is itself support for its strictly jurisdictional nature. Nor would the

10. The statute has been slightly modified on a number of occasions since its original enactment. It now reads in its entirety: "The district courts shall have original jurisdiction of any civil action by an alien for a tort only, committed in violation of the law of nations or a treaty of the United States." 28 U.S.C. §1350.

distinction between jurisdiction and cause of action have been elided by the drafters of the Act or those who voted on it. . . . In sum, we think the statute was intended as jurisdictional in the sense of addressing the power of the courts to entertain cases concerned with a certain subject.

But holding the ATS jurisdictional raises a new question, this one about the interaction between the ATS at the time of its enactment and the ambient law of the era. Sosa would have it that the ATS was stillborn because there could be no claim for relief without a further statute expressly authorizing adoption of causes of action. *Amici* professors of federal jurisdiction and legal history take a different tack, that federal courts could entertain claims once the jurisdictional grant was on the books, because torts in violation of the law of nations would have been recognized within the common law of the time. We think history and practice give the edge to this latter position.

1

"When the United States declared their independence, they were bound to receive the law of nations, in its modern state of purity and refinement." *Ware* v. *Hylton*, 3 U.S. 199 (1796). In the years of the early Republic, this law of nations comprised two principal elements, the first covering the general norms governing the behavior of national states with each other: *"the science which teaches the rights subsisting between nations or states, and the obligations correspondent to those rights,"* E. de Vattel, The Law of Nations (J. Chitty et al. transl. and ed. 1883) (hereinafter Vattel). . . . This aspect of the law of nations thus occupied the executive and legislative domains, not the judicial. See 4 W. Blackstone, Commentaries on the Laws of England 68 (1769) (hereinafter Commentaries) ("[O]ffenses against" the law of nations are "principally incident to whole states or nations").

The law of nations included a second, more pedestrian element, however, that did fall within the judicial sphere, as a body of judge-made law regulating the conduct of individuals situated outside domestic boundaries and consequently carrying an international savor. To Blackstone, the law of nations in this sense was implicated "in mercantile questions, such as bills of exchange and the like . . . ; [and] in all disputes relating to prizes, to shipwrecks, to hostages, and ransom bills." The law merchant emerged from the customary practices of international traders and admiralty required its own transnational regulation. And it was the law of nations in this sense that our precursors spoke about when the Court explained the status of coast fishing vessels in wartime grew from "ancient usage among civilized nations, beginning centuries ago, and gradually ripening into a rule of international law. . . ." *The Paquete Habana*, 175 U.S. 677, 686 (1900).

There was, finally, a sphere in which these rules binding individuals for the benefit of other individuals overlapped with the norms of state relationships. Blackstone referred to it when he mentioned three specific offenses against the law of nations addressed by the criminal law of England: violation of safe conducts, infringement of the rights of ambassadors, and piracy. An assault against an ambassador, for example, impinged upon the sovereignty of the foreign nation and if not adequately redressed could rise to an issue of war. It was this narrow set of violations of the law of nations, admitting of a judicial remedy and at the same time threatening serious consequences in international affairs, that was probably on minds of the men who drafted the ATS with its reference to tort.

2

Before there was any ATS, a distinctly American preoccupation with these hybrid international norms had taken shape owing to the distribution of political power from independence through the period of confederation. The Continental Congress was hamstrung by its inability to "cause infractions of treaties, or of the law of nations to be punished," J. Madison, Journal of the Constitutional Convention 60 (E. Scott ed. 1893), and in 1781 the Congress implored the States to vindicate rights under the law of nations. . . .

. . . During the [Constitutional] Convention itself, . . . Secretary Jay reported to Congress . . . that "the federal government does not appear . . . to be vested with any judicial Powers competent to the Cognizance and Judgment of such Cases."

The Framers responded by vesting the Supreme Court with original jurisdiction over "all Cases affecting Ambassadors, other public ministers and Consuls." U.S. Const., Art. III, §2, and the First Congress followed through. The Judiciary Act reinforced this Court's original jurisdiction over suits brought by diplomats, see 1 Stat. 80, ch. 20, §13, created alienage jurisdiction, §11 and, of course, included the ATS, §9.

3

Although Congress modified the draft of what became the Judiciary Act, it made hardly any changes to the provisions on aliens, including what became the ATS. There is no record of congressional discussion about private actions that might be subject to the jurisdictional provision, or about any need for further legislation to create private remedies; there is no record even of debate on the section. . . . [D]espite considerable scholarly attention, it is fair to say that a consensus understanding of what Congress intended has proven elusive.

Still, the history does tend to support two propositions. First, there is every reason to suppose that the First Congress did not pass the ATS as a jurisdictional convenience to be placed on the shelf for use by a future Congress or state legislature that might, some day, authorize the creation of causes of action. . . . The anxieties of the preconstitutional period cannot be ignored easily enough to think that the statute was not meant to have a practical effect. . . .

The second inference to be drawn from the history is that Congress intended the ATS to furnish jurisdiction for a relatively modest set of actions alleging violations of the law of nations. Uppermost in the legislative mind appears to have been offenses against ambassadors, violations of safe conduct were probably understood to be actionable, and individual actions arising out of prize captures and piracy may well have also been contemplated. But the common law appears to have understood only those three of the hybrid variety as definite and actionable, or at any rate, to have assumed only a very limited set of claims. . . .

B . . .

In sum, although the ATS is a jurisdictional statute creating no new causes of action, the reasonable inference from the historical materials is that the statute was intended to have practical effect the moment it became law. The jurisdictional grant is best read as having been enacted on the understanding that the common law would provide a cause of action for the modest number of international law violations with a potential for personal liability at the time.

IV [Six Justices]

We think it is correct, then, to assume that the First Congress understood that the district courts would recognize private causes of action for certain torts in violation of the law of nations, though we have found no basis to suspect Congress had any examples in mind beyond those torts corresponding to Blackstone's three primary offenses: violation of safe conducts, infringement of the rights of ambassadors, and piracy. We assume, too, that no development in the two centuries from the enactment of §1350 to the birth of the modern line of cases beginning with *Filartiga* v. *Pena-Irala*, 630 F.2d 876 (CA2 1980), has categorically precluded federal courts from recognizing a claim under the law of nations as an element of common law; Congress has not in any relevant way amended §1350 or limited civil common law power by another statute. Still, there are good reasons for a restrained conception of the discretion a federal court should exercise in considering a new cause of action of this kind. Accordingly, we think courts should require any claim based on the present-day law of nations to rest on a norm of international character accepted by the civilized world and defined with a specificity comparable to the features of the 18th-century paradigms we have recognized. This requirement is fatal to Alvarez's claim.

A

A series of reasons argue for judicial caution when considering the kinds of individual claims that might implement the jurisdiction conferred by the early statute. First, the prevailing conception of the common law has changed since 1789 in a way that counsels restraint in judicially applying internationally generated norms. When §1350 was enacted, the accepted conception was of the common law as "a transcendental body of law outside of any particular State but obligatory within it unless and until changed by statute." *Black and White Taxicab & Transfer Co.* v. *Brown and Yellow Taxicab & Transfer Co.*, 276 U.S. 518, 533 (1928) (Holmes, J., dissenting). Now, however, in most cases where a court is asked to state or formulate a common law principle in a new context, there is a general understanding that the law is not so much found or discovered as it is either made or created. Holmes explained famously in 1881 that

> "in substance the growth of the law is legislative . . . [because t]he very considerations which judges most rarely mention, and always with an apology, are the secret root from which the law draws all the juices of life. I mean, of course, considerations of what is expedient for the community concerned." The Common Law 31-32 (Howe ed. 1963).

One need not accept the Holmesian view as far as its ultimate implications to acknowledge that a judge deciding in reliance on an international norm will find a substantial element of discretionary judgment in the decision.

Second, along with, and in part driven by, that conceptual development in understanding common law has come an equally significant rethinking of the role of the federal courts in making it. *Erie R. Co.* v. *Tompkins*, 304 U.S. 64 (1938), was the watershed in which we denied the existence of any federal "general" common law, which largely withdrew to havens of specialty, some of them defined by express congressional authorization to devise a body of law directly, *e.g.*, *Textile Workers* v. *Lincoln Mills of Ala.*, 353 U.S. 448 (1957) (interpretation of collective-bargaining agreements); Fed. Rule Evid. 501 (evidentiary privileges in federal-question cases). Elsewhere, this Court has thought it was in order to create federal common law rules in interstitial areas of particular federal interest. And although we have even assumed competence to make judicial rules of decision of particular importance to foreign relations, such as the act of state doctrine, see *Banco Nacional de Cuba* v. *Sabbatino*, 376 U.S. 398, 427 (1964), the general practice has been to look for legislative guidance before exercising innovative authority over substantive law. It would be remarkable to take a more aggressive role in exercising a jurisdiction that remained largely in shadow for much of the prior two centuries.

Third, this Court has recently and repeatedly said that a decision to create a private right of action is one better left to legislative judgment in the great majority of cases. The creation of a private right of action raises issues beyond the mere consideration whether underlying primary conduct should be allowed or not, entailing, for example, a decision to permit enforcement without the check imposed by prosecutorial discretion. Accordingly, even when Congress has made it clear by statute that a rule applies to purely domestic conduct, we are reluctant to infer intent to provide a private cause of action where the statute does not supply one expressly. While the absence of congressional action addressing private rights of action under an international norm is more equivocal than its failure to provide such a right when it creates a statute, the possible collateral consequences of making international rules privately actionable argue for judicial caution.

Fourth, the subject of those collateral consequences is itself a reason for a high bar to new private causes of action for violating international law, for the potential implications for the foreign relations of the United States of recognizing such causes should make courts particularly wary of impinging on the discretion of the Legislative and Executive Branches in managing foreign affairs. It is one thing for American courts to enforce constitutional limits on our own State and Federal Governments' power, but quite another to consider suits under rules that would go so far as to claim a limit on the power of foreign governments over their own citizens, and to hold that a foreign government or its agent has transgressed those limits. Yet modern international law is very much concerned with just such questions, and apt to stimulate calls for vindicating private interests in §1350 cases. Since many attempts by federal courts to craft remedies for the violation of new norms of international law would raise risks of adverse foreign policy consequences, they should be undertaken, if at all, with great caution.

The fifth reason is particularly important in light of the first four. We have no congressional mandate to seek out and define new and debatable violations of the law of nations, and modern indications of congressional understanding of the judicial role in the field have not affirmatively encouraged greater judicial creativity. It is true that a clear mandate appears in the Torture Victim Protection Act of 1991 . . . providing authority that "establish[es] an unambiguous and modern basis for" federal claims of torture and extrajudicial killing, H. R. Rep. No.102-367, pt. 1, p 3 (1991). But that affirmative authority is confined to specific subject matter, and although the legislative history includes the remark that §1350 should "remain intact to permit suits based on other norms that already exist or may ripen in the future into rules of customary international law," Congress as a body has done nothing to promote such suits. Several times, indeed, the Senate has expressly declined to give the federal courts the task of interpreting and applying international human rights law, as when its ratification of the International Covenant on Civil and Political Rights declared that the substantive provisions of the document were not self-executing.

B

These reasons argue for great caution in adapting the law of nations to private rights . . . [A] word is in order to summarize where we have come so far and to focus our difference with [Justice Scalia] on whether some norms of today's law of nations may ever be recognized legitimately by federal courts in the absence of congressional action beyond §1350. All Members of the Court agree that §1350 is only jurisdictional. We also agree, or at least Justice Scalia does not dispute, *post*, that the jurisdiction was originally understood to be available to enforce a small number of international norms that a federal court could properly recognize as within the common law enforceable without further statutory authority. . . .

. . . [O]ther considerations persuade us that the judicial power should be exercised on the understanding that the door is still ajar subject to vigilant doorkeeping, and thus open to a narrow class of international norms today. *Erie* did not in terms bar any judicial recognition of new substantive rules, no matter what the circumstances, and post-*Erie* understanding has identified limited enclaves in which federal courts may derive some substantive law in a common law way. For two centuries we have affirmed that the domestic law of the United States recognizes the law of nations. See, *e.g., Sabbatino,* 376 U.S., at 423 ("[I]t is, of course, true that United States courts apply international law as a part of our own in appropriate circumstances"); *The Paquete Habana,* 175 U.S., at 700 ("International law is part of our law, and must be ascertained and administered by the courts of justice of appropriate jurisdiction, as often as questions of right depending upon it are duly presented for their determination"). . . . It would take some explaining to say now that federal courts must avert their gaze entirely from any international norm intended to protect individuals.

. . . The First Congress, which reflected the understanding of the framing generation and included some of the Framers, assumed that federal courts could properly identify some international norms as enforceable in the exercise of §1350 jurisdiction. . . . The position we take today has been assumed by some federal courts for 24 years, ever since the Second Circuit decided *Filartiga* v. *Pena-Irala,* 630 F.2d 876 (CA2 1980). . . . Congress . . . has not only expressed no disagreement with our view of the proper exercise of the judicial power, but has responded to its most notable instance by enacting legislation supplementing the judicial determination in some detail. See *supra* (discussing the Torture Victim Protection Act).

While we agree with Justice Scalia to the point that we would welcome any congressional guidance in exercising jurisdiction with such obvious potential to affect foreign relations, nothing Congress has done is a reason for us to shut the door to the law of nations entirely. It is enough to say that Congress may do that at any time (explicitly, or implicitly by treaties or statutes that occupy the field) just as it may modify or cancel any judicial decision so far as it rests on recognizing an international norm as such.

C

We must still, however, derive a standard or set of standards for assessing the particular claim Alvarez raises, and for this case it suffices to look to the historical antecedents. Whatever the ultimate criteria for accepting a cause of action subject to jurisdiction under §1350, we are persuaded that federal courts should not recognize private claims under federal common law for violations of any international law norm with less definite content and acceptance among civilized nations than the historical paradigms familiar when §1350 was enacted. See, *e.g., United States* v. *Smith,* 18 U.S. 153, 163-180 (1820) (illustrating the specificity with which the law of nations defined piracy). This limit upon judicial recognition is generally consistent with the reasoning of many of the courts and judges who faced the issue before it reached this Court. See *Filartiga, supra,* at 890 ("[F]or purposes of civil liability, the torturer has become — like the pirate and slave trader before him — *hostis humani generis,* an enemy of all mankind"); *Tel-Oren, supra,* at 781 (Edwards, J., concurring) (suggesting that the "limits of section 1350's reach" be defined by "a handful of heinous actions — each of which violates definable, universal and obligatory norms"); see also *In re Estate of Marcos Human Rights Litigation,* 25 F.3d 1467, 1475 (CA9 1994) ("Actionable violations of international law must be of a norm that is specific, universal, and obligatory"). And the determination whether a norm is sufficiently definite to support a cause of action[20] should (and, indeed, inevitably must) involve an element of judgment about the practical consequences of making that cause available to litigants in the federal courts.[21]

Thus, Alvarez's detention claim must be gauged against the current state of international law, looking to those sources we have long, albeit cautiously, recognized.

20. A related consideration is whether international law extends the scope of liability for a violation of a given norm to the perpetrator being sued, if the defendant is a private actor such as a corporation or individual. Compare *Tel-Oren* v. *Libyan Arab Republic,* 726 F.2d 774, 791-795 (CADC 1984) (Edwards, J., concurring) (insufficient consensus in 1984 that torture by private actors violates international law), with *Kadic* v. *Karadzic,* 70 F.3d 232, 239-241 (CA2 1995) (sufficient consensus in 1995 that genocide by private actors violates international law).

21. This requirement of clear definition is not meant to be the only principle limiting the availability of relief in the federal courts for violations of customary international law, though it disposes of this case. For example, the European Commission argues as *amicus curiae* that basic principles of international law require that before asserting a claim in a foreign forum, the claimant must have exhausted any remedies available in the domestic legal system, and perhaps in other fora such as international claims tribunals. . . . [C]f. Torture Victim Protection Act of 1991, §2(b), 106 Stat 73 (exhaustion requirement). We would certainly consider this requirement in an appropriate case.

Another possible limitation that we need not apply here is a policy of case-specific deference to the political branches. For example, there are now pending in federal district court several class actions seeking damages from various corporations alleged to have participated in, or abetted, the regime of apartheid that formerly controlled South Africa. The Government of South Africa has said that these cases interfere with the policy embodied by its Truth and Reconciliation Commission, which "deliberately avoided a 'victors' justice' approach to the crimes of apartheid and chose instead one based on confession and absolution, informed by the principles of reconciliation, reconstruction, reparation and goodwill." Declaration of Penuell Mpapa Maduna, Minister of Justice and Constitutional Development, Republic of South Africa. The United States has agreed. See Letter of William H. Taft IV, Legal Adviser, Dept. of State, October 27, 2003. In such cases, there is a strong argument that federal courts should give serious weight to the Executive Branch's view of the case's impact on foreign policy. Cf. *Republic of Austria* v. *Altmann,* 541 U.S. 677, 701-702 (2004) (discussing the State Department's use of statements of interest in cases involving the Foreign Sovereign Immunities Act of 1976, 28 U.S.C. §1602 *et seq.*).

"[W]here there is no treaty, and no controlling executive or legislative act or judicial decision, resort must be had to the customs and usages of civilized nations; and, as evidence of these, to the works of jurists and commentators, who by years of labor, research and experience, have made themselves peculiarly well acquainted with the subjects of which they treat. Such works are resorted to by judicial tribunals, not for the speculations of their authors concerning what the law ought to be, but for trustworthy evidence of what the law really is." *The Paquete Habana*, 175 U.S., at 700.

To begin with, Alvarez cites two well-known international agreements that, despite their moral authority, have little utility under the standard set out in this opinion. He says that his abduction by Sosa was an "arbitrary arrest" within the meaning of the Universal Declaration of Human Rights (Declaration), G. A. Res. 217A (III)(1948). And he traces the rule against arbitrary arrest not only to the Declaration, but also to article nine of the International Covenant on Civil and Political Rights (Covenant), Dec. 19, 1996,[22] to which the United States is a party, and to various other conventions to which it is not. But the Declaration does not of its own force impose obligations as a matter of international law. See Humphrey, The UN Charter and the Universal Declaration of Human Rights, in The International Protection of Human Rights 39, 50 (E. Luard ed. 1967) (quoting Eleanor Roosevelt calling the Declaration " 'a statement of principles . . . setting up a common standard of achievement for all peoples and all nations' " and " 'not a treaty or international agreement . . . impos[ing] legal obligations' ").[23] And, although the Covenant does bind the United States as a matter of international law, the United States ratified the Covenant on the express understanding that it was not self-executing and so did not itself create obligations enforceable in the federal courts. Accordingly, Alvarez cannot say that the Declaration and Covenant themselves establish the relevant and applicable rule of international law. He instead attempts to show that prohibition of arbitrary arrest has attained the status of binding customary international law.

Here, it is useful to examine Alvarez's complaint in greater detail. As he presently argues it, the claim does not rest on the cross-border feature of his abduction. . . . [T]he Court of Appeals rejected that ground of liability. . . . Instead, it relied on the conclusion that the law of the United States did not authorize Alvarez's arrest, because the DEA lacked extraterritorial authority under 21 U.S.C. §878, and because Federal Rule of Criminal Procedure 4(d)(2) limited the warrant for Alvarez's arrest to "the jurisdiction of the United States." It is this position that Alvarez takes now: that his arrest was arbitrary and as such forbidden by international law not because it infringed the prerogatives of Mexico, but because no applicable law authorized it.

Alvarez thus invokes a general prohibition of "arbitrary" detention defined as officially sanctioned action exceeding positive authorization to detain under the domestic law of some government, regardless of the circumstances. Whether or not

22. Article nine provides that "[n]o one shall be subjected to arbitrary arrest or detention," that "[n]o one shall be deprived of his liberty except on such grounds and in accordance with such procedure as are established by law," and that "[a]nyone who has been the victim of unlawful arrest or detention shall have an enforceable right to compensation." 999 U. N. T. S., at 175-176.

23. It has nevertheless had substantial indirect effect on international law. See Brownlie, *supra*, at 535 (calling the Declaration a "good example of an informal prescription given legal significance by the actions of authoritative decision-makers").

this is an accurate reading of the Covenant, Alvarez cites little authority that a rule so broad has the status of a binding customary norm today.[27] He certainly cites nothing to justify the federal courts in taking his broad rule as the predicate for a federal lawsuit, for its implications would be breathtaking. His rule would support a cause of action in federal court for any arrest, anywhere in the world, unauthorized by the law of the jurisdiction in which it took place, and would create a cause of action for any seizure of an alien in violation of the Fourth Amendment. . . . It would create an action in federal court for arrests by state officers who simply exceed their authority; and for the violation of any limit that the law of any country might place on the authority of its own officers to arrest. And all of this assumes that Alvarez could establish that Sosa was acting on behalf of a government when he made the arrest, for otherwise he would need a rule broader still.

Alvarez's failure to marshal support for his proposed rule is underscored by the Restatement (Third) of Foreign Relations Law . . . (1987), which says in its discussion of customary international human rights law that a "state violates international law if, as a matter of state policy, it practices, encourages, or condones . . . prolonged arbitrary detention." *Id.*, §702. Although the Restatement does not explain its requirements of a "state policy" and of "prolonged" detention, the implication is clear. Any credible invocation of a principle against arbitrary detention that the civilized world accepts as binding customary international law requires a factual basis beyond relatively brief detention in excess of positive authority. Even the Restatement's limits are only the beginning of the enquiry, because although it is easy to say that some policies of prolonged arbitrary detentions are so bad that those who enforce them become enemies of the human race, it may be harder to say which policies cross that line with the certainty afforded by Blackstone's three common law offenses. In any event, the label would never fit the reckless policeman who botches his warrant, even though that same officer might pay damages under municipal law.

Whatever may be said for the broad principle Alvarez advances, in the present, imperfect world, it expresses an aspiration that exceeds any binding customary rule having the specificity we require.[29] Creating a private cause of action to further that aspiration would go beyond any residual common law discretion we think it appropriate to exercise. It is enough to hold that a single illegal detention of less than a day, followed by the transfer of custody to lawful authorities and a prompt

27. Specifically, he relies on a survey of national constitutions; a case from the International Court of Justice, *United States* v *Iran*, 1980 I. C. J. 3, 42; and some authority drawn from the federal courts. None of these suffice. The . . . survey does show that many nations recognize a norm against arbitrary detention, but that consensus is at a high level of generality. The *Iran* case, in which the United States sought relief for the taking of its diplomatic and consular staff as hostages, involved a different set of international norms and mentioned the problem of arbitrary detention only in passing; the detention in that case was, moreover, far longer and harsher than Alvarez's. And the authority from the federal courts, to the extent it supports Alvarez's position, reflects a more assertive view of federal judicial discretion over claims based on customary international law than the position we take today.

29. It is not that violations of a rule logically foreclose the existence of that rule as international law. Cf. *Filartiga v. Pena-Irala*, 630 F.2d 876, 884, n.15 (CA2 1980) ("The fact that the prohibition of torture is often honored in the breach does not diminish its binding effect as a norm of international law"). Nevertheless, that a rule as stated is as far from full realization as the one Alvarez urges is evidence against its status as binding law; and an even clearer point against the creation by judges of a private cause of action to enforce the aspiration behind the rule claimed.

arraignment, violates no norm of customary international law so well defined as to support the creation of a federal remedy.

The judgment of the Court of Appeals is *Reversed.*

Justice SCALIA, with whom THE CHIEF JUSTICE and Justice THOMAS join, concurring in part and concurring in the judgment.

There is not much that I would add to the Court's detailed opinion, and only one thing that I would subtract: its reservation of a discretionary power in the Federal Judiciary to create causes of action for the enforcement of international-law-based norms. Accordingly, I join Parts I, II, and III of the Court's opinion in these consolidated cases. Although I agree with much in Part IV, I cannot join it because the judicial lawmaking role it invites would commit the Federal Judiciary to a task it is neither authorized nor suited to perform. . . .

We Americans have a method for making the laws that are over us. We elect representatives to two Houses of Congress, each of which must enact the new law and present it for the approval of a President, whom we also elect. For over two decades now, unelected federal judges have been usurping this lawmaking power by converting what they regard as norms of international law into American law. Today's opinion approves that process in principle, though urging the lower courts to be more restrained.

This Court seems incapable of admitting that some matters — *any* matters — are none of its business. . . . In today's latest victory for its Never Say Never Jurisprudence, the Court ignores its own conclusion that the ATS provides only jurisdiction, wags a finger at the lower courts for going too far, and then — repeating the same formula the ambitious lower courts *themselves* have used — invites them to try again.

It would be bad enough if there were some assurance that future conversions of perceived international norms into American law would be approved by this Court itself. (Though we know ourselves to be eminently reasonable, self-awareness of eminent reasonableness is not really a substitute for democratic election.) But in this illegitimate lawmaking endeavor, the lower federal courts will be the principal actors; we review but a tiny fraction of their decisions. And no one thinks that all of them are eminently reasonable.

American law — the law made by the people's democratically elected representatives — does not recognize a category of activity that is so universally disapproved by other nations that it is automatically unlawful here, and automatically gives rise to a private action for money damages in federal court. That simple principle is what today's decision should have announced. . . .

Justice BREYER, concurring in part and concurring in the judgment.

I join . . . the Court's opinion in respect to the Alien Tort Statute (ATS) claim. The Court says that to qualify for recognition under the ATS a norm of international law must have a content as definite as, and an acceptance as widespread as, those that characterized 18th-century international norms prohibiting piracy. The norm must extend liability to the type of perpetrator (*e.g.*, a private actor) the plaintiff seeks to sue. . . . The Court also suggests that principles of exhaustion might apply, and that courts should give "serious weight" to the Executive Branch's view of the impact on foreign policy that permitting an ATS suit will likely have in a given case or type of case. I believe all of these conditions are important.

I would add one further consideration. Since enforcement of an international norm by one nation's courts implies that other nations' courts may do the same, I would ask whether the exercise of jurisdiction under the ATS is consistent with those notions of comity that lead each nation to respect the sovereign rights of other nations by limiting the reach of its laws and their enforcement. In applying those principles, courts help assure that "the potentially conflicting laws of different nations" will "work together in harmony," a matter of increasing importance in an ever more interdependent world. *F. Hoffmann-La Roche Ltd.* v. *Empagran S. A.*, [542 U.S. 155 (2004)]. . . . .

Taking these matters into account, . . . I can find no similar procedural consensus supporting the exercise of jurisdiction in this case. That lack of consensus provides additional support for the Court's conclusion that the ATS does not recognize the claim at issue here—where the underlying substantive claim concerns arbitrary arrest, outside the United States, of a citizen of one foreign country by another.

Notes and Questions

1. What specifically seem to be the standards that the Court's opinion in *Sosa* establishes for a norm of customary international law ("law of nations") to qualify as a cause of action under the Alien Tort Statute? See especially Part IV.C. of the Court's opinion. Do you believe these standards are sufficiently precise to resolve most questions?

2. Given the *Sosa* standards, do you think that any or all of the following activities provide a federal cause of action under the ATS: genocide (or the killing of all or part of a national, ethnic, racial, or religious group); torturing enemy soldiers or terrorists after capturing them in order to obtain important information; a government or private employer engaging in racial discrimination in the workplace; substantial pollution of a major river that flows into the ocean; and failing to obtain informed consent from a group of adults in a developing country before testing a not yet fully approved medicine on them? (These activities were also raised in Chapter 2 as to the threshold question of what qualifies as a norm of customary international law.)

3. How does one characterize the causes of actions that the Court says are allowed under the "law of nations" part of the Alien Tort Statute? Are they norms of customary international law that directly become federal causes of action under the ATS? Or, are they norms of customary international law that have also met the *Sosa* criteria and have become part of federal common law? (See the discussion in the majority opinion at pages 261-263 above.) If it is the first explanation, then what prevents *any* norm of customary international law that might be a tort from becoming a federal cause of action?

4. In the examples in Question 2 above, does it matter whether the perpetrator of the acts is the government or a private person? See footnote 20 in the Court's opinion. Why should it matter, if at all? Should some acts (e.g., racial discrimination or cruel and degrading treatment) only be actionable, or more easily qualify for a

suit, if the state is the perpetrator or if there is "state action," rather than if a private party is the sole actor. See Kadic v. Karadzic, 70 F.3d 232 (2d Cir. 1995), discussed above at page 252.

5. Should it matter if the private person is an individual or a corporation? See discussion about the recent split of courts re: an individual versus a corporation, at id. at Note 5 and also in Chapter 8.B.8.d.

6. The *Kadic* decision on the liability of private individuals, and not just a government or its officials, relied, in part, on Sections 404 and 702 the Restatement. Section 404 addresses universal jurisdiction to define and punish certain offenses, including by individuals. It provides:

> A state has jurisdiction to define and prescribe punishment for certain offenses recognized by the community of nations as of universal concern, such as piracy, slave trade, attacks on or hijacking of aircraft, genocide, war crimes, and perhaps certain acts of terrorism, even where none of the bases of jurisdiction indicated in §402 is present.

Section 702 is titled The Customary International Law of Human Rights. It provides:

> A state violates international law if, as a matter of state policy, it practices, encourages, or condones
> a. genocide,
> b. slavery or slave trade,
> c. the murder or causing the disappearance of individuals,
> d. torture or other cruel, inhuman, or degrading treatment or punishment,
> e. prolonged arbitrary detention,
> f. systematic racial discrimination, or
> g. a consistent pattern of gross violations of internationally recognized human rights.

7. As indicated in *Kadic* and the Restatement, a government or person connected with the state is held to a higher standard on international human rights than private persons—for example, on racial discrimination and on cruel, inhuman, or degrading treatment. However, if a foreign state is the perpetrator of the tort that injures an alien, it would be hard to sue the state in U.S. courts because most states will be protected in most instances by the Foreign Sovereign Immunities Act, discussed in Chapter 6.

Given foreign state immunities, plaintiffs often seek to sue private persons (individuals or corporations) because they were somehow allegedly involved with the state's activities. What should be the basis for finding a private party liable under the more demanding human rights standards for a state? Should the basis be found in international law? See footnote 20 in *Sosa.* If not, should it be based on U.S. federal law (e.g., 42 U.S.C. §1983) or on a U.S. state's law (e.g., California's) where the court is sitting? Whatever the source of the law, should the relevant liability concepts be based on an aiding and abetting theory? Agency? Joint venture liability? Partnership? Accomplice? "State action"? On the last set of questions regarding liability concepts, see the discussion in Chapter 8.B.8.d.

2. *The* Charming Betsy *Canon and Statutory and Constitutional Interpretation*

International law is invoked at times to help in interpreting U.S. law. In Murray v. The Schooner Charming Betsy, 6 U.S. (2 Cranch) 64 (1804), the Supreme Court avoided a conflict between a statute prohibiting "commercial intercourse with France or her dependencies" by "any person or persons, resident within the United States or under their protection," id. at 118, and customary international law rules regarding neutral rights by determining that the statute did not apply to a ship owner living abroad who was a dual citizen of the United States and Denmark. Id. at 116-120. In his opinion, Chief Justice Marshall identified the principle "that an act of Congress ought never to be construed to violate the law of nations if any other possible construction remains. . . ." Id. at 118. This principle, which also applies to international agreements, has come to be called the "*Charming Betsy* canon" of interpretation of federal statutes. See also Justice Scalia's dissent in Hartford Fire Insurance Co. v. California, 509 U.S. 764 (1993) and the notes following it in Chapter 7; Serra v. Lappin, 600 F.3d 1191, 1198 (9th Cir. 2010); Restatement, Section 114 ("Where fairly possible, a United States statute is to be construed so as not to conflict with international law or with an international agreement of the United States.").

Similarly, some recent U.S. Supreme Court decisions have cited international law or the laws and practices of other countries when interpreting specific provisions of the U.S. Constitution. See e.g., Lawrence v. Texas, 539 U.S. 558, 573 (2003) (citing a European Court of Human Rights decision in the course of overruling the Supreme Court's 1986 decision holding that a U.S. state's criminalizing consensual homosexual conduct was constitutional under the Due Process Clause); Grutter v. Bollinger, 539 U.S. 306, 344 (2003) (Ginsburg, J., concurring) (citing the International Convention on the Elimination of All Forms of Racial Discrimination and the Convention on the Elimination of All Forms of Discrimination against Women in concurring that a law school's affirmative action policies should be upheld under the Equal Protection Clause); Atkins v. Virginia, 536 U.S. 304, 316 n.21 (2002) (citing overwhelming disapproval among the world community of the execution of the mentally retarded in the course of determining the practice is prohibited as cruel and unusual punishment under the Eighth Amendment).

In Roper v. Simmons, 543 U.S. 551, 578 (2005), in addition to other reasons, Justice Kennedy's majority opinion for five Justices used international practice and law to "provide a respected and significant confirmation for [the Court's] conclusion" that juvenile executions violated the Eighth Amendment because they are cruel and unusual punishments under the "evolving standards of decency that mark the progress of a maturing society." 543 U.S. at 561, 578. Noting that the United States was one of only two countries that failed to ratify the U.N. Convention on the Rights of the Child, which prohibits juvenile execution, and was one of only seven countries that have executed juveniles since 1990, Justice Kennedy concluded:

> It is proper that we acknowledge the overwhelming weight of international opinion against the death penalty. . . . The opinion of the world community, while not controlling our outcome, does provide respected and significant confirmation for our own conclusions.

> Over time, from one generation to the next, the Constitution has come to earn the high respect and even, as Madison dared to hope, the veneration of the American people. The document sets forth, and rests upon, innovative principles original to the American experience, such as federalism; a proven balance in political mechanisms through separation of powers; specific guarantees for the accused in criminal cases; and broad provisions to secure individual freedom and preserve human dignity. These doctrines and guarantees are central to the American experience and remain essential to our present-day self-definition and national identity. Not the least of the reasons we honor the Constitution, then, is because we know it to be our own. It does not lessen our fidelity to the Constitution or our pride in its origins to acknowledge that the express affirmation of certain fundamental rights by other nations and peoples simply underscores the centrality of those same rights within our own heritage of freedom. [543 U.S. at 578.]

In his dissent, Justice Scalia responded:

> [T]he basic premise of the Court's argument — that American law should conform to the laws of the rest of the world — ought to be rejected out of hand. . . . In many significant respects the laws of most other countries differ from our law — including not only such explicit provisions of our Constitution as the right to jury trial and grand jury indictment, but even many interpretations of the Constitution prescribed by this Court itself. . . . I do not believe that approval by "other nations and peoples" should buttress our commitment to American principles any more than (what should logically follow) disapproval by "other nations and peoples" should weaken that commitment. More importantly, however, the Court's statement flatly misdescribes what is going on here. Foreign sources are cited today, *not* to underscore our "fidelity" to the Constitution, our "pride in its origins," and "our own [American] heritage." To the contrary, they are cited *to set aside* the centuries-old American practice — a practice still engaged in by a large majority of the relevant States — of letting a jury of 12 citizens decide whether, in the particular case, youth should be the basis for withholding the death penalty. What these foreign sources "affirm," rather than repudiate, is the Justices' own notion of how the world ought to be, and their diktat that it shall be so henceforth in America. [543 U.S. at 624, 628.]

Which view is more persuasive? When evaluating "evolving standards of decency," should the Court use international law and/or the law and practice of other countries to assist it? Is international law and/or practice particularly useful or inappropriate when the laws of U.S. states vary and many diverge from what appears to be an international consensus? By citing international law and practice, does the U.S. Supreme Court help identify and further establish universal norms?

The Court's turn to non-U.S. legal sources and practice in cases like *Simmons* has produced vociferous academic discourse, extensive media coverage, and congressional criticisms. For a detailed look at the historical use of international law and practice in constitutional interpretation, see, for example, Sarah H. Cleveland, Our International Constitution, 31 Yale J. Int'l L. 1 (2006) and The U.S. Supreme Court and International Law: Continuity and Change (David L. Sloss, Michael D. Ramsey & William S. Dodge eds., 2011).

D. THE FIFTY STATES AND FOREIGN AFFAIRS

One of the perceived defects of the Articles of Confederation (the agreement among the 13 states in place prior to the Constitution) was that they did not give the federal government sufficient authority to conduct foreign relations. The Constitution addressed this problem in a variety of ways: Article I, Section 10 prohibits the states from performing certain foreign relations functions, such as treaty making; Article I, Section 8 and Article II broadly authorize the federal political branches to conduct foreign relations through the enactment of federal statutes and treaties; the Supremacy Clause in Article VI establishes that these federal enactments are supreme over state law; Article III extends the federal judicial power to cases involving these federal enactments and to other transnational controversies; and the "take care" clause in Article II authorizes the President to enforce federal enactments.

Despite these constitutional provisions, it cannot be said that federalism is irrelevant to the conduct of U.S. foreign relations. As confirmed by the Tenth Amendment, the Constitution vests the federal government with only limited and enumerated powers, and this principle might apply even when the government is regulating foreign affairs. Further, state law has traditionally governed many aspects of a foreign national's activities in the United States. This is true, for example, of private law issues such as tort, contract, and family law, as well as issues of criminal law. In addition, states sometimes take positions on international economic and political issues, and the federal government often declines to preempt the states on these issues.

The relationship between foreign affairs and federalism has become a more significant issue in recent years, for three reasons. First, there has been increasing overlap between certain areas of international law, such as international trade law and international human rights law, and areas of traditional state regulation. Second, as discussed earlier in this chapter, the Supreme Court has imposed some federalism restraints on the national government in the domestic context. It is conceivable that, notwithstanding Missouri v. Holland, the Court would apply some of these limitations to the foreign affairs context. Third, states and cities increasingly are expressing their own views regarding foreign policy.

Crosby v. National Foreign Trade Council

U.S. Supreme Court
530 U.S. 363 (2000)

Justice Souter delivered the opinion of the Court.

The issue is whether the Burma law of the Commonwealth of Massachusetts, restricting the authority of its agencies to purchase goods or services from companies doing business with Burma, is invalid under the Supremacy Clause of the National Constitution owing to its threat of frustrating federal statutory objectives. We hold that it is.

I

In June 1996, Massachusetts adopted "An Act Regulating State Contracts with Companies Doing Business with or in Burma (Myanmar)." The statute generally bars state entities from buying goods or services from any person (defined to include a business organization) identified on a "restricted purchase list" of those doing business with Burma. Although the statute has no general provision for waiver or termination of its ban, it does exempt from boycott any entities present in Burma solely to report the news, or to provide international telecommunication goods or services, or medical supplies. . . .

There are three exceptions to the ban: (1) if the procurement is essential, and without the restricted bid, there would be no bids or insufficient competition; (2) if the procurement is of medical supplies; and (3) if the procurement efforts elicit no "comparable low bid or offer" by a person not doing business with Burma, meaning an offer that is no more than 10 percent greater than the restricted bid. . . .

In September 1996, three months after the Massachusetts law was enacted, Congress passed a statute imposing a set of mandatory and conditional sanctions on Burma. The federal Act has five basic parts, three substantive and two procedural.

First, it imposes three sanctions directly on Burma. It bans all aid to the Burmese Government except for humanitarian assistance, counternarcotics efforts, and promotion of human rights and democracy. The statute instructs United States representatives to international financial institutions to vote against loans or other assistance to or for Burma, and it provides that no entry visa shall be issued to any Burmese government official unless required by treaty or to staff the Burmese mission to the United Nations. These restrictions are to remain in effect "until such time as the President determines and certifies to Congress that Burma has made measurable and substantial progress in improving human rights practices and implementing democratic government."

Second, the federal Act authorizes the President to impose further sanctions subject to certain conditions. He may prohibit "United States persons" from "new investment" in Burma, and shall do so if he determines and certifies to Congress that the Burmese Government has physically harmed, rearrested, or exiled Daw Aung San Suu Kyi (the opposition leader selected to receive the Nobel Peace Prize), or has committed "large-scale repression of or violence against the Democratic opposition." "New investment" is defined as entry into a contract that would favor the "economical development of resources located in Burma," or would provide ownership interests in or benefits from such development, but the term specifically excludes (and thus excludes from any Presidential prohibition) "entry into, performance of, or financing of a contract to sell or purchase goods, services, or technology."

Third, the statute directs the President to work to develop "a comprehensive, multilateral strategy to bring democracy to and improve human rights practices and the quality of life in Burma." He is instructed to cooperate with members of the Association of Southeast Asian Nations (ASEAN) and with other countries having major trade and investment interests in Burma to devise such an approach, and to pursue the additional objective of fostering dialogue between the ruling State Law and Order Restoration Council (SLORC) and democratic opposition groups.

As for the procedural provisions of the federal statute, the fourth section requires the President to report periodically to certain congressional committee chairmen. . . . And the fifth part of the federal Act authorizes the President "to waive, temporarily or permanently, any sanction [under the federal Act] . . . if he determines and certifies to Congress that the application of such sanction would be contrary to the national security interests of the United States."

On May 20, 1997, the President issued the Burma Executive Order, Exec. Order No. 13047. He certified . . . that the Government of Burma had "committed large-scale repression of the democratic opposition in Burma" and found that the Burmese Government's actions and policies constituted "an unusual and extraordinary threat to the national security and foreign policy of the United States," a threat characterized as a national emergency. The President then prohibited new investment in Burma "by United States persons," any approval or facilitation by a United States person of such new investment by foreign persons, and any transaction meant to evade or avoid the ban. The order generally incorporated the exceptions and exemptions addressed in the statute. Finally, the President delegated to the Secretary of State the tasks of working with ASEAN and other countries to develop a strategy for democracy, human rights, and the quality of life in Burma, and of making the required congressional reports. . . .

III

A fundamental principle of the Constitution is that Congress has the power to preempt state law. Art. VI, cl. 2. Even without an express provision for preemption, we have found that state law must yield to a congressional Act in at least two circumstances. When Congress intends federal law to "occupy the field," state law in that area is preempted. And even if Congress has not occupied the field, state law is naturally preempted to the extent of any conflict with a federal statute. . . . We will find preemption where it is impossible for a private party to comply with both state and federal law, and where "under the circumstances of [a] particular case, [the challenged state law] stands as an obstacle to the accomplishment and execution of the full purposes and objectives of Congress." Hines [v. Davidowitz, 312 U.S. 52, 67 (1941)]. What is a sufficient obstacle is a matter of judgment, to be informed by examining the federal statute as a whole and identifying its purpose and intended effects. . . .

Applying this standard, we see the state Burma law as an obstacle to the accomplishment of Congress's full objectives under the federal Act. We find that the state law undermines the intended purpose and "natural effect" of at least three provisions of the federal Act, that is, its delegation of effective discretion to the President to control economic sanctions against Burma, its limitation of sanctions solely to United States persons and new investment, and its directive to the President to proceed diplomatically in developing a comprehensive, multilateral strategy towards Burma.[8]

8. We leave for another day a consideration in this context of a presumption against preemption. Assuming, *arguendo*, that some presumption against preemption is appropriate, we conclude, based on our analysis below, that the state Act presents a sufficient obstacle to the full accomplishment of Congress's objectives under the federal Act to find it preempted. See Hines v. Davidowitz, 312 U.S. 52, 67 (1941).

Because our conclusion that the state Act conflicts with federal law is sufficient to affirm the judgment below, we decline to speak to field preemption as a separate issue, . . . or to pass on the First Circuit's rulings addressing the foreign affairs power or the dormant Foreign Commerce Clause. See Ashwander v. TVA, 297 U.S. 288, 346-347 (1936) (concurring opinion).

A

First, Congress clearly intended the federal act to provide the President with flexible and effective authority over economic sanctions against Burma. Although Congress immediately put in place a set of initial sanctions (prohibiting bilateral aid, support for international financial assistance, and entry by Burmese officials into the United States), it authorized the President to terminate any and all of those measures upon determining and certifying that there had been progress in human rights and democracy in Burma. It invested the President with the further power to ban new investment by United States persons, dependent only on specific Presidential findings of repression in Burma. And, most significantly, Congress empowered the President "to waive, temporarily or permanently, any sanction [under the federal act] . . . if he determines and certifies to Congress that the application of such sanction would be contrary to the national security interests of the United States."

This express investiture of the President with statutory authority to act for the United States in imposing sanctions with respect to the government of Burma, augmented by the flexibility to respond to change by suspending sanctions in the interest of national security, recalls Justice Jackson's observation in [*Youngstown*] . . . : "When the President acts pursuant to an express or implied authorization of Congress, his authority is at its maximum, for it includes all that he possesses in his own right plus all that Congress can delegate." . . . Within the sphere defined by Congress, then, the statute has placed the President in a position with as much discretion to exercise economic leverage against Burma, with an eye toward national security, as our law will admit. And it is just this plenitude of Executive authority that we think controls the issue of preemption here. The President has been given this authority not merely to make a political statement but to achieve a political result, and the fullness of his authority shows the importance in the congressional mind of reaching that result. It is simply implausible that Congress would have gone to such lengths to empower the President if it had been willing to compromise his effectiveness by deference to every provision of state statute or local ordinance that might, if enforced, blunt the consequences of discretionary Presidential action.

And that is just what the Massachusetts Burma law would do in imposing a different, state system of economic pressure against the Burmese political regime. As will be seen, the state statute penalizes some private action that the federal Act (as administered by the President) may allow, and pulls levers of influence that the federal Act does not reach. But the point here is that the state sanctions are immediate, and perpetual, there being no termination provision. This unyielding application undermines the President's intended statutory authority by making it impossible for him to restrain fully the coercive power of the national economy when he may choose to take the discretionary action open to him, whether he believes that the national interest requires sanctions to be lifted, or believes that the promise of lifting sanctions would move the Burmese regime in the democratic direction. Quite simply, if the Massachusetts law is enforceable the President has less to offer and less economic and diplomatic leverage as a consequence. In Dames & Moore v. Regan, 453 U.S. 654 (1981), we used the metaphor of the bargaining chip to describe the President's control of funds valuable to a hostile country; here, the state Act reduces the value of the chips created by the federal statute. It thus "stands as an obstacle to the accomplishment and execution of the full purposes and objectives of Congress." *Hines*, 312 U.S. at 67.

B

Congress manifestly intended to limit economic pressure against the Burmese Government to a specific range. The federal Act confines its reach to United States persons, imposes limited immediate sanctions, places only a conditional ban on a carefully defined area of "new investment," and pointedly exempts contracts to sell or purchase goods, services, or technology. These detailed provisions show that Congress's calibrated Burma policy is a deliberate effort "to steer a middle path," *Hines*, supra.

. . . The State has set a different course, and its statute conflicts with federal law at a number of points by penalizing individuals and conduct that Congress has explicitly exempted or excluded from sanctions. . . . It restricts all contracts between the State and companies doing business in Burma, except when purchasing medical supplies and other essentials (or when short of comparable bids). It is specific in targeting contracts to provide financial services, and general goods and services, to the Government of Burma, and thus prohibits contracts between the State and United States persons for goods, services, or technology, even though those transactions are explicitly exempted from the ambit of new investment prohibition when the President exercises his discretionary authority to impose sanctions under the federal Act.

As with the subject of business meant to be affected, so with the class of companies doing it: the state Act's generality stands at odds with the federal discreteness. . . .

The conflicts are not rendered irrelevant by the State's argument that there is no real conflict between the statutes because they share the same goals and because some companies may comply with both sets of restrictions. The fact of a common end hardly neutralizes conflicting means, and the fact that some companies may be able to comply with both sets of sanctions does not mean that the state Act is not at odds with achievement of the federal decision about the right degree of pressure to employ. Sanctions are drawn not only to bar what they prohibit but to allow what they permit, and the inconsistency of sanctions here undermines the congressional calibration of force.

C

Finally, the state Act is at odds with the President's intended authority to speak for the United States among the world's nations in developing a "comprehensive, multilateral strategy to bring democracy to and improve human rights practices and the quality of life in Burma." . . . As with Congress's explicit delegation to the President of power over economic sanctions, Congress's express command to the President to take the initiative for the United States among the international community invested him with the maximum authority of the National Government, cf.

Youngstown Sheet & Tube Co., 343 U.S. at 635, in harmony with the President's own constitutional powers, U.S. Const., Art. II, §2, cl. 2("[The President] shall have Power, by and with the Advice and Consent of the Senate, to make Treaties" and "shall appoint Ambassadors, other public Ministers and Consuls"); §3 ("[The President] shall receive Ambassadors and other public Ministers"). . . .

Again, the state Act undermines the President's capacity, in this instance for effective diplomacy. It is not merely that the differences between the state and federal Acts in scope and type of sanctions threaten to complicate discussions; they compromise the very capacity of the President to speak for the Nation with one voice in dealing with other governments. . . .

While the threat to the President's power to speak and bargain effectively with other nations seems clear enough, the record is replete with evidence to answer any skeptics. First, in response to the passage of the state Act, a number of this country's allies and trading partners filed formal protests with the National Government. . . . Second, the EU and Japan have gone a step further in lodging formal complaints against the United States in the World Trade Organization (WTO), claiming that the state Act violates certain provisions of the Agreement on Government Procurement, and the consequence has been to embroil the National Government for some time now in international dispute proceedings under the auspices of the WTO. . . . Third, the Executive has consistently represented that the state Act has complicated its dealings with foreign sovereigns and proven an impediment to accomplishing objectives assigned it by Congress. . . . This evidence in combination is more than sufficient to show that the state Act stands as an obstacle in addressing the congressional obligation to devise a comprehensive, multilateral strategy. . . .

IV

The State's remaining argument is unavailing. It contends that the failure of Congress to preempt the state Act demonstrates implicit permission. . . .

The argument is unconvincing on more than one level. A failure to provide for preemption expressly may reflect nothing more than the settled character of implied preemption doctrine that courts will dependably apply, and . . . the existence of conflict cognizable under the Supremacy Clause does not depend on express congressional recognition that federal and state law may conflict. . . . [T]he silence of Congress is ambiguous. . . .

American Insurance Association v. Garamendi

U.S. Supreme Court
539 U.S. 396 (2003)

[Before and during World War II, the Nazi Government of Germany not only engaged in genocide and enslavement, but it confiscated Jewish assets, including life insurance policies held by Jews. Insurance companies were also ordered to pay the Nazi Government for claims on such policies, instead of the policyholders. After the war, even a life insurance policy that had not been confiscated was likely to be dishonored because the insurance companies denied the existence of the policies or claimed that policies had lapsed, or because the German Government would not provide heirs with documentation of the policyholders' deaths. Various reparations measures adopted in the years after the war still left out many claimants and certain categories of claims.

[After German courts began to interpret the 1990 treaty reunifying German as lifting a moratorium on Holocaust claims by foreign nationals imposed by a previous reparations agreement, Holocaust-related lawsuits flooded into U.S. courts. This led to negotiations among the U.S. and German Governments and other parties.

[While these negotiations were underway, California enacted the Holocaust Victim Insurance Relief Act of 1999 (HVIRA), which required any insurer doing business in California to disclose information about all policies sold in Europe between 1920 and 1945 by the company or any company "related" to it. If an insurer failed to disclose, the mandatory penalty for default was suspension of the company's license to do business in California.

[After HVIRA was enacted, the U.S. Deputy Secretary of the Treasury, Stuart Eizenstat, wrote California officials that HVIRA "has the unfortunate effect of damaging the one effective means now at hand to process quickly and completely unpaid insurance claims from the Holocaust period," the International Commission on Holocaust Era Insurance Claims (ICHEIC). As explained in Justice Souter's opinion below, the ICHEIC was "a voluntary organization formed in 1998 by several European insurance companies, the State of Israel, Jewish and Holocaust survivor associations, . . . and the organization of American state insurance commissioners. The job of the ICHEIC . . . includes negotiation with European insurers to provide information about unpaid insurance policies issued to Holocaust victims and settlement of claims brought under them." In spite of these statements of national interest, the California commissioner of insurance announced in December 1999 that he would fully enforce HVIRA.

[In July 2000, the U.S.-German negotiations resulted in the two countries signing the German Foundation Agreement, whereby the German Government agreed to establish a foundation to be funded with 10 billion deutsch marks contributed equally by the German Government and German companies. According to the agreement, the funds would be used to compensate all those "who suffered at the hands of German companies during the National Socialist era." Specifically for the insurance claims, the agreement provided that the German Foundation would work with the ICHEIC. The U.S. Government agreed to try to persuade the U.S. courts, as well as state and local governments, that the foundation should be "the exclusive forum and remedy" for the resolution of claims against German companies "arising from their involvement in the National Socialist era and World War II."

[The German Foundation agreement then served as a model for similar agreements with Austria and France.

[In response to the California commissioner's announced intention to enforce the California law, American and European insurance companies and a national trade association, the American Insurance Association, sued to enjoin the commissioner from enforcing HVIRA. The district court granted the preliminary injunction and later granted petitioners summary judgment, but the U.S. Court of Appeals for the Ninth Circuit reversed. It held, inter alia, that HVIRA did not violate the federal foreign affairs power.]

Justice SOUTER delivered the opinion of the Court.

. . . The issue here is whether HVIRA interferes with the National Government's conduct of foreign relations. We hold that it does, with the consequence that the state statute is preempted. . . .

The principal argument for preemption made by petitioners and the United States as *amicus curiae* is that HVIRA interferes with foreign policy of the Executive Branch, as expressed principally in the executive agreements with Germany, Austria, and France. . . . There is, of course, no question that at some point an exercise of state power that touches on foreign relations must yield to the National Government's policy, given the "concern for uniformity in this country's dealings with foreign nations" that animated the Constitution's allocation of the foreign relations power to the National Government in the first place. Banco Nacional de Cuba v. Sabbatino, 376 U.S. 398, 427, n.25 (1964).

Nor is there any question generally that there is executive authority to decide what that policy should be. Although the source of the President's power to act in foreign affairs does not enjoy any textual detail, the historical gloss on the "executive Power" vested in Article II of the Constitution has recognized the President's "vast share of responsibility for the conduct of our foreign relations." Youngstown Sheet & Tube Co. v. Sawyer, 343 U.S. 579, 610-611 (1952) (Frankfurter, J., concurring). While Congress holds express authority to regulate public and private dealings with other nations in its war and foreign commerce powers, in foreign affairs the President has a degree of independent authority to act.

At a more specific level, our cases have recognized that the President has authority to make "executive agreements" with other countries, requiring no ratification by the Senate or approval by Congress. . . . See Dames & Moore v. Regan, 453 U.S. 654, 679, 682-683 (1981); United States v. Pink, 315 U.S. 203, 223, 230 (1942). Making executive agreements to settle claims of American nationals against foreign governments is a particularly longstanding practice, the first example being as early as 1799. . . . Given the fact that the practice goes back over 200 years and has received congressional acquiescence throughout its history, the conclusion "[t]hat the President's control of foreign relations includes the settlement of claims is indisputable." *Pink*, supra, at 240 (Frankfurter, J., concurring).

The executive agreements at issue here do differ in one respect from those just mentioned insofar as they address claims associated with formerly belligerent states, but against corporations, not the foreign governments. But the distinction does not matter. . . . As shown by the history of insurance confiscation . . . , untangling government policy from private initiative during wartime is often so hard that diplomatic action settling claims against private parties may well be just as essential in the aftermath of hostilities as diplomacy to settle claims against foreign governments. . . .

Generally, then, valid executive agreements are fit to preempt state law, just as treaties are, and if the agreements here had expressly preempted laws like HVIRA, the issue would be straightforward. But petitioners and the United States as *amicus curiae* both have to acknowledge that the agreements include no preemption clause, and so leave their claim of preemption to rest on asserted interference with the foreign policy those agreements embody. Reliance is placed on our decision in Zschernig v. Miller, 389 U.S. 429 (1968).

Zschernig dealt with an Oregon probate statute prohibiting inheritance by a nonresident alien, absent showings that the foreign heir would take the property "without confiscation" by his home country and that American citizens would enjoy reciprocal rights of inheritance there. . . . [B]y the time Zschernig (an East German resident) brought his challenge, it was clear that the Oregon law in practice had invited "minute inquiries concerning the actual administration of foreign law," and so was providing occasions for state judges to disparage certain foreign regimes, employing the language of the anti-Communism prevalent here at the height of the Cold War. [The Court invalidated] the law as an "intrusion by the State into the field of foreign affairs which the Constitution entrusts to the President and the Congress."

The *Zschernig* majority relied on statements in a number of previous cases open to the reading that state action with more than incidental effect on foreign affairs is preempted, even absent any affirmative federal activity in the subject area of the state law, and hence without any showing of conflict. . . .

Justice Harlan, joined substantially by Justice White, disagreed with the *Zschernig* majority on this point, arguing that its implication of preemption of the entire field of foreign affairs was at odds with some other cases suggesting that in the absence of positive federal action "the States may legislate in areas of their traditional competence even though their statutes may have an incidental effect on foreign relations." Thus, for Justice Harlan it was crucial that the challenge to the Oregon statute presented no evidence of a "specific interest of the Federal Government which might be interfered with" by the law. He would, however, have found preemption in a case of "conflicting federal policy," and on this point the majority and Justices Harlan and White basically agreed: state laws "must give way if they impair the effective exercise of the Nation's foreign policy."

It is a fair question whether respect for the executive foreign relations power requires a categorical choice between the contrasting theories of field and conflict preemption evident in the *Zschernig* opinions, but the question requires no answer here. For even on Justice Harlan's view, the likelihood that state legislation will produce something more than incidental effect in conflict with express foreign policy of the National Government would require preemption of the state law. And since on his view it is legislation within "areas of . . . traditional competence" that gives a State any claim to prevail, it would be reasonable to consider the strength of the state interest, judged by standards of traditional practice, when deciding how serious a conflict must be shown before declaring the state law preempted. Judged by these standards, we think petitioners and the Government have demonstrated a sufficiently clear conflict to require finding preemption here.

IV . . .

To begin with, resolving Holocaust-era insurance claims that may be held by residents of this country is a matter well within the Executive's responsibility for foreign affairs. . . .

The exercise of the federal executive authority means that state law must give way where, as here, there is evidence of clear conflict between the policies adopted by the two. The foregoing account of negotiations toward the . . . settlement agreements is enough to illustrate that the consistent Presidential foreign policy has been to encourage European governments and companies to volunteer settlement funds in preference to litigation or coercive sanctions. As for insurance claims in particular, the national position, expressed unmistakably in the executive agreements signed by the President with Germany and Austria, has been to encourage European insurers to work with the ICHEIC to develop acceptable claim procedures, including procedures governing disclosure of policy information. . . . The approach taken serves to resolve the several competing matters of national concern apparent in the German Foundation Agreement: the national interest in maintaining amicable relationships with current European allies; survivors' interests in a "fair and prompt" but nonadversarial resolution of their claims so as to "bring some measure of justice . . . in their lifetimes"; and the companies' interest in securing "legal peace" when they settle claims in this fashion. As a way for dealing with insurance claims, moreover, the voluntary scheme protects the companies' ability to abide by their own countries' domestic privacy laws limiting disclosure of policy information.

California has taken a different tack of providing regulatory sanctions to compel disclosure and payment. . . . The situation created by the California legislation calls to mind the impact of the Massachusetts Burma law on the effective exercise of the President's power, as recounted in the statutory preemption case, Crosby v. National Foreign Trade Council, 530 U.S. 363 (2000). HVIRA's economic compulsion to make public disclosure, of far more information about far more policies than ICHEIC rules require, employs "a different, state system of economic pressure," and in doing so undercuts the President's diplomatic discretion and the choice he has made exercising it. Whereas the President's authority to provide for settling claims in winding up international hostilities requires flexibility in wielding "the coercive power of the national economy" as a tool of diplomacy, HVIRA denies this, by making exclusion from a large sector of the American insurance market the automatic sanction for noncompliance with the State's own policies on disclosure. . . . The law thus "compromise[s] the very capacity of the President to speak for the Nation with one voice in dealing with other governments" to resolve claims against European companies arising out of World War II.[14]

Crosby's facts are replicated again in the way HVIRA threatens to frustrate the operation of the particular mechanism the President has chosen. The letters from Deputy Secretary Eizenstat to California officials show well enough how the portent of further litigation and sanctions has in fact placed the Government at a disadvantage in obtaining practical results from persuading "foreign governments and foreign companies to participate voluntarily in organizations such as ICHEIC." In addition to thwarting the Government's policy of repose for companies that pay through the ICHEIC, California's indiscriminate disclosure provisions place a handicap on the ICHEIC's effectiveness (and raise a further irritant to the

14. It is true that the President in this case is acting without express congressional authority, and thus does not have the "plenitude of Executive authority" that "controlled the issue of preemption" in Crosby v. National Foreign Trade Council, 530 U.S. 363, 376 (2000). But in *Crosby* we were careful to note that the President possesses considerable independent constitutional authority to act on behalf of the United States on international issues, and conflict with the exercise of that authority is a comparably good reason to find preemption of state law.

European allies) by undercutting European privacy protections. It is true, of course, as it is probably true of all elements of HVIRA, that the disclosure requirement's object of obtaining compensation for Holocaust victims is a goal espoused by the National Government as well. But "[t]he fact of a common end hardly neutralizes conflicting means," *Crosby*, supra, at 379, and here HVIRA is an obstacle to the success of the National Government's chosen "calibration of force" in dealing with the Europeans using a voluntary approach.

B

The express federal policy and the clear conflict raised by the state statute are alone enough to require state law to yield. If any doubt about the clarity of the conflict remained, however, it would have to be resolved in the National Government's favor, given the weakness of the State's interest, against the backdrop of traditional state legislative subject matter, in regulating disclosure of European Holocaust-era insurance policies in the manner of HVIRA. . . .

Indeed, there is no serious doubt that the state interest actually underlying HVIRA is concern for the several thousand Holocaust survivors said to be living in the State. But this fact does not displace general standards for evaluating a State's claim to apply its forum law to a particular controversy or transaction, under which the State's claim [based on the victims' change of residence to California] is not a strong one. . . .

But should the general standard not be displaced, and the State's interest recognized as a powerful one, by virtue of the fact that California seeks to vindicate the claims of Holocaust survivors? The answer lies in recalling that the very same objective dignifies the interest of the National Government in devising its chosen mechanism for voluntary settlements, there being about 100,000 survivors in the country, only a small fraction of them in California. As against the responsibility of the United States of America, the humanity underlying the state statute could not give the State the benefit of any doubt in resolving the conflict with national policy. . . .

The basic fact is that California seeks to use an iron fist where the President has consistently chosen kid gloves. . . . The question relevant to preemption in this case is conflict, and the evidence here is "more than sufficient to demonstrate that the state Act stands in the way of [the President's] diplomatic objectives." *Crosby*, supra, at 386. . . .

V

[The Court concludes here that Congress has not authorized HVIRA-like state laws in any congressional legislation. The Court goes on to observe:] Indeed, it is worth noting that Congress has done nothing to express disapproval of the President's policy. . . .

In sum, Congress has not acted on the matter addressed here. Given the President's independent authority "in areas of foreign policy and national security, . . . congressional silence is not to be equated with congressional disapproval." Haig v. Agree, 453 U.S. 280, 291 (1981). . . .

The judgment of the Court of Appeals for the Ninth Circuit is reversed.

Justice GINSBURG, with whom Justice STEVENS, Justice SCALIA, and Justice THOMAS join, dissenting. . . .

Although the federal approach differs from California's, no executive agreement or other formal expression of foreign policy disapproves state disclosure laws like the HVIRA. Absent a clear statement aimed at disclosure requirements by the "one voice" to which courts properly defer in matters of foreign affairs, I would leave intact California's enactment. . . .

III . . .

Together, *Belmont, Pink,* and *Dames & Moore* confirm that executive agreements directed at claims settlement may sometimes preempt state law. The Court states that if the executive "agreements here had expressly preempted laws like HVIRA, the issue would be straightforward." One can safely demur to that statement, for, as the Court acknowledges, no executive agreement before us expressly preempts the HVIRA. Indeed, no agreement so much as mentions the HVIRA's sole concern: public disclosure.

B

Despite the absence of express preemption, the Court holds that the HVIRA interferes with foreign policy objectives implicit in the executive agreements. I would not venture down that path.

The Court's analysis draws substantially on Zschernig v. Miller. . . .

We have not relied on *Zschernig* since it was decided, and I would not resurrect that decision here. The notion of "dormant foreign affairs preemption" with which *Zschernig* is associated resonates most audibly when a state action "reflect[s] a state policy critical of foreign governments and involve[s] 'sitting in judgment' on them." L. Henkin, Foreign Affairs and the United States Constitution 164 (2d ed.1996). The HVIRA entails no such state action or policy. It takes no position on any contemporary foreign government and requires no assessment of any existing foreign regime. It is directed solely at private insurers doing business in California, and it requires them solely to disclose information in their or their affiliates' possession or control. I would not extend *Zschernig* into this dissimilar domain.[4]

Neither would I stretch *Belmont, Pink,* or *Dames & Moore* to support implied preemption by executive agreement. In each of those cases, the Court gave effect to the express terms of an executive agreement. . . .

To fill the agreements' silences, the Court points to statements by individual members of the Executive Branch. But we have never premised foreign affairs preemption on statements of that order. We should not do so here lest we place the considerable power of foreign affairs preemption in the hands of individual sub-Cabinet members of the Executive Branch. . . . The displacement of state law by

4. The Court also places considerable weight on Crosby v. National Foreign Trade Council, 530 U.S. 363 (2000). As the Court acknowledges, however, *Crosby* was a statutory preemption case. . . . That statutory decision provides little support for preempting a state law by inferring preclusive foreign policy objectives from precatory language in executive agreements.

preemption properly requires a considerably more formal and binding federal instrument.

Sustaining the HVIRA would not compromise the President's ability to speak with one voice for the Nation. To the contrary, by declining to invalidate the HVIRA in this case, we would reserve foreign affairs preemption for circumstances where the President, acting under statutory or constitutional authority, has spoken clearly to the issue at hand. . . . As I see it, courts step out of their proper role when they rely on no legislative or even executive text, but only on inference and implication, to preempt state laws on foreign affairs grounds. . . .

Notes and Questions

1. Although *Crosby* and *Garamendi* both involve state legislation that affects foreign affairs, the Supreme Court decided *Crosby* on a theory of statutory preemption and *Garamendi* on a theory of foreign affairs preemption. What was the basis for the Court's finding of statutory preemption in *Crosby*? Was there a conflict or conflicts between the federal and state statutes? If not, what was the problem(s)?

2. How does the preemption holding of *Crosby* compare with the preemption holding of *Zschernig*? *Zschernig*, discussed in *Garamendi*, applied what has been called "dormant foreign affairs preemption." The idea is that some state laws or activities relating to foreign affairs are preempted as a result of the national government's unexercised, or "dormant," foreign affairs powers.

3. The Court in *Garamendi* discusses the differing views of the *Zschernig* majority and Justice Harlan's opinion regarding the nature of foreign affairs preemption. The *Zschernig* majority supported field preemption, concluding that any state action that had more than incidental effect in the field of foreign affairs should be preempted. Justice Harlan in that case instead espoused conflict preemption, arguing that state legislation should be upheld, even if it affects foreign affairs, unless it conflicts with a federal policy. Does the *Garamendi* majority adopt one of these views, attempt to reconcile both, or replace both with a new framework of analysis? If the *Zschernig* majority opinion's field preemption still applies, what is the scope of its prohibition on state activity? What matters in answering this question: Foreign relations effects? The state's purpose in engaging in the activity? Both? Neither?

4. *Garamendi* recognizes that the Executive Branch has broad foreign relations powers. The majority and dissent agree that the President has the power to conclude executive agreements and that at least some executive agreements should preempt state legislation. The dissent, however, concludes that courts should only find preemption when an executive agreement expressly preempts conflicting state laws, while the majority concludes that preemption may be implied from the foreign policy motivating the executive agreements. In terms of separation of powers considerations, what might be problematic about the majority's application of implied preemption to executive agreements? Was the majority's deference to an Executive Branch official at the level of Deputy Secretary of the Treasury appropriate?

5. In addition to statutory preemption and foreign affairs preemption, state legislation may also be invalidated under a theory of "dormant foreign commerce clause" preemption. Foreign commerce clause preemption is similar to foreign affairs preemption. In Barclays Bank v. Franchise Tax Board of California, 512 U.S. 298 (1994), the Supreme Court held that California's "worldwide combined

reporting" method of taxing multinational corporations was not subject to dormant foreign commerce clause preemption, even though it was different from the federal government's method of taxation and even though it had generated significant protest from foreign governments. The Court rejected the argument that an interference by a state with the nation's ability to "speak with one voice when regulating commercial relations with foreign governments" was sufficient to trigger preemption. The Court explained:

> The Constitution does "'not make the judiciary the overseer of our government.'" Dames & Moore v. Regan, 453 U.S. 654,660 (1981), quoting Youngstown Sheet & Tube Co. v. Sawyer, 343 U.S. at 594 (Frankfurter, J., concurring). Having determined that the taxpayers before us had an adequate nexus with the State, that worldwide combined reporting led to taxation which was fairly apportioned, nondiscriminatory, fairly related to the services provided by the State, and that its imposition did not result inevitably in multiple taxation, we leave it to Congress — whose voice, in this area, is the Nation's — to evaluate whether the national interest is best served by tax uniformity, or state autonomy. Id. at 330.

Is *Garamendi* a turn away from *Barclays Bank*?

6. Some states have enacted "Buy American" statutes requiring state agencies to buy only U.S.-made goods. Lower courts have split on the issue whether these statutes should be invalidated by dormant foreign affairs preemption. Compare Trojan Technologies, Inc. v. Pennsylvania, 916 F.2d 903, 913 (3d Cir. 1990) (upholding Pennsylvania's Buy American law, because, unlike *Zschernig*, it "provides no opportunity for state administrative officials or judges to comment on . . . the nature of foreign regimes") and K.S.B. Technical Sales v. New Jersey District Water Supply Commission, 75 N.J. 272 (1977) (upholding a N.J. Buy American law, which had exceptions, such as if the cost were "unreasonable") with Bethlehem Steel Corp. v. Board of Commissioners, 276 Cal. App. 2d 221, 225 (Ct. App. 2d Dist. 1969) (invalidating the California Buy American Act, because it "amounts to a usurpation by this state of the power of the federal government to conduct foreign trade policy"). Should state "Buy American" statutes be upheld after *Garamendi*?

7. For recent commentary on *Crosby* and *Garamendi*, see Leanne M. Wilson, The Fate of the Dormant Foreign Commerce Clause After Garamendi and Crosby, 107 Colum. L. Rev. 746 (2007) (recommending *Crosby* as a model for future cases involving the balance of federal-state foreign relations power). For a broader article on federal-state relations, see Julian G. Ku, Gubernational Foreign Policy, 115 Yale L.J. 2380 (2006).

Bibliography

For additional discussion of the relationship between international law and U.S. law, and of U.S. foreign relations law more generally, see Michael J. Glennon, Constitutional Diplomacy (1999); Louis Henkin, Foreign Affairs and the United States Constitution (2d ed. 1996); Phillip R. Trimble, International Law: United States Foreign Relations Law (2002); and Harold Hongju Koh, Setting the World Right, 115 Yale L. J. 2350 (2006).

4

International Dispute Resolution

In Chapters 1 and 2 you were introduced to the ways in which the rules of public international law are formed, mostly through the conclusion of treaties and the development of customary international law. Inevitably there are disputes over the meaning of those rules and their enforcement. Those disputes can range from the classic cases of boundary disputes and expropriations of foreign investment to disagreements over the implementation of trade agreements or compliance with environmental or arms control treaties.

In the earlier chapters you saw some examples of international dispute resolution, such as through negotiation, arbitration, and domestic courts. This chapter will analyze the principal methods for resolving international disputes. In reality, there are a wide variety of methods and institutions for dealing with these conflicts. While these possible approaches do not add up to the relatively organized and comprehensive systems found in most countries for resolving domestic disputes, they often provide effective and reasonable avenues for resolving international disagreements and for enforcing decisions. And, as will be seen in this chapter, some international approaches — notably regional courts, specialized courts, and arbitral bodies — hold even greater promise for the future. Indeed, when one looks at the problems with domestic dispute resolution in many countries — such as the often overlapping jurisdiction and the backlog of cases in U.S. courts or the limits on the powers of domestic courts — the weaknesses in the international system are not as glaring as some critics have suggested.

This chapter begins with a section on how parties often work out disagreements through negotiation, occasionally supplemented by mediation or conciliation (Section A). If a dispute is not resolved through these methods, parties often resort to more formal institutions — the International Court of Justice, regional or specialized courts, international arbitration, or domestic courts — which are discussed in the next sections of this chapter.

Section B examines the International Court of Justice, sometimes known as the World Court. It is the International Court of Justice that most people first hear about, though for a variety of reasons it handles only a relatively modest number of cases. Section C considers the important role of regional or specialized courts. The materials there focus on the Court of Justice of the European Communities.

Additional examples are covered in later chapters, such as the European Court of Human Rights, with its increasingly important role (Chapter 8); the International Tribunal for the Law of the Sea (Chapter 9); and the International Criminal Court (Chapter 12).

Section D addresses the rapidly growing field of international arbitration. It considers briefly the history of international arbitration and then looks at its present uses and outstanding issues, with considerable focus on the enforcement of arbitral awards. Section E then considers a number of tailored dispute resolution systems designed for particular contexts that draw heavily from the structure and experience of courts and arbitration. Examples include the dispute resolution provisions in the North American Free Trade Agreement and the dispute resolution arrangement in the World Trade Organization, which became effective in 1995 and has been very active.

Finally, Section F notes the expanding role of domestic courts in international issues. You have already begun to see in Chapter 3 how U.S. courts have applied international law, such as in cases addressing human rights issues. Other countries' domestic courts also frequently hear and decide important questions of international law.

A. NEGOTIATION, MEDIATION, AND CONCILIATION

Most disputes involving international law are resolved through negotiation. In some situations a negotiation is supplemented by mediation or conciliation.

J.G. Merrills, International Dispute Settlement

2-3, 6-13, 15-16, 28-29, 44, 64, 90 (4th ed. 2005)

1. Negotiation

. . . [I]n practice, negotiation is employed more frequently than all the other methods [of dispute settlement] put together. Often, indeed, negotiation is the only means employed, not just because it is always the first to be tried and is often successful, but also because states may believe its advantages to be so great as to rule out the use of other methods, even in situations where the chances of a negotiated settlement are slight. On the occasions when another method is used, negotiation is not displaced, but directed towards instrumental issues, the terms of reference for an inquiry or conciliation commission, for example, or the arrangements for implementing an arbitral decision. Thus in one form or another negotiation has a vital part in international disputes. But negotiation is more than a possible means of settling differences, it is also a technique for preventing them from arising. Since prevention is always better than cure, this form of negotiation, known as "consultation," is a convenient place to begin.

Consultation

When a government anticipates that a decision or a proposed course of action may harm another state, discussions with the affected party can provide a way of heading off a dispute by creating an opportunity for adjustment and accommodation. Quite minor modifications to its plans, of no importance to the state taking the decision, may be all that is required to avoid trouble, yet may only be recognised if the other side is given a chance to point them out. The particular value of consultation is that it supplies this useful information at the most appropriate time — before anything has been done. For it is far easier to make the necessary modifications at the decision-making stage, rather than later, when exactly the same action may seem like capitulation to foreign pressures or be seized on by critics as a sacrifice of domestic interests.

A good example of the value of consultation is provided by the practice of the United States and Canada in antitrust proceedings. Writing of the procedure employed in such cases, a recent commentator has noted that:

> While it is true that antitrust officials of one state might flatly refuse to alter a course of action in any way, it has often been the case that officials have been persuaded to modify their plans somewhat. After consultation, it may be agreed to shape an indictment in a less offensive manner, to change the ground rules of an investigation so as to require only "voluntary" testimony from witnesses, or that officials of the government initiating an investigation or action will keep their antitrust counterparts informed of progress in the case and allow them to voice their concerns. . . .

Consultation between states is usually an *ad hoc* process and except where reciprocity provides an incentive, as in the cases considered, has proved difficult to institutionalise. . . .

Whether voluntary or compulsory, consultation is often easier to implement for executive than legislative decision making, since the former is usually less rigidly structured and more centralised. But legislative action can also cause international disputes, and so procedures designed to achieve the same effect as consultation can have an equally useful part to play. Where states enjoy close relations it may be possible to establish machinery for negotiating the coordination of legislative and administrative measures on matters of common interest. There are clear advantages in having uniform provisions on such matters as environmental protection, where states share a common frontier, or commerce, if trade is extensive. The difficulties of achieving such harmonisation are considerable, as the experience of the European Economic Community has demonstrated, though if uniformity cannot be achieved, compatibility of domestic provisions is a less ambitious alternative. In either case the rewards in terms of dispute avoidance make the effort well worthwhile. . . .

Forms of Negotiation

Negotiations between states are usually conducted through "normal diplomatic channels," that is by the respective foreign offices, or by diplomatic representatives, who in the case of complex negotiations may lead delegations including representatives of several interested departments of the governments concerned. As an alternative, if the subject matter is appropriate, negotiations may be carried out by what are termed the "competent authorities" of each party, that is by representatives of the particular ministry or department responsible for the matter in question — between trade departments in the case of a commercial agreement, for example, or between defence ministries in negotiations concerning weapons procurement. Where the competent authorities are subordinate bodies, they may be authorised to take negotiations as far as possible and to refer disagreements to a higher governmental level. . . .

In the case of a recurrent problem or a situation requiring continuous supervision, states may decide to institutionalise negotiation by creating what is termed a mixed or joint commission. Thus neighbouring states commonly employ mixed commissions to deal with boundary delimitation, or other matters of common concern. . . .

Mixed commissions usually consist of an equal number of representatives of both parties and may be given either a broad brief of indefinite duration, or the task of dealing with a specific problem. An outstanding example of a commission of the first type is provided by the Canadian-United States International Joint Commission, which, since its creation in 1909, has dealt with a large number of issues including industrial development, air pollution and a variety of questions concerning boundary waters. . . .

The public aspect of negotiations which is exemplified in summit diplomacy is also prominent in the activity of international organisations. In the United Nations General Assembly and similar bodies states can, if they choose, conduct diplomatic exchanges in the full glare of international attention. This is undoubtedly a useful way of letting off steam and, more constructively, of engaging the attention of outside states which may have something to contribute to the solution of a dispute. It has the disadvantage, however, that so visible a performance may encourage the striking of attitudes which are at once both unrealistic and difficult to abandon. It is therefore probable that for states with a serious interest in negotiating a settlement, the many opportunities for informal contact which international organisations provide are more useful than the dramatic confrontations of public debate. . . .

For a negotiated settlement to be possible, the parties must believe that the benefits of an agreement outweigh the losses. If their interests are diametrically opposed, an arrangement which would require one side to yield all or most of its position is therefore unlikely to be acceptable. . . .

There are a number of ways in which such an impasse may be avoided. If negotiations on the substantive aspects of a dispute are deadlocked, it may be possible for the parties to agree on a procedural solution. . . .

Another approach is to consider whether the issue at the heart of a dispute can be split in such a way as to enable each side to obtain satisfaction. A solution of this kind was recently devised to the problem of maritime delimitation between Australia and Papua New Guinea in the Torres Strait. Having identified the different strands of the dispute, the parties succeeded in negotiating an agreement which dealt separately with the interests of the inhabitants of islands in the Strait, the status of the islands, seabed jurisdiction, fisheries jurisdiction, conservation and navigation rights. The virtue of this highly functional approach to the problem is underlined by the fact that earlier attempts to negotiate a single maritime boundary for the area had all ended in failure.

If splitting the dispute is not possible, a procedural agreement may be used to compensate one side for yielding on the substantive issue. In 1961 the United Kingdom and Iceland ended a dispute over the latter's fishing limits with an agreement which provided for the recognition of Iceland's claims in return for phasing out arrangements to protect British interests and an undertaking that future disputes could be referred to the International Court [of Justice]. . . .

It often happens that the nature of a dispute and the parties' interests are such that in any agreement one side is bound to gain at the other's expense. A possible way of providing compensation in such a situation is to give the less-favoured party control of details such as the time and place of the negotiations. The latter in particular can assume considerable symbolic importance and thus constitutes an element which may be used to good effect. A more radical solution is to link two disputes together so that a negotiated settlement can balance gains and losses overall and be capable of acceptance by both sides. Such "package deals" are particularly common in multilateral negotiations such as the Third United Nations Conference on the Law of the Sea, where the large number of states involved and the broad agenda made the trading of issues a conspicuous feature of the proceedings.

The fact that today the public dimension of diplomacy has much greater importance than in the past is another factor with a bearing on the substance of international negotiations. For if negotiation is a matter of exchanging proposals and counter-proposals in an attempt to arrive at an agreement from which both sides can derive a measure of satisfaction, the parties' awareness of an audience consisting of the general public in one or both of the states concerned, and the international community as a whole, can seriously affect the outcome. The element of give and take which is usually an essential part of a successful negotiation is likely to be inhibited if every step is being monitored by interested pressure groups at home, while the suspicion that the other side may simply be interested in eliciting a favourable audience reaction may lead serious proposals to be dismissed as mere propaganda. . . .

2. Mediation

When the parties to an international dispute are unable to resolve it by negotiation, the intervention of a third party is a possible means of breaking the impasse and producing an acceptable solution. Such intervention can take a number of different forms. The third party may simply encourage the disputing states to resume negotiations, or do nothing more than provide them with an additional channel of communication. In these situations he is said to be contributing his "good offices." On the other hand, the assignment may be to investigate the dispute and to present the parties with a set of formal proposals for its solution. As we shall see . . . this form of intervention is called "conciliation." Between good offices and conciliation lies the form of third-party activity known as "mediation."

Like good offices, mediation is essentially an adjunct of negotiation, but with the mediator as an active participant, authorised, and indeed expected, to advance his own proposals and to interpret, as well as to transmit, each party's proposals to the other. What distinguishes this kind of assistance from conciliation is that a mediator generally makes his proposals informally and on the basis of information supplied by the parties, rather than his own investigations, although in practice such distinctions tend to be blurred. In a given case it may therefore be difficult to draw the line between mediation and conciliation, or to say exactly when good offices ended and mediation began.

Mediation may be sought by the parties or offered spontaneously by outsiders. Once under way it provides the governments in dispute with the possibility of a solution, but without any antecedent commitment to accept the mediator's suggestions. Consequently it has the advantage of allowing them to retain control of the dispute, probably an essential requirement if negotiations are deadlocked on a matter of vital interest. On the other hand, if a face-saving compromise is what is needed, it may be politically easier to make the necessary concessions in the course of mediation than in direct negotiation. If a dispute concerns sensitive issues, the fact that the proceedings can be completely confidential is an advantage in any case. As with other means of dispute settlement, however, not every international dispute is suitable for mediation. . . .

. . . [M]ediation can only be as effective as the parties wish it to be, and this is governed largely by their immediate situation. Although this is a major limitation on the usefulness of mediation, it is important to retain a sense of perspective. It would be quite wrong to think that a mediator is merely someone who lends his authority to an agreement that is already virtually made. On the contrary, by facilitating the parties' dialogue, providing them with information and suggestions, identifying and exploring their aims and canvassing a range of possible solutions, mediation can play a vital role in moving them towards agreement. Although success will often be incomplete and failure sometimes inevitable, the mediator's job is to spare no effort for the parties and trust that they will reciprocate. . . .

3. Conciliation

Conciliation has been defined as:

> A method for the settlement of international disputes of any nature according to which a Commission set up by the Parties, either on a permanent basis or an *ad hoc* basis to deal with a dispute, proceeds to the impartial examination of the dispute and attempts to define the terms of a settlement susceptible of being accepted by them, or of affording the Parties, with a view to its settlement, such aid as they may have requested.

The eclectic character of the method is at once apparent. If mediation is essentially an extension of negotiation, conciliation puts third party intervention on a formal legal footing and institutionalises it in a way comparable, but not identical, to . . . arbitration. . . . [T]he search for terms "susceptible of being accepted" by the parties, but not binding on them, provides a sharp contrast with arbitration and a reminder of the link between conciliation and mediation. . . .

Currently, . . . conciliation is regularly included in provisions dealing with dispute settlement and retains a modest place among the procedures actually used by states when disputes arise. . . . [C]onciliation offers a procedure adaptable to a variety of needs and demonstrates the advantage to be derived from the structured involvement of outsiders in the settlement of international disputes.

The following materials will give you a sense of how an international negotiation works. First there is the account of former Secretary of State Henry Kissinger on how he approached a complicated negotiation. Then there is an excerpt from

Professor Phillip Trimble on the process by which the U.S. government negotiates treaties. His description deals with arms control, which is more complex and more important than many negotiations. For example, the President and cabinet officers are personally involved in arms control, unlike the situation in many international claims and disputes. And arms control involves the national security side of the bureaucracy, rather than officials handling trade, financial, agricultural, business, and labor issues. Nevertheless, you should get a sense of how the foreign affairs bureaucracy operates and how complex the dynamics of a negotiation can be.

Henry A. Kissinger, Years of Upheaval

214 (1982)

The opening of a complicated negotiation is like the beginning of an arranged marriage. The partners know that the formalities will soon be stripped away as they discover each other's real attributes. Neither party can yet foretell at what point necessity will transform itself into acceptance; when the abstract desire for progress will leave at least residues of understanding; which disagreement will, by the act of being overcome, illuminate the as-yet undiscovered sense of community and which will lead to an impasse destined to rend the relationship forever. The future being mercifully veiled, the parties attempt what they might not dare did they know what was ahead.

Almost invariably I spent the first session of a new negotiation in educating myself. I almost never put forward a proposal. Rather, I sought to understand the intangibles in the position of my interlocutor and to gauge the scope as well as the limits of probable concessions. And I made a considerable effort to leave no doubt about our fundamental approach. Only romantics think they can prevail in negotiations by trickery; only pedants believe in the advantage of obfuscation. In a society of sovereign states, an agreement will be maintained only if all partners consider it in their interest. They must have a sense of participation in the result. The art of diplomacy is not to outsmart the other side but to convince it either of common interests or of penalties if an impasse continues.

Phillip R. Trimble, Arms Control and International Negotiation Theory

25 Stan. J. Int'l L. 543, 549-563 (1989)

I. The Process of International Negotiation

An international negotiation is significantly different from its more familiar domestic counterparts.[26] The most important differences stem from the fact that an international negotiation is much more than an exercise between two autonomous individuals seeking to reach a compromise on mutually accepted goals,

26. Part I, the description of the international negotiation process, is based on the author's experience in international economic negotiations and on published accounts of arms control negotiations. See generally . . . McNeill, U.S.-U.S.S.R. Arms Negotiations: The Process and the Lawyer, 79 Am. J. Int'l L. 52 (1985) (an especially valuable account of the process itself).

and it is also significantly more complicated than the typical labor or corporate negotiation. It involves several interlocking processes, intragovernmental as well as international. Initially, the government bureaucracies involved formulate positions through intricate interagency negotiations. In the case of the American government, an administration may pursue additional negotiations, or at least discussions, with congressional committees and affected nongovernmental interests, such as the nuclear weapons laboratories. The ensuing exchange of positions at the intergovernmental level then normally stimulates further domestic bureaucratic negotiations to produce counterproposals.

In the domestic negotiation each agency has a distinctive perspective from which it views the process and which influences the position it advocates. For example, in a negotiation regarding numbers of strategic nuclear missiles, the Pentagon and the Joint Chiefs of Staff (JCS) would likely propose a position that accommodates current production plans, especially if the United States is producing a new missile while [the other country] is not. Thus, their preferred agreement would permit the United States to carry out its plans but also place some future constraint on the [other country]. . . . The Department of State is concerned with improvement of the overall political relationship and may therefore also want to reach an agreement that can contribute to the maintenance of a good relationship. In this light they are likely to look to what *can* be negotiated and thus favor a result that accommodates both sides' interests. The Central Intelligence Agency (CIA) may want an agreement that can be monitored easily. Some members of Congress may want to assure that any proposed position does not foreclose production of a favored new system that is important to their constituencies. The weapons laboratories may favor a position that requires the development of new warheads.

All these interests must either be accommodated, compromised or overridden by the President before a position can even be put on the negotiating table. Moreover, since the resulting treaty must be approved by Congress or the Senate, the President would be reluctant to override a strong congressional preference or the position of the Pentagon or JCS, whose views carry great weight in the Congress. Hence, accommodation of all competing interests is frequently the order of the day, with the most powerful domestic constituencies having a particularly influential role. The complicated, bureaucratic nature of position formulation distinguishes this type of negotiation from almost all domestic counterparts.

There are, of course, many similar features. Labor and business negotiators also have multiple constituencies with differing interests to satisfy. Even a person negotiating a lease may also have to take account of the separate interests of a spouse. In an international negotiation, however, the members of the constituencies seem to have more sharply divergent interests than the typical members of a labor, corporate or family constituency. . . . [T]he interests within a government may include a wide range of political, military, economic and ideological preferences. . . . In the context of arms control, it is also less likely that both parties want or need an agreement. Simply appearing to negotiate may be enough to satisfy the political needs of the parties. . . .

One major consequence of these differences is that an international negotiation is likely to be a more formal and time-consuming exercise than its domestic counterpart. Carefully negotiated government positions are stated and restated in a stylized fashion. Responses and changes of position are coordinated through sometimes cumbersome national bureaucracies comprised of officials who may be slow to reach agreement on how to proceed. A variety of congressional forces and nongovernmental constituencies subject the negotiators and their supporting bureaucracies to further pressures and delays. Because of this bureaucratic process, negotiators cannot engage in the freewheeling style that one may expect in a domestic context. In international negotiations, personalities thus tend to be less important. Positions represent compromises of basic institutional interests and can be changed only by another compromise of those interests. The individual negotiator therefore normally operates under strict instructions and has much less flexibility or opportunity for creative diplomacy. . . . In addition, international agreements, especially in arms control, do not rest on trust. The personal relationships that presidents often refer to in glowing terms . . . may make a difference in a marginal situation, but those relationships do not deeply influence the outcome of the governmental decisionmaking process.

Moreover, the positions advanced generally reflect compromises with interests dedicated to the status quo, or to no agreement at all. Negotiating positions frequently embody the lowest common denominator of conflicting agency positions. Results therefore tend not to deviate radically from the status quo. Bureaucrats with differing institutional interests will often seek to accommodate all of them. Hence, in the example outlined above regarding strategic missiles, the position finally agreed upon might permit full deployment of current systems, but allow only a single new system or modernization within limits, with provisions for on-site inspection. The military gets its current system. Congress, the defense industry and the weapons labs get the opportunity to develop a new system. The JCS get some limits and some predictability. . . . The State Department would be satisfied because the proposal would seem negotiable. . . . Thus all the institutional interests are to a large degree satisfied by an approach that represents the lowest common denominator. . . . Bureaucrats also prefer to negotiate a compromise themselves, especially if they get most of what they want, rather than permitting a decision to go to a higher level where they may lose everything. . . .

The Formal Negotiation . . .

A large delegation headed by an individual with ambassadorial rank conducts an arms control negotiation. In the American case, the President appoints the ambassador to serve as his or her representative. . . . The delegation itself consists of representatives of the same (or at least most of the same) agencies represented in the interagency working group. In addition, the House and Senate have often designated representatives to negotiations. These representatives have access to some of the papers involved and sometimes sit in on plenary negotiating sessions. Although they do not normally have any impact on the day-to-day negotiations, the specter of congressional consideration of a negotiated agreement can be quite important.

Another important participant in any arms control negotiation is the working group maintained in Washington to "back-stop" the delegation. It is comprised of the same agencies that participated in the initial work on the negotiations and that are represented in the delegation, principally State, . . . Defense, JCS, CIA and the

NSC. The working group is responsible for receiving daily reporting cables, reacting to proposals from the other side and drafting instructions for high-level approval. The interaction of the delegation and the backstop group is extensive. Since each daily development must normally be reported back to Washington and may elicit new instructions or guidance, a regular exchange of cables, phone calls and personal visits is generated between the delegation and the working group and between the ambassador and the White House. . . .

The result of this wealth of interchange among various governmental and nongovernmental entities is an abundance of more interagency negotiation with further opportunity to shape and reshape the original negotiating position. . . .

The formality of highly stylized arms control negotiations imposes further constraints. Each ambassador normally reads an opening statement setting forth the position and making the best arguments available. . . . The responses to the opening statements tend also to be "set pieces" restating fixed positions and refuting the other side's arguments. Each delegate must follow instructions that . . . are likely to be inflexible in the beginning. . . .

The movement from formal exchanges of positions in plenary sessions to the conclusion of an agreed text — the heart of the negotiation process — can take place in a variety of other environments. Negotiators can more easily negotiate in informal settings, such as one-on-one meetings of the delegation heads, social occasions, or smaller working groups growing out of the formal session. Frequently, small working groups dealing with specialized "technical" topics or problems can make progress toward resolving disputes that would be unimaginable in a more formal and conspicuous setting. Agreements can be reached on these matters, while larger, more political differences persist until a high-level decision is made to remove those obstacles to a settlement.

While informal discussions are a central feature of international negotiations, they scarcely resemble the free-wheeling deal-making that the reader may associate with business negotiations. The international negotiator's latitude is considerably restricted by the limited authority delegated in negotiating instructions and the close supervision of working groups in the capital. . . .

The importance of individual negotiating skills and personality in the international context is frequently overstated and is certainly insufficient to change basic government positions; nevertheless, the international negotiator is not entirely without room to maneuver and bring personal skills to bear. Even detailed instructions cannot provide guidelines sufficiently specific to provide minute-by-minute guidance in actual negotiations. Items inevitably arise on which the instructions are silent or at least ambiguous. The ambassador must decide, within the parameters of the instructions, a variety of matters that eventually will determine the pace, and even the success, of the negotiations. For example, the negotiator must decide how and when to present a position, how to support it, when to resort to a fall-back position and when to seek new instructions. The negotiator must exploit ambiguity or silence in the instructions, and must decide whether and when to explore possible compromises without express authority. In doing this, the negotiator must have a sense of the process back home, a command of the interagency delegation structure, and an understanding of the positions of the other side. The negotiator may also use skillful negotiating tactics, such as claiming to lack authority actually possessed to create the appearance of having achieved a "difficult" compromise. Above all, a sound sense of timing is crucial. These skills distinguish the brilliant from the mediocre negotiator and are the most difficult to impart and articulate. . . .

Notes and Questions

1. What are the advantages and disadvantages for states of negotiation, as opposed to adjudication or arbitration, of a dispute?

2. Which agency of the U.S. government would be most inclined to stand up for the interests of autoworkers? The computer industry? The Trimble excerpt describes the different bureaucratic actors in an arms control negotiation. Consider a negotiation about an international trade agreement. In the United States, farmers benefit from substantial governmental subsidies. Which U.S. government agency would be most inclined to oppose reducing farm subsidies? Which agency would be most inclined to favor reducing those subsidies? If there are competing domestic interests, are the President and the Congress likely to balance them in similar ways, or in different ways?

3. What role do international legal rules play in the process of negotiation? Does the frequent resort by countries to negotiation or other informal dispute-resolution mechanisms imply that international legal rules do not really affect the behavior of states? Or does international law influence the positions taken by the parties? In a domestic setting, the parties to a negotiation are likely to realize that if the negotiations fail, either side may resort to a formal dispute resolution institution, such as a court, that will apply the relevant legal rules. For a seminal study in the domestic context on the impact of law on negotiations and bargaining that occur outside a court, see Robert H. Mnookin & Lewis Kornhauser, Bargaining in the Shadow of the Law: The Case of Divorce, 88 Yale L.J. 950 (1979)

Does the international legal system similarly provide a framework for negotiations? Does it depend on whether or not there is a compulsory third-party dispute resolution process to which the parties can submit the dispute? Are legal rules likely to influence the positions of the parties even in the absence of a mandatory dispute resolution mechanism?

4. Given the complicated interagency process discussed in the excerpt above, why might a president ask one of his closest advisers during ongoing negotiations to undertake, without resorting to the interagency process or formal negotiations, private negotiations with a high-level representative from the other country—for example, to try out a new position or to break a deadlock? Operating outside of normal diplomatic channels in this way is sometimes referred to as using the "back channel." India and Pakistan, for example, are reported to have made efforts to address their bitter conflict over Kashmir though back-channel talks.

> For several years, special envoys from Pakistan and India had been holding talks in hotel rooms in Bangkok, Dubai, and London. [Pakistani President Pervez] Musharraf and Manmohan Singh, the Prime Minister of India, had encouraged the negotiators to seek what some involved called a "paradigm shift" in relations between the two nations. The agenda included a search for an end to the long fight over Kashmir, a contest that is often described by Western military analysts as a potential trigger for atomic war. . . . The two principal envoys—for Pakistan, a college classmate of Musharraf's

> named Tariq Aziz, and, for India, a Russia specialist named Satinder Lambah — were developing what diplomats refer to as a "non-paper" on Kashmir, a text without names or signatures which can serve as a deniable but detailed basis for a deal. [Steve Coll, The Back Channel, The New Yorker, May 2, 2009, at 38.]

Progress toward an agreement ended with the political decline and eventual fall of Pakistan's President Musharraf.

What are the advantages of back-channel negotiations? The disadvantages? What effect will they have on the regular negotiating team, and on the interagency process? Can the President be confident that a result achieved through back-channel negotiations will have the support of the government bureaucracies or of key figures in Congress? Might the President in some situations combine regular negotiations with occasional resort to the back channel?

5. When conflict between two countries is particularly intense, it may not be politically possible for the parties even to meet directly to conduct official negotiations. In some of these cases, private elites from each side may meet to discuss the issues dividing their countries. Such unofficial dialogues are referred to as "Track Two" diplomacy. Particularly if the participants in these unofficial policy dialogues have access to the official policy-making process, Track Two diplomacy can enable states to negotiate indirectly. Track Two talks can also open the door to official talks. The negotiations in Oslo, Norway, that produced the Oslo Accords between Israel and the Palestinian Authority in 1993 initially involved non-official but influential Israelis and Palestinians; they were later broadened to include official representatives of the two parties. More recently, a Track Two process known as the Geneva Initiative has brought together Israeli, Palestinian, and other civil society actors who have developed a proposed Israeli-Palestinian peace agreement in an effort to, in the words of its organizers, "bring that moment of peace closer, by showing the way and preparing public opinion and leadership to be accepting of the real compromises required to solve the conflict." For a discussion of Track Two diplomacy on security issues in two politically volatile regions, see Dalia Dassa Kaye, RAND National Security Research Division, Talking to the Enemy: Track Two Diplomacy in the Middle East and South Asia (2007).

6. Based on the brief descriptions in the Merrills excerpt, when do you think that a state might be interested in supplementing negotiations with a mediator, a conciliator, or some other form of alternative dispute resolution?

7. A wide range of actors can offer "good offices" or serve as mediators. Officials from a single country can attempt to mediate a conflict, as Algeria did during the 1979-1981 hostage crisis involving Iran and the United States, and as Qatar undertook to do in 2010 to resolve a border dispute between Djibouti and Eritrea. Sometimes, a group of states will mediate a dispute; beginning in 1994, the "Contact Group," comprising France, Germany, Italy, Russia, the United Kingdom, and the United States, engaged in mediation efforts in the war in Bosnia and later in the Serbia-Kosovo conflict. International organizations and their officials frequently mediate international disputes. The United Nations and the African Union in 2008 appointed Djibril Yipènè Bassolé as Joint African Union-United Nations Chief Mediator to facilitate efforts to negotiate an end to the conflict in Darfur. Even individuals can serve as mediators. Former President Jimmy Carter, acting as a private citizen, has mediated numerous international conflicts, including brokering

a 1994 agreement for the military authorities who had unconstitutionally ousted Haitian President Aristide to step down and permit Aristide to return to office. For more information regarding mediation and other forms of alternative dispute resolution, see Mediation: Theory, Policy and Practice (Carrie Menkel-Meadow ed., 2001); see also Lars Kirchhoff, Constructive Interventions: Paradigms, Process and Practice of International Mediation (2008); Kyle Beardsley, Politics by Means Other than War: Understanding International Mediation (2006); and War Over Words: Mediation and Arbitration to Prevent Deadly Conflict (Melanie C. Greenberg, John H. Barton & Margaret E. McGuinness eds., 2000).

8. The World Trade Organization Dispute Settlement Understanding (DSU) provides that member states may voluntarily undertake procedures such as good offices, conciliation, and mediation, as well as seeking the more binding approach of a panel and the Appellate Body, to resolve disputes. (Article 5.) See Section E for discussion of the WTO dispute settlement system and the Documentary Supplement for the text of the DSU.

9. Inquiry, another international dispute resolution method, centers on fact-finding. The Convention for the Pacific Settlement of International Disputes adopted at the Hague Peace Conference of 1899 and its 1907 successor (discussed further in Section D) provide for Commissions of Inquiry, which are formally constituted panels assigned the limited task of issuing a nonbinding report concerning disputed matters of fact between states. A total of five cases have been submitted to Commissions of Inquiry at the Permanent Court of Arbitration. Why would states elect to use inquiry to resolve a dispute?

10. Many U.S. courts have utilized with varying degrees of success a variety of alternative dispute resolution programs. These programs encompass a wide range of approaches, including mediation and conciliation. See, for example, Ettie Ward, Court-Annexed Alternative Dispute Resolution in the United States Federal Courts: Panacea or Pandemic?, 81 St. John's L. Rev. 77 (2007); Wayne D. Brazil, Comparing Structures for the Delivery of ADR Services by Courts: Critical Values and Concerns, 14 Ohio St. J. on Disp. Resol. 715 (1999).

B. INTERNATIONAL COURT OF JUSTICE

The International Court of Justice, often called the ICJ or the World Court, was created by the U.N. Charter in 1945 and designed to be the principal judicial organ of the United Nations. The ICJ's main function is to decide legal disputes between states. The Court is also empowered to render advisory opinions on certain questions submitted to it by designated organs or specialized agencies of the United Nations.

1. The Structure and Organization of the ICJ

Located in the Netherlands at The Hague, the ICJ is the successor to the Permanent Court of International Justice (PCIJ), which was created by the League of Nations in 1920. The PCIJ was most active from 1922 to 1939. During those 18 years it heard 65 cases, issued 27 advisory opinions, and rendered 32 judgments. Its efforts, for example, effected the settlement of several boundary disputes and a dispute between Denmark and Norway over the sovereignty of eastern Greenland. The PCIJ was dissolved in 1946, soon after the formation of the ICJ. The ICJ's Statute is substantially the same as the PCIJ's Statute, and the ICJ has frequently referred to its predecessor's precedents.

The ICJ is governed by its Statute, which is an annex to and integral part of the U.N. Charter. (See Articles 92 to 96 of the U.N. Charter and the Statute of the International Court of Justice in the Documentary Supplement.) As a result, all U.N. member states are automatically parties to the Statute of the ICJ.

The Court is composed of 15 judges, who are elected to serve nine-year terms. Elections are staggered, so that one-third of the court is elected, or re-elected, every three years. Article 2 of the ICJ Statute sets forth the required qualifications for ICJ judges; they must be "independent" and "persons of high moral character, who possess the qualifications required in their respective countries for appointment to the highest judicial offices, or are jurisconsults of recognized competence in international law." ICJ judges are elected by the U.N. General Assembly and Security Council from among candidates nominated by national groups appointed by individual governments; to win election, a judge must win a majority of the votes cast in both the General Assembly and the Security Council. No two judges may be nationals of the same state. (Articles 2 to 14 of the ICJ Statute govern the process for electing judges.)

Article 9 of the ICJ Statute exhorts the states electing judges to "bear in mind" that the composition of the Court should be representative of "the main forms of civilization and of the principal legal systems of the world." To further such representative balance, an informal "understanding" has emerged under which the geographic distribution of seats on the Court "should roughly parallel the regional distribution of seats on the Security Council." Terry D. Gill, Rosenne's The World Court: What It Is and How It Works 44-45 (6th ed. 2003). Currently, the distribution of seats is as follows: Africa—3 seats; Asia—3 seats; Latin America—2 seats; Western Europe and others (including the United States, Canada, Australia, and New Zealand)—5 seats; Eastern Europe—2 seats. It is also customary that a national of each of the five permanent members of the Security Council—China, France, Russia, the United Kingdom, and the United States—serve on the Court.

The Court's rules and practice reflect somewhat inconsistent assumptions about judges' relationships with the states that appoint them. Candidates for the Court are not formally nominated by governments, but through the "national groups" of up to four individuals who have been appointed to serve as "members" of the Permanent Court of Arbitration, which is discussed in Section D. As one commentator observed, "[t]he purpose of [nominating through 'national groups'], evidently, is to make the role of governments appear somewhat less intrusive. . . . The process also mildly encourages judicial independence. . . ." Thomas M. Franck, Judging the World Court 6 (1986).

Article 31 of the Statute reflects the position that judges are independent and do not necessarily represent the views of the countries that appointed them. It provides that "[j]udges of the nationality of each of the parties shall retain their right to sit in the case before the Court." If, however, only one of the parties to a case has a national on the Court, the other party is allowed to choose a judge to sit on that case. If neither party has a judge of its nationality on the Court, both parties may designate a judge. The appointment of such *ad hoc* judges seems to reflect a view of judges as representatives or advocates for the state that names them.

The role of states in electing judges has generated debate about whether ICJ decision making is fair and impartial. In her study, Professor Edith Brown Weiss concluded:

> This chapter reports the results of a quantitative analysis of the voting behavior of judges in all contentious cases before the International Court of Justice since its inception through 1986. If the Court were according grossly unequal treatment to parties appearing before it, it should show up in the voting patterns of the judges. But the record does not reveal significant alignments, either on a regional, political, or economic basis. There is a high degree of consensus among the judges on most decisions. The most that can be discerned is that some judges vote more frequently together during certain periods than do others, and that in rare instances, notably with the Soviet and Syrian judges, they have always voted the same way. But there have not been persistent voting alignments which have significantly affected the decisions of the Court. [Edith Brown Weiss, Judicial Independence and Impartiality: A Preliminary Inquiry, in The International Court of Justice at a Crossroads 134 (Lori F. Damrosch ed., 1987).]

A more recent study, which purports to use more sophisticated empirical methods than previous studies of ICJ judges' voting behavior, concludes that judges are more likely to vote for their own country or for countries that share certain characteristics, such as level of wealth and political systems, with their home country. See Eric A. Posner & Miguel F.P. de Figueiredo, Is the International Court of Justice Politically Biased?, 34 J. Legal Studies 599 (2005).

The Court ordinarily sits in plenary sessions, with all 15 judges—plus any judges *ad hoc*—participating in a case. The Court's Statute also allows for a smaller chamber (of three or more judges) to hear a case. (Article 26.) The chamber approach is seen as one way to introduce more flexibility into the Court's proceedings and to make it more attractive to the parties to a dispute, who are empowered to determine the chamber's size and to consult with the president of the Court about the identity of the judges who will comprise the chamber. In practice, the decision to refer a case to a chamber is driven principally by the wishes of the parties. As of February 2011, only six ICJ cases had been referred to chambers, mostly in cases involving boundary disputes (including a disagreement between the United States and Canada over the Gulf of Maine).

Under Article 94(1) of the Charter, all U.N. member states undertake to comply with a judgment of the Court in any case to which they are parties. According to Article 59 of the ICJ Statute, the Court's judgments are only binding on the parties to that case. If a country fails to comply with a judgment, the other party may refer the matter to the Security Council, which "may, if it deems it necessary," take measures to enforce the judgment.

As of February 2011, a total of 150 cases had been presented to the Court. Of these, 123 cases were contentious cases and 27 involved advisory opinions. The Court has resolved a considerable number of boundary and territorial disputes and has rendered decisions on such topics as navigational rights of warships through the Corfu Channel; asylum rights; the hostage-taking of American diplomats in Iran; American support for the armed "*contra*" insurgency in Nicaragua; investment rights of shareholders in a foreign company; and the sovereign immunity of diplomats. In recent years, the Court has addressed an increasingly wide range of international law questions, many of which have involved sensitive political issues, such as allegations of genocide and the unlawful use of force.

Sixteen contentious cases were pending before the Court as of February 2011. The cases are listed on the Court's Web site at http://www.icj-cij.org.

2. *Jurisdiction of the ICJ in Contentious Cases*

Article 34(1) of the ICJ Statute provides that "[o]nly states may be parties in cases before the Court." Under Article 35(1), the Court is "open to the parties to the [ICJ] Statute," namely, the 192 members of the United Nations. Yet not every dispute between two countries falls within the Court's jurisdiction. Instead, jurisdiction depends on the consent of the parties, manifested in one of the ways described in Article 36 of the Statute.

Statute of the International Court of Justice

Article 36

1. The jurisdiction of the Court comprises all cases which the parties refer to it and all matters specially provided for in the Charter of the United Nations or in treaties and conventions in force.

2. The states parties to the present Statute may at any time declare that they recognize as compulsory *ipso facto* and without special agreement, in relation to any other state accepting the same obligation, the jurisdiction of the Court in all legal disputes concerning:

a. the interpretation of a treaty;
b. any question of international law;
c. the existence of any fact which, if established, would constitute a breach of an international obligation;
d. the nature or extent of the reparation to be made for the breach of an international obligation.

3. The declarations referred to above may be made unconditionally or on condition of reciprocity on the part of several or certain states, or for a certain time.

4. Such declarations shall be deposited with the Secretary-General of the United Nations, who shall transmit copies thereof to the parties to the Statute and to the Registrar of the Court.

5. Declarations made under Article 36 of the Statute of the Permanent Court of International Justice and which are still in force shall be deemed, as between the parties to the present Statute, to be acceptances of the compulsory jurisdiction of the International Court of Justice for the period which they still have to run and in accordance with their terms.

6. In the event of a dispute as to whether the Court has jurisdiction, the matter shall be settled by the decision of the Court.

The question of whether a country is a member of the United Nations, and consequently a party to the Statute of the ICJ, rarely arises. It proved to be contentious — and gave rise to seemingly inconsistent outcomes — in cases involving the Federal Republic of Yugoslavia (FRY), later known as "Serbia and Montenegro," and today as the Republic of Serbia. After the former Socialist Federal Republic of Yugoslavia (SFRY) disintegrated, the former Yugoslav Republics of Serbia and Montenegro in 1992 designated themselves as the "Federal Republic of Yugoslavia"; that state claimed to continue the international legal personality of the SFRY, including the SFRY's status as a U.N. member state. In Resolution 777 (1992), the Security Council decided that the FRY could not automatically continue the SFRY's membership and should apply to join the United Nations, as had the other states that emerged from the break-up of Yugoslavia. Eventually, in 2000, the FRY requested, and was granted, admission to membership in the U.N., effective November 1 of that year.

In 1999, before the FRY's application for membership in the U.N. was approved, it brought suit in the ICJ against eight NATO states challenging the legality of NATO's bombing campaign against the FRY during the Kosovo crisis. The Court found that the FRY "was not a Member of the United Nations, and in that capacity a State party to the Statute of the International Court of Justice, at the time of filing its Application." Legality of Use of Force (Serbia and Montenegro v. Belgium), Preliminary Objections Judgment, 2004 I.C.J. 279, 311 (Dec. 15) (similar judgments were issued in cases brought against Canada, France, Germany, Italy, the Netherlands, Portugal, and the United Kingdom). The ICJ accordingly dismissed the case for lack of jurisdiction. Id. at 328.

The Court employed a different approach in its November 2008 judgment in a case brought in 1999 against the FRY by Croatia. The judges acknowledged that FRY was not a Member of the United Nations when Croatia initiated the case, but noted that it would have been possible for Croatia to file a new application — over which the Court *would* have had jurisdiction — at any time after the FRY became a member of the United Nations in November 2000. Under the circumstances, the Court elected to show "realism and flexibility . . . [where] the conditions governing . . . jurisdiction were not fully satisfied when proceedings were initiated but were subsequently satisfied, before the Court ruled on its jurisdiction." The ICJ accordingly rejected the argument that it did not have jurisdiction over the FRY (by then called Serbia). Application of the Convention on the Prevention and Punishment of the Crime of Genocide (Croatia v. Serbia), Preliminary Objections Judgment, 2008 I.C.J. 412, 438, 440 (Nov. 18).

a. Jurisdiction by Special Agreement

Once a dispute between countries has arisen, they may conclude a special agreement to submit the matter to the ICJ. Such an agreement, also known as a *compromis,* will define the question or dispute the parties wish the Court to resolve.

Although the parties' intent to submit a case to the ICJ is ordinarily clear, in some cases this has itself been disputed. The question arose in the context of a dispute between Qatar and Bahrain regarding sovereignty over certain islands and the maritime boundary between the two countries. In 1987, with the mediation assistance of King Fahd of Saudi Arabia, Qatar and Bahrain agreed in an exchange of letters to submit the dispute to the ICJ. The countries remained divided, however, about the scope of the dispute, namely, precisely which of their territorial conflicts to submit to the ICJ. Bahrain, Qatar, and Saudi Arabia continued to negotiate to define the scope of the dispute, but failed to reach agreement.

Renewed efforts to resolve the question were made at a meeting in December 1990, when Qatar indicated it was prepared to accept the formulation of the scope of the dispute that Bahrain had proposed ("the Bahraini formula"). The parties agreed that Saudi Arabia would continue to mediate in hopes of negotiating a settlement, but set a May 1991 deadline for those efforts. After the December 1990 meeting, the Foreign Ministers of Bahrain, Qatar, and Saudi Arabia signed "Minutes" recording the consultations that had taken place among them. The text of the Minutes was in Arabic, and Qatar and Bahrain submitted slightly different English translations. According to Qatar, the Minutes included the following provision regarding what would happen in the event no settlement was concluded by May 1991:

> "The following was agreed: . . .
>
> After [May 1991], the parties may submit the matter to the International Court of Justice in accordance with the Bahraini formula, which has been accepted by Qatar, and the proceedings arising therefrom. . . ."

Bahrain's translation was in most respects identical to Qatar's, but provided as follows on the question of recourse to the ICJ:

> "The two parties may, [after May 1991], submit the matter to the International Court of Justice in accordance with the Bahraini formula, which the State of Qatar has accepted, and with the procedures consequent on it. . . ."

On the basis of the 1987 exchange of letters and the 1990 Minutes, Qatar filed an application in the ICJ in July 1991. Bahrain argued that the 1990 Minutes did not constitute a legally binding instrument manifesting its consent to the Court's jurisdiction, and that the Minutes did not in any event enable Qatar to initiate a case unilaterally.

The Court concluded that the Minutes were "not a simple record of a meeting," but rather constituted an international agreement. It also rejected Bahrain's argument that the 1990 Minutes contemplated that the two states would have to act jointly to submit their dispute to the ICJ. The Court found that the instruments negotiated by the parties "left open the possibility for each of the Parties to present its own claims to the Court, within the framework thus fixed." Maritime Delimitation and Territorial Questions between Qatar and Bahrain (Qatar v. Bahrain), Preliminary Objections Judgment, 1994 I.C.J. 112, 121, 123 (July 1).

Notes and Questions

1. Consider the discussion in Chapter 2 about the difference between treaties and political commitments. Are you persuaded that the Foreign Ministers of Qatar, Bahrain, and Saudi Arabia intended to conclude a legally binding instrument when they signed the Minutes of the December 1990 meeting?

2. In 2001, the ICJ issued its merits judgment in the *Qatar v. Bahrain* case. The judgment was a partial victory for each side; the Court awarded certain disputed

islands (the Hawar Islands and Qit'at Jaradah) to Bahrain, but others (Zubarah and Janan Island) to Qatar. The Court determined the maritime boundary between the two states and affirmed the right of innocent passage of Qatari vessels in Bahrain's territorial sea, as delimited by the Court's judgment. Despite the long-standing intransigence of the parties concerning their claims to all of the disputed territories, the governments of Qatar and Bahrain both accepted the ICJ's judgment "and declared the following day a national holiday to celebrate the end of the dispute and better relations between the countries." Colter Paulson, Compliance with Final Judgments of the International Court of Justice since 1987, 98 Am. J. Int'l L. 434, 455 (2004).

b. Jurisdiction under a Dispute Settlement Clause in a Treaty

When states negotiate a treaty, they may agree in advance that any party may submit a dispute concerning the interpretation or application of that treaty to the ICJ. Over 300 treaties, both bilateral and multilateral, contain such ICJ dispute resolution clauses, also known as "compromissory clauses." Consider the following examples of ICJ dispute settlement clauses.

Treaty of Amity, Economic Relations, and Consular Rights Between the United States of America and Iran Signed August 15, 1955

Article XXI

2. Any dispute between the High Contracting Parties as to the interpretation or application of the present Treaty, not satisfactorily adjusted by diplomacy, shall be submitted to the International Court of Justice, unless the High Contracting Parties agree to settlement by some other pacific means.

Convention on the Prevention and Punishment of the Crime of Genocide Opened for Signature December 9, 1948

Article 9

Disputes between the Contracting Parties relating to the interpretation, application or fulfilment of the present Convention, including those relating to the responsibility of a State for genocide or for any of the other [prohibited] acts enumerated in article III, shall be submitted to the International Court of Justice at the request of any of the parties to the dispute.

Oil Platforms (Islamic Republic of Iran v. United States of America)

Int'l Court of Justice
Preliminary Objections Judgment, 1996 I.C.J. 803 (Dec. 12)

[Iran challenged the lawfulness of the destruction by U.S. military forces of a number of Iranian oil production platforms in the Persian Gulf. The attacks arose during the last stages of the 1980-1988 war between Iran and Iraq, when

Iranian forces increased attacks against ships engaged in commercial trade with Arab Persian Gulf countries. In Iran's view, these states were supporting Iraq, even though they formally retained neutral status. The United States, which sought to ensure that commercial shipping in the Gulf was not impeded, concluded that Iran was using the oil platforms as command and control centers for Iranian attacks against neutral commercial vessels.

[Iran grounded jurisdiction on the ICJ dispute resolution clause in Article XXI of the 1955 U.S.-Iran Treaty of Amity, Economic Relations, and Consular Rights. It argued that the destruction of the platforms violated several articles of the Treaty, including: (a) Article I, which provided that there "shall be firm and enduring peace and sincere friendship between the United States of America and Iran"; (b) Article IV(1), which provided that the parties "shall at all times accord fair and equitable treatment to nationals and companies of the other High Contracting Party, and to their property and enterprises"; and (c) Article X(1), which provided that there "shall be freedom of commerce and navigation" between the territories of the two parties.

[In objecting to the ICJ's jurisdiction, the U.S. argued that the dispute over the destruction of the platforms was governed by the law regulating the use of force and self-defense, and did not fall within the ambit of the Treaty of Amity.]

16. . . . [T]he Parties differ on the question whether the dispute between the two States with respect to the lawfulness of the actions carried out by the United States against the Iranian oil platforms is a dispute "as to the interpretation or application" of the Treaty of 1955. In order to answer that question, the Court cannot limit itself to noting that one of the Parties maintains that such a dispute exists, and the other denies it. It must ascertain whether the violations of the Treaty of 1955 pleaded by Iran do or do not fall within the provisions of the Treaty and whether, as a consequence, the dispute is one which the Court has jurisdiction . . . to entertain, pursuant to [the compromissory clause in] Article XXI, paragraph 2. . . .

28. . . . Article I cannot be interpreted as incorporating into the Treaty all of the provisions of international law concerning [peaceful and friendly] relations. Rather, by incorporating into the body of the Treaty the form of words used in Article I, the two States intended to stress that peace and friendship constituted the precondition for a harmonious development of their commercial, financial and consular relations and that such a development would in turn reinforce that peace and that friendship. It follows that Article I must be regarded as fixing an objective, in the light of which the other Treaty provisions are to be interpreted and applied. . . .

31. . . . Article I is thus not without legal significance . . . but cannot, taken in isolation, be a basis for the jurisdiction of the Court. . . .

36. . . . Article IV, paragraph 1, states that the nationals and companies of one of the contracting parties, as well as their property and enterprises, must be treated by the other party in a "fair and equitable" manner. This text prohibits unreasonable or discriminatory measures that would impair certain rights and interests of those nationals and companies. It concludes by specifying that their legitimately acquired contractual rights must be afforded effective means of enforcement. The whole of these provisions is aimed at the way in which the natural persons and legal entities in question are, in the exercise of their private or professional activities, to be treated by the State concerned. In other words, these detailed provisions concern

the treatment by each party of the nationals and companies of the other party, as well as their property and enterprises. Such provisions do not cover the actions carried out in this case by the United States against Iran. Article IV, paragraph 1, thus does not lay down any norms applicable to this particular case. This Article cannot therefore form the basis of the Court's jurisdiction. . . .

37. It remains to consider what consequences, in terms of the jurisdiction of the Court, can be drawn from Article X, paragraph 1, of the Treaty of 1955 [, which provides:]

> "Between the territories of the two High Contracting Parties there shall be freedom of commerce and navigation."

38. . . . [T]he question the Court must decide, in order to determine its jurisdiction, is whether the actions of the United States complained of by Iran had the potential to affect "freedom of commerce" as guaranteed by the provision quoted above. . . . [The United States argued that the attacks on the platforms did not fall within the scope of Article X on the grounds that the term "commerce" in that provision: (1) was confined to maritime commerce; (2) was limited to commerce between the United States and Iran; and (3) referred solely to the actual sale or exchange of goods.]

43. . . . [Regarding the first argument,] the view that the word "commerce" in Article X, paragraph 1, is confined to maritime commerce does not commend itself to the Court.

44. [Regarding the second argument, the] Court does not have to enter into the question whether this provision is restricted to commerce "between" the Parties. It is not contested between them that oil exports from Iran to the United States were — to some degree — ongoing at least until after the destruction of the first set of oil platforms.

45. [Regarding the third argument, the] Court must now consider the interpretation according to which the word "commerce" in Article X, paragraph 1, is restricted to acts of purchase and sale. According to this interpretation, the protection afforded by this provision does not cover the antecedent activities which are essential to maintain commerce as, for example, the procurement of goods with a view to using them for commerce.

In the view of the Court, there is nothing to indicate that the parties to the Treaty intended to use the word "commerce" in any sense different from that which it generally bears. The word "commerce" is not restricted in ordinary usage to the mere act of purchase and sale; it has connotations that extend beyond mere purchase and sale to include "the whole of the transactions, arrangements, etc., therein involved."

In legal language, likewise, this term is not restricted to mere purchase and sale because it can refer to

> "not only the purchase, sale, and exchange of commodities, but also the instrumentalities and agencies by which it is promoted and the means and appliances by which it is carried on, and transportation of persons as well as of goods, both by land and sea."

Similarly, the expression "international commerce" designates, in its true sense, "all transactions of import and export, relationships of exchange, purchase, sale, transport, and financial operations between nations" and sometimes even "all economic, political, intellectual relations between States and between their nationals."

Thus, whether the word "commerce" is taken in its ordinary sense or in its legal meaning, at the domestic or international level, it has a broader meaning than the mere reference to purchase and sale. . . .

49. The Court concludes from all of the foregoing that it would be a natural interpretation of the word "commerce" in Article X, paragraph 1, of the Treaty of 1955 that it includes commercial activities in general, not merely the immediate act of purchase and sale, but also the ancillary activities integrally related to commerce. . . .

51. . . . On the material now before the Court, it is indeed not able to determine if and to what extent the destruction of the Iranian oil platforms had an effect upon the export trade in Iranian oil; it notes nonetheless that their destruction was capable of having such an effect and, consequently, of having an adverse effect upon the freedom of commerce as guaranteed by Article X, paragraph 1, of the Treaty of 1955. It follows that its lawfulness can be evaluated in relation to that paragraph. . . .

Notes and Questions

1. The ICJ's judgment in the *Oil Platforms* case concerned only the preliminary question of whether the Court had jurisdiction under the ICJ dispute settlement clause in the Treaty of Amity. The Court's Rules provide that when presented with a preliminary objection, the Court "shall either uphold the objection, reject it, or declare that the objection does not possess, in the circumstances of the case, an *exclusively preliminary character.*" Rules of Court, Article 79(6) (emphasis added). Was the Court's interpretation of the relevant Treaty provisions "exclusively preliminary," or did the Court essentially have to decide the merits of Iran's claims in ascertaining whether the destruction of the oil platforms was covered by the Treaty? Was the Court's extensive analysis of the meaning of the phrase "freedom of commerce" in Article X of the treaty jurisdictional, or was it substantive?

In a later decision, the Court described the scope of its inquiry at the preliminary objections stage as follows:

> In principle, a party raising preliminary objections is entitled to have these objections answered at the preliminary stage of the proceedings unless the Court does not have before it all facts necessary to decide the questions raised or if answering the preliminary objection would determine the dispute, or some elements thereof, on the merits. . . . The determination by the Court of its jurisdiction may touch upon certain aspects of the merits of the case. [Territorial and Maritime Dispute (Nicaragua v. Colombia), Preliminary Objections Judgment, 2007 I.C.J. 832, 852 (Dec. 13).]

2. Nearly seven years later after its judgment on jurisdiction, the Court issued a merits judgment in the *Oil Platforms* case. Informed by a full presentation of evidence at the merits stage, the ICJ concluded that at the time of the U.S. attacks, no oil produced through the platforms could have been shipped from Iran to the

United States, either because the platforms were already damaged and out of production or because of the adoption by the United States of trade restrictions that barred the importation of Iranian oil. Since the attacks did not interrupt ongoing commerce in oil "between the territories of" the parties, the Court concluded that the attacks did not violate Article X(1) of the Treaty. Oil Platforms (Islamic Republic of Iran v. United States of America), 2003 I.C.J. 161, 204-208 (Nov. 6). Before reaching this conclusion, however, the Court found that the United States actions did not satisfy the requirements for the use of force in self-defense. Id. at 199.

3. If both parties to a dispute agree that one state has violated an obligation owed to the other under a treaty with an ICJ dispute settlement clause, but they disagree about the remedy, would that be a dispute about the interpretation of application of the treaty over which the Court would have jurisdiction? Or would it be a dispute about general principles of state responsibility? In the *LaGrand Case (Germany v. United States of America)*, law enforcement authorities in the United States failed to notify two German nationals arrested for murder — a crime of which they were later convicted and for which they were sentenced to death — of their right of access to German consular officials, as is required under the Vienna Convention on Consular Relations. One of Germany's "submissions," or claims for relief, sought an assurance from the United States that it would not repeat any breaches of its consular notification obligations under the Vienna Convention. In rejecting the U.S. argument that the Court had no jurisdiction over this submission, the Court concluded that:

> a dispute regarding the appropriate remedies for the violation of the Convention alleged by Germany is a dispute that arises out of the interpretation or application of the Convention and thus is within the Court's jurisdiction. Where jurisdiction exists over a dispute on a particular matter, no separate basis for jurisdiction is required by the Court to consider the remedies a party has requested for the breach of the obligation. [LaGrand Case (Germany v. United States of America), 2001 I.C.J. 466, 485 (June 27).]

4. In 2004, the Court decided the *Avena and other Mexican Nationals (Mexico v. United States of America)* case; this was the third case brought against the United States, beginning in 1998, concerning criminal convictions of foreign nationals who had not been notified of their consular access rights, as guaranteed by the Vienna Convention on Consular Relations. Jurisdiction in these cases was based on an optional protocol to the Vienna Convention that provided for compulsory ICJ jurisdiction over "[d]isputes arising out of the interpretation or application of the Convention." In the two cases that culminated in merits judgments (*Avena* and the *LaGrand* case mentioned in the previous note), the Court ruled that the United States had breached its Vienna Convention obligations. As a remedy, the Court ordered the United States to provide judicial "review and reconsideration" of the convictions of foreign nationals whose Vienna Convention rights were violated to determine whether those violations had caused prejudice at trial. LaGrand Case (Germany v. United States of America), 2001 I.C.J. 466 (June 27); Avena and other Mexican Nationals (Mexico v. United States of America), 2003 I.C.J. 12 (Mar. 31). Implementation of these decisions under domestic U.S. law gave rise to serious difficulties and led to the Supreme Court's decision in *Medellin v. Texas*, discussed in Chapter 3.

In March 2005, U.S. Secretary of State Condoleezza Rice sent a letter to the Secretary-General of the United Nations announcing the withdrawal by the United States from the Optional Protocol Concerning the Compulsory Settlement of Disputes to the Vienna Convention on Consular Relations. "As a consequence of this withdrawal," the letter stated, "the United States will no longer recognize the jurisdiction of the International Court of Justice reflected in that Protocol."

5. In a case between the Democratic Republic of the Congo (DRC) and Rwanda, the Court upheld Rwanda's reservation to the ICJ dispute resolution clause of the Genocide Convention, even though it characterized the prohibition against genocide itself as a non-derogable *jus cogens* norm. In *Armed Activities on the Territory of the Congo (New Application: 2002) (Democratic Republic of the Congo v. Rwanda)*, the DRC sought to base jurisdiction in part on Article IX of the Genocide Convention, quoted above. Although Rwanda is a party to the Genocide Convention, it had taken a reservation to Article IX. The DRC argued that Rwanda's reservation was incompatible with the object and purpose of the Genocide Convention because "its effect is to exclude Rwanda from any mechanism for the monitoring and prosecution of genocide, whereas the object and purpose of the Convention are precisely the elimination of impunity for this serious a violation of international law." The Court concluded that

> the fact that a dispute relates to compliance with a norm having such a [*jus cogens*] character, which is assuredly the case with regard to the prohibition of genocide, cannot of itself provide a basis for the jurisdiction of the Court to entertain that dispute. Under the Court's Statute that jurisdiction is always based on the consent of the parties. . . .
>
> Rwanda's reservation to Article IX of the Genocide Convention bears on the jurisdiction of the Court, and does not affect the substantive obligations relating to acts of genocide themselves under that Convention . . . [T]he Court cannot conclude that the reservation of Rwanda in question, which is meant to exclude a particular method of settling a dispute relating to the interpretation, application or fulfilment of the Convention, is to be regarded as incompatible with the object and purpose of the Convention. [Armed Activities on the Territory of the Congo (New Application: 2002) (Democratic Republic of the Congo v. Rwanda), Preliminary Objections Judgment, 2006 I.C.J. 6, 30-3 (Feb. 3).]

c. Jurisdiction under the Optional Clause

Under Article 36(2) of the Statute of the ICJ, sometimes referred to as the "Optional Clause," countries may consent in advance to compulsory ICJ jurisdiction over any claim concerning an international legal dispute. That *ex ante* consent, however, extends only to disputes with other states that have also accepted the compulsory jurisdiction of the ICJ under Article 36(2). States that have accepted the compulsory jurisdiction of the Court in this fashion have, in essence, created a subset of states that are prepared, as against one another, to accept mandatory third-party resolution of their international law disputes.

The Comment to section 903 of the Restatement provides further explanation of the Court's compulsory jurisdiction under the Optional Clause.

> *Compulsory jurisdiction under Article 36(2).* Under the Statute of the Court, a state may declare that it recognizes as compulsory the jurisdiction of the Court with respect to all

> legal disputes concerning the interpretation of a treaty, any question of international law, the existence of any fact constituting a breach of an international obligation, or the nature or extent of the reparation for such a breach. Such a declaration by a state applies only in relation to another state that has made a similar declaration. A declaration may accept the jurisdiction of the court for all legal disputes, or may exclude certain categories of disputes. A declaration is, however, subject to reciprocity, and a defendant state against which a proceeding is brought may invoke an exclusion or other reservation not stipulated in its own declaration but included in the declaration of the plaintiff state. A declaration may be of indefinite duration, or for a limited time only. A declaration for a given time is binding for the period indicated. . . . [Restatement section 903 Comment b.]

As of September 2010, 66 states had declarations in force under Article 36(2) accepting compulsory jurisdiction of the Court. As indicated in the Reporters' Notes to section 903 of the Restatement:

> Several of the declarations antedate the International Court of Justice and originally conferred jurisdiction on the Permanent Court of International Justice, but under Article 36(5) of the Statute of the International Court of Justice such declarations are deemed to be acceptances of the jurisdiction of the successor Court.
>
> Some of the declarations are without limit of time; others are for a specific period (usually five or ten years), in many instances with an automatic renewal clause. Many declarations reserve the right to terminate by a notice of withdrawal effective upon receipt by the Secretary-General of the United Nations. Some declarations specify that they apply only to disputes arising after the declaration was made or concerning situations or facts subsequent to a specified date. Seventeen declarations are without any reservation; the remaining declarations are accompanied by a variety of reservations. Many states have modified their reservations, some of them several times.
>
> The most common reservation excludes disputes committed by the parties to other tribunals or which the parties have agreed to settle by other means of settlement. Another common reservation excludes disputes relating to matters that are "exclusively" or "essentially" within the domestic jurisdiction of the declarant state; some of these reservations provide in addition that the question whether a dispute is essentially within the domestic jurisdiction is to be determined by the declaring state (a so-called "self-judging" clause). Several declarations exclude disputes arising under a multilateral treaty "unless all parties to the treaty affected by the decision are also parties to the case before the Court" or, more broadly, "unless all parties to the treaty are also parties to the case before the Court." . . . [Reporters' Note 2.]

States that have accepted the compulsory jurisdiction of the ICJ may be concerned that other states, which have not accepted the Court's jurisdiction under Article 36(2), may file such a declaration solely for the purpose of initiating a particular case. Consider how the declaration of the United Kingdom — the only one of the five permanent members of the U.N. Security Council that accepts the compulsory jurisdiction of the ICJ — addresses this problem.

United Kingdom

5 July 2004

1. The Government of the United Kingdom of Great Britain and Northern Ireland accept as compulsory ipso facto and without special convention, on condition

of reciprocity, the jurisdiction of the International Court of Justice, in conformity with paragraph 2 of Article 36 of the Statute of the Court, until such time as notice may be given to terminate the acceptance, over all disputes arising after 1 January 1974, with regard to situations or facts subsequent to the same date, other than:

(i) any dispute which the United Kingdom has agreed with the other Party or Parties thereto to settle by some other method of peaceful settlement;
(ii) any dispute with the government of any other country which is or has been a Member of the Commonwealth;
(iii) any dispute in respect of which any other Party to the dispute has accepted the compulsory jurisdiction of the International Court of Justice only in relation to or for the purpose of the dispute; or where the acceptance of the Court's compulsory jurisdiction on behalf of any other Party to the dispute was deposited or ratified less than twelve months prior to the filing of the application bringing the dispute before the Court.

2. The Government of the United Kingdom also reserves the right at any time, by means of a notification addressed to the Secretary-General of the United Nations, and with effect as from the moment of such notification, either to add to, amend or withdraw any of the foregoing reservations, or any that may hereafter be added.

The ICJ addressed the validity and legal effect of reservations in a state's Optional Clause declaration in the following case:

Certain Norwegian Loans (France v. Norway)

Int'l Court of Justice
1957 I.C.J. 9 (July 6)

[French nationals owned bonds issued before World War I by the Kingdom of Norway and two Norwegian banks. These bonds initially contained varying clauses that France claimed expressly promised and guaranteed payment in gold. Norway later passed legislation allowing payment of the bonds with Bank of Norway notes, which were not convertible into gold.

[The French government espoused the claims of its nationals, and proposed to resolve the matter through an international dispute resolution mechanism. The Norwegian government maintained that the bondholders' claims were within the jurisdiction of the Norwegian courts and that these claims were solely matters of domestic law. The French government then brought the case to the ICJ.

[Both parties had declared their acceptance of the compulsory jurisdiction of the ICJ under Article 36(2). The French declaration, however, was not unconditional.]

It will be recalled that the French Declaration accepting the compulsory jurisdiction of the Court contains the following reservation:

> This declaration does not apply to differences relating to matters which are essentially within the national jurisdiction as understood by the Government of the French Republic.

In the Preliminary Objections filed by the Norwegian Government it is stated:

> The Norwegian Government did not insert any such reservation in its own Declaration. But it has the right to rely upon the restrictions placed by France upon her own undertakings.
>
> Convinced that the dispute which has been brought before the Court by the Application of July 6th, 1955, is within the domestic jurisdiction, the Norwegian Government considers itself fully entitled to rely on this right. Accordingly, it requests the Court to decline, on grounds that it lacks jurisdiction, the function which the French Government would have it assume.

In considering this ground of the Objection the Court notes in the first place that the present case has been brought before it on the basis of Article 36, paragraph 2, of the Statute and of the corresponding Declarations of acceptance of compulsory jurisdiction; that in the present case the jurisdiction of the Court depends upon the Declarations made by the Parties in accordance with Article 36, paragraph 2, of the Statute on condition of reciprocity; and that, since two unilateral declarations are involved, such jurisdiction is conferred upon the Court only to the extent to which the Declarations coincide in conferring it. A comparison between the two Declarations shows that the French Declaration accepts the Court's jurisdiction within narrower limits than the Norwegian Declaration; consequently, the common will of the Parties, which is the basis of the Court's jurisdiction, exists within these narrower limits indicated by the French reservation. . . .

France has limited her acceptance of the compulsory jurisdiction of the Court by excluding beforehand disputes "relating to matters which are essentially within the national jurisdiction as understood by the Government of the French Republic." In accordance with the condition of reciprocity to which acceptance of the compulsory jurisdiction is made subject in both Declarations and which is provided for in Article 36, paragraph 3, of the Statute, Norway, equally with France, is entitled to except from the compulsory jurisdiction of the Court disputes understood by Norway to be essentially within its national jurisdiction. . . .

For these reasons, the Court, by twelve votes to three, finds that it is without jurisdiction to adjudicate upon the dispute which has been brought before it by the Application of the Government of the French Republic of July 6th, 1955.

Questions

1. The Norwegian Optional Clause declaration stated that Norway recognized the Court's jurisdiction as compulsory "in relation to any other State accepting the same obligation, that is to say, on condition of reciprocity." Was that essential to the Court's decision? What if the Norwegian declaration did not include the reciprocity condition—that is, what if it had been made unconditional? Based on the reasoning in the opinion above, would the Court have found jurisdiction? Professor Rosenne concludes, "[W]here two declarations are in different terms, jurisdiction exists only to the extent that they coincide." Gill, Rosenne's The World Court, supra, at 74.

2. The Court in the *Norwegian Loans* case did not examine the legality of France's "within the national juridiction" reservation because neither of the parties questioned the validity of the reservation. If the facts in the case were reversed so that Norway sued France in the ICJ over French bonds, would Norway have any basis for challenging the reservation in response to a claim by France that the matters were "essentially within [its] national jurisdiction?" What if France, in the *Nuclear Tests* cases discussed in Chapter 2, claimed that it understood the nuclear tests to be essentially within its national jurisdiction? Should the Court always accept the invocation of a self-judging reservation of this type?

3. Judge Lauterpacht, in a separate opinion in the *Norwegian Loans* case, argued that France's self-judging reservation, which he called the "automatic reservation," was invalid. In his view, the reservation was incompatible with Article 36(6) of the ICJ Statute, which provides that "[i]n the event of a dispute as to whether the Court has jurisdiction, the matter shall be settled by the decision of the Court." Judge Lauterpacht also concluded that France's declaration accepting the Court's jurisdiction did not constitute a legal obligation. In his view:

> The effect of the French reservation relating to domestic jurisdiction is that the French Government has . . . undertaken an obligation to the extent to which it, and it alone, considers that it has done so. This means that it has undertaken no obligation. An instrument in which a party is entitled to determine the existence of its obligation is not a valid and enforceable legal instrument of which a court of law can take cognizance. It is not a legal instrument. It is a declaration of a political principle and purpose. [Certain Norwegian Loans, 1957 I.C.J. 34, 48 (July 6) (separate opinion of Judge Lauterpacht).]

If Judge Lauterpacht had persuaded a majority of the Court to declare a self-judging reservation to be invalid, what would the result be? Would the Court have jurisdiction?

4. What law would the Court have applied if it had decided that it had jurisdiction in this case? What legal documents or sources would the Court have looked to?

5. What precedential value would an ICJ judgment on the merits have? See Article 59, which provides that "[t]he decision of the Court has no binding force except between the parties and in respect of that particular case."

d. Jurisdiction Under the Optional Clause Applied: The Nicaragua Litigation

The Court faced a contentious dispute regarding its Optional Clause jurisdiction when Nicaragua sued the United States in 1984 over U.S. support of the "*contras*," an insurgent group seeking to overthrow the Soviet-supported Sandinista Nicaraguan government. (As we shall see, the case also proved to be a challenge to respect for the ICJ's judgments.) In its application initiating proceedings, Nicaragua alleged that the United States "is using military force against Nicaragua and intervening in Nicaragua's internal affairs. . . . The United States has created an 'army' of more than 10,000 mercenaries . . . installed them in more than ten base camps in Honduras along the border with Nicaragua, trained them, paid them, supplied them with arms, ammunition, food and medical supplies, and directed their attacks against human and economic targets inside Nicaragua."

Nicaragua claimed the ICJ had jurisdiction under Article 36(2) of the ICJ Statute. At the time the case was brought, the following Optional Clause declarations were in force for the United States and Nicaragua:

United States of America

26 VIII 46.

I, Harry S Truman, President of the United States of America, declare on behalf of the United States of America, under Article 36, paragraph 2, of the Statute of the International Court of Justice, and in accordance with the Resolution of 2 August 1946 of the Senate of the United States of America (two-thirds of the Senators present concurring therein), that the United States of America recognizes as compulsory ipso facto and without special agreement, in relation to any other State accepting the same obligation, the jurisdiction of the International Court of Justice in all legal disputes hereafter arising concerning

(a) the interpretation of a treaty;
(b) any question of international law;
(c) the existence of any fact which, if established, would constitute a breach of an international obligation;
(d) the nature or extent of the reparation to be made for the breach of an international obligation;

Provided, that this declaration shall not apply to

(a) disputes the solution of which the parties shall entrust to other tribunals by virtue of agreements already in existence or which may be concluded in the future; or
(b) disputes with regard to matters which are essentially within the domestic jurisdiction of the United States of America as determined by the United States of America; or
(c) disputes arising under a multilateral treaty, unless (1) all parties to the treaty affected by the decision are also parties to the case before the Court, or (2) the United States of America specially agrees to jurisdiction; and

Provided further, that this declaration shall remain in force for a period of five years and thereafter until the expiration of six months after notice may be given to terminate this declaration.

Done at Washington this fourteenth day of August 1946.

(Signed) Harry S Truman

Nicaragua

[*Translation from the French*] 24 IX 29.

On behalf of the Republic of Nicaragua I recognize as compulsory unconditionally the jurisdiction of the Permanent Court of International Justice.

Geneva, 24 September 1929.

(*Signed*) T. F. Medina

Nicaragua also claimed jurisdiction under a compromissory clause in a 1956 bilateral Treaty of Friendship, Commerce and Navigation (FCN Treaty), contending that U.S. military and paramilitary activities (including the alleged mining of Nicaraguan ports) violated various provisions of the treaty, particularly those related to freedom of commerce and navigation.

Military and Paramilitary Activities in and Against Nicaragua (Nicaragua v. United States of America)

Int'l Court of Justice
Preliminary Objections Judgment, 1984 I.C.J. 392 (Nov. 26)

1. On 9 April 1984 the Ambassador of the Republic of Nicaragua to the Netherlands filed in the Registry of the Court an Application instituting proceedings against the United States of America in respect of a dispute concerning responsibility for military and paramilitary activities in and against Nicaragua. In order to found the jurisdiction of the Court the Application relied [in part] on declarations made by the Parties accepting the compulsory jurisdiction of the Court under Article 36 of its Statute. . . .

13. . . . The United States made a declaration, pursuant to [Article 36, paragraph 2 of the Statute of the ICJ], on 14 August 1946, containing certain reservations, to be examined below, and expressed to

> "remain in force for a period of five years and thereafter until the expiration of six months after notice may be given to terminate this declaration".

On 6 April 1984 the Government of the United States of America deposited with the Secretary-General of the United Nations a notification, signed by the United States Secretary of State, Mr. George Shultz, referring to the Declaration deposited on 26 August 1946, and stating that:

> "the aforesaid declaration shall not apply to disputes with any Central American State or arising out of or related to events in Central America, any of which disputes shall be settled in such manner as the parties to them may agree.
>
> Notwithstanding the terms of the aforesaid declaration, this proviso shall take effect immediately and shall remain in force for two years, so as to foster the continuing regional dispute settlement process which seeks a negotiated solution to the interrelated political, economic and security problems of Central America."

This notification will be referred to, for convenience, as the "1984 notification."

14. In order to be able to rely upon the United States Declaration of 1946 to found jurisdiction in the present case, Nicaragua has to show that it is a "State accepting the same obligation" within the meaning of Article 36, paragraph 2, of the Statute. For this purpose, Nicaragua relies on a Declaration made by it on 24 September 1929 pursuant to Article 36, paragraph 2, of the Statute of the Permanent Court of International Justice. . . . Nicaragua relies further on paragraph 5 of Article 36 of the Statute of the present Court, which provides that:

> Declarations made under Article 36 of the Statute of the Permanent Court of International Justice and which are still in force shall be deemed, as between the parties to the present Statute, to be acceptances of the compulsory jurisdiction of the International Court of Justice for the period which they still have to run and in accordance with their terms.

[The Court then recounted the unusual facts regarding Nicaragua's Declaration under Article 36 of the Statute of the PCIJ, which allowed for Optional Clause declarations similar to those provided for in Article 36(2) of the Statute of the ICJ. In 1939, Nicaragua notified the League of Nations by telegram that it had ratified the Statute of the PCIJ, but the country's instrument of ratification never reached the depository League of Nations, possibly because the document might have been lost at sea during World War II (¶¶15-16). Although Nicaragua had, at the time it signed the PCIJ Statute in 1929, declared its acceptance of the compulsory jurisdiction of the PCIJ, the Court concluded that this declaration "had not acquired binding force" because Nicaragua could not demonstrate that it had become a party to the Statute of the PCIJ. (¶26) In 1945, Nicaragua became a party to the United Nations Charter and the Statute of the ICJ. (¶16)]

27. . . . [W]hile the declaration had not acquired binding force, it is not disputed that it could have done so, for example at the beginning of 1945, if Nicaragua had ratified the . . . Statute of the Permanent Court. . . . It follows that such a declaration as that made by Nicaragua had a certain potential effect which could be maintained indefinitely. This durability of potential effect flowed from a certain characteristic of Nicaragua's declaration: being made "unconditionally", it was valid for an unlimited period. . . . In sum, Nicaragua's 1929 Declaration was valid at the moment when Nicaragua became a party to the Statute of the new Court; it had retained its potential effect because Nicaragua, which could have limited the duration of that effect, had expressly refrained from doing so.

32. . . . [With respect to the object and purpose of Article 36, paragraph 5,] the primary concern of those who drafted the Statute of the present Court was to maintain the greatest possible continuity between it and its predecessor. [The Court also examined the practice of the parties and found that the "constant acquiescence of Nicaragua in affirmations, to be found in United Nations and other publications, of its position as bound by the optional clause constitutes a valid manifestation of its intent to recognize the compulsory jurisdiction of the Court." (¶109).

[The Court then turned to the question of the 1984 notification by the United States that disputes with Central American states were excluded from the coverage of the 1946 U.S. declaration, effective immediately. It rejected the U.S. effort to characterize the instrument as a "modification" of the scope of U.S. acceptance of the Court's jurisdiction which — unlike a notice of termination — would not trigger the six-month notice requirement. The Court found that the 1984 notification "is intended to secure a partial and temporary termination, namely to exempt, with immediate effect, the United States from the obligation to subject itself to the Court's jurisdiction with regard to any application concerning disputes with Central American States, and disputes arising out of events in Central America." (¶58).]

59. Declarations of acceptance of the compulsory jurisdiction of the Court are facultative, unilateral engagements, that States are absolutely free to make or not to make. In making the declaration a State is equally free either to do so unconditionally and without limit of time for its duration, or to qualify it with conditions or reservations. In particular, it may limit its effect to disputes arising after a certain date; or it may specify how long the declaration itself shall remain in force, or what notice (if any) will be required to terminate it. However, the unilateral nature of declarations does not signify that the State making the declaration is free to amend the scope and the contents of its solemn commitments as it pleases. . . .

61. . . . Although the United States retained the right to modify the contents of the 1946 Declaration or to terminate it, a power which is inherent in any unilateral act of a State, it has, nevertheless assumed an inescapable obligation towards other States accepting the Optional Clause, by stating formally and solemnly that any such change should take effect only after six months have elapsed as from the date of notice.

62. The United States has argued that the Nicaraguan 1929 Declaration, being of undefined duration, is liable to immediate termination, without previous notice, and that therefore Nicaragua has not accepted "the same obligation" as itself for the purposes of Article 36, paragraph 2, and consequently may not rely on the six months' notice proviso against the United States. The Court does not however consider that this argument entitles the United States validly to act in non-application of the time-limit proviso included in the 1946 Declaration. The notion of reciprocity is concerned with the scope and substance of the commitments entered into, including reservations, and not with the formal conditions of their creation, duration or extinction. It appears clearly that reciprocity cannot be invoked in order to excuse departure from the terms of a State's own declaration, whatever its scope, limitations or conditions. . . .

63. Moreover, since the United States purported to act on 6 April 1984 in such a way as to modify its 1946 Declaration with sufficiently immediate effect to bar an Application filed on 9 April 1984, it would be necessary, if reciprocity is to be relied on, for the Nicaraguan Declaration to be terminable with immediate effect. But the right of immediate termination of declarations with indefinite duration is far from established. It appears from the requirements of good faith that they should be treated, by analogy, according to the law of treaties, which requires a reasonable time for withdrawal from or termination of treaties that contain no provision regarding the duration of their validity. Since Nicaragua has in fact not manifested any intention to withdraw its own declaration, the question of what reasonable period of notice would legally be required does not need to be further examined: it need only be observed that from 6 to 9 April would not amount to a "reasonable time." . . .

65. In sum, the six months' notice clause forms an important integral part of the United States Declaration and it is a condition that must be complied with in case of either termination or modification. Consequently, the 1984 notification, in the present case, cannot override the obligation of the United States to submit to the compulsory jurisdiction of the Court vis-à-vis Nicaragua, a State accepting the same obligation. . . .

67. The question remains to be resolved whether the United States Declaration of 1946, though not suspended in its effects vis-à-vis Nicaragua by the 1984 notification, constitutes the necessary consent of the United States to the jurisdiction of the Court in the present case, taking into account the reservations which were attached to the declaration. Specifically, the United States has invoked proviso *(c)* to that declaration, which provides that the United States acceptance of the Court's compulsory jurisdiction shall not extend to

> "disputes arising under a multilateral treaty, unless (1) all parties to the treaty affected by the decision are also parties to the case before the Court, or (2) the United States of America specially agrees to jurisdiction."

This reservation will be referred to for convenience as the "multilateral treaty reservation." . . . As for proviso (b), excluding jurisdiction over "disputes with regard to matters which are essentially within the domestic jurisdiction of the United States of America as determined by the United States of America," the United States has informed the Court that it has determined not to invoke this proviso, but "without prejudice to the rights of the United States under that proviso in relation to any subsequent pleadings, proceedings, or cases before this Court".

68. The United States points out that Nicaragua relies in its Application on four multilateral treaties, namely the Charter of the United Nations, the Charter of the Organization of American States, the Montevideo Convention on Rights and Duties of States of 26 December 1933, and the Havana Convention on the Rights and Duties of States in the Event of Civil Strife of 20 February 1928. . . .

73. . . . [T]he multilateral treaty reservation could not bar adjudication by the Court of all Nicaragua's claims because Nicaragua . . . does not confine those claims only to violations of [these] four multilateral conventions. . . . On the contrary, Nicaragua invokes a number of principles of customary and general international law that, according to the Application, have been violated by the United States. The Court cannot dismiss the claims of Nicaragua under principles of customary and general international law, simply because such principles have been enshrined in the texts of the conventions relied upon by Nicaragua. The fact that the above-mentioned principles, recognized as such, have been codified or embodied in multilateral conventions does not mean that they cease to exist and to apply as principles of customary law, even as regards countries that are parties to such conventions. Principles such as those of the non-use of force, non-intervention, respect for the independence and territorial integrity of States, and the freedom of navigation, continue to be binding as part of customary international law, despite the operation of provisions of conventional law in which they have been incorporated. Therefore, since the claim before the Court in this case is not confined to violation of the multilateral conventional provisions invoked, it would not in any event be barred by the multilateral treaty reservation in the United States 1946 Declaration. . . .

113. For these reasons, the Court,

(1) (a) *finds,* by eleven votes to five, that it has jurisdiction to entertain the Application filed by the Republic of Nicaragua on 9 April 1984, on the basis of Article 36, paragraphs 2 and 5, of the Statute of the Court. . . .

(b) *finds,* by fourteen votes to two, that it has jurisdiction to entertain the Application filed by the Republic of Nicaragua . . . , in so far as that Application relates to a dispute concerning the interpretation or application of the Treaty of Friendship, Commerce and Navigation between the United States of America and the Republic of Nicaragua . . . [of] 1956, on the basis of Article XXIV of that Treaty. . . .

Notes and Questions

1. Less than two months after the ICJ decision on jurisdiction and admissibility, the United States announced that, because the ICJ's ruling was "contrary to law and fact," the United States had "[w]ith great reluctance" decided not to participate in further proceedings in the case. The Court continued its proceedings without U.S. participation and, in 1986, ruled against the United States on the merits of Nicaragua's claims. By substantial majorities, the Court decided that the United States had violated customary international law and the FCN Treaty between the two countries by a number of acts, including laying mines in Nicaraguan territorial waters; attacking Nicaraguan ports and other facilities; and training, arming, equipping, financing, and supplying the insurgent *contra* forces. (For a fuller discussion of the substantive aspects of the merits decision, see Chapter 11 on the use of force.) The Reagan Administration took no steps to change U.S. activities in Central America in response to the Court's judgment.

The Court's 1986 merits decision contemplated a further round of proceedings to determine the amount of damages that the United States owed Nicaragua. Following the election in 1990 of a new Nicaraguan government led by President Violeta Barrios de Chamarro, however, Nicaragua renounced all rights of action under the Court's judgment and requested the ICJ to remove the case from its list.

2. The U.S. reaction to the ICJ's jurisdiction judgment in the *Nicaragua* case was not limited to refusing to participate in further proceedings. In December 1985, the United States gave formal notice that it was terminating its 1946 declaration of acceptance of the Court's compulsory jurisdiction under Article 36(2). In a statement explaining the U.S. action, the State Department's Legal Adviser noted that only a small number of states had accepted the Court's compulsory jurisdiction. As a result, he stated:

> the hopes originally placed in compulsory jurisdiction by the architects of the Court's Statute have never been realized and will not be realized in the foreseeable future. We had hoped that widespread acceptance of compulsory jurisdiction and its successful employment in actual cases would increase confidence in judicial settlement of international disputes and, thus, eventually lead to its universal acceptance.

The statement also expressed concerns about the ICJ's assertion of jurisdiction in the *Nicaragua* case, particularly over a controversy "related to an ongoing use of armed force." Terminating U.S. acceptance of the Court's compulsory jurisdiction, the statement concluded, "was a regrettable but necessary measure taken in order to safeguard U.S. interests." Statement by the Legal Adviser, Abraham D. Sofaer, to the Senate Foreign Relations Committee (Dec. 4, 1985), reprinted in Department of State Bulletin, January 1986, at 67, 68, 70-71.

3. Article 36(5) of the ICJ Statute effectively treats declarations accepting the compulsory jurisdiction of the Permanent Court of International Justice as Optional Clause declarations for purposes of Article 36(2) of the ICJ Statute, provided that the PCIJ declarations "are still in force." Is the Court's conclusion that Nicaragua's 1929 declaration "had retained its potential effect" persuasive? Assume that Nicaragua intended to bring its PCIJ declaration into force as binding obligation. Is the failure to complete the ratification process merely a technical failure? Was the Court correct to overlook this, given Nicaragua's evident intent? If the United States had sued Nicaragua and argued that its unperfected 1929 declaration provided a basis for jurisdiction, would the Court have agreed?

4. Do you agree with the Court that the United States did not have the right to modify its acceptance of the Court's jurisdiction because the six-month notice clause was applicable? Should that clause have been effective even when Nicaragua had no notice period in its acceptance? Could Nicaragua have terminated its acceptance without advance notice?

5. Why doesn't the reciprocity principle apply to the U.S. acceptance of the Court's compulsory jurisdiction? Is the Court's *Nicaragua* decision consistent with its analysis in the *Norwegian Loans* case? Or, since under Article 59 of the ICJ Statute cases have binding force only between the parties and in respect of a particular case, should inconsistency not matter? Would the answer to these questions affect your view as to whether a state should adhere to the ICJ?

6. Was the 1946 U.S. declaration a unilateral act? Could the Court have plausibly held that one unilateral act could be amended by another? Is the Court's conclusion that the U.S. could not modify the terms of its Optional Clause declaration with immediate effect consistent with the premise that the Court's jurisdiction is based on state consent?

7. What possible grounds could you identify for concluding that the United States was legally prohibited from modifying its Optional Clause declaration on less than six months' notice? Is a declaration under Article 36(2) the kind of unilateral act that creates international legal obligations? Consider the ICJ's decision in the *Nuclear Tests* case, noted in Chapter 2, in which the Court concluded that certain unilateral declarations by French officials regarding the cessation of atmospheric nuclear tests were legally binding. Could a reliance theory support such a conclusion? Is reliance a source of legal obligation under international law?

8. The Court noted in paragraph 67 of its opinion that the United States did not invoke the "domestic jurisdiction" proviso in its 1946 declaration accepting the Court's compulsory jurisdiction, although the United States reserved the right to raise the matter later. If the United States had invoked the proviso, would the Court have had to accept it? See the discussion of self-judging "domestic jurisdiction" reservations above. Why do you think the United States did not invoke the proviso? How credible would it have been?

9. As paragraph 67 also notes, the United States did invoke another proviso in its 1946 declaration, which said that its acceptance of the Court's compulsory jurisdiction did not extend to "disputes arising under a multilateral treaty, unless (1) all

parties to the treaty affected by the decision are also parties to the case before the Court, or (2) the United States of America specially agrees to jurisdiction." The violations of customary international law invoked by Nicargua, especially those concerning the use of force and intervention, involved rules that are to a very large degree equivalent to those governed by the multilateral treaties cited in paragraph 68 of the Court's judgment. Does applying customary international law rules that are co-extensive with a multilateral treaty frustrate the intent of a state making such a multilateral treaty reservation?

10. When Nicaragua filed its suit in April 1984, the then-Legal Adviser to the U.S. Secretary of State reportedly predicted that the ICJ would not take jurisdiction over the lawsuit, probably because the Court had traditionally taken a cautious view of its jurisdiction. Do you read the ICJ's decision above to be a conservative approach to jurisdiction? If not, why might the Court have been aggressive in asserting its jurisdiction? Could it have been based in part on a shared perception of the Court's majority that the Court needed to become more assertive in addressing controversial political and security questions to reverse a declining caseload and, arguably, a diminishing international stature? Or a perception by the Court's majority that the United States was so committed to the rule of law that it would accept any decision by the Court? Or a perception that if it the Court did not hear Nicaragua's claims on the merits, it would give a green light to what many saw as a disregard of international law by the United States? Or a concern that the Court would be seen as unwilling to carry out its responsibilities because of a fear about American political power? Do you think judges think in these ways? Should they?

11. Notwithstanding its withdrawal from the Optional Clause, the United States has, since 1986, continued to participate in litigation before the ICJ. Even as the U.S. was announcing its intention to terminate its acceptance of the Court's compulsory jurisdiction, it announced that Italy and the United States were by special agreement submitting a longstanding dispute regarding the 1968 seizure by Italian authorities of an electronics plant owned by an Italian subsidiary of two U.S. corporations to a chamber of the Court. In a 4-1 decision in July 1989 (with the U.S. judge dissenting), the ICJ chamber ruled that the seizure did not violate the treaty between the two countries. See Elettronica Sicula S.p.A. (ELSI) (United States of America v. Italy), 1989 I.C.J. 15 (July 20). Since then, the United States has participated in seven cases before the ICJ, each time as a respondent.

e. Forum Prorogatum

A final jurisdictional basis for the ICJ is found in Article 38, paragraph 5, of the Rules of Court, which provides:

> When the applicant State proposes to found the jurisdiction of the Court upon a consent thereto yet to be given or manifested by the State against which such application is made, the application shall be transmitted to that State. It shall not however be entered in the General List, nor any action be taken in the proceedings, unless and until the State against which such application is made consents to the Court's jurisdiction for the purposes of the case.

Known as the doctrine of *forum prorogatum*, this enables a party to a dispute to invite its adversary to resolve the case before the ICJ by submitting an application with the Court. Article 38(5) of the Rules of Court, which came into force in 1978, did not serve as a basis for jurisdiction in any ICJ cases until 2003, when France consented to jurisdiction after the Republic of the Congo filed an application in what was subsequently designated as the *Certain Criminal Proceedings in France (Republic of the Congo v. France)* case. France again consented to *forum prorogatum* jurisdiction in a case initiated in 2006 by Djibouti, which similarly concerned the extra-territorial exercise of French criminal jurisdiction.

Notes and Questions

1. Why would a state seek to secure the Court's jurisdiction by filing an application and hoping the respondent state will consent to jurisdiction? Would it not make more sense for the claimant state to attempt to negotiate a special agreement? Why would a respondent state agree to participate in a case on the basis of the claimant's unilateral application? Is it relevant in this regard that the two cases in which France has consented to jurisdiction under the *forum prorogatum* doctrine involve actions of the French criminal justice system, which is largely independent of the Executive Branch?

2. In 1992, Hungary attempted to invoke Article 38(5) of the Court's Rules by filing an application against what was then Czechoslovakia concerning major public works projects on the Danube river. Czechoslovakia did not consent, but in 1993 Hungary and Slovakia—the successor state to Czechoslovakia for these issues—concluded a special agreement to refer their dispute to the Court. See Gabcikovo-Nagymaros Project (Hungary v. Slovakia), 1997 I.C.J. 7 (Sept. 25).

3. Procedure in the ICJ

Litigation before the ICJ is highly formal and deliberate. Except in cases involving a special agreement, the process begins when a country files an application with the Court. Thereafter, the parties submit lengthy responsive written pleadings. Evidence is, for the more part, presented in documentary form as part of the written pleadings, although infrequently witnesses appear and give oral testimony at the oral proceedings stage of the case. Depending on the nature of the case and the views of the parties, the case may be decided in phases, with a phase for (1) "preliminary objections" concerning the Court's jurisdiction or the "admissibility" of the case, discussed below; (2) the merits of the case; and (3) reparation (or damages). There is also the possibility for a preliminary "provisional measures" stage, discussed below.

When briefing in a case, or a phase, has been fully completed, the Court holds oral proceedings. Oral proceedings can range from several days to several weeks, depending on the complexity of the case. At the conclusion of the oral hearings, the Court deliberates, and in due course issues a written judgment. The Court employs highly formal procedures for its deliberations and opinion drafting. Judgments are often lengthy and are frequently accompanied by multiple separate and dissenting opinions. Because of the slow pace at which countries brief cases, the length of oral proceedings, and the formality of the Court's decision-making process, it typically completes no more than two or three cases per year, although it issues many procedural orders in other pending cases. Scholars and judges have developed and debated proposals to streamline the Court's work, and the Court has made some changes to its procedures and working methods. See The International Court of Justice: Efficiency of Procedures and Working Methods, 45 Int'l & Comp. L.Q. Supplement S1 (1996), which reports on the recommendations of a study group established by the British Institute of International and Comparative Law; D.W. Bowett et al., The International Court of Justice: Process, Practice and Procedure (1997).

a. Provisional Measures

The ICJ may, at the request of either party or on its own initiative, issue a preliminary order that grants some interim relief to one of the parties or, in some circumstances, that directs the parties to refrain from acts that would aggravate the dispute while it is pending before the Court. In the words of one authority on the ICJ: "This enables the Court to take steps roughly corresponding to an interim injunction which domestic courts are frequently empowered to issue pending the final determination." Gill, Rosenne's The World Court, supra, at 79. The ICJ Statute provides:

Article 41

1. The Court shall have the power to indicate, if it considers that circumstances so require, any provisional measures which ought to be taken to preserve the respective rights of either party.

2. Pending the final decision, notice of the measures suggested shall forthwith be given to the parties and to the Security Council.

The use of the terms "indicate" and "ought to be taken" in Article 41(1), as well as "measures suggested" in Article 41(2), for many years created doubt about whether the Court's provisional measures were legally binding, or whether they were merely hortatory. The Court took up this issue in the *LaGrand Case (Germany v. United States of America)*, involving the failure by the United States to notify foreign nationals who had been convicted of capital crimes of their right to consular access. There, the ICJ has issued a provisional measures order indicating that the United States "should take all measures at its disposal to ensure that Walter LaGrand [one of the German nationals on behalf of whom Germany had brought the case] is not executed pending the final decision in these proceedings." Germany sought an emergency stay of execution before the U.S. Supreme Court based, in part, on the ICJ's provisional measures order. The U.S. Executive Branch took the position before the Supreme Court that the ICJ's provisional measures orders were not legally binding, and LaGrand was subsequently executed by the state of Arizona.

In evaluating whether its provisional measures are legally binding, the Court noted that the plain language of its statute is unclear, in that the French version of

Article 41 conveys a more mandatory character for provisional measures orders than the English text does. Accordingly, the Court turned to the object and purpose of the Statute as an interpretive guide:

> The object and purpose of the Statute is to enable the Court to fulfil the functions provided for therein, and in particular, the basic function of judicial settlement of international disputes by binding decisions in accordance with Article 59 of the Statute. The context in which Article 41 has to be seen within the Statute is to prevent the Court from being hampered in the exercise of its functions because the respective rights of the parties to a dispute before the Court are not preserved. It follows from the object and purpose of the Statute, as well as from the terms of Article 41 when read in their context, that the power to indicate provisional measures entails that such measures should be binding, inasmuch as the power in question is based on the necessity, when the circumstances call for it, to safeguard, and to avoid prejudice to, the rights of the parties as determined by the final judgment of the Court. The contention that provisional measures indicated under Article 41 might not be binding would be contrary to the object and purpose of that Article. [LaGrand Case (Germany v. United States of America), 2001 I.C.J. 466, 502-503 (June 27).]

Notes and Questions

1. Article 94(1) of the United Nations Charter requires each U.N. member state "to comply with the decision of the International Court of Justice in any case to which it is a party." Before the Court issued its judgment in *LaGrand*, would you have interpreted the use of the singular term "the decision" to mean that only the Court's final judgment, and not an interim order such as a provisional measures order, is legally binding?

2. Requests for provisional measures typically are submitted with the application, and the Court ordinarily reaches a decision on whether to order provisional measures before the Court has resolved any challenge to its jurisdiction. The consensual nature of ICJ jurisdiction raises questions about the Court's power to issue provisional measures orders before its jurisdiction has been confirmed. And yet the need for urgency that frequently justifies provisional measures may preclude full deliberation of jurisdictional questions.

This tension between the need for urgent action and respect for the consensual nature of the ICJ's jurisdiction was faced in 2008, when the Republic of Georgia brought a case—and a request for provisional measures—in the ICJ against the Russian Federation arising out of Russia's military operations against Georgian forces in South Ossetia and Abkhazia and its eventual August 2008 invasion of Georgia. Georgia based jurisdiction on the ICJ dispute resolution clause in Article 22 of the Convention on the Elimination of All Forms of Racial Discrimination (CERD), claiming that Russia's actions constituted racial discrimination "through attacks against, and mass-expulsion of, ethnic Georgians, as well as other ethnic groups," in South Ossetia and Abkhazia. Application of the International Convention on the Elimination of All Forms of Racial Discrimination (Georgia v. Russian Federation), 2008 I.C.J. 353, 354 (Provisional Measures Order of Oct. 15). Russia denied that the Court had jurisdiction under CERD; it argued that to the extent there was a dispute between Russia and Georgia, it "relate[s] to the use of force, humanitarian law, territorial integrity, but in any case not to racial discrimination." Id. at 375.

The ICJ explained that at the provisional measures stage, "the Court need not finally satisfy itself . . . that it has jurisdiction on the merits of the case," but that it could not indicate provisional measures "unless the [jurisdictional bases] invoked by the Applicant appear, prima facie, to afford a basis on which the jurisdiction of the Court might be founded." Id. at 377. The Court concluded that "the acts alleged by Georgia appear to be capable of contravening rights provided for by CERD, even if certain of these alleged acts might also be covered by other rules of international law, including humanitarian law." Id. 387. The existence of a dispute "capable of falling within the provisions of CERD" satisfied the Court's requirement for a finding of prima facie jurisdiction. The Court adopted a provisional measures order that required both parties — not just Russia — to, among other things, refrain from racial discrimination. Id. at 398.

b. Admissibility

Along with challenges to jurisdiction, respondent states may try to dispose of cases on preliminary grounds by objecting to the "admissibility" of a claim. In raising such an argument,

> . . . the objecting State argues that the claim cannot be admitted, is "inadmissible", often on the ground that some other applicable rule of general international law has not been complied with — for instance the substantive condition of the law for the exercise of the right of diplomatic protection, such as the failure to exhaust local remedies before the institution of proceedings. Questions of admissibility can also include such matters as the failure to attempt to reach an agreement through diplomatic negotiations where this is called for in a treaty or under rules of general international law. "Admissibility" can also isolate such matters as whether the dispute is a "legal" dispute capable of being settled by judicial means, or whether it involves questions which fall within the exclusive competence of the Security Council. These types of objection involve questions of judicial policy as much as they do issues of strict law. [Gill, Rosenne's The World Court, supra, at 83.]

At the preliminary objections phase of the *Nicaragua* litigation, the United States argued that the case was inadmissible because it dealt with politically sensitive use of force issues committed to the political, not judicial, organs of the United Nations.

Military and Paramilitary Activities In and Against Nicaragua (Nicaragua v. United States of America)

Int'l Court of Justice
Preliminary Objections Judgment, 1984 I.C.J. 392 (May 10)

84. The Court now turns to the question of the admissibility of the Application of Nicaragua. The United States of America contended in its Counter-Memorial that Nicaragua's Application is inadmissible on five separate grounds, each of which, it is said, is sufficient to establish such inadmissibility, whether considered as a legal bar

to adjudication or as "a matter requiring the exercise of prudential discretion in the interest of the integrity of the judicial function". . . .

89. . . . [T]he United States regards the Application as inadmissible because each of Nicaragua's allegations constitutes no more than a reformation and restatement of a single fundamental claim, that the United States is engaged in an unlawful use of armed force, or breach of the peace, or acts of aggression against Nicaragua, a matter which is committed by the Charter and by practice to the competence of other organs, in particular the United Nations Security Council. . . .

91. It will be convenient to deal with this alleged ground of inadmissibility together with the [next] ground advanced by the United States namely that the Court should hold the Application of Nicaragua to be inadmissible in view of the subject-matter of the Application and the position of the Court within the United Nations system, including the impact of proceedings before the Court on the ongoing exercise of the "inherent right of individual or collective self-defence" under Article 51 of the Charter. . . .

93. The United States is thus arguing that the matter was essentially one for the Security Council since it concerned a complaint by Nicaragua involving the use of force. However, having regard to the *United States Diplomatic and Consular Staff in Tehran* case, the Court is of the view that the fact that a matter is before the Security Council should not prevent it being dealt with by the Court and that both proceedings could be pursued *pari passu*. In that case the Court held: . . .

> Whereas Article 12 of the Charter expressly forbids the General Assembly to make any recommendation with regard to a dispute or situation while the Security Council is exercising its functions in respect of that dispute or situation, no such restriction is placed on the functioning of the Court by any provision of either the Charter or the Statute of the Court. The reasons are clear. It is for the Court, the principal judicial organ of the United Nations, to resolve any legal questions that may be in issue between parties to the dispute; and the resolution of such legal questions by the Court may be an important, and sometimes decisive, factor in promoting the peaceful settlement of the dispute. This is indeed recognized by Article 36 of the Charter, paragraph 3 of which specifically provides that:
>
> > In making recommendations under this Article the Security Council should also take into consideration that legal disputes should as a general rule be referred by the parties to the International Court of Justice in accordance with the provisions of the Statute of the Court. . . .

95. It is necessary to emphasize that Article 24 of the Charter of the United Nations provides that

> In order to ensure prompt and effective action by the United Nations, its Members confer on the Security Council *primary* responsibility for the maintenance of international peace and security. . . .

The Charter accordingly does not confer *exclusive* responsibility upon the Security Council for the purpose. . . .

96. It must also be remembered that, as the *Corfu Channel* case shows, the Court has never shied away from a case brought before it merely because it had political implications or because it involved serious elements of the use force. . . .

Notes and Questions

1. Are the "admissibility" issues raised by the United States similar to "justiciability" or "political question" arguments in domestic U.S. judicial practice? Should the Court decide cases raising sensitive political issues and even the use of force? Does it matter if they are pending before the U.N. Security Council? Or are these provincial notions derived from U.S. constitutional law? Should the ICJ exhibit what Alexander Bickel called the "passive virtues" of the U.S. Supreme Court — the "jurisdictional techniques" — that enable the Court to avoid controversial public policy questions? See Antonio Perez, The Passive Virtues and the World Court: Pro-Dialogic Abstention by the International Court of Justice, 18 Mich. J. Int'l L. 285 (1986).

2. How would you assess the long-run effect of the Court's decision to adjudicate the sensitive use of force issues in the *Nicaragua* case? Would you focus on the U.S. reaction, including its withdrawal from the compulsory jurisdiction of the Court? Or would you attempt to assess the affect of the *Nicaragua* decision on the subsequent willingness of states to use the Court?

3. The role of the veto means that the Security Council is unlikely to condemn or impose sanctions on any of the five permanent members of the Council or their very close allies for violations of international law. Does that affect the role the Court should play in cases that are politically sensitive or involve the use of force?

c. Request for an Interpretation of a Judgment

Although judgments of the ICJ are not subject to appeal, the parties may, if they disagree about the meaning of a judgment, request an interpretation from the Court. The ICJ Statute provides:

Article 60

The judgment is final and without appeal. In the event of dispute as to the meaning or scope of the judgment, the Court shall construe it upon the request of any party.

After the U.S. Supreme Court held in *Medellin v. Texas* (discussed in Chapter 3) that the ICJ's 2004 judgment in the *Avena* case (discussed above) was not entitled to "direct enforcement in domestic [U.S.] courts," 552 U.S. 491, 513 (2008), Mexico filed an Application with the Court seeking an interpretation of the *Avena* judgment. Mexico argued that under the correct interpretation of *Avena,* the United States was "required to guarantee that no . . . Mexican national entitled to review and reconsideration under the *Avena* Judgment is executed unless and until that review and reconsideration is completed and it is determined that no prejudice resulted from the violation." The Court concluded that while its earlier judgment imposed "an obligation of result [to provide review and reconsideration] which clearly must be performed unconditionally," it "nowhere lays down or implies that the courts in the United States are required to give direct effect" to that obligation:

> [T]he Judgment leaves it to the United States to choose the means of implementation, not excluding the introduction within a reasonable time of appropriate legislation, if

deemed necessary under domestic constitutional law. Nor moreover does the *Avena* Judgment prevent direct enforceability of the obligation in question, if such an effect is permitted by domestic law. In short, the question is not decided in the Court's original Judgment and thus cannot be submitted to it for interpretation under Article 60 of the Statute.

Mexico's argument . . . concerns the general question of the effects of a judgment of the Court in the domestic legal order of the States parties to the case in which the judgment was delivered, not the "meaning or scope" of the *Avena* Judgment, as Article 60 of the Court's Statute requires. By virtue of its general nature, the question underlying Mexico's Request for interpretation is outside the jurisdiction specifically conferred upon the Court by Article 60. [Request for Interpretation of the Judgment of 31 March 2004 in the Case Concerning Avena and Other Mexican Nationals (Mexico v. United States of America), Judgment, ¶¶44-45 (Jan. 19, 2009), reprinted in 48 I.L.M. 199 (2009).]

4. *Advisory Opinions*

In addition to its jurisdiction in contentious cases between states, the International Court of Justice is empowered under the United Nations Charter and its Statute to render advisory opinions on legal questions presented by various international organizations.

U.N. Charter, Article 96

1. The General Assembly or the Security Council may request the International Court of Justice to give an advisory opinion on any legal question.

2. Other organs of the United Nations and specialized agencies, which may at any time be so authorized by the General Assembly, may also request advisory opinions on legal questions arising within the scope of their activities.

ICJ Statute, Article 65

1. The Court may give an advisory opinion on any legal question at the request of whatever body may be authorized by or in accordance with the Charter of the United Nations to make such a request. . . .

Currently, the Economic and Social Council (as a U.N. organ) and 16 specialized agencies are authorized to seek advisory opinions from the Court in accordance with Article 96(2) of the Charter.

a. Jurisdiction

In 1993, the World Health Organization (WHO) — one of the specialized agencies empowered to request an advisory opinion under Article 96(2) of the U.N. Charter — requested an opinion on the question of whether, in view of the anticipated health and environmental effects, "the use of nuclear weapons by a State in war or other armed conflict [would] be a breach of its obligations under international law including the WHO Constitution." The request required the Court to determine the scope of its advisory opinion jurisdiction.

> [T]he provisions of [the WHO Constitution] may be read as authorizing the Organization to deal with the effects on health of the use of nuclear weapons, or of any other hazardous activity, and to take preventive measures aimed at protecting the health of populations in the event of such weapons being used or such activities engaged in.
>
> The question put to the Court in the present case relates, however, *not to the effects* of the use of nuclear weapons on health, but to the *legality* of the use of such weapons *in view of their health and environmental effects.* Whatever those effects might be, the competence of the WHO to deal with them is not dependent on the legality of the acts that caused them. Accordingly, it does not seem to the Court that the provisions of . . . the WHO Constitution, interpreted in accordance with the criteria referred to above, can be understood as conferring upon the Organization a competence to address the legality of the use of nuclear weapons, and thus in turn a competence to ask the Court about that. . . .
>
> [T]he Charter of the United Nations laid the basis of a "system" designed to organize international co-operation in a coherent fashion by bringing the United Nations, invested with powers of general scope, into relationship with various autonomous and complementary organizations, invested with sectorial powers. The exercise of these powers by the organizations belonging to the "United Nations system" is co-ordinated, notably, by the relationship agreements concluded between the United Nations and each of the specialized agencies. . . .
>
> . . . And there is no doubt that questions concerning the use of force, the regulation of armaments and disarmament are within the competence of the United Nations and lie outside that of the specialized agencies. Besides, any other conclusion would render virtually meaningless the notion of a specialized agency; it is difficult to imagine what other meaning that notion could have if such an organization need only show that the use of certain weapons could affect its objectives in order to be empowered to concern itself with the legality of such use. [Legality of the Use by a State of Nuclear Weapons in Armed Conflict, Advisory Opinion, 1996 I.C.J. 66, 76, 80 (July 8).]

Notes and Questions

1. How is the ICJ's advisory opinion function consistent with the notion that the Court's jurisdiction must be grounded in consent? Won't almost any advisory opinion issued by the Court address the rights and obligations of—or at least affect the interests of—states, including states that may not have consented to the Court's jurisdiction under the Optional Clause?

2. Independently of the WHO, the General Assembly also requested an advisory opinion from the Court on the legality of the use of nuclear weapons. Because the General Assembly is authorized by Article 96(1) of the U.N. Charter to request an advisory opinion "on any legal question," the General Assembly's request did not confront the same jurisdictional barrier as the WHO's request. In its response to the General Assembly's request, the Court noted that nuclear weapons were not specifically prohibited under existing treaties and obligations. It nevertheless indicated that the use of such weapons "seems scarcely reconcilable with" international law rules governing the conduct of warfare. The Court nevertheless concluded that that

it did not have "sufficient elements to enable it to conclude with certainty that the use of nuclear weapons would necessarily be at variance with the principles and rules of law applicable in armed conflict in any circumstance," particularly in extreme cases of self-defense "in which the very survival of a State would be at stake." The Court further advised that nuclear weapons states that are parties to the Nuclear Nonproliferation Treaty are obligated "to pursue in good faith and bring to a conclusion negotiations leading to nuclear disarmament in all its aspects under strict and effective international control." Legality of the Threat or Use of Nuclear Weapons, Advisory Opinion, 1996 I.C.J. 226 (July 8).

b. Discretionary Grounds for Declining to Give an Opinion

Unlike the specialized agencies, the General Assembly and Security Council may seek advisory opinions on "any" legal question, not merely those arising within the scope of their activities. In the *Status of Eastern Carelia* case, the Permanent Court of International Justice, the ICJ's predecessor, declined to answer a request for an advisory opinion, even though it had jurisdiction. The League of Nations, to which Russia did not belong, sought an opinion regarding the legal status of disputed territory under a bilateral treaty between Finland and Russia. The Court concluded that since the requested opinion "bears on an actual dispute between Finland and Russia," rendering an opinion would be inconsistent with the principle that states cannot be compelled to submit their disputes to arbitration without their consent. The Court declined to answer the question submitted to it. Status of Eastern Carelia, P.C.I.J. (ser. B) No. 5 (1923).

Since then, the ICJ has reiterated that it retains "a discretionary power to decline to give an advisory opinion even if the conditions of jurisdiction are met." Legal Consequences of the Construction of a Wall in the Occupied Palestinian Territory, Advisory Opinion, 2004 I.C.J. 136, 156 (July 9). In practice, however, the current ICJ has never declined to answer a request for an advisory opinion over which it concluded it had jurisdiction. In response to the General Assembly's request for an advisory opinion about Israel's construction of a wall as a security barrier in occupied Palestinian territory, the Court noted:

> 44. . . . The Court . . . is mindful of the fact that its answer to a request for an advisory opinion "represents its participation in the activities of the Organization, and, in principle, should not be refused". Given its responsibilities as the "principal judicial organ of the United Nations" (Article 92 of the Charter), the Court should in principle not decline to give an advisory opinion. In accordance with its consistent jurisprudence, only "compelling reasons" should lead the Court to refuse its opinion. . . .
>
> 49. . . . [Regarding the contention that the Court should on discretionary grounds decline to exercise its jurisdiction because the request concerns a contentious matter between Israel and Palestine in respect of which Israel has not consented to the Court's jurisdiction,] the Court does not consider that the subject-matter of the General Assembly's request can be regarded as only a bilateral matter between Israel and Palestine. Given the powers and responsibilities of the United Nations in questions relating to international peace and security, it is the Court's view that the construction of the wall must be deemed to be directly of concern to the United Nations. The

responsibility of the United Nations in this matter also has its origin in the Mandate and the Partition Resolution concerning Palestine. This responsibility has been described by the General Assembly as "a permanent responsibility towards the question of Palestine until the question is resolved in all its aspects in a satisfactory manner in accordance with international legitimacy" (General Assembly resolution 57/107 of 3 December 2002). Within the institutional framework of the Organization, this responsibility has been manifested by the adoption of many Security Council and General Assembly resolutions, and by the creation of several subsidiary bodies specifically established to assist in the realization of the inalienable rights of the Palestinian people.

50. The object of the request before the Court is to obtain from the Court an opinion which the General Assembly deems of assistance to it for the proper exercise of its functions. The opinion is requested on a question which is of particularly acute concern to the United Nations, and one which is located in a much broader frame of reference than a bilateral dispute. In the circumstances, the Court does not consider that to give an opinion would have the effect of circumventing the principle of consent to judicial settlement, and the Court accordingly cannot, in the exercise of its discretion, decline to give an opinion on that ground. [Legal Consequences of the Construction of a Wall in the Occupied Palestinian Territory, Advisory Opinion, 2004 I.C.J. at 156, 158-59.]

Notes and Questions

1. Is the Court's discretionary power to decline to provide an advisory opinion comparable to its power to determine that a contentious case is inadmissible? If one of the U.N.'s political bodies requests an advisory opinion, should the Court ever decline to provide an answer? If so, under what circumstances?

2. In the Legality of the Threat or Use of Nuclear Weapons Advisory Opinion, 1996 I.C.J. 226 (July 8), some states urged the Court to decline to render an opinion because doing so might adversely affect disarmament negotiations. In *Legal Consequences of the Construction of a Wall in the Occupied Palestinian Territory*, the Advisory Opinion excerpted above, some participants argued in a similar spirit that an advisory opinion from the Court could impede a political, negotiated solution to the Israeli-Palestinian conflict. In both cases, the Court noted that states were divided about the role an advisory opinion might play in the ongoing political processes; it concluded that the potential political impact was not a compelling reason to decline to give an opinion. In its 2010 Advisory Opinion on the legality of Kosovo's unilateral declaration of independence, some states argued that the Court's opinion "might lead to adverse political consequences." The Court again rejected this reason for declining on discretionary grounds to render an opinion, stating: "[The Court] cannot — in particular where there is no basis on which to make such as assessment — substitute its own view as to whether an opinion would be likely to have an adverse effect." Accordance with International Law of the Unilateral Declaration of Independence in Respect of Kosovo, Advisory Opinion, at ¶35 (July 22, 2010), reprinted in 49 I.L.M. 1404 (2010). This case is discussed further in Chapter 5 on the question of what constitutes a state under international law.

3. In answering the General Assembly's request for an advisory opinion on the legality of the wall being constructed by Israel to separate the occupied Palestinian territories from Israel, the Court noted that a substantial portion of the wall would

be built within the occupied territories. The Court determined that construction of the wall creates "a 'fait accompli' on the ground that could well become permanent, in which case . . . it would be tantamount to de facto annexation" in violation of Israel's obligations as an occupying power under the Fourth Geneva Convention of 1949. The ICJ also found that the construction of the wall "gravely infringe[s] a number of rights of Palestinians residing in the territory occupied by Israel" and consequently "constitutes breaches by Israel of various of its obligations under the applicable international humanitarian law and human rights instruments." The Court rejected Israel's claim that the wall was a permissible exercise of its right of self-defense to combat a growing Palestinian terrorist threat. The Court suggested that the right of self-defense was available only in response to armed attacks by a state, not by non-state actors. It also indicated that construction of the wall could not be justified by the doctrine of "necessity" because the Court was "not convinced that the construction of the wall along the route chosen was the only means to safeguard the interests of Israel against the peril which it has invoked as justification for that construction." By a vote of 14-1, the Court stated that Israel was obligated to dismantle certain portions of the wall that had already been built, to stop further construction in the Palestinian territories, and to make reparations for damages caused by its illegal acts. Legal Consequences of the Construction of a Wall in the Occupied Palestinian Territory, Advisory Opinion, 2004 I.C.J. 136 (July 9).

Some commentators sharply criticized various aspects of the ICJ's Advisory Opinion. Some objected to the Court's failure to exercise judicial restraint by declining to answer the General Assembly's request for an opinion in view of, among other things, the "improper and glaringly unbalanced" formulation of the request. Michla Pomerance, The ICJ's Advisory Jurisdiction and the Crumbling Wall Between the Political and the Judicial, 99 Am. J. Int'l L. 26, 31 (2005). Others questioned the Court's summary assertion that Israel may not invoke its right of self-defense to combat terrorist attacks originating from the occupied territories. See, e.g., Sean D. Murphy, Self-Defense and the Israeli Wall Advisory Opinion: An *Ipse Dixit* from the ICJ?, 99 Am. J. Int'l L. 62, 62 (2005); Ruth Wedgwood, The ICJ Advisory Opinion on the Israeli Security Fence and the Limits of Self-Defense, 99 Am. J. Int'l L. 52, 58 (2005). Other commentators, however, expressed general support for the ICJ's ruling, see, e.g., Richard A. Falk, Toward Authoritativeness: The ICJ Ruling on Israel's Security Wall, 99 Am. J. Int'l L. 42 (2005); Ardi Imseis, Critical Reflections on the International Humanitarian Law Aspects of the ICJ *Wall* Advisory Opinion, 99 Am. J. Int'l L. 102 (2005), and in particular for its interpretation of the principles of international humanitarian law. See, e.g., David Kretzmer, The Advisory Opinion: The Light Treatment of International Humanitarian Law, 99 Am. J. Int'l L. 88, 101 (2005).)

4. Although advisory opinions themselves are not binding, states may, by agreement, decide to treat advisory opinions as binding. The parties to the 1946 Convention on the Privileges and Immunities of the United Nations, for example, have agreed that in the event of a dispute between a state and the U.N. about the interpretation of the treaty, the U.N. is to seek an advisory opinion from the Court. Article 30 of the Convention provides: "The opinion given by the Court shall be accepted as decisive by the parties." This provision was most recently applied in the context of a dispute between the United Nations and Malaysia in Difference

Relating to Immunity from Legal Process of a Special Rapporteur of the Commission on Human Rights, Advisory Opinion, 1999 I.C.J. 62 (April 29).

5. *Assessment of the ICJ and Future Directions*

In the past 20 years, the ICJ, while continuing to settle traditional border and maritime jurisdiction cases, has seen an increase in controversies involving an expanding range of international legal claims, including cases involving sensitive political, security, and humanitarian issues. For example, the Court in 2007 ruled on Bosnia's allegations that the state then known as the Federal Republic of Yugoslavia (FRY) was responsible for the commission of genocide against Bosnian Muslims during the 1991-1995 war in Bosnia. The Court concluded that Bosnia has not established, with respect to most of the killings that took place during the war, that the perpetrators had acted with the required intent to destroy the Bosnian Muslim group in whole or substantial part. The Court did find that the 1995 massacre of Bosnian Muslims at Srebrenica constituted genocide, but that the acts of the Bosnian Serb army at Srebrenica were not attributable to the FRY. The Court nevertheless noted that the FRY was in a position of influence over the Bosnian Serbs who perpetrated genocide at Srebrenica, and accordingly concluded that the FRY had violated its obligation under the Genocide Convention to prevent genocide. Application of the Convention on the Prevention and Punishment of the Crime of Genocide (Bosnia and Herzegovina v. Serbia and Montenegro), Judgment (Feb. 26, 2007), reprinted in 46 I.L.M. 188 (2007).

The Court addressed another set of sensitive security issues in a 2005 judgment in a case brought by the Democratic Republic of the Congo (DRC) against Uganda for violations of its territorial integrity and sovereignty, interference in its internal affairs, and violations of international human rights and humanitarian law. The controversy stemmed from an attempt by the new Kabila government in the DRC to expel all foreign powers — including some that had helped Kabila oust former President Mobutu from power — from the DRC's territory. The Court held that Uganda had violated the sovereignty and territorial integrity of the Congo, and that Uganda's actions also violated the prohibition of use of force under Article 2(4) of the U.N. Charter. The Court further found that Uganda's military forces, through their attacks against Congolese civilians, committed human rights and international humanitarian law violations. See Armed Activities on the Territory of the Congo (Democratic Republic of the Congo v. Uganda), 2005 I.C.J. 168 (Dec. 19, 2005).

The Court has also issued decisions addressing areas of growing interest to the international community, such as universal criminal jurisdiction. In 2000, the Democratic Republic of the Congo brought suit against Belgium for issuing an arrest warrant against Abdulaye Yerodia Ndombasi, then the DRC's Foreign Minister, charging him with war crimes and crimes against humanity. Belgium asserted jurisdiction under a controversial Belgian law enabling Belgium to assert universal jurisdiction over serious violations of international humanitarian law. The Court found that Belgium's actions violated the inviolability and immunity from criminal process of sitting foreign ministers under customary international law. Arrest Warrant of 11 April 2000 (Democratic Republic of the Congo v. Belgium), 2002 I.C.J. 3 (Feb. 14).

In the realm of international environmental law, the Court's 1997 decision in the case between Hungary and Slovakia regarding a major infrastructure project on the Danube River, discussed in Chapter 2, gave prominence to environmental protection, specifically highlighting the need to ensure sustainable development in the course of development. The Court's 2010 decision concerning Uruguay's planned construction of major pulp mills on the Uruguay River, which forms the international boundary between Uruguay and Argentina, helped develop the understanding of international obligations regarding sustainable development, the equitable use of transboundary rivers, and the performance of environmental impacts assessments. Pulp Mills on the River Uruguay (Argentina v. Uruguay), Judgment (April 20, 2010), reprinted in 49 I.L.M. 1118 (2010).

Even though many of its decisions have been important, the Court has not lived up to the hopes of many of its early supporters that the Court, along with the United Nations, would evolve into the judicial branch of an international government. To begin with, even though the Court's docket has become more active recently, 150 cases in over 65 years is not a heavy caseload. Many of the cases before the Court have involved territorial disputes; although these have undoubtedly been of significance to the parties, they have not necessarily been of great international importance generally. And, in more than 35 contentious cases, jurisdiction over or admissibility of the claim was challenged, with the Court dismissing many of these cases.

Acceptance by states of the Court's authority, as reflected by consent to its compulsory jurisdiction under Article 36(2) of the ICJ Statute, is limited. As noted above, only 66 out of 192 parties to the ICJ Statute have Article 36(2) declarations in force.

The reasons for the Court's limited influence are varied. Some commentators, as noted above, suggest that the Court lacks judicial independence and decides cases on political grounds. But it may be that the opposite is true; countries may wish to preserve the flexibility to interpret the law in a way that suits their interests. It may be the prospect of a neutral and independent legal evaluation of their behavior by the Court that states seek to avoid. Whatever the reason for the reluctance of states to submit their disputes to the ICJ, the consensual nature of the Court's jurisdiction is a profound limitation.

The Court's effectiveness is also hampered by its rigid procedures and the long time period cases consume. It took the Court ten years to decide all phases of the *Qatar v. Bahrain* case. The case concerning the *Application of the Convention on the Prevention and Punishment of the Crime of Genocide* between Croatia and Serbia was filed in 1999 and was still pending in February 2011. In fairness to the Court, this is often due to the deliberate schedule favored by the parties for the submission of their written pleadings and requests for additional rounds of written submissions.

Concerns about the enforceability of the Court's rulings may also serve as a constraint on its influence. When the Court reaches a judgment on the merits, the affected parties have generally complied with it. In 1994, for instance, Libya withdrew its military forces from territory it had occupied and purported to annex that the Court later determined belonged to Chad. In 2006, Nigeria similarly withdrew from regions in the contested and oil-rich Bakassi Peninsula that the Court had determined were part of Cameroon. Studies of the record of compliance with ICJ decisions have concluded that the ICJ's final judgments "receive a great deal of deference" by states, and that the "Court's compliance record is good, though not perfect." Paulson, Compliance with Final Judgments of the International Court of Justice since 1987, supra, 98 Am. J. Int'l L. at 460; see also Constanze Schulte, Compliance with Decisions of the International Court of Justice (2004) (noting a "generally satisfactory compliance record for judgments"). There have, however, been a number of instances in which recalcitrant states have refused to comply with the Court's judgments. In such cases, the U.N. Security Council, hampered in part by its veto-wielding members, has yet to take measures to enforce an ICJ judgment.

In 1980, for example, Iran refused to comply with the Court's judgment to release U.S. hostages being held in the American Embassy in Tehran. And the United States continued to support the Nicaraguan *contras* in spite of the Court's 1986 decision saying that this support violated international law. More recently, in the *Breard*, *LaGrand*, and *Avena* cases, the United States did not comply with ICJ provisional measures orders that directed a stay of execution for certain foreign nationals who were not informed of their right to consular assistance under the Vienna Convention on Consular Relations. See Chapter 3.

Recent years have witnessed a substantial increase in the number of formal international disputes resolution bodies, which also affects the international role of the ICJ. Even when a court is the preferred approach, states are relying more on regional and specialized courts (as discussed in Section C). Possibly the most important alternative is the increasing use of international arbitration (as discussed in Section D). In addition to the ICJ, the twentieth century produced various other international tribunals to which states are increasingly resorting, including the European Court of Justice, the European Court of Human Rights, the dispute settlement forums of the WTO, and the Inter-American Court of Human Rights. The uncertainty and potential inconsistency that may result from the recent proliferation of international courts and tribunals raises additional questions not only about the future role of the ICJ, but about the integrity of the international legal system more generally. The following excerpt highlights ways in which international courts have themselves taken steps to minimize the fragmentation of international law, at least on questions of procedure and remedies.

Chester Brown, The Cross-Fertilization of Principles Relating to Procedure and Remedies in the Jurisprudence of International Courts and Tribunals

30 Loy. L.A. Int'l & Comp. L. Rev. 219, 219-222 (2008)

It is undeniable that the multiplication of international judicial bodies . . . has had implications for the international legal order. The "proliferation" of international courts and tribunals might be regarded as a positive development in that it evidences a trend toward the peaceful settlement of disputes, and away from non-peaceful means of regulating differences. This increase in courts, however, has not come without complications.

As is well known, the growth in the number of international courts has occurred in the absence of an overarching framework: there are no formal links between different international courts, and there is no structural hierarchy within which they operate. This means that international tribunals essentially operate in isolation from each other. This led the Appeals Chamber of the International Criminal Tribunal for the former Yugoslavia (ICTY) to observe in its Prosecutor v. Tadic decision:

> International law, because it lacks a centralised structure, does not provide for an integrated judicial system operating an orderly division of labour among a number of tribunals, where certain aspects or components of jurisdiction as a power could be centralised or vested in one of them but not the others. In international law, every tribunal is a self-contained system (unless otherwise provided).

The proliferation of these so-called "self-contained systems" has had various problematic effects on the administration of international justice. One problem is the "fragmentation" of international law through the emergence of doctrinal inconsistencies. In addition, the proliferation creates overlapping jurisdictions among different international courts, giving rise to the problem of parallel competing proceedings concerning the same dispute. . . .

A review of the practice of international courts and tribunals on a range of issues relating to procedure and remedies reveals evidence suggesting that there is a tendency, or at least an instinct, on the part of international courts and tribunals to adopt common approaches. These universal approaches have led to increasing commonality in the case law of international courts. This commonality concerns both the existence of procedural and remedial powers and the manner in which those powers are exercised. The practice has given rise to the emergence of what might be called a "common law of international adjudication."

The emergence of commonalities is significant because it was unclear whether the proliferation of international tribunals would give rise to the convergence in their approach to procedure and remedies. Moreover, there was the potential for the emergence of inconsistent approaches to result. . . . Nonetheless, the case law of international courts and tribunals reveals convergent rather than divergent practices on these issues. It demonstrates that while international courts seek to apply the provisions of their statutes and rules of procedure, these instruments do not foresee every procedural issue that may arise in the course of international proceedings. Additionally, most are silent on the nature of the remedies that can be awarded. Where lacunae exist in these instruments and where their provisions might be interpreted and applied in various ways, international courts often turn for guidance to the practice of other international tribunals, and many examples can be cited to illustrate this.

Notes and Questions

1. Should the ICJ try to hear the full range of international law issues, or should it focus on certain areas, such as boundary disputes? Should the advisory jurisdiction of the ICJ be expanded and international organizations be encouraged to seek the Court's opinions? Should individuals be allowed to sue foreign states or even their own state? Should a process such as the referral proceeding in the European Union (EU), where a national court refers EU law issues to the European Court of Justice (discussed in the next section), be developed so that national courts can refer international law issues to the ICJ for decision?

2. Should there be a formal hierarchy among the existing international tribunals? If so, should the ICJ act as an international supreme court? Could the ICJ fulfill such a role? Is a formal structure necessary? Professor Charney has noted the practice of "judicial dialogue" between the ICJ and other tribunals, reflected in the practice of those tribunals to cite ICJ jurisprudence on such diverse subjects as the law of treaties, the sources of international law, the law of state responsibility, nationality, compensation for injury to aliens, and maritime boundary law. Jonathan L. Charney, Is International Law Threatened by Multiple International Tribunals?, 217 Recueil des Cours 101 (1998). For more on concerns about the "fragmentation" of international law stemming from the proliferation of international courts and tribunals, see Yuval Shany, The Competing Jurisdictions of International Courts and Tribunals (2003); Ruti Teitel & Robert Howse, Cross-Judging: Tribunalization in a Fragmented but Interconnected Global Order, 41 N.Y.U.J.Int'l L. & Pol. 959 (2009).

3. What relationship should the United States have with the ICJ? Should it accept compulsory jurisdiction again, along the lines of its 1946 declaration? Should it accept compulsory jurisdiction, but with more extensive reservations to limit the scope of its consent? Or should the United States accept ICJ jurisdiction only for disputes under specific bilateral or multilateral treaties? If so, for what kinds of treaties? Or should the United States resort to the Court only by special agreement in a specific dispute?

4. Should the enforceability of ICJ judgments be improved? How could this be done? Or is it enough to depend on the voluntary acquiescence of the losing party, international pressure, or the yet-to-be-used enforcement by the U.N. Security Council under Article 94(2) of the Charter?

5. For an excellent and comprehensive treatise on the ICJ, see Shabtai Rosenne, The Law and Practice of the International Court 1920-2005 (4th ed. 2006). The Court itself maintains an up-to-date Web site at http://www.icj-cij.org. You might want to keep your answers to the questions above a little tentative until you are more familiar with some of the other methods of formal dispute resolution in the international arena — notably, regional and specialized courts, arbitration, and domestic courts, which we discuss below.

C. REGIONAL AND SPECIALIZED COURTS

Since World War II, several regional and specialized courts have been created and some have grown in importance, notably in Europe. The similar societies there, combined with the searing experience of two world wars, have helped foster major efforts to integrate the economies and societies. One important result of these efforts was the creation of the Court of Justice for the European Union. This judicial arm of the European Union has broad powers, including the authority to rule invalid the national legislation of member states.

Europe also is the home of the European Court of Human Rights, which has a major role in the interpretation and application of the European Convention for the Protection of Human Rights and Fundamental Freedoms. Almost all European countries have agreed to abide by the decisions of this court. (See discussion in Chapter 8 on human rights.)

Outside Europe, regional and specialized courts are still rare and are less well-developed. There is an Inter-American Court of Human Rights, but its jurisdiction is more limited than that of its European counterpart. (See also Chapter 8.)

One notable development is the International Tribunal for the Law of the Sea, which was established in 1996 under the Law of the Sea Convention. This tribunal is available for disputes under the detailed provisions of the Convention governing the use of the seas, which cover approximately three-quarters of the world's surface. The Tribunal, however, is only one of four formal methods that states can choose to resolve disputes under the Convention. The other three approaches are international arbitration, special technical arbitral tribunals, and the ICJ. Moreover, if the states concerned have selected different methods of dispute resolution, the dispute may be submitted "only to arbitration." (See Chapter 9.)

Another major development is the International Criminal Court (ICC), which was established to try suspected war criminals and perpetrators of genocide or crimes against humanity. The ICC was established in the Rome Statute, a treaty that emerged in 1998 from a conference attended by representatives from 127 countries. The treaty obtained the necessary ratifications for entry into force in July 2002, despite strong United States opposition, and the ICC began operations in 2003. The Court is designed to be the permanent successor to the temporary war crimes tribunals set up after World War II and the special tribunals created to handle the more recent situations in the former Yugoslavia and in Rwanda. (See Chapter 12 for a discussion of individual responsibility, war crimes tribunals, and the International Criminal Court.)

The material below will focus on the especially successful judicial institution for the European Union. The other regional and specialized courts mentioned above will be considered further in the indicated chapters.

1. *The Court of Justice of the European Union*

The Court of Justice of the European Union is the sole judicial institution of the European Union (EU). It is made up of three courts: the Court of Justice, the lower General Court, and the Civil Service Tribunal.

The Court of Justice is the most important of these. It was originally established in 1958 when the European Community and the Court, as the Community's judicial arm, were created when the Treaty Establishing the European Community (commonly known as the Treaty of Rome) came into force.* The EU was then created by the Treaty on European Union (EU Treaty), which entered into force in 1993 and provided new momentum for European integration. The Lisbon Treaty modified this system in late 2009 by restructuring and reorganizing many of the EU institutions.

*Three European Communities were established in the 1950s — the European Economic Community, the European Coal and Steel Community, and the European Atomic Energy Community. Some of their nonjudicial institutions were merged in 1967. With further changes, the Communities came to be collectively referred to as the "European Community" or "European Communities," but are now referred to as the European Union. For further discussion of the evolution of the European Communities into the European Union, see Chapter 5.C.

As of January 2011, the 27 members of the EU are: Austria, Belgium, Bulgaria, Cyprus, Czech Republic, Denmark, Estonia, Finland, France, Germany, Greece, Hungary, Ireland, Italy, Latvia, Lithuania, Luxembourg, Malta, Poland, the Netherlands, Portugal, Romania, Slovakia, Slovenia, Spain, Sweden, and the United Kingdom.

The EU is involved in determining a vast range of activities by its member states or their citizens, including not only tariffs, exchange controls, and investment, but also foreign policy, human rights issues, and, for some countries, a common currency and monetary policy. The present role of the EU is broad, and it is growing. (For more information on the EU, see Chapter 5.[**])

The Court of Justice is considered a central force in this process of European integration and is not answerable to any other entity for its decisions. The following excerpt by Professor T.C. Hartley provides a useful overview of the purposes, structure, and procedure of the court. He sometimes refers to the Court of Justice as the European Court.

T.C. Hartley, The Foundations of European Union Law

47-56, 58, 70 (7th ed. 2010)

[Under the new terminology introduced by the Treaty of Lisbon in 2009] 'Court of Justice of the European Union' is an umbrella term covering all the judicial bodies set up by the Treaties. These are:

- the Court of Justice (generally known as the 'European Court');
- the General Court (formerly known as the 'Court of First Instance'); and
- specialized courts (at the moment, only the Civil Service Tribunal).

The main functions of these courts are: to ensure that the law is enforced (especially against Member States); to act as referee between the Member States and the Union as well as between the Union institutions *inter se*; and to ensure the uniform interpretation and application of Union law throughout the Union.

The European Court

Judges

There is one Judge from each Member State: twenty-seven at present. They are appointed by the common accord of the Member States. It is stated in the Treaties that Judges must be 'persons whose independence is beyond doubt and who possess the qualifications required for appointment to the highest judicial offices in their respective countries or who are jurisconsults of recognized competence'. . . .

Judges are appointed for staggered terms of six years. . . . They are eligible for re-appointment and this frequently occurs; there is no retirement age. The Member States cannot remove a Judge during his (or her) term of office, but he may be dismissed if, in the unanimous opinion of the other Judges and Advocates general,

**Also, excerpts of the consolidated versions of the "Treaty on European Union" (TEU) and "Treaty on the Functioning of the European Union" (TFEU) (also known as the revised "Treaty of Rome") are contained in the Documentary Supplement.

'he no longer fulfils the requisite conditions or meets the obligations arising from his office'. So far this procedure has never been put into operation.

The President of the Court is elected by his brother Judges for a renewable term of three years. The election is by secret ballot. The President's function is to direct the judicial and administrative business of the Court and to preside at sessions of the full Court. The Court is divided into Chambers. . . .

. . . [T]he Court reaches decisions by a majority. . . .

The Court normally sits in Chambers; it sits as a full Court only in exceptional cases. In addition to Chambers of three or five Judges, there is provision for a Grand Chamber, consisting of at least thirteen Judges. It is presided over by the President of the Court. The Court will sit as Grand Chamber where a Member State or a Union institution which is a party to the proceedings so requests. The Court will normally sit in plenary formation (full Court) only in the special case laid down in the Statute — for example, the compulsory retirement of a member of the Commission for misconduct. However, a Chamber will be able to refer a case of exceptional importance to the full Court.

It might be thought that the comparatively short terms of office, as well as the appointment procedure, would lessen the independence of the Judges. . . . [O]n the contrary, the Court is generally regarded as one of the most 'European-minded' institutions in the Union.

The most important protection the Judges have against national pressure is the fact that there is always just one 'judgment of the Court' without any separate concurring or dissenting judgments. Since, moreover, the Judges swear to uphold the secrecy of their deliberations, it is never known how individual Judges voted. Therefore it is impossible to accuse a Judge of being insufficiently sensitive to national interests or of having 'let his Government down'; no one outside the Court can ever know whether he vigorously defended the position adopted by his own country or was in the forefront of those advocating a 'Union solution'.

The background of the Judges is varied: some previously held political or administrative offices; some were in private practice or were members of the national judiciary; others had academic appointments.

Advocates General

In addition to the Judges, there are also eight Advocates General. Although not required by law, this normally includes one from each of the big countries. They have the same status as Judges: the same provisions regarding appointment, qualifications, tenure, and removal apply to them as to Judges; they receive the same salary, and they rank equally in precedence with the Judges according to seniority in office. One Advocate General is appointed First Advocate General. . . . [T]he Advocates General play no part in the Court's deliberations regarding cases.

. . . In the words of the Treaty [of Lisbon], 'It shall be the duty of the Advocate-General, acting with complete impartiality and independence, to make, in open court, reasoned submissions on cases which in accordance with the Statute of the Court of Justice of the European Union, require his involvement.' When each new case comes to the Court, it is assigned by the First Advocate General to one of the Advocates General. The Advocate General to whom the case is assigned, together with his (or her) legal secretary . . . , will study the issues involved and undertake any legal research they think necessary. After the parties have concluded their submissions to the Court, the Advocate General will give his opinion. This opinion is not binding on the Court, but will be considered with great care by the Judges when they make their decision. It is printed, together with the judgment, in the law reports.

Impartiality and independence are important characteristics of the Advocate General's office. He represents neither the Union nor any Member State: he speaks only for the public interest. He works quite separately and independently from the Judges; one could say that he gives a 'second opinion' which is in fact delivered first. This opinion shows the Judges what a trained legal mind, equal in quality to their own, has concluded on the matter before them. It could be regarded as a point of reference, or starting point, from which they can begin their deliberations. In many cases they follow the Advocate General fully; in others they deviate from his opinion either wholly or in part. . . .

One feature of the European Court which has sometimes given rise to comment is that there is no appeal from its judgments. In most cases it may be regarded as a court of first and last resort. . . . In these circumstances, the role of the Advocate General is especially important. His opinion could in fact be regarded as a judgment of first instance which is subject to instant and invariable appeal. It is, however, an appeal of a special nature, since the parties normally have no opportunity to comment on the opinion before the Court begins its deliberations. . . .

The General Court

The General Court was established in 1989, following amendments contained in the Single European Act. It was originally called the 'Court of First Instance', before being renamed by the Treaty of Lisbon. The aim when creating this court was to lessen the workload of the European Court by relieving it of some of the cases with no political or constitutional importance, especially those involving complex facts. The European Court could then concentrate on the task of deciding the more important cases and maintaining the unity of Union law. A right of appeal to the European Court on points of law would ensure that the General Court stayed in line. It was hoped that the establishment of the General Court would reduce the backlog of cases pending before the European Court. The General Court has indeed relieved the European Court of a significant number of cases, but the unremitting build-up of new cases has meant that delays in getting cases heard (and decided) by the European Court have not been significantly shortened. . . .

The General Court consists of at least one Judge from each Member State. At present, there are twenty-seven Judges. The provisions regarding their . . . terms of office are the same as those for the European Court . . . [T]hey must possess the 'ability required for appointment to high judicial office'.

The General Court usually sits in Chambers of three or five Judges. It may also be constituted by a single Judge. It sits in plenary sessions in certain special instances. . . .

The Civil Service Tribunal

Article 257 TFEU [Treaty on the Functioning of the European Union] makes provision for the establishment of specialized courts, which are intended to lessen the workload of the General Court by relieving it of some of the less important cases. Acting under this provision, the Council has established the European Civil Service Tribunal, which hears disputes involving the European Union Civil Service. At present, it consists of seven Judges, appointed by the Council acting unanimously. They are appointed for a renewable period of six years and are chosen from among persons who 'possess the ability required for appointment to judicial office.' An appeal from their decisions (on points of law only) lies to the General Court.

Jurisdiction

This section is concerned with the jurisdiction of the European Court, the General Court, and the Civil Service Tribunal. Initially, no distinction will be made between them and, for ease of explanation, they will all be referred to as 'the European Court'.

The Treaties give the European Court only limited jurisdiction. There are a number of specific heads of jurisdiction and a case must be brought within one of them if the Court is to hear it. . . .

There are several criteria according to which the Court's jurisdiction may be classified. The most basic distinction is between judgments, on the one hand, and opinions or rulings, on the other hand. The latter are very much rarer than the former, but they occur in a number of situations, for example where the Council, the Commission, or a Member State requests an opinion on whether an international agreement which the Union intends to conclude with a non-Member State is compatible with the EU Treaties. . . .

As far as judgments are concerned, the most fundamental distinction is between actions begun in the European Court (direct actions) and actions begun in a national court from which a reference for a preliminary ruling is made to the European Court. This distinction is important because, if an action is begun in the European Court, it will end in the European Court: the Court's judgment will constitute a final determination of the dispute between the parties and will grant any remedies that may be appropriate; it is not subject to appeal.

If, on the other hand, the action is begun in a national court, it will end in a national court: the European Court's ruling will be transmitted to the national court and the latter will then decide the case. Here the European Court's ruling, though binding and not subject to appeal, is merely a determination of an abstract point of law: the European Court does not decide the case as such. The national court decides any relevant questions of fact and then applies the law — including relevant provisions of Union law as interpreted by the European Court — to the facts; it also exercises any discretion it may have as to the remedy to be given.

In spite of the limited role played by the European Court, preliminary rulings are of great importance because they concern the relationship between Union law and national law. It is only to the extent that it penetrates the national legal systems and confers rights and imposes obligations directly on private citizens that Union law can be really effective. It is through its power to give preliminary rulings that the European Court has established the doctrine of direct effect and the doctrine of the supremacy of Union law over national law. The European Court will give a preliminary ruling only when requested to do so by a national court which considers that a question of Union law is relevant to its decision: any court or tribunal *may* make such a request; a court or tribunal from which there is no appeal *must* do so.

The issues which may be referred to the European Court are of three kinds: the interpretation of a provision of Union law, the effect of such a provision in the national legal system (which, in theory, is also a question of interpretation), and, in the case of a measure passed by the Union itself, the validity of such a provision.

Direct actions may be divided into two categories: those over which the Court has jurisdiction by virtue of an agreement between the parties and those where the Court's jurisdiction is conferred by direct operation of the law. The former are not very important in practice; the main example is actions arising out of a contract concluded by the Union which contains a clause giving jurisdiction to the European Court.

Direct actions where the Court's jurisdiction does not depend on consent may be classified according to whether the defendant is the Union or a Member State. A number of different kinds of action may be brought against the Union. The two most important are actions for judicial review and actions for damages for non-contractual liability (tort). Actions for judicial review may be brought either to annul a Union measure or to oblige a Union institution to pass a measure which it had previously refused to pass. Such proceedings are brought against the relevant Union institution; they may be brought by a Member State, another Union institution, or—in certain special cases—by a private individual.

Actions for damages for non-contractual liability may be brought against the Union by either a Member State or a private individual. The applicant must prove that he has suffered loss as a result of Union action (or inaction).

Other proceedings in which a Union institution is the defendant include appeals against penalties imposed under Union regulations (if the regulation in question so provides), and employment disputes between the Union and its staff.

Actions against a Member State are called enforcement actions. They may be brought against a Member State alleged to have violated Union law. The applicant may be either the Commission or another Member State; in practice it is almost always the Commission. There is a preliminary procedure in which an opinion is given by the Commission after the Member State has explained its position: if the Member State refuses to abide by this opinion, the Commission (or the other Member State) brings the action before the Court. . . .

Jurisdiction of the General Court

The European Court (Court of Justice) has jurisdiction in all the above instances except where jurisdiction has been conferred on the General Court or the Civil Service Tribunal.

The rules governing the jurisdiction of the General Court are to be found in Article 256 TFEU, and Article 51 of the Statute. They are rather complex. The Treaty Articles confer jurisdiction on the General Court in a fairly wide range of cases . . . however, they also provide, first, that the Statute may reserve some of these cases for the European Court, and, secondly, that it may give the General Court jurisdiction in other cases. . . . The result is that cases before the General Court consist mainly, though not entirely, of cases brought by private persons (usually companies) against the Union (usually the Commission). Competition cases, anti-dumping cases, and trade mark cases are the most important. . . .

There is a right of appeal, on points of law only, from the General Court to the European Court.

Jurisdiction of the Civil Service Tribunal and Appeals from It

The jurisdiction of the Civil Service Tribunal is limited to disputes between the Union and its staff. There is a right of appeal on points of law from its decisions to the General Court. . . .

Precedent

Does the doctrine of precedent apply in the European Court? The answer is that there is no legal doctrine of *stare decisis*, but the Court does follow its previous decisions in almost all cases. The case law of the European Court is just as important for the development of Union law as that of English courts is for modern English law. . . . However, though lawyers and Advocates General have always cited copious precedents, the Court itself used to refer to its previous decisions only in rare instances. One almost got the impression that it was trying to disguise the extent to which it followed precedent. . . . Today the position has changed, though the Court usually cites precedents only when they support its reasoning: it does not normally cite them in order to distinguish them.

There are a number of important instances where the Court has not followed precedent. These are the result of changing circumstances or a change of opinion among the Judges, possibly following criticism by Advocates General or academic writers. Where this happens, the Court does not normally overrule the earlier case as an English court would: it simply ignores it.

[In 2009, there were 561 new cases brought before the ECJ (including 302 references for preliminary rulings, 143 direct actions, and 104 appeals), and 588 cases were completed. Among the completed cases, there were 259 preliminary rulings, 215 direct actions, and 97 appeals. The Court had 741 cases pending at the end of 2009. The Court of First Instance received 568 new cases and completed 555 cases. It had 1191 cases pending. (See the Court of Justice's Annual Report at http://curia.europa.eu/jcms/jcms/Jo2_7000/ (2010).)]

2. *The Relationship of European Union Law to National Law*

There are several sources of European Union law. Written sources can be subdivided into categories. First, there is the "primary legislation," which is created directly by the Member States. It includes the Union's constitutive treaties and their annexes, schedules, protocols, and amendments.

"Secondary legislation" consists of the law created by the Union institutions, which are expressly empowered by the primary legislation to make binding, juridical acts. (See, e.g., Article 288 (ex Art. 249)* in the Consolidated Version of the Treaty on the Functioning of the European Union (TFEU Treaty), excerpted in the

*The European treaties have been amended over time and the article numbers changed. Current material, like that above, first provides the article number in its present location in the cited treaty. The second number is the article number in the earlier Treaty. With the cases excerpted below, the article the Court actually cited comes first with the bracketed reference being the location of the present article.

Documentary Supplement.) "Secondary" is used in a chronological sense and does not indicate that this legislation is somehow inferior in its legal effects to the constitutive treaties. Finally, there are the international agreements concluded by the European Union, which is an entity with an international legal personality. Several experts on European Union law explain these sources as follows:

> In the continental European tradition it is customary to identify the authoritative "sources" of law for any given legal system. Within the EU, the constitutive treaties, along with the other basic treaties we have identified, clearly constitute the primary sources of law. Secondary sources consist chiefly of the legally binding acts adopted by the EU institutions. . . . [T]hese acts include the many regulations, directives and decisions issued from time to time by the Council, the Parliament and the Council, or the Commission. Secondary sources also include the treaties to which the EU is a party, including trade and association agreements with third countries. . . . The EU has also acquired more and more "soft law," chiefly as a result of the informal lawmaking methods know [sic] as the "open method of coordination". . . .

Judgments of the Court of Justice and its accessory Court of First Instance also constitute important sources of EU law. . . . The Court of Justice considers the institutions and the Member States alike to be bound by the Court's interpretations of EU law and also by certain "general principles of law," such as the principles of proportionality and legitimate expectations . . . and various fundamental rights which the Court has recognized in its case law. . . . These principles not only constitute sources of EU law, but sources superior in rank to the EU's secondary legislation." [George A. Bermann, Roger J. Goebel, William J. Davey & Eleanor M. Fox, Cases and Materials on European Union Law 35 (2010). European Union law has a complex relationship with the laws of the Member States. To begin with, the fact that the European Union is based on treaties has interesting consequences for the relationship between Union law and national law. As Professor Hartley explains:

> Since Union law is based on a set of treaties, the important issue for our purposes is the application of a treaty in the domestic law of the States that are parties to it. If a treaty (or a provision in it) applies in the legal system of such a State without that State having to adopt any legislation specifically providing for the application of that treaty, the treaty is said to be "directly effective" or to have "direct effect". A treaty that is directly effective is automatically part of the legal system of the State in question. If, on the other hand, it is not directly effective, it cannot be applied in the domestic law of that State without the adoption of legislation to make provision for this. . . .
>
> If direct effect is given to a provision of Union law, that provision is applied by the national court as part of the law of the land. No rule of national law *specifically* referring to it is necessary. . . . [H]owever, a rule of national law making general provision for direct effect *is* necessary. The *Van Gend en Loos* case was the first decision by the European Court on direct effect; it is also one of the most important judgments ever handed down by the Court. The case arose when a private firm sought to invoke Union law against the Dutch customs authorities in proceedings in a Dutch tribunal. The tribunal made a reference [for a preliminary ruling] to the European Court. The main issue was whether Article 12 of the EEC Treaty was directly effective. [Hartley, supra. at 204, 209.]

Van Gend en Loos v. Nederlandse Administratie der Belastingen

European Court of Justice
Case 26/62, [1963] ECR 1

[In September 1960 Van Gend en Loos imported ureaformaldehyde into the Netherlands from the Federal Republic of Germany. This product was then subject to an 8 percent import duty under a 1958 protocol between Belgium, Luxembourg, and the Netherlands. Van Gend en Loos challenged the application of the 8 percent duty by lodging an objection with the Inspector of Customs and Excise at Zaandam and argued that as of January 1, 1958 (the date the EEC Treaty came into force), this product had been subject to a 3 percent duty. The 1958 protocol resulted in a higher duty and was thus an infringement of Article 12 [now Art. 38] of the EEC [now TFEU] Treaty. Article 12 [now Art. 38] provides that Member States are to refrain from introducing new duties on imports and from increasing existing duties.

[Countering Van Gend en Loos' argument, the Nederlandse Administratie der Belastingen, the Dutch customs collectors, stated that the product's classification as of January 1, 1958, had subjected it to a 10 percent duty; therefore, the protocol did not result in a higher duty. The Tariefcommissie, a Dutch court, without resolving the question of which duty the product had originally been subject to, requested a preliminary ruling from the Court of Justice on the following two questions:]

> 1. Whether Article 12 of the EEC Treaty [now Art. 38 of the TFEU] has direct application within the territory of a Member State, in other words, whether nationals of such a State can, on the basis of the Article in question, lay claim to individual rights which the courts must protect;
>
> 2. In the event of an affirmative reply, whether the application of an import duty of 8% to the import into the Netherlands by the applicant in the main action of ureaformaldehyde originating in the Federal Republic of Germany represented an unlawful increase within the meaning of Article 12 of the EEC Treaty [now Art. 38 of the TFEU]. . . .

[The Court answered the first question in the affirmative, giving the following reasoning:] The objective of the EEC Treaty [now TFEU], which is to establish a Common Market, the functioning of which is of direct concern to interested parties in the Community, implies that this Treaty is more than an agreement which merely creates mutual obligations between the contracting states. This view is confirmed by the preamble to the Treaty which refers not only to governments but to peoples. It is also confirmed more specifically by the establishment of institutions endowed with sovereign rights, the exercise of which affects Member States and also their citizens. Furthermore, it must be noted that the nationals of the states brought together in the Community are called upon to cooperate in the functioning of this Community through the intermediary of the European Parliament and the Economic and Social Committee.

In addition the task assigned to the Court of Justice under Article 177 [now Art. 267 providing for preliminary rulings], the object of which is to secure uniform interpretation of the Treaty by national courts and tribunals, confirms that the states have acknowledged that Community law has an authority which can be invoked by their nationals before those courts and tribunals.

The conclusion to be drawn from this is that the Community constitutes a new legal order of international law for the benefit of which the states have limited their sovereign rights, albeit within limited fields, and the subjects of which comprise not only Member States but also their nationals. Independently of the legislation of Member States, Community law therefore not only imposes obligations on individuals but is also intended to confer upon them rights which become part of their legal heritage. These rights arise not only where they are expressly granted by the Treaty, but also by reason of obligations which the Treaty imposes in a clearly defined way upon individuals as well as upon the Member States and upon the institutions of the Community. . . .

The wording of Article 12 [now Art. 38] contains a clear and unconditional prohibition which is not a positive but a negative obligation. This obligation, moreover, is not qualified by any reservation on the part of states which would make its implementation conditional upon a positive legislative measure enacted under national law. The very nature of this prohibition makes it ideally adapted to produce direct effects in the legal relationship between Member States and their subjects. . . .

. . . The fact that . . . Articles 169 [now Art. 258] and 170 [now 259] of the [TFEU] Treaty enable the Commission and the Member States to bring before the Court a State which has not fulfilled its obligations does not mean that individuals cannot plead these obligations, should the occasion arise, before a national court. . . .

A restriction of the guarantees against an infringement of Article 12 [now Art. 38] by Member States to the procedures under Article 169 [now Art. 258] and 170 [now Art. 259] would remove all direct legal protection of the individual rights of their nationals. There is the risk that recourse to the procedure under these Articles would be ineffective if it were to occur after the implementation of a national decision taken contrary to the provisions of the Treaty.

The vigilance of individuals concerned to protect their rights amounts to an effective supervision in addition to the supervision entrusted by Articles 169 [now Art. 226] and 170 [now Art. 259] to the diligence of the Commission and of the Member States.

It follows from the foregoing considerations that, according to the spirit, the general scheme and the wording of the Treaty, Article 12 [now Art. 38] must be interpreted as producing direct effects and creating individual rights which national courts must protect. . . .

[The Court of Justice then concluded that, regarding the second question, the Tariefcommissie was the proper court to make the determination as to whether the import duty charged was higher after January 1, 1958 or not.]

3. *The Supremacy of Union Law and the Restriction of National Powers*

What happens when Union law and national law come into conflict? Which law prevails? As Professor Hartley explains:

> It is a basic rule of Union law that (subject to one exception) a directly effective provision of Union law always prevails over a provision of national law. This rule,

which is **not found in any of the Treaties** but has been proclaimed with great emphasis by the Court, applies irrespective of the nature of the Union provision (constitutive Treaty, Union act, or agreement with a non-member State) or that of the national provision (constitution, statute, or subordinate legislation); it also applies irrespective of whether the Union provision cam before, or after, the national provision: in all cases the national provision must give way to Union law. [Hartley, supra. at 243 (emphasis added).]

The *Simmenthal* case below was an important decision in establishing that Union law prevailed over national law.

Amministrazione delle Finanze dello Stato v. Simmenthal S.p.A.

European Court of Justice
Case 106/77, [1978] ECR 629

[In July 1973, Simmenthal imported beef for human consumption from France into Italy. Pursuant to Italian domestic law, the Italian government charged the importer a fee for veterinary and public health inspection. Believing that such fees were contrary to Community law, Simmenthal sued in Italian court for a refund. The Italian court, the Pretore di Susa, referred the question of the validity of the fees under Community law to the ECJ. The Court ruled that the fees were the equivalent of a quantitative restriction and thus invalid under Article 30 of the EEC Treaty [now Art. 34 of the TFEU]. In light of this ruling, the Pretore di Susa ordered the Italian government to refund the fees charged. The Italian government appealed, contending that the Italian court had to apply Italian domestic law, absent repeal by the national legislature or invalidation by the Italian Constitutional Court. This latter argument was based on the principle that the Italian Constitution Court needed to determine the constitutionality of Italian laws. The case was then referred again to the ECJ.]

The Pretore . . . held that the issue before him involved a conflict between certain rules of Community law and a subsequent national law, namely the said Law No. 1239/70.

The Pretore . . . referred to the Court two questions framed as follows:

> (a) Since, in accordance with Article 189 of the EEC Treaty [now Art. 288 of the TFEU] and the established case-law of the Court of Justice of the European Communities, directly applicable Community provisions must, notwithstanding any internal rule or practice whatsoever of the Member States, have full, complete and uniform effect in their legal systems in order to protect subjective legal rights created in favour of individuals, is the scope of the said provisions to be interpreted to the effect that any subsequent national measures which conflict with those provisions must be forthwith disregarded without waiting until those measures have been eliminated by action on the part of the national legislature concerned (repeal) or of other constitutional authorities (declaration that they are unconstitutional) especially, in the case of the latter alternative, where, since the national law continues to be fully effective pending

such declaration, it is impossible to apply the Community provisions and, in consequence, to ensure that they are fully, completely and uniformly applied and to protect the legal rights created in favour of individuals? . . .

[The second question did not need to be addressed because of the European Court's answer to the first question.]

The main purpose of the *first question* is to ascertain what consequences flow from the direct applicability of a provision of Community law in the event of incompatibility with a subsequent legislative provision of a Member State.

Direct applicability in such circumstances means that rules of Community law must be fully and uniformly applied in all the Member States from the date of their entry into force and for so long as they continue in force.

These provisions are therefore a direct source of rights and duties for all those affected thereby, whether Member States or individuals, who are parties to legal relationships under Community law.

This consequence also concerns any national court whose task it is as an organ of a Member State to protect, in a case within its jurisdiction, the rights conferred upon individuals by Community law.

Furthermore, in accordance with the principle of the precedence of Community law, the relationship between provisions of the Treaty and directly applicable measures of the institutions on the one hand and the national law of the Member States on the other is such that those provisions and measures not only by their entry into force render automatically inapplicable any conflicting provision of current national law but — in so far as they are an integral part of, and take precedence in, the legal order applicable in the territory of each of the Member States — also preclude the valid adoption of new national legislative measures to the extent to which they would be incompatible with Community provisions.

Indeed any recognition that national legislative measures which encroach upon the field within which the Community exercises its legislative power or which are otherwise incompatible with the provisions of Community law had any legal effect would amount to a corresponding denial of the effectiveness of obligations undertaken unconditionally and irrevocably by Member States pursuant to the Treaty and would thus imperil the very foundations of the Community.

The same conclusion emerges from the structure of Article 177 of the Treaty [now Art. 267 of the TFEU] which provides that any court or tribunal of a Member State is entitled to make a reference to the Court whenever it considers that a preliminary ruling on a question of interpretation or validity relating to Community law is necessary to enable it to give judgment.

The effectiveness of that provision would be impaired if the national court were prevented from forthwith applying Community law in accordance with the decision or the case-law of the Court.

It follows from the foregoing that every national court must, in a case within its jurisdiction, apply Community law in its entirety and protect rights which the latter confers on individuals and must accordingly set aside any provision of national law which may conflict with it, whether prior or subsequent to the Community rule. . . . .

On those grounds the Court, in answer to the questions referred to it by the Pretore di Susa by order of 28 July 1977, hereby rules:

> A national court which is called upon, within the limits of its jurisdiction, to apply provisions of Community law is under a duty to give full effect to those provisions, if necessary refusing of its own motion to apply any conflicting provision of national legislation, even if adopted subsequently, and it is not necessary for the court to request or await the prior setting aside of such provisions by legislative or other constitutional means.

4. *The Charter of Fundamental Rights*

One result of the Lisbon Treaty was to add the Charter of Fundamental Rights to the European Union's "primary legislation," discussed above.

George A. Bermann, Roger J. Goebel, William J. Davey & Eleanor M. Fox, Cases and Materials on European Union Law

208-10, 214-15 (2010)

As the European Community, and later the European Union, steadily gained increasing political, economic and social powers in the 1980s and 1990s, it seemed increasingly anomalous that its "constitution" lacked any bill of rights. . . .

Prompted by the German Presidency, the European Council decided at Cologne in 1999 to prepare a Charter of its own that would set forth the fundamental rights applicable at the Union level. . . . [The] committee, calling itself a Convention, began meeting in Brussels in December 1999, working independently of the intergovernmental conference that was at the same time preparing the Treaty of Nice. Considering the sensitivity of some of the issues, extraordinary progress was made, with a complete first draft available by July 2000. After receiving critical comments from Parliament, organized labor and non-governmental organizations, the Convention presented a second draft in September 2000. . . .

The Charter sets out a concise, yet comprehensive statement of fundamental rights, divided among six chapters corresponding to six fundamental values: dignity, freedoms, equality, solidarity, citizens' rights and justice. The chapter on dignity declares the inviolability of human dignity, forbids the death penalty and outlaws trafficking in human beings. It also establishes innovative, if vague, guarantees against the abuse of genetic engineering and biotechnology, for example expressly prohibiting "the reproductive cloning of human beings." The chapter on freedoms proclaims, among other things, the right of privacy (including data privacy protection), freedom of expression and assembly, pluralism of the media, the right of property, the right to education and freedom to choose an occupation. Conspicuous in the chapter on equality are prohibitions of discrimination on the basis of "sex, race, colour, ethnic or social origin, genetic features, language, religion or belief, political or other opinion, membership of a national minority, property, birth, disability, age or sexual orientation," as well as the inclusion of provisions on the rights of children and the elderly, and the right to cultural diversity. The chapter on solidarity provides for various rights of employees, the right to health care, and the goals of high levels of environmental and consumer protection. Citizens' rights in chapter five include the right of access to documents and the right of petition. Chapter six on justice promises, among other things, the right to a fair trial and an effective remedy, as well as certain rights for criminal defendants. . . .

The Charter's principal weakness has been that the Protocol annexing it to the Nice Treaty expressly declared it to be judicially unenforceable. In applauding the Charter, both then President Romano Prodi of the Commission and President Nicole Fontaine of the Parliament cited this as a serious shortcoming. . . .

The Treaty of Lisbon's TEU Article 6(1) finally gives the Charter of Fundamental Rights . . . "the same legal value as the Treaties," . . . The Charter having "legal value" presumably means that its provisions have become binding on the courts of the EU and the Member States. The number and breadth of the rights enumerated, and the complex balancing of values they require, guarantee that the EU courts will shoulder a substantial interpretive burden.

Notes and Questions

1. Besides the Court of Justice of the European Union discussed above, the rest of the structure of the European Union will be considered in Chapter 5. Note for now, however, TFEU Article 344 provides that "Member States undertake not to submit a dispute concerning the interpretation or application of this Treaty to any method of settlement other than those provided for therein."

2. What is the significance of the power of the Court of Justice to render preliminary rulings on issues of Union law arising during litigation before member state courts? Does this enhance the power of the court? Does it contribute to the overall harmonization of Union policies?

3. Did the Court's decisions in *Van Gend en Loos* and *Simmenthal* (which have been followed in later cases) enhance the authority of the European Union? What is the effect on member state legislatures?

4. In another landmark case, Costa (Flaminio) v. ENEL, Case 6/64, [1964] ECR 585, the Court of Justice wrote:

> By contrast with ordinary international treaties, the EEC Treaty has created its own legal system which, on the entry into force of the Treaty, became an integral part of the legal systems of the Member States and which their courts are bound to apply.
>
> By creating a Community of unlimited duration, having its own institutions, its own personality, its own legal capacity and capacity of representation on the international plane and, more particularly, real powers stemming from a limitation of sovereignty or a transfer of powers from the States to the Community, the Member States have limited their sovereign rights, albeit within limited fields, and have thus created a body of law which binds both their nationals and themselves.

5. The ECJ has played a significant role in encouraging member states to comply with their treaty obligations. First, in Andrea Frankovich v. Italy, Joined Cases 6 & 9/90, [1991] I ECR 5357, [1993] 2 CMLR 66, the Court held Italy liable for damages to individuals caused by its failure to implement an EU directive (an EU act that is binding on identified member states, but leaves to the national authorities of each member state the choice of form and methods to reach the required result).

Second, Article 258 of the TFEU provides that the Commission can bring to the ECJ a matter where the Commission believes that the member state "has failed to fulfill an obligation under the Treaties." Under Article 260, the Commission can then ask the ECJ to fine a member state that does not comply with the Court's judgment. The Commission is to specify the amount of the lump sum or penalty payment, and the ECJ may impose it.

In 1997, the Commission opened legal proceedings against six member states (Belgium, France, Germany, Spain, Italy, and Greece) for fines for failing to follow the Court's decisions on wild birds and other environmental matters. The Commission opened additional proceedings against member states in 1998, including Ireland, for failing to implement an EU directive on water pollution. The EU Commission has used the threat of fines to bring recalcitrant member states to prompt compliance. The more common procedure by far is for the Commission to bring an action under Article 258 and use the ECJ judgment, along with the threat of action under Article 260 to ensure compliance.

However, the ECJ has handed down fines against member states. For example, in Commission v. Greece, Case C-387/97, [2000] ECR I-5407, the ECJ ordered Greece to pay the Commission 20,000 euros* per day until Greece fully complied with an ECJ judgment that waste be disposed of without endangering human health and without harming the environment. In Commission v. French Republic, Case C-177/04, 2006 ECJ CELEX 604J0177 (Mar. 14, 2006), the ECJ fined France a penalty payment of 31,650 euros per day until it took the necessary measures to comply fully with a judgment declaring that French products liability law was inconsistent with a Community directive limiting the liability of a supplier of a defective product.

The ECJ for the first time imposed a lump sum fine, in addition to the periodic penalty payments it had imposed in prior cases, in Commission v. French Republic, Case C-304/02, 2005 ECJ CELEX 602J0304 (July 12, 2005). France had failed to comply with an ECJ judgment concerning Community regulations controlling fishing activities because France did not impose adequate controls to prevent the sale of undersized fish and because French authorities were lax in punishing infringements of those measures. Because of public and private interests and because France's breach of obligations had persisted for a long period of time, the ECJ ordered France to pay a lump sum of 20 million euros, in addition to a periodic penalty payment of 57,761,250 euros for each six-month period of noncompliance.

In 2008, France was fined again for violating a Directive on the regulation of the use of genetically modified organisms (GMOs). France failed to implement the directive in a timely way. When the Commission took France to Court, France immediately complied. Because of France's immediate reaction, the Court did not impose an ongoing penalty and instead decided to fine France with a lump-sum fine of 10 million Euros for France's initial delay.

6. Compare the European Court of Justice with the U.S. Supreme Court and the International Court of Justice. Consider, for example, (a) the power of these courts to enforce their rulings and (b) the sources of law to which these courts refer in

*The value of the euro to the dollar has varied widely since the euro's introduction in 2002 in 12 EU member states, ranging from 86 cents in 2002 and reaching a high in 2008 of $1.59 in July 2008. As of November 23, 2010, the exchange rate for one euro was about $1.34.

rendering their decisions. Would you consider the ECJ more similar to the U.S. Supreme Court or to the ICJ? Why do you think that the ECJ has been viewed as more successful than the ICJ? In light of what you learned in Chapter 3, how do *Van Gend en Loos* and *Simmenthal* compare with what a U.S. court would do when confronted with a conflict between national legislation and a treaty? Is the concept of direct effects similar to the U.S. law regarding self-executing treaties?

7. Might the position of Advocate General that exists for the European Court of Justice have potential benefit for a U.S. court, such as the U.S. Supreme Court? Does any equivalent or similar position exist that provides submissions to the U.S. Supreme Court?

8. In July 1998, four U.S. Supreme Court Justices (Justices Sandra Day O'Connor, Anthony M. Kennedy, Ruth Bader Ginsburg, and Stephen G. Breyer) visited the ECJ in Luxemburg for the first time as a group on a mission to share common legal ideas and to cultivate judicial cooperation. During this mission, the Justices emphasized the significance of the ECJ decisions. Justice O'Connor said, "We certainly are going to be more inclined to look at the decisions of [the European Court of Justice] on substantive issues . . . and perhaps use them and cite them in future decisions." Justice Breyer added, "Lawyers in America may cite an EU ruling to our court to further a point, and this increases the cross-fertilization of U.S.-EU legal ideas." (Washington Post, July 9, 1998, at A6.) (See discussion of international law, including European human rights law, being cited in U.S. Supreme Court opinions in Chapter 3.C.2.)

9. Why do you think the European states have taken the lead in the world in allowing regional courts (the ECJ and the European Court of Human Rights) to have a major say regarding an individual state's economic and other policies? Do you expect that other regions might be willing to create and accept a court like the ECJ in the near future? What about the countries of North and South America, or the ASEAN countries in Asia (discussed in Chapter 5)?

10. Although recent EU treaties, including the Lisbon Treaty, have expanded the ECJ's jurisdiction considerably (for example, into the areas of free movement of persons with the EU, and fundamental rights), the jurisdiction of other regional and specialized courts is usually more limited. The jurisdiction of the European Court of Human Rights is limited to human rights. The newest international courts, the Law of the Sea Tribunal and the International Criminal Court, are focused on the special issues of the law of the sea and serious violations of international humanitarian law, respectively. Do you think that an international court with a specialized jurisdiction has more chance of gaining the support of states and other international entities than does a court with a theoretically broad jurisdiction such as the ICJ? If so, what other specialized areas would seem particularly appropriate for an international court whose decisions would be enforced by individual states?

11. The ECJ has an excellent Web site at http://curia.europa.eu/.

D. INTERNATIONAL ARBITRATION

Arbitration between countries or between a country and a private party (such as an investor) has had a mixed history over the centuries. In recent years it has taken on new life and led to the creation of new arrangements.

For instance, even while the United States and Iran have often traded insults and sometimes hostile fire since 1981, the Iran-United States Claims Tribunal continued to proceed steadily (though slowly) through its caseload left over from the 1979-1981 hostage crisis. Also, the World Bank's International Centre for the Settlement of Investment Disputes (ICSID) has experienced a steady increase in its caseload of arbitrations between host countries and investors.

In the analogous area of commercial arbitration among private parties, business is booming as the number of international transactions grows and as arbitration increasingly becomes the preferred method of formal dispute resolution for many types of business deals. Although this book's focus is about arbitration involving one or more states (and possibly private entities as well), the activity in private commercial arbitration is often relevant. Arbitral panels—whether a country is a party or not—are likely to select from among the same sets of procedural rules and face similar choice-of-law questions. Moreover, the enforcement of most, though not all, arbitral awards looks to the same convention—the New York Convention on the Recognition and Enforcement of Foreign Arbitral Awards, which over 140 countries have ratified.

This section explores the history of arbitration, then analyzes the current uses and some outstanding issues in arbitration, including the question of enforcement of arbitral awards. The next section will then examine some examples of international dispute resolution systems tailored to particular circumstances.

1. *History of Arbitration*

Arbitration has had a long, and mixed, history. In his book, International Arbitration and Procedure (1911), Robert Morris (hereafter Morris) provides some of the earliest history.

Arbitration was used by the ancient Greeks to settle internal quarrels (e.g., between the city states). Disputes with the outside world, however, were settled through war or other means. Conditions in ancient Greece were especially favorable to arbitration—the Greeks shared a common religion, language, and an affinity for athletic games. The only thing they lacked was a unified political identity. Specific procedures were established and followed in arbitration proceedings. The Delphic oracle was often chosen as an arbitrator, as were poets, statesmen, and athletic victors. Alliances also were made between cities, which included clauses to ensure that any subsequent dispute between them would be subject to arbitration.

Early Roman history, when Italy was made up of many independent states, also contains many instances of arbitration. However, after Rome asserted sovereignty over all of Italy, arbitration became less frequent, finally ceasing with the assertion of dominion by Rome over all the world. "This conception [of Rome as the only sovereignty in the world] is necessarily antagonistic to the idea of [public] arbitration." (Morris, at 6.)

Upon the disintegration of the Roman Empire, arbitration once more became common. Unlike in ancient Greece, common procedures for arbitration proceedings were not established. Popes, monarchs, emperors, and lords all arbitrated disputes. "Perhaps the most famous instance [of Papal arbitration] was the decision of Alexander VI between Spain and Portugal in their quarrel over the newly discovered lands in the new world. . . . The Pope finally decided [in 1493] that Spain should hold everything west of a line somewhere between the forty-first and forty-fourth degrees of longitude, and Portugal everything east." (Morris, at 12.) That essentially limited Portugal to the eastern part of Brazil. Penalties against those entities that did not respect arbitration decisions ranged from monetary fines to excommunication.

With the appearance of (more or less) stable monarchies in Europe, arbitration between nations became less common, while arbitration of business disputes became more so. "[I]n a treaty between France and England in 1606, two arbitral courts were established, each consisting of two Englishmen and two Frenchmen, one court holding at London, the other at Paris. Aggrieved French shipowners presented their protests at London, and aggrieved Englishmen at Paris." An arbitration board was also established in 1652 to resolve "commercial disputes that had accumulated for many years" between merchants of England and Holland. (Morris, at 16-17.)

The following excerpt provides a survey of the development of public arbitration and some of its use from 1794 through 1955.

J. L. Simpson & Hazel Fox, International Arbitration: Law and Practice

1-40 (1959)

The Early Anglo-American Arbitrations, 1794-1842

In 1794 there was concluded between the United Kingdom and the United States the General Treaty of Friendship, Commerce and Navigation. . . . It provided a new starting point for the development of international [public] arbitration, after the process, in the preceding period of a century or more, had come to be regarded as virtually in desuetude. Of the various questions which had been outstanding between the United Kingdom and the United States, since the latter proclaimed their independence in 1776, the . . . Treaty settled all but three. These were referred to arbitration. The form chosen was that of mixed commissions, consisting of one or two commissioners appointed by each party, who were together to choose a third or fifth by agreement or by drawing lots. [One commission was able to agree on the exact position of the Saint Croix River between the United States and the British possessions in what is now Canada.]. . . .

Later experience was to confirm that the success of a mixed commission often depended on the ability of the commissioners appointed by the parties to give agreed decisions on the questions submitted to them without recourse to the umpire or arbitrator. This in turn meant that the mixed commission worked best where the subject-matter of the dispute allowed or encouraged the commissioners to act to some extent as negotiators rather than as judges, to temper justice with diplomacy, to give a measure of satisfaction to both sides, for example, in a territorial dispute. . . .

The Alabama Claims Arbitration, 1871-72

. . . [T]he *Alabama Claims* arbitration — also between the United Kingdom and the United States — gave the [arbitral] process a new impetus, and introduced a number of rules and practices which were gradually to command general acceptance. . . . The *Alabama* claims arose from the failure, real or alleged, of the United Kingdom in her duties as a neutral during the American Civil War—in particular, in permitting *Alabama* and her supply ship, *Georgia*, to be built in British yards for the use of the Southern States, whose belligerency, to the chagrin of the Northern States, had been recognised. References to heads of state had been shown to have certain disadvantages, while the issues were too large for a mixed commission of the traditional type. Accordingly, a new type of tribunal had to be constituted. This consisted of one member appointed by each side and members appointed, respectively, by the King of Italy, the President of the Swiss Confederation and the Emperor of Brazil. Thus, a collegiate international court, which was to set the pattern for many others, had emerged.

Continuance of the Older Forms, 1871-89

. . . In the last two decades of the nineteenth century there were no fewer than ninety international arbitrations between various states. . . .

The Hague Peace Conferences, 1899 and 1907

By the end of the nineteenth century, arbitration had become a widely spread international custom; and it was natural that its discussion should occupy a considerable place in the deliberations of the Hague Peace Conferences of 1899 and 1907. The conclusion of the Convention for the Pacific Settlement of International Disputes was the most positive of the achievements of the Conference of 1899.

The Convention established . . . the misnamed Permanent Court of Arbitration [PCA]. It is little more than a panel of names from which arbitrators may be selected, when the occasion arises. The Convention allows governments party to it to nominate a maximum of four persons "of known competency in questions of international law, of the highest moral reputation and disposed to accept the duties of Arbitrator." . . . When a dispute arises between parties to the Convention, which they wish to refer to a tribunal of the [PCA], each appoints two arbitrators from the panel. The four arbitrators thus chosen select an umpire. If the four arbitrators are evenly divided on the selection of the umpire, the [Convention provided a series of steps for the] choice of umpire. . . .

The only permanent feature of the [PCA] is the Bureau established in accordance with Article 22 of the Convention. The services of the Bureau are available for tribunals formed from the Permanent Court of Arbitration, and may also be placed at the disposal of other tribunals and commissions of inquiry. [The Convention also] lays down the rules of procedure which apply in default of agreement to the contrary between the parties. The formulation of these rules in 1899 was a valuable corrective to the extreme informality of some of the earlier arbitrations. As amended in 1907, they are still today cited as authority when disputes arise upon points of procedure, and they have influenced the drafting of many *compromis*.

Between 1902 and 1905, recourse was had to the machinery established by the Convention of 1899 for the settlement of four disputes. . . . In all these cases, the issues were of secondary importance. They served, however, to put the provisions of the Convention of 1899 to the test, and to show where improvements might be attempted. . . .

The Convention of 1899 declared in Article 16 that:

> In questions of a legal nature, and especially in the interpretation or application of International Conventions, arbitration is recognised by the Signatory Powers as the most effective, and at the same time the most equitable, means of settling disputes which diplomacy has failed to settle.

The Conference of 1907 cautiously added to Article 16 the words:

> Consequently, it would be desirable that, in disputes regarding the above-mentioned questions, the Contracting Powers should, if the case arise, have recourse to arbitration, in so far as circumstances permit.

The Final Act of the Conference of 1907, with a magnificence of language masking the disappointment of high hopes, stated that the Conference was unanimous in admitting the principle of compulsory arbitration, in declaring that certain disputes, in particular those relating to the interpretation and application of international agreements, might be submitted to compulsory arbitration without any restriction. . . . [The Conference, however, was unable to agree on any specific proposal for the acceptance of compulsory arbitration.]

The Mixed Arbitral Tribunals and Claims Commissions Following the War of 1914-18

The Treaty of Versailles provided . . . for the establishment of mixed arbitral tribunals between each of the Allied and Associated Powers on the one hand and Germany on the other. Each tribunal consisted of one member appointed by each Government, and a president appointed by the two Governments jointly. If the two Governments failed to agree upon a president, he was selected by the Council of the League of Nations. The jurisdiction of the mixed arbitral tribunals included claims by nationals of the Allied or Associated Power arising out of exceptional war measures taken by Germany in respect of property, and also, in a large variety of contractual matters, cases between nationals of the Allied or Associated Power and nationals of Germany. . . .

By an Agreement of August 10, 1922, between the United States and Germany, a Mixed Claims Commission was set up to deal with claims of U.S. citizens against Germany for damage to property, rights and interests in Germany, other claims for injury to persons or property as a consequence of war, and debts due to U.S. citizens by the German Government or German nationals. . . .

Post-War Tribunals

Most of the peace treaties which followed the Second World War and the treaties embodying the provisional settlement with Germany made elaborate provision for the settlement of disputes.

A procedure closely resembling the older practice of appointing a mixed commission, consisting of two national commissioners, who tend in fact to be negotiators rather than arbitrators in the strict sense, and have resort to a "neutral" umpire only in the event of their disagreeing, is provided for in the Peace Treaties with Italy, Rumania, Bulgaria, Hungary and Finland, and the State Treaty with Austria. . . .

The divided state of Germany necessitated a different form of post-war settlement. . . . That settlement produced a series of tribunals, each with jurisdiction over different classes of matters. . . .

Ad Hoc Tribunals

. . . In modern practice an arbitrator is expected to give a decision on his personal and undivided responsibility. Since this is so, it is only rarely that states are willing to place the entire responsibility for a decision upon the shoulders of one man.

The collegiate court, consisting of a national member appointed by each party and an uneven number of "neutral" members, not nationals of either of the parties and appointed by agreement between the parties or by an outside authority, is the normal form in present-day practice. . . .

In a tribunal constituted on this pattern the determination of the number of "neutral" members and their selection are of crucial importance. Not only will the presidency go to a "neutral" member, but it is also a fair working assumption that the two national members of the tribunal will disagree, and that the decision will, in effect, be that of the "neutral" member or members. When large issues have arisen between states, there may be reluctance to entrust the effective decision to one "neutral" member. The tribunal of three "neutral" members offers the advantages of shared responsibility for the effective decision of large issues and detached consideration of the merits by several minds, and is the more usual form.

Recent public arbitrations. Arbitral tribunals have been used to settle disputes between nations in the last few decades, though private commercial arbitration is much more common. The following is a summary of some recent awards in public arbitrations that were recorded in the Permanent Court of Arbitration, the International Law Reports series, the International Arbitration Reports, or the Reports of International Arbitral Awards.

Date	*Parties*	*Issue*
1988	Egypt/Israel	Boundary dispute
1990	France/New Zealand	Return of two Frenchmen who bombed Greenpeace ship
1992	United States/Chile	Assassination of Orlando Letelier
1992	United States/United Kingdom	User fees at Heathrow Airport

Date	Parties	Issue
1994	Argentina/Chile	Determination of land boundary
1998–1999	Eritrea/Yemen	Territorial sovereignty and maritime boundaries
2004	Netherlands/France	Rhine River pollution
2005	Belgium/Netherlands	Reactivation of the Iron Rhine Railway
2006	Barbados/Republic of Trinidad and Tobago	Delimitation of the exclusive economic zone and the continental shelf between them
2007	Guyana/Suriname	Maritime delimitation between states with adjacent coasts
2007	England/France/Private parties	Issues regarding construction and operation of Eurotunnel
2000–2009	Eritrea/Ethiopia Boundary Commission and Claims Commission	Border delimitation based on colonial treaties and claims from armed conflict

One should note here an important recent entity that helped influence the attitudes of the United States and other governments toward international arbitration.

The Iran-U.S. Claims Tribunal was established pursuant to the 1981 Algiers Accords, which dealt with several issues stemming from the Iranian seizure of 52 Americans, primarily diplomatic personnel, in November 1979. The Accords provided for Iran's releasing the hostages and the United States' lifting the freeze on about $12 billion in Iranian funds. The Claims Tribunal was designed to resolve a number of outstanding monetary claims by U.S. and Iranian citizens, as well as their governments, that arose from the events during that period. (See the *Dames & Moore* case and the discussion of IEEPA in Chapter 3.)

The Tribunal was established in The Hague, Netherlands. The United States appointed three arbitrators and the Iranians three, and these six picked three more arbitrators. After some initial delays and wrangling among the arbitrators, The Tribunal ruled on procedural matters, helped settle some claims, and ruled on the merits of other claims. The Algiers Accords provided for a $1 billion Security Account (created from some of the frozen Iranian funds) to ensure payments of awards against Iran. Iran had frequently replenished the account through accumulated interest on the original $1 billion and through sales of crude oil to U.S. companies.

The Tribunal has completed its adjudication of all the private claims of U.S. nationals against Iran. The cases remaining on the Tribunal's docket are official claims between the Iranian and U.S. governments. As of December 31 2009, the Tribunal had rendered 601 awards and other decisions. Over $2.166 billion plus interest was awarded to U.S. parties (excluding interest), and about $1 billion plus interest was awarded to Iran and Iranian parties. Iran-United States Claims Tribunal, Quarterly Communiqué (2010), http://www.iusct.org/communique-english.pdf.

The generally successful functioning of the Claims Tribunal demonstrates that two countries, even when faced with continuing diplomatic and military friction, can set up an arbitral system that could handle many business and property claims in a relatively businesslike manner.

2. *Arbitration: How It Works and Common Pitfalls*

The following excerpt by Gary Born provides a sense of how arbitration works and what common pitfalls need to be avoided. In addition to addressing the advantages and disadvantages of arbitration, the excerpt also provides an introduction to leading arbitral institutions and rules. Although the focus is on international commercial arbitration, states or state-owned entities are often parties in these arbitrations, and the procedures and enforcement methods discussed here are often relevant to public international arbitrations.

Gary Born, International Commercial Arbitration: Commentary and Materials

1-26 (2d ed. 2001)

A. What Is International Arbitration?

International arbitration is a means by which international disputes can be definitively resolved, pursuant to the parties' agreement, by independent, non-governmental decision-makers. There are almost as many other definitions of international arbitration as there are commentators on the subject.

1. Defining Characteristics of Commercial Arbitration

Commercial arbitration is common in both international and domestic contexts. In each, it has several defining characteristics. First, arbitration is generally *consensual*— in most cases, the parties must agree to arbitrate their differences. Second, arbitrations are resolved by *non-governmental decision-makers*— arbitrators do not act as state judges or government agents, but are private persons ordinarily selected by the parties. Third, arbitration produces a *binding award*, which is capable of enforcement through national courts — not a mediator's or conciliator's non-binding recommendation. Finally, arbitration is comparatively *flexible*, as contrasted to most court procedures. . . .

3. Legal Framework for International Commercial Arbitration

Although international arbitration is a consensual means of dispute resolution, it has binding effect only by virtue of a complex framework of national and international law. As we discuss below, international conventions, national arbitration legislation, and institutional arbitration rules provide a specialized legal regime for most international arbitrations. This legal regime enhances the enforceability of both arbitration agreements and arbitral awards, and seeks to insulate the arbitral process from interference by national courts or other governmental authorities.

On the most universal level, the United Nations Convention on Recognition and Enforcement of Foreign Arbitral Awards (the "New York Convention") has been ratified by more than [140] nations, including all significant trading states and most major developing states. The Convention obliges member states to recognize and enforce both international commercial arbitration agreements and awards, subject to limited exceptions. Other international conventions impose comparable obligations on member states with respect to particular categories of disputes or with respect to particular bilateral or regional relationships.

In addition, most developed trading states (and many other countries) have enacted national arbitration legislation that provides for the enforcement of international arbitration agreements and awards, that limits judicial interference in the arbitration process, and that authorises specified judicial support for the arbitral process. National arbitration legislation typically affirms the capacity of parties to enter into valid and binding agreements to arbitrate future commercial disputes, provides mechanisms for the enforcement of such arbitration agreements (through orders to stay litigation or (less frequently) to compel arbitration), and requires the recognition and enforcement of arbitration awards. In addition, most modern arbitration legislation narrowly limits the power of national courts to interfere in the arbitration process, either when arbitral proceedings are pending or in reviewing ultimate arbitration awards. In many cases, national arbitration statutes also authorize limited judicial assistance to the arbitral process. This assistance can include selecting arbitrators or arbitral situses, enforcing a tribunal's orders with respect to evidence-taking or discovery, and granting provisional relief in aid of arbitration. . . .

4. Institutional Arbitration Rules

International commercial arbitration frequently occurs pursuant to institutional arbitration rules, which are often incorporated by reference into parties' arbitration agreements. The leading international arbitration institutions include the International Chamber of Commerce, the London Court of International Arbitration, and the American Arbitration Association, each of which has adopted its own set of rules governing the procedural aspects of arbitration.* These institutions, as well as another several dozen or so less widely-known bodies, supervise international arbitrations when parties agree to dispute resolution under their auspices. In addition, the UNCITRAL Commercial Arbitration Rules are widely used in so-called *ad hoc* (or non-institutional) arbitrations. . . .

B. An Overview of the Advantages and Disadvantages of International Arbitration

The popularity of arbitration as a means for resolving international commercial disputes has increased significantly over the past several decades. This popularity reflects important advantages of international arbitration as a means of resolving

*[Another leading arbitral institution is the International Centre for the Settlement of Investment Disputes (ICSID). It is specifically designed to handle disputes in which one party is a state entity and the other is a private concern. See further discussion below. — Eds.]

international commercial disputes. Despite these advantages, however, international arbitration also has significant shortcomings. These strengths and weaknesses are summarized below.

First, international arbitration is often perceived as ensuring a genuinely neutral decision-maker in disputes between parties from different countries. International disputes inevitably involve the risk of litigation before a national court of one of the parties, which may be biased, parochial, or unattractive for some other reason. Moreover, outside an unfortunately limited number of industrialized nations, local court systems simply lack the competence, experience, resources, and traditions of even-handedness satisfactorily to resolve many international commercial disputes.

International arbitration offers a theoretically competent decision-maker satisfactory to the parties, who is, in principle, independent of either party or any national or international governmental authority. On the other hand, private arbitrators can have financial, personal, or professional relations with one party (or its counsel). . . .

Second, a carefully-drafted arbitration clause generally permits the resolution of disputes between the parties in a single forum pursuant to an agreement that most national courts are bound by international treaty to enforce. This mitigates the expense and uncertainty of multiple judicial proceedings in different national courts.

On the other hand, incomplete or otherwise defective arbitration clauses can result in judicial and arbitral proceedings where the scope or enforceability of the provision, as well as the merits of the parties' dispute, must be litigated. Moreover, even well-drafted arbitration agreements cannot entirely exclude the expense and delay of a litigant determined to confound the arbitral process.

Third, arbitration agreements and arbitral awards are generally (but not always) more easily and reliably enforced in foreign states than forum selection clauses or foreign court judgments. As described elsewhere, [over 140] nations have acceded to the New York Convention, which obliges contracting states to enforce arbitration agreements and awards (subject to specified, limited exceptions). In contrast, there are no world-wide treaties relating to either forum selection agreements or judicial judgments. The perceived ease of enforceability of arbitral awards has contributed to fairly substantial voluntary compliance with arbitral awards, although there is little empirical data comparing such compliance with that applicable to judicial judgments.

In some developing and other countries, there has been a perception that international commercial arbitration was developed by, and was biased in favor of, Western commercial interests. As a consequence, national law in many countries was historically hostile towards international arbitration. . . . In general, this hostility has waned somewhat over the past decade, with many states acceding to the New York Convention and enacting "pro-arbitration" legislation.

Fourth, arbitration tends to be procedurally less formal and rigid than litigation in national courts. As a result, parties have greater freedom to agree on neutral and appropriate procedural rules, set realistic timetables, select technically expert and neutral decision-makers, involve corporate management in dispute-resolution, and the like. On the other hand, the lack of a detailed procedural code or decision-maker with direct coercive authority may permit party misconduct or create opportunities for an even greater range of procedural disputes between the parties.

Fifth, international arbitration typically involves less extensive discovery than is common in litigation in some national courts (particularly common law jurisdictions). This is generally attractive to international businesses because of the attendant reduction in expense, delay, and disclosure of business secrets.

Sixth, international arbitration is usually more confidential than judicial proceedings — as to submissions, evidentiary hearings, and final awards. This protects business and commercial confidences and can facilitate settlement by reducing opportunities and incentives for public posturing. On the other hand, few arbitrations are entirely confidential, with disclosures often occurring by means of judicial enforcement actions, unilateral party action, regulatory inquiries, or otherwise.

Seventh, the existence of an arbitration clause, a workable arbitral procedure, and an experienced arbitral tribunal may create incentives for settlement or amicable conciliation. The cooperative elements that are required to constitute a tribunal and agree upon a procedural framework can sometimes help foster a climate conducive to settlement. . . . On the other hand, where relations are irrevocably soured, the need for some measure of cooperation between the parties in conducting the arbitration can permit party misconduct greatly to impede dispute resolution.

Finally, arbitration is often lauded as a prompt, inexpensive means of dispute resolution. That can sometimes be the case, but international arbitration is also frequently criticized as both slow and expensive. The difficulties in scheduling hearing dates (with busy arbitrators, lawyers, and clients in different countries), the need to agree upon various procedural steps, and other factors often give international arbitrations a fairly stately pace. Nonetheless, national court proceedings are also often slow, and the existence of appellate review (and possible re-trials) introduces additional delays not ordinarily encountered in arbitration.

Likewise, although sometimes advertised on grounds of economy, even its proponents rightly acknowledge that "[i]nternational arbitration is an expensive process." Both private arbitrators (unlike judges) and arbitral institutions (unlike most courts) must be paid by the parties. And there is a perception that some institutional fees, charged for "administrative" services, are unnecessarily high. Nonetheless, these expenses generally will be less than the legal fees and other costs required for lengthy appellate proceedings or (in some jurisdictions) discovery. . . .

. . . At bottom, if generalizations must be made, international arbitration is much like democracy; it is nowhere close to ideal, but it is generally better than the existing alternatives. To those who have experienced it, litigation of complex international disputes in national courts is often distinctly unappealing. Despite the daunting procedural complexities and other uncertainties, arbitration often offers the least ineffective way to finally settle the contentious disputes that arise when international transactions go awry.

Gary Born, International Commercial Arbitration

90-109, 147-51, 153, 154-158, 160, 172-73, 194 (2009)

1. International Arbitration Conventions

Over the past century, major trading nations have entered into a number of international treaties and conventions designed to facilitate the transnational enforcement of arbitration awards and agreements and to promote the use of arbitration in international matters. They have done so for the specific purpose of providing an effective mechanism for resolving international commercial disputes, and thereby promoting international trade and investment. These instruments have, for the most part, contributed to a stable and effective legal framework for arbitration between international businesses. . . .

a. The New York Convention

The . . . United Nations Convention on the Recognition and Enforcement of Foreign Arbitral Awards . . . [generally] referred to as the "New York Convention," . . . is by far the most significant contemporary legislative instrument relating to international commercial arbitration. It provides what amounts to a universal constitutional charter for the international arbitral process, whose sweeping terms have enabled both national courts and arbitral tribunals to develop durable, effective means for enforcing international arbitration agreements and arbitral awards. . . .

b. European Convention on International Commercial Arbitration

The 1961 European Convention on International Commercial Arbitration is one of the world's most important regional commercial arbitration treaties. . . . The European Convention entered into force in 1964, and 31 states are currently party to it. . . . The Convention's impact in actual litigation has not been substantial (owing to the limited number of Contracting States, all of whom are also party to the New York Convention). . . . The Convention is currently somewhat dated— reflecting its origins during the Cold War—and efforts are underway to revise its provisions. . . .

d. The ICSID Convention

The International Center for the Settlement of Investment Disputes ("ICSID") is a specialized arbitration institution, established pursuant to the so-called "ICSID Convention" or "Washington Convention" of 1965. ICSID was established at the initiative of the International Bank for Reconstruction and Development ("IBRD" or "World Bank"), and is based at the World Bank's Washington headquarters. The ICSID Convention is designed to facilitate the settlement of "investment disputes" (*i.e.*, "legal dispute[s] arising directly out of . . . investment[s]") that the parties have agreed to submit to ICSID. Investment disputes are defined as controversies that arise out of an "investment" and are between a Contracting State or designated state entity (but not merely a private entity headquartered or based in a Contracting State) and a national of another signatory state. As to such disputes, the Convention provides both conciliation and arbitration procedures. ICSID arbitrations are governed by the ICSID Convention and the ICSID Arbitration Rules. . . . Until recently, however, relatively few cases had been brought under the Convention. ICSID's caseload has very significantly increased in the past two decades, particularly as a consequence of arbitrations brought pursuant to bilateral investment treaties ("BITs") or investment protection legislation. . . .

e. Bilateral Investment Treaties or Investment Protection Agreements

Bilateral investment treaties ("BITs") or investment protection agreements ("IPAs") became common during the 1980s and 1990s, as a means of encouraging capital investment in developing markets. Capital-exporting states (including the United States, most Western European states, and Japan) were the earliest and most vigorous proponents of the negotiation of BITs, principally with countries in developing regions. More recently, states from all regions of the world and in all stages of development have entered into BITs. A recent tally indicated that more than 2500 BITs are presently operative.

Most BITs provide significant substantive protections for investments made by foreign investors, including guarantees against expropriation and denials of fair and equitable treatment. BITs also frequently contain provisions which permit foreign investors to require international arbitration (typically referred to as "investor-State arbitration") of specified categories of investment disputes with the host state—including in the absence of a traditional contractual arbitration agreement with the host state. . . .

f. Bilateral Friendship, Commerce and Navigation Treaties

A number of nations have entered into bilateral treaties dealing principally with commercial relations and incidentally with international arbitration. These treaties generally provide for the reciprocal recognition of arbitral awards made in the territory of the Contracting States. For example, the United States includes an article relating to arbitration between private parties in many of its bilateral Friendship, Commerce and Navigation treaties. For the most part, these treaty provisions have been effectively superseded by the terms of the New York Convention and other multilateral treaties, which generally provide substantially more expansive protections. . . . .

3. Overview of Leading International Arbitration Institutions and Rules

. . . [A] central objective of contemporary international arbitration conventions and national arbitration legislation has been to give effect to commercial parties' international arbitration agreements, including agreements on arbitral procedures. A vital means by which parties exercise their autonomy in this context is through the inclusion, in their commercial contracts, of arbitration agreements incorporating institutional or *ad hoc* arbitration rules.

International arbitration can be either "institutional" or "*ad hoc.*" There are vitally important differences between these two alternatives. Institutional arbitrations are conducted pursuant to institutional arbitration rules, almost always overseen by an administrative authority with responsibility for various aspects relating to constituting the arbitral tribunal, fixing the arbitrators' compensation and similar matters. In contrast, *ad hoc* arbitrations are conducted without the benefit of an appointing and administrative authority or (generally) pre-existing arbitration rules, subject only to the parties' arbitration agreement and applicable national arbitration legislation.

a. Institutional Arbitration

A number of organizations, located in different countries, provide institutional arbitration services, often tailored to particular commercial or other needs. As indicated above, the best-known international commercial arbitration institutions are the International Chamber of Commerce ("ICC"), the American Arbitration Association ("AAA") and its International Centre for Dispute Resolution ("ICDR"), and the London Court of International Arbitration ("LCIA"). . . .

There are also a number of less widely-known regional or national arbitral institutions, as well as the International Centre for the Settlement of Investment Disputes ("ICSID"), dealing with investment disputes, and industry-specific institutions.

These (and other) arbitral institutions have promulgated sets of procedural rules that apply where parties have agreed to arbitration pursuant to such rules. Among other things, institutional rules set out the basic procedural framework and timetable for the arbitral proceedings. Institutional rules also typically authorize the arbitral institution to select arbitrators in particular disputes (that is, to serve as "appointing authority"), to resolve challenges to arbitrators, to designate the place of arbitration, to fix or influence the fees payable to the arbitrators and (sometimes) to review the arbitrators' awards to reduce the risk of unenforceability on formal grounds. Each arbitral institution has a staff (with the size varying significantly from one institution to another) and a decision-making body.

It is fundamental that arbitral institutions do not themselves arbitrate the merits of the parties' dispute. This is the responsibility of the particular individuals selected as arbitrators. Arbitrators are virtually never employees of the arbitral institution, but instead are private persons selected by the parties. If parties cannot agree upon an arbitrator, most institutional rules provide that the host institution will act as an "appointing authority," which chooses the arbitrators in the absence of the parties' agreement.

b. Ad Hoc Arbitration

Ad hoc arbitrations are not conducted under the auspices or supervision of an arbitral institution. Instead, parties simply agree to arbitrate, without designating any institution to administer their arbitration. *Ad hoc* arbitration agreements will sometimes choose an arbitrator (or arbitrators), who is (or are) to resolve the dispute without institutional supervision or assistance. The parties will sometimes also select a pre-existing set of procedural rules designed to govern *ad hoc* arbitrations. For international commercial disputes, the United Nations Commission on International Trade Law ("UNCITRAL") has published a commonly-used set of such rules, the UNCITRAL Arbitration Rules.

Where *ad hoc* arbitration is chosen, parties usually will (and certainly should) designate an appointing authority, that will select the arbitrator(s) if the parties cannot agree (or if their chosen arbitrator is unable to serve) and that will consider any subsequent challenges to members of the tribunal. If the parties fail to select an appointing authority, then the national arbitration statutes of many states permit national courts to appoint arbitrators (but this is less desirable than selection of an experienced appointing authority).

c. Relative Advantages and Disadvantages of Institutional and Ad Hoc Arbitration

Both institutional and *ad hoc* arbitration have strengths. Institutional arbitration is conducted according to a standing set of procedural rules and supervised, to a greater or lesser extent, by a professional staff. This reduces the risks of procedural breakdowns, particularly at the beginning of the arbitral process, and of technical defects in the arbitral award. The institution's involvement can be particularly constructive on issues relating to the appointment of arbitrators, the resolution of challenges to arbitrators, the selection of an arbitral seat and fixing the arbitrators' fees, where professional, specialized staff provide better service than *ad hoc* decisions by national courts with little, if any, experience or institutional resources for such matters.

Equally important, many institutional rules contain provisions that make the arbitral process more reliable and expeditious. This includes provisions concerning . . . separability, provisional measures, disclosure, arbitrator impartiality, corrections and challenges to awards, replacement of arbitrators . . . , costs and the like. Less directly, an arbitral institution lends its standing to any award that is rendered, which may enhance the likelihood of voluntary compliance and judicial enforcement.

On the other hand, *ad hoc* arbitration is typically more flexible, less expensive (since it avoids sometimes substantial institutional fees) and arguably more confidential than institutional arbitration. Moreover, the growing size and sophistication of the international arbitration bar, and the efficacy of international legislative frameworks for commercial arbitration, have partially reduced the relative advantages of institutional arbitration. Nonetheless, most experienced international practitioners fairly decisively prefer the more structured, predictable character of institutional arbitration, and the benefits of institutional rules and appointment mechanisms, at least in the absence of unusual circumstances arguing for an *ad hoc* approach. . . .

e. Leading International Arbitral Institutions

If institutional arbitration is desired, the parties must choose a particular arbitral institution and refer to it in their arbitration clause. Parties ordinarily rely on one of a few established international arbitration institutions. This avoids the confusion and uncertainty that comes from inexperienced arbitrator appointments and administrative efforts.

All leading international arbitration institutions are prepared to, and routinely do, administer arbitrations sited almost anywhere in the world, and not merely in the place where the institution itself is located. There is therefore no need to select an arbitration institution headquartered in the parties' desired arbitral seat. . . .

A number of organizations provide institutional arbitration services. Some of the best known of these organizations are described briefly below.

The services rendered by professional arbitration institutions come at a price, which is in addition to the fees and expenses of the arbitrators. Every arbitral institution has a fee schedule that specifies what that price is. The amounts charged by institutions for particular matters vary significantly, as does the basis for calculating such fees. For example, some institutions use hourly charges while others charge based upon a percentage of the amount in dispute. . . .

i. International Chamber of Commerce International Court of Arbitration

The ICC's International Court of Arbitration was established in Paris in 1923. . . . The ICC remains the world's leading international commercial arbitration institution, and has less of a national character than any other leading arbitral institution.

The ICC's annual case load was well above 300 cases per year during much of the 1990s, and it now approaches 600 cases per year. Most of these cases are international disputes, many involving very substantial sums. The ICC's caseload includes disputes between parties from around the world, with parties outside Western Europe being involved in more than 50% of all ICC cases in many recent years.

The ICC has promulgated a set of ICC Rules of Arbitration (which are periodically revised, most recently in 1998) as well as the ICC Rules of Optional Conciliation, the ICC Rules for Expertise, the ICC Dispute Board Rules and the ICC Rules for a Pre-Arbitral Referee Procedure. Under the ICC Rules, the ICC (through the International Court of Arbitration ("ICC Court")) is extensively involved in the administration of individual arbitrations. Among other things, the ICC Court and its Secretariat are responsible for . . . confirming the parties' nominations of arbitrators; appointing arbitrators if a party defaults or if the parties are unable to agree upon a presiding arbitrator or sole arbitrator; considering challenges to the arbitrators including on the basis of lack of independence; reviewing and approving so-called "Terms of Reference," which define the issues and procedures for the arbitration; reviewing a tribunal's draft award for formal and other defects; and fixing the arbitrators' compensation.

The ICC's International Court of Arbitration is not, in fact, a "court," and does not itself decide disputes or act as an arbitrator. Rather, the ICC Court is an administrative body that acts in a supervisory and appointing capacity under the ICC Rules. . . .

ii. London Court of International Arbitration

Founded in 1892, the LCIA is, by many accounts, the second most popular European institution in the field of international commercial arbitration. The LCIA's annual caseload, which is generally increasing, has exceeded 100 disputes in recent years. . . . Most LCIA arbitrations are sited in London. . . .

iii. American Arbitration Association and International Centre for Dispute Resolution

. . . The AAA is the leading U.S. arbitral institution, and reportedly handles one of the largest numbers of arbitral disputes in the world. The primary arbitration rules administered by the AAA are the AAA Commercial Arbitration Rules. These rules are used in a large majority of domestic U.S. commercial arbitrations. . . . Although there are questions about methodology, the AAA reports increases in its international case load from 453 cases filed in 1999 to more than 580 new international filings in 2005. On any measure, these statistics place the AAA among the world's most active international arbitration institutions. . . .

5. Overview of Elements of International Arbitration Agreements

As already discussed, international commercial arbitration is almost always consensual: arbitration generally occurs only pursuant to an arbitration agreement between the parties. It is, of course, possible for parties to agree to submit an existing dispute to arbitration, pursuant to a "submission agreement" or "*compromise.*" Typically, however, disputes are arbitrated as a consequence of pre-existing arbitration clauses in the parties' underlying commercial contract.

Parties are largely free to draft their arbitration agreements in whatever terms they wish and in practice this freedom is liberally exercised. Like other contractual clauses, the terms of arbitration agreements are largely a product of the parties' interests, negotiations and drafting skills.

International arbitration agreements often—and advisedly—address a number of critical issues. These are: (a) the agreement to arbitrate; (b) the scope of the disputes submitted to arbitration; (c) the use of an arbitration institution and its rules; (d) the seat of the arbitration; (e) the method of appointment, number, and qualifications of the arbitrators; (f) the language of the arbitration; and (g) a choice-of-law clause. In particular cases, other provisions may be either vital to an effective international arbitration agreement or advantageous to one or both parties. . . .

Notes and Questions

1. There were 145 parties to the New York Convention on the Recognition and Enforcement of Foreign Arbitral Awards (New York Convention), as of January 2011. It is easily the most-used convention dealing with the recognition and enforcement stage of these awards. For more information on the New York Convention, visit the Web site at http://www.uncitral.org/uncitral/en/uncitral_texts/arbitration/NYConvention.html. See also the U.N. Web site at http://untreaty.un.org.

2. As of November 2010, the ICSID Convention had 144 states that were parties to the Convention. The Centre had 123 cases pending and had concluded 206. The Centre's Web site is at http://icsid.worldbank.org.

3. The international arbitration business continues to boom at the ICC. The ICC Court received 817 new arbitration requests in 2009. During 2009, over 2,000 parties from 128 different countries were involved. Arbitrators appointed or confirmed under the ICC Rules were of 73 different nationalities, and the place of arbitration occurred in 53 countries throughout the world.

4. Business is also flourishing at the American Arbitration Association (AAA). Its cases are primarily domestic, but the AAA is expanding its international efforts, having established a new International Center for Dispute Resolution in 1996. The Center has established cooperative agreements with 62 arbitral institutions in 43 countries worldwide, maintains a worldwide panel of more than 400 independent arbitrators and mediators, and maintains several hundred multinational cases each year.

5. In 1990, the United States ratified the 1975 Inter-American Convention on International Commercial Arbitration and enacted implementing legislation. The Inter-American Convention is similar in form and substance to the New York

Convention, except that it usually provides for the use of the rules of the Inter-American Commercial Arbitration Commission. Supporters of the Inter-American Convention hoped that U.S. ratification would help promote Western Hemisphere economic cooperation because they expected more Latin American countries to accept this convention than the New York Convention. Eighteen nations had ratified the convention as of November 2010, but all were also parties to the New York Convention.

6. In recent years there has been a significant but fluctuating growth in the number of international commercial arbitrations in Asia. The globalization of Asian economies has led to more commercial arbitrations and stronger commercial dispute resolution systems. For a discussion of the recent development of Asian-based arbitration, see Simon Greenberg et al., International Commercial Arbitration: Asia-Pacific Perspectives (2010).

7. What do you see as the advantages and disadvantages of international arbitration? In what kinds of international disputes where at least one of the parties is a government or governmental entity do you think it is most advantageous? In national security issues between two countries? In boundary disputes between countries? In trade disputes between two countries? In an investment dispute between a country and a foreign private investor? Do you think the public visibility of a particular dispute or the monetary amount involved might affect the decision whether or not to arbitrate? Why, for example, do you believe that the Iran-United States Claims Tribunal has functioned in a reasonably satisfactory manner? (For details on the Iran-U.S. Tribunal, see the paragraphs below the table above just before the start of section 4.D.2.

8. Should the U.S. government or another country's government want to allow disputes between private parties arising under that country's securities or antitrust laws to be settled by arbitration? Would the policies served by those laws be more aggressively enforced by an international arbitrator or a judge in that country? What are the policies behind arbitration? How would you balance any conflicting policies?

Problem. You are the general counsel to Modern Copper, Inc. (MCI). MCI wants to invest $500 million in Chile to develop new copper mines. MCI, however, is cautious about making the investment, partly because of past expropriations of U.S. investments by Chile. As a result, MCI will take a number of actions to minimize its exposure — such as adding politically influential Chilean investors, borrowing heavily from U.S. and foreign banks, planning to locate its processing and fabricating plants in other countries, and purchasing insurance against expropriation. Nevertheless, MCI will have some of its own money tied up in the investment and is not fully protected from an expropriation.

In the negotiations between MCI and the Chilean government, Chile has refused to agree to allow disputes over the investment to be heard by U.S. courts or to have U.S. law apply. MCI does not want to rely for protection on the Chilean courts or Chilean law.

The president of MCI asks you to draft arbitration provisions that would protect MCI in case Chile tries to expropriate MCI's new copper mines. The president says she does not need the exact legal language now, but she would like to have a clear statement of the key provisions that should be included if MCI is to be adequately protected. She notes that the proposed provisions must be ones that MCI could reasonably try to get the Chilean government to accept. She also says that you should explain the rationale for the proposals.

3. Judicial Attitudes Toward International Arbitration

An article by Robert von Mehren provides a brief historical survey of judicial attitudes toward international arbitration through 1980s. Following that article is the U.S. Supreme Court's 1985 landmark opinion in Mitsubishi Motors v. Soler Chrysler-Plymouth, which provides an authoritative statement on the attitude of the U.S. judiciary toward international arbitration, a statement which is still good today.

Arthur T. Von Mehren, From *Vynior's Case* to *Mitsubishi*: The Future of Arbitration and Public Law

12 Brook. J. Int'l L. 583 (1986)

B. United States . . .

1. Judicial Attitudes Toward Arbitration: 1776-1920

From the early nineteenth century, the Supreme Court pursued a policy of enforcing arbitral awards rendered before a judicial proceeding was commenced. . . . [T]he Supreme Court assumed a position that would later shape the distinctive American statutory scheme for arbitration when it gave wide latitude not only to an arbitrator's findings of fact but also to his conclusions of law. Arbitration, the Court said, should receive judicial encouragement and courts should not set aside arbitral awards for mistakes of law or of fact, so long as the award represents the "honest decision, of the arbitrators, after a full and fair hearing of the parties" and conforms to the terms of the arbitration agreement.

The positive attitude of the Supreme Court and of the state and lower federal courts, however, did not extend to clauses in agreements that mandated arbitration for future disputes under a contract. These courts simply assumed that such clauses were revocable and non-enforceable. . . . It was left first to some state legislatures such as New York and then to the Congress to overrule the common law courts' reluctance to give full effect to executory agreements for arbitration.

The Federal Arbitration Act was passed in 1925, to enhance "the great value of voluntary arbitrations" as well as "the practical justice in the enforced arbitration of disputes where written agreements for that purpose have been voluntarily and solemnly entered into." The Act allows both a stay of court proceedings when the issue involved in such a suit should be referred to arbitration by terms of an agreement as well as specific enforcement of a written arbitration clause in maritime contracts and contracts bearing on interstate or foreign commerce. Furthermore the Act provides some gap-filling power, judicial authority to compel the attendance of witnesses and a limited set of bases for overturning an award at the enforcement stage consistent with the policy enunciated [long ago] . . . of giving "every reasonable intendment" to uphold the award. . . .

The old argument against ousting courts from their jurisdiction was briefly revived in a 1970 case involving judicial enforcement of the forum selection clause in an international contract for the towing by a German corporation of an American drilling barge from the United States to Italy.[62] [T]he Court of Appeals for the Fifth Circuit ordered the German company to stay the proceedings it had commenced in England pursuant to the forum selection clause in the towage contract and to bring all claims before the American court. The Supreme Court reversed.[65] Chief Justice Burger characterized the "ouster" argument as "hardly more than a vestigial legal fiction". . . .

> No one seriously contends in this case that the forum-selection clause "ousted" the District Court of jurisdiction over [the American company's] action. The threshold question is whether that court should have exercised its jurisdiction to do more than give effect to the legitimate expectations of the parties, manifested in their freely negotiated agreement, by specifically enforcing the forum clause.

Citing "compelling reasons why a freely negotiated private international agreement, unaffected by fraud, undue influence, or overweening bargaining power . . . should be given full effect," the Court concluded that courts should specifically enforce forum clauses.

The Court's decision in *The Bremen* came fast on the heels of the United States' ratification of the New York Convention on the Recognition and Enforcement of Foreign Arbitral Awards. In *The Bremen* the court supported judicial deference to private international agreements that choose the courts of one state over other states with equally valid claims to jurisdiction over a contractual dispute. As a result, the Court provided the foundation for a generous and unstinting construction of the Convention's requirement, under Article II-3, that the courts of contracting states, when seized of an action in a matter governed by an arbitration agreement, "at the request of one of the parties, [shall] refer the parties to arbitration, unless it finds that the said agreement is null and void, inoperative or incapable of being performed."[The Convention is in the Documentary Supplement.]

C. Other Legal Traditions

Arbitration has become a welcome method of resolving disputes in almost all the legal systems of the world. . . .

D. Trends Regarding the Domain of Arbitration

Conceived largely as forums for the resolution of disputes under private law, arbitral panels are increasingly being asked to consider claims that involve substantial issues of public law and policy. As arbitration becomes a broadly sanctioned and even favored method of dispute resolution the world over, the question of the range of legal issues that may be submitted to arbitral settlement becomes more pressing. . . .

62. Zapata Off-Shore Co. v. M/S Bremen, 428 F.2d 888 (5th Cir. 1970), *aff'd on reh'g*, 446 F.2d 907 (5th Cir. 1971), *cert. granted sub. nom.*, The Bremen v. Zapata Off-Shore Co., 407 U.S. 1 (1972).

65. *The Bremen*, 407 U.S. 1.

Issues arising under three areas of American public law—bankruptcy, securities trading, and antitrust— . . . engendered considerable litigation and debate in the context of arbitration. . . .

. . . [However, in] Mitsubishi Motors Corp. v. Soler Chrysler-Plymouth, Inc. [see below], the Supreme Court held that a party to an international agreement with a general executory arbitration clause may not seek the aid of the federal courts for relief in a claim under the antitrust laws but must submit the claims to an arbitral tribunal. . . .

Mitsubishi Motors Corp. v. Soler Chrysler-Plymouth

U.S. Supreme Court
473 U.S. 614 (1985)

BLACKMUN, J., delivered the opinion of the Court, in which BURGER, C.J., and WHITE, REHNQUIST, and O'CONNOR, J.J., joined. STEVENS, J., filed a dissenting opinion, in which BRENNAN, J., joined, and in which MARSHALL, J., joined except as to Part II. POWELL, J., took no part in the decision of the cases.

Justice BLACKMUN delivered the opinion of the Court.

The principal question presented by these cases is the arbitrability, pursuant to the Federal Arbitration Act, 9 U.S.C. §1 et seq., and the [New York] Convention on the Recognition and Enforcement of Foreign Arbitral Awards (Convention), of claims arising under the Sherman Act, 15 U.S.C. §1 et seq., and encompassed within a valid arbitration clause in an agreement embodying an international commercial transaction.

I

Petitioner-cross-respondent Mitsubishi Motors Corporation (Mitsubishi) is a Japanese corporation which manufactures automobiles and has its principal place of business in Tokyo, Japan. Mitsubishi is the product of a joint venture between, on the one hand, Chrysler International, S.A. (CISA), a Swiss corporation . . . wholly owned by Chrysler Corporation, and, on the other, Mitsubishi Heavy Industries, Inc., a Japanese corporation. The aim of the joint venture was the distribution through Chrysler dealers outside the continental United States of vehicles manufactured by Mitsubishi and bearing Chrysler and Mitsubishi trademarks. Respondent-cross-petitioner Soler Chrysler-Plymouth, Inc. (Soler), is a Puerto Rico corporation with its principal place of business in . . . Puerto Rico.

On October 31, 1979, Soler entered into a Distributor Agreement with CISA which provided for the sale by Soler of Mitsubishi-manufactured vehicles within a designated area, including metropolitan San Juan. On the same date, CISA, Soler, and Mitsubishi entered into a Sales Procedure Agreement (Sales Agreement) which . . . provided for the direct sale of Mitsubishi products to Soler and governed the terms and conditions of such sales. Paragraph VI of the Sales Agreement, labeled "Arbitration of Certain Matters," provides:

> All disputes, controversies or differences which may arise between [Mitsubishi] and [Soler] out of or in relation to Articles I-B through V of this Agreement or for the

breach thereof, shall be finally settled by arbitration in Japan in accordance with the rules and regulations of the Japan Commercial Arbitration Association.

Initially, Soler did a brisk business in Mitsubishi-manufactured vehicles. . . . In early 1981, however, the new-car market slackened. Soler ran into serious difficulties in meeting the expected sales volume, and by the spring of 1981 it felt itself compelled to request that Mitsubishi delay or cancel shipment of several orders. About the same time, Soler attempted to arrange for the transshipment of a quantity of its vehicles for sale in the continental United States and Latin America. Mitsubishi and CISA, however, refused permission for any such diversion, citing a variety of reasons, and no vehicles were transshipped. Attempts to work out these difficulties failed. Mitsubishi eventually withheld shipment of 966 vehicles, apparently representing orders placed for May, June, and July 1981 production, responsibility for which Soler disclaimed in February 1982.

The following month, Mitsubishi brought an action against Soler in the United States District Court for the District of Puerto Rico under the Federal Arbitration Act and the Convention.[2] Mitsubishi sought an order, pursuant to 9 U.S.C. §§4 and 201,[3] to compel arbitration in accord with ¶VI of the Sales Agreement. Shortly after filing the complaint, Mitsubishi filed a request for arbitration before the Japan Commercial Arbitration Association.

Soler denied the allegations and counterclaimed against both Mitsubishi and CISA. It alleged numerous breaches by Mitsubishi of the Sales Agreement,[5] . . . and asserted causes of action under the Sherman Act. In the counterclaim premised on the Sherman Act, Soler alleged that Mitsubishi and CISA had conspired to divide markets in restraint of trade. To effectuate the plan, according to Soler, Mitsubishi had refused to permit Soler to resell to buyers in North, Central, or South America vehicles it had obligated itself to purchase from Mitsubishi; had refused to ship ordered vehicles or the parts, such as heaters and defoggers, that would be necessary to permit Soler to make its vehicles suitable for resale outside Puerto Rico; [etc.]. . . .

2. The complaint alleged that Soler had failed to pay for 966 ordered vehicles; that it had failed to pay contractual "distress unit penalties," intended to reimburse Mitsubishi for storage costs and interest charges incurred because of Soler's failure to take shipment of ordered vehicles; that Soler's failure to fulfill warranty obligations threatened Mitsubishi's reputation and goodwill; . . . and that the Distributor and Sales Agreements had expired by their terms or, alternatively, that Soler had surrendered its rights under the Sales Agreement.

3. . . . Section 201 provides: "The Convention on the Recognition and Enforcement of Foreign Arbitral Awards of June 10, 1958, shall be enforced in United States courts in accordance with this chapter." Article II of the Convention, in turn, provides:

> 1. Each Contracting State shall recognize an agreement in writing under which the parties undertake to submit to arbitration all or any differences which have arisen or which may arise between them in respect of a defined legal relationship, whether contractual or not, concerning a subject matter capable of settlement by arbitration. . . .
>
> 3. The court of a Contracting State, when seized of an action in a matter in respect of which the parties have made an agreement within the meaning of this article, shall, at the request of one of the parties, refer the parties to arbitration, unless it finds that the said agreement is null and void, inoperative or incapable of being performed.

5. The alleged breaches included wrongful refusal to ship ordered vehicles and necessary parts, failure to make payment for warranty work and authorized rebates, and bad faith in establishing minimum sales volumes.

After a hearing, the District Court ordered Mitsubishi and Soler to arbitrate . . . the federal antitrust issues[. I]t recognized that the Courts of Appeals, following American Safety Equipment Corp. v. J.P. Maguire & Co., 391 F.2d 821 (CA2 1968), uniformly had held that the rights conferred by the antitrust laws were " 'of a character inappropriate for enforcement by arbitration.' " The District Court held, however, that the international character of the Mitsubishi-Soler undertaking required enforcement of the agreement to arbitrate even as to the antitrust claims. It relied on Scherk v. Alberto-Culver Co., 417 U.S. 506, 515-520 (1974), in which this Court ordered arbitration, pursuant to a provision embodied in an international agreement, of a claim arising under the Securities Exchange Act of 1934. . . .

The United States Court of Appeals for the First Circuit affirmed in part and reversed in part. . . .

. . . [A]fter endorsing the doctrine of *American Safety*, precluding arbitration of antitrust claims, the Court of Appeals concluded that neither this Court's decision in *Scherk* nor the Convention required abandonment of that doctrine in the face of an international transaction. Accordingly, it reversed the judgment of the District Court insofar as it had ordered submission of "Soler's antitrust claims" to arbitration. . . .

We granted certiorari primarily to consider whether an American court should enforce an agreement to resolve antitrust claims by arbitration when that agreement arises from an international transaction.

II. . . .

. . . By agreeing to arbitrate a statutory claim, a party does not forgo the substantive rights afforded by the statute; it only submits to their resolution in an arbitral, rather than a judicial, forum. It trades the procedures and opportunity for review of the courtroom for the simplicity, informality, and expedition of arbitration. . . . Having made the bargain to arbitrate, the party should be held to it unless Congress itself has evinced an intention to preclude a waiver of judicial remedies for the statutory rights at issue. Nothing, in the meantime, prevents a party from excluding statutory claims from the scope of an agreement to arbitrate.

. . . [T]he Court of Appeals correctly conducted a two-step inquiry, first determining whether the parties' agreement to arbitrate reached the statutory issues, and then, upon finding it did, considering whether legal constraints external to the parties' agreement foreclosed the arbitration of those claims.

III

We now turn to consider whether Soler's antitrust claims are nonarbitrable even though it has agreed to arbitrate them. . . . As in Scherk v. Alberto-Culver Co., 417 U.S. 506 (1974), we conclude that concerns of international comity, respect for the capacities of foreign and transnational tribunals, and sensitivity to the need of the international commercial system for predictability in the resolution of disputes require that we enforce the parties' agreement, even assuming that a contrary result would be forthcoming in a domestic context.

Even before *Scherk*, this Court had recognized the utility of forum-selection clauses in international transactions. In [The Bremen v. Zapata Off-Shore Co.,

407 U.S. 1 (1972)], an American oil company, seeking to evade a contractual choice of an English forum and, by implication, English law, filed a suit in admiralty in a United States District Court against the German corporation which had contracted to tow its rig [from the United States] to a location in the Adriatic Sea. Notwithstanding the possibility that the English court would enforce provisions in the towage contract exculpating the German party which an American court would refuse to enforce, this Court gave effect to the choice-of-forum clause. It observed:

> The expansion of American business and industry will hardly be encouraged if, notwithstanding solemn contracts, we insist on a parochial concept that all disputes must be resolved under our laws and in our courts. . . . We cannot have trade and commerce in world markets and international waters exclusively on our terms, governed by our laws, and resolved in our courts. 407 U.S., at 9.

Recognizing that "agreeing in advance on a forum acceptable to both parties is an indispensable element in international trade, commerce, and contracting," the decision in *The Bremen* clearly eschewed a provincial solicitude for the jurisdiction of domestic forums.

Identical considerations governed the Court's decision in *Scherk*, which categorized "[a]n agreement to arbitrate before a specified tribunal [as], in effect, a specialized kind of forum-selection clause that posits not only the situs of suit but also the procedure to be used in resolving the dispute.". . . . This Court [enforced] the arbitration agreement even while assuming for purposes of the decision that the controversy [involving alleged fraud under Section 10(b) of the 1934 Securities Exchange Act] would be nonarbitrable . . . had it arisen out of a domestic transaction. Again, the Court emphasized:

> A contractual provision specifying in advance the forum in which disputes shall be litigated and the law to be applied is . . . an almost indispensable precondition to achievement of the orderliness and predictability, essential to any international business transaction. . . .
>
> A parochial refusal by the courts of one country to enforce an international arbitration agreement would not only frustrate these purposes, but would invite unseemly and mutually destructive jockeying by the parties to secure tactical litigation advantages. . . . [It would] damage the fabric of international commerce and trade, and imperil the willingness and ability of businessmen to enter into international commercial agreements. . . .

The Bremen and *Scherk* establish a strong presumption in favor of enforcement of freely negotiated contractual choice-of-forum provisions. Here, as in *Scherk*, that presumption is reinforced by the emphatic federal policy in favor of arbitral dispute resolution. And at least since this Nation's accession in 1970 to the Convention,* and the implementation of the Convention in the same year by amendment of the Federal Arbitration Act,[16] that federal policy applies with special force in the field of

*[New York Convention on the Recognition and Enforcement of Foreign Arbitral Awards. See the Documentary Supplement—Eds.]

16. Act of July 31, 1970, Pub. I, 91-368, 84 Stat. 692, codified at 9 U.S.C. §§201-208.

international commerce. Thus, we must weigh the concerns of *American Safety* against a strong belief in the efficacy of arbitral procedures for the resolution of international commercial disputes and an equal commitment to the enforcement of freely negotiated choice-of-forum clauses.

At the outset, we confess to some skepticism of certain aspects of the *American Safety* doctrine. . . .

. . . The mere appearance of an antitrust dispute does not alone warrant invalidation of the selected forum on the undemonstrated assumption that the arbitration clause is tainted. A party resisting arbitration of course may attack directly the validity of the agreement to arbitrate. Moreover, the party may attempt to make a showing that would warrant setting aside the forum-selection clause — that the agreement was "[a]ffected by fraud, undue influence, or overweening bargaining power"; that "enforcement would be unreasonable and unjust"; or that proceedings "in the contractual forum will be so gravely difficult and inconvenient that [the resisting party] will for all practical purposes be deprived of his day in court." But absent such a showing — and none was attempted here — there is no basis for assuming the forum inadequate or its selection unfair.

Next, potential complexity should not suffice to ward off arbitration. . . . [A]daptability and access to expertise are hallmarks of arbitration. The anticipated subject matter of the dispute may be taken into account when the arbitrators are appointed, and arbitral rules typically provide for the participation of experts either employed by the parties or appointed by the tribunal. Moreover, it is often a judgment that streamlined proceedings and expeditious results will best serve their needs that causes parties to agree to arbitrate their disputes. . . .

For similar reasons, we also reject the proposition that an arbitration panel will pose too great a danger of innate hostility to the constraints on business conduct that antitrust law imposes. International arbitrators frequently are drawn from the legal as well as the business community; where the dispute has an important legal component, the parties and the arbitral body with whose assistance they have agreed to settle their dispute can be expected to select arbitrators accordingly.[18] . . .

We are left, then, with the core of the *American Safety* doctrine — the fundamental importance to American democratic capitalism of the regime of the antitrust laws. Without doubt, the private cause of action plays a central role in enforcing this regime. . . .

The importance of the private damages remedy, however, does not compel the conclusion that it may not be sought outside an American court. . . .

There is no reason to assume at the outset of the dispute that international arbitration will not provide an adequate mechanism. To be sure, the international arbitral tribunal owes no prior allegiance to the legal norms of particular states; hence, it has no direct obligation to vindicate their statutory dictates. The tribunal, however, is bound to effectuate the intentions of the parties. Where the parties have agreed that the arbitral body is to decide a defined set of claims which includes, as in these cases, those arising from the application of American antitrust law, the

18. We are advised by Mitsubishi and *amicus* International Chamber of Commerce, without contradiction by Soler, that the arbitration panel selected to hear the parties' claims here is composed of three Japanese lawyers, one a former law school dean, another a former judge, and the third a practicing attorney with American legal training who has written on Japanese antitrust law.

tribunal therefore should be bound to decide that dispute in accord with the national law giving rise to the claim. . . .[19] And so long as the prospective litigant effectively may vindicate its statutory cause of action in the arbitral forum, the statute will continue to serve both its remedial and deterrent function.

Having permitted the arbitration to go forward, the national courts of the United States will have the opportunity at the award-enforcement stage to ensure that the legitimate interest in the enforcement of the antitrust laws has been addressed. The Convention reserves to each signatory country the right to refuse enforcement of an award where the "recognition or enforcement of the award would be contrary to the public policy of that country." Art. V(2) (b). . . . While the efficacy of the arbitral process requires that substantive review at the award-enforcement stage remain minimal, it would not require intrusive inquiry to ascertain that the tribunal took cognizance of the antitrust claims and actually decided them.

As international trade has expanded in recent decades, so too has the use of international arbitration to resolve disputes arising in the course of that trade. The controversies that international arbitral institutions are called upon to resolve have increased in diversity as well as in complexity. Yet the potential of these tribunals for efficient disposition of legal disagreements arising from commercial relations has not yet been tested. If they are to take a central place in the international legal order, national courts will need to "shake off the old judicial hostility to arbitration," and also their customary and understandable unwillingness to cede jurisdiction of a claim arising under domestic law to a foreign or transnational tribunal. To this extent, at least, it will be necessary for national courts to subordinate domestic notions of arbitrability to the international policy favoring commercial arbitration.

Accordingly, we "require this representative of the American business community to honor its bargain," Alberto-Culver Co. v. Scherk, 484 F.2d 611, 620 (CA7 1973) (Stevens, J., dissenting), by holding this agreement to arbitrate "enforce [able] . . . in accord with the explicit provisions of the Arbitration Act." *Scherk*, 417 U.S., at 520.

It is so ordered. . . .

Justice Stevens, with whom Justice Brennan joins, and with whom Justice Marshall joins except as to Part II, dissenting.

19. In addition to the clause providing for arbitration before the Japan Commercial Arbitration Association, the Sales Agreement includes a choice-of-law clause which reads: "This Agreement is made in, and will be governed by and construed in all respects according to the laws of the Swiss Confederation as if entirely performed therein." The United States raises the possibility that the arbitral panel will read this provision not simply to govern interpretation of the contract terms, but wholly to displace American law even where *it* otherwise would apply. Brief for United States as *Amicus Curiae* 20. At oral argument, however, counsel for Mitsubishi conceded that American law applied to the antitrust claims and represented that the claims had been submitted to the arbitration panel in Japan on that basis. The record confirms that before the decision of the Court of Appeals the arbitral panel had taken these claims under submission.

We therefore have no occasion to speculate on this matter at this stage in the proceedings, when Mitsubishi seeks to enforce the agreement to arbitrate, not to enforce an award. Nor need we consider now the effect of an arbitral tribunal's failure to take cognizance of the statutory cause of action on the claimant's capacity to reinitiate suit in federal court. We merely note that in the event the choice-of-forum and choice-of-law clauses operated in tandem as a prospective waiver of a party's right to pursue statutory remedies for antitrust violations, we would have little hesitation in condemning the agreement as against public policy.

One element of this rather complex litigation is a claim asserted by an American dealer in Plymouth automobiles that two major automobile companies are parties to an international cartel that has restrained competition in the American market. Pursuant to an agreement that is alleged to have violated §1 of the Sherman Act, 15 U.S.C. §1, those companies allegedly prevented the dealer from transshipping some 966 surplus vehicles from Puerto Rico to other dealers in the American market.

The petitioner denies the truth of the dealer's allegations and takes the position that the validity of the antitrust claim must be resolved by an arbitration tribunal in Tokyo, Japan. This Court's holding rests almost exclusively on the federal policy favoring arbitration of commercial disputes and vague notions of international comity arising from the fact that the automobiles involved here were manufactured in Japan. . . . I respectfully dissent. In my opinion, (1) a fair construction of the language in the arbitration clause in the parties' contract does not encompass a claim that auto manufacturers entered into a conspiracy in violation of the antitrust laws; (2) an arbitration clause should not normally be construed to cover a statutory remedy that it does not expressly identify; (3) Congress did not intend §2 of the Federal Arbitration Act to apply to antitrust claims; and (4) Congress did not intend the [New York] Convention on the Recognition and Enforcement of Foreign Arbitral Awards to apply to disputes that are not covered by the Federal Arbitration Act. . . .

II. . . .

Nothing in the text of the 1925 Act, nor its legislative history, suggests that Congress intended to authorize the arbitration of any statutory claims.

Until today all of our cases enforcing agreements to arbitrate under the Arbitration Act have involved contract claims. . . . But this is the first time the Court has considered the question whether a standard arbitration clause referring to claims arising out of or relating to a contract should be construed to cover statutory claims that have only an indirect relationship to the contract. . . .

III

The Court has repeatedly held that a decision by Congress to create a special statutory remedy renders a private agreement to arbitrate a federal statutory claim unenforceable. The special interest in encouraging private enforcement of the Sherman Act has been reflected in the statutory scheme ever since 1890. . . .

International Comity

It is clear then that the international obligations of the United States permit us to honor Congress' commitment to the exclusive resolution of antitrust disputes in the federal courts. The Court today refuses to do so, offering only vague concerns for comity among nations. The courts of other nations, on the other hand, have applied the exception provided in the Convention, and refused to enforce agreements to arbitrate specific subject matters of concern to them.[35]

Notes and Questions

1. Why might U.S. federal judges see international arbitration as a method of formal dispute resolution that deserves their support? As a threat to them?

2. Do you think that the arbitration in Japan will fully consider Soler's antitrust complaint? How will the arbitrators know about U.S. antitrust law? (See footnote 18 of the opinion.)

3. What substantive law did the agreement to arbitrate provide for? (See footnote 19 of the opinion.) Would the arbitrators consider Soler's U.S. antitrust complaint? What did the majority of the Supreme Court say about that in the footnote? Suppose that the contract included a provision that "general principles of international commercial law" would apply. Would the arbitrators consider Soler's U.S. antitrust law complaint?

4. What did the majority opinion describe as the U.S. policy in favor of enforcement of freely negotiated contractual choice-of-forum provisions and arbitration in particular? Is there any special policy toward international arbitration? Does the Court suggest that as long as an agreement to international arbitration is valid and Congress has not forbidden it, any claim may be arbitrated. Is this a good policy? If not, what should be the limits on the parties' ability to agree to arbitrate?

5. The majority opinion seems to rely partly on the ability of the courts to review arbitral awards at the enforcement stage. The majority notes, though, that "substantive review at the award-enforcement stage remain minimal." As discussed in the next section, some review is permitted when recognizing and enforcing a foreign arbitral award. Many of the awards, however, are often made without an extensive opinion by the arbitrator(s). How can legitimate public policy concerns be safeguarded at the enforcement stage if the court does not know the arbitrator's considerations or reasoning? For example, suppose the arbitrator issued a one-line decision denying Soler's claims. Could Soler then pursue an antitrust claim in U.S. courts? If the decision included an award of $500,000 in favor of Mitsubishi, would Soler have any defense? (The next section should shed some light on the questions in this Note.)

6. Arguably the presumption in favor of arbitration noted in *Mitsubishi* was further strengthened by the Supreme Court in Carnival Cruise Lines v. Shute, 499 U.S. 585 (1991). The Court there upheld a forum-selection clause contained in small print on a ticket that a Washington State couple (the Shutes) received after purchasing passage on a ship owned by a Florida-based cruise line. The clause designated Florida courts as the agreed-upon forum for the resolution of disputes.

35. For example, the Cour de Cassation in Belgium has held that disputes arising under a Belgian statute limiting the unilateral termination of exclusive distributorships are not arbitrable under the Convention in that country, Audi-NSU Auto Union A.G. v. S.A. Adelin Petit & Cie. (1979), in 5 Yearbook Commercial Arbitration 257, 259 (1980), and the Corte di Cassazione in Italy has held that labor disputes are not arbitrable under the Convention in that country, Compagnia Generale Construzioni v. Piersanti, [1980] Foro Italiano I 190, in 6 Yearbook Commercial Arbitration 229, 230 (1981).

Mrs. Shute was injured when she slipped on a deck mat while the ship was in international waters off the Mexican coast. The Shutes filed suit in a U.S. district court in the state of Washington. The Supreme Court held that the U.S. Court of Appeals for the Ninth Circuit erred in not enforcing the forum-selection clause.

Since *Mitsubishi,* the U.S. Supreme Court has reaffirmed its support for enforcing agreements to arbitrate, both international and domestic. For example in Vaden v. Discover Bank 129 S.Ct. 1262, 1274-75 (2009), the Court affirmed *Mitsubishi* and said that agreements to arbitrate were valid, irrevocable and enforceable just as any other contract.

4. *Enforcement of International Arbitral Awards*

a. In General

What happens when a tribunal has issued an award? How can the winning party collect on its award? In his treatise, Gary Born describes some of the most important considerations regarding the enforcement of international arbitral awards.

Gary Born, International Commercial Arbitration

2327-31, 2333-34, 2346 (2009)

The final steps in the arbitration proceedings involve the arbitral award. Once a final arbitral award is made, the tribunal's original mandate is substantially concluded. The tribunal becomes *functus officio* and its remaining responsibilities (and powers) are highly circumscribed. Thereafter, compliance with, and enforcement of, the award becomes a matter for the parties and national courts.

Arbitral awards are not "advisory" instruments. In most cases, parties voluntarily comply with international arbitral awards: empirical studies and anecdotal evidence indicates that the percentage of voluntary compliance with arbitral awards exceeds 90% of international cases. This reflects the parties' contractual undertakings to arbitrate and to comply with the resulting arbitral award, the efficacy of the arbitral process (which leaves parties believing that their dispute has been fairly resolved) and the likelihood that the award can be coercively enforced. Moreover, in particular contexts, there are specific commercial or related pressures for parties to comply with arbitral awards, such as with ICSID awards (issued under World Bank auspices) or awards under the arbitration rules of various trade associations.

Nevertheless, not all international arbitral awards are voluntarily complied with. The ultimate test of any arbitration is therefore its ability to render an award which, if necessary, will be recognized and enforced in relevant national courts — including, if necessary, through coercive mechanisms of execution, attachment and garnishment. If an award cannot be successfully enforced, then the parties' arbitration agreement and investment in the arbitral proceedings will have been for naught and the entire process will be questioned. Fortunately, in most cases, the recognition and enforcement of arbitral awards is straightforward and speedy.

At the same time, like other legal proceedings, arbitrations may be imperfect and can leave one party feeling aggrieved. A party in this position may wish to take steps to have the arbitral award corrected or, alternatively, judicially reviewed and set aside—just as a party that has lost in first instance litigation proceedings may seek appellate review. In contrast to the relative ease and efficiency of recognizing and enforcing foreign arbitral awards, efforts to set aside or annul an international arbitral award frequently face substantial obstacles and succeed only in rare cases.

After an international arbitral award is made, international arbitration conventions and national arbitration statutes provide five basic legal avenues which may be taken with respect to the award in the national courts in the arbitral seat. These five avenues can be taken independently or, on occasion, pursued in parallel, sometimes with different parties initiating different proceedings.

First, a party to the arbitration may seek a "correction" or "interpretation" of the arbitral award by the tribunal. The circumstances in which such relief is available are very limited (and constitute one of the narrow exceptions to the general principle that an arbitral tribunal becomes *functus officio* after making its final award). If an award is corrected or interpreted, the correction or interpretation becomes a part of the tribunal's final award, then subject to further actions in national courts, as detailed below. Second, the prevailing party in the arbitration may commence proceedings in the national courts of the arbitral seat to "confirm" or "recognize" the award (*e.g.*, to obtain *exequatur*). The successful confirmation of the award will usually provide the basis for the entry of a judgment of the local national court based upon the underlying award. The confirmation of an award in the arbitral seat may occasionally be a defensive act (for example, to comply with local law requirements providing that awards can only be confirmed within a certain period after they are made); much more frequently, confirmation is a step towards further actions, and specifically, towards "enforcement" of the relief granted in the award (for example, execution against the award-debtor's assets). In most jurisdictions, procedures for the confirmation of awards made locally are summary in nature and expedited in timing.

After confirmation of an award in the arbitral seat, the resulting judgment can typically either be "enforced" in local courts (typically in the same manner as a domestic court judgment) or it can be taken to another state for "recognition" and enforcement in accordance with that state's legislation for recognizing and enforcing foreign judgments. As this description indicates, and notwithstanding occasional imprecisions in terminology, "recognition" refers to judicial acceptance or confirmation of an arbitral award (or foreign court judgment) and the entry of a local court judgment accepting or confirming the operative terms of the foreign award, while "enforcement" refers to the subsequent reliance of local national courts on this judgment for execution, attachment, garnishment and similar remedies under local law.

Third, an award can be taken to a state outside the arbitral seat, to be "recognized" (and then enforced) in the courts of that state, without first being confirmed or recognized in the arbitral seat. Recognition of a foreign arbitral award occurs in the form of a local national court judgment, which gives the award full legal force within the local legal system (in the same manner that a foreign judgment is recognized).

. . . [O]ne of the fundamental reforms of the New York and European Conventions was to remove the requirement of "double *exequatur*," which had required an award to be confirmed in the arbitral seat before it could be recognized or enforced abroad. Under the New York and European Conventions, an award is capable of recognition outside the arbitral seat even if it has not been recognized or confirmed in the arbitral seat. Indeed, as discussed below, there will be circumstances in which an arbitral award may (and will) be recognized abroad even if it has been set aside in the arbitral seat.

Once the award is recognized in a foreign state, the resulting judgment can then ordinarily be given effect in the local courts of that State in the same manner as a judgment of that state's courts. This includes coercively "enforcing" the award/judgment against the assets of the award/judgment-debtor, in accordance with local legislation governing the execution and enforcement of judgments. It also includes giving the award/judgment preclusive effect in the courts of the foreign state (presumptively in accordance with local legislation regarding the preclusive effects of foreign awards and/or judgments).

Fourth, the unsuccessful party in the arbitration may commence proceedings, in the national courts of the arbitral seat, to "set aside," "vacate," or "annul" the award. If successful, such an action generally has the legal effect of nullifying the award within the domestic legal regime of the arbitral seat, in much the way that an appellate decision vacates a trial court judgment. After an award is annulled, it cannot be enforced locally in the courts of the arbitral seat.

Nonetheless, despite the annulment of an arbitral award, the better view is that the award still exists — both as a matter of fact and (potentially) as a matter of law in other legal systems outside the arbitral seat. It remains open in principle to the successful party in the arbitration to attempt to have the award recognized and enforced, notwithstanding its annulment in the arbitral seat, in courts outside the arbitral seat. Equally, it remains open in principle to the successful party in the arbitration to rely on the award for preclusive effects in foreign court proceedings, irrespective of the award's annulment in the arbitral seat. In both instances, the annulment of the award in the arbitral seat, and the reasons for that annulment, may be relied upon to resist recognition and enforcement of the award, but the annulment is not necessarily independently sufficient to preclude recognition of the award in other states.

Finally, in some instances, it is not possible for an arbitral award to be recognized or enforced as an award. This can result from a failure timely to confirm it in the arbitral seat or to recognize it elsewhere, from formal defects, or from valid substantive grounds for resisting confirmation or recognition of the award. Even in such cases, the award may nonetheless continue to have limited legal effect under national law. For example, under local law, the award may be the basis for a contract action under national law, or may be admissible as evidence in an action on the merits of the parties' underlying dispute. . . .

Chapter 21. Legal Framework for International Arbitral Awards. . . .

A. Introduction

The legal effects of international arbitral awards are subject to a complex legal framework of both international and national sources. On the international level, . . . the New York Convention and other international conventions address various substantive and forum selection aspects of the annulment, recognition and enforcement of international arbitral awards. On the national level, . . . contemporary arbitration statutes provide procedural mechanisms and substantive criteria for making, annulling, correcting, confirming, recognizing and enforcing international arbitral awards. The overall effect of these national and international instruments is to establish a strongly "pro-enforcement" legal regime for the recognition and enforcement of those international arbitral awards to which these instruments apply. These provisions broadly parallel the similar pro-arbitration provisions of national and international legal regimes with regard to international arbitration agreements and international arbitral proceedings. . . .

B. Applicability of International Arbitration Conventions and National Arbitration Legislation to International Arbitral Awards

Critical to the legal effects, annulment, recognition and enforcement of an international arbitral award is determining what (if any) international arbitration convention and what national arbitration legislation is applicable to the award. . . .

---

b. Under the New York Convention

Most of the cases involving enforcement of an arbitral award arise under the New York Convention on the Recognition and Enforcement of Foreign Arbitral Awards. Let us look more closely at Articles I and V of that convention. (Additional excerpts from the Convention are in the Documentary Supplement.)

New York Convention

Article I

1. This Convention shall apply to the recognition and enforcement of arbitral awards made in the territory of a State other than the State where the recognition and enforcement of such awards are sought, and arising out of differences between persons, whether physical or legal. It shall also apply to arbitral awards not considered as domestic awards in the State where their recognition and enforcement are sought. . . .

3. When signing, ratifying or acceding to this Convention, or notifying extension under article X hereof, any State may on the basis of reciprocity declare that it will apply the Convention to the recognition and enforcement of awards made only in the territory of another Contracting State. It may also declare that it will apply the Convention only to differences arising out of legal relationships, whether contractual or not, which are considered as commercial under the national law of the State making such declaration.

Article V

1. Recognition and enforcement of the award may be refused, at the request of the party against whom it is invoked, only if that party furnishes to the competent authority where the recognition and enforcement is sought, proof that:

(a) The parties to the agreement referred to in article II were, under the law applicable to them, under some incapacity, or the said agreement is not valid under the law to which the parties have subjected it or, failing any indication thereon, under the law of the country where the award was made; or

(b) The party against whom the award is invoked was not given proper notice of the appointment of the arbitrator or of the arbitration proceedings or was otherwise unable to present his case; or

(c) The award deals with a difference not contemplated by or not falling within the terms of the submission to arbitration, or it contains decisions on matters beyond the scope of the submission to arbitration, provided that, if the decisions on matters submitted to arbitration can be separated from those not so submitted, that part of the award which contains decisions on matters submitted to arbitration may be recognized and enforced; or

(d) The composition of the arbitral authority or the arbitral procedure was not in accordance with the agreement of the parties, or, failing such agreement, was not in accordance with the law of the country where the arbitration took place; or

(e) The award has not yet become binding on the parties, or has been set aside or suspended by a competent authority of the country in which, or under the law of which, that award was made.

2. Recognition and enforcement of an arbitral award may also be refused if the competent authority in the country where recognition and enforcement is sought finds that:

(a) The subject matter of the difference is not capable of settlement by arbitration under the law of that country; or

(b) The recognition or enforcement of the award would be contrary to the public policy of that country.

The leading U.S. case on the enforcement of international arbitral awards under the New York Convention is the *Parsons & Whittemore* opinion of the U.S. Court of Appeals for the Second Circuit.

Parsons & Whittemore Overseas Co. v. Societe Generale de L'Industrie du Papier (RAKTA)

U.S. Court of Appeals
508 F.2d 969 (2d Cir. 1974)

SMITH, Circuit Judge:

Parsons & Whittemore Overseas Co., Inc., (Overseas), an American corporation, appeals from the entry of summary judgment [in 1974 by a U.S. federal district court judge] on the counterclaim by Societe Generate de L'lndustrie du Papier (RAKTA), an Egyptian corporation, to confirm a foreign arbitral award holding Overseas liable to RAKTA for breach of contract. . . . Jurisdiction is based on

9 U.S.C. §203, which empowers federal district courts to hear cases to recognize and enforce foreign arbitral awards, and 9 U.S.C. §205, which authorizes the removal of such cases from state courts, as was accomplished in this instance. We affirm the district court's confirmation of the foreign award. . . .

In November 1962, Overseas consented by written agreement with RAKTA to construct, start up and, for one year, manage and supervise a paperboard mill in Alexandria, Egypt. The Agency for International Development (AID), a branch of the United States State Department, would finance the project by supplying RAKTA with funds . . . Among the contract's terms was an arbitration clause, which provided a means to settle differences arising in the course of performance, and a "force majeure" clause, which excused delay in performance due to causes beyond Overseas' reasonable capacity to control.

Work proceeded as planned until May, 1967. Then, with the Arab-Israeli Six Day War on the horizon, recurrent expressions of Egyptian hostility to Americans—nationals of the principal ally of the Israeli enemy—caused the majority of the Overseas work crew to leave Egypt. On June 6, the Egyptian government broke diplomatic ties with the United States and ordered all Americans expelled from Egypt except those who would apply and qualify for a special visa.

Having abandoned the project for the present with the construction phase near completion, Overseas notified RAKTA that it regarded this postponement as excused by the force majeure clause. RAKTA disagreed and sought damages for breach of contract. Overseas refused to settle and RAKTA, already at work on completing the performance promised by Overseas, invoked the arbitration clause. Overseas responded by calling into play the clause's option to bring a dispute directly to a three-man arbitral board governed by the rules of the International Chamber of Commerce. After several sessions in 1970, the tribunal issued a preliminary award, which recognized Overseas' force majeure defense as good only during the period from May 28 to June 30, 1967. In so limiting Overseas' defense, the arbitration court emphasized that Overseas had made no more than a perfunctory effort to secure special visas and that AID's notification that it was withdrawing financial backing did not justify Overseas' unilateral decision to abandon the project.[3] After further hearings in 1972, the tribunal made its final award in March, 1973: Overseas was held liable to RAKTA for $312,507.45 in damages for breach of contract and $30,000 for RAKTA's costs; additionally, the arbitrators' compensation was set at $49,000, with Overseas responsible for three-fourths of the sum.

Subsequent to the final award, Overseas in the action here under review sought a declaratory judgment to prevent RAKTA from collecting the award out of a letter of credit issued in RAKTA's favor by Bank of America at Overseas' request. . . . RAKTA . . . counterclaimed to confirm and enter judgment upon the foreign arbitral award. Overseas' defenses to this counterclaim, all rejected by the district court, form the principal issues for review on this appeal. Four of these defenses are derived from the express language of the applicable . . . Convention on the Recognition and Enforcement of Foreign Arbitral Awards (Convention), and a fifth is arguably implicit in the Convention. These include: enforcement of the

3. RAKTA represented to the tribunal that it was prepared to finance the project without AID's assistance.

award would violate the public policy of the United States, the award represents an arbitration of matters not appropriately decided by arbitration; the tribunal denied Overseas an adequate opportunity to present its case; the award is predicated upon a resolution of issues outside the scope of the contractual agreement to submit to arbitration; and the award is in manifest disregard of law. . . .

I. Overseas' Defenses Against Enforcement

In 1958 the Convention was adopted by 26 of the 45 states participating in the United Nations Conference on Commercial Arbitration held in New York. For the signatory states, the New York Convention superseded the Geneva Convention of 1927. . . . The 1958 Convention's basic thrust was to liberalize procedures for enforcing foreign arbitral awards: While the Geneva Convention placed the burden of proof on the party seeking enforcement of a foreign arbitral award and did not circumscribe the range of available defenses to those enumerated in the convention, the 1958 Convention clearly shifted the burden of proof to the party defending against enforcement and limited his defenses to seven set forth in Article V. Not a signatory to any prior multilateral agreement on enforcement of arbitral awards, the United States declined to sign the 1958 Convention at the outset. The United States ultimately acceded to the Convention, however, in 1970, and implemented its accession with 9 U.S.C. §§201-208. Under 9 U.S.C. §208, the existing Federal Arbitration Act, 9 U.S.C. §§1-14, applies to the enforcement of foreign awards except to the extent to which the latter may conflict with the Convention. . . .

A. Public Policy

Article V(2) (b) of the Convention allows the court in which enforcement of a foreign arbitral award is sought to refuse enforcement, on the defendant's motion or *sua sponte*, if "enforcement of the award would be contrary to the public policy of [the forum] country." The legislative history of the provision offers no certain guidelines to its construction. Its precursors in the Geneva Convention and the 1958 Convention's ad hoc committee draft extended the public policy exception to, respectively, awards contrary to "principles of the law" and awards violative of "fundamental principles of the law." In one commentator's view, the Convention's failure to include similar language signifies a narrowing of the defense. On the other hand, another noted authority in the field has seized upon this omission as indicative of an intention to broaden the defense.

Perhaps more probative, however, are the inferences to be drawn from the history of the Convention as a whole. The general pro-enforcement bias informing the Convention . . . points toward a narrow reading of the public policy defense. An expansive construction of this defense would vitiate the Convention's basic effort to remove preexisting obstacles to enforcement. Additionally, considerations of reciprocity—considerations given express recognition in the Convention itself[4]—counsel courts to invoke the public policy defense with caution lest foreign courts

4. "A Contracting State shall not be entitled to avail itself of the present Convention against other Contracting States except to the extent that it is itself bound to apply the Convention." (Article XIV.)

frequently accept it as a defense to enforcement of arbitral awards rendered in the United States.

We conclude, therefore, that the Convention's public policy defense should be construed narrowly. Enforcement of foreign arbitral awards may be denied on this basis only where enforcement would violate the forum state's most basic notions of morality and justice.

Under this view of the public policy provision in the Convention, Overseas' public policy defense may easily be dismissed. Overseas argues that various actions by United States officials subsequent to the severance of American-Egyptian relations — most particularly, AID's withdrawal of financial support for the Overseas-RAKTA contract — required Overseas, as a loyal American citizen, to abandon the project. Enforcement of an award predicated on the feasibility of Overseas' returning to work in defiance of these expressions of national policy would therefore allegedly contravene United States public policy. In equating "national" policy with United States "public" policy, the appellant quite plainly misses the mark. To read the public policy defense as a parochial device protective of national political interests would seriously undermine the Convention's utility. This provision was not meant to enshrine the vagaries of international politics under the rubric of "public policy." Rather, a circumscribed public policy doctrine was contemplated by the Convention's framers and every indication is that the United States, in acceding to the Convention, meant to subscribe to this supranational emphasis.

To deny enforcement of this award largely because of the United States' falling out with Egypt in recent years would mean converting a defense intended to be of narrow scope into a major loophole in the Convention's mechanism for enforcement. We have little hesitation, therefore, in disallowing Overseas' proposed public policy defense.

B. Non-Arbitrability

Article V(2)(a) authorizes a court to deny enforcement, on a defendant's or its own motion, of a foreign arbitral award when "[t]he subject matter of the difference is not capable of settlement by arbitration under the law of that [the forum] country." . . .

The court below was correct in denying relief to Overseas under the Convention's non-arbitrability defense to enforcement of foreign arbitral awards. There is no special national interest in judicial, rather than arbitral, resolution of the breach of contract claim underlying the award in this case. . . .

C. Inadequate Opportunity to Present Defense

Under Article V(1)(b) of the Convention, enforcement of a foreign arbitral award may be denied if the defendant can prove that he was "not given proper notice . . . or was otherwise unable to present his case." This provision essentially sanctions the application of the forum state's standards of due process.

Overseas seeks relief under this provision for the arbitration court's refusal to delay proceedings in order to accommodate the speaking schedule of one of Overseas' witnesses, David Nes, the United States Charge d'Affairs in Egypt at the time of the Six Day War. This attempt to state a due process claim fails for several reasons.

First, inability to produce one's witnesses before an arbitral tribunal is a risk inherent in an agreement to submit to arbitration. By agreeing to submit disputes to arbitration, a party relinquishes his courtroom rights — including that to subpoena witnesses — in favor of arbitration "with all of its well known advantages and drawbacks." Secondly, the logistical problems of scheduling hearing dates convenient to parties, counsel and arbitrators scattered about the globe argues against deviating from an initially mutually agreeable time plan unless a scheduling change is truly unavoidable. In this instance, Overseas' allegedly key witness was kept from attending the hearing due to a prior commitment to lecture at an American university — hardly the type of obstacle to his presence which would require the arbitral tribunal to postpone the hearing as a matter of fundamental fairness to Overseas. Finally, Overseas cannot complain that the tribunal decided the case without considering evidence critical to its defense and within only Mr. Nes' ability to produce. In fact, the tribunal did have before it an affidavit by Mr. Nes in which he furnished, by his own account, "a good deal of the information to which I would have testified." Moreover, had Mr. Nes wished to furnish *all* the information to which he would have testified, there is every reason to believe that the arbitration tribunal would have considered that as well.

The arbitration tribunal acted within its discretion in declining to reschedule a hearing for the convenience of an Overseas witness. Overseas' due process rights under American law, rights entitled to full force under the Convention as a defense to enforcement, were in no way infringed by the tribunal's decision.

D. Arbitration in Excess of Jurisdiction

Under Article V(1)(c), one defending against enforcement of an arbitral award may prevail by proving that:

> The award deals with a difference not contemplated by or not falling within the terms of the submission to arbitration, or it contains decisions on matters beyond the scope of the submission to arbitration. . . .

This provision tracks in more detailed form §10(d) of the Federal Arbitration Act, 9 U.S.C. §10(d), which authorizes vacating an award "[w]here the arbitrators exceeded their powers." Both provisions basically allow a party to attack an award predicated upon arbitration of a subject matter not within the agreement to submit to arbitration. This defense to enforcement of a foreign award, like the others already discussed, should be construed narrowly. Once again a narrow construction would comport with the enforcement-facilitating thrust of the Convention. In addition, the case law under the similar provision of the Federal Arbitration Act strongly supports a strict reading.

In making this defense as to three components of the award, Overseas must therefore overcome a powerful presumption that the arbitral body acted within its powers. Overseas principally directs its challenge at the $185,000 awarded for loss of production. Its jurisdictional claim focuses on the provision of the contract reciting that "[n]either party shall have any liability for loss of production." The tribunal cannot properly be charged, however, with simply ignoring this alleged limitation on the subject matter over which its decision-making powers extended. Rather, the arbitration court interpreted the provision not to preclude jurisdiction on this matter. As in United Steelworkers of America v. Enterprise Wheel & Car Corp., the court may be satisfied that the arbitrator premised the award on a construction of the contract and that it is "not apparent," 363 U.S. 593 at 598, that the scope of the submission to arbitration has been exceeded.

The appellant's attack on the $60,000 awarded for start-up expenses and $30,000 in costs cannot withstand the most cursory scrutiny. In characterizing the $60,000 as "consequential damages" (and thus proscribed by the arbitration agreement), Overseas is again attempting to secure a reconstruction in this court of the contract—an activity wholly inconsistent with the deference due arbitral decisions on law and fact. The $30,000 in costs is equally unassailable, for the appellant's contention that this portion of the award is inconsistent with guidelines set by the International Chamber of Commerce is twice removed from reality. First of all, contrary to Overseas' representations, these guidelines (contained in the Guide to ICC Arbitration . . .) do not require, as a precondition to an award of expenses, express authority for such an award in the arbitration clause. The arbitration agreement's silence on this matter, therefore, is not determinative in the case under review. Secondly, since the parties in fact complied with the Guide's advice to reach agreement on this matter prior to arbitration—i.e., the request by each for such an award for expenses amounts to tacit agreement on this point—any claim of fatal deviation from the *Guide* is disingenuous to say the least.

Although the Convention recognizes that an award may not be enforced where predicated on a subject matter outside the arbitrator's jurisdiction, it does not sanction second-guessing the arbitrator's construction of the parties' agreement. . . .

E. Award in "Manifest Disregard" of Law

Both the legislative history of Article V, see supra, and the statute enacted to implement the United States' accession to the Convention[6] are strong authority for treating as exclusive the bases set forth in the Convention for vacating an award. On the other hand, the Federal Arbitration Act, specifically 9 U.S.C. §10, has been read to include an implied defense to enforcement where the award is in "manifest disregard" of the law.

This case does not require us to decide, however, whether this defense stemming from dictum in *Wilko* obtains in the international arbitration context. For even assuming that the "manifest disregard" defense applies under the Convention, we would have no difficulty rejecting the appellant's contention that such "manifest disregard" is in evidence here. Overseas in effect asks this court to read this defense as a license to review the record of arbitral proceedings for errors of fact or law—a role which we have emphatically declined to assume in the past and reject once again. . . .

Insofar as this defense to enforcement of awards in "manifest disregard" of law may be cognizable under the Convention, it . . . fails to provide a sound basis for

6. ". . . The court shall confirm the award unless it finds one of the grounds for refusal or deferral of recognition or enforcement specified in the said Convention." (9 U.S.C. §207.)

vacating the foreign arbitral award. We therefore affirm the district court's confirmation of the award. . . .

Notes and Questions

1. Do you agree with the *Parsons & Whittemore* court on the public policy issue? When do you believe that public policy should be a defense?

2. What was the strongest argument by Overseas to deny enforcement of the award?

3. Does the $185,000 awarded for loss of production fall "within the terms of the submission to arbitration" given that the arbitration agreement stated that "[n]either party shall have any liability for loss of production"? Why or why not? If it does not seem to fall within the terms, what were the court's reasons for still upholding that part of the award?

4. United States courts have set a high threshold for finding that an award was made in "manifest disregard of the law." In Kanuth v. Prescott, Ball & Turben, Inc., 949 F.2d 1175, 1182 (D.C. Cir. 1991), the court said: " 'manifest disregard' means much more than failure to apply the correct law. 'Manifest disregard' may be found, for example, if the [arbitration] panel understood and correctly stated the law but proceeded to ignore it." See also Kurke v. Oscar Gruss and Son, Inc., 454 F.3d 350, 354 (D.C. Cir. 2006).

5. Given the *Parsons & Whittemore* case (which reflects the state of the law in the United States), do you believe that it is generally easy to enforce international arbitral decisions in U.S. courts? Is the enforcement situation what you think it should be? For other cases following the *Parsons* approach, see Aasma v. American Steamship Owners Mutual Protection and Indemnity, 238 F. Supp. 2d 918 (N.D. Ohio 2003) (confirming international arbitral award of over $500,000 in costs and fees against asbestos plaintiffs under the default rules of the United Kingdom's Arbitration Act 1996, even though such an award was contrary to the so-called American Rule that each party should pay its own attorneys' fees); Matter of Chromalloy Aeroservices and the Arab Republic of Egypt, 939 F. Supp. 907 (D.D.C. 1996) (granting Chromalloy's petition to recognize and enforce an international arbitral award that had been made in Egypt against the Egyptian government, even though the Egyptian Court of Appeal said the award was nullified because it found the arbitral panel had used the wrong substantive law of Egypt); and National Oil Corp. v. Libyan Sun Oil Co., 733 F. Supp. 800, 819-820 (D. Del. 1990) (upholding an international arbitral award against a U.S. oil company in favor of an oil company owned by the Libyan government). For an example of a court holding that the annulment of an award means that the award cannot be enforced see, for example, Termorio SA v. Electranta SP, 487 F.3d 928 (D.C. Cir. 2007). For a case of non-enforcement of an arbitral award, see Iran Aircraft Industries v. Avco Corp., 980 F.2d 141 (2d Cir. 1992) (found that losing party in an early arbitration by the Iran-U.S. Claims Tribunal was, because of some unique circumstances, "unable to present [its] case" within the meaning of Article V(1)(b) of the N.Y. Convention).

6. Article I of the New York Convention states that the enforcement regime of the Convention only applies to arbitral awards that are international. For the

Convention to apply, the arbitral award in question must either have been granted outside the country where enforcement is sought or the award must be considered "non-domestic" in the country where enforcement is sought.

7. Most frequently, like U.S. courts, most foreign courts enforce international arbitral awards under the N.Y. Convention. In L'Aiglon S.A. v. Téxtil União S.A., Case No. SEC 856, May 18, 2005, the Brazilian Superior Court of Justice enforced a foreign arbitral award of $900 million against Téxtil União, a Brazilian company. The underlying dispute related to a contract between Téxtil União and a Swiss company to purchase crude cotton. The Brazilian court confirmed the award against Téxtil União, even though Téxtil União did not sign the arbitration clause, because neither the New York Convention nor Brazilian arbitration law required that the arbitration clause be signed by the parties, and Téxtil União's participation in the arbitration constituted consent to it. And, the Lam Dong People's Court in Vietnam upheld an arbitral award rendered by an ICC arbitral tribunal against a Vietnamese company. The underlying dispute related to a contract between a South Korean silk company and the Vietnam Sericulture Corporation (Viseri). The Vietnamese court confirmed the award against Viseri, holding that it "conformed to international practices, the Vietnam Trade Law, and the ordinance on international arbitration in Vietnam." For more information, see World Arbitration & Mediation Report, vol. 17, no. 3 (March 2006) and vol. 13. no. 2 (March 2002), respectively.

8. Efforts by domestic courts to enjoin arbitration proceedings or to refuse to recognize or enforce the proceedings sometimes tend to occur when a country undergoes political and financial turmoil. For example, in 1997-1998 after the Indonesian economy was hit hard in the Asian financial crisis and the long-lived regime of President Suharto collapsed, a local court tried to enjoin one arbitration proceeding over a major energy project and other arbitration proceedings encountered difficulties in obtaining recognition and enforcement of awards. One of the cases was finally settled only after courts in several countries and many international banks had become involved. For a detailed analysis and further instances of difficulties in enforcing arbitration awards, see Mark Kantor, International Project Finance and Arbitration with Public Sector Entities: When Is Arbitrability A Fiction?, 24 Fordham Int'l L.J. 1122, 1171-72 (2001).

For information on difficulties with arbitrations involving Argentina after the country went through economic problems, see Carlos Alfaro & Pedro Lorenti, The Growing Opposition of Argentina to ICSID Arbitral Tribunals: A Conflict Between International and Domestic Law?, 6 J. World Inv. & Trade 417 (2005).

9. There is an extensive literature on international arbitration. Some recent publications include: Thomas E. Carbonneau, The Law and Practice of Arbitration (2004); David D. Caron & John R. Crook, The Iran-United States Claims Tribunal and the Process of International Claims Resolution (2000); Yves Derains & Eric A. Schwartz, *A Guide to the ICC Rules of Arbitration* (2d ed. 2005); William W. Park, Arbitration of International Business Disputes: Studies in Law and Practice (2006); Jan Paulsson (ed.), I-IV *International Handbook on Commercial Arbitration* (Update 2008).

E. TAILORED DISPUTE RESOLUTION SYSTEMS

The past three sections in this Chapter on the ICJ, regional and specialized courts, and arbitration have studied examples of courts or of international arbitration. The international community of states, international organizations, and private parties have, however, also creatively developed some tailored systems of formal dispute resolution to deal with particular circumstances. These tailored systems have drawn heavily from the structure and experience of courts and arbitration.

Leading examples of these tailored systems are the dispute resolution provisions in the North American Free Trade Agreement (NAFTA) and the World Trade Organization (WTO). NAFTA provides three different approaches to address a wide variety of issues, including some matters that would otherwise have been under the exclusive jurisdiction of Canadian, Mexican, or U.S. courts. And, compared to its predecessor General Agreement on Tariffs and Trade (GATT), the WTO has a very strong dispute resolution system for a wide range of trade disputes among its 150-plus members. As we will see, if consultations fail, a dispute under the WTO system first goes to a panel that is similar to arbitration, but then there is an automatic right of appeal to an appellate body that is similar to an appellate court.

1. North American Free Trade Agreement (NAFTA)

The United States, Canada, and Mexico are parties to the important North American Free Trade Agreement (NAFTA), which came into force on January 1, 1994. NAFTA is a comprehensive free trade agreement negotiated among regional countries, though it is not as comprehensive as a common market (such as the European Union).* It was also the first free trade agreement between industrial countries and a developing country (Mexico) where the obligations are reciprocal.

NAFTA involves a large regional market, comparable to the European Union. The combined population of the three countries in 2009 was about 448 million (307 million for the United States, 107 million for Mexico, and 34 million for Canada). The 2009 gross domestic product of the NAFTA countries was approximately $16.5 trillion ($14.3 trillion for the United States, $1.3 trillion for Canada, and $875 billion for Mexico).

The United States and Canada are each other's largest trading partners. In 2009, total two-way trade in goods between them equaled about $433.1 billion. In comparison, trade in goods between the United States and China, the second largest trading partner of the United States, was about $404.4 billion

As a result of economic reforms in Mexico during the late 1980s and early 1990s, U.S. trade with Mexico had been growing rapidly even before NAFTA. In 2009, the United States exported about $129 billion in goods to Mexico and imported about $178.3 billion. Mexico has become the United States's third largest trading partner. Trade between Canada and Mexico had been small, but it has increased substantially under NAFTA. Since NAFTA came into effect, U.S. trade

*A free trade agreement eliminates most, if not all, tariffs between its members, but its members retain their own external tariffs toward third countries. A common market goes at least one step further and creates equal external tariffs for its members for goods coming from third countries. The European Union is a common market and it involves a number of further steps toward regional integration.

with Canada and Mexico has grown substantially faster in percentage terms than U.S. trade with the rest of the world. (For more data regarding the NAFTA countries, the European Union, and other countries, see Table 5-1 at the start of Chapter 5.)

NAFTA followed upon the United States-Canada Free Trade Agreement (FTA) that became effective in January 1989. The FTA had been designed to remove most, though not all, trade barriers between the United States and Canada.

In the following excerpt, economists Gary Hufbauer and Jeffrey Schott provide a summary analysis of the basic NAFTA agreement negotiated in 1992.

Gary Clyde Hufbauer & Jeffrey J. Schott, NAFTA: An Assessment

2-6 (1993)

In essence, the NAFTA is a new, improved, and expanded version of the Canada-US FTA. In large part, the agreement involves commitments by Mexico to implement the degree of trade and investment liberalization promised between its northern neighbors in 1988. However, the NAFTA goes further by addressing unfinished business from the FTA, including protection of intellectual property rights, rules against distortions to investment (local-content and export performance requirements), and coverage of transportation services.

The NAFTA provides for the phased elimination of tariff and most non-tariff barriers on regional trade . . . [The phase-in periods of up to 15 years have now passed.] In addition, the NAFTA extends the innovative dispute settlement procedures of the FTA to Mexico (in return for a substantial revamping of Mexican trade laws that injects more transparency into the administrative process and brings Mexican antidumping and other procedures closer to those of the United States and Canada); contains precedent-setting rights and obligations regarding services and investment; and takes an important first step in addressing cross-border environmental issues.

The agreement contains notable commitments with regard to liberalization of trade and investment. First, the NAFTA establishes . . . free trade in agricultural products between the United States and Mexico . . . an impressive achievement considering the dismal track record of other trade talks in reducing long-standing farm trade barriers.

Second, the investment obligations of the NAFTA (and related dispute settlement provisions) accord national treatment to NAFTA investors, remove most performance requirements on investment in the region, and open up new investment opportunities in key Mexican sectors such as petrochemicals and financial services. The investment provisions provide a useful model for future GATT trade accords, despite the notable exceptions for primary energy and Canadian cultural industries.

Third, the pact sets important precedents for future regional and multilateral negotiations by substantially opening the financial services market in Mexico to US and Canadian participants . . . and by removing significant obstacles to land transportation and telecommunications services.

Finally, the NAFTA offers a schizophrenic result in textiles and apparel. On the one hand, the pact calls for the elimination of [almost] all tariffs and quotas on regional trade in textiles and apparel. . . . This is the first time in this heavily protected sector that imports from an important developing-country supplier have been significantly liberalized by the United States and Canada. However, the rules of origin established to qualify for duty-free treatment are highly restrictive. . . .

The NAFTA is a noteworthy achievement, but its implications for Mexico, Canada, and the United States should not be exaggerated. By widening the scope of the market and enlarging the range of available labor skills, the NAFTA enables North American firms and workers to compete more effectively against foreign producers both at home and in world markets. But the ability of the NAFTA partners to gain maximum benefits from the pact with minimum adjustment costs depends importantly on maintaining domestic economic policies that ensure growth. Firms will still look first and foremost at the macroeconomic climate in each country in setting their investment priorities.

Implications for Mexico, the United States, and Canada

For Mexico, the NAFTA reinforces the extensive market-oriented policy reforms implemented since 1985. These reforms have promoted real annual growth of 3 to 4 percent in the 1990s and a falling rate of inflation. The NAFTA portends a continuation of the fast pace of change in the Mexican economy by extending the reform process to sectors such as autos, textiles and apparel, finance, telecommunications, and land transportation. Mexican exporters will also benefit in two distinct ways: the relatively unfettered access to the US market that they already enjoy under various unilateral US programs will be sustained, and the few remaining US trade barriers will be liberalized. . . .

For the United States, the NAFTA reforms should enhance an already-important export market. . . . Over time, the NAFTA should impel industrial reorganization along regional lines, with firms taking best advantage of each country's ability to produce components and assembled products and thus enhancing competitiveness in the global marketplace.

In addition, the NAFTA meets key US foreign policy objectives. . . . The NAFTA should anchor achievements already made in Mexico and reinforce efforts to promote economic growth and political pluralism in that country.

For Canada, the NAFTA reinforces, and in some cases strengthens, its FTA preferences in the US market. . . . In addition, the NAFTA improves Canada's access to the Mexican market. . . .

NAFTA "Lowlights"

Despite its attractions, the NAFTA does contain warts and blemishes. For example, basic energy remains immune to free trade. . . .

But the main area where the NAFTA is open to criticism is its enunciation of restrictive rules of origin. These arcane trade provisions have been aptly labeled "tools of discrimination": they are used to determine which goods qualify for preferential treatment under the NAFTA and to deny NAFTA benefits to those goods that contain significant foreign-sourced components.

Rules of origin are an integral part of all free trade pacts, but the NAFTA provisions pose two distinct dangers. First, to an undue extent, they penalize regional producers by forcing them to source from less efficient suppliers located in the region, thereby undercutting the global competitiveness of the buying firms. Second, the NAFTA rules could establish an unhappy precedent for other preferential trading pacts, which may choose to emulate the restrictive practices articulated in the NAFTA to the disadvantage of the original perpetrators. . . .

During the 1992 Presidential campaign, then-Governor Clinton identified some problems with the basic NAFTA agreement that the Bush Administration had negotiated. In 1993, the Clinton Administration promptly negotiated with Canada and Mexico three "side agreements" to the basic NAFTA agreement before submitting the whole package to the U.S. Congress for approval.

The most important side agreements dealt with environmental concerns and labor problems. The environment agreement was an attempt to ensure that none of the three countries could gain a competitive advantage in trade by failing to enforce environmental laws. The agreement created a trilateral Commission on Environmental Cooperation with a broad agenda and some dispute resolution powers.

The labor agreement created a trilateral Commission for Labor Cooperation. The Commission has powers to gather and publish information and to coordinate cooperative activities. The Commission also had limited enforcement powers. For a detailed discussion of these two agreements, see, for example, Thomas Schoenbaum, The North American Free Trade Agreement (NAFTA): Good for Jobs, for the Environment, and for America, 23 Ga. J. Int'l & Comp. L. 461 (1993). (The third side agreement dealt with the potential problem of import surges as a result of NAFTA hurting one of the member countries, but added very little substance to existing U.S. laws.) Recent assessments indicate that these side agreements have not achieved much in the difficult areas of labor and environment, and recommendations have been made for further steps, including on climate change. See Gary Clyde Hufbauer & Jeffrey J. Schott, NAFTA Revisited, Pol'y Options, Oct. 2007.

Even with the side agreements, the whole NAFTA package encountered heavy resistance in the U.S. Congress. The AFL-CIO and other labor groups were particularly unhappy with the arrangement. They believed that, even with the side agreement on labor standards, the NAFTA package provided inadequate protection for U.S. workers. President Clinton and his administration, however, mounted a successful effort to obtain approval for the agreement in the House of Representatives and the Senate in the fall of 1993. Canada and Mexico encountered less legislative opposition and also obtained approval in 1993. As noted earlier, NAFTA went into force in January 1994.

Gary Clyde Hufbauer & Jeffrey J. Schott, NAFTA Revisited

Pol' Options 83, 83-84 (Oct. 2007)

Throughout its duration, NAFTA has been hailed by some and derided by others. Proponents laud the pact's contribution to regional trade and investment and argue for an acceleration of the integration process. Critics focus on NAFTA's impact on wages and jobs because of growing competition and immigration; some fear that increased cooperation will lead to a loss of sovereignty . . .

Much of what was promised from NAFTA could never be achieved solely through a free trade deal; much of what has occurred since NAFTA cannot be attributed to the agreement. Trade pacts create opportunities; they don't guarantee results. . . .

Energy and border security have captured the political spotlight, yet minimal progress has been achieved on both files. Additionally, Mexican GDP growth has averaged only 3 percent per annum since 1993. . . . The Mexican political system has not delivered the tax and energy reforms that would generate new resources to fund investments in physical infrastructure, social services, and education. Mexico has neither rousted the drug lords nor eradicated the corruption mentality. These factors have limited Mexico's ability to take full advantage of NAFTA . . .

A trade agreement can be assessed against many standards . . . We apply a straightforward test: How well did the three countries meet the objectives set out in NAFTA . . . NAFTA succeeded in advancing economic integration and achieving the goals agreed to in the pact—though not in reaching the inflated promises of politicians when the pact entered into force. While the pact is comprehensive compared to other trade agreements, in some areas its footprint is small. . . .

NAFTA lacks the medicinal powers to cure important ills of North America, including high levels of illegal immigration and trafficking of illegal drugs, slow progress on environmental problems, growing income disparities (particularly within Mexico), and weak growth in real wages. Some of these problems are correlates of economic integration and higher incomes, though NAFTA is only a small part of the story.

NAFTA was and is foremost a commercial agreement. . . . Between 1993 and 2006, trilateral merchandise trade rose almost three-fold, now exceeding $800 billion annually. US-Mexico trade has expanded at a particularly rapid clip, much faster than US merchandise trade with the world . . . Much of NAFTA commerce is concentrated in autos and parts, and energy, which together account for a third of regional trade. By contrast, cross-border services trade flows (not including remittances to Mexico) have grown at a more measured pace . . . One of the key Mexican objectives in NAFTA was to increase foreign direct investment (FDI), and here again the pact has had a positive impact. The stock of FDI in Mexico from all sources has increased more than four-fold since 1993.

Among the most important aspects of NAFTA are the numerous mechanisms established for dispute resolution. These were "state of the art" tailored mechanisms that built upon the successful procedures that had existed under the United States-Canada Free Trade Agreement (FTA).

NAFTA established three principal mechanisms for resolving disputes. First, there is the Chapter 11 procedure for disputes between an investor of one party and another party. Second, there is the special Chapter 19 mechanism for disputes under the antidumping and countervailing duty laws. Third, there is a Chapter 20 general mechanism for resolving many disputes among the parties that do not fall within the second category.

"Dumping" is defined under U.S. law as the sale of foreign merchandise in the United States at less than its fair value, usually measured by comparing (with adjustments) the price in the United States with that in the home market at the same stage of the production process. Such sales must cause or threaten "material injury" to a U.S. industry or materially retard the establishment of an industry. The International Trade Commission (ITC), an independent agency in the U.S. government (whose six commissioners are appointed for staggered nine-year terms), is charged with making the essential determination regarding injury. The U.S. Department of Commerce makes the initial determination regarding whether there has been dumping and, if so, by how much. If Commerce finds dumping and the ITC finds injury, then Commerce can make a determination of increased tariffs or other relief to offset the price discrimination. These determinations can usually be appealed to the U.S. federal courts. However, for sales from Mexico or Canada that are covered by NAFTA, an appropriate party can request a review by a NAFTA panel as a substitute for judicial review.

Similarly, "countervailing duties" under U.S. law can be imposed on foreign merchandise if the foreign manufacture, production, or export of that merchandise is being subsidized, directly or indirectly. For most cases, there is a requirement of real or threatened injury similar to that under the dumping laws, and the ITC is again charged with making this determination. The Department of Commerce determines the existence and amount of the subsidies. If the ITC finds injury and Commerce finds the subsidies, then Commerce determines the amount of countervailing duties that are to be imposed. Again, for cases not covered by NAFTA, these determinations can be appealed to the U.S. federal courts.

The following analysis by Gary Horlick and Amanda DeBusk provides an excellent overview of the principal dispute-resolution procedures in NAFTA.

Gary Horlick & Amanda DeBusk, Dispute Resolution Under NAFTA

27 J. World Trade 21-41 (1993)

I. Introduction

. . . NAFTA . . . contains numerous mechanisms for resolving disputes. This article focuses on the three dispute resolution mechanisms that are the most fully elaborated in the NAFTA:

(1) the Chapter 11, Subchapter B mechanism for resolving disputes between a party and an investor in another party;
(2) the Chapter 19 mechanism for resolving disputes under the antidumping and countervailing duty laws; and
(3) the Chapter 20 mechanism for resolving disputes among the parties. . . .

II. Investor Disputes

(A) Description of Investor Dispute Resolution Mechanism

NAFTA breaks new ground with the Chapter 11 investor dispute resolution mechanism. It permits investors to resort to binding international arbitration if a host government violates the investment provisions of the NAFTA.[6] An investor may seek arbitration if a party (e.g. the United States, Mexico, or Canada) violates its commitment to afford treatment to investors of another party that is no less favourable than it accords its own investors and investors of other countries.[7] NAFTA prohibits the parties from imposing specific performance requirements such as minimum export levels, domestic content rules, preferences for domestic sourcing, trade balancing and technology transfer requirements.[8] Expropriations are prohibited unless certain conditions are met.[9] Investors are guaranteed the right to convert local currency into foreign currency at the prevailing market rate and freely transfer the currency.[10] There are various exceptions to NAFTA's investment provisions covering areas such as investment in telecommunications, maritime services, Mexico's oil industry and others. An investor may use the NAFTA to assert its own claims or those of an enterprise under its ownership or control in the host country.

The NAFTA dispute resolution mechanism for investor disputes does not establish a new procedural regime but instead permits investors to seek arbitration for violations of NAFTA under:

— the ICSID Convention, provided that both the disputing party and the party of the investor are parties to the Convention;[13]

— the Additional Facility Rules of ICSID, provided that either the disputing party or the party of the investor, but not both, is a party to the ICSID Convention;[14]

— or the United Nations Commission on International Trade Law (UNCITRAL) Arbitration Rules.

ICSID panels are established under the auspices of the World Bank to hear disputes between governments and private investors. The Additional Facility Rules of ICSID are designed, inter alia, for investment arbitrations where one of the disputing parties is a member of the ICSID Convention but the other is not. The UNCITRAL Arbitration Rules are optional rules that parties can choose to use to govern disputes arising out of contracts or other disputes. . . .

There are several preconditions to use of the NAFTA investor dispute resolution mechanism. First, the investor must have incurred a loss or damage by reason

6. NAFTA, Article 1116.

7. Ibid., Article 1102 (national treatment); Article 1103 (most-favoured-nation treatment).

8. Ibid., Article 1106.

9. Ibid., Article 1110. There is an exception for expropriations for a public purpose provided that they are done on a non-discriminatory basis in accordance with the due process of law and upon payment of fair compensation; id., Article 1110(1).

10. Ibid., Article 1109.

13. Of the three parties, only the United States is a signatory of the ICSID Convention. Therefore, the option of arbitration under the ICSID Convention will be available only if another party becomes a signatory.

14. This provision would be applicable if the dispute involves the United States (or a U.S. investor) and another party (or another party's investor).

of, or arising out of a breach of, certain NAFTA provisions protecting investors. Second, the claim must be timely lodged. . . . Third, the aggrieved investor must attempt consultation and negotiation prior to resorting to arbitration. . . .

(D) Binding Nature of Investor Panel Decisions

NAFTA provides that the investor dispute resolution panel's decision will be binding. NAFTA Article 1135(5) states that each party undertakes to provide for the enforcement in its territory of an award. . . . In addition, a disputing investor may seek enforcement of an arbitration under the ICSID Convention, [the New York Convention, or the Inter-American Convention]. . . .

III. Resolution of Antidumping/Countervailing Duties

(A) Introduction

Chapter 19 of the NAFTA provides for the resolution of trade disputes concerning antidumping and countervailing duty investigations. . . . In this article, the Chapter 19 panels of the NAFTA and FTA are referred to as the "AD/CVD panels." . . .

. . . The NAFTA . . . permits dispute resolution through a panel of experts from the exporting and importing nations as a substitute for judicial review of AD/CVD cases.

NAFTA panels must apply the same standard of review that a reviewing court of the country whose decision is challenged would apply. In the United States, the standard is whether the decision is: (a) unsupported by substantial evidence on the record; or (b) otherwise not in accordance with law . . . *

(C) NAFTA Structured for Impartial Decision-Making

NAFTA provides for each of the two involved parties to select two panelists, with the fifth panelist to be selected by mutual agreement, or, failing agreement, by lot. . . .

(D) NAFTA AD/CVD Panel Decisions Will Be Binding

. . . NAFTA AD/CVD panel decisions are binding. NAFTA Article 1904(9) provides: "The decision of a panel under this Article shall be binding on the involved parties with respect to the particular matter between the parties that is before the panel." . . .

(F) NAFTA AD/CVD [Extraordinary Challenge Committee for Challenges to Panel Decisions] . . .

NAFTA has a system for challenging AD/CVD panel decisions. . . .

NAFTA Article 1904.13 allows a party to challenge the decision of a binational panel in the following limited circumstances:

*[See Note 3 below for the exact statutory language. — Eds.]

(a) (i) a member of the panel was guilty of gross misconduct, bias, or a serious conflict of interest, or otherwise materially violated the rules of conduct;

(ii) the panel seriously departed from a fundamental rule of procedure; or

(iii) the panel manifestly exceed its powers, authority or jurisdiction set forth in this Article, for example by failing to apply the appropriate standard of review.

In addition, under NAFTA Chapter 19, the party must show that the situation is so serious that at least one of the actions in subparagraph (a) materially affected the panel's decision *and* poses a continued threat to the integrity of the binational panel review process. . . .

IV. Disputes of the Parties

(A) Introduction

NAFTA Chapter 20 establishes a dispute mechanism for disputes of the parties. . . . It covers disputes concerning the interpretation or application of NAFTA, alleged violations of NAFTA and the nullification or impairment of the benefits of NAFTA. . . .

The NAFTA Chapter 20 panels are structured similarly to NAFTA AD/CVD panels, although there are some important distinctions. While the parties delegated to private parties the right to request Chapter 19 reviews, only the three national governments can request Chapter 20 reviews. . . .

. . . Chapter 20 panels produce an initial report, which includes recommendations for resolution of the dispute. Then, the panel will consider comments and issue a final report.

. . . [T]he parties can override a Chapter 20 panel's report. Upon receipt of the report, the parties "shall agree" on resolution of the dispute, which "normally" will conform with the panel's determination and recommendations.[141] These provisions give the panel "moral" influence over resolution of the dispute.

While the AD/CVD panels may only affirm or remand agency decisions, the Chapter 20 panels have broader discretion in finding a remedy. . . . NAFTA expansively defines potential remedies as the "non-implementation or removal of a measure not conforming with this Agreement or causing nullification or impairment in the sense of Annex 2004 or, failing such a resolution, compensation."[142] NAFTA does not limit dispute resolution to these broadly-defined remedies. Rather, it provides that they are to be used "wherever possible."

There is no [Extraordinary Challenge Committee] for Chapter 20 panels. If the parties do not agree with the recommendation of a panel and cannot resolve a dispute within 30 days . . . , then the final recourse for the aggrieved party is "to suspend the application to the party complained against of benefits of equivalent effect until such time as they have reached agreement on a resolution of the dispute."[144] . . .

141. Article 2018 (1).
142. Ibid., Article 2018 (2).
144. Ibid., Article 2019 (1).

(C) NAFTA Improves on FTA Panel Selection Process

. . . NAFTA establishes an innovative system whereby a party selects panelists from nationals of another party. If the dispute involves two parties, they are to endeavour to agree on the chair of the panel and then each party is to select two panelists who are citizens of the other dispute party. If the parties cannot agree on the chair, the chair is to be chosen by lot. . . .

Notes and Questions

The NAFTA dispute resolution provisions are not simple. To help you understand them, consider the following questions:

1. Under the NAFTA dispute resolution procedures for trade disputes concerning antidumping and countervailing duty (AD/CVD) investigations (Chapter 19), are the determinations of the panels binding?

2. Can a private party (e.g., a U.S. importer) challenge a U.S. antidumping duty investigation before a NAFTA panel?

3. What exactly is the standard of review under Chapter 19? What if the U.S. Executive Branch correctly applied existing U.S. law to find that Canadians were dumping timber in the United States and should face higher tariffs? Even if Canada felt that the U.S. law was wrong, does the dispute mechanism of the binational arbitration panel offer any relief?

The standard of review for U.S. cases is adopted from U.S. import laws, specifically 19 U.S.C. §1516A(b) (1). It provides:

> The court shall hold unlawful any determination, finding, or conclusion found—
>
> (A) in an action brought [against certain determinations by a government agency], to be arbitrary, capricious, an abuse of discretion, or otherwise not in accordance with the law, or
>
> (B) in an action [against agency determinations usually made at a later point in the fact-finding process], to be unsupported by substantial evidence on the record, or otherwise not in accordance with law.

4. Turn to the general dispute resolution procedures of NAFTA under Chapter 20. Once the matter is before the panel, does it proceed directly to rendering a decision or are there interim steps? What if a Chapter 20 panel issues a final report that a party does not implement? What are the remedies of the other party? (See Articles 2018-2019.)

5. Why do you think that the Chapter 20 panel's findings were not simply made binding? Why is the Chapter 20 process more drawn out than the Chapter 19 panels for AD/CVD cases? Could it turn upon the potential importance, sensitivity, or uniqueness of issues that fall under the general dispute resolution chapter? The scope of potential remedies?

6. Additional dispute-resolution procedures are available through the North American Commission for Environmental Cooperation (CEC) for environmental disputes. As discussed above, the CEC was established to implement the objectives of one of NAFTA's side agreements — the North American Agreement on Environmental Cooperation (NAAEC). The CEC's dispute-settlement procedures, however,

are different from those of Chapter 20; they make a CEC procedure longer, more expensive, and more difficult to initiate.

7. The NAFTA countries also negotiated a labor side agreement known as the North American Agreement on Labor Cooperation (NAALC). The main objectives of the NAALC are (1) to monitor national labor laws in each member country, (2) to promote joint programs to improve labor practices, and (3) to establish a dispute-resolution forum for labor cases when domestic procedures are insufficient. Although modest improvements have been made under NAALC, political pressure in all three NAFTA countries has made enforcement difficult. Specifically, the NAFTA parties continue to be reluctant to surrender authority on labor issues to a supranational institution.

8. The dispute-resolution system of NAFTA Chapter 19 has seen frequent use.

> From the standpoint of U.S. exporters to Mexico, Chapter 19 ensured that Mexico observed due process guarantees. From the standpoint of Canada and Mexico, Chapter 19 was meant to ensure that US administrative decisions are closely scrutinized. In most cases, panel decisions have lowered US CVD and AD duties against Canadian and Mexican exports. . . .
>
> As of June 2005, 103 panel reviews have been initiated under NAFTA Chapter 19. But it is important to note that intra-NAFTA cases are increasingly appealed to the WTO rather than Chapter 19 panels. . . . An important reason is that the WTO has enunciated common standards and procedures for AD, CVD, and safeguard remedies, whereas NAFTA requires that national agencies faithfully apply their own standards and procedures. [Gary Clyde Hufbauer & Jeffrey J. Schott, NAFTA Revisited: Achievements and Challenges, 212-13 (2005)]

Of these 103 panel reviews, the United States was a defendant in 69 cases, Canada in 19, and Mexico in 15. As of August 2005, there were three reviews by the Extraordinary Challenge Committee.

Chapter 20 has been utilized less frequently. "As of June 2005, Chapter 20 panel consultations reportedly have occurred only 10 times." *Id.* at 214. For further details about NAFTA cases under these chapters, see http://www.nafta-sec-alena.org.

9. Investment disputes brought under NAFTA's Chapter 11 have been some of the most interesting and controversial developments under the agreement. Here are some examples of these cases.

In January 1997, Metalclad Corporation, a U.S. company, filed a Chapter 11 claim against Mexico. Early in the 1980s, Metalclad bought an existing waste disposal site in Mexico with the intentions of building a new hazardous waste facility. However, in 1995, local governments in Mexico passed environmental regulations that denied Metalclad permission to operate the hazardous waste landfill. The arbitral tribunal ruled in August 2000 that Mexico's actions constituted an unjustified expropriation and that such behavior denied Metalclad national treatment and the minimum standard of treatment required for investors under international law. The tribunal awarded Metalclad $16.7 million in damages. (See Chapter 10.B.)

In July 1998, a Canadian funeral conglomerate called The Loewen Group initiated an arbitration against the U.S. government for $725 million, claiming that a Mississippi jury verdict violated its investor rights under Chapter 11. In 1995, Loewen was sued by a small Mississippi funeral home operator and funeral insurance provider over the terms of an insurance contract. After Loewen refused to settle the routine contract dispute that probably was worth less than $20 million, the local company sued in state court. After being allowed to hear, among other allegations, that Canadians were racist, the rural Mississippi jury returned a $500 million verdict against the Loewen Group, of which $400 million was for punitive damages. Loewen was prevented from filing an appeal in the Mississippi courts because Mississippi required that defendant post a bond of 125 percent of the total award, which was beyond Loewen's resources. As a result, Loewen chose to settle the case with the Mississippi plaintiff for about $175 million.

The Loewen Group and its one-time owner, Mr. Richard Loewen, then filed a case with ICSID against the United States for violations of Chapter 11. Specifically, they claimed that the Mississippi trial violated international norms of fairness and amounted to an expropriation and denial of justice under Chapter 11. The ICSID panel rendered its opinion in June 2003. Although the tribunal criticized the Mississippi trial as a "disgrace" and "antithesis of due process," it nonetheless dismissed the Loewen Group's claim because the entity had already become an American company by the time it submitted its claims for arbitration and it was thus ineligible to claim jurisdiction under NAFTA Chapter 11. The tribunal determined that it also lacked jurisdiction over Mr. Loewen, the Canadian owner of the Loewen Group in the past, because it was not shown that he owned or controlled the Loewen Group at the time its claims were submitted for arbitration. Award of June 26, 2003, 42 I.L.M. 811 (2003); Adam Liptak, Review of U.S. rulings by Nafta Tribunals Stirs Worries, N.Y. Times, April 18, 2004, at 20.

Should NAFTA's expropriation provisions be comparable to, or more or less restrictive than, the U.S. domestic law on government takings? And, how should NAFTA balance investment protection with environmental and labor concerns? For more information about the Chapter 11 arbitrations, consult http://www.state.gov/s/l/c3439.htm. See also, for example, Vicki Been & Joel C. Beauvais, The Global Fifth Amendment: NAFTA's Investment Protections and the Misguided Quest for an International "Regulatory Takings" Doctrine, 78 N.Y.U. L. Rev. 30 (2003). For a summary and analysis of all NAFTA dispute resolution mechanisms, including Chapter 11, see Armand de Mestral, NAFTA Dispute Resolution: Creative Experiment or Confusion?, in Regional Trade Agreements and the WTO Legal System, 359 (Lorand Bartels & Federico Ortino eds., 2006).

10. As indicated in the second Hufbauer-Schott excerpt above, there has been much debate about the effects of NAFTA. For examples of a more critical view of the agreement, see Robert Scott, The High Price of Free Trade, Economic Policy Institute Briefing Paper 147 (2003); Isabel Studer, Obstacles to Integration: NAFTA's Institutional Weakness, in Requiem or Revival? The Promise of North American Integration 53 (Isabel Studer & Carol Wise eds., 2007). For a response to such criticisms, see Gary Clyde Hufbauer & Jeffrey J. Schott, NAFTA's Bad Rap, Int'l Econ. 19 (Summer 2008).

2. *Dispute Resolution Under the World Trade Organization (WTO) and the General Agreement on Tariffs and Trade (GATT)*

The World Trade Organization (WTO), which was the result of the Uruguay Round negotiations, came into being in 1995 and includes a major dispute resolution system. This system represents a substantial strengthening of what existed under the General Agreement on Tariffs and Trade (GATT), which came into effect in 1947.

As an introduction, the following excerpt provides an overview of the Uruguay Round agreement and the WTO. (The WTO is discussed in more detail in Chapter 5.C.)

IMF Survey, Trade Agreement Mandates Broad Changes

Jan. 10, 1994, at 2-3

The Final Act would, after ratification . . . , cut tariffs on industrial goods by an average of more than one third, progressively liberalize trade in agricultural products, and convert the GATT from a provisional agreement into a formal international organization, to be called the World Trade Organization (WTO).

The WTO will serve as a single institutional framework encompassing the GATT and all the results of the Round. It will be directed by a Ministerial Conference that will meet at least once every two years, and its regular business will be overseen by a General Council. Countries must accept all of the results of the Uruguay Round, without exception, to become WTO members.

The Final Act's 550 pages include about 15 separate agreements, annexes, decisions, and understandings that would, among other things, bring trade in agricultural products, services, textiles and clothing, and intellectual property within the ambit of the WTO. The agreement would also discipline the use of subsidies and countervailing measures, and technical barriers; tighten antidumping rules and eliminate certain restrictive trade-related investment measures; strengthen existing measures to open up government procurement to foreign suppliers; regulate the use of restrictive safeguard actions; strengthen and clarify procedures for the settlement of trade disputes among WTO members; and increase the transparency of national trade policies by confirming and widening the scope of the Trade Policy Review Mechanism.

Of special interest here is the WTO's dispute resolution system. Compared to the GATT system, the new arrangement is more centralized and its streamlined procedures are set out with greater specificity. Moreover, under GATT, a panel decision had to be adopted by the consensus of the contracting parties, which meant that the losing party could oppose its adoption. In the WTO, there must be a consensus against the adoption of the report of the panel or the Appellate Body—a complete reversal. The following excerpt outlines the WTO's dispute resolution mechanism. (The Documentary Supplement includes Articles XXII and XXIII of the original GATT agreement and excerpts from Dispute Settlement Understanding that was part of the Uruguay Round agreement.)

John H. Jackson, William J. Davey & Alan O. Sykes, Jr., Legal Problems of International Economic Relations

266-276, 284 (5th ed. 2008)

Section. 7.3 The WTO Dispute Settlement Understanding

The WTO Agreement provides that one of the principal functions of the WTO is the administration of the Understanding on Rules and Procedures Governing the

Settlement of Disputes, which is Annex 2 to the WTO Agreement. . . . Indeed, the Dispute Settlement Understanding (DSU) states that the dispute settlement system "is a central element in providing security and predictability to the multilateral trading system" (art. 3.2). The DSU sets forth a comprehensive statement of dispute settlement rules and, while it builds on the past GATT practices, it makes several fundamental changes in the operation of the system. The DSU is administered by the Dispute Settlement Body (DSB), which is the WTO General Council acting in a specialized role under a separate chair. The DSU regulates dispute settlement under all covered WTO agreements, although under some agreements special rules and procedures will be applicable.

The general philosophy of WTO dispute settlement is set out in Article 3 of the DSU. Among the principles that are enshrined in that article are the following:

> First, it is recognized that the system serves to preserve the rights and obligations of Members and to clarify the existing provisions of the WTO agreements in accordance with the customary rules of interpretation of public international law. . . .
>
> Second, it is agreed that the results of the dispute settlement process cannot add to or diminish the rights and obligations provided in the WTO agreements. . . .

Third, several provisions highlight that the aim of dispute settlement is to secure a positive solution to a dispute and that a solution that is acceptable to the parties and consistent with the WTO agreements is clearly to be preferred.

Fourth, although the DSU provides for the eventuality of non-compliance, it is explicitly stated in DSU Article 3.7 that "the first objective of the dispute settlement mechanism is usually to secure the withdrawal of the measures concerned if these are found to be inconsistent with the provisions of any of the covered agreements." Retaliatory action is described as the last resort.

(A) The DSU Procedures

. . . . There are four major phases of WTO dispute settlement: First, the parties must attempt to resolve their differences through consultations. Second, if that fails, the complaining party may demand that a panel of independent experts be established to rule on the dispute. Third, and new under the DSU, is the possibility of an appeal by any party to the dispute to the Appellate Body. Finally, if the complaining party succeeds, the DSB is charged with monitoring the implementation of its recommendations. If the recommendations are not implemented, the possibility of negotiated compensation or authorization to withdraw concessions arises. . . .

(1) Consultations

The requirement that disputing parties consult with a view toward satisfactorily adjusting the matter is contained in Article XXIII itself. The hope is that the parties will resolve their dispute without having to invoke the formal dispute settlement procedures. The rules regarding consultations are set out in article 4 of the DSU. The manner in which the consultations are conducted is up to the parties. The DSU has no rules on consultations beyond that they are to be entered into in good faith and are to be held with 30 days of a request. . . . [A] significant number of cases end at the consultations stage (either through settlements or abandonment of a case).

If consultations fail to settle a dispute within 60 days after the request therefor, the complaining party may request the establishment of a panel. Art. 4.7. In fact, consultations often go on for more than 60 days.

(2) Panel Process

Under the DSU, the right of party to have a panel established is clearly set out in article 6.1. If consultations fail to resolve a dispute within the 60-day time frame specified in article 4, a complainant may insist on the establishment of a panel and, at the meeting following that at which the request first appears on the DSB's agenda, the DSB is required to establish a panel unless there is a consensus in the DSB not to establish a panel. Since the complaining party may prevent the formation of this "reverse" consensus, there is effectively a right to have a panel established. . . .

(a) Setting Up the Panel

Once a panel is established, it is necessary to select the three individuals who will serve as panelists. DSU article 8 provides for the Secretariat to propose potential panel members to the parties, who are not to object except for compelling reasons. In practice, parties are relatively free to reject proposed panelists, but if the parties do not agree on panel members within 20 days of establishment, any party may request the WTO Director-General to appoint the panel on his or her own authority. Art. 8.7. In recent years, the Director-General has appointed some members of almost one-half of the panels composed.

Article 8.1 of the DSU provides [the criteria for membership on a panel]. . . . These criteria could be roughly summarized as establishing three categories of panelists: government officials (current or former), former Secretariat officials and trade academics or lawyers. It is specifically provided that panelists shall not be nationals of parties or third parties, absent agreement of the parties. It is also specified that in a case involving a developing country, one panelist must be from a developing country (if requested). Of the individuals actually chosen for panel service, it appears that the vast majority (over 80%) are current or former government officials.

The DSU provides that panelists serve in their individual capacities and that Members shall not give them instructions or seek to influence them. In addition, the DSB has adopted rules of conduct applicable to participants in the WTO dispute settlement system. The rules require that panelists "be independent and impartial, shall avoid direct or indirect conflicts of interest and shall respect the confidentiality of proceedings." . . .

(b) The Task of Panels

The DSU provides in article 7.1 for standard terms of reference (absent agreement to the contrary). The standard terms direct a panel "To examine, in the light of the relevant provisions in (name of the covered agreement/s cited by the parties to the dispute), the matter referred to the DSB by (name of party) in document DS/ . . . and to make such findings as will assist the DSB in making the recommendations or in giving the rulings provided for in that/those agreement/s." . . .

More generally, DSU Article 11 provides that a panel shall make an objective assessment of the matter before it, including an objective assessment of the facts of the case and the applicability of and conformity with the relevant WTO agreements. . . .

(c) Panel Procedures

A panel normally meets with the parties shortly after its selection to set its working procedures and time schedule. The DSU's standard proposed timetable for panels makes provision for two meetings between the panel and the parties to discuss the substantive issues in the case. Each meeting is preceded by the filing of written submissions. The DSU permits other WTO members to intervene as third parties and present arguments to the first meeting of the panel. While panel and Appellate Body proceedings have traditionally not been open to the public, since 2005 several panel meetings have been open to the public pursuant to the agreement of the parties. A party is free to choose the members of its delegation to hearings. Thus, parties may be assisted, and often are, by private counsel.

Among the most fundamental issues that arise in assessing a complaint is the assignment of the burden of proof. Generally speaking, the decisions of the Appellate Body have held that the burden of proof rests upon the party who asserts the affirmative of a particular claim or defense. If that party adduces sufficient evidence to raise a presumption that what is claimed is true, then the burden shifts to the other party to rebut the presumption. The Appellate Body has also spoken in terms of the need for a claimant to establish a *prima facie* case.

In GATT dispute settlement, it was often the case that factual issues were not that important. The basic issue was typically whether a particular governmental measure violated GATT rules. To date, comparatively more WTO disputes have involved disputed factual issues. In order to establish facts, panels normally ask oral and written questions to which the parties are expected to respond. The parties often bring government experts versed in the relevant field to panel meetings. Some parties have submitted affidavit evidence to establish facts. . . .

One area in which panels have already become more sophisticated is in the use of experts in scientific matters. In this regard, the DSU provides that if a panel deems it appropriate, it may consult either individual experts or form an expert review group to advise it on technical and scientific issues. . . .

One basic issue faced by panels is what sort of standard of review should be applied in reviewing challenged measures. Of course, in some cases that issue is not particularly significant. The only issue is whether the measure violates a WTO rule. But in an increasing number of cases, the assessment of a measure's consistency with WTO rules involves an assessment of the justification for a measure, for example, of whether a measure is "necessary" within the terms of an exception contained [in] GATT Article XX or whether a measure is "based on" or rationally related to a risk assessment in the case of an SPS (health) measure. In such a case, to what extent should a panel or the Appellate Body defer to the challenged government's assessment of necessity or rationality? The DSU gives no guidance on this issue beyond directing panels to make an objective assessment of the matter before them. . . .

After hearings and deliberations, the panel prepares a report detailing its conclusions. Traditionally, the panel has submitted its description of the dispute and of the parties' arguments to the parties for comment. Under the DSU, panels are required to submit an interim report containing their legal analysis for comment as well. Art. 15. Appendix 3 of the DSU specifies time limits for implementations of the various stages in the panel process. Those time limits suggest that the panel report should normally be issued within six to eight months of the establishment of the panel. In practice, cases typically take more time than that.

(d) Consideration and Adoption of Panel Reports

Under GATT dispute settlement practice prior to conclusion of the Uruguay Round, after a panel issued its report, it was considered for adoption by the GATT Council. Traditionally, decisions in the Council were made by consensus, which meant that any party—including the losing party—could prevent the Council from adopting a panel report. If unadopted, a report would represent only the view of the individual panel members. While parties did not often permanently block adoption of reports, some reports were never adopted (even when the underlying dispute was resolved) and others were adopted only after months of delay. Many commentators felt that this was a major failing in what was otherwise a fairly successful GATT dispute settlement system. Indeed, it is difficult to explain to someone new to the subject why the losing party by itself should be able to prevent adoption of a panel report.

The DSU fundamentally changed this procedure. It eliminates the possibility of blockage by providing in Article 16 that a panel report shall be adopted unless there is an appeal (see below) or a "reverse consensus," i.e., a consensus *not* to adopt the report. This switch from requiring a consensus for adoption to requiring a consensus to block adoption is a very significant change. It appears that it was adopted in hopes that it would satisfy US complaints about weaknesses in the GATT system and thereby result in the United States using the system in the future instead of taking unilateral action as it had done sometimes in the past. Basically, other GATT parties were willing to make the change as a way to rein in US unilateralism in trade matters. Indeed, article 23.1 of the DSU requires WTO members to use the WTO dispute settlement system exclusively if they "seek the redress of a violation of obligations or other nullification or impairment of benefits under the covered agreements." . . .

(3) The Appellate Body

The change in the consensus rule described above was paired with the introduction of a right to appeal a panel decision. The DSU creates a standing Appellate Body with seven members, appointed for four-year terms and representative of WTO membership. Only one reappointment is permitted. The Appellate Body is authorized to draw up its own working procedures, . . . in consultation with the Chairman of the DSB and the Director-General. These procedures . . . are available at the WTO website.

The Appellate Body hears appeals of panel reports in divisions of three, although its rules provide for the division hearing a case to exchange views with the other four Appellate Body members before the division finalizes its report. The members of the division that hears a particular appeal are selected by a secret procedure that is based on randomness, unpredictability and the opportunity for all members to serve without regard to national origin. The Appellate Body is required to issue its report within 60 (at most 90) days from the date of the appeal, and its report is to be adopted automatically by the DSB within 30 days, absent consensus to the contrary (as explained above). The appealed panel report is also adopted at that time, as modified by the Appellate Body report.

The Appellate Body's review is limited to issues of law and legal interpretation developed by the panel. However, the Appellate Body has taken a broad view of its power to review panel decisions. It has the express power to reverse, modify or affirm panel decisions, but the DSU does not include a possibility of remanding a case to a panel. Partly as a consequence, the Appellate Body has adopted the practice, where possible in light of a panel's factual findings, of completing the analysis of particular issues in order to resolve cases where it has significantly modified a panel's reasoning. This avoids requiring a party to start the whole proceeding over as a result of those modifications . . .

Although the Appellate Body has never articulated a standard of review that it will apply on appeals of panel reports, it has engaged in fairly intensive review of such reports. In doing so, it has in general left its stamp clearly on most areas of WTO law. . . . While strict notions of "stare decisis" do not apply in the WTO, it is clear that prior cases do play an important role in dispute settlement, especially those considered to be well-reasoned and persuasive. Indeed, the Appellate Body noted early on that adopted GATT panel reports created "legitimate expectations" that similar matters would be handled similarly, and both panels and the Appellate Body frequently support their decisions by extensive citation and quotation of prior decisions. Thus, it is appropriate to speak of the Appellate Body's effect on "WTO law."

Generally speaking, the Appellate Body tends to rely heavily on close textual interpretation of the WTO provisions at issue, stressing that a treaty interpreter must look to the ordinary meaning of the relevant terms, in their context and in light of the object and purpose of the relevant agreement (a requirement of Article 31 of the Vienna Convention of the Law of Treaties) and must not interpret provisions so as to render them devoid of meaning. The Appellate Body has expressed the need to respect due process and procedural rights of Members in the dispute settlement process, but by and large it has recognized considerable discretion on the part of panels, which has led it in the end to reject most procedural/due process challenges. On the whole, it is difficult to characterize the Appellate Body as being more or less deferential to Member discretion than panels. While it has significantly cut back on the scope of panel rulings in some cases, it has significantly expanded the scope of liability in others.

(4) Implementation and Suspension of Concessions

If it is found that a complaint is justified, the panel/Appellate Body report typically recommends that the offending member cease its violation of WTO rules, normally by bringing the offending measure into conformity with its obligations. After it adopts a report, the DSB monitors whether or not its recommendations are implemented. The DSU requires a losing respondent to indicate what actions it plans to take to implement the panel's recommendations. If immediate implementation is impracticable, then implementation is required within a reasonable period of time. Art. 21.3. The reasonable period of time is normally set by agreement of the contending parties, or, absent agreement, by arbitration, typically by a member of the Appellate Body. Normally, the period is not to exceed 15 months; a range of 8-10 months is average.

If the recommendations are not implemented, the prevailing party is entitled to seek compensation from the non-complying member or request DSB authority to suspend concessions previously made to that member (sometimes referred to as "retaliation"). Art. 22.1. . . . [U]nder the DSU, suspension of concessions is to be authorized automatically in the absence of implementation or compensation, absent a consensus in the DSB to the contrary. Art. 22.6. There are specific arbitration procedures for determining the level of such a suspension if no agreement can be reached.

The DSU provides: "Prompt compliance with recommendations or rulings of the DSB is essential in order to ensure the effective resolution of disputes to the benefit of all Members" (art. 21.1). The DSB will normally recommend the withdrawal of any measure found to be inconsistent with a member's obligations, and the DSU explicitly provides that withdrawal of a nonconforming measure is preferred to compensation or suspension of concessions. Art. 22.1. Compensation and suspensions of concessions are viewed as "temporary measures," to be used when a report is not implemented in a reasonable time. The preference for withdrawal is also found in the WTO Agreement itself, where article XVI:4 provides that "[e]ach Member shall ensure the conformity of its laws, regulations and administrative procedures with its obligations as provided in the annexed Agreements." Thus, there would appear to be an international law obligation to implement recommendations to withdraw inconsistent measures.

The application of the foregoing procedures on implementation and retaliation has been controversial. . . .

. . . [The record] suggests a successful implementation rate of 83%. It should be mentioned, however, that there have been a number of cases, now resolved, where there were long-running disputes over implementation. . . . Moreover, the record of successful implementation must also be tempered by the fact that in some cases, the complaining parties have accepted what they have claimed was less than full implementation. Nonetheless, for an international system of dispute settlement in which any case may be brought, this is an impressive record. . . .

The former Chairman of the WTO Appellate Body provided some insight and humanity into this dispute-resolution process in a 2002 speech excerpted below.

James Bacchus, Remarks at the Woodrow Wilson International Center for Scholars

(May 1, 2002)

I am often asked:

What is it like to be one of the "faceless foreign judges" of the World Trade Organization in Geneva, Switzerland? Today, I will try to answer that question, or at least part of it. . . .

We are seven around the table. We are from seven different countries. We are from seven different regions of the world. We are from seven different legal traditions. We are, in the words of the WTO treaty, "broadly representative of membership in the WTO." . . .

The subject of these discussions is what we call the "covered agreements." The "covered agreements" are the more than 27,000 pages of international concessions and obligations that comprise the WTO treaty and that bind all WTO members. . . .

We do not even have titles. The WTO treaty speaks only of a "standing Appellate Body." The treaty does not say what the seven "persons" who are members of the Appellate Body should be called. So we call ourselves simply "Members of the Appellate Body." . . .

Technically, the Appellate Body is rightly described as "quasi-judicial." To have legal effect, our rulings must be adopted by the Members of the WTO. But a ruling by the Appellate Body in an international trade dispute will *not* be adopted only if *all* the Members of the WTO decide "by consensus" that it should *not* be — including the Member or Members in whose favor we may have ruled. Thus far, this has never happened.

But whether our work is described as "judicial" or "quasi-judicial," and whatever we may be called, we have much to do around our table in Geneva. We have much to do because . . . the Appellate Body of the WTO is unique in two important ways.

The first way in which we are unique is that we have what we lawyers call "compulsory jurisdiction." All WTO Members have agreed in the WTO treaty to resolve all their disputes with other WTO Members involving matters that are covered by the WTO treaty in the WTO dispute settlement system.

The second way in which the Appellate Body is unique is that we make judgments that are enforced. Our judgments are enforced, not by us, but by the Members of the WTO themselves through the power of economic suasion.

The Members of the WTO are sovereign countries and customs territories. No Member of the WTO can ever be required to comply with any judgment in WTO dispute settlement. Yet, under the WTO treaty, if a Member chooses not to comply, it pays an economic price. That price is what the treaty describes as "compensation and the suspension of concessions."

This is a form of "damages" to the other Member injured in that trade dispute. These "damages" consist of either additional access for the injured Member to the market of the "non-complying" Member in other sectors of trade, or reduced access for the "non-complying" Member to the market of the injured Member in other sectors of trade. As this can sometimes be a very high price to pay, WTO Members have considerable economic incentive to choose to comply with WTO judgments. And they almost always do.

These two ways in which we are unique help keep us busy around our round table in Geneva in an effort to help provide what the WTO treaty calls "security and predictability to the multilateral trading system." Our jurisprudential uniqueness is, of course, the culmination of more than half a century of building the multilateral trading system, first under the GATT, and now under the Dispute Settlement Understanding that is the legal linchpin of the WTO treaty.

We are also kept busy because WTO Members know that, when they bring a case in WTO dispute settlement that eventually reaches the Appellate Body, they will receive a *legal* judgment, and not a *political* judgment. . . .

The parties to the proceedings in WTO dispute settlement that arise from these trade disputes are exclusively the countries and other customs territories that are Members of the WTO. . . .

Given the broad scope and sway of the WTO treaty, the disputes that are resolved in WTO dispute settlement can involve manufacturing, agriculture, services, intellectual property, investment, taxation, and virtually every other area of world commerce. The appeals we have judged thus far have involved everything from apples to computers, from automobiles to semiconductors, from shrimp to satellites, and from bananas to chemicals to oil to aerospace. . . .

We do not render advisory opinions on the Appellate Body. We render opinions only when there are specific trade disputes. By treaty, all WTO Members that are parties to a dispute have the automatic right to appeal "issues of law covered in the panel report and legal interpretations developed by the panel" to the Appellate Body. On appeal, we seven "shall address each of the issues raised . . . during the appellate proceeding." We "may uphold, modify or reverse the legal findings and conclusions of the panel." . . .

Thus, we cannot choose the disputes that are appealed to us. Unlike the Supreme Court of the United States, we have no discretionary jurisdiction. Further, we have no power to remand a dispute to a panel for further consideration. We have no authority whatsoever to decline to hear an appeal. Moreover, we have no authority whatsoever to refrain from "addressing" a legal issue that has been properly raised in an appeal. The WTO treaty says that we "shall address" every legal issue raised in an appeal. So we do.

And we do so within strict deadlines established by the treaty. Most other international tribunals have no deadlines. But, no matter how complicated the issues may be that are raised on appeal, generally we have no more than 90 days in which to hear and decide an appeal. . . . As our record reflects, we take seriously the need to "address" the legal issues . . .

. . . Using [our] working procedures, in each appeal, we review the panel record and the panel report, we review submissions by the WTO Members that are interested parties and third parties, we conduct an oral hearing on the legal issues that have been raised, and we deliberate and write a final report containing our judgment. And generally we do all this within no more than 90 days. (My colleagues would no doubt urge me to add that this is, actually, no more than 75 days, as we must allow two weeks for mandatory translation.) . . .

We have been able to meet our deadlines in part because we have shared our growing workload among the seven. By treaty, three of us sit as a "division" to hear and decide each appeal. Those three sign the report of the Appellate Body in that appeal. Before a decision is reached, the three on the "division" in the appeal engage in an "exchange of views" with the four others who are not on the "division." One of the three serves as "Presiding Member" of the "division." By treaty, all seven of us "serve in rotation" in all these roles, and, by rule, we do so on an anonymous and random basis that tends to equalize our individual workloads.

Whatever our individual role may be in any particular appeal, each of us strives always to reach a "consensus" in every appeal. We are not required to do so. The treaty does not prohibit dissents. The treaty provides only that "opinions expressed" by individuals serving on the Appellate Body must be "anonymous." But, thus far, in all our years of working together, and in about fifty appeals, there has not been even one dissent to the conclusions in any report of the Appellate Body. Thus far, all our decisions have been by "consensus."

I do not believe that I betray the "confidentiality" of our table talk in any way by saying that the "consensus" we have achieved in the many appeals that have been made, thus far, to the Appellate Body has not always been achieved easily. . . .

The disputes that are appealed to us and are discussed around the table are about the meaning of the obligations that are contained in the "covered agreements" that comprise the WTO treaty. These obligations are found in the words of the treaty. The meaning of the words of the treaty is thus our constant focus in rendering our judgments. As we noted in our very first appeal, this focus is in keeping with the international rules of treaty interpretation found in the Vienna Convention on the Law of Treaties.

Our focus on the words of the WTO treaty is as it should be. The WTO treaty contains WTO rules. The Appellate Body exists to construe WTO rules in WTO dispute settlement. Yet, as we also noted in our very first appeal, WTO rules cannot, in WTO dispute settlement, be viewed in "clinical isolation" from other international law.

Our responsibility in every appeal is to say everything about the meaning of the words of the treaty that must be said in order to "address" the legal issues "raised" in that appeal and thus assist the WTO Members in resolving that dispute in a "positive solution." Our aim in every appeal is to do that, only that, and no more. . . .

. . . [S]ome may say as well that some decisions have been made in appeals in WTO dispute settlement that should, ideally, have been made instead by the Members of the WTO through multilateral negotiations leading to WTO rulemaking. Here, too, in some instances, I might agree. Yet it is neither my role nor my place to make suggestions to the Members of the WTO about their rulemaking. The Members of the WTO have established an effective system for settling disputes about existing rules. It is for the Members of the WTO to decide how best to establish an effective system for making new rules.

You tell me. Which makes better sense? Should the Members of the WTO unravel an effective system for settling disputes about existing rules because they have not yet established an effective system for making new rules? Or, should the Members of the WTO try instead to establish a system for making new rules that will be as effective as the system they already have for settling disputes about existing rules? To intone one of the many truisms of which we sometimes seem so enamored in international law, but without the usual, obligatory Latin phrasing: don't fix what ain't broke; fix only what needs fixing.

In sum, I will say this to the critics of the various outcomes of various cases thus far in WTO dispute settlement. . . . I will trust *every* Member of the WTO to remember that the entire national interest of *no* Member is to be found in the outcome of any one, single case. Rather, the overriding and abiding national interest of *every* Member of the WTO is to be found instead in the shared international interest of *all* Members in the continued success and strengthening of the WTO dispute settlement system. And, because I am an American, I will be so bold as to add: This is especially true of the largest economy in the world and the largest trading nation in the world — the United States of America. And we Americans must never forget it. . . .

This will not always be easy. . . . [I]n 1990, . . . journalist Michael Kinsley in *The New Republic* . . . wrote . . . good advice for all Members of the WTO, and for all of us who support the work of the WTO, as, together, we seek and serve the international rule of law: . . . "Law that need not be obeyed if you disagree with it is not law. If we want meaningful international law to be available when we find it useful, we must respect it even when we don't." . . .

Notes and Questions

1. How similar were the old GATT panels to arbitration (i.e., where the panel's decision is binding)? How similar are the new WTO panels to arbitral panels? To an international court?

2. Unlike the old GATT system, the WTO system provides for a layer for appeals. The standing Appellate Body should help ensure consistency in panel decisions. If a case is appealed and the appellate panel makes its decision, how similar is that decision to an arbitration? Or to the highest appellate court in a jurisdiction?

3. Some Uruguay Round negotiators thought that the appeal mechanism also provided a little more "political cover" to a losing party back home. The losing state could appeal an adverse panel decision. Even if it lost again, the state could argue to legislators and various interest groups back home that it had fought the matter as hard as possible, that it had "gone the extra mile." This would be part of the justification for changing practices or laws that had been found in violation of the WTO agreements.

4. What are the allowed time periods for the panel and Appellate Body proceedings under the DSU? See Article 20. The panels and especially the Appellate Body have generally adhered to the allowed time periods. How long then is the losing party allowed to take to comply with the panel's or Appellate Body's recommendations? See Article 21.

5. Does the panel or Appellate Body have the authority to rule a country's law or regulation void because it is inconsistent with a WTO agreement? How would a panel's or the Appellate Body's decision differ in language and effect from those of the U.S. Supreme Court if the Supreme Court found the law of a U.S. state (e.g., California) inconsistent with the U.S. Constitution? How would a WTO decision differ from the decision of the European Court of Justice if it found the law of a member state (e.g., France) inconsistent with the EC Treaty? See DSU, Article 19.

6. What are the remedies under the WTO? Review GATT Articles XXII and XXIII and Articles 21 and 22 of the WTO's dispute procedure in the Documentary Supplement. Are punitive damages allowed? Are the remedies limited to a decision that the offending practice be changed or to steps by the injured party to obtain compensation or suspension of concessions or other obligations? Is compensation limited to the amount of harm suffered (see Article 22.4)?

7. How effective are these remedies for a small country that is being injured by the illegal practices of a much larger trading partner? What if the large trading partner decides that it is upset enough with the other country (possibly for foreign policy reasons) that it is willing to accept an equivalent suspension of concessions or other obligations rather than change its practices?

8. Near the end of the excerpt from Professors Jackson, Davey, and Sykes, the authors contend: "Thus, there would appear to be an international law obligation to implement recommendations to withdraw inconsistent measures." Countries have generally complied with the panel/Appellate Body reports.

However, what if a country (or countries) feels strongly that its national interests do not justify changing its laws or regulations to make them consistent with the WTO agreements as interpreted by the panel/Appellate Body? For example, in the *Beef Hormones* case, the Appellate Body found in 1998 that the European Union did not have the requisite scientific basis under the Agreement on the Application of Sanitary and Phytosanitary Measures (SPS Agreement) for preventing the importation of American beef that had been fed hormones. However, the EU continued to refuse to allow the importation of the American beef, even after the WTO had authorized the United States to retaliate by imposing new tariffs on a variety of EU imports worth over $100 million. The EU countries continued to resist, in part because of political pressures in their countries from various groups that were genuinely concerned about the health effects of consuming beef that had once been treated with hormones, even though the scientific basis for their fears might not have been sufficient for the WTO panel and Appellate Body. This decision also took place in the context of England's troubles with mad-cow disease in its cattle and an outbreak of hoof-and-mouth disease in livestock in England and some other EU countries.

Should the WTO require the EU leaders to ignore these domestic concerns and accept the WTO decision as its legal obligation without any exceptions, thus allowing the importation of the American beef? Or, in certain special cases, should the WTO recognize that its members have the sovereign right essentially to decide not to comply and to accept the retaliatory measures indefinitely? If the WTO should not accept any "escape valve" whereby a country can decline to comply and accept retaliation, how can the WTO force compliance? Are these forcing measures now provided for in the DSU? (See Article 22.) Might the elimination of any escape value be counter-productive in terms of building support for the WTO?

After over a decade of wrangling and consultations, the United States and EU signed a Memorandum of Understanding in May 2009 that would reduce American sanctions in return for a tariff rate quota with a zero duty for imports of hormone-free beef to the EU, with the possibility for eventual suspension of all sanctions. This arrangement may become permanent.

Similar issues might be raised in the future by attempts by countries to prohibit or limit the importation of food that has been grown with genetically modified seed. This seed has been developed to grow strains of crops that are more resistant to disease and/or have higher yields. Critics question whether the effects, if any, on the health of people who consume these crops are completely known.

A panel report issued in September 2006 concluded that a general *de facto* moratorium on approval of genetically modified products (GMO) by the European Communities violated the SPS Agreement because the moratorium resulted in undue delay in the completion of approval procedures for the products. The panel noted that the parties bringing the case did not question whether the European Communities could consider possible risks of GMOs in implementing this general moratorium. This panel's decision did not examine whether biotech products in general are safe or not. The EU was given until November 2007 to comply with the panel's decision, but did not lift the moratorium. As a result, the United States initiated further proceedings against the EU, but then suspended them in favor of further negotiations. As of October 2010, the EU had settled with the other two parties challenging the moratorium, Canada and Argentina, but a resolution with the United States had not been reached.

9. The frequent and diverse use of the WTO dispute resolution system continues. From January 1995 through October 2010, there had been over 400 complaints filed with the WTO. There were over 30 active cases in October 2010. About 70 percent of the panel reports were appealed. Over 130 Appellate Body and panel reports had been adopted by the Dispute Settlement Body.

10. To give you a sense of the diversity of the WTO cases, here are some of the first cases for which the whole process has been completed and the report of the Appellate Body adopted: a complaint by the United States and EU against Japan's discriminatory internal taxes on alcoholic beverages; a complaint by Costa Rica against U.S. restrictions on imports of cotton and man-made fiber underwear; a complaint by the Philippines against Brazil for measures affecting desiccated coconut; a complaint by the United States against Canada regarding certain measures on periodicals; a complaint by the United States and several Latin American countries against the European Union's regime for the importation, sale, and distribution of bananas; and a complaint by the United States against India's patent protection for pharmaceutical and agricultural chemical products. More recently, reports have been adopted on: a complaint by the EU against Brazil regarding imports of retreaded tires; a complaint by the United States and Taiwan against the EU for tariff treatment of intellectual property; a complaint by the United States against China for trade restrictions on films, recordings and publications; and a complaint by India against the United States regarding rules of origin on textiles.

11. As the incomplete list above suggests, the United States has brought more cases than any other country. It has also been sued more frequently than any other country. The United States has lost some cases, including one regarding billions of dollars in tax benefits for U.S. corporations who formed special foreign sales corporations, one involving increased tariffs on steel imports, one involving a cross-border prohibition on gambling and betting services, and one involving subsidies on cotton that affects billions of dollars in U.S. agricultural subsidy programs. Nevertheless, more often than not, the United States has been successful in the WTO cases, reflecting in part its relatively open domestic market.

From what you know now, do you think that it is generally in the interest of the United States to have a strong WTO (with rules, an institutional framework, and a strong dispute resolution system) that is designed to open markets for goods and services, to encourage foreign investment, and to protect intellectual property rights? What concerns might you have regarding a strong WTO vis-à-vis other international institutions, the U.S. government, or other entities? (The institutional structure and role of the WTO will be discussed further in Chapter 5.)

12. In November 2001, the Fourth Ministerial Conference on the WTO was held in Doha, Qatar. The Conference issued the Doha Declaration, which called for negotiations on various aspects of WTO structure and implementation procedure, including negotiations to revise the Dispute Settlement Understanding. The negotiations bogged down, however, over several disputes, including complaints by developing countries about the agricultural subsidies of developed countries that

protected the developed countries' domestic farmers and markets. Reaching an agreement on any of the major issues was hampered in part by the WTO's requirement that there be unanimity among member states on new agreements. In November 2010, the Seventh Ministerial Conference officially avoided negotiating at all, focusing instead on a "review" of WTO activities.

13. The WTO has an excellent, up-to-date Web site at http://www.wto.org. In addition, there is now a voluminous array of books, journals, and articles about the WTO. For example, besides the sources cited above, see John H. Jackson, The Jurisprudence of GATT and the WTO (2000); The Law, Economics and Politics of Retaliation in WTO Dispute Settlement (Chad Bown & Joost Pauwelyn, eds., 2010); The WTO and International Trade Law/Dispute Settlement (Petros C. Mavroidis & Alan O. Sykes eds., 2005).

3. *Mass Claims Processing*

Other examples of the tailored dispute resolution system include the extensive developments in mass claims processing. Similar to the circumstances that led to the Iran-U.S. Claims Tribunal, there have been other situations where an event or cluster of events have given rise to many claims, and policymakers are able to agree on an international claims process that involves some variant on arbitration or other form of international dispute resolution and that can address the claims or at least most of them.

Examples include the mass claims processes established to handle claims arising from Iraq's 1990 invasion of Kuwait (the U.N. Compensation Commission or UNCC); from the Eritrean-Ethiopian strife (Eritrea-Ethiopia Claims Commission); from the breakup of Yugoslavia (the Commission for Real Property Claims in Bosnia and Herzegovina); and from the Holocaust, expropriations, and other activities during the World War II period (e.g., Austrian General Settlement Fund and the Holocaust Victim Assets Programme). More recent examples include the Kosovo Property Claims Commission (KPCC), the Iraq Property Claims Commission, and the Marshall Islands Nuclear Claims Tribunal.

For further examples and updated information about these various mass claims processes, see the Web site of the Permanent Court of Arbitration at http://www.pca-cpa.org. See also Redressing Injustices Through Mass Claims Process: Innovative Responses to Unique Challenges (International Bureau of the Permanent Court of Arbitration ed., 2006).

F. DOMESTIC COURTS

1. *The Role of International Law*

Federal and state courts in the United States and domestic courts in other countries often adjudicate cases involving international issues. These cases might range from a claim of violation of internationally recognized human rights to the enforcement of a contract for the sale of goods across national boundaries.

In determining these cases, U.S. courts might apply state law, a federal statute or common law, the law of another country, or international law. International treaties to which the United States is a party are part of U.S. law. Moreover, as seen earlier with the *Paquete Habana* and *Sosa* cases (in Chapter 3.C), U.S. courts sometimes apply customary international law as part of U.S. law. Indeed, U.S. courts seem to be encountering such international law questions more frequently in recent decades. (See Chapter 3. Questions of choice of law and of the applicability of another nation's laws are discussed further in Chapter 7.)

Similarly, another nation's domestic courts might decide cases by applying that nation's laws, the law of another state, or international law. As discussed in the following excerpt, the role of international law in other countries varies. As in the United States, there are often important differences between the role of treaties and customary international law. Notwithstanding the variations, both treaties and customary international law appear to play an important role in many countries.

I.A. Shearer, Starke's International Law

67, 76-77 (11th ed. 1994)

The object of the present discussion is to ascertain in what manner and to what extent municipal courts do apply a rule of international law. How far do they give effect to it automatically, and how far is some specific municipal measure of statutory or judicial incorporation required before that rule can be recognised as binding within the municipal sphere? A further question is, how far a rule of international law will be applied by a municipal court if it actually conflicts with a rule of municipal law judge-made or statutory rule. The answers to these questions will be found to require distinctions to be made, on the one hand, between customary and treaty rules of international law; and on the other between statutory and judge-made municipal law. . . .

Practice of States Other than Great Britain and the United States

The practice of states other than Great Britain and the United States reveals wide variations both in the requirements of constitutional law, and in the attitudes of municipal courts concerning the application therein of customary international law and of treaties.

So far as one can sum up this practice, and despite the hazard of generalisation on so complex a matter, the following propositions may be ventured:

1. In a large number of states, customary rules of international law are applied as part of internal law by municipal courts, without the necessity for any specific act of incorporation, provided that there is no conflict with existing municipal law.
2. Only a minority of states follow a practice whereby, without the necessity for any specific act of incorporation, their municipal courts apply customary rules of international law to the extent of allowing these to prevail in case of conflict with a municipal statute or municipal judge-made law.

3. There is no uniform practice concerning the application of treaties within the municipal sphere. Each country has its own particularities as regards promulgation or publication of treaties, legislative approval of treaty provisions, and so on. Moreover, certain treaties, such as informal administrative arrangements, are never submitted to the legislature. Also the courts in some countries, for example the German Federal Republic, will, like American courts, give effect to self-executing treaties, that is to say, those capable of application without the necessity of legislative implementation. In other countries, for example, Belgium, legislative enactment or legislative approval is necessary for almost all treaties, particularly those which affect the status of private citizens. As to conflicts between the provisions of treaties and earlier or later statutes, it is only in relatively few countries that the superiority of the treaty in this regard is established. France is a case in point, for if a treaty has been duly ratified in accordance with law, French tribunals, both judicial and administrative, will give effect to it, notwithstanding a conflict with internal legislation. But in most countries, for example, Norway, treaties do not per se operate to supersede state legislation or judge-made law. Exceptionally, however, there are some countries the courts of which go so far as to give full force to treaties, even if contrary to the provisions of the constitution of the country concerned.
4. In general, there is discernible a considerable weight of state practice requiring that in a municipal court, primary regard be paid to municipal law, irrespective of the applicability of rules of international law, and hence relegating the question of any breach of international law to the diplomatic domain.

Reference should be made in this connection to certain modern constitutions, containing far-reaching provisions to the effect that international law shall be treated as an integral part of municipal law. A current example is article 25 of the Basic Law for the Federal Republic of Germany which lays down that the general rules of public international law shall form part of federal law, and shall take precedence over the laws of and create rights and duties directly for the inhabitants of the federal territory. It has been claimed that this and similar constitutional provisions reflect a growing tendency among states to acknowledge the supremacy of international law within the municipal sphere. Be that as it may, it is none the less curious that these constitutional provisions appear to support the positivist thesis that before international law can be applicable by municipal courts some specific adoption by municipal law is required, since it is only in virtue of these provisions of municipal constitutional law that the rules of international law are valid and applicable within the municipal sphere. . . .

Questions

1. Based on your knowledge of practice in the United States and other countries, do you think that domestic courts should recognize an increased role for customary international law? Should customary international law take precedence over acts by a country's chief executive or the chief executive's delegates? Over acts that a country recognizes as exclusively or primarily the responsibility of

the chief executive—for example, recognition of new governments? Should newly developed customary international law have precedence over a country's prior statutes? Should later domestic statutes override a rule of customary international law?

2. Why do you think that the practice regarding international treaties varies so much among states? Might this reflect the relative roles of the chief executive and the national legislature in law making? Should each state have a presumption that any treaty (or certain types of treaties) is self-executing? Or should the presumption be that a treaty is non-self-executing? What effect might such a presumption have on the relative roles of the chief executive and the national legislature?

3. Should domestic courts be the arbiters of the role of customary international law? Similarly, should domestic courts have the final say on whether a treaty is self-executing or not? Or should the courts defer to the chief executive or the legislature on various matters?

2. *Enforcement of Another State's Civil Judgments*

Once you have a judgment, you might need to enforce it if the other party does not voluntarily comply. One possible approach to enforce a civil judgment is through the domestic courts of another country. This is another way in which domestic courts participate in the international arena.

United States courts are required by the Full Faith and Credit clause of the Constitution to recognize and enforce the judgments of sister states (e.g., New York, California, Virginia). Article VI, section 1 provides: "Full Faith and Credit shall be given in each State to the public Acts, Records, and Judicial Proceeding of every other State."

Foreign judgments, however, do not have the support of the constitutional command. The usual starting point for analysis of the duty of U.S. courts to enforce judgments is the principle of comity among nations, enunciated in the old case of Hilton v. Guyot, 159 U.S. 113, 202-203 (1895). And, since Erie v. Tompkins, 304 U.S. 64 (1938), it has been accepted that in the absence of a federal statute or treaty or some other basis for federal jurisdiction (e.g., admiralty), recognition and enforcement of foreign country judgments is a matter of a state law, and an action to enforce a foreign country judgment is not an action arising under federal laws. Thus, state courts, and federal courts applying state law, recognize and enforce foreign country judgments without regard for federal rules.

The following excerpt from the Restatement briefly notes the diversity of practice among foreign countries regarding recognition and enforcement.

Restatement, Part IV, Chapter 8: Foreign Judgments and Awards

Introductory Note

. . . There are no agreed principles governing recognition and enforcement of foreign judgments, except that no state recognizes or enforces the judgment of another state rendered without jurisdiction over the judgment debtor. . . .

State practice varies widely. Some states require a treaty or proof of reciprocity (e.g., the Federal Republic of Germany), some have no such requirement (e.g., France), and some do not enforce foreign judgments at all in the absence of a treaty. . . . Some states (e.g., the United States) treat default judgments and contested judgments substantially alike for purposes of enforcement; others (e.g., Great Britain) enforce default judgments in limited circumstances only. Some states distinguish sharply between civil judgments ordering the payment of money and other judgments, such as those determining status of persons; others treat different types of judgments substantially alike. Some states recognize foreign judgments directly; others require "validation" by local courts (e.g., Italy). Some states (e.g., France) permit intermediate provisional measures, such as attachment of the judgment debtor's assets, prior to decision on enforcement. All states decline to recognize some judgments on the basis of conflict with their public policy or *ordre public*, but these terms have different meaning from state to state. Courts of some states (e.g., France) recognize a foreign judgment only if they would have applied the same law to the controversy as that chosen by the rendering court, or if the choice of law did not affect the result. Some states (e.g., Belgium) reserve the right to review the merits of a foreign judgment, though they do not always do so. It appears that the country most receptive to recognition of foreign judgments is the United States, in which the principles and practices engendered by the Full Faith and Credit clause in the United States Constitution in respect of sister-State judgments have to a large extent been carried over to recognition and enforcement of judgments of foreign states. . . .

The next excerpt expands on U.S. practice regarding the recognition and enforcement of foreign civil judgments and then discusses in some detail the practices of Germany and England.

Gary B. Born and Peter B. Rutledge, International Civil Litigation in United States Courts

1009-1017 (4th ed. 2007)

A. Introduction

In most circumstances, the judgment of a national court has no independent force outside the forum's territory. Thus, most courts will (and can) enforce their own money judgments only against assets located within their territorial jurisdiction; likewise, most courts will only infrequently attempt to preclude re-litigation in foreign forums already decided in a domestic proceeding. As a general rule, therefore, a judgment *will* operate in foreign states only if the courts of those states are willing to provide assistance by recognizing or enforcing the judgment. . . .

1. Recognition and Enforcement Distinguished

"Recognition" and "enforcement" of foreign judgments are related but distinct concepts. The recognition of a foreign judgment occurs when a U.S. court relies upon a foreign judicial ruling to preclude litigation of a particular claim, or issue, on the ground that it has been previously litigated abroad. Recognition is akin to the domestic U.S. doctrines of *res judicata* and collateral estoppel. In contrast, the enforcement of a foreign judgment occurs when a court affirmatively uses its coercive powers to compel a defendant ("judgment debtor") to satisfy a judgment rendered abroad. The enforcement of foreign judgments is typically sought by a plaintiff ("judgment creditor") who has obtained a money judgment in foreign proceedings that the judgment debtor refuses to satisfy.

2. Recognition and Enforcement of Sister State Judgments Under the U.S. Full Faith and Credit Clause

Before examining the recognition and enforcement of "foreign" judgments, it is useful to consider briefly the treatment of this issue in domestic U.S. litigation, where the judgments of one state's courts are routinely enforced in sister states. . . . Article IV, §1 of the U.S. Constitution requires that "Full Faith and Credit shall be given in each State to the public Acts, Records, and Judicial Proceedings of every other State." The full faith and credit clause *requires* state courts, as a matter of federal constitutional law, to recognize any valid final judgment rendered in another state of the Union.

The enforceability of state court judgments under the Full Faith and Credit Clause is subject to limited exceptions. These permit nonenforcement only where a state judgment was rendered by a court without personal or subject matter jurisdiction, where the defendant did not receive adequate notice or an opportunity to be heard, or where the state judgment was obtained by fraud. . . . Recognition or enforcement of a sister state judgment is required even where the underlying claim is contrary to the public policy of the state where enforcement is sought. . . .

The Full Faith and Credit Clause reflects fundamental national policies. The clause rests on the belief that national unity will be promoted by requiring individual states to give effect to the judicial decisions of other states. . . . The clause also reflects the public interest in judicial finality. . . .

B. Recognition and Enforcement of Foreign Judgments by U.S. Courts

1. No Express Federal Law Governing Recognition and Enforcement of Foreign Judgments

There is presently no federal standard governing the enforcement of judgments rendered by foreign courts in the United States.[21] Unlike sister state judgments, foreign judgments are not governed by the Full Faith and Credit Clause. Likewise, although federal statutes have been tabled,[23] there is no federal statute generally applicable to the enforcement of foreign court judgments in U.S. courts.

Unlike many foreign states, the United States is not a party to any international agreement regarding the mutual recognition of judgments. (In contrast, the United States is a party to the New York Convention, dealing among other things with the

21. This distinguishes the recognition and enforcement of foreign court judgments from the enforcement of international arbitral awards, where most issues are governed by federal statute (the Federal Arbitration Act) or by treaty (the New York Convention).

23. . . . [T]he American Law Institute recently approved a proposed federal statute governing the recognition and enforcement of foreign judgments. . . .

recognition and enforcement of foreign arbitral awards.) Indeed, the United States has made few attempts to conclude treaties with other countries on the reciprocal recognition and enforcement of judgments, and those attempts have failed. . . .

. . . [A]t the initiative of the United States, the Hague Conference on Private International Law made efforts to produce an acceptable text of a multilateral judgments convention between 1992 and 2001. These negotiations eventually failed and the Hague Conference instead turned its attention to the much more limited proposed Convention on Choice of Courts Agreement [which, as discussed in the Notes below, is not in force and which the United States has not ratified]. . . .

2. Contemporary Approaches to Enforceability of Foreign Judgments in the United States

Although the United States lacks a uniform nationwide standard for enforcing foreign judgments, there are surprisingly few fundamental differences in the approaches taken by the various states. In some 20 states, the recognition of foreign judgments is governed by state common law, derived from the Supreme Court's 1895 decision in Hilton v. Guyot [159 U.S. 113 (1895)]. Thirty other states* have adopted the UFMJRA ["Uniform Foreign Money Judgments Recognition Act"], modeled largely on *Hilton's* standards.

a. *Hilton v. Guyot: International Comity and the Presumptive Enforceability of Foreign Judgments.*

Most state courts have adopted the basic approach to foreign judgments taken almost a century ago in Hilton v. Guyot. There, a French citizen sought to enforce in the United States a judgment of a French court against two New York residents arising out of the New Yorkers' business in France. The Supreme Court reviewed a New York federal court's enforcement of the judgment.

Writing for the Court, Justice Gray began by suggesting that the enforceability of a foreign judgment required looking to international law, citing the *Paquete Habana* rule that international law "is part of our law, and must be ascertained and administered by the courts of justice, as often as such questions are presented in litigation." With this explanation, Justice Gray turned to prevailing territorial limits on national jurisdiction as a ground for denying the French judgment any independent effect in the United States: "No law has any effect, of its own force, beyond the limits of the sovereignty from which its authority is derived."

The Court went on to consider what rationale would justify a U.S. court in giving effect to a foreign court's judgment. It reasoned that international comity was the relevant source of authority:

> . . . "Comity," in the legal sense, is neither a matter of absolute obligation, on the one hand, nor of mere courtesy and good will, upon the other. But it is the recognition which one nation allows within its territory to the legislative, executive or judicial acts of another nation, having due regard both to international duty and convenience, and

*[And the District of Columbia. — Eds.]

> to the rights of its own citizens or of other persons who are under the protection of its laws.

Based upon this principle of comity, *Hilton* fashioned a rule of general common law governing when U.S. federal courts should enforce foreign judgments:

> [W]here there has been opportunity for a full and fair trial abroad before a court of competent jurisdiction, conducting the trial upon regular proceedings, after due citation or voluntary appearance of the defendant, and under a system of jurisprudence likely to secure an impartial administration of justice between the citizens of its own country and those of other countries, and there is nothing to show either prejudice in the court, or in the system of laws under which it was sitting, or fraud in procuring the judgment, or any other special reason why the comity of this nation should not allow it full effect, the merits of the case should not, in an action brought in this country upon the judgment, be tried afresh, as on a new trial or an appeal, upon the mere assertion by the party that the judgment was erroneous in law or in fact.

The Court rejected earlier U.S. (and other) authorities which had concluded that foreign judgments were only prima facie evidence of the defendant's liability and were subject to rebuttal in the court where recognition was sought. On the facts in *Hilton*, the Court found that the French decree satisfied the above requirements, but nonetheless refused to enforce the judgment, citing a "reciprocity requirement." In a 5-4 decision, Justice Gray reasoned that international comity did not require enforcement of the French judgment because French courts would not reciprocally enforce a U.S. judgment in reverse circumstances.

Hilton's basic rule continued to be followed in the United States, with various modifications, for the next century. . . .

b. Statutory Mechanisms for the Enforcement of Foreign Judgments: Uniform Foreign Money Judgments Recognition Act and Uniform Foreign-Country Money Judgments Recognition Act.

Although [many] states follow *Hilton's* common law approach, [most] have instead enacted statutes setting forth the circumstances in which their courts will enforce foreign money judgments. Each of these states has adopted some form of the UFMJRA, which was developed in 1962 by the National Conference of Commissioners on Uniform State Laws and the American Bar Association. The Act was based closely on common law principles derived from Hilton v. Guyot. . . .

As with the common law, foreign judgments are presumptively entitled to recognition under the UFMJRA if they are "final and conclusive and enforceable where rendered even though an appeal therefrom is pending or it is subject to an appeal."[50] If a foreign judgment does satisfy this standard, then it is "conclusive between the parties to the extent that it grants or denies recovery of a sum of money." Again like *Hilton*, however, the Act sets forth a number of specific exceptions to the general enforceability of foreign money judgments. . . .

50. Uniform Foreign-Money Judgments Recognition Act, §2.

The National Conference of Commissioners on Uniform State Laws recently approved the Uniform Foreign-Country Money Judgments Recognition Act ("UFCMJRA"). The Purpose of the UFCMJRA was "to update the [UFMJRA], to clarify its provisions and to correct problems created by the interpretation of the [UFMJRA] since its promulgation." [As of July 2010, 14 states have adopted the UFCMJRA, but] the UFMJRA continues to be the main statutory source governing the enforcement of foreign judgments in the United States.

3. Foreign Approaches to the Enforceability of U.S. and Other Judgments

There is no uniform practice among foreign states regarding the recognition and enforcement of foreign judgments. In many states (particularly civil law jurisdictions), the recognition of foreign judgments has been dealt with by bilateral or multilateral international agreements. Where no international agreement exists (as is the case where United States judgments are concerned), recognition of foreign judgments is often difficult.

This difficulty can be particularly acute with regard to U.S. judgments, because of the complexity of U.S. litigation procedures, the size of damage awards, and the nature of U.S. jurisdictional claims. . . . In the words of a leading European commentator, who was intimately involved in negotiations for the abortive Hague judgments convention, "everybody fears to be obliged to enforce what they consider to be excessive judgments coming out of U.S. courts".

In Germany, the recognition of foreign judgments is generally governed by §328 of the German Code of Civil Procedure. Section 328 provides:

Recognition of a judgment of a foreign court shall not be permitted:

1. if the courts of the relevant foreign state would not have jurisdiction pursuant to German law;
2. if the defendant, who did not appear in the proceeding and objects on that basis, was not properly served or served in sufficient time to allow him to defend himself;
3. if the judgment is inconsistent with a German judgment or with a prior foreign judgment whose recognition is sought or with a pending proceeding concerning the same facts;
4. if recognition of the judgment would manifestly lead to a result which is incompatible with fundamental principles of German law (ordre public), particularly, if recognition would be incompatible with constitutional principles;
5. if reciprocity is not assured. . . .

In England, the recognition and enforcement of foreign judgments is, in the absence of an international agreement, generally subject to common law standards. These standards can be summarized as follows:

> The basic rule under English law is that any foreign judgment for a debt or definite sum of money (not being a sum payable in respect of taxes, or other charges of a like nature, a fine or other penalty) which is final and conclusive on the merits, may be enforced at Common Law in the absence of fraud or some other overriding consideration of public

> policy provided that the foreign court had jurisdiction over the defendant in accordance with conflict of law principles.

In cases involving default judgments, English law imposes strict jurisdictional limits. In particular, a foreign court will be found to have properly exercised jurisdiction only if the defendant was physically present in the foreign state at the time of the action, or if the defendant voluntarily appeared in the action, or if the defendant contractually submitted to the jurisdiction of the foreign court.

The Restatement notes that there are some exceptions to U.S. recognition and enforcement of foreign court judgments—notably for tax and penal judgments.

§483. Recognition and Enforcement of Tax and Penal Judgments

Courts in the United States are not required to recognize or to enforce judgments for the collection of taxes, fines, or penalties rendered by the courts of other states.

Comment

a. Nonrecognition not required but permitted. This section states a principle that has long been accepted both in international and in United States practice. However, the rationale for the rule has been questioned, particularly with respect to tax judgments. No rule of United States law or of international law would be violated if a court in the United States enforced a judgment of a foreign court for payment of taxes or comparable assessments. . . .

b. Penal judgments defined. A penal judgment, for purposes of this section, is a judgment in favor of a foreign state or one of its subdivisions, and primarily punitive rather than compensatory in character. A judgment for a fine or penalty is within this section; a judgment in favor of a foreign state arising out of a contract, a tort, a loan guaranty, or similar civil controversy is not penal for purposes of this section. . . .

c. Tax judgment defined. For purposes of this section, a tax judgment is a judgment in favor of a foreign state or one of its subdivisions based on a claim for an assessment of a tax, whether imposed in respect of income, property, transfer of wealth, or transactions in the taxing state. . . .

e. Recognition and enforcement of public law judgments distinguished. Judgments not entitled to enforcement under this section may nevertheless be recognized for certain purposes. For instance, a foreign conviction of a crime may be recognized for purposes of denying the convicted person a visa or naturalization; a conviction for extortion or blackmail maybe recognized as a defense to an action by the convicted person on the debt in question; a conviction in a foreign bastardy or paternity proceeding may be recognized in an action for child support.

Questions of the enforceability of a judgment can affect the choice of the forum where a party might be inclined to bring an action that involves international issues.

The discussion above provides the essential situation for the enforcement of a foreign court's civil judgment in U.S. courts.

As discussed in Section D above, decisions by an international arbitral panel can be enforced relatively easily in the many states that have ratified the New York Convention on the Recognition and Enforcement of Foreign Arbitral Awards or the International Convention for the Settlement of Investment Disputes. However, as is also true of foreign court judgments, if the recalcitrant party is a state (and if it has not waived its immunity), there still might be problems executing on specific assets because of the doctrine of foreign sovereign immunity. (See Chapter 6.A.)

Notes and Questions

1. As of 2010, 17 states, the District of Columbia, and the Virgin Islands had adopted some version of the Uniform Foreign Money Judgments Recognition Act. Among the states were Alaska, Connecticut, Delaware, Florida, Georgia, Illinois, Maine, Maryland, Massachusetts, Missouri, New Jersey, New York, North Dakota, Ohio, Pennsylvania, Texas, and Virginia. As of 2010, 14 states had adopted the newer Uniform Foreign-Country Money Judgments Recognition Act (UFCMJRA), including California, Colorado, Hawaii, Idaho, Iowa, Michigan, Minnesota, Montana, Nevada, New Mexico, North Carolina, Oklahoma, Oregon, and Washington. See www.nccusl.org/Update.

2. Looking to the empirical evidence, whether it be under common law or under the UFMJRA/UFCMJRA, it appears that U.S. courts generally uphold foreign court civil judgments, though there have been exceptions. At the same time, although it has been said that the *Hilton* reciprocity requirement "is no longer followed in the great majority of State and federal courts in the United States" (Restatement Section 481, cmt. *d*), a recent treatise finds that "the reciprocity requirement has recently enjoyed a resurgence of sorts. Some states, such as Ohio and Texas, include a reciprocity requirement as a discretionary ground for denying enforcement to a foreign judgment, while others, such as Georgia and Massachusetts, mandate reciprocal treatment for recognition of foreign judgments." Gary B. Born and Peter B. Rutledge, International Civil Litigation in United States Courts 1027 (4th ed. 2006) (footnote omitted). Some eight U.S. states that have adopted the Uniform Act included a provision concerning reciprocity.

3. As indicated in footnote 23 of the Born excerpt above, the American Law Institute approved in 2005 a proposed federal law relating to the enforcement and recognition of foreign court judgments. After considerable discussion within the ALI, the proposal does include a qualified reciprocity requirement. ALI, The Foreign Judgments Recognition and Enforcement Act (2005). Congress has yet to take action on the proposed statute.

4. Would you favor a uniform rule in the United States for the enforcement of foreign court judgments? Should states be encouraged to adopt uniform acts such as the Uniform Foreign Money Judgments Recognition Act? Or should Congress, pursuant to the commerce clause and other constitutional provisions, pass a statute establishing uniform standards as it did with the statute implementing the New York Convention? Or should matters be left as they are?

5. The United States has been involved in negotiations seeking a multinational convention on the recognition of foreign court judgments. The negotiations

have met with only limited success. In 2005, the Hague Conference on Private International Law reached agreement on a proposed new multilateral treaty, the Convention on Choice of Court Agreements. As explained by Professor Ronald Brand:

> The Convention sets out three basic rules:
>
> 1) the court chosen by the parties in an exclusive choice of court agreement has jurisdiction;
> 2) if an exclusive choice of court agreement exists, a court not chosen by the parties does not have jurisdiction, and must decline to hear the case; and
> 3) a judgment resulting from jurisdiction exercised in accordance with an exclusive choice of court agreement must be recognized and enforced in the courts of other Contracting States. [Brand, The New Hague Convention on Choice of Court Agreements, ASIL Insight, July 26, 2005.]

As of November 2010, the Convention has not yet come into force. Only Mexico has ratified it. See status table at the Hague Convention Web site, http://www.hcch.net/index_en.php?act=conventions.text&cid=98.

6. Since 1978, the European Union countries have had arrangements dealing with jurisdiction and enforcement of foreign judgments, first in the Convention on Jurisdiction and Enforcement of Judgments in Civil and Commercial Matters (known as the Brussels Convention), and more recently in the European Community Council Regulation on Jurisdiction and the Recognition and Enforcement of Judgments in Civil and Commercial Matters.* The Regulation deals with the recognition of foreign judgments and the permissible bases for establishing jurisdiction among member states of the EU. All EU member states are covered by the Regulation.

The Regulation applies in civil and commercial matters, except for revenue, customs, and administrative matters, and a few other areas. The Regulation first provides the basic rules for jurisdiction for a member state's court. The basic principle is that jurisdiction is exercised by the state where the defendant is domiciled, regardless of nationality. The Regulation does have a provision prohibiting member states from using designated "exorbitant" bases to establish jurisdiction over persons. In the case of legal persons or firms, their domicile is based on where they have their statutory basis, central administration, or principal place of business.

The Regulation then provides for automatic recognition and enforcement of a judgment given by a court in another member state that has jurisdiction under the Regulation. If a party contests the recognition of a judgment against it, provision is made for a special procedure to obtain a declaration of enforceability. Essentially the sole ground for nonrecognition or nonenforcement is that the recognition or enforcement would be manifestly contrary to public policy. Are the Regulation's provisions similar in this respect to those of the Full Faith and Credit Clause in U.S. practice?

7. The Internet poses complex problems for the enforcement of foreign court judgments. Several French associations brought suit in France in 2000 against Yahoo!, Inc., an Internet service provider (ISP) based in California, for failing to

*Council Regulation (EC) No 44/2001 of 22 December 2000 on jurisdiction and the recognition and enforcement of judgments in civil and commercial matters.

prevent the sale of Nazi memorabilia on an automated auction Web site. Because the sale of Nazi propaganda is a violation of the French Criminal Code, the High Court of Paris ordered Yahoo to eliminate French citizens' access to any Yahoo auction site advertising such products. The court also ordered Yahoo to post warnings alerting French citizens to the illegal content on the auction site.

Before the French plaintiffs brought an action to enforce the French order in U.S. courts, Yahoo sought a declaratory judgment in a U.S. district court in California against enforcement of the French judgment in the United States. Yahoo argued, among other issues, that it was technologically impossible to block French citizens from accessing Yahoo.com without banning Nazi-related material from Yahoo.com altogether. Hence, abiding by the French order would infringe impermissibly upon the rights of U.S. citizens under the First Amendment of the U.S. Constitution.

In November 2001, the U.S. district court granted a declaratory judgment against enforcing the French judgment against Yahoo. A very divided en banc Court of Appeals for the 9th Circuit eventually dismissed Yahoo's case in 2006, with three of the judges in the majority concluding the matter was not ripe for decision and three finding a lack of personal jurisdiction over the defendants. Yahoo! Inc. v. La Ligue Contre Le Racisme et L'Antisemitisme, 433 F.3d 1199 (9th Cir. 2006), *cert. denied*, 126 S. Ct. 2332 (2006).

The U.S. district court's reasoning is worth noting, however. The court held:

> [T]he French order's content and viewpoint-based regulation of web pages and auction site on Yahoo.com, while entitled to great deference as an articulation of French law, clearly would be inconsistent with the First Amendment if mandated by a court in the United States. What makes this case uniquely challenging is that the Internet in effect allows one to speak in more than one place at the same time. Although France has the sovereign right to regulate what speech is permissible in France, this court may not enforce a foreign order that violates the protections of the United States Constitution by chilling protected speech that occurs simultaneously within our borders. [Yahoo! Inc. v. La Ligue Contre Le Racisme et L'Anti-semitisme, 169 F. Supp. 2d 1181, 1192 (N.D. Cal. 2001).]

Do you agree with the U.S. district court's statement? In addition to enforcement problems, are there potential issues arising from the ubiquitous nature of the Internet with respect to ISPs such as Yahoo or AOL or Internet search engines such as Google, which are now subject to service of process in most countries of the world, where libel and censorship laws might well differ from those in the United States? (Jurisdictional issues, including regarding the Internet, are discussed further in Chapter 7.)

8. What current justifications are there for the rule stated in section 483 of the Restatement? If a court enforces other foreign judgments out of a sense of comity, why should it not enforce a tax or penal judgment? Wouldn't that please the foreign government plaintiff?

9. Why should tax judgments be treated differently from any other money judgment?

10. Even if the rule in section 483 still seems right for hard-core crime, are there not good arguments for applying some foreign criminal laws (as distinct from

enforcing foreign judgments), at least for purposes of collecting a fine, in areas like fraud and antitrust? Why shouldn't a U.S. court enforce the antitrust laws of Japan, particularly against an American national? Or would it be easier to apply those laws to a Japanese national? Wouldn't that relieve some of the impetus for extraterritorial application of U.S. law?

11. Given the possible problems of enforcing a foreign court's judgment, should a potential plaintiff be advised to sue in a jurisdiction where the defendant has assets sufficient to satisfy a judgment?

12. What impact, if any, do you think that there will be on a party's selection of a particular forum by possible concerns over whether a U.S. court will recognize and enforce a foreign court's judgment? Do these questions about foreign court judgments encourage the use of international arbitration? If so, do you favor this tendency? Do you think that the decision of an international arbitral panel should be more easily enforceable in the United States than the decision of the highest court of another country (say, France or Germany), even when the arbitral panel might have consisted only of, say, one arbitrator acting under relatively simple procedures and subject to no right of appeal? What policies underlie U.S. support for international arbitration?

13. If the defendant has assets in the United States, do concerns over the possible enforcement of foreign court judgments encourage the initial resort to U.S. courts rather than to foreign courts? As you will see, the answer to this question might turn on some issues addressed in later chapters — for example, the status of foreign sovereign immunity and the act of state doctrine in U.S. courts (discussed in Chapter 6) or the jurisdictional reach of U.S. courts (treated in Chapter 7).

Problem. Much has been happening in the area of formal resolution of international disputes — ranging from increased activity at the International Court of Justice, to the emergence of specialized courts, to major new decisions by regional courts, and to increased use of international arbitration.

You are the new Legal Adviser to the U.S. Secretary of State. She is trying to determine priorities and goals in foreign policy for the Administration. The Secretary of State asks you what the U.S. emphases should be in approaches to international dispute resolution. For example, in discussions with the European Union over the effects of its further integration or with Russia over future arms control treaties or with various states in the world over enforcement of possible new environmental conventions to combat the greenhouse effect or other environmental problems, how might disputes be best handled if diplomacy is unable to resolve an issue?

The Secretary asks you to prepare a memorandum that analyzes possible approaches to dispute resolution and that proposes some specific steps. The more comprehensive your proposals, the better. However, although you should try to develop some general recommendations or principles, you should recognize how and when different situations might require different approaches.

5

States and Other Major International Entities

States, international organizations, individuals, corporations, and other entities have varying legal status under international law. Each may be a "person" or "subject" of international law in some sense or another, with recognized rights and duties.

States are the principal persons under international law. As we saw in Chapter 2, states can create international law by entering into international agreements or through practice that can lead to customary international law. A state also has considerable rights and duties under international law, including the right to regulate its territory and nationals as well as the duty to accord internationally recognized fair treatment to its nationals and to aliens within its territory.

In this chapter we initially focus on what a "state" is and who determines this status. We also consider groups that fall short of being states, such as territories. We then turn to entities other than states that can also be persons under international law. An international or regional organization, such as the United Nations or the European Union,

> has the legal capacity and personality and the rights and duties given it by the international agreement that is its charter and governs its activities. Other capacities, rights and duties may be given it by particular international agreements, by agreements applicable to international organizations generally or by customary international law. International organizations, when they act within their constitutional authority, sometimes make and often contribute to international law. [Restatement, Introductory Note to Part II, at 70.]

We briefly examine the major international and regional organizations — such as the United Nations, the World Bank, the International Monetary Fund, the European Union, and the Association of Southeast Asian Nations — and some of the current issues surrounding them.

Individuals and corporations also have some status under international law.

> In the past it was sometimes assumed that individuals, [as well as] corporations, companies or other juridical persons created by the laws of a state, were not persons under (or subjects of) international law. In principle, however, individuals and private juridical entities can have any status, capacity, rights or duties given them by international law or

> agreement, and increasingly individuals and private entities have been accorded such aspects of personality in varying measures. For example, international law and numerous international agreements now recognize human rights of individuals and sometimes give individuals remedies before international bodies. Individuals may be held liable for offenses against international law, such as piracy, war crimes or genocide. Corporations frequently are vehicles through which rights under international economic law are asserted. [Id. at 70-71.]

Chapter 4 analyzes the alternative forums where individuals and private juridical entities, as well as states, can seek to protect their rights. Chapter 8 focuses on the internationally recognized human rights that individuals, corporations, and other juridical persons have within a state.

A. STATES AND THEIR GOVERNMENTS

1. *What Is a State?*

A "state" in international law is what we often refer to as a nation or country (such as the United States of America or Japan) and is not one of the 50 U.S. states (such as California). As illustrated in Table 5-1 on pages 432-433, states come in all sizes and shapes, with great variations among them in population and in their level of economic development. States also vary tremendously in their cultures, political systems, educational levels, natural resources, and many other attributes. There are now over 190 states in the world.

Whether an entity is a state or not is a question that arises only occasionally, such as in the event of secession when a part of a state splits off and seeks to be a state. How would you characterize, though, the European Union? The Vatican and the Holy See? Kosovo? Taiwan? Antarctica?

The 1933 Montevideo Convention on the Rights and Duties of States, ratified by 16 Western Hemisphere countries (including the United States), provides in Article I: "The state as a person of international law should possess the following qualifications: (a) a permanent population; (b) a defined territory; (c) government; and (d) capacity to enter into relations with other states."

The Restatement essentially repeats these qualifications, and its Comment elaborates on them:

Restatement Section 201

Comment

b. Defined territory. An entity may satisfy the territorial requirement for statehood even if its boundaries have not been finally settled, if one or more of its boundaries are disputed, or if some of its territory is claimed by another state. An entity does not necessarily cease to be a state even if all of its territory has been occupied by a foreign power or if it has otherwise lost control of its territory temporarily.

c. Permanent population. To be a state an entity must have a population that is significant and permanent. Antarctica, for example, would not now qualify as a state even if it satisfied the other requirements of this section. . . .

d. Government. A state need not have any particular form of government, but there must be some authority exercising governmental functions and able to represent the entity in international relations.

e. Capacity to conduct international relations. An entity is not a state unless it has competence, within its own constitutional system, to conduct international relations with other states, as well as the political, technical and financial capabilities to do so. An entity that has the capacity to conduct foreign relations does not cease to be a state because it voluntarily turns over to another state control of its foreign relations, as in the "protectorates" of the period of colonialism, the case of Liechtenstein, or the "associated states" of today. States do not cease to be states because they have agreed not to engage in certain international activities or have delegated authority to do so to a "supranational" entity, e.g., the European Communities. Clearly, a state does not cease to be a state if it joins a common market.

Notes and Questions

1. What should be the minimum population for an entity to be a state? Are the 305,000 people in Iceland (in the North Atlantic) sufficient? The 83,000 inhabitants of Andorra, a mountainous co-principality between France and Spain? The 12,000 inhabitants of Tuvalu, a group of South Pacific islands best known for leasing out the rights to its Internet domain name (.tv) for $4 million a year, effectively doubling its GDP?

2. How permanent must the population be? Does the Vatican qualify with about 900 residents and perhaps 3,000 more day workers who are nonresidents?

3. Is the European Union (EU) a state because it conducts some international activities on behalf of its members — for example, setting external tariffs and negotiating with non-EU states on many economic issues? Alternatively, are England and France still states despite their participation in the EU?

4. On October 3, 1990, Germany was formally reunified. Essentially what happened was that the government of the German Democratic Republic (East Germany) dissolved, and East Germany was absorbed as new states (*länder*) into the Federal Republic of Germany (FRG). The reunited nations acceded to the name, constitution, political structure, parties, parliamentary system, and administrative system of the FRG. The expanded FRG continued to respect the FRG's existing treaty obligations, including its membership in the European Union and the North Atlantic Treaty Organization (NATO). (See discussion of these entities later in this chapter.)

5. If you and your classmates could find an uninhabited, unclaimed island in the middle of the ocean (perhaps formed by recent volcanic activity), might you try to form a new state? Would it be in your interest to do this, rather than claim the island for the country where you are a citizen? (As discussed in Chapter 9, the Law of the Sea Convention and customary international law provide that a state has sovereignty over the ocean and seabed that extend 12 nautical miles from its shores and substantial sovereignty over the minerals and fish found in its exclusive economic zone that can extend 200 nautical miles from its shores.)

6. Review Table 5-1, which provides some useful geopolitical facts. Which are the five biggest states listed in the table in terms of population? GDP? Exports? Imports? If the European Union is treated as one entity, where does it rank relative to non-EU states in terms of population and GDP?

TABLE 5-1 Illustrative States and Other Entities[1]

	Population (Millions)	Land Area (Thousand Sq. Km.)	Gross Domestic Product (Billion U.S.$)	Exports (Billion U.S.$)	Imports (Billion U.S.$)
North and Central America					
United States	307	9,162	14,256	1,057	1,604
Canada	34	9,094	1,336	316	353
Mexico	107	1,944	875	230	258
Europe					
European Union (EU27)[2]	499	4,333	16,389	1,537[3]	1,681[3]
France	63	548	2,649	484	560
Germany	82	349	3,347	1,122	931
Italy	60	294	2,113	406	412
Poland	38	304	430	135	147
Spain	46	499	1,460	218	288
United Kingdom	62	242	2,175	353	482
Other EU States	148	2,060	4,215	1,866[4]	1,814[4]
Russia	142	16,378	1,231	282	164
Turkey	75	770	617	102	141
Ukraine	46	579	114	40	45
Asia					
China, P.R.[5]	1,308	9,291	4,605	1,523	1,356
India	1,155	2,973	1,310	163	257
Indonesia	230	1,812	540	119	117
Japan	128	365	5,068	582	552
Pakistan	170	771	162	18	32
South Korea	49	97	833	358	344
Taiwan[6]	23	36[7]	379	204	175
Vietnam	87	310	92	56	85
South America					
Argentina	40	2,737	309	57	42

(continued)

TABLE 5-1 (*Continued*)

	Population (Millions)	*Land Area (Thousand Sq. Km.)*	*Gross Domestic Product (Billion U.S.$)*	*Exports (Billion U.S.$)*	*Imports (Billion U.S.$)*
Brazil	194	8,459	1,571	151	139
Colombia	46	1,110	231	34	33
Venezuela	28	882	327	76	42
Africa					
Egypt	83	995	188	23	45
Libya	6	1,760	62	36	21
Nigeria	155	911	169	52	45
South Africa	49	1,214	286	54	74
Sudan	42	2,376	55	7	8
Middle and Near East					
Iran	68	1,629	331	71	60
Iraq	31	437	66	34	23
Israel	7	22	195	48	47
Saudi Arabia	25	2,000	369	177	95
Syria	21	184	52	11	22
World Total	6,775	129,612	58,228	12,373	12,887

[1]The figures for population, gross domestic product, and land area are from World Bank, http://data.worldbank.org/, unless otherwise indicated. The data for population, land area, and GDP are from 2009. The figures for exports and imports of goods are also for 2009 and are from International Monetary Fund, Direction of Trade Statistics (August 2010), unless otherwise indicated. The data for exports are calculated as an aggregation of goods exports, f.o.b. The data for imports include cost of goods, insurance, and freight (c.i.f.).

[2]The World Bank data for GDP for EU members Cyprus and Malta are for 2008 and 2007, respectively, rather than 2009.

[3]2009 statistics from IMF Direction of Trade Statistics database. The European Union data include only trade with non-EU members and do not include internal trade.

[4]2009 statistics from IMF Direction of Trade Statistics database. The data for Other EU States include both internal and external trade.

[5]The figures for China include Hong Kong and Macao, but not Taiwan.

[6]Source for Taiwan trade data is IMF International Financial Statistics database, August 2010.

[7]Source for Taiwan's land area is the Taiwanese government Web site which directs to http://www.gio.gov.tw/taiwan-website/5-gp/yearbook/ch01.html.

2. *Who Decides What Is a State?*

Restatement Section 201

Comment h

Whether an entity satisfies the requirements for statehood is ordinarily determined by other states when they decide whether to treat that entity as a state. Ordinarily, a new state is formally recognized by other states, but a decision to treat an entity as a state may be manifested in other ways. Since membership in the principal international organizations is constitutionally open only to states, admission to membership in an international organization such as the United Nations is an acknowledgement by the organization, and by those members who vote for admission, that the entity has satisfied the requirements of statehood.

While there is some dispute, many believe that a state is under no duty to formally recognize another entity as a state. Professor Brownlie writes:

> Recognition, *as a public act of state,* is an optional and political act and there is no legal duty in this regard. However, in a deeper sense, if an entity bears the marks of statehood, other states put themselves at risk legally if they ignore the basic obligations of state relations. . . . Even recognition is not determinant of diplomatic relations, and absence of diplomatic relations is not in itself non-recognition of the state. [Ian Brownlie, Principles of Public International Law 89-90 (7th ed. 2008).]

Even if a state does not formally recognize another state, the Restatement agrees that the state is required to treat an entity as a state if it meets the standards of section 201. The Restatement does include the important caveat that the requirement does not apply if the entity "has attained the qualifications for statehood as a result of a threat or use of armed force in violation of the United Nations Charter." (Id. §202.)

The Reporters' Note to section 202 indicates:

> 1. *Statehood and recognition*. The literature of international law reflects disagreement as to the significance of the recognition of statehood. Under the "declaratory" theory, an entity that satisfies the requirements of §201 is a state with all the corresponding capacities, rights and duties, and other states have the duty to treat it as such. Recognition by other states is merely "declaratory," confirming that the entity is a state, and expressing the intent to treat it as a state. Another view has been that recognition by other states is "constitutive," i.e., that an entity is not a state in international law unless it is generally recognized as such by other states. Some writers, . . . while adopting the "constitutive" theory, argued that states had an obligation to recognize an entity that met the qualifications set forth in §201.
>
> This section tends towards the declaratory view, but the practical differences between the two theories have grown smaller. Even for the declaratory theory, whether an entity satisfies the requirements for statehood is, as a practical matter, determined by other states. On the other hand, the constitutive theory lost much of its significance when it was accepted that states had the obligation to treat as a state any entity having the characteristics set forth in §201. . . . Delays in recognizing or accepting statehood

have generally reflected uncertainty as to the viability of the new state, or the view that it was created in violation of international law, in which case there is a duty not to recognize or accept the entity's statehood.

In the past, when a state treated an entity as a state without formal recognition it was sometimes said to be extending "de facto" as opposed to "de jure" recognition. Those terms, used with varying and uncertain meaning, are avoided in this Restatement.

In U.S. law, the President has the exclusive authority to recognize or not to recognize a foreign state (and, as will be discussed later, the particular government of that state). This is implied in the President's express constitutional powers under Article II to appoint and to receive ambassadors. In addition, the President has authority to conclude international agreements related to recognition without participation of the Senate or both houses of Congress. United States v. Belmont, 301 U.S. 324 (1937) (upholding executive agreement that recognized the new government of the Soviet Union).

The President can recognize a foreign state (or its government) either expressly or by implication. As indicated in the Restatement:

> Recognition of a state has been effected by express official declaration, by the conclusion of a bilateral agreement with the state, by the presentation of credentials by a United States representative to the authorities of the new state, and by receiving the credentials of a diplomatic representative of that state. The fact that the United States is a member of an international organization of which a state it does not recognize is also a member does not imply recognition of that state by the United States. . . . [Section 202, Reporters' Note 2.]

The disintegration of the Soviet Union and Yugoslavia in the early 1990s led to statements by U.S. officials and steps regarding the recognition of states by the European Community (now European Union). The Community issued on December 19, 1991, a Declaration on the Guidelines on the Recognition of the New States in Eastern Europe and in the Soviet Union. The Declaration "affirm[ed] their readiness to recognize, subject to the normal standards of international practice and the political realities in each case, those new states which . . . have constituted themselves on a democratic basis, have accepted the appropriate international obligations and have committed themselves in good faith to a peaceful process and to negotiations." The declaration went on to require, among other matters, "respect . . . for the rule of law, democracy and human rights." 31 I.L.M. 1486 (1992). On the other hand, the United States and the EC member states quickly recognized the new states, including countries such as Kazakhstan, Turkmenistan, and Ukraine where observers questioned the commitment then to democracy and human rights.

To address specifically the recognition of new states arising from the breakup of Yugoslavia, the European Community established in August 1991 an "Arbitration Commission" comprising five presidents from among the Constitutional Courts of the EC countries. The Commission became known as the Badinter Commission after the name of the French lawyer appointed its president. Although its opinions were not legally binding, the Badinter Commission proceeded to issue a number of legal opinions that were influential and provided generally consistent interpretations regarding the status of the various successor states to Yugoslavia.

3. *What Is the Effect of Being a State?*

Statehood entails certain rights and duties. The Restatement says:

Restatement

Section 206. Capacities, Rights and Duties of States

Under international law, a state has:

(a) sovereignty over its territory and general authority over its nationals;

(b) status as a legal person, with capacity to own, acquire and transfer property, to make contracts and enter into international agreements, to become a member of international organizations, and to pursue, and be subject to, legal remedies;

(c) capacity to join with other states to make international law, as customary law or by international agreement.

These capacities, rights, and duties that derive from statehood are significant. This will become clearer as you study later materials in this chapter (such as the materials in Section 5) and those in Chapter 6 on foreign sovereign immunity and the act of state doctrine and in Chapter 7 on jurisdictional issues. It is worth pausing, however, to consider an arguably special case that highlights some of the problems of classifying an entity as a state.

Note on the International Legal Status of the Holy See and the State of Vatican City

In international relations, the Pope is the head of the Roman Catholic Church, the Holy See is its government and diplomatic agent, and its independent territory is the State of Vatican City. This State of Vatican City is surrounded by Italy, possesses 0.44 square miles of territory, has a resident population of about 900 people, is a full member of several United Nations specialized agencies, participates in international conferences, and is a party to treaties with many states.

Over 170 countries now recognize and maintain diplomatic relations with the Holy See and the State of Vatican City. In 1984, for example, the United States government and the Holy See established reciprocal diplomatic relations at the level of an embassy and of a nunciature, respectively. As of January 2011, however, the Holy See and China did not have diplomatic relations, and the Holy See recognized Taiwan. There have been some recent positive gestures between the Holy See and China, but no formal rapprochement.

The Holy See and the State of Vatican City do not readily fit into any established category of international legal status.

> Traditionally, the Pope's sovereign rule over the Papal States provided a basis for the secular authority of the Holy See. However, following the annexation of the Papal States by the Kingdom of Italy in 1870, the secular position of the Pope assumed an uncertainty that the Holy See and the State of Italy only settled in 1929 under the terms of the Lateran Treaty and the Concordat. The Treaty re-established within the city of Rome an independent State of the Vatican City, governed absolutely by the Holy See, which like all other states exercises a sovereign right to engage in foreign relations. . . .

> As both the sovereign of the State of the Vatican City and the spiritual authority of the Church, the Holy See joins the separate secular and ecclesiastical personalities established by these two documents. The status of the Vatican in international law thus remains difficult to define in practical terms, since most states conduct foreign relations not with the State of the Vatican City, but with the Holy See. [Note, Diplomatic Relations, 25 Harv. Int'l LJ. 445-446 (1984).]

The Holy See and some analysts have taken the position that its international personality is derived from its religious and spiritual authority, rather than from Vatican City's small territory. See Robert John Araujo, S.J., The International Personality and Sovereignty of the Holy See, 50 Cath. U. L. Rev. 291 (2001). Others highlight the effect of territorial holdings on the Holy See's status in international law.

A 1987 decision by Italy's highest court, the Supreme Court of Cassation, helped clarify the status of Vatican City vis-à-vis Italy. In a victory for the Vatican, the Italian court annulled Italian arrest warrants accusing an American archbishop and two other Vatican bank executives of fraudulent complicity in the billion dollar collapse of a Milan-based bank. The three officials had lived behind Vatican walls for almost five months. The court reasoned that, pursuant to the Lateran Treaty of 1929, the affairs of the Vatican Bank were outside Italian jurisdiction.

Questions

1. What prompts states to establish diplomatic relations with the Holy See? Because it meets the traditional criteria, cited earlier, for a state? Because of its ecclesiastical influence? Political influence? A combination of all these factors? Why, for example, do you think the Polish government made considerable efforts in the 1980s to become the first communist government to establish diplomatic relations with the Vatican?

2. Is discussion concerning recognition of the Holy See in part a question regarding the status of micro-states, such as Monaco (0.73 square miles) and Nauru (8 square miles)?

4. *Who Governs the State?*

Recognition of a state, as noted above, is a formal acknowledgment by another state that the entity qualifies for statehood. But who governs that state? It is important to note that the question of recognition of governments is conceptually distinct from that of recognition of states. Recognizing a specific government is "formal acknowledgment that a particular regime is the effective government of a state." Restatement, section 203, comment a.

Usually no problems arise when a change of government occurs in accord with the domestic law of a state. For example, when a new U.S. President is elected, relations with other countries are unaffected. Other countries do not go through the formalities of recognizing the new U.S. government.

Questions of recognition do arise, however, when a new government assumes power in a manner that violates domestic law. The change can occur in a variety of ways, including a revolution, a civil war, or a military *coup d'état*. Sometimes it is not so clear that there has been an extra-constitutional switch in government. For example, a government or the chief executive may resign under military duress and be replaced by leadership that the military prefers. In such situations, the decision to recognize the new foreign government often involves an interesting combination of international law and international politics.

In recent years, there have been two major approaches to recognition — the traditional approach and the Estrada Doctrine — plus a less well-accepted approach called the Tobar Doctrine.

P.K. Menon, The Law of Recognition in International Law

65-79 (1994)

(1) The Traditional Approach

Under the traditional approach, a State considering recognition seeks to determine

(a) Effectiveness of control;
(b) Stability and permanence;
(c) Popular support; and
(d) Ability and willingness to fulfill obligations.

(a) Effectiveness of Control

The principle of effectiveness of control is a fundamental concept and uncontroverted. Recognition of a Government which is not in effective control of the territory would constitute premature recognition and would be considered intervention with domestic affairs of the State. . . .

(b) Stability and Permanence

. . . [S]tability and permanence is another important requirement of a political body to confer upon it the legal quality of Government. The rationale of this requirement is the need for a certain measure of continuity in inter-State relations.

The quality of stability is taken in a broad sense. It is difficult to quantify it. Lauterpacht refers to a "reasonable prospect of permanency." The decision of third States as to stability is influenced by political conditions prevailing in the particular country when the change of Government has taken place. . . .

(c) Popular Support

Another requirement for recognition of a Government is the popular support for it, otherwise known as the consent of the governed. . . .

"Popular support" does not necessarily suggest that the new Government should command the voluntary and positive support of the people. It may suffice to have "the ability to exact habitual, though not willing, obedience." . . .

Popular support, in this context, means apparent acquiescence of the people. . . .

(d) Ability and Willingness to Fulfill Obligations . . .

The ability to fulfill international obligations . . . is implied in the ability to govern. As Chen remarks, "A government which is unable to represent the will of the nation internationally and to compel the enforcement of its international obligations is no government."

The test of willingness to fulfill international obligations is of comparatively recent origin. . . .

(2) The Tobar Doctrine

In 1907, Carlos R. Tobar, former Minister of Foreign Affairs of Ecuador, proposed the following which has since become known as the Tobar Doctrine:

> The American republics, for the good name and credit of all of them, if not for other humanitarian and "altruistic" considerations should intervene, at least mediately and indirectly, in the internal dissensions of the republics of the continent. This intervention might be, at least, by denying recognition to governments *de facto* born of revolutions against the constitutional order. . . .

. . . [T]he Tobar Doctrine has never enjoyed widespread acceptance.

(3) The Estrada Doctrine

. . . [The Estrada Doctrine] is contained in a declaration of Senor Don Genaro Estrada, Secretary of Foreign Relations of Mexico, on September 27, 1930 in which it was stated that, the granting of recognition being an insulting practice implying judgment upon the internal affairs of foreign States, the Mexican Government would henceforth confine itself to the maintenance or the non-maintenance of diplomatic relations with foreign governments without pronouncing judgment upon the legality of those governments. . . .

In effect, the Doctrine is an extreme form of *de factoism.* It discards the distinction between changes of Government by peaceful ballots and changes of Government by blood-thirsty bullets.

In accordance with the Estrada Doctrine, the recognition of Governments that come to power through extra constitutional means is eliminated. Only new States are recognized; when a new Government comes to power either through constitutional means or otherwise, its relations with other States remain unchanged. Thus, the Doctrine "is in accord with the principles of the continuity of the state and of the juridical equality of states." It brushes aside all issues of a political, legal or moral character as irrelevant to the right of a Government to be the representative of the State; rejects intervention in the internal affairs of other States, and eliminates the practice of granting recognition to Governments. A good number of States have adopted the Doctrine either officially or in practice. . . .

See also Restatement section 203. The Reporters' Notes provide a succinct history of the U.S. practice on recognition through 1986:

> 1. *United States practice as to recognizing governments.* United States practice long reflected the view that recognition of governments was not a matter of international obligation but could be granted or withheld at will, to further national policy. United States policy has varied as to whether recognition should be withheld from a regime that has obtained power other than through constitutional processes. The case for withholding recognition was classically stated by President Wilson on March 11, 1913 after General Huerta overthrew the government of President Madero in Mexico. Based on the premise that a "just government rests always upon the consent of the governed," Wilson's view was that a regime taking control by force should not be dealt with on equal terms by other governments. . . .
>
> At other times, however, United States policy has been to recognize the government in power despite distaste for the way it acceded to power, or for its ideology, policies, or personnel. The constitutionality of a regime's coming to power was often legally and factually difficult to determine and, in any event, the inquiry might seem improper and insulting to the country involved. It could also become awkward to continue to refuse to deal with a regime that was thriving in spite of non-recognition. . . .
>
> Since 1970 . . . "U.S. practice has been to deemphasize and avoid the use of recognition in cases of changes of governments and to concern ourselves with the question of whether we wish to have diplomatic relations with the new governments." . . . In some situations, however, the question cannot be avoided, for example, where two regimes are contending for power, and particularly where legal consequences within the United States depend on which regime is recognized or accepted. . . .
>
> 2. *Government established in violation of international law.* In 1979-80, many governments, including the United States, withheld recognition of the regime established in Afghanistan by the U.S.S.R. following invasion in violation of Article 2 (4) of the United Nations Charter. . . . Similarly, the United States refused to recognize the Heng Samrin regime imposed upon Kampuchea (Cambodia) by the armed forces of Vietnam; a majority of the General Assembly has voted against treating the Heng Samrin delegation as the representative of Kampuchea.

5. *What Is the Significance of Recognition of a Government?*

An unrecognized regime lacks some of the important benefits of a recognized government. The recognized government is able to designate representatives for the state in international organizations, and the recognized government's diplomatic representatives are able to speak on behalf of the state and to exercise the prerogatives of statehood. (See section 3 above.) Reflecting this situation, Restatement section 205 indicates:

Restatement Section 205

Under the law of the United States:

(1) an entity not recognized as a state, or a regime not recognized as the government of a state, is ordinarily denied access to courts in the United States;

(2) a regime not recognized as the government of a state is not entitled to property belonging to that state located in the United States;

(3) courts in the United States ordinarily give effect to acts of a regime representing an entity not recognized as a state, or of a regime not recognized as the government of a state, if those acts apply to territory under the control of that regime and relate to domestic matters only.

For example, before it was recognized by the United States in 1933, the communist regime of the Soviet Union was regularly denied access to U.S. courts. See also Republic of Vietnam v. Pfizer, 556 F.2d 892 (8th Cir. 1977) (upholding dismissal of suit by the Republic of Vietnam, which was not then recognized by the United States), but see National Petrochemical Co. of Iran v. M/T Stolt Sheaf, 860 F.2d 551 (2d Cir. 1988), cert. denied, 489 U.S. 1081 (1989) (allowing an Iranian corporation wholly owned by Iran to bring a diversity suit even though the U.S. government had not yet formally recognized the Khomeini government of Iran). The courts are, however, open to recognized governments with which the United States does not maintain diplomatic relations, such as that of Cuba. See, e.g., Banco Nacional de Cuba v. Sabbatino, 376 U.S. 398, 408-412 (1964) (severance of diplomatic relations, commercial embargo, and freezing of Cuban assets in the United States did not bar Cuban state-owned corporation from U.S. courts).

Nonrecognition was used in 1988 by the Reagan Administration as a legal tool to help impose economic sanctions against the regime of General Manuel Antonio Noriega of Panama. In late February 1988, the then President of Panama, Eric Arturo Delvalle, tried to force General Noriega to step down as commander of the armed forces. Noriega refused and obtained a vote in the legislature that ousted Delvalle instead and installed a new president acceptable to Noriega. Delvalle went into hiding at a U.S. military base in Panama.

Nevertheless, in March 1988 the Reagan Administration certified that Delvalle was still the legitimate president of Panama. As a result, under a World War II statute, U.S. banks could not release to the Noriega regime about $60 million that were on deposit in the accounts of the government of Panama (12 U.S.C. §632 (1982)). Rather, the deposits were blocked by the U.S. government, which approved payments to Delvalle's representatives for governmental activities. In April 1988 the financial sanctions against the Noriega regime were made more extensive when President Reagan declared a national emergency and invoked his powers under the International Emergency Economic Powers Act (IEEPA). (See Chapter 3.) When Delvalle's term of office expired in 1989 under Panamanian laws, the U.S. government ended his representatives' access to the blocked accounts.

A more recent case involves the Taliban regime in Afghanistan. After the Taliban had fought and effectively obtained control of about 90 percent of Afghanistan in the late 1990s, the Taliban was only recognized as the government of Afghanistan by three countries: Pakistan, Saudi Arabia, and the United Arab Emirates. The United States and other countries objected to many of the policies of the very fundamentalist Taliban (e.g., their treatment of prisoners, women, and other religious groups) and its refusal to accept some of the obligations of the predecessor governments. Throughout the period of Taliban control, Afghanistan's seat at the United Nations and in other international organizations was held by the previous government of Burhanuddin Rabbani. The United States closed the Afghan embassy in Washington to the Taliban government and denied it access to approximately $217 million in frozen assets.

After September 11, 2001, two of the countries that had recognized the Taliban withdrew their recognition, with Pakistan maintaining relations primarily as a channel for negotiations. Opposition forces led by other Afghan leaders, as well as military forces from the United States, Britain, and other countries, routed the Taliban in late 2001. The United States and other countries soon recognized Hamid Karzai's interim authority as the government of Afghanistan in 2002, and the United States released the frozen assets to the new government.

The Ivory Coast in 2010-2011 provided a situation in which the question of recognition of a government involved a temporary standoff between the government of President Laurent Gbagbo and the 16-nation West African group known as ECOWAS the United Nations, France, the United States, and essentially the rest of the world community. Gbagbo refused to step down after international election monitors and other observers determined that he clearly lost a November 28, 2010, election to his rival, Alassane Ouattara. There was international concern that the election dispute might trigger a renewal of the civil war that led to the death of thousands of people in 2002 and 2003. The United States and other democratic countries were also concerned that allowing the election results to be ignored would be a bad precedent as several other African countries prepared for elections, including in southern Sudan (see discussion of Sudan in section 7 below).

The U.N. Security Council formally recognized Ouattara's election in Resolution 1962 on December 20, 2010. Acting under its broad powers under Article VII of the U.N. Charter, the Security Council: "*urges* all the Ivorian parties and stakeholders to respect the will of the people and the outcome of the election in view of ECOWAS and African Union's recognition of . . . Ouattara as President-elect of Côte d'Ivoire and representative of the freely expressed voice of the Ivorian people as proclaimed by the Independent Electoral Commission." The Resolution also included teeth — it renewed the mandate of the U.N. Operations in Côte d'Ivoire (UNOCI) and determined that UNOCI should maintain its total authorized strength of 8,650 military and policy personnel, it authorized the U.N. Secretary-General to extend the deployment of up to 500 additional personnel, and it authorized the temporary redeployment of additional military forces. Then, the U.N. General Assembly decided unanimously to recognize the list of diplomats whom Ouattara submitted as the Ivory Coast's sole official representatives at the United Nations. Also, ECOWAS, the United States, and other countries began imposing economic sanctions in December. After four months of bloody fighting, involving not only the forces of the two leaders but also U.N. and French forces supporting Ouattara, Gbagbo was captured in early April 2011. Ouattara was formally inaugurated as president on May 21, 2011.

Looking at recognition from another perspective, a state often effectively withdraws recognition from one regime when it recognizes another regime as the government. A somewhat unique example of this was the 1979 U.S. recognition of the

People's Republic of China as the Chinese government. As a result, the regime on Taiwan, called the Republic of China, lost its recognition.

Note on the Special Status of Taiwan

In 1978, President Jimmy Carter announced that the United States would normalize diplomatic relations with the government of the People's Republic of China (PRC) and that present diplomatic relations with the government of the Republic of China (ROC or Taiwan) would end as of January 1, 1979. The withdrawal of recognition from the Republic of China in favor of the PRC ended nearly 30 years of a complicated relationship between the United States, Taiwan, and the PRC, but also began the problem of the "special status of Taiwan" that continues to the present.

The China policy of the United States after World War II reflected the U.S. historic ties to the Nationalist ROC regime over a communist PRC regime. Thus, the Republic of China was recognized as a sovereign state representing all the people in mainland China as well as on Taiwan. However, beginning with President Richard Nixon's 1972 visit to Beijing, the United States began a process of normalizing U.S.-PRC relations. A joint U.S.-PRC communique, known as the Shanghai Communique, was one of the results of this visit and represented the basis for future U.S.-PRC relations. The Communique stated in part:

> The two sides reviewed the long-standing serious disputes between China and the United States. The Chinese reaffirmed its position: The Taiwan question is the crucial question obstructing the normalization of relations between China and the United States; the Government of the People's Republic of China is the sole legal government of China; Taiwan is a province of China which has long been returned to the motherland; the liberation of Taiwan is China's internal affair in which no other country has the right to interfere; and all U.S. forces and military installations must be withdrawn from Taiwan. The Chinese Government firmly opposes any activities which aim at the creation of "one China, one Taiwan," "one China, two governments," "two Chinas," and "independent Taiwan" or advocate that "the status of Taiwan remains to be determined."
>
> The U.S. side declared: The United States acknowledges that all Chinese on either side of the Taiwan Strait maintain there is but one China and that Taiwan is a part of China. The United States Government does not challenge that position. It reaffirms its interest in a peaceful settlement of the Taiwan question by the Chinese themselves. With this prospect in mind, it affirms the ultimate objective of the withdrawal of all U.S. forces and military installations from Taiwan. In the meantime, it will progressively reduce its forces and military installations on Taiwan as the tension in the area diminishes.

But the normalization process stalled for awhile. The PRC maintained that it was the sole government of all China, of which Taiwan was a province; the United States continued to recognize the ROC as the government of all China. The disagreement was resolved under the Carter Administration by the "Joint Communique on the Establishment of Diplomatic Relations Between the United States of America and the People's Republic of China," pursuant to which the two governments mutually recognized one another. The United States concurrently withdrew its recognition of the Republic of China on Taiwan.

Since withdrawing its recognition of Taiwan, the United States has maintained "nonofficial ties" with "the people of Taiwan." These ties are extensive — in 2009 the

United States exported about $18 billion worth of goods to Taiwan and imported about $24 billion in Taiwanese goods. (In comparison, the United States exported about $69 billion to the much larger PRC and imported about $302 billion.)

The Taiwan Relations Act, 22 U.S.C. §§3301 et seq., is the statutory basis for maintaining these ties. Under the act Taiwan receives essentially all the privileges and immunities normally extended to an officially recognized government.

Taiwan Relations Act

Application of Laws: International Agreements

Sec. 4. (a) The absence of diplomatic relations or recognition shall not affect the application of the laws of the United States with respect to Taiwan, and the laws of the United States shall apply with respect to Taiwan in the manner that the laws of the United States applied with respect to Taiwan prior to January 1, 1979.

(b) The application of subsection (a) of this section shall include, but shall not be limited to, the following:

1. Whenever the laws of the United States refer or relate to foreign countries, nations, states, governments, or similar entities, such terms shall include and such laws shall apply with respect to Taiwan. . . .

7. The capacity of Taiwan to sue and be sued in courts in the United States, in accordance with the laws of the United States, shall not be abrogated, infringed, modified, denied, or otherwise affected in any way by the absence of diplomatic relations or recognition. . . .

(c) For all purposes, including actions in any court in the United States, the Congress approves the continuation in force of all treaties and other international agreements, including multilateral conventions, entered into by the United States and the governing authorities on Taiwan recognized by the United States as the Republic of China prior to January 1, 1979, and in force between them on December 31, 1978, unless and until terminated in accordance with law. . . .

The American Institute in Taiwan

Sec. 6. (a) Programs, transactions, and other relations conducted or carried out by the President or any agency of the United States Government with respect to Taiwan shall, in the manner and to the extent directed by the President, be conducted and carried out by or through —

(1) The American Institute in Taiwan, a nonprofit corporation incorporated under the laws of the District of Columbia. . . .

Sec. 10. . . . (c) Upon the granting by Taiwan of comparable privileges and immunities with respect to the Institute and its appropriate personnel, the President is authorized to extend with respect to the Taiwan instrumentality and its appropriate personnel, such privileges and immunities (subject to appropriate conditions and obligations) as may be necessary for the effective performance of their functions.

In October 1980, the American Institute in Taiwan and the Coordination Council for North American Affairs (CCNAA), the Taiwanese instrumentality, entered an agreement whereby both unofficial organizations are given diplomatic privileges and immunities that are similar to the privileges and immunities given to official diplomats. In October 1994, the CCNAA was renamed as the Taipei Economic and Cultural Representative Office in the United States (TECRO).

Notes and Questions

1. Since the Taiwan Relations Act treats Taiwan in essentially the same way as it was treated before January 1979, should Taiwan be considered a state with a recognized government under U.S. domestic law?

2. The ROC moved away from its claim over mainland China during the 1990s and began to focus on the status of Taiwan and some nearby islands over which it had effective control. The issue became whether Taiwan and the nearby islands would try to become an independent state under the ROC government. The PRC has made clear that it would resort to military action and forcible reunification if Taiwan declared its independence. The presidency of Chen Shui-bian (2000-2008) represented the highpoint of the ROC's claims to independence.

After the election of President Ma Ying-jeou in 2008, the ROC ceased pursuing de jure recognition as an independent state. The position of the ROC, as articulated by Ma Ying-jeou in 2009, is "no unification, no independence." If an entity has not declared its own statehood, can it be treated by other states as being a state? How is Taiwan similar to a sovereign state? Comment f of Restatement section 201 takes the view that "[w]hile the traditional definition does not formally require it, an entity is not a state if it does not claim to be a state."

3. As part of its progress toward democracy, Taiwan held its first parliamentary elections in December 1995 and its first direct presidential election in March 1996. In the ROC's second direct presidential election, in 2000, Chen Shui-bian of the Democratic Progressive Party (DPP) defeated the incumbent Kuomintang (KMT) party, which had held power since 1949, marking the first democratic transition of power in Taiwanese history. In 2006, the Taiwanese democracy hit a rough patch. President Chen was put on trial on corruption charges, and he resigned his post shortly before he was convicted and sentenced to life in prison. Elections in 2008 brought the KMT party back to power, led by Ma Ying-jeou. He has held power peacefully and was reelected in 2009.

4. In recent years, the relationship between the PRC and the ROC has varied greatly, with relations having improved substantially after the 2008 elections in Taiwan. Cross-strait movements of people, which had begun in small numbers in 2007, grew to 4.5 million people from Taiwan visiting the mainland in 2009 and millions visiting Taiwan from the mainland. This cross-straits travel and rapidly increasing trade and investment were aided by a growing number of agreements between the mainland and Taiwan. For example, the Cross-Straits Economic Cooperation Framework Agreement (ECFA) of June 2010 was designed to facilitate liberalization of trade and other economic relations. It calls for the progressive reduction of tariffs on most goods and increased cross-straits investment.

5. From the Shanghai Communique of 1972 through January 2011, the U.S. policy toward Taiwan was generally unchanged. For example, during his major visit

to China in June 1998, President Clinton reaffirmed that the United States does not "support independence for Taiwan, or two Chinas; or one Taiwan-one China. And we don't believe that Taiwan should be a member in any organization [such as the U.N.] for which statehood is a requirement." President Clinton added that matters should be handled peacefully. The Clinton Administration, however, backed Taiwan's as well as China's entry into the World Trade Organization in 2001 because the WTO allows "custom areas" (e.g., Taiwan), as well as states, to be members. (See WTO section later in this chapter.)

As for military support to Taiwan, officially the United States "acknowledges" China's claim that Taiwan is a part of China, but the United States remains a major supplier of arms to Taiwan and it has maintained a policy of "strategic ambiguity" on the question of whether it would come to Taiwan's assistance militarily if the PRC attempted to take the island by force. This policy has deterred China from using force, while leaving Taiwan hesitant to rely on the availability of the American deterrent if Taiwan were to consider a declaration of independence.

The Obama Administration has continued this line of approach. In January 2010, the United States approved the sale to Taiwan of approximately $6.4 billion worth of military equipment. The Obama Administration stated that the sale was not an indication of a departure from previous U.S. policy toward the ROC or the PRC.

6. *Hong Kong.* After approximately 150 years of British colonial rule, Hong Kong was returned to China on July 1, 1997. Britain had formally leased the territory from China in 1898 for a period of 99 years. The Chinese regained much more than 365 square miles of land. Hong Kong had about 7 million residents, and it ranked as the world's eleventh-largest trading economy. The two entities were already bound together economically; China was Hong Kong's largest trading partner.

In 1984, as the lease was nearing its expiration, Britain and China signed a joint Declaration on Hong Kong in preparation for the transfer. The Declaration propounds a "one country, two systems" standard, preserving a degree of freedom for Hong Kong. The Chinese incorporated the principles of the Declaration into the 1990 Basic Law, which provides the framework for the future status of Hong Kong.

The Basic Law allows Hong Kong to remain a semiautonomous Special Administrative Region for 50 years. Hong Kong will continue as a free-market economy, although the Beijing government has assumed exclusive control of international relations and defense. The region is considered a "free port" and directs its own monetary and fiscal policies. For instance, in 2010 Hong Kong signed a trade agreement with Oregon and Washington State to facilitate wine imports. Also in 2010, Hong Kong and mainland China signed the Closer Economic Partnership Arrangement (CEPA), which liberalized trade and investment policies between the two areas. In addition, Hong Kong retains the British common law legal system, and a supreme appeals court has been established for the region.

As for political developments, despite the Basic Law's promise of universal suffrage as the "ultimate aim," many democrats in Hong Kong believe that Chinese leaders have been slow to move on major changes to the present system. The chief executive and most legislators are elected indirectly, allowing Beijing to intervene in the process. In 2010, the Legislative Council did pass a set of reforms that would modestly increase the popular representation in the legislature in the next round of elections in 2012. While the Hong Kong media remain under private control, self-censorship has increased. In addition, recent years have seen China overruling

Hong Kong court decisions, the expulsion of dissidents, and the passage of anti-sedition acts. Hong Kong still retains more freedom than the Chinese mainland, a benefit from the end of British rule there, but the difference is narrowing.

6. *And Then the Recognized Government Changes: Who Is Responsible for What?*

Governments often change, both through normal processes such as elections and through extraconstitutional means.* Assuming that the new government is recognized, what are its international rights and obligations that stem from the rights and duties of the preceding government? Is the state bound by commitments entered into by governments that have ceased to exist? As concrete examples, will the U.S. government after President Barack Obama be liable for the U.S. debt caused by the deficits during the Bush and Obama Administrations? Was the Iranian government of Ayatollah Khomeini liable for the contracts with foreigners made by the Shah of Iran when he was in power?

The traditional international law theory has been that changes in the government or ideology of a state do not change the state or affect its international rights and obligations. See Restatement Section 208, comment a and Reporters' Note 2. However, does it matter how the new government came to power? Or how much of a change the new government represents? Or what was the nature of the past commitments?

In a 1982 case, 240 U.S. citizens sued in a class action the PRC government to recover the principal and interest on bearer bonds issued in 1911 by the Imperial Chinese Government and sold in the United States.

> These bonds were issued as part of a larger Manchu modernization program aimed at constructing the Hukuang Railway, still an important part of the transportation system of the People's Republic of China.
>
> Interest payments were to be made on the bonds twice yearly. At the earliest, the principal was due in 1951. The face of the bond expressly stated that "[t]he Imperial Government of China pursuant to an Imperial Edict . . . engages that the principal moneys and interest hereby secured shall duly be paid in full. . . ."
>
> In 1912, the Imperial Chinese government was overthrown and replaced by the Republic of China. Up to 1930, timely interest payments were made on the bonds. After 1930, only two fractional interest payments were made to the bondholders.
>
> Before mid-1937, Chiang Kai-Shek's Republican government attempted to salvage the debt instruments, proposing the extension on the payment of principal until 1976. The Sino-Japanese War in 1937 preempted further attempts at settlement. The domestic tumult continued until the end of World War II.
>
> As late as 1947, the Chinese government, long defaulting on interest payments, reaffirmed its continuing debt. However, in 1949, history intervened. The Republic of China was overthrown in favor of the People's Republic of China. The former government fled to Taiwan; the bonds were never paid. [Note, Defaulting of Foreign States and an Expansive Role for the Act of State Doctrine, 6 Whittier L. Rev. 177, 177-178 (1984).]

*The issues associated with succession of governments are separate from those related to succession of states, which are discussed in the following section.

The U.S. district court concluded:

> It is an established principle of international law that "[c]hanges in the government or the internal policy of a state do not as a rule affect its position in international law. A monarchy may be transformed into a republic, or a republic into a monarchy; absolute principles may be substituted for constitutional, or the reverse; but, though the government changes, the nation remains, with rights and obligations unimpaired." . . . Moore, Digest of International Law, vol. 1, p.249. The People's Republic of China is the successor government to the Imperial Chinese Government and, therefore, the successor to its obligations. The People's Republic of China has made no provision for payment of the principal due on the Hukuang bonds. . . . [Jackson v. People's Republic of China, 550 F. Supp. 869, 872 (N.D. Ala. 1982), *rev'd on other grounds*, 596 F. Supp. 386 (1984), *aff'd*, 794 F.2d 1490 (11th Cir. 1986), *cert. denied*, 480 U.S. 917 (1987).]

The district court ruled for the plaintiffs, entering a $41 million default judgment against the PRC because the PRC had received proper service of process and had failed to appear or plead within the requisite time. (This decision was later reversed on foreign sovereign immunity grounds, which is discussed extensively in Chapter 6.)

Despite its reiteration in this Jackson case, the theory of universal succession of governments to the international obligation of their predecessors is not always followed in the face of pragmatic modern state practice.

> Perhaps more acceptable from a modern point of view are equitable theories which call for a concrete look at the benefits and burdens of successor [governments]. Under such theories, a successor [government's]liability (or degree of liability) for a loan to a predecessor turns upon whether the successor government would be "unjustly enriched" if it did not assume a debt. In the case of the Huguang bonds, for instance, the benefit accruing to the Chinese from the construction of railways in China due to the Huguang loan could be material to a determination of the PRC's liability. [Eugene A. Theroux & Thomas Peele, China and Sovereign Immunity: The Huguang Railway Bonds Case, 2 China Law Reporter 129, 147 (1982-83).]

The position of the Chinese government throughout the *Jackson* case was that it did not recognize and had no obligation to repay "debts incurred by the defunct Chinese governments." *Aide memoire* to the Ministry of Foreign Affairs, reprinted in 22 I.L.M. 81 (1983). However, Theroux and Peele, supra at 133-134, note that:

> The Chinese position . . . does not appear to be that a successor government can never, or even rarely, be liable for the debts of predecessor governments. Instead, their position appears to be that obligations incurred by former Chinese regimes belong to the category of "odious debts," which successor governments may (the *aide memoire* implies) decline to assume. The *aide memoire* avers that the Huguang bonds were "one of the means" which the Qing Government, "in collusion with the imperialist powers who were carving out spheres of influence in China," used "to bolster its reactionary rule and repress the people." . . .
>
> [Two historical instances illustrate the principle of repudiation of odious debts.] One of these instances was the American refusal to assume, after the Spanish-American War of 1898, the Cuban debt, which arose from the sale of bonds on the international market. During negotiations, Spain argued that the debts were Cuban, and that as part

of the transfer of sovereignty from Spain to the United States, the United States was bound to assume those obligations. The Americans regarded the debts as "a mass of Spanish obligations and charges . . . the burden of which, imposed upon the people of Cuba without their consent and by force of arms, was one of the principal wrongs for the termination of which the struggles for Cuban independence were taken."

Another example . . . is that of the repudiation by Soviet Russia of the debts of previous Russian governments, including the debts of the former Tsarist regime. . . .

The Soviet actions are elaborated on in Restatement section 208, Reporters' Note 2:

> The new regime insisted that it was not merely a new government but represented a new state, and that therefore the U.S.S.R. was not responsible for the international obligations assumed by the previous regime, including its debts. Other states rejected that position and continued to call on the U.S.S.R. to carry out the obligations of the previous regime. The Soviet government itself frequently claimed rights belonging to Czarist Russia and accepted treaties to which Czarist Russia had adhered as effective, even if it sometimes invoked the defense of *rebus sic stantibus* to escape obligations under them.

In July 1986, the Soviet Union and Britain signed an agreement that ended a 60-year dispute over the liability of the communist government for bonds issued internationally by the Czarist government that preceded it. The agreement did not result in large amounts of money changing hands, because both countries essentially waived the claims against each other and retained what they previously had of each other's property. As a result, the British bondholders were not expected to recover much of the Czarist bonds' $75 million face value. At the time, this agreement was, however, of considerable practical significance to the U.S.S.R.:

> . . . Moscow's borrowing needs are increasing. In European financial markets, there have been persistent rumors recently that Moscow, through its foreign trade bank . . . wants to raise money in the international credit markets.
>
> "If the Soviets do want to issue bonds, this agreement should clear the way for them to do it," said Michael Gough, director of Britain's Council of the Corporation for Foreign Bondholders. . . ." [N.Y. Times, July 16, 1986, at D2, col. 5.]

Theroux and Peele conclude that "the history of . . . government succession issues illustrates 'an almost Bismarckian *Realpolitik*: expediency is the international "principle" which determines whether a successor will or will not assume the debts of a predecessor.' " (Supra at 148.)

A claim of "odious debts" arose again after the fall of Saddam Hussein in 2003. Saddam had incurred huge debts to finance Iraq's wars and its leadership had lived extravagantly. There was some uncertainty about how much Iraq owed to foreign government and other foreign creditors, with estimates ranging from $120 to $200 billion. Many outside financial experts thought the burden was far beyond the capacity of the Iraqi people to repay in a reasonable period. As The Financial Times reported in December 2003, "Some U.S. officials have suggested most of this huge stock should be written off as 'odious debts'—borrowings incurred without the consent of Iraqis and from which they have not benefited."

In late 2003 the Paris Club, an informal group of industrial nations, forgave 80 percent of Iraq's nearly $40 billion in debt owed to the member countries, including the United States, France, Germany, Japan, and Russia. Iraq's other major creditors, including its Middle Eastern neighbors, some non-Paris Club countries, and some commercial debtors felt the pressure to accept the 80 percent debt-forgiveness formula on the more than $80 billion owed them. Most of these other creditors had done so by 2006.

Notes and Questions

1. Some commentators note that the *Jackson* court failed to consider the potential liability of the government of the Republic of China on Taiwan for the railway bonds. If the court had considered this issue, how should it be decided? How does it fit with the international legal principles of succession of governments?

2. After a period of turmoil in 1978-1979, the conservative religious government of Ayatollah Khomeini took control in Iran without any formal elections, displacing a moderate interim government that had come into power after the self-imposed exile of the Shah of Iran. Should private U.S. corporations have been able to enforce long-term contracts entered into with the Shah's government? (See discussion of the Iran-U.S. Claims Tribunal in Chapter 4.D.1.).

3. In late 2001, a new interim government under Hamid Karzai came into power in Afghanistan and was recognized immediately by most countries. The new government replaced the defeated Taliban government, which had taken control in the late 1990s of about 90 percent of the territory of Afghanistan during a civil war, but had only been recognized by three countries. Most countries and the United Nations had continued to recognize the Northern Alliance during the late 1990s until 2002. Should the Karzai government be responsible for the debts of the Taliban? Or of the Northern Alliance?

4. As you review the preceding materials in this chapter, why do you think there should be a difference between recognition of states, recognition of governments, and establishment of diplomatic relations?

5. If you were advising a government of a new state, what would you say are the most practical consequences of recognition and diplomatic relations? Which are the most important? Are those consequences legal or political?

6. Would you favor an objective determination of statehood (based on the facts) and a subjective determination for recognizing a government? Given the criteria for statehood, is an objective determination possible? Is an objective determination possible with respect to a set of criteria for recognition of governments?

7. In view of the recent trend toward democratic governments, should the United States revive the Tobar Doctrine? If so, should it do so unilaterally or seek multilateral recognition, such as through a treaty or a General Assembly resolution? (See also the European Community Declaration after the break up of the Soviet Union and Yugoslavia.)

8. Reflecting on state practice regarding recognition of states and governments, Professor Henkin concluded:

> An entity that is a state in fact is a state in law. A regime that is a government in fact is a government in law. A very different question is whether other governments must establish relations with a new state or a new regime. Maintaining relations with other

governments is normal behaviour within the international system, but there is no legal obligation to maintain diplomatic relations with another government. Some governments refrain from maintaining relations with particular governments because they see no need for such relations, or find it too costly; some because they wish to show their disapproval of those governments. [Louis Henkin, International Law: Politics and Values 15-16 (1995).]

7. *State Succession*

Succession of states is one state replacing another state with respect to the territory, capacities, rights, and duties of the predecessor state. A clear distinction must be drawn between a state succeeding another and the changing of governments within a state. For example, the United States succeeded to the former 13 colonies, whereas President Bush's election changed the government of the United States.

Types of succession can include a new state totally absorbing the first (e.g., through conquest, annexation, or merger), becoming independent of the first state (as with former colonies), or taking only part of the territory of another (including both secession and movement of boundaries), or a state dissolving into two or more states (as with the former Soviet Union and Yugoslavia). Thus, the total number of states can decrease, increase, or remain constant. Types of treaties can include bilateral or multilateral agreements that relate to trade, military, international organizations, or boundaries.

Recent examples of entities at least trying to become independent of existing states are Kosovo, which declared independence from an unaccepting Serbia in February 2008, and southern Sudan, whose population voted overwhelmingly in January 2010 to be independent of Sudan. Both are discussed at the end of this section.

State succession raises important questions as to the ownership of public property, obligations for public debts, and burdens and privileges under international agreements. The answers to these questions are uncertain and subject to considerable debate.

Three competing theories attempt to provide an answer. The theories of universal succession, "clean slate," and partial succession respectively provide for the new state succeeding to all, none, or part of the preceding state's rights and responsibilities. Often the theory used in practice depends on the type of succession or, in the case of international agreements, the type of treaty involved.

Drawing heavily upon the experience with the decolonization following World War II, the Restatement (1986) adopted the view that succession had varying effects on the rights and duties of states. Some of the applicable Restatement provisions follow.

Restatement

Section 209. State Succession: State Property and Contracts

(1) Subject to agreement between predecessor and successor states, title to state property passes as follows:

(a) where part of the territory of a state becomes territory of another state, property of the predecessor state located in that territory passes to the successor state;

(b) where a state is absorbed by another state, property of the absorbed state, wherever located, passes to the absorbing state;

(c) where part of a state becomes a separate state, property of the predecessor state located in the territory of the new state passes to the new state.

(2) Subject to agreement between predecessor and successor states, responsibility for the public debt of the predecessor, and rights and obligations under its contracts, remain with the predecessor state, except as follows:

(a) where part of the territory of a state becomes territory of another state, local public debt, and the rights and obligations of the predecessor state under contracts relating to that territory, are transferred to the successor state;

(b) where a state is absorbed by another state, the public debt, and rights and obligations under contracts of the absorbed state, pass to the absorbing suite;

(c) where part of a state becomes a separate state, local public debt, and rights and obligations of the predecessor state under contracts relating to the territory of the new state, pass to the new state.

Comment

a. Public and private properly distinguished. Subsection (1) deals with property belonging to a state. In general, private property rights are not affected by a change in sovereignty over the territory in which the property is located or in which its owner resides.

Section 210. State Succession: International Agreements

(1) When part of the territory of a state becomes territory of another state, the international agreements of the predecessor state cease to have effect in respect of that territory and the international agreements of the successor state come into force there.

(2) When a state is absorbed by another state, the international agreements of the absorbed state are terminated and the international agreements of the absorbing state become applicable to the territory of the absorbed state.

(3) When part of a state becomes a new state, the new state does not succeed to the international agreements to which the predecessor state was party, unless, expressly or by implication, it accepts such agreements and the other party or parties thereto agree or acquiesce.

(4) Pre-existing boundary and other territorial agreements continue to be binding notwithstanding Subsections (l)-(3).

The following excerpt provides an overview of different theories and possible legal norms. Consider how each theory balances the international community's interest in stability against the new state's interest in sovereignty.

Geoffrey Watson, The Law of State Succession

Contemporary Practice of Public International Law, 115-127 (Ellen Schaffer & Randall J. Snyder Eds., 1997)

When one state succeeds to part or all of the territory of another state, a number of practical problems arise. One set of questions relates to succession in respect of treaties. . . . A second set of succession questions relates to state property and debt. . . .

Yet another problem is state succession in respect of international organizations. . . .

With the breakup of the Soviet Union and Yugoslavia, these last questions have recently taken on new urgency. . . .

I. State Succession in Respect of Treaties

This section considers two important sources on treaty succession: the 1978 Vienna Convention on State Succession in Respect of Treaties, and customary international law. The Vienna Convention is a useful starting point for analysis. The Convention is [now in force with 22 states as parties as of January 2011.] [T]he Convention [also] has importance as a codification of customary law; for example, the Legal Adviser to the U.S. Department of State has said that the Convention's provisions are "generally regarded as declarative of existing customary law by the United States." . . .

The preliminary articles of the Convention define its terms and scope of application. Article 1 provides that the Convention applies to the "effects of a succession of States in respect of treaties between States." Several other provisions, however, significantly limit the Convention's sphere of application. For example, . . . Article 6 makes clear that the Convention applies only to state succession "occurring in conformity with international law," in particular the U.N. Charter. This provision is apparently intended to ensure that the Convention does not bestow any legitimacy on conquest or other acquisition of territory by the unlawful use of force. . . .

Much of the Convention favors continuity in treaty relations. That is, the Convention often provides that a successor state continues to be bound by the treaties of its predecessor. For example, Article 11 provides flatly that state succession "does not as such affect" a boundary treaty. Similarly, Article 12 takes the position that succession does not affect certain rights and obligations pertaining to the use of territory. Article 31 provides that wh[...] [t]wo or more states unite, the newly-united successor state is bound by the trea[...] predecessor states with respect to the territory formerly covered by t[...] [pote]ntially with respect to the entire territory of the new state[...] [a]gree. Conversely, Article 34 provides for continui[...] the new, smaller successor states are pre[...] [predece]ssor state. . . .

Still, some provisions of [...] In particular, the Conventi[...] [...]nt State." Article 16 of the C[...] [...]not bound to maintain in forc[...] [...]e of the succession of States t[...] [...]n the succession of States rela[...] [...]cessor State the territory of w[...] [...] States was a dependent terri[...] [pre]decessor State was responsible[...] [...] designed to acknowledge tha[...] [pr]edecessor treaty in any meaningful [...] [th]at a newly independent state may consent [...] [tr]eaty, either multilateral or bilateral. Thus even the rules for "newly independent states" leave room for continuity in treaty relations. This accommodation for continuity is plainly consistent with state practice. . . .

Taken as a whole, the Convention is a useful contribution to the law of succession in respect of treaties, but it hardly represents the only source of law on the matter. . . .

The customary international law of state succession, like the Vienna Convention, generally supports continuity in treaty relations. Just as the Convention supports continuity in boundary treaties, customary international law has traditionally adhered to [a similar] rule. . . . Just as the Vienna Convention contemplates some continuity when two or more states unite, state practice also seems to recognize that the new larger state is bound by treaties of all its predecessors. . . . The practice on this point is somewhat variegated, however. In the most prominent recent case, the reunification of Germany, the Federal Republic of Germany did not flatly consent to be bound by all treaties applicable to East Germany. . . . In any event, the Vienna Convention's endorsement of continuity in cases of merger has a solid foundation in state practice.

The same can be said of the Vienna Convention's emphasis on continuity of treaty relations in connection with the dismemberment of states (as opposed to the creation of "newly independent" states). A preference for continuity has characterized much commentary and at least some state practice relating to the dissolution of states. Thus it is often said that the former Soviet Republics are bound by the arms-control and other agreements of their predecessor state, the Soviet Union. Likewise, it has been argued that the former Yugoslav republics are bound by Yugoslavia's treaties. Interestingly, the third U.S. Restatement of Foreign Relations Law rejects a rule of continuity in such circumstances. It has instead endorsed a "clean slate" for all new states that have broken off from a larger state, regardless of whether the new states are ex-colonies. . . .

The Vienna Convention's "clean slate" rule for "newly independent" states seems as much an exercise in progressive development as codification of customary law. To be sure, there have been instances in which new states have claimed a clean slate. . . . [E]xamples include Poland and Czechoslovakia, which claimed a clean slate upon seceding from the Austro-Hungarian Empire, and Pakistan, which claimed a clean slate when leaving India in 1947.

But many new states have foregone a clean slate and have consented to be bound by some or all of the treaties of the predecessor state. [Examples include] the dissolution of the union of Sweden and Norway in 1905, the separation of Austria and Hungary, and the separation of Syria and Egypt following the dissolution of the United Arab Republic. Moreover, this type of continuity has not been limited to new states born out of the dismemberment of a larger state. It has also extended to so-called "newly independent" states, as when a new state and its former colonial master enter into a devolution agreement. . . . In any event, state practice does not uniformly support the Vienna Convention's distinction between newly-independent states, which get a clean slate, and other new states, which do not. . . .

. . . This area does not lend itself well to codification because states tend to resolve succession questions on an *ad hoc*, case-by-case basis, in which practical concerns outweigh theoretical ones, giving rise to divergent solutions. . . .

II. Succession of State Property and Debt

If a state inherits its predecessors' treaties, does it also inherit the predecessors' property—and debt? As with treaty succession, analysis of the succession of state property begins with a multilateral convention, in this case the Vienna Convention on Succession of States in Respect of State Property, which was concluded in 1983. . . . [T]he Property Convention is not in force. [As of January 2011, only seven states have ratified] it, well short of the fifteen [ratifications] required before the Convention enters into force. . . . [T]he Property Convention rarely seems to dictate states' decisions in questions of property succession, but again it is a useful starting place for analysis. . . .

The Property Convention's substantive provisions begin with twelve articles on succession in respect of state property. Article 16 provides that when two or more states unite, the successor inherits the state property of the predecessors. . . . When part of the territory of a state is transferred to another, Article 14(1) provides that succession of state property should be accomplished by agreement between the predecessor and successor states. In the absence of such agreement, Article 14(2) provides that immovable state property in the transferred territory should pass to the successor, and that movable state property should pass if it is "connected with the activity of the predecessor State in respect of the territory" in question. Articles 17 and 18 establish similar but not identical rules for separating and dissolving states, respectively. Like Article 14, these Articles provide that successor states in such circumstances do succeed to . . . movable property connected with the "activity" of the predecessor state in respect of that territory. But they also provide, more vaguely, that other movable property should pass to the successors "in equitable proportion."

Like the Treaty Convention, the Property Convention establishes different rules on the property of "newly independent" states. Article 15 reverses the presumptions established in Article 14. A newly independent state is entitled to immovable state property in the transferred territory unless the new state and its predecessor otherwise agree, and even then such agreement "shall not infringe the principle of the permanent sovereignty of every people over its wealth and natural resources." . . .

The Property Convention also establishes interesting rules relating to succession of debt. Again, the easy case is that in which two or more states unite. In such circumstances, the new, larger state simply inherits the debts of its predecessors. Otherwise, the debt is to be settled by agreement or, failing that, split in "equitable proportion." . . .

Again, the Convention's rules on succession of debt contain a striking (and controversial) exception for "newly-independent states." Under the Convention, such states are liberated from debt, just as they are liberated from their colonial masters. Article 38(1) provides: "[N]o State debt of the predecessor State shall pass to the newly independent State, unless an agreement between them provides otherwise. . . ." Any such agreement must not infringe on the "permanent sovereignty" of such a state, and its implementation may not "endanger the fundamental economic equilibria" of the new state. . . .

III. Succession in Respect of International Organizations

In recent years, the most widely-publicized succession problems have involved successor states' efforts to claim the U.N. seats of their predecessors. These questions

are governed primarily by the Charter and practice under the Charter, not by the Vienna Convention on Treaty Succession. . . .

It is now clear that a new state can sometimes succeed to its predecessor's seat in the United Nations without applying for readmission. Russia's succession to the Soviet seat in the United Nations is the most prominent example. Russia inherited the Soviet seat on the Security Council with surprisingly little fuss, and without an amendment of the U.N. Charter, which identifies the USSR—not "Russia"—as one of the five permanent members of the Council. This was possible in part because the other members of the Commonwealth of Independent States acquiesced in the outcome.* Supporters of this result can point to some U.N. precedent for it. When India and Pakistan emerged from British India, for example, the new Republic of India was permitted to assume the U.N. membership of the former Indian Union, though the new state of Pakistan was required to apply for U.N. membership. But this result also comported with a devolution agreement among Britain, India, and Pakistan. . . .

But other recent state practice makes it equally clear that new states do not always succeed to the U.N. seats of their predecessors. The most prominent example is the new "Federal Republic of Yugoslavia," the rump Yugoslavia composed of Serbia and Montenegro. The Federal Republic of Yugoslavia was denied full rights of succession to the seat of the former Yugoslavia in the U.N. General Assembly. Other examples point in the same direction. The new Czech and Slovak republics were not permitted to succeed automatically to Czechoslovakia's seat in the United Nations, even though the two new states had entered into a devolution agreement calling for them to "alternate the continuity of Czechoslovakia for purposes of membership in international organizations. . . ." Even so, the two new states were required to apply for admission as new Members of the United Nations, and both were admitted on January 19, 1993. . . .

Can these cases be reconciled? . . . One explanation is that a successor state is more likely to succeed to the U.N. seat of its predecessor if other successors acquiesce in or otherwise consent to the succession. In the Soviet case, the Alma Ata Declaration—signed by the leaders of the former Soviet republics—formally endorsed Russia's continuance in the Soviet seat at the United Nations. In the India case, a devolution agreement bequeathed the Indian Union's membership on the new Republic of India. By contrast, the former Yugoslav republics did not concede that the new rump Federal Republic of Yugoslavia of Serbia and Montenegro should succeed to the former Yugoslavia's U.N. seat.

Second, a successor state is more likely to inherit a predecessor's U.N. seat if the successor was the "dominant" part of the predecessor state in size or population or both. By this test, Russia was the dominant member of the Soviet Union, just as India was the dominant member of the Indian Union. By contrast, Serbia constituted only about "40% of the area and 44% of the population of the former Yugoslavia."

Third, a successor state is more likely to succeed to a U.N. seat if other states acquiesce. Again, most states acquiesced in the Russian case, whereas many objected

*[The other permanent member states of the Security Council supported this outcome. Giving Russia the seat and the accompanying veto in December 1991 avoided problems of re-opening the Charter, thus effectively postponing action on demands by Germany, Japan, and several large developing countries for permanent membership on the Security Council.—Eds.]

in the Yugoslav case. This last factor may ultimately be the decisive one. A formerly "dominant" state is not as likely to succeed to its predecessor's U.N. seat if a majority of states in the General Assembly or the Security Council oppose that result—even if its fellow successors support its succession. . . .

Thus it appears that the law in this area will unfold on a case-by-case basis, and that it will be influenced at least as much by state practice as by Charter norms or either of the Vienna Conventions on state succession. . . .

Notes and Questions

1. The issues of state succession are often governed by international agreements. An example is the 1991 agreement establishing the Commonwealth of Independent States in which Belarus, Ukraine, and Russia divided the responsibility for the results of the Chernobyl accident.

2. As discussed in the Watson excerpt, in practice, successor states never start with a "clean slate." History shows that most successor states acknowledge some obligations of the prior state. New states find that the value of the preexisting state's rights and duties outweighs their cost, or they succumb to pressure from the other contracting states. For example, before the formal dissolution of the Soviet Union, the need to bolster the credit of the ailing Soviet Union and the promise of assistance from industrialized nations was sufficient pressure for eight of the republics to agree to take responsibility for a portion of the Soviet Union's public debt. Further, President George H. W. Bush linked U.S. formal diplomatic recognition of Ukraine to its acceptance of preexisting arms control commitments.

3. If you were the leader of a new state created from a part of the former Soviet Union or Yugoslavia, what would be your attitude toward assuming the past rights and obligations of the predecessor state for its embassies abroad? Public debts? Treaties regarding the protection of diplomatic and consular personnel? Trade agreements? Arms control agreements?

If you were the U.S. Secretary of State, what would be your attitude toward the rights and obligations of this new state on the same types of matters?

4. As discussed above, one issue in state succession is a new state's membership in international organizations such as the U.N. In May 1992, the United States objected to the rump of Yugoslavia (the Federal Republic of Yugoslavia consisting then of Serbia and Montenegro) succeeding to the U.N. seat of Yugoslavia after the secession of Slovenia, Bosnia and Herzegovina, and Croatia. U.S. objections helped result in U.N. General Assembly Resolution 47/1, which declared that the Federal Republic of Yugoslavia could not automatically continue the U.N. membership of the former Socialist Federal Republic of Yugoslavia and that it should apply for membership in the United Nations. Given the case of Russia, is this a double standard? Is requiring the new Yugoslavia to reapply consistent with the standard for membership established when India and Pakistan separated?

After the successful U.S. and NATO operations in 1999 against the Federal Republic of Yugoslavia (Serbia and Montenegro) over its repression of Albanians in Kosovo and after the ouster of President Slobodan Milosevic in 2000, the government that came to power in the FRY changed the FRY's policies on key issues such as improving respect of democracy and human rights and beginning to cooperate with the International Criminal Tribunal for the Former Yugoslavia. The new government also elected to apply for membership in the United Nations and other international organizations as a new member. The FRY was admitted to the United Nations and the Organization of Security and Cooperation in Europe (OSCE) in November 2000. In June 2006, Serbia and Montenegro officially severed ties and became independent states. In the United Nations, Serbia continued the FRY's membership, but now as Serbia. Montenegro applied for admission to the U.N. and was promptly admitted as a new member.

5. *Kosovo.* Kosovo presents an ongoing question of whether a disputed area is a state. Kosovo is a landlocked area with a population of nearly two million people, primarily of Albanian descent. After the breakup of Yugoslavia, Kosovo became an autonomous province of Serbia. The Serbian repression of Albanians in Kosovo led to the NATO bombing campaign in 1999 and U.N. Security Council Resolution 1244, authorizing the interim international administration of Kosovo by the U.N. Mission in Kosovo (UNMIK) and some provisions for self-government. The resulting Constitutional Framework for Provisional Self-Government in Kosovo led to the establishment of local, democratic political institutions.

On February 2008, the popularly elected Assembly of Kosovo formally declared Kosovo to be an independent and sovereign state. A number of countries, including the United States and most of the European Union countries, recognized Kosovo's independence. Serbia, Russia, and other states denounced the declaration as illegal.

In October 2008, the U.N. General Assembly voted to request an advisory opinion from the International Court of Justice (ICJ). On July 22, 2010, the ICJ by a 10-4 vote opined that Kosovo's declaration of independence did not violate general international law, Security Council Resolution 1244, or the Constitutional Framework. The Court was clear, however, that it was just responding to that narrow question about the declaration; the Court was not asked, nor was it deciding, whether Kosovo had achieved statehood or what were the legal consequences of that. Accordance with International Law of the Unilateral Declaration of Independence, Advisory Opinion (July 22, 2010), reprinted in 49 I.L.M. 1404 (2010); see Bart M.J. Szewczyk, Lawfulness of Kosovo's Declaration of Independence, ASIL Insight, August 17, 2010.

As of January 2011, it appears that 73 states, including the United States, 22 of the 27 EU members, and all of Kosovo's neighbors, except Serbia, had recognized Kosovo. (There were at least 193 states in the world at that time — the 192 members of the U.N. plus the State of Vatican City, which has not applied for U.N. membership but which is recognized as a state by most countries.) Kosovo is not a U.N. member, and membership is unlikely, at least for now, because of Russia's opposition. U.N. membership requires approval by the U.N. General Assembly and the Security Council, where Russia has a veto. (China has not taken a stand on Kosovo's independence.)

Is Kosovo a state, and why or why not? Who decides? Should a U.S. district court judge treat Kosovo as a state — for example, entitled to immunity under the Foreign Sovereign Immunities Act (which will be analyzed in Chapter 6)? Should the U.S. President and the State Department treat a person that the government of Kosovo sends to be its emissary as an ambassador or a private citizen?

6. *Southern Sudan.* Pursuant to a peace agreement in 2005 that the government of Sudan and various warring groups accepted, a referendum on self-determination occurred in southern Sudan in January 2011. The people of that region voted heavily in favor of independence. As of February 2011, some fighting had broken out in southern Sudan between the southern Sudanese military forces and various

groups. Neverthless, the southern Sudanese government and military reportedly believe their control in the area was sufficient for them to declare independence from Sudan in July 2011.

If the government of Sudan resists that vote and objects to the independence of the South, with its substantial oil reserves, what might southern Sudan do to strengthen its claim to independence? What might countries that support the referendum and its results do?

As of February 2011, Kosovo's claim to statehood remained contested, whereas it appears that southern Sudan's will be accepted. Is this because southern Sudan presents a stronger factual claim to satisfying the requirements for statehood than Kosovo does? Or is it because Sudan and key states in the international community have accepted southern Sudan's independence, whereas Serbia, Russia, and other states have opposed Kosovo's independence? Is this consistent with the legal rules governing the recognition of states identified above in section 1? What does this say about the role of the "constitutive" and "declaratory" theories of statehood discussed in Section 2 above?

6. Besides the attempts by Kosovo and southern Sudan to become independent in 2008 and 2010, there have been a number of other cases in the last few decades. In 1990, North and South Yemen unified after two decades of hostilities following their independence from European colonialism. Also in 1990, Namibia broke away from South Africa, which had administered the former German colony since World War I. In 1993, after 30 years of armed struggle and a U.N. supervised referendum, Eritrea achieved independence from Ethiopia. In Asia, East Timor (or Timor-Leste) gained independence from Indonesia in 2002. Future state successions around the globe seem inevitable, and the related international law issues will continue to arise.

B. TERRITORIES AND OTHER ENTITIES

The substantial territorial holdings of the United Kingdom, France, the United States, and other Western industrialized countries shrunk during the past century as their former territories and colonies became independent. Besides new states being created, a variety of other new entities were formed. Although not precisely fitting the traditional definition of a state, they are capable of acting and interacting on the international level.

At the end of World War II, the British Empire encompassed 62 dependencies. Today, only tiny possessions containing around 300,000 people are left. Since the beginning of the twentieth century, most British colonies have evolved toward self-rule. This process has often produced several unique ties between the British monarchy and her former dependencies, such as Australia and Canada, but almost all these former dependencies are now considered independent states.

For the United States, the status of relations with Puerto Rico and the former Trust Territory of the Pacific Islands are noteworthy.

1. *Puerto Rico*

Puerto Rico, a four-island chain with a population of about 4 million, was ceded by Spain to the United States in 1898 at the end of the Spanish-American War. During the first half of the twentieth century, Puerto Rico and the United States managed, not without difficulty, to define the former's status as a U.S. territory. In 1952 Congress passed Public Law 600, which authorized Puerto Rico to draft its own constitution. The law was approved by the Puerto Rican people as well as by Congress and established the Commonwealth of Puerto Rico.

> [The Commonwealth] acquired the type of local governmental autonomy associated with the States in the United States federal structure. Presently, Puerto Rico has its own Constitution, pursuant to which it elects the Governor and legislature; appoints judges, cabinet officials, and lesser officials in the executive branch; sets its own educational policies; determines its own budget; and amends its own civil and criminal codes. [Arnold H. Leibowitz, The Commonwealth of Puerto Rico: Trying to Gain Dignity and Maintain Culture, 11 Ga.J. Int'l & Comp. L. 211, 232 (1981).]

Puerto Rico has had a Resident Commissioner in the House of Representatives since 1904. While he may speak in Congress and in committee and may introduce legislation, he cannot vote on the House floor. Although U.S. citizens since 1917, Puerto Ricans cannot vote in presidential elections. Under the commonwealth relationship, the United States determines the foreign and defense affairs of Puerto Rico.

For several decades, political parties in Puerto Rico have questioned the concept of "commonwealth" as the final status for Puerto Rico, with some instead seeking either statehood or independence. The official U.S. position remains that the people of Puerto Rico are self-governing and that the decision to alter their present status rests with them alone.

Puerto Rico's international status is ambiguous partly because the parameters of its association with the United States remain uncertain. Puerto Rico is often treated as one of the U.S. states in U.S. judicial opinions as well as by the Executive Branch. At other times, its commonwealth status sets it apart from the federal states. For example, residents of Puerto Rico are exempt from federal income taxes and from full-scale application of minimum wage laws. Puerto Rico is also the recipient of substantial federal assistance.

Notes and Questions

1. Is the Commonwealth of Puerto Rico more like one of the federal states than like a sovereign nation? Is Puerto Rico's lack of capacity to conduct foreign affairs enough to deny it the classification of a sovereign nation?

2. On December 13, 1998, Puerto Rico held a plebiscite on status. The resulting vote was interpreted as the majority rejecting the statehood idea. The results were 50.2 percent for "none of the above," the option favored by supporters for Puerto Rico remaining a U.S. commonwealth. Another 46.5 percent backed a measure to seek statehood status through the U.S. Congress. Options offering full or partial independence received less than 3 percent of the vote.

3. As noted earlier, the British Commonwealth still has its interesting ties. In September 1990, Britain's Queen Elizabeth II, who is nominally Canada's sovereign as well, approved a request from Canada's Prime Minister to add eight new seats to its appointive Senate. Prime Minister Brian Mulroney was seeking to ensure passage of a controversial sales tax that might have been blocked by the

appointed Senate, even though it passed in the popularly elected House of Commons.

The Queen's authority stemmed from a provision of the 1867 British North America Act. Royal assent to the Prime Minister's request can only be given if the Senate is deadlocked on an important issue and if there is no other way to break the impasse. Since 1990, the Queen's relationship with Canada has returned to its normal, quiet routine — for example, occasionally visiting the country and participating in ceremonies.

In Australia, 54 percent of Australians voted in 1999 against replacing Queen Elizabeth as their head of state with a president elected by parliament. Australia would have still remained in the Commonwealth if the proposal had succeeded. Many commentators saw the result not as a vote in favor of the monarchy, but as expressing a preference for a president elected directly by the people rather than indirectly by parliament.

2. *Trust Territory of the Pacific Islands*

The former Trust Territory of the Pacific Islands (Micronesia) was administered by the United States beginning in 1947, pursuant to a U.N. Strategic Trusteeship Agreement. The Trust Territory had been administered by Japan under a League of Nations mandate after World War I. The Pacific Islands Trust was established after the United States wrested the islands from Japanese occupation during World War II.

The Trust Territory encompassed an area of considerable strategic importance, including over 2,000 islands with a total population of about 140,000. While the total land area of the islands is only about 716 square miles, the islands are scattered over an ocean area as large as the continental United States. The number of islands and their location entitle the state(s) that have sovereignty over them to claim large amounts of adjoining ocean area, particularly under the boundary lines accepted under the Law of the Sea Convention. (See Chapter 9.) Moreover, important ship and aircraft routes between Asia and the United States traverse the region.

Although relying on the United States for military and economic assistance, the Micronesians moved toward self-government beginning in the mid-1960s. In 1969 the United States started negotiations with the peoples of Micronesia in order to redefine the relationship between itself and the Trust Territory. The extensive and complex negotiations resulted in two distinct results — commonwealth status for the Northern Mariana Islands and free association for Palau, the Marshall Islands, and Federated States of Micronesia.

The Covenant to Establish a Commonwealth of the Northern Mariana Islands in Political Union with the United States of America was signed in 1975 and became U.S. law one year later. As a result, the people of the Northern Marianas became U.S. citizens (though they do not receive all of the constitutional rights of mainland citizens), and the Northern Marianas obtained self-governing commonwealth status under U.S. sovereignty. Unlike Puerto Rico, the Mariana Islands have no representative in Congress. Designated provisions of the U.S. Constitution and certain federal laws, including income tax laws, apply to the Marianas under the covenant.

In 1982 representatives of the other three Trust Territory components and the United States signed the Compact of Free Association. In U.N.-observed plebiscites conducted in 1983, the peoples of the Republic of the Marshall Islands and the Federated States of Micronesia (FSM) approved the compact and in 1986 gained independence. Palau approved its compact in 1993, and became independent in 1994, bringing the Trust Territory to an end. U.S. financial support has remained a mainstay of these islands' economies, although the United States has been phasing out aid to Micronesia. Under the free association arrangements, the United States maintains major defense rights, including the right to deny access there to any nation that the United States considers a threat.

The 1982 Compact of Free Association between the United States and the Marshall Islands and FSM provides in Section 121 that: "The Governments of the Marshall Islands and the Federated States of Micronesia have the capacity to conduct foreign affairs and shall do so in their own name and right. . . ." On the other hand, Section 311 provides, in part, that: "The Government of the United States has full authority and responsibility for security and defense matters in or relating to the Marshall Islands and the [FSM] . . ." Section 313 then provides, in part: "The Governments of the Marshall Islands and the [FSM] shall refrain from actions which the Government of the United States determines, after appropriate consultation with those Governments, to be incompatible with its authority and responsibility for security and defense matters in or relating to the Marshall Islands and the [FSM]."

Free association is relatively unique in international practice. Two other examples are the Cook Islands and Niue. They have free association status with New Zealand, since 1965 and 1974, respectively.

> Free association differs from independence in that one of the parties to the bilateral agreement willingly binds itself, by its own constitutional process—whether by delegation or otherwise—to cede to the other a fundamental sovereign authority and responsibility for the conduct of its own affairs. Specifically, this distinction is exemplified by the reservation to the United States of plenary defense authority (as contrasted with treaty rights to exercise certain defense functions), and the ensuing limitation on Micronesian freedom of action. Free association is distinguished from integration into a metropolitan power by the retention by the freely associated government of the power to assert itself domestically and internationally without reference to the legal authority of another state. [Arthur John Armstrong, Strategic Underpinnings of the Legal Regime of Free Association: The Negotiations for the Future Political States of Micronesia, 7 Brook. J. Int'l L. 179,182 (1981).]

Notes and Questions

1. The ability of the FSM, Marshall Islands, and Palau to act in the international realm could potentially bring the freely associated states into conflict with U.S. national security interests in the Pacific. How might this potential conflict be resolved, given that the United States retains control over the security and defense affairs of these states, while they retain authority over their foreign affairs? To what extent might "foreign affairs" be subsumed by "security and defense matters"? Is the United States being given a de facto voice in the foreign affairs of these states?

2. Under Article 4(1) of the U.N. Charter, an entity applying for U.N. membership must be a state that is willing to accept the obligations of the Charter and is able and willing to carry out these obligations. Under this standard should the

Micronesian freely associated states qualify for membership? Will these entities be able to carry out their U.N. obligations if the United States retains control over their defense and security affairs? In 1991 the FSM and the Marshall Islands became U.N. members, and Palau was admitted in 1994.

C. INTERNATIONAL AND REGIONAL ENTITIES

International and regional organizations, such as the United Nations or the European Union, can also be persons under international law. Indeed, their role in international activities and in the making of international law is growing rapidly. Organizations that have been in existence for decades have often continued to evolve, and new entities are coming into being in response to new needs.

To discuss all of these organizations in depth is beyond the scope of this book. In this section we briefly describe the principal international and regional entities and highlight a few of the major contemporary issues. Other chapters also contain considerable material on some of these entities. For example, the International Court of Justice is discussed in Chapter 4 on dispute resolution. There are often references to these entities because of their major impact on international law.

1. An Overview

Even before the end of World War II in 1945, the Allies and other countries were actively discussing the creation of international institutions that would provide more security and stability in the world.

The central institution was to be the United Nations. The name was devised by President Franklin D. Roosevelt and was first used in the Declaration of the United Nations of January 1942, when representatives of 26 nations pledged to continue fighting together against the Axis powers. In a real sense the origins of the United Nations can be traced far back in history to several attempts — from the Achaean League in ancient Greece to the League of Nations after World War I — to create an organization that would prevent military conflict among its members and settle international disputes. The International Court of Justice (ICJ) was designed as the formal judicial body to resolve legal disputes.

Other key international institutions included the International Monetary Fund (IMF), which was designed to promote international monetary cooperation and stability in foreign exchange. The period prior to World War II had experienced tremendous financial instability, caused in part by rapid changes in the value of individual nations' currencies and numerous currency restrictions. The International Bank for Reconstruction and Development (or World Bank) was created to help provide funds for the reconstruction of war-ravaged nations and to promote economic development.

The International Trade Organization (ITO) was envisioned as an institution to provide a structure and enforcement for rules that would regularize and encourage international trade. The worldwide economic problems of the 1930s had been caused in part by the protectionist policies adopted by the United States and other countries. United States congressional opposition to the ITO, however, caused it to be a stillbirth. A subsidiary agreement, the General Agreement on Tariffs and Trade (GATT), was left to fill the void.

The creators of these international institutions also assumed that regional organizations might develop to supplement the efforts of the international entities. For example, the U.N. Charter specifically assumes the active existence of regional groups (Articles 52-54), as does the GATT for customs unions and free trade areas (Article XXIV).

In establishing these international institutions, the planners and policymakers tried to avoid the mistakes of the past. There was a consensus that the United States would have to be a member. The U.S. failure to join the League of Nations had clearly not been helpful for the health of that institution. Similarly, the majority view that emerged in the early years of these institutions was that the defeated Axis powers—Germany, Japan, and Italy—had to be given a role. Indeed, many believed that it was important that those countries be thoroughly entwined in international and regional groups. The policy after World War I of extracting heavy reparations from Germany and slating it for harsh treatment for future decades was one of the justifications that Adolf Hitler had used to gain the support of the German people and to break the post-World War I agreements.

The post-World War II institutions continue to exist today, except for the ITO. They have failed, however, to achieve some of their original objectives. Although the successful U.N. response to the Iraqi invasion of Kuwait in 1990 helped revive hopes for the future of the institution, the United Nations has been much less successful at preventing war and settling disputes than its creators had hoped. Also, as discussed in Chapter 4, the ICJ has been less active and successful as the judicial body to help resolve disputes than was envisioned.

In the decades since World War II each of the institutions has also evolved, some much more than others. In the 1970s the IMF saw the United States go off the gold standard and the major industrial countries of the world switch to flexible exchange rates. The World Bank has changed its focus from reconstructing the war-torn economies of Europe to encouraging the development of countries in Latin America, Africa, Asia, and Eastern Europe. The GATT has been transformed into the World Trade Organization (WTO), a formal international trade institution that has become very active.

While the initial set of institutions was growing and evolving, a wide range of other institutions and separate agreements has developed. These include regional organizations such as the European Union and Asia-Pacific Economic Cooperation (APEC); regional courts such as the European Union's Court of Justice and the European Court of Human Rights; international arbitration through institutions like the International Center for the Settlement of Investment Disputes; the quasi-formal operations of countries with similar interests, such as the Group of 8 (G-8) countries (the United States, Japan, Germany, France, United Kingdom, Italy, Canada, and Russia); and more recently the Group of 20 (G-20) countries (the G-8 plus other important countries, such as China, India, and Brazil); and a vast array of multilateral and bilateral agreements for various purposes—from combating terrorism, to protecting diplomatic personnel, to enforcement of arbitral awards.

These new institutions and agreements have often supplemented the work of the older institutions. For example, the regional development banks (such as the Inter-American Development Bank and the Asian Development Bank) have helped to increase the availability of public development funds and to target them on specific regions.

For some problems and activities, the newer entities have essentially supplanted the older institutions. For instance, the finance ministers of the G-8 and G-20 countries discuss exchange rates among themselves and take steps that sometimes have more impact on these rates than the IMF. Also, the active caseloads of the two European regional courts include at least a few cases that could well have gone to the ICJ.

Often the role of the newer entities vis-à-vis the older institutions is complicated. For example, the European Union (EU) helps further the aim of the WTO by reducing trade barriers among the member states of the Union. However, to the extent that the EU might be slower to reduce barriers against non-member states (e.g., to protect the EU's farmers) than one of the individual member states might otherwise have been, the EU is delaying progress in the WTO. Another example is the Law of the Sea Convention. Although it provides for resort to the ICJ as one means of resolving disputes, it also established a new international court (the International Tribunal for the Law of the Sea) as well as two arbitral mechanisms.

2. *International Institutions*

a. The United Nations: Its Structure, Purposes, and Future

The United Nations, which formally came into existence in 1945, is the principal international organization designed to prevent military confrontations among its members and to help resolve international disputes. It has also embarked on numerous other tasks, from simplifying international air travel to the eradication of malaria and smallpox. The following excerpt provides a useful introduction to the U.N.'s structure and activities.

United Nations, The United Nations Today

3-22 (2008)

[Updated in brackets by this casebook's authors through January 2011.]

The Charter is the constituting instrument of the Organization, setting out the rights and obligations of member states, and establishing the United Nations organs and procedures. An international treaty, the Charter codifies at the international level the major principles of international relations — from the sovereign equality of States to prohibition of the use of force in international relations. . . .

Membership

Membership of the United Nations is open to all peace-loving nations which accept the obligations of the Charter and are willing and able to carry out these obligations. [As of January 2011, there were 192 member states in the United Nations. This number includes the 2006 admission of Montenegro, which separated from Serbia. Switzerland and Timor-Leste joined in 2002.]

The General Assembly admits new Member States on the recommendation of the Security Council. The Charter provides for the suspension or expulsion of a Member for violation of the principles of the Charter, but no such action has ever been taken. . . .

Structure of the Organization

The Charter established six principal organs of the United Nations: the General Assembly, the Security Council, the Economic and Social Council, the Trusteeship Council, the International Court of Justice and the Secretariat. The United Nations family, however, is much larger, encompassing 15 agencies and several programmes and bodies.

General Assembly

The General Assembly is the main deliberative organ. It is composed of representatives of all Member States, each of which has one vote. Decisions on important questions, such as those on peace and security, admission of new Members and budgetary matters, require a two-thirds majority. Decisions on other questions are by simple majority.

Functions and Powers

Under the Charter, the functions and powers of the General Assembly include:

- to consider and make recommendations on the principles of cooperation in the maintenance of international peace and security, including the principles governing disarmament and arms regulation;
- to discuss any question relating to international peace and security and, except where a dispute or situation is being discussed by the Security Council, to make recommendations on it;[1]
- to discuss and, with the same exception, make recommendations on any question within the scope of the Charter or affecting the powers and functions of any organ of the United Nations;
- to initiate studies and make recommendations to promote international political cooperation, the development and codification of international law, the realization of human rights and fundamental freedoms for all, and international collaboration in economic, social, cultural, educational and health fields;
- to make recommendations for the peaceful settlement of any situation, regardless of origin, which might impair friendly relations among nations;

1. Under the "Uniting for Peace" resolution, adopted by the General Assembly in November 1950, the Assembly may take action if the Security Council, because of lack of unanimity of its permanent members, fails to act where there appears to be a threat to international peace, breach of the peace or act of aggression. The Assembly is empowered to consider the matter immediately with a view to making recommendations to Members for collective measures, including, in case of a breach of the peace or act of aggression, the use of armed forces when necessary to maintain or restore international peace and security.

- to receive and consider reports from the Security Council and other United Nations organs;
- to consider and approve the United Nations budget and to apportion the contributions among Members;
- to elect the non-permanent members of the Security Council, the members of the Economic and Social Council . . . (when necessary); to elect jointly with the Security Council the Judges of the International Court of Justice; and, on the recommendation of the Security Council, to appoint the Secretary-General.

Sessions

The General Assembly's regular session begins each year on Tuesday in the third week of September. . . .

At the beginning of each regular session, the Assembly holds a general debate, often addressed by heads of state and government, in which Member States express their views on the most pressing international issues. Most questions are then discussed in its six Main Committees. . . .

Some issues are considered directly in plenary meetings while others are allocated to one of the six Main Committees. Resolutions and decisions, including those recommended by the committees, are adopted in plenary meetings—usually before the recess of the regular session in December. They may be adopted with or without a vote. . . .

While the decisions of the Assembly have no legally binding force for governments, they carry the weight of world opinion, as well as the moral authority of the world community.

The work of the United Nations year-round derives largely from the decisions of the General Assembly—that is to say, the will of the majority of the Members as expressed in resolutions adopted by the Assembly. That work is carried out:

- by committees and other bodies established by the Assembly to study and report on specific issues, such as disarmament, peace-keeping, development and human rights;
- in international conferences called for by the Assembly; and
- by the Secretariat of the United Nations—the Secretary-General and his staff of international civil servants.

Security Council

The Security Council has primary responsibility, under the Charter, for the maintenance of international peace and security.

The Council has 15 members; five permanent members—China, France, the Russian Federation, the United Kingdom and the United States—and 10 elected by the General Assembly for two-year terms.

Each member has one vote. Decisions on procedural matters are made by an affirmative vote of at least 9 of the 15 members. Decisions on substantive matters require nine votes and the absence of a negative vote by any of the five permanent members.

All five permanent members have exercised the right of veto at one time or another. If a permanent member does not fully agree with a decision but does not wish to cast its veto, it may choose to abstain — thus the resolution to be adopted if it obtains the required number of nine votes in favour.

Under Article 25 of the Charter, all members of the United Nations agree to accept and carry out the decisions of the Security Council. While other organs of the United Nations make recommendations to governments, the Council alone has the power to take decisions which Member States are obligated under the Charter to implement.

Functions and Powers

Under the Charter, the functions and powers of the Security Council include the following:

- to maintain international peace and security in accordance with the principles and purposes of the United Nations;
- to formulate plans for establishing a system to regulate armaments;
- to call upon the parties to a dispute to settle it by peaceful means;
- to investigate any dispute or situation which might lead to international friction, and to recommend methods of adjusting such disputes or the terms of settlement;
- to determine the existence of a threat to the peace or act of aggression and to recommend what action should be taken;
- to call upon the parties concerned to comply with such provisional measures as it deems necessary or desirable to prevent an aggravation of the situation;
- to call on members of the United Nations to take measures not involving the use of armed force — such as sanctions — to give effect to the Council's decisions;
- to resort to or authorize the use of force to maintain or restore international peace and security;
- to encourage the peaceful settlement of local disputes through regional arrangements and to use such regional arrangements for enforcement action under its authority;
- to recommend to the General Assembly the appointment of the Secretary-General and, together with the Assembly, to elect the Judges of the International Court of Justice.
- to request the International Court of Justice to give an advisory opinion on any legal question;
- to recommend to the General Assembly the admission of new members to the United Nations.

The Security Council is so organized as to be able to function continuously, and a representative of each of its members must be present at all times at United Nations Headquarters. The Council may meet elsewhere: in 1972, it held a session in Addis Ababa, Ethiopia; in 1973 it met in Panama City, Panama; and in 1990 it met in Geneva, Switzerland.

When a complaint concerning a threat to peace is brought before it, the Council's first action is usually to recommend that the parties try to reach agreement by peaceful means. The Council may set forth principles for a peaceful settlement.

In some cases, the Council itself undertakes investigation and mediation. It may dispatch a mission, appoint special representatives or request the Secretary-General to use his good offices.

When a dispute leads to hostilities, the Council's first concern is to bring it to an end as soon as possible. The Council may issue ceasefire directives that can be instrumental in preventing an escalation of the conflict.

The Council may also dispatch military observers or a peacekeeping force to help reduce tensions, keep opposing forces apart and create conditions of calm in which peaceful settlements may be sought. Under Chapter VII of the Charter, the Council may decide on enforcement measures, including economic sanctions, arms embargoes, financial sanctions, travel bans or collective military action.

The sanctions instrument is an important tool available to the Security Council in seeking to promote international peace and security. Each of the sanctions regimes currently in existence features "smart" or targeted sanctions—arms embargoes, financial sanctions, and travel bans—designed to eliminate or minimize unintended effects by focusing on those responsible for the policies condemned by the international community, while leaving other parts of the population and international trade relations unaffected. . . .

[For example, in 2010, the Security Council passed a resolution imposing additional sanctions upon Iran for that state's continued failure to comply with its international obligation to cease its efforts toward obtaining nuclear weapons. Those sanctions contained exceptions for humanitarian aid.]

The Council has established two international criminal tribunals to prosecute crimes against humanity in the former Yugoslavia and in Rwanda. The tribunals are subsidiary organs of the Council. . . .

[There have been proposals for changing the membership and voting structure of the Security Council. However, the only time the Security Council's composition has been changed was in 1965, when it was enlarged from 11 to 15 members by the addition of four more rotating members, which serve two-year terms. Supporters of change contend that the present five permanent members (P-5) (the United States, Great Britain, France, Russia, and China) reflect the world powers of 1945, not of today.

[A number of other countries—including Brazil, Germany, India, and Japan—want to have permanent seats rather than act as occasional rotating members. (Unless there is an expansion in the Council's total membership of 15 states, this would reduce the opportunities for other nonpermanent members to occasionally sit on the Council.) These aspirants have differing views on whether they also seek a veto.

[Eliminating the veto for the present permanent members as part of a change in voting structure seems highly unlikely, at least for the time being. At least some of the permanent members (very likely including the United States) would be opposed to it and would have their vetoes available to prevent the change.

[Note that the use of vetoes has been rare since 1990. There were 24 vetoes from May 1990 through December 2009—including one by Russia objecting to the renewal of the U.N. observer mission in Georgia and several by the United States on resolutions against Israel. However, the veto remains a powerful tool. For example, during the efforts led by the United States and United Kingdom against Iraq in 2002-2003 for Iraqi breaches of previous resolutions, the text and actual passage of new resolutions was very much affected by the possibility of vetoes by France, Russia, and China.

[In November 2009, the General Assembly held a debate on possible reform measures aiming to expand the membership of the Security Council. Although there is widespread support for expanding membership, there is something far short of consensus on which states should enjoy a new seat on the Council and whether or not veto power should be expanded to new members. In 2010, President Obama proposed that India be given a permanent seat without addressing the role of other aspirants or the veto. See discussion below in the excerpt from a Council on Foreign Relations report.]

Economic and Social Council

The Charter established the Economic and Social Council as the principal organ to coordinate the economic and social work of the United Nations and the specialized agencies and institutions — known as the United Nations family of organizations. The Council has 54 members, who serve for three-year terms. Voting in the Council is by simple majority; each member has one vote. . . .

Relations with Nongovernmental Organizations

Under the Charter, the Economic and Social Council consults with nongovernmental organizations (NGOs) concerned with matters within its competence. Over 2,870 NGOs have consultative status with the Council. The Council recognizes that these organizations should have the opportunity to express their views, and that they possess special experience or technical knowledge of value to its work. . . .

Trusteeship Council

The Trusteeship Council was established by the Charter in 1945 to provide international supervision for 11 Trust Territories placed under the administration of 7 Member States, and ensure that adequate steps were taken to prepare the Territories for self-government or independence. . . .

By 1994, all Trust Territories had attained self-government or independence, either as separate States or by joining neighbouring independent countries. . . .

Its work completed, the Trusteeship Council — its membership reduced now to the five permanent members of the Security Council . . . — has amended its rules of procedure to meet as and where occasion may require.

International Court of Justice

Located at The Hague, in the Netherlands, the International Court of Justice is the principal judicial organ of the United Nations. It settles legal disputes between states and gives advisory opinions to the United Nations and its specialized agencies. Its Statute is an integral part of the United Nations Charter. [See Chapter 4.B.]. . . .

Secretariat

The Secretariat — consisting of international staff working in duty stations around the world — carries out the diverse day-to-day work of the Organization. It services the other principal organs of the United Nations and administers the programmes and policies laid down by them. At its head is the Secretary-General, who is appointed by the General Assembly on the recommendation of the Security Council for a five-year, renewable term. . . .

The Secretariat has some 25,530 staff members on contracts of one year or more, of whom some 17,630 are paid from extrabudgetary resources. Staff on short-term contracts bring the total to some 30,550 staff from 182 countries. As international civil servants, staff members and the Secretary-General answer to the United Nations alone for their activities and take an oath not to seek or receive instructions from any government or outside authority. Under the Charter, each member state undertakes to respect the exclusively international character of the responsibilities of the Secretary-General and the staff and to refrain from seeking to influence them improperly.

The United Nations, while headquartered in New York, maintains a significant presence in Addis Ababa, Bangkok, Beirut, Geneva, Nairobi, Santiago and Vienna, and has offices all over the world.

Secretary-General

Equal parts diplomat and advocate, civil servant and CEO, the Secretary-General is a symbol of United Nations ideals and a spokesman for the interests of the world's peoples, in particular the poor and vulnerable. Mr. Kofi Annan of Ghana completed two five-year terms as Secretary-General on 31 December 2006 and was succeeded by the eighth Secretary-General, Mr. Ban Ki-moon of the Republic of Korea.

The Charter describes the Secretary-General as "chief administrative officer" of the Organization, who shall act in that capacity and perform "such other functions as are entrusted" to him or her by the Security Council, General Assembly, Economic and Social Council and other United Nations organs. The Charter also empowers the Secretary-General to "bring to the attention of the Security Council any matter which in his opinion may threaten the maintenance of international peace and security." These guidelines both define the powers of the office and grant it considerable scope for action. . . .

One of the most vital roles played by the Secretary-General is the use of his "good offices"—steps taken publicly and in private, drawing upon his independence, impartiality and integrity, to prevent international disputes from arising, escalating or spreading. . . .

Budget of the United Nations

The regular budget of the United Nations is approved by the General Assembly for a two-year period. The budget is initially submitted by the Secretary-General. . . .

The budget approved for the biennium [2010-2011 is $5.16] billion. . . . The budget covers the costs of the United Nations programmes in areas such as political affairs, international justice and law, international cooperation for development, public information, human rights and humanitarian affairs. . . .

The main source of funds for the budget is the contributions of Member States. These are assessed on a scale approved by the Assembly on the recommendation of the Committee on Contributions, made up of 18 experts who serve in their personal capacity and are selected by the General Assembly. . . .

The fundamental criterion on which the scale of assessments is based is the capacity of countries to pay. This is determined by considering their relative shares of total gross national product, adjusted to take into account a number of factors, including their per capita incomes. . . . In 2000, the Assembly fixed a maximum of 22 percent of the budget for any one contributor.

The overall financial situation of the United Nations has been precarious for several years because of the continuing failure of many Member States to pay, in full and on time, their assessed contributions. The United Nations has managed to continue to operate thanks to voluntary contributions from some countries and to its Working Capital Fund (to which Member States advance sums in proportion to their assessed contributions), and by borrowing from peacekeeping operations.

Member states' unpaid contributions to the regular budget totaled $362.0 million at the end of 2006. Out of 191 assessed member states, 134 had paid their assessments in full, while the remaining 57 had failed to meet their statutory financial obligations to the Organization.

In addition to the regular budget, Member States are assessed for the costs of the International Tribunals . . . , and, in accordance with a modified version of the basic scale, for the costs of peacekeeping operations.

Peacekeeping costs peaked at $3 billion in 1995, reflecting in particular the expense of operations in Somalia and the former Yugoslavia, but were down to $889 million in 1999. By the end of 2001, the annual cost of United Nations peacekeeping had again risen to just over $2.5 billion — reflecting major new missions in Kosovo, East Timor (now Timor-Leste), Sierra Leone, the Democratic Republic of the Congo, and Eritrea and Ethiopia.

Since July 2005, the annual cost of United Nations peacekeeping has experienced more than a twofold increase, reflecting major new missions in Côte d'Ivoire, Liberia, Haiti, the Sudan, and Timor-Leste and the expansion in Lebanon. For the year beginning 1 July 2007, the . . . budgets totaled some $5.3 billion, excluding separate financing for the hybrid African Union/United Nations mission in Darfur. Nevertheless, this amount represents half of 1 percent of world military spending (more than $1 trillion annually).

United Nations funds and programmes — such as the United Nations Children's Fund (UNICEF), the United Nations Development Programme (UNDP) and the High Commissioner for Refugees — have separate budgets. The bulk of their resources is provided on a voluntary basis by governments, and also by individuals, as in the case of UNICEF. The United Nations specialized agencies also have separate budgets. . . .

The United Nations Family of Organizations

The United Nations family of organizations (the "United Nations system") consists of the **United Nations Secretariat**, the United Nations **funds and programmes** (such as UNICEF and UNDP), the specialized agencies (such as UNESCO and WHO) and **related organizations**. The funds and programmes are subsidiary bodies of the General Assembly. The specialized agencies are linked to the United Nations through special agreements and report to the Economic and Social Council and/or the General Assembly. The related organizations — including IAEA and the World Trade Organization — address specialized areas and have their own legislative bodies and budgets. Together, the organizations of the UN system address all areas of economic and social endeavour. . . .

[The 15 specialized agencies related to the United Nations include: International Labour Organization (ILO); Food and Agriculture Organization of the United Nations (FAO), United Nations Educational, Scientific and Cultural Organization (UNESCO), World Health Organization (WHO), the World Bank Group, International Monetary Fund (IMF), International Civil Aviation Organization (ICAO), Universal Postal Union (UPU), International Telecommunication Union (ITU), World Meteorological Organization (WMO), International Maritime Organization (IMO), World Intellectual Property Organization (WIPO), International Fund for Agricultural Development (IFAD), United Nations Industrial Development Organization (UNIDO).]

Notes and Questions

1. What should be the role of the United Nations? First, do you think that the United Nations can successfully play the role initially envisioned for it of preventing military conflict among its members and of settling international disputes? How does the voting system in the Security Council help or hurt these efforts? Can we expect the Security Council to be more effective in situations where none of the permanent members has a vital interest that the Security Council action might threaten? Might the United Nations be particularly useful when there are regional crises or conflicts that the permanent members would prefer to have resolved? (See Chapter 11 for further discussion of U.N. peacekeeping efforts and other Security Council actions.)

2. How does the growing threat of international terrorism change the role of the United Nations? Should terrorism affect the definition of "self-defense" under Chapter 51 of the U.N. Charter? How should the U.N. and the international community of nations define terrorism? Given the nebulous character of many terrorist organizations, what level of connection should the U.N. seek to establish for allowing a state that has been attacked by terrorists to retaliate against another state for sponsoring terrorist activity? (These questions are also addressed in Chapter 11.)

3. What other roles should the United Nations have besides peacekeeping? Encouraging worldwide efforts to preserve the environment? Stopping drug traffic? Dealing with international health problems, such as AIDS? Acting as a regular and convenient meeting place when new problems arise? Does the organization have greater potential in these other areas compared to peacekeeping, particularly peacekeeping among the major powers? Why or why not?

4. The U.N. General Assembly voted to create a Human Rights Council in 2006 to replace the Human Rights Commission, which had been widely criticized for a membership that included repressive regimes and which had done little that was constructive. Each of the 47 members of the Human Rights Council were selected by an absolute majority of the General Assembly with the member states expected to take into consideration candidates' contribution to the promotion and protection of human rights, a standard that did not exist for the earlier Human Rights Commission. In spite of this standard, besides a number of countries with solid human rights records — such as Canada, Finland, France, Japan, and Switzerland — the new members also included, among others, China, Cuba, Russia, and Saudi Arabia. The Bush Administration opposed the resolution creating the new Council, fearing that the reform was inadequate. (For further discussion of the Council, see Chapter 8.B.5.)

5. Why do you think that the United Nations has spawned so many specialized agencies? Are there benefits to having complex, continuing problems handled by a permanent agency with an expert staff? Or is this bureaucracy running amok?

6. The United Nations has been under continuing pressure, particularly from the United States, to tighten its budget and personnel policies and to implement cost-cutting measures. The U.N.'s financial difficulties arise not only from increased demands for its services but also, in part, from the continuing failure of many member states to pay their assessed contributions to the regular budget or to peacekeeping operations.

Throughout the 1980s and 1990s, the U.S. Congress regularly withheld much of the dues owed to the United Nations on the grounds that the organization was inefficient and poorly managed. At one point, the United States had a $1.3 billion debt to the U.N., which comprised 65 percent of the total debt by member states. Besides creating problems for U.N. operations, the U.S. arrears also threatened to cost the United States its vote in the General Assembly. Under Article 19 of the U.N. Charter, if a country owes the equivalent of two years' worth of assessed dues, the country loses its right to vote in the General Assembly, though this sanction is not automatically enforced.

In 1999, Congress passed the Helms-Biden Act, which required the U.N. to accept $926 million in full satisfaction of the U.S. debt, a reduction in the U.S. share of the regular budget from 25 percent to 22 percent, and an additional reduction to 20 percent by 2002. Moreover, the law required a reduction in the U.S. peacekeeping share from 31 to 25 percent by 2001. The goal of the Helms-Biden Act was also to make U.S. payment of dues contingent upon U.N. reforms, including the revision of the assessment scale.

Such unilateral action by the United States encountered criticism from abroad. After many months of negotiations, an agreement was adopted by the General Assembly in December 2000 and called for the reduction of the U.S. share of the general budget from 25 to 22 percent. Also, the deal reduced the U.S. share of peacekeeping costs to 26 percent by 2003.

The agreement, however, did not end the U.S. budgetary problems with the U.N. The deal fell just short of the requirements set forth in the Helms-Biden Act. As a result, an amendment to the Helms-Biden Act reflecting the differences between the original statute and the agreement was required before the United States could pay its outstanding debt to the U.N. The amendment was enacted into law in 2001, and substantial payments were made. Since then, the U.S. has made headway on closing the gap between assessed dues and actual contributions. As of December 31, 2009, the U.S. owed $859 million in arrears. See Majorie Ann Browne, United Nations System Funding: Congressional Issues, Congressional Reference Service 30 (August 9, 2010).

7. In 2005, Congress funded the U.S. Institute for Peace to create a task force to study the U.N. and recommend an action agenda for the United States. The Task Force, cochaired by former House Speaker Newt Gingrich and former Senate majority leader, George Mitchell, issued a report in June 2005. It recommendations included, among others, the creation of an Independent Oversight Board and a Chief Operating Officer, establishing sunset provisions for all programs; requiring disclosure standards for top officials, and giving more independence to the U.N.'s Department of Peacekeeping.

8. The following excerpt addresses further the question of possibly expanding the membership on the U.N. Security Council, with special consideration of U.S. policy. As noted in the previous excerpt from the U.N. publication, President Obama did propose in 2010 that India be given a permanent seat on the Security Council.

Kara C. McDonald & Stewart M. Patrick, UN Security Council Enlargement and U.S. Interests

Council on Foreign Relations Special Report 5-10 (Dec. 2010)

The UN Charter, as amended in 1965, creates a fifteen-member council with the authority to impose binding decisions on all UN member states. The UNSC's power resides with the five permanent members — China, France, Russia, the United Kingdom, and the United States — designated in 1945 as the primary guardians of world order. The charter . . . provides ten additional seats elected for two-year terms based on contributions to peace and security, with consideration to geographic parity (in practice the elected seats have been divvied up among the regional blocs).

Proponents of [Security Council] enlargement observe that the distribution of global power has dramatically changed since 1945, and that the number of UN member states has surged from 51 to 192 without a parallel expansion of the UNSC. The UNSC's permanent membership, for example, excludes major UN funders like Japan and Germany, emerging power like India and Brazil, and all of Africa and Latin America. Enlargement proponents warn that the UNSC's global authority will erode if it fails to expand membership from underrepresented regions. Moreover, skillfully accomplished enlargement could provide a near-term opportunity to manage power transitions, "socializing" today's regional leaders into security. If expansion is inevitable, proponents believe, the United States should lead it now . . . rather than get dragged along by others later.

Opponents of enlargement dispute that the UNSC is experiencing a crisis of legitimacy, arguing that it remains the most effective of all UN organs and that the UNSC's permanent structure still reflects the leading political and military powers. Enlargement would dilute U.S. power, increase gridlock, encourage lowest-common-denominator actions, and empower antagonistic leaders of the non-aligned movement (NAM). The expectation that permanent UNSC membership will tame obstreperous state behavior at the UN is naive. . . . In any case, UNSC reform is unlikely to be achieved, given the two-thirds United Nations General Assembly (UNGA) and unanimous P5 support required for charter revision. The United States would thus be foolish to take the lead on UNSC reform, which would only alienate the main aspirants or the next tier of countries — many of which are U.S. allies. It would be wiser to let multilateral negotiations continue along an inconclusive path than risk blame for a failed negotiation or conclude a reform that jeopardizes U.S. interest.

A Closer Look

A closer look suggests that while many arguments often offered in support of enlargement are flawed, the case for expanding the UN Security Council is a compelling one. A common claim, particularly in the developing world, is that the UNSC is increasingly illegitimate and ineffective, given its inequitable geographic composition, declining relevance to today's security threats, inability to ensure compliance with its ostensibly blinding resolutions, and exclusion of countries that could contribute to international security. According to this analysis, the UNSC is in poor and even terminal condition.

In truth, the situation is nowhere near so dire. The actual behavior of member states . . . suggests the UNSC's legitimacy, credibility, and effectiveness are more robust than critics claim. Nevertheless, failure to enlarge the UNSC is problematic, for it excludes from permanent membership powerful countries that could contribute to international security and offer long-term political support for the United Nations.

Dwindling Legitimacy?

From the perspective of the United States and other permanent members, the legitimacy of the UNSC as currently constituted is clear: it emanates from the UN Charter. As long as the charter remains in force and unamended, the existing UNSC structure is legitimate.

To date, critiques of the UNSC's legitimacy have been couched primarily in terms of equitable geographic representation. According to regional blocs, the UNSC's domination by Western countries and failure to include permanent members from Africa and Latin America give it dwindling authority to issue binding international decisions, particularly in settings like sub-Saharan Africa, where the majority of UN peace operations occur. The lack of perspectives from the global South reinforces perceptions that the UNSC is a neocolonial club, determining questions of war and peace for the poor without their input.

Such talking points pack a political punch in the developing world. But these arguments confront two inconvenient truths. First, regional representation and parity were never the basis for designing the UNSC's permanent members, which were chosen primarily as guarantors of world peace. The same should be true, presumably, of any additional permanent seats. The charter suggests that the candidacies of emerging powers such as Brazil or India (as well as established ones like Germany and Japan) should be weighed not on their role as regional leaders, but on their ability to help safeguard international peace. The place to address regional balance is clearly in the UNSC's elected seats, since Article 23 of the UN Charter explicitly mentions "equitable geographic distribution" as a secondary consideration.

Second, designating new permanent members will not likely sate demands for greater regional representation. Indeed, opposition to the main aspirants (Brazil, Germany, India, and Japan) is strongest from their regional rivals (Argentina, Mexico, Italy, Pakistan, and South Korea). . . .

Decreasing Relevance?

The UNSC's relevance is not declining; it remains the premier multilateral institution for matters of international security. To be sure, UN member states exploit a range of frameworks—including regional organizations, ad hoc coalitions, and interest-based partnerships—to advance their national and collective security. Examples range from the African Union to the Six Party Talks on North Korea. But in the last five years, the UNSC has spent comparatively less time rubber-stamping diplomatic agreements made outside its chambers and more time forging agreements within its own remarks. UNSC Resolution 1701 to end the Lebanon war, the P5+ Germany negotiations on Iran, and the UNSC's sanctions against North Korea are all examples. The UNSC's continued relevance is also illustrated by states' desire to serve on it. Every October the UNGA is filled to capacity when delegations elect the new rotating UNSC member amid an orgy of vote-buying. . . .

Weakening Implementation?

Some critics claim that the lack of geographic balance in the council's permanent membership and its failure to include regional leaders erode its perceived authority, complicating the implementation and enforcement of its resolutions, and causing states to turn to other frameworks to address security problems.

With rare exceptions, however, UN members continue to regard the UNSC as the most authoritative international institution in matters of global peace and security. To be sure, states are sometimes slow to align national laws and practices with new UNSC resolutions, and bureaucratic inertia contributes to deficiencies in implementation. But the resolutions most commonly flouted today are those imposing sanctions and other punitive measures, and the violators tend to be the targeted states and their sympathizers. These are cases less of weak implementation than of political defiance. Examples include the arms embargoes on Sudan and Somalia, resolutions condemning violence in eastern Congo, and the sanctions resolutions against Iran and North Korea. A change in UNSC composition would probably not address noncompliance by offending states, like North Korea, Iran, or Syria.

A More Compelling Case for Reform: Shifting Concepts and Realities of Power

The UNSC, then, faces no immediate crisis of legitimacy, credibility, or relevance. At the same time, however, there is a powerful geopolitical argument for compositional reform. The primary consideration for permanent membership should be power—the ability and willingness to deploy it in service of global security. Openness to UNSC enlargement is justified by the changing nature of threats to international peace and by the need to harness the power of emerging and established states as pillars of an open, rule-bound global system.

In 1945, permanent UNSC membership was primarily justified by political-military power, including a capacity to prevent—and, if necessary, conduct and win—interstate war. But in today's more diffuse security environment, national military power is no longer the sole or necessarily supreme qualification. Combating transnational threats, ranging from terrorism to nuclear proliferation to climate change, requires not only military but also diplomatic, economic, and technological capabilities. Strategies to contain, manage, and solve global challenges depend as much on the cohesion of multilateral responses as on military might—and they require the contributions of all major emerging and established powers.

In this new environment, the relevant question is: What composition does the UNSC need to fulfill its mandate to maintain international peace and security?

The past six decades have witnessed significant shifts in the relative size of the world's largest economies, alongside more modest shifts in relative defense spending. These trends suggest the emergence of new countries able to contribute to international peace and security. The hurdle to UNSC permanent membership must remain high, and aspirant countries should demonstrate an ability to broker and deliver global solutions to transnational threats.

Skillfully accomplished, UNSC expansion could be an investment in global stability. While the UNSC is not presently in crisis, there are persuasive practical and geopolitical grounds for the United States to support a modest enlargement of its permanent membership. To fulfill its mandate the UNSC needs to draw on the collective authority and capabilities of many states. The Obama administration has an opportunity to shift the reform debate from one of entitlement to one of responsibility and action. . . . By spearheading reform that gives emerging nations (as well as important established powers) a stake in the current order, the United States can increase global political support for (or at least acquiescence to) existing arrangements and leverage the contributions of capable states willing to provide a larger share of global public goods.

Historically, the task of accommodating rising powers has been among the most difficult challenges of world politics. International relations tend to be particularly turbulent when the global distribution of power changes and international structures fail to keep pace. The interwar years (1919-39) provide a case in point. While it is impossible to predict the future, failure to adjust the UNSC's composition could well complicate multilateral security cooperation in the decades ahead. . . .

Any efforts to enlarge the UNSC will be difficult, but it will get harder with time as power diffuses around the world and calls for reform increase. By acting now, the United States can help harness the capabilities of new global actors and create incentives for their responsible behavior.

Notes and Questions

1. Do you agree with the excerpt above that the United States should work with other countries to try to enlarge the U.N. Security Council, including the addition of new permanent members? If not, why not? Could it be because the effort is unlikely to succeed and not worth the commitment of time and prestige? What vote is required in the Security Council and in the General Assembly to enlarge the Security Council?

2. The excerpt above does not address the question of whether the new permanent members should be given a veto. If one or, more likely, a few new permanent members were to be added to the Security Council, do you think that each of them should have a veto? If not, is it likely that each of the present P-5 countries could be convinced to give up their veto? On what terms should the United States support the enlargement of the Security Council?

3. Besides the issues above regarding possible enlargement of the Security Council, what should be the approach of the United States toward the U.N.? Should the United States continue to pay its dues promptly? Should the United States lend combat forces to U.N. peacekeeping missions? If so, under whose command?

4. As we continue through the list of other international and regional entities, consider what the alternatives are to an active United Nations. Depending on the

problem or issue, do the other entities have the necessary breadth of membership and resources? Are some problems or issues better handled by the whole international community (i.e., through the United Nations), while other problems or issues are better addressed by regional entities (such as the European Union) or by groups of countries with similar interests (e.g., the G-8)?

Bibliography

The literature on the United Nations and its specialized agencies is vast. Besides the sources already cited in this section and the many official publications of the United Nations, recent studies include David L. Bosco, Five to Rule Them All: The UN Security Council and the Making of the Modern World (2009); Michael W. Doyle & Nicholas Sambanis, Making War and Building Peace: United Nations Peace Operations (2006); James Traub, The Best Intentions: Kofi Annan and the UN in the Era of American World Power (2006). The United Nations has an excellent Web site at http://www.un.org.

b. The International Monetary Fund and the World Bank Group

In a 1944 wartime conference in Bretton Woods, New Hampshire, representatives of 44 countries formed two international organizations to promote economic cooperation and development, the International Monetary Fund (IMF or Fund) and the International Bank for Reconstruction and Development (World Bank). Now, over 65 years later, each institution has more than 185 members, including all the major countries. In the past decades, both institutions have changed as the monetary system went off the gold standard and fixed exchange rates and as the focus of development aid shifted from post-war destruction in Europe to the Third World. The economic problems in Asia, Russia, and Latin America starting in the mid-1990s required further changes. More recently, the IMF has taken on a leading role in lending to countries suffering from the economic crisis that struck the world in 2008.

Both the IMF and the World Bank are supposed to be apolitical. The World Bank charter, for example, provides that the Bank and its officers "shall not interfere in the political affairs of any member; nor shall they be influenced in their decisions by the political character of the member or members concerned. Only economic considerations shall be relevant to their decisions." (IBRD Articles of Agreement, art. IV, §10.)

(1) IMF: Purpose and Function

The IMF is the world's central monetary institution and in recent years has been at the forefront of the cooperative international debt strategy. As indicated on the IMF's excellent Web site in December 2010:

> The IMF's primary purpose is to ensure the stability of the international monetary system — the system of exchange rates and international payments that enables countries (and their citizens) to transact with one another. This system is essential for promoting sustainable economic growth, increasing living standards, and reducing

> poverty. Following the recent global crisis, the Fund is clarifying and updating its mandate to cover the full range of macroeconomic and financial sector issues that bear on global stability. . . .
>
> The IMF's resources are provided by its member countries, primarily through payment of quotas. . . . At the April 2009 G-20 Summit, world leaders pledged to support a tripling of the IMF's lending resources from about US$250 billion to US$750 billion. http://www.imp.org/external/np/exr/facts/glance.htm.

Among its major activities, the IMF administers the funds in various accounts and financial arrangements, which provide an asset pool that members can draw on to finance deficits in their balance of payments (discussed later); administers special drawing rights (SDRs), an international reserve asset created by the IMF; and provides "surveillance" of the member countries (i.e., advice on "policies that foster economic stability, reduce vulnerability to economic and financial crises, and raise living standards"). Id.

Each nation has a quota, which determines how much it needs to contribute (or subscribe) to the IMF's General Reserve Account (GRA). Quotas are usually reviewed every five years and broadly reflect a country's economic strength. The size of a nation's quota determines not only the amount of its subscription, but also its drawing rights in the GRA, its share of SDR allocations, and its voting power within the IMF. Members pay in their quotas using both SDRs and other currencies.

The SDR, or special drawing right, is an international monetary reserve asset created by the IMF in 1969 to supplement existing reserve assets and provide a common unit of account. Its value is set using a weighted basket of four currencies: the U.S. dollar, Japanese yen, British pound sterling, and the euro. The relative weight of the currencies in the basket is adjusted every five years based on their roles in international trade and finance. In November 2010, the IMF reassigned the weight of currencies so that the U.S. dollar decreased from 44 percent to 41.9 percent, the euro increased from 34 percent to 37.4 percent, the pound sterling increased from 11 percent to 11.3 percent, and the Japanese yen decreased from 11 percent to 9.4 percent. As of January 12, 2011, one SDR was equal to approximately $1.53.

When a country joins the IMF, besides contributing its quota, the country's responsibilities are to cooperate with both the Fund and with other members to assure orderly exchange arrangements. It is also required to promote exchange rate stability and to avoid exchange rate restrictions that would harm national and international prosperity. Another "rule of good conduct" requires a member to provide the Fund with financial and economic information about itself. The Fund monitors the compliance of member countries with these obligations through surveillance over members' exchange rate policies and over the international monetary system.

(2) The World Bank Group: Purpose and Function

Formed as a sister organization to the IMF, the initial goal of the International Bank for Reconstruction and Development (IBRD, or World Bank) was to provide long-term financing to those countries in need of reconstruction after World War II. Its purpose now is to promote economic and social progress in developing nations by providing financial and technical assistance. The World Bank Group is now composed of the IRBD and its affiliates, the International Development Association (IDA), which is sometimes grouped in with the IBRD as the World Bank; the International Finance Corporation (IFC); the International Centre for the Settlement of Investment Disputes (ICSID); and the Multilateral Investment Guarantee Agency (MIGA).

The IBRD finances its lending operations, primarily by borrowing money in the private international capital markets, backed by guarantees of its member governments. The IBRD aims to reduce poverty in middle-income and creditworthy poorer countries by promoting sustainable development through loans, guarantees, risk management products, and advisory services. Loans are generally repayable over 12-15 years, and carry a near-market interest rate (commensurate with that paid by the Bank on its borrowings). Each loan must be made to or guaranteed by the government concerned.

The IDA was established in 1960 to provide assistance to the world's poorest countries on softer terms than those of IBRD loans. Funds lent by the IDA come principally from contributions by its richer members but also from transfers of net earnings from the IBRD. Loans generally have no interest charge and require repayment in 35 to 40 years.

The IBRD and the IDA share the same staff, and they use the same criteria for funding projects. Together they provide more development assistance than any other single agency, multilateral or bilateral, in the world. In fiscal year 2009, they approved new loans of $46.9 billion for a variety of projects.

In financing a project, the Bank does not compete with other sources of funding. Rather, it is a "lender of last resort": it funds only those projects for which the necessary capital is not available from other sources on reasonable terms. However, once the Bank is involved, most projects then receive financial support from other multilateral or bilateral agencies or commercial banks, which reflects the Bank's role as a catalyst for capital funding.

The IFC was established in 1956. Its function is to assist the economic development of less developed countries by promoting growth in their economies' private sectors via both direct lending and encouragement of private investment. The IFC is a separate entity from the Bank and has its own operating and legal staff; however, it uses the Bank for administrative and other services. Membership in the IFC totals over 180 members.

The IFC complements the work of the Bank. It is required to make loans without a government guarantee. The IFC and the Bank have jointly financed projects, and it is not uncommon for IFC projects to be dependent on infrastructure projects financed by the Bank.

ICSID, which was created by the Convention on the Settlement of Investment Disputes Between States and Nations of Other States in 1965, provides a voluntary mechanism for settling disputes between host governments and foreign investors through conciliation and arbitration. As of January 2011, 144 nations were parties to the Convention. (See discussion in Chapter 4.D.)

MIGA, established in 1988, has the mission to promote foreign direct investment (FDI) into developing countries. It seeks to do this by providing political risk insurance for foreign investments (covering, for example, expropriation or political violence), dispute resolution services for guaranteed investments, and technical assistance. services. In January 2011, MIGA had 175 member countries.

(3) The IMF and the World Bank: Structure

The IMF and the World Bank possess similar membership and structures. Only states may be members of the IMF or the World Bank Group. A state need not be a member of the United Nations in order to join the IMF, but membership in the Fund is a prerequisite to joining the World Bank. Within the World Bank Group, most members of the IBRD are members of the IDA and the IFC as well.

The two institutions are each governed by a board of governors and an executive board. The board of governors is the senior organ and is composed of one governor and one alternate governor from each member. In practice, the executive board is the most important organ. It meets in continuous session and is responsible for general operations.

The World Bank executive board has 24 executive directors in addition to a president (traditionally an American). The IMF has 24 executive directors, three deputy managing directors, and a managing director (usually a European). Those members with the largest quotas each appoint its own executive director. As of December 2010, the United States had the largest voting bloc at the IBRD with 16.36 percent, followed by Japan (7.85 percent), Germany (4.48 percent), France, and the United Kingdom (4.30 percent each). In the IMF, the United States also had the largest voting power, with 16.74 percent. Japan and Germany followed with 6.01 percent and 5.87 percent, respectively, and France and Britain with 4.85 percent each. China also has its own elected executive director with 3.65 percent of the votes. The remaining executive directors are elected by groups of the remaining countries. Also, the two largest creditor members may also appoint a director (if they don't have one already).

The IMF and the Bank use a weighted voting system based on members' quotas. However, Fund and Bank organs rarely resort to formal votes except when required to do so. Rather, most work is done by consensus.

Although the IMF and World Bank are primarily state-centric organizations, in recent years they have become more responsive to the concerns of non-state actors.

(4) U.S. Influence over International Financial Institutions

Although the United States was an important participant in the negotiations leading to the Bretton Woods agreement and the United States continues to support exchange rate stability and development efforts in less-developed countries, the IMF and World Bank have not been very instrumental in promoting specific U.S. foreign policy objectives. This is due to two factors: first, these institutions are apolitical in nature and focus only on economic realities within the borrowing countries; second, the U.S. quota does not give the United States even close to a majority position in either organization. Rather, the United States must rely on informal lobbying to further its objectives.

(5) The Changing Roles and Relationship of the IMF and the World Bank Since 1970

In August 1971 the United States ended the convertibility of the U.S. dollar into gold at an officially fixed price A few months later the United States devalued the dollar. By March 1973 most major currencies were floating in value. The system that emerged was one of flexible exchange rates.

During the decade following the collapse of fixed exchange rates, the IMF was occupied with adapting to the new system. It created for itself a supervisory role over the floating system as monitor of members' economic policies. It also continued to lend to countries experiencing temporary balance-of-payments deficits.

In 1982 the IMF stepped in with short-term funds to enable Mexico to meet its debt repayment obligations. That step opened the door to a new role—providing funds and encouraging new private bank lending to heavily indebted countries in exchange for IMF-supervised economic restructuring within those counties. An Economist article in February 1988 reported that the IMF lent more than $22 billion between 1982 and 1984.

The task of restoring creditworthiness to countries was a more difficult task than first envisioned, however, and required more than the short-term loans then offered by the IMF. It prompted the IMF to alter its offerings to include longer-term lending.

During this same period of the 1970s and 1980s, the World Bank found that with floating exchange rates, currency exchange risks had a greater impact than before on the profitability of proposed development projects. The Bank's concern with domestic currency values increased. Likewise, its involvement in the general economic health of developing countries grew, as many oil-importing countries encountered major financial shocks from the sharp oil price rises.

Although the Articles of Agreement for both the World Bank and the IDA specify that loans made or guaranteed by these organizations shall be for specific projects, "except in special circumstances" (see IBRD art. III, §4(vii) and IDA art. V, §1(b)), the Bank Group has interpreted "specific projects" and "special circumstances" broadly. The steady growth in the breadth of their interpretation allowed the Bank in 1980 to begin offering "structural adjustment" loans. Rather than for a specific project, such as a dam or a factory, these loans can be for general macroeconomic or structural programs that will have a more widespread impact on the economy or a segment of it.

Both the World Bank and the IMF encountered new challenges in the 1990s as a result of the breakup of the Soviet Union, instability in Eastern Europe, the 1995 economic crisis in Mexico, and then the Asian and Russian financial crises of 1997-1998.

For the World Bank, these challenges led to record lending and raised questions about the Bank's lending practices. With the breakup of the Soviet Union and the attempts at market and social reform in former communist countries, the World Bank made large loans to Russia and other countries. In 1998, the Asian financial crisis pushed the Bank's lending to record levels, which included assistance in the areas of financial reforms, social security, technology, education, and health. The events in Asia also led to questions about the Bank not having imposed stricter lending conditions in prior years on countries with institutional problems, such as a weak banking structure and corruption in Indonesia.

The IMF was also very active. For example, recognizing the problems that former communist countries had in transitioning to market economies, the IMF established a temporary systemic transformation facility in 1993. It loaned funds to countries so that they could institute policies that would then allow them to borrow under the other permanent IMF programs.

The challenges for the IMF—and questions about its performance—were probably even more demanding than for the World Bank. The situation might best be understood by delving further into how IMF lending occurs and then analyzing how the IMF initially reacted to the 1997-1998 Asian financial crisis. In an IMF publication, David Driscoll explains the Fund's basic lending process.

David D. Driscoll, What Is the International Monetary Fund?

14-17 (1997) [with updates added]

Although the IMF was founded primarily as a cooperative institution to oversee the international monetary system, it also supports that system by occasionally injecting into it sums of money, sometimes on a very large scale, through loans to its members. Indeed, the IMF is perhaps best known to the general public for pumping billions of dollars into the system during the debt crisis of the 1980s and for the vast amounts it committed to Mexico and to Russia during the 1990s. . . . In 1995, it extended to Mexico a credit of over $17 billion and to Russia more than $6.2 billion to help tide these countries over a difficult period of reform. . . .

The quota subscriptions . . . constitute the largest source of money at the IMF's disposal. Quotas are now in theory worth about [$755 billion in 2011], although in practice this sum is deceptively large. Because member countries pay 75 percent of their quotas in domestic money, and because most national currencies are rarely in demand outside the countries issuing them, approximately half of the money on the IMF's balance sheets cannot be used. . . . [M]ost potential borrowers from the IMF want only the major convertible currencies: the U.S. dollar, the Japanese yen, . . . the pound sterling, and [now the euro].

As each member has a right to borrow from the IMF several times the amount it has paid in as a quota subscription, quotas might not provide enough cash to meet the borrowing needs of members in a period of great stress in the world economy. To deal with this eventuality, the IMF has had since 1962 a line of credit . . . with a number of governments and banks throughout the world. This line of credit, called the General Arrangements to Borrow, is renewed every five years. The IMF pays interest on whatever it borrows under these arrangements and undertakes to repay the loan in five years. These arrangements have been strengthened by a decision on the New Arrangements to Borrow . . . .

In addition to these arrangements, the IMF also borrows money from member governments or their monetary authorities for specific programs of benefit to its members. Over the past decade, using its good credit rating, the IMF has borrowed to provide needy members with more money for longer periods and under more favorable terms than they could obtain on their own. Borrowing these large amounts has to a certain extent changed the nature of the IMF, making it more like a bank, which is essentially an institution in the business of borrowing from one group and lending to another. . . .

The IMF lends money only to member countries with payments problems, that is, to countries that do not take in enough foreign currency to pay for what they buy from other countries. The money a country takes in comes from what it earns from exports, from providing services (such as banking and insurance), and from what tourists spend there. Money also comes from overseas investment and, in the case of poorer countries, in the form of aid from better-off countries. Countries, like people, however, can spend more than they take in, making up the difference for a time by borrowing until their credit is exhausted, as eventually it will be. When this happens, the country must face a number of unpleasant realities, not the least of which are commonly a loss in the buying power of its currency and a forced reduction in its imports from other countries. A country in that situation can turn for assistance to the IMF, which will for a time supply it with sufficient foreign exchange to allow it to put right what has gone wrong in its economic life, with a view to stabilizing its currency and strengthening its trade.

A member country with a payments problem can immediately withdraw from the IMF the 25 percent of its quota that it paid in gold or a convertible currency. If the 25 percent of quota is insufficient for its needs, a member in greater difficulty may request more money from the IMF. . . .

As a country draws increasingly on these funds, conditions might be attached. This conditionality is part of the IMF's attempts to stabilize the financial situations in borrowing countries and thereby reduce their need for Fund resources. The conditions might include such items as new taxes, reductions in government employment, reductions in subsidies, sale of government enterprises, devaluation of the currency, and limitations on the importation of luxury goods. Although these conditions are intended to eliminate the country's balance-of-payments deficits without imposing unnecessarily harsh restrictions on trade or causing adverse effects on economic growth, the measures sometimes prove to be unpopular domestically. These conditions have made the Fund—and the domestic leaders who accept its austerity measures—the targets of criticism.

This general description of the IMF lending process can be put in context by considering the Asian financial crisis of 1997-1998 and the more recent crisis in 2008-2010. The article by economist Adam Posen applies the 1997-1998 Korean situation and its lessons to the European problems in 2008-2010. The second excerpt is from a 2010 speech by Dominique Strauss-Kahn, the Managing Director of the IMF, discussing how the IMF has reformed its process.

Adam Posen, One Fiscal Size Does Not Fit All

Eurointelligence June 22, 2010

Twelve years ago, the Asian Financial Crisis hit. The International Monetary Fund took a common approach across the crisis countries, prioritizing fiscal austerity. In retrospect, outside observers and the Fund itself came to the conclusion this was a mistake—while appropriate for Indonesia, the "It's Mostly Fiscal" approach made the situation worse than it needed to be in South Korea, with negative spillovers for the rest of the region.

[I]n 1997-98, a few small East Asian economies came up against limits after extended booms funded by capital inflows. Indonesia and Thailand had run large current account deficits* and accumulated public debt. They also had significant

*[The balance on a country's current account is essentially the sum of a country's balance in trade of goods and services and its balance on income receipts and payments. —Eds.]

structural problems that made their high rates of growth unsustainable. Just as in the euro area today, financial markets suddenly woke up to this reality, and began pulling out money. Interest rates rose for these countries and their solvency problems turned into shortages of liquidity. As usual, ratings agencies had backed their borrowing on the way up, and turned on these economies accelerating their difficulties on the way down.

So far, so simple, though also sad. Similar to Greece and arguably Portugal, today, the Asian economies that had lived beyond their means found it had caught up with them. Their creditors, public and private, were understandably upset—though of course the creditors were the ones that made the mistaken assumption that exchange rate pegs assured repayment of debts, justifying the loans at low interest rates. The IMF came in to perform its primary role of financing and designing adjustment plans, with an appropriate emphasis on austerity in Indonesia and Thailand.

The much bigger and much sounder South Korean economy then fell into difficulties. The direct effects of contraction in its neighboring trading partners hurt Korea. Despite being far more advanced in what it produced and at a higher income level than the rest of non-Japan Asia, Korea also suffered competitively from depreciations and wage falls in its region. Worst of all, financial panic prompted in part by worries about the exposures and funding of Korean banks fed a downward spiral. And thus the IMF came in there, too.

Yet, then the austerity treatment was taken too far. Rather than differentiating its requirements of South Korea to reflect the better fundamentals of the economy (and its size), sharp fiscal tightening was made a requirement of IMF lending there as well. The austerity had significant contractionary effects, because lack of confidence in Korean solvency beyond the panic was unjustified. No benefit accrued from these measures. . . . The contraction in South Korea was longer and deeper than it had to be as a result.**

**As another respected economist, Professor Martin Feldstein, detailed in 1998 during the crisis:

> The Korean economy was performing well: real GDP grew at eight percent per year in the 1990s, . . . inflation was below five percent, and the unemployment rate was less than three percent. . . . Korea got in trouble in mid-1997 because its business and financial institutions had incurred short-term foreign debts that far exceeded Korea's foreign exchange assets. By October, U.S. commercial banks estimated that Korea's short-term debts were $110 billion—more than three times Korea's foreign exchange reserves. With investors nervous about emerging markets in general and Asia in particular, it is not surprising that the Korean won came under attack.
>
> Since Korea's total foreign debt was only about 30 percent of GDP (among the lowest of all developing nations), this was clearly a case of temporary illiquidity rather than fundamental insolvency. Moreover, since the current account deficit was very small and rapidly shrinking, there was no need for the traditional IMF policy of reduced government spending, higher taxes, and tight credit. Yet something needed to be done to stop the loss of foreign exchange and to maintain bank lending to the country and its healthy businesses. . . .
>
> What Korea needed was coordinated action by creditor banks to restructure its short-term debts, lengthening their maturity and providing additional temporary credits to help meet the interest obligations. . . . The IMF could have helped by providing a temporary bridge loan. . . .
>
> Instead, the IMF organized a pool of $57 billion from official sources—the IMF, the World Bank . . . and others—to lend to Korea so that its private corporate borrowers could meet their foreign currency obligations to U.S., Japanese, and European banks. In exchange for those funds, the IMF demanded a fundamental overhaul of the Korean economy and a contractionary macroeconomic policy of higher taxes, reduced spending, and high interest rates. . . . [Martin Feldstein, Foreign Affairs, Mar./Apr. 1998, at 20-33.]

The effects were not limited to this honest though costly mistake, which the IMF — to its credit — has since recognized and not repeated. The deeper contraction in Korea sent around the world the effects of the Asian financial crisis with renewed force. It arguably led, in part, to the Russian default and global difficulties of October 1998. Less obviously, but probably doing more lasting damage, this set of policies in Korea also gave renewed vigor to the complaints among Asian emerging markets that the IMF was unfair and autocratic. Desire to avoid future IMF involvement has fed the accumulation of reserves through exchange rate undervaluation, and thus mercantilist or protectionist policies, from Beijing to Kuala Lumpur, and beyond. That in turn has contributed to the global imbalances we have today, the ongoing political fragility of the open world economy, and the inability of the G-20 to gain agreements beyond immediate crisis response.

That is an awful lot of damage from one misguided application of austerity to a country that could have had a less costly adjustment. But those are the facts. That kind of costly mistake is what the governments of the euro area are now potentially repeating in their treatment of Spain. Spain is not Greece or Portugal. Spain has much stronger fundamentals and has suffered less justifiably from financial panic than its neighbors or Ireland. . . .

Yet, if excessive austerity is imposed on Spain, the result will be even more miserable than for Korea, with at least as bad an international impact. South Korea in the end was able to recover through a significant currency devaluation and expansion of trade. That is not available to Spain, especially if its major trading partners within the euro area contract their own demand and compress their own wages. The unfairness, perceived and actual, of such an outcome for the Spanish economy will promote political resentment across borders, if not outright conflict — and that is much more harmful within a political union than with regard to some far off international institution like the IMF. There is still time for the euro area to learn from and avoid repeating the South Korean mistake. The IMF did.

As this illustration of the Korean example and its application to the European situation show, the IMF has areas where it can improve. Some of these areas have been characterized by the Managing Director of the IMF, Dominique Strauss-Kahn.

Dominique Strauss-Kahn, Crisis and Beyond — The Next Phase of IMF Reform

Prepared Remarks at the Peterson Institute for International Economics, Washington, D.C. (June 29, 2010)

Drawing on the lessons from the crisis [that began in 2008], the IMF is looking at how we might further clarify and improve our "mandate" and the way we work. The goal is to become even more responsive and effective in addressing the new realities facing our membership, especially in the world beyond the crisis. . . .

Let me start by talking very briefly about the Fund's response to the crisis. We acted as a vehicle for policy coordination and were among the earliest to call for a global fiscal stimulus — a globally coordinated effort that helped the world avoid a second Great Depression.

On the financing side, the G-20 leaders' commitment to triple our resources played a major role in restoring confidence. We committed over $200 billion, and pumped another $283 billion in Special Drawing Rights (SDRs) into the system. Our new Flexible Credit Line (FCL) provided a strong safety net for countries with a good track record. We tripled our concessional lending commitments to low-income countries, charging zero interest through 2012. And we enhanced country ownership by making our lending programs more flexible, streamlining policy conditions, and being responsive to the needs of the most vulnerable groups in crisis countries.

In these countries, output losses were smaller relative to past crises, and the kinds of wrenching adjustment seen in the past—large movements in exchange rates and interest rates—were avoided. [Interest rate spreads] narrowed for the countries under the Flexible Credit Line. And in most cases, including among low-income countries, fiscal policy was able to act as a brake on the economic downturn.

The crisis also changed the way the IMF works with regional entities. The first step was our close collaboration with the European Union in providing financing to countries outside the eurozone. Later, when the Greek crisis broke, the eurozone was—understandably perhaps—reluctant to entertain a similar IMF role. But it soon became clear that IMF resources, and above all experience in dealing with such crises, was needed, and so we stepped in, establishing a new kind of relationship with our European partners. I hope that we may be able to consider similar modes of partnership with other organizations throughout the world. . . .

This crisis has shown clearly that globalization is not merely theoretical. It is real. What starts in a single country can have repercussions far beyond that country, and we could even see an economic "butterfly effect" in action. . . .

Because we adapted to meet the needs of our members during the crisis, the IMF played a useful role. But now we need to think about our role in the future—in "peace time," if you will, beyond the crisis—especially since globalization is here to stay.

Surveillance

Let me begin with IMF surveillance and our dual role as ruthless truth-teller and trusted policy advisor. Before the crisis, surveillance lagged behind global economic and financial developments. We did things pretty much as we always did, focusing mostly on individual countries rather than systemic issues. Even the format of our reports has barely changed over the decades, limiting their effectiveness.

We need a new toolkit for a new era. We have made a good start. Our revamped Early Warning Exercise—run jointly with the Financial Stability Board—looks more at systemic effects, tail risks, and vulnerabilities. But we need to put macro-financial stability at the front and center of IMF surveillance. . . .

Lending

Let me now turn to our lending. Clearly, there are still gaps in the global financial safety net. The FCL was a successful step in the right direction, and we are considering enhancing it by expanding its duration and removing the cap on access.

It also might be useful to establish a framework for dealing with systemic crises — a coordinated mechanism to proactively channel liquidity to countries under pressure. To be effective, resources should be deployed as quickly as possible, and focus on countries that can propagate the shock, whatever its origin, across the world — to stop the falling dominoes. Of course, no country may want to move first, as that might risk sending the wrong message to markets. To get around this chicken-and-egg problem, we could think about providing multicountry assistance simultaneously.

The IMF is also exploring ways of cooperating more closely with regional financing arrangements, including in the context of global liquidity provision. This has the dual benefit of increasing the available resources and country ownership. Our recent partnership with Europe represents a new and innovative mode of cooperation, and could provide a useful precedent for working with other regions in the future. . . .

Governance

What I have set out here is an ambitious agenda. For it to work, we need enhanced legitimacy. Legitimacy depends on a governance structure that reflects today's global reality. When the Fund was founded in 1944, we had 45 members. Today, we have 187. Back then, a small team of countries powered the global economy. Today, there are many engines across many countries. So obviously, increased effectiveness means increased legitimacy, and governance reforms are the key to unlocking legitimacy.

Reforming IMF governance goes hand-in-hand with modernizing our mandate. The 2008 Quota and Voice reform was a first step. We are now committed to . . . give a greater voice to dynamic emerging markets and developing countries. . . .

Conclusion

I call upon our members to support these reforms. We must have the tools necessary to avoid future crises to the best of our ability and to address them effectively once they arrive. . . .

Our role begins with economic stability, but it ends with the goal of all multilateral institutions — a stable and peaceful world.

Notes and Questions

1. What are the advantages of developed countries banding together to form apolitical international financial institutions rather than acting independently or bilaterally to achieve the same goals?

2. Should the United States (or other nations) use the Fund and the World Bank to advance its own international political/economic agenda? Do actions based on ideological grounds threaten the effectiveness of the institutions? Should U.S. policymakers ignore the effects that the institutions' actions might have on specific U.S. foreign policy and economic interests when making decisions on U.S. contributions? (See also the discussion in Chapter 8 regarding the use of these institutions to promote human rights.)

3. Do you think that the IMF pursued appropriate policies during the Asian financial crisis and the 2007-2010 crisis? Did the IMF have the right emphasis on major structural and institutional reforms?

4. Many experts have suggested that the IMF loan guarantees in the past may have encouraged creditors to invest excessively in high-risk projects and countries. Should some of the major international private lenders have been required to "take a haircut" in, say, Korea — this is, should they be required to absorb some losses on their loans — or should they essentially be made whole through government loan guarantees and other provisions? Why or why not?

5. Learning from its experience in Asia in 1997-1998 and hearing the criticisms, the International Monetary Fund allowed Ecuador to go into default on some of its outstanding debt in 1999. In part, this appeared to be a warning to the international private lenders that the IMF would not always protect them. On a much larger scale, the IMF was limited in its support of Argentina when that country had a severe financial crisis starting in 2001.

6. If you were a U.S. Senator asked to approve increased U.S. contributions to the IMF (in order to increase the size of the U.S. quota), would you want to add any conditions to the authorization?

Bibliography

The annual reports of the institutions discussed in this section are very informative, as are their Web sites: http://www.imf.org and http://www.worldbank.org. See also the annual reports of the National Advisory Council on International Monetary and Financial Policies, which provide a wealth of information about these institutions and U.S. international economic activities.

c. The World Trade Organization (WTO) and the General Agreement on Tariffs and Trade (GATT)

The substantial growth of international trade and its related economic benefits can be attributed in part to the World Trade Organization (WTO) and its predecessor, the General Agreement on Tariffs and Trade (GATT). Indeed, the WTO has become one of the most influential international institutions. For example, see the discussion in Chapter 4 of the frequency and diversity of cases brought before its strong dispute resolution system. What follows is a brief history of the GATT and an analysis of the WTO.

(1) The GATT

When the proposed International Trade Organization (ITO) was stillborn after World War II, in part because of opposition in the U.S. Senate, the GATT metamorphosed from just a trade agreement into an international organization that administered the agreement and provided the forum where nations could promote trade liberalization. The GATT continued to play that role as an institution until the WTO came into being in January 1995. The GATT agreement continues in the new WTO framework as an important trade agreement with key principles and provisions.

The purpose of GATT was to promote trade liberalization through the elimination of both tariff barriers and nontariff barriers (such as quotas or quantitative trade restrictions). Members had four fundamental obligations. Upon joining the GATT, members undertook to (1) apply trade barriers on a nondiscriminatory basis; (2) limit tariffs on items at the levels set forth in the GATT tariff schedules; (3) refrain from circumventing trade concessions through the use of other barriers to trade; and (4) settle trade conflicts via consultation and a special dispute resolution process.

Central to nondiscrimination are two principles: most-favored-nation treatment (MFN) and national treatment obligation (NTO). The GATT agreement starts with an unconditional most-favored-nation provision: "[A]ny advantage, favour, privilege or immunity granted by any contracting party to any product originating in or destined for any country shall be accorded immediately and unconditionally to the like product originating in or destined for the territories of all other contracting parties." (Article I, para. 1.) In short, it prohibits discrimination between goods from different foreign countries. As for national treatment obligation, the principle prohibits discrimination between goods that are domestically produced and those that are imported. (See Article III.)

Exceptions to these GATT rules and principles, however, do exist. Exceptions can be obtained, for instance, by granting of a waiver by the GATT members; by using safeguard measures that allow a nation under certain conditions to impose restrictions or increase a tariff in order to prevent or limit serious injury to domestic producers (although the other country retains a right to claim redress); or by claiming a balance-of-payments crisis. The formation of a customs union or free trade area also allows some exceptions to GATT. Additionally, developing countries are exempted from many GATT obligations.

To further their stated goals, GATT members held periodic rounds of trade negotiations. Eight rounds of negotiations took place between 1947 and 1994. The first six rounds focused primarily on the reduction of tariff barriers to trade. They were quite successful: the average level of tariffs on products in major industrial countries fell to about 13 percent by the early 1960s and then to about 4 percent in 1986.

As tariffs were successfully reduced in the 1970s, nontariff barriers (NTBs) became more prominent as impediments to free trade. The Tokyo Round, which lasted from 1973 to 1979, resulted in a series of "Codes" on subsidies, technical barriers to trade, and government procurement, but the Round did not fully resolve these issues.

By the mid-1980s, changes in the international economy, coupled with frustration over the continued prevalence of NTBs, threatened the international trade system. The prospect of increased use of protectionist national trade policies and bilateral trade agreements prompted GATT members to call for a new round of multilateral trade negotiations.

In September 1986, the trade ministers of GATT's member nations opened the Uruguay Round of trade negotiations (named for the location where the opening declaration was issued). The Round, which ended in December 1993, resulted in the most comprehensive agreements ever completed under the GATT. The Final Act of the Uruguay Round was formally signed in Morocco on April 15, 1994.

The Uruguay Round had many major achievements. Tariffs on industrial goods were reduced on average by more than one-third, barriers to agricultural trade were eased, and the provisional GATT institutional arrangements were changed into a formal international institution, the WTO. Previously uncovered areas (e.g., trade in services, textiles and clothing, and intellectual property) were brought under the auspices of the WTO under new agreements — including, among others, the General Agreement on Trade in Services (GATS) and the Agreement on Trade-Related Aspects of Intellectual Property Rights (TRIPS). New or strengthened rules were developed for a number of areas of trade and investment, and (as discussed in Chapter 4) a strong dispute resolution system was created.

(2) *The World Trade Organization*

The creation of the WTO was the most significant result of the Uruguay Round. The WTO is designed to help implement the agreements negotiated during the Round. It continues to work toward the objectives of GATT — most notably, the expansion of world trade. The WTO is also the forum for multilateral trade negotiations and administers the dispute resolution system.

The following excerpt from a final GATT publication provides some essential details on the transition from the GATT to the WTO:

What Is the WTO?

GATT Focus, May 1994, at 11-12

In its Preamble, the Agreement establishing a World Trade Organization reiterates the objectives of the GATT, namely raising standards of living and incomes, ensuring full employment, expanding production and trade, and optimal use of the world's resources, while at the same time extending them to services and making them more precise:

- it introduces the idea of "sustainable development" in relation to the optimal use of the world's resources . . . ;
- it recognizes that there is a need for positive efforts designed to ensure that developing countries, and especially the least-developed among them, secure a better share of the growth in international trade.

Decision-Making

The WTO will continue the decision-making practice followed under the GATT: decision by consensus which is deemed to exist if no member formally objects. Recourse to voting, where a decision cannot be reached by consensus, is institutionalized, whereas previously it was exceptional. Decisions will still be taken by a majority of the votes cast, on the basis of "one country, one vote."

However, in two cases — *interpretation* of the provisions of the agreements and *waiver* of a member's obligations — conditions imposed by the Agreement are more severe. The majority required is then three quarters of the members, whereas under the GATT it was only two thirds of the votes cast representing at least half of the members. Moreover, the granting of waivers will be more strictly controlled (justification, time-limits, possibility of recourse to dispute settlement). . . .

Original and New Members

The member countries of the GATT as of the date of entry into force of the WTO Agreement will become original members of the WTO. However, the least-developed countries recognized as such by the United Nations will only be required to undertake commitments and concessions to the extent consistent with their individual development.

The accession procedures and the majority of two thirds of the members required remain the same as under the GATT.

Status and Budget

The WTO will have legal personality and will be accorded privileges and immunities similar to those accorded to the specialized agencies of the United Nations. . . .

The establishment of the World Trade Organization will reinforce the status and the image of the principal institution with responsibility for international trade, by placing it on the same footing as the IMF and the World Bank.

The Director-General of the WTO will be appointed by the Ministerial Conference which will also adopt regulations setting up his powers and duties. . . .

The WTO has been met with wide acceptance. As of January 2011, the WTO had 153 members. Twenty-nine other governments have applied for membership, and accession talks are ongoing in many cases. All the large countries are members, except for Russia. It is possible that Russia will be allowed to join the WTO as early as 2011.

Joining the WTO requires a commitment to adhere in the future to all WTO agreements, except for three plurilateral ones (the Agreement on Trade in Civil Aircraft, the Agreement on Government Procurement, and the Information Technology Agreement).[8] Moreover, an applicant usually will need to make substantial changes in its existing tariffs and other economic regulations (e.g., market access), rather than being allowed to maintain high tariffs and closed markets. For example, the WTO talks with China occupied several years because China resisted undertaking the market-opening steps that the United States, European Union countries, and other WTO members thought were necessary. The final accession agreement, completed in 2001, reflected a hard-fought compromise.

All WTO members may participate in all councils and committees, except the Appellate Body, dispute settlement panels, textiles monitoring body, and the plurilateral committees. (See the Chart.) Present WTO members have been quick to resort to the powerful new WTO dispute system, as noted in Chapter 4.

8. The International Dairy Agreement and the International Bovine Meat Agreement, plurilateral agreements at the WTO's founding, were terminated in 1997. The issues covered in these agreements were subsumed in the multilateral agreements on Agricultural and on Sanitary and Phytosanitary Standards.

WTO structure

All WTO members may participate in all councils, committees, etc, except Appellate Body, Dispute Settlement panels, and plurilateral committees.

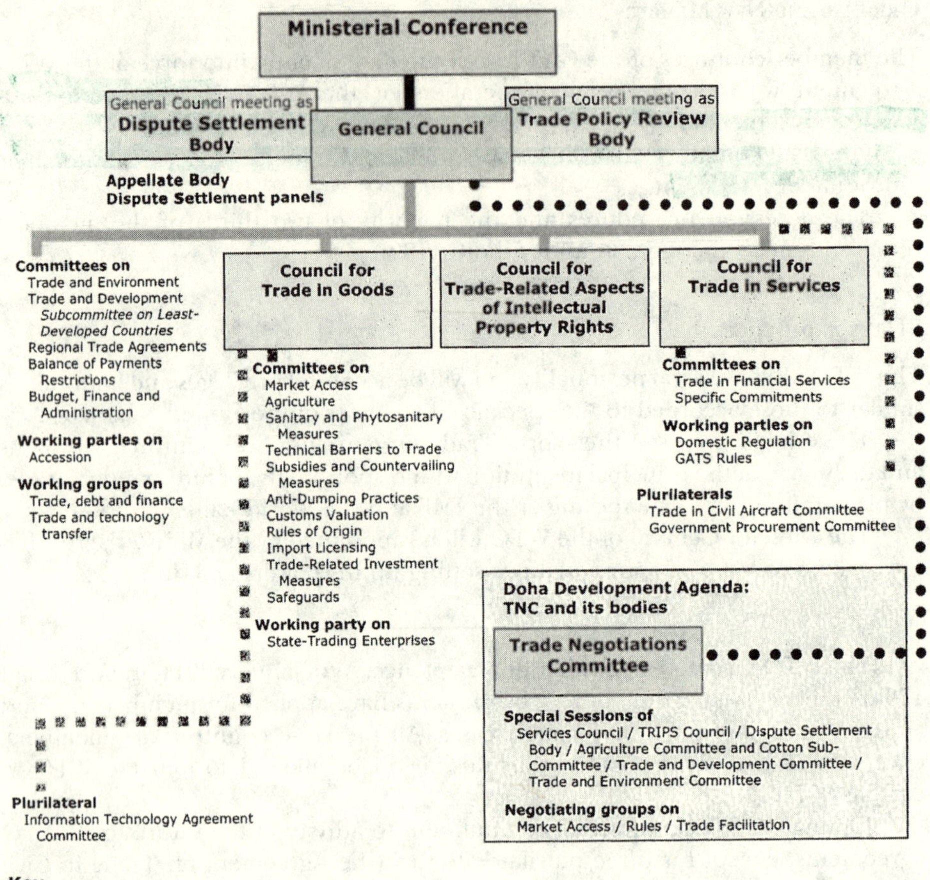

Key

Reporting to General Council (or a subsidiary)

Reporting to Dispute Settlement Body

Plurilateral committees inform the General Council or Goods Council of their activities, although these agreements are not signed by all WTO members

Trade Negotiations Committee reports to General Council

The General Council also meets as the Trade Policy Review Body and Dispute Settlement Body

In a major speech to the WTO in May 1998, President Clinton noted the impact already of the Uruguay Round and the WTO. He pointed out that, because of the tariff cuts and other market-opening measures initiated in 1995, "world trade had increased by 25 percent." However, President Clinton cautioned:

> In order to build a trading system for the 21st century that honors our values and expands opportunity, we must do more to ensure that spirited economic competition among nations never becomes a race to the bottom — in environmental protections, consumer protections, or labor standards. We should be leveling up, not leveling down. Without such a strategy, we cannot build the necessary public support for continued expansion of trade. Working people will only assume the risks of a free international market if they have the confidence that the system will work for them.

At the WTO's Fourth Ministerial Conference in Doha, Qatar, in fall 2001, the WTO members agreed on the Doha Declaration that called for new negotiations aimed to make progress on a wide range of matters, ranging from agriculture to intellectual property to trade in services. In short, the WTO members launched the follow-up to the Uruguay Round: the Doha Round. The declaration set January 1, 2005, as the date for completing the Doha negotiations. Some labeled the negotiations the Doha Development Round because many members agreed that the primary focus should be on improving the economic situation of developing states.

The negotiations ran into trouble, however. As of winter 2010, no end was in sight. Explanations abound for the struggles. One respected scholar argues there is no single explanation for the Round's slow movement, but the most important factors include: (a) the growth of developing countries, like China, India, and Brazil, who are wielding their new-found bargaining power; (b) growing skepticism toward global trade among policymakers in the United States and European Union, who until the Doha Round were the pacesetters of further trade liberalization; (c) earlier trade rounds, like the Tokyo and Uruguay Round settled the "easier" issues, leaving the more intractable issues for the Doha Round; and (d) a tactical mistake early on by the Round's negotiators to require progress on agriculture liberalization, traditionally the toughest area of trade politics, before the discussions could proceed substantially in other areas like services.[9]

Others simply claim the overall economic benefits from the Round are far too limited to compensate for the political hurdles of trade liberalization. Avoidance of important economic issues, like undervalued exchange rates, that can have a substantial impact on trade is also blamed. Finally, in the wake of the Doha Round's struggles many scholars have begun the march for WTO reform, calling for, among many things, a stronger WTO Secretariat and modifications to the consensus voting procedures.

Throughout the Doha Round, the opposition of many countries effectively blocked two contemporary issues from being on the table: (1) the relationship between trade and the environment and also (2) the relationship between trade and labor standards.

9. Jeffrey J. Schott, The Future of the Multilateral Trading System in a Multi-polar World, Discussion Paper, Deutsches Institut für Entwicklungspolitik (2008).

If the Doha Round should ultimately fail, many commentators have called for a host of plurilateral or multilateral sectoral agreements on issues like trade facilitation, information technology goods, chemical goods, and environmental goods. A good deal of negotiating has already occurred on these issues, and countries would probably like to come away from the table with some accomplishments.

It should be noted explicitly that if the Doha Round fails to reach a conclusion it does not mean the end of the WTO. Although a failure would have substantial political and legitimacy costs for the WTO, the existing agreements and framework of the organization, including the successful dispute settlement mechanism, would be unchanged.

The Warwick Commission convened an international panel of experts to take an independent look at the WTO's past accomplishments and challenges ahead. Their assessment is broader than the Doha Round's struggles and is relevant to the WTO should the Doha Round succeed or not.

The Multilateral Trade Regime: Which Way Forward?

The Report of the First Warwick Commission, 2, 7-8 (2007) [figures updated]

From the 23 countries that were contracting parties to the original GATT, the WTO has grown to include [153 Members as of January 2011]. . . . No Member of the WTO has ever sought to leave and, indeed, there is still a queue to join. . . . [D]isputes between WTO Members are almost invariably settled. Importantly, few disputes result in the imposition of trade sanctions and rarely do harm to wider international ties. . . . Expectations — in both the public and private sectors — are effectively shaped by the widely accepted WTO principles of nondiscrimination, reciprocity and transparency. . . .

The four key functions of the WTO are:

- *Reducing discrimination and furthering market-access opportunities in international commerce.* The successes of the GATT/WTO system are exemplified in the progressive liberalization of tariffs since 1947 and the near-universal membership of the WTO today. The entry requirements faced by new WTO Members are stringent; mirroring the significant recent broadening of the multilateral trading system's substantive remit. Yet the fact that [twenty-five] countries have nonetheless chosen to meet them since 1995 suggests that they see benefits in joining the system.
- *Formulating rules for the conduct of international trade.* The depth and range of rules on cross-border trade and investment have grown significantly over the 60-year life of the GATT/WTO. Parties to the agreement have not always agreed on the desirable content of the rules but nobody contests the value of multilateral rules in fostering certainty and predictability in trade and in helping to dilute the role of power in determining trade outcomes.
- *Promoting transparency in national laws and regulations.* Through its various agreements, the GATT/WTO has enhanced the transparency of

commerce-related national laws and regulations through the requirement for Members to publish changes to their trade measures and notify any changes in rules. . . .

- *Settling commercial disputes.* The Dispute Settlement Understanding (DSU) of the WTO has given an unprecedented enforceability to agreements. It is one of the most successful, and the busiest, state-to-state dispute settlement systems in the history of international law. As of [January 31, 2011], WTO members had filed [420] complaints through the DSU. While the WTO's accomplishments are no mean achievement, the current multilateral trading system, as governed by the WTO, also faces serious challenges. . . .

The first challenge is to counter growing opposition to further multilateral trade liberalization in industrialized countries. . . .

That the bipolar global trade regime dominated primarily by the United States and Western Europe has given way to a multipolar alternative [with the United States, European Union, Japan, China, India and Brazil as major poles] is now an established fact. The second challenge is to ensure that this evolving configuration does not lapse into longer term stalemate or worse, disengagement.

In this changing environment, the third challenge is to forge a broad-based agreement among the membership about the WTO's objectives and functions, which in turn will effectively define the "boundaries" of the WTO.

The fourth challenge is to ensure that the WTO's many agreements and procedures result in benefits for its weakest Members. This requires that the membership addresses the relationships between current trade rules and fairness, justice, and development.

The fifth challenge relates to the proliferation of preferential trading agreements and what steps can be taken to ensure that the considerable momentum behind these initiatives can be eventually channeled to advance the long-standing principles of non-discrimination and transparency in international commerce. . . .

Notes and Questions

1. Why is a more open, nondiscriminatory trading system (i.e., free trade) beneficial? If it is beneficial, why do countries maintain trade barriers?

2. Do nations need international trading agreements and institutions like the GATT and WTO? Why? Why not enter into bilateral agreements with various countries?

3. In terms of budget, the WTO is much smaller than other major international organizations. The WTO's operating budget is approximately $200 million per year. This figure pales in comparison with the World Bank's ($1.7 billion) and the IMF's ($900 million) budgets. The WTO's staff is roughly 600 people compared to 10,000 for the World Bank and 2,700 for the IMF.

4. As the Warwick Commission excerpt mentions, there has been an increasing tendency toward more free trade areas and customs unions. The European Union is the largest example (although it involves more than just free trade, as discussed later in this chapter). The North American Free Trade Agreement, effective in 1994, is

another example. (See Chapter 4.) There are also many bilateral free trade agreements in existence, with more being negotiated. As of January 2011, the European Union had notified 21 active free trade agreements to the WTO. Their partners include, among others, Chile, Egypt, Israel, and Mexico. Besides NAFTA, the United States had active free trade agreements with Australia, Bahrain, Chile, Israel, Jordan, Morocco, Oman, Peru, and Singapore. The United States is also a member of the Dominican Republic-Central America FTA (CAFTA-DR), which includes Costa Rica, Dominican Republic, El Salvador, Guatemala, Honduras, and Nicaragua. The United States has also concluded free trade agreements with Columbia, Panama, and South Korea, but all three agreements still require approval by the U.S. Congress as of January 2011. The European Union meanwhile has had ongoing trade agreement negotiations with Canada, South Korea, India, and Ukraine.

Although Article XXIV of the GATT agreement specifically recognizes the possibility of free trade areas and customs unions, do you see how there might be some tension between an international system of open, nondiscriminatory trading and several bilateral or regional free trade arrangements? Should the United States give priority to negotiating further reductions in tariffs and NTBs and new agreements in the WTO, or should it try to work out special arrangements with individual countries, such as Japan or Turkey?

5. WTO membership is open as follows:

> A government not party to this Agreement, or a government acting on behalf of a separate customs territory possessing full autonomy in the conduct of its external commercial relations and of the other matters provided for in this Agreement, may accede to this Agreement, on its own behalf or on behalf of that territory, on terms to be agreed between such government and the Contracting Parties. Decisions of the Contracting Parties under this paragraph shall be taken by a two-thirds vote. [GATT, Art. XXXIII.]

In 1990 Taiwan applied for GATT membership as the "Separate Customs Territory of Taiwan, Penghu, Kinmen and Matsu." In a carefully negotiated and choreographed process that took into account the strong views of China regarding Taiwan (see the discussion earlier in this chapter), China was admitted to membership in the WTO on December 11, 2001, and Taiwan (under the name "Chinese Taipei") and became a member on January 1, 2002. Chinese Taipei joined another customs territory, Hong Kong, which has been a longstanding and active member of the GATT and then WTO, even after its transfer to China.

6. The WTO's excellent Web site is at http://www.wto.org, and there are voluminous GATT and WTO documents. The literature also includes the several recent books on the WTO that are cited at the end of Chapter 4.D.

Besides the formal international institutions such as the United Nations, World Bank, IMF, and WTO, there are more informal international groupings or coalitions that have a major impact on international life. Two of the more important are the Group of Eight and the Group of Twenty, with the latter taking on an increasingly major role. There is also the Group of 77 (this organization now actually has over 130 members). Although the exact legal status of these groups is hazy, one should be aware of their existence.

d. The Group of Eight (and Sometimes Seven)

The Group of Eight (G-8) refers to eight major industrialized countries—Canada, France, Germany, Italy, Japan, Russia, the United Kingdom, and the United States. The heads of state of these eight countries, plus the President of the EU's European Council, meet in annual summits to discuss issues of common concern and to develop cooperative approaches. The emphasis has been on economic matters, although the international environment emerged as a new major issue at the July 1989 summit in Paris.

Starting in 1991, the then-Group of Seven (G-7) edged toward becoming the Group of Eight, at least for summits, as the leader of Russia was invited to some parts of the summit meetings, despite the weak Russian economy. By June 2006, Russia hosted the G-8 summit, marking its equal membership in the group.

The G-7, however, continues to exist as well because the finance ministers and central bank governors of the seven countries sometimes meet without Russia to consider certain international financial issues. For example, the G-7 finance ministers met in October 2001 to discuss steps to combat the financing of terrorists. More broadly, the G-7 developed arrangements for coordination of economic policies. This intergovernmental coalition often meets to work out positions ahead of the Group of Twenty (G-20) or IMF meetings.

The nations work to achieve consistent and mutually compatible economic policies and accept considerable multilateral surveillance of their economies. Coordination has helped to change the pattern of exchange rates and to change interest rates. The G-7 also was instrumental in resolving trade conflicts in preparation for the establishment of the WTO.

Although the G-7 nations are aware of the advantages of intergovernmental economic cooperation, competing domestic demands pose formidable obstacles. Because of these competing considerations, the record of the group is mixed. Its greatest success probably came in 1986-1987 when the group reached major agreements affecting interest rates and the exchange rate (bringing the U.S. dollar substantially down in value).

By the late 1990s, the financial muscle of the G-8 and its approach of making policy privately and often in advance of larger international meetings generated criticism from other nations. The other countries argued that their influence is diminished and that the broader consultations envisioned in the IMF are being undercut by the secret negotiations of a few beforehand.

e. The Group of Twenty

In the aftermath of the 1997 Asian financial crisis, members of the G-8 recognized the need to bring into discussions a more representative sampling of the world's major economies. The first meeting of the Group of Twenty (G-20) took place in Berlin in 1999.

The membership of the G-20 includes the G-8 countries, plus Argentina, Australia, Brazil, China, India, Indonesia, Mexico, Saudi Arabia, South Africa, the Republic of Korea, Turkey, and the European Union. (Brazil, Russia, India, and China are sometimes referred to collectively as the "BRIC" economies, highlighting the rapid economic expansion these states achieved in recent years.) These countries represent about 90 percent of the world's economic output.

The purpose of the G-20 is "to bring together systemically important industrialized and developing economies to discuss key issues in the global economy." www.g20.org. While the G-20 has not insulated the world from global financial downturns, it has facilitated greater communication and cooperation among the financial regulators of member states. They have discussed measures to promote the world's financial stability and to achieve sustainable economic growth and development. For instance, after the collapse of the American subprime mortgage market in 2008, the G-20 became a focal point of efforts designed to ameliorate the international ramifications of those events.

Reflecting the economic importance of the 20 countries, the G-20 announced in September 2009 that it would become the new group for developing international economic cooperation. It essentially eclipsed on financial issues the G-8, which will continue to meet on security issues but carry less influence.

As the G-20 grew in importance, there was also criticism. Some nonmember countries noted that there were no formal criteria for membership in the G-20. Rather, it is a self-appointed group that has no formal process for adding new members. Another line of criticism is that informal organizations, like the G-20 and the G-8, tend to undermine the legitimacy and effectiveness of the IMF, World Bank, and other international and regional financial institutions. However, the G-20 meetings regularly include representatives from these institutions and sometimes are a prelude to the IMF-World Bank meetings.

f. The Group of 77

The Group of 77 (G-77) is a coalition of about 130 nations that have bound together to coordinate their efforts and to protect the interests of the developing African, Asian, and Latin American countries. Organized in the 1960s, the group was the first major effort at Third World unity in the economic area.

> [O]ur coming together in the Group of 77 has the purpose of enabling us to deal on terms of greater equality with an existing Centre of Power. Ours is basically a unity of opposition. And it is a unity of nationalism. . . .
>
> The Group of 77 does not share an ideology. . . . We are not necessarily friendly with each other. . . .
>
> What we have in common is that we are all, in relation to the developed world, dependent, not interdependent, nations. . . . We are not the prime movers of our own destiny.
>
> The unity of the entire Third World is necessary for the achievement of fundamental change in the present world economic arrangements. . . .
>
> For the object is to complete the liberation of the Third World countries from external domination. . . . And unity is our instrument—our only instrument—of liberation. [Mwalimu Julius K. Nyerere, former President of Tanzania, in a 1979 speech, quoted in Karl P. Sauvant, The Group of 77: Evolution, Structure, Organization 132-135 (1981).]

The Group of 77 has continued to function as a caucus for the developing countries on both economic and political concerns before various U.N. bodies. Although most of the countries are poor, there are a few members, such as the

United Arab Emirates and Qatar, whose per capita incomes have at times exceeded that of the United States.

The grievances of the Group of 77 are varied. The group, however, has developed some objectives and policies that have enjoyed broad consensus among its members. Many of these appeared initially in the program for change that was labeled the New International Economic Order (NIEO). The NIEO, which was enunciated in various Group 77 statements and in some U.N. documents, included calls for a country's right to expropriate property subject only to its own domestic law; less protection for patents, copyrights, and other intellectual property; greater protection for the prices of raw materials through commodity agreements and buffer stocks; and special tariff treatment by the developed countries for the products of developing countries.

Many of these policies have reflected the fact that the developed countries possess most of the world's capital, including the intellectual property, and are heavily industrialized. The developing countries often are dependent on the export of raw or partially finished materials, and they want to reduce that dependence. The NIEO also envisioned procedural changes, including reform of the voting procedures in the IMF, World Bank, and other world economic institutions so that the developing nations have greater representation.

Recently, the focus of the Group of 77 has shifted somewhat. The economic problems of the early 1990s created an atmosphere that made it difficult for the G-77 nations to stand united against developed nations. As a result, the Group struggled in its attempts to pressure the North, as many G-77 nations opted for bilateral negotiations with the industrialized states. G-77 leaders began to call for greater "South-South" cooperation. The G-77 has a Web site at http://www.g77.org.

3. *Regional Institutions*

A wide variety of regional entities exist, with different purposes and in varying stages of institutional development. This section first looks to Europe, where it discusses the European Union and its impressive progress, and also briefly considers the North Atlantic Treaty Organization (NATO) and the Organization on Security and Co-operation in Europe (OSCE). The section then addresses two regional entities that continue to develop, the Association of Southeast Asian Nations (ASEAN) and the Asia-Pacific Economic Cooperation (APEC). Lastly, two of the more traditional regional political organizations—the Organization of American States (OAS) and the African Union (AU)—are briefly described. Although not discussed, it should be noted that there are regional development banks for Latin America, Africa, Asia, and Eastern Europe, which are modeled on the World Bank, though their assets are substantially less. The membership of these banks typically includes many of the industrialized countries in addition to the countries in the bank's region. There are also emerging free trade areas and common markets such as Mercosur in South America.

a. The European Union

Emerging from the rubble and memories of World War II, the European Union today is a vibrant, vital entity on the international scene. It not only maintains common external trade policies, but succeeded by 1993 in implementing an internal market among its member states. Four fundamental freedoms within the Union are generally recognized: (1) the free movement of goods, (2) the free movement of capital, (3) freedom of movement of persons, and (4) the right of establishment and to provide services.

In November 1993, the Treaty on European Union, or Maastricht Treaty, went into force. The Maastricht Treaty added two so-called pillars to the first pillar of then European Community's largely economic activities, and it adopted the all-encompassing term of "European Union" for the three pillars. The new pillars dealt with Common Foreign and Security Policy (including defense) and Justice and Home Affairs (including cooperation on crime, terrorism, and immigration issues).

Then the Treaty of Amsterdam, which came into force in 1999, laid the groundwork for enlarging the Union membership. This was followed by the Treaty of Nice, which came into effect in early 2003 and resolved a number of outstanding issues left unresolved in Amsterdam, especially the issues of voting practices and the representation of the existing and new member states after the Union's expansion. Most recently, the Treaty of Lisbon came into effect in December 2009 and considerably improved the EU's decision-making processes and furthered the integration that was particularly needed after the Union's enlargements.

The Treaty of Lisbon ended the distinction between the European Union and the Economic Community, embracing all within the European Union (EU). It also essentially combined the "three pillars." The Treaty of Lisbon and the earlier treaties are now consolidated in the revised Treaty on European Union (TEU) and the Treaty on the Functioning of the European Union (TFEU), with the latter replacing the Treaty Establishing the European Community (or EC or Rome Treaty). (Excerpts of the consolidated versions of the TEU and TFEU treaties are contained in the Documentary Supplement. Note that the articles have been renumbered as a result of the Lisbon Treaty.)

As a result, since the Maastricht Treaty in 1993, the EU has expanded its scope to include monetary union (the euro), a legally binding Charter of Fundamental Rights, a rotating presidency, cooperation in many areas, a common foreign and security policy (CFSP), and even a military "rapid reaction force" for use in humanitarian and peacekeeping operations and crisis management. The EU today is a comprehensive, multifaceted institution, far more than merely an economic entity.

As of January 2011, the European Union included 27 member states: Austria, Belgium, Bulgaria, Cyprus, the Czech Republic, Denmark, Estonia, the Federal Republic of Germany, Finland, France, Greece, Hungary, Ireland, Italy, Latvia, Lithuania, Luxembourg, Malta, the Netherlands, Poland, Portugal, Romania, Slovakia, Slovenia, Spain, Sweden, and the United Kingdom. There are 23 official languages. Although other countries have indicated their interest in joining, the EU itself has indicated very mixed interest in admitting other larger countries like Turkey. Smaller countries like Croatia, Macedonia, and Iceland, however, have good chances of being admitted in the next few years.

The EU has a population of about 500 million, or about 190 million more than the United States and 370 million more than Japan. As an economic force, the EU rivals the United States. The EU's gross domestic product (GDP) exceeds the United States' GDP by about $2 trillion and by China's or Japan's by about

$10-11 trillion. Moreover, estimates indicate that the Union's external exports and imports account for a greater share of world trade than does the United States' trade. When Canada's and Mexico's statistics are added to the U.S. figures, the three NAFTA countries combined approximate the EU in GDP, but not in population. (For additional data, see Table 5-1 at the beginning of this chapter.)

Besides the EU member states, since January 1994 the EU has been a party to the European Economic Area (EEA) Agreement, which extends the four freedoms of the European Union — that is, movement of goods, capital, and persons, and the right of establishment — to Norway, Iceland, and Lichtenstein.

The following materials examine in detail the structure of the Union and its function within the international system.

(1) Foundations and Development of the European Union

Although the dream of a unified Europe had existed for centuries, the events of World War II created new reasons for steps toward a Community.

> If we cast our minds back to the early post-war days we will realise that a Community approach was the practical answer to many problems. Europe was in ruins politically and economically; the European colonial empires faced liquidation; the importance of the single European states which dominated the League of Nations was diminished; the "dollar-gap" resulted in great influence of the USA not only as a benevolent saviour but also as a potential master; an "iron curtain" was drawn across Europe and the world cowered in the shadows of great powers: the USA and Soviet Russia facing each other menacingly across Europe. Only rapid recoveries in concert could restore Europe's self-respect. . . . As for grand designs, the architects of the Community soon realised that great ideologies and elaborate blueprints were of little practical use and that nothing could be achieved at one stroke. [K.P.E. Lasok & D. Lasok, Law and Institutions of the European Union 5 (7th ed. 2001).]

Definitely in the minds of the European architects of the Community was the perception that the new Federal Republic of Germany had to be entwined in economic and political arrangements with the rest of Western Europe. The other countries did not want a repeat of World War I and II. In the words of Robert Schuman, the French foreign minister, the goal was to make any future war among these nations "not merely unthinkable, but materially impossible."

Although collectively referred to as the "European Community" from 1978 until 1993, there were three European Communities within the pre-Maastricht structure: the European Coal and Steel Community (ECSC), the European Economic Community (EEC), and the European Atomic Energy Community (Euratom).

T.C. Hartley, The Foundations of European Union Law

3-4 (7th ed. 2010)

[The European Coal and Steel Community was] the first to be established. . . . The ECSC Treaty was signed on 18 April 1951. . . . It entered into force on 23 July 1952 and terminated in 2002.

The signatories to the ECSC Treaty were the six original Member States: Germany, Belgium, France, Italy, Luxembourg, and the Netherlands. The United Kingdom was invited to take part, but declined to do so. . . . Four principal institutions were created: the Council (representing the member states); the Commission (a supranational executive, which was originally called the 'High Authority'); the Assembly; and the Court. . . .

Next came the European Economic Community (EEC) (subsequently renamed the "European Community" or "EC") and the European Atomic Energy Community ("EAEC" or "Euratom"). The EEC Treaty and the EAEC Treaty were both signed in Rome on 25 March 1957 and entered into force on 1 January 1958. . . . The United Kingdom was again invited to participate but dropped out of the preliminary discussions. The signatories were therefore the same six States. . . . Separate Commissions and Councils were created for each of the new Communities, but all three shared the same Assembly and Court. . . .

It was . . . illogical and inconvenient for the two most important institutions to be triplicated, so a Merger Treaty (officially known as the Treaty Establishing a Single Council and a Single Commission of the European Communities) was signed in Brussels on 8 April 1965 and entered into force on 1 July 1967. This Treaty did not merge the Communities themselves but merged the three Commissions to form a single Commission and merged the three Councils to form a single Council.

Progress in the three Communities bogged down in the late 1970s and early 1980s. The solution was the Single European Act (SEA), which came into force July 1, 1987. It amended the three original treaties. Some of the Act's more notable amendments provided for changes in the decision-making processes of the Community and brought areas such as the environment within the scope of the previous treaties. The amendments also provided for the establishment of a court of first instance for the Court of Justice (discussed in Chapter 4 and now called General Court) and furnished a legal basis for foreign policy cooperation by the members. Additionally, the amendments formally adopted the name "European Parliament" for the originally named Assembly, a switch that the Assembly had made by itself in 1962.

In a further major step toward greater economic and political integration, the member states signed the Treaty on European Union at Maastricht in December 1991. The Maastricht Treaty changed the framework of the existing treaties in five significant ways. First, it set a goal of 1999 for the implementation of a common European currency. Second, it established EU citizenship, in theory giving a Union citizen the right to live anywhere within the Union and to vote in local and European elections. Third, the Treaty gave the Commission greater authority to regulate, among other areas, education, the environment, and health and consumer protections. Fourth, the powers of the EU's democratically elected body, the European Parliament, were expanded to give it a greater voice in the appointments process and proposals for new EU directives. Fifth, the Treaty added two new pillars, one on Common Foreign and Security Policy (including defense) (CFSP) and one on the Justice and Home Affairs institution, which would provide for cooperation among the member states on volatile issues such as immigration and terrorism.

In 1997, the leaders of member states met in Amsterdam to set a target date for a unified currency and to make institutional reforms to allow for the inclusion of new members. The resulting Treaty of Amsterdam scheduled the euro, the single European currency, for initial accounting use in 1999 and began the negotiation process with the ten Eastern European nations applying for the EU membership.

The Nice Treaty in 2000 resolved many of the so-called Amsterdam leftovers, bringing changes that were needed before new members could be admitted. These included changing the makeup of Union institutions and modifying voting procedures to take into account the larger number of member states, and increasing the power of the European Parliament and Commission President vis-à-vis the Council.

In order to achieve a thorough overhaul of the structure of the European Union, a draft Constitutional Treaty was agreed upon by the heads of state and was signed ceremonially on October 29, 2004. In 2005, however, the Constitutional Treaty was rejected by referenda in France and the Netherlands, and it became clear that the Constitutional Treaty could not be implemented.

In 2007, the German presidency restarted negotiations by removing the symbolic elements of the Constitution and reducing it to its substantive elements. These were approved in October 22, 2007, in Lisbon. Despite an initial rejection of the Lisbon Treaty in Ireland, the Irish approved the Treaty in a second referendum on October 2, 2009. The Treaty of Lisbon officially came into effect on December 1, 2009.

As noted above, the Lisbon Treaty made major changes in the structure and operation of the European Union. It made the term European Union (EU) all inclusive, ending the distinction between the EU and the Economic Community. It essentially combined the "three pillars." Further changes are detailed below.

(2) Political

Institutions of the European Union. Besides the Court of Justice (discussed in Chapter 4), three main institutions make and implement European Union law: the Commission, the Council, and the European Parliament. Also, the European Council (which is distinct from the Council) and the European Central Bank became official institutions of the EU when the Lisbon Treaty acknowledged a position that they had effectively held in prior years. The European Council meets several times a year at the head-of-state level to resolve issues on a government-to-government basis that the other institutions lack either the authority or the political will to resolve.

George A. Bermann, Roger J. Goebel, William J. Davey & Eleanor M. Fox, Cases and Materials on European Union Law

44-49, 54-58, 37-44, 59-60 (2010)

A. The Commission

The central administrative body of the Union, the European Commission, bears a striking but imperfect resemblance to a Government. Often referred to as the Community's executive organ, the Commission does in fact perform many tasks commonly identified with the executive: formulating a general legislative program, initiating the legislative process by drafting specific pieces of legislation, exercising regulatory powers delegated to it by the Council, taking administrative decisions, carrying out administrative policies and programs, and overseeing (and if need be enforcing) compliance with the law. . . .

1. The Commission's Role and Powers

[The earlier Treaty Establishing the European Community] Article 211 described the role of the Commission in very general terms. Probably most important was "its own power of decision" and participation in the legislative process, indicating both the Commission's power to take administrative decisions in the implementation of agricultural and competition policy, and its right to initiate all legislative drafts. The Commission was also to "ensure that the provisions of this Treaty" are enforced, notably through its power to bring proceedings in the Court of Justice for infringements by Member States of the Treaty and its secondary law. The Commission often proudly refers to this as its role of "guardian of the Treaties."

[Lisbon's Treaty of European Union or TEU] Article 17 is more precise and detailed. It declares that the "Commission shall promote the general interest of the Union," "ensure the application of the Treaties," and oversee the application of Union law under the control of the Court of Justice. The Commission is also to exercise "coordinating, executive and management functions," executing the budget and managing programs, as well as providing the Union's "external representation" except in the CFSP.

Thus, the Commission plays a vital role in setting policy and drafting legislation, as well as in conducting operations and executing regulatory decisions. The Commission's significant monopoly on the initiation of legislation and the subsequent drafting of text throughout the legislative process, granted by . . . [Lisbon's Treaty on the Functioning of the European Union or] TFEU Article 294 . . . , enables [the Commission] to set the legislative agenda. (The Parliament, Court and Member States have very limited rights to initiate legislation.) The Commission's delegated regulatory power and ability to take legally binding administrative decisions is particularly important in the fields of agriculture, fisheries, competition, technical standards, customs and trade. The Commission's regulation of agricultural policy is particularly complex, as it regulates product standards, marketing and prices for many different commodities at frequent intervals. . . .

[The Commission currently consists of 27 Commissioners, one from each Member State. The appointments are for a renewable period of five years. A Protocol to the 2000 Nice Treaty envisioned that the Commission would be reduced in size, and Lisbon's TFEU Article 244 provided that the European Council would unanimously decide upon a method for rotation determining which State was entitled to a Commissioner at a particular time, treating each State equally. However, several states were unhappy with this. And, to encourage a favorable vote in the second Irish referendum on the Lisbon Treaty in 2009, the European Council indicated to Ireland that Ireland would continue to have its Commissioner. It appears likely that, through amendment or otherwise, each Member State will continue to be entitled to a Commissioner indefinitely.

[Commissioners are appointed according to the procedures in TEU Article 17. First, the President of the Commission is selected. Acting by qualified majority (discussed below), the European Council proposes a candidate for President to the European Parliament, which must elect the candidate by a majority vote. Then, the Council, acting by "common accord" with the President, adopts a list of the other proposed Commissioners, based on suggestions made by the Member States. The European Parliament then needs to vote to consent to them. After that, the Commissioners are appointed by the European Council, voting by a qualified majority.]

. . . TFEU Article 245 . . . imposes a strong obligation of independence upon Commissioners. Member States are also bound by the Treaty not to influence them in the performance of their duties. Although this obligation is usually respected, Commission Presidents have had occasion to remind State governments that they should not try to pressure their Commissioners when the Commission is taking a decision on some controversial issue.

2. *The President of the Commission*

The President's formal authority within the Commission has been progressively strengthened. As noted, he or she participates in the designation of the other Commissioners. Under . . . TEU Article 17(6) . . . , the President is given the power to allocate and reallocate portfolios among the Commission's members and "lay down guidelines" for the Commission's work. Moreover, the President may require a Commissioner to resign, and the text does not indicate that this power is limited to cases of misconduct. . . .

Probably the President's greatest influence on Commission operations is the ability to set the agenda for its program of action. Indeed, each January the President presents to the Parliament the Commission's agenda for the year. The President also chairs Commission meetings, setting their agenda as well. Another vital role of the President is to serve as the Commission's customary spokesman to the other institutions, the ECB, business sectors and the public at large. . . . [T]he President is a member of the European Council, enabling him or her to present Commission views directly to the Union's highest political leaders and to participate in their deliberations. There is no question but that the Commission President has always been the most prominent leader and spokesperson of the EU up to the present time.

B. The European Parliament

The [original] EEC Treaty's Article 189 had described the Parliament's role as purely "advisory and supervisory." Although the Council was required by the Treaty to consult the Parliament in some fields, Parliament had no power to make binding amendments, much less cast a veto. Indeed, the EEC Treaty originally designated the Parliament as the "Assembly," but almost at once it began to call itself the Parliament, and the SEA formally changed its name in 1987. . . .

Quite naturally, Parliament's size increased with each successive enlargement. In an effort to keep the Parliament's size within limits of operational efficiency, . . . [t]he Treaty of Lisbon's TEU Article 14 makes the maximum 750 seats, and prescribes that the European Council shall decide on Parliament's composition, acting unanimously and with Parliament's consent. [Elections are held every five years. The Member States employ a system of proportional representation in which members of Parliament (MEPs) are elected nationally or in large districts in a country, with the victorious political parties allocated members according to each party's proportion of the total vote.]

Unlike the US House of Representatives, the number of MEPs allocated to each State does not closely correspond to its population. Traditionally the largest States have been underrepresented and the smaller ones overrepresented. This continues under the Lisbon TEU, whose Article 14(2) specifically prescribes that every State shall have at least six MEPs, with the largest limited to 96. Thus Germany is permitted only 96 MEPs, although its population would entitle it to around 40 more if MEPs were allocated purely on the basis of population. France, Italy, Poland, Spain and the UK are also substantially underrepresented, while Cyprus, Estonia, Luxembourg and Malta are guaranteed 6 MEPs, and many other smaller States are overrepresented as well.

MEPs are elected in the various Member States on the basis of their national political party affiliation. They then form coalitions to constitute party groups in the Parliament. From 1979 to 1994, the Socialists were the largest party, but in 1999 and subsequent elections the conservative group, the European Peoples Party, has been the largest group, averaging around 200 MEPs, while the Socialists average around 180, and the Liberals and Greens have 40-60. The remainder represent smaller left or right wing factions or are independent.

The Parliament elects its own President for a two-and-a-half year term, once renewable, by tradition alternating representatives of the two larger parties. . . . The Parliament also elects 14 vice-presidents who join the President in the Bureau, which organizes Parliament's meetings and appoints the committees and their chairs. Most of Parliament's work is performed within the committees, with plenary sessions frequently merely voting to approve committee reports. . . . Unlike the US Congress, the Parliament has a rather small staff of around 5000, not counting accredited parliamentary assistants whom MEPs may hire and fire on their own. . . .

One might expect a parliament to adopt all legislation and do so on its own. However, even today the European Parliament shares legislative power with the Council. . . . Indeed, in some sensitive fields, such as taxation and competition, Parliament still only exercises the consultative role that it possessed originally, giving only advisory opinions to the Council. The Lisbon Treaty did give the Parliament an equal voice with the Council in adopting legislation concerning agriculture and fisheries, . . . and in a number of other fields . . . .

Moreover, as we previously observed, it is the Commission that exercises the power of initiative in proposing legislation, although Parliament does have the right to request the Commission to propose specific legislation. . . . In a July 2000 Inter-institutional Agreement, the Commission agreed to respond promptly to any such parliamentary request and to give close attention to any amendments Parliament proposes during the legislative process. (An Inter-institutional Agreement has the status of soft law, and is unlikely to be violated.)

Apart from its part in the legislative process, Parliament gained over time an important role in the Union's international relations. In this sphere, the Parliament has the right of assent regarding the accession of new Member States . . . (TEU Article 49 [now] . . . uses the word consent rather than assent). . . . [T]he Parliament may either approve or veto, acting by an absolute majority of all of its members. Parliament also has the right of assent with regard to association agreements for close relations with third countries as well as agreements that entail substantial budgetary commitments or create institutional structures. See . . . TFEU Article 218. For other international agreements, Parliament has only a right to be consulted under TFEU Article 218, and to be kept informed in the field of the CFSP. . . .

Recent years have witnessed efforts to enable national parliaments to become more involved in EU affairs. . . . The Lisbon TEU's Article 18 on the role of national parliaments requires that they be notified in advance of draft legislative acts, applications for accession, and any proposals for Treaty amendments. The Lisbon Treaty's Protocol on Subsidiarity elaborates on this by increasing the minimum period for comment by national parliaments on draft legislation to eight weeks, and by enabling any national parliament to provide the Commission, Council and Parliament with a "reasoned opinion" whenever it believes that a proposal would violate the subsidiarity principle.

C. The Council

1. Institutional Role and Composition

The Council (or the Council of Ministers, as it is often called) does not have a perfect analogue among conventional government structures at the nation-state level. . . . [T]he Council's formal name is the Council of the European Union.

Prior to the Lisbon Treaty, EC Treaty Article 202 described the Council's role as to "ensure coordination of the general economic policies of the Member States," to "take decisions" and grant the Commission delegated powers of implementation. In fact, the Council's most important power has always been to adopt legislation, alone until the Single European Act, and thereafter, jointly with the Parliament in many fields. The Council also decides external trade policies and concludes international agreements concerning trade, investment aid, fisheries, etc. The Lisbon's TEU Article 16 provides a good description: the Council shall "jointly with the Parliament, exercise legislative and budgetary functions," and, on its own, "carry out policy-making and coordinating functions." . . .

. . . Lisbon TEU Article 16 (2) . . . states that the Council is to be composed of a representative of each Member State "at ministerial level" authorized to commit that Member State's government. . . .

Often the Ministers of Foreign Affairs comprise the Council. When they meet as the Council on institutional or internal affairs, they are known as the "General Affairs Council," as distinct from the "External Relations Council," the name used when they meet for purposes of action under the Common Commercial Policy (i.e. external trade and economic relations) or the Common Foreign and Security Policy. When a meeting concerns a specialized subject, such as transport, agriculture or employment, the Council may consist of the relevant ministers (or pairs of ministers, when two distinct matters—foreign affairs and agriculture, for example—are involved). With the advent of Monetary Union, Council meetings of the economic and finance ministers (known for short as the Ecofin Council) became increasingly common. . . .

. . . Lisbon TEU Article 16(9) retains [the approach that the Presidency of the Council rotates among Member States every six months.] Acting as President of a Council configuration has significant practical consequences, because the President largely sets the agenda for actions at meetings, which can be used to concentrate attention on a policy proposal or draft legislation of interest to the

President or his or her State. The current Council President also chairs all Council meetings. A skillful chair can promote the efficiency of decision-making, while a chair lacking in skill may be unable to bring a meeting to a successful conclusion. . . .

The Council's most important role is that of legislature. In a very few fields (notably in the CFSP), the Council alone legislates, although it must usually obtain the Parliament's views in the consultation procedure. . . .

Currently, the Council mostly legislates jointly with the Parliament, with each having an equal voice, in what the Lisbon Treaty denominates the "ordinary legislative procedure," previously called codecision. . . . Legislation to achieve the internal market, or to adopt most rules concerning employment or social policy, consumer protection, environmental protection, health, education and culture, are all adopted jointly by the Council and Parliament. The Lisbon Treaty added to this list agriculture and fisheries, as well as some other fields in which the Council had previously acted alone. Note also that . . . the Commission plays a critical role in the legislative process, because in almost all fields the Treaty accords it the sole power of initiative to present the first draft, and subsequently to present successive drafts incorporating Council or Parliament amendments.

In international affairs, the Council plays a leading role. Not only does the Council ultimately enter into international agreements on behalf of the Union, but it establishes policy guidelines for the Commission in the latter's negotiation of agreements. The most important field is that of trade, but the EU also enters into many fisheries agreements, and agreements involving financial and technical assistance. The Treaty provisions concerning the final conclusion of international agreements are complex. . . .

The Amsterdam Treaty created the post of the High Representative for the CFSP. . . . The Lisbon Treaty has substantially augmented the authority and responsibilities of this official. Lisbon TEU Article 18 prescribes that the High Representative, named by the European Council by a qualified majority vote, shall preside over the Foreign Affairs Council (ending the rotation of that Council according to the six-month Presidencies) and shall "conduct the Union's common foreign and security policy." Moreover, the High Representative serves simultaneously as Vice-president of the Commission, with the foreign affairs portfolio. Inasmuch as the High Representative will head a new External Affairs Service, merging the prior services of the Commission and Council and responsible for all Union delegations to third states, the post will have substantially enhanced power. In November 2009, the European Council chose Baroness Ashton . . . as the High Representative.

The Council is greatly aided in its work by a body called the COREPER, an acronym for the French term for Committee of Permanent Representatives. . . . COREPER, consisting of two representatives from each Member State customarily holding ambassadorial rank, usually meets weekly in two groups to review all draft legislation and other measures before their consideration by the Council itself. If COREPER is able to agree on a course of action, it recommends it to the Council, which usually endorses the recommendation with little or no debate. If COREPER is unable to agree, but believes certain policy issues concerning the proposed measure can be resolved by the Council, it will refer the issues to the Council for deliberation, and then accept the Council's views as the basis for further work. COREPER's work obviously greatly facilitates the taking of Council action. . . .

2. Council Voting

The EEC Treaty had required the Council to act unanimously in some fields, but enabled it to act by a special majority vote, called qualified majority voting (QMV), in many other fields (and by way of great exception by simple majority vote, as on budgetary matters). . . .

The Lisbon Treaty TEU's Article 24 continues to require Council unanimity for CFSP action. The TFEU also continues to require unanimity to adopt measures to harmonize taxation, sensitive environmental or social policy legislation, or measures pursuant to TFEU Article 352, the article relied on to adopt measures to achieve the common market when no Treaty provision expressly enables them. In a Union now consisting of 27 Member States, achieving unanimity in any of these is likely to be rare. The Council is authorized to act by a simple majority of all Member States only when adopting its rules of procedure or requesting the Commission to prepare studies or proposals, pursuant to . . . TFEU Articles 240-41. . . .

QMV voting dates back to the original EEC Treaty. The essential idea is easy to understand. The Treaty stipulates that each State has a specific number of votes and then requires a stated total number of affirmative votes to take action on adopting policies, legislation or decisions by QMV. When there were only six Member States, the calculations were simple, and QMV voting operated smoothly, unless a State claimed a veto by virtue of the Luxembourg Compromise [which no longer exists]. This remained essentially true as the Community grew to fifteen States.

At the time of the European Council in Nice in December 2001, allocating votes to the current and prospective Member States and setting the formula to act via QMV proved one of the most difficult issues to resolve. The ultimate compromise is complicated. Although Germany has about one-third more people than France, Italy and the UK, all four states were allotted 29 votes, while Spain and Poland received 27. Going down in function of population, the Netherlands received 13 votes, Belgium 12, and so on down to the six States with the smallest population, which each received three (Malta), or four (the others). The QMV formula then required that 72% of the total weighted votes had to be affirmative to adopt a measure. In practice, this could mean that up to four of the six larger States could be outvoted. To prevent this, a so-called double majority vote was required: any State could request a calculation to determine whether States having 62% of the Union's population were in favor, and, if not, the proposed action would fail. . . . Although complicated, this QMV system has operated satisfactorily. In practice, even when the Treaty stipulates QMV voting, the Council generally prefers to act by quasi-unanimity.

The Lisbon Treaty prescribes a new QMV system. Its TEU Article 16(4) requires for action the affirmative vote of 55% of all the ministers, (i.e. States) comprising at least fifteen of them, and representing 65% of the Union population. By requiring the concurrence of States having 65% of the Union population, the Lisbon Treaty slightly increases the influence of Germany and other large States and makes it less likely that they would be outvoted. However, Article 16(4) stipulates that a blocking minority must consist of at least four States. Moreover, due to opposition from smaller States, a Protocol on Transitional Provisions retains the

Nice formula until November 1, 2014, and permits any State to invoke it until March 31, 2017. . . .

D. The European Council

In 1987, the Single European Act first formally recognized the European Council as an informal policy-maker. Subsequently, the Maastricht TEU's Article 4 declared that the European Council shall "provide the Union with the necessary impetus for its development and define the general guidelines thereof." The European Council could not, however, take legally binding decisions, although its authoritative status enabled it in effect to direct the Council or Commission to do so.

Over the years, the European Council has resolved difficult policy issues that the Council lacked the political capacity to resolve. The European Council has set long-term policy guidelines for the Community, endorsed institutional reforms, embraced the idea of an Economic and Monetary Union (EMU), supported German reunification within the Community, set the criteria for accession of the central and eastern European states, scheduled successive intergovernmental conferences in contemplation of treaty amendments, commissioned and eventually endorsed the EU's Charter of Fundamental Rights, and of course, reached the agreement necessary to achieve the Treaty of Lisbon.

Among the European Council's most prominent functions is the coordination of Member State foreign policy, a process that evolved into the Common Foreign and Security Policy. The European Council may now unanimously establish guidelines which enable the Council of Ministers itself to take foreign policy decisions on a qualified majority voting basis. . . .

The Lisbon Treaty's designation of the European Council as an institution of the Union with the capacity to take binding decisions confirms its crucial policy-setting role. The Lisbon TEU's Article 15 retains the description of the European Council's composition, political guidance role, and meetings. Article 15 expressly bars the European Council from exercising any legislative functions. Its decisions are generally taken by consensus, but it can act by simple majority or qualified majority vote in certain decisions. Thus, TEU Article 48 enables the European Council to act by simple majority in deciding to launch a treaty amendment procedure, and TFEU Article 235 enables the European Council to act by qualified majority vote (using the Council mode of QMV) to nominate the President of the Commission, designate the High Representative, and fix the list of Council configurations and the rotation of the Council President. The President of the Commission has no vote in the European Council. . . .

The Lisbon Treaty created a major new post, that of a full-time President of the European Council. Its TEU Article 15(6) states that the President shall serve a two-and-a-half year term, renewable once, with the European Council using a QMV vote under TFEU 235 to elect its President. In November 2009, the European Council chose Herman Van Rompuy, the Prime Minister of Belgium, as its first President.

The President of the European Council has several important duties: to chair the meetings and "drive forward" the European Council's work, to ensure continuity, to "endeavour to facilitate cohesion and consensus," and to report to Parliament after each meeting. The President also represents the Union externally in its common foreign and security policy, but "without prejudice" to the powers of the High Representative for Foreign Affairs and Security Policy.

Although the media has often called the post the "President of the European Union" instead of President of the European Council, it remains to be seen whether the President will become more of a spokesperson on Union affairs than is the President of the Commission. The basic idea behind creating the post was to promote continuity in European Council affairs by ending the shifts in views and emphasis due to the six-month rotation of the Council Presidency. Again, only time will tell whether the President of the European Council will be very successful in achieving this.

Note on the Ombudsman

Another innovation of the Maastricht Treaty was the creation of the office of Ombudsman, based on the Scandinavian model. See . . . TFEU Article 228. . . . The Ombudsman reviews complaints of maladministration brought to it by MEPs or by any EU national or resident. He or she may compel the cooperation of any institution (except the Court of Justice) in an investigation, and ultimately makes findings and recommendations, supported by reports to the Parliament. Each new Parliament names an Ombudsman for the parliamentary term of office.

The Treaty requires that the Ombudsman be completely independent . . . and engaging in no other occupation while in office. In 1994, Parliament imposed as an eligibility requirement that the Ombudsman have the qualifications for exercising the highest judicial office in his or her country and possess "the acknowledged competence and experience to undertake the duties" of the office.

Any EU citizen or person resident or established in an EU Member State may complain to the Ombudsman, either directly or through an MEP, about maladministration on the part of the EU's political institutions. Any such complaint must be filed within two years of the underlying act and must show that efforts were made to remedy the problem through direct contact with the institution or body responsible. . . . Even without having received a complaint, the Ombudsman is free to conduct all the inquiries he or she deems necessary to "clarify" a possible instance of maladministration. The institution complained about is entitled to be informed immediately of the complaint; on the other hand, it is required to cooperate fully in furnishing information and files (except where needs of secrecy dictate otherwise) and in making officials available to testify. The Ombudsman has no means of enforcing its investigative powers, though Parliament may make representations on the Ombudsman's behalf. All information supplied to the Ombudsman is deemed confidential. If, however, information relates to possible criminal violations, it must be reported to the competent authorities. The Ombudsman may only examine acts of the EU institutions, and not of national institutions, even when the latter act in implementation of EU law.

If the Ombudsman finds there to be a prima facie case of maladministration, he or she must inform the institution or body and give it a period of three months in which to respond. Eventually, the Ombudsman issues a report to the Parliament (and to the institution in question, with notice to the complainant) as appropriate. The Ombudsman may propose (though not impose) corrective action. . . .

(3) Decision-making in the European Union

T.C. Hartley, The Foundations of European Union Law

105-106 (7th ed. 2010)

Article 288 TFEU lists five different kinds of acts that may be adopted if other provisions confer the power to do so. They are:

1. regulations;
2. directives;
3. decisions;
4. recommendations;
5. opinions.

Article 288 also contains a short statement of the characteristics each kind of act is supposed to have. A regulation is essentially normative in character: it lays down general rules which are binding both at the Union level and at the national level. Directives and decisions differ from regulations, in that they are not binding in quite the same way. Directives may be addressed only to Member States and they are binding only as to the result to be achieved: they leave to the national authorities 'the choice of form and methods'. This suggests that they lay down an objective and allow each national Government to achieve it by the means it regards as most suitable. A decision, on the other hand, is binding in its entirety; however, if it specifies those to whom it is addressed (which it usually does), it is binding only on them. Recommendations and opinions are not binding at all. [A recommendation suggests the addressee take a specific course of action; an opinion lays the groundwork for subsequent legal proceedings.] . . .

These provisions appear to form a neat and tidy system in which formal designations correspond to differences in function. The differences suggest a hierarchy. . . .

Unfortunately, things are not as simple as this. The first complication is that the formal designation of an act—the label given to it by its author—is not always a reliable guide to its contents. An act may be called a regulation but bear all the characteristics of a decision; or it may be called a directive but leave very little choice as to form and methods. Faced with this situation, the European Court has sometimes rejected the formal designation and looked instead at the substance of the act. If an act in the form of a regulation does not lay down general rules but is concerned with deciding a particular case, the Court may call it a 'disguised decision' and treat it for certain purposes as if it were a decision. . . . It is not clear, however, how far the Court will go in this 'relabelling' process. . . .

A second complication is that in practice the difference between the various kinds of acts are not as great as might appear from the Treaty provisions. In particular, judgments of the European Court have had the effect of upgrading directives so that they are now much closer to regulations: even if they have not been implemented by the Member State to which they are addressed, they can directly confer rights on private citizens which may be invoked against public authorities.

A third complication is that the European Court has ruled that the list in what is now Article 288 is not exhaustive: it is possible to have a legally binding act which does not fall into any of the categories enumerated in the Treaty. Acts falling into this residual category are usually called, for want of a better name, acts *sui generis.*

The decision-making process. The path of legislation in the Union varies from the straightforward to the Byzantine. It depends on the legal basis for the legislation (i.e., the provision under which it is being proposed). Note the discussion above in the Bermann excerpt at C.1. about the Council and the "ordinary legislature procedure." Usually the Commission prepares a proposal, which goes to the Parliament and the Council. If the latter two agree with the Commission, the proposal is adopted. More likely, the process can get very complicated. There can be a back-and-forth between the Commission, Parliament, and Council. There are even provisions for a Conciliation Commission between the Parliament and Council, with the Commission acting as a conciliator. The details of the legislative process are beyond the scope of this casebook. For further discussion, see Hartley, supra, at 36-42, or Bermann, et al., supra, at 80-87.

(4) *What Does It All Add Up To?*

The preceding overview of the Union's structure should indicate that the Union is a unique, still-developing entity. Comparisons between it and other international and national entities are difficult. For example, look again at the three EU political institutions and consider what interests each institution represents. In the Council the interests of member states are represented. In the Commission those of the Union as a whole, somehow defined, take precedence. And in the European Parliament the concerns of the citizens of the Union are considered.

Additionally, the member states have given up certain aspects of their sovereignty to Union institutions. However, the Amsterdam Treaty introduced the concept of variable-speed integration, called "Closer Cooperation," which allows (with a number of conditions) some member states to cooperate closely with other members to move toward greater integration; while allowing other member states the option to join them at a later stage. This happened, for example, when the United Kingdom, Denmark, and Sweden decided not to join the euro zone or when the United Kingdom and Poland received a special assurance that the Charter of Fundamental Rights would not be extended to their countries.

Notes and Questions

1. Because of their composition, which of the EU's key institutions — the Commission, European Parliament, Council, European Council, and the Court of Justice — seem more likely to favor greater integration in the Union? Which seem more likely to be inclined to promote the interests of the individual member states?

2. Is the Union a very democratic entity? Consider how Commission members are selected. Who are the delegates to the Council? What institution is the most democratic? Do you believe it beneficial that the Maastricht, Amsterdam, and Lisbon treaties have given the Parliament a somewhat expanded role? Is it relevant that the governments of all the member states are democratically elected and hence in theory are subject to the people?

3. How would you categorize the Union? Is it a state? A supranational entity? Is the Union more similar to a federal system like the United States, a regional organization like the Organization of American States (discussed below), or an international organization like the United Nations? As you try to describe the Union, how would you categorize the "member states"—are they still states? Have they become something less? For example, is France still a state?

4. To what extent can the key Union institutions be analogized to the tripartite structure of the U.S. government? How clearly delineated are the executive and legislative functions of the Union?

5. Professor Andrew Moravscik provides another perspective.

> Let us appreciate how much Europe has achieved. We should not be trapped by rhetoric or fears about what it aspires to be. The EU is not a United States of Europe in the making. Instead, it should be seen for what it is—the most successful international organization in history. The secret of that success lies not only in the Europeans' willingness to centralize certain types of political power, but also in knowing how to mold and limit that power [Andrew Moravcsik, In Defence of the "Democratic Deficit": Reassessing Legitimacy in the European Union, 40 J. Common Mkt. Stud. 603, 607 (2002).]

(5) Budget

One area where the Parliament has considerable say is in the EU's budget. The Union's main sources of revenue are customs duties on imports from outside the Union, a portion of proceeds of the value added tax (VAT) imposed by the member states, and a direct levy based on the GNP of the member states. The size and composition of the budget has posed many problems for the Community over the years.

As explained by Professor Bermann and his coauthors:

> The Treaty of Lisbon has significantly modified the prior Treaty provisions in favor of the Parliament. TFEU Article 311 prescribes that the Council, acting unanimously and after consulting the Parliament, shall decide upon the EU's system of own resources. . . . [T]he process for adopting the annual budget, under the TFEU Article 314 requires a conciliation committee whenever the Council and Parliament cannot agree, and ultimately grants Parliament the decisive voice, provided 60% of the votes cast by an absolute majority of its members endorse an approach on disputed budget items. The Commission implements the budget, pursuant to TFEU Article 317. For several years, the annual budget has exceeded 100 billion Euros.
>
> Budgetary politics can produce divisions along Member State lines. . . .
>
> Once the budget is adopted, the Commission has responsibility for administering the receipt of revenues, the control of cash flow and the disbursement of expenditures. Its administration of EU finances is reviewed by the Court of Auditors. . . . The Court of Auditors in effect carries out an annual audit and reports to the Council and the Parliament. [Bermann, et al., supra, at [102-03].]

The European Union's budget compared to the US budget. The general budget in 2010 for the European Union was about 141.5 billion euros (approximately US$190 billion, although the exchange rate varies). Although the agricultural portion used to be around 55 percent of the total budget, its proportion has dwindled to about 30 percent as the EU has focused on new areas. For example, the EU has allocated 1.4 billion euros to the social inclusion of disabled people, migrants, and minorities. It has also offered 500 million euros for one-on-one guidance training and job placement for people who have lost their jobs. In addition, 7.5 billion euros have been dedicated to scientific research and 1.1 billion euros to internet and energy grids. Only 6 percent of the total budget is paid for EU administration.

Expenditures for military forces and many entitlement programs, such as the equivalent of social security, unemployment compensation, and Medicare in the United States, are not included in the Union budget, but are in the national budgets of the member states. This helps explain the small EU budget relative to, say, that of the United States. (The U.S. federal budget for FY2010 was about $3.5 trillion.)

The more limited size of the EU government compared to the U.S. federal government can also be appreciated by the relative employment numbers. The U.S. government has about 2.8 million employees. The EU government employees (often derogatively called "eurocrats") number about 35,000. This is less than the state government employment in Maryland (about 81,000) and less than the city government employment in major U.S. cities. Moreover, the EU total includes a substantial number of interpreters because of the EU's 23 official languages. Many official proceedings and documents require interpretation in most, if not all, of the languages.

Besides not having an EU military or social security system, the EU is able to operate with much smaller numbers than the U.S. government because of much greater reliance on the government bureaucracies of member states. The Union will often issue a directive, which the member state governments are expected to implement. This is partly because the member state governments were well established even before the creation of the European Community and then the European Union. This also reflects the considerable political pressures in the Union against the growth of a large bureaucracy in Brussels.

(6) Important EU Principles

The EU's size and method of operation are influenced by the important principles of subsidiarity and harmonization and the related concept of mutual recognition.

Subsidiarity. This principle was first introduced in the Maastricht Treaty. It means that in areas where the EU does not have exclusive jurisdiction, the EU takes action only when the member states have insufficient means to reach the objectives of the proposed action. The principle of subsidiarity assigns decision making to national, regional, or local levels as much as possible. It is supposed to be taken into account at every stage of the EU legislative process. As Bermann, et al., illustrate:

> Lisbon TEU Article 5 . . . sets out the principle of subsidiarity. . . . [The second paragraph] reads as follows:
>
> In areas which do not fall within its exclusive competence, the Community shall take action, in accordance with the principle of subsidiarity, only if and insofar as the objectives of the proposed action cannot be sufficiently achieved by the Member States

> and can therefore, by reason of the scale or effects of proposed action, be better achieved by the Community.
>
> The third paragraph of Article 5 adds the principle of proportionality: Community action "shall not go beyond what is necessary to achieve the objectives of this Treaty." . . .
>
> The term, "subsidiarity," does not appear in US constitutional analysis, although the application of the Tenth Amendment and the "states' rights" doctrine does present certain analogies. The concept of subsidiarity is therefore not so easy to grasp. The basic notion behind subsidiarity is that the EU should not exercise a legislative or other power shared with the Member States if, upon examination, the underlying purpose can be achieved as well, or perhaps even better, by the Member States. EU action must be shown to be more effective or efficient than Member State action. Moreover, the reference to Member State action does not indicate only national action, but includes also regional or local action, which should often be preferred in order to keep government closer to the people. . . . [Bermann, et al., supra, at 117-18].

Harmonization and mutual recognition. The EU's method of operation and size are also affected by the principle of harmonization and the related concept of mutual recognition. The principle of harmonization was first introduced in the EC's Treaty of Rome in an effort to create an open internal market that was free from competition. The principle seeks to coordinate national legislation of the member states in order to remove trade barriers. The establishment of common external tariffs and the prohibition of import quotas within the union are examples of methods used to achieve a single European market. The adoption of uniform environmental standards in the areas of automobile emissions, chemical substances, and pesticides also facilitates free movement of goods.

However, in a significant movement away from attempts to overharmonize national legislation, the Court of Justice introduced the concept of mutual recognition. Mutual recognition allows a product that is legally produced and sold in one member state to move freely in all other member states. The case that established this concept, Rewe v. Bundesmonopolverwaltung fur Branntwein, Case 120/78, [1979] E.C.R. 649, [1979] 3 C.M.L.R. 494 (usually referred to by its common name, *Cassis de Dijon*), was brought to the court by a company that wanted to import a French liqueur into the Federal Republic of Germany. The company could not import the French liqueur, Cassis de Dijon, into the country because its alcohol content was lower than the German requirement of 25 percent. Even though the alcohol content requirement was applied equally to German liqueurs, the court found Germany to be in violation of Article 28 (ex Art. 30), which prohibits "any national measure capable of hindering, directly or indirectly, actually or potentially, intra-Community trade."

The ruling in *Cassis de Dijon* facilitated the EU's movement toward a single market and reduced the need for a large EU administrative bureaucracy because it allowed for free movement of goods without having to wait for harmonization directives from the EU institutions. The concept of mutual recognition is limited by the national need to impose restrictions for the protection of consumers, health, and the environment as well as for the maintenance of fair commercial transactions. However, the effects of the court's decision have been far-reaching. In 1998, Austria, Belgium, France, Greece, Ireland, Italy, the Netherlands, and Sweden faced infringement proceedings (which may subject member states to fines) for creating trade barriers for a range of products, including alcoholic beverages, car spare parts, chocolate, diet supplements, margarine, precious metals, road tankers, salami, telecommunications equipment, and vitamin-enriched foods. Specifically in the case of the Italy, the national legislation restricted imports of chocolate containing vegetable fats other than cocoa butter. Italy allowed those chocolates to be sold only if they were labeled as a chocolate substitute. The Commission determined that the Italian legislation violated the concept of mutual recognition and went beyond the consumer protection exception under *Cassis de Dijon*, since the consumers can be informed by less restrictive labeling.

Notes and Questions

1. Do you think the United States should adopt such a principle of subsidiarity as well? Has it perhaps already adopted something similar? Is this the idea behind the Tenth Amendment? Who do you think likes the subsidiarity principle and who dislikes it?

2. Assume the French and German regulations regarding the minimum amount of alcohol for a liqueur are the same as existed at the time of the *Cassis de Dijon* decision. If a U.S. or Japanese company wanted to sell its liqueur in the EU, including in France and Germany, what EU country's alcohol requirement should the U.S. or Japanese company have to meet? Should it depend on the location of the EU port where the goods might first arrive in the EU? Or should the requirement vary by whether the non-EU liqueur is being sold in France or Germany? Consider the Court of Justice's rationale for mutual recognition. Would not varying requirements for a non-EU liqueur also hinder trade in the EU? And, realizing that goods move freely among the EU countries once the goods are within the EU, would not enforcement be a problem if the requirements varied?

(7) The European Economic and Monetary Union (EMU)

A prominent symbol of European integration is the adoption between 1999 and 2002 of a single currency—the euro. In January-February 2002, euro notes and coins were introduced into 12 EU states and their respective national currencies were taken out of circulation, leaving the euro as the sole official currency. These states were: Austria, Belgium, Finland, France, Germany, Greece, Ireland, Italy, Luxembourg, the Netherlands, Portugal, and Spain. The United Kingdom, Denmark, and Sweden opted to remain outside the European Monetary Union, at least for the time being. Additionally, non-EU states, including Monaco, Vatican City, and San Marino, have adopted the euro as their national currency.

The ten states that joined the EU in 2004 (Cyprus, the Czech Republic, Estonia, Hungary, Latvia, Lithuania, Malta, Poland, Slovakia, and Slovenia) and the two that joined in 2007 (Romania and Bulgaria) are expected to adopt the euro when they are economically prepared to do so. In January 2007, Slovenia became the first new member to introduce the euro and since then Cyprus, Malta, Slovakia, and Estonia have adopted the euro.

With the new monetary union, a European Central Bank (ECB) was created in 1998. Responsibility for monetary policy among the euro countries passed to the ECB. The conversion rates between those countries' currencies and the new euro were fixed (to the sixth decimal point) in January 1999. Relative to the U.S. dollar, the euro was initially worth about $1.167. Although the euro's value initially declined, fluctuating between 86 cents and one dollar in 2002, its value has appreciated significantly since 2003 and reached 1.588 to $1 in July 2008. As of November 2010, the euro was about 1.37 to $1.

In a political sense, the EMU is a significant step toward the goal of a unified Europe, as the member states have ceded a substantial amount of their sovereignty in monetary and fiscal policy to the ECB for the benefits of a common currency. The euro was expected to save people and entities in the EU over €20-25 billion yearly in the transaction costs that multiple currencies caused. The additional savings from the improved ability to compare prices easily across borders probably saved even more. Moreover, in an economic sense, the size and wealth of the EMU will have important implications for the world economy.

With respect to global economics, the euro has become a serious alternative to the dollar as a global reserve currency.

> At the end of 2008, some 45 per cent of international debt securities were denominated in dollars compared to 32 per cent in euros. The dollar was used in 86 per cent of all foreign exchange transactions compared to 38 per cent in which the euro was used, and 66 countries used the dollar as their exchange-rate anchor, compared with 27 that used the euro. The EU and the European Central Bank also play a key role in financial stabilization efforts even outside the euro zone. Andrew Moravcsik, Europe: The Quiet Superpower, 7 French Politics 411 (September-December 2009).

The euro, however, encountered rough going during the worldwide financial crisis of 2007-2011, that was caused in part by real estate price bubbles not only in the United States but also in some European countries. Just as the United States and much of the world was emerging from the crisis in late 2009, "the European crisis entered a new phase. First Greece, then Ireland, then Spain and Portugal suffered drastic losses in investor confidence and hence a significant rise in borrowing costs." Paul Krugman, Can Europe Be Saved?, N.Y. Times, Jan. 12, 2011.

How the European crisis will play out is uncertain as of January 2011. Various approaches are possible for the countries, including fiscal austerity and/or debt restructuring. The participation of these countries (e.g., Greece, Ireland, Spain, and Portugal) in the euro zone limits the ability of each country to devalue its currency as an alternative approach to stabilizing their economy by encouraging increased exports and a drop in imports. Iceland, which is not a part of the euro zone, followed the devaluation path with some success just a few years before. Some international economists have publicly suggested that some of the beleaguered EU countries might need to consider at some point the drastic approach of exiting or ending their participation in the euro and returning to a national currency.

(8) Free Movement of Workers

One of the EU's four fundamental freedoms is the free movement of persons, and the EU has made significant progress in this area. EU citizens have the right to move and reside freely within the member states. EU citizens also have the right to work in any member state under the same conditions as the citizens of that member state.

As one measure to further internal freedom of movement, the Schengen Area was created in 1985 by a separate agreement among France, Germany, Belgium, Luxembourg, and the Netherlands and later incorporated into the EU by the Treaty of Amsterdam. The Schengen Area is a passport-free zone in which internal borders between the Schengen member states are eliminated. Immigration checks are conducted at external borders of the EU. As of August 2010, 22 EU member states (Austria, Belgium, Czech Republic, Denmark, Estonia, Finland, France, Germany, Greece, Hungary, Italy, Latvia, Lithuania, Luxembourg, Malta, Netherlands, Poland, Portugal, Slovak Republic, Slovenia, Spain, Sweden), plus three non-EU states, Norway, Iceland, and Switzerland fully apply the provisions of the Schengen agreement. The United Kingdom and Ireland are only partial participants in the Schengen Area.

Although citizens of EU member states have the right to work anywhere in the Union, barriers to their free movement remain in practice. For example, supplementary pension schemes have become a significant practical barrier to free movement. Workers often find that they can move from state to state, but their pensions do not. Regulations provide for coordination of statutory social security schemes, guaranteeing workers and students the same treatment as nationals of the host Member State, but EU law has not yet addressed supplementary pension schemes.

Professionals have also encountered problems with recognition of their qualifications in other member states. The EU has taken measures to address these problems in Directive 2005/36/EC, which took effect in October 2007. This Directive allows citizens to provide professional services on a temporary and occasional basis in another member state without having to apply for recognition of their qualifications. Additionally, for a professional who seeks to relocate to another member state on a more permanent basis, the Directive sets forth a general system for the recognition of professional qualifications. It involves general mutual recognition unless there are substantial differences between the professional's training and the member state's requirements; a system of automatic recognition of qualifications attested by professional experience in industrial, craft, and commercial activities; and a system of automatic recognition of the qualifications for doctors, nurses, dental practitioners, veterinary surgeons, midwives, pharmacists, and architects.

(9) The External Activities of the European Union

The provisions of the Treaty on European Union establishing a common foreign and security policy were the result of a gradual process of greater EU action outside its own economic area. Since the 1960s, the EU has been involved in international economic issues. In conjunction with its role in setting common external trade barriers and reducing internal trade barriers, the Community acted as the negotiator for its member states in the GATT and WTO negotiating rounds.

With the Lisbon Treaty, the common foreign and security policy (CFSP) has become integrated within the scope of the EU. As Professor Hartley describes:

> For many years, the Union has been an active player in the foreign-policy and defence areas, though a striking feature of its activity in the beginning was that this took place entirely outside the institutional framework established by the Treaties. This gradually began to change, but, until the coming into force of the Treaty of Lisbon,

the common foreign and security policy (together with police and judicial co-operation in criminal matters) were kept separate from other activities. This was done through the distinction between the European Community (EC) and the European Union: the common foreign and security policy (CFSP) and policy and judicial co-operation in criminal matters, while falling within the scope of the Union, were outside that of the EC, the entity under which the other policies were conducted. Now that the EC has been abolished, there is no longer any conceptual difference between the CFSP and other areas of Union activity. Nevertheless, the CFSP still retains distinctive features: legislative powers are lacking; the jurisdiction of the European Court is largely excluded; and decision-making is based on the principle that no Member State should be bound against its will.

This latter principle finds expression in the rule that decisions in the European Council and the Council must be taken by unanimity. However, there is a rule that a Member State may abstain from voting while making a formal declaration referring to Article 31(1), second sub-paragraph. The effect of this is that the measure will be passed—an abstention by a Member State that is present does not prevent its adoption—but, by virtue of Article 31(1), second sub-paragraph, the Member State in question will not itself be bound. This allows individual Member States to opt out of EU policies without preventing the others from going ahead. Nevertheless, the Member State in question must accept that the Union is bound, and it must not itself actively undermine the policy.

. . . The Common Security and Defence Policy

The common security and defence policy could be said to contain the seeds of a future European Army, though this will not come into being for a long time, if indeed it comes into being at all. According to the Treaties, the common security and defence policy, which is an integral part of the CFSP, is intended to provide the Union with an operational capacity which can be used in military operations outside the Union. It involves the progressive framing of a Union defence policy. There is also a European Defence Agency charged with the task of improving the military capabilities of the Member States.

. . . The High Representative of the Union for Foreign Affairs and Security Policy

This office was newly created by the Treaty of Lisbon. Under Article 18 TEU, the High Representative is appointed by the European Council (acting by a qualified majority), with the agreement of the President of the Commission. He or she (the first appointee was a woman, Baroness Cathy Ashton, a British politician who was previously a member of the Commission) has the task of conducting the CFSP: she contributes to its development and carries it out as mandated by the Council. She presides over the Foreign Affairs Council (the Council in its foreign affairs configuration) and is one of the Vice-Presidents of the Commission. She is assisted by a European External Action Service, a kind of embryonic EU diplomatic service, which operates in co-operation with the diplomatic services of the Member States, and consists of officials from the relevant departments of the Council Secretariat and the Commission, as well as staff seconded from the national diplomatic services of the Member States." [Hartley, supra, at 32-34]

The EU's sanctions against Iran's nuclear program are an active example of EU involvement in foreign policy. In summer and fall 2009, the EU followed up on U.N. sanctions (which its member states supported) with thoroughgoing sanctions that went beyond the U.N. sanctions.

Notes and Questions

1. Why do you think the member states believe there are benefits in jointly developing and implementing a European foreign policy? Is there something to the old adage about "strength in numbers"?

2. What limits do you see regarding the benefits of CFSP from the standpoint of the individual member states? Do they all share the same views and policies—for example, toward Turkey, Serbia, or the Middle East?

3. What seem to be the relative roles of the EU's political institutions in making and implementing international agreements on behalf of the Union?"

(10) The Future of the European Union

Where is the European Union headed? The EU has been adding new member states, while also further integrating many activities. Some experts have worried whether widening and deepening can occur simultaneously. However, the Amsterdam, Nice, and Lisbon Treaties appear to be attempts to do just that—to welcome new member states into the Union while further integrating the members into a more closely knit Union. For a new member state to join the EU, the Commission must determine that state has met the required political and economic criteria, that is:

> The stability of institutions guaranteeing democracy, the rule of law, human rights and respect for and protection of minorities (the *political criterion*);
>
> The existence of a functioning market economy as well as the capacity to cope with competitive pressure and market forces within the Union (the *economic criterion*);

and will be able to enact and implement the *acquis communitaire* (the Union's legislation).

Other states may join the EU in the more distant future. The EU began accession negotiations with Turkey and Croatia in October 2005 and signed a pre-membership agreement with Albania and Montenegro. In December 2005, the EU granted Macedonia the status of candidate country but did not open accession negotiations. Iceland applied for membership in July 2009. Large expansions of the Union similar to those in the past are unlikely to occur in the near term. Although some smaller states might join the EU in the next few years, their impact on the EU would not be as significant as for previous expansions. Future big expansions that include, say, Turkey face many more hurdles.

There are indications that the Union is likely to remain in its current operational form for the next few decades. As Professor Andrew Moravcsik notes:

> [The] situation appears stable. The truth is that today no plausible "grand projet" for Europe can be found—nothing, at least, on the projects that powered major constitutional reform in the past, such as the CAP [Common Agricultural Policy],

> the single market, the single currency, or the recent enlargement. Polls show that most Europeans are broadly satisfied with the current scope of the EU. . . .
>
> [T]he EU has quietly struck a "European constitutional settlement". Barring a very large exogenous shock, it is unlikely to be upset by functional challenges, autonomous institutional evolution, or demands for democratic accountability. . . .
>
> The EU is now older than most existing democracies. Its multilevel governance system is the only distinctively new form of state organization to emerge and prosper since the rise of the democratic social welfare state at the turn of the twentieth century—and it works remarkably well. We learn far more by viewing the EU as the most advanced model for international cooperation, a vantage point from which it appears as an unambiguous success story, rather than as a nation-state in the making, which encourages cycles of overambition and disappointment. [Andrew Moravcsik. The European Constitutional Settlement, in Making History: European Integration and Institutional Change at Fifty 23, 27-28, 47 (Sophie Meunier & Kathleen R. McNamara—Eds., 2007).]

It remains to be seen, however, whether the ongoing crisis in the euro zone in early 2011 might lead to changes in at least the European Economic and Monetary Union.

Notes and Questions

1. Is there a potential tension between "widening" (enlarging the number of members) and "deepening" the institutions (greater integration)? Can these two goals continue to exist coextensively? If not, is one more desirable than the other in the case of the European Union? For example, will the wealthier member states be amenable to further diluting their sovereignty to a Union that includes states with which they have much less common history? Should the Union slow down its integration process to allow the new members to catch up?

2. What role will a European Union, with a greater or lesser degree of "federalism," have in the larger world? Will it be primarily an economic superpower only, unable to turn its financial strength into foreign policy and defense leverage because of internal divisions? Or, will the European Union increasingly speak with one powerful voice across the international stage, as it does now in the World Trade Organization?

3. In addition to the works cited in this section and in Chapter 4, there is an extensive literature on the European Union both generally and on specific aspects of it. The EU has a very comprehensive and current Web site, http://europa.eu.

b. North Atlantic Treaty Organization (NATO)

The North Atlantic Treaty Organization originally was the security organization designed to provide for the defense of Western Europe. NATO was formed in 1949 in response to growing concern over actions taken by the Soviet Union, including its consolidation of communist rule in Eastern Europe after World War II.

As of January 2011, NATO had 28 full members, including the United States, Canada, Iceland, Turkey, and most of the countries of Western Europe (though not Austria and Switzerland). Poland, Hungary, and the Czech Republic had joined the

Alliance in 1999. Seven additional countries (Bulgaria, Estonia, Latvia, Lithuania, Romania, Slovakia, and Slovenia) became members in 2004, and Albania and Croatia joined NATO in 2009. Georgia is also under consideration for future membership. Its inclusion in NATO, however, would likely anger Russia (see below). In 2008, the Former Yugoslav Republic of Macedonia's ascension into NATO was blocked by Greece because of a 17-year dispute over Macedonia's name. Deliberations on its membership will resume after the naming dispute has been resolved.

The original purpose of NATO was collective self-defense. The North Atlantic Treaty, however, does not obligate a member to come to the aid of any other member if an attack occurs. Article 5, which authorizes collective self-defense in the event of an armed attack, provides that NATO members agree to consider an armed attack against one or more of them in Europe or North America as "an attack against them all," but requires only that a member take "such action as it deems necessary" to restore and maintain the security of the North Atlantic area. Each state's response must be in accord with its own constitutional processes. Nevertheless, there has been a substantial measure of integration of military forces and military planning, including unified commands and regional planning groups.

Article 5 has only been invoked once in NATO's history, namely after the events of September 11, 2001, when NATO demonstrated its support for the United States. (See the discussion in the case study in Chapter 1.E.)

With the fall of the Berlin Wall in late 1989 and the disintegration of the Soviet Union in 1991-1992, the Cold War thawed and geopolitics changed in Europe. NATO began its own transformation from being just a collective self-defense entity for Western Europe. In addition to opening its door to new members from the former Warsaw Pact, NATO made major changes in its military and political structures, and has increased cooperation with nonmember states in a wide range of areas.

First, to deepen its engagement with the neutral and formerly communist states of Central and Eastern Europe, NATO instituted the Partnership for Peace (PFP) program in 1991. While the PFP program is aimed at enhancing cooperation between NATO and non-NATO states, it does not provide full NATO membership or security guarantees. In 1997, NATO created the Euro-Atlantic Partnership Council (EAPC) to establish political and military cooperation between NATO members and PFP states. The EAPC membership is open to all members of PFP and the Organization on Security and Cooperation in Europe (OSCE) (discussed below). The EAPC currently includes all 28 NATO members and all 22 PFP countries.

Also, in May 2002, NATO and Russia replaced the NATO-Russia Permanent Joint Council, set up in 1997 to allow bilateral consultation, with a new NATO-Russia Council. Russia now sits as an equal with the 28 NATO members and participates in the consensus, although it lacks veto power. Relations between NATO and Russia became seriously strained in 2008 following the Russia-Georgia crisis. While tensions remain between NATO and Russia, dialogue and cooperation have resumed. Efforts are being made to cooperate in a number of key areas, including antiterrorism, crisis management, arms control, missile defense, military cooperation, and civil emergencies.

Second, NATO continues to work to make its military capability more flexible and increasingly focuses on "out-of-area" capability. Because an invasion of Western

Europe is no longer a concern, NATO forces are being adapted to address security problems in other volatile areas. Indeed, it was NATO that conducted the military efforts, which were largely an air campaign, in 1999 against Serbia over its repression of the Albanians in Kosovo. (See the discussion of the Kosovo campaign in Chapter 11.)

In August 2003, NATO took over command and coordination of the International Security Assistance Force (ISAF) in Afghanistan. This is NATO's first mission outside the European-Atlantic area. Initially restricted to providing security in and around Kabul, ISAF has expanded its mission to cover all of the country. ISAF's main role is to assist the Afghan government and its security forces in the establishment of a secure and stable environment. ISAF forces are directly involved in conducting counterinsurgency operations and training the Afghan National Army. NATO also facilitates reconstruction and development projects. As of December 2010, NATO was leading about 132,000 from 48 countries.

Although there has been some tension among the security functions of NATO, the EU, and the OSCE, NATO remains as the primary European security institution. In November 2010, NATO adopted a new "Strategic Concept" for the next ten years. It reaffirms the Alliance's commitment to collective defense and paves the way for the Alliance to modernize its defense and deterrence capabilities, while continuing to promote international stability. NATO has an excellent Web site at http://www.nato.int.

c. The Organization on Security and Cooperation in Europe (OSCE)

As a new Europe emerges, one important question is: which regional organizations will play major roles? Besides the institutions already discussed in this chapter or elsewhere — the European Union, NATO, and the European Court of Human Rights — other regional entities exist. One that seems likely to play a continuing role is the Organization on Security and Cooperation in Europe (OSCE).

The OSCE is the world's largest regional security organization. Its membership consists of all the European states (including the former republics of the Soviet Union), plus the United States and Canada. An OSCE Fact Sheet provides basic background information:

> The Organization traces its origins to the early 1970s, to the Helsinki Final Act and the creation of the Conference on Security and Co-operation in Europe (CSCE), which at the height of the Cold War served as an important multilateral forum for dialogue and negotiation between East and West.
>
> The fall of the Berlin Wall in 1989 and the collapse of the Soviet Union in 1991 heralded the start of a new era for a "Europe whole and free", and the participating States called upon the CSCE to respond to the emerging challenges. The CSCE acquired its first permanent structures, including a Secretariat and institutions, and established the first field missions. In 1994 the CSCE, more than a conference, was renamed the Organization for Security and Co-operation in Europe.
>
> The complex security challenges of the 21st century — from climate change to the spectre of terrorism — have made it clear that co-operation fostered by the OSCE is needed more than ever.

> These combine with the challenges inherited from the past—resolving conflicts in the former Soviet Union, embedding stability in the Balkans, promoting military transparency—to make the OSCE agenda ambitious and full. [What is the OSCE?, Factsheet, http://www.osce.org/ (October 2010).]

The 1994 transition from "conference" to regional security organization has made the OSCE a more active participant in European affairs. Now comprising 56 countries, the OSCE works for "early warning, conflict prevention, crisis management and post-conflict rehabilitation." The OSCE maintains 18 field missions in several states, including high-profile missions to Bosnia-Herzegovina, Kosovo, and in Central Asia. Among the tasks of these missions is overseeing elections and helping to ensure the rule of law and protection of minorities.

In the twenty-first century, the OSCE's greatest contribution is likely to be in conflict prevention and de-escalation. By acting quickly and quietly, OSCE missions and field operations have defused conflicts in Ukraine and Macedonia at a fraction of the cost of its peacekeeping missions to Bosnia and Kosovo. Where conflict prevention has failed, OSCE missions have been helpful in rebuilding war-torn societies, particularly in the former Yugoslav and Soviet republics.

Notes and Questions

1. Would the OSCE, with its larger membership than NATO, provide a more comprehensive framework for the security of the entire continent? The United States has opposed such a belief as unworkable at the present time. It has rebuffed an independent security role for the OSCE, preferring to have it act in concert with the United Nations or NATO.

2. Besides those regional institutions mentioned in the preceding sections, Europe has a number of other regional entities of varying scope and purpose. These include the Council of Europe and the Economic Commission for Europe.

The Council of Europe is a parliamentary organization aimed at furthering democracy and human rights. It played a role in the establishment of the European Court of Human Rights, and membership in it is a precondition for participation in that court. The Council of Europe had 47 member states, including Russia, as of October 2010. With its expanded membership encompassing a large number of different nationalities, the Council has turned its attention to such issues as migration, the right to citizenship, social exclusion, minorities, cybercrime, terrorism, and human trafficking. More information on the Council is available at its Web site: http://www.coe.int. Although the United States is not a member, the Council has extended an invitation for the United States to participate in some of its functions. Canada, Japan, Mexico, and the Holy See also have observer status with the Council.

The Economic Commission for Europe (ECE) is one of the more active regional commissions under the United Nations, covering both Europe and North America. Headquartered in Geneva, the Council has helped develop common policies and programs in trade, in scientific and technological cooperation, and for environmental problems such as acid rain and air pollution. Its membership includes the European countries plus the United States, Canada, and most of the former Soviet republics.

There is also the Organization of Economic Cooperation and Development (OECD), but its scope has expanded beyond Western Europe and North America to include other industrial democracies, such as Japan, Korea, Mexico, Australia, and New Zealand. It works toward developing policies on a range of economic, scientific, and social issues. It has played a leading international role since the 1990s in encouraging the passage of national laws to outlaw bribery of foreign officials, with the OECD Convention on Combatting Bribery of Foreign Officials in International Business Transactions. Its Web site is at http://www.oecd.org.

4. Which regional entity or entities should have the major role in helping develop coordinated policies toward regional issues in Europe such as the movement of people or transboundary air and water pollution? Which entity or entities should have the major role in helping resolve disputes between two or more European countries, such as the ethnic dispute between Hungary and Romania over the treatment of minorities? How should issues of trade and investment be handled? Does it matter what the particular problem is? Do international institutions and bilateral agreements as well as regional entities have a role to play?

5. From the U.S. standpoint, which regional entities should it encourage to develop further? Should the United States especially encourage those entities of which it is a member?

In sharp contrast to the many regional entities in Europe, including some very strong ones, the development of regional organizations in the rest of the world is spottier. However, in the rapidly developing Pacific Rim, two major organizations — the Association of Southeast Asian Nations (ASEAN) and the broadly based Asia-Pacific Economic Cooperation (APEC) coalition — are playing an increasingly important role.

d. The Association of Southeast Asian Nations (ASEAN)

The Association of Southeast Asian Nations is a coalition of ten rapidly developing countries in Southeast Asia. Its membership includes Brunei, Cambodia, Indonesia, Laos, Malaysia, Myanmar (formerly Burma), the Philippines, Singapore, Thailand, and Vietnam. As of July 2010, these countries had a combined population of about 590 million and a gross domestic product of about $1.5 trillion.

As stated in the Bangkok Declaration of 1967 announcing the group's creation, ASEAN was designed to

> accelerate the economic growth, social progress and cultural development in the region through joint endeavours . . . ; [t]o promote regional peace and stability . . . ; [t]o promote active collaboration and mutual assistance . . . in the economic, social, cultural, technical, scientific and administrative fields; . . . [t]o collaborate more effectively for the greater utilization of their agriculture and industries, the expansion of their trade . . . and the raising of the living standards of their peoples.

Malaysia, the Philippines, and Thailand were the founding members of ASEAN in 1967, with Indonesia and Singapore joining next. ASEAN lay dormant between 1967 and 1975. The fall of Saigon to North Vietnam in 1975 prompted the Bali Summit of February 1976 and marked the emergence of the entity as a functional institution. The Summit yielded the establishment of a modest but permanent ASEAN secretariat in Jakarta, Indonesia, and the signing of two key documents, the Treaty of Amity and Cooperation in Southeast Asia and the Declaration of ASEAN Concord, the latter mandating the elevation of economic matters to the same status as political and social concerns. In December 2008, the ASEAN Charter came into force, establishing a new legal and institutional framework for the burgeoning community.

To support cooperation on basic commodities, promote industrial products, and promote inter-ASEAN trade, ASEAN introduced preferential trading arrangements (PTAs) to reduce tariffs on selected products of member states. In January 1992, ASEAN members made significant progress by entering into a trade agreement that set a goal of gradually dismantling intra-regional trade barriers and forming an Asia Free Trade Area (AFTA) within 15 years.

To varying degrees, the ASEAN countries encountered serious economic problems in 1997-1998 during the Asian economic crisis. In response to the crisis, ASEAN established an economic surveillance group to monitor economic and financial data within the bloc and exert peer pressure for corrective measures as necessary. Since 1999, the region has rebounded economically and accelerated its integration among its members and with Northeast Asia.

Although improving its members' economic well-being is a major goal, ASEAN has broader objectives as well. Some have compared it to the European Union at a much earlier stage of development. In addition to its economic programs, ASEAN has become an important entity where Asia-Pacific security is discussed. Moreover, in the mid-1990s, the ASEAN members cooperated on a variety of political and general welfare issues. The countries signed in 1995 a treaty declaring Southeast Asia a Nuclear Free Zone.

Since 1997 the group has also cooperated on a number of environmental issues to ensure sustainable development in the region. In 2007, member countries signed the Cebu Declaration on East Asian Energy Security, which vowed to develop alternative energy sources. ASEAN also provides relief and assistance to member states suffering from emergencies.

The past several years have seen greater integration within Southeast Asia and increased ties with China, Japan, and South Korea (known as ASEAN +3), as well as New Zealand, Australia, and India. Barriers to trade in the ASEAN Free Trade Area (AFTA) have come down ahead of schedule — the original six members have eliminated tariffs on 99 percent of products and the newer members are not far behind.

Since the 1990s, ASEAN meetings have frequently included China, Japan, Korea, and other countries. Japan has long been ASEAN's largest external trade partner, and trade with Korea and China is increasing rapidly. Senior officials of ASEAN +3 countries meet several times a year to discuss a variety of economic and financial matters, and there is a strong force for expanding some parts of AFTA to include these three regional giants. The ASEAN-Japan Comprehensive Economic Partnership, which came into force in December 2008, is a free trade pact that hopes to establish an ASEAN-Japan Free Trade Area within ten years. And, in January 2010, ASEAN entered into separate Free Trade Agreements with China, India, Korea, and New Zealand and Australia. The China-ASEAN Free Trade Area is the world's biggest in terms of population size and the third largest agreement in economic value. The ASEAN Web site is at http://www.aseansec.org.

e. Asia-Pacific Economic Cooperation (APEC)

The organization for Asia-Pacific Economic Cooperation, which convened for the first time in 1989, consists of 21 Pacific Rim members — seven ASEAN members (Brunei, Indonesia, Malaysia, the Philippines, Singapore, Thailand, and Vietnam), plus Australia, Canada, Chile, China, Hong Kong, Japan, Mexico, New Zealand, Papua New Guinea, Peru, Russia, South Korea, the United States, and Taiwan. The members account for over 54 percent of the world's gross domestic product, over 43 percent of the world's trade, approximately 40 percent of the world's population, and 48 percent of the earth's land area, thus giving them a substantial impact on the international arena.

APEC facilitates economic growth, cooperation, trade, and investment. APEC is not a formal organization and does not establish any treaty rights or obligations for its members. Instead, all decisions are followed on a voluntary basis. APEC conducts annual ministerial meetings and organizes working groups try to develop solutions to the world's trade and economic problems. These groups address issues such as energy, telecommunications, technology transfer, transportation, and investment. Between annual ministerial meetings, a group of senior officials from each member meets to oversee the forum's programs. APEC also supports programs that promote public health, mitigate the effects of climate change, provide disaster relief, and maximize the benefits of globalization in other ways.

To better define its mission, APEC developed the "Bogor Goals," which call for free and open trade to be achieved in all industrialized nations by 2010 and in all developing nations by 2020. In November 2010, the APEC members concluded that significant progress had been made toward the Bogor goals, including major reductions in tariffs among industrialized countries, but more work remained.

As an example of APEC's efforts, at the APEC 1996 summit meeting, the United States and most of the other major APEC members agreed to eliminate tariffs on information technology equipment. Their undertaking was then broadened to include other countries in the WTO to create a major International Technology Agreement (ITA) that removed among those countries all tariffs on computers, software, semiconductors, and telecommunications equipment by 2000. The ITA covers over $600 billion in world trade and benefits consumers and companies through lower prices on information technology products. This experience, among others, led many to hope that APEC would be not only a force for liberalized trade in the Asia-Pacific region but also a model for the rest of the world. When the WTO's Doha Round of world trade talks stalled, APEC leaders took matters into their own hands and turned their focus to the possibility of creating a Free Trade Area of the Asia-Pacific. APEC's Web site is http://www.apec.org.

f. The Organization of American States (OAS)

The Organization of American States was envisioned to allow the countries of the Western Hemisphere collectively to pursue economic cooperation, human development, and hemispheric security. The OAS is considered a regional organization under Article 52 of the U.N. Charter. The OAS had 35 members as of January 2011. The essential purposes of the OAS are stated in the OAS Charter, which came into force in 1951. Specifically, the entity exists

> to strengthen the peace and security of the continent; . . . to ensure the pacific settlement of disputes that may arise among the Member States; . . . to provide for common action on the part of those States in the event of aggression; . . . to seek the solution of political, juridical and economic problems that may arise among them; . . . [and] to promote, by cooperative action, their economic, social and cultural development.

The OAS owes its formation largely to the Cold War. The United States foresaw that a strong regional organization of the Western Hemisphere would act as an opposing force against the Soviet bloc in the United Nations and in other strategically relevant contexts.

Although the Latin American states were less worried about the Soviet threat, they welcomed the OAS Charter as a means to inhibit the interventionist impulses of their North American neighbor. Indeed, the United States has historically acted unilaterally in the Latin American region, due to perceived threats to national security interests and to feelings that Latin America was within the U.S. sphere of influence. The principle of nonintervention embodied in the Charter has consequently been the cardinal doctrine of Latin Americans in their dealings with the United States.

Human rights. One area in which the OAS has made some progress has been its effort to improve human rights within the region. In 1959, the OAS created the Inter-American Commission on Human Rights (IACHR), which routinely prepares reports on human rights situations in the region. In 1969, the OAS adopted the American Convention on Human Rights, which led to the establishment of the Inter-American Court of Human Rights. (See Chapter 8.) During the Haitian crisis of the 1990s, the OAS and the United Nations set up a joint observer mission in Haiti to monitor human rights abuses by the military government. In 2010, the IACHR issued a 300-page report rebuking Venezuela and President Hugo Chávez for violating human rights, often by punishing citizens for their political beliefs and stifling free expression. The OAS itself, however, has remained silent on the issue.

Hemispheric security. The OAS role in ensuring stability in the Americas has varied. The OAS played a major role in demonstrating hemispheric opposition to the location of Soviet missiles in Cuba in 1962. It authorized a peacekeeping force (including U.S. troops) for the Dominican Republic after the United States intervened there in 1965, provided a forum for debates over the U.S. intervention in Grenada in 1983, and expressed "regret" over the U.S. invasion of Panama in 1989.

OAS action concerning Honduras. In June 2009, Honduran president Manuel Zelaya was ousted in an army coup d'etat. Reflecting its interest in promoting democracy, the OAS voted to suspend Honduras's right to participate in the OAS. Honduras elected a new president, Porfirio Lobo Sosa, in November 2009. Lobo established a national unity cabinet with members from all parties. In June 2011, the OAS General Assembly voted to lift the suspension of Honduras.

OAS and Cuba. In 1962, the OAS voted to suspend Cuba from participation because of its communist form of government. In 2009, nearly half a century later,

OAS members agreed to lift the suspension. The United States supported the measure but had asked that Cuba show commitment to democracy and human rights before being reinstated. Cuba, however, announced that it did not wish to return to participation as a member.

Other activities. In recent years, the OAS has continued to send electoral observation missions to monitor elections in various countries, helping to ensure transparency and integrity in elections. Special OAS missions have also worked to support the peace process in various local disputes. The OAS carries out technical cooperation programs to promote sustainable development and particular needs such as river basin management and natural disaster mitigation. The OAS has also adopted conventions against corruption, illegal arms trafficking, and violence against women. The OAS Web site is at http://www.oas.org.

g. The African Union (AU)

The African Union came into operation in July 2002, in Durban, South Africa, replacing the discredited Organization of African Unity (OAU). The OAU was seen in much of Africa as a "President's Trade Union," with little relevance to most Africans, in a continent where many of its presidents ruled dictatorially.

The OAU also lacked coercive powers. Indeed, the only power implicit in the system was that of the opinion of member states, a power that could conceivably influence compliance. The OAU Charter emerged as a compromise between two factions. The radicals, who desired a unified Africa with a powerful, continent-wide organization, obtained agreement on an all-Africa organization. The moderates, who opposed any surrender of sovereignty, ensured that the Charter gave scant powers to the new organization. Thus, although an instrument of unity, the Charter sanctified each state's individuality.

At the suggestion of Colonel Qadaffi, the heads of state of Africa met in Libya in 1999, where they called for the establishment of an African Union. The Constitutive Act was completed in July 2000. The Act is intended to restore the credibility that the OAU lacked. Article 4(h) in theory gives the Union the right to intervene in a member state in cases of war crimes, genocide, and crimes against humanity. It also stresses the importance of human rights and democratic principles and includes peer review mechanisms that require adherence to principles of good governance and transparency to participate in the benefits of the Union.

As of January 2011, all 53 member states of the OAU had signed the AU Constitutive Act. Morocco is the only African country that is not an AU member. Some member states, such as Guinea, Madagascar, and Niger, have been suspended from the Union due to a coup d'etat or other political upheavals. After Madagascar was reinstated, the AU imposed sanctions on the nation's leaders when they failed to meet deadlines for setting up a new government. This was the first time the AU had taken such measures against any African nation.

It remains to be seen whether the AU will avoid the pitfalls of its predecessor, and even if it does, whether it will become the powerful unifying force or force for democracy that some hope for.

An important test of the AU's effectiveness will be how it handles the conflict in Darfur, Sudan, which has been labeled "genocide" by many observers. Under the authority of AU, the Darfur Ceasefire Commission (CFC), which is responsible for the monitoring of the execution of the Darfur Peace Agreement and other agreements between the Sudanese parties, was inaugurated in June 2006. The AU has also sent a joint AU/U.N. peacekeeping force, UNAMID, to the Sudan. The increasing efforts of the AU and United Nations are discussed in Chapter 11.C.3. The AU has also deployed a peacekeeping mission to Somalia, with the U.N.'s approval. The situations in Darfur and Somalia highlight the important need to provide reliable and sustainable resources to AU peacekeeping missions. The Web site of the African Union is at http://www.africa-union.org.

Although most of the major international and regional organizations are discussed above, there are many others covering a wide range. These others will be noted as they appear elsewhere in the text.

Questions

1. What are the relative advantages of regional versus international organizations? Do they depend on the entity's objectives?

2. For international or regional organizations, is there a greater chance of success if the objectives are kept narrow or specialized — for example, military security, economic growth, or protection of the environment? Or, again, does it depend on what objectives are being sought?

3. Which international organization or organizations seem to have been the most successful? Which have been the least successful? Can we draw some lessons for the future from their experience?

4. Similarly, which regional organization or organizations seem to have been the most successful? Which have been the least successful? Can we draw any lessons from their experience?

5. Are there any compelling problems that present international and regional organizations should become more active in tackling? Which organization(s)? And are there any compelling problems that could better be handled by a new organization?

6

Foreign Sovereign Immunity and the Act of State Doctrine

This chapter explores two especially significant consequences of statehood. They are the rules in international and domestic law regarding (a) the immunity of a state from the jurisdiction of the domestic courts of another state (called foreign sovereign immunity) and (b) the legal effect of certain acts of a foreign state (called the act of state doctrine). These rules exist to varying degrees in many countries, although we will study them primarily from a U.S. perspective.

In the section on foreign sovereign immunity, we address the immunities of foreign states and briefly discuss the related issues of the legal status of embassies and consulates. We also discuss personal immunities for foreign government officials, diplomats, consuls, and for present and former heads of state. These various categories for immunities for foreign officials can sometimes overlap.

A. THE IMMUNITY OF FOREIGN STATES

Under both international and domestic law a state is immune in many situations from the jurisdiction of foreign courts. The immunity of foreign states was particularly broad throughout the world until the twentieth century, and then it began to erode in various states. The United States was slow to adjust, generally adhering to the broader, or "absolute," theory of immunity until 1952. Now existing in the United States, and generally elsewhere, is a limited scope for state immunity, often termed the "restrictive" theory.

1. Absolute Immunity

Joseph M. Sweeney, The International Law of Sovereign Immunity

20-21 (U.S. Dept. of State Publication (1963))

Until about 1900, the immunity of a state from the judicial process of another—or immunity from jurisdiction as it is frequently called for convenience—was broad, but not without limitations. It was not granted when the litigation involved ownership or other interests in immovables in the territory or when it involved an interest in an estate locally administered. Even though these limitations were well recognized, the immunity was usually stated in terms giving it an absolute character.

In Spanish Government v. Lambege et Pujol, decided in 1849, the Supreme Court of France stated the rule thus:

> The reciprocal independence of states is one of the most universally respected principles of international law, and it follows as a result therefrom that a government cannot be subjected to the jurisdiction of another against its will, and that the right of jurisdiction of one government over litigation arising from its own acts is a right inherent to its sovereignty that another government cannot seize without impairing their mutual relations. [1849] D, 1, 5, 9. . . . .

About 1900, a judicial practice developed in some states of denying immunity from jurisdiction to a foreign state when it was made a respondent with respect to an act of a commercial or so-called private nature. The courts involved reasoned that the traditional rule of immunity from jurisdiction covered only litigation arising from public acts of a foreign state and did not extend to litigation arising from other types of acts. The courts of other states did not draw this distinction and extended immunity from jurisdiction to a foreign state irrespective of the nature of the act involved.

In Societe Anonyme des Chemins de Fer Liegeois Luxembourgeois v. the Netherlands, decided in 1903, the Supreme Court of Belgium stated the distinction between public and commercial or private acts as follows:

> Sovereignty is involved only when political acts are accomplished by the state. . . . However, the state is not bound to confine itself to a political role, and can, for the needs of the collectivity, buy, own, contract, become creditor or debtor, and engage in commerce. . . . In the discharge of these functions, the state is not acting as public power, but does what private persons do, and as such, is acting in a civil and private capacity. When after bargaining on a footing of equality with a person or incurring a responsibility in no way connected with the political order, the state is drawn in litigation, the litigation concerns a civil right, within the sole jurisdiction of the courts, . . . and the foreign state as civil person is like any other foreign person amenable to the Belgian courts. [1903] Pas. 1, 294, 301.

. . . Thus two concepts of sovereign immunity from jurisdiction came to coexist by the late 1930's: the one termed "absolute" because of its broader scope, and the other termed "restrictive" because of its narrower scope. . . .

Until 1952, the U.S. Executive Branch and courts generally accepted the absolute theory of immunity. The seminal case was The Schooner Exchange v. M'Faddon, 11 U.S. (7 Cranch) 116 (1812). There, the question was whether U.S. citizens could lay claim to a French warship that had been seized in U.S. waters. The citizens claimed that they had earlier been the owners of the ship when it had been seized on the high seas by the French and that they were entitled to have the vessel restored to them through a proceeding in admiralty.

The Supreme Court unanimously decided that the French government should be immune from the jurisdiction of U.S. courts and should therefore be able to retain the vessel. Justice Marshall presumed a "perfect equality and absolute independence of sovereigns, and [a] common interest impelling them to mutual intercourse, and an interchange of good offices with each other." Id. at 136. He further noted that

> the Exchange being a public armed ship, in the service of a foreign sovereign, with whom the government of the United States is at peace, and having entered an American port open for her reception, on the terms on which ships of war are generally permitted to enter the ports of a friendly power, must be considered as having come into the American territory, under an implied promise, that . . . she should be exempt from the jurisdiction of that country. [Id. at 147.]

In the twentieth century, the absolute theory came under some attack in the lower court proceedings in Berizzi Bros. Co. v. The Pesaro, 271 U.S. 562 (1926). The Pesaro was a merchant ship owned and operated by the Italian government and was used to carry merchandise for hire. While so employed, the vessel allegedly failed to deliver artificial silk picked up at a port in Italy for delivery to New York. A "libel in rem" proceeding in admiralty was begun in the U.S. courts for damages for the failure to deliver.

The Italian government asked the U.S. Department of State to intercede in the suit to get it dismissed. The U.S. response was "The Department is of the opinion that vessels owned by a state and engaged in commerce are not entitled . . . to the immunity accorded vessels of war." (2 Hackworth, Digest of International Law 437 (1941).) A U.S. district court then denied immunity, relying in part on the Department of State's position. The Pesaro, 277 F. 473, 479-480 n.3 (S.D.N.Y. 1921). However, this decision was vacated because of a Supreme Court decision in an unrelated case dealing with the procedures for claiming immunity. Another U.S. district court judge then granted immunity to the ship.

The Supreme Court unanimously affirmed the grant of immunity. After quoting extensively from its opinion in *The Schooner Exchange*, the Court stated:

> We think the principles [for immunity enunciated in *The Schooner Exchange*] are applicable alike to all ships held and used by a government for a public purpose, and that when, for the purpose of advancing the trade of its people or providing revenue for its treasury, a government acquires, mans and operates ships in the carrying trade, they are public ships in the same sense that warships are. We know of no international usage which regards the maintenance and advancement of the economic welfare of a people in time of peace as any less a public purpose than the maintenance and training of a naval force. [Berizzi Bros. Co. v. The Pesaro, 271 U.S. at 574.]

As the *Pesaro* litigation illustrates, although courts sometimes considered the views of the Executive Branch in making sovereign immunity determinations, they did not feel obligated to accept those views. They deferred to the Executive Branch's decisions as to which governments should be recognized, but they felt free to make their own determinations regarding sovereign immunity.

This view changed starting in the late 1930s. In Compania Espanola de Navegacion Maritima, S.A. v. The Navemar, 303 U.S. 68, 74 (1938), the Supreme Court stated for the first time that Executive Branch suggestions of immunity were binding on the courts. Subsequently, in Ex parte Peru, 318 U.S. 578 (1943), and Mexico v. Hoffman, 324 U.S. 30 (1945), the Court made clear that, if the Executive Branch expressed its views regarding whether immunity should be granted, courts were bound to accept those views. Thus, the Court stated in *Hoffman* that "[i]t is therefore not for the courts to deny an immunity which our government has seen fit to allow, or to allow an immunity on new grounds which the government has not seen fit to recognize." Id. at 35. Under this regime, "if the Executive announced a national policy in regard to immunity generally, or for the particular case, that policy was law for the courts and binding upon them, regardless of what international law might say about it." Louis Henkin, Foreign Affairs and the United States Constitution 56 (2d ed. 1996).

2. *Restrictive Immunity*

A number of states had begun to shift toward restrictive immunity in the period prior to World War II, as noted earlier. Thus, the United States increasingly found itself subject to the restrictive theory of immunity in foreign courts, even though U.S. courts would grant absolute immunity to these same foreign nations. In addition, as an increasing number of nations engaged in international commerce through state-controlled enterprises, the absolute theory of immunity was perceived as undermining U.S. business interests. In response to these developments, the State Department began negotiating bilateral treaties requiring nations to waive sovereign immunity for state-controlled enterprises engaged in business activities within the territory of the other party. Between 1948 and 1958, the Department of State negotiated 14 such treaties.

Absolute immunity also was perceived as inconsistent with limitations that had been imposed by Congress on the U.S. government's immunity from suit in its own courts. These statutes included the 1887 Tucker Act, which gave the Court of Claims (now the United States Claims Court) jurisdiction over a variety of contract and other commercial claims against the U.S. government, and the 1946 Federal Tort Claims Act, which allowed the federal courts to hear certain suits against the U.S. government for common law torts committed by its employees.

The Department of State reexamined its policy toward foreign sovereign immunity in 1952. The importance of this rethinking reflected the State Department's major role since 1938 in determining whether a foreign country should receive immunity. The result was the well-known "Tate Letter" by the acting Legal Adviser, Jack B. Tate. He set forth the Department's position in future cases.

May 19, 1952

My Dear Mr. Attorney General:

The Department of State has for some time had under consideration the question whether the practice of the Government in granting immunity from suit to foreign governments made parties defendant in the courts of the United States without their consent should not be changed. The Department has now reached the conclusion that such immunity should no longer be granted in certain types of cases. In view of the obvious interest of your Department in this matter I should like to point out briefly some of the facts which influenced the Department's decision.

A study of the law of sovereign immunity reveals the existence of two conflicting concepts of sovereign immunity, each widely held and firmly established. According to the classical or absolute theory of sovereign immunity, a sovereign cannot, without his consent, be made a respondent in the courts of another sovereign. According to the newer or restrictive theory of sovereign immunity, the immunity of the sovereign is recognized with regard to sovereign or public acts (*jure imperil*) of a state, but not with respect to private acts (*jure gestionis*). There is agreement by proponents of both theories, supported by practice, that sovereign immunity should not be claimed or granted in actions with respect to real property (diplomatic and perhaps consular property excepted) or with respect to the disposition of the property of a deceased person even though a foreign sovereign is the beneficiary.

The classical or virtually absolute theory of sovereign immunity has generally been followed by the courts of the United States, the British Commonwealth, Czechoslovakia, Estonia, and probably Poland.

The decisions of the courts of Brazil, Chile, China, Hungary, Japan, Luxembourg, Norway, and Portugal may be deemed to support the classical theory of immunity if one or at most two old decisions anterior to the development of the restrictive theory may be considered sufficient on which to base a conclusion.

The position of the Netherlands, Sweden, and Argentina is less clear since although immunity has been granted in recent cases coming before the courts of those countries, the facts were such that immunity would have been granted under either the absolute or restrictive theory. However, constant references by the courts of these three countries to the distinction between public and private acts of the state, even though the distinction was not involved in the result of the case, may indicate an intention to leave the way open for a possible application of the restrictive theory of immunity if and when the occasion presents itself.

A trend to the restrictive theory is already evident in the Netherlands where the lower courts have started to apply that theory. . . .

The German courts . . . have held to the classical theory, but it should be noted that the refusal of the Supreme Court in 1921 to yield to pressure by the lower courts for the newer theory was based on the view that that theory had not yet developed sufficiently to justify a change. In view of the growth of the restrictive theory since that time the German courts might take a different view today.

The newer or restrictive theory of sovereign immunity has always been supported by the courts of Belgium and Italy. It was adopted in turn by the courts of Egypt and of Switzerland. In addition, the courts of France, Austria, and Greece, which were traditionally supporters of the classical theory, reversed their position in the 20's to embrace the restrictive theory. Rumania, Peru, and possibly Denmark also appear to follow this theory.

Furthermore, . . . in most of the countries still following the classical theory there is a school of influential writers favoring the restrictive theory and the views of writers, at least in civil law countries, are a major factor in the development of the law. Moreover, the leanings of the lower courts in civil law countries are more significant in shaping the law than they are in common law countries where the rule of precedent prevails and the trend in these lower courts is to the restrictive theory.

Of related interest to this question is the fact that ten of the thirteen countries which have been classified above as supporters of the classical theory have ratified the Brussels Convention of 1926 under which immunity for government owned merchant vessels is waived. In addition the United States, which is not a party to the Convention, some years ago announced and has since followed, a policy of not claiming immunity for its public owned or operated merchant vessels. Keeping in mind the importance played by cases involving public vessels in the field of sovereign immunity, it is thus noteworthy that these ten countries (Brazil, Chile, Estonia, Germany, Hungary, Netherlands, Norway, Poland, Portugal, Sweden) and the United States have already relinquished by treaty or in practice an important part of the immunity which they claim under the classical theory.

It is thus evident that with the possible exception of the United Kingdom little support has been found except on the part of the Soviet Union and its satellites for continued full acceptance of the absolute theory of sovereign immunity. There are evidences that British authorities are aware of its deficiencies and ready for a change. The reasons which obviously motivate state trading countries in adhering to the theory with perhaps increasing rigidity are most persuasive that the United States should change its policy. Furthermore, the granting of sovereign immunity to foreign governments in the courts of the United States is most inconsistent with the action of the Government of the United States in subjecting itself to suit in these same courts in both contract and tort and with its long established policy of not claiming immunity in foreign jurisdictions for its merchant vessels. Finally, the Department feels that the widespread and increasing practice on the part of governments of engaging in commercial activities makes necessary a practice which will enable persons doing business with them to have their rights determined in the courts. For these reasons it will hereafter be the Department's policy to follow the restrictive theory of sovereign immunity in the consideration of requests of foreign governments for a grant of sovereign immunity.

It is realized that a shift in policy by the executive cannot control the courts but it is felt that the courts are less likely to allow a plea of sovereign immunity where the executive has declined to do so. There have been indications that at least some Justices of the Supreme Court feel that in this matter courts should follow the branch of the Government charged with responsibility for the conduct of foreign relations.

In order that your Department, which is charged with representing the interests of the Government before the courts, may be adequately informed it will be the Department's practice to advise you of all requests by foreign governments for the grant of immunity from suit and of the Department's action thereon.

Sincerely yours,

For the Secretary of State:
Jack B. Tate
Acting Legal Adviser

Notes and Questions

1. What might explain the worldwide shift toward the restrictive theory of immunity in the early to mid-twentieth century? Was the United States advantaged or disadvantaged by adhering to the absolute theory of immunity until 1952?

2. What seemed to be the principal reasons leading to the shift in the U.S. position to the restrictive theory? Was it just that most other countries adhered to that position? Or did it have practical implications, notably the exposure of the United States in foreign courts versus the exposure of other states in U.S. courts?

3. What states would have benefited most if the United States had continued its policy of absolute immunity? Those states with large private sectors or those states with state trading companies and socialist economies? Do you think it was relevant that the Cold War was at its height in 1952, with the Soviet Union having installed friendly governments in Eastern Europe and U.S. troops fighting in Korea?

For a few years after the Tate Letter, the State Department usually made decisions on sovereign immunity claims by a foreign state on the basis of the foreign government's submission. Criticism of this procedure, however, led the Department's Office of Legal Adviser to conduct quasi-judicial hearings on whether a particular claim of immunity was within the Tate Letter's criteria.

This regime, under which the State Department made some immunity determinations and the courts made others, did not always produce consistent decisions. A pair of Second Circuit cases, Victory Transport, Inc. v. Comisaria General de Abastecimientos y Transportes, 336 F.2d 354 (2d Cir. 1964), and Isbrandtsen Tankers v. President of India, 446 F.2d 1198 (2d Cir. 1971), illustrates this point. In *Victory Transport*, a ship owner sued a department of the Spanish government for damages sustained in connection with the department's charter of the ship to transport wheat to Spain. Because the State Department did not take a position in the case, the court made its own determination of whether immunity was warranted. After considering the purposes of the restrictive theory of immunity, international practice, and past State Department positions, the court concluded that the governmental actions in question were properly considered private and commercial and thus not entitled to immunity.

By contrast, in *Isbrandtsen Tankers*, the Second Circuit granted immunity in a similar situation. There, a ship owner sued the Indian government for damages associated with the government's detention of vessels being used to ship grain to India. The key difference from *Victory Transport* was that here the State Department submitted a suggestion of immunity. The court noted that, if it proceeded to make its own determination of immunity, "we might well find that the actions of the Indian government were, as appellant contends, purely private commercial decisions." Id. at 1200. Instead, it accepted the State Department's suggestion, stating that "once the State Department has ruled in a matter of this nature, the judiciary will not interfere." Id. at 1201.

Unhappiness with the process for deciding immunity under the Tate Letter and a desire for greater predictability led private lawyers, scholars, and the Department of State to push for legislation establishing more precise criteria. Some of the reasons are set out in the following testimony by the Legal Adviser.

Testimony of the Legal Adviser of the U.S. Department of State on the Foreign Sovereign Immunities Act of 1976

Hearings on H.R. 11315, 94th Cong., 2d Sess. 24, 26-27 (1976)

[Monroe Leigh:]

The Tate letter was based on a realization that the prior absolute rule of sovereign immunity was no longer consistent with modern international law.

The Tate letter, however, has not been a satisfactory answer. From a legal standpoint, it poses a devil's choice. If the Department follows the Tate letter in a given case, it is in the incongruous position of a political institution trying to apply a legal standard to litigation already before the courts.

On the other hand, if forced to disregard the Tate letter in a given case, the Department is in the self-defeating position of abandoning the very international law principle it elsewhere espouses.

From a diplomatic standpoint, the Tate letter has continued to leave the diplomatic initiative to the foreign state. The foreign state chooses which case it will bring to the State Department and in which case it will try to raise diplomatic considerations.

Leaving the diplomatic initiative in such cases to the foreign state places the United States at a disadvantage. This is particularly true since the United States cannot itself obtain similar advantages in other countries. In virtually every other country in the world, sovereign immunity is a question of international law decided exclusively by the courts and not by institutions concerned with foreign affairs.

For this reason, when we and other foreign states are sued abroad, we realize that international law principles will be applied by the courts and that diplomatic relations will not be called into play.

Moreover, from the standpoint of the private citizen, the current system generates considerable commercial uncertainty. A private party who deals with a foreign government entity cannot be certain of having his day in court to resolve an ordinary legal dispute. He cannot be entirely certain that the ordinary legal dispute will not be artificially raised to the level of a diplomatic problem through the government's intercession with the State Department.

The purpose of sovereign immunity in modern international law is not to protect the sensitivities of 19th-century monarchs or the prerogatives of the 20th-century state. Rather, it is to promote the functioning of all governments by protecting a state from the burden of defending law suits abroad which are based on its public acts.

However, when the foreign state enters the marketplace or when it acts as a private party, there is no justification in modern international law for allowing the foreign state to avoid the economic costs of the agreements which it may breach or the accidents which it may cause.

The law should not permit the foreign state to shift these everyday burdens of the marketplace onto the shoulders of private parties.

Notes and Questions

1. As indicated in the testimony excerpted above, the U.S. Legal Adviser supported the then-proposed Foreign Sovereign Immunities Act (FSIA). Since

his office usually had the day-to-day responsibility then for deciding whether to recommend to courts that a foreign state or its agencies be granted immunity, the Legal Adviser was effectively giving up considerable power. Does this suggest that the problems the Legal Adviser mentioned in his testimony had become truly vexing ones? Was it difficult to make a determination based on diplomatic as well as legal grounds without producing seemingly inconsistent results?

2. On the other hand, are there still reasons why the Executive Branch might prefer to make some individual sovereign immunity decisions? What might those be? As developed in the next section, Congress enacted the FSIA, in part, to address the problems associated with Executive Branch determinations of immunity. The FSIA has served as the legal framework for establishing subject matter jurisdiction over foreign sovereigns in U.S. courts since 1976. However, as also developed below, the recent Supreme Court decision in Republic of Austria v. Altmann, 541 U.S. 677 (2006), may have reintroduced a degree of federal court deference to Executive Branch statements of interest.

3. *The Foreign Sovereign Immunities Act: An Overview*

After over a decade of discussion, the Foreign Sovereign Immunities Act of 1976 was enacted. It went into effect in January 1977. The text, as amended, is in the Documentary Supplement.

As indicated in the House Report accompanying the bill that became the FSIA, the bill "would codify the so-called 'restrictive' principle of sovereign immunity, as presently recognized in international law." The Report also said that the bill would "transfer the determination of sovereign immunity from the executive branch to the judicial branch, thereby reducing the foreign policy implications of immunity determinations and assuring litigants that these often crucial decisions are made on purely legal grounds and under procedures that insure due process." The Report also indicated that the bill would provide the "sole and exclusive standards to be used in resolving questions of sovereign immunity raised by foreign states" before U.S. federal or state courts. H.R. Rep. No. 1487, 94th Cong., 2d Sess. 7, 12.

The FSIA is essentially a jurisdictional statute. Under it, issues of personal jurisdiction, subject matter jurisdiction, and immunity from suit are intertwined. If proper service is made on a foreign state defendant, personal jurisdiction exists with respect to any claim for which there is federal subject matter jurisdiction. Federal subject matter jurisdiction in turn exists "as to any claim for relief in personam with respect to which the foreign state is not entitled to immunity." 28 U.S.C. §1330(a).

Under the statute, "foreign states" are presumptively entitled to immunity. However, the FSIA also contains various exceptions to sovereign immunity. Under this structure, a court must determine whether the foreign state defendant is immune from suit in order to determine whether the court has personal and subject matter jurisdiction. If the court finds that the defendant is immune, the court lacks personal and subject matter jurisdiction. Conversely, if the court finds that there is an exception to immunity, and that proper service has been made, the court automatically has personal and subject matter jurisdiction (assuming no violation of due process requirements).

The FSIA also has a number of provisions dealing with procedural matters. These include service of process, enforcement of judgments, and other issues. The important ones will be discussed below.

A useful starting point for studying the FSIA is the U.S. Supreme Court's first consideration of the Act, where the Court provided a careful description of the statute. This case also suggests far-reaching implications for the possible jurisdiction of the U.S. federal courts. However, a full discussion of the issue of Article III federal question jurisdiction is outside the scope of this casebook. (Article III provides, in part, for jurisdiction of the U.S. courts in cases "arising under" federal law.) In reading this excerpt, you should not get bogged down in the question of the scope of Article III, but note rather the practical effect of the decision on who can sue a foreign sovereign in U.S. courts and on what grounds.

Verlinden B.V. v. Central Bank of Nigeria

U.S. Supreme Court
461 U.S. 480 (1983)

Chief Justice BURGER delivered the opinion for a unanimous Court. . . .

On April 21, 1975, the Federal Republic of Nigeria and petitioner Verlinden B.V., a Dutch corporation . . . , entered into a contract providing for the purchase of 240,000 metric tons of cement by Nigeria. The parties agreed that the contract would be governed by the laws of the Netherlands and that disputes would be resolved by arbitration before the International Chamber of Commerce, Paris, France.

The contract provided that the Nigerian Government was to establish an irrevocable, confirmed letter of credit for the total purchase price through Slavenburg's Bank in Amsterdam. According to [Verlinden's] amended complaint, however, respondent Central Bank of Nigeria, an instrumentality of Nigeria, improperly established an unconfirmed letter of credit payable through Morgan Guaranty Trust Co. in New York.[1] [See Note 1 following this case regarding letters of credit.]

In August 1975, Verlinden subcontracted with a Liechenstein corporation, Interbuco, to purchase the cement need to fulfill the contract. Meanwhile, the ports of Nigeria had become clogged with hundreds of ships carrying cement, sent by numerous other cement suppliers with whom Nigeria also had entered into contracts.[2] In mid-September, Central Bank unilaterally directed its correspondent banks, including Morgan Guaranty to adopt a series of amendments to all letters of credit issued in connection with the cement contracts. Central Bank also directly notified the suppliers that payment would be made only for those shipments approved by Central Bank two months before their arrival in Nigerian waters. [The parties did not seriously dispute that Central Bank's actions violated the applicable legal rules for letters of credit.]

Verlinden then sued Central Bank in the United States District Court . . . , alleging that Central Bank's actions constituted an anticipatory breach of the letter of credit. Verlinden alleged jurisdiction under the Foreign Sovereign Immunities

1. Morgan Guaranty acted solely as an advising bank; it undertook no independent responsibility for guaranteeing the letter of credit.

2. In 1975, Nigeria entered into 109 cement contracts with 68 suppliers. . . .

Act, 28 U.S.C. §1330. [Central Bank] moved to dismiss for, among other reasons, lack of subject-matter and personal jurisdiction. . . .

[The district court held that a foreign instrumentality is entitled to sovereign immunity unless one of the Act's exceptions applies.] After carefully considering each of the exceptions upon which petitioner relied, the District Court concluded that none applied, and accordingly dismissed the action.[5]

[The court of appeals affirmed, but on different grounds. The court held that Act exceeded the scope of Article III of the Constitution. The U.S. Supreme Court granted certiorari, and it reversed and remanded.]

For more than a century and a half, the United States generally granted foreign sovereigns complete immunity from suit in the courts of this country. . . .

As [The Schooner Exchange v. M'Faddon, 7 Cranch 116 (1812)] made clear, however, foreign sovereign immunity is a matter of grace and comity on the part of the United States, and not a restriction imposed by the Constitution. . . .

In 1976, Congress passed the Foreign Sovereign Immunities Act in order to free the Government from the case-by-case diplomatic pressures, to clarify the governing standards, and to "assur[e] litigants that . . . decisions are made on purely legal grounds and under procedures that insure due process," H.R. Rep. No. 94-1487, p.7 (1976). To accomplish these objectives, the Act contains a comprehensive set of legal standards governing claims of immunity in every civil action against a foreign state or its political subdivisions, agencies, or instrumentalities.

For the most part, the Act codifies, as a matter of federal law, the restrictive theory of sovereign immunity. A foreign state is normally immune from the jurisdiction of federal and state courts, 28 U.S.C. §1604, subject to a set of exceptions specified in §§1605 and 1607. Those exceptions include actions in which the foreign state has explicitly or impliedly waived its immunity, §1605(a)(l), and actions based upon commercial activities of the foreign sovereign carried on in the United States or causing a direct effect in the United States, §1605(a) (2).[11] When one of these or the other specified exceptions applies, "the foreign state shall be liable in the same manner and to the same extent as a private individual under like circumstances,"§1606.[12]

The Act expressly provides that its standards control in "the courts of the United States and of the States,"§1604, and thus clearly contemplates that such suits may be brought in either federal or state courts. However, "[i]n view of the potential sensitivity of actions against foreign states and the importance of

5. The District Court dismissed "for lack of personal jurisdiction." Under the Act, however, both statutory subject-matter jurisdiction (otherwise known as "competence") and personal jurisdiction turn on application of the substantive provisions of the Act. Under §1330(a), federal district courts are provided subject-matter jurisdiction if a foreign state is "not entitled to immunity either under sections 1605-1607 . . . or under any applicable international agreement"; §1330(b) provides personal jurisdiction wherever subject-matter jurisdiction exists under subsection (a) and service of process has been made under 28 U.S.C. §1608. Thus, if none of the exceptions to sovereign immunity set forth in the Act applies, the District Court lacks both statutory subject-matter jurisdiction and personal jurisdiction. The District Court's conclusion that none of the exceptions to the Act applied therefore signified an absence of both competence and personal jurisdiction.

11. The Act also contains exceptions for certain actions "in which rights in property taken in violation of international law are in issue,"§1605 (a) (3); actions involving rights in real estate and in inherited and gift property located in the United States, §1605(a)(4); actions for certain noncommercial torts within the United States, §1605(a)(5); certain actions involving maritime liens, $1605(b); and certain counterclaims, §1607.

12. Section 1606 somewhat modifies this standard of liability with respect to punitive damages and wrongful death actions.

developing a uniform body of law in this area," H.R. Rep. No. 94-1487, supra, at 32, the Act guarantees foreign states the right to remove any civil action from a state court to a federal court, §1441 (d). The Act also provides that any claim permitted under the Act may be brought from the outset in federal court, §1330(a).[13] If one of the specified exceptions to sovereign immunity applies, a federal district court may exercise subject-matter jurisdiction under §1330(a); but if the claim floes not fall within one of the exceptions, federal courts lack subject-matter jurisdiction.[14] In such a case, the foreign state is also ensured immunity from the jurisdiction of state courts by §1604.

III

The District Court and the Court of Appeals both held that the Foreign Sovereign Immunities Act purports to allow a foreign plaintiff to sue a foreign sovereign in the courts of the United States, provided the substantive requirements of the Act are satisfied. We agree.

On its face, the language of the statute is unambiguous. The statute grants jurisdiction over "any nonjury civil action against a foreign state . . . with respect to which the foreign state is not entitled to immunity," 28 U.S.C. §1330(a). The Act contains no indication of any limitation based on the citizenship of the plaintiff.

The legislative history is less clear in this regard. The House Report recites that the Act would provide jurisdiction for "any claim with respect to which the foreign state is not entitled to immunity under sections 1605-1607," H.R. Rep. No. 94-1487, supra, at 13 (emphasis added), and also states that its purpose was "to provide when and how parties can maintain a lawsuit against a foreign state or its entities," id., at 6 (emphasis added). At another point, however, the Report refers to the growing number of disputes between "American citizens" and foreign states, id., at 6-7, and expresses the desire to ensure "our citizens . . . access to the courts," id., at 6 (emphasis added).

Notwithstanding this reference to "our citizens," we conclude that, when considered as a whole, the legislative history reveals an intent not to limit jurisdiction under the Act to actions brought by American citizens. Congress was aware of concern that "our courts [might be] turned into small 'international courts of claims[,]' . . . open . . . to all comers to litigate any dispute which any private party may have with a foreign state anywhere in the world." Testimony of Bruno A. Ristau, Hearings on H.R. 11315, at 31. As the language of the statute reveals, Congress protected against this danger not by restricting the class of potential plaintiffs, but rather by enacting substantive provisions requiring some form of substantial contact with the United States. See 28 U.S.C. §1605.[15] If an action

13. "[To] encourage the bringing of actions against foreign states in Federal courts," H. R. Rep. No. 94-1487, p. 13 (1976), the Act specifies that federal district courts shall have original jurisdiction "without regard to amount in controversy." §1330(a).

14. In such a situation, the federal court will also lack personal jurisdiction.

15. Section 1605(a) (1), which provides that sovereign immunity shall not apply if waived, may be seen as an exception to the normal pattern of the Act, which generally requires some form of contact with the United States. We need not decide whether, by waiving its immunity, a foreign state could consent to suit based on activities wholly unrelated to the United States. The Act does not appear to affect the traditional doctrine of *forum non conveniens.*

satisfies the substantive standards of the Act, it may be brought in federal court regardless of the citizenship of the plaintiff. . . .[16]

IV

We now turn to the core question presented by this case: whether Congress exceeded the scope of Art. III of the Constitution by granting federal courts subject matter jurisdiction over certain civil actions by foreign plaintiffs against foreign sovereigns where the rule of decision may be provided by state law.

This Court's cases firmly establish that Congress may not expand the jurisdiction of the federal courts beyond the bounds established by the Constitution. Within Art. III of the Constitution, we find two sources authorizing the grant of jurisdiction in the Foreign Sovereign Immunities Act: the Diversity Clause and the "Arising Under" Clause. The Diversity Clause, which provides that the judicial power extends to controversies between "a State, or the Citizens thereof, and foreign States," covers actions by citizens of States. Yet diversity jurisdiction is not sufficiently broad to support a grant of jurisdiction over actions by foreign plaintiffs, since a foreign plaintiff is not "a State, or [a][Citizen] thereof." . . . We conclude, however, that the "Arising Under" Clause of Art. III provides an appropriate basis for the statutory grant of subject-matter jurisdiction to actions by foreign plaintiffs under the Act. . . .

. . . [A] suit against a foreign state under this Act necessarily raises questions of substantive federal law at the very outset, and hence clearly "arises under" federal law, as that term is used in Art. III.

By reason of its authority over foreign commerce and foreign relations, Congress has the undisputed power to decide, as a matter of federal law, whether and under what circumstances foreign nations should be amenable to suit in the United States. Actions against foreign sovereigns in our courts raise sensitive issues concerning the foreign relations of the United States, and the primacy of federal concerns is evident. See, e.g., Banco Nacional de Cuba v. Sabbatino, 376 U.S. 398, 423-425 (1964). . . .

To promote these federal interests, Congress exercised its Art. I powers[19] by enacting a statute comprehensively regulating the amenability of foreign nations to suit in the United States. The statute must be applied by the district courts in every action against a foreign sovereign, since subject-matter jurisdiction in any such action depends on the existence of one of the specified exceptions to foreign sovereign immunity, 28 U.S.C. §1330(a).[20] At the threshold of every action in a district court against a foreign state, therefore, the court must satisfy itself that

16. Prior to passage of the [FSIA], which Congress clearly intended to govern all actions against foreign sovereigns, state courts on occasion had exercised jurisdiction over suits between foreign plaintiffs and foreign sovereigns. . . . Congress did not prohibit such actions when it enacted the Foreign Sovereign Immunities Act, but sought to ensure that any action that might be brought against a foreign sovereign in state court could also be brought in or removed to federal court.

19. In enacting the legislation, Congress relied specifically on its powers to prescribe the jurisdiction of federal courts, Art. I, §8, cl. 9; to define offenses against the "Law of Nations," Art. I, §8, cl. 10; to regulate commerce with foreign nations, Art. I, §8, cl. 3; and to make all laws necessary and proper to execute the Government's powers, Art. I, §8, cl. 18.

20. The House Report on the Act states that "sovereign immunity is an affirmative defense which must be specially pleaded," H.R; Rep. No. 94-1487, p.17 (1976). Under the Act, however, subject-matter jurisdiction turns on the existence of an exception to foreign sovereign immunity, 28 U.S.C. §1330(a). Accordingly, even if the foreign state does not enter an appearance to assert an immunity defense, a district court still must determine that immunity is unavailable under the Act.

one of the exceptions applies — and in doing so it must apply the detailed federal law standards set forth in the Act. Accordingly, an action against a foreign sovereign arises under federal law, for purposes of Art. III jurisdiction. . . .

[I]n enacting the Foreign Sovereign Immunities Act, Congress expressly exercised its power to regulate foreign commerce, along with other specified Art. I powers. See n.19, supra. As the House Report clearly indicates, the primary purpose of the Act was to "se[t] forth comprehensive rules governing sovereign immunity," H.R. Rep. No. 94-1487, p.12 (1976); the jurisdictional provisions of the Act are simply one part of this comprehensive scheme. The Act thus does not merely concern access to the federal courts. Rather, it governs the types of actions for which foreign sovereigns may be held liable in a court in the United States, federal or state. The Act codifies the standards governing foreign sovereign immunity as an aspect of substantive federal law, . . . and applying those standards will generally require interpretation of numerous points of federal law. Finally, if a court determines that none of the exceptions to sovereign immunity applies, the plaintiff will be barred from raising his claim in any court in the United States — manifestly, "the title or right set up by the party, may be defeated by one construction of the . . . laws of the United States, and sustained by the opposite construction." . . . That the inquiry into foreign sovereign immunity is labeled under the Act as a matter of jurisdiction does not affect the constitutionality of Congress' action in granting federal courts jurisdiction over cases calling for application of this comprehensive regulatory statute.

Congress, pursuant to its unquestioned Art. I powers, has enacted a broad statutory framework governing assertions of foreign sovereign immunity. In so doing, Congress deliberately sought to channel cases against foreign sovereigns away from the state courts and into federal courts, thereby reducing the potential for a multiplicity of conflicting results among the courts of the 50 States. The resulting jurisdictional grant is within the bounds of Art. III, since every action against a foreign sovereign necessarily involves application of a body of substantive federal law, and accordingly "arises under" federal law, within the meaning of Art. III.

V

A conclusion that the grant of jurisdiction in the Foreign Sovereign Immunities Act is consistent with the Constitution does not end the case. An action must not only satisfy Art. III but must also be supported by a statutory grant of subject-matter jurisdiction. As we have made clear, deciding whether statutory subject-matter jurisdiction exists under the Foreign Sovereign Immunities Act entails an application of the substantive terms of the Act to determine whether one of the specified exceptions to immunity applies.

In the present case, the District Court, after satisfying itself as to the constitutionality of the Act, held that the present action does not fall within any specified exception. The Court of Appeals, reaching a contrary conclusion as to jurisdiction under the Constitution, did not find it necessary to address this statutory question.[23]

23. In several related cases involving contracts between Nigeria and other cement suppliers, the Court of Appeals held that statutory subject-matter jurisdiction existed under the Act. In those cases, the court held that Nigeria's acts were commercial in nature and "cause [d] a direct effect in the United States," within the meaning of 28 U.S.C. §1605(a). Texas Trading & Milling Corp. v. Federal Republic of Nigeria, 647 F.2d, at 310-313. Each of those actions involved a contract with an American supplier

Accordingly, on remand the Court of Appeals must consider whether jurisdiction exists under the Act itself. If the Court of Appeals agrees with the District Court on that issue, the case will be at an end. If, on the other hand, the Court of Appeals concludes that jurisdiction does exist under the statute, the action may then be remanded to the District Court for further proceedings.

It is so ordered.

Notes and Questions

1. The facts in *Verlinden* indicate the contract provided for the use of a letter of credit. A short explanation might be useful:

> The letter of credit is a bank's commitment that it will, under certain circumstances, make a payment to the latter's beneficiary, typically the seller or its bank. " In the trade transaction, the stated condition of payment is that the bank will pay when it sights specified documents, including those evidencing title such as the bill of lading. . . .
>
> . . . The letter of credit is governed by a combination of domestic law, particularly the Uniform Commercial Code in the United States, and of international principles stated in the Uniform Customs and Practice for Documentary Credit. . . . [J. Barton & Fisher, International Trade and Investment 44 (1986).]

A letter of credit may be "revocable" or "irrevocable." These terms refer to the issuing bank's power to cancel or modify the letter of credit. Often the credit is irrevocable for a designated period of time. A letter of credit may also be "confirmed" or "unconfirmed." These terms refer to the absence or presence of a second bank's obligation in addition to that of the issuing bank. A confirmed letter of credit means that the second bank adds its guarantee to that of the issuing bank. An unconfirmed irrevocable credit is one which the issuing bank has undertaken not to revoke, but under which the second (or correspondent) bank has no direct liability to the exporter. See Harold J. Berman and Colin Kaufman, The Law of International Commercial Transactions (Lex Mercatoria), 19 Harv. Int'l L.J. 221 (1978).

In *Verlinden*, how responsible was the U.S. bank, Morgan Guaranty Trust Company, to use its funds to pay the letter of credit? See footnote 1 in the excerpt above.

2. The *Verlinden* case was remanded to determine if it fell within any of the FSIA's specified exceptions to immunity, which would mean that U.S. courts had jurisdiction. Given the facts as stated, what should be the result below? What connections did the case have to the United States? (See the discussion above in the preceding Note and footnotes 1 and 23 in the excerpt.) You might wait to answer this question until you have studied the commercial activity exception, discussed below. As it turned out, *Verlinden* was settled before any further decisions in the lower courts. Nigeria apparently paid Verlinden an undisclosed sum of money.

3. Should foreigners be allowed to sue foreign states in U.S. courts? In what cases? What are the benefits? The dangers? (In thinking about this question, recall the Alien Tort Statute litigation discussed in Chapter 3 and Chapter 8.B.)

---

operating within the United States, however. In the present case, the District Court found that exception inapplicable, concluding that the repudiation of the letter of credit "caused no direct, substantial, injurious effect in the United States." 488 F. Supp., at 1299-1300.

4. What safeguards exist to protect U.S. courts from being opened up to claims that have no connection to the United States? What safeguards exist under the FSIA? What safeguards exist otherwise? The Court noted in footnote 15 that the Act "does not appear to affect the traditional doctrine of *forum non conveniens.*" (See the discussion in Chapter 7.B of doctrines—such as forum non conveniens, comity, and exhaustion of local remedies—that might limit a U.S. court from adjudicating a case.)

5. In December 2004, the U.N. General Assembly adopted the U.N. Convention on Jurisdictional Immunities of States and Their Property. As discussed below at the end of [subsection 13], the Convention is both similar to and different from the FSIA. As of January 2011, only 11 of the 30 countries necessary for the Convention to come into force had ratified it. The United States has not yet signed the Convention, much less ratified it, and U.S. ratification is reportedly not imminent.

6. Regarding the Article III question in *Verlinden*: Beyond its importance in upholding the constitutional validity of the FSIA, *Verlinden* provides a "reaffirmation of the breadth of Congress' power to grant federal jurisdiction over cases requiring the application of any federal law that does more than govern access to the courts." Note, The Supreme Court, 1982 Term, 97 Harv. L. Rev. 70, 215 (1983). Because the *Verlinden* Court construed the FSIA to include claims brought by foreign plaintiffs, the statute failed to meet Article III's requirements for diversity jurisdiction. "Arising under" jurisdiction is, therefore, the basis for permitting access to the courts under the FSIA. However, purely jurisdictional statutes cannot serve as the basis for establishing "arising under" jurisdiction. See, e.g., Mesa v. California, 489 U.S. 121, 136 (1989) ("[P]ure jurisdictional statutes which seek to do nothing more than grant jurisdiction over a particular class of cases cannot support Art. III 'arising under' jurisdiction."). What aspects of the FSIA did the Court identify as substantive in nature? Keep this question in mind when reading the Court's decision in Republic of Austria v. Altman, 541 U.S. 677 (2004), excerpted later in this section.

The U.S. Supreme Court later considered the relationship between the FSIA and the Alien Tort Statute, as well as other jurisdictional statutes, in its 1989 decision in Argentine Republic v. Amerada Hess Shipping Corp., 488 U.S. 428 (1989). That case arose from an Argentine military aircraft bombing an oil tanker in international waters during the 1982 war between Great Britain and Argentina over the Falklands Islands (or the Islas Malvinias to the Argentineans). The tanker, which was traveling between the U.S. Virgin Islands and Alaska, had to be scuttled in the South Atlantic.

Two Liberian corporations—the owner of the tanker and the entity that chartered it—sued the Argentine Republic in a U.S. district court, pursuant to the Alien Tort Statute (ATS), to recover damages for a tort allegedly committed by its armed forces on the high seas in violation of international law. (The ATS is discussed in Chapter 3.) The Supreme Court upheld the dismissal of the suit. Writing for himself and six other Justice, Chief Justice Rehnquist decided:

> We think that the text and structure of the FSIA demonstrate Congress' intention that the FSIA be the sole basis for obtaining jurisdiction over a foreign state in our courts. Section 1604 and §1330(a) work in tandem: §1604 bars federal and state courts from

exercising jurisdiction when a foreign state is entitled to immunity, and §1330(a) confers jurisdiction on district courts to hear suits brought by United States citizens and by aliens when a foreign state is not entitled to immunity. As we said in *Verlinden*, the FSIA "must be applied by the district courts in every action against a foreign sovereign, since subject-matter jurisdiction in any such action depends on the existence of one of the specified exceptions to foreign sovereign immunity." . . .[3]

. . . Congress had violations of international law by foreign states in mind when it enacted the FSIA. For example, the FSIA specifically denies foreign states immunity in suits "in which rights in property taken in violation of international law are in issue." 28 U.S.C. §1605 (a) (3). Congress also rested the FSIA in part on its power under Art. I, §8, cl. 10, of the Constitution "[t]o define and punish Piracies and Felonies committed on the high Seas, and Offenses against the Law of Nations." From Congress' decision to deny immunity to foreign states in the class of cases just mentioned, we draw the plain implication that immunity is granted in those cases involving alleged violations of international law that do not come within one of the FSIA's exceptions. . . .

Having determined that the FSIA provides the sole basis for obtaining jurisdiction over a foreign state in federal court, we turn to whether any of the exceptions enumerated in the Act apply here. . . . We agree with the District Court that none of the FSIA's exceptions applies on these facts. . . .

We hold that the FSIA provides the sole basis for obtaining jurisdiction over a foreign state in the courts of this country, and that none of the enumerated exceptions to the Act applies to the facts of this case.

Questions

1. Do you agree with the U.S. Supreme Court? Is its opinion consistent with the comprehensive scheme that Congress had created in the FSIA?

2. If the case had been remanded (as Justices Blackmun and Marshall urged in a concurring opinion), is it likely that the plaintiffs would have been able to establish that one of the FSIA's exceptions applied? If so, which one? (These exceptions will be discussed in more detail in the rest of this section.)

3. Did the plaintiffs in *Amerada Hess* meet the requirements for jurisdiction under the Alien Tort Statute? If so, why did the Court nevertheless order dismissal of their suit? What is left of Alien Tort Statute litigation after this decision? Can a foreign citizen still maintain an action against a private citizen for a tort that violates the law of nations? Against a present or former foreign officials? (See the discussion in Chapter 3.C and 8.B about the ATS and human rights cases.) The excerpt in the next section from 'the Supreme Court's decision in Samantar v. Yousuf, 1308 S. Ct. 2278 (2010), may help answer the questions about foreign officials—present and past.

3. . . . Our conclusion here is supported by the FSIA's legislative history. See, e.g., H.R. Rep. No. 94-1487, p.12 (1976) (H.R. Rep.); S, Rep, No. 94-1310, pp.11-12 (1976) (S. Rep.), U.S. Code Cong. & Admin. News 1976, pp. 6604, 6610 (FSIA "sets forth the sole and, exclusive standards to be used in resolving questions of sovereign immunity raised by sovereign states before Federal and State courts in the United States," and "prescribes . . . the jurisdiction of U.S. district courts in cases involving foreign states").

4. Entities Covered by the FSIA

The FSIA covers suits against three types of entities: foreign states proper, their political subdivisions, and their agencies and instrumentalities. See 28 U.S.C. §1603(a). While all of these entities qualify as "foreign states" for purposes of FSIA immunity, the statute treats foreign states proper and their political subdivisions differently than it treats agencies and instrumentalities for purposes of service of process, venue, the scope of the Section 1605(a)(3) exception, punitive damages, and execution of judgments. With respect to each of these issues, foreign states proper and their political subdivisions receive more protection than do their agencies and instrumentalities.

It is thus sometimes important to distinguish between political subdivisions and agencies and instrumentalities. In making this distinction, courts generally apply a "core functions" test or a "legal characteristics" test. The core functions test looks at whether the functions of the entity are governmental or commercial. See, e.g., Garb v. Republic of Poland, 440 F.3d 579, 591-594 (2d Cir. 2006); Magness v. Russian Fed'n, 247 F.3d 609, 613 n.7 (5th Cir. 2001). Thus, an entity whose core functions are predominantly governmental is treated as the foreign state itself, while an entity the structure and core function of which are commercial qualifies as an agency or instrumentality and receives different treatment under the FSIA from a political subdivision of a government.

Under the legal characteristics test, courts balance three facets of legal status that are enumerated in the statute's legislative history. Specifically, courts look at whether the entity can sue and be sued in its own name, contract in its own name, or hold property in its own name. See, e.g., Hyatt Corp. v. Stanton, 945 F. Supp. 675, 681 (S.D.N.Y. 1996).

To qualify as an agency or instrumentality of a foreign state, an entity must, among other things, be "a separate legal person, corporate or otherwise," and be "an organ of a foreign state or a political subdivision thereof," or have a majority of its shares or other ownership interests "owned by a foreign state or political subdivision thereof." 28 U.S.C. §1603(b). Thus, corporations that are majority owned by a foreign state qualify as agencies or instrumentalities.

What if a corporation is not directly majority owned by a foreign state but instead is majority owned by another corporation that, in turn, is directly majority owned by a foreign state? In Dole Food Co. v. Patrickson, 538 U.S. 468 (2003), the U.S. Supreme Court held that a foreign state must itself own a majority of a corporation's shares if the corporation is to be deemed an instrumentality of the state under the FSIA. Among other things, the Court (in a decision authored by Justice Kennedy) reasoned that Congress had corporate formalities in mind when it drafted the definition of instrumentalities, and that "[a] basic tenet of American corporate law is that the corporation and its shareholders are distinct entities." Justices Breyer and O'Connor dissented on that issue, arguing that the FSIA was designed to offer legal protection to a foreign state "not only when it acts directly in its own name but also when it acts through separate legal entities," and that the majority's decision was inconsistent with this purpose.

To what extent are the actions of an agency or instrumentality attributable to the foreign state or vice versa? The Supreme Court addressed this attribution question in First National City Bank v. Banco Para El Comercio Exterior de

Cuba, 462 U.S. 611 (1983), also known as the "*Bancec*" case. In that case, the Cuban government had expropriated Citibank's assets in Cuba. Subsequently, Bancec, a Cuban government-owned bank, sued Citibank in a U.S. court to collect on a letter of credit. Citibank filed a counterclaim, seeking a setoff for the value of its expropriated assets. The issue was whether the Cuban government's expropriation could be attributed to Bancec for purposes of the setoff. The Court first concluded that the FSIA does not itself address this question. The Court also declined to apply state law, concluding that a uniform federal standard was desirable. Instead, the court looked to internationally recognized principles of corporate law and equity as "informed both by international law principles and by articulated congressional policies." Id. at 623.

Applying these principles, the Court in *Bancec* adopted a presumption that government instrumentalities that are established as separate entities should be treated as such, something the Court said was supported by "[d]ue respect for the actions taken by foreign sovereigns and for principles of comity between nations." Id. at 626. The Court further held that this presumption could be overcome in two situations: first, "where a corporate entity is so extensively controlled by its owner that a relationship of principal and agent is created"; and, second, where treating the entity as separate from the foreign state "would work fraud or injustice." Id. at 629. Under the facts of that case, the Court held that the presumption was overcome because Bancec had been dissolved early in the litigation and its capital divided between Cuba's central bank and other government enterprises, such that "the Cuban Government and [Cuba's central bank], not any third parties that may have relied on Bancec's juridical identity, would be the only beneficiaries of any recovery [under the letter of credit]." Id. at 631.

The presumption of separateness adopted in *Bancec* has barred recovery in a number of FSIA cases. For example, in the *Letelier* case, discussed below in subsection [8], where the U.S. district court had found the Republic of Chile liable for political assassination in Washington, D.C., the plaintiffs were not able to execute successfully against the assets of the Chilean government-owned airline because the airline was found to be a separate entity. See Letelier v. Republic of Chile, 748 F.2d 790 (2d Cir. 1984).

Immunity of foreign officials. The FSIA does not expressly address the immunity of individual foreign officials. Rather, it covers suits against "foreign states." A growing split developed in the circuit courts in the late 1990s to 2010 over whether "foreign states" included foreign officials. Concerns over plaintiffs' circumventing the limitations of the FSIA by suing the foreign state's officials rather than the foreign state itself, as well as the foreign relations implications of suits against high-level foreign officials, led some courts to hold that the FSIA extends to suits against foreign officials acting within their official capacity. These courts also held, however, that the FSIA does not apply when the official is acting outside the scope of his or her authority. See, e.g., Velasco v. Government of Indonesia, 370 F.3d 392 (4th Cir. 2004); Jungquist v. Nahyan, 115 F.3d 1020 (D.C. Cir. 1997); Chuidian v. Philippine National Bank, 115 F.3d 1020 (9th Cir. 1997). By contrast other courts rejected the FSIA's application to foreign officials. See, e.g., Enahoro v. Abubakar, 408 F.3d 877 (7th Cir. 2005). The Supreme Court addressed the applicability of the FSIA to foreign officials in 2010 in the case below.

Mohamed Ali Samantar v. Bashe Abdi Yousuf et al.

U.S. Supreme Court
130 S. Ct. 2278 (2010)

Justice STEVENS delivered the opinion of the Court.

From 1980 to 1986 petitioner Mohamed Ali Samantar was the First Vice President and Minister of Defense of Somalia, and from 1987 to 1990 he served as its Prime Minister. Respondents are natives of Somalia who allege that they, or members of their families, were the victims of torture and extrajudicial killings during those years. They seek damages from petitioner based on his alleged authorization of those acts. The narrow question we must decide is whether the Foreign Sovereign Immunities Act of 1976 (FSIA or Act), 28 U.S.C. §§1330, 1602 *et seq.*, provides petitioner with immunity from suit based on actions taken in his official capacity. We hold that the FSIA does not govern the determination of petitioner's immunity from suit.

I

Respondents are members of the Isaaq clan, which included well-educated and prosperous Somalis who were subjected to systematic persecution during the 1980's by the military regime then governing Somalia. They allege that petitioner exercised command and control over members of the Somali military forces who tortured, killed, or arbitrarily detained them or members of their families; that petitioner knew or should have known of the abuses perpetrated by his subordinates; and that he aided and abetted the commission of these abuses. Respondents' complaint sought damages from petitioner pursuant to the Torture Victim Protection Act of 1991, 28 U.S.C. §1350, and the Alien Tort Statute, 28 U.S. C. §1350. Petitioner, who was in charge of Somalia's armed forces before its military regime collapsed, fled Somalia in 1991 and is now a resident of Virginia. The United States has not recognized any entity as the government of Somalia since the fall of the military regime.

Respondents filed their complaint in November 2004. . . . The District Court stayed the proceedings to give the State Department an opportunity to provide a statement of interest regarding petitioner's claim of sovereign immunity. . . . In 2007, having received no response from the State Department, the District Court reinstated the case [and] . . . concluded that it did not have subject-matter jurisdiction and granted petitioner's motion to dismiss.

The District Court's decision rested squarely on the FSIA. . . . Although characterizing the statute as silent on its applicability to the officials of a foreign state, the District Court followed appellate decisions holding that a foreign state's sovereign immunity under the Act extends to " 'an individual acting in his official capacity on behalf of a foreign state,' " but not to " 'an official who acts beyond the scope of his authority.' " The court rejected respondents' argument that petitioner was necessarily acting beyond the scope of his authority because he allegedly violated international law.

The Court of Appeals reversed. . . . [It] concluded, "based on the language and structure of the statute, that the FSIA does not apply to individual foreign government agents like [petitioner]." Having found that the FSIA does not govern whether petitioner enjoys immunity from suit, the Court of Appeals remanded the case for further proceedings, including a determination of whether petitioner is entitled to immunity under the common law. We granted certiorari.

II

The doctrine of foreign sovereign immunity developed as a matter of common law long before the FSIA was enacted in 1976. . . .

Following *Schooner Exchange*, a two-step procedure developed for resolving a foreign state's claim of sovereign immunity. . . . Under that procedure, the diplomatic representative of the sovereign could request a "suggestion of immunity" from the State Department. *Ex parte Peru*, 318 U.S., at 581. If the request was granted, the district court surrendered its jurisdiction. But "in the absence of recognition of the immunity by the Department of State," a district court "had authority to decide for itself whether all the requisites for such immunity existed." In making that decision, a district court inquired "whether the ground of immunity is one which it is the established policy of the [State Department] to recognize." *Hoffman*, 324 U.S., at 36. Although cases involving individual foreign officials as defendants were rare, the same two-step procedure was typically followed when a foreign official asserted immunity. See, *e.g.*, *Heaney*, 445 F.2d, at 504-505.[6] . . .

Congress responded to the inconsistent application of sovereign immunity by enacting the FSIA in 1976. Section 1602 describes the Act's two primary purposes: (1) to endorse and codify the restrictive theory of sovereign immunity, and (2) to transfer primary responsibility for deciding "claims of foreign states to immunity" from the State Department to the courts. After the enactment of the FSIA, the Act—and not the pre-existing common law—indisputably governs the determination of whether a foreign state is entitled to sovereign immunity.

What we must now decide is whether the Act also covers the immunity claims of foreign officials. We begin with the statute's text and then consider petitioner's reliance on its history and purpose.

III

The FSIA provides that "a foreign state shall be immune from the jurisdiction of the courts of the United States and of the States" except as provided in the Act. §1604. Thus, if a defendant is a "foreign state" within the meaning of the Act, then the defendant is immune from jurisdiction unless one of the exceptions in the Act applies. See §§1605-1607 (enumerating exceptions). The Act, if it applies, is the "sole basis for obtaining jurisdiction over a foreign state in federal court." *Argentine Republic* v. *Amerada Hess Shipping Corp.*, 488 U.S. 428, 439 (1989). The question we face in this case is whether an individual sued for conduct undertaken in his official capacity is a "foreign state" within the meaning of the Act.

6. Diplomatic and consular officers could also claim the "specialized immunities" accorded those officials, Restatement (Second) of Foreign Relations Law of the United States §66, Comment *b* (1964-1965) (hereinafter Restatement), and officials qualifying as the "head of state" could claim immunity on that basis.

The Act defines "foreign state" in §1603 as follows:

"(a) A 'foreign state' . . . includes a political subdivision of a foreign state or an agency or instrumentality of a foreign state as defined in subsection (b).

"(b) An 'agency or instrumentality of a foreign state' means any entity—

"(1) which is a separate legal person, corporate or otherwise, and

"(2) which is an organ of a foreign state or political subdivision thereof, or a majority of whose shares or other ownership interest is owned by a foreign state or political subdivision thereof, and

"(3) which is neither a citizen of a State of the United States as defined in section 1332(c) and (e) of this title, nor created under the laws of any third country."

The term "foreign state" on its face indicates a body politic that governs a particular territory. . . . In §1603(a), however, the Act establishes that "foreign state" has a broader meaning, by mandating the inclusion of the state's political subdivisions, agencies, and instrumentalities. Then, in §1603(b), the Act specifically delimits what counts as an agency or instrumentality. . . .

We turn first to the term "agency or instrumentality of a foreign state," §1603(b). It is true that an individual official could be an "agency or instrumentality," if that term is given the meaning of "any thing or person through which action is accomplished," *In re Terrorist Attacks on Sept. 11, 2001*, 538 F. 3d 71, 83 (CA2 2008). But Congress has specifically defined "agency or instrumentality" in the FSIA, and all of the textual clues in that definition cut against such a broad construction.

First, the statute specifies that "'agency or instrumentality . . . ' means any *entity*" matching three specified characteristics, §1603(b) (emphasis added), and "entity" typically refers to an organization, rather than an individual. See, *e.g.*, Black's Law Dictionary 612 (9th ed. 2009). Furthermore, several of the required characteristics apply awkwardly, if at all, to individuals. The phrase "separate legal person, corporate or otherwise," §1603(b)(1), could conceivably refer to a natural person, solely by virtue of the word "person." But the phrase "separate legal person" typically refers to the legal fiction that allows an entity to hold personhood separate from the natural persons who are its shareholders or officers. It is similarly awkward to refer to a person as an "organ" of the foreign state. See §1603(b)(2). And the third part of the definition could not be applied at all to a natural person. A natural person cannot be a citizen of a State "as defined in section 1332(c) and (e)," §1603(b)(3), because those subsections refer to the citizenship of corporations and estates. Nor can a natural person be "created under the laws of any third country." Thus, the terms Congress chose simply do not evidence the intent to include individual officials within the meaning of "agency or instrumentality."[9]

. . . It is true that use of the word "include" [as used in the definition of "foreign state" in §1603(a)] can signal that the list that follows is meant to be illustrative rather than exhaustive. . . . But even if the list in §1603(a) is merely illustrative, it still suggests that "foreign state" does not encompass officials, because the types of defendants listed are all entities.

9. Nor does anything in the legislative history suggest that Congress intended the term "agency or instrumentality" to include individuals. On the contrary, the legislative history, like the statute, speaks in terms of entities.

Moreover, elsewhere in the FSIA Congress expressly mentioned officials when it wished to count their acts as equivalent to those of the foreign state, which suggests that officials are not included within the unadorned term "foreign state." For example, Congress provided an exception from the general grant of immunity for cases in which "money damages are sought against a foreign state" for an injury in the United States "caused by the tortious act or omission *of that foreign state or of any official* or employee of that foreign state while acting within the scope of his office." §1605(a)(5) (emphasis added).... If the term "foreign state" by definition includes an individual acting within the scope of his office, the phrase "or of any official or employee ..." in 28 U.S. C. §1605(a)(5) would be unnecessary....

In sum, "[w]e do not ... construe statutory phrases in isolation; we read statutes as a whole." *United States* v. *Morton*, 467 U.S. 822, 828 (1984). Reading the FSIA as a whole, there is nothing to suggest we should read "foreign state" in §1603(a) to include an official acting on behalf of the foreign state, and much to indicate that this meaning was not what Congress enacted.[12] The text does not expressly foreclose petitioner's reading, but it supports the view of respondents and the United States that the Act does not address an official's claim to immunity.

IV

As discussed at the outset, one of the primary purposes of the FSIA was to codify the restrictive theory of sovereign immunity, which Congress recognized as consistent with extant international law. See §1602. We have observed that a related purpose was "codification of international law at the time of the FSIA's enactment," *Permanent Mission of India to United Nations* v. *City of New York*, 551 U.S. 193, 199 (2007), and have examined the relevant common law and international practice when interpreting the Act....

[T]he relationship between a state's immunity and an official's immunity is ... complicated, ... although we need not and do not resolve the dispute among the parties as to the precise scope of an official's immunity at common law.... *Permanent Mission*, 551 U.S., at 200, states that the immunity of individual officials is subject to a caveat not applicable to any of the other entities or persons[15] to which the foreign state's immunity extends. The Restatement provides that the "immunity of a foreign state ... extends to ... any other public minister, official, or agent of the state with respect to acts performed in his official capacity *if the effect of exercising jurisdiction would be to enforce a rule of law against the state.*" Restatement §66

12. Nor is it the case that the FSIA's "legislative history does not even hint of an intent to exclude individual officials," *Chuidian*, 912 F. 2d, at 1101. The legislative history makes clear that Congress did not intend the FSIA to address position-based individual immunities such as diplomatic and consular immunity. H. R. Rep., at 12 ("The bill is not intended ... to affect either diplomatic or consular immunity"). It also suggests that general "official immunity" is something separate from the subject of the bill. See *id.*, at 23 ("The bill does not attempt to deal with questions of discovery.... [I]f a plaintiff sought to depose a diplomat in the United States or a high-ranking official of a foreign government, diplomatic and official immunity would apply").

15. The Restatement does not apply this caveat to the head of state, head of government, or foreign minister. See Restatement §66. Whether petitioner may be entitled to head of state immunity, or any other immunity, under the common law is a question we leave open for remand. See 552 F. 3d 371, 383 (CA4 2009). We express no view on whether Restatement §66 correctly sets out the scope of the common law immunity applicable to current or former foreign officials.

(emphasis added).[16] And historically, the Government sometimes suggested immunity under the common law for individual officials even when the foreign state did not qualify. There is therefore little reason to presume that when Congress set out to codify state immunity, it must also have, *sub silentio*, intended to codify official immunity.

We have recognized, in the context of the act of state doctrine, that an official's acts can be considered the acts of the foreign state, and that "the courts of one country will not sit in judgment" of those acts when done within the territory of the foreign state. See *Underhill* v. *Hernandez*, 168 U.S. 250, 252, 254 (1897).* Although the act of state doctrine is distinct from immunity, and instead "provides foreign states with a substantive defense on the merits," *Altmann*, 541 U.S., at 700, we do not doubt that in some circumstances the immunity of the foreign state extends to an individual for acts taken in his official capacity. But it does not follow from this premise that Congress intended to codify that immunity in the FSIA. . . .

Petitioner would have a stronger case if there were any indication that Congress' intent to enact a comprehensive solution for suits against states extended to suits against individual officials. But to the extent Congress contemplated the Act's effect upon officials at all, the evidence points in the opposite direction. As we have already mentioned, the legislative history points toward an intent to leave official immunity outside the scope of the Act. See n. 12, supra. And although questions of official immunity did arise in the pre-FSIA period, they were few and far between.[18] The immunity of officials simply was not the particular problem to which Congress was responding when it enacted the FSIA. The FSIA was adopted, rather, to address "a modern world where foreign state enterprises are every day participants in commercial activities," and to assure litigants that decisions regarding claims against states and their enterprises "are made on purely legal grounds." H. R. Rep., at 7. We have been given no reason to believe that Congress saw as a problem, or wanted to eliminate, the State Department's role in determinations regarding individual official immunity.[19]

Finally, our reading of the FSIA will not "in effect make the statute optional," as some Courts of Appeals have feared, by allowing litigants through "artful pleading . . . to take advantage of the Act's provisions or, alternatively, choose to proceed under the old common law." Even if a suit is not governed by the Act, it may

16. Respondents contend that this caveat refers to "the compulsive effect of the judgment on the state," Brief for Respondents 42, but petitioner disputes that meaning, Reply Brief for Petitioner 17-18. We need not resolve their dispute, as it is enough for present purposes that the Restatement indicates a foreign official's immunity may turn upon a requirement not applicable to any other type of defendant.

*[Chapter 6.B explores the act of state doctrine. — Eds.]

18. A study that attempted to gather all of the State Department decisions related to sovereign immunity from the adoption of the restrictive theory in 1952 to the enactment of the FSIA reveals only four decisions related to official immunity, and two related to head of state immunity, out of a total of 110 decisions. . . .

19. The FSIA was introduced in accordance with the recommendation of the State Department. H. R. Rep., at 6. The Department sought and supported the elimination of its role with respect to claims against foreign states and their agencies or instrumentalities. See Hearings on H. R. 11315. . . . (1976) (testimony of Monroe Leigh, Legal Adviser, Dept. of State). But the Department has from the time of the FSIA's enactment understood the Act to leave intact the Department's role in official immunity cases. See Digest 1020 ("These decisions [of the Department regarding the immunity of officials] may be of some future significance, because the Foreign Sovereign Immunities Act does not deal with the immunity of individual officials, but only that of foreign states and their political subdivisions, agencies and instrumentalities").

still be barred by foreign sovereign immunity under the common law. And not every suit can successfully be pleaded against an individual official alone.[20] Even when a plaintiff names only a foreign official, it may be the case that the foreign state itself, its political subdivision, or an agency or instrumentality is a required party, because that party has "an interest relating to the subject of the action" and "disposing of the action in the person's absence may . . . as a practical matter impair or impede the person's ability to protect the interest." Fed. Rule Civ. Proc. 19(a)(1)(B). If this is the case, and the entity is immune from suit under the FSIA, the district court may have to dismiss the suit, regardless of whether the official is immune or not under the common law. See *Republic of Philippines* v. *Pimentel*, 553 U.S. 851, 867 (2008)("[W]here sovereign immunity is asserted, and the claims of the sovereign are not frivolous, dismissal of the action must be ordered where there is a potential for injury to the interests of the absent sovereign"). Or it may be the case that some actions against an official in his official capacity should be treated as actions against the foreign state itself, as the state is the real party in interest. Cf. *Kentucky* v. *Graham*, 473 U.S. 159, 166 (1985) ("[A]n official-capacity suit is, in all respects other than name, to be treated as a suit against the entity. It is *not* a suit against the official personally, for the real party in interest is the entity" (citation omitted)).

We are thus not persuaded that our construction of the statute's text should be affected by the risk that plaintiffs may use artful pleading to attempt to select between application of the FSIA or the common law. And we think this case, in which respondents have sued petitioner in his personal capacity and seek damages from his own pockets, is properly governed by the common law because it is not a claim against a foreign state as the Act defines that term. Although Congress clearly intended to supersede the common-law regime for claims against foreign states, we find nothing in the statute's origin or aims to indicate that Congress similarly wanted to codify the law of foreign official immunity.

Our review of the text, purpose, and history of the FSIA leads us to the conclusion that the Court of Appeals correctly held the FSIA does not govern petitioner's claim of immunity. The Act therefore did not deprive the District Court of subject-matter jurisdiction. We emphasize, however, the narrowness of our holding. Whether petitioner may be entitled to immunity under the common law, and whether he may have other valid defenses to the grave charges against him, are matters to be addressed in the first instance by the District Court on remand. The judgment of the Court of Appeals is affirmed, and the case is remanded for further proceedings consistent with this opinion.

Notes and Questions

1. The Court's decision was unanimous. However, Justices Scalia, Alito, and Thomas filed concurring opinions questioning the need for, and propriety of resorting to legislative history.

20. Furthermore, a plaintiff seeking to sue a foreign official will not be able to rely on the Act's service of process and jurisdictional provisions. Thus, a plaintiff will have to establish that the district court has personal jurisdiction over an official without the benefit of the FSIA provision that makes personal jurisdiction over a foreign state automatic when an exception to immunity applies and service of process has been accomplished in accordance with 28 U.S.C. §1608.

2. In *Samantar,* why did the Court hold that the FSIA does not govern whether an individual foreign official enjoys immunity from civil suits?

3. What did the Court then say about whether present or past foreign officials are entitled to immunity under common law and whether there may be other defenses that would be available to him? Note the Court's statement that "[a]lthough Congress clearly intended to supersede the common-law regime for claims against foreign states, we find nothing in the statute's origin or aims to indicate that Congress similarly wanted to codify the law of foreign official immunity." On remand, the U.S. district court would need to make a determination as to whether Samantar is "entitled to immunity under the common law, and whether he may have other valid defenses to the grave charges against him."

4. *Samantar* did not describe the manner in which district courts should determine foreign officials' amenability to suit under the "common law." The United States' amicus brief contended that the "FSIA left in place the pre-existing practice of recognizing official immunity in accordance with suggestions of immunity by the Executive Branch." In this regard, the brief further stated that individual immunity determinations are "properly founded on non-statutory principles articulated by the Executive Branch," which in turn "are informed by customary international law and practice."

The Supreme Court appeared to endorse the position of the government when it noted that "[w]e have been given no reason to believe that Congress saw a problem, or wanted to eliminate the State Department's role in determinations regarding individual official immunity." Indeed, in the second paragraph of part II of its decision (see above), the Court referred to the two-step procedure existing before passage of the FSIA. If that procedure were to be followed post-*Samantar,* should a court follow the State Department's suggestion as to whether there should be immunity or not? If the State Department is silent, should a court make its own determination of whether there should be immunity, or should the court try to decide in accord with the Department's policies?

5. Postscript. On remand in *Samantar,* the U.S. district court (Brinkema, J.) decided on February 15, 2011: "The government has determined [as indicated in an amicus brief] that the defendant does not have foreign official immunity. Accordingly, defendant's common law sovereign immunity defense is no longer before the Court, which will now proceed to consider the remaining issues in defendant's Motion to Dismiss." Does the district court's language indicate its view that the court should follow the government's view?

6. Note that, even before *Samantar,* the FISA was usually not used for situations involving diplomats, consular officials, officials who qualified as "heads of state," or some special cases, such as special envoys or missions. Diplomats and consuls are covered by Vienna Convention on Diplomatic Relations (VCDR) and the Vienna Convention on Consular Relations (VCCR), respectively. For diplomats and consuls, the traditional approach of the courts would be to defer to Executive Branch suggestions of immunity and to divest themselves of jurisdiction if State suggested that. There were exceptions when the State Department simply certified the defendant's general qualification for diplomatic or consular immunity but left it to the court to make the factual determination as to whether the conduct alleged either qualified as an exception to the broad diplomatic immunity under the VCDR or for a limited "official acts" immunity under the VCCR. Immunity for diplomats and

consuls is discussed in subsection 16. Where heads of state or government are involved, customary international law principles are applicable as well as the views of the State Department. (See subsection 17 below. For some special cases, see subsection 18 below.)

Hence, *Samantar's* impact is primarily on present or former foreign officials who are not able to claim the specialized diplomatic or consular immunities and who are not covered by head of state immunity. These officials might range from lower level foreign officials in the United States who do not qualify for diplomatic or consular immunities, or they could be a wide range of officials in the foreign country who do not qualify under head of state immunity, but upon whom there has been proper service of process. In determining immunity claims of these officials, courts may look to the Executive's two-step procedure before the FSIA practice, as discussed above in Note 4. One factor that might further complicate the determination of immunity claims by foreign officials would be the extent of immunity to accord *former* foreign officials such as Samantar. (See also the discussion under subsections 16-17 below.)

Whether Executive Branch suggestions of immunity will prove to be determinative in all cases involving foreign officials, and the extent to which customary international law will play a role in cases where the Executive Branch refrains from providing a suggestion of immunity, remains to be seen.

7. What impact does *Samantar* have on the ability of foreign and domestic citizens to maintain actions against foreign officials under the Alien Tort Statute? (The ATS is discussed in Chapter 3.C and 8.B.8.d.)

8. Similarly, what impact does *Samantar* have on the ability of foreign and domestic citizens to maintain actions against foreign officials under the Torture Victims Protection Act, respectively? (This statute is also discussed in Chapter 3.C.) The Torture Victims Protection Act creates a civil cause of action against any individual who under actual or apparent authority, or color of law, of any foreign nation subjects an individual to torture or extrajudicial killing. Does this Act, which does not address immunity but creates a civil cause of action, indicate a congressional intent to override somehow the "common law" of foreign official immunity, at least in cases involving official torture or extrajudicial killing?

9. Do you think that an individual should be held accountable for egregious violations of international law such as torture, genocide, war crimes, or crimes against humanity when his or her responsibility is based only on actions taken in an official governmental capacity? The Supreme Court did not reach this argument in *Samantar,* noting that the district court had rejected the argument that Samantar had necessarily acted beyond the scope of his official capacity by allegedly violating international law. Earlier, in Wei Ye v. Jiang Zemin, 383 F. 3d 620 (7th Cir. 2004), the court decided that it should defer to the Executive Branch suggestion of immunity for the former President of China even though the complaint, based on the Alien Tort Statute, alleged that the defendant had violated *jus cogens* norms of international law. For a discussion of immunity of officials for certain acts that qualify as crimes under international law, see Chapter 12.B.2.a.

10. The Supreme Court was careful to emphasize that in some cases where individual foreign officials are sued, the "sovereign immunity" of the state itself might be relevant. For example, the court stated that, "we do not doubt that in some circumstances the immunity of the foreign state extends to an individual for acts taken in his official capacity." In which circumstances do you think the immunity

of the sovereign state would (or should) extend to the individual official? What factors should be relevant to making this distinction? Do you think *Samantar* presents the type of factual scenario where the immunity of the state should be extended to the official?

5. Retroactivity

The next case addresses the question whether the FSIA applies retroactively to conduct that took place before the statute's enactment.

Republic of Austria v. Altmann

U.S. Supreme Court
541 U.S. 677 (2004)

[Maria Altmann filed this action in 2000 against Austria and its instrumentality, the Austrian Gallery. She sought to recover certain Gustav Klimt paintings expropriated after Nazi Germany's invasion and claimed annexation of Austria. Altmann is the sole heir of Ferdinand Bloch-Bauer, who, along with his wife Adele (the subject of two Klimt portraits), had owned the paintings prior to World War II. The Bloch-Bauers were close friends of Klimt. Adele Bauer died in 1925.

[During the German "Anschluss," Ferdinand Bloch-Bauer's sugar company and home were "Aryanized" by the Nazis. A patron of the arts, his collection of paintings was parceled out amongst Nazi officials. The Austrian Gallery eventually obtained possession of five of the Klimt paintings.

[After the end of the war, Austria voided all Nazi confiscations. However, as a condition of receiving the required export papers for some of Bloche-Bauer's art, a lawyer for the heirs allegedly agreed, without Maria Altmann's permission, to acknowledge the validity of the Austrian Gallery's possession of the Klimt paintings. The Austrian government's practice of conditioning the issuance of export papers on the "donation" of other valuable artwork was allegedly commonplace. Even after Austria passed a new restitution law returning all artwork that was coercively donated to state museums, the Austrian Gallery allegedly continued to claim that Adele Bloch-Bauer left the paintings to the Gallery in her will. In 1998, a journalist discovered documents demonstrating that the Austrian Gallery knew that neither of the Bloch-Bauers had, in fact, donated the Klimts to the Gallery.

[Austria refused to arbitrate Ms. Altmann's claims of ownership of the Klimt paintings. Ms. Altmann initially sued in Austrian courts, but Austrian court costs are a percentage of the damages sought and suing in an Austrian court was excessively expensive because of the $150 million estimated value of the paintings. Even with a possible waiver that might have been available under Austrian law but that the Austrian government opposed in court, the cost would have been about $350,000. Ms. Altmann filed suit instead in the U.S. federal district court in Los Angeles and sought to establish jurisdiction over her claims through the expropriation exception, Section 1605(a)(3), of the Foreign Sovereign Immunities Act.]

STEVENS, J., delivered the opinion of the Court, in which O'CONNOR, SCALIA, SOUTER, GINSBURG, and BREYER, J.J., joined. SCALIA, J., filed a concurring opinion. BREYER, J. filed a concurring opinion, in which SOUTER, J. joined. KENNEDY, J., filed a dissenting opinion, in which REHNQUIST, C.J. and THOMAS, J. joined.

Justice STEVENS delivered the opinion of the Court. . . .

The District Court agreed with [the plaintiff] that the FSIA's expropriation exception covers [defendants'] alleged wrongdoing, and the Court of Appeals affirmed that holding. As noted above, however, we declined to review this aspect of the courts' opinions, confining our grant of certiorari to the issue of the FSIA's general applicability to conduct that occurred prior to the Act's 1976 enactment, and more specifically, prior to the State Department's 1952 adoption of the restrictive theory of sovereign immunity. We begin our analysis of that issue by explaining why . . . the [retroactivity] default rule announced in our opinion in Landgraf v. USI Film Products, 511 U.S. 244 (1994), does not control the outcome in this case.

In *Landgraf* we considered whether §102 of the Civil Rights Act of 1991, which permits a party to seek compensatory and punitive damages for certain types of intentional employment discrimination . . . applied to an employment discrimination case that was pending on appeal when the statute was enacted. The issue forced us to confront the " 'apparent tension' " between our rule that " 'a court is to apply the law in effect at the time it renders its decision,' " and the seemingly contrary "axiom that '[r]etroactivity is not favored in the law' " and thus that " 'congressional enactments . . . will not be construed to have retroactive effect unless their language requires this result". . . .

Acknowledging that, in most cases, the antiretroactivity presumption is just that — a presumption, rather than a constitutional command — we examined the rationales that support it. . . .

Balancing these competing concerns, we described the presumption against retroactive application in the following terms:

> "When a case implicates a federal statute enacted after the events in suit, the court's first task is to determine whether Congress has expressly prescribed the statute's proper reach. If Congress has done so, of course, there is no need to resort to judicial default rules. When, however, the statute contains no such express command the court must determine whether the new statute would have retroactive effect, *i.e.*, whether it would impair rights a party possessed when he acted, increase a party's liability for past conduct, or impose new duties with respect to transactions already completed. If the statute would operate retroactively, our traditional presumption teaches that it does not govern absent clear congressional intent favoring such a result." [*Landgraf*, 511 U.S. at 280.]

Though seemingly comprehensive, this inquiry does not provide a clear answer in this case. Although the FSIA's preamble suggests that it applies to preenactment conduct, that statement by itself falls short of an "expres[s] prescri[ption of] the statute's proper reach." Under *Landgraf*, therefore, it is appropriate to ask whether the Act affects substantive rights (and thus would be impermissibly retroactive if applied to preenactment conduct) or addresses only matters of procedure (and thus may be applied to all pending cases regardless of when the underlying conduct occurred). But the FSIA defies such categorization. To begin with, none of the three examples of retroactivity mentioned in the above quotation fits the FSIA's clarification of the law of sovereign immunity. Prior to 1976 foreign states had a justifiable expectation that, as a matter of comity, United States courts would grant them immunity for their public acts (provided the State Department did not recommend otherwise), but they had no "right" to such immunity. Moreover, the FSIA merely opens United States courts to plaintiffs with pre-existing claims against foreign states; the Act neither' increase[s those states'] liability for past conduct" nor "impose[s] new duties with respect to transactions already completed." Thus, the Act does not at first appear to "operate retroactively" within the meaning of the *Landgraf* default rule.

That preliminary conclusion, however, creates some tension with our observation in [*Verlinden*] that the FSIA is not simply a jurisdictional statute "concern[ing] access to the federal courts" but a codification of "the standards governing foreign sovereign immunity as an aspect of *substantive* federal law." Moreover, we noted in *Verlinden* that in any suit against a foreign sovereign, "the plaintiff will be barred from raising his claim in *any* court in the United States" unless one of the FSIA's exceptions applies. . . .

Thus, *Landgraf's* default rule does not definitively resolve this case. In our view, however, *Landgraf's* antiretroactivity presumption . . . is most helpful in that context. The aim of the presumption is to avoid unnecessary *post hoc* changes to legal rules on which parties relied in shaping their primary conduct. But the principal purpose of foreign sovereign immunity has never been to permit foreign states and their instrumentalities to shape their conduct in reliance on the promise of future immunity from suit in United States courts. Rather, such immunity reflects current political realities and relationships, and aims to give foreign states and their instrumentalities some *present* "protection from the inconvenience of suit as a gesture of comity." Dole Food Co. v. Patrickson, 538 U.S. 468, 479 (2003). Throughout history, courts have resolved questions of foreign sovereign immunity by deferring to the "decisions of the political branches . . . on whether to take jurisdiction." In this *sui generis* context, we think it more appropriate, absent contraindications, to defer to the most recent such decision — namely, the FSIA — than to presume that decision *inapplicable* merely because it postdates the conduct in question.

V

This leaves only the question whether anything in the FSIA or the circumstances surrounding its enactment suggests that we should not apply it to petitioners' 1948 actions. Not only do we answer this question in the negative, but we find clear evidence that Congress intended the Act to apply to preenactment conduct.

To begin with, the preamble of the FSIA expresses Congress' understanding that the Act would apply to all postenactment claims of sovereign immunity. That section provides: "*Claims* of foreign states to immunity should *henceforth* be decided by courts of the United States and of the States in conformity with the principles set forth in this chapter." Though perhaps not sufficient to satisfy *Landgraf's* "express command" requirement, this language is unambiguous: Immunity "claims" — not actions protected by immunity, but assertions of immunity to suits arising from those actions — are the relevant conduct regulated by the Act; those claims are "henceforth" to be decided by the courts. . . .

The FSIA's overall structure strongly supports this conclusion. Many of the Act's provisions unquestionably apply to cases arising out of conduct that occurred before 1976. In [*Dole Food*], for example, we held that whether an entity qualifies as an "instrumentality" of a "foreign state" for purposes of the FSIA's grant of immunity depends on the relationship between the entity and the state at the time suit is brought rather than when the conduct occurred. In addition, *Verlinden* . . . ' involved a dispute over a contract that predated the Act. And there has never been any doubt that the Act's procedural provisions relating to venue, removal, execution, and attachment apply to all pending cases. Thus, the FSIA's preamble indicates that it applies "henceforth," and its body includes numerous provisions that unquestionably apply to claims based on pre-1976 conduct. In this context, it would be anomalous to presume that an isolated provision (such as the expropriation exception on which respondent relies) is of purely prospective application absent any statutory language to that effect.

Finally, applying the FSIA to all pending cases regardless of when the underlying conduct occurred is most consistent with two of the Act's principal purposes: clarifying the rules that judges should apply in resolving sovereign immunity claims and eliminating political participation in the resolution of such claims. . . . The [FSIA], freed from *Landgraf's* antiretroactivity presumption, clearly applies to conduct, like petitioners' alleged wrongdoing, that occurred prior to 1976 and, for that matter, prior to 1952 when the State Department adopted the restrictive theory of sovereign immunity. . . .

VI

We conclude by emphasizing the narrowness of this holding. To begin with, although the District Court and Court of Appeals determined that §1605(a)(3) covers this case, we declined to review that determination. Nor do we have occasion to comment on the application of the so-called "act of state" doctrine to petitioners' alleged wrongdoing. Unlike a claim of sovereign immunity, which merely raises a jurisdictional defense, the act of state doctrine provides foreign states with a substantive defense on the merits. . . .

Finally, while we reject the United States' recommendation to bar application of the FSIA to claims based on pre-enactment conduct, Brief for United States as *Amicus Curiae,* nothing in our holding prevents the State Department from filing statements of interest suggesting that courts decline to exercise jurisdiction in particular cases implicating foreign sovereign immunity. The issue now before us . . . concerns interpretation of the FSIA's reach — a "pure question of statutory construction . . . well within the province of the Judiciary." While the United States' views on such an issue are of considerable interest to the Court, they merit no special deference. In contrast, should the State Department choose to express its opinion on the implications of exercising jurisdiction over *particular* petitioners in connection with *their* alleged conduct, that opinion might well be entitled to deference as the considered judgment of the Executive on a particular question of foreign policy.[23] See, e.g., American Ins. Assn. v. Garamendi, 539 U.S. 396, 414 (2003)

23. . . . We do not hold, however, that executive intervention could or would trump considered application of the FSIA's more neutral principles; we merely note that the Executive's views on questions within its area of expertise merit greater deference than its opinions regarding the scope of a congressional enactment. . . .

(discussing the President's " 'vast share of responsibility for the conduct of our foreign relations' "). We express no opinion on the question whether such deference should be granted in cases covered by the FSIA. . . .

. . .

Justice BREYER, with whom Justice SOUTER joins, concurring.

I join the Court's opinion and judgment, but I would rest that judgment upon several additional considerations. . . .

Second, the legal concept of sovereign immunity, as traditionally applied, is about a defendant's *status* at the time of suit, not about a defendant's *conduct* before the suit. . . . *Sixth,* other legal principles, applicable to *past conduct,* adequately protect any actual past reliance and adequately prevent (in the dissent's words) "open[-ing] foreign nations worldwide to vast and potential liability for expropriation claims in regard to conduct that occurred generations ago, including claims that have been the subject of international negotiation and agreement:

For one thing, statutes of limitations, personal jurisdiction and venue requirements, and the doctrine of *forum non conveniens* will limit the number of suits brought in American courts. . . .

Moreover, the act of state doctrine requires American courts to presume the validity of "an official act of a foreign sovereign performed within its own territory." . . .

Further, the United States may enter a statement of interest counseling dismissal. . . . Such a statement may refer, not only to sovereign immunity, but also to other grounds for dismissal, such as the presence of superior alternative and exclusive remedies. . . .

Finally, a plaintiff may have to show an absence of remedies in the foreign country sufficient to compensate for any taking. . . .

Justice KENNEDY, with whom the Chief Justice [REHNQUIST] and Justice THOMAS join, dissenting.

. . . As the Court's careful opinion illustrates, the case is difficult. In my respectful view, however, its decision in incorrect.

At the outset, here is a summary of my primary concerns with the majority opinion: To reach its conclusion the Court must weaken the reasoning and diminish the force of the rule against the retroactivity of statutes, a rule of fairness based on respect for expectations; the Court abruptly tells foreign nations this important principle of American law is unavailable to them in our courts; . . . as if to mitigate this harsh result, the Court adds that the Executive Branch has inherent power to intervene in cases like this; this, however, is inconsistent with the congressional purpose and design of the FSIA; the suggestion reintroduces, to an even greater degree than before, the same influences the FSIA sought to eliminate from sovereign immunity determinations; . . . the ultimate effect of the Court's inviting foreign nations to pressure the Executive is to risk inconsistent results for private citizens who sue, based on changes and nuances in foreign affairs, and to add prospective instability to the most sensitive area of foreign relations. . . .

Notes and Questions

1. After the Supreme Court denied Austria's claim that the FSIA did not apply retroactively, an arbitration panel in Austria awarded Maria Altmann possession of

five of the Klimt paintings. In June of 2006, the most famous of the five, Adele Bloche-Bauer I, was sold for a reported $135 million. At the time, the amount represented the highest price paid for a painting, surpassing the $104 million received for Picasso's 1905 *Boy with a Pipe (The Young Apprentice).* In November 2006, Ms. Altmann placed the remaining four Klimt paintings up for auction and the final bidding for these four paintings totaled $192.2 million.

2. What was the holding of *Altmann*? Was the Court's rationale for not applying *Landgraf's* presumption of anti-retroactivity persuasive? Does giving the FSIA retroactive effect upset the immunity expectations of foreign nations who engaged in the type of conduct that satisfies the statute's exceptions? What expectations of immunity would Austria have had prior to the 1952 Tate letter? What expectations would it have had between 1952 and the 1976 enactment of the FSIA? Will the application of the FSIA to conduct that occurred prior to its enactment in 1976 lead to an increase in litigation against foreign sovereigns related to atrocities such as the holocaust or genocide in the Balkans?

3. What were the possible limits that Justice Souter's majority opinion and Justice Breyer's concurrence identified for suits against foreign sovereigns for conduct that occurred prior to the enactment of the FSIA?

4. In Part VI of *Altmann*, the Court suggests that a State Department statement of interest in cases involving particular litigants might warrant deference from the courts. Although the Court avoided expressing an opinion on this issue, the language of Part VI elicited a sharp dissent from Justice Kennedy, joined by Chief Justice Rehnquist and Justice Thomas.

Why do you think that the majority discussed possible deference to the Executive Branch if the decision in *Altmann* did not require resolution of that issue? Is deference warranted if the Executive Branch countenances a result that appears to conflict with the provisions of the FSIA? Note that the Solicitor General argued against the retroactivity of the FSIA on purely legal, rather than foreign policy, grounds. Recall from *Verlinden* that some of the reasons for congressional enactment of the FSIA were to eliminate diplomatic pressure for an Executive Branch recommendation of immunity, avoid inconsistent immunity decisions that conflicted with the restrictive theory, and supply definitive legal standards for ensuring due process. Should courts defer to the Executive Branch, or should courts follow the FSIA as enacted by Congress? Does the FSIA represent an agreement between the political branches on a solution for the problems that arose when the Executive Branch made recommendations on immunity? If so, why should the Supreme Court unilaterally alter the balance agreed upon by the President and Congress by now suggesting a role for the Executive Branch going beyond the terms of the FSIA? In Sosa v. Alvarez-Machain (discussed in Chapter 3), which was decided several weeks after *Altmann*, the Court relied on the language of Part VI to reiterate that "there is a strong argument that federal courts should give serious weight to the Executive Branch's view of the case's impact on foreign policy." 542 U.S. 692, 732 n.21 (2004). Might both *Altmann* and *Sosa* indicate a willingness by the Court to permit Executive Branch recommendations of immunity similar to those issued in the period between the issuance of the 1952 Tate letter and the enactment of the FSIA?

After its decision in *Altmann*, the Court granted certiorari and vacated the judgments of the circuit courts in four pending cases whose resolution also required a determination of the retroactivity of the FSIA. The cases were remanded to the circuit courts of appeal for disposition not inconsistent with the *Altmann* decision. In two of these cases, Whiteman v. Dorotheum GMBH & Co., 431 F.3d 57 (2d Cir. 2005), and Hwang Geum Joo v. Japan, 413 F.3d 45 (D.C. Cir. 2005), the appellate courts combined the language of Executive Branch deference in Part VI of *Altmann* and footnote 21 of *Sosa* with the political question doctrine to dismiss the plaintiff's claims on the basis of nonjusticiability. (The political question doctrine is a justiciability doctrine invoked when resolution of the issue is better suited for the political process or the Constitution itself delegates the particular power in dispute to another branch of government.) In both court cases, the Executive Branch submitted a statement of interest that argued, among other things, that U.S. foreign policy interests counseled dismissal. In the other two cases, Abrams v. Société Nationale des Chemins de Fer Francais, 389 F.3d 61 (2d Cir. 2004), and Garb v. Republic of Poland, 400 F.3d 579 (2d Cir. 2006), the courts determined that the FSIA exceptions were not satisfied and dismissed the cases, rather than relying on deference to the Executive Branch or the political question doctrine.

Which situation is preferable: Executive Branch intervention that incorporates geopolitical ramifications into sovereign immunity decisions, or determinations made by the courts based upon the purely legal criteria enacted by Congress in the FSIA? Because the Court in both *Altmann* and *Sosa* failed to explicitly state that Executive Branch statement of interests are entitled to deference, the degree to which courts will ultimately take the Executive Branch statements into account is yet unclear. In analyzing Executive Branch statements, however, courts may look at the thoroughness and specificity of the statement and whether the statement specifically requests dismissal. See, e.g., City of New York v. Permanent Mission of India to the U.N., 446 F.3d 365 (2d Cir. 2006) and Doe v. Exxon Mobil Corp. 473 F.3d 345 (D.C. Cir. 2007), respectively.

Additionally, it appears that some courts and commentators generally believe that the reference to case-specific deference in *Sosa* and *Altmann* is not a creation of a new doctrine, but rather refers to the traditional practice of using Executive Branch statements to inform preexisting norms of judicial restraint such as the political question, act of state doctrine (discussed in section B of this Chapter), or comity doctrines. See, e.g., Khulumani v. Barclay Nat'l Bank, Ltd., 504 F.3d 254, 262 n.10 (2d Cir. 2007) (per curiam) (noting that "[t]he parties agree that Sosa's reference to 'case-specific deference' implicates either the political question or international comity doctrine"), aff'd due to lack of a quorum sub nom., Am. Isuzu Motors, Inc. v. Ntsebeza, 553 U.S. 1028 (2008).

5. For analyses of *Altmann* and the ramifications of reintroducing deference into foreign sovereign immunity determinations, see Mark J. Chorazak, Clarity and Confusion: Did the Republic of Austria v. Altmann Revive State Department Suggestions of Foreign Sovereign Immunity?, 55 Duke L.J. 373 (2005); Charles H. Brower II, Republic of Austria v. Altmann, 99 Am. J. Int'l L. 236 (2005).

6. The *Altmann* Court included a discussion of Dole Food Co. v. Patrickson, 538 U.S. 468 (2003). In that case the Court held that an entity's relationship with a foreign sovereign—i.e., whether it is a political subdivision, instrumentality, or agency under Section 1332—is ascertained from the relationship at the time of the suit, rather than at the time the injury occurred.

7. Another case involving thousands of valuable Jewish religious books, manuscripts, and other documents allegedly expropriated by the Bolshevik government during the 1917 October Revolution in Russia led to a U.S. court decision against Russia in 2008 and then a default judgment in 2010. Agudas Chasidei Chabad v. Russian Fed'n, 528 F.3d 934 (D.C. Cir. 2008); [same case], 729 F. Supp. 2d 141 (D.C.D.C. 2010) (granting default judgment after Russia declined to participate further in the litigation). In response, state-run Russian art museums expressed concerns that the judgment might lead to the seizure of their artwork on loan in the United States despite assurances from U.S. diplomats. The Russians canceled long-scheduled loans to American institutions—including one of Cézanne's famous card player paintings that was going to New York City's Metropolitan Museum of Art and several Gauguin paintings that were headed to the National Gallery of Art in Washington, DC. The diplomatic feud was still underway in February 2011. Carol Vogel & Clifford J. Levy, Dispute Derails Art Loans from Russia, N.Y. Times, Feb. 2, 2011, at C1.

6. *Waiver Exception*

Under the FSIA's waiver exception, a foreign state is not immune from suit if it "has waived its immunity either explicitly or by implication." 28 U.S.C. §1605(a) (1). Explicit waivers of immunity, such as a waiver in a treaty or contract, present relatively few problems. Such waiver provisions are very common in the legal documents used when a foreign state borrows money from a bank or purchases goods or services from a sophisticated company. See Capital Ventures Int'l v. Republic of Argentina, 552 F.3d 289 (2d Cir. 2009).

But what constitutes a waiver "by implication"? The legislative history of the FSIA states as follows:

> With respect to implicit waivers, the courts have found such waivers in cases where a foreign state has agreed to arbitration in another country or where a foreign state has agreed that the law of a particular country should govern a contract. An implicit waiver would also include a situation where a foreign state has filed a responsive pleading in an action without raising the defense of foreign sovereign immunity. [H.R. Rep. No. 94-1487, at 18.]

What does this statement suggest about the scope of the implicit waiver exception? In general, courts have construed the FSIA's implicit waiver exception narrowly, limiting it to situations in which the foreign state defendant has indicated a willingness to be sued in U.S. courts. The selection of U.S. law to govern a contract is generally treated as a waiver of FSIA immunity. See, e.g., Eckert Int'l, Inc. v. Fiji, 32 F.3d 77 (4th Cir. 1994). But a selection of foreign law is generally not viewed as a waiver. See, e.g., Eaglet Corp. v. Banco Central de Nicaragua, 839 F. Supp. 232 (S.D.N.Y. 1993), aff'd, 23 F.3d 641 (2d Cir. 1994). Nor is an agreement to submit to the jurisdiction of a foreign state generally viewed as a waiver of FSIA immunity. See, e.g., Ohntrup v. Firearms Center, 516 F. Supp. 1281, 1285 (E.D. Pa. 1981), aff'd, 760 F.2d 259 (3d Cir. 1985).

Does a foreign state implicitly waive its immunity by engaging in egregious conduct—for example, by violating *jus cogens* norms of international law? Despite an argument to this effect by one judge, see Princz v. Federal Republic of Germany, 26 F.3d 1166, 1176 (D.C. Cir. 1984) (Wald, J., dissenting), courts have uniformly held that egregious conduct does not itself constitute a waiver. In addition to the majority opinion in *Princz*, see, for example, Sampson v. Federal Republic of Germany, 250 F.3d 1145 (7th Cir. 2001); Smith v. Socialist People's Libyan Arab Jamahiriya, 101 F.3d 239, 344-345 (2d Cir. 1996). There have been a number of proposals presented to Congress to create a *jus cogens* exception to immunity, but so far none of those proposals has been enacted. Should Congress create such an exception? If so, how should *jus cogens* be defined? What problems might courts encounter in applying such an exception? (For a discussion of the *jus cogens* concept, see Chapter 2.A.)

7. *Counterclaim Exception*

The FSIA also has an exception to immunity for counterclaims. See 28 U.S.C. §1607. If a foreign state brings a lawsuit in a U.S. court, it is denied immunity under this section for (a) any claim that falls within an exception to immunity; (b) any claim that arises out of the same transaction or occurrence as the sovereign's claim; and (c) any claim up to the amount of the foreign state's claim. The FSIA's legislative history indicates that Congress intended by this exception to codify the Supreme Court's decision in National City Bank v. Republic of China, 348 U.S. 356 (1955), which held that the *Schooner Exchange* decision did not apply to counterclaims because such claims do not involve "an attempt to bring a recognized foreign government into one of our courts as a defendant and subject it to the rule of law to which nongovernmental obligors must bow." Id. at 361.

8. *Commercial Activity Exception*

One of the most widely invoked exceptions to immunity under the FSIA is the commercial activity exception in 28 U.S.C. §1605(a) (2). A suit can satisfy this exception in three different ways: either the suit must be "based upon a commercial activity carried on in the United States by the foreign state," based upon "an act performed in the United States in connection with a commercial activity of the foreign state elsewhere," or based upon "an act outside the territory of the United States in connection with a commercial activity of the foreign state elsewhere and that act causes a direct effect in the United States."

The 1976 House Report for the FSIA notes the following regarding the FSIA's definition of "commercial activity":

House Report No. 94-1487

Paragraph [(d)] of section 1603 defines the term "commercial activity" as including a broad spectrum of endeavor, from an individual commercial transaction or act to a regular course of commercial conduct. A "regular course of commercial conduct" includes the carrying on of a commercial enterprise such as a mineral extraction company, an airline or a state trading corporation. Certainly, if an activity is customarily carried on for profit, its commercial nature could readily be assumed. At the other end of the spectrum, a single contract, if of the same character as a contract which might be made by a private person, could constitute a "particular transaction or act."

As the definition indicates, the fact that goods or services to be procured through a contract are to be used for a public purpose is irrelevant; it is the essentially commercial nature of an activity or transaction that is critical. Thus, a contract by a foreign government to buy provisions or equipment for its armed forces or to construct a government building constitutes a commercial activity. The same would be true of a contract to make repairs on an embassy building. Such contracts should be considered to be commercial contracts, even if their ultimate object is to further a public function.

By contrast, a foreign state's mere participation in a foreign assistance program administered by the Agency for International Development (AID) is an activity whose essential nature is public or governmental, and it would not itself constitute a commercial activity. By the same token, a foreign state's activities in and "contacts" with the United States resulting from or necessitated by participation in such a program would not in themselves constitute a sufficient commercial nexus with the United States so as to give rise to jurisdiction (see sec. 1330) or to assets which could be subjected to attachment or execution with respect to unrelated commercial transactions (see sec. 1610(b)). However, a transaction to obtain goods or services from private parties would not lose its otherwise commercial character because it was entered into in connection with an AID program. Also public or governmental and not commercial in nature, would be the employment of diplomatic, civil service, or military personnel, but not the employment of American citizens or third country nationals by the foreign state in the United States.

The courts would have a great deal of latitude in determining what is a "commercial activity" for purposes of this bill. It has seemed unwise to attempt an excessively precise definition of this term, even if that were practicable. Activities such as a foreign government's sale of a service or a product, its leasing of property, its borrowing of money, its employment or engagement of laborers, clerical staff or public relations or marketing agents, or its investment in a security of an American corporation, would be among those included within the definition.

. . . As paragraph [(e)] of section 1603 indicates, a commercial activity carried on in the United States by a foreign state would include not only a commercial transaction performed and executed in its entirety in the United States, but also a commercial transaction or act having a "substantial contact" with the United States. This definition includes cases based on commercial transactions performed in whole or in part in the United States, import-export transactions involving sales to, or purchases from, concerns in the United States, business torts occurring in the United States (cf. §1605(a)(5)), and an indebtedness incurred by a foreign state which negotiates or executes a loan agreement in the United States, or which receives financing from a private or public lending institution located in the United States — for example, loans, guarantees or insurance provided by the Export-Import Bank of the United States. It will be for the courts to determine whether a particular commercial activity has been performed in whole or in part in the United States. This definition, however, is intended to reflect a degree of contact beyond that occasioned simply by U.S. citizenship or U.S. residence of the plaintiff.

The Supreme Court first considered the scope of the commercial activity exception in Republic of Argentina v. Weltover, Inc., 504 U.S. 607 (1992). In that case, Argentina attempted, pursuant to a presidential decree, to reschedule the payments that were due on debt instruments (called "Bonods") that it had issued to foreign creditors. These Bonods provided for payment of interest and principal in U.S. dollars, and also provided that payment was to be made in London, Frankfurt, Zurich, or New York, at the election of the creditor. The plaintiffs, two Panamanian corporations and a Swiss bank, collectively held $1.3 million of Bonods, and the plaintiffs refused to accept the rescheduling and insisted on full payment, specifying New York as the place where payment should be made. Argentina did not pay, and the plaintiffs brought a breach-of-contract action in federal court in New York, relying on the third clause of the commercial activity exception, which applies if the suit is based upon "an act outside the territory of the United States in connection with a commercial activity of the foreign state elsewhere and that act causes a direct effect in the United States."

In an opinion written by Justice Scalia, the Court first held that Argentina's issuance of the bonds was "commercial activity." The Court explained that, "when a foreign government acts, not as a regulator of a market, but in the manner of a private player within it, the foreign sovereign's actions are 'commercial' within the meaning of the FSIA." Id. at 614. The Court also emphasized that it is the nature of the foreign government's actions, not their purpose, that determines whether they are commercial. "[T]he issue," said the Court, "is whether the particular actions that the foreign state performs (whatever the motive behind them) are the type of actions by which a private party engages in 'trade and traffic or commerce.' " Id. (quoting Black's Law Dictionary 270 (6th ed. 1990)). In this case, the Court reasoned that "[t]he commercial character of the Bonods is confirmed by the fact that they are in almost all respects garden-variety debt instruments: They may be held by private parties; they are negotiable and may be traded on the international market (except in Argentina); and they promise a future stream of cash income." Id. at 615.

Second, the Court concluded that Argentina's unilateral rescheduling of the Bonods had a "direct effect" within the United States as required by the third clause of section 1605(a) (2). The Court rejected the argument, which had some support in the legislative history, that the effect must be "substantial" and "foreseeable." All that is required, said the Court, is that the effect be direct—i.e., that it "follow as an immediate consequence of the defendant's activity." Id. at 618. Because the plaintiffs in this case had designated New York as the place of payment under the Bonods, the Court reasoned, Argentina's rescheduling of the obligations had a direct effect in New York: "Money that was supposed to have been delivered to a New York bank for deposit was not forthcoming." Id.

The Supreme Court considered other aspects of the commercial activity exception in the following decision.

Saudi Arabia v. Nelson

U.S. Supreme Court
507 U.S. 349 (1993)

Justice SOUTER delivered the opinion of the Court.

The Foreign Sovereign Immunities Act of 1976 entitles foreign states to immunity from the jurisdiction of courts in the United States, 28 U.S.C. §1604, subject to certain enumerated exceptions. §1605. One is that a foreign state shall not be immune in any case "in which the action is based upon a commercial activity carried on in the United States by the foreign state."§1605(a) (2). We hold that respondents' action alleging personal injury resulting from unlawful detention and torture by the Saudi Government is not "based upon a commercial activity" within the meaning of the Act, which consequently confers no jurisdiction over respondents' suit.

I

Because this case comes to us on a motion to dismiss the complaint, we assume that we have truthful factual allegations before us, though many of those allegations are subject to dispute. Petitioner Kingdom of Saudi Arabia owns and operates petitioner King Faisal Specialist Hospital in Riyadh, as well as petitioner Royspec Purchasing Services, the Hospital's corporate purchasing agent in the United States. The Hospital Corporation of America, Ltd. (HCA), an independent corporation existing under the laws of the Cayman Islands, recruits Americans for employment at the Hospital under an agreement signed with Saudi Arabia in 1973.

. . . HCA placed an advertisement in a trade periodical seeking . . . a monitoring systems engineer at the Hospital. The advertisement drew the attention of respondent Scott Nelson in September 1983, while Nelson was in the United States. After interviewing for the position in Saudi Arabia, Nelson returned to the United States, where he signed an employment contract with the Hospital, satisfied personnel processing requirements, and attended an orientation session that HCA conducted for Hospital employees. In the course of that program, HCA identified Royspec as the point of contact in the United States for family members who might wish to reach Nelson in an emergency.

In December 1983, Nelson went to Saudi Arabia and began work at the Hospital, monitoring all "facilities, equipment, utilities and maintenance systems to insure the safety of patients, hospital staff, and others." He did his job without significant incident until March 1984, when he discovered safety defects . . . 'that posed fire hazards and otherwise endangered patients' lives. Over . . . several months, Nelson repeatedly advised Hospital officials of the safety defects and reported the defects to a Saudi Government commission as well. Hospital officials instructed Nelson to ignore the problems.

". . . [O]n September 27, 1984, [however,] Hospital employees summoned him to the Hospital's security office where agents of the Saudi Government arrested him.[1] The agents transported Nelson to a jail cell, in which they "shackled, tortured and bea[t]" him, and kept him four days without food. . . . Government agents forced him to sign a statement written in . . . [Arabic], the content of which he did not know; a Hospital employee who was supposed to act as Nelson's interpreter advised him to sign "anything" the agents gave him to avoid further beatings. Two days later, Government agents transferred Nelson to the Al Sijan Prison "to await trial on unknown charges."

1. Petitioners assert . . . Nelson [was arrested] because he had falsely represented to the Hospital that he had received a degree from the Massachusetts Institute of Technology and had provided the Hospital with a forged diploma to verify his claim. The Nelsons concede these misrepresentations, but dispute that they occasioned Scott Nelson's arrest.

At the Prison, Nelson was confined in an overcrowded cell area infested with rats, where he had to fight other prisoners for food and from which he was taken only once a week for fresh air and exercise. Although police interrogators repeatedly questioned him in Arabic, Nelson did not learn the nature of the charges, if any, against him. For several days, the Saudi Government failed to advise Nelson's family of his whereabouts, though a Saudi official eventually told Nelson's wife, respondent Vivian Nelson, that he could arrange for her husband's release if she provided sexual favors.

Although officials from the United States Embassy visited Nelson twice during his detention, they concluded that his allegations, of Saudi mistreatment were "not credible" and made no protest to Saudi authorities. It was only at the personal request of a United States Senator that the Saudi Government released Nelson, 39 days after his arrest. . . . Seven days later, . . . the Saudi Government allowed Nelson to leave the country.

In 1988, Nelson and his wife filed this action against petitioners . . . seeking damages for personal injury. The Nelsons' complaint sets out 16 causes of action, which fall into three categories: [1] various intentional torts, including battery, unlawful detainment, wrongful arrest and imprisonment, false imprisonment, inhuman torture, disruption of normal family life, and infliction of mental anguish. [2][N]egligently failing to warn Nelson of otherwise undisclosed dangers of his employment, namely, that if he attempted to report safety hazards the Hospital would likely retaliate against him and the Saudi Government might detain and physically abuse him without legal cause. . . .

. . . For there to be jurisdiction . . . the Nelsons' action must be "based upon" some "commercial activity" by petitioners that had "substantial contact" with the United States within the meaning of the Act. Because we conclude that the suit is not based upon any commercial activity by petitioners, we need not reach the issue of substantial contact. . . .

We begin our analysis by identifying the particular conduct on which the Nelsons' action is "based" for purposes of the Act. Although the Act contains no definition of the phrase "based upon," and the relatively sparse legislative history offers no assistance, guidance is hardly necessary. In denoting conduct that forms the "basis," or "foundation," for a claim, see Black's Law Dictionary 151 (6th ed. 1990) (defining "base") . . . , the phrase is read most naturally to mean those elements of a claim that, if proven, would entitle a plaintiff to relief under his theory of the case.

What the natural meaning of the phrase "based upon" suggests, the context confirms. . . . §1605(a) (2) contains two clauses following the one at issue here. The second allows for jurisdiction where a suit "is based . . . upon an act performed in the United States in connection with a commercial activity of the foreign state elsewhere," and the third speaks in like terms, allowing for jurisdiction where an action "is based . . . upon an act outside the territory of the United States in connection with a commercial activity of the foreign state elsewhere and that act causes a direct effect in the United States." Distinctions among descriptions juxtaposed against each other are naturally understood to be significant, and Congress manifestly understood there to be a difference between a suit "based upon" commercial activity and one "based upon" acts performed "in connection with" such activity.

The only reasonable reading of the former term calls for something more than a mere connection with, or relation to, commercial activity.[4]

In this case, the Nelsons have alleged that petitioners recruited Scott Nelson for work at the Hospital, signed an employment contract with him, and subsequently employed him. While these activities led to the conduct that eventually injured the Nelsons, they are not the basis for the Nelsons' suit. Even taking each of the Nelsons' allegations about Scott Nelson's recruitment and employment as true, those facts alone entitle the Nelsons to nothing under their theory of the case. The Nelsons have not, after all, alleged breach of contract, but personal injuries caused by petitioners' intentional wrongs and by petitioners' negligent failure to warn Scott Nelson that they might commit those wrongs. Those torts, and not the arguably commercial activities that preceded their commission, form the basis for the Nelsons' suit.

Petitioners' tortious conduct itself fails to qualify as "commercial activity" within the meaning of the Act, although the Act is too " 'obtuse' " to be of much help in reaching that conclusion. We have seen already that the Act defines "commercial activity" as "either a regular course of commercial conduct or a particular commercial transaction or act," and provides that "[t]he commercial character of an activity shall be determined by reference to the nature of the course of conduct or particular transaction or act, rather than by reference to its purpose." 28 U.S.C. §1603(d). If this is a definition, it is one distinguished only by its diffidence; as we observed in our most recent case on the subject, it "leaves the critical term 'commercial' largely undefined." Republic of Argentina v. Weltover, Inc., 504 U.S. 607 (1992). . . . [C]ongressional diffidence necessarily results in judicial responsibility to determine what a "commercial activity" is for purposes of the Act.

We took up the task just last Term in *Weltover*. . . . We . . . held that the meaning of "commercial" for purposes of the Act must be the meaning Congress understood the restrictive theory to require at the time it passed the statute.

. . . We explained in *Weltover* that a state engages in commercial activity under the restrictive theory where it exercises " 'only those powers that can also be exercised by private citizens,' " as distinct from those " 'powers peculiar to sovereigns.' " Put differently, a foreign state engages in commercial activity for purposes of the restrictive theory only where it acts "in the manner of a private player within" the market. . . .

We emphasized in *Weltover* that whether a state acts "in the manner of" a private party is a question of behavior, not motivation. . . . We did not ignore the difficulty of distinguishing " 'purpose' (i.e., the reason why the foreign state engages in the activity) from 'nature' (i.e., the outward form of the conduct that the foreign state performs or agrees to perform)," but recognized that the Act "unmistakably commands" us to observe the distinction. . . .

Unlike Argentina's activities that we considered in *Weltover*, the intentional conduct alleged here (the Saudi Government's wrongful arrest, imprisonment, and torture of Nelson) could not qualify as commercial under the restrictive theory.

4. We do not mean to suggest that the first clause of §1605(a) (2) necessarily requires that each and every element of a claim be commercial activity by a foreign state, and we do not address the case where a claim consists of both commercial and sovereign elements. We do conclude, however, that where a claim rests entirely upon activities sovereign in character, as here, jurisdiction will not exist under that clause regardless of any connection the sovereign acts may have with commercial activity.

The conduct boils down to abuse of the power of its police by the Saudi Government, and however monstrous such abuse undoubtedly may be, a foreign state's exercise of the power of its police has long been understood for purposes of the restrictive theory as peculiarly sovereign in nature. Exercise of the powers of police and penal officers is not the sort of action by which private parties can engage in commerce. . . .

The Nelsons and their amici urge us to give significance to their assertion that the Saudi Government subjected Nelson to the abuse alleged as retaliation for his persistence in reporting Hospital safety violations, and argue that the character of the mistreatment was consequently commercial. . . . But this argument does not alter the fact that the powers allegedly abused were those of police and penal officers. In any event, the argument is off the point, for it goes to purpose, the very fact the Act renders irrelevant to the question of an activity's commercial character. Whatever . . . the Saudi Government's motivation for its allegedly abusive treatment of Nelson, it remains the case that the Nelsons' action is based upon a sovereign activity immune from the subject-matter jurisdiction of United States courts under the Act.

In addition to the intentionally tortious conduct, the Nelsons claim a separate basis for recovery in petitioners' failure to warn Scott Nelson of the hidden dangers associated with his employment. The Nelsons allege that, at the time petitioners recruited Scott Nelson and thereafter, they failed to warn him of the possibility of severe retaliatory action if he attempted to disclose any safety hazards he might discover on the job. In other words, petitioners bore a duty to warn of their own propensity for tortious conduct. . . . For aught we can see, a plaintiff could recast virtually any claim of intentional tort committed by sovereign act as a claim of failure to warn, simply by charging the defendant with an obligation to announce its own tortious propensity before indulging it. To give jurisdictional significance to this feint of language would effectively thwart the Act's manifest purpose to codify the restrictive theory of foreign sovereign immunity. . . .

Justice White, with whom Justice Blackmun joins, concurring in the judgment. . . .

To run and operate a hospital, even a public hospital, is to engage in a commercial enterprise. The majority never concedes this point, but it does not deny it either, and to my mind the matter is self-evident. By the same token, warning an employee when he blows the whistle and taking retaliatory action, such as harassment, involuntary transfer, discharge, or other tortious behavior, although not prototypical commercial acts, are certainly well within the bounds of commercial activity. . . . Nelson alleges that petitioners harmed him in the course of engaging in their commercial enterprise, as a direct result of their commercial acts. His claim, in other words, is "based upon commercial activity."

Indeed, I am somewhat at a loss as to what exactly the majority believes petitioners have done that a private employer could not. As countless cases attest, retaliation for whistle-blowing is not a practice foreign to the marketplace. . . . On occasion, private employers also have been known to retaliate by enlisting the help of police officers to falsely arrest employees. . . . More generally, private parties have been held liable for conspiring with public authorities to effectuate an arrest, . . . and for using private security personnel for the same purposes. . . .

Nevertheless, I reach the same conclusion as the majority because petitioners' commercial activity was not "carried on in the United States." The Act defines such conduct as "commercial activity . . . having substantial contact with the United States." 28 U.S.C. §1603(e). Respondents point to the hospital's recruitment efforts in the United States, including advertising in the American media, and the signing of the employment contract in Miami. . . . [W]hile these may very well qualify as commercial activity in the United States, they do not constitute the commercial activity upon which respondents' action is based. Conversely, petitioners' commercial conduct in Saudi Arabia, though constituting the basis of the Nelsons' suit, lacks a sufficient nexus to the United States. Neither the hospital's employment practices, nor its disciplinary procedures, has any apparent connection to this country. . . .

Justice KENNEDY, with whom Justice BLACKMUN and Justice STEVENS join as to Parts I-B and II, concurring in part and dissenting in part.

I join all of the Court's opinion except the last paragraph of Part II, where, with almost no explanation, the Court rules that, like the intentional tort claim, the claims based on negligent failure to warn are outside the subject-matter jurisdiction of the federal courts. These claims stand on a much different footing from the intentional tort claims for purposes of the Foreign Sovereign Immunities Act (FSIA). In my view, they ought to be remanded to the District Court for further consideration. . . .

. . . The Nelsons' claims alleging that the Hospital, the Kingdom, and Royspec were negligent in failing during their recruitment of Nelson to warn him of foreseeable dangers are based upon commercial activity having substantial contact with the United States. As such, they are within the commercial activity exception and the jurisdiction of the federal courts. Unlike the intentional tort counts of the complaint, the failure to warn counts do not complain of a police beating in Saudi Arabia; rather, they complain of a negligent omission made during the recruiting of a hospital employee in the United States. . . .

Omission of important information during employee recruiting is commercial activity as we have described it. See Republic of Argentina v. Weltover, Inc., 504 U.S. 349 (1992). . . .

Having met the jurisdictional prerequisites of the FSIA, the Nelsons' failure to warn claims should survive petitioners' motion under Federal Rule of Civil Procedure 12(b) (1) to dismiss for want of subject-matter jurisdiction.

Notes and Questions

1. As should be clear from the materials above, it is important to read carefully the relevant sections of the FSIA, including section 1603 (d) and (e) and section 1605(a)(2). (See the Documentary Supplement.)

2. In light of section 1603 and *Weltover* and *Nelson,* how would you define "commercial activity"? Is changing the currency exchange rates by a central bank a commercial activity? Is purchasing a pistol for the police a commercial act?

3. As indicated in the two cases above, in determining whether a foreign state's conduct is commercial, the FSIA directs the courts to look to the nature of the conduct rather than to the foreign state's purpose. See section 1603(d). Why do

you think the FSIA requires this? Is it difficult to determine a foreign state's purpose(s) behind its acts? How do you discern the nature of an activity? Do you agree with the Court in *Nelson* that there is "difficulty" in sometimes distinguishing between purpose and nature? Compare the purchase by the government of South Korea from a U.S. company of 100 screwdrivers versus 100 missiles with a range of over 300 miles and capable of carrying nuclear warheads. (Major weapons sales such as these missiles would require a U.S. government license.) Are both sales commercial acts?

4. In *Nelson*, the plaintiffs attempted to establish jurisdiction under the first clause of section 1605(a) (2) ("in which the action is based upon a commercial activity carried on in the United States by the foreign state"). Why did the Nelsons not sue on a theory of breach of contract? What activities did the majority say the plaintiff's suit was based upon?

5. In their separate opinion, Justices Kennedy, Blackmun, and Stevens would have allowed jurisdiction because of commercial activity having substantial contact with the United States on the theory that the defendants were negligent in failing during their recruitment of Nelson to warn him of foreseeable dangers. Did the majority persuasively deny this aspect of the plaintiffs' claim?

6. Why does it seem that the plaintiffs did not sue under the FSIA's noncommercial tort exception (which is discussed in the following section)?

7. In *Weltover*, the plaintiffs successfully relied on the third clause of section 1605(a)(2)—i.e., "upon an act outside the territory of the United States in connection with a commercial activity of the foreign state elsewhere and that causes a direct effect in the United States." After determining Argentina's issuance of "garden-variety" bonds was a commercial activity, the *Weltover* Court "reject[ed] the suggestion that §1605(a)(2) contains any unexpressed requirement of 'substantiality' or 'foreseeability.'" 504 U.S. at 618. Rather, the Court concluded that an "effect is 'direct' if it follows "as an immediate consequence of the defendant's . . . activity." Id. at 618 (internal quotations omitted).

There has been extensive litigation regarding the interpretation of the phrase, "direct effect in the United States." See, e.g, Virtual Countries, Inc. v. Republic of South Africa, 300 F.3d 230, 238-241 (2d Cir. 2002); Corzo v. Banco Cent. de Reserva del Peru, 243 F.3d 519, 525-526 (9th Cir. 2001); Byrd v. Corporacion Forestal y Industrial de Olancho SA, 182 F.3d 380, 390-391 (5th Cir. 1999). Courts appear to have had some difficulty in translating this phrase into a consistent approach. Compare Voest-Alpine Trading USA, Corp. v. Bank of China, 142 F.3d 887, 897 (5th Cir. 1998) (holding "that a financial loss incurred in the United States by an American plaintiff . . . constitutes a direct effect sufficient to support jurisdiction" under section 1605(a)(2)), with United World Trade, Inc. v. Mangyshlakneft, 33 F.3d 1232, 1238 (10th Cir. 1994) ("[W]e must conclude that [plaintiff's] allegation that it lost profits . . . as a result of the defendants' actions does not meet the requirements of §1605(a)(2)").

Circuit courts are also split over whether a legally significant act—i.e., the act that gives rise to the cause of action—must occur in the United States. See, e.g., Keller v. Central Bank of Nigeria, 277 F.3d 811, 817 (6th Cir. 2002), which discusses the split.

8. As discussed earlier, personal jurisdiction is established under the FSIA when the foreign state has been properly served under section 1608 and when one of

the FSIA exceptions to immunity have been met. More generally in the United States, establishing personal jurisdiction that is consistent with constitutional due process standards involves a determination of whether the defendant has "certain minimum contacts with [the forum] such that the maintenance of the suit does not offend 'traditional notions of fair play and substantial justice,' " International Shoe Co. v. Washington, 326 U.S. 310, 316 (1945) (quoting Milliken v. Meyer, 311 U.S. 457, 463 (1940)). This has been interpreted to require that a defendant has purposely availed itself of the benefits and protections of the forum and that finding jurisdiction is reasonable. In *Weltover,* however, the Supreme Court left open the question whether a foreign state is "a person" for the purposes of the Due Process Clause. 504 U.S. at 619.

Usually this question would not arise because the FSIA statutory language has the effort of requiring minimum contacts with the United States. However, in a few cases, the statutory language might permit a finding of jurisdiction where a due process analysis would not. Possible exceptions include where a court interprets "direct effect" in the United States broadly enough that it encompasses commercial activity abroad that has few ties to the United States. Another example is the (a)(1) waiver exception, discussed above, which does not specify any requirement for contacts with the United States. However, an explicit waiver should not create due process concerns because personal jurisdiction defenses are capable of being waived by defendants. See Fed. R. Civ. 12(h) (waiver of personal jurisdiction). Implicit waivers, which can be found under (a)(1), could raise problems, though, if the exception were construed loosely. A third example is the Section 1605A exception for state sponsors of terrorism (discussed below). It establishes jurisdiction in some circumstances if a single victim of a terrorist attack is a U.S. citizen, even if the attack is outside the United States.

In Price v. Socialist People's Libyan Arab Jamahiriya, 294 F.3d 82 (D.C. Cir. 2002), the D.C. Circuit concluded that foreign states are not "persons" within the meaning of the Fifth Amendment, and thus do not receive the same due process protections as natural people and corporations. The court based its decision on the Supreme Court's determination that U.S. states were not "persons" entitled to the due process protections of the Fifth Amendment. See South Carolina v. Katzenbach, 383 U.S. 301, 323-324 (1966). In 2009, the Second Circuit agreed with *Price's* holding. See Frontera Res. Azerbaijan Corp. v. State Oil Co. of the Azerbaijan Republic, 582 F.3d 393, 399 (2nd Cir. 2009).

9. *Noncommercial Torts*

Section 1605(a)(5) provides that there shall not be immunity in an action, not otherwise encompassed within the commercial activity exception, "in which money damages are sought against a foreign state for personal injury or death, or damage to or loss of property, occurring in the United States and caused by the tortious act or omission of that foreign state or of any official or employee of that foreign state while acting within the scope of his office or employment." This exception does not apply, however, to "(A) any claim based upon the exercise or performance or the failure to exercise or perform a discretionary function regardless of whether the discretion be abused, or (B) any claim arising out of malicious prosecution, abuse of process, libel, slander, misrepresentation, deceit, or interference with contract rights."

The House Report for the FSIA states that this exception was directed "primarily at the problem of traffic accidents but is cast in general terms as applying to all tort actions for monetary damages, not otherwise encompassed by section 1605(a)(2) relating to commercial activities." By its terms, the noncommercial tort exception does not apply to claims based upon the exercise or failure to exercise a discretionary function. The following decisions consider the scope of this limitation.

Letelier v. Republic of Chile

U.S. District Court
488 F. Supp. 665 (D.D.C. 1980)

[In 1976, Orlando Letelier, a former ambassador from Chile, and Ronni Moffitt were killed by a car bomb in Washington, D.C. Their families brought suit against the Republic of Chile, its intelligence agency, and various Chilean officials, alleging that they were responsible for the bombing.]

Green, District Judge. . . .

In the instant action, relying on section 1605(a) (5) as their basis for combatting any assertion of sovereign immunity, plaintiffs have set forth several tortious causes of action arising under international law, the common law, the Constitution, and legislative enactments, all of which are alleged to spring from the deaths of Orlando Letelier and Ronni Moffitt. The Republic of Chile, while vigorously contending that it was in no way involved in the events that resulted in the two deaths, further asserts that, even if it were, the Court has no subject matter jurisdiction in that it is entitled to immunity under the Act, which does not cover political assassinations because of their public, governmental character.

. . . It is clear from [the legislative history], the Chilean government asserts, that the intent of Congress was to include only private torts like automobile accidents within the exclusion from immunity embodied in section 1605(a) (5).

Prominently absent from defendant's analysis, however, is the initial step in any endeavor at statutory interpretation: a consideration of the words of the statute. . . . Subject to the exclusion of these discretionary acts defined in subsection (A) and the specific causes of action enumerated in subsection (B), neither of which have been invoked by the Republic of Chile, by the plain language of section 1605 (a) (5) a foreign state is not entitled to immunity from an action seeking money damages "for personal injury or death . . . caused by the tortious act or omission of that foreign state" or its officials or employees. Nowhere is there an indication that the tortious acts to which the Act makes reference are to only be those formerly classified as "private," thereby engrafting onto the statute, as the Republic of Chile would have the Court do, the requirement that the character of a given tortious act be judicially analyzed to determine whether it was of the type heretofore denoted as *jure gestionis* or should be classified as *jure imperil.* Indeed, the other provisions of the Act mandate that the Court not do so, for it is made clear that the Act and the principles it sets forth in its specific provisions are henceforth to govern all claims of sovereign immunity by foreign states. 28 U.S.C. §§1602, 1604.

Although the unambiguous language of the Act makes inquiry almost unnecessary, further examination reveals nothing in its legislative history that contradicts or qualifies its plain meaning. The relative frequency of automobile accidents and their potentially grave financial impact may have placed that problem foremost in the minds of Congress, but the applicability of the Act was not so limited, for the committees made it quite clear that the Act "is cast in general terms as applying to all tort actions for money damages" so as to provide recompense for "the victim of a traffic accident or other noncommercial tort." . . .

Examining then the specific terms of section 1605 (a) (5), despite the Chilean failure to have addressed the issue, the Court is called upon to consider whether either of the exceptions to liability for tortious acts found in section 1605(a) (5) applies in this instance. It is readily apparent, however, that the claims herein did not arise "out of malicious prosecution, abuse of process, libel, slander, misrepresentation, deceit, or interference with contract rights," 28 U.S.C. §1605(a) (5) (B) (1976), and therefore only the exemption for claims "based upon the exercise or performance or the failure to exercise or perform a discretionary function regardless of whether the discretion be abused," id. §1605(a) (5) (A), can be applicable.

As its language and the legislative history make apparent, the discretionary act exemption of subsection (A) corresponds to the discretionary act exception found in the Federal Tort Claims Act. As defined by the United States Supreme Court in interpreting the Federal Tort Claims Act, an act that is discretionary is one in which "there is room for policy judgment and decision." Dalehite v. United States, 346 U.S. 15, 36 (1953). Applying this definition to the instant action, the question becomes, would the alleged determination of the Chilean Republic to set into motion and assist in the precipitation of those events that culminated in the deaths of Orlando Letelier and Ronni Moffitt be of the kind in which there is "room for policy judgment and decision."

While it seems apparent that a decision calculated to result in injury or death to a particular individual or individuals, made for whatever reason, would be one most assuredly involving policy judgment and decision and thus exempt as a discretionary act under section 1605(a) (5) (A), that exception is not applicable to bar this suit. As it has been recognized, there is no discretion to commit, or to have one's officers or agents commit, an illegal act. Whatever policy options may exist for a foreign country, it has no "discretion" to perpetrate conduct designed to result in the assassination of an individual or individuals, action that is clearly contrary to the precepts of humanity as recognized in both national and international law. Accordingly there would be no "discretion" within the meaning of section 1605(a) (5) (A) to order or to aid in an assassination and were it to be demonstrated that a foreign state has undertaken any such act in this country, that foreign state could not be accorded sovereign immunity under subsection (A) for any tort claims resulting from its conduct. As a consequence, the Republic of Chile cannot claim sovereign immunity under the Foreign Sovereign Immunities Act for its alleged involvement in the deaths of Orlando Letelier and Ronni Moffitt.

Risk v. Halvorsen

U.S. Court of Appeals
936 F.2d 393 (9th Cir. 1991)

BRUNETTI, Circuit Judge. . . .

In 1977 Plaintiff Larry Risk married Elisabeth Antonsen Risk, a native and citizen of Norway. In 1983 the Risk family—Larry, Elisabeth and their two children—moved to Norway for a period. After an attempt by Larry to remove the children to the United States, Elisabeth received a temporary order from a Norwegian County Court providing ordinary visitation rights for the father. During the first visitation period Larry returned with the children to the United States.

In 1984 Elisabeth filed a petition in the Superior Court of San Francisco seeking custody of the two children. The parties were awarded joint custody and the superior court order prohibited the parents from removing the children from the five San Francisco Bay Area counties. In addition, the parties were required to surrender their children's passports and their own to Larry Risk's attorney, and were prohibited from applying for replacement passports without a court order. In July 1984, apparently with the assistance of various Norwegian government officials, Elisabeth Risk returned to Norway with her children.

Larry Risk filed this action in April, 1988, alleging that the Norwegian government and its consular officials conspired to violate and in fact violated the 1984 California custody order by suggesting to Elisabeth Risk that she return to Norway with the children; by providing travel documentation for Elisabeth and the children; by providing financial assistance to Elisabeth to make the trip; and, finally, by obstructing Larry Risk in his effort to Locate and contact his children. . . .

The district court rejected jurisdiction over Norway under the FSIA because of an exception to the general jurisdiction provision, section 1605 (a) (5), which excludes claims based on the exercise or performance, or failure to exercise or perform, a discretionary function.

Whether the acts of the Norwegian officials are within the discretionary function exception to the FSIA is controlled by principles developed under the Federal Tort Claims Act ("FTCA"). First, we "must determine whether the government employee had any discretion to act or if there was an element of choice as to appropriate conduct." Liu v. Republic of China, 892 F.2d 1419, 1431 (9th Cir. 1989). . . . Second, we consider "whether the decisions were grounded in social, economic, and political policy," concentrating on "the nature of the conduct, rather than the status of the actor. . . ." MacArthur Area Citizens Ass'n v. Peru, 809 F.2d 918,922 (D.C. Cir. 1987), vacated on other grounds, 823 F.2d 606 (1987).

In *MacArthur*, a neighborhood association sued the Republic of Peru for occupation and use of a building in violation of a zoning ordinance. The circuit court for the District of Columbia held that the discretionary function exception to the FSIA applied because the establishment of a chancery in a particular building, and modification of that building for security purposes, is a discretionary act of public policy, both political and economic in nature.

In Joseph v. Nigeria, [830 F.2d 1018, 1026 (9th Cir. 1987)], we declined to apply the discretionary function exception to acts of officials of the Nigerian government which lead to a tort suit. In that case, the government officials were accused of destruction of the property in which the Nigerian Consulate was located. We held that while acquisition and operation of the property was a discretionary function, purely destructive acts are not part of the policy decision to establish the consulate and thus fall outside the scope of the discretionary function exception.

The acts of the agents of the Norwegian government are closer to those of the officials in *MacArthur* and thus the discretionary function exception applies.

The Norwegian officials are accused of advising and assisting a Norwegian citizen and her children in leaving the United States. There can be no doubt the officials here were exercising discretion. . . .

Appellant argues that because the acts of the Norwegian officials may constitute a violation of California criminal law,[3] the acts should fall outside the scope of the discretionary function exception to the FSIA, and thus that the district court should have retained jurisdiction over Norway. . . .

[Among other things], appellant relies on Letelier v. Republic: of Chile, 488 F. Supp. 665 (D.D.C. 1980). In that case, members of the families of a Chilean national and his assistant who were ordered assassinated by members of the Chilean government brought a tort action against Chile in federal court. The district court refused to apply the discretionary function exception to the FSIA, stating that "there is no discretion to commit, or to have one's officers or agents commit, an illegal act. . . . Whatever policy options may exist for a foreign country, it has no 'discretion' to perpetrate conduct designed to result in the assassination of an individual or individuals." Id. at 673.

While the *Letelier* court apparently considered "action that is clearly contrary to the precepts of humanity" outside the scope of the discretionary function exception, id., the nature of the act in that case obviously influenced the court. In this case, the most that can be said is that Norwegian officials issued travel documents to a Norwegian citizen and her children, also citizens of Norway; that they provided funds for her travel; and that they protected her from contact by her former husband. Although these acts may constitute a crime under California law, it cannot be said that every conceivably illegal act is outside the scope of the discretionary function exception. *MacArthur,* 809 F.2d at 922 n.4.

The district court correctly held that the discretionary function exception to the FSIA applies in this case and that it has no jurisdiction to hear the claims against Norway.

Notes and Questions

1. By its terms, section 1605(a)(5) has a territorial requirement. It is for claims "in which money damages are sought against a foreign state for personal injury of death, or damage to or loss of property, occurring in the United States and caused by the tortious act or omission." Section 1603(c) defines "United States" as including "all territory and waters, continental, or insular, subject to the jurisdiction of the United States."

3. Intentional violation of a custody order, or of the rights of a parent under such an order is a felony in California. Cal. Penal Code §278.5 (West 1988).

In Argentine Republic v. Amerada Hess Shipping Corp., 489 U.S. 428 (1989) (discussed above), the U.S. Supreme Court ruled that the high seas (where the oil tanker was attacked) did not fit within this definition, even though U.S. courts might exercise admiralty jurisdiction over some events on the high seas. As a result, the Court ruled that because the injury to the ship "unquestionably occurred well outside the 3-mile limit then in effect for the territorial waters of the United States, the exception for noncommercial torts cannot apply." In dicta, the Court also stated the noncommercial tort exception "covers only torts occurring within the territorial jurisdiction of the United States." Id. at 441.

Even before *Amerada Hess,* a number of courts had held that the tortious act or omission must occur in the United States. See, e.g., Persinger v. Islamic Republic of Iran, 729 F.2d 835 (D.C. Cir. 1984). These courts emphasized the legislative history, which not only refers to traffic accidents but also states that "the tortious act or omission must occur within the jurisdiction of the United States."

After the Supreme Court's 1992 decision in *Amerada Hess,* at least the Second and Sixth Circuits have joined the D.C. circuit in holding that the "entire tort" must occur in the United States. See, e.g., O'Bryan v. Holy See, 556 F.3d 361, 382 (6th Cir. 2009) ("concluding that in order to apply the tortious act exception, the 'entire tort' must occur in the United States"); Calibri v. Gov't of the Republic of Ghana, 165 F.3d 193, 200 n.3 (2d Cir. 1999) ("Although cast in terms that may be read to require that only the injury rather than the tortious acts occur in the United States, the Supreme Court has held that this exception 'covers only torts occurring within the territorial jurisdiction of the United States' " (quoting Amerada Hess, 488 U.S. at 441)).

In contrast, by relying in part on the statutory language, in Olsen ex rel. Sheldon v. Government of Mexico, 729 F.2d 641 (9th Cir. 1984) (a case decided prior to *Amerada Hess*) the Ninth Circuit did not accept the theory that the entire tort must occur within U.S. jurisdiction for a case to come within the noncommercial tort exception. In 2009, the Ninth Circuit did not take a position on the issue post *Amerada Hess.* See Doe v. Holy See, 557 F.3d 1066, 1085 n.11 (9th Cir. 2009). Can you think of situations where an act of commission or omission might occur, in part, outside of the United States but result in injuries to American nationals in the United States? For example, what if a foreign intelligence agency plans an assassination and builds a bomb in the agency's own country, but then the killers with the bomb come to the United States and carry out the assassination? Is it difficult to determine the location of a tortious comission?

2. What is a discretionary function? As indicated in *Risk,* above, the limitation on the FSIA (a)(5) exception is based upon and tracks the language of the Federal Tort Claims Act (FTCA), 28 U.S.C. §2860(a). Generally, the analysis is two pronged. First, the court must determine whether the act "involves an element of judgment or choice." Berkovitz v. United States, 486 U.S. 531, 536 (1988). This determination does not depend on the status of the actor, but rather the nature of the conduct in question. Second, the choice must be based on social, political, or economic policy. Id. Evaluate the decisions in *Letelier* and *Risk* in light of this two part test. Did Chilean officials' conduct involve an element of choice? What about the Norwegian officials' conduct? Were their actions based upon policy decisions?

3. The court in *Letelier* concluded that Chilean officials lacked the discretion to commit an illegal act—in that case, political assassination. The Ninth Circuit in *Risk*

concluded that, even though the Norwegian officials allegedly violated California criminal law, their acts were discretionary. Which court was right? The Court in *Risk* noted *Letelier's* language categorizing political assassination as "clearly contrary to the precepts of humanity." Should an "illegality" exception to the discretionary function exception be limited to serious criminal or other illegal activity? Contrary to *Risk,* should facilitating a mother fleeing a jurisdiction with a child in violation of state law come within that exception?

4. Note also that the noncommercial tort exception contains an exclusion for "any claim arising out of malicious prosecution, abuse of process, libel, slander, misrepresentation, deceit, or interference with contractual rights." Section 1605(a)(5)(B). Why might the U.S. government want to preclude claims against a foreign sovereign based on these torts? Might these lawsuits often involve particular sensitive issues for a foreign sovereign?

5. Exception (a)(5) includes specific language addressing the liability of a foreign state for the "tortious act or omission . . . of any official or employee of that foreign state while acting within the scope of his office or employment." FSIA section 1606 provides that a foreign state shall be "liable in the same manner and to the same extent as a private individual under like circumstances." For discussion of this scope of employment issue, and questions about the approach in *Liu,* see Gary B. Born and Peter B. Rutledge, International Civil Litigation in United States Courts 307-308 (4th ed. 2007).

10. Expropriation

Section 1605(a)(3) denies immunity in two categories of expropriation cases where "rights in property taken in violation of international law are in issue." The limiting conditions regarding the location of the property and the identity of its possessor need to be studied carefully. (See Documentary Supplement.) The FSIA Committee Report notes:

> The term "taken in violation of international law" would include the nationalization or expropriation of property without payment of the prompt, adequate and effective compensation required by international law. It would also include takings which are arbitrary or discriminatory in nature. Since, however, this section deals solely with issues of immunity, it in no way affects existing law on the extent to which, if at all, the "act of state" doctrine may be applicable. See 22 U.S.C. 2370(e)(2) (Footnote omitted.)

(See the discussion of the act of state doctrine later in this chapter.)

By way of example, this section was found to deny immunity in Agudas Chasidei Chabad v. Russian Fed'n, 528 F.3d 934 (D.C. Cir. 2008) and Kalamazoo Spice Extraction Co. v. Provisional Military Government of Socialist Ethiopia, 616 F. Supp. 660 (W.D. Mich. 1985). Although the U.S. Supreme Court did not address the applicability of the (a)(3) exception in Republic of Austria v. Altmann, supra, if the allegations in that case were true, would the exception be satisfied when the case was remanded to the lower courts? Note that, in his concurrence, Justice Breyer noted that "[n]or can Austria now deny that the Gallery is 'engaged in commercial activity in the United States.' "

11. Enforcement of Arbitral Agreements

Section 1605(a) was amended in 1988 to include a new subsection (6). Its purpose was to remove the immunity of foreign states in actions seeking to enforce arbitration agreements or arbitral awards in a number of situations. These include agreements or awards made pursuant to the New York Convention on the Recognition and Enforcement of Arbitral Awards or the ICSID Convention.

The amendment also added a subsection (6) to section 1610 to ensure that property in the United States of a foreign state that was used for a commercial activity in the United States could be executed against or attached to satisfy an arbitral award rendered against the foreign state. (Section 1610 will be discussed in more detailed in subsection 13, below.) Moreover, another section of the 1988 law provided that "[e]nforcement of arbitral agreements, confirmation of arbitral awards, and execution upon judgments based on orders confirming such awards shall not be refused on the basis of the act of state doctrine." (This doctrine will be discussed in a later section.)

The combined effect of these provisions is to allow U.S. courts to enforce international arbitration agreements and to order appropriate execution against the losing party's property, even if the party is a foreign state.

Besides the FSIA exceptions discussed above, section 1605 also includes: subsection (a) (4) for certain rights in property in the United States and subsection (b) for certain admiralty suits. (The statute is in the Documentary Supplement.)

12. Terrorist Acts

Congress added section 1605A to the FSIA in 2008. This provision allows suits for damages against certain foreign states for engaging in specified terrorist acts or providing material support for these acts. The eligible states are ones designated by the U.S. Secretary of State as state sponsors of terrorism. As of January 2011, there were four such states: Cuba, Iran, Sudan, and Syria. This new terrorism exception, which replaces former subsection (7) of section 1605(a), denies immunity where a designated state sponsor of terrorism is sued

> for personal injury or death that was caused by an act of torture, extrajudicial killing, aircraft sabotage, hostage taking, or the provision of material support or resources for such an act if such act or provision of material support or resources is engaged in by an official, employee, or agent of such foreign state while acting within the scope of his or her office, employment, or agency.

One of Congress's main reasons for passing section 1605A was that the former terrorism exception under subsection 1605(a)(7) had been held by some courts not to provide a separate right of action against foreign states for victims of terrorism. While the statute stripped foreign states of immunity, these courts found that plaintiffs still had to find another provision of law under which to sue, such as state tort law. For acts occurring abroad, a plaintiff might well have trouble finding an applicable federal or U.S. state statute, and in any case might have trouble meeting the elements of a separate cause of action.

In response, section 1605A explicitly creates a statutory private right of action. The provision provides:

> A foreign state that is or was a state sponsor of terrorism . . . and any official, employee or agent of that foreign state while acting within the scope of his or her office, employment, or agency, shall be liable to — (1) a [U.S.] national . . . , (2) a member of the armed forces, (3) an employee of the [U.S.] Government . . . , or of an individual performing a contract awarded by the United States Government, acting within the scope of the employee's employment, or (4) the legal representative of [such persons], for personal injury or death caused by [the specified terrorist acts] of that foreign state, or of an official, employee or agent of that foreign state, for which the courts of the United States may maintain jurisdiction under [Section 1605A] for money damages.

Section 1605A contains certain exceptions and limitations. As quoted above, the claimant or victim must be a U.S. national, member of the armed forces, U.S. government employee or contractor, or their legal representative. In cases in which the act occurred in the foreign state, the court may only hear claims if "the claimant has afforded the foreign state a reasonable opportunity to arbitrate the claim in accordance with the accepted international rules of arbitration." New claims under section 1605A are also subject to a ten-year statute of limitations.

As for the type of damages allowed, the FSIA generally prohibits the award or recovery of punitive damages against the foreign state itself, though they are allowed against an agency or instrumentality. (Section 1606.) However, section 1605A explictly provides that money damages against both foreign states and their officials, employees, or agents under the terrorism exception may include "economic damages, solatium, pain and suffering, and punitive damages." Foreign states are also vicariously liable for the acts of their officials, employees or agents.

The following case discusses the scope of the 1605A exception and the effect of the 2008 amendments.

Murphy v. Islamic Republic of Iran

U.S. District Court
740 F. Supp. 2d 51 (D.D.C. 2010)

Lamberth, Chief Judge.

This case arises out of the October 23, 1983, bombing of the United States Marine barracks in Beirut, Lebanon ("the Beirut bombing"), where a suicide bomber murdered 241 American military servicemen in the most deadly state-sponsored terrorist attack upon Americans until the tragic attacks on September 11, 2001. . . .

II. Background

[This case contains two complaints: one by the plaintiffs, the other by the plaintiffs in intervention. The FSIA terrorism exception applies retroactively to claims made by both plaintiffs and intervenors. This excerpt will focus on the plaintiffs.] The Court has taken judicial notice of the findings and conclusions entered in a related case. The Court will enter default judgment against defendants and in favor of all plaintiffs. . . . Plaintiffs . . . have brought various claims of wrongful death, assault, battery, and intentional infliction of emotional distress (IIED), for which they seek compensatory and punitive damages.

A. Retroactive Application of Recently Amended Provisions of the FSIA to Plaintiffs . . .

This case comes to the Court following final judgment in Peterson v. Islamic Republic of Iran, See Peterson v. Islamic Republic of Iran, 515 F. Supp. 2d 25 (D.D.C. 2007) (Lamberth, J.) [hereinafter *Peterson II*] (final judgment); Peterson v. Islamic Republic of Iran, 264 F. Supp. 2d 46 (D.D.C. 2003) (Lamberth, J.) [hereinafter *Peterson I*] (default judgment). Peterson established the liability of Iran and MOIS [the Iranian Ministry of Information and Security] in the terrorist attack out of which this case also arise, but did so under [the former] §1605(a)(7), thus reaching "inconsistent and varied result[s]" when various states' tort laws differed. Congress responded to this inconsistency and the unavailability of punitive damages by replacing §1605(a)(7) with §1605A, a new terrorism exception that provides an independent federal cause of action and makes punitive damages available to plaintiffs. Plaintiffs now seek to retroactively take advantage of these changes. . . .

Parties seeking to take advantage of this new federal cause of action and punitive-damages allowance must proceed under one of three procedural approaches. These three approaches are prior actions, related actions, or stand-alone actions. [Ed. Note: Plaintiffs filed here as a action related to Valore v. Islamic Republic of Iran [2010], a consolidation of four cases which were commenced under §1605(a)(7) and which arose out of the same act or incident as this case: the Beirut Bombing.]

III. Facts

Based on the plaintiffs' . . . uncontroverted factual assertions in their complaints and with due reference to facts found in *Peterson*, the Court finds the following:

A. The Relationship Between Hezbollah and Iran . . .

. . . Hezbollah began its existence as a faction within a group of moderate Lebanese Shi'ites known as Amal. Following the 1982 Israeli invasion of Lebanon, the Iranian government sought to radicalize the Lebanese Shi'ite community, and encouraged Hezbollah to split from Amal. Having established the existence of Hezbollah as a separate entity, the government of Iran framed the primary objective of Hezbollah: to engage in terrorist activities in furtherance of the transformation of Lebanon into an Islamic theocracy modeled after Iran. . . .

B. The Beirut Bombing

The complicity of Iran in the 1983 attack was established conclusively . . . [by a] message [that] had been sent from MOIS to [the] Iranian ambassador to Syria. . . . The message directed the Iranian ambassador to contact . . . the leader of the terrorist group Islamic Amal, and to instruct him to have his group instigate attacks against the multinational coalition in Lebanon, and "to take a spectacular action against the United States Marines."

> Hezbollah members formed a plan to carry out simultaneous attacks against the American and French barracks in Lebanon. . . .
>
> At approximately 6:25 a.m. Beirut time, the truck drove past the Marine barracks. As the truck circled in the large parking lot behind the barracks, it increased its speed. The truck crashed through a concertina wire barrier and a wall of sandbags, and entered the barracks. When the truck reached the center of the barracks, the bomb in the truck detonated. . . .
>
> . . . The four-story Marine barracks was reduced to fifteen feet of rubble. *Peterson I,* 264 F. Supp. 2d at 54-58 (footnotes omitted.)

"As a result of the . . . explosion, 241 servicemen were killed, and many others suffered severe injuries." *Id.* at 58.

IV. Jurisdiction

The FSIA "is the sole basis of jurisdiction over foreign states in our courts." The FSIA concerns both subject-matter jurisdiction and personal jurisdiction. The Court has both.

A. Subject-Matter Jurisdiction

Several sections of the FSIA and related statutes set forth several specific requisites that must be satisfied for the Court to have jurisdiction over the subject matter of this case. These requisites may be broken down into four categories: grant of original jurisdiction, waiver of sovereign immunity, requirement that a claim be heard, and limitations. Plaintiffs . . . have satisfied all subject-matter jurisdictional requisites.

1. Grant of Original Jurisdiction.

The FSIA grants U.S. district courts "original jurisdiction without regard to amount in controversy of any nonjury civil against a foreign state . . . as to any claim for relief in personam with respect to which the foreign state is not entitled to immunity." §1330(a). . . .

. . . [Plaintiffs] have instituted this action against Iran and MOIS. . . . Iran, of course, is considered to be a foreign state. . . . MOIS is a political subdivision of Iran.

. . . [B]ecause this is a nonjury civil action against a foreign state for relief in personam to which the defendants are not immune, the Court has original jurisdiction over this case.

2. Waiver of Sovereign Immunity. . . .

. . . Under the FSIA terrorism exception, sovereign immunity is waived when (1) a foreign state (2) committed "an act of torture, extrajudicial killing, aircraft sabotage, hostage taking, or [provided] material support or resources for such an act if such act or provision of material support or resources is engaged in by an official, employee, or agent of such foreign state while acting within the scope of his or her office, employment, or agency," (3) which "caused" (4) "personal injury or death" (5) for which "money damages are sought." §1605A(1). . . .

. . . [Plaintiffs] allege that defendants committed torture, committed extrajudicial killing, and provided material support and resources therefor by providing operational control over and financial and technical assistance to Iranian agents of Hezbollah who constructed, deployed, and exploded the truck bomb, injuring and killing hundreds. . . .

. . . [C]oncerning causation, "there is no 'but-for' causation requirement" for claims made under the FSIA. In Kilburn v. Socialist People's Libyan Arab Jamahiriya [2004], a case which interpreted the substantially similar §1605(a)(7) that is now §1605A, this Circuit noted that in the FSIA, "the words 'but for' simply do not appear; only 'caused by' do." Adopting the Supreme Court's approach to a different but similarly worded jurisdictional statute, the Circuit interpreted the causation element "to require only a showing of 'proximate cause.' Plaintiffs . . . have sufficiently alleged causation.

. . . [Plaintiffs] allege several instances of personal injury and death for which money damages have been sought. The FSIA does not restrict the personal injury or death element to injury or death suffered directly by the claimant; instead, such injury or death must merely be the bases of a claim for which money damages are sought. §1605A(1). In this case, plaintiffs . . . alleged, of course, the deaths of 241 servicemen and numerous other physical injuries suffered by those who survived the attack, but also emotional and financial injury to survivors, decedents, decedent's estates, and decedent's family members, for which plaintiffs . . . seek millions of dollars in money damages. . . .

Accordingly, because plaintiffs . . . have brought suit against a foreign state for acts of torture and extrajudicial killing and the provision of material resources for the same which caused personal injury and death for which money damages have been sought, defendants are not entitled to sovereign immunity.

3. Requirement That a Claim Be Heard.

A federal district court "shall hear a claim" under the FSIA terrorism exception when certain conditions are met. §1605A(2). One such set of conditions applies where (1) "the foreign state was designated as a state sponsor of terrorism at the time the act" giving rise to the claim occurred "or was so designated as a result of such act," . . . (2) "the claimant or the victim was, at the time the act" giving rise to the claim, "a [U.S.] national . . . [,] a member of the armed forces[,] or otherwise an employee of the Government of the United States[ ] or of an individual performing a contract awarded by the United States Government . . ."; and (3) "in a case in which the act occurred in the foreign state against which the claim has been brought, the claimant has afforded the foreign state a reasonable opportunity to arbitrate the claim in accordance with the accepted international rules of arbitration." The FSIA elaborates on the first element by defining "state sponsor of terrorism" to mean "a country the government of which the Secretary of State has determined . . . is a government that has repeatedly provided support for acts of international terrorism" . . . .

First, concerning designation as a state sponsor of terrorism, Iran was so designated by the Secretary of State in partial response to the Beirut bombing. . . .

Second, concerning claimants and victims, the Court identifies victims as those who suffered injury or died as a result of the attack and claimants as those whose claims arise out of those injuries or deaths but who might not be victims themselves.

In this case, victims include the 241 members of the U.S. armed forces who were killed, the many more who were physically and emotionally injured, and the family members alleging injury suffered from intentional infliction of emotional distress, all of whom are [U.S.] nationals. . . . Claimants include the same groups or the estates thereof. . . .

Third and finally, because the Beirut bombing occurred in Lebanon, not the defendant-state, the arbitration requirements of §1605A(a)(2)(A)(iii) do not apply.

Accordingly, because Iran was designated a state sponsor of terror by the U.S. State Department as a partial result of the Beirut bombing . . . ; all victims and claimants were or are members of the U.S. armed forces, U.S. nationals, or the estates thereof; and arbitration need not be attempted, the Court is required by the FSIA to hear plaintiffs' claims.

4. Limitations.

All cases brought under §1605A face a 10-year limitations period. . . . The action to which this action is related — *Valore*— was commenced in 2003, well within the 10-year period after April 24, 1996. . . .

B. Personal Jurisdiction

The FSIA provides specific statutory rules controlling when a federal district court shall have personal jurisdiction over a foreign state, see §1608, and ordinary minimum-contacts requirements of the Fifth Amendment do not apply to non-person foreign entities, see TMR Energy, 411 F.3d at 299-302. . . . Applying these distinctions, the Court has personal jurisdiction under the FSIA over Iran . . . and MOIS . . . and the minimum-contacts test does not apply. . . .

V. Liability. . . .

In this case, both defendants are considered a foreign state and were and are designated state sponsors of terrorism at all times and for reasons giving rise to liability under the FSIA. Additionally, the bases for the alleged liability of these defendants are actions of their officials, employees, and agents. Defendants are therefore subject to liability under the FSIA-created cause of action. Further, plaintiffs . . . are or were nationals of the United States. . . . Finally, though not liable for torture, defendants are liable for extrajudicial killing and the provision of material support and resources for such killing, which was committed by officials, employees, and agents of defendants; which caused injury under several theories of liability; and for which the Court has jurisdiction for money damages. Therefore, plaintiffs . . . may recover the appropriate amount of damages as determined by the Court *infra* Part VI.

VI. Damages. . . .

Survivors of the Beirut Bombing are entitled to damages for the pain and suffering they endured and continue to endure to this day, as well as damages for economic losses. . . . Family members of victims of the Beirut Bombing are entitled to solatium. Finally, those plaintiffs who have requested them are entitled to punitive damages.

VIII. Conclusion

Iran and MOIS are responsible for the deaths and injuries of hundreds of American servicemen; are liable for physical, emotional, and pecuniary injuries suffered as a result; and deserve to be punished to the fullest legal extent possible. In a recent interview, Iranian President Mahmoud Ahmadinejad declared that he and his country "oppose terrorism. We strongly oppose" it. The Court sincerely hopes that the compensatory damages awarded today help to alleviate plaintiffs' . . . injuries, and that the punitive damages also awarded inspire Iran to adhere to its professed opposition to terrorism.

Notes and Questions

1. What seem to be the legislative purposes behind the 1605A exception? Do the offenses covered in the exception for foreign states that are designated state sponsors of terrorism seem to be the appropriate ones? Do you agree with the requirement that the victim or claimant be a U.S. national or employed by the U.S. government?

2. Do you agree with the provision requiring that the defendant state be given the opportunity to first arbitrate claims, in accordance with accepted international rules of arbitration, if the act occurred in the foreign state against which the claim has been brought? Might a state that the United States has designated as supporting terrorists be concerned about receiving a fair hearing in U.S. courts? If the foreign state can seek arbitration for acts within its own territory, why should that state not also be able to resort to arbitration for acts it has allegedly committed or supported in a third country—for example, Lebanon or Israel? Does the statute seem inconsistent here? Alternatively, if the country where the act allegedly occurred has a judicial system that provides a reasonable opportunity to a fair judicial proceeding, should a plaintiff first be required to exhaust the opportunity in that third country?

3. The text of Section 1605A specifically makes it retroactive. However, a ten-year statute of limitations applies. How do you think that the 1605A exception, enacted in 2008, is affected by the 2004 decision of the U.S. Supreme Court in Republic of Austria v. Altmann, supra, which determined that other provisions of the FSIA could be applied retroactively? Could a plaintiff argue that events that predate the ten-year statute of limitations are covered by the *Altmann* decision? Or, does the later-in-time rule apply?

4. In June of 2010, the Supreme Court held that an individual foreign official sued for conduct undertaken in his official capacity is not a "foreign state" and therefore is not entitled to immunity under the FSIA. See Samantar v. Yousuf, 130 S.Ct. 2278 (2010). Section 1605A provides that both a foreign state sponsor of terrorism and "any official, employee or agent" of such foreign state are liable under a private right of action. What are the implications of *Samantar* for individual foreign officials under 1605A? Should the text of Section 1605A creating a cause of action against both the "foreign state" and "any official, employee, or agent" of that state indicate that both the state and the individual can be sued under this FSIA section? (See the excerpt from and discussion of *Samantar* earlier in this section.)

5. In May of 2006, the State Department announced that the Bush Administration was removing Libya from the list of state sponsors of terrorism. Administration

spokespersons cited the Libyan government's destruction of chemical weapons stock and the cessation of a clandestine nuclear weapons program as reasons for lifting the designation. The issue was pressed by relatives of 230 of the victims of Libya's bombing of a Pam Am Flight over Lockerbie, Scotland. The payment of the final 20 percent of a $2.7 billion settlement, which provided about $10 million to the beneficiaries of each victim, was contingent on the removal of Libya from the list. The Libyan Claims Resolution Act, enacted on August 4, 2008, provides a blanket exception to the FSIA terrorism provisions for Libya upon the signing of an international agreement with the United States that settles all outstanding terrorism claims from a designated amount of money. The U.S.-Libya Claims Agreement was signed on August 14, 2008. This meant that Libya could no longer be sued under Section 1605A.

6. The pursuit of damages for terrorism under the FSIA often involves complex competing interests. On the one hand, Congress has a strong interest in compensating the victims of terrorist acts. However, Executive Branch considerations of foreign policy and security may prefer that claims be handled through diplomacy or even dropped entirely. For example, Iraq was removed from the list of state sponsors of terrorism in 2004 following the U.S. invasion and regime change. President Bush subsequently vetoed the first version of the 2008 amendments to the FSIA on the grounds that the enhanced provisions would open up Iraq to substantial liability, which could damage relations with the new government and jeopardize the security of American troops. The version that was ultimately signed into law included a provision authorizing the President to waive its application with respect to Iraq. The Bush administration immediately exercised the waiver.

7. Besides the *Murphy* decision, there have been numerous cases brought under section 1605A and its predecessor (a)(7), and many of them have resulted in large damage awards, sometimes amounting to up to about $300 million per deceased U.S. victim. These cases have concerned, among other things, the 1995 suicide bombing of a bus in Israel, see Flatow v. Islamic Republic of Iran, 999 F. Supp. 1 (D.D.C. 1998) (linking Iran to the terrorist group that was responsible for the attack); the bombing of Pan Am Flight 103 over Lockerbie, Scotland, in 1988, see Rein v. Socialist People's Libyan Arab Jamahiriya, 162 F.3d 748 (2d Cir. 1998); and the kidnapping and murder of American contractors by Al-Qaeda in Iraq, see Gates v. Syrian Arab Republic, 580 F.Supp.2d 53 (D.D.C. 2008).

8. Once a plaintiff secures a damage award against a state sponsor of terrorism, it remains difficult, if not impossible, to recover from the foreign state. Naturally, these states are not inclined to voluntarily pay the large punitive damage awards. These states also try to keep any attachable assets out of U.S. jurisdiction unless the U.S. government has already frozen the assets. To overcome this problem, early plaintiffs attempted to recover damage awards by attaching Iranian embassy properties and funds awarded to Iran through the Iran-U.S. Claims Tribunal. However, the Clinton Administration argued such attachments violated U.S. treaty obligations and exposed U.S. assets abroad, such as embassy and consulate buildings, to the risk other countries would take similar action.

Congress responded to this problem in 1998 by amending the FSIA section 1610 to add subsection (f). The amendment permitted execution or attachment by plaintiffs of property of state sponsors of terrorism in the United States frozen subject to the International Emergency Economic Powers Act (IEEPA) or the

Trading with the Enemy Act (TWEA). The amendment also required that State Department and Treasury officials "assist any [plaintiff] . . . in identifying, locating, and executing against the property" of a foreign state found responsible for terrorist acts under section 1605(a)(7). However, because of Executive Branch opposition, Congress inserted a provision that allowed the President to waive the ability to attach frozen property "in the interests of national security." Section 1610(f)(2)(B)(iii). President Clinton immediately invoked the waiver provision when he signed the legislation. He explained his reasons as follows:

> If this section were to result in attachment and execution against foreign embassy properties, it would encroach on my authority under the Constitution to "receive Ambassadors and other public Ministers." Moreover, if applied to foreign diplomatic or consular property, section 117 would place the United States in breach of its international treaty obligations. It would put at risk the protection we enjoy at every embassy and consulate throughout the world by eroding the principle that diplomatic property must be protected regardless of bilateral relations. . . . It would also effectively eliminate use of blocked assets of terrorist states in the national security interests of the United States, including denying an important source of leverage. In addition, [the section] could seriously affect our ability to enter into global claims settlements that are fair to all U.S. claimants, and could result in U.S. taxpayer liability in the event of a contrary claims tribunal judgment. [Statement by President William J. Clinton upon signing H.R. 4328, 34 Weekly Comp. Pres. Doc. 2108 (Nov. 2, 1998).]

With this avenue effectively foreclosed by Presidential waiver, Congress again came to the aid of certain victims with outstanding judgments against state sponsors of terrorism. In section 2002 of the Victims of Trafficking and Violence Protection Act of 2000, P.L. 106-386, Congress created a compensation system for plaintiffs whose cases against Cuba and Iran were decided prior to July 20, 2000 or were instituted on five dates actually specified in the bill. Of all the cases affected, one was against Cuba and the other ten were against Iran. The Act allowed payments of damages in the Cuban case of $96.7 million from frozen Cuban funds. Over $380 million in damages from the ten cases against Iran were to be paid out of the U.S. Treasury. After payment, these claims were then subrogated to the U.S. government, which was to "pursue these [claims] . . . in appropriate ways, including any negotiation process." Did Congress pursue the correct course in designing legislation to compensate U.S. terror victims? An original justification of the FSIA terrorism exception was the deterrent effect potential judgments would have on state sponsors of terrorism. Does the foregoing legislation accomplish that goal? And, when (if ever) is the U.S. government likely to obtain reimbursement from Iran of the funds the U.S. government paid out of the U.S. Treasury to the U.S. victims?

The Terrorism Risk Insurance Act (TRIA) of 2002 added several cases to the list that were compensable under section 2002 above. The TRIA also made any blocked assets available to satisfy outstanding judgments for compensatory, but not punitive, damages. As a nod to U.S. treaty obligations, Congress added a narrow waiver provision permitting the President to prevent attachment of "property subject to the Vienna Convention on Diplomatic Relations or the Vienna Convention on Consular Relations."

Finally, the 2008 terrorism amendments attempted to make it easier for plaintiffs to recover against state sponsors of terrorism by creating special procedures for attachment and execution of assets in cases under section 1605A, as discussed in the next section.

Does the ad hoc compensation system currently in effect seem like the best way to permit recovery of damage awards? Should victims of terrorism, some of whom were tourists or business people knowingly traveling in troubled places, receive many millions more in compensation than, say, police officers or military killed while on active duty? Or more than the victims of the September 11 attacks, whose surviving families received awards varying between $250,000 and $7.1 million from the September 11th Victim Compensation Fund, which was financed by the U.S. government? Can you think of a better system?

9. Outstanding judgments under section 1605A against a country might well come to exceed the country's assets now frozen in the United States, as has already occurred with the outstanding judgments against Iran. Pending cases could also lead to this situation occurring against Cuba. If U.S. diplomatic and commercial relations were then to improve with regard to one of these countries, possibly because of a change of government there, could the successful plaintiffs still go after that country's assets were they to come under U.S. jurisdiction? For example, if a Cuban or Iranian government-owned oil company in a moderate Cuba or Iran were to do business with U.S. customers, would the customers' payments awaiting transfer from U.S. banks be attachable? (See Chapter 5.A.6. regarding the obligations of successor governments.) If these assets were vulnerable, would this not put a damper on improving business relations between the United States and new, moderate governments? Would it put the United States at a disadvantage with other Western countries seeking to do business with new governments in the former terrorist states? Might these outstanding judgments be part of negotiations on a claims settlement agreement between the United States and the other country when relations were improving? (See the discussion about these agreements in *Dames & Moore* in Chapter 3.B.) Might section 1605A be amended so that judgments against a terrorist state would be conditioned to lapse upon a major change in the government of the state? Should the President be able to waive its provisions in the interests of national security, as Congress specifically allowed for Iraq? See generally Anne-Marie Slaughter & David Bosco, Plaintiff's Diplomacy, Foreign Affairs, Sept.-Oct. 2000, at 102.

10. In most of the cases brought under section former 1605(a)(7) and now section 1605A, the defendants have refused to show up for the case, and the courts have proceeded to enter default judgments. The FSIA requires that, before a default judgment can be entered against a foreign state, the claimant must "establish[] his claim or right to relief by evidence satisfactory to the court." 28 U.S.C. §1608(e). Even with this requirement, what effect might these default judgments have on the case law of foreign sovereign immunity?

11. Should the terrorism exception apply only to foreign states designated as state sponsors of terrorism, or should its scope be expanded to include more states? Perhaps all foreign states? For example, should Scott Nelson have been allowed to sue Saudi Arabia in the U.S. courts in the circumstances in the *Nelson* case, excerpted above? What are the practical implications of opening up American courts to suits under the 1605A exception against *any* foreign sovereign?

12. In November 2000, Iran's Parliament enacted a law that allows Iranian "victims of US interference since the 1953 coup d'etat" to sue the United States

in Iranian courts. This law was enacted as a "measure of reciprocity" in response to the suits allowed in U.S. courts against Iran. See Iran MPs Cry "Down with America," Approve Lawsuits Against United States, Agence France Presse, Nov. 1, 2000. In February 2003, an Iranian court entered a judgment of over $100 million against the U.S. government in a case brought by an Iranian businessman who was apprehended in 1992 in the Bahamas by undercover U.S. Customs agents for allegedly violating U.S. sanctions laws. Hossein Alikhani was flown to Florida where he was interrogated, which he claimed involved battery and abuse, and then jailed for three months. Commentators immediately drew a connection between Iran's allowance of this suit and the recent suits allowed against Iran in U.S. courts.

Should the United States be concerned about such "reciprocal" actions in foreign courts in response to broad U.S. claims of jurisdiction under such provisions as 1605A? What about Sudan allowing the owner of the chemical plant that U.S. cruise missiles destroyed in 1998 following the terrorist bombing of U.S. embassies in east Africa to sue the U.S. government for damages, including punitive damages, in Sudan's courts. (See discussion of the Al-Shifa case in U.S. courts in Chapter 3.A.2.d. There was apparently a lack of evidence showing a link between the chemical plant and terrorists.) Or, should Cuba allow its citizens to sue the U.S. government in Cuban courts for injuries allegedly caused by the U.S. trade embargo against Cuba?

13. Section 1605A is not the only statutory provision relevant to suits involving terrorism. Foreign plaintiffs may be able to use the Alien Tort Statute (discussed in Chapter 3) to sue non-state actors and foreign government officials for acts of terrorism, if the plaintiffs can establish that such acts violate customary international law or a U.S. treaty. In addition, both foreign and domestic plaintiffs may be able to use the Torture Victim Protection Act (also discussed in Chapter 3) to sue foreign government officials or others who commit acts of torture or extrajudicial killing "under actual or apparent authority, or color of law, of any foreign nation." In addition, in the early 1990s, Congress enacted a statute that provides a civil cause of action for U.S. nationals injured by an "act of international terrorism." See 18 U.S.C. §2333. The cause of action, however, does not include suits against states or against an officer or employee of a state who is acting "within his or her official capacity or under color of legal authority." 18 U.S.C. §2337. (This statute is discussed further in Chapter 7.)

14. For additional discussion of the state sponsor of terrorism exception, see Jennifer K. Elsea, Suits Against Terrorist States by Victims of Terrorism, CRS Report for Congress (updated August 8, 2008); Barry E. Carter, Terrorism Supported by Rogue States: Some Foreign Policy Questions Created by Involving U.S. Courts, 36 New Eng. L. Rev. 933 (2002); and Debra M. Strauss, Reaching Out to the International Community: Civil Lawsuits as the Common Ground in the Battle Against Terrorism, 19 Duke J. Comp. & Int'l L. 307 (2009).

15. Consider at this point all the exceptions, discussed above, to foreign sovereign immunity that are now in the FSIA. Can you fit them all into the public/private act distinction enunciated in the 1952 Tate letter? Which might not fit? Do you think all the FSIA exceptions are appropriate exceptions to foreign sovereign immunity? Which might not be?

13. Immunity from Attachment or Execution

The FSIA also contains important provisions regarding immunity from attachment or execution. As described in the House FSIA Report:

House Report No. 94-1487

Section 1609. Immunity from Attachment and Execution of Property of a Foreign State

As in the case of section 1604 of the bill with respect to jurisdiction, section 1609 states a general proposition that the property of a foreign state, as defined in section 1603(a), is immune from attachment and from execution, and then exceptions to this proposition are carved out in sections 1610 and 1611, Here, it should be pointed out that neither section 1610 nor 1611 would permit an attachment for the purpose of obtaining jurisdiction over a foreign state or its property. For this reason, section 1609 has the effect of precluding attachments as a means for commencing a lawsuit. . . .

Attachments for jurisdictional purposes have been criticized as involving U.S. courts in litigation not involving any significant U.S. interest or jurisdictional contacts, apart from the fortuitous presence of property in the jurisdiction. Such cases frequently require the application of foreign law to events which occur entirely abroad.

Such attachments can also give rise to serious friction in United States' foreign relations. In some cases, plaintiffs obtain numerous attachments over a variety of foreign government assets found in various parts of the United States. This shotgun approach has caused significant irritation to many foreign governments.

At the same time, one of the fundamental purposes of this bill is to provide a long-arm statute that makes attachment for jurisdictional purposes unnecessary in cases where there is a nexus between the claim and the United States. Claimants will clearly benefit from the expanded methods under the bill for service on a foreign state (sec. 1608), as well as from the certainty that section 1330(b) of the bill confers personal jurisdiction over a foreign state in Federal and State courts as to every claim for which the foreign state is not entitled to immunity. The elimination of attachment as a vehicle for commencing a lawsuit will ease the conduct of foreign relations by the United States and help eliminate the necessity for determinations of claims of sovereign immunity by the State Department.

Section 1610. Exceptions to Immunity from Attachment or Execution

Section 1610 sets forth circumstances under which the property of a foreign state is not immune from attachment or execution to satisfy a judgment. Though the enforcement or judgments against foreign state property remains a somewhat controversial subject in international law, there is a marked trend toward limiting the immunity from execution.

A number of treaties of friendship, commerce and navigation concluded by the United States permit execution of judgments against foreign publicly owned or controlled enterprises (for example, Treaty with Japan, April 2, 1953, art. 18(2), 4 UST 2063 . . .). The widely ratified Brussels Convention for the Unification of

Certain Rules relating to the Immunity of State-Owned Vessels, April 10, 1926, 196 L.N.T.S. 199, allows execution of judgments against public vessels engaged in commercial services in the same way as against privately owned vessels. Although not a party to this treaty, the United States follows a policy of not claiming immunity for its publicly-owned merchant vessels, both domestically, 46 U.S.C. 742, 781, and abroad, 46 U.S.C. 747. . . . Articles 20 and 21 of the Geneva Convention on the Territorial Sea and the Contiguous Zone, April 29, 1958, to which the United States is a party, recognize the liability to execution under appropriate circumstances of state-owned vessels used in commercial service.

However, the traditional view in the United States concerning execution has been that the property of foreign states is absolutely immune from execution. Even after the "Tate Letter" of 1952, this continued to be the position of the Department of State and of the courts. . . . Sections 1610(a) and (b) are intended to modify this rule by partially lowering the barrier of immunity from execution, so as to make this immunity conform more closely with the provisions on jurisdictional immunity in the bill. . . .

Section 1611. Certain Types of Property Immune from Execution

Section 1611 exempts certain types of property from the immunity provisions of section 1610 relating to attachment and execution.

Questions

1. Do the FSIA provisions increase or decrease the use of attachment of assets to obtain jurisdiction against a foreign state?

2. From the plaintiff's standpoint, is the FSIA system for obtaining jurisdiction usually preferable to the use of pre-judgment attachments? Why or why not?

3. Do the FSIA provisions increase or decrease the use of attachment or execution to satisfy a judgment against a foreign state? How?

4. If a plaintiff obtains a judgment for damages against a foreign state in the U.S. courts, is the plaintiff likely to be able to execute successfully against that sovereign's assets in the United States? See Letelier v. Republic of Chile, 748 F.2d 790 (2d Cir. 1984), *cert. denied*, 471 U.S. 1125 (1985) (plaintiffs were unable to execute against a commercial passenger jet of the state-owned Chilean airline, in part because the airline was deemed a separate entity and plaintiffs had failed to name it as a defendant in the initial suit on liability).

5. The 2008 amendments to the FSIA added several significant provisions intended to make it easier for plaintiffs to attach and execute on the property of state sponsors of terrorism. Section 1605A contains a novel procedure under which plaintiffs may file a lien of *lis pendens*.

> In every action filed in a United States district court [under Section 1605A] . . . the filing of a notice of pending action . . . shall have the effect of establishing a lien of lis pendens upon any real property or tangible personal property that is (A) subject to attachment in aid of execution, or execution, under section 1610; (B) located within that judicial district; and (C) titled in the name of any defendant. . . .

Originally a common law doctrine, liens of *lis pendens* do not by themselves act as prejudgment attachments, but serve as constructive notice of pending action concerning the property. They have the practical effect of limiting the potential transferability of the assets named in the notice. The 1605A procedure is very broad, allowing plaintiffs to file notice against any assets, without enumeration, in any district where they believe assets may be located. See Estate of Heiser v. Islamic Republic of Iran, 605 F.Supp.2d 248 (2009).

The 2008 amendments also added a new subjection (g) to section 1610. It provides that the property of a foreign state subject to a claim under section 1605A and the property of an agency or instrumentality of such a state

> including property that is a separate juridicial entity or is an interest held directly or indirectly in a separate juridicial entity, is subject to attachment in aid of execution, upon that judgment as provided in this section, regardless of (A) the level of economic control over the property by the government of the foreign state; (B) whether the profits of the property go to that government; (C) the degree to which officials of that government manage the property or otherwise control its daily affairs; (D) whether that government is the sole beneficiary in interest of the property; or (E) whether establishing the property as a separate entity would entitle the foreign state to benefits in United States courts while avoiding its obligations.

The purpose of this provision is to make any property in which state sponsors of terrorism have a beneficial ownership subject to execution, with some exceptions, such as for diplomatic and consular property. Congress therefore greatly expanded in terrorism cases the potential entities that might be subject to execution in contrast to the familiar, but more demanding test of extensive control. (See discussion of the so-called *Bancec* case in Section A.4. above.)

6. For further discussion of the FSIA generally, see, for example, Gary B. Born & Peter B. Rutledge, International Civil Litigation in United States Courts 297-344 (4th ed. 2007).

14. The Current Status of Foreign Sovereign Immunity Outside the United States

As noted in the 1952 Tate Letter above, with the exception of the Soviet Union and its allies, most other industrial countries adopted the restrictive theory of sovereign immunity even before the United States. The trend toward reduced immunity by foreign sovereigns continued in a large number of jurisdictions, including Great Britain, France, Germany, and Italy. Moreover, the FSIA rules on attachment and execution draw on and have many similarities with the European Convention on State Immunity and Additional Protocol, adopted in 1972, and the United Kingdom's State Immunity Act of 1978.

Professor Dellapenna describes these and other developments in the following excerpt.

Joseph W. Dellapenna, Suing Foreign Governments and Their Corporations

8-21 (2d ed. 2003)

§1.2 The Emergence of Restrictive Immunity Internationally

. . . While the immunity of foreign states in common law jurisdictions today is determined by a statute that purportedly codifies the whole law of the topic, in civil law countries foreign state immunity (and the immunities of the domestic sovereign as well) largely remains, as it nearly always has been in the civil law tradition, a judicial construct discoverable only from study of the *"jurisprudence"* (case law) of the relevant courts. Thus one must examine the cases in civil law countries if one is to predict how a current case will come out—despite the fact that civil law courts generally are not bound by a rule of precedent. Considerable debate emerged . . . [in civil law countries] over how to determine when a state acts in a private capacity or in a public capacity. The theories coalesced around two approaches hinging on the purpose, or on the nature, of the act. Gradually most [civil law countries] accepted the nature of the act as dispositive, but without universal agreement on what acts were by their nature public or private. Courts in each particular state have generally followed the more developed domestic immunity jurisprudence to determine the nature (or the purpose) of the act in question. . . .

French jurisprudence long leaned toward the purpose test for public acts, but more recent decisions have accepted the nature test. French courts have not been troubled by the private nature of state contracts relating to the development of natural resources, such as exploration for oil. On the other hand, French courts classify the expropriation of property without compensation as a public act. Such decisions further support the conclusion that French courts now classify acts as public or private according to their nature rather than their purpose.

. . . [French] courts [have] announced that the nature of the act determined immunity, and not the status of the entity that performs it. This principle has been applied to uphold immunity for a foreign national bank carrying out exchange controls, and in a suit against an Algerian state-owned corporation holding property expropriated without compensation. . . .

French courts now generally limit the property of the foreign state subject to execution according to whether the foreign state holds the property for public or private uses. On this basis, some courts have refused execution in the absence of proof of the precise purpose for which the assets are held. . . .

The German Law on the Constitution of Courts (*Gerichtsverfassungsgesetz*) declares that German courts cannot exercise jurisdiction over entities immune by virtue of general rules of international law. This provision became the basis for adopting the restrictive theory in Germany. . . .

German courts are definitely committed to the nature test for determining whether the specific act that is the basis for the suit is public or private. By this approach, the German courts have seldom sustained claims of immunity. Unlike courts in most other countries, German courts do not even require that the non-immune acts have a significant contact with Germany before permitting the proceeding to go forward. The major class of cases for which German courts have upheld immunity are instances involving the expropriation of property. The provision of information by New Scotland Yard to German police has also been held to be a public act. The one perhaps surprising decision in this jurisprudence was a decision that the performance of ordinary secretarial duties in a consulate was a public act.

German courts also held the USSR immune from claims for the loss of agricultural crops due to contamination from fallout from Chernobyl. The court held that German courts lacked jurisdiction because there was no non-immune property in Germany from which the court could derive jurisdiction, the USSR's regulatory responsibilities were a sovereign activity that did not in themselves give rise to liability, and the USSR did not itself operate the plant. Presumably suit could have been brought against the agency or instrumentality that operated the plant based on injuries in Germany, but how one would ever be able to enforce any resulting judgment remained highly unlikely.

The German practice regarding whether a secondary entity shares the immunity of a foreign state is in stark contrast with the French practice. While the French practice is functional, the German practice is structuralist, generally rejecting any claim of immunity on behalf of any juridically separate entity. The court in which most of these cases were decided, however, later conceded that a separate entity might share the state's immunity if it were performing public functions. The Federal Constitutional Court declined to consider the question, however, because the funds in question would not have been immune in any event.

The German practice is similarly straightforward towards immunity from execution, a matter that German courts have declared to be entirely derivative from immunity from suit. Possible future use of the funds for public purposes is simply irrelevant. . . .

§1.3 The British State Immunity Act

The acceptance of the restrictive theory of foreign state immunity came more slowly in common law nations. A transition from an absolute theory [was difficult] . . . owing to the doctrine of *stare decisis*. . . . Change in this regard generally required a statute rather than the development of the caselaw. The British State Immunity Act exemplifies the common law approach to the problem of state immunity outside the United States. . . .

The British State Immunity Act provides that states are "immune from the jurisdiction of the courts of the United Kingdom" except as provided elsewhere in the Act. Furthermore, the Act precludes jurisdiction if the action is between states regardless of the nature of the claim. The Act provides further that the immunity is to apply even if the foreign state does not appear in the proceeding. The State Immunity Act goes on to provide exceptions to immunity based upon (listed alphabetically):

(1) arbitrations involving foreign states and private parties;
(2) business associations issues;
(3) commercial transactions and contracts linked to the United Kingdom;
(4) damage or loss to tangible property caused by an act or omission in the United Kingdom;

(5) employment contracts made, and to be at least partly performed, in the United Kingdom;
(6) intellectual property rights perfected in the United Kingdom;
(7) maritime claims arising from the commercial use of a ship;
(8) personal injuries or death;
(9) property claims;
(10) submission to the jurisdiction of the courts of the United Kingdom; and
(11) tax claims arising from British taxes.

While the substantive core of the British State Immunity Act resembles our own Foreign Sovereign Immunities Act, in several respects the British Act is different and might even be superior. Most significantly, it provides a relatively clear definition of "commercial transaction":

(1) any contract for the supply of goods or services;
(2) any loan or other transaction for the provision of finance and any guarantee or indemnity in respect of any such transaction or of any other financial obligation; and
(3) any other transaction or activity (whether of a commercial, industrial, financial, professional or other similar character) into which a state enters or in which it engages otherwise than in the exercise of sovereign authority.

The definition, while leaving some residual uncertainty in its last clause, would have prevented some of the considerable difficulties our courts encountered under the "definition" provided in our Foreign Sovereign Immunities Act, although those problems can resurface when the residual clause "any other transaction or activity . . . into which a state enters or in which it engages otherwise than in the exercise of sovereign authority" applies. . . .

Torts, whether commercial or otherwise, pose some particular problems. The British State Immunity Act excludes torts arising out of nuclear injuries or the activities of foreign armed forces in the United Kingdom. The territorial requirement that injury or loss of property is actionable only if caused by an act or omission in the United Kingdom presumably precludes suits based on transboundary pollution directly affecting Britain. . . .

The Act expansively defines a "state" as including:

(1) the sovereign or other head of the state;
(2) the government of the state;
(3) any department of the government without a separate juridical personality; and
(4) juridically separate entities when exercising sovereign authority.

The Secretary of State for Foreign and Commonwealth Affairs has the authority to grant a conclusive certificate on such questions as whether a particular country is a "state" or whether a person is a head of state or government. . . . Absent a certification by the Secretary of State, the courts will decide the question through a factual inquiry into the actual status of the claimed state. . . .

§1.4 International Conventions on State Immunity

As the foregoing discussion indicates, the patterns regarding the immunity of foreign states found in the different states spread across Europe are not uniform. . . . [T]here could only be considerable uncertainty among the states of the emerging European Union as well as across Europe generally. To respond to this concern, the member states of the Council [of] Europe completed the drafting of the European Convention on State Immunity in 1972. . . . [It entered into force in 1976 with three ratifications. As of February 2011, however, it had been ratified by only eight nations: Austria, Belgium, Cyprus, Germany, Luxembourg, the Netherlands, Switzerland, and the United Kingdom.] In part, this slow acceptance reflects the willingness of many European states to await the completion of a treaty based on the work of the International Law Commission.

Superficially, the European Convention appears to have had even less impact than the handful of ratifications might suggest. According to British practice, for example, the British State Immunity Act controls over any inconsistent provisions of the Convention even though the Convention was ratified about a year after the Act was adopted. The Convention, however, had a significant impact on the drafting of the British State Immunity Act, and in fact the goal of making British law on the topic consistent with the Convention was one of the stated purposes for enactment of the statute.

Structurally, the European Convention takes the opposite approach from both the Foreign Sovereign Immunities Act and the British State Immunity Act, both of which start from a presumption of state immunity. The European Convention begins in 14 articles by declaring that foreign states are not immune, and leaves the rule of immunity as a residual rule for cases not covered by the provisions precluding immunity. This perhaps suggests that the presumption is to be against immunity, but there are no precedents to settle the question.

With only a few exceptions, immunity is precluded for claims under the same circumstances as provided in the British Act. . . .

The European Convention has no general rule precluding immunity for commercial activities, although it does preclude immunity when the litigation concerns "industrial, commercial, or financial activity" that the state conducts through . . . "an office, agency, or other establishment" created on the territory of the forum state for such purposes. The Convention's provision on non-immunity for torts adds a requirement that the tortfeasor must have been in the forum state when the facts giving rise to the litigation occurred.

As an example of international practice, the European Court of Human Rights found that it was "unable to discern in the international instruments, judicial authorities or other materials before it any firm basis for concluding that, as a matter of international law, a State no longer enjoys immunity from civil suit in the courts of another State where acts of torture are alleged," even assuming the peremptory nature of the prohibition on torture, Al-Adsani v. United Kingdom, App. No. 35763/97 (Nov. 21, 2001).

A potentially important international treaty, the U.N. Convention on Jurisdictional Immunities of States and Their Property, was adopted by the U.N. General

Assembly in December 2004. The Convention is now awaiting the required 30 ratifications, acceptances, approvals, or accessions to come into force. As of February 2011, only 11 countries had done so. The United States has not yet signed nor ratified it. Reportedly, a U.S. signature is not imminent, in part because of concerns about the lack of some exceptions (e.g., terrorism) and because of concerns about the implications of U.S. signature (but a slow ratification process) under Article 18 of the Vienna Convention on the Law of Treaties. (See Chapter 2.A.)

The Convention is the first modern multilateral agreement (beyond the countries of Europe) to provide for a comprehensive approach to questions of sovereign immunity in foreign courts. It is based on the restrictive theory of immunity. As described by David P. Stewart, who was on the U.S. delegation to the negotiations:

> Substantively, [the Convention] provides that, subject to certain specified exceptions, a state enjoys immunity from the jurisdiction of foreign courts in respect of itself and its property. The express exceptions include, inter alia, claims arising from: commercial transactions; contracts of employment; personal injury and damage to property; ownership, possession, and use of property; intellectual and industrial property; . . . certain matters relating to arbitration proceedings; and situations involving consent to jurisdiction. . . . Separate articles provide criteria for service of process and rendering default judgments. . . .
>
> . . . The term "state" is defined broadly [to include the state itself, its organs, political subdivisions, and agencies and instrumentalities when the last category is] "entitled to perform and are actually performing acts in the exercise of sovereign authority of the State."
>
> The definition of "state" also explicitly embraces "representatives of the State acting in that capacity." By including individuals who represent the state (in addition to heads of state, whose immunity . . . is specifically dealt with . . . , the convention clearly endorses the broader principle of "foreign official liability." [David P. Stewart, The UN Convention on Jurisdictional Immunities of States and Their Property, 99 Am. J. Int'l L. 194, 195-96 (2005).]

In addition, it is generally understood that the Convention's provisions do not cover criminal proceedings. The Convention contains an explicit general rule that it is not retroactive.

For a discussion of sovereign immunity in China, which still purports to follow the absolute theory of immunity, see James V. Feinerman, Sovereign Immunity in the Chinese Case and Its Implications for the Future of International Law, in Essays in Honour of Wang Tieya 251 (R. St. John MacDonald ed., 1993). Chinese authorities, however, have reportedly been more willing recently to negotiate contractual provisions that waive the sovereign immunity of Chinese government entities in foreign courts or international arbitral arrangements.

15. The Legal Status of Embassies and Consulates

Related to the issue of foreign sovereign immunity and the FSIA is the question of the legal status of embassies and consulates. These premises are generally immune under international and U.S. law from attachment or execution. Even more than that, these premises often enjoy a special status in the United States as well as in other countries.

Contrary to popular belief, however, diplomatic mission and consular post properties are not extensions of the sending state's territory. Both in fact and in law, diplomatic premises are within the territory of the receiving state. Nevertheless, as section 466 of the Restatement states: "The premises . . . of an accredited diplomatic mission or consular post [in the territory of another state] are inviolable, and are immune from any exercise of jurisdiction by the receiving state that would interfere with their official use."

This summary is drawn from the Vienna Convention on Diplomatic Relations of April 18, 1961, 23 U.S.T. 3227, and the Vienna Convention on Consular Relations of April 24, 1963, 21 U.S.T. 77. (Both Conventions are in the Documentary Supplement.) The Conventions have been widely adopted, including by the United States. The United States has also adopted statutes extending key provisions of the Convention on Diplomatic Relations to the diplomatic missions of nonratifying countries.

The Conventions' concept of "inviolability" imposes two separate obligations on the receiving, or host, state. The first is to refrain from acting within the diplomatic premise. Diplomatic missions are immune from searches, seizures, attachment, execution, or any other form of enforcement jurisdiction that might interfere with the premise's official use. In practical terms, the receiving state can rarely exercise enforcement jurisdiction within a diplomatic premise. See, e.g., 767 Third Avenue Associates v. Permanent Mission of the Republic of Zaire to the United Nations, 988 F.2d 295 (2d Cir. 1993) (holding that the Zaire mission to the United Nations could not be evicted from its property in New York, despite having failed to pay its rent).

The second duty imposed on receiving states is protecting diplomatic premises from private interference. In the United States, the District of Columbia and the federal government have enacted statutes for this purpose, curtailing permissible activity within 500 feet of diplomatic premises. The statutes are aimed at preventing private group interference with diplomatic property. Violation of any of the statutes can result in a fine or imprisonment. See Boos v. Barry, 485 U.S. 312 (1988). (The Supreme Court upheld a clause of a D.C. statute that makes it unlawful "to congregate" within 500 feet of an embassy "and refuse to disperse after having been ordered to do so by the police." The Court, however, struck down as violating the First Amendment another clause of the statute that made it unlawful to display any sign that tends to bring the foreign government into "public odium" or "public disrepute.")

While a number of underlying theories have been offered for granting these immunities (e.g., respect for an equal sovereign, reciprocity, or ancient custom), the most common justification is functional necessity. Diplomats and consuls carry out functions that are often highly confidential, sensitive, or unpopular. Diplomatic premises are necessary for these functions. If diplomatic premises were subject to the receiving state's enforcement jurisdiction and not protected, diplomats would encounter additional obstacles to fulfilling their responsibilities.

Inviolability does not, however, exempt diplomatic premises from legislative jurisdiction. While the laws of the receiving state cannot be enforced, these laws apply with equal force within diplomatic premise walls. Whether an action triggers criminal or civil liability is determined by the receiving state's law.

For example, when criminal acts occur on diplomatic premises and inviolability either does not apply or is not invoked, those acts may be prosecuted under local law. In Fatemi v. United States, 192 A.2d 525 (D.C. 1963), for example, protestors refused to leave the Iranian embassy in Washington. The head of the mission authorized local police to arrest the demonstrators. In defense, the protestors contended that the local court lacked jurisdiction because the crime occurred in the Iranian embassy and therefore in Iranian territory. In rejecting this claim, the D.C. Court of Appeals held that diplomatic premises are part of the territory of the receiving state and when inviolability is not invoked, prosecution under municipal law is permissible.

When inviolability is invoked or applicable, the conflict between municipal law violations and the receiving state's inability to prosecute can result in disputes. For instance, diplomatic missions in Washington are required to conform to District of Columbia building and fire codes; conformance, however, cannot be enforced due to diplomatic premise inviolability. As a result, there is a continuing tension between municipal authorities and resident diplomatic missions. Under the Foreign Missions Act of 1982, 22 U.S.C. §§4301 et seq., the Secretary of State is authorized to withhold "benefits" (e.g., utilities, construction permits, American workers) from missions that violate local law.

While there is a firm consensus on the core issues of diplomatic premise inviolability, a number of issues remain in dispute. No consensus has been reached regarding either the propriety of grants of diplomatic asylum on diplomatic premises or about entry by receiving state officials in the event of an emergency. Both Vienna Conventions expressly avoided these issues.

Notes and Questions

1. What good reasons are there for making an embassy inviolable? What are the drawbacks? Do the present provisions of the Vienna Convention on Diplomatic Relations seem to strike the right balance? If the United States does not adhere to these provisions, what might the ramifications be for U.S. embassies abroad?

2. *A*, a diplomat from country *X* to country *Y*, is caught stealing documents from country *X*'s embassy. Country *X* waives any personal diplomatic immunity that *A* might enjoy and does not invoke its premise inviolability. May *A* avoid prosecution for theft in country *Y* by asserting that the crime was committed on "foreign soil"? See Rex v. A. B., 1 KB. 454 (1941) (United Kingdom).

3. After the American hostages in Iran were released, a number of former hostages and their families attempted to obtain compensation from the Islamic Republic of Iran based in part on the FSIA's noncommercial tort exception. (This was before Congress enacted the exception for state sponsors of terrorism.) This act denies the sovereign immunity defense with respect to certain injuries or other damages occurring within U.S. territory. Could the former hostages maintain their action under the FSIA? See Persinger v. Islamic Republic of Iran, 729 F.2d 835 (D.C. Cir. 1983), and McKeel v. Islamic Republic of Iran, 722 F.2d 582 (9th Cir. 1983) (U.S. embassy was not part of U.S. territory for FSIA purposes.) Even with the new exception for state sponsors of terrorism, the American hostages have

been unsuccessful in their suits against Iran. See Roeder v. Islam Republic of Iran, 333 F.3d 228 (D.C. Cir. 2003) and Roeder v. Islamic Republic of Iran, No. 08-487 (EGS), 2010 U.S. Dist. LEXIS 104905, at *1 (D.D.C. Sept. 10, 2010). Federal courts have held that Congress has not acted definitively and unambiguously to abrogate the Algiers Accords, which prohibited suits by the hostages against Iran.

4. After the United States invaded Panama in December 1989, General Manuel Noriega, the Panamanian leader, took refuge from U.S. troops in the Vatican embassy (or nunciature) in Panama City. For a day or two while Noriega was inside the embassy, U.S. soldiers outside directed speakers at the embassy and played rock music at very high decibel levels. Was that activity consistent with the principles in the Vienna Convention on Diplomatic Relations? Noriega later left the Vatican embassy voluntarily, surrendered to U.S. officials, and was flown to the United States to stand trial on charges of drug smuggling. (For a discussion of the U.S. invasion of Panama, see Chapter 11.)

16. Personal Immunity for Diplomats and Consuls

At least as well protected as the embassies and consulates are the diplomats themselves. Diplomatic personal inviolability in some form has been universally recognized. Ancient civilizations, both Western and Eastern, accorded envoys personal inviolability.

By the end of the Middle Ages, diplomatic personal immunity from criminal and civil liability was entrenched in international law. Although occasionally criticized by commentators and violated by sovereigns, this personal inviolability has remained essentially unchanged. One justification for this inviolability was put forward by Grotius in the seventeenth century. Known as "extraterritoriality," it created the fiction that a diplomat (and his residence) legally remained in the sending state. This theory remained popular until the late nineteenth century.

In more contemporary times, personal inviolability of diplomatic agents has been codified in the Vienna Convention on Diplomatic Relations, which went into force in 1964 and the United States ratified in 1972. Rather than using the word "extraterritoriality," the preamble to the Convention couches the diplomatic privileges and immunities in terms of functional necessity—that is, helping the diplomat perform his duties. (See Documentary Supplement.) However, personal immunity is very broad. For example, Article 29 provides: "The person of a diplomatic agent shall be inviolable. He shall not be liable to any form of arrest or detention. The receiving State shall treat him with due respect and shall take all appropriate steps to prevent any attack on his person, freedom or dignity."

Article 31 then provides, in part, that "[a] diplomatic agent shall enjoy immunity from [the receiving State's] criminal[,] . . . civil[,] and administrative jurisdiction, except in the case of . . . an action relating to any professional or commercial activity exercised by the diplomatic agent in the receiving State outside his official functions." Courts have interpreted the commercial activity exception in this article narrowly to cover only trade or business engaged in for personal profit, not business relationships that are incidental to the daily life of a diplomat. See, e.g., Tabion v. Mufti, 73 F.3d 535 (4th Cir. 1996) (holding that diplomatic immunity extended to suit brought by a present diplomat's domestic servant concerning her employment relationship with the diplomat).

The scope of immunity provided for diplomats after their period of service has ended (residual diplomatic immunity) is much narrower. Article 39(2) extends immunity only to acts performed by the diplomat "in the exercise of his functions as a member of the mission." See, e.g., Swarna v. Al-Awadi 622 F.3d 123 (2d. Cir. 2010) (refusing to extend residual diplomatic immunity to former Kuwaiti diplomat because his employment of a domestic servant was a private act unrelated to "his functions as a member of the mission").

Consular immunity can be substantially different from diplomatic immunity. The modern consul derives from the practice of thirteenth- and fourteenth-century Venetian merchants in foreign ports choosing one of their number to represent them. Consuls were gradually given other responsibilities, such as adjudicating disputes between countrymen abroad. While this practice declined during the sixteenth century, it reemerged at the end of the seventeenth century and became very popular as trade between nations increased during the late eighteenth and throughout the nineteenth centuries.

Consuls were rarely granted any immunity, although they were accorded a great amount of respect. This was primarily due to the nature of the consuls themselves; they were merchants who carried out their duties as consuls in addition to carrying out their trade. Professional or career consuls are a relatively recent phenomena, first becoming common in the nineteenth century. Their present roles include issuing passports and visas, helping the nationals of their own (or the sending) state, and promoting the development of commercial, cultural, and other ties between the countries.

As more career consuls appeared, specific immunities were negotiated between nations as part of their consular agreements. Normally, career consuls were considered inviolable, while honorary or nonprofessional consuls were immune from liability for official acts. This dichotomy is continued in the Vienna Convention on Consular Relations. Like diplomats, career consuls are generally inviolable. Honorary consuls are accorded immunity for their official acts but remain liable for their acts not related to consular business.

Notes and Questions

1. In 1997, a Georgian diplomat, Gueorgui Makharadze, killed an American teenager in a car accident in Washington, D.C. The diplomat was very drunk and driving at a high rate of speed on a city street. Under diplomatic immunity, Makharadze could have escaped prosecution in the United States. However, Georgia's president, Eduard Shevardnadze, decided to waive his immunity. The Georgian diplomat was convicted and sentenced by a D.C. court to 7 to 21 years for involuntary manslaughter.

The waiver of the Georgian diplomat's immunity extended only to criminal prosecution and not to civil litigation. The D.C. District Court held that Georgia's waiver of Makharadze's immunity was limited to criminal prosecution because neither the Department of State's request to Georgia for a waiver of immunity nor the actual waiver expressly mentioned civil litigation. The court reasoned that "Article 31 of the Convention does not confer immunity in a single blanket statement, but confers criminal immunity in one sentence and civil and administrative immunity separately, in another sentence. This suggests that the Convention considers immunity from criminal jurisdiction and immunity from civil and administrative jurisdiction to be distinct privileges." The court also stated that although Makharadze was no longer a diplomat when the civil suit was filed, he nevertheless had "residual immunity" because he was attending a business dinner at the time of the crash. Should there be distinctive civil and criminal immunities? Do you think that express waiver of civil immunity was necessary in Makharadze's case? See Knab v. Republic of Georgia, Civ. No. 97-3118, 1998 U.S. Dist. LEXIS 8820 (D.D.C. May 29, 1998).

2. If a foreign state refuses to waive a diplomat's immunity, does this mean that injured parties in the United States are left without a remedy? What about diplomatic remedies? Remedies in the courts of the foreign state?

17. *Head-of-State Immunity*

Related to the doctrines of foreign sovereign immunity, common law foreign official immunity, and diplomatic immunity is the question of immunity for heads of state and other high-level foreign officials. This question is one of common law and is not specifically addressed in either the FSIA or in the treaties and statutes governing diplomatic immunity. In the decision below, the court considered a defense of head-of-state immunity raised on behalf of General Manuel Noriega of Panama, whom the U.S. government had seized in Panama and brought back to the United States for trial on drug trafficking charges.

United States v. Noriega

U.S. Court of Appeals
117 F.3d 1206 (11th Cir. 1997)

KRAVITCH, Senior Circuit Judge:

Manuel Antonio Noriega appeals: (1) his multiple convictions stemming from his involvement in cocaine trafficking; and (2) the district court's denial of his motion for a new trial based on newly discovered evidence. In attacking his convictions, Noriega asserts that the district court should have dismissed the indictment against him due to his status as a head of state. . . .

On February 4, 1988, a federal grand jury indicted Manuel Antonio Noriega on drug-related charges. At that time, Noriega served as commander of the Panamanian Defense Forces in the Republic of Panama. Shortly thereafter, Panama's president, Eric Arturo Delvalle, formally discharged Noriega from his military post, but Noriega refused to accept the dismissal. Panama's legislature then ousted Delvalle from power. The United States, however, continued to acknowledge Delvalle as the constitutional leader of Panama. Later, after a disputed presidential election in Panama, the United States recognized Guillermo Endara as Panama's legitimate head of state.

On December 15, 1989, Noriega publicly declared that a state of war existed between Panama and the United States. Within days of this announcement by Noriega, President George Bush directed United States armed forces into combat in Panama for the stated purposes of "safeguard[ing] American lives, restor[ing] democracy, preserv[ing] the Panama Canal treaties, and seiz[ing] Noriega to face federal drug charges in the United States." . . . The ensuing military conflagration resulted in significant casualties and property loss among Panamanian civilians. Noriega lost his effective control over Panama during this armed conflict, and he surrendered to United States military officials on January 3, 1990. Noriega then was brought to Miami to face the pending federal charges.

Following extensive pre-trial proceedings and a lengthy trial, a jury found Noriega guilty of eight counts in the indictment and not guilty of the remaining two counts. The district court entered judgments of conviction against Noriega upon the jury's verdict and sentenced him to consecutive imprisonment terms of 20, 15 and five years, respectively. . . .

Noriega first argues that the district court should have dismissed the indictment against him based on head-of-state immunity. He insists that he was entitled to such immunity because he served as the *de facto*, if not the *de jure*, leader of Panama. The district court rejected Noriega's head-of-state immunity claim because the United States government never recognized Noriega as Panama's legitimate, constitutional ruler.

The Supreme Court long ago held that "[t]he jurisdiction of courts is a branch of that which is possessed by the nation as an independent sovereign power. The jurisdiction of the nation within its own territory is necessarily exclusive and absolute. It is susceptible of no limitation not imposed by itself." The Schooner Exchange v. McFaddon, 11 U.S. (7 Cranch) 116, 136 (1812). The Court, however, ruled that nations, including the United States, had agreed implicitly to accept certain limitations on their individual territorial jurisdiction based on the "common interest impelling [sovereign nations] to mutual intercourse, and an interchange of good offices with each other. . . ." Id. at 137. Chief among the exceptions to jurisdiction was "the exemption of the *person of the sovereign* from arrest or detention within a foreign territory." Id. (emphasis added).

The principles of international comity outlined by the Court in *The Schooner Exchange* led to the development of a general doctrine of foreign sovereign immunity. . . . As this doctrine emerged, the "Court consistently [] deferred to the decisions of the political branches — in particular, those of the Executive Branch — on whether to take jurisdiction over actions against foreign sovereigns and their instrumentalities."

In 1976, Congress passed the Foreign Sovereign Immunities Act ("FSIA"). . . . Because the FSIA addresses neither head-of-state immunity, nor foreign sovereign immunity in the criminal context, head-of-state immunity could attach in cases, such as this one, only pursuant to the principles and procedures outlined in *The Schooner Exchange* and its progeny. As a result, this court must look to the Executive Branch for direction on the propriety of Noriega's immunity claim.

Generally, the Executive Branch's position on head-of-state immunity falls into one of three categories: the Executive Branch (1) explicitly suggests immunity; (2) expressly declines to suggest immunity; or (3) offers no guidance. Some courts have held that absent a formal suggestion of immunity, a putative head of state should receive no immunity. See, e.g., In re Doe, 860 F.2d 40, 45 (2d Cir. 1988). In the analogous pre-FSIA, foreign sovereign immunity context, the former Fifth Circuit accepted a slightly broader judicial role. It ruled that, where the Executive

Branch either *expressly* grants or denies a request to suggest immunity, courts must follow that direction, but that courts should make an independent determination regarding immunity when the Executive Branch neglects to convey clearly its position on a particular immunity request. See Spacil v. Crowe, 489 F.2d 614, 618-19 (5th Cir. 1974) (granting petition for writ of mandamus directing district court to follow government's suggestion of immunity in civil case).

Noriega's immunity claim fails under either the *Doe* or the *Spacil* standard. The Executive Branch has not merely refrained from taking a position on this matter; to the contrary, by pursuing Noriega's capture and this prosecution, the Executive Branch has manifested its clear sentiment that Noriega should be denied head-of-state immunity. . . . Moreover, given that the record indicates that Noriega never served as the constitutional leader of Panama, that Panama has not sought immunity for Noriega and that the charged acts relate to Noriega's private pursuit of personal enrichment, Noriega likely would not prevail even if this court had to make an independent determination regarding the propriety of immunity in this case. . . . Accordingly, we find no error by the district court on this point. . . .

Notes and Questions

1. Noriega's U.S. prison sentence ended in September 2007. His release from prison, however, was halted by pending extradition requests from both France and Panama. In April 2010, U.S. Secretary of State Hillary Rodham Clinton signed off on Noriega's extradition to France. He subsequently stood trial there for money laundering charges and was sentenced to seven years in prison.

2. Do you think there should be immunity for heads of states for actions taken while they are heads of state? Should it be absolute immunity or should it be a restrictive immunity under which certain actions are not immune — for example, commercial activity or noncommercial torts?

3. Should head-of-state immunity extend to other high ranking officials, such as the Secretary of State (or Foreign Minister), other Cabinet officers, or chiefs of police? Should it extend to their spouses or children?

4. After the U.S. Supreme Court's decision in Samantar v. Yousuf, 130 S. Ct. 2278,(2010), foreign officials — including foreign heads of state — are unable to claim immunity as a foreign state or as an agency or instrumentality under the Foreign Sovereign Immunities Act. This lack of statutory guidance will make it even more likely that U.S. courts will generally then look to the Executive Branch for suggestions of immunity. For cases in which the courts have followed Executive Branch guidance in the past, see, for example, Doe I v. State of Israel, 400 F. Supp. 2d 86 (D.D.C. 2005) (granting head of state immunity to Israeli Prime Minister Ariel Sharon when the executive branch filed a suggestion of immunity with the court), Tachiona v. United States, 386 F.3d 205 (2d Cir. 2004) (granting immunity to the president and foreign minister of Zimbabwe); Wei Ye v. Jiang Zemin, 383 F.3d 620 (7th Cir. 2004) (head of state immunity recognized for president of China because of U.S. government suggestion of immunity was conclusive).

When the Executive Branch offers no guidance, courts diverge. Some courts have held that in the absence of Executive Branch suggestions of immunity, courts are to determine on their own whether a head of state should be granted immunity. In some cases, the Executive Branch's failure to offer any guidance seems to have played a role in denying head of state immunity. See, e.g., First America Corp. v. Al-Nahyan, 948 F. Supp. 1107 (D.D.C. 1996).

5. In 2000 Belgium issued an international arrest warrant for Foreign Minister Abdulaye Yerodia Ndombasi of the Democratic Republic of the Congo. The Congolese government replied by instituting an action in the ICJ claiming the arrest warrant violated several international law principles, including the diplomatic immunity of ministers of foreign affairs. See Case Concerning the Arrest Warrant of 11 April 2000 (Democratic Republic of the Congo v. Belgium), 2002 I.C.J. 3 (Feb. 14). The Court held that, under customary international law, Belgium had violated Congo's rights in issuing the arrest warrant.

The Court noted that "in international law it is firmly established that . . . certain holders of high-ranking office in a State, such as the Head of a State, Head of Government and Minister for Foreign Affairs, enjoy immunities from jurisdiction in other States, both civil and criminal." After examining state practice, the Court also concluded that "[N]o distinction can be drawn between acts performed by a Minister for Foreign Affairs in an 'official' capacity, and those claimed to have been performed in a 'private capacity.' " It further stated that "it [was] unable to deduce from this [State] practice that there exists under customary international law any form of exception to the rule according immunity from criminal jurisdiction . . . where they are suspected of having committed war crimes or crimes against humanity."

6. What about immunity for a former head of state? Similar to the situation with the present head of state, most U.S. courts look to the executive branch for guidance. In most cases, though, the claims for former head-of-state immunity have been resolved because the new government has waived the immunity of the former head of state's country and because it is generally accepted that the foreign government can do this. See, e.g., In re Doe, 860 F.2d 40, 45-46 (2d Cir. 1988) (former Philippine president's immunity waived by new Philippine government).

7. Augusto Pinochet, the former president of Chile, was placed under house arrest while visiting Great Britain on an extradition warrant issued at the request of Spanish authorities charging Pinochet with torture, hostage taking, abduction, and murder. The case ultimately reached the British House of Lords. The Law Lords drew a distinction between the immunity enjoyed by a sitting head, which renders him immune from claims whether or not they relate to matters done for the benefit of the state (immunity *ratione personae*), and the more limited immunity of a former head of state, which extends only to his official acts during his tenure in office (immunity *ratione materiae*). Regina v. Bow Street Metropolitan Stipendiary Magistrate and Others, Ex parte Pinochet Ugarte, [2000] 1 A.C. 147, 201-202 (1999) (opinion of Lord Browne Wilkinson).

A majority of the Law Lords concluded that the 1984 Torture Convention abrogated any of Pinochet's claims of head-of-state immunity rooted in customary international law. However, doctors examined Pinochet and found him unfit to stand trial in Spain, and he returned to Chile. Should a former, or even a sitting, head of state be given immunity against allegations of torture, hostage taking, and murder under customary international law? Are these crimes not serious enough to abrogate head of state immunity, or other the immunity of other foreign officials, even in the absence of an applicable treaty? See Chapter 12.B.

18. *Other Immunities*

Besides the diplomatic, consular, and head of state immunities discussed in the immediately preceding subsections and foreign officials' common law immunity discussed after *Samantar* in subsection 4 above, other immunities might be available in certain situations.

Most countries, including the United States, are parties to the General Convention on the Privileges and Immunities of the United Nations, which went into effect in September 1946 and has 157 parties as of February 2011. The Convention expanded upon and helped implement in some states Article 105 of the U.N. Charter. Article 105 provides that the representatives of U.N. members and U.N. officials shall "enjoy such privileges and immunities as are necessary for the independent exercise of their functions in connection" with the United Nations.

Similarly, in addition to the General Convention, there is the Convention on the Privileges and Immunities of the Specialized Agencies, which provides for immunities of organizations related to the United Nations under Articles 57 and 63 of the U.N. Charter. As of February 2011, the Convention has 116 parties, though not the United States. Also, many international and regional organizations have provisions in their charters providing for some immunities.

Also, some countries recognize immunities for temporary missions and special envoys from another country. For example, there is a Convention on Special Missions, which came into force in June 1985. As of February 2011, the Convention had 38 parties, not including the United States. The Convention provides that officials from a foreign state on special missions are entitled to immunity to the extent required by the performance of the person's official duties. For further information about the immunities of international organizations and their personnel, see, for example, Hazel Fox, The Law of State Immunity 724 (2008).

B. THE ACT OF STATE DOCTRINE

Besides the question of whether a foreign sovereign is immune from the jurisdiction of the court, statehood can raise special questions when a court begins to address the substantive issues in the dispute. A defendant foreign sovereign or other party can argue that the plaintiff has no basis for its claims because the challenged acts of the foreign sovereign are valid, and the plaintiff thereby loses.

As detailed below, the act of state doctrine, which is sometimes invoked in U.S. courts, provides that certain acts of a foreign state will be presumed to be valid, and the court will not sit in judgment on them. The doctrine can arise in a surprisingly wide variety of situations. Note, for example, that unlike foreign sovereign immunity, private parties can seek to rely on the doctrine.

Also unlike foreign sovereign immunity, which was codified by Congress in 1976, the act of state doctrine is still essentially a judicial doctrine—and it can be a complicated one at that. Defining its scope and the possible exceptions to it is a challenge.

Although the act of state doctrine is particularly strong in the United States, the courts in most foreign states have exercised some restraint in adjudicating challenges to the acts of other states, such as on the issue of expropriation. The status of the act of state doctrine in other countries is noted in a number of U.S. opinions.

The current status of the doctrine in other countries is addressed at the end of this chapter.

Another way to look at the act of state doctrine is that it is a special rule for conflict-of-law situations. A court will usually apply the law of the state where the principal acts occurred or where the center of gravity of the relevant act is. (See Chapter 7.C.) However, this usual approach may be set aside where the law would violate an important public policy of the forum state, such as allowing an expropriation of private property without just compensation. (See Restatement (Second) of Conflict of Laws §90 (1971); cf. Restatement of Foreign Relations Law (Third) §469, Reporters' note 1 (1987).) When a foreign state's acts are involved, the act of state doctrine may even prevent the use of a public policy exception under the host country's laws to stop applicability of the foreign law. The end result is that the foreign law is left controlling.

1. Historical Background

In this chapter we examine the development and current status of the act of state doctrine in U.S. courts. The doctrine can be traced to early decisions granting foreign governments and their leaders immunity from suit. See, e.g., The Schooner Exchange v. M'Faddon, 11 U.S. (7 Cranch) 116 (1812).

The U.S. Supreme Court first clearly invoked the doctrine in Underhill v. Hernandez, 168 U.S. 250 (1897), a case that arose out of the events of the Venezuelan revolution of 1892. George Underhill was an American citizen who had been living in Bolivar, Venezuela. He had constructed a waterworks system for the city and was engaged in supplying the place with water and carrying on a machinery repair business.

On August 13, 1892, anti-government forces under the command of General Hernandez entered the city and took control. Sometime after that, Underhill applied to General Hernandez for a passport to leave the city. Hernandez refused this request and requests by others on Underhill's behalf in order, the lower courts found, "to coerce [Underhill] to operate his waterworks and his repair works for the benefit of the community and the revolutionary forces." Finally, on October 18, Underhill was given a passport and left the country.

In the meantime, the revolutionary forces had been generally successful and took control of the Venezuelan capital. On October 23, the so-called Crespo government was formally recognized by the United States as the legitimate government of Venezuela.

Underhill sued General Hernandez to recover damages for the detention caused by the general's refusal to grant the passport, for Underhill's alleged confinement to his own house, and for certain alleged assaults and affronts by the soldiers of Hernandez's army.

Chief Justice Fuller delivered the opinion of the Court and affirmed the dismissal of Underhill's suit. In the opinion, whose first paragraph has often been quoted since, the Court stated:

> Every sovereign state is bound to respect the independence of every other sovereign state, and the courts of one country will not sit in judgment on the acts of the government of another, done within its own territory. Redress of grievances by reason of such

> acts must be obtained through the means open to be availed of by sovereign powers as between themselves.
>
> Nor can the principle be confined to lawful or recognized governments, or to cases where redress can manifestly be had through public channels. The immunity of individuals from suits brought in foreign tribunals for acts done within their own states, in the exercise of governmental authority, whether as civil officers or as military commanders, must necessarily extend to the agents of governments ruling by paramount forces as a matter of fact. Where a civil war prevails . . . foreign nations do not assume to judge of the merits of the quarrel. If the party seeking to dislodge the existing government succeeds, and the independence of the government it has set up is recognized, then the acts of such government from the commencement of its existence are regarded as those of an independent nation. . . .
>
> . . . We think the Circuit Court of Appeals was justified in concluding "that the acts of the defendant were the acts of the government of Venezuela, and as such are not properly the subject of adjudication in the courts of another government." . . . Id. at 252-253.

The Supreme Court reaffirmed the act of state doctrine in a number of decisions in the early 1900s. Two of the important ones were decided on the same day in 1918. Oetjen v. Central Leather Co., 246 U.S. 297 (1918) and Ricaud v. American Metal Co., 246 U.S. 304 (1918). As later described by the U.S. Supreme Court:

> *Oetjen* involved a seizure of hides from a Mexican citizen . . . by General Villa, acting for the forces of General Carranza, whose government was recognized by this country subsequent to the trial but prior to decision by this Court. The hides were sold to a Texas corporation which shipped them to the United States and assigned them to defendant. As assignee of the original owner, plaintiff replevied the hides, claiming that they had been seized in violation of the Hague Conventions. In affirming a judgment for the defendant, the Court. . . . chose to rest its decision on other grounds. It described the designation of the sovereign as a political question to be determined by the legislative and executive departments rather than the judicial department, invoked the established rule that such recognition operated retroactively to validate past acts, and found the basic tenet of *Underhill* to be applicable to the case before it. . . .
>
> In *Ricaud* the facts were similar . . . except that the property taken belonged to an American citizen. The Court found *Underhill* . . . and *Oetjen* controlling. . . . [Banco Nacional de Cuba v. Sabbatino, 376 U.S. 398, 417-418 (1964)]

In *Ricaud* itself, the Court also noted that the act of state doctrine was not a refusal to exercise jurisdiction, but rather a situation where the "details of such action or the merit of the result cannot be questioned but must be accepted by our courts as a rule for their decision." 246 U.S. at 309.

The Supreme Court also followed *Underhill* in two cases involving expropriation of property by the Soviet Union. United States v. Belmont, 301 U.S. 324 (1937) and United States v. Pink, 315 U.S. 203 (1942). (The latter case is excerpted in Chapter 3.)

2. *The Sabbatino Decision*

A more recent, seminal case on the act of state doctrine is Banco Nacional de Cuba v. Sabbatino, 376 U.S. 398 (1964). Like several later cases, it arose from the events surrounding the breakdown of relations between the United States and Fidel

Castro's Cuba, notably Castro's nationalization of many U.S. interests in Cuba. In 1959 Castro's revolution ousted the government of Fulgencio Batista. Since many viewed the Batista dictatorship as harsh and corrupt, the initial U.S. reaction to Castro was a cautious and mixed one. Matters, however, became increasingly strained as leftists and communists asserted themselves in the new government and as many Cubans fled to the United States. In 1961, the United States supported, not very covertly, an attempted invasion of Cuba by Cuban exiles at the Bay of Pigs. The attackers were routed. In 1962, the United States imposed a trade embargo against Cuba under the Trading with the Enemy Act. (See Chapter 3 regarding emergency powers.) In October 1962, President Kennedy ordered a quarantine of Cuba to keep out Soviet offensive nuclear missiles, which the Cubans and Soviets were installing there. (See Chapter 11 regarding the Cuban missile crisis.)

Banco Nacional de Cuba v. Sabbatino, Receiver

U.S. Supreme Court
376 U.S. 398 (1964)

[As relations grew increasingly hostile between the United States and Cuba in 1960, the United States reduced the sugar quota* for Cuba on July 6. In response, on the same day Cuba adopted Law No. 851, which denounced the U.S. action and authorized the Cuban leaders to expropriate any property or enterprise in which American nationals had an interest. "Although a system of compensation was formally provided, the possibility of payment under it was deemed illusory," according to the Court.

[Among the companies that were nationalized was Compania Azucarera Vertientes-Camaguey de Cuba (C.A.V.), a Cuban corporation whose stock was owned principally by U.S. residents. Its wholly owned subsidiary had contracted to sell Cuban sugar to Farr, Whitlock & Co., a U.S. commodities broker. After nationalization of C.A.V.'s sugar (on the day it was being loaded onto the ship), Farr, Whitlock entered into a second contract, identical to the one with C.A.V., with an instrumentality of the Cuban government.

[The ship then sailed for Morocco. Farr, Whitlock received payment for the sugar from its customers. The company refused to pay the representative of the Cuban government, however; rather, it turned over the proceeds to the receiver for C.A.V.'s assets (Sabbatino), who had been appointed by a New York court. The court also ordered Farr, Whitlock not to take any step that would allow the funds to leave the state. C.A.V. made it easy for Farr, Whitlock by agreeing to indemnify the company for any loss in the ensuing litigation.

[Banco Nacional de Cuba, which had been assigned the Cuban government's right to payment under the second contract, filed suit in the U.S. District Court against Farr, Whitlock, and Sabbatino. The defendants responded that title to the sugar had never passed to the Cuban government because the expropriation violated international law.]

*[Sugar quotas limit the amount of sugar that a foreign country can sell to the United States. The U.S. price is generally well above the world price because the U.S. price is set in part to help higher-cost U.S. domestic producers. — Eds.]

Mr. Justice Harlan delivered the opinion of the Court [for himself and Justices Warren, Black, Douglas, Clark, Brennan, Stewart, and Goldberg]. . . .

While acknowledging the continuing vitality of the act of state doctrine, the [district] court believed it inapplicable when the questioned foreign act is in violation of international law. Proceeding on the basis that a taking invalid under international law does not convey good title, the District Court found the Cuban expropriation decree to violate such law in three separate respects: it was motivated by a retaliatory and not a public purpose; it discriminated against American nationals; and it failed to provide adequate compensation. Summary judgment against petitioner was accordingly granted.

The Court of Appeals, affirming the decision on similar grounds, relied on two letters (not before the District Court) written by State Department officers which it took as evidence that the Executive Branch had no objection to a judicial testing of the Cuban decree's validity. The court was unwilling to declare that any one of the infirmities found by the District Court rendered the taking invalid under international law, but was satisfied that in combination they had that effect. We granted certiorari because the issues involved bear importantly on the conduct of the country's foreign relations and more particularly on the proper role of the Judicial Branch in this sensitive area. For reasons to follow we decide that the judgment below must be reversed. . . .

II

It is first contended that this petitioner, an instrumentality of the Cuban Government, should be denied access to American courts because Cuba is an unfriendly power and does not permit nationals of this country to obtain relief in its courts. . . .

Under principles of comity governing this country's relations with other nations, sovereign states are allowed to sue in the courts of the United States. This Court has called "comity" in the legal sense "neither a matter of absolute obligation, on the one hand, nor of mere courtesy and good will, upon the other." Hilton v. Guyot, 159 U.S. 113,163-164. . . .

Respondents, pointing to the severance of diplomatic relations, commercial embargo, and freezing of Cuban assets in this country, contend that relations between the United States and Cuba manifest such animosity that unfriendliness is clear, and that the courts should be closed to the Cuban Government. We do not agree. This Court would hardly be competent to undertake assessments of varying degrees of friendliness or its absence, and, lacking some definite touchstone for determination, we are constrained to consider any relationship, short of war, with a recognized sovereign power as embracing the privilege of resorting to United States courts. Although the severance of diplomatic relations is an overt act with objective significance in the dealings of sovereign states, we are unwilling to say that it should inevitably result in the withdrawal of the privilege of bringing suit. . . .

IV . . .

In deciding the present case the Court of Appeals relied in part upon an exception to the unqualified teachings of *Underhill*, *Oetjen*, and *Ricaud*. . . . In Bernstein v. Van

Heyghen Freres Societe Anonyme, 163 F.2d 246, suit was brought to recover from an assignee property allegedly taken, in effect, by the Nazi Government because plaintiff was Jewish. Recognizing the odious nature of this act of state, the court, through Judge Learned Hand, nonetheless refused to consider it invalid on that ground. Rather, it looked to see if the Executive had acted in any manner that would indicate that United States Courts should refuse to give effect to such a foreign decree. Finding no such evidence, the court sustained dismissal of the complaint. In a later case involving similar facts the same court again assumed examination of the German acts improper, Bernstein v. N. V. Nederlandsche-Amerikaansche Stoomvaart-Maatschappij, 173 F.2d 71, but, quite evidently following the implications of Judge Hand's opinion in the earlier case, amended its mandate to permit evidence of alleged invalidity, 210 F.2d 375, subsequent to receipt by plaintiff's attorney of a letter from the Acting Legal Adviser to the State Department written for the purpose of relieving the court from any constraint upon the exercise of its jurisdiction to pass on that question.[18]

This Court has never had occasion to pass upon the so-called *Bernstein* exception, nor need it do so now. For whatever ambiguity may be thought to exist in the two letters from State Department officials on which the Court of Appeals relied, is now removed by the position which the Executive has taken in this Court on the act of state claim; respondents do not indeed contest the view that these letters were intended to reflect no more than the Department's then wish not to make any statement bearing on this litigation.[19]

The outcome of this case, therefore, turns upon whether any of the contentions urged by respondents against the application of the act of state doctrine in the premises is acceptable: (1) that the doctrine does not apply to acts of state which violate international law, as is claimed to be the case here; (2) that the doctrine is inapplicable unless the Executive specifically interposes it in a particular case; and

18. The letter stated:

1. This government has consistently opposed the forcible acts of dispossession of a discriminatory and confiscatory nature practiced by the Germans on the countries or peoples subject to their controls. . . .

3. The policy of the Executive, with respect to claims asserted in the United States for the restitution of identifiable property (or compensation in lieu thereof) lost through force, coercion, or duress as a result of Nazi persecution in Germany, is to relieve American courts from any restraint upon the exercise of their jurisdiction to pass upon the validity of the acts of Nazi officials. State Department Press Release, April 27, 1949.

19. Abram Chayes, the Legal Adviser to the State Department, wrote on October 18, 1961, in answer to an inquiry regarding the position of the Department by Mr. John Laylin, attorney for amici:

> The Department of State has not, in the *Bahia de Nipe* case or elsewhere, done anything inconsistent with the position taken on the Cuban nationalizations by Secretary Herter. Whether or not these nationalizations will in the future be given effect in the United States is, of course, for the courts to determine. Since the *Sabbatino* case and other similar cases are at present before the courts, any comments on this question by the Department of State would be out of place at this time. As you yourself point out, statements by the executive branch are highly susceptible of misconstruction.

A letter dated November 14, 1961, from George Ball, Under Secretary For Economic Affairs, responded to a similar inquiry by the same attorney:

> I have carefully considered your letter and have discussed it with the Legal Adviser. Our conclusion, in which the Secretary concurs, is that the Department should not comment on matters pending before the courts.

(3) that, in any event, the doctrine may not be invoked by a foreign government plaintiff in our courts.

V

Preliminarily, we discuss the foundations on which we deem the act of state doctrine to rest, and more particularly the question of whether state or federal law governs its application in a federal diversity case.

We do not believe that this doctrine is compelled either by the inherent nature of sovereign authority, as some of the earlier decisions seem to imply, see *Underhill*, supra; or by some principle of international law. If a transaction takes place in one jurisdiction and the forum is in another, the forum does not by dismissing an action or by applying its own law purport to divest the first jurisdiction of its territorial sovereignty; it merely declines to adjudicate or makes applicable its own law to parties or property before it. . . .

That international law does not require application of the doctrine is evidenced by the practice of nations. Most of the countries rendering decisions on the subject fail to follow the rule rigidly.[21] No international arbitral or judicial decision discovered suggests that international law prescribes recognition of sovereign acts of foreign governments. . . . If international law does not prescribe use of the doctrine, neither does it forbid application of the rule even if it is claimed that the act of state in question violated international law. The traditional view of international law is that it establishes substantive principles for determining whether one country has wronged another. Because of its peculiar nation-to-nation character the usual method for an individual to seek relief is to exhaust local remedies and then repair to the executive authorities of his own state to persuade them to champion his claim in diplomacy or before an international tribunal. . . . Although it is, of course, true that United States courts apply international law as a part of our own in appropriate circumstances, Ware v. Hylton, 3 Dall. 199, 281; The Nereide, 9 Cranch 388, 423; The Paquete Habana, 175 U.S. 677, 700, the public law of nations can hardly dictate to a country which is in theory wronged how to treat that wrong within its domestic borders.

Despite the broad statement in *Oetjen* that "The conduct of the foreign relations of our Government is committed by the Constitution to the Executive and Legislative . . . Departments," 246 U.S., at 302, it cannot of course be thought that "every case or controversy which touches foreign relations lies beyond judicial cognizance." Baker v. Carr, 369 U.S. 186, 211. The text of the Constitution does not

21. In English jurisprudence, in the classic case of Luther v. James Sagor & Co., [1921] 3 K.B. 532, the act of state doctrine is articulated in terms not unlike those of the United States cases. But see Anglo-Iranian Oil Co. v. Jaffrate, [1953] 1 Weekly L.R. 246, [1953] Int'l L. Rep. 316 (Aden Sup. Ct.) (exception to doctrine if foreign act violates international law). Civil law countries, however, which apply the rule make exceptions for acts contrary to their sense of public order. See, e.g., *Ropit* case, Cour de Cassation (France), [1929] Recueil Général Des Lois et Des Arrêts (Sirey) Part I, 217; 55 Journal Du Droit International (Clunet) 674 (1928), [1927-1928] Ann. Dig., No. 43; Graue, Germany: Recognition of Foreign Expropriations, 3 Am. J. Comp. L. 93 (1954); Domke, Indonesian Nationalization Measures Before Foreign Courts, 54 Am. J. Int'l L. 305 (1960) . . . Anglo-Iranian Oil Co. v. S.U.P.O.R. Co., [1955] Int'l L. Rep. 19 (Ct. of Venice), 78 Il Foro Italiano Part I, 719. . . . See also Anglo-Iranian Oil Co. v. Idemitsu Kosan Kabushiki Kaisha, [1953] Int'l L. Rep. 312 (High Ct. of Tokyo).

require the act of state doctrine; it does not irrevocably remove from the judiciary the capacity to review the validity of foreign acts of state.

The act of state doctrine does, however, have "constitutional" underpinnings. It arises out of the basic relationships between branches of government in a system of separation of powers. It concerns the competency of dissimilar institutions to make and implement particular kinds of decisions in the area of international relations. The doctrine as formulated in past decisions expresses the strong sense of the Judicial Branch that its engagement in the task of passing on the validity of foreign acts of state may hinder rather than further this country's pursuit of goals both for itself and for the community of nations as a whole in the international sphere. Many commentators disagree with this view. . . . Whatever considerations are thought to predominate, it is plain that the problems involved are uniquely federal in nature. If federal authority, in this instance this Court, orders the field of judicial competence in this area for the federal courts, and the state courts are left free to formulate their own rules, the purposes behind the doctrine could be as effectively undermined as if there had been no federal pronouncement on the subject.

We could perhaps in this diversity action avoid the question of deciding whether federal or state law is applicable to this aspect of the litigation. . . .

However, we are constrained to make it clear that an issue concerned with a basic choice regarding the competence and function of the Judiciary and the National Executive in ordering our relationships with other members of the international community must be treated exclusively as an aspect of federal law.[23] It seems fair to assume that the Court did not have rules like the act of state doctrine in mind when it decided Erie R. Co. v. Tompkins. . . .

. . . We conclude that the scope of the act of state doctrine must be determined according to federal law.[25]

VI

If the act of state doctrine is a principle of decision binding on federal and state courts alike but compelled by neither international law nor the Constitution, its continuing vitality depends on its capacity to reflect the proper distribution of functions between the judicial and political branches of the Government on matters bearing upon foreign affairs. It should be apparent that the greater the degree of codification or consensus concerning a particular area of international law, the more appropriate it is for the judiciary to render decisions regarding it, since the courts can then focus on the application of an agreed principle to circumstances of fact rather than on the sensitive task of establishing a principle not inconsistent with the national interest or with international justice. It is also evident that some aspects of international law touch much more sharply on national nerves than do others;

23. At least this is true when the Court limits the scope of judicial inquiry. We need not now consider whether a state court might, in certain circumstances, adhere to a more restrictive view concerning the scope of examination of foreign acts than that required by this Court.

25. Various constitutional and statutory provisions indirectly support this determination, see U.S. Const, Art. I, §8, cls. 3, 10; Art. II, §§2, 3; Art. III, §2; 28 U.S.C. §§1251 (a) (2), (b) (1), (b) (3), 1332(a) (2), 1333,1350-1351, by reflecting a concern for uniformity in this country's dealings with foreign nations and indicating a desire to give matters of international significance to the jurisdiction of federal institutions.

the less important the implications of an issue are for our foreign relations, the weaker the justification for exclusivity in the political branches. The balance of relevant considerations may also be shifted if the government which perpetrated the challenged act of state is no longer in existence, as in the *Bernstein* case, for the political interest of this country may, as a result, be measurably altered. Therefore, rather than laying down or reaffirming an inflexible and all-encompassing rule in this case, we decide only that the Judicial Branch will not examine the validity of a taking of property within its own territory by a foreign sovereign government, extant and recognized by this country at the time of suit, in the absence of a treaty or other unambiguous agreement regarding controlling legal principles, even if the complaint alleges that the taking violates customary international law.

There are few if any issues in international law today on which opinion seems to be so divided as the limitations on a state's power to expropriate the property of aliens. There is, of course, authority, in international judicial and arbitral decisions, in the expressions of national governments, and among commentators for the view that a taking is improper under international law if it is not for a public purpose, is discriminatory, or is without provision for prompt, adequate, and effective compensation. However, Communist countries, although they have in fact provided a degree of compensation after diplomatic efforts, commonly recognize no obligation on the part of the taking country. Certain representatives of the newly independent and underdeveloped countries have questioned whether rules of state responsibility toward aliens can bind nations that have not consented to them and it is argued that the traditionally articulated standards governing expropriation of property reflect "imperialist" interests and are inappropriate to the circumstances of emergent states.

The disagreement as to relevant international law standards reflects an even more basic divergence between the national interests of capital importing and capital exporting nations and between the social ideologies of those countries that favor state control of a considerable portion of the means of production and those that adhere to a free enterprise system. It is difficult to imagine the courts of this country embarking on adjudication in an area which touches more sensitively the practical and ideological goals of the various members of the community of nations.[34]

When we consider the prospect of the courts characterizing foreign expropriations, however justifiably, as invalid under international law and ineffective to pass title, the wisdom of the precedents is confirmed. While each of the leading cases in this Court may be argued to be distinguishable on its facts from this one — *Underhill* because sovereign immunity provided an independent ground and *Oetjen, Ricaud,* and *Shapleigh* because there was actually no violation of international law — the plain implication of all these opinions . . . is that the act of state doctrine is applicable even if international law has been violated. . . .

The possible adverse consequences of a conclusion to the contrary of that implicit in these cases is highlighted by contrasting the practices of the political branch with the limitations of the judicial process in matters of this kind. Following

34. There are, of course, areas of international law in which consensus as to standards is greater and which do not represent a battleground for conflicting ideologies. This decision in no way intimates that the courts of this country are broadly foreclosed from considering questions of international law.

an expropriation of any significance, the Executive engages in diplomacy aimed to assure that United States citizens who are harmed are compensated fairly. Representing all claimants of this country, it will often be able, either by bilateral or multilateral talks, by submission to the United Nations, or by the employment of economic and political sanctions, to achieve some degree of general redress. Judicial determinations of invalidity of title can, on the other hand, have only an occasional impact, since they depend on the fortuitous circumstance of the property in question being brought into this country. Such decisions would, if the acts involved were declared invalid, often be likely to give offense to the expropriating country; since the concept of territorial sovereignty is so deep seated, any state may resent the refusal of the courts of another sovereign to accord validity to acts within its territorial borders. Piecemeal dispositions of this sort involving the probability of affront to another state could seriously interfere with negotiations being carried on by the Executive Branch and might prevent or render less favorable the terms of an agreement that could otherwise be reached. Relations with third countries which have engaged in similar expropriations would not be immune from effect.

The dangers of such adjudication are present regardless of whether the State Department has, as it did in this case, asserted that the relevant act violated international law. If the Executive Branch has undertaken negotiations with an expropriating country, but has refrained from claims of violation of the law of nations, a determination to that effect by a court might be regarded as a serious insult, while a finding of compliance with international law, would greatly strengthen the bargaining hand of the other state with consequent detriment to American interests.

Even if the State Department has proclaimed the impropriety of the expropriation, the stamp of approval of its view by a judicial tribunal, however impartial, might increase any affront and the judicial decision might occur at a time, almost always well after the taking, when such an impact would be contrary to our national interest. Considerably more serious and far-reaching consequences would flow from a judicial finding that international law standards had been met if that determination flew in the face of a State Department proclamation to the contrary. When articulating principles of international law in its relations with other states, the Executive Branch speaks not only as an interpreter of generally accepted and traditional rules, as would the courts, but also as an advocate of standards it believes desirable for the community of nations and protective of national concerns. In short, whatever way the matter is cut, the possibility of conflict between the Judicial and Executive Branches could hardly be avoided. . . .

Another serious consequence of the exception pressed by respondents would be to render uncertain titles in foreign commerce, with the possible consequence of altering the flow of international trade.[38] If the attitude of the United States courts were unclear, one buying expropriated goods would not know if he could safely import them into this country. Even were takings known to be invalid, one would

38. This possibility is consistent with the view that the deterrent effect of court invalidations would not ordinarily be great. If the expropriating country could find other buyers for its products at roughly the same price, the deterrent effect might be minimal although patterns of trade would be significantly changed.

have difficulty determining after goods had changed hands several times whether the particular articles in question were the product of an ineffective state act.[39]

Against the force of such considerations, we find respondents' countervailing arguments quite unpersuasive. Their basic contention is that United States courts could make a significant contribution to the growth of international law, a contribution whose importance, it is said, would be magnified by the relative paucity of decisional law by international bodies. But given the fluidity of present world conditions, the effectiveness of such a patchwork approach toward the formulation of an acceptable body of law concerning state responsibility for expropriations is, to say the least, highly conjectural. . . .

It is contended that regardless of the fortuitous circumstances necessary for United States jurisdiction over a case, involving a foreign act of state and the resultant isolated application to any expropriation program taken as a whole, it is the function of the courts to justly decide individual disputes before them. Perhaps the most typical act of state case involves the original owner or his assignee suing one not in association with the expropriating state who has had "title" transferred to him. But it is difficult to regard the claim of the original owner, who otherwise may be recompensed through diplomatic channels, as more demanding of judicial cognizance than the claim of title by the innocent third party purchaser, who, if the property is taken from him, is without any remedy.

Respondents claim that the economic pressure resulting from the proposed exception to the act of state doctrine will materially add to the protection of United States investors. We are not convinced, even assuming the relevance of this contention. Expropriations take place for a variety of reasons, political and ideological as well as economic. When one considers the variety of means possessed by this country to make secure foreign investment, the persuasive or coercive effect of judicial invalidation of acts of expropriation dwindles in comparison. The newly independent states are in need of continuing foreign investment; the creation of a climate unfavorable to such investment by wholesale confiscations may well work to their long-run economic disadvantage. Foreign aid given to many of these countries provides a powerful lever in the hands of the political branches to ensure fair treatment of United States nationals. Ultimately the sanctions of economic embargo and the freezing of assets in this country may be employed. Any country willing to brave any or all of these consequences is unlikely to be deterred by sporadic judicial decisions directly affecting only property brought to our shores. . . .

It is suggested that if the act of state doctrine is applicable to violations of international law, it should only be so when the Executive Branch expressly stipulates that it does not wish the courts to pass on the question of validity. . . . We should be slow to reject the representations of the Government that such a reversal of the *Bernstein* principle would work serious inroads on the maximum effectiveness of United States diplomacy. Often the State Department will wish to refrain from taking an official position, particularly at a moment that would be dictated by the development of private litigation but might be inopportune diplomatically. . . . We

39. Were respondents' position adopted, the courts might be engaged in the difficult tasks of ascertaining the origin of fungible goods, of considering the effect of improvements made in a third country on expropriated raw materials, and of determining the title to commodities subsequently grown on expropriated land or produced with expropriated machinery. . . .

do not now pass on the *Bernstein* exception, but even if it were deemed valid, its suggested extension is unwarranted.

However offensive to the public policy of this country and its constituent States an expropriation of this kind may be, we conclude that both the national interest and progress toward the goal of establishing the rule of law among nations are best served by maintaining intact the act of state doctrine in this realm of its application. . . .

The judgment of the Court of Appeals is reversed and the case is remanded to the District Court for proceedings consistent with this opinion.

It is so ordered.

Mr. Justice WHITE, dissenting.

I am dismayed that the Court has, with one broad stroke, declared the ascertainment and application of international law beyond the competence of the courts of the United States in a large and important category of cases. I am also disappointed in the Court's declaration that the acts of a sovereign state with regard to the property of aliens within its borders are beyond the reach of international law in the courts of this country. However clearly established that law may be, a sovereign may violate it with impunity, except insofar as the political branches of the government may provide a remedy. This backward-looking doctrine, never before declared in this Court, is carried a disconcerting step further: not only are the courts powerless to question acts of state proscribed by international law but they are likewise powerless to refuse to adjudicate the claim founded upon a foreign law; they must render judgment and thereby validate the lawless act. . . . [T]he Court expressly extends its ruling to all acts of state expropriating property. . . . No other civilized country has found such a rigid rule necessary for the survival of the executive branch of its government; the executive of no other government seems to require such insulation from international law adjudications in its courts; and no other judiciary is apparently so incompetent to ascertain and apply international law.[1]

I do not believe that the act of state doctrine, as judicially fashioned in this Court, and the reasons underlying it, require American courts to decide cases in disregard of international law and of the rights of litigants to a full determination on the merits. . . .

The position of the Executive Branch of the Government charged with foreign affairs with respect to this case is not entirely clear. As I see it no specific objection by the Secretary of State to examination of the validity of Cuba's law has been interposed at any stage in these proceedings, which would ordinarily lead to an adjudication on the merits. Disclaiming, rightfully, I think, any interest in the outcome of

1. The courts of the following countries, among others, and their territories have examined a fully "executed" foreign act of state expropriating property:

England: Anglo-Iranian Oil Co. v. Jaffrate, [1953] Int'l L. Rep. 316 (Aden Sup. Ct.). . . .

Germany: N.V. Verenigde Deli-Maatschapijen v. Deutsch-Indonesische Tabak-Handelsgesellschaft m.b.H. (Bremen Ct. App.), excerpts reprinted in Domke, supra, at 313-314 (1960). . . .

Japan: Anglo-Iranian Oil Co. v. Idemitsu Kosan Kabushiki Kaisha, [1953] Int'l L. Rep. 305 (Dist. Ct. of Tokyo), aff'd, [1953] Int'l L. Rep. 312 (High Ct. of Tokyo). . . .

The Court does not refer to any country which has applied the act of state doctrine in a case where a substantial international law issue is sought to be raised by an alien whose property has been expropriated. This country and this Court stand alone among the civilized nations of the world in ruling that such an issue is not cognizable in a court of law.

the case, the United States has simply argued for a rule of nonexamination in every case, which literally, I suppose, includes this one. If my view had prevailed I would have stayed further resolution of the issues in this Court to afford the Department of State reasonable time to clarify its views in light of the opinion. In the absence of a specific objection to an examination of the validity of Cuba's law under international law, I would have proceeded to determine the issue and resolve this litigation on the merits.

Notes and Questions

1. After reading *Underhill* and *Sabbatino*, how would you define the act of state doctrine? What acts by a foreign sovereign would the act of state doctrine cover? Are there any exceptions?

2. In *Underhill*, how formal were the acts of General Hernandez that Underhill complained about? Were they actual laws or formal decrees? Is it even clear whether there were written orders?

3. What was the position of the executive branch in *Sabbatino*? (See text at pages 618 and 622 and the dissent by Justice White, above.) How did the executive branch's position differ from the *Bernstein* case, discussed in the opinion? What position did the U.S. Supreme Court take on the so-called *Bernstein* exception?

4. What were the Court's reasons for finding the act of state doctrine applicable? Was it required by international law? Was it required by the Constitution?

5. Did the Court view the doctrine as one of state or federal law? Why?

6. What did the Supreme Court majority believe was the international law regarding expropriation of property? Would the result have been different if the then-current state of international law had been different or more clear? What if Cuba's taking had been found to violate customary international law? Does the Court believe that the act of state doctrine would not be applicable then? What if Cuba's taking had violated a treaty with the United States?

7. Note that courts have held that a government's confiscation, within its territory, of the property of its *own citizens* does not violate customary international law. See, e.g., FOGADE v. ENB Revocable Trust, 263 F.3d 1274 (11th Cir. 2001); see Odyssey Marine Exploration, Inc. v. Unidentified, Shipwrecked Vessel, 675 F.Supp.2d 1126, 1147 (M.D. Fla. 2009).

8. Regardless of the executive branch's position during the *Sabbatino* litigation, the Court's decision was not popular with Congress. The decision came after relations with the Castro government in Cuba had distinctly cooled. Castro had expropriated U.S. properties of substantial value. On its part, the U.S. government had provided major support for the abortive Bay of Pigs invasion of Cuba.

Soon after the decision, Congress adopted the so-called *Sabbatino* Amendment, or Second Hickenlooper Amendment. 22 U.S.C. §2370(e)(2). This amendment was added to the initial 1962 Hickenlooper Amendment, §2370(e)(1), sponsored by Senator Burton Hickenlooper (R.-Iowa). Also, as discussed below, some of the second amendment's operative language depends on criteria in the First Hickenlooper Amendment. The *Sabbatino* Amendment provides:

> Notwithstanding any other provision of law, no court in the United States shall decline on the ground of the federal act of state doctrine to make a determination on the merits

> giving effect to the principles of international law in a case in which a claim of title or other right to property is asserted by any party including a foreign state (or a party claiming through such state) based upon (or traced through) a confiscation or other taking after January 1, 1959, by an act of that state in violation of the principles of international law, including the principles of compensation and the other standards set out in this subsection: *Provided*, That this subparagraph shall not be applicable (1) in any case in which an act of a foreign state is not contrary to international law or with respect to a claim of title or other right to property acquired pursuant to an irrevocable letter of credit of not more than 180 days duration issued in good faith prior to the time of the confiscation or other taking, or (2) in any case with respect to which the President determines that application of the act of state doctrine is required in that particular case by the foreign policy interests of the United States and a suggestion to this effect is filed on his behalf in that case with the court. [22 U.S.C. §2370(e)(2).]

The reference in the amendment above to the "principles of compensation and the other standards set out in this subsection" was to the First Hickenlooper Amendment's standards that included, among others:

> appropriate steps . . . to discharge its obligations under international law toward such citizen or entity, including speedy compensation for such property in convertible foreign exchange, equivalent to the full value thereof, as required by international law, or fails to take steps designed to provide relief from such taxes, exactions, or conditions, as the case may be.

On remand, the U.S. court of appeals applied the statute retroactively to the *Sabbatino* case and, as a result, Cuba's claim was dismissed. The court did note that the *Sabbatino* Amendment provided that it make a determination of the taking on the merits "giving effect to the principles of international law." The court specifically noted, however, that "[i]t is clear that if these domestic statutory standards are different from the international law standards which we applied when we decided this case formerly, the statutory standards tend to be more exacting upon the expropriating nations." Banco Nacional de Cuba v. Farr, 383 F.2d 166, 185 (2d Cir. 1967), *cert. denied*, 390 U.S. 956, *rehearing denied*, 390 U.S. 1037 (1968) (this case is the same as *Sabbatino* except for the change in the name of one of the named parties).

Although the *Sabbatino* Amendment was quickly applied to the very case that gave it one of its names, later decisions by courts have consistently interpreted it narrowly to require only nonapplication of the act of state doctrine when there are claims of title involving specific property actually before the court, such as when there are claims of title of property (rather than mere breach of contract claims), and that property or its proceeds is presently located in the United States. The amendment has been held not to apply to claims for compensation for taking of specific property that is not before the court. See, e.g., Glen v. Club Mediterranee, S.A., 365 F. Supp. 2d 1263, 1268 (S.D. Fla. 2005), aff'd on other grounds, 450 F.3d 1251 (11th Cir. 2006); Compania de Gas de Nuevo Laredo, S.A. v. Entex, Inc., 686 F.2d. 322 (5th Cir. 1982); Menendez v. Saks & Co, 485 F.2d 1355 (2d Cir. 1973), *cert. denied*, 491 U.S. 991 (1976); Restatement section 444.

Why might the courts have narrowly construed the *Sabbatino* Amendment? Could there be an element of the courts not being happy with Congress trying to limit their discretion? Does the amendment provide a particularly good basis for deciding whether or not to apply the act of state doctrine? What is the statute's standard for determining whether an expropriation is in violation of international law?

In addition to the *Sabbatino* Amendment, the Helms-Burton Act of 1996, enacted after Cuban fighter planes shot down two unarmed aircraft over international waters, also contains a provision prohibiting courts from denying claims on the basis of the act of state doctrine in some claims against traffickers of property expropriated by Cuba. 22 U.S.C. §6082(a)(6). (See discussion of the Helms-Burton Act in Chapter 7.)

3. Limitations and Exceptions

The materials below consider some of the limitations on, and possible exceptions to, the act of state doctrine.

In First National City Bank v. Banco Nacional de Cuba, 406 U.S. 759 (1972), the Cuban bank, which was government owned, sued First National City Bank to obtain the excess from the U.S. bank's sale of collateral securing a loan to the government-owned Cuban bank. The U.S. bank had promptly sold the collateral for a profit of at least $1.8 million dollars after the Cuban government seized all the branches of First National City Bank in Cuba in 1960.

The Supreme Court decided by a 5-4 majority that the act of state doctrine did not apply to prevent the U.S. bank from using the counterclaim in U.S. courts to challenge the Cuban government's expropriation of the U.S. bank's assets in Cuba. The defendant U.S. bank was allowed to recover on its counterclaim up to the amount that Banco Nacional was awarded on its complaint. (First National City Bank had waived any recovery above this amount during the proceedings in the district court.) The Department of State had taken the position that the act of state doctrine should not apply in this counterclaim situation.

The basis of the Supreme Court's decision was unclear because of the four different opinions by the Justices. Briefly, Justice Rehnquist announced the judgment of the Court and delivered an opinion in which only Chief Justice Burger and Justice White joined. The three Justices followed the recommendation of the Executive Branch, explicitly acknowledging that they were "adopt[ing] and approv[ing] the so-called *Bernstein* exception." (See discussion of that exception in the *Sabbatino* case.) They also noted that the result was "consonant with the principles of equity set forth" in the Court's decision in National City Bank v. Republic of China, (348 U.S. 356 (1955). There the Court had denied foreign sovereign immunity to the Republic of China when it had taken the initiative of bringing a lawsuit in a U.S. court. (See discussion in Section A.6. above regarding FSIA Section 1607.)

Justice Douglas concurred in the result, on the basis of *National City Bank*. He specifically declined to adopt the *Bernstein* exception.

Justice Powell concurred in the result, but he seemed to reject *Bernstein* and did not rely on *National City Bank*. He was for a narrow reading of *Sabbatino*.

The four dissenters, in an opinion by Justice Brennan, "unequivocally" rejected *Bernstein* and interpreted Justices Douglas and Powell as having done so also.

The dissenters also said that *National City Bank*, a foreign sovereign immunity case, is "not at all on point." In their view, *Sabbatino* was still controlling and that the circumstances of the case raised a "political question."

So, although there were five votes for finding that the act of state doctrine did not apply in this counterclaim situation, only three Justices based their vote on the *Bernstein* exception and six rejected it.

First National City Bank was followed by Alfred Dunhill of London, Inc. v. Republic of Cuba, 425 U.S. 682 (1976). The facts were briefly as follows. In 1960, the Cuban government nationalized the five leading manufacturers of Havana cigars. None of the owners were U.S. citizens. These companies, however, sold large quantities of cigars to U.S. customers, including Alfred Dunhill of London, Inc. (Dunhill), Saks, and Faber.

The Cuban government named "interventors" to operate the businesses of the nationalized Cuban concerns. The interventors continued to ship cigars, including to U.S. customers. The U.S. customers paid the interventors for new purchases and also on old accounts receivable, on the assumption that the interventors were entitled to collect the accounts receivable of the seized businesses. The former owners of the Cuban businesses, most of whom had fled to the United States, sued the U.S. companies in U.S. district court on various counts. Cuba was allowed to intervene.

The U.S. district court ruled that the Cuban interventors were entitled to collect from the U.S. importers all amounts due and unpaid with respect to shipments *after* the date of expropriation. However, the court concluded that the situs of the accounts receivable was with the importers, so that the 1960 expropriation did not reach the pre-intervention accounts. As the Supreme Court recited, "Dunhill—and at last we arrive at the issue in this case—was entitled to more from interventors—$148,000—than it owed for postintervention shipments—$93,000—and to be made whole, asked for and was granted judgment against the interventors for the full amount of its claim, from which would be deducted the smaller judgment entered against it." Id. at 688.

In its majority opinion by Justice White and four other Justices, the Court concluded it would not give effect to the interventors' refusal to honor their quasi-contractual obligation to repay the funds the U.S. importers had paid to them on the pre-intervention accounts receivable. The Court concluded that "[n]o statute, decree, order, or resolution of the Cuban Government itself was offered in evidence indicating that Cuba had repudiated its obligations in general or any class thereof or that it had as a sovereign matter determined to confiscate the amounts due three foreign importers." Id. at 695. In other words, in the view of five Justices, only formal acts would qualify for the act of state doctrine.

Three Justices joined Justice White in Part III of his opinion, which concluded that "the concept of an act of state should not be extended to include the repudiation of a purely commercial obligation owed by a foreign sovereign or by one of its commercial instrumentalities." Id. So, the arguments for a "commercial activity" exception attracted four Justices.

In short, the status of different possible exceptions to the act of state doctrine varied and was not clear when the Supreme Court made its last major decision on the doctrine in the case below.

W.S. Kirkpatrick & Co. v. Environmental Tectonics Corp.

U.S. Supreme Court
493 U.S. 400 (1990)

Justice SCALIA delivered the opinion of the [unanimous] Court.

In this case we must decide whether the act of state doctrine bars a court in the United States from entertaining a cause of action that does not rest upon the asserted invalidity of an official act of a foreign sovereign, but that does require imputing to foreign officials an unlawful motivation (the obtaining of bribes) in the performance of such an official act.

The facts as alleged in respondent's complaint are as follows: In 1981, Harry Carpenter, who was then Chairman of the Board and Chief Executive Officer of petitioner W.S. Kirkpatrick & Co., Inc. (Kirkpatrick) learned that the Republic of Nigeria was interested in contracting for the construction and equipment of an aeromedical center at Kaduna Air Force Base in Nigeria. He made arrangements with Benson "Tunde" Akindele, a Nigerian citizen, whereby Akindele would endeavor to secure the contract for Kirkpatrick. It was agreed that, in the event the contract was awarded to Kirkpatrick, Kirkpatrick would pay to two Panamanian entities controlled by Akindele a "commission" equal to 20% of the contract price, which would in turn be given as a bribe to officials of the Nigerian Government. In accordance with this plan, the contract was awarded to petitioner W.S. Kirkpatrick & Co., International (Kirkpatrick International), a wholly owned subsidiary of Kirkpatrick; Kirkpatrick paid the promised "commission" to the appointed Panamanian entities; and those funds were disbursed as bribes. All parties agree that Nigerian law prohibits both the payment and the receipt of bribes in connection with the award of a government contract.

Respondent Environmental Tectonics Corporation, International, an unsuccessful bidder for the Kaduna contract, learned of the 20% "commission" and brought the matter to the attention of the Nigerian Air Force and the United States Embassy in Lagos. Following an investigation by the Federal Bureau of Investigation, the United States Attorney for the District of New Jersey brought charges against both Kirkpatrick and Carpenter for violations of the Foreign Corrupt Practices Act of 1977, 91 Stat. 1495, as amended, 15 U.S.C. §78dd-l et seq., and both pleaded guilty.

Respondent then brought this civil action in the United States District Court for the District of New Jersey against Carpenter, Akindele, petitioners, and others, seeking damages under the Racketeer Influenced and Corrupt Organizations Act, 18 U.S.C. §1961 et seq., the Robinson-Patman Act, 49 Stat. 1526, 15 U.S.C. §13 et seq., and the New Jersey Anti-Racketeering Act, N.J. Stat. Ann. §2C:41-2 et seq. (West 1982). The defendants moved to dismiss the complaint under Rule 12 (b) (6) of the Federal Rules of Civil Procedure on the ground that the action was barred by the act of state doctrine.

The District Court, having requested and received a letter expressing the views of the legal advisor to the United States Department of State as to the applicability of the act of state doctrine, treated the motion as one for summary judgment under Rule 56 of the Federal Rules of Civil Procedure, and granted the motion. The District Court concluded that the act of state doctrine applies "if the inquiry presented for judicial determination includes the motivation of a sovereign act which would result in embarrassment to the sovereign or constitute interference in the conduct of foreign policy of the United States." . . . Applying that principle to the facts at hand, the court held that respondent's suit had to be dismissed because in order to prevail respondents would have to show that "the defendants or certain of them intended to wrongfully influence the decision to award the Nigerian Contract by payment of a bribe, that the Government of Nigeria, its officials or other representatives knew of the offered consideration for awarding the Nigerian Contract to Kirkpatrick, that the bribe was actually received or anticipated and that 'but for' the payment or anticipation of the payment of the bribe, ETC would have been awarded the Nigerian Contract."

The Court of Appeals for the Third Circuit reversed. . . . [I]t found application of the doctrine unwarranted on the facts of this case. The Court of Appeals found particularly persuasive the letter to the District Court from the legal advisor to the Department of State, which had stated that in the opinion of the Department judicial inquiry into the purpose behind the act of a foreign sovereign would not produce the "unique embarrassment, and the particular interference with the conduct of foreign affairs, that may result from the judicial determination that a foreign sovereign's acts are invalid." The Court of Appeals acknowledged that "the Department's legal conclusions as to the reach of the act of state doctrine are not controlling on the courts," but concluded that "the Department's factual assessment of whether fulfillment of its responsibilities will be prejudiced by the course of civil litigation is entitled to substantial respect." In light of the Department's view that the interests of the Executive Branch would not be harmed by prosecution of the action, the Court of Appeals held that Kirkpatrick had not met its burden of showing that the case should not go forward; accordingly, it reversed the judgment of the District Court and remanded the case for trial. We granted certiorari.

II

This Court's description of the jurisprudential foundation for the act of state doctrine has undergone some evolution over the years. We once viewed the doctrine as an expression of international law, resting upon "the highest considerations of international comity and expediency," Oetjen v. Central Leather Co., 246 U.S. 297, 303-304 (1918). We have more recently described it, however, as a consequence of domestic separation of powers, reflecting "the strong sense of the Judicial Branch that its engagement in the task of passing on the validity of foreign acts of state may hinder" the conduct of foreign affairs, Banco Nacional de Cuba v. Sabbatino, 376 U.S. 398, 423 (1964). Some Justices have suggested possible exceptions to application of the doctrine, where one or both of the foregoing policies would seemingly not be served: an exception, for example, for acts of state that consist of commercial transactions, since neither modern international comity nor the current position of our Executive Branch accorded sovereign immunity to such acts, see Alfred Dunhill of London, Inc. v. Republic of Cuba, 425 U.S. 682, 695-706 (1976) (opinion of White, J.); or an exception for cases in which the Executive Branch has represented that it has no objection to denying validity to the foreign sovereign act, since then the courts would be impeding no foreign policy goals, see First National City Bank v. Banco Nacional de Cuba, 406 U.S. 759, 768-770 (1972) (opinion of Rehnquist, J.).

The parties have argued at length about the applicability of these possible exceptions, and, more generally, about whether the purpose of the act of state doctrine would be furthered by its application in this case. We find it unnecessary, however, to pursue those inquiries, since the factual predicate for application of the act of state doctrine does not exist. Nothing in the present suit requires the court to declare invalid, and thus ineffective as "a rule of decision for the courts of this country," Ricaud v. American Metal Co., 246 U.S. 304, 310 (1918), the official act of a foreign sovereign.

In every case in which we have held the act of state doctrine applicable, the relief sought or the defense interposed would have required a court in the United States to declare invalid the official act of a foreign sovereign performed within its own territory. In Underhill v. Hernandez, 168 U.S. 250, 254 (1897), holding the defendant's detention of the plaintiff to be tortious would have required denying legal effect to "acts of a military commander representing the authority of the revolutionary party as government, which afterwards succeeded and was recognized by the United States." In Oetjen v. Central Leather Co., supra, and in Ricaud v. American Metal Co., supra, denying title to the party who claimed through purchase from Mexico would have required declaring that government's prior seizure of the property, within its own territory, legally ineffective. In *Sabbatino*, upholding the defendant's claim to the funds would have required a holding that Cuba's expropriation of goods located in Havana was null and void. In the present case, by contrast, neither the claim nor any asserted defense requires a determination that Nigeria's contract with Kirkpatrick International was, or was not, effective.

Petitioners point out, however, that the facts necessary to establish respondent's claim will also establish that the contract was unlawful. Specifically, they note that in order to prevail respondent must prove that petitioner Kirkpatrick made, and Nigerian officials received, payments that violate Nigerian law, which would, they assert, support a finding that the contract is invalid under Nigerian law. Assuming that to be true, it still does not suffice. The act of state doctrine is not some vague doctrine of abstention but a "*principle of decision* binding on federal and state courts alike." *Sabbatino* (emphasis added). As we said in *Ricaud*, "the act within its own boundaries of one sovereign State . . . becomes . . . a rule of decision for the courts of this country." Act of state issues only arise when a court must decide — that is, when the outcome of the case turns upon — the effect of official action by a foreign sovereign. When that question is not in the case, neither is the act of state doctrine. That is the situation here. Regardless of what the court's factual findings may suggest as to the legality of the Nigerian contract, its legality is simply not a question to be decided in the present suit, and there is thus no occasion to apply the rule of decision that the act of state doctrine requires. Cf. Sharon v. Time, Inc., 599 F. Supp. 538, 546 (SDNY 1984) ("The issue in this litigation is not whether [the alleged] acts are valid, but whether they occurred"). . . .

Petitioners insist, however, that the policies underlying our act of state cases — international comity, respect for the sovereignty of foreign nations on their own territory, and the avoidance of embarrassment to the Executive Branch in its conduct of foreign relations — are implicated in the present case because, as the District Court found, a determination that Nigerian officials demanded and accepted a bribe "would impugn or question the nobility of a foreign nation's motivations," and would "result in embarrassment to the sovereign or constitute interference in the conduct of foreign policy of the United States." The United States, as amicus curiae, favors the same approach to the act of state doctrine, though disagreeing with petitioners as to the outcome it produces in the present case. We should not, the United States urges, "attach dispositive significance to the fact that this suit involves only the 'motivation' for, rather than the 'validity' of, a foreign sovereign act," Brief for United States as Amicus Curiae 37, and should eschew "any rigid formula for the resolution of act of state cases generally." In some future case, perhaps, "litigation . . . based on alleged corruption in the award of contracts or other commercially oriented activities of foreign governments could sufficiently touch on 'national nerves' that the act of state doctrine or related principles of abstention would appropriately be found to bar the suit," id., at 40 (quoting *Sabbatino*) and we should therefore resolve this case on the narrowest possible ground, viz., that the letter from the legal advisor to the District Court gives sufficient indication that, "in the setting of this case," the act of state doctrine poses no bar to adjudication, ibid.*

These urgings are deceptively similar to what we said in *Sabbatino,* where we observed that sometimes, even though the validity of the act of a foreign sovereign within its own territory is called into question, the policies underlying the act of state doctrine may not justify its application. We suggested that a sort of balancing approach could be applied — the balance shifting against application of the doctrine, for example, if the government that committed the "challenged act of state" is no longer in existence. But what is appropriate in order to avoid unquestioning judicial acceptance of the acts of foreign sovereigns is not similarly appropriate for the quite opposite purpose of expanding judicial incapacities where such acts are not directly (or even indirectly) involved. It is one thing to suggest, as we have, that the policies underlying the act of state doctrine should be considered in deciding whether, despite the doctrine's technical availability, it should nonetheless not be invoked; it is something quite different to suggest that those underlying policies are a doctrine unto themselves, justifying expansion of the act of state doctrine (or, as the United States puts it, unspecified "related principles of abstention") into new and uncharted fields.

The short of the matter is this: Courts in the United States have the power, and ordinarily the obligation, to decide cases and controversies properly presented to them. The act of state doctrine does not establish an exception for cases and controversies that may embarrass foreign governments, but merely requires that, in the process of deciding, the acts of foreign sovereigns taken within their own jurisdictions shall be deemed valid. That doctrine has no application to the present case because the validity of no foreign sovereign act is at issue.

The judgment of the Court of Appeals for the Third Circuit is affirmed.

It is so ordered.

* Even if we agreed with the Government's fundamental approach, we would question its characterization of the legal advisor's letter as reflecting the absence of any policy objection to the adjudication. The letter . . . did not purport to say whether the State Department would like the suit to proceed, but rather responded (correctly, as we hold today) to the question whether the act of state doctrine was applicable.

Notes and Questions

1. How persuasive is the Court's conclusion in *Kirkpatrick* that the act of state doctrine had no application there because the "validity of no foreign sovereign act is at issue"? What about *Kirkpatrick*'s argument that Environmental Tectonics could prevail only if it proved that Nigerian officials had received payments that violated Nigerian law and that supported a finding that the resulting contract was invalid under Nigerian law?

2. What weight did the lower federal courts appear to give to the position of the Department of State? What weight does the Supreme Court give to the Executive Branch's position? Is the Court more willing than the Executive Branch to give dispositive significance to the distinction between "motivation for," rather than "validity of," a foreign sovereign act?

3. Could *Kirkpatrick* have been decided the same way by use of a "commercial" exception to the act of state doctrine? After *Kirkpatrick,* what is the status of this commercial exception, which received the support of some Justices in the *Dunhill* case discussed above?

4. What did the Court in *Kirkpatrick* mean by the statement that the "act of state doctrine is not some vague doctrine of abstention but a 'principle of decision' " (citing *Sabbatino*)? Was the Court saying that the doctrine is not a variant on the political question doctrine, but is rather a conflict-of-laws principle? (See introduction to this Section B.) If so, what is the significance of this statement?

5. Review the last four Supreme Court cases above — *Sabbatino, First National City Bank, Dunhill,* and *Kirkpatrick.* What is the status of the various possible exceptions to the applicability of the act of state doctrine — e.g., for a treaty, for less than formal acts, for counterclaims, for commercial activity, and for the views of the Department of State (*Bernstein*)? Have some exceptions received more support than others?

6. The "treaty exception" in the act of state doctrine, as suggested in *Sabbatino,* was recognized and followed in Kalamazoo Spice Extraction Co. v. Provisional Military Government of Socialist Ethiopia, 729 F.2d 422 (6th Cir. 1984). In that case, the Ethiopian government had expropriated the shares of an Ethiopian company held by an American corporation. The U.S. court of appeals analyzed an article in the 1953 Treaty of Amity and Economic Relations between the United States and Ethiopia, which provided that "property shall not be taken except for a public purpose, nor shall it be taken without prompt payment of just and effective compensation." The court concluded that the article made the act of state doctrine inapplicable in that case because it established a standard of compensation for expropriated property.

7. After *Kirkpatrick,* some observers have noted that most lower courts narrowly interpreted the act of state doctrine. For example, see discussions and cases cited in Gary B. Born & Peter B. Rutledge, International Civil Litigation in United States Courts 783 (4th ed. 2007); see also Provincial Gov't of Marinduque v. Placer Dome, Inc., 582 F.3d 1083, 1091 (9th Cir. 2009) (finding act of state doctrine not applicable because none of the alleged acts of state were "essential" to the claims). The doctrine is still found applicable in a variety of situations, however. E.g., Nocula v. UGS Corporation, 520 F.3d 719 (7th Cir. 2008) (act of state doctrine applies to foreign government's seizure of goods during criminal investigation); Glen v. Club Mediterranee, 450 F.3d 1251, 1256-1257 (11th Cir. 2006) (act of state doctrine held

applicable in a case involving the alleged expropriation by the Cuban government of property held in Cuba by then-Cuban citizens); World Wide Minerals, Ltd. v. Republic of Kazakhstan, 296 F.3d 1154, 1165-1166 (D.C. Cir. 2002) (act of state doctrine applies when issue is the "legality" of a state's denial of an export license).

8. From the plaintiff's standpoint, what is the difference between a court's dismissal of a case based on foreign sovereign immunity and a court's dismissal of a case based on its application of the act of state doctrine? Consider res judicata and collateral estoppel. For an example of a case in which the court found that it had jurisdiction under the commercial activity exception to the Foreign Sovereign Immunities Act, but then dismissed the case based on its application of the act of state doctrine, see Callejo v. Bancomer, 764 F.2d 1101 (5th Cir. 1985).

4. *The Act of State Doctrine in Other States*

Oppenheim's International Law

365, 368-376 (Robert Jennings & Arthur Watts Eds., 9th ed. 1992)

§112 State Equality and Recognition of Foreign Official Acts: 'Act of State'. . . .

This restraint upon the questioning of foreign state acts, known especially in the United States of America as the act of state doctrine, may be known differently in other states. In particular, English law uses that term in a somewhat different sense; nevertheless, substantively the same general rule of judicial restraint is applied by English courts although perhaps more restrictively than in the United States.

It is not clear how far this doctrine may properly be regarded as a rule of public international law or whether it belongs essentially to the province of private international law. Considerations of public policy have often prevented a full recognition of the validity of foreign legislation. There is probably no international judicial authority in support of the proposition that recognition of foreign official acts is affirmatively prescribed by international law. . . .

The Italian Court of Cassation has, however, held the non-justiciability of acts of foreign states to be a principle of international law, forming part of the Italian legal system.

§113 Foreign Legislation Contrary to International Law

Whatever may be the rule of international law as to the duty of states (and their courts) to recognize the effects of foreign legislation within the foreign country concerned, it would appear that there is no such obligation with respect to foreign legislation, whatever the place of its purported effect, which is in itself contrary to international law.

The matter most frequently arises in connection with the seizure of property without compensation, and courts have varied in their approach and their conclusions. Sometimes the foreign expropriation law is denied effect on grounds which may have little, if anything, to do directly with its violation of international law. Thus irrespective of its compatibility with international law, it may be held that the law does not have extra-territorial effect, or that to give effect to it would be contrary to the public policy of the forum. Similarly, where effect is given to the law, the court may not have expressly considered its possible incompatibility with international law, or may have inquired into the matter and concluded that the law, or at least its application in the case before the court, did not involve any violation of international law. However, in Banco National de Cuba v. Sabbatino the United States Supreme Court denied the permissibility even of making such an inquiry, thus precluding any possible finding that a foreign law in violation of international law should be denied effect. . . .

Other courts have not held themselves inhibited from inquiring into the extent to which a foreign expropriation law is contrary to international law, and their conclusions justify the assertion that foreign legislation which is contrary to international law may properly be treated as a nullity and, with regard to rights of property, as incapable of transferring title to the state concerned either within its territory or outside it. Where courts have expressly reached the conclusion that the law (or the action taken under it) was contrary to international law, they have in most cases declined to give effect to it. However, some courts, while not expressly deciding that the foreign legislation in question violated international law (and thus not actually giving effect to it despite such a violation) have suggested that even if it were contrary to international law effect should nevertheless be given to it; or, having found the law contrary to international law, have said that on that ground alone it should not be denied effect, although going on to deny it effect on some other ground. In such cases the court has tended to regard questions of the violation of international law, and suitable redress therefore, as an inter-governmental rather than a judicial matter, particularly since the international remedy for a taking of property pursuant to legislation in breach of international law is not necessarily invalidity of that law or non-recognition of a private law tied to property, but more often the payment of damages to the injured state.

Courts may be under a constitutional compulsion to give effect to the law of their own sovereign legislature even if violative of international law—although they will not lightly impute to it the intention to violate international law and although in some countries courts have in fact the power to refuse to give effect to national legislation contrary to international law—but there is no compelling reason why they should assist in giving effect to violations of international law by a foreign legislature. In the absence of compulsory jurisdiction of international tribunals and having regard to the prohibition, under the Charter of the United Nations and elsewhere, of compulsive means of enforcement of international law by national action, municipal courts may on occasions provide the only means for securing respect for international law in this and other spheres. Principle does not countenance a rule which, by reference to international law, obliges courts to endow with legal effect legislative and other acts of foreign states which are in violation of international law; and in practice no such international obligation is regarded as existing. However, in view of the practice of states as revealed by the actions of their courts, some of which have been prepared to acknowledge legal effects of foreign acts in violation of international law, it probably cannot be said that international law forbids courts to give effect to such a foreign act when to do so is in accordance with their own national laws. It is in any case consistent with the principle that such violations of international law on the part of foreign states ought not to be assumed in the absence of evidence of a cogent character.

Notes and Questions

1. Do the practices of other states suggest U.S. courts should continue at least some applications of the act of state doctrine?

2. What are the strongest arguments for the doctrine? The strongest arguments against it?

3. Related to the act of state doctrine in the United States is the doctrine of foreign sovereign compulsion. It protects from liability under U.S. law certain actions by individuals or entities that are compelled by foreign governments. The doctrine has been found only infrequently by U.S. courts, primarily in the antitrust context. See Trugman-Nash, Inc. v. New Zealand Dairy Bd., 954 F.Supp. 733 (S.D.N.Y. 1997); Interamerican Refining Corp. v. Texaco Maracaibo, Inc., 307 F. Supp. 1291 (D. Del. 1970); Restatement sections 441-442. The Department of Justice and the Federal Trade Commission formally recognize the doctrine as a narrow defense to antitrust liability. See Department of Justice and Federal Trade Commission, Antitrust Enforcement Guidelines for International Operations, Apr. 1995, available at http://www.justice.gov/atr/public/guidelines/internat.htm.

Problem. Assume you are a clerk for a U.S. Supreme Court Justice. He is a thoughtful moderate. He calls you into his office and presents you with the following project:

The Court has before it a case involving the act of state doctrine. In the past the Court has heard arguments on whether to reconsider *Sabbatino* and eliminate the act of state doctrine but decided against the step. This Justice wants you to prepare a memorandum that addresses whether the Court might use this case or others on which certiorari could be granted to eliminate or make substantial modifications in the act of state doctrine. For now, the Justice is not concerned with the particulars of the specific case that is pending; rather, he wants to develop a constructive analysis of what should be done with the doctrine.

He asks that your memorandum address in detail whether or not the doctrine should be eliminated or substantially modified. Although he expects you to identify and address a range of issues, he says that you should (among other matters) include the following issues: What kind of cases would be affected by a change in the law? What types of parties would be benefited or hurt? What would be the likely impact on U.S. foreign policy and on the effective diplomacy of the U.S. Executive Branch?

The Justice asks that you give him your recommendation on whether the doctrine should be eliminated or not. If not, then do you have recommendations on how the doctrine should be modified? If you do propose elimination or changes, what would be the legal theory (or theories) that could be used to justify these changes?

7

Allocation of Legal Authority Among States

To advise a client on the legal implications of a course of action involving more than one country, a lawyer must obviously focus on the government or governments that may authorize, regulate, or prohibit the conduct. Even in those parts of the world where no government asserts sovereignty, such as Antarctica and outer space, there are international agreements concluded by governments that define the applicable legal regime. Moreover, while individuals and corporations as well as governments may "create" law through contract, and while international organizations may exercise law-making authority, those acts are supported by the authority of governments. A contract is valid and enforceable because some national legal system says so. Arbitral awards, even those applying international law or general principles of law, have force in part because they are enforceable under national legal systems. International organizations take their power from international agreements entered into by governments. In short, we still work in a world dominated in large part by the power of the state. States control borders, regulate conduct, and claim power over access to resources.

Consequently, an international lawyer is centrally concerned with the allocation of power and authority among states in the world. Much of this casebook can be viewed as an examination of the bases for exercise of authority by governments and the limitations expressed in legal norms on the exercise of that authority. Law performs both functions. It legitimates claims of authority, such as the right of a government to regulate all conduct within its territory, as well as the conduct of its nationals anywhere in the world. It also limits that authority. Thus, for example, a state may claim the authority to tax its nationals on their worldwide income, but the state may have limited itself from taxing their foreign income by norms established in a treaty or a statute.

The legal universe is frequently divided into public and private spheres. Public law concerns the relationship of government and its subjects, such as criminal law, tax law, and other economic regulation such as the antitrust and securities laws. By contrast, private law, such as contract, tort, and property law, concerns the relationships of persons, natural and juridical, among themselves. There are also rules that define which state's law applies to transactions having a relationship to more than one state. Thus public international law is concerned with whether a state has authority to apply its drug laws, tax laws, or antitrust laws to conduct by persons in another state (e.g., a U.S. criminal prosecution of French and German companies that agree in the Bahamas to fix the prices of goods to be exported to the United States). Private international law (or conflict of laws), on the other hand, is concerned with whether a state may apply its tort, contract, or property rules to events or transactions that have significant connections with it and another state (e.g., a California court deciding which jurisdiction's law applies to determine the validity of a contract between Mitsubishi of Japan and Chrysler to sell cars manufactured in Korea for delivery in Hong Kong).

In Sections A and B of this chapter we examine public international law—first, the permissible bases on which a state may justify application of its law and the limitations imposed by international law on that application, and, second, the stricter rules dealing with the authority of a state to enforce its law. In Section C we outline the principal approaches of private international law (or conflict of laws) in choosing applicable private law. The types of analysis sometimes used in resolving conflicts of private law are similar to those used in the public international law materials dealing with limitations on a state's ability to apply its law.

In its sphere, public international law distinguishes between three different types of authority (or "jurisdiction," as it is usually called)—a state's right to *prescribe* or apply law to certain persons or activities, a state's right to *enforce* that law by applying sanctions to a violator, and a state's right to *adjudicate* the legality of conduct. (The 1987 Restatement of Foreign Relations Law added the third category.)

An example will help illustrate the differences: A terrorist kills three pedestrians when he explodes by remote control a bomb he has placed in a parked car just outside a shopping mall in Chicago. He flees to Syria, where the Syrian authorities claim that they cannot find him. The United States has prescriptive jurisdiction regarding the terrorist's conduct in its territory. Hence, under accepted principles of international law, the United States has jurisdiction to outlaw the killings in its territory. However, it does not have adjudicatory jurisdiction to try him or enforcement jurisdiction to compel compliance with the law or to punish him, because he is not present in U.S. territory and is beyond the reach of U.S. officials. Moreover, all three bases of jurisdiction are limited by an international law principle of reasonableness, in addition to whatever limitations may be found in U.S. constitutional or statutory law.

For background, consider the following excerpt:

Restatement

Part IV—Introductory Note

Statements of the international law of jurisdiction traditionally have tended to distinguish between jurisdiction to prescribe—the authority of a state to make its substantive laws applicable to particular persons and circumstances—and jurisdiction to enforce law against particular persons or in particular circumstances. Since jurisdiction to prescribe was seen principally as a function of national legislation, it was sometimes referred to as legislative jurisdiction. Since enforcement was often thought of as exercised essentially by judicial process, jurisdiction to enforce was often equated with jurisdiction to adjudicate.

Increasingly, however, it has become clear that the identification of prescription with legislation, and of enforcement with adjudication, is too simple. In principle, substantive regulation derives its authority from legislation, . . . but much regulation is effected through administrative rules and regulations, through executive acts and orders, and sometimes by court decree. Enforcement is often carried out through executive or administrative rather than judicial action; enforcement is thus not merely an aspect of adjudication, and the rules of jurisdiction applicable to nonjudicial enforcement are different in several respects from those that govern judicial enforcement. At the same time, adjudication is often used for purposes that are not strictly "enforcement," but rather for declaration of rights and vindication of private interests. The process of adjudication, whatever the purposes for which it is used, is a significant category in the foreign relations law of the United States.

Accordingly, this Restatement deals with jurisdiction under the following headings: (a) jurisdiction to prescribe, i.e., the authority of a state to make its law applicable to persons or activities; (b) jurisdiction to adjudicate, i.e., the authority of a state to subject particular persons or things to its judicial process; and (c) jurisdiction to enforce, i.e., the authority of a state to use the resources of government to induce or compel compliance with its law. See §401.

These categories of jurisdiction are often interdependent, and their scope and limitations are shaped by similar considerations. Jurisdiction to prescribe may be more acceptable where jurisdiction to adjudicate or to enforce is plainly available; jurisdiction to adjudicate may be more acceptable where the state of the forum also has jurisdiction to prescribe by virtue of its links to the persons, interests, relations, or activities involved. However, the purposes and consequences of the different categories of jurisdiction are not necessarily congruent, and balancing the competing interests in the different contexts can lead to different results.

A. JURISDICTION TO PRESCRIBE PUBLIC LAW

Typically, five bases of prescriptive jurisdiction are recognized:

(1) territory (including conduct having effects in territory)
(2) nationality
(3) protective
(4) passive personality
(5) universal

Before we analyze each of these bases in some detail, Professor Starke's treatise provides an overview.

I. A. Shearer, Starke's International Law

183-212 (11th ed. 1994)

The practice as to the exercise by states of jurisdiction over persons, property, or acts or events varies for each state, and these variations are due to historical and geographical factors which are nonetheless coming to play a less important role in measure as . . . countries have become geographically more knit together. Historically, states, such as Great Britain, in which sea frontiers predominated, paid primary allegiance to the territorial principle of jurisdiction, according to which each state might exercise jurisdiction over property and persons in, or acts or events occurring within its territory; this was because the free or unrestricted movement of individuals or of property to or from other countries did not in the past occur so readily or frequently as between states bounded for the most part by land frontiers. On the other hand, most European states took a much broader view of the extent of their jurisdiction precisely because the continent is a network of land or river frontiers, and acts or transactions of an international character were more frequent owing to the facility and rapidity of movement across such frontiers.

However, with the increasing speed of communications, the more sophisticated structure of commercial organisations or enterprises with transnational ramifications, and the growing international character of criminal activities . . . there has been a noticeable trend towards the exercise of jurisdiction on the basis of criteria other than that of territorial location.

. . . [In] the much discussed *Lotus* Case (1927), . . . the Permanent Court of International Justice [decided] there is no restriction on the exercise of jurisdiction by any state unless that restriction can be shown by the most conclusive evidence to exist as a principle of international law. In that case the Permanent Court did not accept the French thesis — France being one of the parties — that a claim to jurisdiction by a state must be shown to be justified by international law and practice. In the Court's opinion, the onus lay on the state claiming that such exercise of jurisdiction was unjustified, to show that it was prohibited by international law.

There is one practical limitation on the exercise of wide jurisdiction by a particular state. . . . "[N]o State attempts to exercise a jurisdiction over matters, persons or things with which it has absolutely no concern." . . . [G]enerally, it will be found that the territorial basis of jurisdiction is the normal working rule.

2. Territorial Jurisdiction

The exercise of jurisdiction by a state over property, persons, acts or events occurring within its territory is clearly conceded by international law to all members of the society of states. The principle has been well put by Lord Macmillan:

> It is an essential attribute of the sovereignty of this realm, as of all sovereign independent States, that it should possess jurisdiction over all persons and things within its territorial limits and in all causes civil and criminal arising within these limits. . . .

For the purposes of the exercise of territorial jurisdiction, it has been customary to assimilate to state territory: (a) the maritime coastal belt or territorial sea; (b) a ship bearing the flag of the state wishing to exercise jurisdiction. . . .

Technical Extensions of the Territorial Jurisdiction

Apart from the assimilation to territory of the territorial sea, of ships at sea, . . . certain technical extensions of the principle of territorial jurisdiction became necessary in order to justify action taken by states in cases where one or more constituent elements of an act or offence took place outside their territory. These extensions were occasioned by the increasing facilities for speedy international communication and transport, leading to the commission of crimes in one state which were engineered or prepared in another state. . . . [S]everal states met the new conditions by technically extending the territorial jurisdiction:

a. Applying the *subjective territorial principle,* these states arrogated to themselves a jurisdiction to prosecute and punish crimes commenced within their territory, but completed or consummated in the territory of another state. Although this principle was not so generally adopted by states as to amount to a general rule of the law of nations, particular applications of it did become a part of international law as a result of the provisions of two international conventions, the Geneva Convention for the Suppression of Counterfeiting Currency (1929), and the Geneva Convention for the Suppression of the Illicit Drug Traffic (1936). Under these conventions, the states parties bound themselves to punish, if taking place within their territory, conspiracies to commit and intentional participation in the commission of counterfeiting and drug traffic offences wherever the final act of commission took place, as also attempts to commit and acts preparatory to the commission of such offences, and in addition agreed to treat certain specific acts as distinct offences and not to consider them as accessory to principal offences committed elsewhere. . . .

b. Pursuant to the *objective territorial principle,* certain States applied their territorial jurisdiction to offences or acts commenced in another state, but: (i) consummated or completed within their territory, or (ii) producing gravely harmful consequences to the social or economic order inside their territory. The objective territorial theory was defined . . . as follows:

> The setting in motion outside of a State of a force which produces as a direct consequence an injurious effect therein justifies the territorial sovereign in prosecuting the actor when he enters its domain.

Illustrations of the theory . . . were:

a. a man firing a gun across a frontier and killing another man in a neighbouring state;
b. a man obtaining money by false pretences by means of a letter posted in Great Britain to a recipient in Germany.

The objective territorial principle was applied in the provisions of the two international conventions just referred to, and has also been recognised in decisions of English, German, and American courts. But the most outstanding example of its application has been the decision of the Permanent Court of International Justice in 1927 in the *Lotus* Case. The facts in that case were shortly, that a French mail steamer, the *Lotus,* collided on the high seas with a Turkish collier, due allegedly to the gross negligence of the officer of the watch on board the *Lotus,* with the result that the collier sank and eight Turkish nationals on board perished. The Turkish authorities instituted proceedings against the officer of the watch, basing the claim to jurisdiction on the ground that the act of negligence on board the *Lotus* had produced effects on the Turkish collier, and thus according to the rule mentioned above, on a portion of Turkish territory. By a majority decision, the Permanent Court held that the action of the Turkish authorities was not inconsistent with international law.

The objective territorial principle plays a recognised role in respect to the exercise of jurisdiction as to multinational corporations. . . . The difficulties in applying to these enterprises traditional notions of jurisdiction have been well expressed as follows:

> The multi-national corporation, by definition, . . . has activities in more than one State. If a strict territorial approach is adopted, each State may regulate only those activities within its borders. Such an approach could have serious effects. It might make it impossible for the corporation to do business by subjecting it to contradictory or confusing legal regimes, or on the other hand, it might allow the corporation to escape liability for conduct whose components are legal in each of the States in which they take place but which, taken as a whole, is illegal under the laws of some or all of the States concerned.

One approach for which there is authority is that the country in the territory of which the effects or results are felt of action taken by the head office (in another country) of the multinational corporation is entitled to exercise jurisdiction, e.g. against the servants or assets of branches or subsidiaries locally situated. It is true that the head office's action may have concurrent effects in a large number of countries, the jurisdiction of all of which could then be attracted without being debarred by international law, so that ultimately it will be necessary to work out some appropriate code or the exercise of jurisdiction under international law over multinational corporations in order to avoid jurisdictional conflicts. . . . Reference should be made to what apparently purports to be an extension by way of degree of the objective territorial principle, namely, the "effects" doctrine adopted by American federal courts under which, especially in anti-trust proceedings, jurisdiction is exercised extra-territorially on the basis of the effects or consequences, however remote, within the United States and which are deemed to be of so reprehensible a nature (provided that they are *direct*), economic or otherwise, as to attract or necessitate such jurisdiction. Having regard to the possible serious results for their trading interests which the awards of American federal courts may involve (triple damages may be awarded); this "effects" jurisdiction has been objected to by the United Kingdom, Australia and other countries, and has led to the passage of local legislation to preclude the enforcement in the objecting countries of any element, evidentiary, procedural or otherwise of the American proceedings or judgments. It is claimed that the "effects" jurisdiction, as asserted by American courts, is contrary to international law, and that the local protective legislation [sometimes called blocking statutes] is validly opposable to such American extra-territorial process.

Territorial Jurisdiction over Aliens

Territorial jurisdiction is conceded by international law as much over aliens as over citizens of the territorial state. . . . [N]o presumption of immunity arises from the fact that the person against whom proceedings are taken is an alien. . . .

3. [Nationality] Jurisdiction . . .

According to present international practice, [nationality] jurisdiction may be exercised on the basis of one or other of the following principles:

A. *Active nationality principle.* Under this principle, jurisdiction is assumed by the state of which the person, against whom proceedings are taken, is a national. The active nationality principle is generally conceded by international law to all states desiring to apply it. . . .

B. *Passive [personality or] nationality principle.* Jurisdiction is assumed by the state of which the person suffering injury or a civil damage is a national. International law recognises the passive [personality or] nationality principle only subject to certain qualifications. . . . The justification, if any, for exercising jurisdiction on this principle is that each state has a perfect right to protect its citizens abroad, and if the territorial state of the locus delicti neglects or is unable to punish the persons causing the injury, the state of which the victim is a national is entitled to do so if the persons responsible come within its power. But as against this, it may be urged that the general interests of a state are scarcely attacked "merely because one of its nationals has been the victim of an offence in a foreign country." The passive nationality principle is embodied in several national criminal codes. . . .

4. Jurisdiction According to the Protective Principle

International law recognizes that each state may exercise jurisdiction over crimes against its security and integrity or its vital economic interests. Most criminal codes contain rules embodying in the national idiom the substance of this principle, which is generally known as the *protective* principle. . . .

The rational grounds for the exercise of this jurisdiction are two-fold:

i. the offences subject to the application of the protective principle are such that their consequences may be of the utmost gravity and concern to the state against which they are directed;

ii. unless the jurisdiction were exercised, many such offences would escape punishment altogether because they did not contravene the law of the place where they were committed (lex loci delicti) or because extradition would be refused by reason of the political character of the offence.

The serious objection to the protective principle is that each state presumes to be its own judge as to what endangers its security or its financial credit. Thus in many cases, the application of the protective principle tends to be quite arbitrary.

5. Jurisdiction According to the Universal Principle . . .

An offence subject to universal jurisdiction is one which comes under the jurisdiction of all states wherever it be committed. Inasmuch as by general admission, the offence is contrary to the interests of the international community, it is treated as a delict jure gentium and all states are entitled to apprehend and punish the offenders. Clearly the purpose of conceding universal jurisdiction is to ensure that no such offence goes unpunished.*

The Restatement summarizes the international law principles of prescriptive jurisdiction as follows:

Restatement

Section 402. Bases of Jurisdiction to Prescribe

Subject to §403, a state has jurisdiction to prescribe law with respect to

(1) (a) conduct that, wholly or in substantial part, takes place within its territory;

(b) the status of persons, or interests in things, present within its territory;

(c) conduct outside its territory that has or is intended to have substantial effect within its territory;

(2) the activities, interests, status, or relations of its nationals outside as well as within its territory; and

(3) certain conduct outside its territory by persons not its nationals that is directed against the security of the state or against a limited class of other state interests.

See also Comment *g* to this section (excerpted in Section A.4 below) (passive personality) and section 404 (excerpted in excerpt A.5 below) (universal jurisdiction).

Notes and Questions

1. As discussed in the Starke excerpt above at pages 640 and 641-642, the Permanent Court of International Justice (the predecessor to the ICJ) concluded that international law did not prevent Turkey from applying its criminal law to the conduct of a French merchant ship officer (Lieutenant Demons) on the high seas. His ship had collided with a Turkish ship, killing eight Turkish nationals. France had argued that Turkey would violate international law. S.S. *Lotus* (France v. Turkey), 1927 P.C.I.J. (Ser, A) No. 10. A longer discussion of the case is in Chapter 1.C, but briefly the court opined:

> International law governs relations between independent States. The rules of law binding upon States therefore emanate from their own free will as expressed in conventions or by usages generally accepted as expressing principles of law and established in order to regulate the relations between these co-existing independent communities or with a view to the achievement of common aims. Restrictions upon the independence of States cannot therefore be presumed.

*[The discussion of universal jurisdiction in Subsection A.5 below will provide more detail about the offences that might come under this principle. — Eds.]

Now the first and foremost restriction imposed by international law upon a State is that—failing the existence of a permissive rule to the contrary—it may not exercise its power in any form in the territory of another State. In this sense jurisdiction is certainly territorial; it cannot be exercised by a State outside its territory except by virtue of a permissive rule derived from international custom or from a convention.

It does not, however, follow that international law prohibits a State from exercising jurisdiction in its own territory, in respect of any case which relates to acts which have taken place abroad, and in which it cannot rely on some permissive rule of international law. Such a view would only be tenable if international law contained a general prohibition to States to extend the application of their laws and the jurisdiction of their courts to persons, property and acts outside their territory, and if, as an exception to this general prohibition, it allowed States to do so in certain specific cases. But this is certainly not the case under international law as it stands at present. Far from laying down a general prohibition to the effect that States may not extend the application of their laws and the jurisdiction of their courts to persons, property and acts outside their territory, it leaves them in this respect a wide measure of discretion which is only limited in certain cases by prohibitive rules; as regards other cases, every State remains free to adopt the principles which it regards as best and most suitable. . . .

In these circumstances, all that can be required of a State is that it should not overstep the limits which international law places upon its jurisdiction; within these limits, its title to exercise jurisdiction rests in its sovereignty.

It follows from the foregoing that the contention of the French Government to the effect that Turkey must in each case be able to cite a rule of international law authorizing her to exercise jurisdiction, is opposed to the generally accepted international law. . . .

Thus, the *Lotus* decision suggests that there is a presumption that an extraterritorial (or any other) assertion of prescriptive jurisdiction by a state is legal unless the target can show that a rule of international law prohibits that assertion. Do you think that this presumption is based on an outmoded celebration of state sovereignty that is inappropriate today?

On the other hand, the court noted that Turkey was "exercising jurisdiction in its own territory"—the trial was in Turkey and the effects of the negligent act in question were felt on board a Turkish vessel. What was the prescriptive jurisdictional basis for the application of Turkish law to the controversy? What was France's claim? Which state had the burden of demonstrating the existence of a rule of international law to support its position? Would international law be strengthened if the rule were the opposite? Whose interests would be advanced, and whose hampered, by the approach taken in the *Lotus* case?

How would you show that international law prohibited a particular extraterritorial assertion of prescriptive jurisdiction? Tax treaties provide an obvious source of such limitations in that they set forth in considerable detail limitations on a state's taxing authority. Limitations based on customary international law seem more difficult to establish. In the materials that follow, describing common foreign reactions to expansive U.S. assertions of prescriptive jurisdiction, consider whether such limitations can be inferred. How would you show that customary international law limits a state's prescriptive jurisdiction in the field of, say, securities regulation? Also consider what is at stake in these controversies. Which states and what interests benefit from strict territorial limits or at least robust customary international law-based limits on prescriptive jurisdiction?

2. Why should a Connecticut theft statute not apply to a theft in Massachusetts? Or France?

3. If Congress passes a law criminalizing the possession of heroin in Malaysia by Malaysian nationals, should a U.S. court apply that law (assuming the defendant was properly before the court)? Would your response be different in the case of a Swiss court applying Swiss law that criminalized the adulteration of chocolates by anyone anywhere in the world? Or a Pakistani court applying a Pakistani law prohibiting the consumption of alcohol to college students drinking vodka in Florida (again assuming the defendants were properly before the court)?

4. Which of the five bases of prescriptive jurisdiction summarized by Starke seem the strongest bases for a state claiming that it can prescribe law to certain persons or activities? What are the sources of your thinking on this question? If territorial jurisdiction seems natural, why is that so? Does nationality also seem strong? Which others?

5. Consider now the implications of the Internet. Would China violate international law if it criminalized the posting of material on the Web about certain religious groups, such as the Falun Gong? Would Saudi Arabia be in violation of international law if it criminalized the posting of photos of unveiled women on the Web? Does it matter, in the examples above, whether the individuals posting the information were in China, Saudi Arabia, or the United States? Similarly, does it matter if the servers that contained the posted information were in China, Saudi Arabia, or the United States?

To take an actual case, did France violate international law when it prohibited the sale of Nazi paraphernalia over the Internet? In fact, such items were for sale at the time on the Yahoo Web site, to which users located in France had access. Does it matter that Yahoo's headquarters and servers were in California? Or, does it matter that Yahoo apparently could not identify and screen out all the users in France who tried to access the part of its Web site that had the Nazi items for sale? Moving for a moment beyond issues of prescriptive jurisdiction, assuming that France made these sales of Nazi items illegal under French law and a French court held that Yahoo had violated the law, how could France enforce the judgment? The *Yahoo* case is discussed in Chapter 4.F.2.

Should a country's laws (statutory or common law) regarding defamation or libel apply to Internet material? Australia's highest court held that Australia's courts had jurisdiction to hear a defamation claim under Australian law (specifically the law of the plaintiff's home state of Victoria) by an Australian businessman against Dow Jones & Co. for a story published on Barron's Online. Mr. Joseph Gutnick claimed that an article defamed him by saying that he had been involved with two Americans in a money-laundering scheme. The challenged material had been edited in New York City and uploaded by Dow Jones onto its server in New Jersey. Barron's Online had an estimated 1,700 subscribers in Australia out of a total of 550,000 subscribers. The Australian High Court unanimously held that "ordinarily, defamation is to be located at the place where the damage to reputation occurs. . . . In the case of material on the World Wide Web, it is not available in comprehensible form until downloaded on to the computer of a person who has used a web browser to pull the material from the web server. It is where that person downloads the material that the damage to reputation may be done." (Para. 44.) Dow Jones & Co. v. Gutnick [2002] HCA56 (10 Dec. 2002) (High Court of Australia).

While recognizing the uniquely broad reach of the World Wide Web, the High Court noted that "those who make information accessible by a particular method do so knowing of the reach that their information may have." (Para. 39.) Rejecting the argument that its approach would make a publisher liable to the defamation laws of every country from "Afghanistan to Zimbabwe," the High Court said this concern was "unreal when it is recalled that in all but the unusual cases, identifying the person about whom material is to be published will readily identify the defamation law to which that person may resort." (Para. 54.) What should be the result if a repressive regime tried to prescribe strict rules regarding libel against authors and publishers on the Internet—for example, limiting any negative comments about that country's government? Its national religion? Its citizens? Its occasional visitors? Any company doing business there?

In the *Dow Jones* case above, which of the jurisdictional principles discussed by Professor Starke is the basis for the Australian court determining that it had jurisdiction? Territorial? Objective territorial? Nationality? Passive nationality or passive personality principle? For another libel case involving the Internet but where a court in Ontario, Canada, did not assume jurisdiction, see Bangoura v. Washington Post, 2005 O.J. No. 3849.

6. A recent criminal libel case caused considerable concern for, among others, editors of law reviews and other publications that have an online component. Dr. Karin Calvo-Goller, an academic in Israel of Israeli and French nationality, chose to bring the action in France against Professor Joseph Weiler, editor in chief of the European Journal of International Law and a professor of law at New York University. Professor Weiler, who is not a French national, had posted a book review written in English on the journal's associated Web site that is on a server in New York. The review itself was written by a German professor in Germany and criticized a book that Dr. Calvo-Goller had written. Dr. Calvo-Goller complained to Weiler, saying that the review contained false factual statements, was libelous, and might cause harm to her professional reputation. She asked that it be removed from the Web site. Citing academic freedom and noting that the reviewer was well-regarded, Weiler refused, indicating that Calvo-Goller could submit her comments to the journal's Web site. Because defendant Weiler did not just want to challenge jurisdiction, but also to affirm the principle of academic freedom, the case went to a full trial in Paris. See http://www.ejiltalk.org/in-the-dock-in paris.

On March 3, 2011, the Tribunal de Grand Instance de Paris issued its decision in favor of the defendant. The court noted that the complainant had engaged in "forum shopping." An unofficial translation of the opinion has the court adding that it was with "just cause, that Joseph Weiler believes that the [complainant] has abused her right to bring legal proceedings, on the one hand by initiating an action for defamation in relations to words that do not go beyond the limits of academic criticism . . . and, on the other hand, by artificially bringing proceedings through the French criminal justice system." She was directed to pay Weiler 8,000 euros (or about $11,320). See Dirk Voorhoof on http://strasbourgobservers.com (March 8, 2011). Although the French court ruled in the defendant's favor, should there be some continuing concern about the possibilities for shopping for a friendly forum against publications that appear online?

The following five sections look more carefully at each of the bases of prescriptive jurisdiction.

1. Territory

In the United States legislation is normally considered to be territorial in scope. In other words, a California statute would normally be construed to apply throughout California, and a U.S. federal statute would normally be construed to apply throughout the United States. However, the California statute would not normally be interpreted to apply to California citizens elsewhere in the world or to the conduct of all people throughout the world who may later stray into California and thus be subject to the in personam jurisdiction of its courts. Nor would the U.S. federal statute normally be construed to apply to U.S. citizens elsewhere in the world or to the conduct of all persons who may in the future be subject to the personal jurisdiction of U.S. courts.

Under a strict application of the territorial theory, each country would have the exclusive right to regulate within its territory and no authority to regulate outside that territory, a neat division of power in the world. Around a hundred years or so ago, the basis for this territorial limitation was found in natural law, international law (or the "law of nations" as it was often styled in the nineteenth century), or just an assumption inherent in the natural order of things. Thus, considering the question of whether the U.S. antitrust laws applied to conduct by American nationals in a foreign country, Justice Holmes remarked:

> [T]he general and almost universal rule is that the character of an act as lawful or unlawful must be determined wholly by the law of the country where the act is done. . . . For another jurisdiction, if it should happen to lay hold of the actor, to treat him according to its own notions rather than those of the place where he did the acts, not only would be unjust, but would be an interference with the authority of another sovereign, contrary to the comity of nations, which the other state concerned justly might resent. . . .
>
> The foregoing considerations would lead in case of doubt to a construction of any statute as intended to be confined in its operation and effect to the territorial limits over which the lawmaker has general and legitimate power. "All legislation is prima facie territorial." . . . We think it entirely plain that what the defendant did in Panama or Costa Rica is not within the scope of the statute so far as the present suit is concerned. . . . [American Banana Co. v. United Fruit Co., 213 U.S. 347, 356-357 (1909).]

Justice Holmes referred to the "comity of nations" as a limiting restraint on the extraterritorial application of law. In Hilton v. Guyot, 159 U.S. 113, 163-164 (1895), the Court defined that concept:

> "Comity" . . . is neither a matter of absolute obligation, on the one hand, nor of mere courtesy and good will, upon the other. But it is the recognition which one nation allows within its territory to the legislative, executive, or judicial acts of another nation, having due regard both to international duty and convenience, and to the rights of its own citizens or of other persons who are under the protection of its laws.

The principle of comity has sometimes been treated as a principle of international law, but more often has been regarded as something short of a legal limitation, more like an act of altruistic deference or an acknowledgment of superior foreign interest (or lesser U.S. interest) in the matter at hand. Comity also refers to two types of limitation: first, the limitations that are self-imposed by a legislature in adopting a statute (or limitations placed by a court in applying the statute); and, second, limitations adopted by a court in fashioning a decision that affects foreign interests. We first examine the international law or comity limitations on application of law, and later look at those limitations on enforcement and adjudicatory jurisdiction.

Since *American Banana*, and especially in the past few decades, Congress has passed many laws whose provisions are explicitly extraterritorial. These include, for example, the 1992 Torture Victim Protection Act (discussed in Chapter 3.C) and 28 U.S.C. §1605A (the 2008 amendment to the Foreign Sovereign Immunities Act discussed in Chapter 6.A). Moreover, U.S. law enforcement agencies and U.S. courts have increasingly applied U.S. law extraterritorially, that is, to persons acting abroad, when their acts have a substantial effect on the United States. For example, a foreign price-fixing conspiracy undertaken abroad, but having an impact on prices in the U.S. market, has been held to be covered by the Sherman Act (the same antitrust statute that Justice Holmes discussed in the *American Banana* case quoted above).

As will be discussed later in this section, this tendency of the U.S. Congress to pass and U.S. courts and agencies to apply U.S. law extraterritorially has often been sharply resisted by foreign courts, governments, and scholars, and continues to generate controversy. For example, the EU, Canada, the United Kingdom, and several other countries have retaliated by passing so-called blocking statutes making it illegal for persons subject to the jurisdiction of those countries to comply with certain extraterritorial laws and regulations, and forbidding enforcement of certain judgments based on them. These blocking laws have sometimes even included "claw back" provisions — that is, remedies with which their nationals could seek to recover the damages imposed by U.S. enforcement efforts. By the 1990s, though, many countries had come to accept and use the "effects" test in carrying out their own national regulation of international commerce.

Against this tendency by U.S. courts and law enforcement agencies to apply many U.S. laws extraterritorially, there remains a longstanding principle or canon of construction that, unless a contrary intent appears, U.S. laws should be construed to only apply within the territorial jurisdiction of the United States.

A leading case that invokes this canon of interpretation is Equal Employment Opportunity Commission (EEOC) v. Arabian American Oil Company (Aramco), 499 U.S. 244 (1991). There the plaintiff, a U.S. citizen of Lebanese descent, was an engineer for an Aramco subsidiary and was working in Saudi Arabia. Both Aramco and its subsidiary were Delaware corporations. Plaintiff sued the two companies under Title VII of the Civil Rights Act of 1964 on the ground that he was harassed and ultimately discharged by the defendants on account of his race, religion, and national origin. (Title VII prohibits discriminatory employment practices based on an individual's race, color, religion, sex, or national origin.)

The court noted both parties conceded that Congress had the authority to enforce its laws beyond the territorial boundaries of the United States. However, the court cited the presumption against extraterritoriality. It found that the plaintiff's claims that Title VII applied extraterritorially to U.S. employers who employ

U.S. citizens abroad failed "both as a matter of statutory language and of our previous case law."

The court's specific decision in *Aramco* was soon overturned by Congress. Congress added a new provision to Title VII that expanded the definition of an employee covered by the law to include U.S. citizens employed abroad by a U.S. corporation or a subsidiary it controls. The amendments, however, made clear that Title VII did not require the employer to take actions that "would violate the law of the foreign country in which such workplace is located." The law also did not apply to foreign employers who were not controlled by an American employer.

An important and more recent decision by the U.S. Supreme Court is the 2010 one below that strongly reaffirmed the presumption against extraterritoriality. In doing so, the Court reversed a number of decisions that stretched over several decades by U.S. courts, especially the Second Circuit Court of Appeals, regarding the statutory provision at issue in the case. Those courts had interpreted the anti-fraud provisions of the 1934 U.S. securities law to apply extraterritorially to actors and transactions outside the United States.

Morrison v. National Australian Bank

U.S. Supreme Court
130 S. Ct. 2869 (2010)

[Justice Scalia delivered the opinion of the Court in which Justice Roberts, Justice Kennedy, Justice Thomas, and Justice Alito join.]

We decide whether §10(b) of the Securities Exchange Act of 1934 provides a cause of action to foreign plaintiffs suing foreign and American defendants for misconduct in connection with securities traded on foreign exchanges.

Respondent National Australia Bank Limited (National) was, during the relevant time, the largest bank in Australia. Its Ordinary Shares—what in America would be called "common stock"—are traded on the Australian Stock Exchange Limited and on other foreign securities exchanges, but not on any exchange in the United States. . . .

The complaint alleges the following facts, which we accept as true. In February 1998, National bought respondent HomeSide Lending, Inc., a mortgage servicing company headquartered in Florida. . . .

. . . [O]n July 5, 2001, National announced that it was writing down the value of HomeSide's assets by $450 million; and then again on September 3, by another $1.75 billion. The prices of [its] Ordinary Shares . . . slumped. . . . According to the complaint, . . . HomeSide [and some HomeSide executives] . . . had manipulated HomeSide's financial models to make the rates of early repayment unrealistically low in order to cause the mortgage-servicing rights to appear more valuable than they really were. The complaint also alleges that National and [its managing director and chief operating officer Frank] Cicutto were aware of this deception by July 2000, but did nothing about it. . . .

[Petitioners had purchased National's Ordinary Shares in 2000 and 2001 before the write-downs. They sued National, HomeSide, Cicutto, and three

HomeSide executives in the U.S. District Court for alleged violations of sections 10(b) and 20(a) of the Securities and Exchange Act of 1934, and SEC Rule 10b-5.

[Respondents moved to dismiss for lack of subject-matter jurisdiction under Federal Rule of Civil Procedure 12(b)(1) and for failure to state a claim under Rule 12(b)(6). The District Court granted the motion to dismiss for lack of subject-matter jurisdiction. The Court of Appeals for the Second Circuit affirmed. The Supreme Court granted certiorari. As discussed in Note 6 below, the Supreme Court decided that the district court did have subject-matter jurisdiction, but went on to consider whether the petitioners' allegations stated a claim under Rule 12(b)]

III

A

It is a "longstanding principle of American law 'that legislation of Congress, unless a contrary intent appears, is meant to apply only within the territorial jurisdiction of the United States.'" EEOC v. Arabian American Oil Co., 499 U.S. 244, 248 (1991) (*Aramco*). This principle represents a canon of construction, or a presumption about a statute's meaning, rather than a limit upon Congress's power to legislate. It rests on the perception that Congress ordinarily legislates with respect to domestic, not foreign matters. Thus, "unless there is the affirmative intention of the Congress clearly expressed" to give a statute extraterritorial effect, "we must presume it is primarily concerned with domestic conditions." The canon or presumption applies regardless of whether there is a risk of conflict between the American statute and a foreign law, see Sale v. Haitian Centers Council, Inc., 509 U.S. 155, 173-74 (1993). When a statute gives no clear indication of an extraterritorial application, it has none.

Despite this principle of interpretation, long and often recited in our opinions, the Second Circuit believed that, because the Exchange Act is silent as to the extraterritorial application of §10(b), it was left to the court to "discern" whether Congress would have wanted the statute to apply. This disregard of the presumption against extraterritoriality did not originate with the Court of Appeals panel in this case. It has been repeated over many decades by various courts of appeals in determining the application of the Exchange Act, and §10(b) in particular, to fraudulent schemes that involve conduct and effects abroad. That has produced a collection of tests for divining what Congress would have wanted, complex in formulation and unpredictable in application. . . .

B

. . . . Petitioners and the Solicitor General contend . . . that three things indicate that §10(b) or the Exchange Act in general has at least some extraterritorial application.

First, they point to the definition of "interstate commerce," a term used in §10(b), which includes "trade, commerce, transportation, or communication . . . between any foreign country and any State." 15 U.S.C. §78c(a)(17). But "we have repeatedly held that even statutes that contain broad language in their definitions of 'commerce' that expressly refer to 'foreign commerce' do not apply abroad."

The general reference to foreign commerce in the definition of "interstate commerce" does not defeat the presumption against extraterritoriality.

Petitioners and the Solicitor General next point out that Congress, in describing the purposes of the Exchange Act, observed that the "prices established and offered in such transactions are generally disseminated and quoted throughout the United States and foreign countries." The antecedent of "such transactions," however, is found in the first sentence of the section, which declares that "transactions in securities as commonly conducted upon securities exchanges and over-the-counter markets are affected with a national public interest." §78b. Nothing suggests that this *national* public interest pertains to transactions conducted upon *foreign* exchanges and markets. The fleeting reference to the dissemination and quotation abroad of the prices of securities traded in domestic exchanges and markets cannot overcome the presumption against extraterritoriality.

Finally, there is §30(b) of the Exchange Act, 15 U.S.C. §78dd(b), which *does* mention the Act's extraterritorial application: "The provisions of [the Exchange Act] or of any rule or regulation thereunder shall not apply to any person insofar as he transacts a business in securities without the jurisdiction of the United States," unless he does so in violation of regulations promulgated by the Securities and Exchange Commission "to prevent . . . evasion of [the Act]." (The parties have pointed us to no regulation promulgated pursuant to §30(b).) The Solicitor General argues that "[this] exemption would have no function if the Act did not apply in the first instance to securities transactions that occur abroad."

We are not convinced. In the first place, it would be odd for Congress to indicate the extraterritorial application of the whole Exchange Act by means of a provision imposing a condition precedent to its application abroad. And if the whole Act applied abroad, why would the Commission's enabling regulations be limited to those preventing "evasion" of the Act, rather than all those preventing "violation"? The provision seems to us directed at actions abroad that might conceal a domestic violation, or might cause what would otherwise be a domestic violation to escape on a technicality. At most, the Solicitor General's proposed inference is possible; but possible interpretations of statutory language do not override the presumption against extraterritoriality. . . .

. . . . Subsection 30(a) contains what §10(b) lacks: a clear statement of extraterritorial effect. Its explicit provision for a specific extraterritorial application would be quite superfluous if the rest of the Exchange Act already applied to transactions on foreign exchanges — and its limitation of that application to securities of domestic issuers would be inoperative. Even if that were not true, when a statute provides for some extraterritorial application, the presumption against extraterritoriality operates to limit that provision to its terms. No one claims that §30(a) applies here.

The concurrence claims we have impermissibly narrowed the inquiry in evaluating whether a statute applies abroad, citing for that point the dissent in Aramco. But we do not say, as the concurrence seems to think, that the presumption against extraterritoriality is a "clear statement rule," ibid., if by that is meant a requirement that a statute say "this law applies abroad." Assuredly context can be consulted as well. But whatever sources of statutory meaning one consults to give "the most faithful reading" of the text there is no clear indication of extraterritoriality here. . . .

IV

A

Petitioners argue that the conclusion that §10(b) does not apply extraterritorially does not resolve this case. They contend that they seek no more than domestic application anyway, since Florida is where HomeSide and its senior executives engaged in the deceptive conduct of manipulating HomeSide's financial models; their complaint also alleged that [two HomeSide executives] made misleading public statements there. This is less an answer to the presumption against extraterritorial application than it is an assertion — a quite valid assertion — that that presumption here (as often) is not self-evidently dispositive, but its application requires further analysis. For it is a rare case of prohibited extraterritorial application that lacks all contact with the territory of the United States. But the presumption against extraterritorial application would be a craven watchdog indeed if it retreated to its kennel whenever some domestic activity is involved in the case. The concurrence seems to imagine just such a timid sentinel but our cases are to the contrary. In *Aramco,* for example, the Title VII plaintiff had been hired in Houston, and was an American citizen. The Court concluded, however, that neither that territorial event nor that relationship was the "focus" of congressional concern, but rather domestic employment.

Applying the same mode of analysis here, we think that the focus of the Exchange Act is not upon the place where the deception originated, but upon purchases and sales of securities in the United States. Section 10(b) does not punish deceptive conduct, but only deceptive conduct "in connection with the purchase or sale of any security registered on a national securities exchange or any security not so registered." Those purchase-and-sale transactions are the objects of the statute's solicitude. It is those transactions that the statute seeks to "regulate"; it is parties or prospective parties to those transactions that the statute seeks to "protec[t]." And it is in our view only transactions in securities listed on domestic exchanges, and domestic transactions in other securities, to which §10(b) applies.

The primacy of the domestic exchange is suggested by the very prologue of the Exchange Act, which sets forth as its object "[t]o provide for the regulation of securities exchanges . . . operating in interstate and foreign commerce and through the mails, to prevent inequitable and unfair practices on such exchanges. . . ." We know of no one who thought that the Act was intended to "regulat[e]" *foreign* securities exchanges — or indeed who even believed that under established principles of international law Congress had the power to do so. The Act's registration requirements apply only to securities listed on national securities exchanges. . . .

Finally, we reject the notion that the Exchange Act reaches conduct in this country affecting exchanges or transactions abroad for the same reason that *Aramco* rejected overseas application of Title VII to all domestically concluded employment contracts or all employment contracts with American employers: The probability of incompatibility with the applicable laws of other countries is so obvious that if Congress intended such foreign application "it would have addressed the subject of conflicts with foreign laws and procedures." Like the United States, foreign countries regulate their domestic securities exchanges and securities transactions occurring within their territorial jurisdiction. And the regulation of other countries often differs from ours as to what constitutes fraud, what disclosures must be made, what damages are recoverable, what discovery is available in litigation, what individual actions may be joined in a single suit, what attorney's fees are recoverable, and many other matters. The Commonwealth of Australia, the United Kingdom of Great Britain and Northern Ireland, and the Republic of France have filed amicus briefs in this case. So have (separately or jointly) such international and foreign organizations as the International Chamber of Commerce, the Swiss Bankers Association, the Federation of German Industries, the French Business Confederation. . . . They all complain of the interference with foreign securities regulation that application of §10(b) abroad would produce, and urge the adoption of a clear test that will avoid that consequence. The transactional test we have adopted—whether the purchase or sale is made in the United States, or involves a security listed on a domestic exchange—meets that requirement. . . .

* * *

Section 10(b) reaches the use of a manipulative or deceptive device or contrivance only in connection with the purchase or sale of a security listed on an American stock exchange, and the purchase or sale of any other security in the United States. This case involves no securities listed on a domestic exchange, and all aspects of the purchases complained of by those petitioners who still have live claims occurred outside the United States. Petitioners have therefore failed to state a claim on which relief can be granted. We affirm the dismissal of petitioners' complaint on this ground.

It is so ordered.

Justice Sotomayor took no part in the consideration or decision of this case.
[Justice Breyer concurred in part and concurred in the judgment.]

Justice Stevens, with whom by Justice Ginsburg joins, concurring in the judgment.

While I agree that petitioners have failed to state a claim on which relief can be granted, my reasoning differs from the Court's. I would adhere to the general approach that has been the law in the Second Circuit, and most of the rest of the country, for nearly four decades.

Today the Court announces a new "transactional test" for defining the reach of §10(b) of the Securities Exchange Act of 1934 (Exchange Act). Henceforth, those provisions will extend only to "transactions in securities listed on domestic exchanges . . . and domestic transactions in other securities." If one confines one's gaze to the statutory text, the Court's conclusion is a plausible one. But the federal courts have been construing §10(b) in a different manner for a long time, and the Court's textual analysis is not nearly so compelling, in my view, as to warrant the abandonment of their doctrine.

The text and history of §10(b) are famously opaque on the question of when, exactly, transnational securities frauds fall within the statute's compass. As those types of frauds became more common in the latter half of the 20th century, the federal courts were increasingly called upon to wrestle with that question. The Court of Appeals for the Second Circuit, located in the Nation's financial center, led the effort. . . . Relying on opinions by Judge Henry Friendly, the Second Circuit eventually settled on a conduct-and-effects test. This test asks "(1) whether the wrongful conduct occurred in the United States, and (2) whether the wrongful conduct had a substantial effect in the United States or upon United States citizens." Numerous cases flesh out the proper application of each prong.

The Second Circuit's test became the "north star" of §10(b) jurisprudence not just regionally but nationally as well. With minor variations, other courts converged on the same basic approach. Neither Congress nor the Securities Exchange Commission (Commission) acted to change the law. To the contrary, the Commission largely adopted the Second Circuit's position in its own adjudications.

I acknowledge that the Courts of Appeals have differed in their applications of the conduct-and-effects test, with the consequence that their respective rulings are not perfectly "cohesive." It is nevertheless significant that the other Courts of Appeals, along with the other branches of Government, have "embraced the Second Circuit's approach." If this Court were to do likewise, as I would have us do, the lower courts would of course cohere even more tightly around the Second Circuit's rule.

In light of this history, the Court's critique of the decision below for applying "judge-made rules" is quite misplaced. This entire area of law is replete with judge-made rules, which give concrete meaning to Congress' general commands. "When we deal with private actions under Rule 10b-5," then-Justice Rehnquist wrote many years ago, "we deal with a judicial oak which has grown from little more than a legislative acorn." The " 'Mother Court' " of securities law tended to that oak. One of our greatest jurists — the judge who, "without a doubt, did more to shape the law of securities regulation than any [other] in the country" — was its master arborist.

It is true that "when it comes to 'the scope of [the] conduct prohibited by [Rule 10b-5 and] §10(b), the text of the statute [has] control[led] our decision[s].' " The problem . . . is that the text of the statute does not provide a great deal of control. As with any broadly phrased, longstanding statute, courts have had to fill in the gaps.

The development of §10(b) law was hardly an instance of judicial usurpation. Congress invited an expansive role for judicial elaboration when it crafted such an open-ended statute in 1934. And both Congress and the Commission subsequently affirmed that role when they left intact the relevant statutory and regulatory language, respectively, throughout all the years that followed. . . .

This Court has not shied away from acknowledging that authority. We have consistently confirmed that, in applying §10(b) and Rule 10b-5, courts may need "to flesh out the portions of the law with respect to which neither the congressional enactment nor the administrative regulations offer conclusive guidance." . . .

. . . . The Second Circuit refined its test over several decades and dozens of cases, with the tacit approval of Congress and the Commission and with the general assent of its sister Circuits. That history is a reason we should give additional weight to the Second Circuit's "judge-made" doctrine, not a reason to denigrate it. . . .

II

The Court's other main critique of the Second Circuit's approach — apart from what the Court views as its excessive reliance on functional considerations and reconstructed congressional intent — is that the Second Circuit has "disregard[ed]" the presumption against extraterritoriality. It is the Court, however, that misapplies the presumption, in two main respects.

First, the Court seeks to transform the presumption from a flexible rule of thumb into something more like a clear statement rule. . . .

. . . [W]hile the Court's dictum that "[w]hen a statute gives no clear indication of an extraterritorial application, it has none," makes for a nice catchphrase, the point is overstated. The presumption against extraterritoriality can be useful as a theory of congressional purpose, a tool for managing international conflict, a background norm, a tiebreaker. It does not relieve courts of their duty to give statutes the most faithful reading possible.

Second, and more fundamentally, the Court errs in suggesting that the presumption against extraterritoriality is fatal to the Second Circuit's test. For even if the presumption really were a clear statement (or "clear indication,") rule, it would have only marginal relevance to this case.

. . . Accordingly, the presumption against extraterritoriality "provides a sound basis for concluding that Section 10(b) does not apply when a securities fraud with no effects in the United States is hatched and executed entirely outside this country." But that is just about all it provides a sound basis for concluding. And . . . no party to the litigation disputes it. No one contends that §10(b) applies to wholly foreign frauds.

Rather, the real question in this case is how much, and what kinds of, domestic contacts are sufficient to trigger application of §10(b). In developing its conduct-and-effects test, the Second Circuit endeavored to derive a solution from the Exchange Act's text, structure, history, and purpose. Judge Friendly and his colleagues were well aware that United States courts "cannot and should not expend [their] resources resolving cases that do not affect Americans or involve fraud emanating from America."

Given its focus on "domestic conditions," I expect that virtually all " 'foreign-cubed' " actions—actions in which "(1) foreign plaintiffs [are] suing (2) a foreign issuer in an American court for violations of American securities laws based on securities transactions in (3) foreign countries,"—would fail the Second Circuit's test. As they generally should. Under these circumstances, the odds of the fraud having a substantial connection to the United States are low. . . .

Thus, while §10(b) may not give any "clear indication" on its face as to how it should apply to transnational securities frauds, it does give strong clues that it should cover at least some of them. And in my view, the Second Circuit has done the best job of discerning what sorts of transnational frauds Congress meant in 1934—and still means today—to regulate. I do not take issue with the Court for beginning its inquiry with the statutory text, rather than the doctrine in the Courts of Appeals. I take issue with the Court for beginning and ending its inquiry with the statutory text, when the text does not speak with geographic precision, and for dismissing the long pedigree of, and the persuasive account of congressional intent embodied in, the Second Circuit's rule.

Repudiating the Second Circuit's approach in its entirety, the Court establishes a novel rule that will foreclose private parties from bringing §10(b) actions whenever the relevant securities were purchased or sold abroad and are not listed on a domestic exchange. . . . And while the clarity and simplicity of the Court's test may have some salutary consequences, like all bright-line rules it also has drawbacks.

Imagine, for example, an American investor who buys shares in a company listed only on an overseas exchange. That company has a major American subsidiary with executives based in New York City; and it was in New York City that the executives masterminded and implemented a massive deception which artificially inflated the stock price—and which will, upon its disclosure, cause the price to plummet. Or, imagine that those same executives go knocking on doors in Manhattan and convince an unsophisticated retiree, on the basis of material misrepresentations, to invest her life savings in the company's doomed securities. Both of these investors would, under the Court's new test, be barred from seeking relief under §10(b).

The oddity of that result should give pause. For in walling off such individuals from §10(b), the Court narrows the provision's reach to a degree that would surprise and alarm generations of American investors—and, I am convinced, the Congress that passed the Exchange Act. Indeed, the Court's rule turns §10(b) jurisprudence (and the presumption against extraterritoriality) on its head, by withdrawing the statute's application from cases in which there is both substantial wrongful conduct that occurred in the United States and a substantial injurious effect on United States markets and citizens.

III

In my judgment, if petitioners' allegations of fraudulent misconduct that took place in Florida are true, then respondents may have violated §10(b), and could potentially be held accountable in an enforcement proceeding brought by the Commission. But it does not follow that shareholders who have failed to allege that the bulk or the heart of the fraud occurred in the United States, or that the fraud had an adverse impact on American investors or markets, may maintain a private action to recover damages they suffered abroad. Some cases involving foreign securities transactions have extensive links to, and ramifications for, this country; this case has Australia written all over it. Accordingly, for essentially the reasons stated in the Court of Appeals' opinion, I would affirm its judgment.

The Court instead elects to upend a significant area of securities law based on a plausible, but hardly decisive, construction of the statutory text. In so doing, it pays short shrift to the United States' interest in remedying frauds that transpire on American soil or harm American citizens, as well as to the accumulated wisdom and experience of the lower courts. I happen to agree with the result the Court reaches in this case. But "I respectfully dissent," once again, "from the Court's continuing campaign to render the private cause of action under §10(b) toothless."

Notes and Questions

1. Does the Congressional amendment of Title VII promptly after the *Aramco* decision indicate that the Court in *Aramco* incorrectly interpreted Title VII? Or, does it demonstrate that the decision put the burden on Congress to indicate how much extraterritorial jurisdiction it wishes to exercise, and that Congress choose to respond?

2. In *Morrison*, is the Supreme Court saying that Congress cannot regulate securities transactions by foreigners on foreign exchanges, or that Congress did not do this in the statute? Should the court have given some deference to the Second Circuit's approach of interpreting Congress' intent? Should it be irrelevant that the Second Circuit and other courts had been applying such an interpretation for 40 years?

3. Congress reacted promptly to the *Morrison* decision. One expert reports that Congressional reaction to the decision was immediate.

> Less than twenty-four hours after the Court handed down its decision, a conference committee completed work on the Dodd-Frank Wall Street Reform and Consumer Protection Act. The bill reported out of conference authorizes the Justice Department and the SEC to bring suits alleging violations of the securities laws with respect to foreign transactions, if there exists "conduct within the United States that constitutes significant steps in furtherance of the violation, or if conduct occurring outside the United States [had] foreseeable substantial effect within the United States." The bill also directs the SEC to study the possibility of extraterritorial enforcement of the securities laws through private litigation. These amendments . . . make clear that, as to private suits such as the *Morrison* litigation, the restrictions read into the securities laws by the Supreme Court remain in effect. . . .
>
> *Morrison* represents one more step, although an especially dramatic one, in the Supreme Court's efforts to shift the responsibility for managing international regulatory conflicts from the judiciary to Congress. Rather than reading legislation as reaching the full range of transactions permitted under "prevailing notions of international comity," the Court left it to Congress to indicate how much of its extraterritorial regulatory authority it wishes to exercise. [Paul B. Stephen, *Morrison v. Nat'l Australia Bank Ltd.*: The Supreme Court Rejects Extraterritoriality, ASIL Insights, vol. 14, issue 22 (Aug. 2, 2010).]

4. What might be the justifications for the presumption against extraterritoriality? To comply with congressional wishes? To defer to the executive? To avoid foreign relations controversy? To comply with international law? Some combination of these? Should the Court abandon the presumption and simply attempt to discern legislative intent? (Legislative history might make the intention clear in some cases, but some Justices, including Justice Scalia, disfavor reference to legislative history.) Why not apply a presumption *in favor* of extraterritoriality?

5. Whose interests would be served by a rigid territorial division of law-prescribing authority? The interests of developing states? Industrialized states? Multinational corporations? Consumers? Human rights advocates?

6. Note: The Supreme Court's opinion "correct[ed] a threshold error in the Second Circuit's analysis." That court had affirmed dismissal under Rule 12(b)(1) because it considered the extraterritorial reach of Section 10(b) to raise a question of subject-matter jurisdiction.

However, the Supreme Court indicated that: "But to ask what conduct §10(b) reaches is to ask what conduct §10(b) prohibits, which is a merits question. Subject-matter jurisdiction, by contrast, 'refers to the tribunal's "power to hear a case."' It presents an issue quite separate from the question whether the allegations the plaintiff makes entitle him to relief. The District Court here had jurisdiction under 15 U.S.C. §78aa." (That section provides that "district courts . . . shall have exclusive jurisdiction of violations of [the Exchange Act] or the rules and regulations thereunder.") The Court then went on to consider whether the petitioners' allegations stated a claim, treating the issues under Rule 12(b)(6).

Even if a domestic statute's text explicitly indicates that it is to apply extraterritorially, or a court determines that there is enough evidence that the presumption against extraterritoriality is overcome, many commentators as well as the Restatement have advanced the argument that the extraterritorial application of a state's law should be limited by an international law rule of "reasonableness."

Restatement

Section 403. Limitations on Jurisdiction to Prescribe

(1) Even when one of the bases for jurisdiction under §402 [page 644 above] is present, a state may not exercise jurisdiction to prescribe law with respect to a person or activity having connections with another state when the exercise of such jurisdiction is unreasonable.

(2) Whether exercise of jurisdiction over a person or activity is unreasonable is determined by evaluating all relevant factors, including, where appropriate:

(a) the link of the activity to the territory of the regulating state, i.e., the extent to which the activity takes place within the territory, or has substantial, direct, and foreseeable effect upon or in the territory;

(b) the connections, such as nationality, residence, or economic activity, between the regulating state and the person principally responsible for the activity to be regulated, or between that state and those whom the regulation is designed to protect;

(c) the character of the activity to be regulated, the importance of regulation to the regulating state, the extent to which other states regulate such activities, and the degree to which the desirability of such regulation is generally accepted;

(d) the existence of justified expectations that might be protected or hurt by the regulation;

(e) the importance of the regulation to the international political, legal, or economic system;

(f) the extent to which the regulation is consistent with the traditions of the international system;

(g) the extent to which another state may have an interest in regulating the activity; and

(h) the likelihood of conflict with regulation by another state.

(3) When it would not be unreasonable for each of two states to exercise jurisdiction over a person or activity, but the prescriptions by the two states are in conflict, each state has an obligation to evaluate its own as well as the other state's interest in exercising jurisdiction, in light of all the relevant factors, Subsection (2); a state should defer to the other state if that state's interest is clearly greater.

Comment

a. *Reasonableness in international law and practice.* The principle that an exercise of jurisdiction on one of the bases indicated in §402 is nonetheless unlawful if it is unreasonable is established in United States law, and has emerged as a principle of international law as well. There is wide international consensus that the links of territoriality or nationality, §402, while generally necessary, are not in all instances sufficient conditions for the exercise of such jurisdiction. Legislatures and administrative agencies, in the United States and in other states, have generally refrained from exercising jurisdiction where it would be unreasonable to do so, and courts have usually interpreted general language in a statute as not intended to exercise or authorize the exercise of jurisdiction in circumstances where application of the statute would be unreasonable.

This approach was endorsed in the dissenting opinion by Justice Scalia and three other Justices in Hartford Fire Insurance Co. v. California, which follows. One of the issues in that case was whether the Sherman Act covered a conspiracy by a group of London reinsurance companies to limit the terms of insurance offered in the United States. The conspiracy allegedly operated by effectively forcing certain U.S. primary insurers to change the terms of their standard domestic liability insurance policies to conform with the policies that the defendants wanted to reinsure.*

It is important to understand that there can be several different concepts of "jurisdiction" involved in a case, including personal jurisdiction of the court over the defendant, subject matter jurisdiction of the court over the type of case presented, and the international law-based concepts of jurisdiction to prescribe, jurisdiction to enforce, and jurisdiction to adjudicate (introduced above). Keep them separate in your mind.

In the *Hartford* case, the London reinsurance companies did not contest personal jurisdiction of the U.S. federal courts. Moreover, both the majority and minority opinions accepted that the U.S. courts had subject matter jurisdiction. The question that Justice Scalia raised in his minority opinion was whether the assertion of prescriptive (or legislative) jurisdiction by the United States under the Sherman Act was reasonable in this case. If not, Justice Scalia would have the courts rule "on the merits that the plaintiff failed to state a cause of action under the relevant [federal] statute."

You should recall from Chapter 3 that an act of Congress may trump an inconsistent rule of international law, so the international law issue may seem moot. However, as Justice Scalia points out, it is a settled rule of statutory construction that an act of Congress is construed to be consistent with international law whenever possible. Because the Sherman Act is arguably ambiguous as to its coverage of acts by foreigners abroad, international law may effectively limit the scope of the Sherman Act through this technique of statutory interpretation. If the law—properly construed to be consistent with international law—does not apply to defendants' foreign conduct, then they have not violated the law.

Justice Souter's majority opinion adopted a different approach. He did not use international law to construe the Sherman Act; he did not even refer to international law. Instead, he referred to possible limits required by "comity," which, as noted above, is less binding than international law. Some commentators have criticized his approach for sharply limiting the situations in which comity would be employed.

*The Sherman Act makes illegal, among other matters, every contract, combination, or conspiracy in unreasonable restraint of interstate or foreign commerce. 15 U.S.C. §1. Its broad language includes conspiracies by competitors to fix prices or the terms of sale or purchase. Passed in 1890, the Sherman Act constitutes an important part of U.S. federal antitrust laws.

Hartford Fire Insurance Co. v. California

U.S. Supreme Court
509 U.S. 764 (1993)

[Justice SOUTER authored the opinion for the majority of five Justices:]

At the outset, we note that the District Court undoubtedly had jurisdiction of these Sherman Act claims, as the London reinsurers apparently concede. See Tr. of Oral Arg. 37 ("Our position is not that the Sherman Act does not apply in the sense that a minimal basis for the exercise of jurisdiction doesn't exist here. Our position is that there are certain circumstances, and that this is one of them, in which the interests of another State are sufficient that the exercise of that jurisdiction should be restrained"). . . . [I]t is well established by now that the Sherman Act applies to foreign conduct that was meant to produce and did in fact produce some substantial effect in the United States. . . . [22] Such is the conduct alleged here: that the London reinsurers engaged in unlawful conspiracies to affect the market for insurance in the United States and that their conduct in fact produced substantial effect.

According to the London reinsurers, the District Court should have declined to exercise such jurisdiction under the principle of international comity. The Court of Appeals agreed that courts should look to that principle in deciding whether to exercise jurisdiction under the Sherman Act. This availed the London reinsurers nothing, however. To be sure, the Court of Appeals believed that "application of [American] antitrust laws to the London reinsurance market would lead to significant conflict with English law and policy," and that "[s]uch a conflict, unless outweighed by other factors, would by itself be reason to decline exercise of jurisdiction." But other factors, in the court's view, including the London reinsurers' express purpose to affect United States commerce and the substantial nature of the effect produced, outweighed the supposed conflict and required the exercise of jurisdiction in this litigation.

. . . [E]ven assuming that in a proper case a court may decline to exercise Sherman Act jurisdiction over foreign conduct (or, as Justice Scalia would put it, may conclude by the employment of comity analysis in the first instance that there is no jurisdiction), international comity would not counsel against exercising jurisdiction in the circumstances alleged here.

The only substantial question in this case is whether "there is in fact a true conflict between domestic and foreign law." Societe Nationale Industrielle Aerospatiale v. United States District Court, 482 U.S. 522, 555 (1987) (Blackmun, J., concurring in part and dissenting in part). The London reinsurers contend that applying the Act to their conduct would conflict significantly with British law, and the British government, appearing before us as amicus curiae, concurs. They assert that Parliament has established a comprehensive regulatory regime over the London reinsurance market and that the conduct alleged here was perfectly consistent with British law and policy. But this is not to state a conflict. . . . No conflict exists, for these purposes, "where a person subject to regulation by two states can comply with the laws of both." Restatement (Third) Foreign Relations Law 403,

22. Justice SCALIA believes that what is at issue in this litigation is prescriptive, as opposed to subject-matter, jurisdiction. . . . The parties do not question litigation jurisdiction, however, and for good reason: it is well established that Congress has exercised such jurisdiction under the Sherman Act.

Comment e. Since the London reinsurers do not argue that British law requires them to act in some fashion prohibited by the law of the United States, or claim that their compliance with the laws of both countries is otherwise impossible, we see no conflict with British law. We have no need in this case to address other considerations that might inform a decision to refrain from the exercise of jurisdiction on grounds of international comity.

[Justice SCALIA wrote a dissenting opinion, which was joined by three other Justices.]

. . . The petitioners . . . various British corporations and other British subjects, argue that certain of the claims against them constitute an inappropriate extraterritorial application of the Sherman Act. It is important to distinguish two distinct questions raised by this petition: whether the District Court had jurisdiction, and whether the Sherman Act reaches the extraterritorial conduct alleged here. On the first question, I believe that the District Court had subject-matter jurisdiction over the Sherman Act claims against all the defendants (personal jurisdiction is not contested). The respondents asserted nonfrivolous claims under the Sherman Act, and 28 U.S.C. §1331 vests district courts with subject-matter jurisdiction over cases "arising under" federal statutes. As precedents such as Lauritzen v. Larsen, 345 U.S. 571 make clear, that is sufficient to establish the District Court's jurisdiction over these claims. . . . The second question — the extraterritorial reach of the Sherman Act — has nothing to do with the jurisdiction of the courts. It is a question of substantive law turning on whether, in enacting the Sherman Act, Congress asserted regulatory power over the challenged conduct. See EEOC v. Arabian American Oil Co., 499 U.S. 244 (1991) (Aramco). If a plaintiff fails to prevail on this issue, the court does not dismiss the claim for want of subject-matter jurisdiction — want of power to adjudicate; rather, it decides the claim, ruling on the merits that the plaintiff has failed to state a cause of action under the relevant statute.

There is, however, a type of "jurisdiction" relevant to determining the extraterritorial reach of a statute; it is known as "legislative jurisdiction," or "jurisdiction to prescribe," 1 Restatement (Third) of Foreign Relations Law of the United States 235 (1987) (hereinafter Restatement (Third)). This refers to "the authority of a state to make its law applicable to persons or activities," and is quite a separate matter from "jurisdiction to adjudicate," see id., at 231. There is no doubt, of course, that Congress possesses legislative jurisdiction over the acts alleged in this complaint: Congress has broad power under Article 1, 8, cl. 3 "[t]o regulate Commerce with foreign Nations," and this Court has repeatedly upheld its power to make laws applicable to persons or activities beyond our territorial boundaries where United States interests are affected. But the question in this case is whether, and to what extent, Congress has exercised that undoubted legislative jurisdiction in enacting the Sherman Act.

Two canons of statutory construction are relevant in this inquiry. The first is the "long-standing principle of American law 'that legislation of Congress, unless a contrary intent appears, is meant to apply only within the territorial jurisdiction of the United States.'" Applying that canon in *Aramco*, we held that the version of Title VII of the Civil Rights Act of 1964 then in force, did not extend outside the territory of the United States even though the statute contained broad provisions extending its prohibitions to, for example, "'any activity, business, or industry in commerce.' " We held such "boilerplate language" to be an insufficient indication to override the presumption against extraterritority. The Sherman Act contains similar "boilerplate language," and if the question were not governed by precedent, it would be worth considering whether that presumption controls the outcome here. We have, however, found the presumption to be overcome with respect to our antitrust laws; it is now well established that the Sherman Act applies extraterritorially.

But if the presumption against extraterritoriality has been overcome or is otherwise inapplicable, a second canon of statutory construction becomes relevant: "[A]n act of congress ought never to be construed to violate the law of nations if any other possible construction remains." Murray v. The Charming Betsy, 2 Cranch 64, 118, 2 L. Ed. 208 (1804) (Marshall, C.J.). This canon is "wholly independent" of the presumption against extraterritoriality. It is relevant to determining the substantive reach of a statute because "the law of nations," or customary international law, includes limitations on a nation's exercise of its jurisdiction to prescribe. See Restatement (Third) §§401-416. Though it clearly has constitutional authority to do so, Congress is generally presumed not to have exceeded those customary international-law limits on jurisdiction to prescribe.

Consistent with that presumption, this and other courts have frequently recognized that, even where the presumption against extraterritoriality does not apply, statutes should not be interpreted to regulate foreign persons or conduct if that regulation would conflict with principles of international law. [Justice Scalia then summarized three cases where statutes were held inapplicable to the case presented in part because to do so would violate the international law of the sea or more important foreign interests.]

In sum, the practice of using international law to limit the extraterritorial reach of statutes is firmly established in our jurisprudence. In proceeding to apply that practice to the present case, I shall rely on the Restatement (Third) . . . for the relevant principles of international law. Its standards appear fairly supported in the decisions of this Court construing international choice-of-law principles (*Lauritzen, Romero,* and *McCulloch*) and in the decisions of other federal courts. . . . Whether the Restatement precisely reflects international law in every detail matters little here, as I believe this case would be resolved the same way under virtually any conceivable test that takes account of foreign regulatory interests.

Under the Restatement, a nation having some "basis" for jurisdiction to prescribe law should nonetheless refrain from exercising that jurisdiction "with respect to a person or activity having connections with another state when the exercise of such jurisdiction is unreasonable." Restatement (Third) §403(1). The "reasonableness" inquiry turns on a number of factors. . . . Rarely would these factors point more clearly against application of United States law. The activity relevant to the counts at issue here took place primarily in the United Kingdom, and the defendants in these counts are British corporations and British subjects having their principal place of business or residence outside the United States. Great Britain has established a comprehensive regulatory scheme governing the London reinsurance markets, and clearly has a heavy "interest in regulating the activity," id., §403(2) (g). Finally, §2(b) of the McCarran-Ferguson Act allows state regulatory statutes to override the Sherman Act in the insurance field, subject only to the narrow "boycott" exception set forth in §3(b)—suggesting that "the importance of regulation to the [United States]," id., §403(2) (c), is slight. Considering these factors, I think it unimaginable that an assertion of legislative jurisdiction by the United States would be considered reasonable, and therefore it is inappropriate to assume, in the absence of statutory indication to the contrary, that Congress has made such an assertion.

It is evident from what I have said that the Court's comity analysis, which proceeds as though the issue is whether the courts should "decline to exercise . . . jurisdiction," rather than whether the Sherman Act covers this conduct, is simply misdirected. I do not at all agree, moreover, with the Court's conclusion that the issue of the substantive scope of the Sherman Act is not in the case. To be sure, the parties did not make a clear distinction between adjudicative jurisdiction and the scope of the statute. . . . In any event, if one erroneously chooses, as the Court does, to make adjudicative jurisdiction (or, more precisely, abstention) the vehicle for taking account of the needs of prescriptive comity, the Court still gets it wrong. It concludes that no "true conflict" counseling nonapplication of United States law (or rather, as it thinks, United States judicial jurisdiction) exists unless compliance with United States law would constitute a *violation* of another country's law. That breathtakingly broad proposition, which contradicts the many cases discussed earlier, will bring the Sherman Act and other laws into sharp and unnecessary conflict with the legitimate interests of other countries—particularly our closest trading partners.

Notes and Questions

1. In *Hartford Fire,* which opinion is more persuasive—Justice Souter's majority opinion or Justice Scalia's dissenting opinion? Souter's opinion superficially seems less respectful of international norms: he refers to comity, not law, and many think he would require an irreconcilable conflict ("a true conflict") of legal commands directed at the defendant before invoking comity. Scalia's opinion squarely applies what he calls "international law" to limit the U.S. legislative reach, as indicated by Restatement section 403(2).

2. Do you agree with the position that many believe Justice Souter adopted—i.e., that there is no conflict here and that comity should apply only if a person is compelled by two sovereigns to take inconsistent action? Or is Justice Scalia's point more persuasive—that there is clearly a conflict in government policy: the United Kingdom tolerates the conduct; the United States condemns it, so a court should choose which policy should prevail. What interests should comity protect? On what basis can a court weigh the conflicting policies?

The U.S. Supreme Court revisited the question of the extraterritorial reach of the federal antitrust laws in the next case. Justice Breyer's opinion for the Court affirms the second canon of statutory construction that Justice Scalia described in *Hartford Fire.* The Court also seems to take an approach that is more consistent with Restatement §403 and Justice Scalia's dissent in *Hartford Fire,* than with Justice Souter's majority opinion there. Worth noting is that Justice Souter is nevertheless one of the five Justices who joined Justice Breyer's opinion.

F. Hoffmann-La Roche Ltd. v. Empagran S.A.

U.S. Supreme Court
542 U.S. 155 (2004)

[Foreign and domestic purchasers of vitamins filed a class action lawsuit alleging that foreign and domestic vitamin manufacturers and distributions had engaged in a price-fixing conspiracy in violation of the Sherman Act (15 U.S.C. §1 et seq.). The conspiracy allegedly raised the price of vitamin products to U.S. and foreign customers.

[Defendants moved to dismiss the suit as to some foreign purchasers who had allegedly bought the vitamin products for delivery outside the United States. The issue on appeal was whether these foreign purchasers could continue their lawsuit given the provisions of the Foreign Trade Antitrust Improvements Act of 1982 (FTAIA) (15 U.S.C. §6).]

Justice Breyer delivered the opinion of the Court. . . .

We here focus upon anticompetitive price-fixing activity that is in significant part foreign, that causes some domestic antitrust injury, and that independently causes separate foreign injury. We ask two questions about the price-fixing conduct and the foreign injury that it causes. First, does that conduct fall within the FTAIA's general rule excluding the Sherman Act's application? That is to say, does the price-fixing activity constitute "conduct involving trade or commerce . . . with foreign nations"? We conclude that it does.

Second, we ask whether the conduct nonetheless falls within a domestic-injury exception to the general rule, an exception that applies (and makes the Sherman Act . . . applicable) where the conduct (1) has a "direct, substantial, and reasonably foreseeable effect" on domestic commerce, and (2) "such effect gives rise to a [Sherman Act] claim." We conclude that the exception does not apply where the plaintiff's claim rests solely on the independent foreign harm.

In more concrete terms, this case involves vitamin sellers around the world that agreed to fix prices, leading to higher vitamin prices in the United States and independently leading to higher vitamin prices in other countries such as Ecuador. We conclude that, in this scenario, a purchaser in the United States could bring a Sherman Act claim under the FTAIA based on domestic injury, but a purchaser in Ecuador could not bring a Sherman Act claim based on foreign harm.

I . . .

Petitioners moved to dismiss the suit as to the *foreign* purchasers (the respondents here), five foreign vitamin distributors located in Ukraine, Australia, Ecuador, and Panama, each of which bought vitamins from petitioners for delivery outside the United States. Respondents have never asserted that they purchased any vitamins in the United States or in transactions in United States commerce, and the question presented assumes that the relevant "transactions occurr[ed] entirely outside U. S. commerce." . . .

II

The FTAIA seeks to make clear to American exporters (and to firms doing business abroad) that the Sherman Act does not prevent them from entering into business arrangements (say, joint-selling arrangements), however anticompetitive, as long as those arrangements adversely affect only foreign markets. It does so by removing from the Sherman Act's reach, (1) export activities and (2) other commercial activities taking place abroad, *unless* those activities adversely affect domestic commerce, imports to the United States, or exporting activities of one engaged in such activities within the United States.

[The FTAIA's] technical language initially lays down a general rule placing *all* (non-import) activity involving foreign commerce outside the Sherman Act's reach. It then brings such conduct back within the Sherman Act's reach *provided that* the conduct *both* (1) sufficiently affects American commerce, *i.e.*, it has a "direct, substantial, and reasonably foreseeable effect" on American domestic, import, or (certain) export commerce, *and* (2) has an effect of a kind that antitrust law considers harmful, *i.e.*, the "effect" must "giv[e] rise to a [Sherman Act] claim."

We ask here how this language applies to price-fixing activity that is in significant part foreign, that has the requisite domestic effect, and that also has independent foreign effects giving rise to the plaintiff's claim. . . .

IV

. . . Because the underlying antitrust action is complex . . . we reemphasize that we base our decision upon the following: The price-fixing conduct significantly and adversely affects both customers outside the United States and customers within the United States, but the adverse foreign effect is independent of any adverse domestic effect. In these circumstances, we find that the FTAIA exception does not apply (and thus the Sherman Act does not apply) for two main reasons.

First, this Court ordinarily construes ambiguous statutes to avoid unreasonable interference with the sovereign authority of other nations. See, *e.g., McCulloch* v. *Sociedad Nacional de Marineros de Honduras*, 372 U.S. 10, 20-22 (1963) (application of National Labor Relations Act to foreign-flag vessels). This rule of construction reflects principles of customary international law — law that (we must assume) Congress ordinarily seeks to follow. See Restatement (Third) . . . §§403(1), 403(2) (1986) (hereinafter Restatement) (limiting the unreasonable exercise of prescriptive jurisdiction with respect to a person or activity having connections with another State); *Murray v. Schooner Charming Betsy*, 6 U.S. 64, 2 Cranch 64, (1804) ("[A]n act of Congress ought never to be construed to violate the law of nations if any other possible construction remains"). *Hartford Fire Insurance Co. v. California*, 509 U.S. 764, 817 (1993) (SCALIA, J., dissenting) (identifying rule of construction as derived from the principle of "prescriptive comity"). This rule of statutory construction cautions courts to assume that legislators take account of the legitimate sovereign interests of other nations when they write American laws. It thereby helps the potentially conflicting laws of different nations work together in harmony — a harmony particularly needed in today's highly interdependent commercial world.

No one denies that America's antitrust laws, when applied to foreign conduct, can interfere with a foreign nation's ability independently to regulate its own commercial affairs. But our courts have long held that application of our antitrust laws to foreign anticompetitive conduct is nonetheless reasonable, and hence consistent with principles of prescriptive comity, insofar as they reflect a legislative effort to redress *domestic* antitrust injury that foreign anticompetitive conduct has caused. See *United States* v. *Aluminum Co. of America*, 148 F.2d 416, 443-444 (CA2 1945) . . .

But why is it reasonable to apply those laws to foreign conduct *insofar as that conduct causes independent foreign harm and that foreign harm alone gives rise to the plaintiff's claim?* Like the former case, application of those laws creates a serious risk of interference with a foreign nation's ability independently to regulate its own commercial affairs. But, unlike the former case, the justification for that interference seems insubstantial. See Restatement §403(2) (determining reasonableness on basis of such factors as connections with regulating nation, harm to that nation's interests, extent to which other nations regulate, and the potential for conflict). Why should American law supplant, for example, Canada's or Great Britain's or Japan's own determination about how best to protect Canadian or British or Japanese customers from anticompetitive conduct engaged in significant part by Canadian or British or Japanese or other foreign companies?

. . .

We recognize that principles of comity provide Congress greater leeway when it seeks to control through legislation the actions of *American* companies, see Restatement §402; and some of the anticompetitive price-fixing conduct alleged here took place in *America.* But the higher foreign prices of which the foreign plaintiffs here complain are not the consequence of any domestic anticompetitive conduct *that Congress sought to forbid,* for Congress did not seek to forbid any such conduct insofar as it is here relevant, *i.e.,* insofar as it is intertwined with foreign conduct that causes independent foreign harm. Rather Congress sought to *release* domestic (and foreign) anticompetitive conduct from Sherman Act constraints when that conduct causes foreign harm. . . .

We thus repeat the basic question: Why is it reasonable to apply this law to conduct that is significantly foreign *insofar as that conduct causes independent foreign harm and that foreign harm alone gives rise to the plaintiff's claim?* We can find no good answer to the question. . . .

Respondents reply that many nations have adopted antitrust laws similar to our own, to the point where the practical likelihood of interference with the relevant interests of other nations is minimal. Leaving price fixing to the side, however, this Court has found to the contrary. See, *e.g., Hartford Fire,* 509 U.S. at 797-799 (1991) (noting that the alleged conduct in the London reinsurance market, while illegal under United States antitrust laws, was assumed to be perfectly consistent with British law and policy). . . .

Regardless, even where nations agree about primary conduct, say price fixing, they disagree dramatically about appropriate remedies. The application, for example, of American private treble-damages remedies to anticompetitive conduct taking place abroad has generated considerable controversy. And several foreign nations have filed briefs here arguing that to apply our remedies would unjustifiably permit their citizens to bypass their own less generous remedial schemes, thereby upsetting a balance of competing considerations that their own domestic antitrust laws embody. *E.g.* [citing briefs from Germany, Canada, and Japan]. . . .

We conclude that principles of prescriptive comity counsel against the Court of Appeals' interpretation of the FTAIA. Where foreign anticompetitive conduct plays a significant role and where foreign injury is independent of domestic effects, Congress might have hoped that America's antitrust laws, so fundamental a component of our own economic system, would commend themselves to other nations as well. But, if America's antitrust policies could not win their own way in the international marketplace for such ideas, Congress, we must assume, would not have tried to impose them, in an act of legal imperialism, through legislative fiat.

Second, the FTAIA's language and history suggest that Congress designed the FTAIA to clarify, perhaps to limit, but not *to expand* in any significant way, the Sherman Act's scope as applied to foreign commerce. And we have found no significant indication that at the time Congress wrote this statute courts would have thought the Sherman Act applicable in these circumstances. . . .

Taken together, these two sets of considerations, the one derived from comity and the other reflecting history, convince us that Congress would not have intended the FTAIA's exception to bring independently caused foreign injury within the Sherman Act's reach. . . .

For these reasons, we conclude that petitioners' reading of the statute's language is correct. That reading furthers the statute's basic purposes, it properly reflects considerations of comity, and it is consistent with Sherman Act history.

Justice O'CONNOR took no part in the consideration or decision of this case.

Justice SCALIA, with whom Justice THOMAS joins, concurring in the judgment.

I concur in the judgment of the Court because the language of the statute is readily susceptible of the interpretation the Court provides and because only that interpretation is consistent with the principle that statutes should be read in accord with the customary deference to the application of foreign countries' laws within their own territories.

Notes and Questions

1. How does the *Empagran* decision deal with the question of comity? Note that Justice Breyer's opinion cites Justice Scalia's dissenting opinion from *Hartford Fire* and also cites Restatement Section 403. Does Justice Breyer require a showing of a "true conflict," as described by Justice Souter in *Hartford Fire*? Does he take into account the effect on other countries' efforts to enforce their antitrust laws?

2. Justice Scalia identified and discussed two important U.S. canons of statutory construction in *Hartford Fire*:

> The first is the "long-standing principle of American law 'that legislation of Congress, unless a contrary intent appears, is meant to apply only within the territorial jurisdiction of the United States.' " . . .
>
> But if the presumption against extraterritoriality has been overcome or is otherwise inapplicable, a second canon . . . becomes relevant: "[A]n act of congress ought never to be construed to violate the law of nations if any other possible construction remains." Murray v. The Charming Betsy [(1804)].

The first canon was discussed earlier in this section in the 2010 *Morrison* case and the notes immediately before and after that case.

3. Justice Scalia's second well-established canon of statutory interpretation, which he says is " 'wholly independent' of the presumption against extraterritoriality," is that a statute should be construed, if possible, not to violate international law. In the Court's later opinion in *Empagran,* 'Justice Breyer phrases the canon somewhat differently—i.e., "this Court ordinarily construes ambiguous statutes to

avoid unreasonable interference with the sovereign authority of other nations." He cites essentially the same earlier cases as Justice Scalia and cites the Scalia opinion. What significance, if any, do you see in this different phrasing of the canons? Is Justice Breyer grounding the canon on comity, rather than "international law"? For his part, Justice Scalia characterized the limits as relevant principles of international law or customary international law limits on the jurisdiction to prescribe.

4. In discussing the second canon, besides citing The Charming Betsy decision (discussed in Chapter 3), both Justice Scalia and Justice Breyer discussed maritime cases, in which U.S. labor and tort legislation was held not to apply to foreign flag vessels carrying cargo from foreign ports to U.S. ports. The contact with U.S. territory would arguably have been sufficient to legitimize U.S. prescriptive jurisdiction, but international law provides that the law of the foreign state whose flag the vessel flies controls and supersedes the territorial principle. Often foreign flag vessels are indirectly owned by U.S. individuals or corporations. In these cases there clearly are conflicts (or at least sharp differences) between the relevant U.S. and foreign laws. Imposition of U.S. labor and tort standards, for example, is more likely to protect the employees on board the ships and make the ships' operations more costly. For a more recent opinion in the area, see Spector v. Norwegian Cruise Line Ltd., 549 U.S. 119 (2004). Should a U.S. corporation be allowed to avoid U.S. legal requirements by conducting operations through foreign subsidiaries?

5. For a good survey of varying interpretations of the *Hartford Fire* and *Empagran* decisions, see Gary B. Born and Peter B. Rutledge, International Civil Litigation in United States Courts 668-674 (4th ed. 2006).

6. Although the United States is certainly among the most active countries in asserting extraterritorial jurisdiction, it is by no means the only one. For example, the European Union, with its 27 member states, has been very active in antitrust enforcement, even when it has extraterritorial impact. In recent years, the EU has challenged several mergers between non-European companies, and has been successful in preventing them or obtaining concessions. The most notable EU challenge effectively blocked the proposed merger of two very large U.S. corporations, GE and Honeywell, because of its impact in Europe, after U.S. antitrust authorities had indicated that the U.S. government would not oppose the merger.

7. Would it be better to limit extraterritorial application of antitrust law or other laws by international agreements, rather than by judicially employed presumptions and comity analysis?

8. The well-regarded authors of a leading antitrust law casebook have observed:

> Perhaps the most important recent development in the area of international comity has been the expansion of the . . . agreements [on procedural cooperation] that exist among some of the major antitrust enforcement authorities of the world. The United States is now a party to a number of such agreements. [These include Germany (1976), Australia (1999), the European Community (1991, supplemented by a 1999 agreement on "positive comity"), and Canada (1995).] In one, the Treaty with Canada . . . (1988), the U.S. Department of Justice and the Canadian Bureau of Competition Policy are empowered actually to conduct joint investigations, including the sharing of confidential information. . . .
>
> Most of the more recent cooperation agreements, such as the U.S.-EC agreement and the 1995 U.S.-Canada agreement, emphasize both traditional comity and so-called positive comity. . . . The concept of positive comity . . . allows the enforcement agency to seek action from the foreign authority in whose territory the alleged anticompetitive

> conduct is taking place, if that conduct would also violate the foreign country's law [, rather than the enforcement agency initially taking action]. In its present form, positive comity has not been made mandatory. . . . Instead, it is an option that is encouraged under the cooperation agreements. [Robert Pitofsky, Harvey J. Goldschmid, & Diane P. Wood, Trade Regulation: Cases and Materials 1248-1250 (6th ed. 2010).]

2. *Nationality*

The right of a state to regulate the conduct of its citizens or nationals anywhere in the world is, like territorial jurisdiction, usually noncontroversial. Congress can thus legislate with respect to the conduct of a U.S. national anywhere in the world. (Note, though, that the Restatement states that jurisdiction to prescribe is limited by a reasonableness requirement with respect to a person or activity having connections with another state. Restatement §403(1).)

A number of U.S. laws specifically extend to the conduct or income of U.S. nationals abroad. For example, the federal income tax laws generally apply to encompass income earned by U.S. nationals anywhere, although the taxpayers might qualify for credits on foreign taxes they paid. The Foreign Corrupt Practices Act prohibits bribery of foreign officials abroad. 15 U.S.C. §78dd-2 (2010). Every male citizen of the United States between the ages of 18 and 26 can be required to register for military service. 18 U.S.C. app. §453(a) (2010).

A recent case addressing the limits on the extraterritorial reach of Congress under the Foreign Commerce Clause of the U.S. Constitution addressed the nationality principle. In United States v. Clark, 435 F.3d 1100 (9th Cir. 2006), the defendant was a 71-year-old U.S. citizen convicted under the Prosecutorial Remedies and Other Tools to End the Exploitation of Children Today Act of 2003 ("Protect Act"), Pub. L. No. 108-21, 117 Stat. 650 (2003). The statute makes it a felony for any U.S. citizen who travels in "foreign commerce"—i.e., to a foreign country—to then engage in an illegal commercial sex act with a minor. 18 U.S.C. §2423(c). On appeal, the defendant did not dispute that he traveled in "foreign commerce," nor did he dispute that he engaged in illicit commercial sexual conduct. Rather, he challenged the congressional authority to regulate his conduct under the Commerce Clause. The court concluded that "[t]he combination of Clark's travel in foreign commerce and his conduct of an illicit commercial sex act in Cambodia shortly thereafter put the statute squarely within the Congress's *Foreign Commerce Clause* authority." Id. at 1116. In upholding the statute and the conviction, the court of appeals held, among other matters, that the extraterritorial reach of the statute was in accord with the nationality principle of international law. Id. at 1106. See also, e.g., Blackmer v. United States, 284 U.S. 421, 436 (1932) (the Supreme Court upheld a contempt fine against a U.S. national living in France who failed to obey a subpoena ordering him to appear as a witness at a U.S. criminal trial; "[b]y virtue of his obligations of citizenship, the United States retained its authority over him, and he was bound by its laws made applicable to him in a foreign country").

The normal practice is to allow each state to determine who its nationals are—for example, a child of a national, no matter where the child is born, or a child born in the state's territory, no matter what the nationality of the child's parents.

The definition of "corporate nationality," however, presents particularly difficult problems. Under U.S. practice, a corporation normally has the nationality or citizenship of the state where it is incorporated. Nevertheless, the Internal Revenue

Code taxes foreign source income of certain foreign corporations when they are "owned or controlled" by U.S. citizens, thereby treating those corporations as if they are U.S. nationals for this limited purpose.

More controversially, some U.S. laws apply to all individuals and corporations that are "subject to the jurisdiction of the United States," a phrase that the U.S. government sometimes interprets, through regulations, to include foreign corporations owned or controlled by U.S. persons. This would include a French subsidiary of a U.S. corporation. The claimed basis for the authority is the nationality principle. For example, one major statute authorizing international economic sanctions is the International Emergency Economic Powers Act (IEEPA). It applies to "any person, or . . . any property, subject to the jurisdiction of the United States." The Treasury regulations implementing the IEEPA provide:

The term, person subject to the jurisdiction of the United States, includes:

(a) Any individual, wherever located, who is a citizen or resident of the United States;
(b) Any person within the United States as defined in [another section];
(c) Any corporation organized under the laws of the United States or of any state, territory, possession, or district of the United States; and
(d) Any corporation, partnership, or association, wherever organized or doing business, that is owned or controlled by persons specified in paragraph (a) or (c) of this section. [31 C.F.R. 500.329 (2010).]

This form of extraterritorial application of U.S. law has long rankled foreign governments, precipitating protests and stimulating countermeasures. For example, in 1965 a French court appointed a temporary administrator to manage Fruehauf-France, a French subsidiary that was 70 percent owned by a U.S. parent, in order to carry out a contract with China that was prohibited under the then applicable U.S. regulations. The controversy is described by Professor Lowenfeld:

Andreas F. Lowenfeld, Trade Controls for Political Ends

92-93 (1983)

Fruehauf had been organized in 1918 in Detroit, had opened a Canadian plant in 1928, and had spread after the War to Europe, Brazil, Australia, and Japan. By 1965, Fruehauf had factories in 10 countries, and 80 distributors sold and serviced Fruehauf products in nearly all parts of the world other than communist countries. . . .

S.A. Fruehauf-France, located about 15 miles south of Paris, was owned 70 percent by Fruehauf Detroit, and 30 percent by French interests. Five of the directors were appointed from Detroit, including the Chairman and the Vice President/International of the parent company, and two other American citizens, all represented by one United States citizen resident in France who carried a permanent proxy from the senior officials of Fruehauf Detroit. The three other directors, all French citizens, were appointed by the holders of the 30 percent interest in the enterprise. One of the French directors, Raoul Massardy, served as President-General Manager.

In early October, 1964 Fruehauf-France was invited to bid on a contract to supply a large order of semi-trailers to the French truck company Berliet. Berliet advised that the transaction would involve exports from France, but no destination was named. Fruehauf-France submitted its bid on October 16, 1964, subject only to the condition that the unknown destination not be one in which another Fruehauf distributor had exclusive rights. Between the middle of October and the end of November a variety of communications flowed between Berliet and Fruehauf-France, dealing with specifications, price, and delivery terms. . . . [B]y November 30, Berliet informed Fruehauf-France that its offer was the most attractive, and that it should begin procuring the necessary materials with a view to commencing delivery by February 15, 1965. The final signed order was received by Fruehauf-France on December 24, 1964, with a contract price of about Fr. 1,800,000 (U.S. $360,000).

At some time during the fall, Fruehauf-France learned that the trailers, together with tractors to be manufactured by Berliet, were destined for the People's Republic of China. It is not clear when or whether this fact was called to the attention of Fruehauf Detroit, but in any case the latter did not notify the United States government or apply for a license.

Early in January, 1965, the U.S. Treasury learned of the proposed transaction, and called in Fruehauf Detroit's top management. Fruehauf Detroit was instructed to cause Fruehauf-France to cancel the Berliet contract forthwith, as execution of the contract would be a violation of the Foreign Assets Control Regulations [promulgated under the predecessor statute to the IEEPA] punishable by heavy criminal penalties. Following several weeks of meetings and telephone calls, Fruehauf Detroit complied with the order of the U.S. Treasury; it formally instructed Fruehauf-France to cancel the contract, and to seek to minimize the damages vis-a-vis Berliet. When Berliet refused to release Fruehauf-France and threatened suit, Massardy resigned as president, and the three French directors petitioned the local commercial court for the appointment of a temporary administrator who would manage the company and carry out the contract. The court granted the petition on February 16, 1965. The corporation, on the basis of a resolution adopted by the five American directors, appealed.

The Court of Appeals of Paris upheld the appointment of the temporary administrator. Societe Fruehauf Corp. v. Massardy, [1968] D.S. Jur. 147 (Ct. App. Paris, May 22, 1965). Among other reasons, the court noted that the damage liability of Fruehauf-France would

> ruin the financial equilibrium and the moral credit of Fruehauf-France, S.A. and provide its disappearance and the unemployment of more than 600 workers; . . . in order to name a temporary administrator the judge-referee must take into account the interests of the company rather than the personal interests of any shareholders even if they be the majority. [The opinion was translated and appeared in 5 Int'l L. Mat. 476 (1966).]

The decision of the French courts to appoint a temporary administrator to take control of a functioning French company created a new precedent in French corporate law. See William Lawrence Craig, Application of the Trading with the Enemy Act to Foreign Corporations Owned by Americans: Reflections on Fruehauf v. Massardy, 83 Harv. L. Rev. 579, 582 (1970).

The U.S. Department of Treasury did not take any further action against the U.S. parent company. This might have reflected, in part, the great French sensitivity at the time to the U.S. effort to extend its laws to a French subsidiary.

Another U.S.-European trade dispute arose in the 1980s over the construction of a Soviet pipeline to carry natural gas from large fields in Siberia to Western Europe. In June 1982, President Reagan announced an unprecedented broadening of trade controls against the Soviet Union. These controls were on exports of oil and gas equipment and technology and were designed at least in part to hamper Soviet construction of the pipeline.

Barry E. Carter, International Economic Sanctions: Improving the Haphazard U.S. Legal Regime

83-85 (1988)

Two controls went beyond any previous assertion of extraterritorial jurisdiction under the foreign policy provisions of the EAA [Export Administration Act]. First, the controls prevented foreign subsidiaries of U.S. firms from exporting equipment and technology even though it was of wholly foreign origin. Second, the controls restricted independent foreign companies from exporting foreign-origin products that were made with technology acquired through licensing agreements with U.S. companies. These controls covered, for example, compressors built by a French Company (e.g. Creusot-Loire) under a licensing agreement with a U.S. company (e.g. General Electric).

The U.S. policy against the pipeline clashed with that of major European countries that were not opposed to its construction—indeed, some were signing contracts to buy gas from the pipeline and many countries were encouraging their companies to participate in its construction. The attempt by the United States to impose its antipipeline policy on companies operating in, say, France, West Germany, England, and Italy drew a strong reaction. The European Economic Community and others argued that the extraterritorial extension of the controls was contrary to international law. Governments in some European countries encouraged companies within their borders to honor their contracts with the Soviets. France even issued formal orders directing businesses to continue to perform. As a result, several companies in Europe, including some U.S. subsidiaries such as Dresser-France, found themselves subject to conflicting orders from the United States and from the country where they were located. Several of these companies complied with the directives from their resident countries and performed under their contracts. The United States reacted swiftly by placing the companies that did not comply with the U.S. orders on a "temporary denial" list, which essentially cut these companies off from all exports from the United States.

Although no U.S. court ruled definitively on the extraterritorial reach of the controls, at least one European court ruled against it. In Compagnie Européenne des Petroles S.A. v. Sensor Nederland B.V., a Dutch district court decided that Sensor, a Dutch subsidiary of a U.S. corporation, could not be excused from performing a sales contract under Dutch law because of the U.S. export regulations. The court determined that the U.S. regulations had no jurisdictional basis under international law that required the court to take the regulations into account.

The President's decision to rescind the regulations was apparently caused by the strong allied reaction, pressures from the U.S. business community and Congress, and the apparent ineffectiveness of the controls since work on the pipeline continued and companies in Europe generally continued to perform under their contracts. Possibly chastened by the pipeline experience, the Reagan Administration [did not assert] such broad extraterritorial jurisdiction since, not even in . . . controls pursuant to IEEPA against Nicaragua, South Africa, and Libya. Nevertheless, the broad statutory authority remains unchanged at this point.

The Netherlands: District Court at the Hague Judgment in Compagnie Européenne des Petroles S.A. v. Sensor Nederland B.V.

22 Int'l Legal Materials 66 (1983)

1. The Facts

From the documents before the Court and the proceedings at the sitting of September 3, 1982, the following facts can so far be taken as having been established between the parties:

—Compagnie Europeenne des Petroles S.A. (C.E.P.) is a company organized and existing under French law and domiciled in Paris.

—Sensor Nederland B.V. (Sensor) is, according to its Articles of Association, domiciled at The Hague and has its business address at Voorschoten.

—The management of Sensor is entirely in the hands of Pierson Trust B.V., domiciled at Amsterdam.

—Sensor is a 100% subsidiary of Geosource International (Nederland) B.V., which is domiciled at Amsterdam and is a 100% subsidiary of Geosource, Inc., a corporation organized and existing under the laws of one of the United States of America and domiciled at Houston, Texas.

—Around February 1982 C.E.P. entered into negotiations with Sensor about the supply of 2,400 strings of geophones with spare parts.

—By telex of May 19, 1982, C.E.P. placed an order with Sensor for the supply of 2,400 strings of geophones with spare parts for the price of Nfls 2,249,369.60. The delivery time was to be 14-16 weeks.

—By telex of May 19, 1982, Sensor confirmed the order placed with it.

—C.E.P.'s official purchase order of June 3, 1982, includes the following terms:
Price: FOB Understood Rotterdam, packing for Sea shipment and delivery included
Delivery: Within 14-16 weeks
Payment: By letter of credit to be opened 8 weeks before delivery
Ultimate Destination: U.S.S.R.

—On June 18, 1982, Sensor confirmed the purchase order in writing; mention was made of delivery before September 20, 1982.

—By telex and letter of June 28, 1982, C.E.P. . . . confirmed its order [without spare parts] to the 2,400 strings of geophones for the price of Nfls 2,103,264.00.

— On July 1, 1982, Sensor confirmed to C.E.P. the receipt of the (revised) order placed by G.E.P. on June 28,1982.

— On July 27, 1982, Sensor informed C.E.P. that it would not be able to meet its delivery obligation in good time, now that, as a subsidiary of an American corporation, it had to respect the export embargo of June 22, 1982, imposed by the President of the United States.

— On August 11, 1982, C.E.P. reminded Sensor that it had been agreed that the goods would be delivered f.o.b. Rotterdam not later than on September 20, 1982.

— On that day—August 11—C.E.P. drew Sensor's attention to the consequences of failure to deliver on time.

— On August 12, 1982, Sensor again informed C.E.P. that as a subsidiary of an American corporation it had to respect the President's embargo.

2. The Claim

After modifying its original claim, C.E.P. is now asking that Sensor be ordered to deliver to C.E.P. by October 18, 1982, at the latest, in the agreed manner, the 2,400 strings of geophones ordered by C.E.B., on pain of a penalty of Nfls 100,000 [about $35,000], payable forthwith to C.E.P., for each day after October 18, 1982, that Sensor fails to deliver the said 2,400 strings of geophones. . . .

4. Applicable Law

The international contract of sale was concluded by telex; the parties made no choice of law.

In the event of failure by the parties to make such a choice, an international contract is governed by the laws of the country with which it is most closely connected.

This is presumed to be the country where the party who is to effect the performance which is characteristic of the contract has its principal place of business at the time of conclusion of the contract.

This principle is embodied in Article 4 of the Convention on the Law applicable to Contractual Obligations, which convention was signed by the Netherlands on June 19, 1980.

Although this Convention has not (yet) been ratified by the Netherlands, its Article 4 should already be applied as valid Netherlands private international law.

Applicability of Netherlands law implies in the present case that the Uniform Act governing the International Sale of Goods (Neth. O.J. 1971 No. 780) is also applicable to the contract.

5. The Defence

Sensor has submitted that it is subject to the [U.S.] Export Administration Regulations and that by virtue of §385.2 (c) of those Regulations it cannot fulfill its obligations towards C.E.P.

According to Sensor, the sanctions with which Sensor and Geosource are threatened in the event of infringement of the Export Administration Regulations constitute *force majeure* and justify a reliance on the "exonerating circumstances" of section 74 of the Uniform Act governing the International Sale of Goods.

6. §385.2(0) of the Export Administration Regulations

6.1 The text of §385.2 (c) of the Export Administration Regulations [would prohibit this sale].

6.2 Under Section 11 of the Export Administration Act, any infringement of the regulation reproduced above is punishable by a fine of up to $100,000, by a term of imprisonment of up to ten years and by withdrawal of export licenses.

7. Assessment of the Extra-Territorial Jurisdiction Rule of §385.2(C)(2)(IV)

7.1 In what follows, it will be assumed that an export transaction such as that agreed upon between C.E.P. and Sensor falls within the scope of section (1) of §385.2(c) and that the U.S. authorities have not granted an export license for that transaction.

It will also be assumed that Sensor is a "corporation" within the meaning of paragraph (iv) of section (2) of the American regulation [which provided that any corporation, wherever it was incorporated or doing business, was subject to U.S. jurisdiction if it were owned or controlled by a U.S. corporation].

7.2 Under point 4 above it has been found that the contract between C.E.P. and Sensor is governed by Netherlands law. To what extent, therefore, is it necessary to take into account a measure under U.S. law that operates in restraint of trade?

In answering that question, the first consideration must be that that measure extends to the transaction between C.E.P. and Sensor simply and solely via the jurisdiction rule of section (2)(iv). The object of that rule is manifestly to endow the [sanctions] measure with effects vis-á-vis corporations located outside the United States which conclude contracts outside the United States with non-American corporations.

That is the situation that arises in the present case. What particularly merits attention is the fact that, under international law as commonly interpreted, Sensor Nederland B.V. has Netherlands nationality, having been organized in the Netherlands under Netherlands law and both its registered office and its real centre of administration being located within the Netherlands. In accordance with this interpretation, the Treaty of Friendship, Commerce and Navigation between the Kingdom of the Netherlands and the United States of America of March 27, 1956, provides in Article XXIII, third paragraph:

> Companies constituted under the applicable laws and regulations within the territories of either Party shall be deemed companies thereof and shall have their juridical status recognized within the territories of the other Party.

7.3 The circumstance that the trade embargo imposed by the American authorities has been endowed with extra-territorial effects as hereinbefore described raises the question as to whether the jurisdiction rule that brings about such effects is compatible with international law.

7.3.1 The starting point for answering such questions is the universally accepted rule of international law that in general it is not permissible for a State to exercise jurisdiction over acts performed outside its borders. Exceptions to this rule are, however, possible, for instance under the so-called "nationality principle" or the "protection principle" (the "universality principle" can be disregarded here).

7.3.2 The American jurisdiction rule would not appear to be justified by the nationality principle in so far as that rule brings within its scope companies of other than U.S. nationality.

The position would be different if, in the first place, the criterion "owned or controlled by persons specified in paragraphs (i), (ii), or (iii) of this section" were . . . a yardstick for the (U.S.) nationality of the corporation . . . but in general, according to the views held outside the United States, this has to be regarded as in itself dubious, and in the relations between the United States and the Netherlands it is out of the question, having regard to the treaty provision hereinbefore cited under 7.2. The consequence of this is that the nationality principle offers insufficient basis for the jurisdiction rule here at issue.

7.3.3 Under the protection principle, it is permissible for a State to exercise jurisdiction over acts—wheresoever and by whomsoever performed—that jeopardize the security or creditworthiness of that State or other State interests. Such other State interests do not include the foreign policy interest that the U.S. measure seeks to protect. The protection principle cannot therefore be invoked in support of the validity of the jurisdiction rule here at issue.

7.3.4 It is also of importance to examine whether the acts of exportation covered by the American embargo, in so far as they are performed outside the United States, have direct and illicit effects within the territory of the United States. If that is the case, then those acts can be regarded as having been performed within the United States and on that ground brought within the jurisdiction of the United States under generally accepted rules of international law.

It cannot, however, be seen how the export to Russia of goods not originating in the United States by a non-American exporter could have any direct and illicit effects within the United States. Via this route too, therefore, the jurisdiction rule cannot be brought into compatibility with international law.

7.3.5 The foregoing does not entail that, measured by international law standards, the jurisdiction rule has to be denied all effects.

It is not unacceptable, for instance, that its effects should extend to American citizens who, wishing to evade the American embargo, to that end set up a non-American corporation outside the United States.

There is, however, no evidence to suggest that this has occurred in the present case. . . .

8. Conclusion

It follows from the foregoing that Sensor's reliance on the American embargo fails and that the claim . . . must be allowed, Sensor being ordered to pay costs.

The imposition of economic sanctions has become a regular feature of U.S. foreign policy. Congress continues frequently to authorize a wide variety of sanctions against a number of target countries and against a great number of individual groups and entities (such as terrorists and drug traffickers). In turn, the Executive

Branch continues to act to impose sanctions on countries, groups, and individuals through executive orders and other determinations. Many of these sanctions have been imposed in connection with measures authorized by the U.N. Security Council, such as those against Iran, North Korea, or Libya. Others are unilateral, as with the Soviet pipeline case and, more recently, with the sanctions against Cuba under the Helms-Burton legislation, and U.S. laws against countries and entities that sell sensitive items related to weapons of mass destruction. Sanctions have also frequently been imposed under general legislation such as IEEPA and the Export Administration Act, often with extraterritorial effect. (For further discussion of economic sanctions, see the Chapter 3.B.3 section on national emergency legislation above and the section on U.S. human rights sanctions in Chapter 8.B.8.b.)

There are two different types of situations where foreign governments have vigorously resisted the extraterritorial application of U.S. rules: first, where foreign operations of foreign-incorporated subsidiaries of U.S. parent corporations are covered by the rule and, second, where foreign operations of independent foreign corporations with only tenuous connections to the United States are involved — for example, using technology originating in the United States or taking advantage of property once owned by U.S. nationals.

European judicial reaction has been hostile (as the *Fruehauf* and *Sensor* cases demonstrate). Another example involved a U.S. attempt in 1987 to freeze Libyan bank deposits in a London branch of a U.S. bank. A U.K. trial court ruled that Bankers Trust Company was obligated to pay the Libyan Arab Foreign Bank $292.5 million in funds that the Libyan bank had deposited with Bankers Trust and that the U.S. bank claimed had been frozen. About half of the money had been in the London branch of Bankers Trust, and the other half was money the U.S. bank had failed to transfer, as directed by the Libyan bank, to its London branch prior to the freeze. In reaching its decision, the trial court concluded that law of the place (i.e., U.K. law) applied to accounts in the United Kingdom, even in the branch of a U.S. bank. Libyan Arab Foreign Bank v. Bankers Trust Co., 26 I.L.M. 1600 (Q.B. Comml. Ct. Sept. 2, 1987). Rather than appeal this unfavorable opinion, Bankers Trust paid the Libyan bank the $292.5 million, plus $28 million in interest. The U.S. Treasury Department granted the necessary license for Bankers Trust to make the payment to a Libyan entity.

As discussed earlier in Chapter 6 before the *Sabbatino* case, the United States has strongly opposed the Cuban government since shortly after Fidel Castro took power in Cuba through a revolution in 1959. Extensive limits on trade and other economic transactions were first imposed in 1962 and have continued to varying degrees. Probably the greatest controversy was sparked by the Helms-Burton Act of 1996. Consider the following analysis of the law.

Andreas F. Lowenfeld, Congress and Cuba: The Helms-Burton Act

90 Am.J. Int'l L. 419 (1996)

On March 12, 1996, President Clinton signed the Cuban Liberty and Democratic Solidarity (Libertad) Act of 1996, generally known by the names of its principal sponsors as the Helms-Burton Act. . . .

Title III of the Act, which embodies the threat to nationals of third countries — Canadians, Spaniards, Argentines or whatever — has drawn the most comment, both because it raises once again the issue of economic sanctions through exercise of extraterritorial jurisdiction, and because it explicitly rejects the act of state doctrine and empowers United States courts to adjudicate claims arising from expropriations carried out in Cuba more than three decades ago. . . .

III. Property in Cuba, Litigation in America

The issue of compensation for property of United States nationals . . . is the focus of title III. The scheme of the Act is to create a right of action in United States courts on behalf of any U.S. national who has a claim for property confiscated by Cuba since January 1,1959, against any person who "traffics" in such property. . . . Whoever "traffics" in property that once belonged to U.S. nationals is to be confronted with the prospect of litigation in the United States, and of exposure to damages equal in the first instance to the value of the property in question, and if the trafficking continues, to treble damages (section 302(a)). "Trafficking," a word heretofore applied in legislation almost exclusively to dealing in narcotics, is defined to include not only selling, transferring, buying, or leasing the property in question, but also "engag[ing] in a commercial activity using or otherwise benefiting from confiscated property" (section 4(13)). Thus the Act contemplates that if an English company purchases sugar from a Cuban state enterprise and the English company also does business in the United States and accordingly is amenable to the judicial jurisdiction of a U.S. court, it would be liable to a U.S. national who could show that some of the English company's purchases consisted of sugar grown on the plantation that the plaintiff once owned. There is no necessary connection between the value of the property on which the claim is based and the value of the transaction on which the assertion of "trafficking" rests. . . .

[T]he President is authorized to suspend the effectiveness of title III for a period of six months if he determines and reports to Congress that the suspension "[i] is necessary to the national interests of the United States and [ii] will expedite a transition to democracy in Cuba" (section 306(b)(1)). The suspension may be extended for additional periods of six months upon further determinations by the President to the same effect. . . . This compromise, which was not contained in either the House or the Senate bill, was accepted, according to the Conference Report, at the request of the executive branch "in order to afford the President flexibility to respond to unfolding developments in Cuba." . . .

. . . It is clear that a suit of the kind contemplated in title III of Helms-Burton would run up against the [act of state] doctrine as set out in *Sabbatino* and succeeding cases. . . . The authors of the Helms-Burton Act dealt with this problem head-on. They provided (in section 302(a) (6)) that the act of state doctrine shall not be applicable to actions brought under the Act. . . .

The *piece de resistance* of the Cuban Liberty and Democratic Solidarity (Libertad) Act, evidently, is the linkage between exposure to litigation in the United States and conduct abroad. The conduct may be in Cuba itself, such as building a hotel or operating a cement works; or it may be in Canada, France, Mexico — anywhere that an embargo against Cuba is not in effect.

The sanction is not quite a prohibition, as now prevails with respect to foreign companies linked by ownership or control to United States firms. But virtually all commercial enterprises in Cuba were taken over by the Government in the years after Fidel Castro came to power, whether they previously belonged to U.S. nationals, Cuban nationals or third-country nationals. It follows that any person that deals with an enterprise that existed prior to January 1, 1959 (by whatever name), or with an enterprise that could be regarded as a successor to such an enterprise, stands exposed to litigation in the United States, if it does business or otherwise can be found in the United States. Of course, not all such litigation, if it took place, would result in a final judgment against the defendant. Plaintiffs would, it seems, have the burden of proving that defendants were dealing in *their* confiscated property, and there might well be different interpretations of what that meant. But no one likes to face a lawsuit with high potential damages, least of all in the United States. And just in case the potential defendant's calculation might come out to prefer continuing the commercial relation with Cuba, even at the risk of litigation in the United States, Helms-Burton provides that . . . damages are to be trebled. In case that deterrent is still not sufficient, section 401 requires that the Secretary of State shall not grant a visa to, and the Attorney General shall not admit into the United States, any person who after the enactment of the Act has confiscated property or traffics in property a claim to which is owned by a U.S. national. This provision by its terms applies also to a corporate officer, principal or shareholder with a controlling interest in such a person, and — I think for the first time in the not always honorable history of U.S. alien exclusion laws — to the spouse, minor child or agent of a person excludable under any of the preceding categories. It is hard to believe that Ms. Jones, the daughter of a corporate executive from Toronto, might be stopped at the border when she returns from her summer vacation for her junior year at Vassar, but that is what the statute says.

In short, for any firm that does business in the United States or is amenable to suit in the United States, the choice is between an ice cream sundae and a root canal treatment. Given the doubtful prospects of business in Cuba in any event, and the huge potential of the American market, the proponents of Helms-Burton are fairly confident that persons who contemplate investment in Cuba or transactions with Cuba will change their minds, and that those who have already made such deals will look for ways to unload their investments or terminate their contracts.

Helms-Burton as a Secondary Boycott

As I see it, the Helms-Burton Act is thus in intent — and probably in effect — a classical secondary boycott, much like the Arab boycott of Israel. State *A* may prohibit trade with (or investment by its nationals in) state *B*. That is the typical embargo or *primary boycott* — the United States vis-á-vis Cuba, Syria (and others) vis-á-vis Israel, many countries against South Africa until 1994. Putting aside the (not insignificant) issue of applying such a boycott to subsidiaries established abroad, a primary boycott does not usually raise issues of international law, because the boycotting state is exercising its jurisdiction in its own territory or over its own nationals.

In a *secondary boycott,* state *A* says that if *X,* a national of state C, trades with state *B, X* may not trade with or invest in *A.* In other words, *X* is required to make a choice between doing business with or in *A*, the boycotting state, and doing business with or in *B*, the target state, although under the law of C where *X* is established, trade with both *A* and *C* is permitted.

After some hesitation, the United States strongly condemned the boycott of Israel maintained by the League of Arab States. U.S. law has prohibited American firms from complying with the Arab boycott, and even from filling out forms supplied by the Boycott Office or otherwise answering questions designed to disclose whether or not the firm has done business with Israel. . . .

It is true that the sanctions imposed by the Helms-Burton Act are distinguishable from the Arab boycott of Israel, in that the sanction for violation under Helms-Burton is not a prohibition, only exposure to litigation and exclusion. But the litigation, as we have seen, may result in damages equal not to defendants' gain but to plaintiffs' loss, plus interest for some thirty-five years, all subject to trebling if the potential defendants do not exercise their Hobson's choice quickly. The objective, in any case, is the same. *X*, a national of state *C* (say Canada), is being coerced by state *A* (the United States) to stop trading with *B* (Cuba) or handling merchandise containing products of state *B*, although the law of *C* makes such trade perfectly legal and may even encourage it. I believe that (in time of peace) the exercise of jurisdiction by the United States for these purposes, to impose a secondary boycott on Cuba, like the exercise of jurisdiction by members of the Arab League to impose a secondary boycott on Israel, is contrary to international law, because it seeks unreasonably to coerce conduct that takes place wholly outside of the state purporting to exercise its jurisdiction to prescribe.

Helms-Burton and the Effects Doctrine

The authors of the Helms-Burton Act were prepared for criticism that they were engaged in extraterritorial legislation. They included in the Findings on which the operative portions of the Act are based, the statement:

> International law recognizes that a nation has the ability to provide for rules of law with respect to conduct outside its territory that has or is intended to have substantial effect within its territory. (Section 301 (9)) . . .

I submit that the effort by the authors of Helms-Burton to build on the *Restatement* is flawed — fundamentally flawed — in two respects. *First*, the effect against which the legislation is directed — even if one can locate it in the United States — was caused by the Government of Cuba, not by the persons over whom jurisdiction is sought to be exercised. Thus, even leaving aside the thirty-six-year interval between conduct and effect on the one hand, . . . the effort to place Helms-Burton within the effects doctrine is no more than a play on words. It does not withstand analysis, and it would carry the effects doctrine farther than it has ever been carried before.

Second, the effort to impose United States policy on third countries or their nationals in the circumstances here contemplated is unreasonable by any standard. I need not here go through the criteria for evaluating reasonableness set out in the *Restatement*; different writers and courts have formulated or understood the criteria in different ways. I think for present purposes the most persuasive way to look at the legislation is to ask how Americans would react if the tables were turned.

Suppose, for instance, Iran were to adopt a law stating that anyone who invests in the Great Satan U.S.A. will be subject to suit in Iran for up to the value of the assets that the former Shah robbed from the Iranian people, as determined by the Majlis. BMW, calculating its litigation exposure in Iran and the value of its investments in the United States, cancels operations about to begin at its new plant in Spartansburg, South Carolina; at the same time, Mercedes Benz cancels its plan to build a sports vehicle plant in Vance, Alabama. I believe all Americans would be outraged, both at Iran for adopting the law I have suggested, and at the German manufacturers for having capitulated. I do not believe we would be hearing Iran's exercise of jurisdiction characterized as reasonable. . . .

Diversion from the Situation in Cuba

In the first few days after the passage of the Cuban Liberty and Democratic Solidarity Act, the press was full of reports of opposition to the Act from America's best friends. . . . [T]here is a real danger that Helms-Burton will have the same effect that President Reagan's famous pipeline regulations had in 1982.

. . . The reaction in Europe was loud, quick, all negative, and much of it invoked international law. . . .

Notes and Questions

1. Who has the final say when two countries disagree on a major project? In the *Fruehauf* case, which country's laws prevailed? Which country's law prevailed in *Sensor* and why? What courts decided the cases? Might the decision in each case have been different if the matter had somehow come up in a U.S. court?

2. Obviously there is great potential for conflict in these situations where the states involved have fundamentally different foreign and economic policies. Should those conflicts be resolved through a political process (such as a diplomatic negotiation) or judicially? If a political agreement cannot be reached, is it unfair to subject a defendant to inconsistent commands of criminal or civil law? If you were counsel to the corporate entities involved, what arguments would you make, and to whom, to prevent that from happening?

3. If you were a senator from a state, such as California, with many exporting multinational companies, would you favor amending these laws to limit extraterritorial application? How? Does your opinion vary according to whether the sanctions are applied to Iran, North Korea, Myanmar (Burma), China, or Nigeria?

4. What would be your attitude toward such an amendment if you were counsel to the State Department? Defense? Commerce? Agriculture? Would it matter to these government agencies (or to multinational companies affected by the sanctions) whether the extraterritorial elements of the sanctions were codified in the sanctions law or were implemented through an Executive Order or other regulation? Which approach is easier to change when relations between the United States and the target country change?

5. Should a U.S. corporation be able to avoid U.S. law by simply incorporating a foreign subsidiary? Was that the situation in the Fruehauf-France case?

6. What would be the result in *Sensor* if there were no FCN Treaty? Apply the Restatement section 403 factors. What result?

7. As a general rule, should U.S. sanctions legislation passed by Congress have some type of presidential waiver provision that allows the President some flexibility in applying economic pressure and adjusting to changed circumstances? (Note the waiver added to Title III of Helms-Burton or the waiver added to the Burma sanctions legislation, discussed in the *Crosby* case in Chapter 3.D.) How hard or easy should Congress make the waiver provision? Should it just require the President to make a determination of "national interest" or "national security," or should it have additional conditions and reporting requirements?

8. The foreign reaction to the Helms-Burton Act was swift and negative, with foreign governments saying that the Act interfered with their national policies for their companies on trade with Cuba. By 1997, so-called blocking or antidote legislation had been passed by Canada, the European Union, Mexico, and Argentina. Each of these laws prohibits private or public cooperation with U.S. implementation of Helms-Burton and establishes sizeable penalties for doing so. They also bar their courts from enforcing judgments awarded under Helms-Burton.

The more innovative element of some of these blocking laws is their "claw back" provisions. These create a cause of action in the foreign state on behalf of a national or corporation of that state who has a judgment rendered against it in U.S. courts under Helms-Burton. That person can sue in his own court for an equivalent amount of damages, enforceable against the assets of the U.S. plaintiff in the defendant's home state. This has the effect both of dissuading potential U.S. litigants, who may lose as much as they gain, even with treble damages, and of indemnifying the EU, Canadian, or other foreign citizens who wish to continue trading with Cuba. For more on these blocking laws, see Jorge F. Perez-Lopez and Matias F. Travieso-Diaz, The Helms-Burton Law and Its Antidotes: A Classic Standoff?, 7 Sw. J.L. & Trade Am. 95 (2000).

9. In part because of these strong foreign reactions to the Helms-Burton Act, the Clinton Administration negotiated an understanding with the EU pursuant to which the President exercised his waiver authority every six months until the end of his presidency to prevent lawsuits under Title III and to use discretion in banning foreign nationals under Title IV. In turn, as its part of the understanding to help promote democracy in Cuba, the EU made some critical statements about Castro's government. As of March 2011, President Bush and President Obama have similarly continued to waive the lawsuit provisions of Title III, despite political pressure from anti-Castro groups in the United States. The Act, however, still remains on the books.

10. The literature on extraterritoriality is extensive. See, e.g., Gary B. Born and Peter B. Rutledge, International Civil Litigation in United States Courts 570-577, 581-584, 914-915 (4th ed. 2006); Andreas F. Lowenfeld, International Litigation and Arbitration 39-143 (2d ed. 2002); Barry E. Carter, International Economic Sanctions: Improving the Haphazard Legal Regime 85, 253-254 (1988); Andreas F. Lowenfeld, International Litigation and Arbitration 55-175 (3d ed. 2006).

The territorial and nationality principles support most legislation a government is likely to want to adopt. However, there are a few situations in which these principles do not cover matters that governments have often felt compelled to regulate, such as currency counterfeiting and visa fraud (conduct that may well be by aliens acting outside national territory). Moreover, some states have considered it desirable to protect their nationals working or traveling abroad by extending their law to offenses against such nationals committed by foreigners on foreign territory. The protective principle and passive personality are the legal doctrines that justify these assertions of prescriptive jurisdiction.

3. *Protective Principle*

Restatement

Section 402(3). Bases of Jurisdiction to Prescribe

Subject to §403, a state has jurisdiction to prescribe law with respect to . . .
(3) certain conduct outside its territory by persons not its nationals that is directed against the security of the state or against a limited class of other state interests.

Comment

f. The protective principle. Subsection (3) restates the protective principle of jurisdiction. International law recognizes the right of a state to punish a limited class of offenses committed outside its territory by persons who are not its nationals— offenses directed against the security of the state or other offenses threatening the integrity of governmental functions that are generally recognized as crimes by developed legal systems, e.g., espionage, counterfeiting of the state's seal or currency, falsification of official documents, as well as perjury before consular officials, and conspiracy to violate the immigration or customs laws. The protective principle may be seen as a special application of the effects principle, but it has been treated as an independent basis of jurisdiction. The protective principle does not support application to foreign nationals of laws against political expression, such as libel of the state or of the chief of state.

United States v. Romero-Galue

U.S. Court of Appeals
757 F.2d 1147 (11th Cir. 1985)

TJOFLAT, Circuit Judge:

Section 955a(c) of Title 21 of the United States Code makes it a crime "for any person on board any vessel within the customs waters of the United States to knowingly or intentionally . . . possess with intent to . . . distribute" marijuana. This appeal questions whether the Congress, in enacting this statute, intended to reach the possession of marijuana by foreigners aboard a foreign vessel on the high seas.[1] The district court held that Congress did not so intend and dismissed the indictment. We reverse.

1. The high seas lie seaward of a nation's territorial sea, which is the band of water that extends up to three miles out from the coast. No nation may assert sovereignty over the high seas. [The United States and almost all other countries now recognize a territorial sea of twelve rather than three nautical miles. (See Chapter 9.) —EDS.]

I

On January 7, 1984, the U.S. Coast Guard cutter *Escape,* while patrolling an area in the Caribbean Sea known as the Mysteriosa Bank of the Yucatan Pass [about 350 miles from any U.S. territory], a thoroughfare used to transport marijuana from Colombia, South America to the United States, sited a shrimp boat, the *El Don,* lying dead in the water, apparently having engine trouble. The Coast Guard suspected that the *El Don* was a smuggling vessel; she was not rigged for fishing, flew no flag, and bore no markings indicating her home port. Exercising the "right of approach,"[3] the *Escape* pulled alongside the *El Don,* and several Coast Guardsmen boarded her to examine her registration papers and determine her identity. In the course of accomplishing this, the Coast Guardsmen discovered a cargo in excess of four and one-half tons of marijuana in the vessel's hold.

The Coast Guardsmen determined that the *El Don* was of Panamanian registry. This information was relayed to the U.S. State Department which, in turn, communicated with the Panamanian government. Thereafter, the Coast Guard, presumably with Panama's approval, instructed the *Escape* to seize the *El Don* and its crew and to take them to Key West, Florida for prosecution. The *Escape* followed this instruction.

On January 20, 1984, in the Southern District of Florida, the *El Don*'s crew, the appellees here, were indicted under the Marijuana on the High Seas Act of 1980. . . . The District Court found that count II failed to state an offense because the defendants' possession of marijuana had taken place on a foreign vessel located on the high seas, i.e., beyond the territorial waters of the United States, and section 955a(c) did not reach such conduct. The government now appeals.

Section 955a(c) states:

> It is unlawful for any person on board any vessel within the customs waters of the United States to knowingly or intentionally . . . possess with intent to . . . distribute [marijuana].

The "customs waters of the United States" are defined as:

> The term "customs waters" means, in the case of a foreign vessel subject to a treaty or other arrangement between a foreign government and the United States enabling or permitting the authorities of the United States to board, examine, search, seize, or otherwise to enforce upon such vessel upon the high seas the laws of the United States, the waters within such distance of the coast of the United States as the said authorities are or may be so enabled or permitted by such treaty or arrangement and, in the case of every other vessel, the waters [within 12 miles]. . . .

Congress' goal when it enacted section 955a(c) of the Marijuana on the High Seas Act was not unlike the one Congress had in mind when it passed the

3. The "right of approach" is a doctrine of international maritime common law that bestows a nation's warship with the authority to hail and board an unidentified vessel to ascertain its nationality. If suspicions as to the vessel's nationality persist, as they well may even after the captain has declared her nation of registry, the inquiring nation may board the vessel and search for registration papers or other identification in order to verify the vessel's nationality. The "right of approach" is codified by article 22 of the Convention on the High Seas. . . .

Anti-Smuggling Act; both statutes authorize the prosecution of smugglers hovering on the high seas beyond the twelve mile limit. Under section 955a(c), the government can now reach narcotics smugglers aboard vessels of nontreaty nations within twelve miles of our coast and those aboard vessels of treaty nations within the area on the high seas designated by treaty or other arrangement. Whether such a treaty or other arrangement existed between the United States and Panama concerning the *El Don* is a mixed question of fact and law which the government should be entitled to address at trial.

The defendants argue Congress did not intend that "customs waters" be established in areas as remote as the one in which the *El Don* was seized, because this would transgress principles of international law. It is true that Congress did not intend to transgress international law; it limited the reach of the Marijuana on the High Seas Act, declaring that the Act was "designed to prohibit all acts of illicit trafficking in controlled substances on the high seas which the United States can reach under international law." This limitation, however, would not have precluded the designation, by treaty or other arrangement, of the place where the El Don was seized as "customs waters."

Nothing in international law prohibits two nations from entering into a treaty, which may be amended by other arrangement, to extend the customs waters and the reach of the domestic law of one of the nations into the high seas. . . . Even absent a treaty or arrangement, the United States could, under the "protective principle" of international law, prosecute foreign nationals on foreign vessels on the high seas for possession of narcotics. The protective principle permits a nation to assert jurisdiction over a person whose conduct outside the nation's territory threatens the nation's security or could potentially interfere with the operation of its governmental functions. The defendants' argument is thus without merit. Count II of the indictment stated a section 955a(c) offense, and the district court erred in dismissing it.

Notes and Questions

1. Traditionally what have been the grounds for the protective principle? See the excerpt from Starke's International Law at page 643 and the Restatement excerpt at beginning of this subsection.

2. Note the last paragraph of the *Romero* opinion. Even accepting the protective principle, what is the basis in the statute for upholding the indictment? Should the indictment stand even if a defendant's possession of marijuana was outside 12 miles and there were *no* treaty or other arrangements with the flag state? Or, more generally, is the court in effect allowing criminal liability to be imposed on a defendant in the absence of a governing statute? Did the court correctly decide the case? Since early times, the U.S. Supreme Court has held that there cannot be federal crimes in the absence of a statute—for example, United States v. Hudson & Goodwin, 11 U.S. (7 Cranch) 32, 34 (1812); United States v. Coolidge, 14 U.S. (1 Wheat) 415, 416-417 (1816).

3. Can exterritorial application of antitrust laws be justified under the protective principle? Can U.S. laws against foreign terrorists acting abroad be justified under the protective principle? Should there be some requirement that the terrorists are intending to have an effect within the United States and/or that the effect

needs to be more than a trivial one — that is, substantial? If so, does the protective principle differ from the effects test under the territorial principle? See Restatement section 402, cmt. *f*: "The protective principle may be seen as a special application of the effects principle, . . . but it has been treated as an independent basis of jurisdiction."

4. Does the dictum in the last paragraph of *Romero* show that the *Lotus* decision, discussed earlier in the Starke excerpt, is correct to hold that there is no limit imposed by international law on prescriptive jurisdiction, except for those established by a rule of international law?

5. The history of international law-based efforts to control drugs dates back at least to the 1912 International Opium Convention. In 1988 the U.N. General Assembly recommended by consensus the U.N. Convention Against Illicit Traffic in Narcotic Drugs and Psychotropic Substances, reproduced at 28 I.L.M. 493 (1989). The United States adhered to the Convention in 1990. As of March 2011, there were 185 parties that were parties to the Convention. The Convention requires each signatory to adopt domestic law criminalizing a defined list of offenses, including money laundering; to provide for confiscation of assets and extradition; and to prohibit trade in prescribed chemicals.

4. *Passive Personality*

The comment to section 402 of the Restatement of Foreign Relations Law states:

Restatement Section 402

Comment

g. The passive personality principle. The passive personality principle asserts that a state may apply law — particularly criminal law — to an act committed outside its territory by a person not its national where the victim of the act was its national. The principle has not been generally accepted for ordinary torts or crimes, but it is increasingly accepted as applied to terrorist and other organized attacks on a state's nationals by reason of their nationality, or to assassination of a state's diplomatic representatives or other officials.

United States v. Columba-Colella

U.S. Court of Appeals
604 F.2d 356 (5th Cir. 1979)

Wisdom, Circuit Judge:

In this case, unfortunately, the legally correct result produces something like declaring an open season on motor vehicles in American border towns — provided that the recipient of the stolen vehicles escapes the clutches of Mexican and Canadian law. Nevertheless, for lack of jurisdiction, we must reverse the district court's judgment entering defendant Francesco Columba-Colella's plea of guilty to the offense of receiving a stolen vehicle in foreign commerce in violation of 18 U.S.C. §2313. The criminal offense occurred in Mexico.

I

On the evening of August 21, 1978, Francesco Columba-Colella met a young man named Keith in Curley's Bar in Juarez, Mexico. The two struck up a conversation and became casual friends. Two days later they met again by chance at five-thirty in the afternoon on a Juarez street. Keith told Francesco he wanted to sell a car, and Francesco, who had lived in Juarez for at least two years, responded that he knew someone who might be interested in buying it. Keith then informed him for the first time that the car had been stolen in El Paso, Texas, and offered Francesco half the proceeds of any sale he could arrange. Francesco assented, took the keys to the car, a Ford Fairmont, and agreed to meet Keith the next day at 2:00 p.m. in The Kentucky Bar in Juarez. The meeting was not to take place. Later, the same evening, as Francesco was approaching the car with his wife, he was arrested by Mexican police.

The defendant, who was nineteen years old, resided in Juarez, where he lived with the Mexican woman whom he had married in 1976. He is a British citizen who was not employed in the United States and did not own property in the United States. He intended to reside permanently in Mexico and become a Mexican citizen.

After the defendant's motion to dismiss was denied, Columba-Colella pleaded guilty, but reserved the right to appeal the jurisdictional issue. The trial court committed him to the custody of the Attorney General for five years.

II

The only question raised on appeal is whether the lower court had jurisdiction over the case. Had the defendant been a United States citizen, there would be no jurisdictional problem, for a country may supervise and regulate the acts of its citizens both within and without its territory.

When an allegedly criminal act is performed by an alien on foreign soil courts in the United States have long held that if jurisdiction is to be extended over that act, it must be supported by either the *protective* or the *objective territorial* theory. Under the protective theory, which does not bear on the resolution of the case before us, a country's legislature is competent to enact laws and, assuming physical power over the defendant, its courts have jurisdiction to enforce criminal laws wherever and by whomever the act is performed that threatens the country's security or directly interferes with its governmental operations. A state/nation is competent, for example, to punish one who has successfully defrauded its treasury, no matter where the fraudulent scheme was perpetrated.

The objective territorial theory looks not to interference with governmental interests but to objective effects within the sovereign slate. The theory requires that before a state may attach criminal consequences to an extraterritorial act, the act must be intended to have an effect within the state. As Mr. Justice Holmes announced the theory, in the context of an interstate extradition:

> Acts done outside a jurisdiction, but intended to produce and producing effects within it, justify a state in punishing the cause of the harm as if he had been present at the effect, if the state should succeed in getting him within its power

Strassheim v. Daily, 1911, 221 U.S. 280, 284-85. Assume, for example, that persons or their agents conspire to rent a boat in Miami, sail it beyond United States coastal waters, and load it with a cargo of illegal drugs. Then, en route to a United States port but while still on the high seas, the conspirators are apprehended. This country may under the objective territorial theory apply its drug laws to punish them if it can establish intent to violate those laws.

III

There is no basis for jurisdiction over the defendant in the present case. He is not a United States citizen. He has not threatened the security of this country or interfered with its governmental function. Although the objective territorial theory applies, the fact that no conspiracy has been alleged means that the theory does not support jurisdiction in the case.

Had a conspiracy been demonstrated, the defendant could be said to have been engaged in a criminal enterprise, an essential element of which, the theft, occurred in the United States. Had Columba-Colella's intent anticipated and embraced the car theft in Texas, that act could be imputed to him. And since the United States is competent to proscribe the theft of property within its borders, it would then have had the jurisdiction it asserts in this case.

The defendant did not conspire to steal the car, and the theft in no way depended on any act or intent of the defendant. Whatever injury the owner of the car suffered was complete before Columba-Colella's chance meeting with Keith on the street in Juarez on the afternoon of August 22, 1978, and the agreement their meeting produced. To put it differently, though Columba-Colella's agreement to fence the car followed Keith's crime, his act, which may have been a crime under Mexican law, is legally unrelated to the prior crime. His act was no constituent element of Keith's act and is not made so by the coincidence that the property subject to their agreement belonged to a citizen of the jurisdiction in which the theft occurred.

The district judge relied on United States v. Fernandez, 5 Cir. 1974, 496 F.2d at 1294, in finding he had jurisdiction over the case. In *Fernandez,* the defendant was charged with possessing, forging, and uttering stolen United States Treasury checks. The defendant argued that this Court lacked jurisdiction because all the criminal acts involved were alleged to have taken place not in the United States but in Mexico. In finding that there was jurisdiction, we noted that the defendant's acts "prevent [ed] the normal disbursement of Social Security Funds to those lawfully entitled to receive such funds." 496 F.2d at 1296. . . . The district court's reliance on *Fernandez* is misplaced in this case, for here there was no interference with a governmental function, and therefore no reason to invoke the protective theory.

IV

There is no question, of course, that Columba-Colella's conduct somehow affected a United States citizen. Had he been successful in his enterprise, he would have prevented the stolen car from finding its way back to its owner. But that an act affects the citizen of a state is not a sufficient basis for that state to assert jurisdiction over the act. It is difficult to distinguish the present case from one in which the defendant had attempted not to fence a stolen car but instead to pick the pockets of American tourists in Acapulco. No one would argue either that Congress would be competent to prohibit such conduct or that the courts of the United States would have jurisdiction to enforce such a prohibition were the offender in their control. Indeed, Congress would not be competent to attach criminal sanctions to the murder of an American by a foreign national in a foreign country, even if the victim returned home and succumbed to his injuries.

These hypothetical cases involve criminal conduct that takes place wholly within a country, and whose character must therefore be determined by the law of the place where the act was done. The present case is similar. We therefore follow the method set out in American Banana Co. v. United Fruit Co., 1909, 213 U.S. 347, 357. We find that because the defendant's act in this case is beyond its competence to proscribe, Congress did not intend to assert jurisdiction here under 18 U.S.C. §2313. . . .

V

The practical problem we face is that our decision may encourage car thefts in border towns. Two facts limit this encouragement. In the ordinary case, as the United States Attorney averred in oral argument before this Court, a conspiracy will be charged and proved. When this is possible, there is no jurisdictional problem. And even where a conspiracy cannot be shown, each sovereign may punish the wrongful act committed in its territory: when we release Columba-Colella, he will be subject to whatever sanctions are applicable under the law of Mexico.

The result we reach is part of the price a nation must pay to support mutuality of comity between sovereign nations.

The judgment is reversed and the charge is dismissed.

Notes and Questions

1. If Congress passes a statute without ascertainable legislative intent on extraterritorial application, making it a felony to murder an American citizen, would the courts apply it in cases invoking murders abroad? Which crime is more prevalent—hostage murder, ordinary murder, or fencing stolen cars? Does it make any sense to conclude that Congress may legitimately punish the first crime (which Congress has done, as discussed below), but not the more common last two?

2. Do you agree with Judge Wisdom's fatalism ("unfortunately, the legally correct result produces something like declaring an open season on motor vehicles in American border towns")? Is that what Congress intended?

3. Why did Mexico not protest in this case? In the absence of such a protest, why should a criminal defendant be able to raise this supposed violation of international law?

4. As enacted in 1948 and continuing through 1984, the applicable statute (18 U.S.C. §2313) in the case above provided:

> Whoever receives, conceals, stores, barters, sells, or disposes of any motor vehicle or aircraft, moving as, or which is a part of, or which constitutes interstate or foreign commerce, knowing the same to be stolen, shall be fined not more than $5,000 or imprisoned not more than five years, or both.

Could the court have interpreted the statute to cover the alleged offense under the passive personality principle? Should such a principle extend to receipt in a foreign country by an alien of a car stolen in the United States?

5. In 1984 Congress amended the statute to read:

> Whoever receives, *possesses*, conceals, stores, barters, sells, or disposes of any motor vehicle or aircraft, *which has crossed a State or United States boundary after being stolen*, knowing the same to have been stolen, shall be fined. . . . [Italicized words indicate 1984 changes.]

Given the same set of facts as in Columba-Colella but assuming they occur in 1985, should the court uphold the jurisdiction of the trial court? Must it? Note that U.S. law requires that:

> Each justice or judge of the United States shall take the following oath or affirmation before performing the duties of his office: "I, _____ _____, solemnly swear (or affirm) that I will administer justice without respect to persons, and do equal right to the poor arid to the rich, and that I will faithfully and impartially discharge and perform all the duties incumbent upon me as _____ under the Constitution and laws of the United States. So help me God."[28 U.S.C. §453.]

6. In 1984, in order to implement the Convention Against the Taking of Hostages, Congress passed legislation, which provides (as amended through 2010):

18 U.S.C. §1203. Hostage Taking

> (a) Except as provided in subsection (b) of this section, whoever, whether inside or outside the United States, seizes or detains and threatens to kill, to injure, or to continue to detain another person in order to compel a third person or a governmental organization to do or abstain from doing any act as an explicit or implicit condition for the release of the person detained, or attempts or conspires to do so, shall be punished by imprisonment for any term of years or for life and, if the death of any person results, shall be punished by death or life imprisonment.
>
> (b) (1) It is not an offense under this section if the conduct required for the offense occurred outside the United States unless—
>
> (A) the offender or the person seized or detained is a national of the United States;
>
> (B) the offender is found in the United States; or
>
> (C) the governmental organization sought to be compelled is the Government of the United States.
>
> (2) It is not an offense under this section if the conduct required for the offense occurred inside the United States, each alleged offender and each person seized or detained are nationals of the United States, and each alleged offender is found in the United States, unless the governmental organization sought to be compelled is the Government of the United States

(a) What theories of prescriptive jurisdiction are reflected in section 1203(b)? Note the two different theories reflected in subsection (b)(1)(A).

(b) What interest does the U.S. government have in criminalizing acts wholly outside the United States solely on the basis that the offender is "found" in the United States? (The Hostages Convention provides for this assertion of prescriptive jurisdiction.)

(c) Could Congress have deleted subsection (b) consistent with international law? U.S. constitutional law?

(d) Would there be any international or constitutional law problems with extending prescriptive jurisdiction by making it a crime to kill an American anywhere in the world?

7. Would the *Columba-Colella* case, if correct, mean that the Hostage Act is not applicable outside the United States? Does the Hostage Act clearly intend to cover crimes outside the United States? Does Congress have the power to pass laws explicitly covering these crimes? (See the Note on the *Clark* case at the beginning of Section A.2 above on nationality.)

If so, is the language in the *Columba-Colella* incorrect that "Congress would not be competent to attach criminal sanctions to the murder of an American by a foreign national in a foreign country, even if the victim returned home and succumbed to this injuries."

8. See also section 1605A of the FSIA and the *Murphy* case discussed in Chapter 6.A.12. Doesn't that provision explicitly cover certain actions against Americans abroad?

9. In a 2002 case, the U.S. court of appeals affirmed the conviction of a foreign citizen who, while working as an employee aboard a foreign cruise ship, engaged in sexual contact with a 12-year-old passenger, who was an American citizen, while the ship was in Mexican territorial waters. The cruise ship departed from and returned to one of California's harbors. Upon her return, the young female victim missed several days of school and underwent psychological counseling. The defendant had argued that the United States did not have extraterritorial jurisdiction over the crime.

The applicable U.S. statute, 18 U.S.C. §2243(a), makes it a criminal offense to "knowingly engage in a sexual act with another person who has attained the age of 12 years but has not attained the age of 16 years." This statute applies in the "special maritime and territorial jurisdiction of the United States," (18 U.S.C. §2243(b) which is defined elsewhere as including, "[t]o the extent permitted by international law, any foreign vessel during a voyage having a scheduled departure from or arrival in the United States with respect to an offense committed by or against a national of the United States"[18 U.S.C. §7(8)]. The court of appeals found that international law supported extraterritorial jurisdiction in this case under the territorial principle and the passive personality principle. United States v. Neil, 312 F.3d 419 (9th Cir. 2002). What would the court's reasoning likely have been? Do you agree? (For further discussion on the law of the sea rules regarding ships, see Chapter 9.)

10. In 1992, in a law making acts of international terrorism federal crimes, Congress enacted provisions allowing U.S. nationals to recover treble damages and attorneys' fees for injury to person, property, or business by reason of an act of international terrorism. As amended, the relevant provisions read:

18 U.S.C. §2331. Definitions

As used in this chapter . . . —

(1) the term "international terrorism" means activities that—

(A) involve violent acts or acts dangerous to human life that are a violation of the criminal laws of the United States or of any State, or that would be a criminal violation if committed within the jurisdiction of the United States or of any State;

(B) appear to the intended—
(i) to intimidate or coerce a civilian population;
(ii) to influence the policy of a government by intimidation or coercion; or
(iii) to affect the conduct of a government by mass destruction, assassination, or kidnapping; and
(C) occur primarily outside the territorial jurisdiction of the United States, or transcend national boundaries in terms of the means by which they are accomplished, the persons they appear intended to intimidate or coerce, or the locale in which their perpetrators operate or seek asylum. . . .
(4) the term "act of war" means any act occurring in the course of—
(A) declared war;
(B) armed conflict, whether or not war has been declared, between two or more nations; or
(C) armed conflict between military forces of any origin;. . . .

18 U.S.C. §2333. Civil Remedies

(a) Action and jurisdiction.—Any national of the United States injured in his or her person, property, or business by reason of an act of international terrorism, or his or her estate, survivors, or heirs, may sue therefore in any appropriate district court of the United States and shall recover threefold the damages he or she sustains and the cost of the suit, including attorney's fees. . . .

18 U.S.C. §2336. Other Limitations

(a) Acts of war. No action shall be maintained under section 2333 of this title for injury or loss by reason of an act of war.

18 U.S.C. §2337. Suits against Government Officials

No action shall be maintained under section 2333 of this title against—
(1) the United States, an agency of the United States, or an officer or employee of the United States or any agency thereof acting within his or her official capacity or under color of legal authority; or
(2) a foreign state, an agency of a foreign state, or an officer or employee of a foreign state or an agency thereof acting within his or her official capacity or under color of legal authority.

(a) What theories of prescriptive jurisdiction are reflected in section 2333 above?

(b) Were the attacks of September 11, 2001, an act of international terrorism (for which a civil remedy is available under section 2333)?

(c) Do the attacks of September 11 come under the limitation for acts of war under section 2336?

(d) Note that the scope of this section 2003 has been litigated extensively, especially regarding the liability of organizations who aid and abet the direct actors. See, e.g., Boim v. Holy Land Found. for Relief and Dev., 549 F.3d 685 (7th Cir. 2008) (en banc). There, the parents of an American citizen killed in Israel allegedly by

Hamas terrorists sued various organizations who supported Hamas. (Hamas has been designated a foreign terrorist organization by the U.S. government.) Among the organizations sued were U.S.-based charitable organizations.

5. *Universal Jurisdiction*

Restatement

Section 404. Universal Jurisdiction to Define and Punish Certain Offenses

A state has jurisdiction to define and prescribe punishment for certain offenses recognized by the community of nations as of universal concern, such as piracy, slave trade, attacks on or hijacking of aircraft, genocide, war crimes, and perhaps certain acts of terrorism, even where none of the bases of jurisdiction indicated in §402 is present.

Comment

a. *Expanding class of universal offenses.* This section, and the corresponding section concerning jurisdiction to adjudicate, §423, recognize that international law permits any state to apply its laws to punish certain offenses although the state has no links of territory with the offense, or of nationality with the offender (or even the victim). Universal jurisdiction over the specified offenses is a result of universal condemnation of those activities and general interest in cooperating to suppress them, as reflected in widely-accepted international agreements and resolutions of international organizations. These offenses are subject to universal jurisdiction as a matter of customary law. Universal jurisdiction for additional offenses is provided by international agreements, but it remains to be determined whether universal jurisdiction over a particular offense has become customary law for states not party to such an agreement. A universal offense is generally not subject to limitations of time.

There has been wide condemnation of terrorism but international agreements to punish it have not . . . been widely adhered to, principally because of inability to agree on a definition of the offense. . . . Universal jurisdiction is increasingly accepted for certain acts of terrorism, such as assaults on the life or physical integrity of diplomatic personnel, kidnapping, and indiscriminate violent assaults on people at large.

b. Universal jurisdiction not limited to criminal law. In general, jurisdiction on the basis of universal interests has been exercised in the form of criminal law, but international law does not preclude the application of non-criminal law on this basis, for example, by providing a remedy in tort or restitution for victims of piracy.

Curtis A. Bradley, Universal Jurisdiction and U.S. Law

2001 U. Chi. Legal F. 323, 326-333 (2001)

There are a number of federal criminal statutes that rely, at least in part, on the universal jurisdiction concept. As one might expect, there is a federal piracy statute, which states simply that "whoever, on the high seas, commits the crime of piracy as defined by the law of nations, and is afterwards brought into or found in the United States, shall be imprisoned for life." . . .

Of more contemporary relevance are a number of terrorism and human rights-related statutes that invoke a form of universal jurisdiction. These statutes criminalize certain acts, such as hostage-taking, aircraft hijacking, and aircraft sabotage, committed outside the United States by citizens of other countries, as long as the offender is "found" within the United States. There is also a statute, enacted in 1994, that criminalizes acts of official torture committed in foreign nations by foreign citizens. . . . Perhaps surprisingly, the federal genocide statute does not assert universal jurisdiction; rather, the offense must occur in the United States or the offender must be a U.S. national. Nor does the federal war crimes statute, enacted in 1996, assert universal jurisdiction. Rather, it requires that the person committing the war crime or the victim of the war crime be a member of the U.S. armed forces or a U.S. national.

In considering Congress's reliance on universal jurisdiction, another relevant statute is the Maritime Drug Law Enforcement Act, which comes close to asserting universal jurisdiction and which has generated a number of decisions addressing Congress's authority to regulate extraterritoriality. The Act makes it "unlawful for any person . . . on board a vessel subject to the jurisdiction of the United States . . . to possess with intent to manufacture or distribute, a controlled substance." The Act includes in its definition of a "vessel subject to the jurisdiction of the United States" both "a vessel without nationality" and "a vessel registered to a foreign nation where the flag nation has consented or waived objection to the enforcement of United States law by the United States." There is no express requirement in these situations of a nexus with the United States, and most courts have declined to read such a requirement into the statute. . . .

. . . Ultimately . . . the exercise of prescriptive jurisdiction by the United States is determined by Congress, not international law or the federal courts. This is so for several reasons.

First, since the early 1800s, it has been settled in the United States that there is no federal common law of crimes. Rather, federal criminal liability can be created in the United States only by a domestic enactment. . . . Nor, as a matter of public policy, will U.S. courts apply foreign criminal law.

Second, courts and scholars have long assumed that, for separation-of-powers and accountability reasons, treaties may not create domestic criminal liability. Thus, even when a treaty calls for the criminalization of conduct or for the exercise of jurisdiction over offenders, the treaty does not by itself create criminal liability under U.S. law. The treaty provisions, in other words, are "non-self-executing" and take effect domestically only when Congress implements them. As a result, a treaty granting universal jurisdiction to prosecute certain crimes does not by itself allow such prosecutions in the United States.

Finally, U.S. law has long allowed federal statutes to supersede earlier inconsistent international law. The Supreme Court has held that when there is a conflict between a federal statute and a treaty, the later in time prevails as a matter of U.S. law. And the lower courts uniformly have held that when there is a conflict between a federal statute and customary international law, the statute prevails, apparently without regard to timing. As a result, Congress is free to override the limitations of international law, including the international law of prescriptive jurisdiction, when enacting a criminal statute. . . .

Despite Congress's control over U.S. exercises of universal jurisdiction, the international law of universal jurisdiction may be relevant to the interpretation of federal criminal statutes. Under the *Charming Betsy* canon of constructions, courts attempt to construe federal statutes, where reasonably possible, so that they do not violate international law. For a variety of reasons, including a desire to avoid conflicts with international law, courts also generally presume that federal statutes do not apply extraterritorially.

The influence of these interpretive rules should not be overstated. The *Charming Betsy* canon does not apply when the reach of a statute is clear. As one court explained in rejecting a prescriptive jurisdiction challenge to a broad anti-terrorism statute, "our duty is to enforce the Constitution, laws, and treaties of the United States, not to conform the law of the land to norms of customary international law." Nor does the *Charming Betsy* canon require the harmonization of U.S. law and international law; it requires simply the avoidance of conflict. As a result, it is not a mandate for extending a statute to the fullest reaches allowed by the international law of universal jurisdiction. In addition, courts are likely to give deference to the views of the executive branch regarding the content of international law.

As for the presumption against extraterritoriality, its effect is limited because it is not applied to all federal statutes. The Supreme Court has not applied it, for example, in the area of antitrust law. More importantly, the Court suggested, in United States v. Bowman, [260 U.S. 94 (1922)], that the presumption against extraterritoriality does not apply to criminal statutes that are, by their nature, focused on extraterritorial matters. As the Court explained, some criminal statutes "are, as a class, not logically dependent on their locality for the government's jurisdiction, but are enacted because of the right of the government to defend itself against obstruction, or fraud wherever perpetrated."[Id. at 98.] Exercises of universal criminal jurisdiction may be especially likely to fall within this exception. Indeed, the district court in [United States v. Bin Laden, 92 F. Supp. 2d 189 (S.D.N.Y. 2000)] relied on this exception as a basis for upholding many of the [criminal charges for 1998 bombings of U.S. embassies in Kenya and Tanzania]. In any event, the presumption against extraterritoriality, like the *Charming Betsy* canon, can be overcome by clear legislative intent. . . .

Notes and Questions

1. In listing the offenses of "universal concern," the Restatement, published in 1987, listed "piracy, slave trade, attacks on or hijacking of aircraft, genocide, war crimes, and perhaps certain acts of terrorism." Section 404. Now, over 20 years later, do you think that "[u]niversal condemnation of those activities and general interest in cooperating to suppress them, as reflected in widely-accepted international agreements and resolutions of international organizations" (id. at cmt. *a*), mean that the "perhaps" can be dropped from the Restatement's statement? Should more acts of terrorism be subject to the principle of universal jurisdiction—e.g., large-scale killing of civilians?

2. Should murder, rape, torture, and/or robbery be included as universal crimes? Why or why not? Could an expansion of universal jurisdiction to such crimes

come into conflict with principles of state sovereignty? If these crimes are not considered universal crimes, can they not still be embodied in national laws and supported, as appropriate, by other principles of jurisdiction — both on a national and an international level?

3. Does the principle of universal jurisdiction extend to support Israel's prosecution of German Nazi officials, such as Adolph Eichmann, who committed war crimes during World War II, even though those crimes were committed at a time when the state of Israel did not yet exist? (Israel became a state in 1948; Germany surrendered in 1945.) See Attorney General of Israel v. Eichmann, 36 Int'l L. Rep. 277, 298-304 (Sup. Ct. Israel 1962).

4. Universal jurisdiction exists or has existed in some European countries' laws. Pursuant to a universal jurisdiction statute, Spain sought to try Augusto Pinochet, former President of Chile, for human rights crimes he allegedly committed in Chile. Spain's unsuccessful efforts to extradite Pinochet from England are discussed in Chapter 6. From 1993 to 2003, Belgium had a law allowing for universal jurisdiction for certain major violations of international law. The law was the basis for the convictions in Belgium of four Rwandans for genocide in Rwanda. Other attempts to use the law to try current and former foreign officials led to international litigation and diplomatic protests from other countries. See the discussion in Chapter 6 of the ICJ decision that Belgium could not arrest and prosecute Congo's Minister for Foreign Affairs because customary international law made him immune.

In response to the growing controversy concerning its universal jurisdiction statute, Belgium adopted restricting amendments to the statute in May 2003 to allow the Belgian prosecutor and courts to dismiss cases when the act did not occur on Belgian territory, the alleged offender is not Belgian nor found on Belgian territory, and the victim is not Belgian or has not resided on Belgian territory in the last three years. The amendment also gives the Belgian government the authority to reject cases in situations, among others, where the accused person is a national of a country with courts that are "competent, independent, impartial and fair."

Although Belgium has limited the scope of its universal jurisdiction law, some other countries continue to conduct criminal prosecutions of non-nationals for crimes committed against non-nationals outside their territory on the basis of universal jurisdiction. See the reference in Note 10 of Chapter 8.B.8.d to prosecutions for genocide, torture, and war crimes in countries such as Canada, France, and the Netherlands.

5. Besides the U.S. laws mentioned in the Bradley excerpt above, the Alien Tort Statute (ATS) is one often-used federal law, pursuant to which many cases have involved conduct and parties with no connection to the United States at the time of the challenged activities. E.g., Filartiga v. Pena-Irala, 630 F.2d 876 (2d Cir. 1980); Kadic v. Karadzic, 70 F.3d 232 (2d Cir. 1995); see Sarei v. Rio Tinto, 550 F.3d 822, 831 (9th Cir. 2008); see Chapter 3.C regarding the ATS generally. The fact that this law is sometimes "an exercise in universal jurisdiction [has] received little consideration in the cases." Donald Francis Donovan and Anthea Roberts, Note and Comment: The Emerging Recognition of Universal Civil Jurisdiction, Am. J. Int'l L. 142, 146 (2006).

6. A recent, careful analysis of universal civil jurisdiction around the world noted that no other states have enacted equivalents to the ATS. However, the authors observed that "case law and commentary on universal civil jurisdiction are beginning to emerge outside the United States." Id. at 149.

B. JURISDICTION TO ENFORCE AND ADJUDICATE PUBLIC LAW

1. Jurisdiction to Enforce

Just because a state's statute is legitimately applicable (on one of the grounds described in Section A above) to a particular person or act, it does not follow that the state may take any action it wants to enforce that law. For example, transborder abductions by a foreign state's agents are rare and generate unfavorable public and diplomatic reactions. And a U.S. federal district court may not be able to subpoena all the evidence it believes it needs in a particular case where that evidence is located abroad. Enforcement jurisdiction is said to be territorial, and the limits seem much more strictly observed than with prescriptive jurisdiction. There are also limits on the power of courts or agencies to serve process across national boundaries as well. The limits may be set by international law, constitutional law, statute, or regulation. The Restatement summarizes its view of the international law rules:

Restatement

Section 431. Jurisdiction to Enforce

(1) A state may employ judicial or nonjudicial measures to induce or compel compliance or punish noncompliance with its laws or regulations, provided it has jurisdiction to prescribe in accordance with §§402 and 403.

(2) Enforcement measures must be reasonably related to the laws or regulations to which they are directed; punishment for noncompliance must be preceded by an appropriate determination of violation and must be proportional to the gravity of the violation.

(3) A state may employ enforcement measures against a person located outside its territory

(a) if the person is given notice of the claims or charges against him that is reasonable in the circumstances;

(b) if the person is given an opportunity to be heard, ordinarily in advance of enforcement, whether in person or by counsel or other representative; and

(c) when enforcement is through the courts, if the state has jurisdiction to adjudicate.

Comment

a. Relation of jurisdiction to enforce to jurisdiction to prescribe and to adjudicate. Under international law, a state may not exercise authority to enforce law that it has no jurisdiction to prescribe. Such assertion of jurisdiction, whether carried out through the courts or by nonjudicial means, may be objected to by both the affected person directly and by the other state concerned. A state that has jurisdiction to prescribe may enforce its law through its courts if it also has jurisdiction to adjudicate, but the fact that it cannot effectively exercise judicial jurisdiction with respect to a person does not preclude enforcement through nonjudicial means, such as those illustrated in Comment *c.* A state that does not have jurisdiction to prescribe is not barred from cooperating in law enforcement by appropriate means with a state that has jurisdiction to prescribe. . . .

b. Judicial enforcement measures. For purposes of this section, judicial enforcement measures include the imposition of criminal sanctions, such as fines and imprisonment, as well as other measures that may be ordered by a court in connection with a judicial proceeding, whether civil, criminal, or administrative, such as an order to produce a document, or a sanction for failure to comply with such an order. A judgment or decree ordering a person to do (or to refrain from doing) an act may have aspects both of prescription and of enforcement. Some measures taken by executive agencies subject to judicial confirmation or annulment, such as seizure of goods by the customs service, freezing of assets by revenue authorities, or execution of a warrant for arrest, have aspects of both judicial and nonjudicial enforcement. A judgment of a court awarding or denying damages in a civil action would generally not be seen as enforcement.

c. Nonjudicial enforcement measures. For purposes of this section, enforcement measures comprise not only the orders of a court, such as those mentioned in Comment b, but also measures such as the following, when used to induce compliance with or as sanctions for violation of laws or regulations of the enforcing state:

— denial of the right to engage in export or import transactions;

— removal from a list of persons eligible to bid on government contracts;

— suspension, revocation, or denial of a permit to engage in particular business activity;

— prohibition of the transfer of assets;

and comparable denial of opportunities normally open to the person against whom enforcement is directed.

This section deals with the imposition of executive, administrative, or police sanctions against persons for violations of law, and is concerned with decisions by officials applying legal standards, both in determining that a violation has occurred and in pursuing procedures leading to the imposition of sanctions. It is not concerned with measures of state policy denying benefits to another state nor with application of general rules, such as a law that refuses entry visas to persons convicted of specified crimes in other states. Imposition of an embargo on trade with a foreign state is not within this section; placing an individual on an export blacklist as a sanction for violation of a law or regulation is an assertion of jurisdiction to enforce covered by this section.

d. Reasonableness as limitation on enforcement jurisdiction. Under Subsection (1), any exercise of jurisdiction to enforce is subject to the principle of reasonableness. For example, it might be reasonable for the United Slates to deny to a foreign company export privileges, i.e., the right to participate in transactions involving export of United States goods, because the company had knowingly reexported a strategic product of United States origin to country X in violation of United States law. It normally would be unreasonable for the United States to deny such export privileges to the same firm simply because it traded with country X in goods not of United States origin, since ordinarily the United States would not have jurisdiction to prescribe with respect to such trade.

There may be a greater limitation on the exercise of jurisdiction to enforce in respect of activity in another state than there is with respect to activity on the high seas.

e. Nonjudicial enforcement measures and fair procedure. Nonjudicial enforcement measures, such as those listed in Comment c, need not meet all the requirements associated with exercise of criminal jurisdiction, but exercise of nonjudicial enforcement jurisdiction is consistent with international law only if it is not arbitrary. The procedures associated with measures of nonjudicial enforcement need not parallel in all respects procedures in courts, but Subsection (3) requires that basic elements of fairness be observed. . . .

Section 432. Measures in Aid of Enforcement of Criminal Law

. . . (2) A state's law enforcement officers may exercise their functions in the territory of another state only with the consent of the other state, given by duly authorized officials of that state.

Comment . . .

b. Territoriality and law enforcement. It is universally recognized, as a corollary of state sovereignty, that officials of one state may not exercise their functions in the territory of another state without the latter's consent. Thus, while a state may take certain measures of nonjudicial enforcement against a person in another state, §431, its law enforcement officers cannot arrest him in another state, and can engage in criminal investigation in that state only with that state's consent. Within a state's own territory, the rules governing arrest and other steps in criminal law enforcement generally apply regardless of the nationality, residence, or domicile of the person accused or investigated, subject only to defined exceptions for persons enjoying diplomatic or consular immunity and to the obligation to observe basic human rights.

c. Consequences of violation of territorial limits of law enforcement. If a state's law enforcement officials exercise their functions in the territory of another state without the latter's consent, that state is entitled to protest and, in appropriate cases, to receive reparation from the offending state. If the unauthorized action includes abduction of a person, the state from which the person was abducted may demand return of the person, and international law requires that he be returned. . . .

Section 433. External Measures in Aid of Enforcement of Criminal Law: Law of the United States

(1) Law enforcement officers of the United States may exercise their functions in the territory of another state only

(a) with the consent of the other state and if duly authorized by the United States;

and

(b) in compliance with the laws both of the United States and of the other state.

One common way that countries cooperate to enforce domestic laws in criminal matters is through extradition. This involves country A sending a person X to country B when X is wanted for trial in country B or has already been convicted of a crime in country B. This process is almost always governed by extradition treaties between the two countries and is discussed in some detail in Chapter 12.A.

. . . Occasionally, though, a state or some of its citizens may undertake to enforce its laws through direct action in the territory of another state. One situation that caused considerable controversy between Mexico and the United States in the 1990s was the abduction of a Mexican doctor, Humberto Alvarez-Machain, from his office in Guadalajara, Mexico, by other Mexicans who had been encouraged to do this by U.S. Drug Enforcement Agency (DEA) officials. The DEA officials believed that Alvarez-Machain had been present during the torture of a DEA agent in Mexico and had acted to prolong the agent's life in order to extend the interrogation.

The situation led to two U.S. Supreme Court cases. In the first case, United States v. Alvarez-Machain, 504 U.S. 55 (1992) (*Alvarez-Machain*), Alvarez-Machain had moved to dismiss the indictment against him, claiming that the U.S. district court lacked jurisdiction to try him because his abduction was in violation of the extradition treaty between the United States and Mexico, and that the abduction constituted "outrageous governmental conduct."

There was a detailed extradition treaty between Mexico and the United States, which the U.S government had not chosen to use. In a sharply divided 6-3 decision by the U.S. Supreme Court, the majority opinion (written by Chief Justice Rehnquist) concluded that the treaty was not the exclusive means for one of the countries to gain custody of a national of the other country for purposes of prosecution and that forcible abductions outside the treaty were not a treaty violation.

The majority concluded:

> Respondent and his amici may be correct that respondent's abduction may be in violation of general international law principles. Mexico has protested the abduction through diplomatic notes, and the decision of whether respondent should be returned to Mexico, as a matter outside of the Treaty, is a matter for the Executive Branch. We conclude, however, that the respondent's abduction was not in violation of the Extradition Treaty between the United States and Mexico, and therefore the rule of Ker v. Illinois [119 U.S. 436 (1886)] is fully applicable in the case. [*Ker* had held that "forcible abduction is no sufficient reason why the party should not answer when brought within the jurisdiction of the court which has the right to try him for such an offence."] The fact of respondent's forcible abduction does not therefore prohibit his trial in a court in the United States for violations of the criminal laws of the United States.

The dissent, authored by Justice Stevens, concluded that the extradition treaty "on its face appears to have been intended to set forth comprehensive and exclusive rules concerning the subject of extradition." The dissent also averred that:

> A critical flaw pervades the Court's entire opinion. It fails to differentiate between the conduct of private citizens, which does not violate any treaty obligation, and conduct expressly authorized by the Executive Branch of the Government, which unquestionably constitutes a flagrant violation of international law, and in my opinion, also constitutes a breach of our treaty obligations.

Notes and Questions

1. What, if any, principle of prescriptive jurisdiction could the United States cite that indicated the United States had jurisdiction over Alvarez-Machain for his alleged

activities in Mexico? If the United States had a basis for asserting jurisdiction in international law, what (if any) other international norms were in dispute in this case?

2. What does it seem are the "general principles of international law principles" referred to near the end of the majority opinion? Why did the Court not apply them? Is this a case where the Executive Branch had acted? (See discussion of customary law in U.S. courts in Chapter 3.C.)

3. What advice would you give Mexico as to its remedies following the *Alvarez-Machain* decision?'

4. Alan J. Kreczko, the Deputy Legal Adviser of the Department of State, testified to a House Judiciary Subcommittee in 1992:

Reactions of Foreign Governments

The Supreme Court's decision has caused considerable concern among a wide range of governments, particularly in the Americas, but elsewhere as well. Many governments have expressed outrage that the United States believes it has the right to decide unilaterally to enter their territory and abduct one of their nationals. Governments have informed us that they would regard such action as a breach of international law. They have also informed us that they would protect their nationals from such action, that such action would violate their domestic law, and that they would vigorously prosecute such violations. Some countries, as well, have told us that they believe that such actions would violate our extradition treaties with them. Some have also suggested that they will challenge the lawfulness of such abductions in international forums. Some have indicated that the decision could affect their parliaments' review of pending law enforcement agreements with the United States. At the same time, some have noted in private that the decision will cause narcotics traffickers to have an increased fear of apprehension by the United States. . . .

The U.S. government has moved actively to isolate the question of whether domestic legal authority exists from the separate question of whether the President will, in fact, exercise that authority. We have reassured other countries that the United States has not changed its policies toward cooperation in international law enforcement, and that the *Alvarez-Machain* case does not represent a "green light" for the United States to conduct operations on foreign territory.

Specifically, immediately following the Supreme Court's decision, the White House issued a public statement reaffirming that:

> . . . The United States strongly believes in fostering respect for international rules of law, including, in particular, the principles of respect for territorial integrity and sovereign equality of states. U.S. policy is to cooperate with foreign states in achieving law enforcement objectives. Neither the arrest of Alvarez-Machain, nor the . . . Supreme Court decision reflects any change in this policy. . . .

At the same time, we are not prepared categorically to rule out unilateral action. It is not inconceivable that in certain extreme cases, such as the harboring by a hostile foreign country of a terrorist who has attacked U.S. nationals and is likely to do so again, the President might decide that such an abduction is necessary and appropriate as a matter of the exercise of our right of self-defense. . . . The Administration has in place procedures designed to ensure that U.S. law enforcement activities overseas fully take into account foreign relations and international law. These procedures require that decisions as to extraordinary renditions from foreign territories be subject to full inter-agency coordination and that they be considered at the highest levels of the government. . . .

In the aftermath of the *Alvarez-Machain* decision, the Mexican Foreign Minister gave a press conference with the following highlights:

- Mexico repudiates as invalid and illegal the decision of the Supreme Court;
- Mexico will consider as a criminal act any attempt by foreign persons or governments to apprehend in Mexican territory any person suspected of a crime; . . .
- Mexico declares that the only legal means for moving persons from one nation to face trial in another are treaties and mechanisms of extradition established under international law; . . .

Mexico sought assurances that further abductions will not take place on Mexican territory and stated that collaboration by Mexicans with foreign governments in criminal acts that violate Mexican sovereignty would be classified as acts of treason against Mexico.

The United States has responded to these Mexican concerns as follows:

- President Bush sent a letter to President Salinas containing unequivocal assurances that his Administration will "neither conduct, encourage nor condone" such trans-border abductions from Mexico.
- The two governments agreed to review the U.S.-Mexico Extradition Treaty. . . .
- There was an exchange of letters between Secretary Baker and Foreign Secretary Solana of Mexico recognizing that trans-border abductions by so-called "bounty hunters" and other private individuals will be considered extraditable offenses by both nations. . . .

[3 U.S. Dept. of State Dispatch 614 (1992).]

5. As noted in the Kreczko testimony above, the United States and Mexico agreed to review their extradition treaty to address Mexico's concerns about such trans-border abductions. In 1994, the Clinton Administration negotiated with Mexico a modification to the bilateral extradition treaty that would explicitly forbid "trans-border abductions" such as the Alvarez-Machain kidnapping. For reasons that are unclear, the treaty amendment was never submitted to the Senate for its advice and consent.

6. After the Supreme Court's ruling in *Alvarez-Machain*, the case was remanded to the district court for a judgment on the merits. Ironically, the case was dismissed for lack of evidence on December 14, 1992. The district judge said the prosecution's case was nothing but the "wildest speculation" that failed to support the charge that Alvarez had participated in the U.S. DEA agent's torture and death. (An informant indicated that a different doctor may have been the culprit.) Alvarez returned to his home in Guadalajara a few days later after having been imprisoned for two and a half years.

Apparently having learned about U.S. law and litigation during his time in U.S. custody, Alvarez then brought a civil damage action under the Federal Tort Claims Act (FTCA) and the Alien Tort Statute (ATS) against the United States, several DEA agents, and several Mexican citizens. He alleged that he had been kidnapped, tortured, and wrongfully imprisoned. In another U.S. Supreme Court decision, the Court dismissed the case. Sosa v. Alvarez-Machain, 542 U.S. 692 (2004). The case is excerpted and analyzed in Chapter 3.C.

7. Even after the *Alvarez-Machain* case, where the defendant was abducted and brought to the United States by foreigners, there still might be a possible "outrageous conduct" limitation on actions by U.S. agents. A 1974 U.S. court of appeals decision held that a federal court must "divest itself of jurisdiction over the person

of a defendant where it had been acquired as a result of the Government's deliberate, unnecessary, and unreasonable invasion" of the accused's constitutional rights. In that case, the defendant alleged that the U.S. court had acquired jurisdiction over him through the actions of U.S. agents, who had kidnapped him in Uruguay, used electronic surveillance and torture, and then brought him to the United States for prosecution. United States v. Toscanino, 500 F.2d 267 (2d Cir), *reh'g denied,* 504 F.2d 1380 (2d Cir.1974); see M. Cherif Bassiouni, International Extradition: United States Law and Practice 273-347 (5th ed. 2007).

8. Turning the clock back to before the 1990 seizure of Alvarez-Machain and the Supreme Court's decision in 1992, the U.S. government had formally determined in 1989 that it was legally permissible for its law enforcement agencies, such as the FBI and DEA, to apprehend individuals who are accused of violating U.S. criminal law in foreign states without the consent of the foreign state in which they are apprehended.

Shortly after the U.S. policy to apprehend individuals abroad appeared in the news, Iran reacted. Members of the Iranian Parliament passed a draft law giving the president of Iran the right to arrest anywhere Americans who take action against Iranian citizens or property anywhere in the world and bring them to Iran for trial. The bill provided that the U.S. citizen would be tried by Iranian courts under Islamic law.

The bill "aims at preserving the prestige and territorial integrity of the Islamic Republic, safeguarding the lives and properties of Iranian nationals abroad and defending the interests of the Islamic Republic."

The Iranian representatives who introduced the bill said it was in response to the U.S. policy and said that they wanted the Iranian law to remain in force for as long as the U.S. law. If you support the 1989 U.S. policy, should the Iranians be allowed a similar policy? It would presumably include seizing U.S. citizens in, say, Chicago for alleged acts against Iranians and spiriting the U.S. citizens back to Iran for trial. If Iran should not be allowed a similar policy as the United States, how does one distinguish between the rights of the two countries? Is the possibility of such reciprocal response by other states a good reason for the United States to curtail its own claims about seizing individuals abroad?

9. In 2003, an Iranian court in Tehran awarded over $100 million in damages to Hossein Alikhani, an Iranian businessman, for his suit against the United States over his 1992 abduction and detention by U.S. Customs agents. Posing as operators of a fishing trip, the agents lured Alikhani onto a private jet in the Bahamas and flew him to Florida for interrogation, which he claimed involved battery and abuse, and then time in jail. Alikhani allegedly had purchased $1.6 million of spare parts for gas generators from a Florida company and planned to ship them through Germany for use in a Libyan government oil field in Libya, which the U.S. government said was a violation of U.S. economic sanctions against Libya. After pleading guilty to a minor charge and being released, Alikhani sued the U.S. government in the Iranian court.

10. After 2001, CIA operatives have allegedly kidnapped terrorist suspects in Italy and elsewhere. The suspects were not being brought to trial, like Alvarez-Machain, but were kept in U.S.-controlled detention facilities abroad or handed over to other countries for interrogation. These abductions led to criminal indictments against the alleged CIA operatives by Italian and German prosecutors. In Italy, a court convicted in absentia 22 CIA operatives and a U.S. Air Force colonel for kidnapping a Muslim cleric off the street in Milan in 2003 and flying him to

Cairo, Egypt, where he was turned over to Egyptian authorities. The defendants in Italy were each sentenced to five years in prison, except for the CIA's former station chief, who received an eight-year sentence. None of the Americans, who were out of the country, have been imprisoned by the Italian authorities. (See also the discussion about foreign renditions and detentions in Chapter 3.B.4.) What should be the appropriate international standard, if any, for another country's agents kidnapping terrorist suspects from a host country? Should it matter whether the host country's intelligence or law enforcement services are informed in advance? Should their permission be required? Should it matter if the abduction is for criminal or simply interrogation purposes?

11. In spite of the incidents above, trans-boundary abductions of those who are suspected of violating a state's laws remain an exceptional means of trying to bring a person before the state's courts or otherwise punishing noncompliance with the law. States have instead developed extensive arrangements, including mutual legal assistance and extradition treaties, to cooperate in the enforcement of laws against crimes with a transnational dimension or against alleged criminal perpetrators who are not within the state's territory. For example, hundreds of alleged criminals are extradited to and from the United States every year. Mutual legal assistance and extradition treaties are discussed in Chapter 12 on international criminal law.

2. *Jurisdiction to Adjudicate*

As you recall, the Restatement asserts that there are limits imposed by customary international law on the right of a state to apply its law (§403). The Restatement also asserts that there are limits on the power of a court to extend its authority abroad:

Restatement

Section 421. Jurisdiction to Adjudicate

(1) A state may exercise jurisdiction through its courts to adjudicate with respect to a person or thing if the relationship of the state to the person or thing is such as to make the exercise of jurisdiction reasonable.

(2) In general, a state's exercise of jurisdiction to adjudicate with respect to a person or thing is reasonable if, at the time jurisdiction is asserted:

(a) the person or thing is present in the territory of the state, other than transitorily;

(b) the person, if a natural person, is domiciled in the state;

(c) the person, if a natural person, is resident in the state;

(d) the person, if a natural person, is a national of the state;

(e) the person, if a corporation or comparable juridical person, is organized pursuant to the law of the state;

(f) a ship, aircraft or other vehicle to which the adjudication relates is registered under the laws of the state;

(g) the person, whether natural or juridical, has consented to the exercise of jurisdiction;

(h) the person, whether natural or juridical, regularly carries on business in the state;

(i) the person, whether natural or juridical, had carried on activity in the state, but only in respect of such activity;

(j) the person, whether natural or juridical, had carried on outside the state an activity having a substantial, direct, and foreseeable effect within the state, but only in respect of such activity; or

(k) the thing that is the subject of adjudication is owned, possessed, or used in the state, but only in respect of a claim reasonably connected with that thing.

(3) A defense of lack of jurisdiction is generally waived by any appearance by or on behalf of a person or thing (whether as plaintiff, defendant, or third party), if the appearance is for a purpose that does not include a challenge to the exercise of jurisdiction.

Notes and Questions

1. The factors are largely drawn from the due process jurisprudence of U.S. constitutional law, except that the Restatement seems to disallow "tag" jurisdiction (i.e., basing jurisdiction on the transitory presence of the defendant). Other states may recognize different tests for adjudicatory jurisdiction, such as the principal place of management of a corporation. Are the problems that could result from an expansive extraterritorial extension of adjudicative jurisdiction by the United States likely to be as severe as those encountered in a broad prescriptive extension of securities or antitrust law?

2. Even when jurisdiction to adjudicate might be reasonable as a matter of due process, there are some reasons why a U.S. court might choose not to exercise its jurisdiction. Among these are the doctrines of *comity, forum non conveniens,* and the rule of customary international law that a litigant must *exhaust the available remedies* provided by the local (or host) state before he may bring suit in a foreign or international court.

The doctrine of *comity* permits a court to decline to exercise jurisdiction in certain circumstances in deference to the laws and interests of a foreign country. Declining jurisdiction under this doctrine is not obligatory, and the question does not arise until the court has already established that it has subject matter and personal jurisdiction. See the discussion above concerning Restatement section 403, *Hartford Fire Insurance,* and *Empagran.*

A similar but distinct doctrine is *forum non conveniens,* which permits a court to dismiss a case where an adequate, alternative forum exists and public and private interests favor having the trial in that forum. Forum non conveniens is available only where the alternate forum provides a real opportunity to be heard, and only in certain circumstances. It is for the court to weigh the factors for and against dismissal and it is within the judge's discretion to deny the motion.

The threshold inquiry of a forum non conveniens analysis is to determine whether the alternate forum is adequate. This includes (1) whether the defendant is amenable to process in the alternate forum, and (2) whether the subject matter of the lawsuit is cognizable there, so as to afford the plaintiff the possibility of relief. The first element is sometimes met by making the dismissal contingent on the defendant's consent to jurisdiction in the alternate forum. The second depends on both the law and procedural safeguards of the alternate forum and the adequacy of the remedy available — although the remedy need not be identical to that available in the U.S. system.

If the court determines that the alternate forum is adequate, it must then balance the public and private interests of trying the case in each forum. Factors to consider are the ease of access to evidence in each forum, the ability to obtain witnesses, the enforceability of a judgment rendered, the interest of each forum in hearing the case and in not filling its docket with unrelated cases, and the interest in having a forum apply its own law where possible. None of these factors is dispositive, but the presumption in U.S. courts is in favor of the plaintiff's choice of forum where that forum is reasonable. In practice, however, the imprecision of the above analysis means that use of the doctrine varies widely from court to court. See, for example, Piper Aircraft Co. v. Reyno, 454 U.S. 235 (1981); In re Union Carbide Corp. Gas Plant Disaster at Bhopal, India, 809 F.2d 195 (2d Cir.), *cert. denied,* 484 U.S. 871 (1987) (affirming dismissal of personal injury claims from industrial disaster in Bhopal, India because India was the more appropriate forum to litigate such claims); Chang v. Baxter Healthcare Corp. 599 F.3d 728 (7th Cir. 2010) (affirming dismissal on forum non conveniens grounds of some of the contract and tort claims of Taiwanese citizens against California manufacturers alleging that the plaintiffs had been infected with the manufacturers' HIV-contaminated blood-clotting factors); but see Wiwa v. Royal Dutch Petroleum Co., 226 F.3d 88 (2nd Cir. 2000), *cert. denied,* 532 U.S. 941 (2001) (reversing district court's forum non conveniens dismissal of a Torture Victim Protection Act case where many of the events had occurred in Nigeria, in part because two of the plaintiffs were U.S. residents and because the TVPA's policies favor U.S. jurisdiction).

A third doctrine that might sometimes be applicable is *exhaustion of local remedies.* It has been described as a domestic prudential standard or a principle of international law. Essentially, it provides in certain situations that a court or international tribunal should not hear a case unless the plaintiff has exhausted its possible remedies available in the local forum. This includes bringing any action authorized by local law and may include nonjudicial remedies. A court may dismiss an action for lack of jurisdiction where the plaintiff has failed to do so. However, a plaintiff is not obligated to pursue remedies where "such remedies are clearly sham or inadequate, or their application is unreasonably prolonged." (Restatement, at section 713, cmt. f. and section 703, cmt. d.; see also Ian Brownlie, Principles of Public International Law 492-501 (7th ed. 2008); Malcolm Shaw, International Law 819-822 (6th ed. 2008).

International court and arbitral decisions have regularly supported the principle of exhaustion of local remedies. As summarized in the Restatement (Third), at §713, Reporters' Notes:

> 5. *Exhaustion of domestic remedies.* In the Interhandel Case (Switzerland v. United States), [1959], I.CJ. Rep. 6, 26-27, the International Court of Justice noted that "[t]he rule that local remedies must be exhausted before international proceedings may be instituted is a well-established rule of customary international law." . . . The Court added that "[b]efore resort may be had to an international court in such a situation, it has been considered necessary that the State where the violation occurred should have an opportunity to redress it by its own means, within the framework of its own domestic legal system."

In that case, the United States had vested the assets of Interhandel during the Second World War, claiming that Interhandel, though incorporated in Switzerland, was controlled by a German company and therefore could properly be considered an enemy alien. Interhandel brought suit in the United States district court in 1946 to recover its assets; a judgment dismissing Interhandel's suit was affirmed in the court of appeals. While a petition for certiorari by Interhandel was pending before the United States Supreme Court in 1959, Switzerland brought a proceeding against the United States in the International Court of Justice.

The Supreme Court of the United States granted Interhandel's petition for certiorari and reversed and remanded the case to the district court. . . . The International Court of Justice dismissed the proceeding before it. The Court said that the exhaustion of local remedies must be observed *a fortiori* when the domestic proceedings are still pending, especially when both the domestic and the international actions are designed to obtain the same result, i.e., the restitution of Interhandel's assets.

As was stated in the Ambatielos Case (Greece v. United Kingdom), 1951, 12 R. Int'l Arb. Awards 91, 120, 122, the phrase "local remedies" should be interpreted broadly, including "the whole system of legal protection, as provided by municipal law," not only the courts and tribunals but also "the use of procedural facilities which municipal law makes available to litigants." There, the claimant lost the case in the lower court because he failed to call a crucial witness, and the Court of Appeals refused "to give leave to adduce [this] evidence." The tribunal held that the claimant had failed to exhaust local remedies, as it was due to his own action that the appeal became futile.

A more recent decision by the International Court of Justice (ICJ or Court), again involving the United States, reaffirmed the rule of exhaustion of local remedies. In Case Concerning Elettronica Sicula S.p.A. (ELSI) (United States of America v. Italy), 1989 I.CJ. 15, the United States instituted proceedings against Italy, alleging that the requisition by the Government of Italy of the plant and related assets of ELSI, a wholly owned subsidiary of a U.S. company (Raytheon), was a violation of a treaty and agreement between the two countries. Prior to concluding on the merits that Italy's actions did not constitute breaches of the treaty or agreement, the Court considered Italy's contention that Raytheon had failed to exhaust its local remedies in Italy. The Court found that the trustee in bankruptcy for ELSI brought a suit against Italian officials in the Court of Palermo, Italy, then the trustee appealed to the Court of Appeal of Palermo, and then appealed to the Court of Cassation which upheld the decision of the Court of Appeal. (Id. at para. 57.) The Court concluded that "Italy has not been able to satisfy the Chamber [of the ICJ] that there clearly remained some remedy which Raytheon . . . ought to have pursued and exhausted." (Id. at para. 63.)

The U.S. Supreme Court has acknowledged the doctrine in a recent major case. In Sosa v. Alvarez-Machain, 542 U.S. 692, 733 n.21 (2004), the majority observed that the European Commission had argued as *amicus curiae* that: "[B]asic principles of international law require that before asserting a claim in a foreign forum, the claimant must have exhausted any remedies available in the domestic legal system, and perhaps in other for a such as international claims tribunals. . . . [C]f. Torture Victim Protection Act of 1991 . . . (exhaustion requirement). We [the Supreme Court] would certainly consider this requirement in an appropriate case." . . . U.S. courts have on occasion required exhaustion of local remedies, either as a rule of customary international law or a domestic prudential consideration. Examples include

Millicom International Cellular v. Republic of Costa Rica, 995 F. Supp. 14, 23 (D.D.C. 1998) (action by three foreign corporations against Costa Rica for alleged unlawful competitive activity; the court cited, among other authorities, *Interhandel*); Greenpeace, Inc. (USA) v. State of France, 916 F. Supp. 773, 783 (C.D. Cal. 1996) (suit by U.S. entities and nationals, among others, against France for seizure of vessels which allegedly constituted a taking or expropriation; the court cited *Interhandel*).

In a recent Ninth Circuit case, former and present residents of Papua New Guinea sued Rio Tinto, a major foreign mining company with subsidiaries in the United States, under the Alien Tort Statute (ATS). Plaintiffs alleged various violations of customary international law, in part because of Rio Tinto's activities with the Papua New Guinea government. In the prolonged ATS litigation, the question arose whether exhaustion of local remedies was required under the ATS. In her plurality opinion for the en banc Court of Appeals, Judge McKeown held that this was an "appropriate case for such consideration under both domestic prudential standards and core principles of international law." Rio Tinto, supra, 550 F.3d at 827. On remand, the district court held that it was inappropriate to impose a prudential exhaustion requirement for certain claims and allowed the plaintiffs to file other claims again and undergo the traditional exhaustion analysis. Sarei v. Rio Tinto, 650 F. Supp. 2d 1004, 1032 (C.D. Ca. 2009).

3. It is important to distinguish between the assertion by a court of its jurisdiction over a person and the application of the forum's law (state or federal) to the dispute. It may be less offensive to hale a Swiss defendant into court if the court applies Swiss law to the case.

4. What are some of the reasons that a foreign plaintiff might prefer to bring a civil action (e.g., under the Alien Tort Statute) in U.S. courts, rather than in a foreign court? The availability of extensive discovery procedures? The possibility of punitive damages (which are not generally allowed in other countries)? The fact that, unlike in many jurisdictions, the losing party is not required to pay the attorneys' fees? The possibility of class actions, which are unusual in most other jurisdictions? A U.S. court system that is generally free of corruption? Conversely, why would a foreign defendant prefer not to face a lawsuit in U.S. courts?

5. Do you think it would be appropriate to have a treaty establishing rules for adjudicatory jurisdiction? Or would it be preferable to harmonize national laws?

The next excerpt from the Restatement is intended to serve as a transition from the principles above, which are generally viewed as being part of public international law, and the choice of law issues in private disputes, which are discussed in the next section.

Restatement

Part IV Chapter 2 — Introductory Note

Traditionally, public international law dealt with judicial jurisdiction only when exercised on government initiative, and treated such jurisdiction as ancillary to jurisdiction to prescribe. The jurisdiction of courts in relation to private controversies was not an important concern of public international law, even when its exercise had transnational implications. In the early development of United States law, both public international law and the conflict of laws between nations were considered part of "the law of nations," as seen, for example, by Marshall and Story. Later, however, the law governing conflict between laws of different nations became a small part of the domestic law of conflict of laws, which primarily focused on conflict between laws of the several States of the United States. In Europe and Latin America the conflict of laws—usually called private international law—was seen as closer to the concerns of public international law, but even there was, until recently, a subject for coordination and harmonization more than for binding international agreements and norms.

The exercise of jurisdiction by courts of one state that affects interests of other states is now generally considered as coming within the domain of customary international law and international agreement. States have long maintained the right to refuse to give effect to judgments of other states that are based on assertions of jurisdiction that are considered extravagant; increasingly, they object to the improper exercise of jurisdiction as itself a violation of international principles. Long before the developments concerning jurisdiction to prescribe, the international law governing the jurisdiction of courts began to give less emphasis to territoriality and nationality. States exercise jurisdiction to adjudicate on the basis of various links, including the defendant's presence, conduct, or, in some cases, ownership of property within the state; conduct outside the state producing certain kinds of injury within the state; or the defendant's nationality, domicile, or residence in the state. Exercise of judicial jurisdiction on the basis of such links is on the whole accepted as "reasonable"; reliance on other bases, such as the nationality of the plaintiff or the presence of property unrelated to the claim, is generally considered "exorbitant."

The development from national law to norms of international law has left the transition incomplete and boundaries blurred. In the United States, and perhaps elsewhere, it is not always clear whether the principles governing jurisdiction to adjudicate are applied as requirements of public international law or as principles of national law.

C. CHOICE OF LAW IN PRIVATE DISPUTES

In Sections A and B we examined the application and enforcement of criminal law and "public" law, such as antitrust and export controls. Comparable problems of allocation of governmental authority in the international system, with similar sources of legal limitation of that authority, can be found in more traditional areas of private law, which we take up in this section.

As indicated above, there are limits to the power of courts to adjudicate with respect to a person or controversy. The rules described in section 421 (Jurisdiction to Adjudicate) of the Restatement are derived from U.S. constitutional law, and they relate to in personam jurisdiction. After a court determines that it has in personam jurisdiction over the defendant (or "jurisdiction to adjudicate" in the Restatement and international law sense), the court must then decide *what law* to apply to the controversy. Thus, in U.S. domestic law if a New York plaintiff injures a New York defendant in an automobile crash in Michigan, the court must decide whether

New York or Michigan rules apply on such questions as the standard of liability, the effect of contributory negligence, punitive damages, spousal immunity, and so on. Similarly, in a case involving a contract negotiated in Illinois and concluded in South Dakota by parties from New York and California, the court must decide whether to apply Illinois, South Dakota, New York, or California rules, on such matters as parol evidence and validity. The same problem can arise in an international context. U.S. courts have normally applied the same rules regarding choice of law among different countries as the choice-of-law rules among the 50 states.

William M. Richman & William L. Reynolds, Understanding Conflict of Laws

157-158 (3d ed. 2002)

A court called upon to resolve a dispute with multi-state aspects must choose a law to apply to the problem. That choice often is not easy to take, and the task is further complicated by the need to select a process to use in choosing the appropriate law. It is not surprising, therefore, that the search for a system for choice of law has occupied a great deal of judicial and academic time and effort. The discussion, especially among the scholars, sometimes seems as though it were being conducted by Byzantine theologians.

Choice of law as a discipline in this country began with the monumental treatise by Justice Joseph Story published in 1834. Story, heavily influenced by the territorial concepts of earlier Dutch thinkers, emphasized the right of a state to control what went on in its courts, subject to notions of comity. American conflicts law in the first half of this century centered on the work of Professor Joseph Beale of the Harvard Law School, an effort culminating in the Restatement (First) of Conflict of Laws in 1934 and Beale's own treatise published in the following year. A territorial imperative lies at the core of Beale's theory, for it is based on the idea that at the moment a cause of action arises, rights vest according to the law of the place where the crucial event occurred. In tort law, for example, *lex loci delicti* ("the law of the place of the wrong") held sway, on the theory that the victim's cause of action had vested according to the law of the place where the injury occurred. . . .

The seeds of the demise of Beale's Restatement, however, had been planted even before it was written. Beginning at the turn of the century Sociological Jurisprudence, and then Legal Realism, had taught that law was and should be functional, and that legal rules should be tailored to serve societal goals. Because Beale's territorial system did not inquire into the purposes behind the competing substantive law rules, the system did not satisfy the mandate of twentieth-century jurisprudence. This problem was recognized by a young Harvard professor, David Cavers, in a path-breaking article in 1933, as well as by Walter Wheeler Cook in a series of articles. . . .

The approach advocated by those and other writers led to the drafting of the Restatement (Second) [of Conflict of Laws]. Work on the project began in 1952 and was essentially complete by 1963, although publication did not occur until 1971. The Reporter was Professor Willis Reese of Columbia. The Restatement (Second) generally eschews hard-and-fast rules in favor of the general principle that the law of the state with the "most significant relationship" to a transaction should control. The goal of that formula is to ensure that the law of the state most concerned with the problem will be applied and lead thereby to a sensible outcome to the litigation. . . .

While work progressed on the Second Restatement, Professor Brainerd Currie of Duke argued that the choice-of-law process should focus on the policies behind state substantive law rules; whether a rule should be applied should depend upon whether the policy underlying that rule would be advanced by its application. Currie's approach, known as "interest analysis," has appeared in various forms and has been incorporated . . . by the Restatement (Second). Some combination of the two systems has been adopted by most courts and commentators in the third of a century since Currie's first articles appeared.

Recent years have seen a partial withdrawal from interest analysis. The specific worry is that the indefinite, almost formless nature of Currie's process has led— perhaps ineluctably— to ad hoc decision-making. To counter that problem, some judges and scholars have suggested that our experience with modern forms of choice of law analysis is broad enough to permit the promulgation of new "rules" that will be both functional and certain.

One way to look at alternative methods of choosing the applicable law is to distinguish between jurisdiction-selecting systems on the one hand, and content- or policy-selecting systems on the other. Jurisdiction-selecting systems choose a state whose law will be applied, regardless of its content or motivating policy. By contrast, content-selecting systems focus on the content and motivating policy of competing substantive laws in making the choice-of-law decision. The First Restatement used jurisdiction-selecting rules. The rules prescribed a jurisdiction whose law was to be invoked once the problem had been properly characterized (as, say, one sounding in tort). The many varieties of interest analysis, by contrast, are content-selecting systems. Choice of law decisions in those systems are functional, in that they seek to assess the impact of a choice on the goals of the substantive law. Of course, the First Restatement and interest analysis are the polar opposites; intermediate positions also exist. An illustration is the Second Restatement, which combines presumptive jurisdiction-selecting rules with tools which can be used to focus on policy considerations. . . .

Under the First Restatement approach the law applicable to a tort claim was the law where the last act necessary to create the cause of action occurred (the "place of the wrong"). If a product is manufactured (but not negligently) in Alberta, Canada, and injures an Alberta resident while that person is visiting Montana, Montana law would apply under the First Restatement approach.

Under interest analysis, on the other hand, the court would analyze the case in terms of the policies underlying the conflicting rules. Thus, if Alberta law provided for strict product liability, while Montana law allowed recovery only for negligence, the court would apply Alberta law. The analysis would be that the policy underlying Alberta's rule of strict liability would seem to be to offer maximum protection to Alberta victims (interest analysis usually assumes that state legislators are only interested in legislating to protect their own constituents, and that state law should run to the benefit, or detriment, of only local residents). The policy behind Montana's law, on the other hand, would perhaps be characterized as subsidizing Montana manufacturers and sellers of manufactured products in Montana, or perhaps assuring Montana residents of reduced product prices (because Montana manufacturers and sellers would not be saddled with strict liability). In this hypothetical case, applying Montana law would not advance either Montana policy because the plaintiffs and defendants are from Alberta, not Montana, and hence are not within the class of intended beneficiaries of the Montana negligence rule. Applying Alberta law, on the other hand, would advance Alberta's policy of giving maximum protection to its residents. Hence, under interest analysis, the Alberta law of strict liability would apply. In this kind of case (sometimes called a "false conflict"), interest analysis offers a sensible, policy-oriented way to avoid application of the First Restatement approach that would mechanically apply the law of the place of injury, which may seem wholly fortuitous. Nevertheless, interest analysis provides an easy answer only to the relatively few cases that present false conflicts, where it is clear that choosing one rule over another advances the policies underlying the former and does not defeat the policies underlying the latter.

As fact situations are varied, and as the characterizations of "policy" become more complex, the cases become much more difficult. If the injured plaintiff in the hypothetical were a Montana resident, what result would follow? If the policy behind Alberta's strict liability rule is characterized as intended to benefit Alberta residents, that policy would not be advanced by applying Alberta law. But if the Montana policy is characterized as intended to protect Montana manufacturers, applying Montana law won't advance that policy either. Neither state's policy would be advanced, and interest analysis gives no guidance as to how to resolve such a case. Professor Currie, the founder of interest analysis, said the forum should apply its own law in such cases, but of course that exposes the potential of forum shopping (but what else is new?). In this hypothetical, however, punishing a Montana plaintiff does seem unjust. Why should a Montana plaintiff have to prove negligence while an Alberta plaintiff gets the benefit of strict liability?

Increasingly, U.S. courts adjudicate disputes having an international dimension. United States plaintiffs may feel that they might get a more sympathetic hearing from a local court (and jury). And foreign plaintiffs may believe that U.S. court procedure — for example, discovery rules — may be more favorable, and U.S. law may offer easier or more generous recovery. The last advantage, of course, should be mitigated by application of choice-of-law rules, especially under the First Restatement approach. Consider, however, the following case:

Pancotto v. Sociedade de Safaris de Mozambique, S.A.R.L.

U.S. District Court
422 F. Supp. 405 (N.D. Ill. 1976)

MARSHALL, District Judge.

The plaintiff, Rosemary Pancotto, has brought this diversity action to recover damages for a personal injury she sustained in 1973 while on a hunting safari in Mozambique. Pending for decision is the motion of defendant Sociedade de Safaris de Mozambique (Safrique), to apply the law of Mozambique to the substantive issues in the action, and for a determination of the relevant Mozambique law. Defendant has complied with the notice provisions of Fed. R. Civ. P. 44.1. Under the rule of Klaxon v. Stentor Electric Mfg. Co., 313 U.S. 487 (1941), a federal court sitting in diversity applies the conflicts law of the state in which it sits. Thus our task regarding the first part of defendant's motion is to determine and apply the Illinois choice of law rule.

Illinois modified its choice of law rules for tort cases in Ingersoll v. Klein, 46 111. 2d 42 (1970). "In our opinion, the local law of the State where the injury occurred should determine the rights and liabilities of the parties, unless Illinois has a more significant relationship with the occurrence and the parties, in which case, the law of Illinois should apply."

The first step in the choice of law analysis is to isolate the substantive legal issues and determine whether the various states' tort rules conflict. If a potential conflict is discovered, the next step is to examine the contacts with the states, evaluating the importance of each contact in relation to the legal issues of the case. Finally, under the Illinois choice of law rule, the law of the state or country of the place of injury is followed, unless Illinois is more significantly interested in the resolution of a particular legal issue.

I. The Defendant's Liability

Defendant's motion identifies the two substantive legal issues to be addressed by this choice of law analysis, each of which will be considered in turn: (1) the defendant's liability; and (2) the appropriate measure of damages. A cursory look at the defendant's materials outlining Mozambique law indicates that the standard of care there was different from Illinois.[1] Briefly, the Mozambique standard of care upon which defendant relies was the "diligence with which a law abiding male head of a family would act." Portuguese Civil Code, Art. 487(2). Although this standard of care bears an analytical similarity to Illinois' reasonable man standard, it may be more or less demanding of an alleged wrongdoer. This putative difference could lead to a different result if Mozambique rather than Illinois law is applied. Consequently, we are faced with a true conflict of laws and must evaluate the parties' contacts with the two states to determine which law should control.

Ingersoll refers us to what is now Restatement (Second) of Conflicts of Laws §145 (1971), for a listing of the contacts to be evaluated in determining which jurisdiction is most significantly concerned with the liability of the alleged tortfeasor. The first of these is the place where the injury occurred. The parties do not dispute that plaintiff sustained her injuries in Mozambique. Mrs. Pancotto accompanied her husband and sons on a hunting safari directed by defendant. She was taking pictures of other members of the hunting party when a swamp buggy driven by a Safrique employee ran into her.

The place of injury has an interest in applying its own tort principles to discourage harmful behavior within its borders. This interest in controlling the tortfeasor's conduct is strongest when the alleged tort is intentional. If the harmful contact is

1. At the time of plaintiff's injury in 1973, Mozambique was a territory of Portugal and applied the Portuguese Civil Code. See Affidavit of Marcel Molins. We take judicial notice that Mozambique in 1975 became an independent nation, with its own law. However, to the extent that Mozambique law is controlling, it is the law as it existed at the time of the alleged wrong.

unintentional, however, the interest of the place of injury is attenuated. Realistically, the negligent tortfeasor is not affected by a state's civil liability laws because he does not premeditate before he acts. Nonetheless, to the extent that such conduct is shaped by legal standards, Mozambique was, at the time of the alleged wrong, interested in the choice of the standard of care to be imposed upon the defendant.

The second contact listed in the Restatement is the place of the conduct which caused injury, which is again clearly Mozambique. The interest of the jurisdiction where the conduct occurred is similar if not identical to that of the place of injury. Again, however, Mozambique's valid interest in controlling harmful conduct assumes less importance when the alleged tortfeasor was not governed by conscious reference to a behavioral standard.

The Restatement's third contact is the domicile or place of business of the parties. This consideration refers us to both Illinois law and that of Mozambique. The plaintiff's domicile, Illinois, is interested in compensating both the victim and her creditors. Mozambique, on the other hand, as the defendant's domicile and principal place of business, is concerned that defendant's conduct conforms to its standards, and may also have an interest in insulating a domiciliary from liability.

The Restatement's final contact point is the place where the parties' relationship is centered. The relationship here has an international flavor. The safari was arranged in large part by intercontinental telephone calls and cables. In addition, certain employees of the defendant visited the plaintiff's husband in Illinois approximately three times prior to the safari, although the parties dispute the business as opposed to personal significance of the visits. Regardless of the nature of the Illinois contacts, they obviously were preparatory to an extended, well-planned interaction in Mozambique. . . . In short, although the relationship had international aspects, it can fairly be characterized as centering in Mozambique.

These contacts and the state interests evoked by them indicate that both Illinois and Mozambique are interested in the resolution of the liability issue. Both jurisdictions' interests are significant. The numerous Mozambique contacts highlight that government's interest in controlling the conduct of those who take action within its borders, and the interest in affording the protection of its laws to its domiciliaries. Illinois, on the other hand, has a strong interest in seeing that its residents are adequately compensated for tortious injuries. The Illinois interest, although based upon a single contact, cannot for that reason be automatically dismissed as less significant. A contact assumes significance only in view of the legal issue to which it relates. Our evaluation of the contacts indicates that both Illinois and Mozambique are validly interested in the resolution of the issue of defendant's liability, and we hesitate to characterize either jurisdiction's interest as more significant.

In general, the Illinois courts have chosen their own law rather than the law of the place of injury only if the majority of the significant contacts were in Illinois, and the tort's occurrence in the foreign state was fortuitous. See e.g., *Ingersoll*, supra. Given that both states here may assert significant although distinct interests in the outcome of the liability issue, the Illinois choice of law rule directs the application of the law of the place of injury, Mozambique.

We now turn to a determination of the Mozambique law governing liability for the acts of misconduct alleged in the complaint.

Rule 44.1 gives district courts wide discretion in the materials to which they may resort to determine the content of foreign law. The defendant has provided copies of the relevant sections of the Portuguese Civil Code, both in that language and in translation. In addition, defendant offers the affidavit of Mr. Marcel Molins, an expert witness conversant with the law of Portugal, who comments upon the law pertinent to the issues of liability and damages. Regarding liability, these combined resources indicate that Portuguese law sets out two standards for liability, either of which might apply to the facts alleged in the complaint. The first standard seems to be a rough equivalent, allowing for cultural differences, of the common law reasonable man standard. Under this standard, "[f]ault is judged, in the absence of another legal criterion, by the diligence with which a law-abiding male head of a family would act in the face of the circumstances of each case." Art. 487(2). . . .

A second standard may be available, however, under the facts alleged here. As in the United States, in Mozambique liability was sometimes imposed without regard to fault. . . . [T]his concept is called objective liability, and appears to be theoretically equivalent to our concept of strict liability in tort. Under the Portuguese Code, the operation of a land vehicle is consider inherently hazardous. . . .

Without further testimony on the matter, we are not prepared to decide at this time which standard of liability would be applied by a Mozambique court. We also need edification on the question whether the common law reasonable man standard and the Mozambique "male head of a family" standard are equivalents or whether the latter imposes a greater or lesser standard of care than does the former. Therefore, in preparation for trial the parties are directed to submit supplemental materials addressing these issues.

II. The Measure of Damages

A brief look at Mozambique's and Illinois' laws on recoverable damages reveals an acute conflict. Illinois permits recovery for medical expenses due to the injury, and, inter alia, compensation for the injury itself, for disfigurement, and for pain and suffering. In contrast, Art. 508 of the Portuguese Civil Code limits liability for travel accidents to 600 contos, or approximately $6,600 in United States dollars. This limit is not inflexible, however. A Mozambique court may apparently, in its discretion, award damages to the full extent of the plaintiff's out-of-pocket loss, although the typical recovery is less generous. And, under Mozambique law, the plaintiff recovers nothing for pain and suffering, disfigurement, or loss of enjoyment of life as she might under Illinois law.

The defendant argues that the Illinois choice of law rule dictates the application of Mozambique law to this issue also. And, in fact, the analysis of the two jurisdictions' interests in the measure of damages leads to such a result. As the place of conduct, injury, defendant's domicile, and the place where the parties' relationship centered, Mozambique has a strong interest in the resolution of this issue. As plaintiff's domicile and the place where the consequences of the injury are felt, Illinois is concerned that plaintiff receives compensation. Plaintiff, however, contends that the application of Mozambique's damage limitation would be so grossly repugnant to Illinois' public and constitutional policy of providing a remedy for all injuries that an Illinois court would refuse to follow Mozambique law, even if the Ingersoll rule would normally dictate its application.

With no Illinois cases in point, the parties discuss certain cases in which the New York courts have faced similar contentions. Of these, Rosenthal v. Warren, 475

F.2d 438 (2d Cir. 1973), is the closest factually to the case here. As a federal court sitting in New York, the *Rosenthal* court was concerned with the proper application of New York's choice of law rule, which differs from the Illinois rule.[3] Despite this difference in orientation, *Rosenthal* points out the important factors to consider in determining whether the forum state's public policy should overrule the law of a foreign jurisdiction.

The plaintiff's decedent in *Rosenthal* was domiciled in New York. Accompanied by the plaintiff, his wife and later his executrix, the decedent traveled to Boston for medical treatment by a physician domiciled in Massachusetts. The decedent died while recuperating in a Massachusetts hospital after surgery performed by the physician. The decedent's wife subsequently sued the physician and the hospital in a New York state court.

The defendants argued that the Massachusetts wrongful death statute, with its $50,000 limit on damages, should apply. The court rejected Massachusetts' statute in favor of New York's full compensation policy. Before doing so, the court confronted and thoroughly analyzed the factors militating against the forum's application of its own public policy. First, the court considered whether the defendants had patterned their conduct upon the Massachusetts statute. . . . Second, the court considered whether the defendants would be unfairly surprised by the application of New York law. . . . Third, the court considered whether defendants had purchased insurance in reliance upon the Massachusetts limitation. . . . Finally, the court evaluated the policy behind the Massachusetts limitation to determine whether application of the New York law would frustrate an important Massachusetts interest. Finding that the few remaining wrongful death limitations are vestiges of the mistaken view that a common law action for wrongful death did not exist, the court declined to apply an archaic and unjust policy, particularly in view of its own policy to assure just and fair compensation for the victims of tortious conduct.

In short, *Rosenthal* indicates that the defendant's reliance, and principles of fundamental fairness and governmental policy should be balanced in determining whether the forum's measure of damages, grounded upon a strong public policy, may be applied against a foreign defendant.

Applying these principles to the factual context here yields some similar conclusions. The tort alleged in the complaint is unintentional, rendering any argument of behavioral reliance untenable. And, as in *Rosenthal*, the defendant here anticipated and welcomed, if not solicited, business contacts with persons outside the jurisdiction. The last two *Rosenthal* considerations, however, are not so easily dismissed. Defendant's counsel has submitted an affidavit attesting that defendant told him it carries no insurance. . . . [T]he lack of insurance suggests that defendant relied upon Mozambique's damage limitation. . . . [W]e have no knowledge of the status of damage limitations for personal injury actions in the world community of nations.

3. New York employs the "interest analysis" approach to conflicts of law, and applies the law of the jurisdiction which because of its relationship to the parties or the occurrence has the greatest concern with the specific issues raised in the case. Rosenthal v. Warren, 475 F.2d 438 (2d Cir. 1973). Applying this rule, the New York courts have attached heavy weight to their state's vital concern that injured domiciliaries are compensated for their loss. E.g., Miller v. Miller, 22 N.Y.2d 12 (1969). In contrast, Illinois follows the approach of the Second Restatement, and applies the law of the place of injury unless Illinois has a more significant interest in the outcome of a specific issue.

Despite these countervailing considerations, our educated prediction is that the Illinois courts would refuse to enforce the Portuguese limitation as unreasonable and contrary to Illinois public policy. Illinois public policy is found in its Constitution, laws, judicial decisions, and also in its customs, morals, and notions of justice. Marchlik v. Coronet Ins. Co., 40 111. 2d 327 (1968). There is perhaps no more compelling Illinois public policy than one expressed in the state's Constitution, which provides that every person should find a certain remedy in the law for injuries to his person. 111. Const. Art. I, §12. . . . [I]'f the right existed at common law, damage limitations without a *quid pro quo* have been disfavored. Moreover, the damage limitations incorporated into Illinois legislation have been more consistent with potential out-of-pocket loss. . . .

Of course, we are not dealing here with a law of Illinois, but one from a foreign country. Recently liberated from foreign rule, the economic and social conditions in Mozambique are quite different from those in Illinois. . . .

In the absence of an articulated national policy, the final inquiry is whether the application of the Illinois law would unfairly prejudice the defendant. Although the defendant is a Mozambique corporation, its trade is international in scope. Safrique allows travel agencies to use its name in advertisements for sporting magazines with national circulation. If Safrique induces residents of other countries to visit Mozambique and profits from the excursions, it is hardly unfair to require Safrique to compensate its clients for tortious injuries inflicted by Safrique employees. Concomitantly, Safrique cannot claim that its clients' residencies take it by surprise. Indeed, Safrique deliberately engages in a business which thrives on international tourism.

A final aspect of the question of prejudice involves counsel's allegation that defendant carries no liability insurance. Safrique's failure to obtain insurance, however, is not alleged to have been motivated by the Mozambique damage limitation. Without supplemental affidavits, this neglect is as easily attributed to oversight as to a calculated business decision that it might cost more in premiums than to directly compensate a victim to the statutory limit.

In conclusion, although the Illinois choice of law rule indicates the application of Mozambique's law to the substantive issues in this action, we feel the Illinois courts would refuse to enforce the Mozambique policy of providing a remedy for personal injuries. Foreign substantive law is not unenforceable simply because it differs from our own law, but because the differences are against public policy. The refusal to enforce a foreign law should not be lightly made. But when no justification is offered for a policy which contravenes a sound public policy of the forum, and the defendant is not unfairly surprised, we believe that the Illinois courts would decline to apply the foreign limitation.

Notes and Questions

1. In *Pancotto,* where did the U.S. district court look for its choice-of-law rules?

2. Applying the selected choice-of-law approach, did the *Pancotto* court then use Illinois's or Mozambique's substantive tort law? Which jurisdiction's law did the court employ for determining damages?

3. As Professors Richman and Reynolds report in 2002, "The Second Restatement [of Conflict of Laws] is the dominant conflicts methodology in American

courts today. Twenty-two jurisdictions follow the Restatement's approach in tort conflicts, and twenty-four do so in contract cases. Additionally several other jurisdictions follow the similar 'significant contacts' approach thus yielding a majority of American jurisdictions. The next most popular American choice-of-law methodology, the traditional First Restatement approach, can claim less than half as many adherents." Understanding Conflict of Laws 213-214 (3d ed. 2002).

4. What law would the *Pancotto* court apply if it followed the First Restatement view? Would it be desirable to prevent forum shopping?

5. Do you see similarities between section 403 of the Restatement (Third) of Foreign Relations Law, which describes limits on a state's right to apply its law to conduct having connections with more than one state (or its jurisdiction to prescribe), and Currie's interest analysis or the "most significant relationship" approach of the Restatement (Second) of Conflict of Laws? Is there any reason that a state should be more or less limited in its right to apply criminal law, regulatory law such as the Sherman Act, or normal tort or contract law?

6. Section 403 assumes that more than one state may have jurisdiction to prescribe law to the same conduct. Section 421 sets forth expansive rules for asserting adjudicatory jurisdiction. Would you expect a U.S. judge ever to decide that the U.S. interest in litigation was less than the competing foreign interest? (See the discussion above after *Hartford Fire* and *Empagran* in Section 7.A.1.) Did the holding in *Pancotto* vindicate U.S. or Mozambique policy?

7. In an international setting, is a vested rights (or territorial) approach better than an interest analysis (section 403-like) approach? At least for potential conflicts of public law? Or is it better in all settings?

8. If it is sometimes illegitimate for the United States to apply sanctions when it applies public law extraterritorially, as suggested by section 403 and *Sensor* (in Section 7.A.2.), should the result be different in the case of the application of U.S. tort law, procedural (discovery) law, or toxic pesticides rules? Why do you think a distinction was drawn in the past between public and private law? Is that distinction still viable?

9. Should a U.S. court have adjudicated the liability of Union Carbide Corporation for the gas leak disaster that occurred at its foreign subsidiary in Bhopal, India? (See discussion of forum non conveniens earlier at page 706.) If the U.S. court kept the case, what law should apply? Could Congress pass an antipollution law applicable to foreign subsidiaries of U.S. corporations anywhere in the world? Should it?

8

International Human Rights and Responsibility for Injuries to Aliens

International human rights law has developed very rapidly in the years since World War II. As noted in Chapter 1, the traditional understanding of international law defined it as the rules that bind states in their relations with one another. In that sense, international law was not concerned either with the state's authority to regulate events within its territory or with the state's relations with individuals. That characterization is in some respects an oversimplification, for even traditional international law established rules concerning a state's treatment of *aliens,* even when it acted within its territory. International law did not, however, apply to the state's treatment of its own nationals.

Since World War II, international human rights law has changed that framework in dramatic ways. Now international law standards are increasingly brought to bear on the conduct of a state within its territory vis-à-vis not only aliens but also its own nationals. Section A begins with an important antecedent to international human rights, the rules of state responsibility for injuries to aliens, and explores the still vibrant issues of international responsibility for injury to alien property. Section B then turns to international human rights law and the ways in which it is implemented and enforced.

A. STATE RESPONSIBILITY FOR INJURIES TO ALIENS

1. The Law of Diplomatic Protection

Under traditional international law doctrine, when a state injured an alien, that injury was viewed as an injury to the state whose national was injured. The resulting claim was therefore made by the injured national's state. In the vocabulary of international law, the injured national's state provides its "diplomatic protection." The following excerpt from a classic text on public international law summarizes the traditional rules of state responsibility (and the one-time opposition by Latin American states to those rules).

J. L. Brierly, The Law of Nations

276-287 (6th ed. 1963)

No state is legally bound to admit aliens into its territory, but if it does so it must observe a certain standard of decent treatment towards them, and their own state may demand reparation for an injury caused to them by a failure to observe this standard. The legal basis of such a demand, in the words of the Permanent Court [of International Justice in the *Panesvezys-Saldutiskis Railway* case], is that

> in taking up the case of one of its nationals, by resorting to diplomatic action or international judicial proceedings on his behalf, a state is in reality asserting its own right, the right to ensure in the person of its nationals respect for the rules of international law. This right is necessarily limited to the intervention on behalf of its own nationals because, in the absence of a special agreement, it is the bond of nationality between the state and the individual which alone confers upon the state the right of diplomatic protection, and it is as a part of the function of diplomatic protection that the right to take up a claim and to ensure respect for the rules of international law must be envisaged.

There is a certain artificiality in this way of looking at the question. No doubt a state has in general an interest in seeing that its nationals are fairly treated in a foreign country, but it is an exaggeration to say that whenever a national is injured in a foreign state, his state as a whole is necessarily injured too. In practice, as we shall see, the theory is not consistently adhered to; for instance, the logic of the theory would require that damages should be measured by reference to the injury suffered by the state, which is obviously not the same as that suffered by the individual, but in fact the law allows them to be assessed on the loss to the individual, as though it were the injury to him which was the cause of action. The procedure, too, is far from satisfactory from the individual's point of view. He has no remedy of his own, and the state to which he belongs may be unwilling to take up his case for reasons which have nothing to do with its merits. . . .

In general a person who voluntarily enters the territory of a state not his own must accept the institutions of that state as he finds them. He is not entitled to demand equality of treatment in all respects with the citizens of the state; for example, he is almost always debarred from the political rights of a citizen; he is commonly not allowed to engage in the coasting trade, or to fish in territorial waters; he is sometimes not allowed to hold land. These and many other discriminations against him are not forbidden by international law. On the other hand, if a state has a low standard of justice towards its own nationals, an alien's position is in a sense a privileged one, for the standard of treatment to which international law entitles him is an objective one, and he need not, even though nationals must, submit to unjust treatment. This statement of the law is denied by certain Latin-American states, which hold that if a state grants equality of treatment to nationals and non-nationals it fulfils its international obligation; but such a view would make each state the judge of the standard required by international law, and would virtually deprive aliens of the protection of their own state altogether. Facts with respect to equality of treatment of aliens and nationals may be important in determining the merits of a complaint of mistreatment of an alien. But such equality is not the ultimate test of the propriety of the acts of the authorities in the light of international law. That test is, broadly speaking, whether aliens are treated in accordance with ordinary standards of civilization. . . .

This international standard cannot be made a matter of precise rules. It is the standard of the "reasonable state," reasonable, that is to say, according to the notions that are accepted in our modern civilization. It was thus described by the U.S.-Mexican Claims Commission [in the *Neers* case]:

> the propriety of governmental acts should be put to the test of international standards, and . . . the treatment of an alien, in order to constitute an international delinquency, should amount to an outrage, to bad faith, to wilful neglect of duty, or to an insufficiency of governmental action so far short of international standards that every reasonable and impartial man would readily recognize its insufficiency. Whether the insufficiency proceeds from deficient execution of an intelligent law or from the fact that the laws of the country do not empower the authorities to measure up to international standards is immaterial.

The standard therefore is not an exacting one, nor does it require a uniform degree of governmental efficiency irrespective of circumstances; for example, measures of police protection which would be reasonable in a capital city cannot fairly be demanded in a sparsely populated territory, and a security which is normal in times of tranquility cannot be expected in a time of temporary disorder such as may occasionally occur even in a well-ordered state. But the standard being an international one, a state cannot relieve itself of responsibility by any provision of its own national law. . . .

It is ordinarily a condition of an international claim for the redress of an injury suffered by an alien that the alien himself should first have exhausted any remedies available to him under the local law. A state is not required to guarantee that the person or property of an alien will not be injured, and the mere fact that such an injury has been suffered does not give his own state a right to demand reparation on his behalf. If a state in which an alien is injured puts at his disposal apparently effective and sufficient legal remedies for obtaining redress, international law requires that he should have had recourse to and exhausted these remedies before his own state becomes entitled to intervene on his behalf. The principle of this rule is that a state is entitled to have a full and proper opportunity of doing justice in its own way before international justice is demanded of it by another state. The local remedies which must be exhausted include administrative remedies of a legal nature but not extra-legal remedies or remedies as of grace. . . .

. . . Although . . . the local remedies rule is applied with a certain strictness, it does not mean that it is necessary for the individual to exhaust remedies which, though theoretically available, would be ineffective or insufficient to redress the injury of which he complains; for example, if the case or statute law binding upon the local courts was such as must compel them to reject his claim, or if, his claim having been lost in a lower court, it was useless to appeal because the critical point was one of fact and the higher court had no power to alter findings of fact. If the local tribunals are notoriously corrupt or notoriously discriminate against foreigners, the individual is not required "to exhaust justice when there is no justice to exhaust." Again, if the wrong has been committed by the legislature itself or by some high official, it not infrequently happens that the local law provides no remedy and in that case there are no local remedies to exhaust. In general, therefore, the prior exhaustion of local remedies is a condition of presenting an international claim unless it can be shown that either there were no local remedies to exhaust or that it was obviously futile to have recourse to those that were available.

Another condition of presenting an international claim is that there should be a bond of nationality between the claimant state and the person injured. So much is the bond of nationality a condition of an international claim that it must not only exist at the date of the original injury but must also continue until the date of the judgment or award. Thus, if the beneficial interest in the claim has meanwhile passed, by death or by assignment, from the person originally injured to a person of a different nationality, the right to bring an international claim will lapse. . . .

A state may incur responsibility by the act or omission of any of its organs, legislative, executive, or judicial. . . .

. . . [For a wrongful act of an official to give rise to the responsibility of his state,] the official must have acted within the scope of his office; otherwise his act would be like that of a private individual. . . .

The term "denial of justice" is sometimes loosely used to denote *any* international delinquency towards an alien for which a state is liable to make reparation. In this sense it is an unnecessary and confusing term. Its more proper sense is an injury involving the responsibility of the state committed by a court of justice, and on the question what acts of this kind do involve the state in responsibility there are two views. Most Latin-American states insist on a very narrow interpretation, and contend in effect that if the courts give a decision of any kind there can be no denial of justice and consequently no responsibility of the state for their conduct. Nothing but the denial to foreigners of access to the courts can be properly regarded as a denial of justice. This view, which involves the virtual rejection of the principle of an international standard applicable to the action of courts of law towards foreigners, cannot be accepted. There are many possible ways in which a court may fall below the standard fairly to be demanded of a civilized state without literally closing its doors. Such acts cannot be exhaustively enumerated, but corruption, threats, unwarrantable delay, flagrant abuse of judicial procedure, a judgment dictated by the executive, or so manifestly unjust that no court which was both competent and honest could have given it, are instances. Possibly it is convenient also to include in the term certain acts or omissions of organs of government other than courts, but closely connected with the administration of justice, such as execution without trial, inexcusable failure to bring a wrongdoer to trial, long imprisonment before trial, grossly inadequate punishment, or failure to enforce a judgment duly given. But no merely erroneous or even unjust judgment of a court will constitute a denial of justice, except in one case, namely where a court, having occasion to apply some rule of international law, gives an incorrect interpretation of that law, or where it applies, as it may be bound by its municipal law to do, a rule of domestic law which is itself contrary to international law.

It will be observed that even on the wider interpretation of the term "denial of justice" which is here adopted, the misconduct must be extremely gross. The justification of this strictness is that the independence of courts is an accepted canon of decent government, and the law therefore does not lightly hold a state responsible for their faults. It follows that an allegation of a denial of justice is a serious step which states, as mentioned above, are reluctant to take when a claim can be based on other grounds.

Restatement

Section 711. Responsibility for Injury to Nationals of Other States

A state is responsible under international law for injury to a national of another state caused by an official act or omission that violates

(a) a human right that . . . a state is obligated to respect for all persons subject to its authority;

(b) a personal right that, under international law, a state is obligated to respect for individuals of foreign nationality; or

(c) a right to property or another economic interest that, under international law, a state is obligated to respect for persons, natural or juridical, of foreign nationality, as provided in §712.

Reporters' Notes

1. *Injury to aliens and human rights standards.* In the early decades of the 20th century, there was substantial agreement among the countries of Europe and North America on basic rules as to the protection to be afforded to foreign nationals. The countries of Latin America, most of which were recipients of foreign persons and capital, rejected these rules. After the Second World War, with the emergence of many new importing states, and with the development of the law of human rights, opposition to special protection for aliens increased. It is generally accepted that states may invoke recognized international human rights standards on behalf of their nationals; attempts to invoke protections going beyond international human rights standards, as in clauses (b) and (c) of this section, might be resisted by some states.

2. *Rights of foreign nationals recognized under customary law.* Before the development of the contemporary law of human rights, states were held responsible for injury to aliens consisting of, or resulting from, various acts or omissions deemed to violate an international standard of justice or other standards accepted in customary international law. The law of responsibility for such injuries was largely developed by claims practice, by negotiation and agreement concerning liability and compensation, and by decisions of arbitral tribunals and claims commissions established pursuant to international agreement. . . .

This body of state practice and decision may be summarized as follows:

A. States have been held responsible for injury due to various actions that have since been accepted as violations of human rights in the Universal Declaration on Human Rights or the Covenant on Civil and Political Rights:

—*Denials of due process in criminal proceedings*:

—arbitrary arrest

—unlawful or prolonged detention or interrogation

—prolonged arbitrary imprisonment

—excessive bail

—delayed trial

—unfair trial

—being tried twice for the same offense

—failure to render a decision

—tribunal manipulated by the executive

—denial of right to defend oneself and confront witnesses

—conviction without diligent and competent counsel

—denial of an interpreter
—denial to accused of communication with representatives of his government

—*Arbitrary use of force by officials:*
—arbitrary or excessive use of force by state officials
—inhuman treatment
—arbitrary molestation of the person; torture to elicit "confession"

—*Other violations of recognized rights*: Claims were also made on behalf of aliens for other actions violating rights later recognized in the Universal Declaration, such as freedom of speech, freedom of religion, freedom to travel within a country, and the right to marry. There is some authority in international law to support such claims, but these freedoms might be restricted to resident aliens, and might be denied in time of national emergency.

There were also claims for injury due to denial to foreign nationals of benefits enjoyed by nationals, such as social security or aid to indigents or incompetents, or due to other discrimination between aliens and nationals or against aliens of particular nationality. International law forbids some such discriminations, but others are permitted. . . .

B. State practice and arbitral decisions have supported state responsibility for several kinds of injury to aliens that have not been recognized as violations of human rights, clause (b) of this section. They include:

—*Failure to protect foreign nationals.* The rule that developed out of the arbitral awards before World War II was that a state was responsible for injuries inflicted upon aliens by private individuals only if the state failed, by intention or neglect, to provide adequate police protection for those aliens. A state incurs no liability for injury to aliens by acts of revolutionary forces if the state is unable to protect the aliens from such injury. If the revolutionary forces succeed, the state may become liable for their actions during the struggle for power. . . .

—*Failure to punish offenses against aliens.* There is support for a rule obligating a state to act vigorously and diligently to punish crimes against aliens. It is argued that failure to punish shows contempt for the alien's state and increases the possibility of harm befalling other nationals of that state. . . .

—*Failure to provide aliens a legal remedy.* It is a wrong under international law for a state to deny a foreign national access to domestic courts. That is the central meaning of "denial of justice." Treaties of friendship, commerce, and navigation generally provide that each party shall give to nationals of the other party access to its courts on the same basis as to its own nationals. However, states reserve the right to deny access to their courts to corporations that have not registered or qualified to do business in the state although they in fact do business within the jurisdiction.

United States law generally affords aliens access to courts even in the absence of international agreement, although in respect of some claims against the United States, the right is conditioned on reciprocity by the alien's country of nationality. . . .

C. States have been deemed not responsible under international law for

—*Certain alleged procedural insufficiencies:*
—witness did not take oath
—reasonable security for costs was required
—court incorrectly but in good faith applied or interpreted the law
—case dismissed for lack of jurisdiction (when another forum was available)
—"technical objections" or "minor irregularities"

—*Such restrictions on aliens as:*
—exclusion from public employment
—limiting access to certain professions and occupations
—denying access to public facilities or resources

—denying right to own or inherit certain property or interests in property
—requiring aliens to register or be otherwise identified
—deporting or expelling aliens pursuant to law
—requiring aliens to serve on juries or testify as witnesses or experts.

Notes and Questions

1. Elihu Root, who served as U.S. Secretary of State in the early 20th century, stated in an address to the American Society of International Law that "[t]here is a standard of justice, very simple, very fundamental, and of such general acceptance by all civilized countries as to form a part of the international law of the world." 4 Am. Soc'y Int'l L. Proc. 16, 20 (1910). How would you articulate the international law standard of treatment? What is the "standard of the 'reasonable state' "? What seemed to have been required by the U.S.-Mexican Claims Commission, quoted in the Brierly excerpt? What is the meaning of a "denial of justice"?

2. Why do you think Latin American states, in the past, resisted the idea of an international standard for the treatment of aliens that would supersede domestic standards? For a discussion of contemporary Latin American attitudes toward the law of diplomatic protection, see Wenhua Shan, Is Calvo Dead?, 55 Am. J. Comp. L. 123 (2007).

3. Historically, the law of state responsibility was primarily reflected in customary international law rather than treaties. How was this customary international law ascertained? If an arbitral commission were adjudicating an alleged violation of the law of state responsibility, what materials would it look to in order to determine the content of this law?

4. As noted in the Brierly excerpt, normally the injured alien must exhaust local remedies before a claim may be brought for a violation of the law of state responsibility. What does exhaustion of local remedies entail? Are there circumstances under which exhaustion will not be required?

Problem. Suppose you have been asked by Singapore's ambassador to the United States to give advice on the options available to his government and the Singapore nationals injured in the following incident that occurred in southern California: A family from Singapore rented a car at Los Angeles airport and drove down to San Diego. While returning that evening to Disneyland, they were detained by the Immigration and Naturalization Service (INS) at a routine immigration checkpoint. The INS officer demanded their passports, which they had left in their hotel in Los Angeles. They produced Singapore identity cards and driving licenses and explained the situation in English (the official language of Singapore). They pointed out that they were driving a car rented in Los Angeles. Nevertheless, apparently thinking they were illegal Mexican immigrants, the officer threw them in a cell and threatened to deport them. Let us assume that they were held overnight (a family of five in a room without sanitation facilities), and then taken to the Mexican border where, although unable to speak Spanish, they were physically deported.

(a) Outline the options available—diplomatic and judicial—and what remedies would be available. How much would a lawsuit cost? Can you get compensation some other way?

(b) As Legal Adviser to the State Department, how would you respond to a diplomatic claim by Singapore? Would you invoke the doctrine of exhaustion of local remedies? If not, would you recommend negotiating an agreement between the United States and Singapore, settling the claim for an agreed amount of compensation? Or agree to arbitrate the dispute? What if the compensation to be paid was nominal? Could you offer a formal apology?

(c) What if, on their return to the United States, the Singapore family was surrounded by an angry mob of detained aliens who attacked and beat them while the INS and local police officers looked on? Suppose instead that the police jailed them, knowing that they would almost certainly be beaten. Would either be a violation of international law?

(d) Assume a U.S. court refused to permit recovery because of domestic constitutional law doctrines regarding official immunity. Would that refusal be a denial of justice and therefore a violation of international law?

2. *Attribution of Conduct to the State*

The following excerpt discusses the circumstances under which conduct is attributed to the state for purposes of state responsibility.

Gordon A. Christenson, Attributing Conduct to the State: Is Anything New?, Remarks on Attribution Issues in State Responsibility

84 Am. Socy. Int'l L. Proc. 51, 52-57 (1990)

The separation of conduct of the state from that of private or nonstate persons became almost universal once feudal collective responsibility receded. The central function of international law in determining this separation has remained unquestioned. Three principles, reflected in all recent codifications and restatements, summarize the tradition.

The first principle says that a state acts through people exercising the state's machinery of power and authority. Acts or omissions of official organs, agents or political subdivisions, including those of successful revolutionary regimes, necessarily are those of the state. These include acts of de facto agents under direct control of those in power in a state or those acting as a government. . . .

The second principle is that international law does not attribute conduct of a nonstate character, such as acts or omissions of private persons, mobs, associations, corporations, trade unions or unsuccessful insurgents, to a state as such. . . .

The third principle is that a state may act through its own independent failure of duty or inaction when an international obligation requires state action in relation to nonstate conduct. This principle properly is a corollary to the first. . . . For example, a state has a duty to take reasonable care to protect aliens from harm and to punish offenders with due diligence. Inaction in the face of this duty is conduct attributable to the state quite independently of the actual wrongful acts. An example, as articulated in the Restatement (Third), of this duty is "to provide aliens reasonable police protection; the state is not responsible for injuries caused by private persons that result despite such police protection. . . ."

Nongovernmental death squads in some countries have systematically eliminated political opposition by the tragic terror of torture and disappearances, not directed by any formal state action but instead allowed by responsible government officials averting their eyes, if not by outright collusion. Tacit approval or complicity by officials would unquestionably be conduct attributable to the state as a breach of human rights or as a crime of state against its own citizens. . . .

Suppose, however, that the link to government is much more difficult to show, that the wink and the nod denoting approval cannot be traced, and that the work of the death squads is seen more as the work of vigilantes or private terrorists. When such action is directed against aliens, the state has a clear affirmative duty under customary international law to protect against criminal acts, and may be held responsible. More often, the victims are nationals of the country as well as foreigners. . . . Failure to protect citizens from "private" death squads in these disappearances by failure to exercise due diligence should be attributable to the state. . . .

In 2001, after decades of study and drafting, the International Law Commission (ILC), the principal law development arm of the United Nations, adopted a set of nonbinding Draft Articles on the Responsibility of States for Internationally Wrongful Acts. The U.N. General Assembly adopted a resolution on December 12, 2001, that "[t]akes note of the articles" and "commends them to the attention of Governments without prejudice to the question of their future adoption or other appropriate action." G.A. Res. 56/83, ¶3, U.N. Doc. A/RES/56/83 (Dec. 12, 2001). Although the ILC undertook both codification and progressive development functions in formulating the Draft Articles, commentators have noted that the rules on attribution "are generally traditional and reflect a codification rather than any significant development of the law." Daniel Bodansky & John Crook, Symposium: The ILC's State Responsibility Articles: Introduction and Overview, 96 Am. J. Int'l L. 773, 782 (2002). The following articles address the issue of attribution:

Article 4

Conduct of Organs of a State

1. The conduct of any State organ shall be considered an act of that State under international law, whether the organ exercises legislative, executive, judicial or any other functions, whatever position it holds in the organization of the State, and whatever its character as an organ of the central government or of a territorial unit of the State.

2. An organ includes any person or entity which has that status in accordance with the internal law of the State.

Article 5

Conduct of Persons or Entities Exercising Elements of Governmental Authority

The conduct of a person or entity which is not an organ of the State under article 4 but which is empowered by the law of that State to exercise elements of the governmental authority shall be considered an act of the State under international law, provided the person or entity is acting in that capacity in the particular instance.

Article 6

Conduct of Organs Placed at the Disposal of a State by Another State

The conduct of an organ placed at the disposal of a State by another State shall be considered an act of the former State under international law if the organ is acting in the exercise of elements of the governmental authority of the State at whose disposal it is placed.

Article 7

Excess of Authority or Contravention of Instructions

The conduct of an organ of a State or of a person or entity empowered to exercise elements of the governmental authority shall be considered an act of the State under international law if the organ, person or entity acts in that capacity, even if it exceeds its authority or contravenes instructions.

Article 8

Conduct Directed or Controlled by a State

The conduct of a person or group of persons shall be considered an act of a State under international law if the person or group of persons is in fact acting on the instructions of, or under the direction or control of, that State in carrying out the conduct.

Article 9

Conduct Carried Out in the Absence or Default of the Official Authorities

The conduct of a person or group of persons shall be considered an act of a State under international law if the person or group of persons is in fact exercising elements of the governmental authority in the absence or default of the official authorities and in circumstances such as to call for the exercise of those elements of authority.

Article 10

Conduct of an Insurrectional or other Movement

1. The conduct of an insurrectional movement which becomes the new government of a State shall be considered an act of that State under international law.

2. The conduct of a movement, insurrectional or other, which succeeds in establishing a new State in part of the territory of a pre-existing State or in a territory under its administration shall be considered an act of the new State under international law.

3. This article is without prejudice to the attribution to a State of any conduct, however related to that of the movement concerned, which is to be considered an act of that State by virtue of articles 4 to 9.

Article 11

Conduct Acknowledged and Adopted by a State as its Own

Conduct which is not attributable to a State under the preceding articles shall nevertheless be considered an act of that State under international law if and to the extent that the State acknowledges and adopts the conduct in question as its own.

Notes and Questions

1. In a decision involving the 1979-1981 hostage situation at the U.S. embassy in Iran, the International Court of Justice found that the student militants who stormed the embassy and seized the U.S. hostages were not initially acting on behalf of Iran, because Iranian authorities had not specifically instructed them to do what they did. Nevertheless, the Court found Iran liable for failing to fulfill its "special duty" under the Vienna Convention on Diplomatic Relations "to take all appropriate steps to protect the premises of [a diplomatic] mission against any intrusion or damage" and to safeguard the personal inviolability of diplomats by taking "all appropriate steps to prevent any attack on [their] person, freedom or dignity." United States Diplomatic and Consular Staff in Tehran (United States of America v. Iran), 1980 I.C.J. 3, 30 (May 24). The inaction of Iranian authorities in attempting to prevent the attack or to end the hostage situation amounted to a breach of Iran's responsibility to protect foreign embassies in its territory. Later on, Iranian authorities officially approved the occupation and declared that the U.S. personnel at the embassy were "under arrest." At that point, reasoned the Court, "The militants, authors of the invasion and jailers of the hostages, had now become agents of the Iranian State for whose acts the State itself was internationally responsible." Id. at 35.

2. In the *Nicaragua* case, discussed in Chapters 4 and 11, the International Court of Justice considered whether the United States was responsible for violations of international humanitarian law allegedly committed by the "*contra*" rebel forces in Nicaragua. The Court found that the United States had provided substantial assistance to the *contras* in the form of financing, training, equipping, and organizing them, and that this assistance violated international law (regarding intervention in another state). Nevertheless, the Court concluded that the United States was not responsible for the specific acts of the *contras*. The Court reasoned:

> [D]espite the heavy subsidies and other support provided to them by the United States, there is no clear evidence of the United States having actually exercised such a degree of control in all fields as to justify treating the *contras* as acting on its behalf. . . . [The United States would not be responsible for the conduct of the *contras*] without further evidence, that the United States directed or enforced the perpetration of the acts contrary to human rights and humanitarian law alleged by the applicant State. Such acts could well be committed by members of the Contras without the control of the United States. For this conduct to give rise to legal responsibility of the United States, it would in principle have to be proved that that State had effective control of the military or paramilitary operations in the course of which the alleged violations were committed. [Military and Paramilitary Activities In and Against Nicaragua (Nicaragua v. United States of America), 1986 I.C.J. 14, 62-65 (June 27).]

3. In its 1999 decision in *Prosecutor v. Tadić,* the Appeals Chamber of the International Criminal Tribunal for the former Yugoslavia adopted a less exacting standard for determining when a state exercises enough control over nonstate actors to be held responsible for their actions. In that case, the Appeals Chamber had to decide whether the actions of the defendant, who was linked to Bosnian Serb forces, had occurred in the context of an international armed conflict, which turned on whether the Federal Republic of Yugoslavia was responsible for the actions of the Bosnian Serb forces. In the context of assessing state control over the actions of organized groups, the Chamber concluded that it is sufficient for attribution "that the Group as a whole be under the overall control of the State." Prosecutor v. Tadić, Case No. IT-94-1-A, Judgment of the Appeals Chamber ¶120 (July 15, 1999). If the group is under the overall control of the State, the Chamber reasoned, "it must perforce engage the *responsibility of that State* for its activities, *whether or not each of them was specifically* imposed, requested or directed by the State." Id. at ¶122. Under this analysis, in order for a state to be responsible for the actions of a military or paramilitary group:

> [I]t must be proved that the State wields overall control over the group, not only by equipping and financing the group, but also by coordinating or helping in the general planning of its military activity. . . . However, it is not necessary that, in addition, the State should also issue, either to the head or to members of the group, instructions for the commission of specific acts contrary to international law. . . . Under international law it is by no means necessary that the controlling authorities should plan all the operations of the units dependent on them, choose their targets, or give specific instructions concerning the conduct of military operations and any alleged violations of international humanitarian law. . . . Acts performed by the group or members thereof may be regarded as acts of *de facto* State organs regardless of any specific instruction by the controlling State concerning the commission of each of those acts. [Id. at ¶¶131-137.]

The ICJ had occasion to reconsider the standard of control in a case brought by Bosnia alleging that the state then known as the Federal Republic of Yugoslavia was responsible for genocide carried out by the armed forces of the self-declared Bosnian Serb Republic, which was attempting to break away from Bosnia. The ICJ took note of the ICTY's decision in the *Tadić* case but elected to retain the "effective control" test articulated in the *Nicaragua* case. The ICJ stated:

> [T]he "overall control" test has the major drawback of broadening the scope of State responsibility well beyond the fundamental principle governing the law of international responsibility: a State is responsible only for its own conduct, that is to say the conduct of persons acting, on whatever basis, on its behalf. . . . [T]he "overall control" test is unsuitable, for it stretches too far, almost to breaking point, the connection which must exist between the conduct of a State's organs and its international responsibility. [Application of the Convention on the Prevention and Punishment of the Crime of Genocide (Bosnia and Herzegovina v. Serbia and Montenegro), Judgment, ¶406 (Feb. 26, 2007), reprinted in 46 I.L.M. 188 (2007).]

4. How does the test for attribution in *Tadić* differ from the one in *Nicaragua?* Which test do the ILC Draft Articles adopt? Based on the Christenson excerpt, the ILC Draft Articles, and the *Nicaragua* and *Tadić* cases, when is a state responsible for the conduct of nonstate actors? For example, when would a state be responsible for

the actions of a terrorist organization that operated from within the state's borders? See Chapter 11.B.e.

5. In a federal state (such as the United States), is the national government responsible for the conduct of sub-national officials? What if the national government lacks the constitutional authority to stop the sub-national officials from engaging in the allegedly wrongful conduct? Should a country be able to avoid its international law obligations by saying that authority for carrying out those obligations rests with subordinate levels of government? In its initial order in the *LaGrand Case* (discussed in Chapters 3 and 4), the International Court of Justice made clear that the United States was responsible for violations of the Vienna Convention on Consular Relations by state or local authorities in the United States, stating that "the international responsibility of a State is engaged by the action of the competent organs and authorities acting in that State, whatever they may be." *LaGrand Case* (Germany v. United States of America), 1999 I.C.J. 9, 16 (Mar. 3) (Provisional Measures Order). The central role of states in the conduct of criminal law under the American federal scheme has generated constitutional questions about how the federal government could implement decisions in *LaGrand* and *Avena and Other Mexican Nationals* (Mexico v. United States of America), 2004 I.C.J. 12 (Mar. 31), which also concerned the criminal convictions in American courts of foreign nationals who had not been notified of their right to consular access under the Vienna Convention on Consular Relations. See Chapter 3.

6. To what extent is a nation responsible under international law for the decisions of its courts? What if the political branches of the nation had no role in the litigation? In an arbitration case brought against the United States under Chapter 11 of the North American Free Trade Agreement (NAFTA), the arbitration panel held that a U.S. judicial decision could constitute an expropriation for purposes of the Agreement. Chapter 11 applies to "measures adopted or maintained by a party" that relate to investors or investment, and NAFTA defines "measure" to include "any law, regulation, procedure, requirement or practice." The Loewen Group, Inc. v. United States, ICSID Case No. ARB(AF)/98/3, Decision on Hearing of Respondent's Objection to Competence and Jurisdiction, ¶¶39-40 (Jan. 5, 2001). The panel noted that this is a broad definition that contains no exclusion for judicial decisions and that the term "measure" has been construed by other tribunals to encompass judicial decisions. The panel also reasoned that interpreting the word "measure" in this way "accords with the general principle of State responsibility." Id. at ¶47. (In 2003, the panel dismissed all claims against the United States on other grounds. See Chapter 4.)

7. For additional discussion of the issue of attribution, see Jan Arno Hessbruegge, The Historical Development of the Doctrines of Attribution and Due Diligence in International Law, 36 N.Y.U. J. Int'l L. & Pol. 265 (2004); Derek Jinks, State Responsibility for the Acts of Private Armed Groups, 4 Chi. J. Int'l L. 83 (2003). For additional discussion of the ILC Draft Articles, see Symposium, The ILC's State Responsibility Articles, 96 Am. J. Int'l L. 773 (2002).

3. *Property Rights*

Property rights issues remain hotly debated in the law of state responsibility. During the 1960s and 1970s, developing countries waged a vigorous attack on multinational corporate behavior and the international economic system in general, in part through advocating in the U.N. General Assembly the declaration of a "New International Economic Order" (NIEO). Their attempts were equally vigorously opposed by the United States and other capital-exporting states. One focus of the debate concerned expropriation of property. Although fewer states today assert a right to expropriate property without meeting international law-based standards of compensation, legal disputes related to foreign investment continue to arise.

Even as the debate about the lawfulness of expropriation has subsided somewhat, the reach of international law into the sphere of transnational economic activity has expanded. Multinational corporate investment today is often characterized more by complex contractual arrangements than by ownership of tangible real property like oil fields and copper mines. The U.S. government has in turn added repudiation of contracts to its list of actions, along with expropriation of property, that U.S. policy opposes, and a body of international investment law has developed. In addition, the concept of "expropriation" itself continues to evolve to address the interference with property rights stemming from regulatory action such as raising taxes, restricting currency exchanges, or strengthening environmental or other regulations. The Restatement describes the traditional U.S. position and some of the challenges to that position.

Restatement

Section 712. State Responsibility for Economic Injury to Nationals of Other States

A state is responsible under international law for injury resulting from:

(1) a taking by the state of the property of a national of another state that

(a) is not for a public purpose, or

(b) is discriminatory, or

(c) is not accompanied by provision for just compensation;

For compensation to be just under this Subsection, it must, in the absence of exceptional circumstances, be in an amount equivalent to the value of the property taken and be paid at the time of taking, or within a reasonable time thereafter with interest from the date of taking, and in a form economically usable by the foreign national;

(2) a repudiation or breach by the state of a contract with a national of another state

(a) where the repudiation or breach is (i) discriminatory; or (ii) motivated by noncommercial considerations, and compensatory damages are not paid; or

(b) where the foreign national is not given an adequate forum to determine his claim of repudiation or breach, or is not compensated for any repudiation or breach determined to have occurred; or

(3) other arbitrary or discriminatory acts or omissions by the state that impair property or other economic interests of a national of another state.

Reporters' Notes

1. *Status of international law on expropriation.* Subsection (1) restates the traditional principles of international law on expropriation. Early in this century these principles were settled law.

The first major challenge to these principles was posed by the U.S.S.R., which rejected the traditional rule, claiming that an alien enters the territory of another state or acquires property there subject wholly to local law. The principles were challenged also by Latin American governments. In 1938, in a famous exchange between Secretary of State Hull and the Minister of Foreign Relations of Mexico, the United States insisted that property of aliens was protected by an international standard under which expropriation was subject to limitations, notably that there must be "prompt, adequate and effective compensation." In contrast, the Government of Mexico insisted that international law required only that foreign nationals be treated no less favorably than were nationals, at least in the case of "expropriations of a general and impersonal character like those which Mexico has carried out for the purpose of redistribution of land." 3 Hackworth, Digest of International Law 655-61 (1942).

After the Second World War, with the coming of many new states and the rise of the "Third World" to influence, opposition to the traditional view received widespread support. For the new majority of states, a people's right to dispose of its national resources became "economic self-determination," and was designated a "human right" and placed at the head of both the International Covenant on Civil and Political Rights and the International Covenant on Economic, Social and Cultural Rights. In 1962, however, the United Nations General Assembly declared that in cases of expropriation of natural resources "the owner shall be paid appropriate compensation . . . in accordance with international law." Resolution on Permanent Sovereignty over Natural Resources, G.A. Res. 1803, ¶4, U.N. GAOR, 17th Sess., Supp. No. 17, at 15, U.N. Doc. A/5327 (Dec. 15, 1962).*

Divisions became sharper in 1974 when the United Nations General Assembly adopted the Charter of Economic Rights and Duties of States, which dealt with the subject without making any reference to international law. The Charter declared that every state has the right

> to nationalize, expropriate or transfer ownership of foreign property, in which case appropriate compensation should be paid by the State adopting such measures, taking into account its relevant laws and regulations and all circumstances that the State considers pertinent. In any case where the question of compensation gives rise to a controversy, it shall be settled under the domestic law of the nationalizing State and by its tribunals . . . [unless otherwise agreed].

The Charter was adopted by 120 in favor, 6 against, and 10 abstentions, the vote reflecting the views of the majority as developing states, with the United States among the dissenters and the other developed Western states either dissenting or abstaining.

The United States and other capital exporting states have rejected the challenge by developing states, have refused to agree to any change in the traditional principles, and have denied that these have been replaced or modified in customary law by state practice. Those states have taken the position that the traditional requirements are solidly based on both the moral rights of property owners and on the needs of an effective international system of private investment. . . .

Both before and after the adoption of the Charter of Economic Rights and Duties of States, many states, including many developing states that supported the Charter (though not generally states in Latin America), concluded bilateral agreements that included provisions for compensation in the case of expropriation. Some of those provisions are contained in treaties of friendship, commerce, and navigation, as part of broader accommodations for foreign trade and investment. Others appear in agreements aimed particularly at the security of foreign investment. . . . Some provisions for

*[The vote on that resolution was 87-2, with 12 abstentions. The United States voted for it. — EDS.]

compensation appear in arrangements whereby a state guarantees the investments of its nationals against loss due to expropriation, after agreement with the state host to the investment. . . .

As noted in the Restatement, the United States has entered into numerous Friendship, Commerce, and Navigation (FCN) treaties and Bilateral Investment Treaties (BITs) that contain provisions protecting property rights. As an example, consider the excerpt of the BIT between the United States and the Republic of the Ukraine that is in the Documentary Supplement. Among other things, that treaty provides, in Article III:

> Investments shall not be expropriated or nationalized either directly or indirectly through measures tantamount to expropriation or nationalization ("expropriation") except: for a public purpose; in a nondiscriminatory manner; upon payment of prompt, adequate and effective compensation.
>
> . . . Compensation shall be equivalent to the fair market value of the expropriated investment immediately before the expropriatory action was taken or became known, whichever is earlier; be calculated in a freely usable currency on the basis of the prevailing market rate of exchange at that time; be paid without delay; include interest at a commercially reasonable rate. . . .

Notes and Questions

1. What was the basis for Soviet and developing country opposition to the traditional international law rules governing expropriation? Recall that in its 1964 decision in *Sabbatino,* excerpted in Chapter 6, the Supreme Court stated that "there are few if any issues in international law today on which opinion seems to be so divided as the limitations of a state's power to expropriate the property of an alien."

2. Why do you think there is less controversy today over the international law rules governing property rights?

3. What investment protections are contained in the U.S.-Ukraine BIT excerpted in the Documentary Supplement? Note that, as of August 2010, the United States had concluded 47 BITs, seven of which had not yet entered into force either because they were awaiting completion of ratification procedures in one or both of the signatory states. These treaties are with a variety of Eastern European, Latin American, Middle Eastern, Asian, and African countries.

4. Congress has adopted a number of measures designed to induce compliance by other countries with U.S. views of appropriate property guarantees. These statutory directives purport to require denial of U.S. foreign development assistance (the Hickenlooper Amendment, 22 U.S.C. §2370(e)(1)) as well as revocation of duty-free tariff treatment (19 U.S.C. §2462(b)(4)) for those states that expropriate American property without paying just compensation. Recall also the congressional limitation on the act of state doctrine for some of these situations. (See Chapter 6.) In addition, Congress has directed the President to vote against loans for those countries by international financial institutions, such as the World Bank, the Inter-American Development Bank, and the Asian Development Bank (22 U.S.C. §2370a(b)).

5. As part of the resolution of the 1979-1981 Iranian hostage crisis, an Iran-U.S. Claims Tribunal was established in The Hague to resolve, among other things, claims of U.S. nationals against Iran and of Iranian nationals against the United States, which arose out of debts, contracts, expropriations, or other measures affecting property rights. As of January 2011, the Tribunal had resolved almost 4,000 claims and had issued 601 awards, the majority of which were in favor of U.S. claimants. The Tribunal's reliance on general principles of international law was discussed in Chapter 2.D. For additional discussion of the Tribunal and its jurisprudence, which addresses a wide variety of international law issues, see the discussion and sources cited in Chapter 4.D.1.

6. Following the defeat of Iraq in the Gulf War in 1991, the U.N. Security Council established a Compensation Commission to adjudicate claims against Iraq arising out of its invasion and occupation of Kuwait. See S.C. Resolution 687 in the Documentary Supplement. Approximately 2.7 million claims were filed with the Commission, completed processing claims in June 2005. The procedures used by this Commission were much less formal (and less costly to administer) than those of the Iran-U.S. Claims Tribunal. Compensation is paid to successful claimants out of a fund that receives a percentage of the proceeds from sales of Iraqi oil; as of January 2011, over $31 billion in compensation has been distributed by the Commission. See Status of Claims Processing at http://www.uncc.ch/status.htm. For background on the Commission's structure and work, see generally The United Nations Compensation Commission: A Handbook (Marco Frigessi di Rittalma & Tullio Treves eds., 1999).

7. Frequently, expropriation claims asserted by the United States under international law have been settled by an international agreement in which the expropriating state pays a "lump sum," often equal to the amount of that state's assets in the United States that had earlier been frozen under IEEPA or similar legislation in response to the nationalization, in exchange for a "discharge" of all claims the United States has against that state under international law. Such a lump-sum agreement was involved in the *Pink* case excerpted in Chapter 3. Since 1992, the United States has signed lump-sum claims settlement agreements with Germany, Albania, Cambodia, and Vietnam. The lump sum typically translates into an amount less, sometimes far less, than the fair value of the claim. In 1990, the United States and Iran agreed to settle the remaining small claims (under $250,000) arising out of the 1979 revolution. As in the case of other lump-sum settlements, the claims involved were then referred for adjudication to the domestic U.S. Foreign Claims Settlement Commission (FCSC), an adjudicative body established by U.S. law to process claims of U.S. nationals against foreign governments. See 22 U.S.C. §§1645 et seq. Its work has normally involved adjudicating claims against governments that have agreed to lump-sum settlements negotiated by the State Department. The FCSC then determines the value of the claims of U.S. nationals who in turn are paid out of the lump sum received for that purpose by the U.S. government. In the case of the small claims against Iran, the FCSC adjudicated approximately 3,100 claims, awarded over $41 million to 1,075 claimants, and denied or dismissed for procedural reasons the rest. Through the end of 2009, the FCSC (and its predecessor agencies) had handled the administration of 45 claims programs, which have included more than 660,000 claims and awards

in excess of $3 billion. Foreign Claims Settlement Commission, U.S. Dept. of Justice, Annual Report 3 (2009).

8. Another way to deal with the risk of expropriation is through insurance. Both the U.S. government, through the Overseas Private Investment Corporation (OPIC), and the World Bank, through the Multilateral Investment Guaranty Agency (MIGA), have sponsored insurance programs under which, for a fee, an investor can be protected against war and expropriation risk, as well as against currency inconvertibility. Similar coverage may also be available in the private market.

Problem. If you were counsel to a corporation considering the establishment of a factory to manufacture aspirin in Indonesia, what legal protections, if any, regarding expropriation would you seek? What issues could be more important than expropriation, and how could you deal with them? How would you describe to your board of directors the relative value of a guarantee of no expropriation (or no currency controls) in (a) the Indonesia constitution, (b) a U.S.-Indonesia treaty, (c) customary international law, (d) insurance from OPIC or MIGA, (e) an individually negotiated agreement between your company and the government of Indonesia, or (f) the threat of U.S. retaliation?

9. As discussed in Chapter 4, the North American Free Trade Agreement contains provisions designed to protect cross-border investors in Canada, the United States, and Mexico. Under Chapter 11 of NAFTA, each of the three NAFTA countries is prohibited from discriminating against investors from the other two countries and from expropriating the property of those investors except in accordance with international law. With respect to expropriation, Chapter 11 provides in relevant part:

> 1. No Party may directly or indirectly nationalize or expropriate an investment of an investor of another Party in its territory or take a measure tantamount to nationalization or expropriation of such an investment ("expropriation"), except:
>
> (a) for a public purpose;
> (b) on a nondiscriminatory basis;
> (c) in accordance with due process of law . . . and
> (d) on payment of compensation. . . .
>
> 2. Compensation shall be equivalent to the fair market value of the expropriated investment immediately before the expropriation took place ("date of expropriation"), and shall not reflect any change in value occurring because the intended expropriation had become known earlier. Valuation criteria shall include going concern value, asset value including declared tax value of tangible property, and other criteria, as appropriate, to determine fair market value. [NAFTA, art. 1110.]

Investors who believe that the Chapter 11 protections have been violated are allowed to initiate an arbitration against the NAFTA country in question. For a list of the cases that have been brought against each of the three NAFTA countries, see the State Department's Web site at http://www.state.gov/s/l/c3439.htm.

10. NAFTA's reference to measures "tantamount" to an expropriation implicates the important question of when regulatory measures qualify as an "indirect" or "creeping" taking of property under international law. Consider the discussion of the problem in the following excerpt.

[I]nternational law prohibits not only formal expropriations or nationalizations of alien property—that is, acts involving a formal transfer of title—but also, in the words of the . . . [Restatement,] "when [a state] subjects alien property to taxation, regulation, or other action that is confiscatory, or that prevents, unreasonably interferes with, or unduly delays, effective enjoyment of an alien's property or its removal from the state's territory."

The apparent clarity of the doctrine blurs, however, when we consider the reality that a great deal of the activity of the modern state entails regulating social and economic activity in ways that interfere substantially with the enjoyment of property rights. Land use regulations, for instance, preclude owners of property zoned for residential purposes from operating businesses or factories, or impose size and setback limitations on the kinds of structures they may erect on their land. Building, fire, and housing codes limit the kinds of materials and architectural designs property owners may employ. Income taxes deprive owners of enterprises of the enjoyment of a portion—often a very substantial portion—of the earnings generated by their property. Occupational health and safety standards, as well as minimum wage requirements, similarly interfere with the ability of owners of enterprises to fully exploit, and enjoy, their property. Environmental regulations, too, can impose substantial costs on businesses and can even require the closure of businesses engaged in environmental hazardous activities. Requiring states to compensate foreign property owners for the costs of such regulatory acts, as customary international law "unreasonable interference" doctrine might seem to mandate, could make them prohibitively expensive. More fundamentally, such a rule would be inconsistent with basic notions of the rights of sovereign states to regulate matters within their territories in the public interest.

The protection accorded to foreign property under international law does not, however, require such a result. For as a corollary to the rules prohibiting "unreasonable interference" with an owner's enjoyment of her property, international law also recognizes that a state need not compensate foreign property owners for interference with property interests that results [—according to the commentary to the Restatement—] from "bona fide general taxation, regulation, forfeiture for crime, or other action of the kind that is commonly accepted as within the police power of states." . . .

States and tribunals in the future will continue to confront situations in which states adopt regulatory measures that injure foreign property interests, and they will have to examine the purpose of the government action. . . . But arbitral tribunals will need to go beyond assessing whether a measure in fact is directed at some stated public welfare purpose. Evaluations of indirect expropriation claims will instead depend to a large degree on an assessment of the legitimacy of public welfare objectives . . . where it is not disputed that those measures have been adopted in good faith.

[Determining] the legitimacy of regulatory purposes will depend on *international* practice. Those regulatory purposes, such as protecting public health, that are recognized by both developed/capital-exporting states and developing/capital-importing states are likely to be accepted as legitimate. Those regulatory purposes accepted by only some states, such as the redistributive and collectivist goals that characterized the New International Economic Order of the 1970s, in comparison, are unlikely to be deemed legitimate for purposes of relieving a state of liability for economic injury to foreign property owners and investors, even if they reflect the territorial state's current standard of behavior. . . .

[In other words,] the question of whether a regulatory measure constitutes an indirect expropriation under international law will depend in part on the extent of international acceptance of the particular substantive public welfare purposes a measure seeks to advance. [Allen S. Weiner, Indirect Expropriations: The Need for a Taxonomy of "Legitimate" Regulatory Purposes, 5 Int'l L. Forum 166, 167-168, 173-175 (2003).]

4. *Nationality*

The rule that a state may assert rights of diplomatic protection only if one of its nationals is injured by another state raises the question of what it takes to be a national of a state in order to enable that state to present a claim or provide its diplomatic protection. The most difficult issues typically involve the nationality of corporate entities.

For most purposes a state itself determines who are its nationals (e.g., persons born in the country, or persons born of parents who are its nationals, or persons who are duly "naturalized"). That determination confers rights (e.g., to vote) and, as we saw in Chapter 7, responsibilities (e.g., the duty to respond to a subpoena) as a matter of domestic law. However, just because a person is a national for purposes of domestic law does not necessarily mean that the person is a national entitled to diplomatic protection. Consider the following excerpts from the Restatement.

Restatement

Section 211. Nationality of Individuals

For purposes of international law, an individual has the nationality of a state that confers it, but other states need not accept that nationality when it is not based on a *genuine link* between the state and the individual. [Emphasis added.]

Comment

. . . *b. Nationality and diplomatic protection.* International law recognizes the right of a state to afford diplomatic protection to its nationals and to represent their interests. Such formal diplomatic protection is generally limited to nationals, but international practice accepts informal intercessions by states on behalf of individuals who are not their nationals. Moreover, a state party to an international human rights agreement has the right to enforce the agreement on behalf of an alien, indeed even a national of the alleged violator-state. . . .

c. "Genuine link". A state is free to establish nationality law and confer nationality as it sees fit. However, under international law other states need not recognize a nationality that is involuntary or that is not based on an accepted "genuine link." The precise contours of this concept, however, are not clear. Laws that confer nationality on grounds of birth in a state's territory (*ius soli*) or of birth to parents who are nationals (*ius sanguinis*) are universally accepted as based on genuine links. Voluntary naturalization is generally recognized by other states but may be questioned where there are no other ties to the state, e.g., a period of residence in the state. The comparative "genuineness" and strength of links between a state and an individual are relevant also for resolving competing claims between two states asserting nationality, or between such states and a third state. . . .

Reporters' Notes

1. "*Genuine link.*" The Nottebohm Case (Liechtenstein v. Guatemala), [1955] I.C.J. Rep. 4, ruled that because there was no genuine link between Nottebohm and Liechtenstein, Guatemala did not have to recognize his Liechtenstein nationality and

Liechtenstein could not bring proceedings before the International Court of Justice on his behalf against Guatemala. Nottebohm, originally of German nationality, was a long-time resident of Guatemala. He had taken a brief trip to Liechtenstein during which he complied with its requirements for naturalization and then returned to Guatemala. Although Liechtenstein's naturalization law required a showing of loss of prior nationality, and German law provided for loss of German nationality upon acquisition of another nationality, Guatemala, at war with Germany, treated Nottebohm as an alien enemy. Liechtenstein objected and brought a proceeding before the International Court of Justice. The Court referred to international arbitral decisions holding that the state to which a dual national has stronger ties is the one entitled to extend protection against third states. It is not clear from the opinion whether a third country would have been entitled to ignore Liechtenstein's naturalization of Nottebohm, since the court stressed the comparative ties of Nottebohm to Liechtenstein and to Guatemala. Nothing in the case suggests that a state may refuse to give effect to a nationality acquired at birth, regardless of how few other links the individual had at birth or maintained later. . . .

Section 213. Nationality of Corporations

For purposes of international law, a corporation has the nationality of the state under the laws of which the corporation is organized.

Comment . . .

b. Relevance of corporate nationality under international law. The nationality of a corporation is relevant under international law for various purposes. A state is responsible for injury to an alien corporation and the state of the corporation's nationality may make a claim for the injury. A state may exercise jurisdiction to prescribe laws for acts of its corporate nationals committed outside of its territory. Corporate nationality is relevant when states claim treaty rights for their nationals.

c. Nationality and state of incorporation. The traditional rule stated in this section, adopted for certainty and convenience, treats every corporation as a national of the state under the laws of which it was created. . . .

As in the case of an individual, a state may refuse to treat a corporation as a national of the state that created it, and reject diplomatic protection by that state, where there is no "genuine link" between them.

d. Significant connections other than nationality. Since a corporation has the nationality of the state that created it, a corporation usually does not have the nationality of more than one state. But connections other than nationality may be significant for the purposes indicated in Comment *b.* In some circumstances, other states may treat as analogous to nationality the fact (i) that the shares of a corporation are substantially owned by nationals of that state; (ii) that the corporation is managed from an office within the state, or (iii) that the corporation has a principal place of business in that state. For example, in time of war, a state may treat a corporation having such ties to the enemy state as an enemy national even though it was incorporated in a non-belligerent state.

The state having such links to a corporation may treat the corporation as its national at least for some purposes. In some circumstances, the state may prescribe law for the corporation even in regard to acts committed outside the state's territory. For a state's limited jurisdiction to prescribe for foreign branches or subsidiaries of its corporations, see §414. . . . The United States has provided diplomatic protection for such companies in case of expropriation or other injury, particularly where the act was directed at the corporation because of its links with the United States. See §713.

e. Special definitions of corporate nationality by international agreement. States are free to depart from the rule of this section by international agreement. Different definitions of corporate nationality are sometimes found in tax treaties, treaties of establishment, treaties of friendship, commerce, and navigation, and in claims settlement agreements.

f. Multinational corporations. The multinational enterprise or corporation (sometimes referred to as a transnational or global corporation) is an established feature of international economic life, but it has not yet achieved special status in international law or in national legal systems. A multinational corporation generally consists of a group of corporations, each established under the law of some state, linked by common managerial and financial control and pursuing integrated policies. (Some writers reserve the term for enterprises that also meet some standard of size in assets, sales, or similar indicator.) In general, the rule stated in this section applies both to the parent company and to its subsidiaries.

Reporters' Notes

1. *Corporate and individual nationality distinguished.* This section applies to corporations the concept of nationality that was developed for individuals, but rules about nationality of individuals can be applied to corporations only with caution. Whereas the individual exists and represents a single mind and body, corporations are a juridical construct and may unite large numbers of individuals having different nationalities. Corporate nationality, moreover, is peculiarly subject to manipulation.

2. *Diplomatic protection of corporations.* A state is entitled to represent and afford diplomatic protection to corporations having its nationality as to individual nationals. However, as indicated in Comment *c*, a respondent state is entitled to reject representation by the state of incorporation where that state was chosen solely for legal convenience, for example as a tax haven, and the corporation has no substantial links with that state, such as property, an office or commercial or industrial establishment, substantial business activity, or residence of substantial shareholders. Compare the Nottebohm Case, §211, Reporters' Note 1.

In the Barcelona Traction Case (Belgium v. Spain), [1970] I.C.J. Rep. 3, the International Court of Justice held that Belgium could not bring proceedings against Spain for injury to a corporation incorporated and having its headquarters in Canada, although most of the company's shares were owned by Belgian nationals, at least where Canada had in the past extended diplomatic protection to the corporation and retained the legal capacity to do so. Id. at 43-45.

3. *Protection of shareholders or subsidiaries against state of incorporation.* Barcelona Traction . . . gave preference to the state of incorporation over a state with other significant links, in representing a company against a third state. The decision does not preclude representation of the company by a state with significant links against the state of incorporation itself. A state cannot, by requiring a foreign enterprise to incorporate locally, compel the enterprise to surrender in advance its right to protection by the state

of its parent corporation or of the parent's shareholders. States have asserted the right to protect the interest of their nationals as shareholders in such a corporation, particularly when the corporation itself is disabled from acting on their behalf, e.g., when the state has dissolved it or placed it in receivership, perhaps because the corporation had claims against the state. The United States and other countries sometimes seek to protect the subsidiary corporation itself rather than its shareholders. The Claims Settlement Declaration of 1981 establishing the Iran-United States Claims Tribunal defines a "national" of Iran or of the United States to include, respectively, a corporation "organized under the laws of Iran or the United States or any of its states . . . , if, collectively, national persons who are citizens of such country hold, directly or indirectly an interest in such corporation or entity equivalent to fifty percent or more of its capital stock."

Notes and Questions

1. What connection must an individual have to a state to satisfy the "genuine link" requirement to establish nationality? What connection must a corporation have?

2. Which states can raise a claim on behalf of an individual or corporation that has more than one nationality? What if the claim is against one of the states of which the individual or corporation is a national? Can any state raise a claim on behalf of a "stateless" individual — that is, an individual who does not have citizenship in any state?

3. Almost one quarter of the large claims (claims of more than $250,000) filed with the Iran-U.S. Claims Tribunal were brought against Iran by claimants with dual American and Iranian nationality. George H. Aldrich, The Jurisprudence of the Iran-United States Claims Tribunal 54 (1996). The Iranian government strenuously argued that the Tribunal, which was empowered to hear claims by "nationals of the United States against Iran and claims of nationals of Iran against the United States," had no jurisdiction over the claims of such dual nationals. Nonetheless, the Tribunal, drawing on the *Nottebohm* decision discussed above, adopted the "dominant and effective" nationality test. In other words, the Tribunal would have jurisdiction over claims against Iran by claimants whose dominant and effective nationality during the relevant time period was American. The Tribunal identified the following factors that would influence the dominant and effective nationality determination: "habitual residence, center of interests, family ties, participation in public life and other evidence of attachment." Id. at 56 (citing Case No. A18 (Iran and United States), Decision No. DEC 32-A18-FT (Apr. 6, 1984)). For more on the Tribunal's jurisprudence on dual national claims, see also Charles H. Brower & Jason D. Brueschke, The Iran-United States Claims Tribunal 32-42 (1998).

4. In 2006, the International Law Commission adopted a set of Draft Articles on Diplomatic Protection. Report of the International Law Commission, 58th Sess., May 1-June 9, July 3-Aug. 11, 2006, U.N. Doc. A/61/10; GAOR, 61st Sess., Supp. No. 10 (2006). How do the following articles on corporate nationality in the ILC's Draft Articles compare with the Restatement's provisions?

Article 9

State of Nationality of a Corporation

For the purposes of the diplomatic protection of a corporation, the State of nationality means the State under whose law the corporation was incorporated. However, when the corporation is controlled by nationals of another State or States and has no substantial business activities in the State of incorporation, and the seat of management and the financial control of the corporation are both located in another State, that State shall be regarded as the State of nationality.

Article 11

Protection of Shareholders

A State of nationality of shareholders in a corporation shall not be entitled to exercise diplomatic protection in respect of such shareholders in the case of an injury to the corporation unless:

(a) The corporation has ceased to exist according to the law of the State of incorporation for a reason unrelated to the injury; or

(b) The corporation had, at the date of injury, the nationality of the State alleged to be responsible for causing the injury, and incorporation in that State was required by it as a precondition for doing business there.

Article 12

Direct Injury to Shareholders

To the extent that an internationally wrongful act of a State causes direct injury to the rights of shareholders as such, as distinct from those of the corporation itself, the State of nationality of any such shareholders is entitled to exercise diplomatic protection in respect of its nationals.

5. In a case involving the alleged expropriation of investments, businesses, and property of a Guinean national living in the Democratic Republic of the Congo (DRC), as well as his arrest, imprisonment, and expulsion from the DRC, the ICJ addressed a number of issues arising under the law of diplomatic protection, including nationality and exhaustion of remedies. Ahmadou Sadio Diallo (Guinea v. Democratic Republic of the Congo), Preliminary Objections Judgment (May 24, 2007), reprinted in 46 I.L.M. 712 712 (2007).

B. INTERNATIONAL HUMAN RIGHTS

1. *Background*

The Nazi atrocities and World War II caused world leaders to reject the traditional assumption that a state's international responsibility is limited to aliens. Today, the treatment by a state of its own nationals is a matter of significant international concern. International human rights law is the vehicle for expression of that concern. The following excerpt describes some of the pre-World War II antecedents of international human rights law.

Louis Henkin, The Age of Rights

13-15 (1990)

The internationalization of human rights, the transformation of the idea of constitutional rights in a few countries to a universal conception and a staple of international politics and law, is a phenomenon of the middle of our century. But it did not spring full-blown.

Historically, how a state treated persons in its territory was indeed its own affair, implicit in its territorial sovereignty. International law developed one early exception when it recognized that how a country treats a national of another state is the proper concern of that state. That exception might be seen as essentially political, not humanitarian, in motivation: if a citizen of the United States is abused elsewhere, the United States is offended. It was widely accepted, therefore, that injustice to a stateless person was not a violation of international law since no state was offended thereby; surely, there was no state that could invoke a remedy for such injustice. But assuming that the doctrine developed because the offended state was concerned for its own rather than for human dignity, it is significant that governments were offended by violations of the "human rights" of their nationals.

In order to determine whether a state could properly claim that its national had been denied "justice," international law developed an international standard of justice. There was no accepted philosophical foundation for such a standard, and no agreed definition of its content; doubtless, it was redolent of "natural rights" and tantamount to a notion of "fairness." Whatever its underpinnings, whatever its substance, the standard for the treatment of foreign nationals that was invoked by their governments and acquiesced in by host governments was often higher than that — if any — applied by these countries to their own citizens at home. The international standard, then, was not a universal human standard, and governments that invoked or accepted it did not suggest that it applied also to how governments treated their own citizens. The treatment accorded by a state to its own citizens was not the concern of international law or the business of other governments, and in fact governments rarely concerned themselves with domestic injustice elsewhere. The few major-power intercessions — for example, that of the United States in the nineteenth century in response to Russian pogroms — did not invoke international law and occurred only when violations were egregious and dramatic. This was usually the case when there was a demand for intercession by a domestic constituency with special affinity for the victims in other country (as in the United States, for example, the Irish, the Jews, and others).

International political considerations inspired other exceptions to the principle that how a government acts towards individuals at home is a matter of domestic concern only. Beginning in the seventeenth century, Catholic and Protestant princes (and others) concluded agreements according freedom of worship and wider toleration to each other's coreligionists. Later, governments assumed international obligations to respect freedoms for ethnic minorities, even those who as a matter of law were nationals of the country in which they lived; in the late nineteenth and early twentieth century, such minority treaties were virtually imposed by the major powers on smaller ones in Central and Eastern Europe because it was believed that violation of minority rights led to intervention by countries that identified with them, and thus to war. Again, the basis for international concern in these cases was some special affinity on the part of some government for some inhabitants of other countries, and concern for international peace, not concern by governments generally for the basic dignity of all human beings, including their own inhabitants. In a different context, the mandate system of the League of Nations following World War I required a commitment by the mandatory power to promote the welfare of the local population. It has been argued that such clauses, too, did not reflect bona fide concern for human rights but were only a "sop" to justify keeping "the natives" in continued tutelage in disregard of commitments to the principle of self-determination. There were authentic humanitarian motivations in the development of "humanitarian law" to mitigate the horrors of war by outlawing certain weapons, protecting the sick and wounded and prisoners of war, and safeguarding civilian populations, but that humanitarian law probably derived from concern by states for their own soldiers and citizens, not for all human beings equally.

The International Labor Organization was an early and noteworthy contributor to international human rights. The ILO was organized after World War I to promote common basic standards of labor and social welfare. In the intervening seventy years, the ILO has promulgated more than a hundred international conventions, which have been widely adhered to and fairly well observed. Again, some might find political-economic rather than humanitarian motivations for what the ILO achieved. The ILO, it is said, was the West's fearful answer to socialism, which had gained its first bridgehead in the USSR; perhaps the conventions reflected also a desire by developed states to reduce "unfair competition" from countries with sub-standard labor conditions.

A less ambiguous example of early international concern for human rights was the movement in the nineteenth century, after major powers abolished slavery in their countries, to outlaw slavery and slave trade by international agreement. Perhaps slavery was sufficiently egregious that no state could be allowed to claim to contain it within its domestic jurisdiction. Moreover, the products of slave labor were sold abroad at a competitive advantage with goods produced by societies that had abolished slavery. Slave trade, surely, was not an internal matter only, involving as it did international trade and colonial competition.

In all, international relations before our time were not impervious to the human conditions inside countries, but concern for individual welfare was framed and confined within the state system. That concern could not spill over state borders except in ways and by means that were consistent with the assumptions of that system, that is, when a state identified with inhabitants of other states on recognized grounds, and that identification threatened international order; when the condition of individuals inside a country impinged on the economic interests of other countries. Whatever the reasons, primitive human rights provisions appeared in international instruments, and the seeds of international human rights were planted.

Much of the discussion in this section focuses on the human rights obligations that states owe to individuals. Bear in mind, however, that individuals may also be held responsible in some circumstances for violating international human rights standards embodied in either treaties or customary international law. Violations of some human rights standards, for example, can give rise to individual criminal liability. The Nuremberg trials after World War II, in which German officials were tried for war crimes and crimes against humanity, were important precedents in establishing the responsibility of government officials for human rights abuses, even abuses committed against their own population. The Charter authorizing those trials defined crimes against humanity as encompassing "murder, extermination, enslavement, deportation, and other inhumane acts committed against any civilian population, before or during the war; or persecutions on political, racial or religious grounds in execution of or in connection with any crime within the jurisdiction of the Tribunal, whether or not in violation of the domestic law of the country where perpetrated." (The Nuremberg trials and international criminal law are discussed in Chapter 12.) Non-state actors (e.g., individuals and possibly corporations) may also in some circumstances be held civilly liable for violating international human rights standards. A prominent example of this is civil litigation in U.S. courts under the Alien Tort Statute (among others) discussed below in Section B.8.d.

2. *U.N. Charter and Universal Declaration*

Article 1 of the U.N. Charter, excerpted in the Documentary Supplement, lists a variety of "purposes" of the United Nations. These purposes include the following:

> To achieve international cooperation in solving international problems of an economic, social, cultural, or humanitarian character, and in promoting and encouraging respect for human rights and for fundamental freedoms for all without distinction as to race, sex, language, or religion. [Article 1(3).]

Consistent with these purposes, Article 55 of the Charter provides specifically for the promotion of human rights by the United Nations:

> With a view to the creation of conditions of stability and well-being which are necessary for peaceful and friendly relations among nations based on respect for the principle of equal rights and self-determination of peoples, the United Nations shall promote:
>
> a. higher standards of living, full employment, and conditions of economic and social progress and development;
>
> b. solutions of international economic, social, health, and related problems; and international cultural and educational cooperation; and
>
> c. universal respect for, and observance of, human rights and fundamental freedoms for all without distinction as to race, sex, language, or religion.

In addition, Article 56 of the Charter states that all members of the United Nations "pledge themselves to take joint and separate action in cooperation with the Organization for the achievement of the purposes set forth in Article 55."

The Charter provisions reflect an important early commitment to promoting human rights, but they do not themselves define those rights. In 1948, the U.N. General Assembly adopted a Universal Declaration of Human Rights that attempted to set forth "a common standard of achievement for all peoples and all nations." The Declaration (which is also excerpted in the Documentary Supplement) lists a variety of political, social, economic, and cultural rights. The Declaration was adopted by the General Assembly without dissent. The vote was 48 to 0, with eight abstentions, primarily by the Soviet Union and the Communist states of Eastern Europe. The Soviet bloc nations subsequently accepted the Declaration when they agreed to the 1975 Final Act of the Conference on Security and Cooperation in Europe, also known as the Helsinki Accords. The Helsinki Accords state, among other things, that "the participating States will act in conformity with the purposes and principles of the Charter of the United Nations and the Universal Declaration of Human Rights."

Although not a legally binding document per se, the Universal Declaration helped give content to the U.N. Charter's general human rights provisions. Together, the U.N. Charter and the Universal Declaration laid the groundwork for a revolutionary change in the focus of international law.

Louis B. Sohn, The New International Law: Protection of the Rights of Individuals Rather Than States

32 Am. U. L. Rev. 1, 14-18 (1982)

As nature abhors a vacuum, constitutional documents abhor strait-jackets. Great ideas cannot be imprisoned; they must be able to move freely from one part of the earth to another. The U.N. Charter contains several such ideas, which revolutionized the world, although no one knew in 1945 how successful the drafters of the Charter would be in planting in that document the seeds from which many mighty trees would grow.

The most influential of these ideas are that human rights are of international concern, and that the United Nations has the duty to promote "universal respect for, and observance of, human rights and fundamental freedoms for all without distinction as to race, sex, language and religion." . . . In the Charter's preamble, the peoples of the United Nations as well as their governments, have reaffirmed their "faith in fundamental human rights, in the dignity and worth of the human person, in the equal rights of men and women and of nations large and small." . . .

Although the U.N. Charter mentions human rights in many places, time constraints at the San Francisco conference made it impossible to prepare a more detailed document paralleling the national bills or declarations of the rights of man and of the citizen. It was promised at that time, however, that the United Nations would commence the drafting of an International Bill of Rights as one of the first items of business. The Commission on Human Rights was established in 1946, only a few months after the Charter came into force, and was asked to prepare such a document. It soon became obvious that the task could take a long time and, in view of the urgency of the matter, that the first step should be a declaration of general principles, to be followed later by a document containing more precise obligations.

Two years later the first document—the Universal Declaration of Human Rights—was ready. On December 10, 1948, the General Assembly, after some amendments, approved it unanimously, with eight abstentions: the Soviet bloc, Saudi Arabia, and the Union of South Africa. Although some delegations emphasized that the Universal Declaration of Human Rights was not a treaty imposing legal obligations, others more boldly argued that it was more than an ordinary General Assembly resolution, that it was a continuation of the Charter and shared the dignity of that basic document. It merely expressed more forcefully rules that already were recognized by customary international law. Under the latter view, the Declaration would possess a binding character. . . . The Declaration itself proclaims that it is "a common standard of achievement for all peoples and all nations." It exhorts every individual and every organ of society to strive, "by progressive measures, national and international, to secure . . . universal and effective recognition and observance [of the rights and freedoms therein]." . . .

The Declaration thus is now considered to be an authoritative interpretation of the U.N. Charter, spelling out in considerable detail the meaning of the phrase "human rights and fundamental freedoms," which Member States agreed in the Charter to promote and observe. The Universal Declaration has joined the Charter of the United Nations as part of the constitutional structure of the world community.

Notes and Questions

1. The U.N. Charter is a binding treaty that has been ratified by almost all states in the world. In light of that fact, what is the legal significance of Articles 55 and 56? What obligations do those Articles impose? How, if at all, can these Articles be enforced? Should individuals have the right to invoke those Articles in domestic courts?

2. The Universal Declaration is not a treaty and, at least originally, was considered nonbinding. As we discuss below, many of the rights set forth in the Declaration have now been codified in treaties. In addition, many commentators have argued that at least some of the provisions of the Declaration reflect customary international law and are therefore binding even on states that have not ratified the relevant treaties. Read through the Declaration. Which rights, if any, do you think should be binding even in the absence of a treaty?

3. Do the rights in the Declaration reflect Western values? In a diverse world of over 190 countries, is it possible to have one universal set of human rights? For a critical perspective, consider these comments by Professor Makau Mutua:

> The adoption in 1948 by the United Nations of the Universal Declaration of Human Rights—the foundational document of the human rights movement—sought to give universal legitimacy to a doctrine that is fundamentally Eurocentric in its construction. Sanctimonious to a fault, the Universal Declaration underscored its arrogance by proclaiming itself the "common standard of achievement for all peoples and nations." The fact that half a century later human rights have become a central norm of global civilization does not vindicate their universality. It is rather a telling testament to the conceptual, cultural, economic, military, and philosophical domination of the European West over non-European peoples and traditions.

> The fundamental texts of international human rights law are derived from bodies of domestic jurisprudence developed over several centuries in Western Europe and the United States. The dominant influence of Western liberal thought and philosophies is unmistakable. No one familiar with Western liberal traditions of political democracy and free market capitalism would find international human rights law unusual. Its emphasis on the individual egoist as the center of the moral universe underlines its European orientation. The basic human rights texts drew heavily from the American Bill of Rights and the French Declaration of the Rights of Man. There is virtually no evidence to suggest that they drew inspiration from Asian, Islamic, Buddhist, Hindu, African, or any other non-European traditions. [Makau Mutua, Human Rights: A Political and Cultural Critique 154 (2002).]

By contrast, Professor Mary Ann Glendon argues that the Universal Declaration of Human Rights reflects non-Western, as well as Western, values:

> It is true that the Declaration's provisions were derived from provisions of the world's existing and proposed constitutions and rights instruments—that is, mostly from countries with well-developed legal traditions. But the label "Western" obscures . . . [features that contributed to] the Declaration's acceptance in non-Western settings. . . .
>
> The Declaration . . . was far more influenced by the modern dignitarian rights tradition of continental Europe and Latin America than by the more individualistic documents of Anglo-American lineage. . . .
>
> Dignitarian rights instruments, with their emphasis on the family and their greater attention to duties, are more compatible with Asian and African traditions [than Anglo-American conceptions of rights]. In these documents, rights bearers tend to be envisioned within families and communities; rights are formulated so as to make clear their limits and their relation to one another as well as to the responsibilities that belong to citizens and the state. . . .
>
> In the spirit of the latter vision, the Declaration's "Everyone" is an individual who is constituted, in important ways, by and through relationships with others. "Everyone" is envisioned as uniquely valuable in himself (there are three separate references to the free development of one's personality), but "Everyone" is expected to act toward others "in a spirit of brotherhood." "Everyone" is depicted as situated in a variety of specifically named, real-life relationships of mutual dependency: families, communities, religious groups, workplaces, associations, societies, cultures, nations, and an emerging international order. Though its main body is devoted to basic individual freedoms, the Declaration begins with an exhortation to act in a "spirit of brotherhood" and ends with community, order, and society. [Mary Ann Glendon, A World Made New: Eleanor Roosevelt and the Universal Declaration of Human Rights 226-227 (2001).]

Professor Jack Donnelly adopts yet a third view. He agrees that few civilizations and cultures, as a historical or anthropological matter, had embraced a vision of equal and inalienable human rights prior to the seventeenth century. But this does not, in his view, undermine the legitimacy of the contemporary application of international human rights norms on a global basis:

> Whatever their past practice, nothing in indigenous African, Asian, or American cultures prevents them from endorsing human rights now. Cultures are immensely malleable. . . . It is an empirical question whether (any, some, or most) members of a culture . . . support human rights as a political conception of justice. . . .

> Today, . . . the moral equality of all human beings is strongly endorsed by most leading comprehensive doctrines in all regions of the world. This convergence, both within and between civilizations, provides the foundation for a convergence on the rights of the Universal Declaration. . . .
>
> . . . People, when given a chance, usually (in the contemporary world) choose human rights, irrespective of region, religion, or culture.
>
> Few "ordinary" citizens in any country have a particularly sophisticated sense of human rights. They respond instead to the general idea that they and their fellow citizens are entitled to equal treatment and certain basic goods, services, protections, and opportunities. . . . [T]he Universal Declaration presents a reasonable first approximation of the list they would come up with, largely irrespective of culture, after considerable reflection. [Jack Donnelly, The Relative Universality of Human Rights, 29 Hum. Rts. Q. 281, 291-292 (2007).]

4. In a 2005 decision, the European Court of Human Rights (discussed below) ruled in a divided judgment that a decree promulgated by Istanbul University in Turkey prohibiting students from wearing Islamic headscarves did not violate guarantees of religious freedom set out in the European Convention on Human Rights. The Court concluded that the headscarf ban was justified in light of Turkey's interest in preserving the secular nature of Turkish institutions and securing the rights of women. Şahin v. Turkey, 44 Eur. Ct. H.R. Rep. 99 (2005). Does this case present an example of a conflict between competing cultural attitudes about human rights?

5. In 2010, a divided Human Rights Council (discussed below) adopted a resolution entitled "Combating Defamation of Religions." Stressing "the need to effectively combat defamation of all religions and incitement to religious hatred in general and against Islam and Muslims in particular," the resolution urged states to provide legal protection against "acts of hatred, discrimination, intimidation and coercion resulting from defamation of religions." Human Rights Council Res. 13/16, Rep. of the Human Rights Council, 13th Sess., March 1-26, 2010, U.N. Doc. A/HRC/RES/13/16 (March 25, 2010). Explaining the U.S. vote against the resolution, the U.S. representative to the Council stated: "We cannot agree that prohibiting speech is the way to promote tolerance, and . . . we continue to see the 'defamation of religions' concept used to justify censorship, criminalization, and in some cases violent assaults and deaths of political, racial, and religious minorities around the world." Does this issue present an example of a conflict between competing cultural attitudes about human rights?

3. The International Covenants

Immediately following the passage of the Declaration, the United Nations Commission on Human Rights began drafting a human rights covenant aimed at converting the nonbinding provisions of the Declaration into binding treaty obligations. This process eventually led to the promulgation of two separate human rights treaties, the International Covenant on Civil and Political Rights (ICCPR) and the International Covenant on Economic, Social and Cultural Rights (ICESCR), both of which are excerpted in the Documentary Supplement. Along with the Universal Declaration, these Covenants are sometimes described as forming an "international bill of rights." The ICCPR entered into force in 1976 and, as of February 2011, had been ratified by 167 parties, including the United States. The ICESCR also took effect in 1976 and, as of February 2011, had been ratified by 160 parties. The United States signed the ICESCR in 1977 but, as of February 2011, had not ratified it.

The ICCPR includes a wide array of civil and political rights, including a right of self-determination, protection against discrimination, a right to life, prohibitions on torture and slavery, procedural rights concerning arrest, trial, and detention, a right of privacy, and rights of association and assembly. The ICESCR also contains a broad list of rights, including rights to work, to join trade unions, to obtain social security, to have an adequate standard of living, and to education. The ICESCR, however, is phrased in more gradual terms than the ICCPR. It provides, for example, that each party "undertakes to take steps . . . to the maximum of its available resources, with a view to achieving progressively the full realization of the rights recognized in the present Covenant by all appropriate means."

As called for by the terms of the ICCPR, a Human Rights Committee was established to monitor state compliance with the treaty. The Committee has 18 members, who are nominated and elected by the parties to the ICCPR; they serve in their individual capacities rather than as government representatives. Parties to the ICCPR are obligated to submit periodic reports to the Committee describing the measures they have taken to give effect to the rights recognized in the treaties. The Committee studies these reports and is authorized to issue "such general comments as it may consider appropriate." The Committee typically issues "concluding observations" about the country reports, including suggestions of ways in which the country can improve its human rights practices.

Under Article 41 of the ICCPR, parties may declare that they recognize a broader role for the Committee, whereby it will "receive and consider communications to the effect that a State Party claims that another State Party is not fulfilling its obligations under the present Covenant." If the parties cannot resolve the matter on their own, the Committee has the authority to "submit a report" on the matter. Over 45 states, including the United States, have issued declarations accepting this role for the Committee, but, as of February 2011, no complaints had actually been made pursuant to Article 41. In a General Comment on the ICCPR, however, the Human Rights Committee stressed that "every State Party has a legal interest in the performance by every other State Party of its obligations" under the Covenant.

> This follows from the fact that the "rules concerning the basic rights of the human person" are *erga omnes* obligations. . . . [T]he mere fact that a formal interstate mechanism for complaints to the Human Rights Committee exists in respect of States Parties that have made the declaration under article 41 does not mean that this procedure is the only method by which States Parties can assert their interest in the performance of other States Parties. On the contrary, the article 41 procedure should be seen as supplementary to, not diminishing of, States Parties' interest in each others' discharge of their obligations. Accordingly, the Committee commends to States Parties the view that violations of the Covenant rights by any State Party deserve their attention. To draw attention to possible breaches of Covenant obligations by other States Parties and to call on them to comply with their Covenant obligations should, far from being regarded as an unfriendly act, be considered as a reflection of legitimate community interest. [U.N. Human Rights Committee, General Comment 31(80), ¶2, U.N. Doc. CCPR/C/21/Rev.1/Add.13 (May 26, 2004).]

In 1976, a First Optional Protocol to the ICCPR took effect. The Protocol empowered the Committee to consider communications from individuals concerning alleged violations of the ICCPR. As of February 2011, 113 parties (but not the United States) had ratified this Protocol.* Unlike the state complaint process under Article 41, the individual communication process under this Protocol has been very active, and the Committee has developed an extensive jurisprudence through its issuance of opinions addressing these communications.

In addition to commenting on country reports and addressing communications under the First Optional Protocol, the Committee has issued a number of general comments interpreting the ICCPR. Many of these comments have been useful in clarifying the ICCPR's scope and have been relatively uncontroversial.

A monitoring committee also was established (in the late 1980s) to administer the ICESCR. This Committee on Economic, Social and Cultural Rights has issued a number of general comments, as well as reports, known as "concluding observations," about the practices of specific countries. In 2008, the General Assembly adopted an Optional Protocol to the IESCR that will, upon entry into force, permit the Committee to receive and consider claims from individuals or groups alleging violations of the economic, social, and cultural rights set forth in the ICESCR. The Protocol will enter into force following ratification by 10 states; as of February 2011, 35 states had signed the Protocol, and 3 states had ratified it.

Notes and Questions

1. Read through the ICCPR. Should any of these rights be controversial? Is the scope of some of these rights unclear? Does Article 6(1) have any relevance to abortion? What is encompassed by Article 7's reference to "cruel, inhuman or degrading treatment or punishment"? What does the word "promptly" mean in Article 9(3)? What constitutes an "arbitrary . . . interference with . . . privacy," referred to in Article 17(1)? Does the "equal protection of the law," referred to in Article 26, have the same scope as the equal protection of the law guaranteed under U.S. constitutional law?

2. Article 4 of the ICCPR allows parties to take measures derogating from their obligations under the treaty "[i]n time of public emergency which threatens the life of the nation." Why do you think the ICCPR contains this derogation clause? Should derogation from human rights obligations ever be permitted? Who decides whether there is the requisite public emergency? Note that no derogation is permitted with respect to certain provisions of the ICCPR, such as the provisions governing the right to life and the prohibitions on torture and slavery. See Article 4(2).

In 2001, the ICCPR's Human Rights Committee issued a general comment designed to "assist States parties to meet the requirements of article 4." The Committee stated, among other things, that (a) "[m]easures derogating from the provisions of the Covenant must be of an exceptional and temporary nature"; (b) "even during an armed conflict measures derogating from the Covenant are allowed only if and to the extent that the situation constitutes a threat to the life of the nation";

*A second Optional Protocol to the ICCPR took effect in 1991. This Protocol calls for abolition of the death penalty. As of February 2011, 73 parties (but not the United States) had ratified the Second Optional Protocol.

(c) parties are required to "provide careful justification not only for their decision to proclaim a state of emergency but also for any specific measures based on such a proclamation"; (d) Article 4 may never be invoked as a basis for "acting in violation of humanitarian law or peremptory norms of international law, for instance by taking hostages, by imposing collective punishments, through arbitrary deprivations of liberty or by deviating from fundamental principles of fair trial, including the presumption of innocence"; (e) elements of certain rights in the Covenant, even though not specifically listed as nonderogable in Article 4, cannot be subject to lawful derogation — for example, there can be no derogation from the prohibitions on taking of hostages, abductions, or secret detentions; and (f) a state availing itself of the right of derogation "must immediately inform the other States parties, through the United Nations Secretary-General, of the provisions it has derogated from and of the reasons for such measures." U.N. Human Rights Committee, General Comment 29, ¶¶2-17, U.N. Doc. CCPR/C/21/Rev.1/Add.11 (Aug. 31, 2001). Are these statements proper interpretations of the ICCPR? Do they go beyond mere interpretation?

3. Read through the ICESCR. Why is the ICESCR phrased in more gradual terms than the ICCPR? Note that the monitoring committee for the ICESCR issued a general comment in 1990 observing that, "while the Covenant provides for progressive realization and acknowledges the constraints due to the limits of available resources, it also imposes various obligations which are of immediate effect." These obligations include, said the committee, the obligation to "take steps" to implement the ICESCR and the obligation to guarantee that the rights under the ICESCR will be exercised without various forms of discrimination. The Committee further explained that, despite the "progressive realization" language in the ICESCR, there is an obligation "to move as expeditiously and effectively as possible towards" realizing the rights in the treaty and that "any deliberatively retrogressive measures in that regard would require the most careful consideration and would need to be fully justified by reference to the totality of the rights provided for in the Covenant and in the context of the full use of the maximum available resources." U.N. Committee on Economic, Social & Cultural Rights, General Comment 3, U.N. Doc. E/1991/23, annex III at 86 (1991).

4. Should the United States ratify the ICESCR? How do its provisions compare with current U.S. law? If the United States became a party, are there any provisions it should decline to accept (through reservations)?

5. The character of the "rights" covered by the ICESCR differs from those in the ICCPR not only in terms of their gradual, aspirational nature, but also with respect to whether states are required to ensure that they be given effect through domestic legal mechanisms. Article 2 of the ICCPR in this regard provides:

> 2. Where not already provided for by existing legislative or other measures, each State Party to the present Covenant undertakes to take the necessary steps, in accordance with its constitutional processes and with the provisions of the present Covenant, to adopt such laws or other measures as may be necessary to give effect to the rights recognized in the present Covenant.
>
> 3. Each State Party to the present Covenant undertakes:
>
> (a) To ensure that any person whose rights or freedoms as herein recognized are violated shall have an effective remedy, notwithstanding that the violation has been committed by persons acting in an official capacity;

(b) To ensure that any person claiming such a remedy shall have his right thereto determined by competent judicial, administrative or legislative authorities, or by any other competent authority provided for by the legal system of the State, and to develop the possibilities of judicial remedy;

(c) To ensure that the competent authorities shall enforce such remedies when granted.

What are the comparable enforcement provisions in the ICESCR?

6. Should the United States ratify the ICCPR's First Optional Protocol? What would be the advantages of doing so? The disadvantages?

7. Do the obligations under the ICCPR to protect human rights apply only to acts by governmental officials, or are states required to safeguard individuals against the violation of rights by private actors? Consider the Human Rights Committee's position on whether the Covenant reaches private, as well as public, conduct.

> [T]he positive obligations on States Parties to ensure Covenant rights will only be fully discharged if individuals are protected by the State, not just against violations of Covenant rights by its agents, but also against acts committed by private persons or entities that would impair the enjoyment of Covenant rights in so far as they are amenable to application between private persons or entities. There may be circumstances in which a failure to ensure Covenant rights as required by article 2 would give rise to violations by States Parties of those rights, as a result of States Parties' permitting or failing to take appropriate measures or to exercise due diligence to prevent, punish, investigate or redress the harm caused by such acts by private persons or entities. States are reminded of the interrelationship between the positive obligations imposed under article 2 and the need to provide effective remedies in the event of breach under article 2, paragraph 3. The Covenant itself envisages in some articles certain areas where there are positive obligations on States Parties to address the activities of private persons or entities. [U.N. Human Rights Committee, General Comment 31(80), ¶8, U.N. Doc. CCPR/C/21/Rev.1/Add.13 (May 26, 2004).]

8. In one of its more controversial General Comments, the ICCPR's Human Rights Committee addressed the issue of reservations taken by states in ratifying the ICCPR. Citing the provision in the Vienna Convention on the Law of Treaties (VCLT) that states may not make a reservation that is incompatible with the object and purpose of a treaty, the Committee stated that "each of the [ICCPR's] many articles, and indeed their interplay, secures the objectives of the Covenant." Although this alone generated controversy, the Committee went further and expressed its view that significant departures from the normal system for evaluating the validity of reservations applied in the context of multilateral human rights treaties:

> Although treaties that are mere exchanges of obligations between States allow them to reserve *inter se* application of rules of general international law, it is otherwise in human rights treaties, which are for the benefit of persons within their jurisdiction. . . .
>
> . . . [T]he Committee believes that [the VCLT's] provisions on the role of State objections in relation to reservations are inappropriate to address the problem of reservations to human rights treaties. Such treaties, and the Covenant specifically, are not a web of inter-State exchanges of mutual obligations. They concern the endowment of individuals with rights. The principle of inter-State reciprocity has no

> place. . . . And because the operation of the classic rules on reservations is so inadequate for the Covenant, States have often not seen any legal interest in or need to object to reservations. The absence of protest by States cannot imply that a reservation is either compatible or incompatible with the object and purpose of the Covenant. . . . [I]t is not safe to assume that a non-objecting State thinks that a particular reservation is acceptable. . . . [U.N. Human Rights Committee, General Comment 24(52), ¶¶8 & 17, U.N. Doc. CCPR/C/21/Rev.l/Add.6 (Nov. 4, 1994)

The Committee suggested that the "compatibility of a reservation with the object and purpose of the Covenant must be established objectively, by reference to legal principles, and the Committee is particularly well placed to perform this task." It accordingly concluded that it "necessarily falls to the Committee," rather than the parties to the ICCPR, "to determine whether a specific reservation is compatible with the object and purpose of the Covenant." In addition, the Committee stated that "[t]he normal consequence of an unacceptable reservation is not that the Covenant will not be in effect at all for a reserving party. Rather, such a reservation will generally be severable, in the sense that the Covenant will be operative for the reserving party without benefit of the reservation." Id. ¶18.

The United States vigorously objected to General Comment 24. Britain and France also filed objections, and the United Nations' International Law Commission criticized General Comment 24 in a 1997 preliminary report. The United States argued, among other things, that: (1) international law empowers the states that are parties to the Covenant, and not the Committee, to determine the permissibility of reservations; (2) it was wrong to imply that a reservation to any of the substantive provisions of the Covenant would contravene its object and purpose; and (3) the Committee's conclusion that reservations it deemed invalid could be severed from the ratification of the state concerned, so that the Covenant would be "operative for the reserving party without benefit of the reservation," was "completely at odds with established legal practice and principles." Observations by the United States on General Comment No. 24, 3 Int'l Hum. Rts. Rep. 265, 266-269 (1996).

Do you agree with the Committee's view that the different nature of multilateral human rights treaties should produce a different system for evaluating reservations? Or should the normal system for evaluating reservations apply? Even if a different approach is warranted, does the Committee have the authority to declare rules that govern the assessment of the validity of reservations to the ICCPR, or does that function remain with states?

9. As noted in Chapter 2, the Human Rights Committee concluded in a general comment issued in 1998 that parties to the ICCPR do not have the right to withdraw from the treaty. The Committee reasoned that the rights under the ICCPR "belong to the people living in the territory of the State party" and that "once the people are accorded the protection of the rights under the Covenant, such protection devolves with territory and continues to belong to them, notwithstanding change in government of the State party, including dismemberment in more than one State or State succession or any subsequent action of the State party designed to divest them of the rights guaranteed by the Covenant." U.N. Human Rights Committee, General Comment 26(61), ¶4, U.N. Doc. CCPR/C/21/Rev.1/Add.8/Rev.1 (Dec. 8, 1997). Is this persuasive? The Secretary-General, in the case of North Korea's notification

that it was withdrawing from the ICCPR, observed that the Covenant does not contain a withdrawal provision and expressed the view that North Korea's withdrawal from the Covenant would not be possible without the consent of all the other parties to the treaty. U.N. Secretary-General, Depository Notification of the Democratic Republic of North Korea, U.N. Doc. C.N.467.1997-TREATIES-10 (Nov. 12, 1997). As a practical matter, can the Committee stop parties to the ICCPR from withdrawing from the treaty?

10. For additional discussion of the ICCPR's Human Rights Committee, see Jakob T. Möller & Alfred de Zayas, The United Nations Human Rights Committee Case Law 1977-2008: A Handbook (2009). For access to the Committee's general comments, jurisprudence, and other documents, see the Web site of the Office of the High Commissioner for Human Rights, at http://www.ohchr.org.

4. *Other Global Human Rights Treaties*

There are a number of other multilateral treaties focused on human rights issues. The most prominent treaties include the following (all of which are excerpted in the Documentary Supplement):

The Convention on the Prevention and Punishment of the Crime of Genocide took effect in 1951 and, as of February 2011, had been ratified by 141 parties. The United States ratified this treaty in 1988. The Convention provides that genocide, "whether committed in time of peace or in time of war, is a crime under international law which they undertake to prevent and to punish." Genocide is defined in the Convention as "any of the following acts committed with intent to destroy, in whole or in part, a national, ethnical, racial or religious group, as such: (a) Killing members of the group; (b) Causing serious bodily or mental harm to members of the group; (c) Deliberately inflicting on the group conditions of life calculated to bring about its physical destruction in whole or in part; (d) Imposing measures intended to prevent births within the group; (e) Forcibly transferring children of the group to another group."

The Convention Against Torture and Other Cruel, Inhuman or Degrading Treatment or Punishment took effect in 1987 and, as of February 2011, had been ratified by 147 parties. The United States ratified this treaty in 1994. The Convention provides that the parties to the Convention "shall take effective legislative, administrative, judicial or other measures to prevent acts of torture in any territory under its jurisdiction." It also provides that "[n]o exceptional circumstances whatsoever, whether a state of war or a threat of war, internal political instability or any other public emergency, may be invoked as a justification of torture." In addition, the Convention obligates parties to prosecute or extradite individuals who are alleged to have committed torture within their jurisdiction. As of February 2011, 57 states were parties to an optional protocol to the Torture Convention that establishes "a system of regular visits undertaken by independent international and national bodies to places where people are deprived of their liberty, in order to prevent torture and other cruel, inhuman or degrading treatment or punishment." The United States is not a party to the protocol to the Torture Convention.

The Convention on the Elimination of All Forms of Racial Discrimination took effect in 1963 and, as of February 2011, had been ratified by 174 parties. The United

States ratified this treaty in 1994. The Convention obligates parties "to prohibit and to eliminate racial discrimination in all its forms and to guarantee the right of everyone, without distinction as to race, color, or national or ethnic origin, to equality before the law." It defines racial discrimination as "any distinction, exclusion, restriction or preference based on race, color, descent, or national or ethnic origin which has the purpose or effect of nullifying or impairing the recognition, enjoyment or exercise, on an equal footing, of human rights and fundamental freedoms in the political, economic, social, cultural or any other field of public life."

The Convention on the Elimination of All Forms of Discrimination Against Women (CEDAW) took effect in 1981 and, as of February 2011, had been ratified by 186 parties. The United States signed this treaty in 1980, but, as of February 2011, had not ratified it. The Convention requires parties to grant equal rights to women and to take appropriate measures to eliminate discrimination against women in a variety of areas, including political life, employment, education, health care, and marriage. It defines discrimination against women as "any distinction, exclusion or restriction made on the basis of sex which has the effect or purpose of impairing or nullifying the recognition, enjoyment or exercise by women, irrespective of their marital status, on a basis of equality of men and women, of human rights and fundamental freedoms in the political, economic, social, cultural, civil or any other field." CEDAW calls upon states not only to eradicate *de jure* discrimination against women, but also to take measures "to modify the social and cultural patterns of men and women, with a view toward achieving the elimination of prejudices and customary and other practices which are based on the idea of the inferiority or superiority of either of the sexes or on stereotyped roles for men and women." CEDAW art. 5. An Optional Protocol to this Convention took effect in 2000, whereby parties to the Protocol recognize the competence of the monitoring committee for this Convention to receive and comment on individual complaints (similar to the First Optional Protocol to the ICCPR). As of February 2011, 102 parties had ratified the Optional Protocol.

The Convention on the Rights of the Child took effect in 1990 and, as of February 2011, had been ratified by 193 parties. The United States signed this treaty in 1995, but, as of February 2011, had not ratified it. The Convention sets forth a variety of rights for children, and defines "child" to mean anyone under the age of 18. The rights in the Convention relate to, among other things, freedom of expression and religion, access to information, adoption, standard of living, health care, education, and criminal punishment. The Convention provides that parties "shall undertake all appropriate legislative, administrative, and other measures for the implementation of the rights recognized in the present Convention," although it also states that, "[w]ith regard to economic, social and cultural rights, States Parties shall undertake such measures to the maximum extent of their available resources and, where needed, within the framework of international co-operation." There are currently two Optional Protocols to the Convention on the Rights of the Child, one prohibiting the use of children in armed conflict and the other prohibiting the sale of children, child prostitution, and child pornography. As of February 2011, these protocols had been ratified by 139 and 142 parties, respectively. (The United States has ratified both protocols, even though it had not ratified the Convention itself.)

Like the ICCPR and ICESCR, all of these treaties, except for the Genocide Convention, have monitoring committees that issue reports and comments.

The international legal regime governing forcibly displaced persons, although sometimes seen as distinct from human rights law, is inspired by comparable humanitarian considerations. The main international law instruments in this area are the 1951 Convention Relating to the Status of Refugees and its 1967 Protocol, which gave universal scope to the rules in the 1951 Convention. As of February 2011, 144 states were parties to both the Convention and the Protocol. (The United States is a party to the 1967 Protocol.) Under these instruments, a refugee is defined as a person who

> owing to well-founded fear of being persecuted for reasons of race, religion, nationality, membership of a particular social group or political opinion, is outside the country of his nationality and is unable or, owing to such fear, is unwilling to avail himself of the protection of that country; or who, not having a nationality and being outside the country of his former habitual residence, is unable or, owing to such fear, is unwilling to return to it. [1951 Refugee Convention, as modified by the 1967 Protocol, art. I(A)(2).]

The Convention establishes rights and duties of refugees in their host country. A central provision of the Convention stipulates: "No Contracting State shall expel or return ("refouler") a refugee in any manner whatsoever to the frontiers of territories where his life or freedom would be threatened on account of his race, religion, nationality, membership of a particular social group or political opinion." Id. art. 33. The U.N. High Commissioner for Refugees (UNHCR) has the lead role in coordinating international action to protect refugees and resolve refugee problems worldwide. Its primary purpose is to safeguard the rights and well-being of refugees. In 2009 there were 10.5 million "refugees of concern to UNHCR" and another 26 million forcibly uprooted persons, known as internally displaced persons or IDPs, living in their own countries.

Notes and Questions

1. Is the widespread codification of human rights norms a positive development? Are there other rights that should be codified?

2. Like the ICCPR, the Convention Against Torture prohibits the use of torture under all circumstances. Should there be any exceptions to this prohibition? What if a suspect had information concerning the location of a bomb that, if not discovered, would kill thousands of people?

Considerable controversy arose over the question of when, if ever, emergency conditions might justify disregarding the prohibition on torture in the wake of the September 11, 2001, attacks by Al Qaeda against the United States. In August 2002, the Office of Legal Counsel in the Department of Justice provided the White House Counsel with a legal memorandum interpreting the criminal U.S. statute implementing the Torture Convention. The memo declared that "[e]ven if an interrogation method arguably were to violate [the statutory prohibition on torture] . . . [a]s Commander-in-Chief, the President has the constitutional authority to order interrogations of enemy combatants to gain intelligence information concerning the military plans of the enemy. . . ." Memorandum from Jay S. Bybee, Assistant Attorney General, to Alberto R. Gonzales, Counsel to the President,

Re: Standards of Conduct for Interrogation under 18 U.S.C. §§2340-2340A, at 31 (Aug. 1, 2002). The memo is discussed in more detail in Chapter 3.

On January 22, 2009, two days after his inauguration, President Obama issued Executive Order 13491, entitled "Ensuring Lawful Interrogations." Citing the Convention on Torture, among other legal sources, it provided that all persons detained by U.S. officials in any armed conflict "shall in all circumstances be treated humanely and shall not be subjected to violence to life and person (including murder of all kinds, mutilation, cruel treatment, and torture), nor to outrages upon personal dignity (including humiliating and degrading treatment)." The executive order prohibited the use of "any interrogation technique or approach, or any treatment related to interrogation, that is not authorized by and listed in" the U.S. Army Field Manual on Human Intelligence Collector Operations. The executive order also prohibited U.S. officials who carry out interrogations from acting in reliance "upon any interpretation of the law governing interrogation — including interpretations of Federal criminal laws, the Convention Against Torture, Common Article 3, [or the] Army Field Manual . . . — issued by the Department of Justice between September 11, 2001, and January 20, 2009." Exec. Order 13491, 74 Fed. Reg. 4893 (Jan. 22, 2009).

3. Look at Article 1(4) of the Convention on the Elimination of All Forms of Racial Discrimination. What implications, if any, does it have for affirmative action programs?

4. Skim the Convention on the Rights of the Child. What are the implications of Article 13(1) of the Convention, which provides that "[t]he child shall have the right to freedom of expression; this right shall include freedom to seek, receive and impart information and ideas of all kinds, regardless of frontiers, either orally, in writing or in print, in the form of art, or through any other media of the child's choice"? How about Article 16, which provides that "[n]o child shall be subjected to arbitrary or unlawful interference with his or her privacy, family, home or correspondence, nor to unlawful attacks on his or her honor and reputation"? Are you surprised that 193 parties have ratified this treaty? Do you think all 193 comply with the treaty's requirements? Even if they do not, might their ratification of the treaty nevertheless be a positive development? Would it be a good idea to provide for expulsion of countries from human rights treaty regimes if they failed to comply with the treaties?

5. Do you think the codification of human rights has improved human rights practices around the world? A seminal and controversial article that examined the practical effect of ratification of human rights treaties found that they may not be correlated with an increase in human rights protections in the ratifying countries. Using a database encompassing the experiences of 166 states over a nearly 40-year period in five areas of human rights law, the author reached the following conclusions:

> Although the ratings of human rights practices of countries that have ratified international human rights treaties are generally better than those of countries that have not, noncompliance with treaty obligations appears to be common. More paradoxically, when I take into account the influence of a range of other factors that affect countries' practices, I find that treaty ratification is not infrequently associated with worse human rights ratings than otherwise expected. [Oona Hathaway, Do Human Rights Treaties Make a Difference?, 111 Yale L.J. 1935, 1940 (2002).]

Hathaway's theory has provoked considerable response among political scientists and the international legal community. Some scholars have challenged Hathaway's methodology and policy analysis, see, e.g., Ryan Goodman & Derek Jinks, Measuring the Effects of Human Rights Treaties, 14 Eur. J. Int'l L. 171 (2003), but a growing body of research suggests that human rights treaties do not by themselves seem to produce significant changes in state behavior. See, e.g., Emilie Hafner-Burton & Tsutsui Kiyoteru, Justice Lost! The Failure of International Human Rights Law to Matter Where Needed Most, 44 J. Peace Res. 407 (2007); Daniel W. Hill, Estimating the Effects of Human Rights Treaties on State Behavior, 72 J. Politics 1161 (2010); and Eric Neumayer, Do International Human Rights Treaties Improve Respect for Human Rights, 49 J. Conflict Resol. 925 (2005).

If Hathaway's findings are correct, what could be the explanation? What is the appropriate solution? Can you think of ways in which enforcement of human rights treaties could be improved?

5. U.N. Human Rights System

The United Nations has been the principal international forum for the promotion of international human rights. Article 68 of the U.N. Charter directs the U.N.'s Economic and Social Council (ECOSOC) to "set up commissions . . . for the promotion of human rights." Pursuant to this directive, ECOSOC established the U.N. Human Rights Commission in 1946. The Commission was empowered to examine, monitor, and publicly report on human rights situations in specific countries and on major phenomena of human rights violations worldwide. Its annual meetings were widely attended by delegates from member nations, from observer nations, and from non-governmental organizations. Each year it issued numerous resolutions on a wide variety of human rights issues.

In 2006, the Commission was disbanded, largely due to criticism about the Commission's performance and the perception that many states sought membership on the Commission not to strengthen human rights, but to protect themselves against criticism and to criticize others. The Commission was replaced with a new Human Rights Council with responsibility for promoting universal respect for human rights. The Council is comprised of 47 states elected by the General Assembly for three-year terms. In electing members, states are to "take into account the contribution of candidates to the promotion and protection of human rights." G.A. Res. 60/251, ¶8, U.N. Doc. A/RES/60/251 (Mar. 15, 2006).

During its sessions, the Council adopts resolutions on a wide range of human rights issues and human rights problems in particular settings, although it does not have the authority to impose legal obligations on states. Among the resolutions adopted by the Council at its 14th session in June 2010 were those condemning attacks against school children in Afghanistan, calling on states to prevent the occurrence of enforced disappearances, and condemning Israel's raid of a flotilla attempting to deliver humanitarian supplies to the Gaza strip. The Council also examines and reports on human rights situations in specific countries (employing procedures known as country mechanisms or mandates) as well as on major phenomena of human rights violations around the world (known as thematic mechanisms or mandates). The Council currently has active country mandates with respect to a variety of countries, including Haiti, North Korea, Somalia, and Sudan. Its thematic mandates include topics such as arbitrary detention, violence against women, child prostitution, contemporary forms of slavery, and the protection of human rights while countering terrorism. Reporting by a body such as the Council can place pressure on regimes to improve human rights practices. In an effort to promote equal treatment of states, the Council has also adopted a "Universal Periodic Review" mechanism under which all states must report on actions they have taken to improve the human rights situations in their countries.

Despite the effort at reform, the Human Rights Council remains subject to criticism over such issues as the election of member states with poor human rights records and bloc voting by regional groups on the basis of geopolitical, rather than human rights, criteria.

In late 1993, the United Nations established the post of the High Commissioner for Human Rights. This High Commissioner is the United Nations official with principal responsibility for United Nations human rights activities. The High Commissioner is appointed by the U.N. Secretary-General with the approval of the General Assembly for a fixed term of four years with the possibility of renewal for a further term of four years. The High Commissioner directs the U.N.'s Office of the High Commissioner for Human Rights, which has an extensive array of responsibilities relating to the promotion of human rights. As of February 2011, the High Commissioner was Navanethem Pillay, former President of the International Criminal Tribunal for Rwanda.

Do you think the United Nations, with its great diversity of members (who vary substantially in their own human rights practices) and a political commitment to balanced geographic representation, can be an effective champion of human rights? How can the Human Rights Council overcome the challenges that plagued the Human Rights Commission? Can you think of ways in which the U.N. human rights system could be improved — for example, in terms of enforcement? For additional discussion of this system, see Henry J. Steiner, Philip Alston & Ryan Goodman, International Human Rights in Context, Ch. 9 (3d ed. 2008).

6. *Customary International Human Rights Law*

In addition to human rights treaties, states are obliged to comply with customary international law with respect to the protection of human rights. The content of the customary international law of human rights is more difficult to discern, however, than the content of treaties. The Restatement, published in 1987, contains the following list of customary international law human rights protections.

Restatement

Section 702. Customary International Law of Human Rights

A state violates international law if, as a matter of state policy, it practices, encourages, or condones

(a) genocide,

(b) slavery or slave trade,

(c) the murder or causing the disappearance of individuals,

(d) torture or other cruel, inhuman, or degrading treatment or punishment,
(e) prolonged arbitrary detention,
(f) systematic racial discrimination, or
(g) a consistent pattern of gross violations of internationally recognized human rights.

The Restatement notes that it includes "only those human rights whose status as customary law is generally accepted (as of 1987) and whose scope and content are generally agreed." It further notes that its list "is not necessarily complete, and is not closed: human rights not listed in this section may have achieved the status of customary law, and some rights may achieve that status in the future." Restatement §702, Comment a. The following excerpts address customary international human rights law and challenges in ascertaining its content.

Christian Tomuschat, Human Rights: Between Idealism and Realism

37-38 (2d ed. 2008)

The classic doctrine of customary international law . . . does not easily lend itself to identifying rules in the field of human rights. Whereas the relations between states can be observed by empirical means, the way in which states behave in their dealings with individual citizens escapes such methods. On the global plane, millions of contacts occur every second. Not even the most sophisticated electronic mechanism would be able to capture and register the human rights-specific features of all these relationships. Therefore, emphasis must be placed on official acts and statements. In particular, in order to get hold of the relevant practice and *opinio juris*, the observer . . . must closely verify to what extent states present their practices as fully corresponding to the international rule of law or whether they simply deny the charges brought against them. Even massive abuses do not militate against assuming a customary rule as long as the responsible author state seeks to hide and conceal its objectionable conduct instead of justifying it by invoking legal reasons. According to this method, there exists today broad agreement to the effect that many of the rules enunciated in the [Universal Declaration of Human Rights] have crystallized as customary law, in particular the right to life, the prohibition of torture (which is the reverse side of a right to physical integrity), the protection of personal freedom, and the prohibition of discrimination on racial grounds. This list of rights and/or forbidden acts and activities is not so much based on actual stock-taking of the relevant state practice but rather on deductive reasoning: if human life and physical integrity were not protected, the entire idea of a legal order would collapse. In searching for customary norms, additional clues can be gained, for instance, from a comparison between the [Universal Declaration on Human Rights] and the [International Covenant on Civil and Political Rights]: rights set forth in the first of these instruments but omitted from the latter — such as the right to asylum and the right to a nationality, as well as the right of ownership — do not easily qualify as having acquired a customary foundation. Over the years, the circle of custom-based rights may increase mainly through discourse in the relevant [human rights treaty] monitoring bodies, much less through real deeds supported by *opinio juris.*

Bruno Simma & Philip Alston, The Sources of Human Rights Law: Custom, *Jus Cogens,* and General Principles

12 Austl. Y.B. Int'l L. 82, 82-85, 88-90 (1988-1989)

In many situations treaty law provides a solid and compelling legal foundation. But despite a steady increase in the number of States Parties to international treaties in recent years, reliance upon treaties alone provides an ultimately unsatisfactory patchwork quilt of obligations and still continues to leave many States largely untouched. Thus treaty law on its own provides a rather unsatisfactory basis on which to ground the efforts of international institutions whose reach is truly universal, such as the General Assembly. . . . The prospects for developing an effective and largely consensual international regime depend significantly on the extent to which those institutions are capable of basing their actions upon a coherent and generally applicable set of human rights norms. . . .

There is thus a strong temptation to turn to customary law as the formal source which provides, in a relatively straight-forward fashion, the desired answers. In particular, if customary law can be construed or approached in such a way as to supply a relatively comprehensive package of norms which are applicable to all States, then the debate over the sources of international human rights law can be resolved without much further ado. Given the fundamental importance of the human rights component of a just world order, the temptation to adapt or reinterpret the concept of customary law in such a way as to ensure that it provides the "right" answers is strong, and at least to some, irresistible. . . .

But while largely endorsing the result that is thereby sought to be achieved, we have considerable misgivings about the means being used. . . . [One important question] is whether this effort to revise or "update" custom does fundamental and irreparable violence to the very concept? As Jennings noted almost a decade ago, much of what many modern commentators characterize as custom "is not only not customary law: it does not even faintly resemble a customary law." . . .

Caution is far from being a characteristic of much of the contemporary human rights literature. Perhaps this has to do with the fact that "human rights lawyers are notoriously wishful thinkers," as John Humphrey once observed. However this may be, it appears that a majority of authors today take the view that international human rights obligations incumbent upon States may, and actually do, also derive from customary international law. This thesis is presented with varying degrees of sophistication. There are writers who state flatly that the entire *corpus* of international human rights law, or, to be slightly more specific, the substance of the 1948 Universal Declaration of Human Rights, is now to be regarded as customary law in its entirety. A recent variation on this approach is that, in order to accommodate all of the desired human rights principles, a "modernized view of customary international law" should be applied. That view would accord "the ability to create custom" to non-state actors such as international organizations and "certain nongovernmental organizations [that] have a distinct, measurable impact on international affairs."

Then there are more moderate, "middle-of-the-road" views, like those of the new Restatement or of Oscar Schachter . . . , according to which something like a "hard core" of human rights obligations exists as customary law today. . . .

According to the traditional understanding of international custom, the emphasis was clearly on the material, or objective, of its two elements, namely State *practice.* Customary international law was generally considered to come about through the emergence of a general (or extensive), uniform, consistent and settled practice, more or less gradually joined by a sense of legal obligation, the *opinio juris.* However, practice had priority over *opinio juris*; deeds were what counted, not just words. What international courts and tribunals mainly did in fact was to trace the subjective element by way of discerning certain recurrent patterns within the raw material of State practice and interpreting those patterns as resulting from juridical considerations. . . .

So much then for the old-style of practice-based custom, *la coutume sage.* Then followed the stage of *la coutume sauvage*: a product grown in the hothouse of parliamentary diplomacy and all too often "sold" as customary law before actually having stood the test of time. What is customary about this cultured pearl version of customary law is not (at least, not necessarily) its consistent application in actual State practice but the fertilizing role it plays through proclamation, exhortation, repetition, incantation, lament. For some writers, practice no longer has any constitutive role to play in the establishment of customary law; rather it serves a purely evidentiary function. After all, the only task practice ever had to perform, the "modernists" would say, was to bring consent or *opinio juris* to the fore; and now that we have all these international bodies, and above all the U.N. General Assembly, generating an almost permanent, intensive flow of communications, consent and *opinio juris* can manifest themselves more or less instantly and without the help of a vehicle as cumbersome and demanding as actual State practice.

For other writers, it is the notion of "practice" itself which has undergone a dubious metamorphosis. It has changed from something happening out there in the real world, after the diplomats and the delegates have had their say, into paper practice: the words, texts, votes and excuses themselves. The process of customary law-making is thus turned into a self-contained exercise in rhetoric. The approach now used is *deductive*: rules or principles proclaimed, for instance, by the General Assembly, as well as the surrounding ritual itself, are taken not only as starting points for the possible development of customary law in the event that State practice eventually happens to lock on to these proclamations, but as a law-making process which is more or less complete in itself, even in the face of contrasting "external" facts. This new, radical customary law has lost the element of retrospection; if its protagonists look back at the past it is a look back in anger, full of impatience with the imperfections and gaps of the old rules. Such impatience also extends to the processes of treaty-making, a field in which delay or a lack of consent simply cannot be argued away by theoretical constructs. Thus the flight into a new, "progressive," more or less instant custom.

The elevation of the Universal Declaration of 1948 and of the documents that have built upon its foundations to the status of customary law, in a world where it is still customary for a depressingly large number of States to trample upon the human rights of their nationals, is a good example of such an approach.

Notes and Questions

1. What rights, if any, should be added to the Restatement's list of human rights protected under customary international law?

2. If the Universal Declaration of Human Rights has assumed the status of binding customary international law, how did this happen? Professor Lillich, in an influential article on customary international human rights, quoted the observation of a leading U.N. human rights official that by the mid-1970s, "the Declaration has been invoked so many times [over the previous past quarter century] both within and without the United Nations that lawyers now are saying that, whatever the intention of its authors may have been, the Declaration is now part of the customary law of nations and therefore is binding on all states." Richard B. Lillich, The Growing Importance of Customary International Human Rights Law, 25 Ga. J. Int'l & Comp. L. 1, 2 (1996). Do you find that persuasive? Does this mean that the economic and social rights identified in the Universal Declaration today reflect customary international law? Or only (some of) the civil and political rights enumerated in it?

3. The contrast in views between Professor Tomuschat, on the one hand, and Bruno Simma (now an ICJ judge) and Professor Alston, on the other, seems to represent a practical illustration of the debate between proponents of "traditional" and "modern" customary international law discussed in Chapter 2. Is all of customary international law of human rights an example of "modern" customary law? To what extent are customary human rights norms supported by state practice? *Opinio juris*? How persuasive are the Simma/Alston criticisms of "modern" customary international law? Does the fact that a vast majority of states are today parties to the main international human rights treaties weaken their claims? Or does it strengthen the objections to efforts to bind the smaller number of states that have not accepted these treaties through the operation of customary international law?

4. What arguments does Professor Tomuschat give for employing a different method for ascertaining customary international human rights law than for ascertaining the content of customary international law in other realms? Are they persuasive?

5. As discussed elsewhere, non-state actors (such as individuals or possibly corporations) might also be held responsible, either as a criminal or civil law matter, for violating some customary norms of international law. Prominent examples of this are found in criminal prosecutions in domestic or international courts for international crimes (discussed in Chapter 12) and civil litigation in U.S. courts under the Alien Tort Statute. See the Notes after *Sosa* in Chapter 3.C and Section B.8.d below on domestic litigation.

6. The U.N. General Assembly in 2007 adopted a "Declaration on the Rights of Indigenous Peoples," a detailed instrument of 47 articles articulating a broad set of individual and collective rights for indigenous peoples. Rights enumerated in the Declaration include rights related to culture, identity, education, health, employment, language, and the right of indigenous peoples to remain distinct and to pursue their own priorities in economic, social, and cultural development. See United Nations Declaration on the Rights of Indigenous Peoples, G.A. Res. 61/295, U.N. Doc. A/RES/61/295 (Oct. 2, 2007). Although the Declaration's introductory provisions characterize the document as "a standard of achievement to be pursued in a spirit of partnership and mutual respect," the Declaration itself employs

language of obligation, declaring, for example, that "[i]ndigenous peoples, in exercising their right to self-determination, have the right to autonomy or self-government in matters relating to their internal and local affairs," id. art. 4, and that "[s]tates shall provide redress through effective mechanisms, which may include restitution, developed in conjunction with indigenous peoples, with respect to their cultural, intellectual, religious and spiritual property taken without their free, prior and informed consent or in violation of their laws, traditions and customs." Id. art. 11(2). Some commentators, though they acknowledge that General Assembly resolutions are non-binding and that states "are not strictly speaking, legally bound to recognize the rights in the Declaration," nevertheless argue that the Declaration "is an official statement by most member countries of the United Nations that these are the legal rights of indigenous peoples in international law. This gives the Declaration considerable political and moral force, creating the basis for it to become binding international law." Robert T. Coulter, The U.N. Declaration on the Rights of Indigenous Peoples: A Historic Change in International Law, 45 Idaho L. Rev. 539, 546 (2009). The United Nations High Commissioner for Human Rights hailed the Declaration as "the most comprehensive statement to date of indigenous peoples' rights."

The United States was one of only four countries (along with Australia, Canada, and New Zealand) to vote against the resolution adopting the Declaration. In a document elaborating on the reasons for its negative vote, the United States commented on the legal character of the Declaration and stressed that it was "aspirational," with "political and moral, rather than legal, force." The U.S. statement emphasized that the Declaration "is not in itself legally binding nor reflective of international law" and asserted:

> The United States rejects any possibility that this document is or can become customary international law. We have continually expressed our rejection of fundamental parts of . . . this text, as have numerous other States. As this declaration does not describe current State practice or actions that States feel obliged to take as a matter of legal obligation, it cannot be cited as evidence of the evolution of customary international law. [Observations of the United States with Respect to the Declaration on the Rights of Indigenous Peoples (Sept. 13, 2007) (released as USUN Press Release 204(07)).]

How would you describe the legal character of the rights articulated in the Declaration on the Rights of Indigenous Peoples? Do all of them reflect customary international law? None of them? Some? What criteria would you use to decide which of those rights, if any, have customary international law status?

The Obama Administration conducted a comprehensive review of the Declaration and in December 2010 announced that the United States had changed its position and would "support" the Declaration. The announcement of support reiterated the U.S. position that the Declaration is "not legally binding or a statement of current international law." Nevertheless, the announcement stated that the Declaration "expresses [the] aspirations of the United States, aspirations that this country seeks to achieve within the structure of the U.S. Constitution, laws, and international obligations, while also seeking, where appropriate, to improve our laws and policies." U.S. Department of State, Announcement of U.S. Support for the United Nations Declaration on the Rights of Indigenous Peoples, Dec. 16, 2010, available at http://www.state.gov/documents/organization/153223.pdf.

7. *Role of NGOs*

States and international institutions are not the only participants in the process of fashioning and enforcing international human rights law. Non-governmental organizations (NGOs) also play an important role. (They also play a prominent role with respect to formation of international law more generally, as discussed in Chapter 2.) Leading human rights NGOs include Amnesty International, Freedom House, Human Rights Watch, and Human Rights First. There are also myriad local human rights NGOs in countries throughout the world. The role of human rights NGOs, and some of the challenges they face, are described below.

Kenneth Roth, Human Rights Organizations: A New Force for Social Change

Realizing Human Rights: Moving from Inspiration to Impact 225, 228-230, 242-243 (Samantha Power & Graham Allison eds., 2000)

The expanded scope of human rights protection has been driven largely by a . . . major development since the adoption of the Universal Declaration: the growth of the human rights movement itself, that is, of nongovernmental organizations (NGOs) devoted to developing and applying international standards on human rights. The human rights movement did not begin with the Declaration. Precursors can be found in the campaigns to abolish slavery, to grant women the right to vote, and to alleviate suffering in time of war. . . . Following World War II, NGOs lobbied for the inclusion of language on human rights in the UN Charter and for the adoption of the Universal Declaration, but there was as yet little in the way of a formal human rights movement.

Since then, however, there has been a veritable explosion in the number and breadth of organizations devoted to human rights, particularly since the 1970s. That is when human rights groups began to emerge in Asia in reaction to repressive governments in Korea, Indonesia, and the Philippines. The Helsinki Accord of 1975, affirming "the right of the individual to know and act upon his rights," helped launch the human rights movement in the Soviet Bloc. Human rights groups emerged throughout Latin America in the 1970s and 1980s in opposition to death squads and "disappearances" under right-wing dictatorships. Much of Asia in the 1990s has seen a stunning proliferation of human rights groups. While growth has been slower in Africa and the Middle East, human rights organizations have established a firm presence in all but the most repressive countries. In many places human rights defenders still face persecution, often severe. . . . Yet despite the danger, this growing movement has become a powerful new source of pressure to uphold human rights. It is the major reason why today the Universal Declaration has so much greater practical breadth and significance than it did fifty years ago. . . .

The reality that people around the globe now assert their rights has helped to underscore the universality of the rights proclaimed in the Universal Declaration. As the "interference in our internal affairs" argument loses its punch, many governments have sought to take refuge in the claim that human rights are a concept that is alien to their cultures. Variations of this argument can be found in the assertion of an

"Asian concept of human rights," the appeal for "African solutions to African problems," the argument that Islam provides the only true basis for human rights, and the U.S. government's distrust of international standards. The emergence of human rights organizations in all parts of the world undercuts these arguments. It shows that rights are not a "foreign imposition" but that people everywhere aspire to the same basic dignity and respect that the rights of the Universal Declaration protect. . . .

Despite its growing strength, the human rights movement has hardly ended serious human rights abuse. There has been much improvement in the last fifty years in most countries of the former Soviet bloc, Latin America, and southern Africa, as well as parts of Asia. But serious problems persist: many governments still resist applying the Universal Declaration to all their people. Repressive governments continue to run such countries as Burma, China, Iraq, North Korea, Saudi Arabia, and Turkmenistan. Abusive warfare is carried out in such places as Afghanistan, Algeria, Colombia, Kosovo, and Sudan. Even genocide, that most universally condemned crime, has been committed in the last decade of the twentieth century, in Bosnia and Rwanda. . . .

. . . The human rights movement cannot promise to end such abuse, but it can generate pressure on governments and insurgents to resist the temptation to violate rights. The goal is to increase the cost of abuse and thus to alter the political calculations that might lead to human rights violations. . . .

In the last half of the twentieth century, seven factors have enabled the human rights movement to become such a substantial force: the [strength of the] human rights ideal, better communications technology, the press, the . . . [willingness of many] influential governments [to make the promotion of human rights an important part of their foreign policy], the development of . . . [internationally recognized human rights law and] standards, the partnership between local and international human rights groups, and the growing professionalism of the human rights movement itself. . . .

As powerful as the human rights movement has become, it is hardly assured of victory in any given case. Certain countries and issues remain stubbornly resistant to the human rights methodology. Some governments are so powerful economically that classic forms of pressure have little impact; Saudi Arabia is an example. Sometimes the human rights movement faces powerful political antagonists, such as the opposition of much of the international business community to forceful advocacy of human rights in China. Geopolitical calculations still lie behind the tolerance of abuses in certain countries, such as the U.S. government's lenient attitude toward persistent atrocities in Rwanda. A cultural tradition of certain forms of abuse can make it difficult to stigmatize a government, as in the case of the repression of women in some Muslim countries. Certain highly repressive governments, such as that of Burma, have prevented the emergence of the local partners that the international human rights movement needs to be most effective. Some elected governments, such as that of Colombia, successfully deflect international opprobrium in part because they are viewed as "democracies" and hence assumed, however falsely, not to commit serious human rights violations. Certain issues are more resistant to the tools of the human rights community . . . while other issues, such as those involving certain economic and social rights, have complicated causes and solutions and cannot be solved easily even where public pressure creates political will to do so.

Of course, steps still can be taken to overcome these obstacles, but they are not easy. In some cases, efforts at public stigmatization can be stepped up. In other cases, new sources of economic or diplomatic pressure can be generated. New allies can be found and innovative partnerships built. But even with such heightened efforts, the human rights methodology is not foolproof. Indeed, we should not expect it to be. The methodology was developed as a way of enforcing rights when traditional resort to a legal system fails. Given the fallibility of many legal systems in protecting rights, even with the coercive power of the state at their disposal, one would hardly expect the less direct methodology of human rights organizations to guarantee success. But it does greatly increase the likelihood that, even in the absence of a functioning legal system, people will have some prospect of securing their rights.

Notes and Questions

1. What are the advantages of NGO participation in the development and enforcement of international human rights law? Are there any disadvantages? Whose interests do the NGOs represent? Does their participation make international human rights law more or less democratic?

2. What obstacles do human rights NGOs face? How can these obstacles be overcome? What are the most effective tools of human rights NGOs?

3. Kenneth Roth, the author of the excerpt above, is the Executive Director of Human Rights Watch, which is now the largest human rights NGO based in the United States. (Amnesty International is based in Great Britain.) The Human Rights Watch Web site offers the following account of the organization's activities:

> Our on-the-ground researchers constantly monitor human rights conditions in some 80 countries around the world. These researchers create the foundations of our work by talking with people who were either abused or who witnessed abuse. Human Rights Watch also speaks with local human rights advocates, journalists, country experts, and government officials. We publish our findings in more than 100 reports and hundreds of news releases each year. In times of crisis, we're at the forefront, releasing up-to-the-minute information and advocating for action. . . .
>
> Because of our insider access and careful fact-checking, international media and concerned governments frequently reference our research. We partner with local human rights groups, making detailed recommendations to governments, rebel groups, international institutions, corporations, policymakers, and the press to adopt reforms. By exposing their actions, we put pressure on human rights abusers to stop violating rights. Our efforts lay the legal and moral groundwork for deep-rooted changes in policy, law, and public opinion. . . .
>
> When we investigate and expose human rights violations, we seek to hold oppressors accountable to their population, to the international community, and to their obligations under international law. We seek to build the case for changes in law or policy, to empower local activism, and to put a name to abusive behaviors that in some local contexts are not identified as such. We work to bring the worst abusers before courts at home or before international tribunals. We seek targeted sanctions — those that harm the abusers but not the population at large. We work to increase the price of human rights abuse. The more tyrants we bring to justice, the more potential abusers will reconsider committing human rights violations. [Human Rights Watch, About Us, http://www.hrw.org/en/about.]

4. Political scientists Thomas Risse and Kathryn Sikkink have emphasized the importance that networks of transnational and domestic human rights NGOs, operating in conjunction with official international regimes, can play in bringing about change in a country's human rights performance.

> . . . We argue that these advocacy networks serve three purposes, which constitute necessary conditions for sustainable domestic change in the human rights area:
>
> 1. They put norm-violating states on the international agenda in terms of moral consciousness-raising. In doing so, they also remind liberal states of their own identity as promoters of human rights.
> 2. They empower and legitimate the claims of domestic opposition groups against norm-violating governments, and they partially protect the physical integrity of such groups from government repression. Thus, they are crucial in mobilizing *domestic* opposition, social movements, and non-governmental organizations (NGOs) in target countries.
> 3. They challenge norm-violating governments by creating a transnational structure pressuring such regimes simultaneously "from above" and "from below". The more these pressures can be sustained, the fewer options are available to political rulers to continue repression. [Thomas Risse & Kathryn Sikkink, The Socialization of International Human Rights into Domestic Practices: Introduction, in The Power of Human Rights: International Norms and Domestic Change 1, 5 (Thomas Risse, Stephen C. Ropp & Kathryn Sikkink eds., 1999).]

5. For additional discussion of the role of NGOs in international human rights law, see Paul J. Nelson & Ellen Dorsey, New Rights Advocacy: Changing Strategies of Development and Human Rights NGOs (2008); and Menno T. Kamminga, The Evolving Status of NGOs Under International Law: A Threat to the Inter-State System, in Non-State Actors and Human Rights 93 (Philip Alston ed., 2005). For a critical perspective on the role of NGOs in the international human rights system, see Robert Charles Blitt, Who Will Watch the Watchdogs? Human Rights Non-governmental Organizations and the Case for Regulation, 10 Buff. Hum. Rts. L. Rev. 261 (2004).

8. The United States and International Human Rights Law

The United States played a leading role in establishing the United Nations and drafting the Universal Declaration of Human Rights. It also frequently expresses concern about human rights violations around the world, and it sometimes uses economic and even military pressure to induce nations to improve their human rights practices. Further, U.S. law reflects a substantial commitment to domestic human rights protections — through, for example, the Bill of Rights. And, as we saw in Chapter 3, U.S. courts have shown a willingness to adjudicate cases involving alleged human rights abuses in other countries, especially in cases (such as *Filartiga*) brought under the Alien Tort Statute. Nevertheless, since the 1950s, the United States has had an uneasy relationship with human rights treaties and institutions, and it is frequently accused of having a double standard, whereby it seeks to enforce international human rights norms against other countries but is unwilling to have its own practices subjected to international regulation.

a. Ratification of Human Rights Treaties

The excerpt below describes the history of U.S. ratification of human rights treaties.

Curtis A. Bradley & Jack L. Goldsmith, Treaties, Human Rights, and Conditional Consent

149 U. Pa. L. Rev. 399, 411-416 (2000)

United States officials played a prominent role in creating the emerging international regime of human rights law [after the Second World War]. Nonetheless, there were intense debates in the United States during the 1950s over whether and to what extent the nation should participate in this regime. These debates focused principally on the domestic implications of ratifying the human rights treaties. Some people were concerned that the U.N. Charter's human rights provisions would give Congress the power to enact civil rights legislation otherwise beyond its constitutional powers. This was a plausible belief in light of the Supreme Court's decision in *Missouri v. Holland*, which held that, when implementing a treaty, Congress is not subject to the federalism limitations applicable to the exercise of its Article I powers. A related concern was that the U.N. Charter would preempt state laws by virtue of the Supremacy Clause. . . . The potentially self-executing nature of the Charter was particularly worrisome to some in the early days of the anticommunist Cold War period because the Universal Declaration, including its very progressive provisions concerning economic, social, and cultural rights, was described by its proponents as giving content to the vague human rights provisions of the U.N. Charter.

Another event that triggered concerns in the United States was President Truman's submission of the Convention on the Prevention and Punishment of the Crime of Genocide to the Senate in 1948. Although the United States had helped to draft the Convention and supported an international prohibition on genocide, many senators and others worried about the domestic consequences of ratifying the treaty. One of their central concerns was the vagueness of the Convention's definition of "genocide." The Convention defined genocide to include certain acts "committed with intent to destroy" covered groups, including the act of causing "mental harm" to members of covered groups. The unease over these definitional provisions related to their possible inconsistency with the First Amendment, their potential use as a basis for prosecuting U.S. military officials abroad, and their foreseeable use in support of a claim that U.S. policies toward African-Americans and Native Americans constituted genocide. There was also a more general concern about the erosion of U.S. sovereignty and independence.

These various concerns led to proposals in the 1950s to amend the Constitution to limit the treaty powers of the United States. Along with leaders of the American Bar Association, a key proponent of such an amendment was Senator John Bricker of Ohio, and the various proposed amendments are commonly referred to jointly as the "Bricker Amendment." In general, the proposed amendments were intended to preclude treaties from being self-executing and to make clear that treaties would not override the reserved powers of the states. . . . There was substantial consideration of these proposals during the 1950s. In fact, one of the proposed amendments fell only one vote short of obtaining the necessary two-thirds vote in the Senate.

To help defeat the Bricker Amendment, the Eisenhower administration made a commitment that it would not seek to become a party to any more human rights treaties. . . . For decades thereafter, presidents did not submit major human rights treaties to the Senate (although they did continue to seek the Senate's advice and consent for the Genocide Convention).

This reticence changed with the Carter administration, which submitted a package of human rights treaties to the Senate in the late 1970s. Since that time, every President has urged the Senate to approve the ratification of major human rights treaties, and the Senate has in fact given its advice and consent to four such treaties.* With respect to the treaties to which the Senate has given its advice and consent, there has been a remarkable consensus across very different administrations and very different Senates about both the desirability of ratifying these treaties and the need to attach [Reservations, Understanding, and Declarations (RUDs)] to the treaties as a condition of ratification to protect domestic prerogatives.

As for the desirability of ratifying human rights treaties, presidents and the Senate have agreed that a failure by the United States to ratify the major human rights treaties would result in at least two kinds of foreign policy costs. First, nonratification would preclude the United States from participating in the treaty-related institutions that, in turn, influence the course of international human rights law. Second, nonratification would create a "troubling complication" in U.S. diplomacy, namely, that the United States could not credibly encourage other nations to embrace human rights norms if it had not itself embraced those norms.

Presidents and the Senate have also agreed, however, that the modern human rights treaties implicate serious countervailing considerations reminiscent of the Bricker Amendment debates. These concerns are easiest to understand with respect to the most ambitious of these treaties, the International Covenant on Civil and Political Rights ("ICCPR"). The ICCPR contains dozens of vaguely worded rights guarantees that differ in important linguistic details from the analogous guarantees under U.S. domestic law. Some of these provisions arguably conflict with U.S. constitutional guarantees. In addition, the ICCPR, if self-executing, would have the same domestic effect as a congressional statute and thus would supersede inconsistent state law and prior inconsistent federal legislation. There was concern that, even if courts ultimately decided that each of the differently worded provisions in the ICCPR did not require a change in domestic law, litigation of these issues would be costly and would generate substantial legal uncertainty. These concerns also arose, although on a narrower scale, with respect to the other human rights treaties.

To address these concerns, President Carter and every subsequent President have included proposed RUDs with their submission of human rights treaties to the Senate. The Senate has given its advice and consent to, and the United States has ratified, four of these treaties: the Genocide Convention, ratified in 1988; the

*[Since this article was written, the United States has, as noted in Section B.4 above, also ratified the Optional Protocol to the Convention on the Rights of the Child on the Involvement of Children in Armed Conflict and the Optional Protocol to the Convention on the Rights of the Child on the Sale of Children, Child Prostitution and Child Pornography (both ratified in 2002). — EDS.]

ICCPR, ratified in 1992; the Torture Convention, ratified in 1994; and the Convention on the Elimination of All Forms of Racial Discrimination, also ratified in 1994. The United States included RUDs in the ratification instruments for each of these treaties as a precondition of U.S. ratification. The Senate usually consented to the RUDs in the form proposed by the President, but sometimes the Senate modified them slightly or requested that the President modify them.

As indicated in the above excerpt, the United States finally began ratifying some of the major human rights treaties in the late 1980s. As of February 2011, however, the United States still had not ratified the ICESCR, the CEDAW, or the Convention on the Rights of the Child. Moreover, as discussed in the excerpt, the United States has conditioned its consent to the human rights treaties that it has ratified with an extensive array of reservations, understandings, and declarations (RUDs). (The RUDs that the United States attached to its ratification of the ICCPR are excerpted in the Documentary Supplement.)

The following excerpt (from the same article) summarizes the typical RUDs attached to U.S. ratification of human rights treaties, and the explanations given by the U.S. treaty makers for these RUDs.

Curtis A. Bradley & Jack L. Goldsmith, Treaties, Human Rights, and Conditional Consent

149 U. Pa. L. Rev. 399, 416-423 (2000)

RUDs are designed to harmonize the [human rights] treaties [the United States ratifies] with existing requirements of U.S. law and to leave domestic implementation of the treaties to Congress. They cover a variety of subjects and take a variety of forms. For purposes of analysis, they can be grouped into five categories:

Substantive Reservations. Some RUDs are reservations pursuant to which the United States declines to consent altogether to certain provisions in the treaties. These reservations are very much the exception to the rule; for each of the four human rights treaties under consideration, the United States consented to a large majority of the provisions. Some substantive reservations are based on potential conflicts between treaty provisions and U.S. constitutional rights. For example, First Amendment concerns led the United States to decline to agree to restrictions on hate speech in the Race Convention "to the extent that [such speech is] protected by the Constitution and laws of the United States." Similarly, the United States attached a reservation to its ratification of the ICCPR, stating that the ICCPR's restriction on propaganda for war and hate speech "does not authorize or require legislation or other action by the United States that would restrict the right of free speech and association protected by the Constitution and laws of the United States."

Other substantive reservations are based not on a constitutional conflict but rather on a political or policy disagreement with certain provisions of the treaties. For example, the United States attached to its ratification of the ICCPR reservations allowing it to impose criminal punishment consistent with the Fifth, Sixth, and Eighth Amendments, including capital punishment of juvenile offenders, notwithstanding limitations on such punishment in the ICCPR.* The United States attached a similar reservation with respect to limitations on punishment in the Torture Convention. It also attached a condition to its ratification of the Race Convention making clear that it was not agreeing to modify the traditional public/private distinction in U.S. civil rights law.

Interpretive Conditions. Some RUDs set forth the United States's interpretation of vague treaty terms, thereby clarifying the scope of United States consent. For example, Articles 2(1) and 26 of the ICCPR prohibit discrimination not only on the basis of "race, colour, sex, language, religion, political or other opinion, national or social origin, property, [and] birth," but also on the basis of any "other status." The United States attached an understanding stating that this open-ended prohibition on discrimination did not preclude legal distinctions between persons "when such distinctions are, at minimum, rationally related to a legitimate governmental objective." It also attached a reservation to both the ICCPR and the Torture Convention stating that the United States considers itself bound by the prohibitions in those treaties on "cruel, inhuman, or degrading treatment or punishment" only to the extent that such treatment or punishment is prohibited by the U.S. Constitution. The United States similarly attached understandings to its ratification of the Genocide and Torture Conventions clarifying the circumstances under which conduct will fall within the terms of these treaties.

Non-Self-Execution Declarations. U.S. treatymakers also have included, when ratifying human rights treaties, declarations stating that the substantive provisions of the treaties are not self-executing. These declarations are designed to preclude the treaties from being enforceable in U.S. courts in the absence of implementing legislation. As the State Department explained in submitting the proposed treaties to President Carter for his transmission to the Senate, "with such declarations, the substantive provisions of the treaties would not of themselves become effective as domestic law."

The treatymakers have given several reasons for these declarations. First, they believe that, taking into account the substantive reservations and interpretive conditions, U.S. domestic laws and remedies are sufficient to meet U.S. obligations under human rights treaties. There is thus no additional need, in their view, for domestic implementation. Second, there is concern that the treaty terms, although similar in substance to U.S. law, are not identical in wording and thus might have a destabilizing effect on domestic rights protections if considered self-executing. Third, there is disagreement about which treaty terms, if any, would be self-executing. The declaration is intended to provide certainty about this issue in advance of litigation. Finally, the treatymakers believe that if there is to be a change in the scope of domestic rights protections, it should be done by legislation with the participation of the House of Representatives. . . .

Federalism Understandings. RUDs for human rights treaties typically contain an understanding or other statement relating to federalism. The RUDs attached to the ICCPR, for example, provide that "the United States understands that this Covenant shall be implemented by the Federal Government to the extent that it exercises

*[In Roper v. Simmons, 543 U.S. 551 (2005), the Supreme Court ruled that the execution of persons who were minors at the time they committed the offense in question violated the Eighth and Fourteenth Amendments of the U.S. Constitution. — EDS.]

legislative and judicial jurisdiction over the matters covered therein, and otherwise by the state and local governments." . . .

ICJ Reservations. U.S. RUDs, like the reservations of many other nations, also typically decline to consent to "ICJ Clauses" in the human rights treaties, pursuant to which claims under the treaties could be brought against the United States in the International Court of Justice. The United States attached a reservation to its ratification of the Genocide Convention, for example, stating that "before any dispute to which the United States is a party may be submitted to the jurisdiction of the International Court of Justice under [Article IX of the Convention], the specific consent of the United States is required in each case." The U.S. treatymakers have explained that the ICJ reservations are designed "to retain the ability of the United States to decline a case which may be brought for frivolous or political reasons." . . .

The RUDs have generated significant criticism. Consider, for example, Professor Henkin's comments, excerpted below.

Louis Henkin, U.S. Ratification of Human Rights Conventions: The Ghost of Senator Bricker

89 Am. J. Int'l L. 341, 344, 345-349 (1995)

By adhering to human rights conventions subject to these reservations, the United States, it is charged, is pretending to assume international obligations but in fact is undertaking nothing. It is seen as seeking the benefits of participation in the convention (e.g., having a U.S. national sit on the Human Rights Committee established pursuant to the [ICCPR]) without assuming any obligations or burdens. The United States, it is said, seeks to sit in judgment on others but will not submit its human rights behavior to international judgment. To many, the attitude reflected in such reservations is offensive: the conventions are only for other states, not for the United States. . . .

The United States has proposed "federalism" clauses in the past, presumably to assuage "states' rights" sensibilities. . . . [The declarations proposed by] the executive branch . . . [state] that the convention shall be implemented by the federal Government to the extent that it "exercises jurisdiction" over matters covered by the treaty, leaving to the states implementation of matters over which the states exercise jurisdiction.

Such a statement is deeply ambiguous. The federal Government exercises jurisdiction over all matters covered in a human rights convention, if only by making the treaty. It exercises jurisdiction over such matters because Congress has the power to legislate, and has legislated, in respect of them. . . .

The "federalism" declarations that have been attached to human rights conventions thus serve no legal purpose. But some see such declarations as another sign that the United States is resistant to international human rights agreements, setting up obstacles to their implementation and refusing to treat human rights conventions as treaties dealing with a subject of national interest and international concern. . . .

The United States [also] has been declaring the human rights agreements it has ratified to be non-self-executing.

The U.S. practice of declaring human rights conventions non-self-executing is commonly seen as of a piece with the other RUDs. As the reservations designed to deny international obligations serve to immunize the United States from external judgment, the declaration that a convention shall be non-self-executing is designed to keep its own judges from judging the human rights conditions in the United States by international standards. To critics, keeping a convention from having any effect as United States law confirms that United States adherence remains essentially empty.

The non-self-executing declaration has been explained — and justified — as designed to assure that changes in U.S. law will be effected only by "democratic processes" — therefore, by legislation, not by treaty. That argument, of course, impugns the democratic character of every treaty made or that will be made by the President with the consent of the Senate.

Whatever may be appropriate in a special case, as a general practice such a declaration is against the spirit of the Constitution; it may be unconstitutional. Article VI of the Constitution provides expressly for lawmaking by treaty: treaties are declared to be the supreme law of the land. The Framers intended that a treaty should become law *ipso facto,* when the treaty is made; it should not require legislative implementation to convert it into United States law. In effect, lawmaking by treaty was to be an alternative to legislation by Congress.

Nothing in the Constitution or in the history of its adoption suggests that the Framers contemplated that some treaties might not be law of the land. That was a later suggestion by John Marshall, because he found that some promises *by their character* could not be "self-executing": when the United States undertook to do something in the future that could be done only by legislative or other political act, the treaty did not — could not — carry out the undertaking. Marshall did not contemplate that treaty undertakings that could be given effect as law by the Executive and the courts, or by the states, should not be carried out by them, but might be converted into promises that Congress would legislate. Surely, there is no evidence of any intent, by the Framers (or by John Marshall), to allow the President or the Senate, by their *ipse dixit,* to prevent a treaty that by its character *could* be law of the land from becoming law of the land. . . .

There is more at issue in the United States RUDs than their effect on a particular treaty; at stake in United States human rights reservation policy is the integrity of the constitutional system for concluding treaties. . . .

. . . [It became apparent] that — apart from the condition of human rights in the United States — United States foreign policy required U.S. support for, if not leadership in, the international human rights movement, and required U.S. adherence to international human rights conventions. Successive administrations slowly abandoned President Eisenhower's commitment [to Senator Bricker not to seek to become a party to additional human rights treaties]. But Senator Bricker's ghost has proved to be alive in the Senate, and successive administrations have become infected with his ideology.

Senator Bricker lost his battle, but his ghost is now enjoying victory in war. For the package of reservations, understandings and declarations achieves virtually what the Bricker Amendment sought, and more. In pressing his amendment, Senator Bricker declared: "My purpose in offering this resolution is to bury the so-called

Covenant on Human Rights so deep that no one holding high public office will ever dare to attempt its resurrection." By its package of RUDs, the United States effectively fulfilled Senator Bricker's purpose, leaving the Covenant without any life in United States law. . . .

U.S. ratification practice threatens to undermine a half-century of effort to establish international human rights standards as international law. Lawyers (and others) committed to the international human rights movement should be on guard to ensure that U.S. ratification policy not set an unfortunate example to other states contemplating adherence, that it not encourage states that have ratified to take their obligations under the conventions lightly. Lawyers in the United States should take arms against the anticonstitutional practice of declaring human rights conventions non-self-executing.

Notes and Questions

1. Should the United States ratify additional human rights treaties, such as the ICESCR, the CEDAW, and the Convention on the Rights of the Child? If so, should it condition its ratification with RUDs? What, according to Professors Bradley and Goldsmith, are the difficulties with international human rights treaties that justify the use of RUDs? How persuasive are these concerns? Is Professor Henkin's suggestion that RUDs make the U.S. ratification of human rights treaties meaningless convincing? Would the United States have ratified the ICCPR and other human rights treaties without the RUDs?

2. Note that, despite its limited embrace of international human rights treaties, the United States has enacted legislation implementing some of the human rights treaties it has ratified. In connection with its ratification of the Genocide Convention, the United States enacted the Genocide Convention Implementation Act, 18 U.S.C. §1091, which makes genocide a federal crime if it is committed in the United States or the alleged offender is a U.S. national. In connection with its ratification of the Torture Convention, the United States enacted a provision making torture outside the United States a federal crime, 18 U.S.C. §2340A. Before ratifying the convention, the United States had also enacted a civil cause of action allowing for the recovery of damages for foreign torture, 28 U.S.C. §1350 note. (The latter statute, known as the Torture Victim Protection Act, is discussed in Chapter 3.) The United States also amended its immigration law to take account of Article 3 of the Torture Convention, which bars the return of a person to another nation "where there are substantial grounds for believing that he would be in danger of being subjected to torture." See Pub. L. No. 105-277, 112 Stat. 2681-822 (1998) (codified as note to 8 U.S.C. §1231).

3. The post-September 11 U.S. practice of "extraordinary rendition" of individuals suspected of involvement in terrorist activity to countries reputed to engage in mistreatment of detainees has given rise to substantial controversy in light of Article 3 of the Torture Convention. Media sources, citing unnamed American sources involved in the rendition program, indicate that U.S. officials were at the time aware that such transferees were likely to be tortured. "According to one [Bush Administration] official who . . . [was] directly involved in rendering captives into foreign hands, the understanding [was], 'We don't kick the [expletive] out of them. We send them to other countries so they can kick the [expletive] out of them.'"

Dana Priest & Barton Gellman, U.S. Decries Abuse But Defends Interrogations; "Stress and Duress" Tactics Used on Terrorism Suspects Held in Secret Overseas Facilities, Wash. Post, Dec. 26, 2002, at A1.

In one prominent case, U.S. authorities detained Maher Arar, a Canadian national suspected of connections to terrorist organizations, while he transited through Kennedy Airport in New York. U.S. authorities later transported him to Syria, where he was held in detention for a year and allegedly tortured by Syrian authorities. Arar brought suit against the U.S. officials he claimed were responsible for his mistreatment, but the Second Circuit affirmed a dismissal of his claim, which was brought as a *Bivens* action. The court concluded that due in part to the "significant diplomatic and national security concerns" raised by Arar's lawsuit, it would not recognize a new type of *Bivens* action in the context of extraordinary rendition. Arar v. Ashcroft, 585 F.3d 559, 575 (2d Cir. 2009) (en banc), cert. denied, 130 S.Ct. 3409 (2010). If the United States had not included a declaration that the Torture Convention was not self-executing when it ratified the treaty, would Arar's case have been actionable under the Convention? Article 14(1) provides that each party "shall ensure in its legal system that the victim of an act of torture obtains redress and has an enforceable right to fair and adequate compensation including the means for as full rehabilitation as possible."

Arar's case also prompted a government investigation in Canada, whose intelligence officials had provided information to the United States about Arar's alleged links to terrorist groups. The investigation concluded that Canadian officials did not in fact possess any information linking Arar to terrorist activities. See Report of the Events Relating to Maher Arar by the Commission of Inquiry into the Actions of Canadian Officials in Relation to Maher Arar 59 (2006). The Canadian government formally apologized to Arar and paid him 10.5 million Canadian dollars in compensation.

As for the broader policy of "extraordinary rendition," press accounts suggest that the Obama Administration "will continue the Bush administration's practice of sending terrorism suspects to third countries for detention and interrogation, but pledges to closely monitor their treatment to ensure that they are not tortured." David Johnston, Rendition to Continue, but with Better Oversight, N.Y. Times, Aug. 25, 2009, at A8.

b. Economic Sanctions

Despite its limited and conditional embrace of international human rights law, the United States has frequently exerted pressure on other nations to improve their human rights practices. Official U.S. foreign assistance is sometimes either targeted, or restricted, with human rights issues in mind. In addition, starting in the 1960s, many U.S. laws have been enacted and Executive Branch decisions made that authorize or impose economic sanctions against target countries for a variety of foreign policy reasons. The sanctions might be intended to oppose terrorism, sanction drug-producing and drug-transit countries, oppose the acquisition of weapons of mass destruction, isolate persons undermining peace agreements, or protect the environment. But they also can be directed at changing the behavior of a country or its nationals in order to combat human rights abuses and/or to promote democracy.

The range of possible U.S. actions can and has included sanctions that limit exports from the United States, imports to the United States, investment in the target country, and private financial transactions between U.S. citizens and the target country's government or citizens. The sanctions can also involve restrictions on U.S. government programs, such as foreign aid and government credit and insurance programs. They can additionally include directions for the United States to vote against loans in international financial institutions (IFIs), such as the World Bank and IMF.

The International Emergency Economic Powers Act (IEEPA), passed in 1977, provides the President with broad powers over exports, imports, and financial transactions whenever the President has declared a national emergency. (IEEPA is analyzed in some detail in Chapter 3.) Presidents have increasingly declared such emergencies, sometimes for human rights reasons. For example, President Reagan invoked IEEPA in 1985 when the United States imposed trade and investment sanctions as well as limits on U.S. government programs against South Africa because of its apartheid policy. Since then, IEEPA has been invoked — sometimes in combination with other, country-specific laws — to impose sanctions against human rights and humanitarian abuses, or to confront interruptions of or threats to democracy, in Myanmar (formerly Burma) (1997), Liberia (2001 and 2004), Zimbabwe (2003), Côte d'Ivoire (2006), Sudan (2006), Belarus (2006), the Democratic Republic of the Congo (2006), Lebanon (2007), Somalia (2010), and Iran (2010), among other cases.

The following excerpt discusses some of the specific laws that have been passed, ranging from limits on military aid and foreign assistance to directing U.S. votes in the international financial institutions.

Barry E. Carter, International Economic Sanctions: Improving the Haphazard U.S. Legal Regime

47-48, 163-164, 172 (1988) [updated through 2006]

[U.S. Government Programs]

2. *Abuse of human rights.* Usually enacted at the initiative of Congress, several laws have attempted to limit foreign assistance to countries that are in gross violation of internationally recognized human rights. The primary legislative efforts have focused on military aid and arms sales, but there have also been efforts to limit economic assistance to these countries.

The first law was passed in 1973. A nonbinding sense of Congress resolution, it was openly ignored by the Nixon and Ford Administrations. Congress responded with several progressive amendments to tighten the law and reduce the President's discretion.

For military assistance and arms sales, the key provision is amended section 502B [22 U.S.C. §2304], which has changed little since 1978. The critical subsection provides that "no security assistance may be provided to any country the government of which engages in a consistent pattern of gross violations of internationally recognized human rights." An exception is permitted if the President certifies in writing to Congress that "extraordinary circumstances exist warranting provision of such assistance." . . .

For economic assistance, the primary provision is amended section 116 [22 U.S.C. §2151n]. Like section 502B, it prohibits assistance to any country that engages in a consistent pattern of gross violations of internationally recognized human rights. It has an important exception—when "such assistance will directly benefit the needy people in such country." . . .

[Congress has also sought to encourage the Executive Branch to apply human rights criteria to U.S. action in various international financial institutions. The following statute is illustrative.

22 U.S.C. §262d

[(a) Policy goals. The United States Government, in connection with its voice and vote in the International Bank for Reconstruction and Development, the International Development Association, the International Finance Corporation, the Inter-American Development Bank, the African Development Fund, the Asian Development Bank, the African Development Bank, the European Bank for Reconstruction and Development, and the International Monetary Fund, shall advance the cause of human rights, including by seeking to channel assistance toward countries other than those whose governments engage in—

[(1) a pattern of gross violations of internationally recognized human rights, such as torture or cruel, inhumane, or degrading treatment or punishment, prolonged detention without charges, or other flagrant denial to life, liberty, and the security of person. . . .]

[In the international financial institutions (IFIs), the] United States can raise . . . foreign policy considerations through its formal votes and by lobbying other member countries and the institution's staff. The decision-making structures at the IMF, World Bank, and regional banks are all similar.

With respect to formal voting, each institution has a board of executive directors, which votes on requests for financial assistance and oversees other operations. . . .

Most decisions on loan requests, however, are made by the executive boards through informal consensus rather than through formal voting procedures. This practice makes it difficult to discern behind-the-scenes maneuvering on loan requests, since records of informal meetings are usually confidential. As a result, it is often difficult to determine when political pressure by one country is instrumental in a loan request being approved, rejected, or never even receiving formal consideration. . . .

Generally, a simple majority of the votes cast is sufficient to resolve a financial request by a member. . . .

[T]he United States lacks the unilateral voting clout to stop assistance from the regular fund of the IDB or from the IMF, World Bank, or . . . regional banks. [The U.S. voting percentages are far less than a majority in each case. Except for the Inter-American Development Bank where the U.S. voting percentage is about 30 percent, the U.S. percentage in the other international financial institutions is 20 percent or less.] . . .

The United States has, then, only limited ability to use the IFIs to impose economic sanctions for its specific foreign policy reasons. This situation results from the nonpolitical purposes and charter provisions of the IFIs and from the limited U.S. voting power. Because U.S. influence is weak in terms of formal voting power, there is greater potential to operate informally through persuasion and coalition building.

There has been considerable debate about the effectiveness of U.S. economic sanctions in combating human rights abuses (or for other foreign policy purposes). There does seem to be substantial agreement among experts that sanctions taken in conjunction with other major countries or with the United Nations (i.e., multilateral sanctions) are more likely to have an impact and come closer to achieving their intended purpose than U.S. unilateral sanctions. For example, probably the most successful economic sanctions for human rights purposes were the fairly comprehensive sanctions imposed by many countries against South Africa.

The South Africa sanctions started with a nonbinding resolution of the U.N. General Assembly in 1962 calling for some sanctions. The progressive adoption of increasingly broad measures by countries gained considerable momentum when the United States and most European Community members imposed sanctions in 1985. After South Africa then released Nelson Mandela and others from prison and repealed some apartheid laws, the United States lifted its sanctions in 1991, followed by other countries and the United Nations in 1991-1994. The authors of a major analytical study of 170 cases of economic sanctions imposed since World War I reached the following conclusions about South Africa:

> Overall, economic and political conditions inside South Africa were clearly the most important factors influencing the outcome in [the South Africa apartheid] case and economic sanctions can be credited with, at best, a modest contribution. The sanctions were obviously useful to the opposition, both as symbolic support and as a lever that the ANC [African National Congress] could use in its negotiations with the government. . . .
>
> In sum, the sanctions added to the already mounting costs of maintaining apartheid. Sanctions clearly did not cause the [governing] National Party to decide to abandon apartheid but they accelerated the inevitable. [Gary Clyde Hufbauer, et al., Case Studies in Sanctions and Terrorism, Case 85-1, at http://www.piie.com/research/topics/sanctions/southafrica.cfm (case study accompanying Gary Clyde Hufbauer, Jeffrey J. Schott, Kimberly Ann Elliott & Barbara Oegg, Economic Sanctions Reconsidered (3d ed. 2007)).]

In another situation, starting in 1988 and continuing into 2011, the United States, the European Community, and Japan progressively imposed sanctions against the government of Myanmar (which was formerly Burma and is still called that in some circles) for its harsh repression of political opponents, including the house arrest of Aung San Suu Kyi in 1989. Her opposition party nevertheless won a majority of the seats in the National Assembly in elections the following year, but the military regime refused to give up power. (Ms. Suu Kyi was awarded a Nobel Peace Prize in 1991 for her efforts to bring democracy to Myanmar.) In 1997 President Clinton, invoking IEEPA and a 1996 law, issued an executive order that bars new U.S. investment in Myanmar. About the same time, U.S. state and local governments also were imposing sanctions, though these were effectively stopped by the U.S.

Supreme Court decision in Crosby v. National Foreign Trade Council, 530 U.S. 363 (2000). (*Crosby* is considered in Chapter 3.D.) Congress passed additional trade and travel sanctions in 2003 and 2008.

The sanctions study cited above notes that although Burma's military has refused to honor the results of Burma's 1990 election, "the decision to hold the elections at all, as well as Burma's decision [in 1995] to release Aung San Suu Kyi from house arrest appear to have been attributable at least in part to . . . the international pressure, including economic sanctions." Hufbauer, Schott, Elliott & Oegg, Case Studies in Sanctions and Terrorism, supra, Case 88-1, at http://www.piie.com/research/topics/sanctions/myanmar.cfm. Nevertheless, the study's assessment of the overall effectiveness of the Burma sanctions is low. Indeed, by 2003, the military junta had again placed Aung San Suu Kyi under house arrest, where she remained until November 2010. She was released a few days after Burma's military government held the country's first elections since 1990. The military-backed Union Solidarity and Development Party won substantial majorities in both houses of parliament in elections widely condemned as unfair.

There also seems to be considerable support for the view that, while unilateral U.S. economic sanctions may express U.S. views and have symbolic value, these unilateral sanctions usually have only limited or negligible economic impact against target countries. This limited economic utility has become increasingly true because, with greater globalization and the industrial growth of a number of countries, a target country can usually find alternative sources of supplies or markets for its goods. Nevertheless, the United States has frequently imposed unilateral sanctions in the past two decades, as well as before.

For example, in 1989, in reaction to the brutal suppression by the Chinese government of students and others in Tiananmen Square in Beijing and elsewhere in China, President George H.W. Bush suspended U.S. arms sales, government-to-government contracts, and certain commercial sales of high-technology items, such as communications satellites. The U.S. sanctions have been steadily relaxed since then, but some restrictions remain in place as of February 2011. The sanctions study mentioned above gives U.S. economic sanctions some credit for combating human rights abuses in China, but overall assesses the sanctions as having largely failed. The study comments: "Economic sanctions have prompted China to release a few individual dissidents and intermittently relax repressive policies. China's leadership, however, maintains the positions that threats to the regime must be quelled." Id., Case 89-2, at http://www.piie.com/research/topics/sanctions/china.cfm.

Concern about the limited effectiveness of unilateral sanctions, as well as the potentially indiscriminate impact of sanctions on the populations of sanctioned countries, has led to an effort to develop targeted, or "smart," sanctions. A number of recent U.S. sanctions programs restrict financial transactions with discrete groups of named individuals — usually political leaders and their supporters — deemed to be responsible for human rights violations. Post-2005 U.S. sanctions programs involving Belarus, Côte d'Ivoire, Liberia, Sudan, Zimbabwe, the Democratic Republic of the Congo, Lebanon, Somalia, and Iran all specify individuals to be sanctioned by virtue of their role in directing human rights abuses, undermining democracy, or fostering civil conflict in which serious human rights abuses have occurred. A study on economic sanctions suggests that "the presence of sanctions against a government leader in a given year makes her or him significantly more likely to lose power in the following year." Nikolay Marinov, Do Economic Sanctions Destabilize Country Leaders?, 49 Am. J. Pol. Sci. 564, 565 (2005).

Notes and Questions

1. Given the broad powers provided to the President by IEEPA, why does Congress still pass specific, new legislation authorizing U.S. economic sanctions? For example, laws have been passed since 1995 authorizing various sanctions against Myanmar, against countries committing religious persecution, against countries practicing female genital mutilation, against countries supporting terrorists, against countries harboring war criminals, and to prohibit the underground trade in rough diamonds used to finance civil war in a number of countries. Possibly these laws might be intended to fill any potential gaps in the President's authority, such as over foreign aid funds. However, the specific laws often overlap the broad IEEPA authorities. It would seem that sometimes those backing the legislation in Congress are using it to call attention to the objectionable activity. Also, the new laws might provide for specific Executive Branch procedures and reporting requirements that the congressional supporters would like to see followed.

2. The Millennium Challenge Act of 2003 was enacted to promote an approach to development assistance that links U.S. assistance to the commitment of recipient countries to ruling justly, encouraging economic freedom, and investing in their people. The Act established a government corporation authorized to provide assistance from the Millennium Challenge Account to eligible countries. Criteria to be considered in determining a county's eligibility for assistance under the Act include whether it has demonstrated a commitment to "just and democratic governance" (including commitment to "political pluralism, equality, and the rule of law") and to "respect [for] human and civil rights." Millennium Challenge Act of 2003, as amended, 22 U.S.C. §7706(b).

3. Assume that proposed unilateral U.S. economic sanctions against, say, a small Asian or African country for egregious abuse of internationally recognized human rights would be likely to have only a limited economic impact on the target country because it could find other suppliers and markets. Should the United States still announce and impose the economic sanction as a symbolic way to emphasize U.S. policies? Should such sanctions be pursued only in conjunction with other countries sanctioning the target country, or at least only after strenuous efforts are made to enlist other countries?

4. Assume you were advising a U.S. senator or representative who wanted to support imposing at least one economic sanction against a country that was seriously violating internationally recognized human rights. Although the impact of various types of economic sanctions obviously depends on the specific circumstances in real cases, assume for now that the economic impact on the target country would be the same whether the sanction were a limit on U.S. exports, a limit on imports from the target country, or a limit on financial transactions between the two countries (e.g., new U.S. loans or investment there). Which type of sanction should the senator or representative prefer? Consider the likely impact on U.S. jobs and on U.S. trade flows.

5. Besides the materials above, for additional discussion of economic sanctions (including U.S. law and practice) and their impact, see Robert Eyler, Economic

Sanctions: International Policy and Political Economy at Work (2007); Michael P. Malloy, Study of New U.S. Unilateral Sanctions: 1997-2006 (2006) (based in part on research by Barry E. Carter), at http://www.usaengage.org; International Sanctions: Between Words and Wars in the Global System (Peter Wallensteen & Carina Staibano eds., 2005).

c. Diplomatic Pressure

In addition to sanctions, the United States often uses diplomatic pressure in an effort to induce changes in human rights practices. Every year, for example, the U.S. State Department is required to prepare and send to Congress a report on each country's human rights record.

The State Department's country report for the year 2009 covered all 192 U.N. member states and other entities like Taiwan, Kosovo, and Western Sahara. The introduction to the report singled out a number of countries that were chosen for "notable developments" during 2009. In that regard, Afghanistan, Burma, the Democratic Republic of the Congo, Iraq, Israel, Nigeria, Pakistan, Russia, Sri Lanka, and Sudan were identified as countries "where conflicts were raging . . . [and] noncombatant civilians faced human rights abuses and violations of international humanitarian law." The report identified Belarus, China, Colombia, Cuba, Iran, North Korea, Russia, Venezuela, Vietnam, and Uzbekistan as countries where either governments or non-state groups had restricted freedom of expression, assembly, and association. The report also provided the following overview of notable settings in which members of vulnerable groups—including racial, ethnic, and religious minorities; the disabled; women and children; migrant workers; and lesbian, gay, bisexual, and transgender individuals—were marginalized and were targets of societal and/or government-sanctioned abuse:

> China continued to exert tight control over activities and peoples that the government perceived as a threat to the Chinese Communist Party. For example, public interest lawyers who took on cases deemed sensitive by the government increasingly were harassed or disbarred, and their law firms often were closed. The government also increased repression of Tibetans and Uighurs. The government tightened controls on Uighurs expressing peaceful dissent and on independent Muslim religious leaders, often citing counterterrorism as the reason for taking action. Following the July [2009] riots that broke out in Urumqi, the provincial capital of Xuar, officials cracked down on religious extremism, "splittism," and terrorism in an attempt to maintain public order. In the aftermath of the violence, Uighurs were sentenced to long prison terms and in some cases were executed, without due process, on charges of separatism. . . . In the Tibetan areas of China, the government's human rights record remained poor as authorities committed extrajudicial killings, torture, arbitrary arrests, and extrajudicial detentions. Authorities sentenced Tibetans for alleged support of Tibetan independence, regardless of whether their activities involved violence. The preservation and development of Tibet's unique religious, cultural, and linguistic heritage also remained a concern.
>
> The [Mubarak-led] government of Egypt failed to respect the freedom of association and restricted freedom of expression, and its respect for freedom of religion remained very poor. Sectarian attacks on Coptic Christians mounted during the year. The government failed to redress laws and government practices that discriminate

> against Christians. The government sponsored "reconciliation sessions" following sectarian attacks, which generally prevented the prosecution of perpetrators of crimes against Copts and precluded their recourse to the judicial system for restitution. This practice contributed to a climate of impunity and may have encouraged further assaults. Members of non-Muslim religious minorities that the government officially recognized generally worshipped without harassment; however, Christians and members of the Baha'i faith, which the government does not recognize, faced personal and collective discrimination in many areas. In a step forward, the government promulgated procedures for members of unrecognized religions, including the Baha'i faith, to obtain national identification documents. . . .
>
> As a growing number of people cross borders to find work, migrant workers have become particularly vulnerable to exploitation and discrimination. In Malaysia, foreign workers were subject to exploitative conditions and generally did not have access to the system of labor adjudication. . . . Some domestic workers alleged that their employers subjected them to inhuman living conditions, withheld their salaries, confiscated their travel documents, and physically assaulted them.
>
> Violence against women, violations of the rights of children, and discrimination on the basis of gender, religion, sect, and ethnicity were common in many countries in the Middle East region. In Saudi Arabia, for example, Muslim religious practices that conflict with the government's interpretation of Sunni Islam are discriminated against and public religious expression by non-Muslims is prohibited. Human rights activists reported more progress in women's rights than in other areas, and the government made efforts to integrate women into mainstream society, for example, through the founding of the Kingdom's first coeducational university in September. However, discrimination against women was a significant problem, demonstrated by the lack of women's autonomy, freedom of movement, and economic independence; discriminatory practices surrounding divorce and child custody; the absence of a law criminalizing violence against women; and difficulties preventing women from escaping abusive environments. There are no laws specifically prohibiting domestic violence. . . . [U.S. Dept. of State, Bureau of Democracy, Human Rights, and Labor, 2009 Country Reports on Human Rights Practices, at http://www.state.gov/g/drl/rls/hrrpt/2009.]

Other forms of discrimination against vulnerable groups identified in the introduction to the State Department's 2009 human rights report included "arbitrary legal restrictions" faced by lesbian, gay, bisexual, and transgender (LGBT) persons in Uganda; "[t]raditional and new forms of anti-Semitism" across Europe, South America, and beyond (some fueled by governments, "most notably Iran's President Ahmadi-Nejad"); increasing discrimination against Muslims in Europe; and killings and incidents of violence against Roma, including in Italy, Hungary, Romania, Slovakia, and the Czech Republic. Id.

The preparation of these country reports can stimulate the U.S. government to take up a particular problem with the state involved. Once published, the reports also provide a basis for pressure from other sources, such as human rights NGOs. In the absence of a centralized enforcement mechanism in the international system, this type of diplomatic and public pressure illustrates the more general phenomenon of state-to-state "horizontal enforcement" of international law. Critics have argued, however, that because of foreign policy concerns, the reports have sometimes been muted in their reporting of human rights abuses.

Diplomatic pressure can take other forms as well. For example, the U.S. government might limit or even terminate its diplomatic relations with a particular regime because of its human rights practices. Or it might decline to engage in cooperative projects with the regime until certain human rights issues are addressed.

Can diplomatic pressure be more effective than formal sanctions? Would it be appropriate to overlook human rights abuses because a nation is cooperating with U.S. foreign policy objectives, such as allowing a U.S. military base on its soil? Cooperating in arresting individuals suspected of international terrorism? Agreeing not to develop nuclear weapons? Supplying oil or other strategic resources to the United States? How should the U.S. government balance its commitment to human rights against other foreign policy interests?

d. Domestic Litigation

Since the *Filartiga* decision in 1980, U.S. courts have exercised jurisdiction over a growing number and variety of civil suits alleging violations of international human rights norms, and the Supreme Court in *Sosa* affirmed that the Alien Tort Statute (ATS), also referred to as the Alien Tort Claims Act (ATCA), confers federal court jurisdiction over widely accepted and specific contemporary international law norms. See Chapter 3.C, including discussion of the ATS and the Torture Victim Protection Act (TVPA).

Plaintiffs have successfully won judgments in a number of prominent cases involving human rights claims, including suits against the President of the self-declared Bosnia Serb Republic in Bosnia-Herzegovina for genocide, war crimes, and other violations of international humanitarian law by Bosnia Serb forces during the Bosnian civil war, Kadic v. Karadzic, 70 F.3d 232 (2d Cir. 1995); against the former Defense Minister of Guatemala based on a campaign of torture, summary execution, disappearance, and arbitrary detention of Guatemala civilians, Xuncax v. Gramajo, 886 F. Supp. 162 (D. Ct. Mass. 1995); against an operative of the Pinochet regime in Chile for the torture and murder of a Chilean citizen killed during the "Caravan of Death," a campaign of repression against suspected opponents of the government, Cabello v. Fernandez-Larios, 205 F.Supp.2d 1325 (S.D. Fla. 2002), aff'd 402 F.3d 1148 (11th Cir. 2005); against Emmanuel "Toto" Constant, the founder and former leader of a notorious death squad that operated under Haiti's 1991-1994 military regime, Doe v. Constant, Civ. No. 04-10108 (S.D.N.Y. Oct. 24, 2006), aff'd, 2009 U.S. App. LEXIS 26052 (2d Cir. 2009); and against a Peruvian military officer for extrajudicial killings during a 1985 massacre of civilians in the course of counter-terrorism operations, Ochoa Lizarbe v. Hurtado, No. 07-21783, 2008 U.S. Dist. LEXIS 109517 (S.D. Fla. Mar 4, 2008).

Some of these cases are default judgments against defendants who did not participate in the litigation, e.g., *Kadic* and *Gramajo*, but in other cases, the defendant has appeared and awards have been issued after a contested trial, e.g., *Fernandez-Larios* and *Hurtado*.

Except for the *Kadic* case, all the cases cited above, including *Filartiga*, were brought against former foreign government officials. Present and former officials are more likely to be subject to ATS or TVPA law suits after the U.S. Supreme Court's decision in 2010 in Samantar v. Yousuf, 130 S.Ct. 2278 (2010). There, a former Prime Minister and Minister of Defense of Somalia argued that he was not liable under the ATS or TVPA because he was immune from the jurisdiction of U.S. courts under the Foreign Sovereign Immunities Act (FSIA) for the acts he committed while he was a government official. The Court held unanimously that the FSIA did not grant immunity to government officials (as opposed to states and their agencies and instrumentalities). The overall effect of *Samantar* is to sharply curtail the availability of FSIA for present or former foreign government officials. The Court did note that government officials might still be able to claim common law immunity for government officials, but did not address its scope. Id. at 2292. Foreign officials might also be able to claim diplomatic or head of state immunity. (See discussion in Chapter 6.A.)

As noted in Chapter 3.C, the *Kadic* case was significant in holding that private individuals could be held liable for violations of at least some rules of international law. Later case law found that private corporations as well as private individuals could be held liable under the ATS either because of the corporation's own conduct or because of its involvement with human rights abuses committed by foreign governments abroad. See, e.g., Doe v. Unocal Corp., 110 F. Supp. 2d 1294 (C.D. Cal. 2000) (settled while on appeal) (suit by Myanmar, or Burmese, citizens against U.S. corporations and their executives for alleged human rights abuses, including forced labor, murder, rape, and torture, that were committed, in least in part by the Myanmar government, in connection with construction of a oil pipeline in Myanmar).

A split has recently developed among the lower federal courts over whether corporations can be sued under the ATS. (The TVPA is specifically limited to cases brought against individuals.) In Kiobel v. Royal Dutch Petroleum, 621 F.3d 111 (2d Cir. 2010), the court dismissed an ATS claim against corporations that allegedly abetted human rights abuses perpetrated against Nigerian residents by the Nigerian government. In a divided ruling, the court recognized that international law had begun to impose responsibility for serious violations of human rights on individuals as well as states. It nevertheless concluded that the notion of *corporate* liability for such violations was not sufficiently recognized under customary international to serve as a basis for a claim under the ATS.

Although Judge Leval concurred in the dismissal of the plaintiff's case in *Kiobel*, he vigorously disagreed with the majority's view, as he put it, "that international law authorizes imposing civil awards of compensatory damages on natural persons but leaves corporations free to violate its rules without legal consequences." Id. at 160 (Leval, J., concurring). He questioned the majority's approach of looking to international law and international cases to determine what kinds of entities could be held civilly liable. "What international law does is it prescribes norms of conduct. . . . And as for civil liability of both natural and juridical persons, . . . the law of nations . . . [provides] that each State is free to decide that question for itself." Id. at 175.

If a private individual or corporation is sued under the ATS before a court that recognizes such suits against corporations, the court may have to consider the extent to which governmental action is required for violations of international human rights law, the circumstances under which governmental action will be imputed to private actors, and whether liability under international law can be grounded on the concept of "aiding and abetting" the direct perpetrators of international law violations.

The question of "aiding and abetting" liability, for example, has generated a number of contested legal questions. One concerns the choice of law to be applied in adjudicating aiding and abetting cases. Should the question of when a defendant is vicariously liable for the acts of another be decided on the basis of international law standards or domestic law standards? Under one view, international law itself must establish that aiding and abetting internationally prohibited conduct gives rise to liability under the ATS. Professor Keitner has referred to this approach as "the 'conduct-regulating rules' approach, because it treats the defendant accomplice's participation as an integral part of the alleged violation." Chimène I. Keitner, Conceptualizing Complicity in Alien Tort Cases, 60 Hastings L.J. 61, 74 (2008). Judge Scheindlin adopted this approach in a case brought by South Africans against a number of corporations alleging that they had aided and abetted international law violations by giving assistance to South Africa's apartheid regime: "As the [ATS] is merely a jurisdictional vehicle for the enforcement of universal norms, the contours of secondary [aiding and abetting] liability must stem from international sources." In re S. African Apartheid Litig., 617 F. Supp. 2d 228, 256 (S.D.N.Y. 2009). Under the other view of aiding and abetting liability, once a court has established that a state has violated international law, the "court can then adjudicate the corporate defendant's liability for contributing to that violation by applying a different body of law—U.S. federal common law." Keitner, supra, 60 Hastings L.J. at 72-73. In an earlier phase of the South Africa apartheid litigation, Judge Hall, in a concurring opinion, observed that both domestic law and international law include aiding and abetting standards. In such cases, he stated, "domestic courts should choose" domestic law. Khulumani v. Barclay Nat'l Bank, Ltd., 504 F.3d 254, 287 (2d Cir. 2007) (Hall, J., concurring). Professor Keitner has criticized this approach, arguing that because the ATS "was intended to provide a federal forum for adjudicating international law violations," courts should use international law standards on accomplice liability, not domestic law standards. Keitner, supra, 60 Hastings L.J. at 77.

For those courts that have relied on international law standards in considering cases involving corporate complicity in international human rights violations, a second issue concerns the precise standard for determining what conduct and associated mental state constitute actionable aiding and abetting under the ATS. In terms of the required conduct, or *actus reus*, the cases have generally held that a corporation must provide "substantial assistance" to the principal perpetrator. See, e.g., Presbyterian Church of Sudan v. Talisman Energy, Inc., 582 F. 3d 244, 247 (2d Cir. 2009). (Despite agreement on the general standard, disagreements about what constitutes substantial assistance have arisen.) On the question of what mental state, or *mens rea*, the defendant corporation must have, there is substantial debate about the underlying doctrinal standard. Some courts have held that it is enough if the defendant corporation has "knowledge" of the impact its actions will have on the commission of abuses by a government. In the case against corporations alleged to have aided and abetted apartheid era violations in South Africa, for instance, Judge Scheindlin held:

> One who substantially assists a violator of the law of nations is equally liable if he or she desires the crime to occur or if he or she knows it will occur and simply does not care. . . . [C]ustomary international law requires that an aider and abettor know that

> its actions will substantially assist the perpetrator in the commissionof a crime or tort in violation of the law of nations. [In re S. African Apartheid Litig., 617 F. Supp. 2d 228, 262 (S.D.N.Y. 2009).]

In other cases, however, courts have rejected the notion that there is international consensus "for imposing liability on individuals who *knowingly* (but not purposefully) aid and abet a violation of international law." *Presbyterian Church,* supra, 582 F.3d at 259. The court in *Presbyterian Church* instead held that to establish aiding and abetting liability under the ATS, "a claimant must show that the defendant provided substantial assistance with the purpose of facilitating" the alleged international law violations. Id. at 247.

Notes and Questions

1. Is U.S. domestic litigation an effective or desirable strategy to improve human rights compliance by other countries? How does it differ from other aspects of U.S. human rights policy, such as economic sanctions and diplomatic pressure?

2. In many of the Alien Tort Statute cases brought against corporations for aiding and abetting human rights violations, the underlying wrongs were committed by a government that is immune from suit in the United States under the Foreign Sovereign Immunities Act. Is it appropriate for a U.S. court to adjudicate aiding and abetting liability when it cannot adjudicate the liability of the principal wrongdoer?

3. Should the Foreign Sovereign Immunities Act be amended to permit more human rights litigation directly against foreign governments? Should the U.S. government be subject to human rights suits in foreign courts?

4. As noted in Chapter 3, the Supreme Court in the *Sosa* case held that federal courts should not recognize new categories of ATS claims "with less definite content and acceptance among civilized nations than the historical paradigms familiar." The Court noted that its ruling was consistent with the approach taken by courts in the past, including *Filartiga,* where the Second Circuit held that a claims of official torture could be brought under the ATCA. In this regard, the Court favorably quoted *Filartiga's* statement that " 'the torturer has become—like the pirate and slave trader before him—*hostis humani generis,* an enemy of all mankind.' " Sosa v. Alvarez-Machain, 542 U.S. 692, 732 (2004) (quoting *Filartiga*). Does the international community also recognize a person or corporation that aids and abets human rights abuses by others as an enemy of all mankind? Does it depend on whether an actor "knowingly" or "purposely" provides substantial assistance to the international law violations?

5. How much guidance do the decisions setting out the test for aiding and abetting liability described above give to corporations in determining what they can and cannot do in other countries? Does it depend on whether the test for liability is "knowingly providing substantial assistance" to international law violations or "purposely providing substantial assistance" to carrying such violation? Should Congress address this issue?

6. Should U.S. courts look to international law standards, including such sources as the decisions of international criminal tribunals, in ascertaining the test for aiding and abetting liability under the Alien Tort Statute? Or should it rely on domestic law principles?

7. Are there reasons to treat corporations differently from individuals in determining whether they can be held liable under the ATS? If international law determines what substantive conduct can be challenged under the ATS, should we look to international law or domestic law to determine whether a particular entity may be held liable? If you believe the question should be answered under international law, would the emerging norms on corporate social responsibility discussed in Chapter 2 provide a basis for corporate responsibility, or do those fall short of the standard set by the Supreme Court in *Sosa*? What other sources might you look to?

8. The practical impact of ATS cases brought against corporations has been growing. According to a March 2010 publication, "there have been more than 140 ATS cases filed against corporations, with 115 of those (82 percent) being filed in the past 15 years." Jonathan Drimmer, Human Rights and the Extractive Industries: Litigation and Compliance Trends, 3 J. World Energy L. & Bus. 121, 122 (2010). Although a few of these cases have produced damages awards, see, e.g., Chowdhury v. WorldTel Bangladesh Holding, Ltd., 588 F. Supp. 2d 375 (E.D.N.Y. 2008) (jury award of $1.75 million to a plaintiff whose business rival helped orchestrate his arrest and torture by paramilitary police), such judgments are still rare. But a number of other prominent ATS cases—including cases such as the *Unocal* case noted above and Wang Xiaoning v. Yahoo! Inc., No. C07-02151 CW (N.D. Cal. Complaint filed Apr. 18, 2007), where the plaintiffs alleged that the provision of information by the defendant corporation of information about its email account holder customers to the Chinese government led to the arbitrary arrest, detention, and torture of authors of pro-democracy writings—have resulted in out-of-court settlements.

9. The Torture Victim Protection Act specifies that U.S. courts may not consider a case "if the claimant has not exhausted adequate and available remedies in the place in which the conduct giving rise to the claim occurred." Although there is no statutory exhaustion requirement under the ATS, the Court in *Sosa* indicated that it "would certainly consider this requirement in an appropriate case." *Sosa,* supra, 542 U.S. at 733 n.21. As noted in the Brierly excerpt above in Section A, the rationale for the exhaustion rule—at least in the context of the law of diplomatic protection—is that "a state is entitled to have a full and proper opportunity of doing justice in its own way before international justice is demanded of it by another state." Should U.S. courts apply an exhaustion requirement in ATS cases? Does the concern about permitting a state to "do justice in its own way" apply where the plaintiffs have not brought suit against a foreign government itself or its officials, but rather against a private corporation that allegedly aided and abetted wrongful acts?

10. As Professor Stephens has noted, the United States is unusual in the extent to which its courts are open to civil cases seeking damages for violations of international human rights law for extraterritorial acts. See Beth Stephens, Translating *Filartiga*: A Comparative and International Law Analysis of Domestic Remedies for International Law Violations, 27 Yale J. Int'l L. 1 (2002); but see Donald Francis Donovan & Anthea Roberts, The Emerging Recognition of Universal Civil Jurisdiction, 100 Am. J. Int'l L. 142, 149 (2006) (suggesting that even though no other states have enacted statutes comparable to the Alien Tort Statute, "case law and commentary on universal civil jurisdiction are beginning to emerge outside the United States"). As discussed in Chapters 7 and 12, however, some countries have exercised broad criminal jurisdiction with respect to human rights abuses—for

example, Spain's effort to try former Chilean leader August Pinochet for torture; the 2009 conviction in Canada of a Rwandan for genocide, crimes against humanity, and war crimes for the 1994 killing of Tutsis in Rwanda; the 2008 conviction (affirmed on appeal in 2010) by a French court of an Algerian police official for the torture of an Algerian citizen in Algeria; and the 2008 conviction in the Netherlands of an Afghan military intelligence official for torture and war crimes in connection with the mistreatment of Afghan detainees between 1985 and 1990, during the civil war in Afghanistan. What explains the openness of the U.S. civil litigation system to international human rights claims? Why has the United States been less open than some countries to using its criminal jurisdiction to adjudicate human rights violations?

11. In addition to conferring criminal jurisdiction over serious human rights violations, the domestic courts of many foreign countries rely extensively on — and give effect to — international human rights law in considering challenges to government conduct. In 2004, for instance, Britain's top court (then part of the House of Lords), declared that the provisions of the U.K.'s Anti-terrorism, Crime and Security Act of 2001, enacted in the wake of the September 11 attacks, that permitted potentially indefinite detention of foreigners violated the European Convention on Human Rights. A v. Secretary of State for the Home Dept. [2004] UKHL 56, [2005] 2 A.C. 68 (appeal taken from Eng.) (U.K.). The Constitutional Court of Colombia in 2006 ruled that Columbia's criminal prohibition of abortion in all circumstances violated the Colombian constitution; the Court concluded that "women's sexual and reproductive rights have . . . been recognized as human rights, and, as such, they have become part of constitutional rights." Decision C-355/06, May 10, 2006 (Const. Ct. Colom.).* Article 232 of South Africa's 1996 constitution provides that "[c]ustomary international law is law in the Republic [of South Africa] unless it is inconsistent with the Constitution or an Act of Parliament," and South African courts "have not hesitated to invoke international law to support their findings." John Dugard, International Law and the South African Constitution, 8 Eur. J. Int'l L. 77, 92 (1997). The Israeli Supreme Court, in reviewing the Israeli military's policy of targeted killings of suspected terrorists in the Occupied Territories, detailed the law of war principles applicable to targeting during armed conflict and ruled that in Israel's "fight against international terrorism, [the state] must act according to the rules of international law." HCJ 769/02 Public Committee Against Torture in Israel v. The Government of Israel [2006] (Isr.). Courts in India have similarly relied on international legal obligations in "construing the nature and ambit of" general constitutional provisions. Vishaka v. Rajastha, 1997 A.I.R. 3011 (Sup. Ct. Ind). In the *Vishaka* case, the Supreme Court cited India's failure to enact legislation to meet its obligations under the Convention on the Elimination of all Forms of Discrimination Against Women (CEDAW) to prevent workplace sexual harassment of women; the Court went so far as to stipulate a set of guidelines for "due observance" by employers to "provide for effective enforcement of the basic human right of gender equality and guarantee against sexual harassment and abuse," pending the enactment of domestic legislation on the subject.

*The original Spanish language text provides: "los derechos sexuales y reproductivos de las mujeres han sido finalmente reconocidos como derechos humanos, y como tales, han entrado a formar parte del derecho constitucional."

Does the practice of non-U.S. courts in cases like these change your opinion about whether human rights treaties ratified in the United States should be self-executing or not?

9. *Regional Human Rights Law*

In addition to the U.N. human rights system, there are several regional international institutions focused on human rights. The European system, the Inter-American system, and the African system are all described below. The European system is regarded as the most "successful" of the three. Its Court has been the most active and has successfully elaborated on the content of a variety of human rights norms. European governments have been quite accommodating to this highly legalized, court-based system, perhaps because of general respect for the rule of law, habitual compliance with the decisions of an independent judiciary, the commitment of participating states to European integration, and general absence of major human rights problems. The Inter-American system has been less active, although in recent years its Commission and Court have produced a number of interesting decisions (including a number of decisions concerning human rights practices in the United States). The African system has done very little to date. Its newly created human rights court is still in its infancy.

a. European System

The European Court of Human Rights, based in Strasbourg, France, is an active regional court. It is a judicial organ of the Council of Europe, a body that is distinct from the European Union (although all 27 members of the European Union are members of the Council of Europe). The Court was established pursuant to the European Convention on Human Rights, which entered into force in 1953. As of February 2011, all 47 members of the Council of Europe had ratified the Convention, under which all parties "undertake to abide by the final judgment of the Court in any case to which they are parties." The following materials describe the Court's evolution into its current structure, its jurisdiction, the growth of its individual complaints procedure, and the effect of its judgments. An excerpt of the Convention is in the Documentary Supplement.

Manfred Nowak, Introduction to the International Human Rights Regime

161, 164-166, 168-171 (2003)

... Gradual Development of the Strasbourg Mechanism

[T]he right of victims of human rights violations to have access to a European Court of Human Rights could only be achieved step by step, as this was regarded by most governments as excessive interference with their national sovereignty. Consequently the [European Convention for the Protection of Human Rights and Fundamental Freedoms (ECHR)] originally contained numerous political compromises. The only mandatory procedure the states committed themselves to by ratifying the

ECHR, was the inter-state complaints procedure . . . before the European Commission of Human Rights and the Committee of Ministers, the highest political body in the Council of Europe. The individual complaints procedure and the jurisdiction of the European Court of Human Rights were optional, i.e. the states parties had the option of recognizing them through additional voluntary declarations, usually only for a limited period. . . .

However even in those cases where states had made the required declarations it did not mean that applicants could turn to the Court directly. [Under the ECHR, individual applications were submitted to the European Commission on Human Rights, which would issue non-binding determinations about whether the respondent state had violated the Convention. Either the Commission or a concerned state could refer the case to the European Court of Human Rights, but the applicant could not. As such, applicants] had to rely on the goodwill of their own government (the party against which the complaint is directed), or that of the Commission. . . .

It took a long time before legal remedies for individuals were extended by . . . amendments to the rules of procedure, as well as by adoption of the 9th and 10th Additional Protocols to the ECHR in the early 1990s. The first radical changes to the Strasbourg mechanism were achieved by the adoption of the 11th Additional Protocol, which entered into force on 1 November 1998. The members of the Commission and the Court, which until then had been working on a voluntary and part-time basis, were replaced by full-time professional judges of a newly established single and permanent European Court of Human Rights. Furthermore, the optional clauses were deleted, which meant that individual complaints and inter-state complaints procedures before an independent court were now compulsory for all states. . . . Thus, the entire procedure has not only been streamlined and accelerated, but also divested of political influence. . . .

. . . Inter-State Complaints Procedure

Although the inter-state complaints procedure has been mandatory since the establishment of the ECHR, few governments have so far availed themselves of the option of taking legal action against other states for violations of human rights. . . .

. . . Individual Complaints Procedure

The real strength and undisputable success of the Council of Europe regarding the protection of human rights is the individual complaints procedure before an independent international court, which decides by a final and binding judgment, whether a state has acted in violation of one or more of the civil and political rights guaranteed by the ECHR. Following a slow start in the first decades, the procedure has really taken off since the 1980s, and even more so since the 1990s. The entry into force of the 11th [Additional Protocol] in November 1998 and the creation of a permanent full-time European Court of Human Rights were major turning points towards making the procedure more professional, more efficient and less political. In total, more than 260,000 individual complaints have been submitted and more than 100,000 applications have been allocated to a decision body . . . since the procedure was introduced. The Court has rendered judgments in more than 3,400 cases. . . .*

The Court is composed of as many judges as there are state parties [currently 47]. . . . The Parliamentary Assembly [of the Council of Europe] elects one judge per state party [from among a list of three candidates nominated by the state] for a period of six years. . . . [Applications by individuals claiming a violation of the ECHR] are examined by judges in their capacity as rapporteurs. Applications may be declared inadmissible or struck on procedural grounds by [judges at a preliminary stage.] Complaints are mostly dismissed if domestic remedies have not been fully exhausted, if [the application has not been filed within six months of the challenged national decision], if alleged human rights violations are insufficiently established ('manifestly ill-founded') or if the complaints are incompatible with the ECHR. . . .

The admissibility and merits of inter-state complaints and individual complaints, which have not been dismissed [at a preliminary stage], are decided on by Chambers composed of seven judges. . . . At this stage again a large portion of the cases are declared inadmissible by the Chamber. The admissibility of complaints is decided either by a separate admissibility decision or together with a judgment on the merits, as is increasingly the case. Cases of major importance (e.g. if existing case law is revised or a serious question affecting the interpretation of the ECHR is raised) may be referred to the Grand Chamber composed of 17 judges. . . .

. . . In exceptional cases, the losing party may appeal to the Grand Chamber, however, appeals are rarely accepted (rare examples include important issues in law of general significance, change in precedent, etc.). . . .

In the event the Court finds a violation of human rights under the Convention, it has limited competence to commit the state party concerned to reparation by means of financial compensation for damages and procedural costs. It does not have any other means of awarding legal redress to the victims of human rights violations, such as by a binding order to take measures of restitution (e.g. releasing prisoners or returning property), measures of rehabilitation, repealing of laws or judgments, criminal prosecution of the persons responsible, etc. . . .

Still, the importance of the Court's judgments for the states concerned, and to some degree also for the other states parties, must not be underestimated. . . . [T]he Court's judgments are precedents that often trigger far-reaching national reforms. . . .

The individual complaints procedure before the European Court of Human Rights is exemplary at the international level not so much because of the individual legal remedies (which are still primarily within the competences of national authorities), but rather because due to the binding jurisdiction and interpretation of ECHR rights by an independent court, it has created a set of common European minimum standards for civil and political rights.

The European Court of Human Rights has issued numerous important decisions, most of which concern human rights practices in Europe. The *Schalk and Kopf*

*[Through the end of 2010, more than 450,000 complaints had been allocated to a judicial body, and the Court had issued judgments in over 13,500 cases. — Eds.]

decision, excerpted below, concerned the right of same-sex couples to marry, an issue that has also attracted considerable attention in this country.

Case of Schalk and Kopf v. Austria

European Court of Human Rights
App. No. 30141/04 (2010), reprinted in 49 ILM 1306 (2010)

[In 2002, the applicants, a same-sex couple living in Vienna, sought to marry. The municipal authorities denied their request on the grounds that "marriage could only be contracted between two persons of opposite sex." In 2010, Austria enacted a Registered Partnership Act that provided same-sex couples with a formal mechanism for recognizing and giving legal effect to their relationships. The rules on the establishment of registered partnership, its effects, and its dissolution resembled the rules governing marriage. Some differences between marriage and registered partnership remained, however. The most important differences concerned parental rights: unlike married couples, registered partners are not allowed to adopt a child, and one partner cannot adopt the other partner's child. Artificial insemination was also excluded.]

37. The Court observes that the gist of the applicants' complaint is that, being a same-sex couple, they do not have access to marriage. This situation still obtains following the entry into force of the Registered Partnership Act. As the [Austrian] Government [has] . . . pointed out, the said Act allows same-sex couples to obtain only a status similar or comparable to marriage, but does not grant them access to marriage, which remains reserved for different-sex couples. . . .

Alleged Violation of Article 12 of the Convention

39. The applicants complained that the authorities' refusal to allow them to contract marriage violated Article 12 of the Convention, which provides as follows:

> "Men and women of marriageable age have the right to marry and to found a family, according to the national laws governing the exercise of this right." . . .

49. According to the Court's established case-law Article 12 secures the fundamental right of a man and woman to marry and to found a family. The exercise of this right gives rise to personal, social and legal consequences. It is "subject to the national laws of the Contracting States", but the limitations thereby introduced must not restrict or reduce the right in such a way or to such an extent that the very essence of the right is impaired. . . .

54. The Court notes that Article 12 grants the right to marry to "men and women". The French version provides *«l'homme et la femme ont le droit de se marier»*. Furthermore, Article 12 grants the right to found a family.

55. The applicants argued that the wording did not necessarily imply that a man could only marry a woman and vice versa. The Court observes that, looked at in isolation, the wording of Article 12 might be interpreted so as not to exclude the marriage between two men or two women. However, in contrast, all other substantive Articles of the Convention grant rights and freedoms to "everyone" or state that

"no one" is to be subjected to certain types of prohibited treatment. The choice of wording in Article 12 must thus be regarded as deliberate. Moreover, regard must be had to the historical context in which the Convention was adopted. In the 1950s marriage was clearly understood in the traditional sense of being a union between partners of different sex. . . .

57. In any case, the applicants did not rely mainly on the textual interpretation of Article 12. In essence they relied on the Court's case-law according to which the Convention is a living instrument which is to be interpreted in present-day conditions. In the applicants' contention Article 12 should in present-day conditions be read as granting same-sex couples access to marriage or, in other words, as obliging member States to provide for such access in their national laws.

58. The Court is not persuaded by the applicants' argument. Although . . . the institution of marriage has undergone major social changes since the adoption of the Convention, the Court notes that there is no European consensus regarding same-sex marriage. At present no more than six out of forty-seven Convention States allow same-sex marriage. . . .

61. . . . [T]he Court would no longer consider that the right to marry enshrined in Article 12 must in all circumstances be limited to marriage between two persons of the opposite sex. Consequently, it cannot be said that Article 12 is inapplicable to the applicants' complaint. However, as matters stand, the question whether or not to allow same-sex marriage is left to regulation by the national law of the Contracting State.

62. In that connection the Court observes that marriage has deep-rooted social and cultural connotations which may differ largely from one society to another. The Court reiterates that it must not rush to substitute its own judgment in place of that of the national authorities, who are best placed to assess and respond to the needs of society.

63. In conclusion, the Court finds that Article 12 of the Convention does not impose an obligation on the respondent Government to grant a same-sex couple like the applicants access to marriage.

64. Consequently, there has been no violation of Article 12 of the Convention.

Alleged Violation of Article 14 Taken in Conjunction with Article 8 of the Convention

65. The applicants complained under Article 14 taken in conjunction with Article 8 of the Convention that they were discriminated against on account of their sexual orientation, since they were denied the right to marry and did not have any other possibility to have their relationship recognised by law before the entry into force of the Registered Partnership Act.

Article 8 reads as follows:

> "1. Everyone has the right to respect for his private and family life, . . .
> 2. There shall be no interference by a public authority with the exercise of this right except such as is in accordance with the law and is necessary in a democratic society in the interests of national security, public safety or the economic well-being of the country, for the prevention of disorder or crime, for the protection of health or morals, or for the protection of the rights and freedoms of others."

Article 14 provides as follows:

> "The enjoyment of the rights and freedoms set forth in [the] Convention shall be secured without discrimination on any ground such as sex, race, colour, language, religion, political or other opinion, national or social origin, association with a national minority, property, birth or other status." . . .

76. The applicants maintained that the heart of their complaint was that they were discriminated against as a same-sex couple. . . . [T]hey asserted that just like differences based on sex, differences based on sexual orientation required particularly serious reasons for justification. In the applicants' contention the Government had failed to submit any such reasons for excluding them from access to marriage. . . .

80. . . . [In reponse,] the [Austrian] Government maintained that it was within the legislator's margin of appreciation whether or not same-sex couples were given a possibility to have their relationship recognised by law in any other form than marriage. The Austrian legislator had made the policy choice to give same-sex couples such a possibility. Under the Registered Partnership Act which had entered into force on 1 January 2010 same-sex partners were able to enter into a registered partnership which provided them with a status very similar to marriage. . . .

94. In view of [the] evolution [of social attitudes towards same-sex couples that has taken place in many member States,] the Court considers it artificial to maintain the view that, in contrast to a different-sex couple, a same-sex couple cannot enjoy "family life" for the purposes of Article 8. Consequently the relationship of the applicants, a cohabiting same-sex couple living in a stable *de facto* partnership, falls within the notion of "family life", just as the relationship of a different-sex couple in the same situation would.

95. The Court therefore concludes that the facts of the present case fall within the notion of "private life" as well as "family life" within the meaning of Article 8. Consequently, Article 14 taken in conjunction with Article 8 applies. . . .

96. The Court has established in its case-law that in order for an issue to arise under Article 14 there must be a difference in treatment of persons in relevantly similar situations. Such a difference of treatment is discriminatory if it has no objective and reasonable justification; in other words, if it does not pursue a legitimate aim or if there is not a reasonable relationship of proportionality between the means employed and the aim sought to be realised. The Contracting States enjoy a margin of appreciation in assessing whether and to what extent differences in otherwise similar situations justify a difference in treatment.

97. On the one hand the Court has held repeatedly that, just like differences based on sex, differences based on sexual orientation require particularly serious reasons by way of justification. On the other hand, a wide margin is usually allowed to the State under the Convention when it comes to general measures of economic or social strategy.

98. The scope of the margin of appreciation will vary according to the circumstances, the subject matter and its background; in this respect, one of the relevant factors may be the existence or non-existence of common ground between the laws of the Contracting States.

99. . . . [T]he Court would start from the premise that same-sex couples are just as capable as different-sex couples of entering into stable committed relationships.

Consequently, they are in a relevantly similar situation to a different-sex couple as regards their need for legal recognition and protection of their relationship. . . .

101. Insofar as the applicants appear to contend that, if not included in Article 12, the right to marry might be derived from Article 14 taken in conjunction with Article 8, the Court is unable to share their view. It reiterates that the Convention is to be read as a whole and its Articles should therefore be construed in harmony with one another. Having regard to the conclusion reached above, namely that Article 12 does not impose an obligation on Contracting States to grant same-sex couples access to marriage, Article 14 taken in conjunction with Article 8, a provision of more general purpose and scope, cannot be interpreted as imposing such an obligation either. . . .

108. The Court starts from its findings above, that States are still free, under Article 12 of the Convention as well as under Article 14 taken in conjunction with Article 8, to restrict access to marriage to different-sex couples. Nevertheless the applicants appear to argue that if a State chooses to provide same-sex couples with an alternative means of recognition, it is obliged to confer a status on them which — though carrying a different name — corresponds to marriage in each and every respect. The Court is not convinced by that argument. It considers on the contrary that States enjoy a certain margin of appreciation as regards the exact status conferred by alternative means of recognition.

109. The Court observes that the Registered Partnership Act gives the applicants a possibility to obtain a legal status equal or similar to marriage in many respects. While there are only slight differences in respect of material consequences, some substantial differences remain in respect of parental rights. However, this corresponds on the whole to the trend in other member States. Moreover, the Court is not called upon in the present case to examine each and every one of these differences in detail. For instance, as the applicants have not claimed that they are directly affected by the remaining restrictions concerning artificial insemination or adoption, it would go beyond the scope of the present application to examine whether these differences are justified. On the whole, the Court does not see any indication that the respondent State exceeded its margin of appreciation in its choice of rights and obligations conferred by registered partnership.

110. In conclusion, the Court finds there has been no violation of Article 14 of the Convention taken in conjunction with Article 8. . . .

For These Reasons, The Court . . .

5. *Holds* unanimously that there has been no violation of Article 12 of the Convention;

6. *Holds* by four votes to three that there has been no violation of Article 14 taken in conjunction with Article 8 of the Convention. . . .

Joint Dissenting Opinion of Judge Rozakis, Spielmann and Jebens

6. The applicants complained not only that they were discriminated against in that they were denied the right to marry, but also — and this is important — that they did not have any other possibility of having their relationship recognised by law before the entry into force of the [Registered Partnership] Act. . . .

7. . . . [I]n our view the violation of [Article 14 taken together with Article 8 of the Convention] occurred . . . prior to the Act.

8. Having identified a "*relevantly similar situation*" (paragraph 99), and emphasised that "*differences based on sexual orientation require particularly serious reasons by way of justification*" (paragraph 97), the Court should have found a violation of Article 14 taken in conjunction with Article 8 of the Convention because the respondent Government did not advance any argument to justify the difference of treatment, relying in this connection mainly on their margin of appreciation (paragraph 80). However, in the absence of any cogent reasons offered by the respondent Government to justify the difference of treatment, there should be no room to apply the margin of appreciation. Consequently, the "*existence or non-existence of common ground between the laws of the Contracting States*" (paragraph 98) is irrelevant as such considerations are only a *subordinate* basis for the application of the concept of the margin of appreciation. Indeed, it is only in the event that the national authorities offer grounds for justification that the Court can be satisfied, taking into account the presence or the absence of a common approach, that they are better placed than it is to deal effectively with the matter.

9. Today it is widely recognised and also accepted by society that same-sex couples enter into stable relationships. Any absence of a legal framework offering them, at least to a certain extent, the same rights or benefits attached to marriage would need robust justification, especially taking into account the growing trend in Europe to offer some means of qualifying for such rights or benefits.

10. Consequently, in our view, there has been a violation of Article 14 in conjunction with Article 8 of the Convention.

Notes and Questions

1. The European Court of Human Rights has issued thousands of decisions, including 1,499 in 2010 alone. These decisions have addressed a wide range of human rights issues, including due process, freedom of expression, family and child custody rights, freedom of association, and the right to privacy. Some of its noteworthy recent decisions include a 2001 decision holding that Great Britain had violated the rights of members of the Irish Republican Army who were shot to death by British security forces; a 2002 decision holding that France had violated the rights of a Nazi collaborator, Maurice Papon, by denying him a right of appeal; a 2003 decision (affirmed by the Grand Chamber in 2005) that Turkey did not accord process to Kurdish separatist leader Abdullah Ocalan during his 1999 trial; a series of judgments beginning in 2005 finding that Russia had committed human rights violations during its armed conflict against separatists in Chechnya and Dagestan; a 2009 decision holding that a British anti-terrorism law permitting the indefinite detention of foreign terrorist suspects violated the Convention; and a 2009 judgment in a case brought by the survivors of a woman abused and eventually killed by her husband holding that Turkey had violated the Convention's guarantee of the right to life because its criminal justice system did not adequately deter domestic violence. In a case of interest to the United States, a man charged with capital murder in Virginia who was later found in the United Kingdom sought a ruling to block his extradition to the United States. The Court concluded that due to the long period of time prisoners convicted of capital crimes spend on death row in

"extreme conditions, with the ever-present and mounting anguish of awaiting execution of the death penalty," his extradition to the U.S. would violate the Convention's guarantee against "inhuman and degrading treatment or punishment." Soering v. United Kingdom, 161 Eur. Ct. H.R. (ser. A) (1989). Despite some occasional grumbling, the member states have generally accepted and complied with the Court's decisions. For access to the Court's case law, see http://www.echr.coe.int/ECHR/EN/Header/Case-Law/HUDOC/HUDOC+database.

2. The 1998 restructuring of the European Court of Human Rights, which today makes it possible for 800 million persons to file direct applications, has resulted in dramatic growth in the Court's docket. This has in turn created a substantial backlog and resulting delays in issuing judgments. In 1997, the last year before the Court's restructuring, it received 4,750 applications. Harry Woolf et al., Review of the Working Methods of the European Court of Human Rights 7-8 (2005). In 2010, in contrast, the Court received over 61,000 applications. The European Court of Human Rights, 2010 Annual Report at 6. Cases now typically take years to decide, and by the end of 2010 the Court's backlog stood at approximately 140,000 cases. Id. Protocol 14, which is meant to streamline the Court's procedures to enable it to manage its docket more efficiently, entered into force in June 2010. Under the Court's amended procedures, a single judge — rather than a panel of three, as was previously the case — will be empowered to make initial admissibility decisions. In addition, the Court will be permitted to "declare inadmissible applications where the applicant has not suffered a *significant disadvantage*."

3. Article 33 of the European Convention on Human Rights provides for compulsory jurisdiction of interstate disputes, but as Professor Nowak notes, such cases have been rare. According to one commentator, from the adoption of the European Convention until January 1, 2004, only 20 interstate complaints were filed. Steven Greer, The European Convention on Human Rights: Achievements, Problems and Prospects 26 (2006). Most of these cases were handled by the European Commission, and through the end of 2010, the European Court of Human Rights had issued judgments in only three interstate cases. In 2007 and 2008, however, Georgia initiated two interstate claims against Russia. The first is based on the alleged harassment of the Georgian immigrant population in Russia following Georgia's arrest of Russian military personal suspected of espionage against Georgia. The second concerns alleged human rights violations committed by Russia during the 2008 armed conflict between Russia and Georgia. Both cases were pending as of February 2011.

4. Why has the European human rights system been so successful? Would it be desirable for the United States to join such a system, either on a regional or worldwide basis?

5. Some of the provisions of the European Convention allow interference with protected rights when "necessary in a democratic society." In addition, the Convention allows nations to derogate from the rights specified in the Convention "in time of war or other emergency threatening the life of the nation." In applying these provisions, the European Court on Human Rights has applied what is called a "margin of appreciation" — that is, it has given some deference to national government determinations about what is necessary. This has been described as an "interpretational tool . . . needed to draw the line between what is properly a matter for each community to decide at a local level and what is so fundamental that it entails

the same requirements for all countries whatever the variations in traditions and culture." Paul Mahoney, Marvellous Richness of Diversity or Invidious Cultural Relativism?, 19 Hum. Rts. L.J. 1, 1 (1998). Does this deference help explain the Court's success? See generally Eva Brems, The Margin of Appreciation Doctrine at the European Court of Human Rights, in Human Rights and Diversity: Area Studies Revisited (David P. Forsythe & Patrice C. McMahon eds., 2004).

6. Other doctrines employed by the European Court of Human Rights stand in contrast to the deferential approach reflected in the "margin of appreciation." The Court interprets the European Convention progressively, as an evolving document that may impose obligations beyond those states anticipated at the time they became parties to the Convention. In finding that Belgian inheritance laws that treated children born out of wedlock differently from legitimate children, the Court observed:

> It is true that, at the time when the Convention . . . was drafted, it was regarded as permissible and normal in many European countries to draw a distinction in this area between the "illegitimate" and the "legitimate" family. However, the Court recalls that this Convention must be interpreted in the light of present-day conditions. In the instant case, the Court cannot but be struck by the fact that the domestic law of the great majority of the member States of the Council of Europe has evolved and is continuing to evolve, in company with the relevant international instruments, towards full juridical recognition of the [legal relationship between mothers and children born out of wedlock]. [Marckx v. Belgium, 31 Eur. Ct. H.R. (ser. A) at 19 (1979).]

What makes this potentially expansive approach to the interpretation of the European Convention of Human Rights acceptable to European states, which remain broadly accepting of the Court's work?

7. Are you persuaded by the *Schalk and Kopf* decision? What provision in the European Convention prohibits discrimination on the basis of sexual orientation? To the extent the Court found that "differences based on sexual orientation require particularly serious reasons by way of justification," what justifications did it rely on as a basis for concluding that same-sex couples do not have a right to marry? Do you agree with the dissent that Austrian law, prior to the adoption of the Registered Partnership Act, violated the European Convention of Human Rights?

8. The parties to the Council of Europe have adopted 14 protocols to the European Convention for the Protection of Human Rights and Fundamental Freedoms. These protocols address a variety of issues, including the expulsion of aliens, criminal procedure, discrimination, and an absolute prohibition on the death penalty. The parties to the Council also have adopted a number of other human rights treaties, including a convention against torture. In addition, they have adopted treaties outside the human rights area, such as an extradition convention. For access to these various treaties, see the Legal Affairs Web site for the Council of Europe, at http://conventions.coe.int.

9. In 2000, the institutions of the European Union (which are distinct from the Council of Europe) adopted a Charter of Fundamental Rights, which sets out a wide range of civil, political, economic, and social rights for European citizens and residents of the European Union. (The Charter is excerpted in the Documentary

Supplement.) The Charter was adopted as nonbinding "soft law" rather than as a binding treaty, but it was significant because it sets out for the first time, in a single text, a comprehensive list of human rights protections for the EU. The Charter of Fundamental Rights acquired legally binding status through its incorporation by reference in the 2007 Treaty of Lisbon, which amended the Treaty on European Union and provides: "The Union recognises the rights, freedoms and principles set out in the Charter of Fundamental Rights . . . which shall have the same legal value as" the EU treaties.

How does the Charter compare with the U.S. Bill of Rights? With the European Convention on Human Rights? Consider, for example, the following provisions in the Charter: Article 2(2), which prohibits the death penalty; Article 21(1), which prohibits discrimination on a wide variety of grounds, including sexual orientation; Article 23, which requires equal treatment of men and women in all areas; Article 25, which concerns the rights of the elderly; and Articles 37 and 38, which require a high level of environmental protection and consumer protection.

10. For additional discussion of the European human rights system, see Donna Gomien, Short Guide to the European Convention on Human Rights (3d ed. 2005); and Robin C.A. White & Clare Ovey, Jacobs, White & Ovey: The European Convention on Human Rights (5th ed. 2010).

b. Inter-American System

In 1948, 21 states in the Western Hemisphere (including the United States) agreed to adopt the Charter of the Organization of American States (excerpted in the Documentary Supplement). Among other things, the Charter established a regional international institution — the Organization of American States (OAS) — which has its headquarters in Washington, DC. Today, all 35 states in the Americas have ratified the Charter. Also in 1948, American states adopted the American Declaration of the Rights and Duties of Man, a nonbinding instrument that sets forth a variety of individual rights and duties.

The OAS Charter called for the establishment of an Inter-American Commission on Human Rights, "whose principal function shall be to promote the observance and protection of human rights and to serve as a consultative organ of the Organization in these matters." The Commission was established in 1959 and held its first session in 1960. Since then, it has carried out numerous visits to the member states to observe the human rights situation in those states and to investigate specific human rights practices. Since 1965, it has been authorized to examine complaints or petitions concerning specific cases of human rights violations, and it has processed thousands of such cases, including a number of cases concerning the United States.

The American Convention on Human Rights took effect in 1978. As of February 2011, 24 states are parties to the Convention; the United States or Canada have not become parties. The Convention is a binding treaty that lists a variety of rights that the parties are required to observe. Among other things, the Convention established an Inter-American Court of Human Rights, based in San Jose, Costa Rica.

The Inter-American human rights system is described in more detail below.

Christian Tomuschat, Human Rights: Between Idealism and Realism

257-259, 261214 (2d ed. 2008)

The Inter-American Court of Human Rights . . . is based on the [American Convention on Human Rights] of 1969, which came into force on 18 July 1978. It has its seat in San José (Costa Rica) and is composed of seven judges. . . .

Generally, the [Court] follows the example set by the [European Court of Human Rights] before the reform brought about by Protocol No. 11. It cannot be seized directly. Only the states parties and the [Inter-American Commission on Human Rights] may submit a case to the Court after the procedures before the [Commission] have been completed ([namely, the Commission has heard an] individual 'petition' in accordance with Article 44 or interstate communication in accordance with Article 45 [of the American Convention]). In contrast to the legal position now prevailing under the ECHR, the jurisdiction of the [Inter-American Court] is not compulsory, but must be specifically accepted (Article 62(1) [of the Convention]). . . .

The [Court] can also deliver advisory opinions. This latter power has played an important role in the history of the Court, while to date [the European Court of Human Rights] had only been asked once for an advisory opinion and that in a case which it deemed to lie outside its jurisdiction. . . .

Although jurisdiction covering contentious cases is still the weightier power, the [Inter-American Court] has not been able to reach the degree of effectiveness of its European counterpart. . . .

[T]he relationship between the [Court] and the [Commission] is not free from tensions. The practice of the Commission to refer to the Court only a few selected cases has provided astounding results. A number count encompassing all the proceedings dealt with by the [Court] from its inception until the end of July 2007 yields no more than 94 cases with 167 judgments. . . . [I]n comparison with the [European Court of Human Rights] the balance sheet may . . . be viewed as rather meagre. . . .

[I]t seems that the [Commission] is still the preponderant element in the institutional structure of the Inter-American system for the protection of human rights. As a latecomer, the [Court] suffers from a natural handicap. It may well be, additionally, that the [Commission] enjoys much better logistical resources than its fellow institution. To a greater extent than the European system, the bodies operating under the [American Convention on Human Rights] would appear to lack sufficiently strong support from the states parties concerned. In situations of major tensions, the pronouncements of the [Commission] do not easily prevail over short-sighted considerations of political expediency.

Other observers of the Inter-American human rights system note that its development "followed a different path from that of its European counterpart."

> Although the institutional structure is superficially very similar and the normative provisions are in most respects very similar, the conditions under which the two systems developed were radically different. Within the Council of Europe, military and other

authoritarian governments have been rare and short-lived, while in Latin America they were close to being the norm until the changes that started in the 1980s.

In contrast to the type of cases and issues that have preoccupied the [European human rights] regime, states of emergency have been common in Latin America, the domestic judiciary has often been extremely weak or corrupt, and large-scale practices involving torture, disappearances and executions have not been uncommon. Many of the governments with which the Inter-American Commission and Court have had to work have been ambivalent towards those institutions at best and hostile at worst. [Henry J. Steiner, Philip Alston & Ryan Goodman, International Human Rights in Context 1021 (3d ed. 2008).]

Notes and Questions

1. Should the United States ratify the American Convention on Human Rights? Should it consent to the jurisdiction of the Inter-American Court?

2. Although the United States has not yet consented to the jurisdiction of the Court, the Court has sometimes issued advisory opinions that relate to the United States. For example, in 1999, the Court issued an advisory opinion concluding that the failure of a nation to comply with the consular notification provisions of the Vienna Convention on Consular Relations when arresting a foreign national violates the due process rights of the arrested person and that, in that situation, imposition of the death penalty is a violation of the person's right not to be deprived of life arbitrarily. The opinion was issued in response to a request by Mexico after it had complained to the United States that a number of its nationals had been sentenced to death by state authorities without having been advised of their right under the Vienna Convention to seek consular assistance. See Advisory Opinion OC-16/99, The Right to Information on Consular Assistance in the Framework of the Guarantees of the Due Process of Law, Inter-Am. Ct. H.R. (ser. A) No. 16 (Oct. 1, 1999).

3. Although the American Declaration of the Rights and Duties of Man was not originally established as a binding treaty, the Inter-American Commission has asserted that its substantive provisions became binding when countries (including the United States) ratified a Protocol to the OAS Charter in 1968. See Case 2141 (United States), Inter-Am. Comm'n H.R., Report No. 23/81, OEA/Ser.L/V/II.54, doc. 9 rev. 1 (1981). Article 112 of the Protocol gave the Commission the "principal function" of promoting "the observance and protection of human rights" and serving as "a consultative organ of the organization in these matters," and Article 150 stated that, "[u]ntil the Inter-American Convention on Human Rights . . . enters into force, the present Inter-American Commission on Human Rights shall keep vigilance over the observance of human rights." In addition, Article 2 of the Statute of the Inter-American Commission provides that, "[f]or purposes of the present Statute, human rights are understood to be . . . [t]he rights set forth in the American Declaration of the Rights and Duties of Man, in relation to the other member states." Do these provisions make the Declaration binding? If not, do they nevertheless reflect or help "crystallize" customary international law?

4. The Inter-American Commission has played an important role in gathering information about human rights practices in Central and South America and in issuing reports concerning these practices. For example, it made a fact-finding visit to Argentina in 1979, while the country was under military rule, and then issued an

extensive report that recommended that Argentina take a number of steps to improve its human rights practices. More recently, a 2008 report examined the problem of inhumane forms of abuse committed against women and girls in Haiti, and a 2009 report on Venezuela highlighted the weakening of the rule of law and democracy in that country. In these and other instances, the Commission's factfinding and reporting may have helped to pressure governments to make human rights reforms. For access to the Commission's country-specific reports, see the Commission's Web site, at http://www.cidh.org/pais.eng.htm.

5. The Inter-American Commission has issued a number of decisions concerning U.S. death penalty practices. In 1987, it ruled that the diversity of capital punishment standards throughout the United States "results in the arbitrary deprivation of life and inequality before the law," in violation of Articles I and II of the American Declaration. See Roach & Pinkerton v. United States, Case 9647, Inter-Am. Comm'n H.R., Report No. 3/87, OEA/Ser.L/V/II.71, doc. 9 rev. 1 (1987). In 1989, it ruled that the U.S. death penalty did not violate the right to life set forth in the American Declaration of Human Rights, notwithstanding statistical evidence suggesting that the race of the defendant and victim affect the likelihood that the death penalty will be imposed. See Celestine v. United States, Case 10.031, Inter-Am. Comm'n H.R., Report No. 23/89, OEA/Ser.L/V/11.77 rev. 1 doc. 7 (1989). In October 2002, the Commission ruled that the United States would violate a general *jus cogens* norm reflected in the American Declaration if it executed an individual who was under 18 years of age at the time of his offense. See Domingues v. United States, Case 12.285, Inter-Am. Comm'n H.R., Report No. 62/02, OEA/Ser.L./V/II.117, doc. 5 rev. 1 (2002). The Commission has decided that capital sentences imposed on foreign nationals who were not notified of their right to consular access under the Vienna Convention on Consular Relations constitute violations of the American Declaration. See, e.g., Fierro v. United States, Case 11.331, Inter-Am. Comm'n H.R., Report No. 99/02, OEA/Ser.L./V/II.118, doc. 70 rev. 2 (2003). In addition, the Commission has ruled that the introduction of evidence of unadjudicated crimes during the sentencing phase of capital trials violates the American Declaration, Suárez Medina v. United States, Case 12.421, Inter-Am. Comm'n H.R., Report No. 91/05, OEA/Ser.L/V/II.124, doc. 5 (2005).

6. The Commission's rulings concerning the United States have not been limited to the death penalty. For example, in 2002, it issued "precautionary measures" urging the United States to "have the legal status of the detainees at Guantanamo Bay [who were being held in connection with the post-September 11 response to terrorism] determined by a competent tribunal." See Inter-American Commission on Human Rights: Decision on Request for Precautionary Measures (Detainees at Guantanamo Bay, Cuba) (March 12, 2002), reprinted at 41 I.L.M. 532 (2002). In another matter related to detainees at Guantanamo, the Commission granted precautionary measures in the case of Djamel Ameziane, a detainee the United States allegedly planned to transfer to his native Algeria. The Commission urged the United States to ensure that Mr. Ameziane was not subject to torture or to cruel, inhumane or degrading treatment while in U.S. custody and to make certain that he was not deported to any country where he might be subjected to torture or other mistreatment. Ameziane v. United States, PM 211/08, Inter-Am. Comm'n H.R., OEA/Ser.L/V/II.134, doc. 5, rev. 1 (2008). (The United States contests the

authority of the Commission to make requests for precautionary measures to states that are not parties to the American Convention on Human Rights.)

The Commission has also determined that the inability of citizens of the District of Columbia to vote for and elect members of the U.S. Congress denies them an effective opportunity to participate in their federal legislature and violates the American Declaration. Statehood Solidarity Committee v. United States, Case 11.204, Inter-Am. Comm'n H.R., Report No. 98/03, OEA/Ser.L./V/II.118, doc. 70 rev. 2 (2003). In another case, the Commission concluded that the United States violated family and due process rights of two lawful U.S. permanent residents with U.S. citizen spouses and children for "failing to duly consider on an individualized basis their rights to family and the best interest of their children" in deporting them following the commission of drug offenses defined as "aggravated felonies" under U.S law. Smith & Armendariz v. United States, Case 12.562, Inter-Am. Comm'n H.R., Report No. 81/10, (Jul. 12, 2010), http://www.cidh.org.

7. Is the Inter-American Commission now acting like a court? Is it appropriate for the Commission to "adjudicate" violations of international human rights norms for a state, such as the United States, that has not consented to the binding international dispute resolution mechanisms of the Inter-American human rights system?

8. For additional discussion of the Inter-American system, see Robert K. Goldman, History and Action: The Inter-American Human Rights System and the Role of the Inter-American Commission on Human Rights, 31 Hum Rts. Q. 856 (2009); Claudio Grossman, The Inter-American System of Human Rights: Challenges for the Future, 83 Ind. L. J. 1267 (2008); and Jo M. Pasqualucci, The Practice and Procedure of the Inter-American Court of Human Rights (2003).

c. African System

The African Charter on Human and Peoples' Rights was adopted in 1981 under the auspices of the Organization of African Unity (now the African Union, or "AU"), and it entered into force in 1986. Among other things, the Charter established the African Commission on Human and Peoples' Rights, which is charged with promoting and protecting human rights on the African continent. More recently, African states have established an African Court of Human and Peoples' Rights. The African human rights system now bears structural similarities to the Inter-American human rights system, although significant differences exist. The Charter, the Commission, and the Court are described below.

Javaid Rehman, International Human Rights Law

306, 309-311, 328, 335-338 (2d ed. 2010)

[H]uman rights have not been the strong point of African governments or African intergovernmental organisations. Effective protection of human rights was rarely a factor influencing the policies of the Organization of African Unity (OAU), the principal regional African organisation. . . .

A major exception to the otherwise genuine distaste for the promotion and implementation of human rights in Africa was the adoption of the African Charter on Human and Peoples' Rights (AFCHPR). . . .

Incorporation of Three Generations of Rights

. . . The Charter contains an elaborate list of traditional civil and political rights. These rights bear strong similarities to the ones contained in other international and regional treaties and include such fundamental rights as the right to equality before the law, the right to liberty, the right to a fair trial, freedom of conscience including religious freedom, freedom of association and freedom of assembly. In addition to the civil and political rights, there is a set of economic, social and cultural rights. These include the right to education, the right to participate in the cultural life of one's community, and the right of the aged and disabled to special measures of protection.

Furthermore, and more exceptionally, the Charter also contains a number of collective rights. . . . The idea of people's rights, in particular, the right to economic and political self-determination, forms a vital element within the constitutional workings of independent African states; it is also strongly represented within the African Charter, which as its title confirms is the only treaty upholding the rights of peoples alongside individual human rights. The Charter contains the important and well-established rights of peoples such as the right to existence and the right to self-determination. . . .

Duties of the Individual

The idea of duties, once again a distinctive feature of African societies, is unprecedented in so far as human rights treaties are concerned. . . . Three general principles emerge from [the] provisions regarding . . . duties. Firstly, that every individual has duties towards his family and society, towards the State, 'other legally recognised communities, and the international community'. Secondly, '[t]he rights and freedoms of each individual shall be exercised with due regard to the rights of others, collective security, morality and common interests'. Thirdly, that everyone has the duty to respect and consider others without discrimination and to promote mutual respect and tolerance. . . .

The African Commission

The African Commission is the main executive organ and is also in charge of implementing the provisions of the Charter. . . .

The African Charter provides for a State reporting procedure, an inter-State complaints procedure, and what it terms as 'Other Communications' procedure. . . .

State Reporting Procedure

The Commission obtains reports from State parties with a view to ascertaining whether or not each State party has taken the necessary administrative, legislative or other measures to implement the Charter. According to Article 62, each State party is obliged to submit every two years . . . 'a report on the [legislative] or other measures taken, with a view to giving effect to the rights and freedoms recognised and guaranteed by the Charter.' . . . The reporting procedure has been treated as 'the back-bone of the mission of the Commission.' . . .

. . . States have been reluctant to produce reports. The Rules of Procedure in the African Commission do not attach sanctions for non-compliance with reporting procedures. The few reports that have been produced are not satisfactory, with only 18 out of 53 States ever having submitted any report. . . .

Inter-State Procedure

In addition to State reporting, the second principal function of the Commission is to ensure the protection of human rights through the complaints procedure. The Charter envisages two modes of inter-State complaints. Firstly, under Article 47 of the Charter if one State party has reason to believe that another State party has violated its obligations under the Charter, it may by written communication refer the matter to the State concerned. . . .

[Under the] alternative mechanism of inter-State complaints . . . a State party may refer the matter directly to the Commission if it considers that another State party has violated any of the provisions of the Charter. . . .

. . . Although a number of attempts were made in the past, in actual effect, the inter-State procedure has thus far only been used once with a complaint being brought forward by the Democratic Republic of the Congo against Burundi, Rwanda and Uganda.

Other Communications

In addition to the inter-State mechanisms . . . , the African Charter also has another complaints procedure which is entitled 'Other Communications.' Much like its [former] European counterpart, this procedure has been more readily used. To date, the Commission had received . . . over 300 communications. . . .

The Commission makes formal findings about whether the respondent state has violated its human rights obligations when it issues reports on individual complaints. Nevertheless, "its decisions are non-binding," and the African Charter "does not provide for any legally enforceable remedies nor have any procedures been established to obtain these remedies." Rehman, International Human Rights Law, supra, at 331. A desire to overcome these weaknesses led to the negotiation in 1998 of a Protocol to the African Charter establishing the African Court of Human and Peoples' Rights. The Protocol entered into force in 2004. The following excerpt describes African Court of Human and People's Rights.

> The African Human Rights Court has both contentious and advisory jurisdiction. Its contentious jurisdiction applies only to states that have ratified the African Human Rights Court Protocol. Generally, contentious individual complaints (including those submitted by NGOs) still have to be submitted to the African Commission. The Commission then decides whether to refer the case to the Court. Exceptionally, if a state has made an optional declaration under Article 34(6) of the Protocol (in addition

to having ratified the Protocol), individual complaints . . . may be submitted directly to the Court. . . .

The AU and its organs, all AU Member States, and 'African organizations recognized by the AU' (which should include NGOs enjoying observer status with the African Commission) have standing to approach the Court directly with requests for advisory opinions.

The substantive scope of the Court's jurisdiction is very wide. Apart from the Charter and the Protocol, it extends to 'other relevant human rights instruments ratified by the states concerned' (in respect of contentious cases) and to 'any other relevant human rights instrument' (in respect of advisory opinions). . . .

Potentially, the Court is a significant improvement on the Commission. It gives binding judgments, has a clear competence to order a wide range of remedies, and will hear cases in open court. Most importantly, the Court Protocol binds states to implement Court decisions, and gives a supervisory role to the AU's political organs. . . .

Currently, a process is underway to amalgamate the African Human Rights Court and the [African] Court of Justice, provided for under the AU Constitutive Act, but never set up. In June 2008, the AU adopted a protocol providing for the 'merger' of these two courts, in the form of the Protocol on the Statute of the African Court of Justice and Human Rights. Once ratified by 15 states, a new institution consisting of two separate chambers, one dealing with human rights and one with general affairs, will replace the existing African Human Rights Court. [Frans Viljoen, The African Regional Human Rights System, in International Protection of Human Rights 503, 513-514 (Catarina Krause & Martin Scheinin, eds., 2009).]

Notes and Questions

1. The African human rights system has been described as "[t]he newest, the least developed or effective (in relation to the European and Inter-American regimes), the most distinctive and the most controversial of the three established regional human rights regimes." Steiner, Alston & Goodman, International Human Rights in Context, supra, at 1062-1063.

2. As of February 2011, 25 countries had become parties to the Protocol establishing the African Court on Human and Peoples' Rights. The Court issued its first, and as of September 2010 its only, judgment in December 2009.

3. As is the case in the Inter-American system, only the African Commission on Human and Peoples' Rights or a state may submit a case to the African Court on Human and Peoples' Rights, unless a state expressly consents to the Court's jurisdiction over individual complaints filed against it. As of January 2010, only two states — Burkina Faso and Malawi — had made declarations under Article 34(6) of the Protocol accepting the Court's jurisdiction over individual claims. In the Court's first judgment, it ruled that it had no jurisdiction over a case brought by an individual against Senegal, which has not made a declaration under Article 34(6). Yogogombaye v. Senegal, Application 001/2008 (Dec. 15, 2009), http://www.african-court.org.

4. Professor Rehman offers the following concluding observations on the African human rights system:

The continent of Africa represents a serious test for those wanting to ensure an effective system of protecting individual and collective group rights. The modern history of

> Africa has been an unfortunate one, and the transition from repressive colonial regimes to independent statehood has not been satisfactory. In many instances, soon after independence, dictatorial and authoritarian regimes took charge of the newly independent States and showed little regard for human dignity and human rights. At the beginning of the new millennium, Africa continues to witness substantial violations of human rights; the recurrent genocidal campaigns in Burundi, Rwanda and Sudan confirm the existence of a major human tragedy. [Rehman, International Human Rights Law, supra, at 349-350.]

Why hasn't the African system been more successful? What could be done to improve it?

5. How does the African Charter compare with other regional human rights conventions, such as the European Convention and the American Convention? What explains the differences? Should human rights be different in different regions of the world? Helen Stacy argues that regional courts can play a particularly useful role in mediating the tension noted above between efforts to achieve universal application of human rights and respect for cultural differences:

> [R]egional institutions can use particular histories as reference points to temper abstract formulations of human rights. . . .
>
> . . . They are well placed to identify rights associated with basic human interests that are neither parochial (the risk associated with national institutions) nor overreaching (the risk with international institutions) when interpreting human rights standards. These factors can lend legitimacy to a regional institution in its support for claims about the existence of human rights and their content. Regional human rights courts are ideally positioned to do the work of cultural interpretation of human rights. They can be an important interlocutor between human rights claims and claims of culture, between the human right to be equal and the human right to be different. [Helen M. Stacy, Human Rights for the 21st Century: Sovereignty, Civil Society, Culture 150-151 (2009).]

10. International Humanitarian Law

International law also protects human rights during times of armed conflict—for example, by giving certain rights to prisoners of war and by prohibiting intentional attacks on noncombatants. This body of international law, known as "international humanitarian law," is discussed in detail in Chapter 11.D. International humanitarian law is reflected in a variety of treaties, most notably the four Geneva Conventions developed after World War II and the subsequent protocols to those Conventions, as well as in customary international law. The requirements of international humanitarian law have been a significant point of discussion in connection with the response to terrorism following the September 11, 2001, terrorist attacks on the United States.

In addition to regulating the actions of nation-states, international humanitarian law imposes individual responsibility. At least since the Nuremberg and Tokyo trials after World War II, it has been recognized that individuals responsible for egregious violations of international humanitarian law can be criminally prosecuted. In the 1990s, ad hoc international tribunals were established to try individuals for violations of international humanitarian law committed during conflicts in the former Yugoslavia and Rwanda. Other ad hoc tribunals have been established to try senior leaders responsible for atrocities committed during Sierra Leone's 1991-2002 civil war and the top leaders of the Khmer Rouge regime responsible for the 1975-1979 genocide in Cambodia. To overcome the need for the use of ad hoc tribunals, a permanent International Criminal Court, based in the Netherlands, was established in 2002. This Court has jurisdiction to adjudicate four types of international crimes: genocide, crimes against humanity, war crimes, and the crime of aggression. Both the ad hoc tribunals and the International Criminal Court are discussed in Chapter 12.

Questions about the scope of application of international human rights law, on the one hand, and international humanitarian law, on the other, can arise in times of armed conflict. The International Court of Justice commented on the relationship between these two bodies of law in wartime:

> [T]he Court considers that the protection offered by human rights conventions does not cease in case of armed conflict. . . . As regards the relationship between international humanitarian law and human rights law, there are thus three possible situations: some rights may be exclusively matters of international humanitarian law; others may be exclusively matters of human rights law; yet others may be matters of both these branches of international law. [Legal Consequences of the Construction of a Wall in the Occupied Palestinian Territory, Advisory Opinion, 2004 I.C.J. Reports 136, 178 (July 9).]

Determining what conduct is governed by which body of law, the Court suggested, depends on the particular circumstances.

Bibliography

For additional discussion of international human rights law, see Michael K. Addo, The Legal Nature of International Human Rights (2010); Jack Donnelly, International Human Rights (3d ed. 2006); Richard B. Lillich et al., International Human Rights: Problems of Law, Policy, and Practice (4th ed. 2006); Dinah Shelton, Regional Protection of Human Rights (2008); Beth A. Simmons, Mobilizing for Human Rights: International Law in Domestic Politics (2009); and David Weissbrodt et al., International Human Rights: Law, Policy, and Process (4th ed. 2009).

9

Law of the Sea

Approximately three-quarters of the world's surface is covered by water, much of it in oceans and seas. As use of the seas intensifies and as it becomes easier to extract oil and minerals from the seabeds, the laws for channeling these burgeoning activities become increasingly important.

This chapter introduces you to the international legal norms for the seas. Even in areas of the seas where countries claim sovereignty, their claims usually reflect generally accepted norms of international law. Moreover, there are vast expanses in the seas where it is generally agreed that no single state or group of states has sovereignty. Here, too, international law is important. Throughout this chapter, remember to keep asking: How well defined are the international legal rules? How did this law develop? Does it bind states that have not agreed to it? Who will enforce the law? How? What should the law be?

A. INTRODUCTION

Much of this chapter will focus on the U.N. Convention on the Law of the Sea (LOS Convention). The LOS Convention is a comprehensive and complicated document that covers issues ranging from the width of a state's territorial waters (and the state's rights there), to rights in zones beyond the territorial waters, to who controls minerals at the bottom of the ocean.

The LOS Convention was completed in 1982 after nine years of intensive multilateral negotiations. It actually came into force in November 1994 after 12 years of diplomatic maneuvering, in part to gain the support of major countries. A key element in the maneuvering was the negotiation in 1994 of a companion Agreement Relating to the Implementation of Part XI of the LOS Convention. It effectively modified the controversial deep seabed mining provisions of the LOS Convention and made the Convention more acceptable to many industrialized countries. As of February 2011, there were 161 parties to the LOS Convention, and 140 of these countries had also become parties to the 1994 Agreement.

The United States is now alone among major industrial countries in not ratifying the LOS Convention and Agreement. Although the United States had actively participated in the negotiations leading up to the LOS Convention, President Reagan opposed the final document, in large part because of the deep seabed mining provisions. The changes made by the 1994 Agreement led the Clinton Administration to submit both the LOS Convention and the Agreement to the U.S. Senate for its advice and consent. This move was supported by a broad coalition that included the U.S. Navy (and more recently, the whole Department of Defense), major industrial groups (e.g., shipping, mining, petroleum, and telecommunications), and environmental organizations. However, in large part because of conservative opposition led by Republican Senator Jesse Helms, the U.S. Senate Foreign Relations Committee did not hold the necessary committee hearings that precede a Senate vote of advice and consent. After Senator Helms' retirement at the end of 2002, the Convention and Agreement moved forward. The Committee, under the chairmanship of Republican Senator Richard Lugar, held hearings and favorably reported unanimously on the Convention and Agreement in February 2004. Then-Majority Leader Senator Bill Frist declined, however, to bring the matter to a vote. In October 2007, the Convention was again reported out of committee favorably, but the full Senate failed to vote on the treaty. Like the Bush and Clinton Administrations, the Obama Administration has expressed its support for the Convention. As of April 2011, however, competing legislative priorities had kept the treaty from entering the full committee process.

President Reagan and succeeding U.S. administrations did selectively embrace, though, many of the Convention's key provisions and made them part of U.S. law, starting even before the new provisions of the LOS Convention had come into force in 1994 for many other countries. 'The United States also remains a party to the four 1958 Geneva conventions, discussed below.

The LOS Convention is the successor not only to the four Geneva conventions, but also to a long line of customary international law and earlier conventions that progressively became more detailed and that reflected technological changes in ships and naval warfare; developments in fishing, oil exploration, and mining; and growing concern about the environment. It is important to have an appreciation of the historical development of the law of the sea to understand the provisions of the LOS Convention. Some of its provisions reflect the customary international law and treaties existing at the time; others represent major expansions or departures from the existing law. Moreover, until the LOS Convention is accepted by all the remaining states (especially the United States), there will be situations in which customary international law and prior treaties still have some weight.

Until the twentieth century, almost all of the law of the sea consisted of customary law that was premised on freedom of the sea. The Justinian Code of 529 A.D., for instance, extended its authority only to the high-water mark, which is the high point reached by tides, and not into the oceans. While several nations, especially Spain and Portugal, purported to control all the world's oceans, these claims were not only short-lived but impossible to enforce. Perhaps the most famous commentary on freedom of the seas is Hugo Grotius's Mare Liberum, first published in 1609. Grotius argued that no nation could legitimately exercise sovereignty over any of the world's oceans, and he generally repudiated the notion of a *mare clausem* (closed sea) as an illegitimate extension of sovereignty.

While widely adhered to, the concept of freedom of the seas was in some conflict with the desires of a coastal state to control the waters immediately adjacent to its coast. For instance, the coastal state would be concerned about smuggling and armed attacks. This conflict continued throughout recent centuries, primarily in debates over the exact breadth of the "territorial sea," the area of adjacent water over which a state could exercise sovereignty. Except for disputes over the territorial sea, however, the freedom of the seas was almost universally accepted.

At the beginning of the twentieth century, there was a growing movement to codify the law of the sea. This was motivated by a number of factors, including the progressive depletion of fishery stocks and the possibility of greater technological exploitation of the oceans. In the 1920s, the League of Nations recognized the law of the sea as an area of international law ripe for codification. A conference was called for this purpose in 1930 at The Hague. Unfortunately, the attending nations were unable to agree on a number of specifics, including the proper breadth of the territorial sea, and the convention disbanded without agreement.

After World War II, the pressures for codification increased. Exploitation of offshore mineral wealth, particularly oil, was a reality, and the depletion of fishery stocks was rapidly increasing. By 1956, the International Law Commission, under the auspices of the United Nations, had drafted a comprehensive report on the subject, and a United Nations Conference on the Law of the Sea was called at Geneva (UNCLOS I).

UNCLOS I produced four treaties in 1958:

1. Convention on the Territorial Sea and Contiguous Zone
2. Convention on the Continental Shelf
3. Convention on the High Seas
4. Convention on Fishing and Conservation of Living Resources of the High Seas

The United States ratified all four, and all four entered into force in the early to mid-1960s.* Each of the Conventions is discussed later.

Although UNCLOS I was considered a great success, a number of issues were left unresolved, including the vital issue regarding the breadth of the territorial sea. In addition, several issues were inadequately resolved due to lack of information, such as the limits of the continental shelf. Consequently, a second conference (UNCLOS II) was convened in 1960. UNCLOS II was not a success. It failed, by only one vote, to adopt a compromise formula that provided for a territorial sea of six nautical miles, plus a six-mile fishery zone.** No formal conventions emerged from the conference.

By 1967 the need for a new agreement was evident. The issues left inadequately resolved by UNCLOS I were increasingly put at issue. Overfishing and pollution in parts of the ocean raised questions about the narrow jurisdictional limits in the 1958

*As of February 2011, there were 52 parties to the first Convention, 58 to the second Convention, 63 to the third, and 38 to the fourth. There was also an Optional Protocol of Signature Concerning the Compulsory Settlement of Disputes to the LOS Conventions of 1958. It extended the compulsory jurisdiction of the International Court of Justice to disputes over the interpretation or application of the conventions. The Protocol entered into force in September 1962. As of February 2011, there were 38 parties to it. Although the United States signed the Optional Protocol in 1958, it has yet to ratify it.

**Unless indicated otherwise, references in this chapter to a "mile" or "miles" are to a nautical mile(s). One nautical mile is equal to 1.151 miles or 1.852 kilometers.

treaty regime. Also, mining of the deep seabed, an issue too remote for UNCLOS I, was thought to be close to practical reality. The mineral wealth of the seabed was thought to be almost limitless, and many were concerned over how it would be developed.

Dr. Arvid Pardo, Malta's representative at the United Nations, was at the fore in calling for a third conference. One of his proposals, adopted as a U.N. resolution in 1967, established an important principle for the conference and the Convention. The resolution declared that the deep seabed and its resources were the "common heritage of mankind." This concept meant that, instead of allowing the deep seabed to be exploited by whoever got there first, the seabed would be developed for the benefit of all mankind. The concept also reinforced the need to define the limits of the territorial sea and national jurisdiction over the seabed.

Once UNCLOS III began in Caracas in 1974 and in Geneva in 1975, the same sense of common concern governed the proceedings. Rather than adopt provisions through a straight majority vote, the conference used a system of consensus. Although this undoubtedly lengthened the proceedings, it guaranteed that no single group of nations could force their will on a minority and thereby attempted to secure the ongoing participation of all nations.

From its inception, the Convention was conceived as a comprehensive agreement. The document, opened for signature in 1982, contains 320 articles and 9 annexes and covers widely divergent subjects, ranging from the nationality of vessels to deep seabed mining. Among other accomplishments, the Convention definitively outlines various zones in the sea where the coastal state and other states have varying rights, such as control of resources or passage of vessels. The regime is divided into areas of descending authority for the coastal state: internal waters, territorial sea, contiguous zone, exclusive economic zone, continental shelf, and high seas. (See the charts on pages 823-825 for a sense of the location of these zones.)

The Convention and its annexes also established a complicated system for the exploitation of the mineral resources in the deep seabed, the so-called Area. (This system will be addressed in later sections.) It was the most controversial aspect of the Convention: while many of the Convention's provisions simply adopted customary international law or have become accepted as international law, the deep seabed mining regime caused considerable dissension. This was the major reason that the Reagan Administration announced in 1982 that the United States would not sign the Convention nor participate in any further negotiations. (President Reagan later said that the United States viewed many of the other LOS Convention provisions as codifying existing customary international law.)

The compromise Agreement reached in 1994 modified the controversial provisions of the deep seabed mining regime and led most hold-out countries, including all the remaining industrial countries except for the United States, to ratify the LOS Convention and the Agreement. Given the widespread ratification of the documents and even the U.S. acceptance of some of the key provisions in them, the LOS Convention and the companion Agreement are now the cornerstone of international law governing the world's oceans.

Even though the United States has only selectively accepted some of the provisions of the Convention and the 1994 Agreement, do all their provisions now constitute customary international law because of their widespread acceptance by other states? Is it now in the interests of the United States to ratify the Convention and

Agreement? At the end of this chapter, we will look for answers to these questions after examining both the U.S. objections to the LOS Convention's provisions on deep seabed mining and the Agreement that was designed to overcome those objections.

A short final section of this chapter focuses on Antarctica. Larger than the combined area of the United States and Mexico but covered almost entirely with ice one mile thick, the development of Antarctica raises some of the same issues as the use of the high seas and the deep seabed.

B. NATIONALITY OF VESSELS

Vessels create particular jurisdictional problems, which should be examined briefly. The rules conferring nationality are, helpfully, almost universally recognized. The excerpts that follow will introduce you to the "law of the flag," recurring problems, and the significance of nationality.

1. *Customary Law*

Lauritzen v. Larsen

U.S. Supreme Court
345 U.S. 571 (1953)

[Larsen, a Danish seaman, brought suit under the Jones Act* to recover for injuries sustained on the Danish ship, the *Randa,* while docked in Havana, Cuba. Larsen based his assertion of federal jurisdiction on a broad reading of the Jones Act that encompassed all sailors and on Lauritzen company's significant New York business contacts. The trial court entered a verdict for Larsen, based on U.S. law. Lauritzen appealed, contending that Danish, not United States, law should apply.** By a vote of 7 to 1, the Supreme Court ruled that U.S. law should not apply. In his opinion for the Court, Justice Jackson addressed a number of factors important for determining choice-of-law questions in maritime tort cases. One of these is the law of the flag.]

Mr. Justice JACKSON delivered the opinion of the Court. . . .

2. Law of the flag. — Perhaps the most venerable and universal rule of maritime law relevant to our problem is that which gives cardinal importance to the law of the

*[At the time of this decision and as of February 2011, the statute read, in part:

> Any seaman who shall suffer personal injury in the course of his employment may, at his election, maintain an action for damages at law, with the right of trial by jury, and in such action all statutes of the United States modifying or extending the common-law right or remedy in cases of personal injury to railway — employees shall apply. . . . [46 App. U.S.C. §688(a).]

In 1982, a subsection (b) was added to the statute that limited the right of action under the statute by a person who was not a U.S. citizen or permanent resident alien at the time of the incident. — EDS.]

**[Under Danish law, seamen's injuries were addressed under a state-operated plan similar to workers' compensation. The Danish plan, unlike American law, did not consider negligence or allow for recovery for pain and suffering. — EDS.]

flag. Each state under international law may determine for itself the conditions on which it will grant its nationality to a merchant ship, thereby accepting responsibility for it and acquiring authority over it. Nationality is evidenced to the world by the ship's papers and its flag. The United States has firmly and successfully maintained that the regularity and validity of a registration can be questioned only by the registering state.[17]

This Court has said that the law of the flag supersedes the territorial principle, even for purposes of criminal jurisdiction of personnel of a merchant ship, because it "is deemed to be a part of the territory of that sovereignty [whose flag it flies], and not to lose that character when in navigable waters within the territorial limits of another sovereignty." On this principle, we concede a territorial government involved only concurrent jurisdiction of offenses aboard our ships. United States v. Flores, 289 U.S. 137, 155-159, and cases cited. Some authorities reject, as a rather mischievous fiction, the doctrine that a ship is constructively a floating part of the flag-state,[18] but apply the law of the flag on the pragmatic basis that there must be some law on shipboard, that it cannot change at every change of waters, and no experience shows a better rule than that of the state that owns her.

It is significant to us here that the weight given to the ensign overbears most other connecting events in determining applicable law. As this Court held in United States v. Flores, supra, at 158, and iterated in Cunard Steamship Co. v. Mellon, supra, at 123:

> And so by comity it came to be generally understood among civilized nations that all matters of discipline and all things done on board which affected only the vessel or those belonging to her, and did not involve the peace or dignity of the country, or the tranquillity of the port, should be left by the local government to be dealt with by the authorities of the nation to which the vessel belonged as the laws of that nation or the interests of its commerce should require. . . .

This was but a repetition of settled American doctrine.

These considerations are of such weight in favor of Danish and against American law in this case that it must prevail unless some heavy counterweight appears.

2. *Flags of Convenience*

"Flag of convenience" (FOC) is a term used to describe ships that bear the flags of countries other than those of the beneficial owners. The most common FOC countries are also often referred to as having "open" registries because their requirements for registration are so minimal.

17. The leading case is The Virginius, seized in 1873 by the Spanish when en route to Cuba. President Grant took the position that "if the ship's papers were irregular or fraudulent, the crime was committed against the American laws and only its tribunals were competent to decide the question." The Attorney General took the same position. The ship was restored.

18. The theoretical basis used by this Court apparently prevailed in 1928 with the Permanent Court of International Justice in the case of The Lotus, P.C.I.J., Series A, No. 10. For criticism of it see Higgins and Colombos, International Law of the Sea (2d ed.), 193-195. We leave the controversy where we find it, for either basis leads to the same result in this case, though this might not be so with some other problems of shipping.

Registering ships under a flag of convenience started in the 1920s and has expanded greatly since World War II. It has been estimated that by 1994 about half of the gross registered tonnage of ships was represented primarily by FOC ships. As of 2009 Panama was the leading FOC country, with an estimated 4,000 vessels of more than 10,000 deadweight tons and a total of about 274 million deadweight tons on its registry, with Liberia next with approximately 137 million deadweight tons. The primary beneficial owners of the FOC ships, based on tonnage, are Greece, Japan, the United States, and Norway. (The U.S. registry itself has just over 9 million tons.)

Owners started to register their vessels in foreign countries as a way to reduce costs and escape regulations. As A.D. Couper highlights in Voyages of Abuse 11-12 (1999):

> The shift to FOC meant renting a foreign flag at a relatively low price. This gave freedom to recruit from any part of the world at reduced wages and conditions. It also allowed companies to escape from national taxation, and from some ship safety and onboard health and social requirements. . . . When all conditions of crew and ship were taken into account, the operating costs of a high-standard ship and crew could be three times greater than those of substandard vessels with deplorable crew conditions.
>
> It was now possible to compete hard on crew costs and to manipulate most costs on a global basis. A single vessel could be financed, mortgaged, built, registered, owned, managed and insured all in different countries. It could be chartered to yet another country, leased back to the country of beneficial ownership and engaged in trading world-wide. . . .

In response, as one expert observed: "[T]he traditional maritime States began to question the validity of the link of nationality established by such 'flag of convenience' registration in 'open registries.' The claim, for which there was certainly some evidence in the early years of this practice, was that safety of shipping and the environment were being endangered by sub-standard ships, manned by ill-paid and inadequately qualified crews and that the flag States concerned had neither the experience nor the administrative machinery to implement shipping legislation in relation to such vessels." 1 Edward Duncan Brown, The International Law of the Sea 288 (1994).

Starting with UNCLOS I in 1958, there were multilateral efforts to deal with the problem of flags of convenience. The primary approach was to add to the long-standing principle that the nationality of a vessel depends on the flag that it is entitled to fly. The result in the LOS Convention was to carry over the key provision in the 1958 Geneva Convention on the High Seas that there must be a "genuine link" between the flag state and the ship. In addition, the LOS Convention began to provide some detail about the duties of the flag state.

Excerpts from the LOS Convention

1833 U.N.T.S. 3, 21 I.L.M. 1261 (1982)

Article 91. Nationality of Ships

1. Every State shall fix the conditions for the grant of its nationality to ships, for the registration of ships in its territory, and for the right to fly its flag. Ships have the nationality of the State whose flag they are entitled to flv. There must exist a genuine link between the State and the ship . . .

Article 92. Status of Ships

1. Ships shall sail under the flag of one State only and, save in exceptional cases expressly provided for in international treaties or in this Convention, shall be subject to its exclusive jurisdiction on the high seas. . . .

Article 94. Duties of the Flag State

1. Every State shall effectively exercise its jurisdiction and control in administrative, technical and social matters over ships flying its flag. . . .

3. Every State shall take such measures for ships flying its flag as are necessary to ensure safety at sea with regard, *inter alia,* to:

(a) the construction, equipment and seaworthiness of ships;

(b) the manning of ships, labour conditions and the training of crews, taking into account the applicable international instruments;

(c) the use of signals, the maintenance of communications and the prevention of collisions. . . .

6. A State which has clear grounds to believe that proper jurisdiction and control with respect to a ship have not been exercised may report the facts to the flag State. Upon receiving such a report, the flag State shall investigate the matter and, if appropriate, take any action necessary to remedy the situation. . . .

Unfortunately, the LOS Convention does not offer a definition of "genuine link." A similar ambiguity, plus the economic benefits reaped by an open registry, led to the widespread abuse of the provision in the earlier High Seas Convention.

In 1986, the Convention on Conditions for Registration of Ships was adopted by a conference in Geneva, and was then opened for signature and ratification. The Convention attempts to define more thoroughly the "genuine link" that should exist between a ship and the state whose flag it flies. The Convention offers flag states the option of maintaining a genuine link, either through the manning of the vessel or through the ownership and management of the vessel. The Convention also mandates that a flag state establish "competent and adequate national maritime administration" in order to exercise effective control over the vessel. The administration is charged with several specific mandatory tasks, such as ensuring that the ship complies with the state's "laws and regulations concerning registration of ships and with applicable international rules and standards concerning, in particular, the safety of ships and persons on board and the prevention of pollution of the marine environment." The Convention, however, does not have any enforcement provisions if the flag state fails to carry out its obligations and responsibilities. As of February 2011, the Convention had been ratified by only 14 states and lacked the required 40 contracting parties to enter into force.

Questions

1. How do Panama and Liberia benefit from making registration easy?

2. What should be the minimum requirement for a ship to fly a state's flag? Ownership by a national? A percentage of nationals on the crew?

3. What responsibilities should the flag state have? Should Panama be held responsible for the actions of one of its flag vessels? How should these obligations be enforced against a flag state?

4. In July 1998, the Carnival cruise ship *Ecstasy*, registered in Liberia, caught fire near the port of Miami. Although no one was hurt, this accident raised questions about the safety standards of ships under the flags of countries with open registries. The International Maritime Organization (IMO), which was established under the United Nations in 1958 and now has 169 member states, provides some safety and pollution standards for ships in international waters. Under the U.N. Convention on the Safety of Life at Sea, the IMO requires flag states to certify that the ships registered under its flag meet certain safety requirements such as sprinkler systems. The IMO also adopted an international safety code, which establishes mandatory safety requirements for shipowners. (See IMO's Web site: http://www.imo.org.)

5. The cruise ship industry presents challenging problems.

> [I]t is likely that many United States citizens who travel on cruises do not realize that when they step onto a cruise ship, even if it embarks from a United States port, they are probably stepping into a floating piece of Panama, or the Bahamas, or whichever foreign country whose flag that ship bears. In fact, aside from three ships operating on the coastwise trade in Hawaii, all of the estimated 200 ocean-going cruise ships worldwide are flagged in countries other than the United States. As such, the same laws and rights that protect United States citizens on U.S. soil do not apply on cruise ships. [Crimes Against Americans on Cruise Ships: Hearing Before the Subcomm. on Coast Guard and Maritime Transportation of H. Comm. on Transportation and Infrastructure, 110th Cong. (2007) (statement of Rep. Elijah E. Cummings).]

For example, Carnival Cruise Lines and Royal Caribbean International are both foreign corporations and register many of their ships in Panama, the Bahamas, or Liberia. Some of the problems that have arisen in recent years have involved cruise ships dumping their wastes in Alaskan territorial waters, allegations of sexual assaults committed by foreign crew members against passengers, outbreaks of communicable diseases in the close quarters of the ships, and unresolved theft of personal items. See, for example, Christopher Elliott, Mystery at Sea: Who Polices the Ships?, N. Y. Times, Feb. 26, 2006 at 9; Denise Grady, Practical Traveler: Staying Well While at Sea, N.Y. Times, Feb. 16, 2003, at E4.

In part because of passenger protests, the foreign cruise lines usually consent to jurisdiction in private lawsuits by U.S. passengers in a U.S. court specified on the ticket. Although this provides jurisdiction in the United States, it might not be a convenient court for the former passengers. For example, see Carnival Cruise Lines v. Shute, 499 U.S. 585 (1991) (discussed in Chapter 4.D.3).

In Spector v. Norwegian Cruise Line Ltd., 545 U.S. 119 (2005), the U.S. Supreme Court held that Title III of the Americans with Disabilities Act of 1990 (ADA) applied, in at least some instances, to the foreign-flag cruise ships departing from, and returning to, U.S. ports. Plaintiffs, who were disabled individuals and their companions, sought to have the ADA's requirements be applicable. These provisions provided, among other matters, for the removal of physical barriers to access in order to accommodate disabled persons. In rendering its opinion, the Court noted that:

> Our cases hold that a clear statement of congressional intent is necessary before a general statutory requirement can interfere with matters that concern a foreign-flag vessel's internal affairs and operations, as contrasted with statutory requirements that concern the security and well-being of United States citizens and territory. While the clear statement rule could limit Title III's application to foreign-flag cruise ships in some instances, . . . it would appear the rule is inapplicable to many other duties Title III might impose. Id. at 125.

The Court remanded the case to determine, among other matters, whether Title III "imposes certain requirements that would interfere with the internal affairs of foreign ships — perhaps, for example, by requiring permanent and substantial structural modifications." If so, "the clear statement rule would come into play." Id. at 142.

As for crimes, individuals can be charged and convicted under U.S. law of certain crimes that they may have committed in international or foreign waters, if the act that occurred was within the "special maritime and territorial jurisdiction of the United States." This jurisdiction is defined as including, "[t]o the extent permitted by international law, any foreign vessel during a voyage having a scheduled departure from or arrival in the United States with respect to an offense committed by or against a national of the United States." 18 U.S.C. §7(8); see United States v. Neil, 312 F.3d 419 (9th Cir. 2002). Moreover, the F.B.I. is authorized to investigate possible crimes within this special jurisdiction. Additionally, Congress passed the Cruise Vessel Safety and Security Act of 2010, which among other things requires cruise ship operators to report promptly serious criminal incidents to the nearest FBI office.

C. INTERNAL AND TERRITORIAL WATERS

This section begins our detailed discussion of maritime boundaries and zones — that is, internal waters, the territorial sea, the contiguous zone, the exclusive economic zone, the continental shelf, and the high seas. Although these terms are undoubtedly still new to you and will be defined as we proceed, three charts that illustrate these terms are included on the next pages. It will be helpful to glance at the charts now, but you will probably only fully understand them as you read through the materials.

To start, the "internal waters" of a state include not only fresh water lakes and rivers, but also parts of the sea. These parts include certain bays and the belt of the sea adjacent to the coast that is within the "baselines." These internal waters are considered part of the territory of the state, and it is generally recognized that a state can exercise the same sovereignty over these waters as over its land area.

From the baselines outward to a now generally accepted distance of 12 nautical miles is the "territorial sea." The coastal state also exercises sovereignty over these waters. (These important rules are in Articles 2 and 3 of the LOS Convention.) Foreign ships, though, have a right of innocent passage.

Additional sea zones, such as the "contiguous zone" and the "exclusive economic-zone," are also measured from the baselines. Obviously critical, then, is how and where the baselines are established, because so much else is measured from them.

CHART 9-1.
LOS Convention: Sea Claims Structure

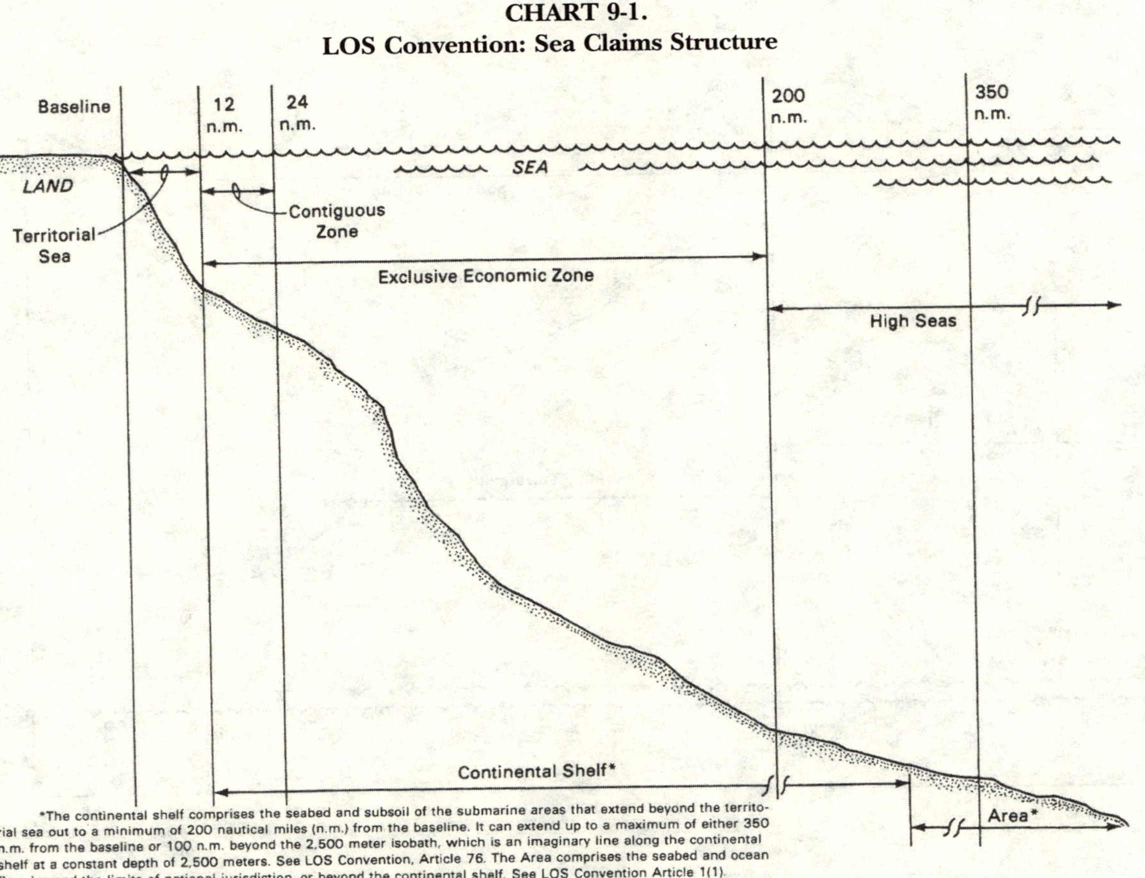

*The continental shelf comprises the seabed and subsoil of the submarine areas that extend beyond the territorial sea out to a minimum of 200 nautical miles (n.m.) from the baseline. It can extend up to a maximum of either 350 n.m. from the baseline or 100 n.m. beyond the 2,500 meter isobath, which is an imaginary line along the continental shelf at a constant depth of 2,500 meters. See LOS Convention, Article 76. The Area comprises the seabed and ocean floor beyond the limits of national jurisdiction, or beyond the continental shelf. See LOS Convention Article 1(1).

CHART 9-2. Uses

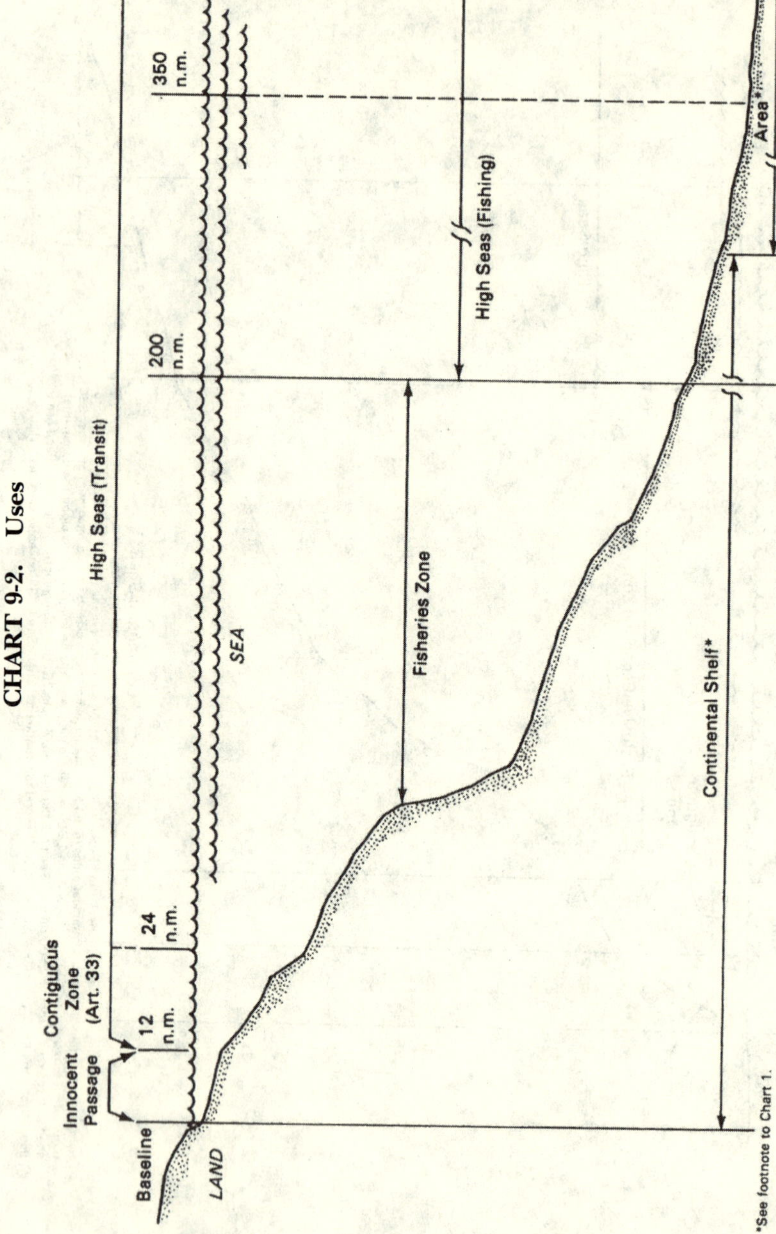

CHART 9-3.
Land-based View: Distance from Shore

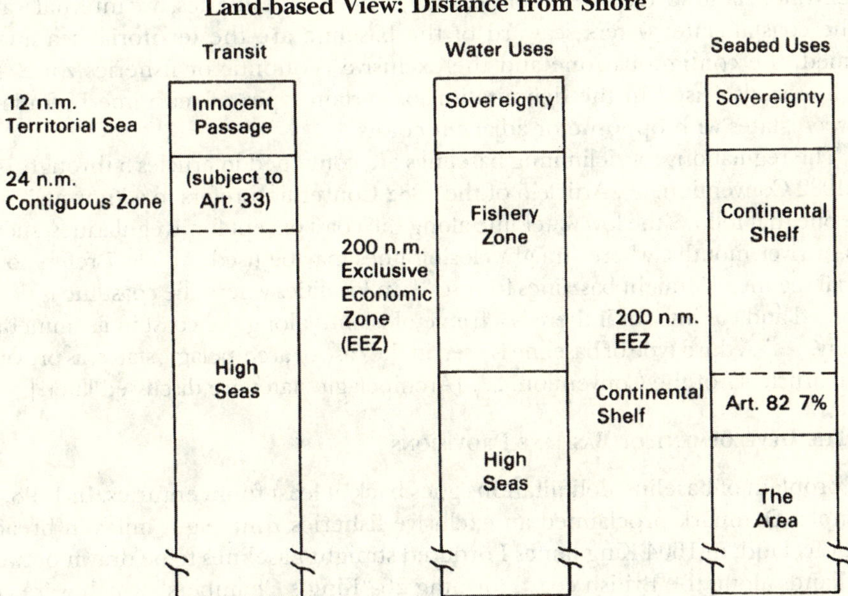

1. *Baselines*

a. General Provisions

Read carefully the relevant provisions of the LOS Convention regarding baselines (Articles 5-10 and 13 are set out in the Documentary Supplement). A discussion of the principal rules concerning baselines and the early historical development of these rules is provided in the following excerpt.

Lewis M. Alexander, Baseline Delimitations and Maritime Boundaries

23 Va. J. Int'l L. 503, 503-506 (1983)

The body of rules and regulations for establishing offshore jurisdictional zones involves three types of geographical issues. One type concerns the width of the various zones, a second issue pertains to the seaward and lateral limits of the zones, and the third involves the baselines along the coast from which the breadth of the zones is measured. The question of baselines is related to the physical nature of the coast itself, a phenomenon which varies greatly from place to place throughout the world. Some coasts are rugged and deeply indented; others are smooth and unbroken; still other coasts are the deltas of rivers where the low-water line can change significantly over short periods of time. Coasts may be fringed by islands, rocks or coral reefs. Given the wide variety of physical conditions which exist world wide, it is somewhat surprising that the 1982 Convention on the Law of the Sea (the Convention or the 1982 Convention) provides for baseline delimitations along almost all types of coastline in a relatively few articles.

The official baseline along the coast is an important juridical feature of the state. Waters landward of the baseline, such as bays and estuaries, are internal waters of the coastal state; waters seaward of the baseline are the territorial sea and, if claimed, the contiguous zone and the exclusive economic or fisheries zone. The baseline is also used in the delimitation of certain types of maritime boundaries between states with opposite or adjacent coasts.

The regulations for delimiting baselines are contained in articles 5 through 14 of the 1982 Convention. . . . Article 5 of the 1982 Convention refers to a "normal" baseline, one that follows the low-water line along the coast except for irregularities, such as bays or river mouths, where straight closing lines may be used. Article 7 refers to the special regime of straight baselines for use "[i]n localities where the coastline is deeply indented and cut into, or if there is a fringe of islands along the coast in its immediate vicinity. . . ." A third type of baseline is used in the case of archipelagic states, as provided for in article 47 of the Convention. . . . [Archipelagic states are discussed later.]

I. The Development of Baseline Provisions

The problem of baseline delimitations goes back at least four centuries. In 1598, for example, Denmark proclaimed an exclusive fisheries zone eight miles in breadth about Iceland; in 1604 King James I ordered straight baselines to be drawn between headlands along the British coast, forming 26 "King's Chambers" which were considered to be British waters. In those early years issues of customs and neutrality were important in determining offshore juridical zones. In 1736 Britain adopted the first of its "Hovering Acts," establishing a customs zone twelve miles in breadth along its coasts; nine years later the Danes defined the breadth of their neutrality zone as four miles, again measured from their coastline.

During the nineteenth and early twentieth centuries baselines tended to follow the sinuosities of the coast. . . .

. . . As early as 1839 . . . ten-mile closing lines were permitted for bays, but problems arose in distinguishing indentations having the configuration of a bay from slight curvatures of the coast. . . .

The International Court of Justice grappled with the baseline issue and related questions in its 1951 decision in the Fisheries Case. The case illustrates some of the problems in drawing a baseline and stands as a statement of the existing customary international law at that time. It also provides a useful comparison with the rules that were developed only 30 years later in the LOS Convention.

Fisheries Case (United Kingdom v. Norway)

Int'l Court of Justice
1951 I.C.J. 116 (Dec. 18)

The facts which led the United Kingdom to bring the case before the Court are briefly as follows.

The historical facts laid before the Court establish that as the result of complaints from the King of Denmark and of Norway, at the beginning of the seventeenth century, British fishermen refrained from fishing in Norwegian coastal waters for a long period, from 1616-1618 until 1906.

In 1906 a few British fishing vessels appeared off the coasts of Eastern Finnmark. From 1908 onwards they returned in greater numbers. These were trawlers equipped with improved and powerful gear. The local population became perturbed, and measures were taken by the Norwegian Government with a view to specifying the limits within which fishing was prohibited to foreigners. The first incident occurred in 1911 when a British trawler was seized and condemned for having violated these measures. . . . In 1932, British trawlers, extending the range of their activities, appeared in the sectors off the Norwegian coast west of the North Cape, and the number of warnings and arrests increased. On July 27th, 1933, the United Kingdom Government sent a memorandum to the Norwegian Government complaining that in delimiting the territorial sea the Norwegian authorities had made use of unjustifiable base-lines. On July 12th, 1935, a Norwegian Royal Decree was enacted delimiting the Norwegian fisheries zone north of 66° 28.8' North latitude. . . .

In 1948, since no agreement had been reached, the Norwegian Government abandoned its lenient enforcement of the 1935 Decree. . . . A considerable number of British trawlers were arrested and condemned. It was then that the United Kingdom Government instituted the present proceedings. . . .

The Norwegian Royal Decree of July 12th, 1935, concerning the delimitation of the Norwegian fisheries zone sets out in the preamble the considerations on which its provisions are based. In this connection it refers to "well-established national titles of right," "the geographical conditions prevailing on the Norwegian coasts," "the safeguard of the vital interests of the inhabitants of the northernmost parts of the country"; it further relies on the Royal Decrees of [1812, 1869, 1881, and 1889].

The [1935] Decree provides that "lines of delimitation towards the high sea of the Norwegian fisheries zone as regards that part of Norway which is situated northward of 66° 28.8' North latitude . . . shall run parallel with straight base-lines drawn between fixed points on the mainland, on islands or rocks, starting from the final point of the boundary line of the Realm in the easternmost part of the Varangerfjord and going as far as Træna in the County of Nordland."

The subject of the dispute is clearly indicated under point 8 of the Application instituting proceedings: "The subject of the dispute is the validity or otherwise under international law of the lines of delimitation of the Norwegian fisheries zone laid down by the Royal Decree of 1935 for that part of Norway which is situated northward of 66° 28.8' North latitude." And further on: "the question at issue between the two Governments is whether the lines prescribed by the Royal Decree of 1935 as the base-lines for the delimitation of the fisheries zone have or have not been drawn in accordance with the applicable rules of international law."

Although the Decree . . . refers to the Norwegian fisheries zone and does not specifically mention the territorial sea, there can be no doubt that the zone delimited by this Decree is none other than the sea area which Norway considers to be her territorial sea. . . .

The coastal zone concerned in the dispute is of considerable length. It lies north . . . of the Arctic Circle, and it includes the coast of the mainland of Norway and all the islands, islets, rocks and reefs, known by the name of the "skjærgaard" (literally, rock rampart), together with all Norwegian internal and territorial waters. The coast of the mainland, which, without taking any account of fjords, bays and minor indentations, is over 1,500 kilometres in length and is of a very distinctive configuration. Very broken along its whole length, it constantly opens out into indentations often penetrating for great distances inland: the Porsangerfjord, for instance, penetrates 75 sea miles inland. To the west, the land configuration stretches out into the sea: the large and small islands, mountainous in character, the islets, rocks and reefs, some always above water, others emerging only at low tide, are in truth but an extension of the Norwegian mainland. The number of insular formations, large and small, which make up the "skjærgaard," is estimated by the Norwegian Government to be one hundred and twenty thousand. From the southern extremity of the disputed area to the North Cape, the "skjærgaard" lies along the whole of the coast of the mainland; east of the North Cape, the "skjærgaard" ends, but the coast line continues to be broken by large and deeply indented fjords.

Within the "skjærgaard," almost every island has its large and its small bays; countless arms of the sea, straits, channels and mere waterways serve as a means of communication for the local population which inhabits the islands as it does the mainland. The coast of the mainland does not constitute, as it does in practically all other countries, a clear dividing line between land and sea. What matters, what really constitutes the Norwegian coast line, is the outer line of the "skjærgaard." . . .

Along the coast are situated comparatively shallow banks, veritable under-water terraces which constitute fishing grounds where fish are particularly abundant. . . .

In these barren regions the inhabitants of the coastal zone derive their livelihood essentially from fishing. . . .

The Parties being in agreement on the figure of 4 miles for the breadth of the territorial sea, the problem which arises is from what base-line this breadth is to be reckoned. . . .

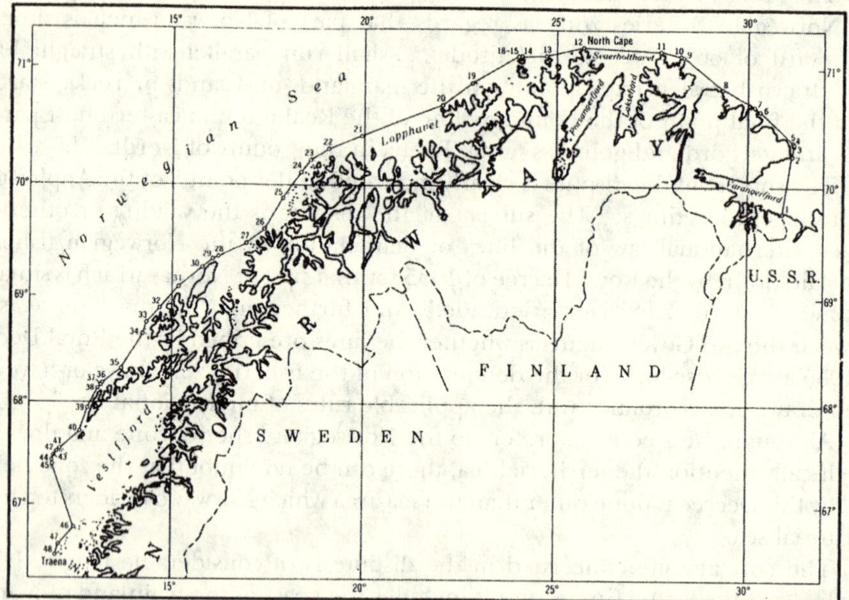

Straight baselines laid down by Norway along its skjaergaard coast under The Norway Royal Decree of 1935.*

*[The map appears as Figure 14 in Aaron Lewis Shalowitz, Shore and Sea Boundaries 69 (Vol. I, 1962).—EDS.]

The Court has no difficulty in finding that, for the purpose of measuring the breadth of the territorial sea, it is the low-water mark as opposed to the high-water mark, or the mean between the two tides, which has generally been adopted in the practice of States. This criterion is the most favourable to the coastal State and clearly shows the character of territorial waters as appurtenant to the land territory. . . . [T]he Parties agree as to this criterion, but that they differ as to its application.

The Parties also agree that in the case of a low-tide elevation (drying rock) the outer edge at low water of this low-tide elevation may be taken into account as a base-point for calculating the breadth of the territorial sea. . . .

The Court finds itself obliged to decide whether the relevant low-water mark is that of the mainland or of the "skjærgaard." Since the mainland is bordered in its western sector by the "skjærgaard," which constitutes a whole with the mainland, it is the outer line of the "skjærgaard" which must be taken into account in delimiting the belt of Norwegian territorial waters. This solution is dictated by geographic realities.

Three methods have been contemplated to effect the application of the low-water mark rule. The simplest would appear to be the method of the *trace parallele,* which consists of drawing the outer limit of the belt of territorial waters by following the coast in all its sinuosities. This method may be applied without difficulty to an ordinary coast, which is not too broken. Where a coast is deeply indented and cut into, as is that of Eastern Finnmark, or where it is bordered by an archipelago such as the "skjærgaard" along the western sector of the coast here in question, the base-line becomes independent of the low-water mark, and can only be determined by means of a geometric construction. In such circumstances the line of the low-water mark can no longer be put forward as a rule requiring the coast line to be followed in all its sinuosities; nor can one speak of exceptions when contemplating so rugged a coast in detail. Such a coast, viewed as a whole, calls for the application of a different method. Nor can one characterize as exceptions to the rule the very many derogations which would be necessitated by such a rugged coast. The rule would disappear under the exceptions.

[The Court briefly considered and dismissed a second method, the "arc of circles" method. It then turned to the "straight base-lines method."]

The principle that the belt of territorial waters must follow the general direction of the coast makes it possible to fix certain criteria valid for any delimitation of the territorial sea; these criteria will be elucidated later. The Court will confine itself at this stage to noting that, in order to apply this principle, several States have deemed it necessary to follow the straight base-lines method and that they have not encountered objections of principle by other States. This method consists of selecting appropriate points on the low-water mark and drawing straight lines between them. . . .

It has been contended, on behalf of the United Kingdom, that Norway may draw straight lines only across bays. The Court is unable to share this view. If the belt of territorial waters must follow the outer line of the "skjærgaard," and if the method of straight base-lines must be admitted in certain cases, there is no valid reason to draw them only across bays, as in Eastern Finnmark, and not also to draw them between islands, islets and rocks, across the sea areas separating them, even when such areas do not fall within the conception of a bay. It is sufficient that they should be situated between the island formations of the "skjærgaard," *inter fauces terrarium*. . . .

In the opinion of the United Kingdom Government, Norway is entitled, on historic grounds, to claim as internal waters all fjords and sunds which have the character of a bay. She is also entitled on historic grounds to claim as Norwegian territorial waters all the waters of the fjords and sunds which have the character of legal straits . . . , and, either as internal or as territorial waters, the areas of water lying between the island fringe and the mainland. . . .

The Court now comes to the question of the length of the base-lines drawn across the waters lying between the various formations of the "skjærgaard." Basing itself on the analogy with the alleged general rule of ten miles relating to bays, the United Kingdom Government still maintains on this point that the length of straight lines must not exceed ten miles.

In this connection, the practice of States does not justify the formulation of any general rule of law. . . .

Furthermore, apart from any question of limiting the lines to ten miles, it may be that several lines can be envisaged. In such cases the coastal State would seem to be in the best position to appraise the local conditions dictating the selection. Consequently, the Court is unable to share the view of the United Kingdom Government, that "Norway, in the matter of base-lines, now claims recognition of an exceptional system." As will be shown later, all that the Court can see therein is the application of general international law to a specific case. . . . Thus the Court, confining itself for the moment to the Conclusions of the United Kingdom, finds that the Norwegian Government in fixing the base-lines for the delimitation of the Norwegian fisheries zone by the 1935 Decree has not violated international law. . . .

It does not at all follow that, in the absence of rules having the technically precise character alleged by the United Kingdom Government, the delimitation undertaken by the Norwegian Government in 1935 is not subject to certain principles which make it possible to judge as to its validity under international law. The delimitation of sea areas has always an international aspect; it cannot be dependent merely upon the will of the coastal State as expressed in its municipal law. Although it is true that the act of delimitation is necessarily a unilateral act, because only the coastal State is competent to undertake it, the validity of the delimitation with regard to other States depends upon international law.

In this connection, certain basic considerations inherent in the nature of the territorial sea, bring to light certain criteria which, though not entirely precise, can provide courts with an adequate basis for their decisions, which can be adapted to the diverse facts in question.

Among these considerations, some reference must be made to the close dependence of the territorial sea upon the land domain. It is the land which confers upon the coastal State a right to the waters off its coasts. It follows that while such a State must be allowed the latitude necessary in order to be able to adapt its delimitation to practical needs and local requirements, the drawing of base-lines must not depart to any appreciable extent from the general direction of the coast.

Another fundamental consideration, of particular importance in this case, is the more or less close relationship existing between certain sea areas and the land formations which divide or surround them. The real question raised in the choice of base-lines is in effect whether certain sea areas lying within these lines are sufficiently closely linked to the land domain to be subject to the regime of internal waters. This idea, which is at the basis of the determination of the rules relating to bays, should be liberally applied in the case of a coast, the geographical configuration of which is as unusual as that of Norway.

Finally, there is one consideration not to be overlooked, the scope of which extends beyond purely geographical factors: that of certain economic interests peculiar to a region, the reality and importance of which are clearly evidenced by a long usage. . . . [The Court went on to discuss the Norwegian practice from 1812 to the present regarding delimitation of baselines.]

From the standpoint of international law, it is now necessary to consider whether the application of the Norwegian system encountered any opposition from foreign States. . . . The general toleration of foreign States with regard to the Norwegian practice is an unchallenged fact.

The notoriety of the facts, the general toleration of the international community, Great Britain's position in the North Sea, her own interest in the question, and her prolonged abstention would in any case warrant Norway's enforcement of her system against the United Kingdom. The Court is thus led to conclude that the method of straight lines, established in the Norwegian system, was imposed by the peculiar geography of the Norwegian coast; that even before the dispute arose, this method had been consolidated by a constant and sufficiently long practice, in the face of which the attitude of governments bears witness to the fact that they did not consider it to be contrary to international law.

For these reasons, the Court . . . Finds

by ten votes to two, that the method employed for the delimitation of the fisheries zone by the Royal Norwegian Decree of July 12th, 1935, is not contrary to international law; and

by eight votes to four, that the base-lines fixed by the said Decree in application of this method are not contrary to international law.

Notes and Questions

1. What was the basis for the Court's holding in the *Fisheries* case? A multilateral treaty? A bilateral agreement? That Norway's claims represented customary international law? That Norway's claims were not inconsistent with customary international law?

2. Note that the Court accepts the parties' agreement that, in those circumstances, the territorial sea was four miles wide and that the issue was to delimit the baseline from which the breadth would be measured.

3. Compare the Court's conclusions in 1951 with the provisions in the LOS Convention for drawing baselines. Do they differ? On a general level, is customary international law now more defined? More specifically, how long a baseline does the LOS Convention allow across the mouth of a bay? (See Article 10, which provides for a maximum line of 24 nm, versus the 10 nm that the United Kingdom alleged in the *Fisheries* case.) Compared to the decision in the *Fisheries* case, do the LOS Convention's baseline provisions expand or reduce the internal waters that a coastal state is likely to have?

b. Dealing with Islands

Islands create special problems in drawing baselines and in determining the territorial sea and other ocean zones. Article 121 of the LOS Convention provides:

LOS Convention

Article 121. Regime of Islands

1. An island is a naturally formed area of land, surrounded by water, which is above water at high tide.

2. Except as provided for in paragraph 3, the territorial sea, the contiguous zone, the exclusive economic zone and the continental shelf of an island are determined in accordance with the provisions of this Convention applicable to other land territory.

3. Rocks which cannot sustain human habitation or economic life of their own shall have no exclusive economic zone or continental shelf.

Questions

1. Under Article 121, how should a coastal state draw the baselines of an island that is part of the state but is located at a distance of, say, 2 nautical miles from the mainland? 11 miles? 23 miles? 300 miles?

2. Does Article 121 mean that even a small island can provide an increase of ocean area that a state can claim for its territorial sea? Which is generally most useful for a state's territorial sea claim—an island 2 nautical miles off the coast, 11 miles, 23 miles, 300 miles, 800 miles? (We ask this question again later, after we have studied the other maritime boundaries and zones, including the exclusive economic zones.)

c. The Special Case of Archipelagic States

A state may be composed of a group of islands that are interrelated geographically, economically, politically, or historically. Important examples include Indonesia and the Philippines, each of which is composed of several thousand islands spread out over more than 1,000 miles. Such archipelagic states created special issues of how to draw baselines and to define the territorial sea and other zones. For example, would a baseline continue from one island to another if the distance between them were 3, 13, or 35 miles? The solution in the LOS Convention was to create a special regime for so-called archipelagic states. (See LOS Articles 46-54.) The key provisions regarding the drawing of the baselines are in Article 47.

LOS Convention

Article 47. Archipelagic Baselines

1. An archipelagic State may draw straight archipelagic baselines joining the outermost points of the outermost islands and drying reefs of the archipelago provided that within such baselines are included the main islands and an area in which the ratio of the area of the water to the area of the land, including atolls, is between 1 to 1 and 9 to 1.

2. The length of such baselines shall not exceed 100 nautical miles, except that up to 3 percent of the total number of baselines enclosing any archipelago may exceed that length, up to a maximum length of 125 nautical miles.

3. The drawing of such baselines shall not depart to any appreciable extent from the general configuration of the archipelago.

4. Such baselines shall not be drawn to and from low-tide elevations. . . .

Notes and Questions

1. Professors Churchill and Lowe provide a brief description of the significance of these archipelagic baselines.

> Archipelagic waters comprise all the maritime waters within archipelagic baselines. One qualification must, however, be made. *Within* archipelagic baselines an archipelagic State can draw closing lines across river mouths, bays and ports on individual islands in accordance with the normal rules on baselines. The waters so enclosed are internal waters, not archipelagic waters [LOS Convention, Article 50]. . . .
>
> The concept of archipelagic waters is a new one in international law. Such waters are neither internal waters nor territorial sea, although they bear a number of resemblances to the latter. An archipelagic State has sovereignty over its archipelagic waters, including their superjacent air space, subjacent sea bed and subsoil, and "the resources contained therein" [Article 49]. This sovereignty is, however, subject to a number of rights enjoyed by third States . . .
>
> [M]ost important, there are the navigational rights of other States. [See discussion of rights of passage in section 4 below.] [R.R. Churchill & A.V. Lowe. The Law of the Sea 125-127 (3d ed. 1999).]

2. Do the baselines permitted for an archipelagic state potentially allow the state to claim sovereignty over a much larger ocean area?

2. *Foreign Vessels in Internal Waters*

Baselines are important not only because they set the landward limits of the territorial sea and the exclusive economic zone, but also because they set the outer limit of internal waters. Internal waters are also referred to as "inland" or "national" waters. As illustrated by Article 2 of the LOS Convention, it is generally accepted that a state may exercise the same sovereignty over these internal waters as it exercises over the land within its borders.

As a result, foreign vessels may only enter a state's inland waters (including its ports) with the state's consent. Usually this consent is freely given and is presumed from the lack of an express prohibition against ships of a foreign flag state, particularly commercial ships. A state can require specific notification, however. Foreign warships, for example, must usually send formal notification through appropriate channels. If no objection is received, the foreign warship is normally thought to have consent to enter the state's inland waters.

In the United States, a number of laws and regulations control access by foreign ships to U.S. ports, with the President being given broad discretion to decide on access. The United States has also entered into bilateral agreements with some countries that further define their rights and the procedures for gaining access. How access is controlled can be important for enforcing laws about terrorism, drug traffic, customs, and immigration.

Once in the inland waters, a foreign vessel is subject to the sovereignty of the host state. All of that country's laws apply with equal force to the vessel. Violations of those laws can be prosecuted in the host state, absent treaty provisions to the contrary or the barrier of diplomatic immunity.

While host states are entitled to exercise jurisdiction over foreign vessels, they rarely do. Instead, most states abide by what is commonly known as the "French modification": host states, based on comity and reciprocity, decline to exercise their jurisdiction over foreign vessels unless activities threaten the "peace of the port" or the "public peace." This modification was adopted by the United States in the Wildenhus's Case, 120 U.S. 1 (1886). Chief Justice Waite, for the Court, said:

> From experience, however, it was found long ago that it would be beneficial to commerce if the local government would abstain from interfering with the internal discipline of the ship, and the general regulation of the rights and duties of the officers and crew towards the vessel or among themselves. And so by comity it came to be generally understood among civilized nations that all matters of discipline, and all things done on board, which affected only the vessel or those belonging to her, and did not involve the peace or dignity of the country, or the tranquillity of the port, should be left by the local government to be dealt with by the authorities of the nation to which the vessel belonged as the laws of that nation, or the interests of its commerce should require. But, if crimes are committed on board of a character to disturb the peace and tranquillity of the country to which the vessel has been brought, the offenders have never, by comity or usage, been entitled to any exemption from the operation of the local laws for their punishment, if the local tribunals see fit to assert their authority. [Id. at 12.]

The United States reaffirmed its adherence to the French modification, but claimed the peace of the port exception, during the Medvid Affair in 1985. Miroslav Medvid, a sailor on a Soviet freighter docked outside New Orleans, Louisiana, jumped ship on the night of October 24-25. United States Immigration and Naturalization Service (INS) officers determined that Medvid was not seeking political asylum and returned him to the freighter. After his initial return sparked a public protest, the United States demanded the opportunity to interview Medvid again to determine if he was being forced to return to the Soviet Union against his will. During the course of the affair, the Legal Adviser to the Department of State wrote Secretary of State Shultz that the United States was well within its rights to remove Medvid, by force if necessary, from the Soviet freighter. Concerning the Wildenhus's Case, the Legal Adviser wrote in part, "Although *Wildenhus* is quite old, it is still good law and is cited as authority in contemporaneous U.S. court decisions."

Questions

1. What types of crimes do you believe disturb the "peace of the port"?

2. Should a state exercise its jurisdiction over public drunkenness? Over use of child labor? Over gambling among crew members? Over possession of heroin or cocaine on the vessel?

3. Breadth of the Territorial Sea

The LOS Convention provides that the territorial sea shall have a breadth of not more than 12 nautical miles from the baseline. This distance, which is now commonly accepted, is a recent development. Note, for example, the four-mile breadth that the parties agreed to in the *Fisheries* case.

Sovereignty over oceans was unknown in the ancient world. The Romans restricted their sovereignty to the high-water mark along the shore. The first recorded exercise of sovereignty over the seas occurred in 1269, when Venice demanded fees for foreign use of the Adriatic Sea. Genoa soon followed by charging fees for the use of the present-day Ligurian Sea. By the end of the fifteenth century, several Papal Bulls and the Treaty of Tordesillas purported to divide most of the world's oceans between Spain and Portugal. England claimed all of the present-day English Channel, the North Sea, and all waters adjacent to France.

In contrast to state practice, many writers denied any legitimate sovereignty over the oceans. Hugo Grotius, apparently as an advocate for the Dutch East India Company, believed that neither the Papal Bulls nor the Treaty of Tordesillas could grant sovereignty over the open sea to either Spain or Portugal. While admitting that sovereignty might extend to waters adjacent to land, Grotius contended that no nation could own the oceans.

The practice of claiming sovereignty over adjacent waters flourished in the seventeenth and eighteenth centuries. Three different methods of delimitation became popular: the line-of-sight rule, the cannon-shot rule, and the marine league.

The "line-of-sight" rule was a vague criterion that was sometimes used in the sixteenth and seventeenth centuries. Because it included distances out to 20-30 miles or more and was also vague, countries came under pressure to adopt more-precise and limited measures. The "cannon-shot" rule, as the name implies, held that a sovereign could exercise authority over the sea that fell within a cannon's range from the shore. Delimitation was easy, if somewhat varied, ranging from a few thousand feet to generally less than three miles.

The third method, the marine league, was the first consistent method of delimitation. Equal to three nautical miles, it had the advantage of being precise and relatively easy to determine. It also was related to the cannon-shot rule, because three miles was considered by some then as the maximum theoretical range of a cannon.

During the nineteenth century Great Britain, as the dominant naval power, proposed and repeatedly sought a three-mile limit. It concluded a number of treaties, beginning with the British-United States Convention of 1818, which called for three-mile delimitation. By the close of the nineteenth century, the three-mile-limit was generally accepted by the major powers as the breadth of the territorial sea, but it was never unanimously accepted. The Scandinavian countries consistently claimed four miles, and several other states claimed larger zones for specific purposes.

The two World Wars and the period between undermined the three-mile limit. First, during the hostilities a number of countries declared vast "neutrality zones" in order to assure their security. For many purposes, these neutrality zones were the equivalent of territorial seas. Second, advances in technology made the three-mile limit economically and militarily too narrow for the waters of the developed states.

Finally, the newly independent nations concluded that the three-mile limit was too narrow. Among other reasons, they resented the situation where developed states (and multinational corporations) exploited the resources just outside the three-mile limit.

At the 1958 Geneva Conference that led to the Convention on the Territorial Sea and Contiguous Zones, the negotiators could not agree on the breadth of the territorial sea, even though they developed careful rules regarding the drawing of baselines and other methods for measurements. There was still substantial support for a three-mile width but also considerable support for six miles. Lacking sufficient consensus, the Convention was silent on this very fundamental issue. The 1960 Geneva Conference then came within one vote of approving a compromise that the United States and Canada proposed. It would have provided for a six-mile territorial sea plus a six-mile exclusive fisheries zone.

Pressures continued to increase for a breadth greater than three miles, and even greater than six miles. In 1970 the United States officially announced its support for the 12-mile limit in the LOS negotiations. (The Soviet Union had adopted such a limit soon after its Revolution of 1918.) By 1982, a majority of nations had acquiesced in the 12-mile limit for the territorial sea, which is what the LOS Convention provides.

In December 1988, President Reagan formally proclaimed that the United States was extending its territorial sea to 12 nautical miles. The proclamation said that the 12 miles were "the limits permitted by international law." Ironically, although Reagan had balked at signing the LOS Convention (for reasons discussed later), the proclamation cited the Convention as reflecting many rules of international law. Indeed, the 12-mile limit is now generally viewed throughout the world as customary international law.

Note

Although President Reagan issued a formal Proclamation and Executive Order in 1988 extending the territorial sea to 12 nautical miles, not all U.S. laws have been amended or interpreted to reflect this change. For example, the Clear Water Act still defines the territorial sea as "extending seaward a distance of three miles." 33 U.S.C. §1362. In United States v. One Big Six Wheel, 166 F.3d 498 (2d Cir. 1999), the court concluded that the Gambling Ship Act, as amended in 1994, did not clearly enough cover the area from 3 to 12 nautical miles to allow the seizure of a gambling device used onboard a cruise ship in this area. The court noted that the 1988 Presidential Proclamation explicitly limited its application by declaring that "nothing in this Proclamation . . . extends or otherwise alters existing Federal or State law or any jurisdiction, rights, legal interest, or obligations derived therefrom. . . ."

On the other hand, the same U.S. Court of Appeals ruled that the meaning of "high seas" in the Death on the High Seas Act (DOSHA) of 1920 was modified by the Presidential Proclamation to extend only to waters past the 12-mile mark, rather than the 3 miles applicable when the law was passed. In In re Air Crash Off Long Island, 209 F.3d 200 (2d Cir. 2000), the plaintiffs were family members or administrators of the estates of some of the 230 passengers who died in the crash of TWA Flight 800 on July 17, 1996. The crash occurred approximately eight nautical miles south of Long Island. Defendants TWA and Boeing contended that DOHSA was the exclusive law governing all damage claims because the deaths occurred over the high seas, which the defendants argued meant waters more than three miles from shore. If DOHSA applied, survivors could not recover nonpecuniary losses because DOHSA excludes damages from loss of society, survivor's grief, and any pre-death pain and suffering of a decedent as well as punitive damages.

The court reasoned that the impact of the Proclamation had to be assessed on a statute-by-statute basis. Analyzing the statutory language, legislative history, and relevant case law, the court concluded that the plaintiffs' interpretation that the "high seas" in the statute now only began beyond 12 nautical miles better reflected the "meaning and purpose" of DOHSA.

In 2000, Congress amended the law to exclude from DOHSA's application any "commercial aviation accident" that occurs within 12 nautical miles from shore. The rest of the law, however, has yet to be amended to specifically incorporate the 12-mile limit adopted in the 1988 Proclamation. The issue of DOHSA's scope arose again after the April 2010 Deepwater Horizon explosion in the Gulf of Mexico. Because the Deepwater rig is considered an oceangoing vessel and because the accident occurred about 50 miles offshore, there were news stories and a Congressional hearing where some people proposed that DOHSA should somehow be amended to not cover the event. Otherwise, DOHSA would limit the 11 victims' families to pecuniary damages.

4. *Rules for Passage*

a. Innocent Passage

Similar to much of the law of the sea, the right of innocent passage developed over the centuries. As Professors Churchill and Lowe observe:

> The existence of a right of innocent passage through the territorial sea for foreign ships was . . . widely conceded throughout the period during which the concept of the territorial sea began to crystallise. . . . This was no well-defined right, around which notions of coastal sovereignty collected, as it were: rather, the concepts of innocent passage and coastal sovereignty developed in parallel, each helping to mould the other. [R.R. Churchill & A.V. Lowe, The Law of the Sea 81 (3d ed. 1999)].

In the Corfu Channel case (United Kingdom v. Albania), 1949 I.C.J. 1 (Dec. 15), the International Court of Justice carefully addressed, among other issues, the question of what passage is "innocent." There, the British Navy had sent warships through the Corfu Channel, an international strait that was partly within the territorial waters of Albania and Greece. On the first occasion in May 1946, Albania had fired on two British cruisers because, Albania claimed, the British had not requested permission. After a series of diplomatic notes, the British decided in October to reassert their right of innocent passage by sending a squadron of warships through the Channel. The warships ran into a minefield and two ships were damaged. In November 1946, the British Navy swept the Channel, including Albania territorial waters, for mines. The British then instituted this suit in the ICJ to recover compensation for its damaged ships.

The ICJ defined the right of innocent passage by considering the "manner" of passage as a decisive test. Looking at the facts, the Court held that the actual British passage in October was "carried out in a manner consistent with the requirements of international law" and did not present a threat to the coastal state. The U.K. was entitled to compensation for the damaged warships. (The Court separately held, based on the facts, that the British mine-clearing operation in November did violate Albanian sovereignty.) The *Corfu Channel* case was followed by attempts to codify the rules for innocent passage.

The LOS Convention built on the *Corfu Channel* case and a few codification attempts to provide considerable specificity to the concept and right of innocent passage in Articles 17 through 26. Article 17 provides that: "Subject to this Convention, ships of all states . . . enjoy the right of innocent passage through the territorial sea." Articles 18 defines passage as "navigation through the territorial sea" for the purpose of traversing that sea without entering internal waters or at a port outside internal waters, or proceeding to or from a port in internal waters. Article 19 then defines "innocent passage" as passage that "is not prejudicial to the peace, good order, or security of the coastal state." That Article goes on to list a number of activities that are not considered innocent—e.g., ranging from "any exercise or practice with weapons of any kind" to "any fishing activities." Articles 20-32 provide further rules about innocent passage. (See the Documentary Supplement.)

Questions

1. Are the articles in the LOS Convention in general accord with the decision in the *Corfu Channel* case? (See especially Articles 17-20.)

2. Under Articles 19-20 can a Russian surface warship traveling between Russia and Cuba sail along the eastern seaboard of the United States at about ten miles from shore? Can a submerged Russian submarine accompany the surface warship? Can a North Korean "fishing trawler" loaded with electronic gear loiter at four miles off the U.S. naval base in Honolulu, Hawaii? At 14 miles?

3. Faced with the following proposed activities in its territorial sea, can the United States, under the LOS Convention, bar a Japanese ship carrying plutonium from Japan to another country; prevent a Liberian ship from cruising up and down the coast while it operates a gambling casino; require all oil tankers to have double-hulled bottoms; and prohibit ship captains and anyone else steering a ship from having more than .02 percent alcohol in their blood?

b. Passage Through International Straits and Archipelagic Sea Lanes

Besides the general rules for innocent passage in the territorial sea, the 1982 LOS Convention recognized the need for special rules for passage through international straits and through the waters of the archipelagic states. These special rules allow less control by the coastal states over passing vessels than does innocent passage, but they do not give ships the same rights as they have on the high seas. As Professors Churchill and Lowe report:

> In the years between UNCLOS I and the close of UNCLOS III many States made claims to wider coastal jurisdiction. . . . While these claims were not inconsistent with

the preservation of rights of passage through international straits, they signalled a growing reluctance to regard passing foreign ships as beyond the jurisdictional reach of coastal States whose security, environmental or economic interests these ships might adversely affect. The major maritime States, on the other hand, considered that their economic well-being and security—particularly in relation to the deployment, and pursuit, of submarines some of which now carried strategic nuclear missiles—depended upon continuing guarantees of passage through international straits such as Dover, Gibraltar, Hormuz, Bab el Mandeb and Malacca. A compromise was reached, based on the creation of two new legal rights of passage: "transit passage" through international straits . . . and "archipelagic sea lanes passage" through archipelagic waters. . . . Both new categories allow less coastal control over passing vessels than does innocent passage, but both also fall far short of granting the same freedom of navigation as would have existed had the waters of the straits constituted high seas.

The regime of transit passage applies to "straits which are used for international navigation between one part of the high seas or an exclusive economic zone and another part of the high seas or an exclusive economic zone"[LOS Convention, Article 37]. . . .

Transit passage is the exercise of freedom of navigation and overflight solely for the continuous and expeditious transit of the strait between one area of high seas or economic zone and another, or in order to enter or leave a State bordering the strait [Article 38(2)]. While there is no criterion of "innocence" to be satisfied, ships and aircraft exercising this right are bound to refrain from the threat or use of force . . . against States bordering the straits . . . [Article 39(f)(b)]. Moreover, there is an obligation to refrain from any activities other than those incidental to their normal modes of continuous and expeditious transit unless rendered necessary *by force majeure* or distress [Article 39(1)(c)]. . . .

. . . As far as submarines are concerned, their apparently common practice of transiting some international straits while submerged seems to be recognised in the requirement that passing vessels engage only in activities "incident to their *normal mode* of continuous and expeditious transit" [Article 39(1)(c); emphasis added]. . . .

[Regarding archipelagic sea lanes,][t]he ships of all States enjoy in archipelagic waters the same right of innocent passage as they enjoy in the territorial sea [Article 52(1)]. . . . In addition, foreign ships and aircraft enjoy the rather more extensive right of "archipelagic sea lanes passage" in sea lanes and air routes designated by the archipelagic State: sea lanes must be designated in consultation with the "competent international organisation" (by which presumably is meant the [International Maritime Organization]) [Article 53]. . . . Archipelagic sea-lanes passage is essentially the same as transit passage through straits. . . . [R.R. Churchill & A.V. Lowe, The Law of the Sea 104-107, 109, 127 (3d ed. 1999).]

Note

The apparent effects of global warming are heating up a long-standing dispute between the United States and Canada over the Northwest Passage. This legendary route between the Atlantic and Pacific across the top of Canada could become a major shipping route if enough ice melts and commercial sea-going ships could make the trip. (Some icebreakers and research ships have recently been able to make the passage more easily than before.) For many shipments between Europe and North America to and from Asia, the Northwest Passage would be much shorter than a route through the Panama Canal or around the tip of South America.

The Canadian view is that the Northwest Passage is under its sole jurisdiction and it can enforce its laws. The Canadians note that this would be the best way to minimize accidental oil spills and unsafe ships in an environment that is pristine and fragile. Although the United States concedes that Canada has sovereignty over much of the Northwest Passage, the United States contends that the Passage is an international strait like other international straits. This would allow Canada less control over passing vessels than do the rules regarding innocent passage. See Doug Struck, Dispute Over NW Passage Revived, Washington Post, Nov. 6, 2006, at A18.

D. CONTIGUOUS ZONES AND HOT PURSUIT

The existence of a contiguous zone is now generally accepted in international law. This is a zone adjacent to the territorial sea where the coastal state is allowed to enforce certain laws, such as customs and immigration. Article 33 of the LOS Convention provides that the contiguous zone may not extend more than 24 nautical miles from the baselines. (This actually makes the contiguous zone 12 miles wide because the territorial sea occupies the first 12 miles from the baselines, and because the contiguous zone is "contiguous," or adjacent, to the territorial sea.)

LOS Convention

Article 33. Contiguous Zone

1. In a zone contiguous to its territorial sea, described as the contiguous zone, the coastal State may exercise the control necessary to:

(a) prevent infringement of its customs, fiscal, immigration or sanitary laws and regulations within its territory or territorial sea;

(b) punish infringement of the above laws and regulations committed within its territory or territorial sea.

2. The contiguous zone may not extend beyond 24 nautical miles from the baselines from which the breadth of the territorial sea is measured.

Notes and Questions

1. In a major U.S. case on smuggling and jurisdictional issues, decided in 1925, the U.S. district court noted that the territorial sea then was a three-mile zone. It also relied on a U.S. statute that extended U.S. jurisdiction to 12 nautical miles from the coast for smuggling. The court then dismissed libels against a seized schooner and its cargo of whiskey, because the whiskey had been unloaded onto another vessel at about 19 miles away from the shore. *The Over the Top* (Schroeder v. Bissell), 5 F.2d 838 (D. Conn. 1925).

2. What appear to be the principal purposes for states recognizing the existence of a contiguous zone?

3. Would you be for a wider or narrower contiguous zone? Why?

4. In August 1999, President Clinton extended the boundaries of the contiguous zone of the United States, a zone of waters "contiguous to the territorial sea of the United States," to 24 nautical miles. He specifically noted that this was "[i]n

accordance with international law, reflected in the applicable provisions of the 1982 Convention on the Law of the Sea." See Presidential Proclamation No. 7219, 64 Fed. Reg. 48,701 (Aug. 2, 1999).

5. *The right of hot pursuit.* A related concept that also has general international acceptance is the right of hot pursuit. This allows a coastal state to pursue into the high seas a foreign ship that the coastal state has reason to believe has violated its laws either within the contiguous zone or within its internal waters or territorial sea. (See LOS Convention Article 111.) When can the coastal state pursue the foreign ship? When can it not?

E. THE EXCLUSIVE ECONOMIC ZONE AND THE CONTINENTAL SHELF

1. *Historical Background*

Under the regime established in the LOS Convention, a state exercises substantial sovereignty in the area known as the exclusive economic zone (EEZ). The EEZ is an area beyond and adjacent to the territorial sea, with a breadth of up to 200 miles from the baseline, in which the coastal state may exercise certain "sovereign rights" over living and nonliving resources. (See Articles 56-57 in the Documentary Supplement.) Assuming a 12-mile-wide territorial sea, the EEZ could be up to 188 nautical miles wide.

The EEZ is in many ways the merger of two previous concepts — the continental shelf regime and the fisheries regime — although the LOS Convention maintains a separate section concerning the continental shelf. The Convention also expands on the two concepts by granting the coastal state rights to exercise jurisdiction with respect to marine scientific research and preservation of the marine environment.

An important balance in the EEZ is granting to the coastal state a variety of rights to the resources in the zone, while protecting the rights of other states to navigate through and over the EEZ, to fish the surplus catch, and to conduct research subject to certain limits. Articles 56 and 57 are carefully balanced by Articles 58 and 87 and by the dispute settlement arrangements provided for in the Convention. (Dispute settlement is discussed in Section G, below.)

A brief history of the two concepts of the continental shelf and a fisheries zone helps explain the EEZ. Prior to World War II, there was no affirmative international law permitting states to claim jurisdiction over the resources of the seas or seabed outside their territorial seas. Several states, particularly in Latin America, had claimed wide "patrimonial" seas, which were essentially the equivalent of the territorial sea. In addition, the practice of the United Kingdom was that countries could claim seabed resources when there was an effective claim and actual exploitation. The customary international law, however, was that a state's sovereignty and jurisdiction almost always stopped at the outer edge of its territorial sea.

The Truman Proclamations of 1945 were the "first positive law on this subject," according to the ICJ in the North Sea Continental Shelf cases, 1969 I.C.J. 3 (Feb. 20). President Truman claimed major new rights for the United States with regard to its continental shelf and fisheries. While similar or greater claims had been made by other countries, the Truman Proclamations were the first such unilateral claim by a major maritime power. Their immediate impact was great, with a number of countries following the U.S. example. By 1958, 20 countries had made similar unilateral claims to their continental shelves. Even more states claimed a right to manage fisheries outside their territorial waters.

The Truman Proclamations

White House Press Release of Sept. 29, 1945
13 Dept. of State Bull. 485-486 (July-Dec. 1945)

The President issued two proclamations on September 28 asserting the jurisdiction of the United States over the natural resources of the continental shelf under the high seas contiguous to the coasts of the United States and its territories, and providing for the establishment of conservation zones for the protection of fisheries in certain areas of the high seas contiguous to the United States. . . .

Policy of the United States with Respect to the Natural Resources of the Subsoil and Sea Bed of the Continental Shelf

By the President of the United States of America

A Proclamation

Whereas the Government of the United States of America, aware of the long range world-wide need for new sources of petroleum and other minerals, holds the view that efforts to discover and make available new supplies of these resources should be encouraged; and

Whereas its competent experts are of the opinion that such resources underlie many parts of the continental shelf off the coasts of the United States of America, and that with modern technological progress their utilization is already practicable or will become so at an early date; and

Whereas recognized jurisdiction over these resources is required in the interest of their conservation and prudent utilization when and as development is undertaken; and . . .

Whereas it is the view of the Government of the United States that the exercise of jurisdiction over the natural resources of the subsoil and sea bed of the continental shelf by the contiguous nation is reasonable and just, since the effectiveness of measures to utilize or conserve these resources would be contingent upon cooperation and protection from the shore, since the continental shelf may be regarded as an extension of the land-mass of the coastal nation and thus naturally appurtenant to it, since these resources frequently form a seaward extension of a pool or deposit lying within the territory, and since self-protection compels the coastal nation to keep close watch over activities off its shores which are of the nature necessary for utilization of these resources. . . .

Now, therefore, I, Harry S Truman, President of the United States of America, do hereby proclaim the following policy of the United States of

America with respect to the natural resources of the subsoil and sea bed of the continental shelf.

Having concern for the urgency of conserving arid prudently utilizing its natural resources, the Government of the United States regards the natural resources of the subsoil and sea bed of the continental shelf beneath the high seas but contiguous to the coasts of the United States as appertaining to the United States, subject to its jurisdiction and control. In cases where the continental shelf extends to the shores of another State, or is shared with an adjacent State, the boundary shall be determined by the United States and the State concerned in accordance with equitable principles. The character as high seas of the waters above the continental shelf and the right to their free and unimpeded navigation are in no way thus affected.

Policy of the United States with Respect to Coastal Fisheries in Certain Areas of the High Seas

By the President of the United States of America

A Proclamation

. . . Now, therefore, I, Harry S Truman, . . . do hereby proclaim the following policy of the United States of America with respect to coastal fisheries in certain areas of the high seas:

In view of the pressing need for conservation and protection of fishery resources, the Government of the United States regards it as proper to establish conservation zones in those areas of the high seas contiguous to the coasts of the United States wherein fishing activities have been or in the future may be developed and maintained on a substantial scale. Where such activities have been or shall hereafter be developed and maintained by its nationals alone, the United States regards it as proper to establish explicitly bounded conservation zones in which fishing activities shall be subject to the regulation and control of the United States. Where such activities have been or shall hereafter be legitimately developed and maintained jointly by nationals of the United States and nationals of other States, explicitly bounded conservation zones may be established under agreements between the United States and such other States; and all fishing activities in such zones shall be subject to regulation and control as provided in such agreements. The right of any State to establish conservation zones off its shores in accordance with the above principles is conceded, provided that corresponding recognition is given to any fishing interests of nationals of the United States which may exist in such areas. The character as high seas of the areas in which such conservation zones are established and the right to their free and unimpeded navigation are in no way thus affected.

The U.S. Congress also addressed these issues. Sections (1) and (2) below were enacted in 1953; section (3) was enacted in 1978.

43 U.S.C. §1332

Congressional Declaration of Policy

It is hereby declared to be the policy of the United States that—

(1) the subsoil and seabed of the outer Continental Shelf appertain to the United States and are subject to its jurisdiction, control, and power of disposition as provided in this subchapter;

(2) this subchapter shall be construed in such a manner that the character of the waters above the outer Continental Shelf as high seas and the right to navigation and fishing therein shall not be affected;

(3) the outer Continental Shelf is a vital national resource reserve held by the Federal Government for the public, which should be made available for expeditious and orderly development, subject to environmental safeguards, in a manner which is consistent with the maintenance of competition and other national needs. . . .

2. *After the Truman Proclamations*

By 1958, unilateral continental shelf claims were common and well established in customary international law. The first U.N. Conference on the Law of the Sea drafted the 1958 Convention on the Continental Shelf (in the Documentary Supplement). By 1974, when the first substantive meeting of the Third U.N. Conference on the Law of the Sea convened, 53 nations were contracting parties to the 1958 Convention.

The Convention on the Continental Shelf recognizes "sovereign rights" of coastal states over the natural resources of the continental shelf. "Natural resources" are the "mineral and other non-living resources of the seabed and subsoil together with living organisms belonging to sedentary species." These sovereign rights did not change the juridical nature of the water above. (Articles 1-3 in the Documentary Supplement.)

Defining the boundaries of the continental shelf encountered some difficulties, however. According to the Convention, the continental shelf encompassed the seabed and subsoil of areas outside and adjacent to the territorial sea, to a depth of 200 metres or, beyond that, to "where the depth of the superjacent waters admits of the exploitation of the natural resources of said areas." (Article 1.) As improvements in technology made it possible to exploit the seabed out to greater and greater distances, it became clear that the outer boundary of the continental shelf needed better definition.

Although a substantial number of nations never signed the Convention, in the North Sea Continental Shelf cases, 1969 I.C.J. 3 (Feb. 20), the ICJ recognized that certain articles of the Convention had become customary international law. This case basically recognized that the coastal state could claim jurisdiction over resources throughout the natural prolongation of the continental landmass.

The LOS Convention substantially adopted the provisions of the Convention on the Continental Shelf. (See Articles 76-85 of the LOS Convention in the Documentary Supplement.) It provided, however, more precise limits on the outer boundary. Whenever it extends beyond 200 nautical miles (n.m.), the outer edge shall not exceed 350 miles from the baseline or 100 n.m. from the 2500-meter isobath, with some qualifications.*

More controversy has surrounded coastal state claims over fisheries beyond their territorial waters. The period after World War II witnessed great advances in fishing technology and rising concern over the depletion of fishing stock. After the Truman Proclamations, a number of states unilaterally claimed broader and broader fisheries jurisdiction. During the 1960s, such unilateral claims were often accompanied by bilateral agreements with nations who traditionally fished in the newly claimed waters. The agreements typically allowed the noncoastal state to gradually reduce its fishing in the newly created fishing zone, rather than having to stop operations immediately.

A consensus proved difficult to reach at both the 1958 and 1960 U.N. conferences on the law of the sea. The developing nations were anxious to maintain control over the fisheries adjacent to their territorial seas, while distant-water fishing nations, such as Japan, were just as anxious to maintain the "high seas" nature of fisheries. The 1958 Convention on the Territorial Sea and the Contiguous Zone provided that the coastal state's sovereignty over the territorial sea, whose breadth was undefined, included sovereignty over the sea (and hence the fish in it). And, although the 1958 Convention on the High Seas defined "freedom of the high seas" to include freedom of fishing, it did not elaborate. (Article 2.)

The 1958 Convention on Fishing and Conservation of Living Resources of the High Seas generally recognized that all states had the right for their nationals to engage in fishing on the high seas. (Article 1.) However, the Convention recognized a coastal state's special interest in the "maintenance of productivity of living resources" in areas of the high seas adjacent to its territorial sea (Article 6.) Of the four 1958 conventions, this particular one has been ratified by the fewest number of parties (38 as of January 2011) and is generally considered the least effective.

The issue of a fisheries regime was on the agenda of the UNCLOS III when it convened in Caracas in 1974. At the same time, the ICJ issued its decision in the Fisheries Jurisdiction case, 1974 I.C.J. 3 (July 25), discussed below.

D.P. O'Connell, The International Law of the Sea

Vol. 1, 539-541 (1982)

The Fisheries Jurisdiction Case

On 25 July 1974, the International Court of Justice handed down its judgment in the cases of United Kingdom v. Iceland and Germany v. Iceland. The United Kingdom and Germany had asked the court to declare that there was no foundation in international law for the claim by Iceland to be able to extend its fisheries jurisdiction to fifty miles from the baseline of the territorial sea and also to decide some ancillary questions to the effect that Iceland could not unilaterally conserve the

*Article 76, §§4-7. The 2500-meter isobath refers to an imaginary line along the continental shelf that is at a constant depth of 2500 meters.

fisheries within this area or exclude British fishing vessels from it outside the twelve-mile limit. . . .

The starting-point for the Court's analysis is the passage in the Anglo-Norwegian Fisheries Case of 1951 in which the Court then said that "the delimination of sea areas has always an international aspect; it cannot be dependent merely upon the will of the coastal State as expressed in its municipal law." This brought international law into the matter. The court reinforced this point by referring to the Geneva Convention on the High Seas which includes fishing among the freedoms of the sea. It pointed out, however, that the freedoms of the high seas are to be exercised, according to the Geneva Convention, "with reasonable regard to the interests of other states in their exercise of the freedom of the high seas." From this the Court concluded that fishing was not an absolute right.

The Court then proceeded to say that two concepts had crystallized in customary law since the Geneva Conference, namely:

(a) the concept of the fishery zone up to twelve miles limit, and
(b) the concept of preferential rights of fishing in adjacent waters of the coastal state beyond the distance of twelve miles.

It regarded the coastal state's absolute right of fishing as restricted to twelve miles, but, at the same time, it did not deny that the coastal state had the right to preferential access to fisheries beyond that limit. The problem which the case presents is whether preferential rights are in practice really distinguishable from absolute rights, and whether the court altogether ruled out unilateral claims beyond twelve miles.

As to the concept of preferential rights, the court based its assertion that these have become part of customary international law upon the history of that proposal at the Geneva Conferences in 1958 and 1960; upon the widespread acceptance of the concept of preferential rights by a large majority at those two conferences, thus showing overwhelming support for the idea that in certain special situations it was fair to recognize that the coastal state had preferential fishing rights; and upon the recognition of preferential rights in various bilateral and multilateral international agreements entered into since 1960. The Court's conclusion on preferential rights is that they are

> not compatible with the exclusion of all fishing activities of other states. A coastal state entitled to preferential rights is not free, unilaterally and according to its own uncontrolled discretion, to determine the extent of those rights. The characterisation of the coastal state's rights as preferential implies a certain priority, but cannot imply the extinction of current rights of other states, and particularly of a state which, like the applicant, has for many years been engaged in fishing in the waters in question, such fishing activity being important to the economy of the country concerned. The coastal state has to take into account and pay regard to other states, particularly when they have established an economic dependence on the same fishing grounds.

The emphasis thus put upon traditional fishing rights led the Court to declare that Iceland's unilateral action constituted an infringement of the principle in the Convention on the High Seas which requires that all States, including coastal states, in exercising their freedom of fishing, pay reasonable regard to the interests of other States. . . .

The Court then indicated that the appropriate method of resolving the dispute was by negotiation on the basis of the facts that Iceland had preferential rights in the fishing, but the United Kingdom had an historic interest. The negotiations between the parties should aim to bring about an equitable apportionment of fishing resources beyond the twelve-mile limit. . . .

This decision by the ICJ was criticized for the imprecision of the concept of preferential rights. The decision also did not help the Court's reputation among many of the developing countries, who were advocating broad coastal state jurisdiction for fisheries in the ongoing Law of the Sea conference. These countries were later joined by some developed countries, including Canada, Australia, and New Zealand. As recounted by Churchill and Lowe in *The Law of the Sea* 288 (3d ed. 1999):

> The USA, and initially Canada, proposed [another] approach to fisheries management based on the migratory characteristics of different species. This proposal categorised fish into sedentary, coastal (i.e. non-sedentary species which inhabit nutrient-rich areas adjacent to the coast), anadromous and wide-ranging species. Access to and management of the first three of these would vest exclusively or primarily in the coastal State, but wide-ranging species would be regulated by international fishery organisations. . . .
>
> The Law of the Sea Convention's provisions on fisheries generally reflect [the broad coastal state jurisdiction position initially pushed by the developing countries], although elements of the species approach can also be seen.

3. *The Law of the Sea Convention and the Current Status of the Exclusive Economic Zone and Continental Shelf*

The key provisions in the LOS Convention for the EEZ and fisheries are found in Part V, especially Articles 55-58 and 61-62. The major provisions for the continental shelf are in Part VI, particularly Articles 76-78 and 82. (See Documentary Supplement.)

The countries that have become parties to the LOS Convention effectively adopted the LOS provisions for their EEZs and continental shelves. In addition, as noted earlier, various economic and fishery zones and continental shelves have been declared. For example, although the United States is not a party to the LOS Convention, the Truman Proclamations in 1945 had made claims about the U.S. continental shelf and fisheries. In 1983, President Reagan proclaimed a U.S. EEZ and announced that the United States would treat those portions of the Convention delimiting various coastal state rights as customary international law on a reciprocal basis. (His statement is excerpted below.)

To give you an appreciation of the substantial area that is included in the exclusive economic zones, some figures are useful. The 200-mile limit encloses 36 percent of the world's total ocean area, or over 37.7 million square nautical miles. Moreover, this area contains the vast majority of the presently exploitable fishery stock and known oil deposits, and 10 percent of the seabed manganese nodules.

The Senkaku Islands provides an illustration of the importance of the EEZ and the critical land that provides a basis for drawing the 200 nautical miles boundaries. The Senkaku (in Japanese), also known as the Diaoyu Islands (in Chinese), are a group of five uninhabited islands and three coral reefs in the East China Sea, located between Okinawa and Taiwan. The islands cover a total land area of only about seven square kilometers.

The islands are at the center of a territorial dispute between China, Taiwan, and Japan. Japan claims that it formally incorporated the islands as part of its territory in 1895, after determining that the land was uninhabited and showed no trace of having been under the control of China. Japan controlled the islands from that time until 1945. After World War II, the United States administered the islands and then later returned administration to Japan in 1972. China and Taiwan, however, maintain that they have had a history of economic use of the islands for centuries.

The islands are located in rich fishing grounds and possibly sit atop significant oil and gas deposits. Territorial control of the islands would add to the EEZ of the claiming country, giving it access to not only the potentially lucrative resources below the islands themselves but also in the surrounding waters. Additionally, Chinese control of the islands could provide the nation with a new route to the Pacific Ocean, an important strategic advantage for the Chinese navy.

The dispute came to a head in September 2010, after the Japanese Coast Guard seized a Chinese fishing vessel operating in the waters off the islands. Both the Chinese government and the Chinese people expressed outrage at the specific incident and Japan's territorial claims to the islands. Chinese individuals protested in front of Japanese diplomatic missions, Chinese travel companies cancelled tours to Japan, Beijing suspended talks between governmental officials, and China halted exports of important rare earth minerals to Japan. By November 2010, the immediate hostilities had ceased and all fishermen were released. The actual territorial dispute, however, remains to be settled and poses the potential for future, escalating conflicts between the two nations, especially as China becomes increasingly assertive in economic and military matters.

Japan has also worked to maintain the control of another island: Okinotorishima. Where is Okinotorishima? The following news article reports the valiant efforts to keep it above water.

Clyde Haberman, Japanese Fight Invading Sea for Priceless Speck of Land

N.Y Times, Jan. 4, 1988, at 1, col. 2

. . . [T]o call Okinotorishima an island is somewhat akin to describing a rowboat as a vessel — true but grandiose. This island has eroded so badly over the years that it now consists of two barren rocks, neither of them much bigger at high tide than a king-size bed.

But Okinotorishima, which means Offshore Bird Island, happens to be [Japan's] southernmost point. And if it disappears beneath the sullen Pacific, as it is almost certain to do unless remedial action is taken, Japan will lose exclusive fishing and mineral rights to 163,000 square miles of ocean.

At high tide, Okinotorishima
is about the size of two big beds.

That, as Japanese officials are painfully aware, is an area bigger than Japan itself. Without Okinotorishima, Japan's exclusive economic zone, which extends 200 nautical miles in all directions from its coastline, would be pushed far back — to either Minami Iwo Jima, an island nearly 400 miles to the northeast, or to Oki Daitojima, another island about the same distance to the northwest.

"Our mission is to conserve Japanese territory," said Masashi Waki, a civil engineer who will oversee the island rescue project for the Construction Ministry.

What Mr. Waki and his colleagues plan to do is to encase Okinotorishima's protruding rocks in large steel-and-concrete blocks that can absorb waves and thereby keep the Japanese outpost afloat. The process is not unlike a dentist putting a tap on a crumbling tooth, only this job is expected to take three years and cost up to $240 million altogether. . . .

Many years ago, Japan thought about putting a weather station there, but the idea never got off the ground. Now, officials are more concerned about Okinotorishima's fishing rights and the possibility that the surrounding waters contain seabed deposits of manganese and cobalt.

But none of that will mean much if the island disappears.

In Storms' Path

Its main problem is that it lies in an area that the Japanese have dubbed Typhoon Ginza, a center of relentless storms that send 60-foot waves pounding against Okinotorishima's twin boulders. By now, they barely endure, two bumps lying 1,400 yards apart and sticking no more than two feet out of the water at high tide.

Beneath the water's surface, they are supported by spindly columns of rock that Government officials fear can collapse at any moment.

Mr. Waki's task of keeping the island above water has persuaded him to build two circular blocks, each 160 feet in diameter, which will surround the deteriorating rocks with protective layers of steel and concrete. In effect, they will create artificial land, designed to stay at least three feet above the water at all times.

It will not be easy, Mr. Waki says.

The most difficult part will be transporting the necessary materials to the site. "This coral reef is in very deep sea," he said, "and it is particularly hard to reach at low tide."

Then, too, Mr. Waki added, there is no way to guarantee the durability of his work. "This should last 50 to 100 years, like any other steel and concrete work," he said. "But I really can't be sure. Out there on the water, conditions are really rough."

Notes and Questions

1. Does saving Okinotorishima automatically provide Japan the exclusive economic zone around it? Does control of the Senkaku Islands provide a country with the exclusive economic zone around it? Consider Article 121 (regime of islands), discussed earlier. See also Article 13.

2. As noted in the article above, Japan's investment of over $75 million was the first installment on a total investment of over $240 million to keep the island above water. In addition, the Japanese government regularly conducted scientific experiments on Okinotorishima, including a four-year study of the durability of a concrete-carbon fiber compound that could be used for building offshore oil rigs.

The investment apparently paid off. As of February 2011, it appears well accepted that Okinotorishima is a Japanese island to which Japan claims not only a territorial sea, but an EEZ.

3. As discussed above in the examples in the text, rival national claims to an island or island grouping takes on potentially huge economic importance, given the control over large ocean areas that the LOS Convention gives to any island (unless there are overlapping boundary claims, which are discussed below). For another example, the Spratly Islands are small, largely uninhabited islands in the South China Sea whose surrounding waters may contain vast deposits of natural gas and oil. The islands are claimed, in whole or part, by China, Taiwan, the Philippines, Brunei, Malaysia, and Vietnam. There have been occasional military confrontations over the islands. In November 2002, at the summit of ASEAN (discussed in Chapter 5), China signed a declaration with ten other Southeast Asian countries in which all parties agreed to exercise self-restraint in the area and to hold future talks. No country, however, relinquished its territorial claims. As of February 2011, China still refused to make the agreement legally binding and tensions remain unsettled.

4. To help you review the various maritime zones under the LOS Convention, which would you consider generally most useful for a state's claims to ocean area for its territorial sea, contiguous zone, and EEZ—an island 2 nautical miles off the state's coast? 11 miles? 23 miles? 300 miles? 800 miles?

5. The boundaries of the Continental Shelf can also raise issues. In August 2007, Russian explorers used a submersible to plant their country's flag on the seabed thousands of feet below the North Pole—a purely symbolic move. Russia claims that some of the seabed under the Pole is actually part of its extended continental shelf. See Marc Benitah, Russia's Claim in the Arctic and the Vexing issue of Ridges in UNCLOS, 11 ASIL Insight, issue 27 (Nov. 8, 2007), at http://www.asil.org/insights.htm.]

Turning to present U.S. policy, we again find the United States selectively adopting some of the legal norms in the LOS Convention.

President Reagan, U.S. Ocean Policy

19 Weekly Comp. Pres. Doc. 383 (Mar. 10, 1983)

The United States has long been a leader in developing customary and conventional law of the sea. Our objectives have consistently been to provide a legal order that will, among other things, facilitate peaceful, international uses of the oceans and provide for equitable and effective management and conservation of marine resources. The United States also recognizes that all nations have an interest in these issues.

Last July I announced that the United States will not sign the United Nations Law of the Sea Convention that was opened for signature on December 10. We have taken this step because several major problems in the Convention's deep seabed mining provisions are contrary to the interests and principles of industrialized nations and would not help attain the aspirations of developing countries. . . .

However, the convention also contains provisions with respect to traditional uses of the oceans which generally confirm existing maritime law and practice and fairly balance the interests of all states.

Today I am announcing three decisions to promote and protect the oceans interests of the United States in a manner consistent with those fair and balanced results in the convention and international law.

First, the United States is prepared to accept and act in accordance with the balance of interests relating to traditional uses of the oceans—such as navigation and overflight. In this respect, the United States will recognize the rights of other states in the waters off their coasts, as reflected in the convention, so long as the rights and freedoms of the United States and others under international law are recognized by such coastal states.

Second, the United States will exercise and assert its navigation and overflight rights and freedoms on a worldwide basis in a manner that is consistent with the balance of interests reflected in the convention. The United States will not, however, acquiesce in unilateral acts of other states designed to restrict the rights and freedoms of the international community in navigation and overflight and other related high seas uses.

Third, I am proclaiming today an Exclusive Economic Zone in which the United States will exercise sovereign rights in living and nonliving resources within 200 nautical miles of its coast. This will provide United States jurisdiction for mineral resources out to 200 nautical miles that are not on the continental shelf. Recently discovered deposits there could be an important future source of strategic minerals.

Within this Zone all nations will continue to enjoy the high seas rights and freedoms that are not resource related, including the freedoms of navigation and overflight. My proclamation does not change existing United States policies concerning the continental shelf, marine mammals, and fisheries, including highly migratory species of tuna which are not subject to United States jurisdiction. The United States will continue efforts to achieve international agreements for the effective management of these species. The proclamation also reinforces this government's policy of promoting the United States fishing industry. . . .

The Exclusive Economic Zone established today will also enable the United States to take limited additional steps to protect the marine environment. In this connection, the United States will continue to work through the International Maritime Organization and other appropriate international organizations to develop uniform international measures for the protection of the marine environment while imposing no unreasonable burdens on commercial shipping.

The policy decisions I am announcing today will not affect the application of existing United States law concerning the high seas or existing authorities of any United States Government agency. . . .

The administration looks forward to working with the Congress on legislation to implement these new policies.

Notes and Questions

1. Why is the Truman Proclamation viewed as so important for the development of customary international law? Was it a unilateral claim, unsupported at the time by any generally accepted principle of international law? Why wasn't the Truman Proclamation seen as a violation of existing customary international law, under which states did not usually claim territorial jurisdiction over the continental shelf, rather than be the basis for a new customary rule of international law? Does it make a difference that the United States at that time was the most powerful maritime nation?

2. Compare the width of the EEZ and the continental shelf under the LOS Convention with what was generally accepted before. Wasn't this an expansion of the sea area that a coastal state had some control over?

3. Why do you think that such a change occurred in the area over which a state has some control? Who benefited the most? Do most states have some sea coasts? From the standpoint of a multinational corporation engaged in offshore drilling for oil and gas, was it that much of a setback that many states extended the outer boundaries of their claims, or did it provide more certainty?

4. For the issues that we have now covered regarding the law of the sea (e.g., the territorial sea, the contiguous zone, the EEZ, the continental shelf), is President Reagan's proclamation of March 1983 generally consistent with the LOS Convention? Where does it differ, if at all, on these issues?

5. The Magnuson Fishery Conservation and Management Act of 1976 asserted U.S. jurisdiction over a fishery conservation zone with a breadth of 200 nautical miles. Reflecting the influence of the LOS Convention, the concept of this zone was later changed by amendment to the Exclusive Economic Zone. This EEZ encompasses approximately 3 million square nautical miles off the coasts of the 50 states, Puerto Rico, and all U.S. territories and possessions. The exact outer limits of the zone had to be negotiated with many neighboring countries that have overlapping boundary claims.

The 1976 Act prohibited foreign fishing within this area unless certain conditions were met. Moreover, the principal fisheries policy of the United States, especially as the Act has been implemented since 1980, has been the "Americanization" of fisheries within the zone. The allocation to foreign countries of allowable catches within the zone was cut by over 90 percent between 1980 and 1989, at the same time that catches by U.S. fishermen within the zone rapidly increased.

In an evolving effort to conserve marine fishery resources, Congress passed several amendments to the Magnuson Fishery Conservation and Management Act. The most recent amendments, signed by President George W. Bush in January 2007, mandate the use of annual catch limits and accountability measures to end overfishing, promote market-based management approaches, and give science a bigger role in fishery conservation. See National Oceanic and Atmospheric Administration Fisheries Feature, at http://www.nmfs.noaa.gov/msa2007/index.html.

6. One effect of the limits on foreign fishing within the U.S. zone and within the EEZs of other countries has been to drive fishing fleets from Japan and other countries further offshore, where they often resort to the use of huge nets, which indiscriminately snare most marine life in their paths.

7. The decline in the world's fish stocks has approached crisis proportions. The U.N' Food and Agricultural Organization (FAO) estimates that 32 percent of world fish stocks are overexploited, depleted, or need to be rebuilt. One response is that nations (such as the United States, discussed above) have taken steps to protect the fish stocks within 200 miles of their shores. Fish, however, do not respect international boundaries. Overfishing on the high seas also is helping cause this depletion of the world's fish stocks.

Besides national measures, some progress in managing the fish stocks can be made through international agreements. For example, 80 countries met in 1993-1995 for the U.N. Conference on Straddling Fish Stocks and Highly Migratory Fish Stocks. In August 1995, the conference reached an agreement to implement the provisions of the LOS Convention relating to the conservation and management of these fish stocks. The agreement provides minimum standards for such fish, which are overharvested by many countries. The agreement entered into force in 2001. As of February 2011, there are 78 parties to the agreement, including (for example) the United States, Canada, Japan, Brazil, and the EU countries, but not China, Peru, or Chile.

For a bilateral example, in 1999, Canada and the United States signed a comprehensive agreement under the existing Pacific Salmon Treaty. The agreement provides a conservation-based approach to the management of the Pacific salmon fisheries, and also contains an equitable sharing of the salmon catch. This agreement came after several years of friction, which included temporary Canadian legislation in 1994 authorizing the seizure of U.S. and other foreign boats in certain situations beyond the 200-mile Canadian EEZ, as well as the actual seizure of three U.S. fishing boats off Vancouver Island in 1997.

4. *Opposite and Adjacent States*

Drawing the outer boundaries of either the EEZ or the continental shelf can encounter problems. These include the situation where the outer boundary would overlap with that of another coastal state or where drawing the outer boundary of a coastal state's continental shelf is unclear due to physical factors. These problems arise on a regular basis. For example, there are over 50 treaties in force delimiting continental shelves between opposite or adjacent states.

In the North Sea Continental Shelf cases, 1969 I.C.J. 1 (Feb. 20), the ICJ was asked to state what international law mandated as the proper method for delimiting the continental shelf between the Federal Republic of Germany, Denmark, and the Netherlands. The continental shelf in that region is particularly shallow, never going below a depth of 200 meters. Most of the boundaries had already been settled between the parties, but the parties could not agree on the method to apply to the contested boundary. Denmark and the Netherlands contended that international law mandated the use of the "equidistance principle" in delimiting the boundary, essentially meaning that every point along the boundary is the same distance from two points chosen on either side of the boundary. Use of this principle, however, would have substantially reduced the German continental shelf. Germany argued that the equidistance principle was not mandated by international law and that more equitable principles should apply.

North Sea Continental Shelf Cases (Federal Republic of Germany v. Denmark; Federal Republic of Germany v. Netherlands)

Int'l Court of Justice
1969 I.CJ. Rep. 1 (Feb. 20) (Summary of the Decision)

The Principles and Rules of Law Applicable

The legal situation was that the Parties were under no obligation to apply the equidistance principle either under the 1958 Convention or as a rule of general or customary international law. . . . It remained for the Court . . . to indicate to the Parties the principles and rules of law in the light of which delimitation was to be effected.

The basic principles in the matter of delimitation, deriving from the Truman Proclamation, were that it must be the object of agreement between the States concerned and that such agreement must be arrived at in accordance with equitable principles. The Parties were under an obligation to enter into negotiations with a view to arriving at an agreement and not merely to go through a formal process of negotiation as a sort of prior condition for the automatic application of a certain method of delimitation in the absence of agreement. . . .

The Parties were under an obligation to act in such a way that in the particular case, and taking all the circumstances into account, equitable principles would be applied. There was no question of the Court's decision being *ex aequo et bono.* It was precisely a rule of law that called for the application of equitable principles, and in such cases as the present ones the equidistance method could unquestionably lead to inequity. Other methods existed and might be employed, alone or in combination, according to the areas involved. Although the Parties intended themselves to apply the principles and rules laid down by the Court some indication was called for of the possible ways in which they might apply them.

For all the foregoing reasons, the Court found in each case that the use of the equidistance method of delimitation was not obligatory as between the Parties; that no other single method of delimitation was in all circumstances obligatory; that delimitation was to be effected by agreement in accordance with equitable principles and taking account of all relevant circumstances, in such a way as to leave as much as possible to each Party all those parts of the continental shelf that constituted a natural prolongation of its land territory, without encroachment on the natural prolongation of the land territory of the other; and that, if such delimitation produced overlapping areas, they were to be divided between the Parties in agreed proportions, or, failing agreement, equally, unless they decided on a régime of joint jurisdiction, user, or exploitation.

In the course of negotiations, the factors to be taken into account were to include: the general configuration of the coasts of the Parties, as well as the presence of any special or unusual features; so far as known or readily ascertainable, the physical and geological structure and natural resources of the continental shelf areas involved; the element of a reasonable degree of proportionality which a delimitation effected according to equitable principles ought to bring about between the extent of the continental shelf areas appertaining to each State and the length of its coast measured in the general direction of the coastline, taking into account the effects, actual or prospective, of any other continental shelf delimitations in the same region. [The vote was 11-6.]

The LOS Convention provided for the delimitation of boundaries between opposite or adjacent states in Article 74 for the EEZ and Article 83 for the continental shelf.

Jonathan I. Charney, Progress in International Maritime Boundary Delimitation Law

88 Am. J. Int'l L. 227, 227 (1994)

Judgments of the International Court of Justice (ICJ) and awards of ad hoc arbitration tribunals carry special weight in international maritime boundary law. On its face, the international maritime boundary law codified in the [LOS Convention] is indeterminate. For the continental shelf and the exclusive economic zone, the legal obligation of coastal states is to delimit the boundary "by agreement on the basis of international law, as referred to in Article 38 of the Statute of the International Court of Justice, in order to achieve an equitable solution." The article on the delimitation of maritime boundaries in the territorial sea is no more determinative despite the fact that it makes direct references to the equidistant line, special circumstances and historic title. In spite of this indeterminacy, if not because of it, coastal states have found that third-party dispute settlement procedures can effectively resolve maritime boundary delimitation disputes. As a consequence, there are more judgments and awards on maritime boundary disputes than on any other subject of international law. . . .

Owing to the relative scarcity of authoritative pronouncements, ICJ judgments and even ad hoc arbitration awards generally assume considerable importance in international law. In international maritime boundary law, the judgments and awards take on even greater salience. There are two reasons for this situation: first, the existence of a unique line of jurisprudence made possible by a continuing series of decisions and, second, the absence of clearer guidance from codification efforts, *opinio juris* and state practice.

Jonathan I. Charney, International Maritime Boundaries

xlii-xlv (1993)

. . . In my opinion . . . no normative principle of international law has developed that would mandate the specific location of any maritime boundary line. The state practice varies substantially. Due to the unlimited geographic and other circumstances that influence the settlements, no binding rule that would be sufficiently determinative to enable one to predict the location of a maritime boundary with any degree of precision is likely to evolve in the near future. . . .

There are, however, trends and practices that are substantial. Surprisingly, it appears from the practice that the equidistant line has played a major role in boundary delimitation agreements, regardless of whether they concern boundaries between opposite or adjacent states. In the vast preponderance of the boundary agreements studied, equidistance had some role in the development of the line and/or the location of the line that was established. . . .

Despite the normative and theoretical uncertainties present in this area, the evidence brought out in this study suggests to me that states seeking to delimit their maritime boundaries ought to consider certain facts and options as they develop their positions and resolve them through negotiation and third party processes.

First, it is clear that primary attention will be placed upon the geography of the coastline.

Second, the equidistant line will be considered in most circumstances as a basis for analyzing the boundary situation. It may very well be used in some form or variant to generate the boundary line itself.

Third, the delimitation of a definitive maritime boundary is not the only option available to states. While different boundaries for different regimes or uses are rare, creative settlements that take certain matters out of contention for boundary delimitation purposes are possible. Thus, joint development or management zones that cross boundaries, revenue sharing, and management cooperation are all possible options which, in the appropriate cases, can facilitate settlement or even make settlement of the maritime boundary irrelevant.

Fourth, even if a definitive boundary cannot be established interim arrangements may be possible. . . .

Ninth, despite the relative indeterminacy of the maritime boundary law there are in state practice and in judicial decisions real limits to the geographical range in which a maritime boundary between two states will be located. These limits are primarily a function of the coastal geography, the size and location of islands, and the waters of the areas in question. What is ultimately considered to be fair or equitable will be largely dictated by a visual conception by the decision-makers of the maps and charts examined for this purpose. As a consequence, focus will be on the division of the water areas in question relative to the coastal states.

Finally, within the above considerations the law and practice permit states and tribunals a range of discretion that allows for the resolution of maritime boundaries in ways that no state need be characterized as a winner or loser, unless a state were itself to stake out an unswervingly doctrinal position. Viewed in isolation, boundary making is a zero sum game. However, the options available to vary the line over extended distances and to resolve related issues on the basis of non-boundary solutions allows for the resolution of maritime boundaries to the maximum advantage of all the participants.

Questions

1. The Court has built further on its general statements in the North Seas Continental Shelf cases in several succeeding cases, such as Maritime Delimitation in the Area Between Greenland and Jan Mayen (Denmark v. Norway), 1993 I.C.J. 38 (June 14); Delimitation of Maritime Boundary in the Gulf of Maine Area (Canada v. United States), 1984 I.C.J. 246 (Oct. 12); and Continental Shelf (Libyan Arab Jamahiriya v. Malta), 1985 I.C.J. 1 (June 3). A recent case is Maritime Delimitation in the Black Sea (Romania v. Ukraine), 2009 I.C.J. 61 (Feb. 9). The Court began by establishing a provisional equidistant line between the adjacent coasts and then considered whether there are any factors that would necessitate changing the line in order to achieve a more equitable result. Finally, the Court checked again to verify that the final delimitation did not lead to an inequitable result for either party.

2. Does there seem to be too much "indeterminancy" to maritime boundary decisions? Should there be more reliance on one standard (e.g., equidistance or equitable standard)? Which standard?

3. How could disputes over the location of a boundary matter between two countries?

F. THE REGIME OF THE HIGH SEAS

The term "high seas" is defined in the LOS Convention as "all parts of the sea that are not included in the exclusive economic zone, in the territorial sea or in the internal waters of a State, or in the archipelagic waters of an archipelagic State." The LOS Convention substantially incorporated the provisions of the 1958 Convention on the High Seas. See Articles 86 and 58 of the LOS Convention. Together, the LOS Convention's provisions on the high seas and EEZ make the EEZ a "sui generis" zone that is neither high seas nor territorial sea. The provisions do preserve the rights of the high seas in the EEZ for states other than the coastal state, unless the Convention specifies to the contrary. A succinct discussion of the high seas provisions of the LOS Convention and the 1958 Convention is provided by the Restatement of Foreign Relations Law.

Restatement

Section 521. Freedom of High Seas

(1) The high seas are open and free to all states, whether coastal or land-locked.

(2) Freedom of the high seas comprises, inter alia:

(a) freedom of navigation;

(b) freedom of overflight;

(c) freedom of fishing;

(d) freedom to lay submarine cables and pipelines;

(e) freedom to construct artificial islands, installations, and structures; and

(f) freedom of scientific research.

(3) These freedoms must be exercised by all states with reasonable regard to the interests of other states in their exercise of the freedom of the high seas.

Source Note

This section is based on Article 2 of the 1958 Convention on the High Seas, and Articles 87 and 89 of the LOS Convention.

Comment

a. Area in which high seas freedoms can be exercised. This section applies to all parts of the sea that are not included in the internal waters, the territorial sea, or the exclusive economic zone of any state, or in the archipelagic waters of an archipelagic state. Certain of these freedoms may be exercised also in the exclusive economic zone of other states. . . .

Section 522. Enforcement Jurisdiction over Foreign Ships on High Seas

(1) A warship, or other ship owned or operated by a state and used only on government noncommercial service, enjoys complete immunity on the high seas from interference by any other state.

(2) Ships other than those specified in Subsection (1) are not subject to interference on the high seas, but a warship or clearly-marked law enforcement ship of any state may board such a ship if authorized by the flag state, or if there is reason to suspect that the ship

(a) is engaged in piracy, slave trade, or unauthorized broadcasting;

(b) is without nationality; or

(c) though flying a foreign flag or refusing to show its flag, is in fact of the same nationality as the warship or law enforcement ship.

Source Note

This section follows with minor modifications Articles 8, 9 and 22 of the 1958 Convention on the High Seas, and Articles 95, 96 and 110 of the LOS Convention.

Comment . . .

b. Enforcement procedure. In cases under Subsection (2), the warship or law enforcement ship may proceed to verify a foreign ship's right to fly its flag by examining its documents and, if necessary, by an examination on board the ship. However, if the suspicions prove to be unfounded, and the boarded ship has committed no act justifying those suspicions, the inspecting state is obligated to pay compensation for any loss or damage. LOS Convention, Article 110.

In specified circumstances warships and law enforcement ships are entitled to engage in hot pursuit.

c. Piracy. Any state may seize a ship or aircraft on the high seas on reasonable suspicion of piracy, arrest the suspected pirates, seize the property on board, try the suspected pirates, and impose penalties on them if convicted. Where the seizure of a ship or aircraft on suspicion of piracy was effected without adequate grounds and the ship was found not to be a pirate ship, the state that made the seizure is liable to the flag state of the seized ship or aircraft for any loss or damage caused by the seizure. LOS Convention, Articles 105-106.

Not every act of violence committed on the high seas is piracy under international law. Only the following acts are considered piratical:

(i) Any illegal acts of violence, detention, or depredation committed for private ends by the crew or the passengers of a private ship or a private aircraft, and directed against another ship or aircraft on the high seas, or against persons or property on board such other ship or aircraft; or against a ship, aircraft, persons, or property in a place outside the jurisdiction of any state;

(ii) any act of voluntary participation in the operation of a ship or of an aircraft with knowledge of facts making it a pirate ship or aircraft;

(iii) any act of inciting or of intentionally facilitating an act described in subparagraphs (1) or (2).

In addition, acts committed by a mutinous crew of a warship or other government ship or aircraft against another ship or aircraft, may also constitute piracy. LOS Convention, Articles 101-102.

d. Slave and drug traffic. Because of the general condemnation of slave trade, international law allows the boarding and inspection of vessels suspected of such trade; it does not permit seizure of the vessel or arrest of the crew unless the flag state has consented. Since slave trade is an offense subject to universal jurisdiction (see §404), the state that boarded the vessel could try members of the crew for violations of its laws, if the flag state consented, and any state could try them later if it obtained jurisdiction over them.

There is movement to extend these rules to illicit traffic in narcotic drugs and psychotropic substances. However, even states, such as the United States, that strongly condemn such traffic do not take steps on the high seas against suspected smugglers except when the ship is without nationality . . . or when permission has been obtained from the flag state (often granted by telegraph or radio) to board, search, and seize the vessel. . . .

Reporters' Notes

1. *Warships and other government ships.* A United States Coast Guard ship is considered a warship. . . . Some convention provisions grant immunity to "government ships operated for non-commercial purpose" (e.g., LOS Convention, Arts. 31-32); others provide immunity to "ships owned or operated by a State and used only on government non-commercial service" (e.g., LOS Convention, Art. 96). It is not clear that any difference was intended. As long as a ship is operated for noncommercial purposes, it is entitled to immunity if it is either owned or operated by the government, for instance, a government-owned ship operated by an oceanographic institute, and engaged on a government-sponsored hydrographic survey, or a private-owned ship chartered by the government for a meteorological service.

2. *Piracy and hijacking.* Acts indicated in Comment *c* are piracy only if they are by private ships and for private ends. Seizure of a ship for political purposes is not considered piracy. See the *Santa Maria* incident in 1961, 4 Whiteman, Digest of International Law 665 (1965). Crew members forced to assist the pirates are not, under the above definition, considered pirates. Wrongful acts by governmental ships are not included in the definition of piracy, but are addressed by general principles of

international law governing state responsibility for violations of international obligations. See §§207 and 901. . . .

5. *Unauthorized broadcasting from high seas.* International law has accepted that any person or ship engaged in unauthorized broadcasting from the high seas may be arrested, and the broadcasting apparatus may be seized, by a law enforcement ship of any of the following states: the flag state of the broadcasting ship; the state of registry of the installation (as some of the broadcasts are made from abandoned platforms built on the continental shelf); the state of which the person is a national; a state where the transmission can be received; and the state where authorized radio communication is suffering interference. See LOS Convention, Art. 109. . . .

Notes and Questions

1. For decades, pirates seemed a thing of the past, but an outbreak of piracy off the coast of Somalia put the issue back into the international spotlight. A notable attack came in April 2009 when four Somali pirates attacked the American cargo ship MV Maersk Alabama, kidnapping the captain. The US Navy pursued the pirates, killed three, and rescued the Maersk's captain. Prior to June 2008, the international law of piracy did not apply to most of the actions of Somali pirates, because the pirates were attacking ships not on the high seas, but rather in the Somali territorial sea. Acting under Charter VII, the U.N. Security Council authorized cooperating states to combat piracy in these waters, in the same way permitted on the high seas. For more information about the international response to the recent increase in piracy, see J. Ashley Roach, Countering Piracy Off Somalia: International Law and International Institutions, 104 Am. J. Int'l L. 397 (2010).

2. Professor Frederic L. Kirgis reports on and analyzes the implications of two Spanish naval vessels stopping and boarding a North Korean vessel on the high seas in December 2002. The boarding appeared to be part of sea patrols that U.S., Spanish, and other ships were engaged in to intercept, among other things, Al Qaeda fighters fleeing from Afghanistan.

> On December 10, two Spanish naval ships stopped and boarded a North Korean cargo vessel on the high seas about 600 miles from the coast of Yemen. The cargo vessel flew no flag. According to a Pentagon official, the vessel took evasive measures in order to avoid inspection. The boarding party found fifteen Scud missiles hidden under sacks of cement. The cargo vessel's manifest said that it was carrying 40,000 sacks of cement, and apparently mentioned no other cargo. The Spanish naval ships were participating in organized patrols of the Indian Ocean and nearby waters keeping watch for Al Qaeda fighters fleeing from Afghanistan. The United States and other countries also participate in the patrols. . . .
>
> Under the [LOS Convention], vessels on the high seas are subject to the exclusive jurisdiction of their flag state and ordinarily may not be boarded by anyone from a foreign naval ship. An exception exists, however, if the boarded ship is without nationality. A vessel that flies no flag and is not otherwise clearly identified with a state of registration is considered a ship without nationality. Consequently it appears that the boarding of the cargo vessel, in and of itself, did not violate international law.

There would still be questions relating to the purpose and consequences of the boarding. The Convention on the Law of the Sea says that when an exception to the no-boarding rule exists, the naval ship may verify the boarded vessel's right to fly its flag or may check its documents and further examine the ship if "suspicion remains." In the context of the Convention, though, the suspicion would have to relate to certain enumerated offenses, which do not include the carrying of weapons. The carrying of weapons at sea, even on a merchant ship, is not a violation of international law unless the carriage is in violation of a treaty obligation of the transporting state. Such does not appear to have been the case here. . . .

The missiles obviously would have military uses, but they appear to have been destined for use by the government of Yemen, which could not reasonably be considered a belligerent despite any terrorist incidents that have occurred there. Nor is there currently a war in the normal sense between the United States (or Spain) and any state involved in the carriage of the missiles.

On December 11, the United States government confirmed that the missiles were destined for the government of Yemen, and released the cargo vessel to complete its voyage. White House spokesperson Ari Fleischer was quoted as saying that "In this instance there is no clear authority to seize the shipment of Scud missiles from North Korea to Yemen." He added, "There is no provision under international law prohibiting Yemen from accepting delivery of missiles from North Korea." Thus the U.S. government appears to have conceded that any justification it might offer under international law for detaining the vessel or seizing the missiles would be unconvincing. [Frederic L. Kirgis, Boarding of North Korean Vessel on the High Seas, 6 ASIL Insight (Dec. 12, 2002), at http://www.asil.org/insights.htm.]

3. Partly in response to the incident above with the North Korean vessel, several countries developed in 2003 the Proliferation Security Initiative (PSI) as a collective, global effort "to strengthen the political commitment, practical capacities, and legal authorities necessary to stop, search, and, if necessary, seize vessels and aircraft believe to be transporting 'weapons of mass destruction, their delivery systems, and related materials.' " Michael Byers, Policing the High Seas: The Proliferation Security Initiative, 98 Am. J. Int'l L. 514 (2004). Due to the secretive nature of many such efforts, it is unclear how successful PSI has been. As of February 2011, over 90 countries have endorsed PSI, which means that the countries commit, among other things, to interdict transfers of proliferation concern to and from states and non-state actors to the extent of their capabilities and legal authorities. For more information about PSI, see id.; Thomas M. Franck et al., Foreign Relations and National Security Law: Cases, Materials, and Simulations 243 (3d ed. 2008); and http://www.wtate.gov/t/isn/c10390.htm.

If you were the U.S. Secretary of State and it came to your attention that there was a likely shipment on a North Korean ship of WMD to Syria, a state that supports terrorists, and North Korea will not consent to an inspection, would you recommend to the President that the U.S. Navy stop and inspect the vessel, and seize any WMD if found? Would these actions likely be allowed under the LOS Convention or customary international law? (Assume none of the U.N. Security Council resolutions imposing sanctions on North Korea, as discussed in Chapter 11.F, apply.) Given the PSI and other treaties and arrangements to limit the spread of WMD, might the Secretary of State be able to argue that customary international law has evolved in this area?

G. DISPUTE SETTLEMENT UNDER THE LOS CONVENTION

One of the many accomplishments of the LOS Convention is the establishment of a comprehensive dispute settlement system. This system is incorporated in Part XV of the Convention.

Louis B. Sohn, Peaceful Settlement of Disputes in Ocean Conflicts: Does UNCLOS III Point the Way?

46 Law & Contemp. Probs. 195, 195-200 (1983)

I. Introduction

One of the important accomplishments of the Third United Nations Law of the Sea Conference is the development of a veritable code for the settlement of the disputes which may arise with respect to the interpretation and application of the Law of the Sea Convention. It was recognized early in the negotiations that if the parties to the Convention had retained the right of unilateral interpretation, then the complex text drafted by the Conference would have lacked stability, certainty, and predictability. It is one of the prerogatives of sovereign equality that in the absence of an agreement on impartial third-party adjudication, the view of one state with respect to the interpretation of the Convention cannot prevail over the views of other member states. . . .

The only effective remedy in such a situation is to provide in advance in the Convention itself for an effective method of settling future interpretation disputes. . . .

II. The General Framework for Dispute Settlement

The resulting system for the settlement of law of the sea disputes is at the same time simple and complex. Its simplicity is due to the fact that the Convention accepts as its guiding principle that in general the will of the parties to a dispute shall prevail and that the parties may by agreement select any dispute settlement method they wish.[6] The more complex provisions apply only if the parties do not agree upon a dispute settlement method.[7]

Even after a dispute has arisen, and even if one of the procedures provided for in the Convention has been started, the parties can agree "at any time" to adopt a special method for settling their dispute.[8] Similarly, if the parties to a dispute have previously agreed, in a bilateral, regional, or general international agreement, to settle disputes (including those relating to the interpretation of international agreements between them) by a procedure entailing a binding decision, this procedure supersedes the procedures provided for in the Law of the Sea Convention.[9]

6. See Convention, art. 280.
7. Id. art. 281(1).
8. Id. art. 280.
9. Id. art. 282.

For example, if the two parties to the dispute have agreed unconditionally to accept the jurisdiction of the International Court of Justice, either of them can refer the dispute to that forum. . . .

Flexibility does not stop at this stage. Unlike most other international instruments, the Law of the Sea Convention does not provide for a unitary system of dispute settlement. Various groups of states have expressed preferences for different methods of settling Convention disputes. Some states have argued for conferring the jurisdiction to interpret the Convention on the International Court of Justice; others have expressed preferences for arbitration; while some have supported special technical commissions; a large group of states has opted for a permanent International Tribunal for the Law of the Sea. After many other solutions were rejected, it was agreed that a state can choose any one of these four methods, but if the two states concerned have chosen different methods, the dispute may be submitted "only to arbitration."[17] All states agreed that if they cannot have the tribunal of their choice they would be willing to go to arbitration. To ensure that this solution will work, an annex to the Convention provides an effective method for selecting the arbitral tribunal.[18]

III. Settlement of Specific Categories of Disputes

Three categories of cases are subject, however, to different procedures: (a) Article 297 governs disputes relating to the exercise by a coastal state of its sovereign rights or jurisdiction in the Exclusive Economic Zone (EEZ); (b) Article 298 governs disputes relating to sea boundary delimitations, to military or law enforcement activities, or to disputes submitted to the Security Council of the United Nations; and (c) Articles 186-91 govern disputes relating to seabed mining. The simplicity of the other provisions of the Convention is matched by the complexity of these three exceptions. . . .

[T]he dispute settlement provisions will be available only to parties to the Convention. Should a dispute arise between a state party to the Convention and a state not a party thereto, such a dispute would have to be resolved in accordance with procedures available to the parties to the dispute outside the Convention. At present, such procedures are seldom available. . . . On the other hand, for disputes between parties to the Convention the system of dispute settlement provided by the Convention, though it appears extremely flexible and provides several options, in the great majority of cases can lead to a binding decision likely to be accepted and complied with by the parties to the dispute. This is the way to the rule of law and to ensuring that the peace of the world will not be jeopardized by a dangerous escalation of law of the sea controversies.

17. Convention, art. 287(1), (5).
18. Id. annex VII.

Notes and Questions

1. As noted above, the LOS Convention allows the parties to choose among different dispute settlement forums. What do you think are the pros and cons of this approach? Did it seem to help obtain the support of the negotiating countries? Does it provide flexibility to the parties? Is it optimal for ensuring consistency in the international law of the sea? (If and when the United States ratifies the LOS Convention, it will likely indicate that arbitration is its preferred dispute settlement alternative. The Clinton Administration's Letter of Transmittal to the U.S. Senate indicated that this was the view of the Executive Branch and the Senate Foreign Relations Committee accepted this.)

2. Note that when the parties cannot agree on a particular dispute settlement forum the default alternative is arbitration. Does this suggest that international arbitration among states is now widely accepted?

3. As indicated above, the LOS Convention did provide for the creation of a new dispute body for at least some of the disputes arising out of the interpretation and application of the Convention. The International Tribunal for the Law of the Sea is an independent judicial body seated in Hamburg, Germany. It is composed of 21 independent members elected by the state parties, with no two members being nationals of the same state and with no fewer than three members from each geographical group.

Disputes over activities in the International Seabed Area are submitted to the Seabed Disputes Chamber of the Tribunal, which consists of 11 judges. Any party to such a dispute may ask the Seabed Disputes Chamber to form an ad hoc chamber composed of three members from the Seabed Disputes Chamber.

The Tribunal has an excellent Web site at http://www.itlos.org.

4. As of February 2011, 18 cases had been filed with the Tribunal since its inception in 1996, with most of the cases dealing with disputes over seized vessels. For example, the Tribunal's first case involved the government of Saint Vincent and the Grenadines instituting proceedings against the government of Guinea because of Guinea's alleged seizure and arrest in October 1997 of the *M/V Saiga* and its crew and cargo off the coast of West Africa. Moving expeditiously, the Tribunal ruled on December 4, 1997, that it had jurisdiction and that Guinea should promptly release the ship and its crew from detention upon the posting of a reasonable bond of some of petroleum cargo and $400,000.

In February 2011, the Tribunal's Seabed Disputes Chamber issued an advisory opinion on the "Responsibilities and Obligations of States Sponsoring Persons and Entities with respect to Activities in the Area." This was the first time that the Tribunal's advisory jurisdiction had been called upon and the first time that the Chamber had a case. The Chamber decided unanimously that, when a state sponsors private contractors who are exploring and exploiting the mineral resources of the seabed, the state is obligated to ensure that such contractors abide by the terms of the contract and the provisions in the LOS Convention. The Chamber interpreted this "obligation to ensure" to entail a high due diligence standard by the state that includes best environmental practices. If a state fails to take "all necessary and appropriate measures to ensure compliance" by the contractor, then the state would be liable for possible environmental or ecological damage. For more about the exploitation of the seabed, see the next section.

H. THE DEEP SEABED MINING REGIME AND THE 1994 AGREEMENT

One of the most controversial parts of the LOS Convention was the deep seabed mining regime it envisioned. In 1958, when the Convention on the High Seas was concluded, the U.N.'s International Law Commission considered the prospect of deep seabed mining to be so remote that it was not material to the agreement.

The rapid advance of technology and the depletion of land-based mineral deposits, however, made deep seabed mining increasingly attractive.

> The discovery of rich deposits of nickel and manganese at the bottom of the oceans, and the development of technologies capable of harvesting such valuable ores in the near future, inaugurated an international legal debate . . . over the rights of the individual states to mine the world's untapped mineral wealth. Specifically, one block, represented by most developing nations, maintain[ed] that the natural resources of the deep oceans [were] the common heritage of mankind, and their exploitation as a consequence, should take place under a communal regime. Conversely, another faction, headed by the United States, and including the most developed nations, argue[d] that the high economic value of the seabed minerals, and their strategic value to the First-World states, require[d] free access by the technologically and financially richer countries as a matter of economic interest. . . . [Arcangelo Travaglini, Reconciling Natural Law and Legal Positivism in the Deep Seabed Mining Provisions of the Convention on the Law of the Sea, 15 Temp. Int'l & Comp. L.J. 313, 313 (2001).]

Given the controversy over the deep seabed mining, there ensued a great deal of international debate, diplomatic maneuvering, and steps by individual states. While negotiations on the LOS Convention were ongoing, Congress in 1980 passed the Deep Seabed Hard Mineral Resources Act, codified at 30 U.S.C. §§1401-1471 (1982). The expressed purpose of the Act was to establish an interim deep seabed regime pending successful completion and entry into force of the Convention. Apparently, passage of the Act was also quietly supported by the then U.S. ambassador to the LOS Convention as a way to pressure the developing countries into agreeing to certain U.S. positions in the negotiations. In addition to licensing and safety provisions, section 118 of the Act called for the negotiation of agreements among "reciprocating states."

This unilateral action was quickly condemned by a number of Convention participants, especially by the Group of 77. The Group of 77, which now numbers more than 120 countries, primarily includes developing countries seeking to protect their interests. (See Chapter 5, C.2.f.) During the Law of the Sea negotiations, the Group often worked out an agreed position in its caucus and then pushed for that position as a bloc in the negotiating sessions. Given its many members, the Group's voice was very influential. Unanimity within the Group on deep seabed mining issues was relatively easy to achieve because the members' interests were generally similar. Unanimity in the international community as a whole, of course, was not easy.

Although criticized, the 1980 U.S. statute regarding reciprocating states was followed by similar legislation in like-minded developed mining states, such as the United Kingdom, West Germany, and Japan. In September 1982, France, West Germany, the United Kingdom, and the United States signed the Interim Arrangements Relating to Polymetalic Nodules of the Deep Seabed.

In December 1982, the LOS Convention was signed by 115 countries and the ratification process began in these countries and in some other countries that signed soon afterward. Essentially because of the deep seabed provisions, however, President Reagan refused to sign the Convention, as did the governments of several other major industrial countries.

When the United States rejected the 1982 Convention, what had previously been thought of as only an interim regime became the potential basis for the permanent U.S. statutory system. The United States moved further toward an alternative to the Convention's deep seabed regime through bilateral and multilateral agreements. This alternative was commonly referred to as the "reciprocating states regime" or the "mini-treaty." In 1984, Belgium, France, West Germany, Italy, the Netherlands, the United Kingdom, and the United States concluded the Provisional Understanding Regarding Deep Seabed Mining, 23 I.L.M. 1354 (1984). Japan joined later. The Provisional Understanding attempted to ensure respect for mining rights granted by reciprocating states and to avoid overlapping mining sites.

Needless to say, many signatories to the LOS Convention condemned this alternative approach. However, a number of the early assumptions underlying the provisions for deep seabed mining changed after the LOS Convention was drafted. First, the end of the Cold War brought a global focus on the advantages of free market economies. Aspects of the Convention taken from the centrally planned economy model were in sharp contrast to ongoing free market reforms. Second, commercial interest in deep seabed mining decreased due to a period of relatively low mineral prices. Industry experts revised their predictions that the mining sites would be fully operational from the mid-1980s to at least the second decade of the twenty-first century. These factors combined to make supporters and opponents of the LOS Convention's provisions on mining more open to accommodation.

In October 1990, consultations among a representative group of countries began under U.N. auspices to determine whether there was enough common ground between the developing and developed countries to seek more generally acceptable arrangements for the governance of deep seabed mining. After the Reagan Administration had consistently refused during 1982-1988 to engage in multilateral discussions about how to deal with the LOS Convention, representatives of the U.S. Department of State during the first Bush Administration and then the Clinton Administration participated in these new consultations. These consultations led to the 1994 Agreement on "interpreting" or implementing the LOS Convention provisions. This Agreement will be examined below.

First, however, it is useful to appreciate what the U.S. concerns had been over the deep seabed mining provisions.

Statement of Ambassador David A. Colson, Deputy Assistant Secretary of State for Oceans

The Law of the Sea Treaty and Reauthorization of the Deep Seabed Hard Mineral Resources Act: Hearings before the Subcomm. on Oceanography, Gulf of Mexico, and the Outer Continental Shelf Deep Seabed Mining, 103rd Cong., 1st Sess. 37 (1994)

The basic flaws of t[he] deep seabed mining regime are manifold. But stated simply, it failed to provide the United States, and other states with major economic interests, a voice commensurate with those interests in decision-making relating to management of deep seabed resources, and it was based on a highly interventionist central economic planning model that was overly bureaucratic and would have preempted private investment in deep seabed mineral resource development, thus, preventing the development of those resources when economic conditions warrant.

In 1982, the Reagan Administration, in its ocean policy statement, reaffirmed support for the rest of the Convention while identifying the specific U.S. objections concerning deep seabed mining. They fell into two broad categories: institutional issues and economic and commercial issues. On the institutional front, we objected to the fact that the U.S. was not guaranteed a seat on the executive council of the international seabed authority (the organization that would administer the deep seabed regime); and we objected that developing countries would dominate the organization based on the rules for decision-making and the relationship between the executive council and the plenary assembly. In addition, we objected to the fact that the convention's provisions on seabed mining could in the future be amended and bind the U.S. without our consent; and we objected to the possibility that future revenues from deep seabed mining might be distributed to national liberation movements over our objections.

On the economic and commercial front we objected to the requirement that commercial enterprises, as a condition to the awarding of mining rights, must undertake to transfer their mining technology to a competing operating arm of the regime known as the Enterprise, or possibly to developing countries. We also objected to the Enterprise benefitting from discriminatory and competitive advantages over commercial enterprises. . . . We also objected to the regime's production control arrangements that limited the level of production from the seabed so as to protect land-based producers of deep seabed minerals. We also objected to the regime's onerous system of financial payments that would have been made by commercial miners, in particular a U.S. $1 million annual fee payable beginning with the exploration stage.

These features made the regime non-viable and led the United States, the United Kingdom and Germany not to sign the convention. Other major industrial countries that signed the convention did not move to ratify, for these same reasons. . . .

The 1994 Agreement was specifically negotiated and designed to cure the defects, indicated above, that the United States and certain other industrialized countries saw in the LOS Convention. What follows is a description of the deep seabed mining regime as it stands presently under the LOS Convention as interpreted or implemented by the 1994 Agreement, which is entitled Agreement Relating to the Implementation of Part XI of the United Nations Convention on the Law of the Sea of 10 December 1982.

R.R. Churchill & A.V. Lowe, The Law of the Sea

238-241, 244-246, 248-253 (3d ed. 1999)

The international law of the deep sea bed has a complexity which readers could be forgiven for thinking is out of proportion to its current practical importance. Given the purpose of this book, and the plethora of detailed treatments of the subject, we will do no more than outline the regime as it stands at present under the 1982 Convention as modified by the 1994 Implementation Agreement.

Principles of the Law of the Sea Convention Regime

The regime governs all activities connected with exploration and exploitation of mineral resources in the Area (LOSC, art. 134(2)). The latter is defined as the "sea bed and ocean floor and subsoil thereof beyond national jurisdiction" (LOSC, art. 1). . . . "[N]ational jurisdiction" for these purposes extends, broadly speaking, to the outer edge of the continental margin, or to a distance of 200 miles from the baseline where the margin does not extend up to that distance. Both the Area itself, which comprises about sixty per cent of the whole sea bed, and its resources (limited by article 133 to mineral resources)[49] are the "common heritage of mankind." As such they are not susceptible of unilateral national appropriation. Rights in the Area and to its resources can be obtained . . . only with the authorisation of the International Sea Bed Authority established by the 1982 Convention (LOSC, arts. 136, 137).

All activities in the Area, which in principle may be conducted both by the Authority itself through its mining arm, the "Enterprise," and by commercial operators, are to be carried out for the benefit of mankind as a whole, taking into particular consideration the interests of developing States and peoples who have not attained self-governing status (LOSC, art. 140). Furthermore, since the superjacent waters and air space remain high seas, reasonable regard must be had to other legitimate uses of those waters and of the Area itself. A succinct (if ungrammatical) account of the core of the regime can be found in article 155(2). . . .

The International Sea Bed Authority[50]

It would be wrong to say that the Area is "governed" by the Authority, because many uses of the Area, such as pipeline and cable laying and scientific research unconnected with the exploitation of sea-bed resources, may be carried out without the need for the Authority's permission. But the Authority is the body through which

49. Living resources and other non-mineral resources (e.g., thermal energy) remain subject to the regime of the high seas.

50. Documents concerning the Authority, and lists of current members of its various organs, are set out on its web site: http://www.isa.org.jm.

States Parties are to organise and control all activities concerned with sea-bed minerals beyond national jurisdiction.

Part XI of the 1982 Convention provides that the Authority has three principal organs: the plenary Assembly, the thirty-six-State Council, and the Secretariat (LOSC, art. 158). The Authority is served by two specialised bodies, the Legal and Technical Commission (LOSC, art. 163) and the Finance Committee (1994IA, Annex, Section 1, paragraph 4, and Section 9). In addition, there is the Authority's mining arm, the Enterprise. Each component of this system has a particular role to play, but it is the Council that is the most important organ, particularly after the amendments effected by the 1994 Implementation Agreement. . . .

The Assembly

All States Parties to the Convention are *ipso facto* members of the Authority and so, too, of the Assembly, wherein each State has one vote. The Assembly is said to be "the supreme organ of the Authority to which the other principal organs shall be accountable," but by depriving it of the power to act alone in crucial areas the 1994 Implementation Agreement has significantly reduced the power of the Assembly, and increased that of the Council. . . . The Assembly formally elects members of the Council, the Governing Body of the Enterprise, and other subsidiary organs of the Authority, and is the forum within which Authority decisions are formally adopted on matters such as the budget and sharing of the costs of the Authority, the rules governing sea-bed mining, and the distribution of the economic benefits of sea-bed mining.

The Council

The Council is responsible for the implementation of the Convention regime within the limits set by the Convention and the general policies established by the Authority, and the establishment of the specific policies of the Authority. Its main specific tasks, listed in article 162, include the supervision of the implementation of Part XI of the Convention; the approval of plans of work submitted by sea-bed miners. . . . ;

The Council has thirty-six members. Its membership is carefully designed both to be representative of the main interest groups concerned with sea-bed mining and to establish a broadly equitable geographical distribution of Council members. . . . Seats for Russia and the USA are guaranteed under the "largest economy" provisions of sub-paragraph (a). . . .

The Enterprise

In the early days of UNCLOS III it was hoped by many that the mining of the riches of the deep sea bed would be primarily the privilege and responsibility of an international mining corporation, the Enterprise, to be established under the auspices of the Authority. The 1982 Convention provided for the establishment of the Enterprise as a separate organ of the Authority, and empowered it to engage in prospecting and mining the Area. . . . Subject to obligations to comply with the Assembly's general policies and the Council's directives and to report to the Authority, the Enterprise was an autonomous organisation, and so would have stood in much the same relationship to the Authority as would commercial operators. . . .

That plan has been radically revised in the face of the commercial realities of seabed mining. No commercial mining of the Area is likely in the near future, and there is therefore no immediate need to establish the Enterprise. Moreover, the Enterprise is required by the 1994 Implementation Agreement to conduct its initial mining operations through joint ventures, not as an independent mining operator. . . .

Decision-making in the International Sea-Bed Authority

The provisions on the composition of the Authority's organs go some way towards safeguarding the interest of the various constituencies concerned with sea-bed mining. It was, however, thought necessary to provide safeguards for the interests of those who might find themselves in a minority in those organs. . . .

. . . The practical result [of the 1994 Implementation Agreement] is that the Council is given the pivotal role in the formation of Authority policy. . . .

The Implementation Agreement stipulates that "as a general rule, decisional-making in the organs of the Authority should be by consensus" (Annex, Section 3, paragraph 2). Consensus means the absence of formal objection. . . .

Some substantive decisions to be taken by the Council *must* be taken by consensus: they cannot be taken by majority vote. These include . . . recommendations to the Assembly on the sharing of the benefits of sea-bed mining; the adoption of rules concerning sea-bed mining; and the adoption of amendments to Part XI of the Convention. . . .

The System of Exploitation

[The substantive provisions of the deep-sea-bed mining regime] are based on the "parallel system," under which the Area may be exploited both by the Enterprise and by commercial operators

Prospecting is the first stage of exploitation under this system. Although the term is not defined, it seems to connote general searches for sea-bed resources, rather than the detailed pre-production surveying which appears to be covered by the term "exploration." Prospecting is essentially free . . . Two or more prospectors may be active in the same area simultaneously. . . .

Exploration and exploitation, in contrast, require specific authorisation by the Authority, which authorisation carries with it exclusive rights. Qualified applicants may submit plans of work for the approval of the Authority. Applicants are "qualified" if they are entities possessing the nationality of a State Party . . . and effectively controlled by them or by their nationals. . . . The applicants must also be sponsored by those States. . . .

Applicants were formerly required to accept the Convention provisions concerning the mandatory transfer of technology. Those provisions were one of the main obstacles to ratification by certain western States. . . . Those provisions were disapplied by the 1994 Implementation Agreement, and replaced with a much simpler provision. It amplifies the general exhortation in article 144 of the 1982 Convention to promote technology transfer and obliges contractors and their sponsoring States to co-operate with the Authority in obtaining technology for the Enterprise and developing States "on fair and reasonable commercial terms and conditions, consistent with the effective protection of intellectual property rights."

The plans of work submitted by qualified applicants (not by the Enterprise) must specify two sites of equal estimated commercial value which may or may not be contiguous, each large enough to support a mining operation. Data concerning both sites and their resources must also be submitted. The Authority may then approve a plan of work relating to one of the two sites, and enter into a contract with the applicant incorporating that plan. If it does so, it must designate the other site as a "reserved site." . . . Where joint ventures are sought (as they must be by the Enterprise in its early days) the contractor that "contributed" the reserved area has the right of first refusal to enter the joint venture arrangement. . . .

Applications are to be dealt with by the Authority in order of receipt. To preclude any possibility of the Authority unreasonably impeding development of the sea bed, it is provided that approval of plans can be refused only in certain specified circumstances. . . .

In all cases it is the Legal and Technical Commission which first reviews the proposed plan. . . . The policies that it is to adopt have been spelled out in the 1994 Implementation Agreement. Deep-sea-bed resources are to be developed in accordance with sound commercial principles; there is to be no subsidisation of sea-bed mining (a provision backed up by the linking of the LOSC regime to the GATT/ World Trade Organisation regime and its provisions on subsidies, procurement, and so on) . . . .

Plans must indicate the maximum mineral production expected, year by year. . . . Under the original 1982 provisions the Authority was required to limit production authorisations to levels that would permit sea-bed minerals to meet a certain proportion of the growth in world nickel demand. That elaborate production ceiling . . . was abandoned in the 1994 Implementation Agreement . . . ; regulation of production is left to the market. . . .

The financial terms of contracts concluded pursuant to approved plans of work and production . . . have been greatly simplified by the 1994 Implementation Agreement. There is an initial fee of $250,000 payable for the processing of the plan application. There will also be an annual fee payable by the contractor once commercial exploitation begins; and the Authority is required to devise a payment system. . . . that "should not be complicated." . . .

The Common Heritage

The "common heritage" will be exploited for the benefit of "mankind as a whole," and not simply of the industrialised States, in a number of ways. The collection and distribution among States — in particular, developing States and peoples — of payments made to the Authority by the commercial operators and perhaps later by the Enterprise is the most obvious. The Convention does not stipulate the manner in which the financial benefits are to be shared out; only that the sharing should be "equitable" (LOSC, art. 140). Precise rules will be decided upon by the Authority. In fact some States will, in effect, have a preferential claim on the monies. These are the developing States that suffer adverse effects on their export earnings or economies as a result of falls in mineral prices caused by sea-bed mining. . . . But it seems clear that the financial benefits of sea-bed exploitation are likely to be modest and not immediate. Commercial mining is still some way off. . . . The claims made in the 1960s of unimaginable wealth seem unlikely ever to be realised. . . .

Notes and Questions

Although the 1994 Agreement may have resolved the objections with the LOS Convention's provisions on deep seabed mining raised by the United States and other developed countries, the debate illustrates fundamental questions regarding the balancing of competing ideologies in international agreements.

1. Do you agree with the fundamental assumption of the Convention that the Area and its resources "are the common heritage of mankind"? (Article 136.) If not, what principle do you support?

2. The Outer Space Treaty, which came into effect in 1967 and has about 100 parties (including the United States), provides that: "The exploration and use of outer space, including the moon and other celestial bodies, shall be carried out for the benefit and in the interests of all countries . . . , and shall be the province of all mankind. . . ." Outer Space Treaty, Jan. 27, 1967, art. 1, 18 U.S.T. 2410, 610 U.N.T.S. 205. Is this similar to the "common heritage of mankind" in the LOS Convention? See also the discussion of Antarctica at the end of this chapter.

3. Prior to the 1994 Agreement, how significant were the provisions about the Area in the overall importance of the Convention? Were problems with those provisions worth opposing the entire Convention?

4. In the absence of an agreement addressing the U.S. objections, would it have been sound policy for the United States to support as customary international law the provisions of the Convention that it liked and disregard the other provisions? Are there any dangers to such a policy?

I. WIDESPREAD ACCEPTANCE OF THE CONVENTION

The successful negotiation of the 1994 Agreement led many countries to move forward with the ratification process for the LOS Convention and the 1994 Agreement. The Convention came into force in November 1994. The Agreement came into force on a provisional basis at the same time and then it acquired the necessary ratifications to come definitively into force in July 1996. Promptly after the 1994 Agreement had been reached, the Clinton Administration announced that the United States would sign the Agreement and that it would submit the Agreement and the Convention to the U.S. Senate for its advice and consent.

Letter of Submittal from the State Department to the President

Message from the President of the United States Transmitting United Nations Convention on the Law of the Sea and the Agreement Relating to the Implementation of Part XI of the United Nations Convention on the Law of the Sea, S. Treaty Doc. No. 103-39 (Oct. 7, 1994)

The Agreement

The achievement of a widely accepted and comprehensive law of the sea convention — to which the United States can become a Party — has been a consistent objective of successive U.S. administrations for the past quarter century.

However, the United States decided not to sign the Convention upon its adoption in 1982 because of objections to the regime it would have established for managing the development of seabed mineral resources beyond national jurisdiction. While the other Parts of the Convention were judged beneficial for U.S. ocean policy interests, the United States determined the deep seabed regime of Part XI to be inadequate and in need of reform before the United States could consider becoming Party to the Convention.

Similar objections to Part XI also deterred all other major industrialized nations from adhering to the Convention. However, as a result of the important international political and economic changes of the last decade—including the end of the Cold War and growing reliance on free market principles—widespread recognition emerged that the seabed mining regime of the Convention required basic change in order to make it generally acceptable. As a result, informal negotiations were launched in 1990, under the auspices of the United Nations Secretary-General, that resulted in adoption of the Agreement on July 28, 1994.

The legally binding changes set forth in the Agreement meet the objections of the United States to Part XI of the Convention. The United States and all other major industrialized nations have signed the Agreement.

The provisions of the Agreement overhaul the decision-making procedures of Part XI to accord the United States, and others with major economic interests at stake, adequate influence over future decisions on possible deep seabed mining. The Agreement guarantees a seat for the United States on the critical executive body and requires a consensus of major contributors for financial decisions.

The Agreement restructures the deep seabed mining regime along free market principles and meets the U.S. goal of guaranteed access by U.S. firms to deep seabed minerals on the basis of reasonable terms and conditions. It eliminates mandatory transfer of technology and production controls. It scales back the structure of the organization to administer the mining regime and links the activation and operation of institutions to the actual development of concrete commercial interest in seabed mining. A future decision, which the United States and a few of its allies can block, is required before the organization's potential operating arm (the Enterprise) may be activated, and any activities on its part are subject to the same requirements that apply to private mining companies. States have no obligation to finance the Enterprise, and subsidies inconsistent with GATT are prohibited.

The Agreement provides for grandfathering the seabed mine site claims established on the basis of the exploration work already conducted by companies holding U.S. licenses on the basis of arrangements "similar to and no less favorable than" the best terms granted to previous claimants; further, it strengthens the provisions requiring consideration of the potential environmental impacts of deep seabed mining.

The Agreement provides for its provisional application from November 16, 1994, pending its entry into force. Without such a provision, the Convention would enter into force on that date with its objectionable seabed mining provisions unchanged. . . . Further, the Agreement provides flexibility in allowing States to apply it provisionally in accordance with their domestic laws and regulations.

In signing the agreement on July 29, 1994, the United States indicated that it intends to apply the agreement provisionally pending ratification. Provisional application by the United States will permit the advancement of U.S. seabed mining interests by U.S. participation in the International Seabed Authority from the outset to ensure that the implementation of the regime is consistent with those interests, while doing so consistent with existing laws and regulations. . . .

As discussed at the beginning of this chapter, despite the 1994 Agreement, the Clinton Administration was unable to obtain the advice and consent of the U.S. Senate to the LOS Convention or the 1984 Agreement. Later Administrations have likewise been unable to obtain Senate advice and consent. As the former Legal Adviser in the George W. Bush Administration observed:

> This multilateral treaty . . . was strongly supported by all branches of the U.S. military, every major U.S. ocean industry and many environmental groups (and even then-Alaska Gov. Sarah Palin). Senior Bush Administration officials testified in favor of the treaty in 2004 and 2007, and the Senate Foreign Relations Committee recommended passage in both years. Despite vigorous efforts by the Bush Administration, the full Senate failed to vote on the convention because of concerns raised by conservative groups.
>
> The Obama administration took office promising a "return" to the U.S. commitment to international law. . . . Sadly, the White House made no effort to obtain Senate approval for the Law of the Sea convention [in 2009]. [John B. Bellinger III, Op-Ed., Our Abandoned Treaties, Wash. Post, June 11, 2010, at A17.

There is still some lingering domestic opposition to the Convention, even after the 1994 Agreement, essentially because of somewhat undefined concerns that the Agreement was insufficient to correct the problems that President Reagan and others perceived in the Convention. Moreover, as discussed above, the United States has selectively adopted many of the provisions of the Convention through laws, executive orders, and presidential proclamations. As a result, it is already enjoying many of the benefits of the Convention without having ratified it.

The United States, though, is now the only major industrialized country that has not ratified the Convention. As noted at the beginning of this chapter, there were 161 parties to the LOS Convention as of February 2011 and 140 of those countries had also become parties to the 1994 Agreement.

Notes and Questions

1. What are some of the more important provisions of the LOS Convention and the 1994 Agreement?

2. Overall, do the LOS Convention and the 1994 Agreement together further the U.S. objective of a widely ratified, comprehensive law of the sea treaty regime that protects and promotes U.S. ocean interests?

3. What major U.S. bureaucracies, constituencies, or interest groups in the United States do you expect would support U.S. ratification of the LOS Convention and the 1994 Agreement? Who was likely to oppose ratification? Why? For example, on which side would you expect to find the U.S. Navy? American fishermen? U.S. deep seabed mining companies? U.S. oil companies?

4. The U.S. Congress passed the Oceans Act of 2000, which went into effect on January 20, 2001. The Act established a 16-member Commission on Ocean Policy to

undertake an 18-month study and to make recommendations to the President and Congress for a national ocean policy for the United States. President George W. Bush appointed the 16 members to the Commission, based on a process that included nominations by both Congress and the President. Admiral James D. Watkins, USN (Ret.), the former Chief of Naval Operations (the Navy's highest uniformed position), was named chairman. Before the Commission expired in 2004, the Commissioners released a final report containing the Commission's findings and recommendations for ocean policy, including the following:

> [I]t is imperative that the nation ratify the United Nations Convention on the Law of the Sea, the preeminent legal framework for addressing international ocean issues. Until that step is taken, the United States will not be able to participate directly in the bodies established under the Convention that make decisions on issues of importance to all coastal and seafaring nations. [See the Commission's Final Report at http://www.oceancommission.gov/documents/full_color_rpt/welcome.html]

5. Do you agree with the Commission's recommendation? Is it preferable for the United States not to ratify the LOS Convention and the 1994 agreement, but continue to select which provisions it will adopt and follow by relying on customary international law, domestic laws, presidential proclamations, and executive orders? What about the Commission's argument that the United States needs to become a full participant in the Convention's decision-making bodies?

6. If a state that was already a party to the LOS Convention refused to approve the 1994 Agreement, would the Convention apply between that state and another state (such as the United States) that ratified the Convention and the Agreement? Would the Convention apply in all respects—as interpreted without the Agreement? (For a possible analogy, see earlier discussion on reservations in Chapter 2.A.4.)

J. ANTARCTICA

> Antarctica is the southernmost continent. Its area of 5.5 million square miles is larger than the United States and Mexico combined, but 93 percent of it is covered with ice an average one-mile thick. Antarctica is colder than any other continent and is a virtual desert, with annual precipitation of less than 3 inches; yet its snow and ice hold [about 70] percent of the world's fresh water. Except for a few bacteria, moss, and insects, the land is lifeless—in contrast with the teeming bird and marine life that includes penguins, seals, whales, fish, and krill (small Antarctic shrimp). [Antarctica Today, Environment, Sept. 1985, at 17.]

For nearly a half century, Antarctica has been a model of international cooperation, though disputes over possible future exploitation of the continent's mineral resources have threatened the harmony. The accomplishments of the past were achieved largely as a result of the Antarctic Treaty System. This system includes the Antarctic Treaty, recommendations adopted pursuant to the Treaty, and separate agreements negotiated under the Treaty.

The Antarctic Treaty was negotiated in 1959 after a year of successful international scientific cooperation by 12 countries. The participants reached this agreement despite the cold war and conflicting land claims. Seven of the countries (Argentina, France, Norway, Britain, Australia, New Zealand, and Chile) claim territorial sovereignty, with some of these claims overlapping. The other five countries (United States, Belgium, Japan, South Africa, and Russia) neither recognize these claims nor assert claims, although the United States and Russia maintain a basis for a claim if they choose to make one. The Treaty suspends all the claims and establishes Antarctica as a zone of peace, demilitarized, denuclearized, and subject to unannounced on-site inspections.

The Antarctic Treaty has a two-tiered status for member states: "contracting status" and "consultative power." Any U.N. member may accede to the Treaty and achieve contracting status. The consultative powers are the decision makers in Antarctica. They include the 12 original signatories and any other state that can show sufficient interest in Antarctica by conducting "substantial scientific research activity." As of February 2011, there were 48 contracting members, 28 of which were also consultative powers.

As the main channel of negotiations for Antarctica, the consultative powers meet regularly to adopt new measures. These resolutions, which require unanimous approval of the consultative powers, provide the flexibility necessary to manage changing interests in Antarctica. The requirement of unanimity assures commitment to the measure by all involved countries. As a result of these meetings, two additional treaties were negotiated: the Convention on the Conservation of Antarctic Marine Living Resources and the Convention for the Conservation of Antarctic Seals.

A problem came to the fore in late 1989, when environmental concerns led two of the consultative powers, France and Australia, to announce that they could no longer support a possible international agreement that would have allowed exploitation, although strictly regulated, of Antarctica's mineral resources.

In 1991, the Antarctic Treaty states approved the Protocol on Environmental Protection to the Antarctic Treaty (the Madrid Protocol). The agreement bans all prospecting, exploration, or commercial exploitation of natural resources on the continent of Antarctica for the next 50 years. As the Department of State explained:

> The new protocol builds on the Antarctic Treaty to provide improved environmental protection measures that can be strengthened in the future as necessary. The protocol sets forth basic principles on the protection of the Antarctic environment, establishes an advisory body, and provides for a system of annexes to incorporate detailed mandatory rules for environmental protection.
>
> The annexes establish legally binding measures on the conservation of Antarctic flora and fauna, waste disposal, marine pollution, and environmental impact assessment procedures that will be subject to compulsory and binding dispute settlement. Future annexes could be added following entry into force of the protocol.
>
> The protocol also prohibits any activities other than scientific research that relate to Antarctic mineral resources. The prohibition can be reviewed at any time after 50 years following entry into force of the protocol.

After 50 years, an amendment to lift the mining ban would have to be approved by three-fourths of the 28 current consultative powers to the Antarctic Treaty. The ban may be lifted prior to the 50-year window only if all the parties to the Treaty agree to do so.

The Protocol went into effect in 1998, after all the consultative parties had ratified it. Obviously, a 50-year moratorium puts a long halt on exploitation of Antarctica.

Notes and Questions

1. Should individual states be allowed to make territorial claims to Antarctica? If so, on what basis? If not, should the continent remain subject to international control? What states should have a voice in the control?

2. Should the mineral and oil resources of Antarctica be considered part of the "common heritage of mankind"? If not, what system for exploitation would be appropriate? If so, how should the states determine whether, and how, exploitation should proceed?

Bibliography

There is an extensive literature on the law of the sea and Antarctica, some excerpted or already cited in this chapter. In addition, for the law of the sea, see Scott G. Borgerson, The National Interest and the Law of the Sea (2009); Law of the Sea (Hugo Caminos ed., 2001); Eric A. Posner & Alan O. Sykes, Economic Foundations of the Law of the Sea, 104 Am. J. Int'l L. 569 (2010). For the latest developments in the law of the sea, see Web site: http://www.un.org/Depts/los.

On Antarctica, see, for example, Christopher C. Joyner, Governing the Frozen Commons: The Antarctic Regime and Environmental Protection (1998); Gillian Triggs & Anna Riddell, Antarctica: Legal and Environmental Challenges for the Future (2007); Protecting the Polar Environment (Davor Vidas ed., 2000). For the latest developments in Antarctica, see the following Web sites: http://www.ats.aq and http://www.asoc.org.

10

International Environmental Law

Traditionally, environmental problems were normally considered to be local or national problems. In recent decades, however, the pace of industrialization and urbanization, together with an enhanced consciousness of the interconnections of the biosphere, have made environmental issues a matter of international concern. As with human rights law, the development of international rules concerning the environment has been hotly contested. Some developing countries regard environmental concerns as problems for the developed world and view environmental regulation as another impediment to their economic development. In addition, environmental regulation may strike at the economic well-being of important industries and states; the United States has cited potential economic harms as a justification for refusing to participate in international agreements aimed at slowing the growth of greenhouse gas emissions that are widely seen as contributing to global climate change. Finally, environmental restrictions can even challenge cultural and social attitudes (as with attempts to ban commercial whaling). In part because the issues are so contentious, there is no general treaty dealing comprehensively with environmental issues. As was the case with human rights, however, concerned organizations and states have used the United Nations as a forum to heighten consciousness of the scope of the problem and to develop "soft law" principles to lay a foundation for the development of customary international law.

In this chapter we start by examining the historical background of international environmental law, learning about the early efforts to deal with international environmental problems. We look at the foundations for the development of customary law, including the key *Trail Smelter* arbitral decision and the work of major international environmental conferences organized by the United Nations.

Most of the law in this area, however, is treaty law. In the last 20 years, several quite revolutionary multilateral treaties have been negotiated that go well beyond previous treaty regimes. These treaties deal with global environmental problems such as ozone depletion, global climate change, biodiversity, and toxic waste disposal on a widely accepted multilateral basis. The creation of these new regimes involves important developments in international law making, such as the participation of NGOs in treaty negotiations and the delegation to international treaty bodies of the power to make decisions that may bind even those states that have not consented to them. We will focus particularly on two treaty regimes dealing with "global commons" problems, ozone depletion and global climate change, and will extract from those regimes the general techniques employed in the international environmental law field. You should of course also think about how these international obligations are implemented domestically, with a view to understanding the most effective techniques to maximize treaty compliance.

A. BACKGROUND AND CUSTOMARY LAW

Many commentators see the 1941 decision in the *Trail Smelter* arbitration between the United States and Canada as a key early source of customary international law in the environmental area.

The history leading up to the arbitration is summarized by the Restatement section 601, Reporters' Note 1:

> The *Trail Smelter* case resulted from injuries caused in the State of Washington by large amounts of sulphur dioxide emitted since 1925 by a smelter plant at Trail, British Columbia. Claims for the injury could not be brought in the courts of British Columbia under a doctrine of nuisance since under the law of that province such claims were "local" and could be brought only in the jurisdiction where the injured property was located. . . . The State of Washington, on the other hand, had no jurisdiction over the polluter, a Canadian company, as it was not engaged in any business in that State. (At that time long-arm jurisdiction was not yet available. . . .) In 1928, the matter was referred to the International Joint Commission established under the Boundary Waters Treaty of 1909, but the Commission's report was rejected by the United States. Further negotiations led to a Convention in 1935 submitting to arbitration two questions: reparation for past injuries and arrangements for the future.

The 1935 Convention established a tribunal empowered to decide: (a) whether the Trail smelter plant had caused damage in Washington and what indemnity should be paid for any such damages; and (2) whether, if the plant had caused damage, "the Trail Smelter should be required to refrain from causing damage in the State of Washington in the future, and if so, to what extent." Article IV of the Convention directed the tribunal to "apply the law and practice followed in dealing with cognate questions in the United States of America as well as international law and practice."

In response to the first question, the Tribunal concluded that the emission of substantial amounts of sulphur dioxide by the smelter plant had caused damage in Washington. The Tribunal determined that "the indemnity to be paid [for this damage] is seventy-eight thousand dollars ($78,000)," plus interest at the rate of six percent per year from the date of the Tribunal's decision until payment was made. The Tribunal then turned to the second question, as shown in the following excerpt.

Trail Smelter Case (United States v. Canada)

Arbitral Tribunal, 1941
III U.N. Rep. Int'l Arb. Awards 1905, 1962-1966 (1950)

Convention for Settlement of Difficulties Arising from Operation of Smelter at Trail, B.C. . . .

The second question under Article III of the Convention is as follows:

In the event of the answer to the first part of the preceding question being in the affirmative, whether the Trail Smelter should be required to refrain from causing damage in the State of Washington in the future and, if so, to what extent? . . .

The first problem which arises is whether the question should be answered on the basis of the law followed in the United States or on the basis of international law. The Tribunal, however, finds that this problem need not be solved here as the law followed in the United States in dealing with the quasi-sovereign rights of the States of the Union, in the matter of air pollution, whilst more definite, is in conformity with the general rules of international law. . . .

As Professor Eagleton puts it (Responsibility of States in International Law, 1928, p. 80): "A State owes at all times a duty to protect other States against injurious acts by individuals from within its jurisdiction." A great number of such general pronouncements by leading authorities concerning the duty of a State to respect other States and their territory have been presented to the Tribunal. These and many others have been carefully examined. International decisions, in various matters, from the Alabama case onward, and also earlier ones, are based on the same general principle, and, indeed, this principle, as such, has not been questioned by Canada. But the real difficulty often arises rather when it comes to determine what . . . is deemed to constitute an injurious act. . . .

No case of air pollution dealt with by an international tribunal has been brought to the attention of the Tribunal nor does the Tribunal know of any such case. The nearest analogy is that of water pollution. But, here also, no decision of an international tribunal has been cited or has been found.

There are, however, as regards both air pollution and water pollution, certain decisions of the Supreme Court of the United States which may legitimately be taken as a guide in this field of international law, for it is reasonable to follow by analogy, in international cases, precedents established by that court in dealing with controversies between States of the Union or with other controversies concerning the quasi-sovereign rights of such States, where no contrary rule prevails in international law and no reason for rejecting such precedents can be adduced from the limitations of sovereignty inherent in the Constitution of the United States.

In the suit of the State of Missouri v. the State of Illinois (200 U.S. 496, 521) concerning the pollution, within the boundaries of Illinois, of the Illinois River, an affluent of the Mississippi flowing into the latter where it forms the boundary between that State and Missouri, an injunction was refused. "Before this court ought to intervene," said the court, "the case should be of serious magnitude, clearly and fully proved, and the principle to be applied should be one which the court is prepared deliberately to maintain against all considerations on the other side." The court found that the practice complained of was general along the shores of the Mississippi River at that time, that it was followed by Missouri itself and that thus a standard was set up by the defendant which the claimant was entitled to invoke. . . .

In the more recent suit of the State of New York against the State of New Jersey (256 U.S. 296, 309), concerning the pollution of New York Bay, the injunction was also refused for lack of proof. . . . "Before this court can be moved to exercise its extraordinary power under the Constitution to control the conduct of one State at the suit of another, the threatened invasion of rights must be of serious magnitude and it must be established by clear and convincing evidence."

What the Supreme Court says there of its power under the Constitution equally applies to the extraordinary power granted this Tribunal under the Convention. What is true between States of the Union is, at least, equally true concerning the relations between the United States and the Dominion of Canada.

In another recent case concerning water pollution (283 U.S. 473), the complainant was successful. The City of New York was enjoined, at the request of the State of New Jersey, to desist, within a reasonable time limit, from the practice of disposing of sewage by dumping it into the sea, a practice which was injurious to the coastal waters of New Jersey in the vicinity of her bathing resorts.

In the matter of air pollution itself, the leading decisions are those of the Supreme Court in the State of Georgia v. Tennessee Copper Company and Ducktown Sulphur, Copper and Iron Company, Limited. . . . [There, the Supreme Court] said (206 U.S. 230):

> . . . [I]t is a fair and reasonable demand on the part of a sovereign that the air over its territory should not be polluted on a great scale by sulphurous acid gas, that the forests on its mountains, be they better or worse, and whatever domestic destruction they may have suffered, should not be further destroyed or threatened by the act of persons beyond its control, that the crops and orchards on its hills should not be endangered from the same source. . . .

The Tribunal, therefore, finds that the above decisions, taken as a whole, constitute an adequate basis for its conclusions, namely, that, under the principles of international law, as well as of the law of the United States, no State has the right to use or permit the use of its territory in such a manner as to cause injury by fumes in or to the territory of another or the properties or persons therein, when the case is of serious consequence and the injury is established by clear and convincing evidence. . . .

Considering the circumstances of the case, the Tribunal holds that the Dominion of Canada is responsible in international law for the conduct of the Trail Smelter. Apart from the undertakings in the Convention, it is, therefore, the duty of the Government of the Dominion of Canada to see to it that this conduct should be in conformity with the obligation of the Dominion under international law as herein determined.

The Tribunal, therefore, answers Question No. 2 as follows: (2) So long as the present conditions in the Columbia River Valley prevail, the Trail Smelter shall be required to refrain from causing any damage through fumes in the state of Washington. . . .

Professor Jacqueline Peel recounts a subsequent stage in the evolution of international environmental law through the development of international "soft law" principles.

Jacqueline Peel, Environmental Protection in the Twenty-First Century: The Role of International Law

The Global Environment: Institutions, Law, and Policy 48, 53-55 (Regina S. Axelrod, Stacy D. VanDeever & David Leonard Downie eds., 3d ed. 2011)

The process of "greening" international law occurred over four periods, responding to particular factors that influenced legal developments. In the early stages of the development of international environmental law, the field lacked a coordinated legal and institutional framework. Attempts to create such a framework came with two global environmental conferences: the 1972 Stockholm Conference and the Rio Earth Summit in 1992. . . .

[Prior to these conference, the] [United Nations] provided a forum for discussing the consequences of technological progress and introduced a period characterized by proliferation of international organizations, engagement with environmental issues, and action to address the causes of pollution and environmental degradation. The relationship between economic development and environmental protection began to be understood. However, the UN Charter did not, and still does not, explicitly address environmental protection or the conservation of natural resources.

Stockholm to Rio. . . . In [the] twenty-year span [beginning with the 1972 Stockholm Conference and concluding with 1992 Earth Summit in Rio,] the UN attempted to put in place a system to address a growing range of environmental issues in a more coordinated and coherent way. A raft of regional and global conventions addressed new issues, and new techniques of regulation were employed.

The 1972 Stockholm Conference, convened by the UN General Assembly, adopted several non-binding instruments, including a Declaration of Twenty-six Guiding Principles. The conference represented the international community's first effort at constructing a coherent strategy for the development of international policy and institutions to protect the environment, and the Stockholm Declaration is generally regarded as the foundation of international environmental law.

One of the most significant contributions of the Stockholm Conference has proved to be the creation of [the United Nations Environment Programme (UNEP)]. UNEP has subsequently been instrumental in the establishment and implementation of important global and regional treaties addressing ozone depletion, trade in hazardous waste, biodiversity, and marine protection.

In addition, the Stockholm Conference catalyzed other global treaties adopted under the UN's auspices, such as the 1982 United Nations Convention on the Law of the Sea (UNCLOS). This treaty establishes a unique, comprehensive framework of global rules for protection of the marine environment and marine living resources, including detailed institutional arrangements and provisions on environmental impact assessment, technology transfer, and liability. These provisions have provided an influential basis for the language and approach of many other environmental agreements.

By 1990, when preparations for Earth Summit formally began, there existed a solid body of rules of international environmental law. States were increasingly subject to limits on the right to allow or carry out activities that harmed the environment. New standards were in place, and a range of techniques sought to implement those standards. Environmental issues, moreover, had begun to intersect with economic matters, especially trade and development lending. But in spite of these relatively impressive achievements, environmental matters remained on the periphery of the international community's agenda and the activities of most institutions.

Earth Summit and Beyond. The 1992 Earth Summit launched a fourth period in the development of international environmental law, requiring that environmental concerns be integrated into all international activities. International environmental law merged with international law in the new field of sustainable development. . . .

Since the Earth Summit, progress in developing and implementing the international concept of sustainable development has not been as promising. The 2002 World Summit on Sustainable Development (WSSD) held in Johannesburg produced a plan of implementation, but in fact it contained few new commitments. This may have been a result of the breadth of the negotiating agenda, which included poverty eradication, agricultural practices, and public health issues. The WSSD's failure to agree on concrete actions for implementing sustainable development suggests that the concept may function best as an overall policy goal, rather than as the basis for prescriptive rules constraining state conduct with respect to the environment.

The 1972 U.N. Stockholm Conference adopted, among other items, the nonbinding Stockholm Declaration of guiding general environmental principles. (The Stockholm Declaration is in the Documentary Supplement.) Of particular relevance to the development of customary international law are Principles 21 and 22:

Stockholm Declaration (1972)

Principle 21

States have, in accordance with the Charter of the United Nations and the principle of international law, the sovereign right to exploit their own resources pursuant to their own environmental policies, and the responsibility to ensure that activities within their jurisdiction or control do not cause damage to the environment of other States or of areas beyond the limits of national jurisdiction.

Principle 22

States shall co-operate to develop further the international law regarding liability and compensation for the victims of pollution and other environmental damage caused by activities within the jurisdiction or control of such states to areas beyond their jurisdiction.

In 1992 the United Nations sponsored the 1992 Rio Conference, formally called the United Nations Conference on Environment and Development (UNCED) and colloquially known as the Earth Summit. The conference adopted a comprehensive set of principles that built on—or perhaps changed—those adopted at Stockholm. Below is the important Rio Principle 2.

Rio Declaration

Principle 2

States have, in accordance with the Charter of the United Nations and the principles of international law, the sovereign right to exploit their own resources pursuant to their own environmental and development policies, and the responsibility to ensure that activities within their jurisdiction or control do not cause damage to the environment of other States or of areas beyond the limits of national jurisdiction.

Earlier, in 1987, the Restatement included the following key section about the then-evolving principles of customary international law in the environmental field. It is notable that the second Restatement of the Foreign Relations Law of the United States, published in 1965, included no express provisions regarding the environment.

Restatement

Section 601. State Obligations with Respect to Environment of Other States and the Common Environment

(1) A state is obligated to take such measures as may be necessary, to the extent practicable under the circumstances, to ensure that activities within its jurisdiction or control

(a) conform to generally accepted international rules and standards for the prevention, reduction, and control of injury to the environment of another state or of areas beyond the limits of national jurisdiction; and

(b) are conducted so as not to cause significant injury to the environment of another state or of areas beyond the limits of national jurisdiction.

(2) A state is responsible to all other states

(a) for any violation of its obligations under Subsection (1)(a), and

(b) for any significant injury, resulting from such violation, to the environment of areas beyond the limits of national jurisdiction.

(3) A state is responsible for any significant injury, resulting from a violation of its obligations under Subsection (1), to the environment of another state or to its property, or to persons or property within that state's territory or under its jurisdiction or control.

Comment:

a. Application of general principles of state responsibility. This Part applies to environmental questions the general principles of international law relating to the responsibility of states for injury to another state or its property or to persons within its territory or their property, or for injury to interests common to all states. . . .

b. "Generally accepted international rules and standards." This phrase is adopted from the law of the sea. The obligation under Subsection (l)(a) refers to both general rules of customary international law (see, e.g., the *Trail Smelter* case . . .) and those derived from international conventions, and from standards adopted by international organizations pursuant to such conventions, that deal with a specific subject, such as oil pollution or radioactive wastes. A state is also obligated to comply with an environmental rule or standard that has been accepted by both it and an injured state, even if that rule or standard has not been generally accepted.

Where an international rule or standard has been violated, any state can object to the violation; where a state has been injured in consequence of such violation, it is entitled to damages or other appropriate relief from the responsible state; where there is a threat of injury, the threatened state, or any state acting on behalf of threatened common interests, is entitled to have the dangerous activity terminated. . . .

d. Conditions of responsibility. A state is responsible under Subsections (2) and (3) for both its own activities and those of individuals or private or public corporations under its jurisdiction. The state may be responsible, for instance, for not enacting necessary legislation, for not enforcing its laws against persons acting in its territory or against its vessels, or for not preventing or terminating an illegal activity, or for not punishing the person responsible for it. In the case of ships flying its flags, a state is responsible for injury due to the state's own defaults under Subsection (1) but is not responsible for injury due to fault of the operators of the ship. In both cases, a state is responsible only if it has not taken "such measures as may be necessary" to comply with applicable international standards and to avoid causing injury outside its territory, as required by Subsection (1). In general, the applicable international rules and standards do not hold a state responsible when it has taken the necessary and practicable measures; some international agreements provide also for responsibility regardless of fault in case of a discharge of highly dangerous (radioactive, toxic, etc.) substances, or an abnormally dangerous activity (e.g., launching of space satellites). . . . In all cases, however, some defenses may be available to the state; e.g., that it had acted pursuant to a binding decision of the Security Council of the United Nations, or that injury was due to the failure of the injured state to exercise reasonable care to avoid the threatened harm. A state is not responsible for injury due to a natural disaster such as an eruption of a volcano, unless such disaster was triggered or aggravated by a human act, such as nuclear explosion in a volcano's vicinity. But a state is responsible if after a natural disaster has occurred it does not take necessary and practicable steps to prevent or reduce injury to other states.

Under Subsections (2)(b) and (3), responsibility of a state for a significant injury entails payment of appropriate damages if the complaining state proves the existence of a causal link between an activity within the jurisdiction of the responsible state and the injury to the complaining state. Determination of responsibility raises special difficulties in cases of long-range pollution where the link between multiple activities in some distant states and the pollution in the injured state might be difficult to prove. Where more than one state contributes to the pollution causing significant injury, the liability will be apportioned among the states, taking into account, where appropriate, the contribution to the injury of the injured state itself.

A state is responsible under this section for environmental harm proximately caused by activity under its own jurisdiction, not for activity by another state. . . .

Under this section, a state is obligated to take all necessary precautionary measures where an activity is contemplated that poses a substantial risk of a significant transfrontier environmental injury; if the activity has already taken place, the state is obligated to take all necessary measures to prevent or reduce pollution beyond its borders. Similarly, where a violation of international environmental rules and standards has already occurred, the violating state is obligated to take promptly all necessary preventive or remedial measures, even if no injury has yet taken place. . . .

Professor Peel provides a more contemporary description of some of the generally accepted norms in the international environmental field. As you read, consider whether these norms represent "soft" or "hard" law.

Jacqueline Peel, Environmental Protection in the Twenty-First Century: The Role of International Law

The Global Environment: Institutions, Law, and Policy 48, 57-62
(Regina S. Axelrod, Stacy D. VanDeever & David Leonard Downie eds., 3d ed. 2011)

International Environmental Law: General Principles

Several general principles of international law have emerged specifically in relation to environmental matters. They are general in the sense that they potentially apply to all members of the international community, span every range of activities, and address the protection of all aspects of the environment. They are principles in the sense that they usually operate as broad, overarching objectives rather than prescriptive rules for state conduct, although if sufficiently well subscribed they may amount to customary international law. In international environmental law, general principles serve an important structural function, providing the common scaffolding upon which more specific rules affecting different environmental resources are built and implemented.

Sovereignty and Responsibility for the Environment

The rules of international environmental law have developed in pursuit of two principles that pull in opposing directions: that states have sovereign rights over their natural resources and that states must not cause damage to the environment. These objectives are reflected in Principle 21 of the Stockholm Declaration and Principle 2 of the Rio Declaration and provide the foundation of international environmental law.

The first element (sovereignty) reflects the preeminent position of states as primary members of the international legal community. It is tempered by the second element (environmental protection), which places limits on the exercise of sovereign rights. In an environmentally interdependent world, activities in one state almost inevitably produce effects in other states or in areas beyond national jurisdiction (such as the high seas).

In the form presented by Principle 21 and Principle 2, the responsibility to prevent damage to the environment of other states or of areas beyond national jurisdiction has been accepted as an obligation by all states. . . . [T]he International Court of Justice has now confirmed that the second element reflects customary international law.[28]

Good Neighborliness and International Cooperation

The principle of "good neighborliness," as enunciated in Article 74 of the UN Charter, concerning social, economic, and commercial matters, has been extended to environmental matters by rules promoting international cooperation. It applies particularly to activities carried out in one state that might have adverse effects on the environment of another state or in areas beyond national jurisdiction. The commitment to environmental cooperation is reflected in many international agreements and is supported by state practice. . . . Specifically, the obligation can require information sharing, notification, consultation or participation rights in certain decisions, the conduct of environmental impact assessments, and cooperative emergency procedures, particularly where activities might be ultrahazardous. The construction of nuclear power plants on borders is an example of an area where cooperative obligations are reasonably well developed. . . .

Sustainable Development

The International Court of justice in the Gabcikovo-Nagymaros case described this principle as expressing the "need to reconcile economic development with protection of the environment." The ideas underlying the concept of "sustainable development" have a long history in international law, dating back at least to the Pacific Fur Seal arbitration in 1893. The concept came of age with Earth Summit and the international agreements that it spawned. It now seems that the principle has acquired harder legal edge. For instance, in 2005 an arbitral tribunal of the Permanent Court of Arbitration in the Iron Rhine Railway case declared:

> Environmental law and the law on development stand not as alternatives but as mutually reinforcing, integral concepts, which require that where development may cause significant harm to the environment there is a duty to prevent, or at least mitigate, such harm. . . . This duty, in the opinion of the Tribunal, has now become a principle of general international law.[33]

What sustainable development means in international law today is a more complicated matter. Where it has been used, it appears to refer to at least four separate but related objectives that, taken together, might constitute the legal elements of the concept of sustainable development. . . . First, as invoked in some agreements such as the [U.N. Framework Convention on Climate Change], it refers to the commitment to preserve natural resources for the benefit of present and future generations (the principles of intragenerational and intergenerational equity). Second, in other agreements, sustainable development refers to

28. "Legality of the Threat or Use of Nuclear Weapons," para. 29. See also "Case Concerning the Gabcikovo-Nagymaros Project" (Hungary/Slovakia), *ICJ Reports* (1997), paras. 53 and 112.

33. "The Iron Rhine (Ijzeren Rijn) Arbitration (Belgium-Netherlands)," *Permanent Court of Arbitration Award Series* (Cambridge, Cambridge University Press, 2005), para. 59.

appropriate standards for the exploitation of natural resources like fisheries based upon sustainable harvest or wise use (the principle of conservation of resources). Third, yet other agreements require an equitable use of natural resources such as international watercourses, suggesting that a state must consider the needs of other states and people (the equitable use principle). A fourth category of agreements requires that environmental considerations be integrated with economic and other development plans, programs, and projects, and that development needs be taken into account in applying environmental objectives (the integration principle).

Common but Differentiated Responsibility

This principle has emerged from applying the broader principle of equity in general international law and recognizing that the special needs of developing countries must be considered if these countries are to be encouraged to participate in global environmental agreements. The principle includes two important elements. First, states have a common responsibility to protect certain environmental resources. Second, it is necessary to take account of differing circumstances, particularly in relation to each state's contribution to causing a particular environmental problem and its ability to respond to the threat.

Application of the principle of common but differentiated responsibility has important, practical consequences. It leads to the adoption and implementation of environmental standards that impose different commitments for states, and it provides a basis for providing financial and technical assistance to developing countries and [least-developed countries] to assist them in implementing their commitments. . . .

Precautionary Principle

This principle emerged in international legal instruments only in the mid-1980s, although it had previously been relied upon in some domestic legal systems. The core of this legal principle, which some believe reflects customary international law, is reflected in Principle 15 of the Rio Declaration, one part of which provides that "[w]here there are threats of serious or irreversible damage, lack of full scientific certainty shall not be used as a reason for postponing cost-effective measures to prevent environmental degradation." The precautionary principle aims to provide guidance to states and the international community in the development of international environmental law and policy in the face of scientific uncertainty and is, potentially, the most radical of environmental principles. Some invoke it to justify preemptive international legal measures to address potentially catastrophic environmental threats such as climate change. Opponents, however, have decried the principle, arguing that it promotes overregulation of a range of human activities.

Notwithstanding the controversy, the principle has been endorsed in a large number of international agreements. . . .

International judicial acceptance of the precautionary principle has been more cautious. The principle was not mentioned in the majority decision in the Gabcikovo-Nagymaros case [before the International Court of Justice], despite considerable scientific uncertainty over the environmental impact of the project. Likewise, the Appellate Body of the [World Trade Organization], in the Beef Hormones and Apple cases, declined to take a position on whether the principle amounts to customary international law, commenting that the international status of the principle is "less than clear." The [International Tribunal for the Law of the Sea] was more forthcoming in the Southern Bluefin Tuna case, citing "prudence and caution" as a basis for its decision requiring Japan to cease an experimental fishing program despite scientific uncertainty as to the impacts of fishing on stocks of the migratory tuna species.

Polluter Pays Principle

This principle states that the costs of pollution should be borne by those responsible for causing the pollution. The precise meaning, international legal status, and effect of the principle remain open to question because international practice based upon the principle is limited. It is doubtful whether it has achieved the status of a generally applicable rule of international law, except perhaps in relation to states in the [European Union (EU], the UN Economic Commission for Europe (UNECE), and the [Organisation of Economic Cooperation and Development (OECD)]. It has nevertheless attracted broad support and underlies rules on civil and state liability for environmental damage . . . and on the permissibility of state subsidies. Developed countries increasingly are acknowledging the "responsibility that they bear in the international pursuit of sustainable development in view of the pressures their societies place on the global environment," as well as the financial and other consequences that flow from this acknowledgment. Supporting instruments include Principle 16 of the Rio Declaration, OECD Council Recommendations, the Treaty of Rome (as amended) and related instrument, and the 1992 agreement establishing the European Economic Area.

Notes and Questions

1. On what basis did the U.S.-Canada arbitral tribunal in the *Trail Smelter* case rely on United States Supreme Court cases as precedential support for its decision? In light of the authorities the tribunal cited, how persuasive is the *Trail Smelter* decision for the assertion of a rule of customary international law?

2. Assuming that Principles 21 and 22 of the Stockholm Declaration excerpted above have become customary international law, what is the exact obligation of a state under these principles? Does the lack of specificity in the Stockholm Principles undermine their practical effect when states must make choices about the trade-offs between development and environmental protection in particular cases?

3. Consider the provisions of Section 601 of the Restatement. Does the formulation there closely follow the Stockholm principles? What about the Restatement's requirement for "significant injury"? Does the "to the extent practicable under the circumstances" qualification in the Restatement reflect a substantive difference from the requirements of the Stockholm Principles?

4. In contrast to Principle 21 of the Stockholm Declaration, Rio Principle 2 includes the additional phrase that states may take their "developmental" policies

into account in balancing environmental and economic concerns. Could this be interpreted as a modification of the *Trail Smelter* result and Stockholm Principle 21? One scholar suggests that

> Rio Principle 2 restates Stockholm Principle 21 with an embellishment that expands [the clause in Principle 21 affirming states' "sovereign right to exploit their own resources"] by authorizing states "to exploit their own resources pursuant to their own environmental and developmental policies."
>
> The addition of the phrase "and developmental" might be interpreted as disrupting and skewing the already delicate balance between the twin clauses juxtaposed in Stockholm Principle 21, and in a manner inconsistent with at least some post-Stockholm sources. Alternatively, one observer commented that the drafters of Rio Principle 2 "simply updated" the Stockholm formulation by clarifying rights of states that are implicit in the earlier text and, indeed, in the international legal regime. . . .
>
> However this modification might be interpreted, the Rio Declaration clearly altered the text of the earlier principle. . . . Whatever the legal effect of this change, given the widespread acceptance and reaffirmance of Principle 21 and, indeed, the numerous documents that have recited it verbatim in the years following the Stockholm Declaration, the only plausible motivation for this modification is a purposeful shift on the part of the drafters of the Rio Declaration in the direction of the development side of the environment/development debate. [David A. Wirth, The Rio Declaration on Environment and Development: Two Steps Forward and One Back, or Vice Versa?, 29 Ga. L. Rev. 599, 621-624 (1995).]

If the substance of Rio Principle 2 differs from that of Stockholm Principle 21, would the adoption of the Rio declaration be sufficient to change customary international law? What is required for the formation and change of customary international law? What political forces might be reflected in the language change in the Rio principle?

5. As noted in the excerpt by Professor Peel, the International Court of Justice in the *Gabcikovo-Nagymaros* case stressed "the great significance that it attaches to respect for the environment, not only for States but also for the whole of mankind." The ICJ continued that:

> The Court is mindful that, in the field of environmental protection, vigilance and prevention are required on account of the often irreversible character of damage to the environment and of the limitations inherent in the very mechanism of reparation of this type of damage.
>
> Throughout the ages, mankind has, for economic and other reasons, constantly interfered with nature. In the past, this was often done without consideration of the effects upon the environment. Owing to new scientific insights and to a growing awareness of the risks for mankind — for present and future generations — of pursuit of such interventions at an unconsidered and unabated pace, new norms and standards have been developed, set forth in a great number of instruments during the last two decades. Such new norms have to be taken into consideration, and such new standards given proper weight, not only when States contemplate new activities but also when continuing with activities begun in the past. This need to reconcile economic development with protection of the environment is aptly expressed in the concept of sustainable development. [Gabcikovo-Nagymaros Project (Hungary v. Slovakia), 1997 I.C.J. 7, 41, 78 (Sept. 25).]

6. The ICJ again had the opportunity to address international environmental law principles — including sustainable development, the need for environmental impact assessments, and the precautionary principle — in a suit brought by Argentina over Uruguay's plans to build large pulp mills on the River Uruguay, where it serves as a border between the two countries. The Court's 2010 judgment turned on the interpretation of a bilateral treaty between Argentina and Uruguay creating a cooperative regime for regulating uses of the river. In interpreting that treaty, however, the Court took account of relevant rules of international law. The Court observed that the parties, in utilizing the river, "should allow for sustainable development which takes account of 'the need to safeguard the continued conservation of the river environment and the rights of economic development of the riparian States.'" Pulp Mills on the River Uruguay (Argentina v. Uruguay), Judgment, ¶75 (April 20, 2010), reprinted in 49 I.L.M. 1123 (2010). According to the Court's interpretation, the treaty regulating utilization of the river required the parties "to strike a balance between the use of the waters and the protection of the river consistent with the objective of sustainable development." Id. ¶177. The Court also indicated that a provision in the treaty requiring the parties to adopt measures to prevent pollution of the river "has to be interpreted in accordance with a practice, which in recent years has gained so much acceptance among States that it may now be considered a requirement under general international law to undertake an environmental impact assessment where there is a risk that the proposed industrial activity may have a significant adverse impact in a transboundary context, in particular, on a shared resource." Id. ¶204.

Nevertheless, the Court concluded that Argentina had failed to provide "conclusive evidence" to show that Uruguay's conduct had caused the pollution Argentina claimed it had. Id. ¶265. Notable in this regard was the Court's statement that "while a precautionary approach may be relevant in the interpretation and application of the provisions of the [treaty], it does not follow that it operates as a reversal of the burden of proof." Id. ¶164.

How is the Court's position on the burden of proof consistent with the precautionary principle described by Professor Peel?

7. Is the kind of damage involved in the *Trial Smelter* arbitration normally compensable under domestic law? Should domestic law, including nuisance law and remedies, be used in the development of customary international law?

8. What remedies besides monetary compensation should be available when there are international environmental harms? What were the remedies provided in *Trail Smelter*? What entity might impose and administer any continuing remedies?

9. What are the weaknesses of customary international environmental law? What are the strengths?

10. In Beanal v. Freeport-McMoran, 197 F.3d 161 (5th Cir. 1999), an Indonesian claimant sued U.S. mining companies under the Alien Tort Statute and the Torture Victim Protection Act for a variety of alleged human rights violations, including environmental abuses, in its operation of an open pit copper, gold, and silver mine situated in Irian Jaya, Indonesia. (Both laws are discussed in Chapter 3.) Analyzing the sources relied on by the plaintiffs, including the specific language of the Rio Declaration's Principle 2, the court concluded that the "sources of international law cited by Beanal and the amici merely refer to a general sense of environmental responsibility and state abstract rights and liberties devoid of

articulable or discernable standards and regulations to identify practices that constitute international environmental abuses or torts." 197 F.3d at 167. In Flores v. Southern Peru Copper Corp., 414 F.3d 233 (2d Cir. 2003), another Alien Tort Statute case, the plaintiffs claimed that the defendant's copper mining, refining, and smelting operations had caused severe lung disease. In rejecting the claims, the court cited an earlier district court judgment that the Stockholm principles do not constitute customary international law "because they 'do not set forth any specific prescriptions, but rather refer only in a general sense to the responsibility of nations,' . . ." Id. at 240. The court also rejected the plaintiffs' reliance on the "broad, aspirational principles regarding environmental protection and sustainable development" in the Rio Declaration. The Court found that the Declaration "includes no language indicating that the States joining in the Declaration intended to be legally bound by it," and that the Declaration accordingly does "not provide reliable evidence of customary international law." Id. at 263.

In a significant decision involving international environmental claims decided after the Supreme Court's decision in Sosa v. Alvarez Machain, 542 U.S. 692 (2004), which interpreted the Alien Tort Statute, a federal district court in Sarei v. Rio Tinto, 650 F. Supp.2d 1004 (C.D. Cal. 2009) considered claims that a mining company violated the rights to life and health of the indigenous population of Papua New Guinea by emitting toxic wastes that contaminated and destroyed the rivers and land. The court concluded that the international norms on which the plaintiffs' environmental destruction claims were based "have not, as yet, achieved the status of 'universal concern.' " Id. at 1025.

11. Plaintiffs have had more success litigating environmental claims before the European Court of Human Rights, which is discussed in Chapter 8.B.9. For instance, a 2009 judgment ruled in favor of a man and his son who alleged that gold-mining operations carried out by an Australian mining company in Romania had endangered the son's life by aggravating his asthma in violation of Article 8 of the European Convention on Human Rights. Article 8 provides that "[e]veryone has the right to respect for his private and family life, his home and his correspondence." The Court observed that pollution could interfere with a person's private and family life by harming his or her well-being. It concluded that Romania was obligated to undertake an assessment of the health risks posed by the mining operations, for which the government has issued a permit, and to adopt suitable measures capable of protecting the rights of individuals to respect for their private lives and homes, "and more generally their right to enjoy a healthy and protected environment." Tătar v. Romania, App. No. 67021/01, at ¶112 (Eur. Ct. H.R., Jan. 27, 2009) (final version issued July 6, 2009).* Although the Court relied largely on provisions of Romanian law in assessing the adequacy of the measures taken by the Romanian government, it also relied heavily on international environmental norms and specifically noted that the precautionary principle has become binding European law. Id. at ¶69(h).**

*The Court's judgment, published in French only at the time of publication of this book, states that Romania failed to protect "le droits de intéressés au respect de leur vie privée et de leur domicile et, plus généralement, à la jouissance d'un environnement sain et protégé."

**The original French text notes that the incorporation of a reference to "le principe de précaution" in the Maastricht Treaty "marque, au niveau européen, l'évolution du principe d'une conception philosophique vers une norme juridique."

B. TREATY LAW: GLOBAL APPROACHES

The following materials illustrate the increasingly important role of treaties in the development of international environmental law since the 1972 Stockholm Conference. States have concluded bilateral and multilateral environmental agreements (both regional and global in scope) to address or regulate such varied problems as pollutants causing transboundary acid rain, the disposal of hazardous chemicals, dumping of waste in the oceans, pollution of international watercourses, and the preservation of biodiversity and protection of endangered species. The materials that follow set the stage by summarizing some of the challenges to international efforts to regulate transnational environmental problems. We next examine some common features of multilateral environmental agreements (MEAs), features that are in part designed to address these challenges. The materials then focus in particular on treaty regimes designed to deal with two major international problems, ozone depletion and global climate change. Considerable progress has been made internationally in limiting ozone depletion, while international efforts to address global climate change have met with less success.

1. Challenges in Developing International Environmental Law

Transnational environmental problems involve a number of special characteristics that affect efforts to develop international legal rules in the field. Professors Bodansky, Brunnée, and Hey highlight some of these challenges:

> *International environmental problems are caused primarily by private conduct.* International law primarily addresses questions of governmental conduct: claiming territory, using force against other states, suppressing human rights, exercising jurisdiction, and so forth. . . . [M]ost pollution and natural resource depletion result from private activities. Consider climate change, for example. Emissions of carbon dioxide and other "greenhouse gasses" result from generating and consuming electricity, driving cars, manufacturing products, growing food, and cutting trees. . . .
>
> The challenge for international environmental law is to develop effective ways of regulating these private activities. Traditionally, international law has governed the conduct of states, not individuals. Thus, in order to control private activities, it must either do so at one step removed, by requiring states to regulate or otherwise influence the behavior of the relevant non-state actors within their borders, or it must find ways to engage private actors more directly. . . .
>
> *International environmental problems involve significant scientific uncertainties.* Although international environmental disputes are often attributable to differences in interests and values among states, they are complicated by uncertainties concerning the facts. Many modern environmental problems have effects that are widely dispersed and long term, with long latency periods. Given the complexity of the physical, economic, and social pressures involved, we often do not know for sure how serious a problem is, what its causes are, how expensive it will be to address, whether it is even a problem at all, and, if it is, whether it is still possible to address. Is the build-up of greenhouse gases in the atmosphere causing global warming, and, if so, how much warming will occur and with what effects? Do genetically modified organisms post a danger to other species and to human health? Are human fertility rates declining, and, if so, to what extent is this decline attributable to persistent organic pollutants?

> On these and many other questions, scientists cannot provide conclusive answers. . . . Decisions [on policy choices] must be made in the face of uncertainty. [Daniel Bodansky, Jutta Brunnée & Ellen Hey, International Environmental Law: Mapping the Field, in The Oxford Handbook of International Environmental Law 1, 6-7 (2007).]

Professor Bodansky in the following excerpt explores additional challenges related to the divergent values and interests of states that can impede cooperation in the international environmental law area.

Daniel Bodansky, The Art and Craft of International Environmental Law

141-145 (2010)

. . . [V]alue differences sometimes concern priorities. Traditionally, developing countries have argued that they cannot devote significant resources to environmental problems, given the multitude of other problems that they face — poverty, infant mortality, and starvation, to name a few. Development, they argue, must take priority over the environment. As the Algerian president reportedly put it in the 1970s, "[I]f improving the environment means less bread for Algerians then I am against it." Developing country views have evolved considerably since then, but they still focus more on economic development than on environmental protection. . . .

Future problems raise a different kind of question [about values]: How should we value the future as compared to the present? If a problem is sufficiently far off, is it really something we need to worry about? If the dangers of climate change, for example, won't manifest themselves for fifty or a hundred years, or longer, wouldn't it make sense to focus on more immediate problems instead?. . . .

Although differences of fact and value are important, differences of interest represent perhaps the most significant obstacle to international environmental cooperation. . . .

Even states with similar scientific and normative views . . . can see their interests very differently based on different national circumstances. States with significant coal or oil resources have different interests with respect to climate change than low-lying island states, which are vulnerable to sea-level rise. Upstream states have different interests from downstream states. States with large areas of tropical forests such as Brazil have different interests from states without forests.

These cases all involve . . . incentive problems. . . . Like individuals, states have no incentive to stop polluting or to protect natural resources, to the extent that the costs and benefits affect other states — that is, to the extent that these costs and benefits represent externalities. The polluting state has different interests from those of the victim state, and states with valuable natural resources have different interests from those of the global community. That is why, in international negotiations, victim states tend to be "pushers," polluting states "draggers," and states that are both polluters and victims, "intermediaries."

. . . [E]ven when states have symmetric interests, cooperation can prove difficult because states' individual interests differ from their collective interest. Collectively, states have an interest in stopping pollution to the extent that the global benefits exceed the costs. As the tragedy of the commons teaches us, however, each individual state nevertheless has an interest in continuing to pollute, if most of the damages from its pollution are externalized. . . . [And states may have difficulty imposing effective sanctions against free riders and violators. If the benefits of the regime are public goods — a slowing of global warming, for example — states cannot punish a violator by excluding it from these benefits. Unless some other sanction can be found, states have an incentive to free ride, inasmuch as they can get the benefits of the agreement regardless of whether they participate or comply.]

. . . Other obstacles to cooperation include distribution issues, strategic factors, and domestic politics.

In some cases, a state may reject an agreement that is in its interest because the agreement seems unfair. Although agreement would provide a collective gain, it founders over how to distribute that gain. In upstream-downstream situations, for example, agreement might require the victim to pay the polluter to stop polluting. This outcome would leave both sides better off, as long as the victim received a bigger benefit from the reduced pollution than the payment needed to get the polluter to stop. Nevertheless, the victim state might still reject such a deal, arguing that, as the injured party, it should not be the one that ends up paying, since that would be unfair. . . .

. . . The importance of equity . . . was brought home to me when I worked in the Clinton Administration on the climate change issue. . . . [T]he Clinton Administration made a major effort to persuade middle income countries to accept emission targets, so that Kyoto would have a wider scope. Our pitch to developing countries was that, through the emission trading system, developing countries would actually come out ahead. . . . Developing countries consistently rejected our arguments . . . [in part because of] their sense of equity: since they were not responsible for creating the climate change problem and had less capacity to respond, they felt they should not be expected to assume any target. . . .

Domestic politics can [also] pose [an] obstacle to agreement. Even when an agreement serves a state's national interests, the state may reject it because of opposition by politically powerful groups. . . .

Public choice theory predicts that such results should be common in environmental law. In the political marketplace, policies tend to lose out when their costs are concentrated and their benefits diffuse. The relatively small number of actors who face high costs have a strong incentive to organize against a policy, whereas the people who benefit, though more numerous, each gain too little to have a strong incentive to act.

Notes and Questions

1. Consider some of the soft law or customary international law environmental principles discussed in the previous section. How do those rules take into account the special characteristics of international environmental problems discussed in the two excerpts above? For instance, does the principle of sustainable development take into account that environmental harm is generated largely by private activity? How do the Restatement rules address the problem of scientific uncertainty?

2. Bear in mind these special characteristics of international environmental problems as you study the following materials on multilateral environmental treaty regimes. How do the treaties attempt to address these challenges? Do they succeed?

2. *Multilateral Environmental Agreements*

As two commentators have observed, the Stockholm Conference on the Human Environment "set off an unprecedented development of new international environmental treaties. Before 1972, only a dozen international treaties with relevance to the environment were in force; twenty-five years later more than a thousand such instruments could be counted." Michael G. Faure & Jürgen Lefevere, Compliance with Global Environmental Policy, in The Global Environment: Institutions, Law, and Policy 172 (Regina S. Axelrod, Stacy D. VanDeever & David Leonard Downie eds., 3d ed. 2011). Professors Shelton and Kiss describe some of the common features of these treaties:

Alexandre Kiss & Dinah Shelton, International Environmental Law

70-84 (3d ed. 2004)

The geographic coverage of environmental treaties varies widely. . . . In fact, a broad global framework of international law has been established for the four "traditional" sectors of the environment: water, soil, atmosphere and biological diversity. . . .

Despite their wide variety in subject matter and geographic scope, environmental treaties have common characteristics, use similar legal techniques, and often are interrelated. The main features they share are: (1) an absence of reciprocity of obligations, (2) interrelated or cross-referenced provisions from one instrument to another, (3) framework agreements, (4) frequent interim application, (5) the creation of new institutions or the utilization of already existing ones to promote continuous cooperation, (6) innovative compliance and non-compliance procedures, and (7) simplified means of modification and amendment.

1. The Nature of Obligations

Each international environmental agreement contains legally binding rules, although such engagements may differ considerably from most traditional norms, for in many treaties there are few precise duties created. Instead, the provisions indicate areas of cooperation and, in some cases, the means states parties should adopt to achieve the goals of the treaty. Environmental treaties often invade traditional spheres of government activities by requiring states to limit pollution emissions, establish licensing systems, regulate and monitor waste disposal, control the export and import of endangered species and hazardous products, and enact penal legislation. Such treaties usually set forth the obligations in general terms, however, and require completion through internal legislative or executive action. For countries like the United States that distinguish between self-executing and non-self-executing treaties — those capable of immediate judicial application and those that require implementing measures — such treaties fall within the latter category. . . .

The principle of reciprocity . . . seeks a legal equilibrium between the obligations accepted by one state and the advantages it obtains from the other contracting party or parties. . . .

Rules of international environmental law, adopted in the common interest of humanity, generally do not bring immediate advantages to contracting states when their objective is to protect species of wild plant and animal life, the oceans, the air, the soil, and the countryside. Even treaties concluded among a small number of states generally lack reciprocity. . . .

Describing these developments, some international jurists have posited the existence in international law of "treaty-laws," distinguished from "treaty-contracts." The distinction may have meaning in the sense that "treaty-laws" are concluded in the common interest of humanity, while "treaty-contracts" are based on the principle of reciprocity. . . .

International environmental obligations also differ from most international law in calling upon the state to regulate the behavior of non-state actors which are the source of most harm to the environment. The obligations must be implemented in national law to control non-state actors within the state's territory and jurisdiction. . . .

The concept of common but differentiated responsibility has been incorporated into all global environmental conventions adopted since the end of the 1980s. . . . [The 1992 UN Framework Convention on Climate Change] illustrates the differentiation by making a distinction between three categories of states:

a. The developed country parties are to take the lead in combating climate change and the adverse effects thereof. They shall provide new and additional financial resources to meet the agreed full costs incurred by developing country parties in complying with their obligations. They shall also assist the developing country parties that are particularly vulnerable to the effects of climate change in meeting costs of adaptation to those adverse effects. They shall facilitate the transfer of environmentally sound technology and know-how to developing countries.
b. Formerly communist countries of Central and Eastern Europe are considered to be undergoing a process of political and economic transition and are granted some flexibility to enhance their ability to address climate change.
c. Developing countries are to receive financial assistance and benefit from the transfer of technology. They have more time to make their initial communication on the measures they have taken to implement the convention and the least-developed parties may make their reports at their discretion. . . .

Two remaining characteristics of international environmental agreements are significant. The first is the deliberate reference to non-party states in many such treaties. To the extent that international environmental agreements impact international trade, it is necessary to include measures to discourage free-riders or provide incentives to compliance. [The Convention on the International Trade in Endangered Species] and the Montreal Protocol [on the Protection of the Ozone Layer], for example, seek to influence the behavior of non-parties by requiring parties to restrict imports from them unless they effectively comply with the provisions of the agreement. . . .

Finally, many environmental agreements . . . prohibit reservations, requiring states to accept them in their entirety. . . . [T]he absence of reservations may reflect the give and take of a multilateral negotiating process where decisions are based upon consensus and bargains. The process would unravel if states could pick and choose their obligations after the fact.

2. Framework Agreements

Since the beginning of the 1970s an increasing number of international treaties have been adopted by procedures that include several phases. The technique of "framework conventions" means that a convention of general scope is adopted, proclaiming the basic principles on which consent can be achieved. The parties foresee the elaboration of additional protocols containing more detailed obligations. . . .

Framework agreements have the advantage that a consensus on basic principles and the need for action which will follow generally is easier to reach than on the details of the action itself, which often have a technical character. Further negotiations can elucidate these measures with the cooperation of scientists, representatives of economic interests, and civil society. New elements can be incorporated as well, as exemplified by the Montreal Protocol on the Protection of the Ozone Layer which reflects the discovery of the ozone "hole" above Antarctica after the Vienna Convention was adopted. Such changes in knowledge and even basic concepts make framework treaties particularly well-adapted to the needs of environmental protection.

3. Interim Application

Several international environmental agreements respond to urgent problems that must be confronted in the shortest possible time. Taking this into account, negotiating states have adopted the technique of approving interim application of the agreements pending their entry into force. . . .

4. Mechanisms and Organs of Cooperation

The previous considerations inevitably lead to a need for permanent international organs of cooperation among states parties to environmental treaties. . . . [T]he importance of acquiring new knowledge, disseminating information and observing the biosphere makes international cooperation . . . necessary and, clearly, permanent. It is not surprising, therefore, that most environmental protection treaties contain institutional provisions, granting varied powers and competence to international organs. Sometimes new functions are confided to organs of already-existing international organizations. . . .

Authority may also be confided to new organizations created by environmental treaties to serve the special needs of the agreement, particularly in the field of regional or sub-regional cooperation. Throughout the world, dozens of Conferences of the Parties (COPs) or international commissions have been created to assure permanent cooperation among contracting parties to treaties concerning, *e.g.*, inland waters, the oceans, and the protection of wildlife. As a general rule these organizations are lightly structured; many do not have permanent secretariats or the secretariat function is handled by another existing inter-governmental or non-governmental organization.

5. Compliance Procedures

. . . International conventions seeking to proclaim and establish the common interest of humanity, distinguished by the restricted role of reciprocity in their provisions, pose particular problems of enforcement. In an international society without institutional strength, bilateral reciprocity has provided an essential guarantee of respect for obligations undertaken, due to the implicit threat of sanctions imposed in the event obligations are breached. . . . [In contrast,] norms against pollution of the sea or the air cannot be enforced by reciprocal pollution. Enforcement must be by other means, especially by international control mechanisms that supervise the implementation of international environmental law by states.

Recent experience shows that compliance with multilateral environmental agreements and even non-binding norms is best ensured at the international level when there is institutional support. Many international environmental agreements create their own institutional framework. . . . Over time, the states drafting international environmental agreements have created a new widely-used pattern of institutions. . . .

6. Adaptation and Evolution of Obligations

One of the principal needs of environmental law, both internal and international, is to adapt to changes in conditions or knowledge altering the requirements of environmental protection. The state of the environment may change rapidly. . . .

Knowledge of the biosphere, its deterioration, renewal and the effects of pollution, evolves quickly. Most authorities viewed atmospheric pollution as a local phenomenon until, during the 1970s, acidity in the lakes of Scandinavia showed that long-range damage could occur. After 1980, the destruction of forests demonstrated that sulfur dioxide (SO_2) was not the only agent responsible for atmospheric pollution, because nitrogen oxide (NO_2) emitted from automobiles may also play a major role in causing damage. Subsequently, discovery that the stratospheric ozone layer is damaged added yet another element to the problem of protecting the atmosphere from pollution. Thus, international action to address one problem necessarily evolved and changed directions in the space of a dozen years.

. . . In addition to using the technique of framework conventions, states have developed an effective response [to the need for evolution] by drafting treaties that establish stable general obligations but also add flexible provisions, especially those prescribing technical norms. The latter may designate the specific products that cannot be dumped or discharged in a given area or may identify the endangered species needing additional protection. The general obligations are set forth in the treaty, which remains stable, while the detailed listing of products or species is reserved to annexes that can be modified easily without amending the principal treaty. The annexes form an integral part of the treaty and thus the modification procedure must be expressly included in the treaty's provisions.

Agreements of this type include the 1979 Bern Convention on the Conservation of European Wildlife and Natural Habitats. . . . [A]ny amendment [to the principal Convention] must be accepted by all the contracting parties. . . . In contrast, the treaty's annexes listing protected species may be modified pursuant to [a] procedure . . . which allows changes to be proposed by a permanent Committee established by the Convention. Proposals are communicated to the contracting parties and at the expiration of three months each modification enters into force for all states that have not filed objections.

Other treaties establish different flexible procedures. . . . These treaties thus establish a bifurcated modification process, in which the structural parts of the treaties are subject to traditional, rather difficult, amendment processes, while the technical details may be altered quickly and less formally. . . .

Some of the same features that make it difficult to conclude multilateral environmental agreements in the first place — that they frequently regulate the behavior of nonstate actors, depend on the collection and analysis of complex scientific data, and do not rest on principles of reciprocity — also give rise to a special set of compliance concerns. The next excerpt highlights how environment treaties attempt to address these challenges.

Michael G. Faure & Jürgen Lefevere, Compliance with Global Environmental Policy

The Global Environment: Institutions, Law, and Policy 172, 178-179, 182, 184-186, 188 (Regina S. Axelrod, Stacy D. VanDeever & David Leonard Downie eds., 3d ed. 2011)

Reporting and Information

The likelihood of compliance [with international environmental treaties] will also depend upon informational issues. Information plays an important role at several stages. First, accurate information on the environmental risks increases the chances of adopting a treaty on the specific subject and also the likelihood of compliance. Second, information, through monitoring or reporting systems, serves to increase the transparency of the implementation and compliance records of states. . . .

Transparency can be achieved through an effective compliance information system that is laid down in the treaty. To a large extent, treaties rely on self-reporting by states. . . . Although reporting procedures can be found in most environmental treaties, they are often vaguely formulated, and the reports are poorly drafted. Hence the reporting procedure is often criticized for its "weak" character and the absence of sanctions in case of noncompliance with the reporting requirements. . . .

The problems with reporting procedures have led to the development of *compliance information systems.* These systems contain elaborate procedures for the provision of information by Member States, the possible review of this information by independent experts, and the availability of this information to the general public. The development of a more elaborate and transparent system for the provision of information on the compliance of Member States automatically increases those states' accountability. . . .

This increased attention to information systems and reporting procedures is part of the transformation from an enforcement to a managerial approach to compliance. Traditionally, the incentives for states to report their own noncompliance were low, since such an admission could only lead to "bad news," such as the imposition of sanctions. The situation totally changes, however, when noncompliance is not necessarily considered as the intentional act of a sovereign state, but may be due, for example, to incapacity. In that case, reporting the problem may lead the other partners in the regime to look for remedies to overcome the difficulty, for example, through a transfer of finances or technology. In this managerial approach, reporting noncompliance should not be threatening but may well be in the state's interest. . . . Thus, the reporting of noncompliance under the Montreal Protocol leads the Implementation Committee to investigate the possibilities of financial and technical assistance instead of threatening with traditional sanctions. . . .

Responses to Noncompliance

. . . [T]raditional treaty mechanisms for noncompliance were restricted to adversarial dispute settlement procedures. These procedures, used generally under international environmental law, mostly involve a sequence of diplomatic and legal means of dispute settlement. [These procedures sometimes provide ultimately for] recourse to legal means of dispute settlement, either arbitration or the International Court of Justice. . . .

The number of cases brought under [these traditional] dispute settlement proceedings is still very limited, especially considering the compliance problems with most environmental treaties. . . . [T]raditional dispute settlement procedures . . . are . . . considered less effective and less appropriate in environmental treaties [than in other fields]. The result of noncompliance with environmental treaties is often damage to the global commons in general, affecting all states, rather than one or several well-identifiable parties.

The ineffectiveness of dispute settlement proceedings in international environmental agreements has led to the development of a new system for responding to noncompliance, called noncompliance procedures (NCPs). Such procedures, rather than "punishing" noncompliance, are aimed at finding ways to facilitate compliance by the state that is in breach of its obligations. They provide a political framework for "amicable" responses to noncompliance that cannot be considered "wrongful." This tendency to use NCPs reflects the new managerial approach, which no longer assumes that noncompliance is the result of a willful desire to violate.

One of the consequences of shifting from an adversarial approach to a more managerial approach is that sanctions play only a minor role in the noncompliance response system. . . . Sanctions against states party to an international treaty, including expulsion or suspension of rights and privileges, are . . . not considered an effective response in the case of noncompliance with an environmental treaty, since one of the aims of these treaties is to achieve global membership. . . .

Toward Comprehensive Noncompliance Response Systems

. . . Increasingly, more recent treaties have included a comprehensive combination of different instruments for responding to noncompliance. These systems, also referred to as comprehensive noncompliance response systems, contain not only methods to sanction violations but, also, and perhaps more important, methods to facilitate compliance, improve transparency and reporting procedures, and prevent violations.

. . . Although the managerial approach is proving successful in treaties such as the Vienna Convention and the Montreal Protocol, one should not forget that we are only at the beginning of new efforts to find solutions to compliance problems. In many other areas it remains difficult to reach any international consensus at all on the protection of our global environment.

International environmental law is increasingly moving from a phase in which the emphasis was on the adoption of standards to one in which the focus is on the implementation of and actual compliance with these standards. One should not forget, however, that it is especially in the phase of adoption that a well-designed noncompliance response system can prove decisive in getting states to agree to new commitments.

Questions

1. Why do you think environmental treaties, more than treaties in other international law fields, focus on efforts to facilitate compliance more than punishing noncompliance? Can this approach work on other areas? Which ones? Human rights? The law governing the use of force?

2. What kinds of sanctions *could* be employed against states that persistently fail to comply with their obligations under multilateral environmental agreements?

3. Protecting the Ozone Layer

Ozone in the earth's stratosphere filters harmful ultra-violet radiation from sunlight. Reacting to a growing body of scientific evidence and analysis as well as pressures from NGOs about the dangers of ozone depletion caused by anthropogenic gases (i.e., gases generated by human activity), most states demonstrated a commendable ability and willingness to act. They negotiated relatively quickly the 1985 Vienna Convention for the Protection of the Ozone Layer, then the 1987 Montreal Protocol on Substances that Deplete the Ozone Layer, followed by successive amendments and adjustments tightening the Protocol's provisions. (Excerpts from both the Vienna Convention and the Montreal Protocol are in the Documentary Supplement.) A rapidly developing situation that could have led to worldwide catastrophic effects has been for the most part contained. The following excerpt provides more details about the problem and the resulting agreements.

Alexandre Kiss & Dinah Shelton, International Environmental Law

559, 575-579 (3d ed. 2004)

The anthropogenic source of ozone depletion was clear by the late 1970s. The utilization of chlorofluorocarbons (CFCs), contained in aerosol sprays and to a lesser extent in solvents and refrigerators, was identified as a major contributing cause. When first developed CFCs were viewed favorably because they are nontoxic, non-flammable, non-corrosive and stable. It is the very stability of CFCs that is the source of the problem because they migrate over long distances and survive for many years. When they reach the stratosphere intact, solar radiation breaks the molecules apart to free reactive chlorine atoms, catalyzing chain reactions that destroy ozone; even if CFC production and use are phased out, ozone depletion will remain for some time, because of the substances already released. By 1985 it was understood that most depletion of the ozone occurs on a seasonal basis above Antarctica and, increasingly, over the Arctic regions. The Antarctic ozone hole has expanded to a size greater than North America and scientists expect it to begin shrinking only in 30 to 50 years as ozone-depleting substances are removed from the atmosphere. . . .

The discovery that widely-used chemical substances were destroying stratospheric ozone induced a number of countries in the 1980s to ban the use of CFCs for aerosol sprays. At the same time, their general use made it obvious that the problems could not be solved unilaterally or even regionally. Thus, the [United Nations Environment Programme (UNEP)] made protection of stratospheric ozone a priority item in its legal action plan and after several years of effort, succeeded in negotiating the [Vienna] Convention for the Protection of the Ozone Layer.

The treaty is a framework convention, providing the basis for systematic cooperation among the states parties respecting protection of stratospheric ozone. The general obligation of states is to take appropriate measures to protect human health and the environment against adverse effects resulting or likely to result from human activities that modify or are likely to modify the ozone layer. . . .

According to Convention Article 8, the Conference of the Parties may adopt protocols to the Convention. Two months after the conclusion of the Vienna Convention, a British Antarctic Survey team published its findings indicating a 40 percent loss of stratospheric ozone over Antarctica. This ozone "hole" stimulated UNEP and the World Meteorological Organization to issue a comprehensive international assessment, which concluded that CFC production trends would lead to dangerous ozone depletion. A subsequent meeting of the parties to the Vienna Convention adopted the Montreal Protocol on Substances that Deplete the Ozone Layer. At the time the Protocol was adopted, scientific uncertainty remained about global ozone loss and increases in [ultra-violet] radiation reaching the earth. The action taken in adopting the Protocol thus represents the first significant application of the precautionary principle.

The Montreal Protocol foresees the control of various forms of chlorofluorocarbons and halons, and their progressive elimination. Industrial countries have agreed to cut production and use of CFCs in half by 1998, and by 1992 to freeze production and use of halons. Countries with an annual consumption of CFCs under 0.3 kilograms per capita, which were mainly developing countries, were given a ten-year period [beyond that established for developed countries] to comply. The Protocol also restricted trade between states parties and non-parties, addressing the "free rider" problem.

The Montreal Protocol came into force on January 1, 1989. The parties to it have met regularly, as foreseen by the agreement. At the first meeting (Helsinki, May 1989), new information indicated that ozone losses were two to three times more severe than had been predicted. Participating states thus adopted a declaration that called for accelerating the phase-out of substances that destroy stratospheric ozone. The meeting also initiated a major revision of the Montreal Protocol.

The second meeting (London, June 1990) considerably tightened the reduction schedule, again in light of scientific findings: it decided on new and shorter deadlines for the complete phaseout of substances. This made even more necessary the effective participation of all significant producers and consumers of ozone depleting substances, in particular countries like China, Brazil and India. In a breakthrough, the London amendments endorsed a financial mechanism and an interim international fund consisting of voluntary contributions from the industrialized nations in order to assist developing countries in meeting the costs of compliance with the Convention and Protocols. For the first time an international environmental treaty called for financial transfers from industrialized to developing countries.

The Fourth Meeting of the Parties (Copenhagen, November 1992) completed the task of adopting the Montreal Protocol and of making it operational. The meeting [delayed] the phase-out dates for industrial countries to 1994 for halons and to 1996 for CFCs, methyl chloroform, and carbon tetrachloride. It also took up the question of hydrochlorofluorocarbons (HCFCs), a proposed substitute for CFCs that is still ozone-depleting but less so than CFCs. The agreement called for their complete phase-out by 2030. A 1995 meeting in Vienna added a phase-out for methyl bromide, to the year 2010 for industrialized countries. The meeting also strengthened requirements for industrialized country use of HCFCs, and added a complete phase-out by 2040 for developing countries. Subsequently in the San José, Costa Rica, meeting [(November 1996)], the states parties adopted new reduction schedules for a number of ozone-depleting substances as well as decisions on illegal trade in such substances and on financial issues. . . .

. . . . [T]he Beijing amendments of 1999 [banned a new substance and also] strengthened compliance measures, in particular by requiring that as of January 1, 2004, each party prohibit the import and export of certain controlled substances listed in Annex C from any state not party to the Protocol. The Colombo annual meeting in 2001 emphasized compliance, with one-third of all decision taken concerning the topic. In addition, [the states parties took a decision that] concerns procedures for assessing the ozone-depleting potential of new substances. Parties are required to request private industry to pay the cost of a preliminary calculation of the ozone-depleting potential for new substances, a strong signal to industry.

. . . The core of the international structure [of the ozone regime] is the annual Meeting of the Parties to the Montreal Protocol which allows the participating states to decide collectively when there is a conflict concerning the interpretation of or the compliance with the treaty obligations accepted. . . .

In spite of [continuing problems with illegal trade in ozone-depleting substances], international efforts to protect the ozone layer have had substantial impact. By 1995, global production of the most significant ozone-depleting substances, the CFCs, was down 76 percent from the peak year of 1988. Several countries and regions advanced beyond the agreements. The EU announced that it will phase out HCFCs by 2015, 15 years before it is legally required to do so. The U.S. Clean Air Act mandates phase-out of methyl bromide nine years ahead of the Protocol requirements. Other countries have similarly accelerated their compliance. Although the task is not yet complete, the international community has responded clearly to the issue.

One of the most significant features of the Montreal Protocol is its law-making and implementation mechanism. Article 2(9) of the Protocol creates a procedure for adjusting the list of controlled substances or permissible levels of production or consumption of controlled substances in a way that can become legally binding for all parties even though not all of them consent to the adjustment. In addition, a great deal of the implementation of the ozone regime takes place through "decisions" taken on a consensus basis at the annual Meetings of the Parties. The parties deem these decisions to be authorized by the general provisions of the Protocol.

Montreal Protocol

Article 2(9)

(a) Based on the assessments made pursuant to Article 9, the Parties may decide whether:

(i) Adjustments to the ozone depleting potentials specified in Annex A, Annex B, Annex C and/or Annex E should be made and, if so, what the adjustments should be; and

(ii) Further adjustments and reductions of production or consumption of controlled substances should be undertaken and, if so, what the scope, amount and timing of any such adjustments should be;

(b) Proposals for such adjustments shall be communicated to the Parties by the Secretariat at least six months before the meeting of the Parties at which they are proposed for adoption;

(c) In taking such decisions, the Parties shall make every effort to reach agreement by consensus. If all efforts at consensus have been exhausted, and no agreement reached, such decision shall, as a last resort, be adopted by a two-thirds majority vote of the Parties present and voting representing a majority of [developing countries] present and voting a majority of the [non-developing Parties] present and voting;

(d) The decisions, which shall be binding on all Parties, shall forthwith be communicated to the Parties by the Depositary . . .

The legal effect in the United States of "decisions" of the Meetings of the Parties was cast into doubt in an important case before the U.S. Court of Appeals for the District of Columbia. The National Resources Defense Council (NRDC) challenged a rule issued by the Environmental Protection Agency regarding the production and consumption of methyl bromide, a substance controlled under the Montreal Protocol. The NRDC argued that the EPA rules violated a "decision" of the Meeting of the Parties to the Montreal Convention regarding methyl bromide production and consumption limits. Noting that the Clean Air Act authorizes the

EPA to allow the production, importation, and consumption of methyl bromide only "[t]o the extent consistent with the Montreal Protocol," the NRDC contended that the EPA rule was not in accordance with the law.

Natural Resources Defense Council v. Environmental Protection Agency

U.S. Court of Appeals
464 F.3d 1, 8-10 (D.C. Cir. 2006)

NRDC fashions the entirety of its argument around the proposition that the "decisions" under the Protocol are "law." This premise is flawed. The "decisions" of the Parties—post-ratification side agreements reached by consensus among 189 nations—are not "law" within the meaning of the Clean Air Act and are not enforceable in federal court . . .

NRDC's interpretation raises significant constitutional problems. If the decisions are "law"—enforceable in federal court like statutes or legislative rules—then Congress either has delegated lawmaking authority to an international body or authorized amendments to a treaty without presidential signature or Senate ratification, in violation of Article II of the Constitution. . . . There is significant debate over the constitutionality of assigning lawmaking functions to international bodies. A holding that the Parties' post-ratification side agreements were "law" would raise serious constitutional questions in light of the nondelegation doctrine, numerous constitutional procedural requirements for making law, and the separation of powers.

We need not confront the "serious likelihood that the statute will be held unconstitutional." It is far more plausible to interpret the Clean Air Act and Montreal Protocol as creating an ongoing international political commitment rather than a delegation of lawmaking authority to annual meetings of Parties. . . .

Article 2H(5) [of the Montreal Protocol, which sets limits on methyl bromide production and consumption "save to the extent the Parties decide to permit the level of production or consumption that is necessary to satisfy uses agreed by them to be critical uses"] thus constitutes an "agreement to agree." The parties agree in the Protocol to reach an agreement concerning the types of uses for which new production and consumption will be permitted, and the amounts that will be permitted. "Agreements to agree" are usually not enforceable in contract. . . . There is no doubt that the "decisions" are not treaties. . . .

. . . Without congressional action . . . side agreements reached after a treaty has been ratified are not the law of the land; they are enforceable not through the federal courts, but through international negotiations.

Further analysis of the ozone regime, including its compliance provisions, is provided by Professors Faure and Lefevere, whose general ideas on compliance with environmental treaties were presented above.

Michael G. Faure & Jürgen Lefevere, Compliance with Global Environmental Policy

The Global Environment: Institutions, Law, and Policy 172, 180-181, 187 (Regina S. Axelrod, Stacy D. VanDeever & David Leonard Downie eds., 3d ed. 2011).

The Montreal Protocol . . . A "Managerial" Primary Rule System

The approach to international environmental treaty design has changed in the past decades, mainly because of the new, more realistic "managerial" approach. Prime examples of this new approach are the Vienna Convention for the Protection of the Ozone Layer and, more important, its subsequent Montreal Protocol on Substances that Deplete the Ozone Layer, adopted under this Convention. . . .

. . . The Vienna Convention and more particularly its Montreal Protocol [concluded only two years later] surprised the international community by their swift adoption, their specific goals, their effectiveness, and the large number of states that have become parties to them. . . . One of the main reasons given for this effectiveness is the design of the treaty system, which has several "modern" characteristics that make it very suitable for dealing with environmental problems in the current international context. In many of the more recent international environmental treaties the Vienna-Montreal system is used as a model, largely because of the flexibility of its primary [i.e., substantive] rule system.

The Vienna Convention establishes the Conference of the Parties (Article 6), which is to meet "at regular intervals," in practice every three to four years. The Montreal Protocol adds a Meeting of the Parties. Montreal protocol meetings are now held annually to discuss the implementation of the commitments and possible improvements to or adoption of new commitments. They are organized by the Ozone Secretariat, set up under Article 7 of the Vienna Convention and Article 12 of the Montreal Protocol. The regular convening of the Meeting of the Parties has proven very useful in keeping the treaty objectives on the political agenda and has ensured a continuous updating of its goals and standards. This updating was made possible by the framework structure chosen by the Vienna Convention. Although not a new structure . . . it has been particularly effective. Whereas the Vienna Convention does no more than establish the framework for further negotiations, the real commitments are laid down in the Montreal Protocol. . . . The provisions of the Montreal Protocol are regularly updated by means of amendments. During the two decades of its existence, the Montreal Protocol has seen a total of five "adjustments" regarding the production and consumption of the controlled substances listed in the Annexes of the Protocol as well as four Amendments. . . . This shows how compliance is likely to be influenced in the treaty design stage by creating a primary rule system that can develop over time, responding to evolving science and the capacity to deal with environmental problems.

The Montreal Protocol also provides an example of how the individual capacities of states may determine their willingness to accept treaty obligations in the first place. India and China would not become parties to the Montreal Protocol until the agreement about compensatory financing had been adopted at the London meeting in 1990. This agreement provided for financial support to developing states in order to allow them to become parties to the protocol and be financially capable of complying with its obligations.

Under the Montreal Protocol, various instruments have been developed to remedy financial incapacity. A Multilateral Fund was set up (Article 10) to provide financial assistance. The fund's implementing agencies — the International Bank for Reconstruction and Development (World Bank), the United Nations Environment Programme, and the United Nations Development Programme — have drawn up country programs and country studies that offer financial support, assistance, and training. Furthermore, the Montreal Protocol provides for the transfer of technology under its Article 10A. On the basis of this article, all states party to the protocol "shall take every practicable step" to ensure that "the best available, environmentally safe substitutes and related technologies are expeditiously transferred" to developing countries (as defined in Article 5[1] of the protocol) and that those transfers "occur under fair and most favourable conditions." . . .

NONCOMPLIANCE PROCEDURES: THE MONTREAL PROTOCOL AND THE KYOTO PROTOCOL

The more recent environmental treaties have new noncompliance procedures, often side by side with the traditional dispute settlement procedures. A prime example of a well-functioning noncompliance procedure is the one set up under Article 8 of the Montreal Protocol. This article states that the parties to the protocol "shall consider and approve procedures and institutional mechanisms for determining noncompliance with the provisions of this Protocol and for treatment of Parties found to be in noncompliance."

At the Copenhagen meeting in November 1992 the Meeting of the Parties adopted the procedure under this article. An Implementation Committee was set up, consisting of ten representatives elected by the Meeting of the Parties, based on equitable geographical distribution. . . . The focus has . . . been on the nonadversarial functions. The procedure allows states, when they believe they are unable to comply with their obligations, to report this inability to the Secretariat and the Implementation Committee. The Implementation Committee also discusses the general quality and the reliability of the data contained in the member states' reports. The Implementation Committee, meeting three to four times a year, has, in fact, assumed a very active role in improving the quality and reliability of the data reported by the member states and, in a cooperative sphere, has sought solutions for parties with administrative, structural, and financial difficulties.

The noncompliance procedure under the Montreal Protocol has served as an important source of inspiration for the development of the compliance regime under the Kyoto Protocol. This regime . . . has both a facilitative and enforcement branch. The enforcement branch will determine whether a country has met its emissions target and, as a result of this determination, apply the consequences for non-compliance that were agreed between countries . . . if this is not the case. The mandate of the facilitative branch is based on the nonadversarial role that the Compliance Committee of the Montreal Protocol has assumed in practice. The facilitative branch has the task of assisting all countries in their implementation of the protocol. Of interest is that the facilitative branch has so far played only a minor role, whereas the enforcement branch has already been requested to deal with two cases (one by Greece and one by Canada).

Notes and Questions

1. The Vienna Convention and the other agreements that comprise the ozone treaty regime have secured widespread international adherence. As of November 2011, there were 196 parties to the Vienna Convention and 196 parties to the Montreal Protocol. In addition, 195 states were parties to the 1992 London amendment to the Protocol; 192 states were parties to the 1994 Copenhagen amendment; 182 states were parties to the 1999 Montreal amendment; and 166 states were parties to the 2002 Beijing amendment.

2. When considering the treaty regime governing ozone, you should examine the Vienna Convention and the Montreal Protocol in the Documentary Supplement. You should extract in general terms what the treaties actually do—for example, how they establish goals, set substantive standards (or "primary rules"), monitor compliance, and enforce their rules. Look particularly at Articles 2-7, 10, and 11 of the Vienna Convention and Articles 4, 5, 6-10, 10A, 11, and 12 of the Montreal Protocol.

3. What are the objectives of the treaties and how do the treaties provide for updating their goals and standards? What are the actual substantive obligations that a state assumes under the Montreal Protocol? Use as examples a developed state like Germany and a developing country, such as Indonesia. Is the Protocol excessively favorable to developing countries? If you think so (or not), what values and assumptions are implicit in your view?

4. How will the meaning of ambiguous provisions in the treaties be ascertained?

5. The parties to the Montreal Protocol, in Article 4, agree not to engage in trade in substances controlled by the treaty and certain products containing such substances with countries that are not parties. What role do such trade restrictions play in the treaty regime? Consider the example of Korea, which elected to join the Protocol in order to continue exporting cars and refrigerators containing controlled substances. Patricia Birnie, Alan Boyle & Catherine Redgwell, International Law and the Environment 353 (3rd ed. 2009).

6. Among the "decisions" the Meetings of the Parties to the Montreal Protocol make each year are formal determinations that particular states are not complying with their obligations under the Protocol. Such decisions serve a public "shaming" function, as well as a caution that continued noncompliance can result in the application of enforcement mechanisms. As noted in the Faure & Lefevere excerpt above, compliance is commonly promoted through cooperative approaches, including multilateral technical assistance programs and financial assistance through the Multilateral Fund for noncompliant states. Compliance can also be encouraged, however, through sanctions. At its Fourth Meeting, the Meeting of the Parties decided on measures that might be taken in the event of noncompliance, including "[s]uspension, in accordance with the applicable rules of international law concerning the suspension of the operation of a treaty, of specific rights and privileges under the Protocol, whether or not subject to time limits, including those concerned with industrial rationalization, production, consumption, trade, transfer of technology, financial mechanism and institutional arrangements." Report of the Fourth Meeting of the Parties to the Montreal Protocol on Substances that Deplete the Ozone Layer, Annex V.C, UNEP/OzL.Pro.4/15 (Nov. 25, 1992). Rights that can be suspended include the right under Article 4

of the Protocol to participate in trade in controlled substances. As of 2009, no countries have been sanctioned for noncompliance with their Montreal Protocol obligations, but "[t]wo developing states, Mauritania and North Korea, have been threatened with loss of Article 5 status [i.e., the entitlement to delay for ten years their compliance with the control measures mandated by the treaty] for failure to report data." Birnie, Boyle & Redgwell, International Law and the Environment, supra, at 354.

7. The development of technology can profoundly affect the economic impact that international environmental rules have on the private actors whose conduct those rules regulate. For example, in the mid-1980s, the DuPont Corporation — originally a major producer of ozone-depleting substances — began to develop alternatives to CFCs. This "is often cited as a critical factor leading to U.S. support for the Montreal Protocol." Daniel Bodansky, The Art and Craft of International Environmental Law, 149 (2010).

8. How does the design of the Vienna Convention and the Montreal Protocol address the "special characteristics" of international environmental problems identified above in subsection 1 of this Section? Which challenges does it address successfully? Which problems does it fail to address?

9. The authors of a thoughtful empirical study of elements that contribute to the success of multilateral environment agreements identified the following as important factors for negotiators to build in to such agreements:

- Ensure that the obligations of the accord are perceived as equitable by parties and potential parties.
- If clearly assessing compliance is a primary concern, make the obligations as precise as possible.
- Try to ensure that the obligations are reinforced rather than contradicted by economic forces.
- Craft the treaty so that the burden of compliance is placed on a manageable number of actors. Target the major actors.
- Ensure that there are leader countries in the negotiations and that early on, they take measures to implement and comply with the agreement.

[Harold K. Jacobson & Edith Brown Weiss, Assessing the Record and Designing Strategies to Engage Countries, in Engaging Countries: Strengthening Compliance with International Environmental Accords 511, 552-553 (Edith Brown Weiss & Harold K. Jacobson eds., 1998).]

How would you assess the Vienna Convention and the Montreal Protocol in light of these considerations?

10. One of the stated advantages of the Montreal Protocol is its flexibility, including the ability of parties to amend the roster of controlled substances, even if not all parties agree, and to take regulatory actions through the relatively informal "decisions" of the Meeting of the Parties. From the standpoint of the United States, does that flexibility raise problems in terms of democratic accountability in view of the way treaties are ratified in the United States? Could there be other ways in which international law is incorporated into U.S. law that is consistent with domestic lawmaking procedures, such as the incorporation of international law principles into a domestic statute? Do you agree with the decision of the court in Natural Resources

Defense Council v. Environmental Protection Agency that a decision of the Meeting of the Parties could only be deemed "law" within the meaning of the Clean Air Act if it is "enforceable in federal court" like a statutes or legislative rule? Does that view conflate the question of whether a norm is legally binding as a matter of international law with the question of whether it is self-executing as a matter of domestic law? For a thoughtful critique of the court's decision, see John H. Knox, International Decisions, Natural Resources Defense Council v. Environmental Protection Agency, 101 Am J. Int'l L. 471 (2007).

11. As an alternative to the Vienna Convention and the Montreal Protocol, would the general norms enunciated in the *Trail Smelter* case, Principle 21 of the Stockholm Declaration, or Principle 2 of the Rio Declaration be sufficient to deal with the problem of ozone depletion?

4. Global Climate Change

Another major problem in the "global commons" is the phenomenon of global climate change caused by the emission of heat-trapping greenhouse gases. The problem of global climate change is much more complicated and controversial than the ozone depletion problem discussed above. Although there is an emerging consensus among scientists that global average temperatures are in fact rising, there is still considerable debate about the likely rate of future warming and the relative importance of various factors that contribute to global warming. There is also considerable debate about how to deal with the problem, with most policymakers recognizing that the costs of action could be substantial (as would be the costs of inaction).

At the Rio Conference in 1992, the participants negotiated a Framework Convention on Climate Change (FCCC). The FCCC went into effect on March 21, 1994. As of February 2011, 193 countries, including the United States, plus the European Union were parties to the Framework Convention.

At the Third Conference of the Parties to the Framework Convention, held in Kyoto, Japan, in December 1997, the parties adopted a controversial Protocol that established some legally binding obligations to reduce greenhouse gas emissions. In these negotiations, as in the Montreal Protocol negotiations, the role of NGOs was especially prominent. The Kyoto Protocol stipulated that it would enter into force only after 55 states, including states responsible for at least 55 per cent of the total carbon dioxide emissions produced in 1990 by developed and eastern and central European states listed in Annex I to the FCCC, had ratified the treaty. The Protocol entered into force on February 16, 2005, following Russia's decision to ratify. As of February 2011, 192 countries plus the European Union were parties. (Excerpts of the Framework Convention and the Kyoto Protocol are in the Documentary Supplement.) Although the United States signed the Protocol in November 1998, the Bush Administration opposed the Protocol and refused to submit it to the Senate for ratification. The Bush Administration objected to the Protocol largely because of concerns about the impact its required emissions reductions would have on the U.S. economy and also because it failed to impose concrete emissions reduction obligations on major developing country sources of greenhouse gases like China and India.

Because the Kyoto Protocol specifies emissions reductions only for a first "reduction commitment period . . . from 2008 to 2012," international attention has shifted to negotiations on a post-2012 emissions reduction regime. The difficulty in finalizing a successor treaty was highlighted at the U.N. Climate Change Conference held in Copenhagen in 2009. That conference resulted in the "Copenhagen Accord," a nonbinding instrument embodying a series of interdependent unilateral emissions reduction commitments by a large number of states. The Conference of the Parties of the FCCC did not adopt the Copenhagen Accord, but merely decided to "take[] note" of it. The following year, however, at the U.N. Climate Change Conference in Cancun, the parties reached a consensus on a document recognizing that emissions reductions would be based on unilateral commitments by states and "recognize[d]" that deep reductions in greenhouse gases are required to hold the increase in global average temperature below 2°C above preindustrial levels. At Cancun, the developed FCCC parties also committed to a "goal" of mobilizing jointly $100 billion per year by 2020 to address the climate change needs of developing countries.

The following materials provide some background to the problem of global climate change and outline the key provisions of the Framework Convention, the Kyoto Protocol, and the Copenhagen Accord.

a. Scientific Aspects and Policy Challenges

The following excerpt provides a helpful introduction to the basic science of climate change and some of its possible effects.

Alexandre Kiss & Dinah Shelton, Guide to International Environmental Law

170-172 (2007)

Since the 1960s scientists have expressed concern that a generalized warming of the planet's atmosphere might lead to changes in the global climate. The global average temperature between 1866 and 1996 increased by more than one degree. The 1990s were the warmest decade on record and included the seven warmest years ever recorded.* The accumulation of gases, such as carbon dioxide, nitrous oxide, methane, chlorofluorocarbons and tropospheric ozone, is viewed as at least partially responsible for the warming. There is evidence that the carbon dioxide concentration in the atmosphere today is 25 to 30 percent higher than what it was in . . . pre-industrial times. In 2001, the Intergovernmental Panel on Climate Change, a network of more than 2,000 scientists and policy experts advising governments on climate policy, concluded that most of the warming observed in the last 50 years has been due to the increase in greenhouse gas concentrations attributable to human activity.

Carbon dioxide is a basic by-product of the combustion of fossil and other natural fuels such as wood, coal, oil, and gasoline. Other significant greenhouse

*[The next decade, from 2000 to 2009, was warmer still. See Note 2 below. — Eds.]

gasses are chlorofluorocarbons, which also contribute to the depletion of the ozone layer, methane, and nitrous oxide. Methane is a metabolic by-product of animals (including humans) and is produced in significant quantities by domestic cattle. It is also a by-product of petroleum production. . . . Nitrous oxide has various industrial applications as an aerosol propellant, and is used as an anesthetic gas. The accumulation of these gases acts as an insulating blanket that traps the energy of sunlight and prevents it from radiating back into outer space. The accumulation of solar energy causes a gradual increase in the average temperature of the earth's surface.

The trend towards increasing temperatures is likely to result in rising sea levels from the melting of the Greenland ice sheet and from the thermal expansion of sea water. A rise in the world's sea levels of approximately 50 centimeters, which is possible during the coming decades, would wreak havoc with the low-lying coastal areas that are home to a substantial portion of the world's population. According to some projections, many small islands would be submerged or become unsafe, and huge areas of heavily populated countries, such as Bangladesh or Indonesia, could become uninhabitable. Louisiana has already lost significant amounts of coastal land because of a recent rise in the Gulf of Mexico. . . . According to one estimate, approximately 5 million square kilometers may be threatened by the year 2075, an area that represents 3 percent of the world's land mass, one-third of global cropland and home to a billion people.

Climate change would also modify the world's agriculture: some areas would become arid, while other regions that are presently too cold would become able to grow cereals, corns, or fruit, and other products needing a warmer climate. Increased water temperatures would disrupt aquatic ecosystems and further burden already distressed fisheries. A particularly sinister consequence of global climate change is the multiplication of violent weather patterns, including severe drought, tropical storms, hurricanes, unusually heavy rainfalls, and the consequential floods and landslides. In addition, a slight rise in average annual air temperature could greatly increase the risk of insect outbreaks. Warmer weather speeds up insect metabolism, making them grow more quickly, breed more frequently, and migrate sooner and further. Tropical diseases carried by pests and micro-organisms, including malaria and dengue fever, may become widely endemic throughout new areas.

The global warming issue exemplifies the principle that all activity in the biosphere is interrelated and interdependent. In addition to industrial and automotive emissions from developed countries, a large part of global warming results from agricultural and resource activities in developing countries. Tropical deforestation is a serious problem that concerns more than the loss of renewable resources and biological diversity; . . . deforestation [also] contribute[s] to global warming. . . . [M]uch of the deforestation that occurs in tropical countries results from land-clearing for agriculture. The topsoil in most tropical countries is so poor that it cannot sustain crops for more than one or two seasons. The famers then move and clear still more forest, typically by means of the "slash and burn" technique. The trees are chopped down or bulldozed, followed by the burning of all the native vegetation and the unusable wood that remains. . . . This unsustainable exploitation of tropical forests contributes to the greenhouse effects, because forests and oceans are natural "sinks" that remove greenhouse gases by absorbing carbon dioxide. Although it is difficult to know the exact proportion of such absorption, deforestation hinders the process and thus enhances global warming.

The nature and causes of global climate change pose different challenges than the problem of ozone-depleting substances and make efforts to negotiate international solutions exceedingly difficult. The excerpt below identifies some of these problems.

> Negotiation of a climate change convention proved to be a much more difficult task than reaching agreement on protection of the ozone layer. The range and complexity of issues involved in containing global warming and uncertainty regarding the nature, severity and timescale of possible climatic effects make the task of phasing out production and consumption of ozone-depleting substances seem relatively simple by comparison. The economic implications of climate change are much greater. Whereas industrial processes that deplete the ozone layer are relatively discrete, greenhouse gas production goes to the heart of energy, transport, agricultural, and industrial policy in all developed states and increasingly in developing ones too. Moreover, the role of carbon sinks means that deforestation, protection of natural habitats and ecosystems, sea-level rise, and sovereignty over natural resources are also important elements of the problem. Thus the sectoral approach, which has traditionally dominated international regulation of the environment, is plainly inappropriate to the interconnected and global character of climate change. Pollution control and the use and conservation of natural resources are both involved, within the broader context of sustainable development. . . . [Patricia Birnie, Alan Boyle & Catherine Redgwell, International Law and the Environment 356 (3rd ed. 2009).]

Notes and Questions

1. The Intergovernmental Panel on Climate Change (IPCC) referred to in the excerpt from Professors Kiss and Shelton released its most recent assessment, the Fourth Assessment Report, in 2007. (The IPCC's Fifth Assessment Report is scheduled to be released between 2013 and 2014.) It concluded that evidence of "warming of the climate system is unequivocal." Intergovernmental Panel on Climate Change, Climate Change 2007: Synthesis Report 30 (2007). It also noted that it is "very likely," i.e., more than 90 percent certain, that "[m]ost of the observed increase in global average temperatures since the mid-20th century is . . . due to the observed increase in anthropogenic [greenhouse gas] concentrations." Id. at 39. One scholar has summarized the environmental consequences that Working Group I of the IPCC projects for the 21st century if greenhouse gas emissions are not abated as follows:

> IPCC Projections for 21st Century:
>
> - Probable atmospheric temperature rise between 1.8°C and 4°C;
> - Possible atmospheric temperature rise between 1.1°C and 6.4°C;
> - Sea level most likely to rise by 28-43 cm;
> - Arctic summer sea ice likely to disappear in second half of 21st century;

- Increase in heat waves very likely;
- Increase in tropical storm intensity likely.

[Jeff Obbard, Climate Change—Living in the Anthropocene, in Crucial Issues in Climate Changes and the Kyoto Protocol 63, 65 (Kheng-Lian Koh, Lin-Heng Lye & Jolene Lin eds., 2010).]

If these projections are accurate, climate change will have potentially catastrophic effects. What are the challenges in persuading countries to act on the basis of such scientific projections? Is it because most people do not understand the science? Because the effects will not be realized until some time in the future? Because the changes take effect gradually?

2. According to a recent NASA analysis, the decade from 2000 to 2009 was the warmest decade since modern records began to be kept in 1880. News Release, Nat'l Aeronautics and Space Admin., Goddard Space Flight Ctr., 2009: Second Warmest Year on Record; End of Warmest Decade (Jan. 21, 2010), http://www.giss.nasa.gov/research/news/20100121/. A separate study considered the likely effects of climate change in the United States and concluded that long heat waves and other hot events could become frequent events by 2039. Noah S. Diffenbaugh & Moetasim Ashfaq, Intensification of Hot Extremes in the United States, 37 Geophys. Res. Lett. L15701 (2010).

3. Despite the findings of the IPCC, some remain skeptical about the phenomenon of global climate change. See, for example, Kenneth P. Green, Countering Kerry's Catastrophic Climate Claims, American Enterprise Institute for Public Policy Research, Energy and Environment Outlook Series, No. 6, at 1 (Dec. 2009), http://www.aei.org/outlook/100096:

> Perhaps the central issue in climate science involves estimates of the sensitivity of the climate to anthropogenic greenhouse gas emissions. Sensitivity refers to just how much warming results from an increased concentration of greenhouse gases in the atmosphere. [A number of] . . . papers demonstrate that the climate's sensitivity to greenhouse gases may be considerably lower than the Intergovernmental Panel on Climate Change (IPCC) claims—so much lower, in fact, that the warming we would expect from doubling the amount of CO_2 in the atmosphere would be quite modest (well below two degrees Celsius) and offer very little risk.

Skepticism about climate change science was exacerbated by a controversy that has come to be known as "Climategate." A recent study describes the controversy:

> On November 19th, 2009, more than 1,000 confidential e-mails from the Climatic Research Unit (CRU) at the University of East Anglia were posted to the Internet. A few of these emails were subsequently cited by climate change critics as evidence that British and American scientists had changed their results to make global warming appear worse than it is, suppressed global warming research they disagreed with, and conspired to delete communications relevant to freedom of information requests. One series of e-mails in particular attracted widespread media interest. In conversations between Phil Jones, director of the CRU and Michal Mann, director of the Earth System Science Center at Pennsylvania State University, Jones described a "trick" employed to allegedly "hide the decline" in warming over the last half century as recorded by some tree ring records. Jones, Mann and other scientists argued that both statements had been taken out of context and misinterpreted. Meanwhile, the story moved from the

> blogosphere into mainstream newspapers and television news and opinion programs. . . . [T]he scandal generated considerable press attention across the United States and around the world, with articles and editorials published in major newspapers and scientific journals, and stories broadcast on major television and radio networks. [Anthony Leiserowitz, et al., Climategate, Public Opinion, and the Loss of Trust 5 (Working Paper, 2010), available at http://www.ssrn.com/.]

The authors of the study found that between 2008 and 2010, skepticism in American attitudes about global warming had increased.

> In 2008, 71 percent of Americans said "yes," global warming is happening. By 2010, however, this number had dropped significantly to 57 percent. Meanwhile the proportion that said "no," global warming is not happening doubled from 10 to 20 percent, while those who said "don't know" increased to 23 percent of the public. [Id. at 3.]

The researchers conclude that "Climategate deepened and perhaps solidified the prior observed declines in public beliefs that global warming is happening, human caused, and of serious concern." Id. at 10. Given the complexity of the science underlying climate change projections, how can policymakers and ordinary citizens resolve questions about whether climate change is occurring and, if it is, whether it is caused by human activity and what its effects will be?

b. The Climate Change Regime: The FCCC, Kyoto, and Beyond

The 1992 United Nations Framework Convention on Climate Change represents broad acknowledgment by states of the need to address the global challenge of climate change. Professors Birnie, Boyle, and Redgwell describe the sharply divided positions states brought to their negotiations in Rio.

> [The Framework Convention on Climate Change adopted at the 1992 Rio Conference] reflects deep differences of opinion among the participating states as to the measures needed and the allocation of responsibility for addressing the problem. Not only was it necessary to acknowledge the differential needs and responsibilities of developed and developing states, but also within each of these groups there were no common positions. Members of the Association of Small Island States, such as Nauru and Vanuatu, which might disappear in the event of modest sea level rise, were much in favour of a strong convention. Their interests were far removed from those of OPEC oil producers such as Saudi Arabia and Kuwait, whose income and economies could seriously suffer if consumption of fossil fuels by developed states were to be reduced. Neither of these groups had much in common with the larger developing states such as China, Brazil, and India, who were mainly concerned not to limit their own economic growth, but had no objection to developed states taking a strong lead. Nor did the developed OECD economies share the same view on the measures that might be needed to tackle climate change. In particular, the United States was not prepared to commit itself to specific emissions reductions or timetables and its opposition resulted in a convention that was significantly weaker than the commitments already voluntarily undertaken by a number of developed states. These divisions among major groups participating in the negotiations must be recalled when assessing and interpreting the Convention. [Birnie, Boyle & Redgwell, International Law and the Environment, supra, at 357.]

The Convention establishes a basic objective of achieving "stabilization of greenhouse gas concentrations in the atmosphere at a level that would prevent dangerous anthropogenic interference with the climate system." Article 2. The Convention calls on all states to implement national programs "to mitigate climate change by addressing anthropogenic emissions"; for developed countries, the Convention further stipulates that their national policies should limit greenhouse gas emissions and protect and enhance greenhouse gas sinks and reservoirs "with the aim of returning . . . [emissions] to their 1990 levels." Arts. 4(1)(b), 4(2)(a), 4(2)(b). Despite this stated goal, the Convention did not impose specific quantitative reduction obligations or deadlines on states. The Convention did create a structure for regular meetings of Conferences of the Parties, which met in Kyoto in 1997 to negotiate a treaty with more detailed and rigorous commitments. The following excerpt describes the key features of the Kyoto Protocol negotiated at that meeting.

Alexandre Kiss & Dinah Shelton, Guide to International Environmental Law

173-176 (2007)

. . . [T]he Kyoto Protocol . . . mov[ed] [the parties to the FCCC] towards the development of precise rules to mitigate anthropogenic climate change. The Protocol specifies different goals and commitments for developed and developing countries concerning future emissions of greenhouse gases. The main features of the Protocol are the reduction targets accepted by the industrialized countries, without corresponding obligations for developing countries; acknowledgment of the role of sinks (seas, forests) of greenhouse gases and their inclusion in the targets; the possible creation of "bubbles" and trading emissions as means for reducing their aggregate emissions and joint implementation agreements with countries that only emit small amounts of greenhouse gases, in principle developing countries.

The Protocol adopts a "big bubble approach": developed countries are allowed to join together and thereby attain their emission reduction commitments jointly by aggregating their anthropogenic carbon dioxide equivalent emissions of greenhouse gases listed in Annex A [to the Protocol]. Emissions should be reduced by at least 5 percent (averaging 5.2 percent) below 1990 levels by the first commitment period of 2008-2012. These reductions cover six greenhouse gasses. . . . Each state of this group [of developed states] shall, by 2005, have made demonstrable progress in achieving its commitments under the Protocol. Former communist countries in economic and political transition benefit from a certain degree of flexibility in the implementation of their commitments. Art. 3(6). They may use, for example, a different base year to determine the reduction of their emissions. Art. 3(5).

Art. 2 lists methods that may be used in order to achieve quantified emission limitation and reduction: enhancement of energy efficiency, protection and enhancement of sinks and reservoirs of greenhouse gases, promotion of sustainable forms of agriculture, increased use of new and renewable forms of energy and environmentally sound technologies, reduction or phasing out of market imperfections, the use of economic instruments, limitation and reduction of emissions of greenhouse gases in the transport sector, and limitation and/or reduction of methane through recovery and use in waste management.

Another specific form of cooperation in the reduction of greenhouse gases is emission trading. According to Art. 6(1), any developed country, for the purpose of meeting its commitments, may transfer to, or acquire from, any other party emission reduction units resulting from projects aimed at reducing emissions. . . . The condition is that any such project provides a reduction in emission by sources or an enhancement of removal by sinks, which is additional to any that would otherwise occur. . . . A developed country may also authorize legal entities to participate, under its responsibility, in actions leading to the generation, transfer, or acquisition of emission reduction units. Art. 6(3). The [Conference of the Parties (COP)] defines the relevant principles, modalities, rules, and guidelines, in particular for verification, reporting, and accountability for emission trading. Art. 16bis.

Any emission reduction units . . . that a party acquires from another party, shall be added to the assigned amount for that party. Art. 3(10). Parallel to this provision, Art. 3(11) foresees that any emission reduction units . . . that a party transfers to another party, shall be subtracted from the assigned amount for that party.

In addition to bubbles and trading, Art. 12 outlines a "clean development mechanism" the task of which is to assist developing countries in achieving sustainable development and in contributing to the ultimate objective of the convention. It also may assist developed countries in achieving compliance with their quantified emission limitation and reduction commitments. On a voluntary basis, emission reduction resulting from each project activity shall be certified by operational entities to be designated by the COP and approved by each party involved. Art. 12(5). Developing countries . . . benefit from project activities resulting in certified emission reductions, while developed countries may use the certified emission reductions accruing from such project activities to contribute to compliance with their quantified emission limitation and reduction commitments. Art. 12(3)(b). The clean development mechanism will assist in arranging funding of certified project activities as necessary. Certified emission reductions obtained during the period 2000 to 2008 can be used by developed countries to assist in achieving compliance in the commitment period 2008 to 2012.

Monitoring of greenhouse gases plays an important role in the Kyoto Protocol. Developed countries must establish national systems to estimate anthropocentric emissions by sources and removals by sinks (Art. 5), as well as annual inventories to incorporate the supplementary information necessary to demonstrate compliance with the commitments accepted under the Protocol (Art. 7). Such information [is] reviewed by teams composed of experts nominated by the parties and the reports of the expert reviews shall be submitted to the COP, which can take decision on any matter required for the implementation of the Protocol. Art. 8.

Arts. 10 and 11 of the Protocol concern developing countries. Their emissions are not limited, but they should formulate, where relevant, cost-effective national and, where appropriate, regional programs to improve the quality of local emission factors, formulate, implement, publish, and regularly update national or regional programs to mitigate climate change, taking into account all relevant economic activities. Developed party cooperation with developing countries shall include the transfer of, or access to, environmentally sound technologies, know-how, practices, and processes pertinent to climate change, as well as capacity-building. New and additional financial resources should be provided to meet the agreed full costs incurred by developing country parties in advancing the implementation of existing commitments.

The COP of the UNFCCC serves as the Meeting of the Parties to the Kyoto Protocol. It keeps under regular review the implementation of the Protocol and makes decisions necessary to promote its effective implementation. It assesses, on the basis of the information made available to it, the overall effects of the measures taken and makes recommendations on any matters necessary for implementation of the Protocol. Art. 13. The COP approves appropriate and effective procedures and mechanisms to determine and address cases of non-compliance with the provisions of the Protocol. Art. 17.

Although the Clinton Administration signed the Kyoto Protocol, the Bush Administration announced that the United States would not ratify the Protocol. In a March 13, 2001, letter to four Republican senators, President Bush wrote that "[m]y Administration takes the issue of global climate change very seriously." However, he indicated that "I oppose the Kyoto Protocol because it exempts 80 percent of the world, including major population centers such as China and India from compliance, and would cause serious harm to the U.S. economy." He called the Protocol "an unfair and ineffective means of addressing global climate change concerns." He went on to note "the incomplete state of scientific knowledge of the causes of, and solutions to, global climate change and the lack of commercially available technologies for removing and storing carbon dioxide." Although President Obama, during remarks at an April 2009 student roundtable in Istanbul, Turkey, characterized the Bush Administration's decision to "opt[] out" of the Kyoto Protocol a "mistake," he has also criticized the Protocol's failure to impose reduction targets on the largest developing states:

> Essentially you have a situation where the Kyoto Protocol . . . called on the developed countries who were signatories to engage in some significant mitigation actions and also to help developing countries. And there were very few, if any, obligations on the part of the developing countries.
>
> Now, in some cases, for countries that are extremely poor, still agrarian and so forth, they're just not significant contributors to greenhouse gases. But what's happened obviously since 1992 is that you've got emerging countries like China and India and Brazil that have seen enormous economic growth and industrialization. So we know that moving forward it's going to be necessary . . . for some changes to take place among those countries. It's not enough just for the developed countries to make changes. Those countries are going to have to make some changes, as well — not of the same pace, not in the same way, but they're going to have to do something to assure that whatever carbon we're taking out of the environment is not just simply dumped in by other parties. . . .
>
> My view was that if we could begin to acknowledge that the emerging countries are going to have some responsibilities, but that those responsibilities are not exactly the same as the developed countries, and if we could set up a financing mechanism to help those countries that are most vulnerable, like Bangladesh, then we would be at least starting to reorient ourselves in a way that allows us to be effective in the future. [The President's News Conference in Copenhagen, Denmark, 2009 Daily Comp. Pres. Doc. 1005, at 4 (Dec. 18, 2009).]

As noted above, the Kyoto Protocol establishes the period from 2008 to 2012 as the first commitment period for cutting greenhouse gas emissions. Article 3(9) of the Protocol obligates the parties to establish reduction commitments "for subsequent periods." As a party to the FCCC, the United States attended the December 2009 Conference of the Parties of FCCC, which also served as the Meeting of the Parties to the Kyoto Protocol. The following excerpt describes the non-legally binding "Copenhagen Accord" produced at the December 2009 Conference.

Daniel Bodansky, The Copenhagen Climate Change Accord

American Society of International Law, ASIL Insights, Vol. 14, Issue 3 (Feb. 12, 2010), http://www.asil.org/insights100212.cfm.

Since the Kyoto Protocol's entry into force in 2005, attention has focused on the question of what to do after 2012, when the Kyoto Protocol's first commitment period ends. Should the Kyoto Protocol be extended through the adoption of a second commitment period, with a new round of emission reduction targets for developed country parties? And, if so, should a new agreement be adopted under the United Nations Framework Convention on Climate Change (UNFCCC), which addresses the emissions of countries that either are not parties to the Kyoto Protocol (the United States) or do not have Kyoto emissions targets (developing countries)? Or should a single new agreement be adopted that replaces the Kyoto Protocol and is more comprehensive in coverage, addressing both developed and developing country emissions?

The Copenhagen Conference of the Parties (COP), which met from December 7-19, 2009, had been intended as the deadline to resolve these questions about the post-2012 climate regime—a view reflected in the unofficial slogan for the conference, "seal the deal." The decision by more than one hundred heads of state or government to attend heightened public expectations that the Copenhagen Conference would result in a major breakthrough; and more than 40,000 people registered, making Copenhagen one of the largest environmental meetings in history. But the lack of progress in the negotiations in the months leading up to Copenhagen suggested that hopes for a full-fledged legal agreement were unrealistic. In the end, the Copenhagen conference resulted only in a political [commitment], the Copenhagen Accord, which was negotiated by the leaders of the world's major economies, but was not formally adopted by the conference, leaving its future prospects uncertain.

The Copenhagen Accord

The Copenhagen Accord is a political rather than a legal document, negotiated by a group of about twenty-five heads of state, heads of government, ministers, and other heads of delegations.

Key elements of the Accord include the following:

Long-term vision—The Copenhagen Accord recognizes the need to limit global temperature increase to no more than 2° Celsius. . . .

Developed country mitigation—Over the past year, general consensus has emerged that developed countries should undertake economy-wide emissions reduction targets for the post-2012 period, although countries have differed about the stringency of these emissions reduction targets, the base-year from which reduction targets should be measured, and whether the targets should be defined using international accounting rules (as in Kyoto) or national legislation (as the U.S. has proposed). The Copenhagen Accord establishes a bottom-up process that allows each Annex I party to define its own target level, base year and accounting rules, and to submit its target in a defined format, for compilation by the UNFCCC Secretariat. Under the terms of the Accord, Annex I countries "commit to implement" their targets, individually or jointly, subject to international monitoring, reporting and verification (MRV).

Developing country mitigation—As with developed country emissions targets, the Copenhagen Accord establishes a bottom-up process by which developing countries will submit their mitigation actions in a defined format, for compilation by the UNFCCC Secretariat. It provides that developing countries will submit greenhouse gas inventories every two years, that [autonomous] developing country mitigation actions will be subject to domestic MRV, and that the results of this domestic MRV will be reported in biennial national communications. . . . The Copenhagen Accord also establishes a registry for listing nationally appropriate mitigation actions (NAMAs) for which international support is sought, and provides that supported NAMAs will be subject to international MRV in accordance with COP guidelines.

Financial assistance—In Copenhagen, the discussions about financial support revolved around the typical issues: how much money, from what sources, and with what governance arrangements? The Copenhagen Accord addresses only the first of these issues, leaving the other two for future resolution. It creates a "collective commitment" for developed countries to provide "new and additional resources . . . approaching $30 billion" for the 2010-2012 period, balanced between adaptation and mitigation, and sets a longer-term collective "goal" of mobilizing $100 billion per year by 2020 from all sources, but links this money to "meaningful mitigation actions and transparency on implementation" (para. 8). It also calls for governance of adaptation funding through equal representation by developing and developed country parties, but does not establish governance arrangement for finance more generally. Finally, it calls for the establishment of a Copenhagen Green Climate Fund (para. 10) as an operating entity of the UNFCCC's financial mechanism, as well as a High Level Panel to consider potential sources of revenue to meet the $100 billion per year goal. . . .

Monitoring, reporting and verification (MRV)—As with the mitigation issue, the MRV discussions have concerned the level of MRV as well as the parallelism/differentiation between developed and developing country MRV. The Copenhagen Accord calls for "rigorous, robust and transparent" MRV of Annex I [developed country] emissions reductions and financing, "in accordance with existing and any further guidelines adopted by the COP." As noted above, [internationally] supported [developing country] NAMAs . . . will be subject to international MRV "in accordance with guidelines adopted by the COP," while so-called "autonomous" mitigation actions will be verified nationally and reported in national communications every two years and subject to "international consultations and analysis under clearly defined guidelines that will ensure that national sovereignty is respected."

The Future of the Copenhagen Accord

Despite agreement on the Copenhagen Accord by the heads of state or government of more than twenty-five countries, including all of the major economies, the conference was unable to "adopt" the Accord due to objections by a small group of countries, led by Sudan, Venezuela, Bolivia, and Nicaragua, which refused to join consensus, arguing that the negotiation of the Copenhagen Accord by a smaller group represented a "coup d'état" against the United Nations because it bypassed the formal meetings. After an all-night session, the impasse was ultimately broken through a decision to "take note of" the Copenhagen Accord, giving it some status in the UNFCCC process but not as much as approval by the COP. Those countries that wish to "associate" themselves with the Copenhagen Accord are to notify the UNFCCC Secretariat for inclusion in the list of countries at the beginning of the Accord.

As of February 10, 2011, the UNFCCC Secretariat had received submissions from more than 120 countries, representing more than 80% of global greenhouse gas emissions (GHG), regarding their plans to reduce their GHG emissions and/or their wish to be "associated" with the Copenhagen Accord. In many cases, countries providing information on their mitigation actions have expressly associated themselves with the Copenhagen Accord, but a number of countries — most notably China, India, Brazil, and South Africa — did not do so expressly.

The Copenhagen Accord asserts that it will be "operational immediately," but fully operationalizing its terms will require further acts — for example, the spelling out of the guidelines for international consultation and analysis of developing country mitigation actions, and the establishment of the various bodies envisioned in the Accord (a High Level Panel to study potential sources of revenue, the Copenhagen Green Climate Fund, and a new Technology Mechanism). Ordinarily, this work would be carried out by the COP. But if some countries continue to block consensus in the COP, as occurred in Copenhagen, then this elaboration of the Copenhagen Accord might need to be done by the "associators" group.

Conclusion

Although the Copenhagen Accord has been criticized by some as inadequate, it represents a potentially significant breakthrough. True, the emission reduction pledges announced thus far do not put the world on a pathway to limiting climate change to 2° C, the ostensible long-term goal of the Accord. But the participating states did agree to list their national actions internationally and to subject their actions to some form of international scrutiny, even when their actions do not receive any international support. Plus, the Accord articulates a quantified long-term goal for the first time (no more than 2° C temperature increase) and puts significant new funds on the table, both for the short and medium terms.

As a political necessity, the Copenhagen Accord continues to reflect the principle of common but differentiated responsibilities and respective capabilities, but in a very different manner than in Kyoto. Developed countries committed to implement economy-wide emission reduction "targets," subject to international MRV, while developing country "actions" will be subject to international MRV only if they receive international support and to national MRV otherwise. Nevertheless, the Copenhagen Accord reflects an apparent shift by China, India, Brazil, and South Africa, which begins to break the so-called "firewall" between developed and developing countries. For the first time, major developing countries have agreed to reflect their national emission reduction pledges in an international instrument, to report on their GHG inventories and their mitigation actions in biennial national communications, and to subject their actions either to MRV (for internationally supported actions) or "international consultation and analysis under clearly defined guidelines that will ensure that national sovereignty is respected" (for domestically supported actions).

This outcome may seem like a rather modest achievement, but it represents some measure of "internationalization" of developing country actions. In any event, if world leaders could not agree to more through direct negotiations, under an intense international spotlight, it is hard to see why mid-level negotiators will be able to achieve more anytime soon. As a result, the Copenhagen Accord may well represent the high-water mark of the climate change regime for some time to come.

In December 2010, at the U.N. Climate Change Conference in Cancun, the parties failed to reach agreement on a new multilateral agreement that would establish binding emissions reduction obligations at the end of the Kyoto's first commitment period in 2012. The Cancun conference built on the "bottom-up" approach in which states make unilateral commitments to "quantified economy-wide emission reduction targets," in the case of developed countries, and "nationally appropriate mitigation actions" in the case of developing countries. The parties "recognize[d]" that "deep cuts in global greenhouse gas emissions are required . . . with a view to reducing global greenhouse gas emissions so as to hold the increase in global average temperature below 2° C above pre-industrial levels," but assumed no binding obligations to reach that goal. The conference produced a significant political commitment by developed states to jointly mobilize $100 billion per year by 2020 to assist developing countries in reducing greenhouse gas emissions and adapting to climate change and created a new "Green Climate Fund" as a financial mechanism to administer assistance funds for developing countries. Building on the commitments in the Copenhagen Accord regarding monitoring, reporting, and verification, the parties at the Cancun conference decided to "enhance" reporting requirements for developing countries and to "conduct a process for international consultations and analysis of biennial reports [from developing countries] in a manner that is non-intrusive, non-punitive and respectful of national sovereignty." The assembled parties also encouraged developing countries to develop national plans to address deforestation.

Notes and Questions

1. In considering the treaty regime governing global climate change, you should examine the Framework Convention and the Kyoto Protocol, which are excerpted in the Documentary Supplement. You should extract in general terms

what the treaties actually do — for example, how they establish goals, set substantive standards, monitor compliance, and enforce norms. Look particularly at Articles 2, 3, and 4 of the Framework Convention and Articles 2-8, 12, 13, 17, and 19 of the Kyoto Protocol.

2. Should the United States ratify the Kyoto Protocol or become a party to a comparable legally binding treaty that mandates specific emissions reductions? Does it depend on whether developing states also agree to reduction targets? Should there be any differences in what is expected of developed and developing countries? Should different developing countries be treated differently?

3. The Clinton Administration was one of the major proponents of the provisions in the Kyoto Protocol allowing states to buy and sell emission rights. Many economists justified this on efficiency grounds. However, does it favor wealthy countries that can afford to buy additional emissions rights? How might the system be made a fair one?

4. What are the advantages of a legally binding treaty like the Kyoto Protocol obligating states to make specific reductions in their emissions of greenhouse gases compared to a political commitment like the Copenhagen Accord in which states coordinate unilateral steps they plan to take on their own to reduce emissions?

5. With complicated problems such as global warming, is the better approach to seek a single treaty to solve the problem or to negotiate a framework convention and a series of protocols and agreements (as was done with the ozone depletion problem)? Would it be better to negotiate either regional treaties or treaties among a subset of the largest sources of greenhouse gas emissions that would take account of their economic concerns?

6. The Kyoto Protocol appears to have had at least some success in regulating greenhouse gas emissions by its parties. According to a report prepared by the UNFCCC Secretariat, "[i]n 2007, the total GHG emissions of 36 Annex B [developed country] Parties from [greenhouse gas] sources [covered by the Protocol] . . . [was] 16.4 per cent lower than the base year level defined under the Kyoto Protocol." For most countries, the base level year was 1990, although, as noted in the excerpt from Professors Kiss and Shelton above, former communist countries had the flexibility to select a different base year to determine their emission reductions. Data on the performance of all developed country parties to the UNFCCC, as opposed to developed country parties to the Kyoto Protocol (i.e., data that includes the United States), reveals a much lower total reduction of greenhouse gas emissions of 5.2 percent, which reflects increases in greenhouse gas emissions in the United States. Data on global greenhouse gases emissions, which also takes into account emissions by developing states (and which is weighted to account for the variable global warming potential of different types of greenhouse gases), indicates that total emissions increased by 24 percent between 1990 and 2007.

7. Why do you think that it has been more difficult to obtain international agreement on the problem of global climate change than on ozone depletion? Might it be a result of the dangers of inaction? Or, might it reflect the complexity of the problem and the difficulties of solutions?

8. How does the design of the regime including the FCCC, the Kyoto Protocol, and the Copenhagen Accord address the "special characteristics" of international environmental problems identified above in subsection 2 of this Section? Which challenges does the regime address successfully? Which problems does it fail to address?

9. Review the factors identified in the Jacobson and Brown Weiss study quoted in note 9 on page 911 that can enhance the prospects for compliance with a multilateral environmental regime. How would you assess the international climate change regime in light of these considerations?

10. In 2009, the U.S. House of Representatives narrowly passed the American Clean Energy and Security Act, which would have established a cap-and-trade system under domestic law for large emitters of greenhouse gases and would for the first time have established mandatory federal obligations to reduce greenhouse gas emissions to be phased in between 2012 and 2050. The Senate did not pass a version of the bill during the 111th Congress that closed in January 2011, and prospects for emissions reduction legislation in the 112th Congress seemed much dimmer.

The House's decision to move forward with legislation regulating greenhouse gas emissions may have been stimulated by a 2007 ruling by the U.S. Supreme Court that the Environmental Protection Agency has statutory authority under the Clean Air Act to regulate the emission of greenhouse gases from new motor vehicles and that it may only decline to exercise this authority if "it determines that greenhouse gases do not contribute to climate change or if it provides some reasonable explanation as to why it cannot or will not exercise its discretion to determine whether they do." Massachusetts v. Environmental Protection Agency, 549 U.S. 497, 533 (2007). Obama Administration officials indicated that they would prefer to have Congress address the climate change issue rather than have the E.P.A. attempt to regulate as an administrative matter. John M. Broder, E.P.A. Clears Path to Regulate Heat-Trapping Gases for First Time in the U.S., N.Y. Times, Apr. 17, 2007, at A15.

Should the United States pursue unilateral efforts to achieve specified emissions reductions if other major emitters, including India and China, do not? Will the costs to U.S. companies place them at a competitive disadvantage compared to other countries? Would enactment of a mandatory emissions reductions law in the United States increase the prospects of persuading other counties to agree to comparable quantified cuts?

11. The substantial challenge of reaching agreement on reducing global emissions of greenhouse gases has given rise to additional approaches to confronting climate change. For example, states are increasingly focusing their attention on strategies to adapt to a world in which average temperatures increase. In its 2007 Assessment Report, the IPCC commented on adaptation:

> Some adaptation is occurring now, to observed and projected future climate change, but on a limited basis. . . . For example, climate change is considered in the design of infrastructure projects such as coastal defence in the Maldives and The Netherlands, and the Confederation Bridge in Canada. Other examples include prevention of glacial lake outburst flooding in Nepal, and policies and strategies such as water management in Australia and government responses to heatwaves in, for example, some European countries. . . .
>
> The array of potential adaptive responses available to human societies is very large, ranging from purely technological (e.g., sea defences), through behavioural (e.g., altered food and recreational choices), to managerial (e.g., altered farm practices) and to policy (e.g., planning regulations). While most technologies and strategies are known and developed in some countries, the assessed literature does not indicate how effective various options are at fully reducing risks, particularly at higher levels of warming and related impacts, and for vulnerable groups. In addition, there are

formidable environmental, economic, informational, social, attitudinal and behavioural barriers to the implementation of adaptation. For developing countries, availability of resources and building adaptive capacity are particularly important.

Adaptation alone is not expected to cope with all the projected effects of climate change, and especially not over the long term as most impacts increase in magnitude. [IPCC, Summary for Policymakers, in Climate Change 2007: Impacts, Adaptation and Vulnerability: Contribution of Working Group II to the Fourth Assessment Report of the Intergovernmental Panel on Climate Change 7, 19 (Martin Parry et al. eds., 2007).]

12. Another possible response to the climate change threat involves not reducing greenhouse gas emissions or adapting to their consequences, but taking affirmative steps to counter the effect of increased atmospheric greenhouse gas concentrations. The following excerpt addresses the nascent phenomenon of "geoengineering," including the potential benefits and risks.

The world's slow progress in cutting carbon dioxide emissions and the looming danger that the climate could take a sudden turn for the worse require policymakers to take a closer look at emergency strategies for curbing the effects of global warming. These strategies, often called "geoengineering," envision deploying systems on a planetary scale, such as launching reflective particles into the atmosphere or positioning sunshades to cool the earth. . . .

Serious research on geoengineering could provide a useful defense for the planet—an emergency shield that could be deployed if surprisingly nasty climatic shifts put vital ecosystems and billions of people at risk. . . . [However,] it is unlikely that all countries will have similar assessments of how to balance the ills of unchecked climate change with the risk that geoengineering could do more harm than good. Governments should immediately begin to undertake serious research on geoengineering and help create international norms governing its use. . . .

The highly uncertain but possibly disastrous side effects of geoengineering interventions are difficult to compare to the dangers of unchecked global climate change. . . .

An effective foreign policy strategy for managing geoengineering is difficult to formulate because the technology involved turns the normal debate over climate change on its head. The best way to reduce the danger of global warming is, of course, to cut emissions of carbon dioxide and other greenhouse gases. But success in that venture will require all the major emitting countries, with their divergent interests, to cooperate for several decades in a sustained effort to develop and deploy completely new energy systems with much lower emissions. Incentive to defect and avoid the high cost of emissions controls will be strong.

By contrast, geoengineering is an option at the disposal of any reasonably advanced nation. A single country could deploy geoengineering systems from its own territory without consulting the rest of the plant. Geoengineers keen to alter their own country's climate might not assess or even care about the danger their actions could create for climates, ecosystems, and economies elsewhere. A unilateral geoengineering project could impose costs on other countries, such as changes in precipitation patterns and river flows or adverse impacts on agriculture, marine fishing, and tourism. And merely knowing that geoengineering exists as an option may take the pressure off governments to implement the policies needed to cut emissions. [David G. Victor, M. Granger Morgan, Jay Apt, John Steinbruner & Katherine Ricke, The Geoengineering Option: A Last Resort Against Global Warming?, 88 For. Aff. 64, 65-66. 70, 71-72 (March/April 2009).]

Do you agree that states should pursue research into geoengineering strategies? Are such approaches too risky? Will they prevent states from making painful commitments to reducing greenhouse gas emissions? What arrangements, if any, could be adopted to minimize the danger that states might employ geoengineering strategies that harm other states?

13. A source of growing concern in the international environmental law field is the potential for tension between the goals of protecting the environment and promoting free trade and investment. Environmental regulations can serve, intentionally or otherwise, as nontariff barriers. Article XX of the General Agreement on Tariffs and Trade (GATT) permits states to adopt measures "(b) necessary to protect human, animal or plant life or health" or "(g) relating to the conservation of exhaustible natural resources if such measures are made effective in conjunction with restrictions on domestic production or consumption." The chapeau to Article XX makes clear, however, such measures are not permissible if they are "applied in a manner which would constitute a means of arbitrary or unjustifiable discrimination between countries where the same conditions prevail, or a disguised restriction on international trade." Similarly, the 1994 Agreement on Sanitary and Phytosanitary Measures affirms the right of states "to take sanitary and phytosanitary measures necessary for the protection of human, animal or plant life or health," but requires that any such measures must be "based on scientific principles and is not maintained without sufficient scientific evidence."

Separate cases were brought before the GATT/World Trade Organization (WTO) dispute settlement mechanism challenging U.S. laws prohibiting the importation of tuna caught with nets that also catch and kill dolphins and laws banning the importation of shrimp from countries whose commercial shrimp trawlers did not use technology to prevent the killing of endangered sea turtles. In both cases, the dispute settlement body found that the laws violated U.S. obligations under GATT, either because GATT-consistent alternatives were available to achieve the environmental goals or because the U.S. measures were applied in a discriminatory fashion. In the shrimp/turtle case, the WTO Appellate Body emphasized that:

> We have not decided that the protection and preservation of the environment is of no significance to the WTO. Clearly it is. We have not decided that the sovereign nations that are members of the WTO cannot adopt effective measures to protect endangered species, such as sea turtles. Clearly, they can and should. And we have not decided that sovereign states should not act together bilaterally, plurilaterally or multilaterally, either within the WTO or in other international fora, to protect endangered species or to otherwise protect the environment. Clearly, they should and do.
>
> . . . What we *have* decided . . . is simply this: although the measure of the United States in dispute in this appeal serves an environmental objective that is recognized as legitimate under Article XX of the GATT . . . , this measure has been applied by the United States in a manner which constitutes arbitrary and unjustifiable discrimination between Members of the WTO, contrary to the requirements of the chapeau of Article XX. [Appellate Body Report, United States—Import Prohibition of Certain Shrimp and Shrimp Products, WT/DS58/AB/R, at ¶¶186-186 (Oct. 12, 1998).]

Following the Appellate Body's decision in the shrimp/turtle case, the United States amended its regulations to permit shrimp imports from any country that adopted shrimp-harvesting practices deemed "comparably effective" in protecting turtles as those practiced by countries from which the United States permitted imports. In response to a renewed challenge to the U.S. measures, the WTO Appellate Body upheld a dispute-resolution panel's conclusion that "conditioning market access on the adoption of a programme *comparable in effectiveness*" did not amount to "arbitrary or unjustifiable discrimination," and thus did not violate U.S. obligations under GATT. United States—Import Prohibition of Certain Shrimp and Shrimp Products, Recourse to Article 21.5 by Malaysia, WT/DS58/AB/RW at ¶144 (Oct. 22, 2001).

Environmental measures have also been challenged under North America Free Trade Agreement (NAFTA) dispute resolution mechanisms aimed at protecting international investment. In the *Metalclad* case, a U.S. waste disposal company that had invested in a hazardous waste landfill project in Mexico challenged a decree issued by a state governor that established a protected natural area and the refusal of the local city council to issue construction permits, which together prevented Metalclad from operating the landfill. An arbitral tribunal established under Chapter 11 of NAFTA concluded that these actions amounted to an expropriation of Metalclad's investment. The tribunal noted that its ruling was not meant to interfere with the right of NAFTA parties to ensure that investments meet environmental standards. The tribunal concluded, however, that environmental considerations did not justify the acts of the Mexican political subdivisions because Mexico's federal authorities, which are vested with authority over the construction and operation of hazardous waste facilities, had approved Metalclad's project. Metalclad v. Mexico, ICSID Case No. ARB(AGF)/97/1 (Aug. 30, 2000).

11

Use of Force and Arms Control

The legal regime regulating the use of military force is a subject that has fascinated, and frustrated, those interested in international law. It has fascinated because the use of force or the threat to use force has often had important and highly visible results in international relations, affecting the fate of nations and individuals. Moreover, the great destructiveness of modern weaponry has made it increasingly important for the world to develop limits on the use of military force and the means by which war is conducted. Nine states are believed to possess nuclear weapons, and a number of other states, including Iran, have the capability to develop them within several years or less. Even non-nuclear, or conventional, weapons are much improved in their ability to kill and maim.

Developing limits on the use of force has also frustrated international law scholars and practitioners. A state's leaders and citizens are particularly hesitant to circumscribe the state's ability to use its military to protect its perceived vital security interests—indeed, in some cases its very existence. These strongly felt concerns have meant that progress toward an effective international legal regime limiting the use of force has been uneven at best.

Nevertheless, the issues are so fundamentally important that we need to examine what has happened in the past, where the law stands at present, and what might be reasonable goals for the future. To do this, this chapter will address six areas.

The first section explores pre-1945 international legal norms regarding the use of force, which continue to influence debate about legal regulation of resort to war today. Second, we will examine the legal framework governing the use of force established in the U.N. Charter after World War II. We will analyze in particular the legal principles about when states may use force without Security Council authorization and how well they have worked. The third section addresses the role of collective security, notably United Nations and regional peacekeeping and peace enforcement efforts, including an examination of the U.N. and U.S. responses to Iraq's 1990 invasion of Kuwait and the U.S.-led invasion of Iraq in 2003, as well as the military strikes authorized by the United Nations in 2011 to protect Libyan civilians from attacks by their own government.

The fourth section will consider important elements of the law of war, or the rules that apply once armed conflict has begun. The fifth section then examines relevant U.S. domestic law, primarily the War Powers Resolution.

Finally, we look at international efforts to combat the proliferation of nuclear, chemical, and biological weapons. This last section includes a discussion of past measures and the recent cases of North Korea and Iran.

A. INTERNATIONAL LEGAL NORMS BEFORE WORLD WAR II

International legal principles regarding the use of force began to emerge in a systematic fashion after the searing experience of the Second World War. Prior to that, there were centuries of sporadic development and decline. The first decade after World War I witnessed some seminal efforts, such as the League of Nations and the Kellogg-Briand Pact, but these efforts failed, and many states found themselves fighting World War II barely 20 years after the end of the previous war.

1. Legal Norms Prior to World War I

The following two excerpts trace the development of international legal norms from the Roman Empire to the start of World War I. First, Malcolm Shaw provides a brief overview of the period up to the Treaty of Westphalia in 1648. The doctrine of the "just war" was at its peak.

Malcolm N. Shaw, International Law

1119-1120 (6th ed. 2008)

The doctrine of the just war arose as a consequence of the Christianisation of the Roman Empire and the ensuing abandonment by Christians of pacificism. Force could be used provided it complied with the divine will. The concept of the just war embodied elements of Greek and Roman philosophy and was employed as the ultimate sanction for the maintenance of an ordered society. St. Augustine (354-430) defined the just war in terms of avenging of injuries suffered where the guilty party has refused to make amends. War was to be embarked upon to punish wrongs and restore the peaceful status quo but no further. Aggression was unjust and the recourse to violence had to be strictly controlled. St. Thomas Aquinas in the thirteenth century took the definition of the just war a stage further by declaring that it was the subjective guilt of the wrongdoer that had to be punished rather than the objectively wrong activity. He wrote that war could be justified provided it was waged by the sovereign authority, it was accompanied by a just cause (i.e., the punishment of wrongdoers) and it was supported by the right intentions on the part of the belligerents.

With the rise of the European nation-states, the doctrine began to change. It became linked with the sovereignty of states and faced the paradox of wars between Christian states, each side being convinced of the justice of its cause. This situation tended to modify the approach to the just war. The requirement that serious attempts at a peaceful resolution of the dispute were necessary before turning to force began to appear. This reflected the new state of international affairs, since there now existed a series of independent states, uneasily co-existing in Europe in a primitive balance of power system. The use of force against other states, far from strengthening the order, posed serious challenges to it and threatened to undermine it. Thus the emphasis in legal doctrine moved from the application of force to suppress wrongdoers to a concern (if hardly apparent at times) to maintain the order by peaceful means. The great Spanish writer of the sixteenth century, Vitoria, emphasised that "not every kind and degree of wrong can suffice for commencing war". . . .

Gradually it began to be accepted that a certain degree of right might exist on both sides, although the situation was confused by references to subjective and objective justice. Ultimately, the legality of the recourse to war was seen to depend upon the formal processes of law. This approach presaged the rise of positivism with its concentration upon the sovereign state, which could only be bound by what it had consented to. . . .

. . . [W]ith positivism and the definitive establishment of the European balance of power system after the Peace of Westphalia, 1648, the concept of the just war disappeared from international law as such. States were sovereign and equal, and therefore no one state could presume to judge whether another's cause was just or not.

Professor Brownlie picks up the story from the Treaty of Westphalia to the start of World War I.

Ian Brownlie, International Law and the Use of Force by States

14, 16, 19-21, 26-28, 40, 45, 49-50 (rev. ed. 1991)

Europe After Westphalia, 1648-1815: Positivism and the Balance of Power . . .

The period 1648 to 1815 is characterized by the relegation of the just war doctrine to the realms of morality or propaganda since in deference to public opinion governments frequently took pains to advance reasons for declaring war which would give the action some colour of righteousness. . . .

Positivist thought on the Law of Nations flourished in the eighteenth century and the maintenance of the Balance of Power [between the various European states or groups of states was] . . . the *ultima ratio* of diplomacy. . . . State practice reflected the . . . doctrine in various ways, not least in the growth of the law of neutrality based on the assumption that the war was lawful on both sides. . . .

Major Features of State Practice in the Period 1815 to 1914

The next century was still dominated by an unrestricted right of war and the recognition of conquests. . . .

The European settlement of 1814 and 1815 and the Final Act of the Congress of Vienna re-established the public law of Europe and the principle of the Balance of Power. Maintenance of the *status quo* against the rising tide of liberalism and national sentiment necessitated close co-operation in support of legitimism and the repression of rebellion. . . . The concept of the Concert of Europe and the Congress system raised a strong presumption against unilateral changes in the *status quo*. . . .

[Despite this presumption, reflected in the 1815 Final Act of the Congress of Vienna,] the right of states to go to war and to obtain territory by right of conquest was [nevertheless] unlimited although some qualifications to this position had appeared by 1914. Situations resulting from resort to force were regarded as legally valid as in the case of the Prussian annexation of the Danish duchies and the annexation of Alsace-Lorraine by the German Empire. Great Britain, France, and Russia made numerous incursions in Asia and Africa, many of which resulted in annexations or the imposition of a protectorate. The United States fought wars in 1846 and 1898 resulting in the annexation of Texas, the Philippines, Cuba, and Puerto Rico. . . . Many contemporary works of authority stated the position by saying that the right to resort to war was a question of morality and policy outside the sphere of law or that it was a means of change aiding the evolution of international society. A large number of writers described war as a judicial procedure involving also execution and punishment; it was looked upon as the "litigation of nations," a means of obtaining redress for wrongs in the absence of a system of international justice and sanctions.

In the latter part of the nineteenth century there appeared a corollary of this view in the form of war as a judicial procedure, a means of settling a dispute. War was stated to be a means of last resort after recourse to available means of peaceful settlement had failed. . . .

The State of War Doctrine

The practice of states since the early nineteenth century has developed a doctrine which might be considered so absurd as not to merit discussion if it were not for the circumstances that governments have frequently used the doctrine and that it has been resorted to even in more recent times. State practice has emphasized that war is not a legal concept linked with objective phenomena such as large-scale hostilities between the armed forces of organized state entities but a legal status the existence of which depends on the intention of one or more of the states concerned. Thus hostilities resulting in considerable loss of life and destruction of property may not result in a state of war, the term commonly applied to this legal status, if the parties contending do not regard a "state of war" as existing. This technical concept is also referred to variously in the sources as "war," "*de jure* war," "war in the legal sense," and "war in the sense of international law." As a legal status it depended on subjective determination by governments of the legal significance of their own actions. . . . [T]he determination did not depend on any objective criteria. In the period between 1798 and 1920 military occupations, invasions, bombardments, blockades, and lesser forms of conflict took place in the absence of any state of war, at least in the opinion of the governments concerned. War became such a subjective concept in state practice that to attempt a definition was to play with words.

In the view of most of the governments there were substantial reasons of policy for avoiding a state of war while at the same time using the desired amount of coercion. In the era of constitutional government the executive was usually bound to observe time-consuming and politically embarrassing procedures before recourse to "war." The process involved preparation of public opinion and the rallying of sufficient support in the legislative assembly. Recourse to "war" incurred a certain odium; "war" was a term which had acquired a deep psychological and emotional significance. "War" implied a full-scale combat which offended pacific sentiment and was wasteful of lives and a nation's resources. . . . The "state of war" involved a termination of commercial intercourse between the contending states and the invalidation or suspension of treaties. In the more modern period, the appearance of restrictions on the right to resort to war in the League Covenant and other instruments was to provide a further reason for avoiding "war." The extreme subjectivity of what may be called the state of war doctrine was tolerable in the period before the League when war was still viewed to some extent as a private duel and not a matter automatically of concern to the community of states. . . .

States often considered that it was desirable to avoid the disruption and embarrassment of full-scale hostilities and war in the legal sense by recourse either to some restricted use of force with a limited object or to extensive operations without any admission of the existence of a "state of war." . . .

The most important conclusion to be drawn from the nineteenth-century experience is the unsatisfactory nature of "war" as a term of art in view of the freedom which the concept conferred on states in characterizing their own actions. It might include situations in which no hostilities were taking place but fail to cover conflicts which though perhaps limited in scope were nevertheless serious threats to peace. . . .

Hostile Measures Short of War

By perhaps the year 1880 it had become recognized in the practice of states that certain legal conditions were to be observed if resort to force was not to be regarded as creating a formal war and the application of the rights and duties of belligerency and neutrality. Reprisals, pacific blockade, and various types of intervention appeared as institutions of customary law. . . . In theory they created a legal regime for the use of force which did not involve a state of war and modern writers refer to them as though they were highly formalized and well defined. The position was in practice affected by the artificiality of the state of war doctrine and both writers and governments failed to provide any adequate means of distinguishing between the various "hostile measures short of war," or between these, the right of self-preservation and self-defence, and the category of "intervention." . . .

The Close of the Period 1815 to 1914: Retrospect and Prospect . . .

. . . [T]he legacies of the state practice in the nineteenth century were of somewhat dubious value for any future development of an effective legal regime relating to resort to force. Trends in state practice toward peaceful settlement of disputes provide a positive feature of the period but it was nevertheless dominated by the right to go to war as an attribute of the sovereign state. It is true that in the latter part of the period between the Congress of Vienna and [World War I] the doctrine that war was an *ultimate* means of enforcing legal rights, peaceful modes of settlement having failed, had developed in the practice of states. But this is not to assert that the "ultimate means" doctrine in any way superseded the assumption that resort to war was a sovereign right of states. There was simply a partial development of the former doctrine and the two doctrines existed side by side in the somewhat contradictory practice of states. The evidence points to a continued dominance of the view that resort to war was a sovereign right. . . .

Although recourse to war—as a means of last resort to enforce a state's claimed legal rights—was seen, prior to 1914, as an inherent aspect of sovereignty, the "right to war" was, according to Professor Brownlie:

> very rarely asserted either by statesmen or works of authority without some stereotyped plea to a right of self-preservation, and of self-defence, or to necessity or protection of vital interests, or merely alleged injury to rights or national honour and dignity. Unilateral interference with the *status quo* was regarded as a *casus belli.* The great variety of *casus belli* admitted in state practice indicates the unreality of any theoretical justification on the ground of a right of self-preservation or on the basis of a doctrine of necessity. Moreover, the essential subjectivity of such concepts was reinforced by the right assumed of individual determination of the factual prerequisites for the resort to war. . . . [Brownlie, International Law and the Use of Force by States, supra, at 41.]

Even during the nineteenth century, Professor Brownlie suggests, "there were some attempts to restrict the right to go to war to cases of direct and immediate danger." Id. at 42. The 1837 *Caroline* incident is an important illustration of this, and the case has remained important in contributing to the present-day understanding of the right to self-defense. The excerpt below cites some of the key correspondence between U.S. and British officials in connection with the *Caroline* incident.

Destruction of the "Caroline"

2 Moore, A Digest of International Law 409-412 (1906)

[During an insurrection in Canada in 1837, which was still a British colony at the time, directed against the British authorities, the insurgents found refuge, recruits, and other private support from the United States, particularly along the border. The U.S. government "adopted active measures for the enforcement of the neutrality laws," but effective enforcement was difficult. In late December 1837, about 1,000 armed insurgents were encamped at Navy Island on the Canadian side of the Niagara River. There was another camp at Black Rock, on the American side.

[The *Caroline* was a small steamer used by the men on Black Rock and Navy Island to travel between the camps and other locations, including the port of Schlosser on the New York side. On December 29, 1837, 23 U.S. citizens were on board the ship in Schlosser when it was boarded at midnight by about 70 or 80 armed men. They attacked the persons on board and "set the steamer on fire, cut her loose, and set her adrift over the Niagara Falls." It was generally reported at the time of the incident that 12 of the U.S. citizens had been wounded on the steamer and "were sent with her over the falls." There were also reports of celebrations by the British forces at Chippewa on the Canadian side. As a result, the incident generated considerable public outcry in the United States.

[A later investigation revised the casualty estimates. It determined that one U.S. citizen had been killed on the dock, that several others were wounded, and that one person was missing. The rest of the people were accounted for. The investigation also determined that the insurgents on Navy Island had fired some shots into Canada the day of the incident and that the force that attacked the *Caroline* was under the command of a British officer. In a letter dated February 6, 1838, Henry Fox, the British ambassador to the United States, justified the British action by stating:

> [The piratical character of the steamboat "Caroline" and the necessity of self-defense and self-preservation, under which Her Majesty's subjects acted in destroying that vessel, would seem to be sufficiently established.

[The United States disagreed, and demanded reparations.]

The case was finally disposed of by [U.S. Secretary of State Daniel] Webster and [Britain's envoy] Lord Ashburton, in the course of their negotiations in 1842, Mr. Webster admitting that the employment of force might have been justified by the necessity of self-defense, but denying that such necessity existed, while Lord Ashburton, although he maintained that the circumstances afforded excuse for what was done, apologized for the invasion of United States territory. . . .

[In his August 6, 1842, letter to Lord Ashburton, Webster stated:]

> "The President sees with pleasure that your Lordship fully admits those great principles of public law, applicable to cases of this kind, which this government has expressed; and that on your part, as on ours, respect for the inviolable character of the territory of independent states is the most essential foundation of civilization. . . . [W]hile it is admitted that exceptions growing out of the great law of self-defence do exist, those exceptions should be confined to cases in which the 'necessity of that self-defence is instant, overwhelming, and leaving no choice of means, and no moment for deliberation.'"

Requirement of proportionality. In an earlier letter to the British, Webster also articulated that the use of force was subject to a requirement of proportionality:

> It will be for [Her Majesty's government] to show, also, that the local authorities of Canada, even supposing the necessity of the moment authorized them to enter the [U.S.] territories . . . at all, did nothing unreasonable or excessive; since the act, justified by the necessity of self-defence, must be limited by that necessity, and kept clearly within it. [Letter from Daniel Webster to Fox (April 24, 1841), in 1 Papers of Daniel Webster: Diplomatic Papers 67 (Kenneth E. Shewmaker, Kenneth R. Stevens & Anita McGurn eds., 1988).]

Reprisals. "Reprisals" were one of the forms of "hostile measures short of war" described in the excerpt from Professor Brownlie. The following excerpt briefly discusses the concept of reprisals and then summarizes the *Naulilaa* case, a prominent example.

Sir Humphrey Waldock, The Regulation of the Use of Force by Individual States in International Law

81 Recueil des Cours 455, 458-460 (1952)

The legal institution of international reprisals goes back to mediaeval times. It has its roots in a system of private reprisals which was in operation from the 14th-18th centuries. An individual, who had suffered injustice abroad and been unable to obtain redress in the State concerned, would obtain his own Sovereign's authority to take reprisals against the nationals of the foreign sovereign. The basis of this form of reprisals was a communal responsibility for injuries done to foreigners. The system was, of course, open to grave abuse and at sea was apt to deteriorate into licensed piracy. Nevertheless, in the absence of other means of redressing injuries to foreigners, it served a purpose and played an important part in the development of the modern right possessed by States of protecting their nationals abroad. By the 19th century all reprisals are public reprisals taken by the State itself and any international wrong done to the State or its nationals is a just cause for reprisals. Again, reprisals having become State acts, they take more often than not the drastic forms of pacific blockade, bombardment or military occupation. . . .

. . . There is, in fact, more legal doctrine surrounding the institution of reprisals than is sometimes appreciated. . . . [For example,] reprisals were not considered legitimate unless the reprisals-taker had previously attempted to obtain redress from the wrongdoer. . . .

The best account of the customary law of reprisals is to be found in the *Naulilaa* case decided in 1928 by a special arbitral tribunal. When Portugal was neutral in the first World War, a small German party crossed the frontier of Portuguese South-West Africa. Owing to a misunderstanding, the Portuguese fired a few shots which killed 3 Germans. Germany immediately sent a punitive force which invaded Portuguese territory, defeated the Portuguese and then withdrew. A native rising followed causing considerable loss to Portugal. The Tribunal, which was established under the Versailles Treaty to hear Portugal's claim, defined reprisals as follows:

> Reprisals are acts of self-help by the injured State, acts in retaliation for acts contrary to international law on the part of the offending State, which have remained unredressed after a demand for amends. In consequence of such measures, the observance of this or that rule of international law is temporarily suspended, in the relations between the two States. They are limited by considerations of humanity and the rules of good faith, applicable in the relations between States. They are illegal unless they are based upon a previous act contrary to international law. They seek to impose on the offending State reparation for the offence, the return to legality and the avoidance of new offences.

It then rejected Germany's pleas of legitimate reprisals saying:

> (1) The *sine qua non* of a legitimate resort to reprisals is that there should have been a previous violation of international law by the other party and in this case the previous act had been not a breach of international law but an accident.
>
> (2) Reprisals are only legitimate when they have been preceded by an unsuccessful demand for redress and in this case there had been no attempt to obtain satisfaction by legal means. The employment of force is only justifiable by a necessity to use it.

(3) Reprisals, when taken, must be reasonably proportionate to the injury suffered and in this case they were out of all proportion to the injury.

This award by three independent Swiss arbitrators is generally accepted as giving a correct interpretation of the customary law of reprisals.

Notes and Questions

1. Consider the circumstances enunciated by Webster in the *Caroline* incident that justify self-defense and incursions into another country's territory. Do you believe that they encompass all the likely cases for allowing self-defense? If the necessity to react is not "instant, overwhelming, and leaving no choice of means, and no moment for deliberation," then is a country barred from using its military force to respond to another country's use of force—for example, a small border incursion, an attack on its military forces abroad, or an attack on its commercial shipping? If a country cannot use its force in response, what other alternatives should it be allowed? The use of economic sanctions? Resort to the International Court of Justice (discussed in Chapter 4)?

2. Do you agree with the conditions for reprisals announced by the arbitral panel in the *Naulilaa* incident? Based on your reading of the historical excerpt from Professor Brownlie, how did reprisals differ traditionally from the use of force in self-defense? Were reprisals more limited in scope? Could some modern theory of reprisals provide a good basis for reacting to attacks by terrorists who are based in another country?

3. When there was a state of war between belligerent states, other states could adopt a status of neutrality. As Professor Oppenheim has written:

> Neutrality may be defined as the attitude of impartiality adopted by third States towards belligerents and recognised by belligerents, such attitude creating rights and duties between the impartial States and the belligerents. Whether or not a third State will adopt an attitude of impartiality at the outbreak of war is not a matter for International Law but for international politics. [2 L. Oppenheim, International Law 653 (7th ed. 1952).]

The neutral state was accorded freedom from belligerent acts and respect for its territory. The traditional rules of neutrality were based on two principles: (1) nonparticipation and (2) nondiscrimination. The nonparticipation requirement was a guarantee to the belligerents that the neutral state would not assist one of the belligerents against the opposing side. Nondiscrimination required the neutral state to deal impartially with all belligerents. The neutral state could continue to interact with the belligerent states in nonmilitary matters, but no belligerent would have trading advantages over the other.

In 1907, the laws of neutrality were codified in the Hague Conventions and were then further elaborated in later conventions. Article 6 of Hague Convention No. XIII, for example, forbade neutral states from furnishing military supplies to a belligerent. Other rules, such as the movement of troops, military equipment, or prizes of war across neutral land, waters, or airspace, were also codified.

Under the neutrality rules of the Hague Convention, neutral states could continue trading with belligerent states in two ways: first, the neutral state could trade in any nonmilitary supplies; second, the neutral state could allow private individuals to supply military goods. A neutral state was not obligated to deter private intervention but was still bound by the nondiscrimination principle. As a result, a neutral state could either impose a total embargo on exports of military goods by private individuals or, alternatively, it could allow the exports but without any discrimination among the belligerents.

2. *Developments from World War I to World War II*

The scope and carnage of World War I had a considerable impact on the attitude of states toward the use of force. As Professor Brownlie relates:

> In the period of the First World War and of the peace settlement and conferences of 1919-1920 there were several indications of the development of increased sensitivity on the part of states to the use of force. The dramatic results of the failure to maintain peace by a system of alliances, the geographical extent of the war, and the enormous loss of life, the chaos which followed, all these tended to create a climate favourable to a new approach. During the currency of the war numerous peace plans appeared and the creation of the League of Nations was an integral part of the peace settlement. [Ian Brownlie, International Law and the Use of Force by States, supra, at 51.]

a. The League of Nations

The major institutional result of the war was the creation of the League of Nations. President Woodrow Wilson was one of the leading figures at the Paris Peace Conference that followed World War I and championed the idea of the League, but the United States failed to join because of opposition in the U.S. Senate. Malcolm Shaw provides a brief analysis of the significance of the League and how it was designed to stop aggression:

> The First World War marked the end of the balance of power system and raised anew the question of unjust war. It also resulted in efforts to rebuild international affairs upon the basis of a general international institution which would oversee the conduct of the world community to ensure that aggression could not happen again. The creation of the League of Nations reflected a completely different attitude to the problems of force in the international order.
>
> The Covenant of the League declared that members should submit disputes likely to lead to a rupture to arbitration or judicial settlement or inquiry by the Council of the League. In no circumstances were members to resort to war until three months after the arbitral award or judicial decision or report by the Council. This was intended to provide a cooling-off period for passions to subside and reflected the view that such a delay might well have broken the seemingly irreversible chain of tragedy that linked the assassination of the Austrian Archduke in Sarajevo with the outbreak of general war in Europe. League members agreed not to go to war with members complying with such an arbitral award or judicial decision or unanimous report by the Council.
>
> The League system did not, it should be noted, prohibit war or the use of force, but it did set up a procedure designed to restrict it to tolerable levels. It was a constant challenge of the inter-war years to close the gaps in the Covenant in an effort to achieve

the total prohibition of war in international law and this resulted ultimately in the signing in 1928 of the General Treaty for the Renunciation of War (the Kellogg-Briand Pact) [discussed below]. [Shaw, International Law, supra, at 1121-1122.]

Professor John Murphy notes one other unique feature of the League, and then relates what happened in the next two decades.

The most important of the novel features were the principle of the guarantee by member states of the political independence and territorial integrity of each member against external aggression, and the use of collective measures—economic, financial, and, perhaps, military—to defeat aggression. . . .

During its first decade the League enjoyed a substantial measure of success in spite of the failure of the United States to become a member. The years 1924 to 1929 were a period of apparent general prosperity, relative peace, and promising cooperative efforts in the economic and social fields. But this veneer of prosperity contributed to the failure of governments to take steps necessary to deal with the basic problems of economic maladjustment and imbalance resulting from the war. The bubble burst in 1929, and the years 1930 to 1936 saw a worldwide depression of unprecedented breadth and depth. The depression helped to bring to power expansionistic, authoritative regimes in Germany, Italy, and Japan. These regimes challenged the peace-keeping capabilities of the League, and the League proved unequal to the challenge.

More properly put, the Great Powers, on whose support the peace-keeping capabilities of the League depended, declined to meet the threat. The United States, as a nonmember, gave only limited support; Great Britain and France, for a variety of political, economic, and social reasons, failed to fulfill their responsibilities as League members. As a result, the League was unable to check Japanese aggression in Manchuria in the early thirties or to sanction Italy effectively after its attack on Ethiopia in October 1935. No attempt whatsoever was made to use League machinery and procedures to prevent German remilitarization of the Rhineland in March 1936 in clear violation of the Treaty of Versailles and the Locarno Pact or the outbreak of war when it became imminent as the result of the Czechoslovakian crisis and the threat to Poland. The expulsion of the Soviet Union in 1939 following its attack on Finland was, in a sense, the League's last gesture as an institution designed to prevent and punish aggression. [John F. Murphy, The United Nations and the Control of International Violence 10-11 (1982).]

b. The Kellogg-Briand Pact

The Kellogg-Briand Pact, one of the most publicized international initiatives of the inter-War period, generated considerable hope about the prospects of maintaining international peace. It contained two brief, substantive articles.

The General Treaty for the Renunciation of War

(commonly called the Kellogg-Briand Pact)
Aug. 27, 1928, 40 Stat. 2343, 94 L.N.T.S. 57

ARTICLE I

The High Contracting Parties solemnly declare in the names of their respective peoples that they condemn recourse to war for the solution of international controversies, and renounce it as an instrument of national policy in their relations with one another.

ARTICLE II

The High Contracting Parties agree that the settlement or solution of all disputes or conflicts of whatever nature or of whatever origin they may be, which may arise among them, shall never be sought except by pacific means.

Notes and Questions

1. Did the Covenant of the League of Nations outlaw war? Outlaw the use of force? What about aggression by one Member State against another?

2. The Kellogg-Briand Pact became effective in July 1929 and is still in force. As of February 2011, it had been ratified by over 60 countries, including the United States.

3. Consider the text of the Kellogg-Briand pact. It renounces war. What about the use of military force that is not called "war"? Is that prohibited? Is this a major loophole? (See the discussion in the Brownlie excerpt above about the "state of war" doctrine and recourse to "hostile measures short of war.") Are uses of force short of war prohibited by the agreement of the parties in Article II "that the settlement or solution of all disputes or conflicts . . . shall never be sought except by pacific means"? What if pacific means fail?

4. The Kellogg-Briand Pact does not include any enforcement mechanisms. Why do you think it did not? How effective can such an agreement be without an enforcement mechanism?

5. The following are two different assessments of the Pact. As you continue through this chapter, decide which assessment you consider more accurate. First, Malcolm Shaw concludes:

> In view of the fact that this treaty has never been terminated and in the light of its widespread acceptance, it is clear that prohibition of the resort to war is now a valid principle of international law. It is no longer possible to set up the legal relationship of war in international society. . . .
>
> However, the prohibition on the resort to war does not mean that the use of force in all circumstances is illegal. Reservations to the treaty by some states made it apparent that the right to resort to force in self-defence was still a recognised principle in international law. Whether in fact measures short of war such as reprisals were also prohibited or were left untouched by the treaty's ban on war was unclear and subject to conflicting interpretations. [Shaw, International Law, supra, at 1122.]

Historian Emanuel Chill offers a considerably more critical assessment:

> The Kellogg-Briand Pact . . . was . . . a brief afterglow of Wilsonian optimism on the darkening horizon of European politics at the close of the period of fulfillment. Calling for the renunciation of aggressive war, but without establishing means of enforcement, the . . . Pact was almost universally subscribed. It stands as an ironic preface to the supervening decades of blood and steel, the 1930's and 1940's. [Emanuel Chill, Commentary, in 2 Major Peace Treaties of Modern History: 1648-1967, at 1225, 1232 (Fred L. Israel ed., 1967).]

B. USE OF FORCE AFTER WORLD WAR II

Two of the most important developments for limiting the use of force that emerged from the cataclysm of World War II were: (1) the Nuremberg trials of Nazi leaders as war criminals; and (2) the adoption of the United Nations Charter.

1. The Nuremberg Charter and Trials

The International Military Tribunal was established at Nuremberg, Germany, in August 1945 by the four major powers — the United States, France, the United Kingdom, and the U.S.S.R. — that defeated Nazi Germany. The Charter of the Tribunal and the ensuing trials before the Tribunal of Nazis charged as war criminals, as well as the trials conducted by the International Military Tribunal for the Far East and a host of other trials and proceedings before other civilian and military tribunals, established important precedents both for the general norms limiting a state's use of force and for the responsibility of individuals. (The issue of individual criminal responsibility under international law is discussed further in Chapter 12.)

For present purposes, it should be noted that the Charter defined certain crimes and authorized the Tribunal to try people for them and to impose judgment and sentence. Article 6 of the Charter defined the crimes.

The Charter of the International Military Tribunal

Article 6

. . . The following acts, or any of them, are crimes coming within the jurisdiction of the Tribunal for which there shall be individual responsibility:

(a) Crimes against peace: namely, planning, preparation, initiation or waging of a war of aggression, or a war in violation of international treaties, agreements or assurances, or participation in a common plan or conspiracy for the accomplishment of any of the foregoing;

(b) War crimes: namely, violations of the laws or customs of war. Such violations shall include, but not be limited to, murder, ill-treatment or deportation to slave labor or for any other purpose of civilian population of or in occupied territory, murder or ill-treatment of prisoners of war or persons on the seas, killing of hostages, plunder of public or private property, wanton destruction of cities, towns or villages, or devastation not justified by military necessity;

(c) Crimes against humanity: namely, murder, extermination, enslavement, deportation, and other inhumane acts committed against any civilian population, before or during the war, or persecutions on political, racial or religious grounds in execution of or in connection with any crime within the jurisdiction of the Tribunal, whether or not in violation of the domestic law of the country where perpetrated.

Leaders, organizers, instigators and accomplices participating in the formulation or execution of a common plan or conspiracy to commit any of the foregoing crimes are responsible for all acts performed by any persons in execution of such plan.

The Charter made it a crime against peace to engage in "planning, preparation, initiation or waging of a war of aggression, or a war in violation of international treaties." Likewise, "wanton destruction of cities, towns or villages" and "devastation not justified by military necessity" were war crimes. Punishment could include death. Defining these crimes in a treaty, and then finding people guilty of them during the war crimes trials, added a new element to the traditional norms regarding the use of force. In response to legal challenges raised by the defendants about how the Tribunal could criminalize wars of aggression, the Tribunal relied heavily on the renunciation of war in the Kellogg-Briand Pact.

The adoption of the United Nations Charter after World War II represented an attempt to address the use of force in international relations in a more comprehensive manner. We turn now to the Charter's use of force regime.

2. *Overview of the U.N. Charter's Use of Force Regime*

The United Nations was created in 1945 primarily to prevent military conflict among its members and to settle international disputes peacefully. (See discussion of the United Nations in Chapter 5.C.) Article 2(3) of the United Nations Charter provides that "[a]ll Members shall settle their international disputes by peaceful means in such a manner that international peace and security, and justice, are not endangered." Among the Charter's key provisions regarding the use of force are Articles 2(4) and 51.

Article 2(4)

All Members shall refrain in their international relations from the threat or use of force against the territorial integrity or political independence of any state, or in any other manner inconsistent with the Purposes of the United Nations.

Article 51

Nothing in the present Charter shall impair the inherent right of individual or collective self-defence if an armed attack occurs against a Member of the United Nations, until the Security Council has taken the measures necessary to maintain international peace and security. . . .

Other important Charter terms governing the use of force are the provisions of Chapter VII under which the Security Council may authorize the use of force in the interests of collective security, as well as the provisions of Chapter VIII regarding the role of regional arrangements, such as the North Atlantic Treaty Organization (NATO). Central to the Council's Chapter VII collective security powers is Article 42, which provides in part that the Security Council "may take such action by air, sea, or land forces as may be necessary to maintain or restore international peace and security." (The U.N. Charter is in the Documentary Supplement. The collective security provisions are set out and discussed in greater depth below in Section C.)

Professor Thomas Franck provides an overview of the Charter's use of force provisions and describes the political and technological developments that began, almost immediately after the Charter's adoption, to challenge the operation of its use of force regime. He also explains his views about the adaptability of the Charter's use of force rules.

Thomas M. Franck, Recourse to Force

1-7 (2002)

After the Second World War, . . . the Nuremberg tribunal was called upon to draw a much brighter line than hitherto against aggression. So, too, at Dumbarton Oaks and San Francisco, a UN Charter was written that makes absolute the obligation of states not to resort to force against each other and to resist collectively any breach of this prohibition.

New remedies, as we know from medicine, tend to produce unexpected side effects. Article 2(4) of the Charter seemingly cures the . . . normative ambiguities [in the League of Nations' Covenant] regarding states' "threat or use of force" against each other. It plugs the loopholes. But did it intend to prevent a state—one facing imminent and overwhelming attack—from striking first in anticipatory self-defense? Did it intend also to immunize against foreign intervention a state whose government is engaged in genocide against a part of its own population? Are there circumstances in which the prohibition on recourse to force in effect endorses that which itself is wholly unconscionable? Did the Charter try to plug too many loopholes? Has the pursuit of perfect justice unintentionally created conditions of grave injustice?

The Use of Force Under the UN Charter System

On its face, the UN Charter, ratified by virtually every nation, is quite clear-eyed about its intent: to initiate a new global era in which war is forbidden as an instrument of state policy, but collective security becomes the norm. Collective security is to be achieved by use of international military police forces and lesser but forceful measures such as diplomatic and economic sanctions. Recourse to such measures is to be the exclusive prerogative of the United Nations, acting in concert. . . .

The Charter text embodies these two radical new concepts: it absolutely prohibits war and prescribes collective action against those who initiate it. We are thereby ushered into the "post-war" era through Charter text: Articles 2(4), 42, and 43.

Article 2(4) essentially prohibits states from using force against one another. Instead, Articles 42 and 43 envisage the collective use of force at the behest of the Security Council upon its determination—Article 39—that there exist what Article 2(4) forbids, a threat to the peace, breach of the peace, or act of aggression: one that must therefore be met by concerted police action. Article 42 sets the parameters for collective measures, including the deployment of military forces. Under Article 43, such forces are to be committed by member states to the service of the Security Council.

In the idealized world of the Charter, no state would ever again attack another: and if one did, its aggression would be met by a unified and overwhelming response made under the authority and control of the Security Council.

Even in 1945, however, there were doubts as to whether this idealized world order was as imminent as the post-San Francisco euphoria predicted. Thus, . . . the Charter provide[s] alternatives, just in case. Article 51 authorizes states to act alone or with their allies in self-defense against any military aggression ("armed attack") that the Security Council might have failed either to prevent or to repel. . . .

In this way, the Charter establishes a two-tiered system.

- The upper tier consists of a normative structure for an ideal world — one in which no state would initiate armed conflict, but in which any acts of aggression that did occur would be met by effective armed force deployed by the United Nations. . . .
- A lower tier is to operate whenever the United Nations is unable to respond collectively against aggression. Subject to certain conditions, states may invoke an older legal principle: the sovereign right of self-defense. Acting alone or with allies, the Charter authorizes members to use force to resist any armed attack by one state on another until UN collective measures come to the victim's rescue. But they may do so only after an actual armed attack. . . .

Both tiers, almost immediately, were seen to fail to address adequately four seismic developments that, even as the Charter was being signed, were beginning to transform the world.

One was the advent of the Cold War, which, because of the veto, froze the Security Council's ability to guarantee collective security under Articles 42 and 43 of the Charter. . . .

Another was the ingenuity with which states effectively and dangerously substituted indirect aggression — the export of insurgency and covert meddling in civil wars — for the sort of traditional frontal military aggression the Charter system was designed to prohibit by Article 2(4) and to repress by Article 42.

The third development was the technological transformation of weaponry (nuclear, chemical, and biological) and of delivery systems (rocketry). These "improvements" tended to make obsolete the Charter's Article 51 provision for states' "inherent" right of self-defense. . . . Article 51 limits "self-defence" to situations where an "armed attack" has occurred. However, the acceleration and escalation of means for launching an attack soon confounded the bright line drawn by the law, effecting a reductio ad absurdum that, literally, seems to require a state to await an actual attack on itself before instituting countermeasures. Inevitably, states responded to the new dangers by claiming a right of "anticipatory self-defence." That claim, however, is not supported by the Charter's literal text. And "anticipatory self-defence," too, is vulnerable to reductio ad absurdum. If every state were free to determine for itself when to initiate the use of force in "anticipation" of an attack, there would be nothing left of Articles 2(4) and 51. . . .

The fourth development was a rising global public consciousness of the importance of human freedom and the link between the repression of human rights and threats to the peace. . . . [T]he text of the Charter puts human rights rather at its periphery while focusing on the prevention of aggression. That deliberate drafting choice reflected the concerns of some states that the cause of human rights might be used to justify intervention in their sovereign affairs. The drafters, of course, did not anticipate the imminent end of colonialism and communism, the rise of a democratic entitlement, and a tectonic shift in public values during the 1990s, each of which altered perceptions of sovereignty and its limits.

All four of these developments might have been (and to some extent were) foreseen, but the Charter's text is not facially responsive to the challenge of change. It, like other grand instruments written for the long term, has had to meet the threat of obsolescence with adaption. . . .

[Change] has come about not by the formal process of amendment but by the practice of the United Nations' principal organs.

Adaptability of the Charter as a Quasi-Constitutional Instrument

The UN Charter is a treaty, one to which almost every state adheres. This universality, alone, distinguishes it from the general run of international agreements. That the drafters of the Charter recognized its special quality is evidenced by Article 103, which purports to establish an unusual principle of treaty law:

> In the event of a conflict between the obligations of the Members of the United Nations under the present Charter and their obligations under any other international agreement, their obligations under the present Charter shall prevail.

This legal primacy of the Charter over subsequent agreements can only be construed as a "quasi-constitutional" feature. Clearly, it illustrates that the drafters intended to create a special treaty different from all others. This difference becomes relevant when we consider the instrument's capacity for adaption through the interpretative practice of its organs and members. . . .

[I]t is the political organs that have done most of this interpretive work. . . . [T]hese interpretations of the Charter are made in the relevant political organ not only by a formal vote but as a merged, or even submerged, part of its "decisions on the matter at issue, and often . . . by implication." . . .

What emerges from the vast legacy of recorded debates and decisions of the principal political organs is that they tend to treat the Charter not as a static formula, but as a constitutive instrument capable of organic growth. Borrowing a phrase coined by the Imperial Privy Council speaking of the Canadian constitution, the Charter is "a living tree." . . .

. . . Two political organs (the General Assembly and the Security Council) were given Charter-implementing powers: Chapters IV and V, respectively. An independent civil service, the Secretariat, headed by a Secretary-General, enjoys autonomous, Charter-based power to construe and apply the Charter and the decisions of the political organs. . . .

Each principal organ and the members thus continuously interpret the Charter and do so in accordance with the requisites of ever-changing circumstances. This necessarily means that the text of the Charter is always evolving. . . .

3. *The Prohibition on the Use of Force*

Unlike the Kellogg-Briand Pact, which banned only "recourse to war," the prohibition on the use of force in Article 2(4) was intended by its drafters to be comprehensive. It was meant to outlaw not only "traditional war, but . . . also other uses of force, whether or not in declared war, whether or not in all-out hostilities." Louis Henkin, How Nations Behave: Law and Policy 139-140 (1979). Some ambiguity arises, however, from the fact that, in Professor Schachter's words, Article 2(4) "is not drafted that way." He continues:

> The last 23 words contain important qualifications. The article requires States to refrain from force or threat of force when that is "against the territorial integrity or political independence of any State" or "inconsistent with the purposes of the United Nations". . . .
>
> One answer to [the] argument [that it would be permissible under Article 2(4) to use force for benign purposes not directed at the territorial integrity or political independence of another state, such as vindicating or securing a legal right] is that the Charter itself requires that disputes be settled by peaceful means (Article 2, para. 3) and that the first declared purpose of the Charter is to remove threats to the peace and to suppress breaches of the peace. Consequently any use of force in international relations [not in self-defense or pursuant to Chapter VII of the Charter] would be inconsistent with a Charter purpose. . . .
>
> A second answer is that any coercive incursion of armed troops into a foreign State without its consent impairs that State's territorial integrity, and any use of force to coerce a State to adopt a particular policy or action must be considered as an impairment of that State's political independence. On these premises it does not matter than the coercive action may have only a short-term effect nor does it matter that the end sought by the use of force is consistent with a stated purpose of the Charter. As long as the act of force involves a non-consensual use of a State's territory or compels a State to take a decision it would not otherwise take, Article 2(4) has been violated. [Oscar Schachter, International Law in Theory and Practice 112-113 (1991).]

Notes and Questions

1. The absence in the Charter of a definition for the term "force" in Article 2(4) presents a threshold question about what conduct the U.N. Charter's use of force regime covers. Does "force" encompass any coercive action taken by states in their international relations? As Professor Schachter notes, the term can be used "in a wide sense to embrace all types of coercion: economic, political and psychological as well as physical." Schachter, International Law in Theory and Practice, supra, at 111. During the San Francisco negotiations on the U.N. Charter, Brazil proposed to broaden the prohibition on the use of force to include economic coercion, but this proposal was rejected. A leading treatise on the U.N. Charter, after conceding that the scope of the term "force" in Article 2(4) is "not undisputed," concludes

that it "does not cover any possible kind of force, but is, according to the correct and prevailing view, limited to armed force." Albrecht Randelzhofer, Article 2(4), in 1 The Charter of the United Nations 117 (Bruno Simma et al. eds., 2d ed. 2002).

2. Although Article 2(4) is concerned with the "use of force," the Charter elsewhere uses different terminology to refer to armed conflict. Article 1, for instance, identifies "the suppression of acts of aggression" as one of the purposes of the United Nations. Article 39 addresses the competence of the Security Council to address a "breach of the peace, or an act of aggression." Are these terms synonymous, or do they have different meanings?

In 1974, after years of discussion, the General Assembly adopted a resolution defining "aggression" as "the use of armed force by a State against the sovereignty, territorial integrity or political independence of another State, or in any other manner inconsistent with the Charter of the United Nations." The resolution lists a series of acts that qualify as acts of aggression, including as the "invasion or attack by the armed forces of a State of the territory of another State," the "[b]ombardment by the armed forces of a State against the territory of another State," and an "attack by the armed forces of a State on the land, sea or air force, or marine and air fleets of another State." The definition further provides that

> the first use of armed force by a State in contravention of the Charter shall constitute *prima facie* evidence of an act of aggression although the Security Council may, in conformity with the Charter, conclude that a determination that an act of aggression has been committed would not be justified in the light of other relevant circumstances, including the fact that the acts concerned or their consequences are not of sufficient gravity. [Definition of Aggression, G.A. Res. 3314 (XXIX), U.N. Doc. U.N. Doc. A/9631 (Dec. 14, 1974).]

The definition of the crime of aggression adopted in 2010 as a proposed amendment to the Statute of the International Criminal Court (ICC) and its relation to the definition of "aggression" in General Assembly Resolution 3314 are addressed in Chapter 12.B.3.d.

3. As states and their citizens become increasingly dependent on computers and information systems, the threat of "cyberattack" is a matter of growing international concern:

> Cyberattack refers to offensive actions to alter, disrupt, deceive, degrade, or destroy computer systems or networks or the information or programs resident in or transiting these systems. Its purpose is to mislead or disable an important network-dependent activity. . . .
>
> The threat of serious cyberattack by state or non-state actors has been on the U.S. security agenda for many years. There have been notable cyberattacks in recent years on the United States and other countries . . . All of these attacks have occurred against an essentially constant background of lower-level probes that are not publicized. A common attack mode is the distributed denial of service (DDOS) blitz, in which tens of thousands of unwittingly cooperating computers are combined into a network (botnet) to flood a target's Web site and thereby disable it. The identity of the organizer and initiator of such an attack can be very difficult to determine, including, importantly, whether it is another government. The public reporting of events almost always speaks only of assumed or likely sources.

> Attacks much more harmful than DDOS, with cascading effects, are technically feasible and are assumed to be under development, certainly at the state level. . . . The threat . . . is expected to grow in scope and sophistication. [David Elliot, Weighing the Case for a Convention to Limit Cyberwarfare, Arms Control Today, Nov. 2009, at 21.]

Do you think that a distributed denial of service attack as described above would be an "armed attack" under the U.N. Charter? A "use of force"? What about the intentional delivery of a computer virus that disables another country's critical computer systems. As a possible example, see the discussion of the Stuxnet virus in Section F.3.d below. Should there be special standards for cyberweapons, or do you think that the traditional international law norms regarding use of force are sufficient?

4. *Exceptions to the Prohibition on the Use of Force: Self-defense*

Although the prohibition on the use of force in Article 2(4) is comprehensive, in that it is intended to cover all uses of armed force between states, the Charter nevertheless recognizes that there may be circumstances in which the use of force is necessary. We examine the use of force under the Charter's collective security provisions in Section C. But first, in this and the following subsections, we explore in greater depth the justifications—some well founded, others less so—that states have relied on in using force based on their own independent or autonomous legal authority. We begin with the following excerpt, which examines the exception that permits force to be used in self-defense.

Allen S. Weiner, The Use of Force and Contemporary Security Threats: Old Medicine for New Ills?

59 Stan. L. Rev. 415, 422-423 (2006)

Fresh from their bitter experience during the Second World War . . . the drafters of the U.N. Charter were not starry-eyed idealists. The League of Nations and the 1928 Kellogg-Briand Pact outlawing war had failed to prevent aggression and global war. As such, the Charter's founders well understood that states might opt to use force despite formal legal prohibitions on their doing so. Accordingly, the U.N. Charter provided two permissible exceptions to Article 2(4)'s prohibition on the use of force: self-defense and collective security measures taken under the authority of the Security Council [discussed in Section C].

. . . SELF-DEFENSE

Article 51 of the U.N. Charter embodies the right to use force in self-defense:

> Nothing in the present Charter shall impair the inherent right of individual or collective self-defence if an armed attack occurs against a Member of the United Nations, until the Security Council has taken measures necessary to maintain international peace and security. . . .

There are several key features to the Article 51 right of self-defense. First, it is a *unilateral* right. A state requires no approval from any external body before it may avail itself of its sovereign right to defend itself. Second, Article 51 allows a state not only to defend itself but also to join others, such as partners in security alliances, in collectively repelling an armed attack launched by another state. Third, the drafters of the Charter contemplated that the right of self-defense would be an interim response; states would be entitled to use force only until such time as the collective security machinery had responded satisfactorily to the initiation of hostilities.

Fourth, and most important, the right of self-defense recognized in the Charter is limited to situations in which an "armed attack" has occurred. In this regard, Article 51, read together with Article 2(4), represents a limitation on the pre-existing customary international law right to use force. Prior to the adoption of the Charter, the existence of an "armed attack" was not a threshold requirement for the use of force. Rather, the right to use force was deemed an inherent element of state sovereignty, and states could resort to force in response to any breach of their legal rights, at least where efforts to resolve the dispute through diplomatic means had failed. Moreover, the concept of self-defense was broadly understood to cover situations in which a state perceived that its "'security' [was] threatened"; at the dawn of the Second World War, customary international law was generally considered to permit the exercise of anticipatory self-defense in the face of imminent danger. However, the prohibition on the use of force in Article 2(4) of the Charter, combined with the limitation on the right of self-defense under Article 51 to cases of armed attacks, served—at least at the time of the Charter's adoption in 1945—to prohibit anticipatory self-defense.

Notes and Questions

1. What is an "armed attack" within the meaning of Article 51 of the Charter? Does any use of military force qualify as an armed attack? In its *Nicaragua* decision, the ICJ drew a distinction between "the most grave forms of the use of force (those constituting an armed attack) [and] other less grave forms." Military and Paramilitary Activities in and Against Nicaragua (Nicaragua v. United States of America), 1986 I.C.J. 14, 101 (June 27). The Court did not elaborate on its view of where the line should be drawn, but contrasted an "armed attack" with a "frontier incident"; the Court suggested that whether a use of force constituted an armed attack would depend on its "scale and effects."

2. Although the right of self-defense is a unilateral right, this does not mean that a state's subjective belief that it is entitled to use force will necessarily be correct. In the *Oil Platforms* case before the ICJ, Iran challenged the destruction by U.S. forces of several Iranian oil production platforms in the Persian Gulf. (The case is discussed further in Chapter 4.) The United States defended its acts as a justifiable exercise of the right of self-defense following a series of attacks on ships engaged in neutral commercial shipping that were American-owned or had been reflagged as U.S. vessels, as well as a missile attack on a U.S.-reflagged oil tanker and the mining of a U.S. warship in international waters. Whether a use of force is necessary in self-defense, the Court stated, "is 'not purely a question for the subjective judgment of the party', and may thus be assessed by the Court." Oil Platforms (Islamic Republic of Iran v. United States of America), 2003 I.C.J. 161, 183 (Nov. 6). The Court said the

requirement that "measures taken avowedly in self-defence must have been necessary for that purpose is strict and objective, leaving no room for any 'measure of discretion.'" Id. at 196.

After reviewing the evidence, the Court concluded that the United States had failed to demonstrate to the Court's satisfaction that the missile that struck a U.S.-reflagged oil tanker had been launched by Iran, and not Iraq, which was at war with Iran. Similarly, the Court noted the "inconclusiveness" of the evidence that Iran was responsible for the mining of a U.S. warship. Id. at 190, 195-196. The Court consequently found that the U.S. attacks against the Iranian oil platforms could not be justified on self-defense grounds.

One commentator has criticized the ICJ's "rigid approach" in adjudicating use of force claims and urges that ex post facto assessments of uses of force should instead take into account the "reasonable perceptions and intentions of decision-makers at the time they resorted to a use of force, including any exceptional circumstances." David Kaye, Adjudicating Self-Defense: Discretion, Perception, and the Resort to Force in International Law, 44 Colum. J. Transnat'l L. 134, 167, 181 (2005).

3. Can nonstate actors commit an "armed attack" that would give rise to a right of self-defense under Article 51 of the Charter? The text of Article 51 itself refers to the right of "self-defence if an armed attack occurs against a Member of the United Nations," and is not limited to circumstances in which an armed attack is launched by another state. In addition, the principles of self-defense elaborated in the Caroline case (discussed above in Section A) arose in the context of a use of force by nonstate actors. More recently, in resolutions addressing the September 11 terrorist attacks against the United States, the Security Council "[r]ecognized the inherent right of individual or collective self-defence in accordance with the Charter." See S.C. Res. 1368, U.N. Doc. S/RES/1368 (Sept. 12, 2001).

In an Advisory Opinion regarding the Israeli security barrier built largely in occupied Palestinian territory, however, the International Court of Justice suggested that the right of self-defense is not available in response to armed attacks by nonstate actors. The Court interpreted Article 51 of the U.N. Charter as recognizing "an inherent right of self-defence in the case of armed attack by one State against another State." Because Palestinian terrorist attacks in Israel were not attacks by a state, the Court concluded that Israel could not justify construction of the security barrier on the basis of self-defense. Legal Consequences of the Construction of a Wall in the Occupied Palestinian Territory, Advisory Opinion, 2004 I.C.J. 136, 194. This view was strongly criticized in separate opinions by Judges Buergenthal, id. at 241-242, Higgins, id. at 215, and Kooijmans, id. at 229. It remains to be seen whether the Court's narrow view of self-defense in its 2004 advisory opinion will gain wide acceptance.

4. In defining the right of self-defense, U.S. Secretary of State Daniel Webster in the *Caroline* case wrote that the right existed when the "necessity of that self-defence is instant, overwhelming, and leaving no choice of means, and no moment for deliberation." Should that standard continue to be applicable? Practically, why should an attacked state be required to respond immediately at the time and place of the attacker's choosing? Should not the attacked country have the opportunity to gather its forces and respond at a time and place that might be more advantageous? For example, if Pakistan were to launch a major surprise attack against India in the mountain passes into Kashmir where Indian forces might

face a tactical disadvantage in mounting a counterattack, should not India have the right to pick a better time and place to launch a counterattack?

5. Article 51 refers to the "inherent right of individual or collective self-defence." As Professor Franck notes, "[b]y adding the term 'collective' to a provision that essentially licenses victims to defend themselves, [Article 51] was also intended to accommodate regional or other mutual defense arrangements." Franck, Recourse to Force, supra, at 48.

Must a state that is the victim of an armed attack ask others to come to its aid, or do states have a right to engage in collective self-defense even when no such request has been made? In the *Nicaragua* case, the International Court of Justice evaluated whether U.S. actions against Nicaragua could be justified on collective self-defense grounds, as a response to Nicaragua's own assistance to leftist rebels fighting against the government of neighboring El Salvador. The Court said:

> It is . . . clear that it is the State which is the victim of an armed attack which must form and declare the view that it has been so attacked. There is no rule in customary international law permitting another State to exercise the right of collective self-defence on the basis of its own assessment of the situation. [Military and Paramilitary Activities in and against Nicaragua (Nicaragua v. United States of America), 1986 I.C.J. 14, 104 (June 27).]

The Court also concluded that "a request by the State which is the victim of the alleged attack" is a requirement for the exercise of collective self defense. Id. at 105. Do you agree that the right of collective self-defense should depend on a request by the state that has been attacked? What would be arguments for or against such a requirement?

5. *Other Claimed Justifications for the Use of Force*

Professor Franck, in the excerpt quoted above, characterizes the U.N. Charter's use of force regime as one capable of adaptation through the practice of the political organs of the United Nations. Since 1945, the members of the United Nations have been faced with efforts by states to justify resort to armed force in circumstances that do not fall squarely within the right of self-defense in Article 51. Professor Franck describes the recurring justifications and the reaction of the U.N.'s political bodies to them.

Thomas M. Franck, Recourse to Force

51-52, 69-70, 76-77, 96-99, 107-110, 131-134 (2002)

In fifty-five years of practice, a pattern of justifications [for resort to armed force] has emerged, sometimes explicitly spelled out, sometimes implicit in the situation. . . .

Five kinds of justifications stand out, each based on a "creative" interpretation of Article 51:

1. The claim that a state may resort to armed self-defence in response to attacks by terrorists, insurgents or surrogates operating from another state;

2. The claim that self-defence may be exercised against the source of ideological subversion from abroad;
3. The claim that a state may act in self-defence to rescue or protect its citizens abroad;
4. The claim that a state may act in self-defence to anticipate and preempt an imminent armed attack; and
5. The claim that the right of self-defence is available to abate an egregious, generally recognized, yet persistently unredressed wrong, including the claim to exercise a right of humanitarian intervention.

These five kinds of claims will be examined [below, with claims to a right to use force to protect citizens abroad, to respond to attacks by terrorists and to engage in humanitarian intervention each discussed in later subsections]. In practice, some are now routinely vindicated, others not. . . .

Self-Defense Against Ideological Subversion . . .

The response of states and international institutions to this justification has been entirely and resoundingly negative. However, the same justification is recently beginning to be heard again, this time in the theological-ideological conflict between forces of Islamic fundamentalism and more tolerant societies, including other more liberal Islamic states, secular India, and the Western societies in which religions have been disestablished. It is too early to judge whether the claim of a right to use force in self-defense against the export of militant theocratic ideology, or of liberal democracy and religious pluralism, will encounter greater acceptance in the practice of states and international organizations than did the Cold War claim to a right to use force against the export of ideological subversion. . . .

Self-Defense Against Attacks on Citizens Abroad . . .

[There have been many] instances in which an expansive concept of "self-defence" has been advanced by a state to justify using force to protect citizens abroad, either by military rescue or by forcibly deterring those who threaten their safety. . . .

These practices [of "humanitarian intervention"* or "citizen rescue"], whatever their currency at [an] earlier time, have now become problematic. They are criticized as a subterfuge used by the strong to interfere in the domestic affairs of the weak. . . . Nevertheless, such [nonconsensual] interventions continue, usually justified by the intervening state as permissible under a flexible reading of Charter Article 51's right of "self-defence." The actual practice of UN organs has tended to be more calibrated, manifesting a situational ethic rather than doctrinaire consistency either prohibiting or permitting all such actions. [Professor Franck proceeds to consider several examples, including the U.S. intervention in the Dominican Republic in 1965 in part to protect U.S. citizens there, the Israeli rescue of hostages

*[The conception of "humanitarian intervention" as Franck uses it here is distinct from the use of military force by a state to stop widespread humanitarian abuses committed by a government against its own population, which is also referred to as "humanitarian intervention." The latter concept it discussed in Section B.5.g below. — Eds.]

aboard a hijacked aircraft at Entebbe, Uganda, in 1976, and the U.S. missile attack against a training camp of Osama bin Laden in Afghanistan after two U.S. embassies were bombed in Africa, with hundreds killed.]

. . . When the facts and their political context are widely seen to warrant a preemptive or deterrent intervention on behalf of credibly endangered citizens abroad, and if the UN itself, for political reasons, is incapable of acting, then some use of force by a state may be accepted as legitimate self-defense within the meaning of Article 51. Military action is more likely to be condoned if the threat to citizens is demonstrably real and grave, if the motive of the intervening state is perceived as genuinely protective, and if the intervention is proportionate and of short duration and likely to achieve its purpose with minimal collateral damage. In practice, whether an action is deemed lawful or not has come to depend on the special circumstances of each case, as demonstrated to, and perceived by, the political and legal institutions of the international system. . . .

. . . Narrowly, recourse to armed force in order to protect nationals abroad may be said to have been condoned as legitimate in specific mitigating circumstances, even though that recourse is still recognized as technically illegal. Or, in a broader interpretation of practice, the system may be said to have adapted the concept of self-defense, under Article 51, to include a right to use force in response to an attack against nationals, providing there is clear evidence of extreme necessity and the means chosen are proportionate.

Anticipatory Self-Defense . . .

Anticipatory self-defense has a long history in customary international law. As early as 1837, it was canvassed by US Secretary of State Daniel Webster in the *Caroline* dispute. In a classical attempt to define but also to limit it, Webster concluded that such a right arises only when there is a "necessity of self-defence . . . instant, overwhelming, leaving no choice of means and no moment for deliberation." He cautioned that it permits "nothing unreasonable or excessive."

Has recourse to such anticipatory self-defense in circumstances of extreme necessity been preserved, or repealed, by the Charter? Common sense, rather than textual literalism, is often the best guide to interpretation of international legal norms. Thus, Bowett concludes that "no state can be expected to await an initial attack which, in the present state or armaments, may well destroy the state's capacity for further resistance and so jeopardise its very existence." In 1996, the International Court of Justice indirectly touched on this question in its Advisory Opinion on the Legality of the Use of Nuclear Weapons in Armed Conflict. A majority of judges was unable to conclude that first-use of nuclear weapons would invariably be unlawful if the very existence of a state were threatened. Despite its ambiguity, the Court appears to have recognized the exceptional nature and logic of a state's claim to use means necessary to ensure its self-preservation. The same reasoning can lead to the logical deduction that no law—and certainly not Article 51—should be interpreted to compel the *reductio ad absurdum* that states invariably must await a first, perhaps decisive, military strike before using force to protect themselves.

On the other hand, a general relaxation of Article 51's prohibitions on unilateral war-making to permit unilateral recourse to force whenever a state feels potentially threatened could lead to another *reduction ad absurdum.* The law cannot have intended to leave every state free to resort to military force whenever it perceived itself grievously endangered by actions of another, for that would negate any role for law. In practice, the UN system has sought, with some success, to navigate between these two conceptual shoals. Three instances may be indicative: the US (and [Organization of American States]) blockade against Cuba during the 1962 missile crisis, Israel's attack on its Arab neighbors in 1967, and Israel's raid on the Iraqi nuclear reactor in 1981. . . .

The problem with recourse to anticipatory self-defense is its ambiguity. In the right circumstances it can be a prescient measure that, at low cost, extinguishes the fuse of a powder-keg. In the wrong circumstances, it can cause the very calamity it anticipates. The 1967 Israeli "first strike" against Egypt's air force was widely seen to be warranted in circumstances where Cairo's hostile intention was evident and Israel's vulnerability patently demonstrable. In the end, the UN system did not condemn Israel's unauthorized recourse to force but, instead, sensibly insisted on its relinquishing conquered territory in return for what as intended to be a securely monitored peace. The system balanced Egypt's illegitimate provocations against Israel's recourse to illegal preventative measures. Most states understood that a very small, densely populated state cannot be expected to await a very probable, potentially decisive attack before availing itself of the right to self-defense.

In the case of the Cuba missile crisis, the international system appears to have been less than convinced that the Soviets' introduction of nuclear-armed missiles—albeit stealthy—genuinely and imminently threatened the US. It was apparent, for example, that deployment of nuclear-armed missiles on US and Russian submarines off each other's coasts had not engendered similar claims to act in "anticipatory self-defence." Still, the covert way Soviet missiles were introduced in Cuba and the disingenuousness with which their deployment had at first been denied, strengthened the US claim to be responding to an imminent threat. That claim was so strongly supported by other states in the Americas as to impede the usual third world rush to judgment against the US. Most important, the forceful countermeasures taken, although probably an act of war in international law and a violation of the literal text of Articles 2(4) and 51, was also seen as cautious, limited, and carefully calibrated. No shots were fired by the ships implementing the blockade. In the end, the outcome—the withdrawal of Soviet missiles from Cuba in return for a reciprocal dismantling of US missiles on the Turkish-Soviet border, together with Washington's promise not again to attempt an invasion of Cuba—was seen by most states (except Cuba) as a positive accomplishment.

Only in the instance of Israel's aerial strike against the Iraqi nuclear plant did the system categorically condemn and deny both the legality and legitimacy of recourse to anticipatory self-defense. In doing so, however, even vociferous critics of Israel made clear that they were not opposed to a right of anticipatory self-defense in principle but, rather that they did not believe that Iraq's nuclear plant was being used unlawfully to produce weapons and that a nuclear attack on Israel was neither probable nor imminent. In this conjecture they may have been wrong, but they were surely right in subjecting to a high standard of probity any evidence adduced to support a claim to use force in anticipation of, rather than as a response to, an armed attack.

Countermeasures and Self-Help . . .

When a right is denied, it is natural to turn to the authority that is the source of that right in the expectation that it will be enforced. When that expectation is not met, there is moral force to the argument that those aggrieved by the failure should themselves be allowed to enforce their legal entitlement as best they can.

In international law, the issue of the legality of countermeasures and self-help arises when, a state having refused to carry out its legal responsibilities and the international system having failed to enforce the law, another state, victimized by that failure, takes countermeasures to protect its interests. "Its interests" in this context denotes the peaceful enjoyment of rights accruing to a state, of which it is deprived by the continuing wrongful acts of another state. It may also be, however, that the notion of a transgressed state interest has expanded to include not only violations of its rights as a sovereign, but also of rights held derivatively as a member of the international system. Thus, for example, every state may enjoy the right *erga omnes* not to have the earth's "commons" — the seas, the air — polluted in violation of globally-applicable norms. Along similar lines, every state may have a right to act to prevent a genocide that, even if not directed at its own people, violates the treaty-based common conscience of humanity. Some recognition has been given to this more extended notion of a state's self-interest by the International Law Commission's Restatement of the Law of State Responsibility.[1] That there are such *erga omnes* norms in international law which, if violated, give rise to a claim by any or all states does not of course resolve the vexed issue of what remedial steps states may take to protect their violated rights against further breaches. Normally, redress would have to be sought through the peaceful means provided by the treaty establishing the violated right or by general international law. The Draft Articles on State Responsibility, in Article 49, permits countermeasures "against a State which is responsible for an internationally wrongful act in order to induce that State to comply with its obligations" but, it adds, such countermeasures "shall not affect (a) The obligation to refrain from the threat or use of force as embodied in the United Nations Charter . . .".

What, exactly, is that "obligation . . . as embodied in the . . . Charter"? Is there an inexorable obligation "to refrain from . . . use of force," when does it arise and what countermeasures are precluded by it? How relevant is the practice of UN organs in construing this limitation on the right to take countermeasures?

These questions are all too relevant because of severe imperfections in the capacity of the international legal system to ensure compliance with its norms and to guarantee a remedy for violations. Reason suggests that self-help and countermeasures remain necessary remedies of last resort. Nevertheless, the text and context of the UN Charter seem to indicate otherwise. . . .

The UN Charter makes no exception to the rule barring states' recourse to violence, not even in situations where an evident and serious wrong has been done that the system, over a protracted period, has failed to redress. The Charter makes

1. Text of Articles, State Responsibility, 31 May 2001, International Law Commission, article 48: "Any State other than an injured State is entitled to invoke the responsibility of another State . . . if: (a) The obligation breached is owed to a group of States including that State, and is established for the protection of a collective interest of the group." The Convention on the Prevention and Punishment of the Crime of Genocide, 78 U.N.T.S. 277 of 1951 is the leading example of a wrong *erga omnes* that accords a right to all states *qua* any violation.

no provision for individual or collective military enforcement of legal rights of states and peoples, as such. In this sense, the Charter may be said to have abrogated states' historic right to deploy force in self-help and to have restricted countermeasures to actions not involving "the threat or use of force" prohibited by Charter Article 2(4). It thus seems to have tilted the balance in the direction of peace and away from justice or, alternatively, in favor of the enunciation of rights but away from their muscular implementation.

On the other hand, a limited right to self-help has long been recognized in customary international law and practice. This has not been specifically repealed by the Charter. It can be argued that, in the absence of new ways to defend or effectuate legal rights, the Charter should not be read to prohibit countermeasures as the remedy of last resort. Indeed, UN practice seems to offer some latitude for states' resort to countermeasures in self-help. In some instances this tolerance has been manifest in UN passivity when faced with actual recourse to force. Israel's capture of Eichmann in Argentina, India's invasion of Goa, as well as Turkey's intervention in Cyprus were met with comparative equanimity, the specific circumstances of each case lending an aura of legitimacy to a recourse to unilateral force and mitigating the system's judgment of self-help in those instances.

On the other hand, those instances in which the UN organs rejected claims of a right to self-help demonstrate that the system mitigates or acquiesces only reluctantly. Self-help may be acknowledged as a remedy of last resort in a situation in which all alternatives for the peaceful vindication of a recognized legal right have been exhausted and the law and the facts indisputably support a plea of extreme necessity. It has not been recognized when used to press less legally convincing claims such as those solely based on geographic contiguity and historic title, especially when the claimed rights are opposable by rights of equal or greater weight, such as that of self-determination.

Nevertheless, in [exceptional] cases the use of force in self-help, while prohibited by the Charter text, may be justified by the evident legitimacy of the cause in which self-help is deployed; and a widespread perception of that legitimacy is likely to mitigate, if not actually to exculpate, the resort to force. . . . The practice of UN organs demonstrates that while the prohibition on forcible self-help is absolute in theory, the principle is more textured in practice. . . .

Obviously, the law of countermeasures and self-help is in flux. . . . Like the [ICJ], the political organs of the United Nations have carefully avoided giving a broad, dogmatic answer to the issues posed by states' recourse to armed countermeasures. Doctrine and principle, here, too, appear subservient to narrower reasons of contextual justice and legitimacy, with the specific facts being given appropriate weight. The invasion of Goa was perceived as the democratic liberation of a part of geographic and cultural India long ruled by a remote and stubborn Iberian dictatorship. The Turkish military occupation of Northern Cyprus in 1974 at first seemed a legitimate reaction to the subterfuge of a despised and expansionist Greek military junta. In the Eichmann case, the strength of Israel's justification was generally acknowledged. The Israelis had argued that a great wrong may sometimes have to be redressed by a much smaller one, and that definition of mitigating circumstances found considerable resonance.

Other arguments based on self-help have fallen on stonier ground. This is exemplified by the rejection of efforts by Argentina's junta to legitimize its invasion of the Falklands, of Indonesia's occupation of East Timor, and of Morocco's suppression of self-determination in the Western Sahara. Each of these cases is different. . . . Each demonstrates the importance of facts, evidence and sensitivity to political context in shaping the systemic response to a claim of self-help, whether that claim is advanced as a legal right or in mitigation of the consequences of a technical wrong.

A larger conclusion may also be teased from this evidence of practice. In interpreting the normative principles of the Charter, the principal organs have made an effort to act as a sort of jury: determining the probative value of alleged facts, assessing claims of extreme necessity, and weighing the proportionality of specific action taken by a party that might otherwise be deprived of any remedy for a serious delict committed against it. This quasi-jury has demonstrated concern to apply the United Nations' quasi-constitution as a "living tree." And, like juries everywhere, the principal organs have tried to bridge the gap, when it appears, between legality and legitimacy, so that the legal order is not seen to suffer from the deficiency that arises when that gap becomes too wide.

Notes and Questions

1. *Security doctrines and international law.* States sometimes articulate doctrines indicating situations in which they are prepared to use force in furtherance of their geopolitical interests or ideological viewpoints, ranging from support of socialism, to protecting a geographical area, to furthering democracy. For example, under the so-called Brezhnev Doctrine, named after Premier Leonid Brezhnev, the Soviet Union asserted the right to intervene in support of any socialist government threatened by antisocialist forces. The Soviet Union relied on this justification when it sent forces into Hungary in 1956 and into Czechoslovakia in 1968. Under the Monroe Doctrine, the United States claimed that efforts by states outside the Americas to extend their spheres of influence in the Western Hemisphere would be deemed a threat to the security of the United States. During the Reagan Administration in the 1980s, under what came to be known as the Reagan Doctrine, the United States appears to have claimed the right generally to use military force or provide other assistance to impose or restore "democracy," particularly where communism existed or threatened.

Are these statements of geopolitical or ideological policy preferences consistent with the text of Article 51? Do such policy statements reflect legal interpretations of the U.N. Charter or policy statements? Could they be seen as acceptable types of "creative" interpretations of Article 51, or should they be rejected as legal grounds for using force? For instance, could the Brezhnev Doctrine have been justified as individual or collective self-defense under Article 51? What about the Reagan Doctrine? Could either doctrine have been justified under any of the exceptions or interpretations discussed by Professor Franck above? Note that he concludes that the view that Article 51 permits self-defense against the source of ideological subversion from abroad has met a strong negative response from other states and from international institutions.

2. Should the United States be able to overthrow a totalitarian or authoritarian government (e.g., North Korea or Syria) to bring democracy to another country? If so, can other countries with democratic governments (e.g., Brazil, France, or India)

use force to bring about democratic governments in other countries, such as neighbors or former colonies? Can Russia use force to reassert its preferred form of government on some of its neighbors (e.g., Ukraine, Kazakhstan, or Georgia)? Can Islamist regimes (e.g., Iran or Saudi Arabia) use some principle of self-defense against ideological subversion to justify their support of Islamist insurgencies in more moderate Islamic countries such as Pakistan, Indonesia, and Malaysia?

3. *Reprisals and other self-help countermeasures.* In the absence of an effective enforcement mechanism in international law, the question arises as to whether a state may have a limited right to use force in self-help if it is unable to remedy a violation of its rights under international law through peaceful means. Many commentators believe that the customary law right of self-help to respond to breaches of international law not involving the use of force was terminated by the U.N. Charter; in the words of Elisabeth Zoller, Article 2(4), "by outlawing the threat or use of force, made resort to armed reprisals legally impossible." Elisabeth Zoller, Peacetime Unilateral Remedies: An Analysis of Countermeasures 38-39 (1984). Moreover, one of the principles set out in the Declaration on Principles of International Law Concerning Friendly Relations and Co-operation among States in accordance with the Charter of the United Nations adopted in General Assembly Resolution 2625 (1970) holds that "States have a duty to refrain from acts of reprisal involving the use of force."

Professor Franck notes above that although the use of force in self-help may be "prohibited by the Charter text," the principle "is more textured in practice." He observes that U.N. practice since the adoption of the Charter "seems to offer some latitude for states' resort to countermeasures in self-help" and notes instances in which "this tolerance has been manifest in UN passivity when faced with actual recourse to force."

Professor Yoram Dinstein has addressed a particular category of "armed reprisals" under international law, in which a state that is the victim of an armed attack does not respond "on the spot," but carefully chooses the place and time of its forcible response. Dinstein notes that since the entry into force of the U.N. Charter, "the record is replete with measures of defensive armed reprisals implemented by many countries." Yoram Dinstein, War, Aggression and Self-Defence 228-229 (4th ed. 2005). He cites as an example U.S. air strikes against Libya launched in 1986 in response to Libyan-sponsored terrorist attacks, especially a bombing Berlin that killed two U.S. servicemen and wounded many more. Is there any difference between what Dinstein refers to as an "armed reprisal" taken "in response to an armed attack" and the exercise of self-defense?

On June 26, 1993, the United States launched a limited strike against Baghdad, Iraq, in response to what U.S. officials concluded was a plot to assassinate former President Bush while he was in Kuwait in April 1993. President Clinton chose one of the most limited options available in order to minimize civilian casualties and to make the response proportionate to the assassination attempt. U.S. officials said the attack was consistent with Article 51 of the U.N. Charter. The United States regarded the attempted assassination as a direct attack on the United States that warranted a direct response.

Do you agree that this U.S. attack satisfied Article 51? Does the fact that the plot was foiled before former President Bush could be attacked undermine the self-defense rationale? Can a measure by the United States two months later be justified as self-defense? Or is it better to view this 1993 attack on Baghdad as a countermeasure or reprisal? Would a use of force taken to punish past transgressions be permissible either as an armed reprisal or as self-defense, or must force be oriented towards preventing future attacks?

More generally, do you believe that the use of force in self-help, as described by Franck, is a permissible use of force under international law today? If not, should it be? Does it depend on whether the breach of international law triggering the reprisal involved the use of force, or other violations of international law? Should measures of self-help in these circumstances be viewed as legitimate, or as technically illegal but where the illegality is mitigated by the circumstances?

4. *Neutrality.* What has happened to the pre-World War I customary law of neutrality, discussed in Section A above? As one commentator observed:

> Since the signing of the United Nations Charter, the customary law of neutrality has been caught between an international legal order which purports to outlaw war and hence make neutrality obsolete, and an international political environment characterized by frequent armed conflicts in which there is a need to regulate the relations of belligerent and non-belligerent states. The results have been confused, if not chaotic. With the juridical status of armed conflicts uncertain, third states have most often refrained from taking a formal stance of neutrality. But where the need for *some* legal rule has been acute and where the particular rule of the customary law has suited their interests, states have invoked that customary law. . . . Neutrality has . . . led a sort of "juridical half-life," suspended between an ideology which denies its premises and a reality which finds it useful, if not necessary. [Patrick M. Norton, Between the Ideology and the Reality: The Shadow of the Law of Neutrality, 17 Harv. Int'l L.J. 249, 249 (1976).]

As noted above in the discussion of the *Oil Platforms* case, during the Iran-Iraq war in the 1980s, the United States and several other countries with important shipping interests in the Persian Gulf emphasized their neutral status as a basis for arguing that their ships should not be attacked by either Iran or Iraq. This did not always deter the belligerents from attacking neutral shipping, but it did provide nonbelligerents with an argument in international organizations. See Maxwell Jenkins, Air Attacks on Neutral Shipping in the Persian Gulf: The Legality of the Iraqi Exclusion Zone and Iranian Reprisals, 8 B.C. Int'l & Comp. L. Rev. 517 (1985). One of the grounds used by the Reagan Administration to justify the need for U.S. Navy escorts for American and other commercial ships going to and from neutral ports in the Gulf was that the Iranians and, to a lesser extent, the Iraqis were illegally attacking neutral shipping.

We turn now to a closer look at some of the claimed justifications for the use of force that might not fit squarely with the text of Article 51.

a. Protection of Citizens Abroad

In a number of cases, states have used military force to rescue their citizens who were being held abroad as hostages or prisoners, where the territorial state was unwilling or unable to intervene. Is such action consistent with the law governing the use of force?

Professor Franck and many other experts agree that there should be some ability for a state to rescue its own citizens. In the excerpt above, Franck concludes that this activity has come to be seen as a justifiable adaptation of the Article 51 concept of self-defense, or at least as legitimate in specific circumstances, even if technically illegal under the Charter. Franck does note that the justification is sometimes a pretext for a strong state to help a friendly regime or to undermine a regime that it does not like.

Professor Dinstein stresses the importance of the link of nationality between a country using force and the persons abroad to be protected or rescued. This, in his view, provides the necessary link to the right of self defense. He writes:

> [T]he use of force by [B] within its own territory, against [A's] nationals, is considered by many to constitute an armed attack against [A]. If that is the case, forcible counter-measures employed by [A] may rate as self-defence, provided that the usual conditions of necessity, proportionality and immediacy are complied with. Sir Humphrey Waldock reiterated these conditions in somewhat different wording, fitting better the specific circumstances of protection of nationals abroad: "There must be (1) an imminent threat of injury to nationals, (2) a failure or inability on the part of the territorial sovereign to protect them and (3) measures of protection strictly confined to the object of protecting them against injury." [Dinstein, War, Aggression and Self-Defense, supra, at 231.]

The Iranian Rescue Mission. In April 1980, a small fleet of U.S. military helicopters and transport planes carrying a specially trained force entered Iranian airspace in the first stage of a planned operation to rescue the 52 American citizens, mostly U.S. diplomats, who had been held hostage in the U.S. Embassy in Tehran since November 1979. (The mission called for the rescue team, after landing at a rendezvous point in the Iranian desert, to fly by helicopter to a location close to Tehran. The force would then travel by trucks to the U.S. Embassy compound where the hostages were held and, using surprise and force, try to free the hostages. The rescuers and the hostages would then move to a nearby field and be flown by helicopters and then aircraft out of Iran.) After three of the eight helicopters developed mechanical troubles, the mission was scrubbed at the first rendezvous point in the Iranian desert. During the subsequent evacuation, two of the aircraft collided, resulting in the death of eight U.S. servicemen. President Carter, in a report to Congress, stated that in carrying out the operation, "the United States was acting wholly within its right, in accordance with Article 51 of the United Nations Charter, to protect and rescue its citizens where the government of the territory in which they are located is unable or unwilling to protect them . . ." President Jimmy Carter, Message to Congress (Apr. 26, 1980), 1 Pub. Papers 779 (1980-1981).

The Panama Invasion. The principle of defense of nationals abroad was also invoked as at least a partial justification for the 1989 U.S. invasion of Panama. The 1989 invasion occurred in the context of sharp deterioration in relations between the United States and Panama and its *de facto* ruler, General Manuel Antonio Noriega. On December 16, members of the Panamanian Defense Force (PDF) killed a U.S. Marine officer at a checkpoint in Panama. Other PDF forces beat a U.S.

naval officer and detained and abused his wife. Bush Administration sources suggested that the two primary legal justifications were the right to protect the lives of U.S. citizens and U.S. rights to protect the Panama Canal, which was owned and operated by the United States until its transfer to Panama in 1999, under the Panama Canal Treaties. The actions of the United States did not meet with international approval. The Organization of American states voted 20 to 1 to express "regret" over the Panama intervention and to urge the United States to withdraw its invasion forces. The U.N. General Assembly voted 75-20, with 39 countries abstaining, in favor of a resolution that "[s]trongly deplore[d]" the U.S. invasion as a "flagrant violation of international law" and demanded an immediate cease-fire and troop withdrawal. The United States, Britain, and France used their vetoes to block the adoption of a similarly worded resolution in the Security Council.

Notes and Questions

1. Should a state be allowed to use military force to free its citizens who are being held hostage if the territorial state will not intervene or cannot do so? If so, under what circumstances? Should an action such as the successful 1976 Israeli mission to free Israeli hostages on a hijacked plane in Entebbe, Uganda, be permissible? If it should be permissible, should it be so under Article 51, or should there be a separate exception to Article 2(4) of the U.N. Charter?

2. In August 2008, armed conflict erupted between Russia and Georgia. The conflict began after Georgia initiated military operations aimed at reasserted Georgian control over the regions of South Ossetia and Abkhazia, secessionist enclaves that Georgia considers to be part of Georgian territory. Russia responded by deploying substantial military forces into the two provinces, and later into Georgia itself, routing Georgian forces in the process. In justifying Russia's military actions, President Medvedev stated, "My duty as Russian president is to safeguard the lives and dignity of Russian citizens, wherever they are. . . . We will not allow the deaths of our compatriots to go unpunished." Some observers contend that Russia's claims in this regard where pretextual, and that Russia had embraced a practice of giving the residents of the two regions Russian passports as "a transparent ploy to justify a later purported need to 'protect' Russian citizens." Russian Troops and Tanks Pour in South Ossetia, The Guardian, Aug. 9, 2008. Russia later recognized the independence of South Ossetia and Abkhazia and has asserted substantial influence over them. Does this case highlight the risk that a right to use force to protect nationals abroad can be abused to advance other foreign policy and strategic goals?

3. Was the abortive U.S. rescue mission in 1980 to free U.S. hostages in Iran justifiable under international law? If so, under what theory? If not, why not? Was it a use of force against the "territorial integrity or political independence" of Iran? Do you agree with President Carter that the mission was a permissible exercise of rights under Article 51 of the U.N. Charter?

4. In addition to invoking Article 51 of the U.N. Charter, President Carter referred to the failed Iranian rescue mission as a "humanitarian mission" and stated: "It was not directed against Iran. It was not directed against the people of Iran." Should this type of "humanitarian intervention," as discussed by Professor Franck in the excerpt above, be a separate exception to Article 2(4) and different from the Article 51 exception of self-defense, or might it be a variant on self-defense?

(Recall that "humanitarian intervention" in this sense is limited to acts taken by a country to protect its own citizens and differs from the use of force by a state to stop widespread abuses committed by another government against its own population; the more general doctrine of "humanitarian intervention is discussed in Section B.5.g below.)

5. Should a right to use force to rescue individuals include a right to act on behalf of nationals of other states, or do you agree with Professor Dinstein that it should be confined to missions to protect a country's own citizens? Is self-defense or humanitarian intervention a better justification for this right to rescue?

6. What if U.S. citizens are held hostage by terrorists in Lebanon and the Lebanese government would like to get them released, but does not have the resources to secure their release in a non-risky way? Does the U.S. government have to wait for Lebanon to request its aid, or can the U.S. President send in a rescue mission on his own initiative?

7. In the Panama case, were the acts of violence directed at U.S. citizens in 1989 sufficient justification for deploying a major military force in a foreign country and changing its regime, as happened after U.S. forces ousted General Noriega from power?

b. Anticipatory or Preemptive Self-defense

By its terms, Article 51 permits a state to use force in self-defense "if an armed attack occurs." However, Article 51 also purports to preserve the "inherent right" of self-defense, which Professor Franck notes has a long history in customary international law. This includes the *Caroline* incident, discussed earlier, where U.S. Secretary of State Daniel Webster recognized a right of anticipatory self-defense but sought to limit it to cases where there is a "necessity of self-defense . . . instant, overwhelming, leaving no choice of means and no moment for deliberation." The customary international law standard of self-defense also included the requirement of proportionality.

In his excerpt above, Professor Franck notes the impracticability in today's world of insisting in all circumstances that a country must await an initial attack that may well defeat or even destroy that country, but also the dangers of permitting "unilateral recourse to force whenever a state feels potentially threatened." Professor Reisman and Andrea Armstrong note that even though Article 51 did not, in their view, originally contemplate a right of anticipatory self-defense, many claim that the Charter, as shaped by state practice, permits a right of anticipatory self-defense in narrow circumstances where there is "palpable evidence of an imminent threat." W. Michael Reisman and Andrea Armstrong, The Past and Future of the Claim of Preemptive Self-Defense, 100 Am. J. Int'l L. 525, 526 (2006). This view was adopted by a panel of prominent experts appointed by the U.N. Secretary-General to address the role of the United Nations in addressing contemporary security challenges. In its report, the panel stated:

> The language of [Article 51] is restrictive: "Nothing in the present Charter shall impair the inherent right of individual or collective self-defense if an armed attack occurs against a member of the United Nations, until the Security Council has taken measures to maintain international peace and security." However, a threatened State, according

to long established international law, can take military action as long as the threatened attack is imminent, no other means would deflect it and the action is proportionate. [United Nations, A More Secure World: Our Shared Responsibility, Report of the High-Level Panel on Threats, Challenges and Change 63 (2004).]

Professor Dinstein favors recognition of an even more limited right to use force to "intercept" an adversary's military strike:

> [I]t is important to pinpoint the exact moment at which an armed attack begins to take place. . . .
>
> In many instances, the opening of fire is an unreliable test of responsibility for an armed attack. . . .
>
> . . . As Sir Humphrey Waldock phrased it:
>
> > "Where there is convincing evidence not merely of threats and potential danger but of an attack actually mounted, then an armed attack may be said to have begun to occur, though it has not passed the frontier."
>
> Interceptive self-defence is lawful, even under Article 51 of the [U.N.] Charter, for it takes place after the other side has committed itself to an armed attack in an ostensibly irrevocable way. Whereas a preventive strike anticipates a latent armed attack that is merely "foreseeable" (or even just "conceivable"), an interceptive strike counters an armed attack which is in progress, even if it is still incipient: the blow is "imminent" and practically "unavoidable." To put it in another way, there is nothing preventive about nipping an armed attack in the bud. But the real (in contradistinction to the suspected) existence of that bud is an absolute requirement. Self-defence cannot be exercised merely on the ground of assumptions, expectations of fear. It has to be demonstrably apparent that the other side is already carrying out an armed attack (even if the attack has not yet fully developed). [Dinstein, War, Aggression and Self-Defence, supra, at 187-188, 191-192.]

Still other commentators argue that while a few states—including the United States, Israel, and the United Kingdom—claim a right of anticipatory self-defense if an attack is imminent, "[t]he majority of states reject anticipatory self-defence." Christine Gray, International Law and the Use of Force 160 (3d ed. 2008).

Notes and Questions

1. In September 2002, the Bush Administration issued a new "National Security Strategy" document, which took a new view of the right of self-defense, at least in the context of preventing U.S. enemies from threatening the United States or its friends with nuclear, chemical, or biological weapons, even where those threats were only emerging. The document noted the settled U.S. view that anticipatory self defense was permissible in the face of "an imminent threat—most often a visible mobilization of armies, navies, and air forces preparing to attack." It went on to state:

> We must adapt the concept of imminent threat to the capabilities and objectives of today's adversaries. . . .
>
> The United States has long maintained the option of preemptive actions to counter a sufficient threat to our national security. The greater the threat, the greater

> the risk of inaction — and the more compelling the case for taking anticipatory action to defend ourselves, even if uncertainty remains as to the time and place of the enemy's attack. To forestall or prevent such hostile acts by our adversaries, the United States will, if necessary, act preemptively. [The National Security Strategy of the United States of America 15 (2002).]

This claimed right to use force preemptively generated widespread debate, both on policy and legal grounds. How does this doctrine differ from the more conventional understanding of "anticipatory" self-defense described above? Do you believe the doctrine of preemptive self-defense represents sound policy? Can it be supported in international law? How precise are the parameters of this policy? What are its limits?

2. The first National Security Strategy document issued by the Obama Administration did not expressly address the issue of anticipatory or preemptive self-defense. It noted only that:

> The United States must reserve the right to act unilaterally if necessary to defend our nation and our interests, yet we will also seek to adhere to standards that govern the use of force. Doing so strengthens those who act in line with international standards, while isolating and weakening those who do not. [The National Security Strategy 22 (2010).]

3. How should the language of Article 51 ("if an armed attack occurs") be interpreted? Should it require that the attacking state has actually fired a weapon or crossed a border? Should the Article include Dinstein's concept of interceptive self-defense? Should a more expansive version of preemptive or anticipatory self-defense be allowed — that is, even when the attacking state has not committed itself in any irrevocable way? For example, what evidence should Israel need before it can invoke the right of self-defense and attack its traditional enemies, say, Syria or Iran? If those states fear such an attack, what evidence should they need before they can invoke the right of self-defense to attack Israel?

4. Could the doctrine of anticipatory self-defense have provided a legitimate justification for the 2003 U.S.-led invasion of Iraq? (See the discussion of the Iraq case below in Section C.2.) Citing explicit statements by senior U.S. government officials that the threat posed by Iraq's suspect weapons of mass destructions programs had not by 2003 become imminent, one commentator argues that the use of force in Iraq cannot be reconciled with the doctrine of anticipatory self-defense, at least as it has traditionally been expressed. See Weiner, The Use of Force and Contemporary Security Threats, supra, 59 Stan. L. Rev. at 439-440.

Does the difficulty of using force against the non-imminent but potentially catastrophic threats posed by nuclear weapons and other weapons of mass destruction under the traditional conception of anticipatory self-defense justify claims for changing that conception, as the Bush Administration sought to do through the policy of preemption set out in the 2002 National Security Strategy? Or does the fact that the forces that invaded Iraq in 2003 found no weapons of mass destruction highlight the dangers of using force before threats are so clear as to be "imminent?" For instance, should the United States have the right to use self-defense against North Korea now that it has detonated a nuclear explosive device? Would either the United States or Israel be justified in attacking Iran in view of its uranium enrichment and reprocessing activities, which the United States and other nations believe are related to a nuclear weapons development program? (See the discussion of nonproliferation and the North Korean and Iranian cases in Section F.3.d below.)

5. In September 2007, Israeli warplanes attacked and destroyed a facility in Syria, later identified as a nearly-completed nuclear reactor secretly under construction since 2001. According to the CIA, the unit was built with North Korean assistance and was modeled on one used by North Korea to produce plutonium for nuclear weapons. Two commentators note:

> What was particularly notable about this attack was what occurred afterward: the near total lack of international comment or criticism of Israel's action. . . . Was the international community tacitly condoning the 2007 Israeli raid even though it appeared that the Syrian reactor did not pose an imminent threat to Israel, the sole justification under international law for the anticipatory use of military force? Were foreign governments, cognizant that the UN Security Council had been unable to halt Iran's continuing development of previously undeclared sensitive nuclear facilities, tacitly endorsing Israel's decision not to invoke the diplomatic tools at its disposal, such as demanding an International Atomic Energy Agency (IAEA) investigation of the site, another traditional prerequisite to the anticipatory use of force? With the case still unfolding, it is premature to draw firm conclusions about its meaning for the future of global nonproliferation efforts, but two issues will bear close watching. Has confidence in the enforcement of nonproliferation norms eroded to the point that the international community is prepared to accept more readily than in the past the preventive use of force to suppress suspected nuclear weapons programs in certain narrowly defined cases? If so, what does this augur for the future use of military force to arrest Iran's weapons-relevant nuclear activities? [Leonard S. Spector & Avner Cohen, Israel's Airstrike on Syria's Reactor: Implications for the Nonproliferation Regime, Arms Control Today, Jul./Aug. 2008, at 15-16]

What do you think explains the international silence following Israel's attack? Might it be that Syria's response was relatively muted? (Syria wrote to the Security Council to protest Israel's request but did not request a Council meeting.) If Israel were to attack Iran's facilities, would Iran adopt a similar profile? And how do you think other states would react?

6. In a crisis between two countries, should the armed attack requirement be different if one of the countries believes that the imminent attack will be with nuclear weapons rather than with conventional ones? A nuclear attack would be much more destructive in most circumstances than one with non-nuclear forces, but wouldn't a preemptive nuclear strike also be much more destructive — and hence an act that requires greater caution than a conventional strike? Also, in one major study of numerous conventional conflicts, the analysis revealed that there were considerable advantages to being able to strike first. The conventional attacker could take advantage of massing its forces and hopefully benefiting from surprise. See Richard Betts, Surprise Attack (1982).

As for a nuclear conflict, does it matter if the potential attacker has many nuclear weapons or not and how vulnerable the weapons are to a preemptive strike?

For example, the United States has thousands of nuclear warheads, which are deployed in different ways, and some are relatively invulnerable to an initial attack. On the other hand, India, Pakistan, or North Korea might have only a few weapons, and they might be vulnerable to a preemptive attack. Would it make sense for an opponent of, say, India to strike first if the opponent thought a nuclear attack by India were "imminent" or "practically unavoidable"? Would it be permissible under international law? Indeed, would the possibility of an imminent attack by any nuclear-armed adversary justify anticipatory or preemptive use of force against that adversary, whether or not its forces were vulnerable?

c. Intervention and Counterintervention

A particularly troublesome set of issues in the international legal regime governing the use of force arises when a state provides support to actors, other than its own regular armed forces, who are engaged in violent acts in or against another country. Such acts are sometimes characterized as "indirect aggression" or as an impermissible form of armed intervention.

In the *Nicaragua* case discussed in Chapter 4.B, the International Court of Justice concluded the United States was not responsible for specific forcible acts of the *contra* resistance groups fighting against the Nicaraguan government that violated human rights or international humanitarian law standards. The Court ruled that Nicaragua had not proved that the United States exercised "effective control of the military or paramilitary operations" in the course of which the alleged violations were committed. (In the *Tadic* case, discussed in Chapter 8.A, the Appeals Chamber of the International Criminal Tribunal for the former Yugoslavia articulated a lower "overall control" standard to determine when a state would be deemed responsible for the acts of organized military groups it supports. It concluded that where a state equips and finances such a group, and coordinates or helps to plan its military activity, it was not necessary for the sponsoring state to issue instructions for the commission of specific acts contrary to international law for those acts to be attributable to the supporting state.)

Nevertheless, the *Nicaragua* Court found that a state could violate the international law prohibition on the use of force even if its involvement with violent nonstate groups did not rise to the level of "effective" control. The ICJ held, by a vote of 12-3, that "by training, arming, equipping, financing and supplying the *contra* forces or otherwise encouraging, supporting and aiding military and paramilitary activities in and against Nicaragua," the United States had breached its duty not to intervene in the affairs of another state. With respect to "those acts of intervention . . . which involve[d] the use of force," the Court concluded that the U.S. had breached the obligation not to use force against another state. Military and Paramilitary Activities in and Against Nicaragua (Nicaragua v. United States of America), 1986 I.C.J. 14, 146-147 (June 27).

In the *Armed Activities on the Territory of the Congo* case, the Democratic Republic of the Congo (DRC) claimed that Uganda had engaged in the unlawful use of force against the DRC through its support for insurgents operating on Congolese territory. The Court found that Uganda had provided training and military support to the Congo Liberation Movement (MLC), a rebel group fighting against the DRC government. Because the DRC had presented insufficient evidence to show that the MLC's conduct was "under the direction or control of" Uganda, the Court concluded that the specific killings and other unlawful acts perpetrated by the MLC were not attributable to Uganda. As in the *Nicaragua* case, the Court nevertheless found that Ugandan support of the MLC constituted "military intervention . . . of such a magnitude and duration that the Court considers it to be a grave violation of the prohibition on the use of force expressed in Article 2, paragraph 4, of the Charter." Armed Activities on the Territory of the Congo (Democratic Republic of the Congo v. Uganda), 2005 I.C.J. 168, 226-227 (Dec. 19).

Notes and Questions

1. Article 3(g) of the Definition of Aggression quoted in Section B.3 above includes as a potential act of aggression "[t]he sending by or on behalf of a State of armed bands, groups, irregulars or mercenaries, which carry out acts of armed force against another State of such gravity as to amount to the [forcible] acts listed above, or its substantial involvement therein." Definition of Aggression, G.A. Res. 3314 (XXIX), U.N. Doc. U.N. Doc. A/9631 (Dec. 14, 1974). Another General Assembly resolution, the Declaration on the Principles of International Law Concerning Friendly Relations and Co-operation among States in Accordance with the Charter of the United Nations, also includes a number of provisions concerning such indirect violence. In elaborating on the principle that states "shall refrain in their international relations from the threat or use of force against the territorial integrity or political independence of any State, or in any other manner inconsistent with the purpose of the United Nations," the Declaration states:

> Every State has the duty to refrain from organizing or encouraging the organization of irregular forces or armed bands, including mercenaries, for incursion into the territory of another State. . . .
>
> Every State has the duty to refrain from organizing, instigating, assisting or participating in acts of civil strife or terrorist acts in another State or acquiescing in organized activities within its territory directed towards the commission of such acts, when the act referred to in the present paragraph involve a threat or use of force. [G.A. Res. 2625 (XXV), U.N. Doc. A/8062 (Oct. 24, 1970).]

2. What is the relationship between the rules of state responsibility (discussed in Chapter 8.A) that govern when a state is deemed responsible for the conduct of nonstate actors, on the one hand, and the commission by a state of indirect aggression or a violation of duty not to assist forcible action by such nonstate actors, on the other? Is the standard of "substantial involvement" by a state in the activities of nonstate actors in paragraph 3(g) of the Definition of Aggression equivalent to "effective" or "overall" control over them?

Intervention can give rise to counterintervention. Countries victimized by violence perpetrated by armed groups with external support frequently claim the right to use force, not only against the armed groups, but also against the sponsoring states. In addition, outside states may decide to deploy their armed forces to assist a government facing insurgent groups on its territory; in some significant cases, third parties have also used force against the sponsoring state. This pattern of intervention and counterintervention can give rise to considerable legal ambiguity.

The United States justified its support for the *contras* in Nicaragua during the 1980s largely as a response to the provision by the Marxist Sandinista regime in Nicaragua of weapons and other support to leftist insurgents fighting against the American-supported government in El Salvador. The United States defended its support for the *contras* as a form of collective self-defense on behalf of El Salvador.

In the excerpt below, after providing some historical background on intervention and counterintervention, Professor Henkin summarizes key aspects of the ICJ opinion relevant to these questions and then goes on to address the issues and legal ambiguities in the area.

Louis Henkin, Use of Force: Law and Policy

Right v. Might: International Law and the Use of Force 46-50, 63 (1991)

Before the UN Charter, the law [regarding intervention and counterintervention] seemed to be that a state may provide military assistance to the government of another state, even to help it suppress rebellion, but a state could not assist rebels against the incumbent government of another state. If rebellion succeeded sufficiently to achieve the status of "belligerent" and constitute a civil war, the law probably forbade assistance to either side. . . .

The United Nations Charter did not expressly address intervention in civil wars. Nothing in article 2(4) forbids sending military assistance to an incumbent government, but the use of force in support of rebels against an incumbent government would be a use of force against the territorial integrity of the state and, presumably, against its political independence. . . . Assistance not involving the use of force, however — for example, providing advice, selling arms, or giving financial assistance to one (or both) sides in a civil war — seems not to be covered by article 2(4), but may violate norms against nonintervention that predate the Charter and have been strongly restated in numerous General Assembly resolutions.

Authoritative Construction of the Law: The Nicaragua Case . . .

In 1986, in the *Nicaragua* case, the International Court of Justice issued . . . its first judgment construing key elements in the law of the Charter.[22] It construed the prohibition in article 2(4) broadly (as imposing strict limitations on the use of force) and the exception in article 51 narrowly (as limiting the circumstances in which force may be used in self-defense). . . .

22. The court concluded that it could not decide the case under the Charter because of a reservation by the United States, and would therefore decide it only under customary international law. But the Court held that customary law and the law of the Charter were essentially congruent in relevant respects, in effect construing the Charter.

[T]he court held (or said) the following:

- The only exception to article 2(4) is article 51: Force against another state that is not justified by a right of self-defense under Article 51 is in violation of Article 2(4) (paragraph 211).
- Whether self-defense is individual or collective, "the exercise of this right is subject to the State concerned having been the victim of an armed attack" (paragraphs 195, 232).
- Armed attack may include acts by armed bands where such acts occur on a significant scale, but "assistance to rebels in the form of the provision of weapons or logistical or other support is not an armed attack justifying the use of force in self-defense" (paragraph 195). . . .
- "States do not have a right of 'collective' armed response to acts which do not constitute an 'armed attack'" (paragraphs 210-11). If no armed attack has occurred, collective self-defense is unlawful, even if "carried on in strict compliance with the canons of necessity and proportionality" (paragraph 237). . . .
- There is no "general right of intervention, in support of an opposition within another state" (paragraph 209). . . .

The court did not resolve important questions as to the law of the Charter. In particular, the *Nicaragua* judgment gave only partial guidance on the difficult issues of intervention and counterintervention. The court denied any right to intervene by force in another state for purposes other than collective self-defense against armed attack; it denied any right to use force against another state in response to the latter's intervention in a third state by means that do not constitute an armed attack. But the court did not address the victim's right of armed response to "less than an armed attack," or what means other than force can be used in response to such interventions by either the victim or its friends (see paragraph 210). The court did not address whether when a state supports one side in a civil war in another country, a third state may "counterintervene" on the other side and, if so, subject to what limitations. . . .

. . . The court's declaration that force may be used only in self-defense against an armed attack reaffirms the original intent of the Charter and the positions commonly held by states (other than the few that have sought to justify their own uses of force). . . .

Less clear, more likely to be reexamined, and requiring much refinement are the court's definition of "armed attack" and its statement of the law as to what is permitted to a victim state (and its friends) in response to violations that do not constitute an armed attack. . . .

The difficult legal issues for the future continue to be those of military intervention and counterintervention. They are not resolved by the court's opinion in the *Nicaragua* case, and there is need — and room — to develop norms within the spirit and the letter of the Charter.

The attempt to regulate military intervention has suffered from asymmetries that are inherent when an international system, consisting of states represented by incumbent governments, is compelled to address internal change and from the difficulties of definition and drawing lines in complex, confused internal and international situations. The governing principles should not be controversial. The international system favors voluntary cooperation between states and between their governments. International law does not forbid one state to sell arms to another state, and upon authentic invitation, a state may introduce military forces into the territory of another to assist the government for various purposes, including maintaining internal order. On the other hand, a state may not introduce arms or armed forces into a country without the consent of its government, surely not to support any groups hostile to the government. . . .

Notes and Questions

1. In *Armed Activities on the Territory of the Congo*, the Court again had the opportunity to consider how a state may respond to military intervention by nonstate actors with connections to an outside state. The Court evaluated whether the deployment and operations of Uganda's regular military forces in the DRC could be justified under principles of self-defense as a response to attacks carried out by the Allied Democratic Forces (ADF), anti-Ugandan rebels operating from Congolese territory. The Court concluded there was no proof of the involvement, direct or indirect, of the government of the DRC in the ADF's attacks.

> The attacks did not emanate from armed bands or irregulars sent by the DRC or on behalf of the DRC, within the sense of Article 3(g) of General Assembly resolution 3314 (XXIX) on the definition of aggression. . . . The Court is of the view that, on the evidence before it, . . . [these attacks] still remained non-attributable to the DRC.
>
> . . . For all these reasons, the Court finds that the legal and factual circumstances for the exercise of a right of self-defence by Uganda against the DRC were not present. Accordingly, the Court has no need to respond to the contentions of the Parties as to whether and under what conditions contemporary international law provides for a right of self-defence against large-scale attacks by irregular forces. [Armed Activities on the Territory of the Congo (Democratic Republic of the Congo v. Uganda), 2005 I.C.J. 168, 223 (Dec. 19).]

2. The former Soviet Union purported to justify its intervention into Afghanistan during 1979-1989 in part on a claimed right of counterintervention. When the Soviet Union began to move large military units into Afghanistan in December 1979, it claimed that its action was prompted by armed intervention by other foreign powers, including the United States. There was, in fact, no evidence of armed intervention by other countries. The Soviet Union also said that its troops entered Afghanistan at the repeated invitation of the Afghanistan government, but Soviet troops summarily executed Afghanistan's President and installed a puppet leader as Afghanistan's new ruler shortly after their intervention.

The Soviet intervention was almost universally condemned by all states other than the Soviet Union and its close allies. A 1980 General Assembly resolution "strongly deplore[d]" the action as a violation of Article 2(4). The resolution passed by a vote of 104 for and 18 against, with 18 abstentions and 12 absent or not voting.

3. In the excerpt above, Professor Henkin states that under international law, "upon authentic invitation, a state may introduce military forces into the territory of another to assist the government for various purposes, including maintaining

internal order." The ICJ in the *Nicaragua* case similarly stated that military intervention is "allowable at the request of the government of a State." 1986 I.C.J. at 126. Elsewhere in the book excerpted above, however, Henkin suggests that where an internal conflict amounts to a civil war, "a state probably may not send troops into the territory of another state to support either side . . . , since that too would violate the latter's territorial integrity and compromise its political independence." Henkin, Right v. Might: International Law and the Use of Force, supra at 47. Do you agree that in cases of civil war, the principle of nonintervention means that states cannot provide military support to the government? If providing assistance to a government to help it "maintain order" is permissible under international law, why would assisting a government in a civil war be impermissible? Would it mean that U.S. military support for the governments in Iraq and Afghanistan that are fighting domestic insurgencies represents impermissible intervention in those countries?

4. If a state engages in intervention against another state that qualifies as a use of force but does not constitute an "armed attack," what legal response should be available to the victim state? Should it not be permitted to use force to defend itself? Particularly if the state engaged in intervention is more powerful than the victim state, does it make sense, as the ICJ held in *Nicaragua*, that third states cannot use force to defend the victim state? What about a situation in which a state is attacked by groups based in a neighboring state whose acts are not attributable to the territorial state? What legal response should be available to the victim state? Do you agree with the Court's conclusion in *Armed Activities on the Territory of the Congo* that there is no right of self-defense in such cases?

d. Vietnam: Intervention, Counterintervention, or Collective Self-defense?

The U.S. involvement in Vietnam during the late 1960s and early 1970s highlights many of the questions regarding the use of force, including collective self-defense and responses to intervention, as well as the difficulty of confining complex real-world events within the conceptual categories of the use of force regime. The conflict had a traumatic effect on many Americans. Large numbers of U.S. citizens opposed the war as it dragged on and as U.S. involvement and casualties increased. Opposition to the war and the fact that the Executive Branch had taken the lead in embroiling the United States in the war were major causes of a resurgence of congressional activity in foreign affairs in the 1970s. For example, the War Powers Resolution, discussed below in Section E, was a direct result of the new congressional activism. In the following excerpt, Professor Henkin addresses the question of the legality of the Vietnam War under principles of international law.

Louis Henkin, How Nations Behave: Law and Foreign Policy

304-308 (2d ed. 1979)

Accusations of violations of law are common weapons in political controversy, often with little warrant. For their part, on the other hand, those who in fact violate the law, commonly plead "not guilty." As regards Vietnam, however, even . . . the judiciously-minded and the impartial were hard put to reach a clear judgment as to the merits of the legal claims of the two sides.

The legal uncertainties about Vietnam revealed uncertainties in the law of the U.N. Charter; they revealed, too, the importance of facts and their characterizations in legal determinations. The legality of the actions of the United States (and those of other parties to the war) turned on difficult issues as to the status and character of the territory and the government of South Vietnam, and their relation to the Vietcong, to North Vietnam, and to the North Vietnamese government. Was the war in Vietnam civil war or international war, and what was the status of the United States in that war? Of course, if the facts were confused, if what they amounted to was disputable, and the governing legal principles uncertain, they were less likely to exercise restraining influence on the policies of governments.

Even the barest, briefest narrative of American involvement in Indochina must go back at least to 1954. At a political conference in Geneva following years of fighting, France signed a cease-fire and agreed to transfer sovereignty to a "State of Vietnam." The Final Declaration of the Conference affirmed the unity of Vietnam and envisioned holding elections in July 1956. But while the rival governments in North and South Vietnam committed themselves to unifying the country, the South Vietnamese government did not accept the Geneva Conference and the United States did not sign the Final Declaration, although it announced that it would abide by the Declaration's terms.

It soon appeared that the South Vietnam government would not agree to general elections, claiming that the elections could not be free in the Communist-controlled North. The United States supported that view. Instead, it led in the establishment of the South-East Asia Collective Defense Treaty (SEATO), and a protocol to that treaty made its provisions applicable to Cambodia, Laos, and "the free territory under the jurisdiction of the state of Vietnam."

General elections were not held in 1956, and in the years that followed Communist-led dissident groups (known as the Vietcong, or later, the National Liberation Front) [engaged] in terroristic activities, rebellion and war against the South Vietnamese government. Supported by Southern Communists trained in North Vietnam, the Vietcong made important headway and by the end of 1960 controlled substantial areas of South Vietnam.

United States support for the South began early and increased slowly. In the early years it helped build up the South Vietnamese army; in 1961 it began to send combat advisers to accompany combat-support units, and by 1963 there were some 16,000 U.S. military personnel in South Vietnam. Following a coup d'état, apparently with U.S. knowledge if not support, President Johnson concluded that stronger U.S. support was necessary. In August 1964 a North Vietnamese attack on two U.S. destroyers in the Gulf of Tonkin led to a resolution by Congress authorizing the President to "take all necessary measures to repel any armed attack against the forces of the United States and to prevent further aggression," and to assist any member or protocol State of SEATO "requesting assistance in defense of its freedom." In October 1964 American aircraft began to attack supply trails in Laos; in March 1965 they began to bomb in North Vietnam; in April 1965 President Johnson sent combat troops. Beginning in the latter months of 1965, North Vietnamese troops entered the South to support the Vietcong. In 1967 the United States began to bomb in Laos, and in 1970 in Cambodia, claiming that the Communists were using those territories to support their aggression, and the local governments were unwilling or unable to prevent them. Despite intermittent efforts by both sides and by third parties to end the war, it continued for years more, terminating finally with the Paris agreements of 1973. . . .

There are at least three possible models to characterize the Vietnam War and the U.S. role in it, and the judgment of international law will largely depend on which characterization it accepts.

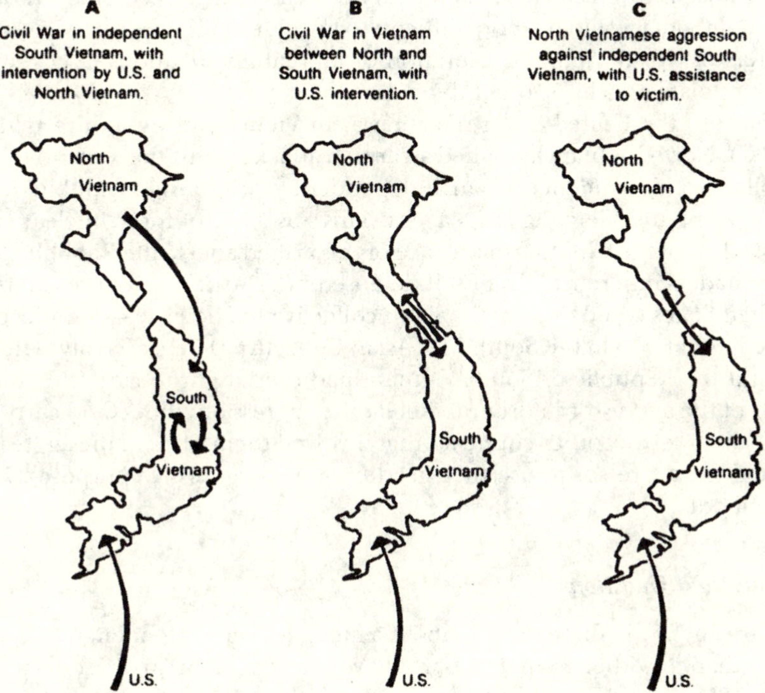

Model A saw the war as civil war within an independent South Vietnam, with North Vietnam an outside state helping one side, the United States another outside state helping the other. Military intervention in civil war was not acceptable under traditional international law, but that law may never have recovered from the wounds it suffered at many hands during the Spanish Civil War [in 1936-39]. On its face at least, such external intervention is not obviously a violation of Article 2(4) of the U.N. Charter as a use of force against the political independence or territorial integrity of another state, if the support was bona fide and the intervenor was not seeking to dominate the side it supported and establish a puppet regime.

On this view of the Vietnam War, neither the United States nor North Vietnam violated a vital contemporary norm of international law, as long as both confined themselves to supporting activity. But U.S. bombing of North Vietnam added an unacceptable dimension, converting an essentially civil war into an international war. (In the Spanish Civil War, intervenors did not, nor claimed the right to, attack each other's territory.) Indeed, world reaction to U.S. participation appeared to harden appreciably after the United States began to bomb in the North, in part perhaps because the world saw the war as an internal affair in South Vietnam and held the United States responsible for expanding it.

A second view (Model B) also saw the war as civil war, not between the Vietcong and the Saigon government in a separate independent South Vietnam, but within the single state of Vietnam, between North Vietnam and the Vietcong on the one hand and Saigon forces on the other. In such a war, U.S. intervention, even bombing North Vietnam, was — again — perhaps a violation of traditional international norms against intervention in civil war, but not clearly of the U.N. Charter. Bombing Laos or Cambodia would be more difficult to justify, even if they were viewed as tacit supporters of North Vietnam; toleration of mutual interventions in civil war does not contemplate attacks by one intervenor against another.

Officially, the United States saw the war in Vietnam in yet a third perspective (Model C). North Vietnam launched an armed attack against the territorial integrity and political independence of an independent country, the Republic of South Vietnam, using the Vietcong as its agent. This was a use of force in clear violation of Article 2(4) of the Charter. In the face of this armed attack, the Republic of South Vietnam had its inherent right of self-defense under Article 51 of the Charter, and the United States could come to its aid in collective self-defense — as indeed, it had obligated itself to do in the South East Asian Collective Defense Treaty. The United States and the Republic of South Vietnam had every right to carry the war to the territory of the aggressor in order to defeat the aggression; they could carry the war to the territory of any other countries that involved themselves in the aggression, or permitted the aggressor to use their territory for its aggressive purposes, *i.e.*, Laos and Cambodia.

Notes and Questions

1. Are any of the three models above a more accurate statement of the Vietnam situation than the others? What facts would you need to know in order to answer that question? How would you answer the question if the relevant facts were genuinely in dispute during the time of the U.S. intervention?

2. Professor Viet Dinh, who escaped from Vietnam by boat with some of his family after the war, believes that the war should be understood as part of the continuing U.S. fight for democracy and capitalism. See Viet D. Dinh, How We Won in Vietnam, Policy Review 51 (Dec. 2000-Jan. 2001). Other attempted explanations for U.S. involvement abound, including that the U.S. decision makers on Vietnam were overly focused on containing communism worldwide and viewed it as monolithic, rather than appreciating the domestic revolutionary character of the Vietnamese opposition. Another explanation was that the U.S. decision makers were operating from the lessons of World War II, when they had come of age and when early British and French attempts to pacify an aggressive country, Nazi Germany, had failed.

3. Under any of the three models described by Professor Henkin, what legal justification is there for the U.S. bombing of Laos and Cambodia? Did it matter whether Laos or Cambodia agreed to permit the Vietcong and North Vietnamese use of their territory or whether they lacked the power to oust them?

In two insightful articles in the 1990 Stanford Law Review analyzing the legality under the U.S. Constitution of the U.S. involvement in Indochina, Professor John Ely undertook an impressive factual analysis of the actual U.S. involvement in Laos and Cambodia. He concludes that much of the U.S. bombing of Laos from 1964 on was to help protect the Laotian government, not just to cut off the North Vietnamese supply routes to South Vietnam. Similarly, the U.S. bombing of parts of Cambodia, which began secretly in March 1969, apparently had at least the acquiescence of Prince Sihanouk, the Cambodian leader. Do Ely's conclusions make it easier to justify the bombings under international law?*

4. If you believe under one theory or another that the U.S. bombing of Laos or Cambodia was justified under international law, would the then-Soviet Union have been justified in attacking Afghan refugee camps in Pakistan during the Soviet intervention in Afghanistan — on the grounds that these refugee camps were acting as training and support bases for the Afghan guerrillas? Was the United States justified in 2010 in attacking militants in Pakistan on the grounds that they were supporting the Taliban insurgency in Afghanistan? Are there important factual differences between the three cases? What kinds of facts or considerations, if any, would you consider relevant in assessing the lawfulness of the use of force in these kinds of cases?

e. Dealing with Terrorists

International law does not deal clearly with how states may respond to international terrorism. An initial question is: Who is a terrorist (versus, say, a freedom fighter)? A further question is: What are the responsibilities of the "host" country (where the terrorist organization or individual is located) to take action? Then there is the issue of what actions a country whose officials or citizens are the target of a terrorist action might take unilaterally against terrorists located in the another country — or against the host country itself. The September 11 attacks and U.S. and world response to them have provided possible answers to some of these questions, while further complicating the issues raised by others.

The initial obstacle to creating a coherent international approach for combating terrorism is the absence of an agreed-upon definition. This obstacle is sometimes expressed by the saying, "One person's terrorist is another person's freedom fighter." This statement has been applied to such groups as Palestinian militants in the Middle East, Kashmiri resistance groups in India and Pakistan, and pro- or anti-Communist rebel groups all over the world during the Cold War. There are also debates about whether any definition of terrorism should include the use of armed force by states against civilians.

*Under U.S. law, Ely concludes that the secret bombing of Cambodia between March 1969 through April 1970 raised very serious constitutional questions, because the Nixon Administration made major efforts to hide what was happening from Congress and the American public. And, for at least the last several months of that bombing, Congress had passed legislative provisions that no money could be spent on bombing targets outside of Vietnam. Ely concludes: "I'd have impeached [President Nixon] for it. Surely it would have been a more worthy ground than the combination of a third-rate burglary and a style the stylish couldn't stomach." John Hart Ely, The American War in Indonesia, Part II, 42 Stan. L. Rev. 1093, 1148 (1990). (The burglary Ely was referring to was the break-in at the Watergate offices of the Democratic Party.)

As a result, U.N. Security Council Resolution 1373, which was adopted in the immediate aftermath of the September 11 attacks and which obligates states to refrain from providing any form of support to terrorists and to take steps to prevent and punish terrorist acts, does not define terrorism. Nor does Security Council Resolution 1624, which calls upon states to adopt domestic measures to "[p]rohibit by law incitement to commit a terrorist act or acts." None of the 13 major multilateral treaties on terrorism adopted since 1963 contains an explicit definition of terrorism; these conventions usually fall back to the next best alternative, the functional approach of defining and outlawing specific acts, such as airplane hijacking, assaults on diplomats, and taking hostages. The definition of these prohibited activities sometimes includes the element that the act be done for the purpose of influencing political authorities in a country. (As of February 2011, the United States was a party to 12 of the 13 major multilateral counterterrorism conventions.) Attempts to develop a more general approach have foundered on the insistence of certain countries and blocs on excluding particular groups from the definition.

Since September 11, some progress on securing international consensus on the definition of terrorism has been made. The U.N. Security Council, in Resolution 1566:

> *Recall[ed]* that criminal acts, including against civilians, committed with the intent to cause serious death or serious bodily injury, or taking of hostages, with the purpose to provoke a state of terror in the general public or in a group of persons or particular persons, intimidate a population or compel a government or an international organization to do or to abstain from doing any act, which constitute offences within the scope of and as defined in the international conventions and protocols relating to terrorism, are under no circumstances justifiable by considerations of a political, philosophical, ideological, racial, ethnic, religious or other similar nature, and *call[ed] upon* all States to prevent such acts and, if not prevented, to ensure that such acts are punished by penalties consistent with their grave nature. [S.C. Res. 1566, ¶3, U.N. Doc. S/RES/1566 (Oct. 8, 2004).]

Despite this progress, it still seems unlikely that a comprehensive convention on terrorism will emerge from the United Nations in the near future.

In October 2001, the United States launched attacks against the Al Qaeda terrorist group that carried out the September 11 attacks against the United States and their Taliban hosts in Afghanistan and participated in the overthrow of the Taliban regime. The idea of punishing a host state for sponsoring terrorism goes back further, however. In 1986, the Reagan Administration sent U.S. planes to bomb targets in Libya in response to a discotheque bombing in Germany that killed two and injured several other U.S. soldiers. While U.S., British, and French vetoes blocked a Security Council resolution, the General Assembly voted 79 to 28, with 33 abstentions, to condemn the U.S. attack on Libya. G.A. Res. 41/83 (1986).

By contrast, the post-September 11 campaign in Afghanistan was widely accepted by the international community, and Professor Franck in 2002 suggested that "there may be emerging in the political organs a greater tolerance for states that carry their wars with terrorists and insurgents across borders to strike at safe havens." Franck, Recourse to Force, supra, at 65. Nevertheless, it may be difficult to extrapolate from the international response to the U.S.-led campaign against the Taliban and Al Qaeda in Afghanistan the recognition of a general entitlement to use force in response to terrorist attacks. Indeed, the recent missile attacks by U.S. forces against Taliban and Al Qaeda militants in Pakistan launched from unmanned aerial vehicles, or drones, has renewed the controversy over this issue. See Section B.5.f below. The following excerpt discusses some of the legal impediments to the unilateral use of force in response to terrorism.

Allen S. Weiner, The Use of Force and Contemporary Security Threats: Old Medicine for New Ills?

59 Stan. L. Rev. 415, 429-437 (2006)

The new security threats [posed by terrorism] present a significant challenge to the legal regime governing the use of force, particularly to the unilateral use of force by states to counter these threats. . . .

1. The Absence of an "Armed Attack"

Uses of force by terrorist actors may not necessarily constitute "armed attacks" that justify the use of self-defense under Article 51. According to the International Court of Justice (ICJ) in the *Nicaragua* case, not all measures that "involve a use of force" are sufficiently "grave" to qualify as an armed attack. In evaluating violence by insurgents in a civil war, the court stated that the key factor was whether their action, "because of its scale and effects, would [be] classified as an armed attack, rather than as a mere frontier incident had it been carried out by regular armed forces." Although the considered view is that the events of September 11, in view of the devastation they wrought, qualified as "armed attacks," not all violent acts committed by terrorists — such as assassinations, hijackings of airplanes, or bombings or shootings taking few lives or causing relatively modest property damage — will be of sufficient scale and effect to constitute armed attacks.

2. Territorial Integrity of the State Where Force Is Used

Using force against terrorists highlights a significant tension in the current international legal regime between a state's right to use force against nonstate actors that have attacked it and the territorial integrity of the state where those terrorists are located. The fact that a terrorist attack is perpetrated by a nonstate actor, rather than by a state, does not necessarily bar the victim state from invoking its right of self-defense. Article 51 refers to the right of "self-defence if an armed attack occurs against a Member of the United Nations." It is not limited to circumstances in which an armed attack is launched by another state.

Nevertheless, a state's use of force against terrorist groups abroad also amounts to a use of force against the state where the terrorists are located when they are attacked. The prohibition in Article 2(4) on the use of force is not limited to uses of force directed against institutions of the state, but to force "against the territorial integrity or political independence of any state." As Schachter writes, "any coercive incursion of armed troops into a foreign state without its consent impairs that State's territorial integrity," and thus violates Article 2(4). In short, the U.N. Charter embodies a tension between the right of a state that is the victim of an armed attack by nonstate terrorists, on the one hand, to exercise the unilateral right of self-defense, and the right of the state where those terrorists reside, on the other, not to be subject to the use of force as long as that state does not itself launch an armed attack.

3. Problematic Justifications: State Responsibility and Harboring

a. State Responsibility

In some cases, the difficulty of using force against a state that has not itself launched an armed attack may be surmounted if the acts of terrorists are attributable to the state itself. According to the . . . [Draft Articles on State Responsibility (discussed in Chapter 8.A)], the conduct of a nonstate actor "shall be considered an act of a State under international law" if the actor "is in fact acting on the instructions of, or under the direction or control of, that State."

The precise degree of control a state must exercise over nonstate actors to establish such de facto responsibility is not entirely settled under international law. . . .

Under either the "effective control" [test from the ICJ's *Nicaragua* decision] or "overall control" standard [from the ICTY's *Tadic* judgment], however, it will typically be difficult to attribute terrorist acts to a sponsoring state. In many instances, the governments of states from which terrorists operate may be affirmatively antithetical to, or at least not share, the ideological goals of terrorist groups present in their territory. In other cases, such as those in which the terrorist group is engaged in an armed insurgency against the government, or the government's security forces otherwise lack the capacity to suppress the terrorist group, there is little the host-state government can do to prevent actions of the terrorist group. Even in the case of Afghanistan, it is difficult to attribute responsibility for the September 11 attacks by Al Qaeda to the Taliban or the state of Afghanistan under either the effective or overall control standards. The Taliban did not seem to have exercised a high degree of control over Al Qaeda, and Al Qaeda was not highly dependent on the Taliban for financing or supplies. Rather, the Taliban essentially made Afghanistan's territory available for Al Qaeda — with which it shared strong ideological ties — to pursue its activities independently.

b. Harboring Terrorists as a Basis for the Use of Force

Even where terrorist acts are not attributable to a state, the use of force against terrorist actors in other states could be defended on alternative legal theories, particularly where the state is harboring or supporting the terrorists. Even though a state with limited control over an armed group operating from its territory may not be deemed responsible for that group's attacks against another state, this does not mean that the harboring state is blameless. The General Assembly has declared that every state has a duty to refrain from "acquiescing in organized activities within its territory directed towards the commission" of forcible "acts of civil strife or terrorist acts in another State."[63] [Scholars also conclude that] . . . international law

63. Declaration on Principles of International Law Concerning Friendly Relations and Co-Operation Among States in Accordance with the Charter of the United Nations, G.A. Res. 2625 (XXV), at 123, U.N. Doc. A/8082 (Oct. 24, 1970). . . .

obligates states to exercise "due diligence" to prevent injuries to aliens caused by terrorists.

The difficulty with this analysis is not the proposition that governments violate customary international law by harboring terrorists. They do. But unless the state exercises the required degree of control over a terrorist group, a violation of the duty not to harbor terrorist groups is legally distinct from the violent acts carried out by the terrorists themselves. The significance of this distinction, of course, is that only a violation of a state's Article 2(4) duty not to engage in a use of force amounting to an armed attack gives rise to the target state's right to use force in self-defense. Since the adoption of the Charter, states may no longer use force by way of reprisal in response to breaches of other legal obligations owed to them, including the duty of states not to allow their territories to be used in a manner injurious to the interests of other states. A state's breach of its obligations not to harbor terrorists would entitle the victim state to demand cessation, to claim reparation, or to seek other remedies available under international law. Under current law, however, a breach of that duty would not entitle the victim state to use force against the harboring government.

4. International Assessment of Claims of Self-Defense Against Terrorism

Although the U.S. invocation of the right of self-defense in response to the September 11 attacks has not provoked much critical commentary, this is an exceptional case. The international community has generally been critical of the use of force in self-defense against nonstate terrorists. Such criticism suggests that the international community favors the territorial inviolability of the states charged with harboring terrorists over the self-defense rights of victims of terrorist attacks. . . .

[The article summarizes a number of past cases between 1968 and 2003 in which assertions of a right to use force in self-defense against terrorist attacks were met with skepticism in the U.N. Security Council.]

. . . [A]lthough the Security Council referred to the right of self-defense in a preambular clause in Resolution 1368, which condemned the September 11 attacks, the Charter does not clearly authorize the use of force in self-defense in response to terrorist acts by nonstate actors located on the territory of other states. Where force has been used against the territory of states from which terrorists operate, but to which the terrorists' conduct is not legally attributable, the international community has generally been skeptical of claims that the use of force was a justifiable exercise of the right of self-defense.[80]

80. This is not to say that the international community's record in condemning uses of force against terrorist groups located on another state's territory has been uniform. As Thomas Franck notes, although Iraq complained in 1995 and 1996 of Turkish military incursions into Iraqi territory in pursuit of Kurdish-secessionist insurgents, "these complaints did not lead to a meeting of, let alone action by, the [Security] Council or the [General] Assembly." Similarly, the missile attacks launched by the United States against Al Qaeda training camps in Afghanistan and a suspected chemical weapons plant in Sudan, in response to the terrorist bombing attacks against American embassies in Tanzania and Kenya, met with only limited condemnation by, and some expressions of support from, other members of the international community. Sudan's formal complaint "was not [even] inscribed on the agenda of the Security Council." . . .

Notes and Questions

1. Who is a terrorist? Do you agree with the approach that has emerged of negotiating treaties that require states to prohibit and punish specified acts, such as aircraft sabotage or detonating an explosive in a public place? If so, which activities should be considered terrorist actions? For example, should suicide bombings of civilians always be considered terrorism?

If a group is oppressed by an authoritarian government or a foreign occupying power, should it have some ability to resist with force? If so, what are the limits of this ability? For example, during the Saddam Hussein regime, should an Iraqi Kurd have had the right to plant a bomb in a civilian part of Baghdad, or is that terrorism? Should the Iraqi Kurd have had the right to attack an isolated Iraqi military outpost, or is this terrorism? Moving to another part of the world, if a member of a Basque separatist group bombs a Spanish army base in northern Spain, should he be considered a terrorist? If he explodes a bomb in a public market in Madrid, Spain, which is outside the Basque region?

2. If the host country does not take action against terrorists found within its borders, should it be required to turn these people over to another country for prosecution for acts committed in the other country or against the target country's citizens? If it does not, what measures should other states be able to take in response? Economic measures? Forcible measures?

3. What should be the standard for using force against a state on the territory of which terrorist groups are based? Do you agree with the excerpt from Professor Weiner above suggesting that the ordinary rules of state responsibility apply and that acts of terrorists are attributable to the host state only if they are acting "on the instructions of, or under the direction or control of," the host state? Should the right of a state to use force against terrorists abroad it depend on whether the host state has the ability to suppress terrorist acts? In a recent article, Professor Tams argues that international law norms regarding the use of force against nonstate terrorist groups have evolved in the past 20 years, and that it is the standard of attribution in particular that has changed:

> . . . [The most] convincing way to accommodate the new practice [regarding unilateral uses of force against terrorists] is to opt for an approach which retains the traditional understanding of self-defence as a justification for the use of force between states, but recognizes the existence of special rules on attribution of terrorist activities. This . . . re-reading indeed seems to be borne out by state practice: states invoking self-defence do make an effort to identify links between the territorial state and the terrorist organization in question. What they no longer seem to do is to identify links that are strong enough to amount to 'effective control' as required by the *Nicaragua* test. Instead, contemporary practice suggests that a territorial state has to accept anti-terrorist measures of self-defence directed against its territory where it is responsible for complicity in the activities of terrorists based on its territory—either because of its support below the level of direction and control or because it has provided a safe haven for terrorists. In short, pursuant to this more moderate re-reading, modern practice points towards a special standard of imputability in relations between terrorist groups and host states, arguably most closely resembling international rules against 'aiding and abetting' illegal conduct. The contours of this new test have yet to be firmly established, and it lies in the nature of things that the broadening of attribution standards increases

> the risk of abuse. However, it is submitted that the concept of 'aiding and abetting' in terrorist activities captures the essence of new practice while still maintaining some degree of predictability. [Christian J. Tams, The Use of Force against Terrorists, 20 European J. Int'l L. 359, 385-386 (2009).]

What are the advantages of permitting states to use force against terrorists abroad if the host state is "aiding and abetting" them — as opposed to permitting the use of force only when the terrorists are under the "direction or control" of the host state? What are the disadvantages? How would the international law standard change from the "direction or control" test to the "aiding and abetting" test?

4. In November 2002, an unmanned Predator aircraft, controlled by U.S. government operators, fired its missile and killed six Al Qaeda members in Yemen, including one who may have helped to plan the attack in 2000 on a U.S. warship, the *U.S.S. Cole*, when it was in a Yemeni port. Another person who may have been a U.S. citizen was also killed in the attack. In January 2007, the U.S. launched at least two airstrikes against Somalis suspected of having ties to Al Qaeda in southern Somalia; the first attack killed eight to ten persons, according to U.S. estimates. Raid Killed Somali Allies of Al Qaeda, U.S. Says, N.Y. Times, Jan. 12, 2007, at A6. Are these uses of force justified under Article 51? Are they necessary and proportionate? Does it depend on the strength of the evidence that the persons killed were members of Al Qaeda? Would a self-defense claim require evidence that they were planning further attacks?

5. The materials excerpted above reflect divergent assessments about the international attitudes toward a state's use of force against terrorists in another country. Professor Franck says there may be an emerging "tolerance for states that carry their wars with terrorists and insurgents across borders to strike at safe havens"; Professor Weiner says the international community has "generally been skeptical of claims that the use of force was a justifiable exercise of the right of self-defense." What kind of information would you seek to attempt to resolve this disagreement? How would you weigh the following series of cases highlighted by Professor Tams and the examples cited in footnote 80 of the Weiner excerpt above?

> - From the mid-1990s, Iran on several occasions invoked Article 51 . . . to justify the use of force against bases of the Mujahedin-e Khalq Organization (MKO) on Iraqi territory. While Iraq denounced the use of force as an act of aggression, the international community did not condemn it. Equally 'uncommented' remained Iran's incursions into Iraqi territory in pursuit of Kurdish armed bands (labeled 'organized terrorist mercenaries'). . . .
> - In 2000 and again in 2004, Russia asserted a right to respond extraterritorially to Islamic terrorists. In 2007, following attacks by Chechen rebels, it conducted air strikes against Chechen bases in the Pankisi Gorge in Georgia, claiming that Georgia 'had been unable to establish a security zone in the area of the [Russian–Georgian] border, continues to ignore Security Council Resolution 1373 and does not put an end to the bandit sorties and attacks on adjoining areas of Russia'. Responses were mixed, but again there was no principled condemnation that would have denied Russia's right to use force extraterritorially.
> - In March 2008, Colombian forces moved into Ecuadorian territory in pursuit of rebels belonging to [the Revolutionary Armed Forces of Colombia, also known as the] FARC (which it considers a terrorist organization). The OAS qualified the operation as a 'violation of [Ecuador's] sovereignty'; other international

organizations were largely silent; the United States expressed support. [Christian J. Tams, The Use of Force against Terrorists, supra, 20 European J. Int'l L. at 379-380.]

6. Should the United States and other countries treat terrorism as a security challenge to be confronted by force — and regulated by the associated legal rules — as opposed to a problem of international crime? This section addresses cases involving the use of force, but there have also been many efforts to cooperate internationally to criminally prosecute terrorists.

In one prominent case, the U.N. Security Council in 1992 demanded that Libya extradite to either the United States or the United Kingdom two Libyans accused of bombing Pan Am flight 103, which blew up in 1988 over Lockerbie, Scotland, killing 270 people, including 189 U.S. citizens. (There are reports that Libya's leader Muammar Qaddafi ordered the bombing in retaliation for the 1986 U.S. bombing attack on Tripoli.) The Council later imposed economic and travel ban sanctions for Libya's failure to comply with the Council's surrender demands. At least in part in response to these pressures, Colonel Qaddafi in 1999 turned over the two accused Libyans in a carefully negotiated arrangement whereby they would be tried by a Scottish court applying Scottish law (because the plane blew up over Scotland), but meeting on more neutral ground in the Netherlands. After a trial lasting nearly nine months, one of the accused — Abdelbaset Ali Mohmed Al Megrahi — was found guilty and sentenced to life in prison. The second accused — Al Amin Khalifa Fhimah — was acquitted. See Her Majesty's Advocate v. Al Megrahi, 40 I.L.M. 582 (High Court of Justiciary at Camp Zeist, The Netherlands, Jan. 31, 2001). Al Megrahi was sentence to life imprisonment, but Scottish authorities granted him release on compassionate grounds in August 2009 after he was diagnosed with terminal prostate cancer.

Does your answer to the question of whether terrorism should be addressed with military force or criminal law sanctions depend on the nature of terrorist threat? Are all terrorist groups alike for these purposes? Professor Waxman argues that it is a mistake to think of "'terrorist threats' as a monolithic category." He suggests that the law of war model may be appropriate in confronting "hierarchical, centralized terrorist organizations operating from geographic safe havens," but much less so for "radicalized individuals conducting a loosely organized, ideologically common but operationally independent fight against western societies." Matthew C. Waxman, The Structure of Terrorism Threats and the Laws of War, 20 Duke J. Comp. & Int'l L. 429, 431 (2010).

7. The United States has a number of laws that can provide jurisdiction to U.S. courts for terrorist acts abroad against U.S. citizens and sometimes even for acts against non-U.S. citizens. (See the Alien Tort Statute and Torture Victim Protection Act, discussed in Chapter 3, and 18 U.S.C. §2333, which is discussed in Chapter 7.) Also, for certain acts, the Foreign Sovereign Immunities Act denies sovereign immunity to those foreign states that have been designated as supporting terrorists (see Chapter 6.A). Note that terrorist acts occurring in the United States would also be subject to U.S. federal and state law regarding the various acts — for example, murder and destruction of property.

8. The case study at Chapter 1.E addresses in some detail the September 11 terrorist attacks and the U.S. and world response to them. Now that you have read and thought more about the international law governing the use of force, was the

U.S. campaign in Afghanistan that began in October 2001 justified under Article 51? Could it be justified under a theory of reprisal? Does the removal of the Taliban and installation of the Karzai government meet the requirement of proportionality?

f. Problems of Application: Afghanistan/Pakistan

In October 2001, as Chapter 1.E recounts, the United States launched Operation Enduring Freedom, a military campaign against Al Qaeda terrorists and the Taliban regime in Afghanistan. As of February 2011, substantial numbers of U.S. forces remained in Afghanistan to fight Al Qaeda and what had become a Taliban insurgency in Afghanistan. U.S. forces grew substantially beginning in 2009 under the Obama Administration's "surge" policy, and as of February 2011, about 100,000 U.S. troops were on the ground in Afghanistan. Many of those troops are part of the NATO forces that comprise the International Security Assistance Force initially authorized pursuant to U.N. Security Council Resolution 1386 (2001), but considerable numbers continue to be deployed as part of U.S.-led Operation Enduring Freedom.

There are important questions about the legal basis for present-day U.S. military operations in Afghanistan and neighboring Pakistan. The United States initially attacked Al Qaeda and Taliban forces in Afghanistan in October 2001 in response to the attacks of September 11. At the time, the Taliban regime exercised effective control over about 90 percent of the territory of Afghanistan, but it was recognized as the de jure government of Afghanistan by only three countries. Although the United States did not recognize the Taliban as the government of Afghanistan, President Bush nevertheless determined in February 2002 that the Geneva Conventions that regulate the conduct of war between state parties to the conventions applied to the armed conflict with the Taliban, which meant that the conflict was an international armed conflict between the United States and Afghanistan. The legal situation probably changed, however, after the fall of the Taliban regime and the installation of the Karzai-led government. Thereafter, in the words of one leading law of war expert, "the 'war' in Afghanistan comprises [an] . . . armed conflict between the Afghan government (supported by foreign States) and various armed groups, most notably the remnants of the Taliban and Al Qaeda." Michael N. Schmitt, Targeting and International Humanitarian Law in Afghanistan, in The War in Afghanistan: A Legal Analysis 307, 308 (Michael N. Schmitt, ed. 2009).

Other commentators suggest that the conflict in Afghanistan is not merely a civil war between the Government of Afghanistan supported by the United States, on one hand, and the Taliban, on the other. They stress that the armed conflict between the United States and the Taliban that was triggered by the September 11 attacks is a distinct and ongoing conflict taking place alongside the civil war in Afghanistan:

> When American and allied troops are fighting the Taliban (and their Al Qaeda ally) on Afghan or adjacent (Pakistani) soil, this is a direct sequel to the hostilities that [that started on October 7, 2001, that] led to the ouster of the Taliban from the seat of power in Kabul. Both segments (past and present) of the hostilities are consecutive scenes in the same drama unfolding in Afghanistan. The . . . war [between the United States

> and the Taliban] will not be over until it is over. And it will only be over once the Taliban are crushed.
>
> We still have in Afghanistan—side by side with the . . . war . . . [between the United States and the Taliban]—an intra-State war (the Taliban [insurgents] versus the Karzai government in Kabul). . . . [Yoram Dinstein, Terrorism and Afghanistan, in The War in Afghanistan: A Legal Analysis 43, 51 (Michael N. Schmitt ed., 2009).]

The conflict in Afghanistan has also spread into Pakistan. Some of the Al Qaeda and Taliban groups have fled from Afghanistan into the "Federally Administered Tribal Areas" in Pakistan where the central Pakistani government exercises little, if any control. Some of these groups support Taliban insurgents in Afghanistan; others conduct their own hit-and-run operations from Pakistani territory into Afghanistan. In addition, an indigenous Pakistan Taliban movement has gained strength in recent years; as of February 2011, the Pakistani Taliban was engaged in an internal insurgency within Pakistan and is also believed to support the insurgency in Afghanistan.

U.S. forces have launched military strikes against insurgents in Pakistan, most prominently missile strikes launched from unmanned aerial vehicles, or drones. Pakistan's government has not publicly consented to U.S. military operations against insurgents, although press reports—including some based on leaked State Department cables—suggest that Pakistan officials have either approved the U.S. attacks or tacitly consented to them.

Professor Murphy discusses self-defense as a potential legal basis for the use of force against insurgents in Pakistan, highlighting that the way the self-defense theory is framed can have significant implications:

> A [potential] basis for finding US cross-border operations into Pakistan permissible . . . relies upon the United States' inherent right of self-defense or its right to engage in collective self-defense at the request of Afghanistan. . . .
>
> In considering this basis, . . . [one must ask:] What was the preceding use of force against which the United States is defending. . . .
>
> . . . There are two candidates for the preceding use of force to which the United States is responding in self-defense. First, the United States might be seen today as still defending against Al Qaeda's attacks of 9/11. . . . If the initial U.S. invasion of Afghanistan was a permissible act of self-defense against the perpetrators of 9/11, . . . then cross-border operations today might be seen as part of a continuous process to accomplish that objective, albeit years later. . . .
>
> An alternative preceding act triggering a right of U.S. self-defense is the more recent cross-border raids into Afghanistan by militants based in Pakistan (mostly Taliban, but with support from Al Qaeda and other foreign fighters) to strike at US or coalition forces, or the government of Afghanistan. This approach does not emphasize the attacks of 9/11 but, rather, the contemporary cross-border operations that are harming coalition and Afghani interests in Afghanistan. [Sean D. Murphy, The International Legality of US Military Cross-Border Operations from Afghanistan into Pakistan, in The War in Afghanistan: A Legal Analysis 109, 123-124 (Michael N. Schmitt ed., 2009).]

Notes and Questions

1. Does it matter whether U.S. military operations in Afghanistan are based on the right of self-defense, as opposed to the consent of the government of

Afghanistan? If the United States is acting on the basis of the consent of the Afghan government, could the Afghan government dictate the kinds of operations U.S. forces would be allowed to engage in? In a November 2010 interview, President Karzai expressed his opposition to nighttime raids carried out by U.S. special forces, stating: "The raids are a problem always. . . . They have to go away. . . . The Afghan people don't like these raids. . . . This is a continuing disagreement between [Afghanistan and the United States]." Joshua Partlow, Karzai Calls on U.S. to Lighten Troop Presence, Wash. Post, Nov. 14, 2010, at A1. If the government of Afghanistan "disagrees" with the United States about such nighttime raids, what legal basis do U.S. forces have for conducting them?

2. Professor Dinstein — who in the essay above argues that the ongoing U.S. conflict against the Taliban is distinct from the civil war between the Karzai government and the Taliban — also writes that the "singular feature" of the conflict between the United States and the Taliban:

> is that it is conducted on Afghan soil with the consent of the Karzai government. This means that, at any point in time, the Karzai government (or, in the future, a successor Afghan government) may withdraw that consent and pull the rug out from under the feet of the United States. . . . [Dinstein, Terrorism and Afghanistan, supra, at 52.]

If this is correct, would this not undermine the ability of the United States to exercise its right of self-defense? Is it consistent with the suggestion by Professor Murphy that the U.S. right to use force against insurgents in Pakistan on self-defense defense grounds is a justification that is distinct from the principle of host state consent? If, on the other hand, the consent of the Afghanistan is not required, can the United States carry out any military actions it wishes to, anywhere in the country, even if the Government of Afghanistan objects? More generally, if the consent of the territorial state is not required for the exercise of self-defense against nonstate groups, does that mean the United States can use force on the territory of any state in the world where Taliban or Al Qaeda forces are located?

3. Could the United States claim a right of anticipatory self-defense against insurgents in Pakistan (or elsewhere) even if they are not linked either to the attacks of September 11 or cross-border raids into Afghanistan? What conditions would have to be met for the use of anticipatory self-defense against nonstate terrorist actors?

4. In a 2010 speech to the American Society of International Law, the State Department's Legal Adviser addressed the question of the U.S. use of force in Afghanistan and elsewhere:

> In the conflict occurring in Afghanistan and elsewhere, we continue to fight the perpetrators of 9/11: a non-state actor, al-Qaeda (as well as the Taliban forces that harbored al-Qaeda). . . .
>
> . . . [A]s a matter of international law, the United States is in an armed conflict with al-Qaeda, as well as the Taliban and associated forces, in response to the horrific 9/11 attacks, and may use force consistent with its inherent right to self-defense under international law. . . . [This legal authority] continues[s] to this day.
>
> As recent events have shown, al-Qaeda has not abandoned its intent to attack the United States, and indeed continues to attack us. Thus, in this ongoing armed conflict, the United States has the authority under international law, and the responsibility to its

> citizens, to use force, including lethal force, to defend itself, including by targeting persons such as high-level al-Qaeda leaders who are planning attacks. [Harold Hongju Koh, The Obama Administration and International Law, Remarks at Annual Meeting of the American Society of International Law, (March 25, 2010), available at http://www.state.gov/s/l/releases/remarks/139119.htm.]

What legal theory for the use of force is reflected in these remarks? Is the theory the same for the use of force against the Taliban as it is for Al Qaeda? Even assuming the United States has a right of self-defense against the Al Qaeda as a result of the September 11 attacks, what is the legal basis for using force against other groups that might be "associated" with them?

5. As discussed in the case study in Chapter 1.E and discussed in Section C below, the International Security Assistance Force (ISAF), a major peacekeeping presence, is deployed in Afghanistan pursuant to Chapter VII Security Council authorization. The resolution establishing ISAF authorizes the force "to take all necessary measures to fulfil its mandate" of assisting the government of Afghanistan in maintaining security. Would that provide broader authority for members of ISAF to use force than either a theory of self-defense or the consent of government of Afghanistan?

6. In Pakistan, does it matter whether U.S. military operations against militants in Pakistan are based on a theory of self-defense linked to the September 11 attacks, as opposed to the insurgency taking place within Afghanistan? Would this affect the targets against whom the United States would be permitted to use force?

7. Professor O'Connell has argued that the use of drone missile attacks in Pakistan violates international law. Mary Ellen O'Connell, Unlawful Killing with Combat Drones: A Case Study of Pakistan, 2004-2009, in Shooting To Kill: The Law Governing Lethal Force in Context (Simon Bronitt ed., forthcoming). As she stated in testimony prepared for an April 28, 2010 hearing before the House of Representatives Subcommittee on National Security and Foreign Affairs, this is due in part to her view that the United States is "using lethal force . . . far from any actual battlefield." She argues: "Armed conflict . . . is a real thing. . . . The fighting or hostilities of an armed conflict occurs within limited zones, referred to as combat or conflict zones. It is only in such zones that killing enemy combatants or those taking a direct part in hostilities is permissible."

Do you agree? Had the United States initiated its October 2001 use of force against Al Qaeda and the Taliban in Afghanistan with drone missile attacks, would that have been lawful? Can the United States claim an ongoing right to exercise self-defense selectively against insurgents in Pakistan, or is the use of force in Pakistan permissible only if there is an active armed conflict taking place to which the United States is a party? Can the U.S. target insurgents much farther away from the "conflict zone" in Afghanistan, as it did in November 2002, when it launched a drone missile attack that killed six Al Qaeda members in Yemen?

g. Humanitarian Intervention

The intractable problems of violent civil wars within a country and the commission of widespread human rights abuses by a government against its own population raise the question of whether states may forcibly intervene in other states for humanitarian purposes. The question of collective responses by the United Nations and regional organizations to humanitarian catastrophes is discussed in a Section C below. In this subsection, we consider whether states may act on their own, without Security Council approval, to use force to halt widespread atrocities in another state.

Professor Franck notes that the categorical prohibition on the use of force in Article 2(4) of the Charter seemingly elevated principles of international order and peace over the principle of using force for "preserving justice and redressing injustice[,] a concept for which the Charter made little provision." Franck, Recourse to Force, supra, at 16. In the except that follows, Professor Franck discusses humanitarian intervention under contemporary international law.

Thomas M. Franck, Recourse to Force

135-136, 137-139, 171-173 (2002)

When a government turns viciously against its own people, what may or should other governments do? The events of the recent past do not permit this to be dismissed as an "academic question." . . .

If the wrong being perpetrated within a state against a part of its own population is of a kind specifically prohibited by international agreement (e.g., the Genocide Convention and treaties regarding racial discrimination, torture, the rights of women and children, and the International Covenant on Civil and Political Rights, as well as agreements on the humanitarian law applicable in civil conflict), humanitarian intervention against those prohibited acts may be thought of as a subspecies of self-help. This is conceptually more persuasive if the wrongful acts have been characterized explicitly or implicitly by the applicable universal treaties as offenses *erga omnes*: that is, against any and all states party to the agreement defining and prohibiting the wrong. In such circumstances, it is possible to argue that every state may claim a right of self-help as a vicarious victim of any violation, at least after exhaustion of institutional and diplomatic remedies. Analogous universal rights to self-help might also arise in the event of violations of certain rules of customary [international] law. . . .

It is . . . difficult conceptually to justify in Charter terms the use of force by one or several states acting without prior Security Council authorization, even when such action is taken to enforce human rights and humanitarian values. The Charter's Article 2(4), strictly construed, prohibits states' unilateral recourse to force. The text makes no exception for instances of massive violation of human rights or humanitarian law when these occur in the absence of an international aggression against another state. In the strict Charter scheme, states are not to use force except in self-defense and regional organizations may not take "enforcement action . . . without the authorization of the Security Council. . . ."

A state using military force without Council authorization against another in "humanitarian intervention" is thus engaging in an action for which the Charter text provides no apparent legal authority. . . .

However, . . . the institutional history of the United Nations — as distinct from the Charter's text — and record of state practice, neither categorically precludes nor endorses humanitarian intervention. Rather, the history and practice support a more nuanced reconciling of the pursuit of peace (as evidenced by Charter Article 2(4)) and of justice through the protection of human and humanitarian rights (as evidenced by the canon of rights-creating universal agreements). In this practical reconciliation we can detect a pragmatic range of systemic responses to unauthorized use of force, depending more on the circumstances than on strictly construed text. This patterned practice suggests *either* a graduated reinterpretation by the United Nations itself of Article 2(4) or the evolution of a subsidiary adjectival international law of mitigation, one that may formally continue to assert the illegality of state recourse to force but which, in ascertainable circumstances, mitigates the consequence of such wrongful acts by imposing no, or only nominal, consequences on states which, by their admittedly wrongful intervention, have demonstrably prevented the occurrence of some greater wrong.

[Franck then examines] eight instances of states' use of force in overtly or implicitly humanitarian interventions. In four of these, an individual state used force without prior Security Council authorization: (India-Pakistan, 1971, Tanzania-Uganda, 1978-79, Vietnam-Kampuchea, 1978-79, France-Central African Empire, 1979). In one, several states jointly participated in such enforcement (France, UK, US-Iraq, 1991-93). In three instances it was regional or collective security organizations that used force in humanitarian crises without prior Council authorization (ECOMOG [Economic Community of West Africa's Cease-Fire Monitoring Group]-Liberia, 1989, ECOMOG-Sierra Leone, 1991, NATO-Yugoslavia (Kosovo), 1999). . . .

. . . [W]hile the UN system aims to substitute its collective security for traditional state reliance on unilateral force, it has had some success in adjusting to a harsher reality. In particular, it has acquiesced, sometimes actively, at other times passively, in the measured expansion of the ambit for discretionary state action and has done so without altogether abandoning the effort evident in Article 2(4) to contain unilateral recourse to force. It has sought balance, rather than either absolute prohibition or license.

This balance is difficult to achieve. If the use of force by NATO in Kosovo is seen as a precedent for a reinterpretation of Article 2(4)'s absolute prohibition on the discretionary use of force by states, the substitution of a more "reasonable" principle, one that accommodates use of force by any government to stop what it believes to be an extreme violation of fundamental human rights in another state, could launch the international system down the slippery slope into an abyss of anarchy. . . .

. . . [T]he law cannot hope to secure acquiescence in a norm that permits its violation at the sole discretion of a party to which it is addressed. Law is strengthened when it avoids absurdly rigid absolutes — for example, by requiring passivity in the face of destruction of entire populations — but only if exceptions intended to prevent such *reductio ad absurdum* are clearly understood and applied in a manner consonant with agreed notions of procedural and evidentiary fairness.

Finally, the instances in which a state or group of states has intervened for humanitarian purposes without incurring significant opposition from the international system may indicate a certain willingness on the part of that community to brook some violation of the law in instances of clearly demonstrated necessity. It does not, however, indicate a fundamental change in the law to give wholesale permission to states to do that which is textually prohibited. Even less does it suggest that conduct which is textually prohibited has, through practice, become legally obligatory. It cannot, on the broadest interpretation of the legal significance of practice, be argued that the law now *requires* states to intervene with or without Security Council authorization, wherever and whenever there is evidence of a massive violation of humanitarian law or human rights. As a former British Foreign Secretary has recently pointed out:

> There is room for much argument about the nature of the cruelties which have been or are being inflicted in Chechnya, Tibet and the Occupied Territories of Palestine. But however great and unwarranted such cruelties, the international community will certainly prove unable or unwilling to intervene to stop them. The distribution of power in the world makes such intervention impossible. . . . The fact that the international community cannot intervene everywhere to protect human rights need not be an argument against helping where we can. . . . It is . . . a reason for not trying to confuse decisions of policy with obligations under international law.

Or, put in lawyers' terms, it is important not to confuse what the law *in some limited circumstances may condone* or excuse with what is *required* by law in every circumstance. . . .

The 1999 bombing campaign by the United States and other members of NATO against the Federal Republic of Yugoslavia (FRY) is viewed by many observers as an important case of humanitarian intervention, although the countries that used force for the most part did not formally claim this as the legal basis for their actions.

After the disintegration of the former Socialist Federal Republic of Yugoslavia in the early 1990s, ethnic Albanians in Kosovo, an autonomous region within Serbia (then one of the constituent republics of the FRY), stepped up a campaign of attacks against Serbians in their effort to split off from Serbia. The Serbs responded with much violence. In March 1998, the Security Council responded to the crisis by adopting Resolution 1160, which called upon the FRY to take steps to resolve the crisis through dialogue and imposed economic sanctions on the FRY. In October, the Security Council adopted Resolution 1199, which went further and explicitly demanded that the FRY "cease all action by [FRY] security forces affecting the civilian population and order the withdrawal of security units used for civilian repression." S.C. Res. 1199, ¶4(a), U.N. Doc. S/RES/1199 (Sept. 23, 1998). Nevertheless, in the winter of 1998-1999, the Serbs conducted a major attack against Kosovo, forcing hundreds of thousands of ethnic Albanians from their homes. NATO warned FRY President Slobodan Milosevic to stop his campaign, but the "ethnic cleansing" continued.

The United States and other countries in NATO felt compelled to stop the FRY's actions, but they met opposition from Russia in the U.N. Security Council. Nevertheless, NATO decided to proceed. On March 24, 1999, NATO forces began air strikes against targets inside Serbia. The attacks continued for 78 days, until Serbia surrendered and Milosevic accepted NATO's terms under which Serbia would withdraw all its military forces from Kosovo and NATO would send 50,000 troops there.

Militarily and politically, NATO's action was a success. However, by intervening militarily inside a sovereign state without the explicit authorization of a Security Council resolution, the NATO campaign raised questions about the U.N. Charter's restrictions on the use of force. It may also have created an important precedent regarding humanitarian intervention.

As Professor O'Connell explains, although leading U.S. officials repeatedly cited the risk of a humanitarian disaster in Kosovo, they did not specifically justify the use of force against the FRY on the basis of the doctrine of humanitarian intervention:

> NATO issued no statement setting out the legal justification for [its bombing campaign], nor did the United States. The US President and Secretary of State made references to humanitarian disaster, though not to a right of humanitarian intervention. . . . In April, Yugoslavia brought a case to the International Court of Justice (ICJ) against ten NATO members arguing that they had used force in violation of international law, including violation of the Genocide Convention. At the ICJ, the Legal Adviser to the US Department of State argued that "[m]embers of the NATO Alliance find their justification in a number of factors. These include: — [t]he humanitarian catastrophe . . . ; [t]he acute threat . . . to the security of neighbouring States . . . ; [t]he serious violation of international humanitarian law and human rights . . . ; and, . . . the resolutions of the Security Council. . . ." He did not, however, argue explicitly that a right of humanitarian intervention justified NATO's action nor that the Security Council resolutions were sufficient on their own to authorize a use of force.
>
> Belgium, alone of the ten states responding to Yugoslavia's case, suggested that at least a nascent right of humanitarian intervention existed when NATO began bombing. Most of the other capitals involved in NATO's use of force argued that the bombing was a justifiable exception to the normal rules. Though their arguments appear related to the defenses of distress or necessity, none explicitly argued either. Some argued that the Security Council Resolutions prior to NATO's . . . use of force provided sufficient authorization to use force. Adding to the lack of clarity of the legal situation, just two days after the start of the bombing, Russia introduced a resolution at the Security Council condemning NATO's bombing as a violation of the Charter and as a threat to international peace. Only Russia, China, and Namibia voted in favor. Even the Secretary General did not condemn NATO's use of force, saying only "normally a U.N. Security Council Resolution is required." [Mary Ellen O'Connell, The UN, NATO, and International Law After Kosovo, 22 Hum. Rts. Q. 57, 80-82 (2000).]

In addition to these statements, President Clinton made a report to Congress, as is consistent with the War Powers Resolution (discussed in Section E) shortly after the NATO bombing began, in which he stated that the military campaign would continue until Milosevic "stop[ped] the repression." He also said:

> The [Federal Republic of Yugoslavia] government has failed to comply with U.N. Security Council resolutions, and its actions are in violation of its obligations under the U.N.

> Charter and its other international commitments. The FRY government's actions in Kosovo are not simply an internal matter. The Security Council has condemned FRY actions as a threat to regional peace and security. The FRY government's violence creates a conflict with no natural boundaries, pushing refugees across borders and potentially drawing in neighboring countries. The Kosovo region is a tinderbox that could ignite a wider European war with dangerous consequences to the United States. . . . [President William J. Clinton, Letter to Congressional Leaders, 1 Pub. Papers 459 (Mar. 26, 1999).]

Professor Stromseth offers the following analysis of the implications of the Kosovo campaign for the doctrine of humanitarian intervention.

Jane Stromseth, Rethinking Humanitarian Intervention: The Case for Incremental Change

Humanitarian Intervention: Ethical, Legal and Political Dilemmas 232, 241-245 (J.L. Holzgrefe & Robert O. Keohane, eds., 2003)

For years to come, NATO's 1999 military intervention in Kosovo will shape international attitudes toward the use of force in response to human rights atrocities. In contrast to the U.S. military action in Afghanistan taken in self-defense against terrorist attacks, the legal basis for NATO's action in Kosovo remains contested. Whether "humanitarian intervention"—the use of force for humanitarian purposes—is lawful or otherwise justified in the absence of state consent or United Nations authorization is a question that has long vexed international lawyers and philosophers. . . .

Four distinct attitudes or approaches to humanitarian intervention in the absence of Security Council authorization can be identified. Each has pros and cons. First is the status quo approach. This view categorically affirms that military intervention in response to atrocities is lawful only if authorized by the UN Security Council or if it qualifies as an exercise of the right of self-defense. Proponents of this view regard NATO's intervention in Kosovo as a clear violation of Article 2(4) that should not be repeated in the future. Defenders of this position include a number of states, most notably Russia and China. . . .

Yet, after Kosovo, it is hard to take a rigid status quo approach. NATO responded to urgent humanitarian circumstances in a situation recognized as a threat to the peace by the Security Council. Furthermore, neither the Council nor the Secretary-General were prepared to condemn NATO's action. . . .

This leads to the "excusable breach" approach to humanitarian intervention. Under this second approach, humanitarian intervention without a UN mandate is technically illegal under the rules of the UN Charter but may be morally and politically justified in certain exceptional cases. In short, it is a violation of the Charter for which states are unlikely to be condemned or punished. . . .

The excusable breach approach has some distinct benefits. It highlights the truly exceptional nature of legitimate non-authorized humanitarian intervention. It contemplates no new legal rules governing the use of force. On the contrary, the existing legal framework, with its various benefits, is affirmed. Yet, in those extraordinary cases that produce a tension between the rules governing the use of force and the protection of fundamental human rights, a "safety valve" is opened. States intervening in such situations are unlikely to be condemned as law-breakers; but they act at their own risk in full awareness that they are violating the rules for a higher-purpose.

This approach has evident drawbacks as well, however. For one thing, it is unsatisfying to label as "illegal" action that the majority of the UN Security Council views as morally and politically justified. . . . Second, the justifications offered by states—and the international responses to state action—are more nuanced than the "excusable breach" approach. NATO states did not argue "we are breaking the law but should be excused for doing so." Instead, NATO states, in sometimes differing ways, explained why they viewed their military action as "lawful"—as having *a legal basis within the normative framework of international law*. . . .

This leads to a third approach: customary law evolution of a legal justification for humanitarian intervention in rare cases. This approach looks to both Security Council and broader international responses to instances of non-authorized humanitarian intervention to ascertain patterns, consistency of rationales, and degrees of acceptance, reflected in practice, if certain conditions are met. This approach asks whether an emerging norm of customary international law can be identified under which humanitarian intervention should be understood not simply as ethically and politically justified but also as legal under the normative framework governing the use of force. The strong non-intervention presumption at the Charter's core is affirmed, but this approach allows for a narrow, evolving legal exception and justification for humanitarian intervention in light of concrete circumstances, and in light of the reasons that states and the UN Security Council find persuasive over time, rather than calling such action flatly illegal or an "excusable breach" of the UN Charter.

The advantages of this approach are considerable and, as I will argue, it offers a more promising path for the future than the alternatives. Nevertheless, the ambiguities inherent in this approach have led some to advocate a fourth, more explicit, approach to humanitarian intervention. Advocates of this fourth approach favor codification of a clear legal doctrine or "right" of humanitarian intervention. Proponents argue that such a "right" or "doctrine" should be established through some formal or codified means such as a UN Charter amendment or a UN General Assembly declaration. The idea is that humanitarian intervention should be a distinct legal basis for using force on a par with the right of self-defense, with fixed criteria or principles spelled out in advance governing legitimate appeal to the right. Although states have been extremely reluctant to advocate a legal right of humanitarian intervention in the absence of Security Council authorization, a number of scholars . . . have made the case for establishing such a right or doctrine with specified criteria to guide assessments of legality. The case for codifying a right of humanitarian intervention rests on a normative attitude towards such interventions, a view about the impact of codification on the legitimacy of international law, a position concerning the role of formalization in curbing abuses, and a view about the relative benefits of clarity versus open-endedness in the evolution of international legal norms.

Notes and Questions

1. What do you believe are the best justifications, if any, for NATO's use of force against the Federal Republic of Yugoslavia over Kosovo? Consider the grievances that President Clinton listed against the FRY or the arguments advanced by the State Department Legal Adviser before the ICJ. Do any provide a legal justification for the use of force by NATO? What principles justifying the use of force can be found in these statements? President Clinton refers to the risk of a "wider European war," but no NATO member claimed that the Kosovo air strikes were justified as self-defense under Article 51. Why not? Could any interpretation of Article 51 permit a state to exercise self-defense against a "threat to regional security"?

2. On March 23, 1999, on the eve of the bombing campaign against the FRY, in response to a question about international legal basis for NATO's use of force, State Department spokesman James P. Rubin cited a series of justifications similar to those later relied on by President Clinton. He concluded that "[o]n the basis of such considerations, we and our NATO allies believe there are legitimate grounds to threaten and, if necessary, use force." What do you think is the significance, if any, of the fact that the State Department spokesman described the use of force as "legitimate," rather than "legal"? Is there a difference between these terms?

Consider in that regard the conclusions reached an independent commission of prominent international legal experts headed by Justice Richard Goldstone of South Africa that reviewed the Kosovo conflict:

> [T]he NATO military intervention was illegal but legitimate. It was illegal because it did not receive prior approval from the United Nations Security Council. However, the Commission considers that the intervention was justified because all diplomatic avenues had been exhausted and because the intervention had the effect of liberating the majority population of Kosovo from a long period of oppression under Serbian rule. [Independent International Commission on Kosovo, The Kosovo report: Conflict, International Response, Lessons Learned 4 (2000).]

3. Like many traditional international law scholars, Professor Dinstein is skeptical about a right of humanitarian intervention:

> Most commentators who favour "humanitarian intervention" studiously avoid the terminology of self-defence and insist that the forcible measures taken are legitimate, not by virtue of compatibility with Article 51 . . . but as a result of being compatible with Article 2(4). . . .
>
> This is a misreading of the Charter. No individual State (or group of States) is authorized to act unilaterally, in the domain of human rights or in any other sphere, as if it were the policeman of the world. [Dinstein, War, Aggression and Self-Defence, supra, at 90-91.]

Compare Professor Dinstein's views with those of Professor Franck in the excerpt that started this subsection. As Franck indicates there, "the institutional history of the United Nations . . . neither categorically precludes nor endorses humanitarian intervention. Rather, the history and practice support a more nuanced reconciling of the pursuit of peace (as evidenced by Charter Article 2(4)) and of justice through the protection of human and humanitarian rights (as evidenced by the canon of rights-creating universal agreements)." Franck, Recourse to Force, supra, at 138-139.

4. Under what circumstances should the international community condone or excuse a state or group of states that intervene, without U.N. authorization, in another state for humanitarian purposes? Should the international community's acceptance of some interventions be limited to instances of demonstrated necessity? Can the circumstances be defined more specifically in advance?

5. At this point, what exceptions do you think should be allowed to the Article 2(4) prohibition on the use of force? Should the exceptions be limited to self-defense under Article 51? What do you interpret that self-defense to allow—anticipatory self-defense? Reprisals? Humanitarian intervention? Do you think that other exceptions should be allowed? If so, for which uses of force? In terms of interpreting the Charter's provisions, do you support strict construction of the Charter, or limited continuing adaptation, or some other approach to regulating the use of force? In considering these questions, how much do your answers depend on your perspective? Would you give the same answers if you were the Secretary of State considering what U.S. government policy should be toward the principles in the U.N. Charter and customary international law limiting the use of force? Should the United States embrace those principles wholeheartedly?

6. Turning back to the first excerpt in this section, Professor Franck expressed his view that because the text of the U.N. Charter "is not facially responsive to the challenge of change," the Charter, "like other grand instruments written for the long term, has had to meet the threat of obsolescence with adaptation." At least one scholar takes a far more pessimistic view of whether the U.N. Charter's provisions have adapted so as to continue to regulate in any meaningful way the international use of force by states. Professor Michael Glennon argues, in effect, that the U.N. Charter's use of force regime has collapsed, and that there are no longer international rules governing the use of force:

> [I]nternational "rules" concerning use of force are no longer regarded as obligatory by states. Between 1945 and 1999, two-thirds of the members of the United Nations—126 states out of 189—fought 291 interstate conflicts in which over 22 million people were killed. This series of conflicts was capped by the Kosovo campaign in which nineteen NATO democracies representing 780 million people flagrantly violated the Charter. The international system has come to subsist in a parallel universe of two systems, one *de jure*, the other *de facto*. The *de jure* system consists of illusory rules that would govern the use of force among states in a platonic world of forms, a world that does not exist. The *de facto* system consists of actual state practice in the real world, a world in which states weigh costs against benefits in regular disregard of the rules solemnly proclaimed in the all-but-ignored *de jure* system. The decaying *de jure* catechism is overly schematized and scholastic, disconnected from state behavior, and unrealistic in its aspirations for state conduct.
>
> The upshot is that the Charter's use-of-force regime has all but collapsed. This includes, most prominently, the restraints of the general rule banning use of force among states, set out in Article 2(4). The same must be said, I argue here, with respect to the supposed restraints of Article 51 limiting the use of force in self-defense. . . .

In one sense, the conclusion that Article 51 has no practical force follows a fortiori from my earlier argument: If there is no authoritative general prohibition of use of force, it makes no sense to consider the breadth of a possible exception. Yet an examination of Article 51 reveals a measure of inconsistency, illogic, and, indeed, incoherence that provides independent grounds for questioning its importuned restraints in decisions concerning use of force. The received interpretation of Article 51 consists in hopelessly unrealistic prescriptions as to how states should behave. Its more concrete sub-rules illustrate why policymakers have come to ignore the Charter's use-of-force regime in fashioning how states behave. . . .

. . . No rules will work that do not reflect underlying geopolitical realities. The use-of-force regime set out in the U.N. Charter failed because the Charter sought to impose rules that are out-of-sync with the way states actually behave. A new use-of-force regime that does work will have to rest far more firmly upon actual patterns of practice that reveal, with solid empirical evidence, what regulation of force is possible and what is not. . . . There is no use in telling ghost stories, Holmes said, to people who do not believe in ghosts. [Michael J. Glennon, The Fog of Law: Self-Defense, Inherence, and Incoherence in Article 51 of the United Nations Charter, 25 Harv. J.L. & Pub. Poly. 539, 540-541, 557-558 (2002).]

Do you agree with Professor Glennon's thesis? Does it matter that even though states may have interpreted the legal norms for their own purposes, no responsible state has been willing to argue that the rules governing the use of force do not apply? Or that states and others typically feel the need to explain how their steps are consistent with international legal norms?

C. COLLECTIVE SECURITY: U.N. AND REGIONAL USE OF FORCE AND PEACEKEEPING EFFORTS

Besides enunciating principles under which states may on their own authority use force, the U.N. Charter allows for the use of force and peacekeeping operations by the United Nations itself. It also empowers the United Nations to authorize the use of force by groups of states and recognizes a security role for regional organizations such as NATO and the Organization of American States. U.N. efforts have been more frequent in recent years, and there have also been activities by both *ad hoc* coalitions of states and the regional groups. Overall, collective intervention has increasingly occurred, particularly in the context of internal conflicts.

This section first analyzes the U.N.'s collective security regime, including consideration of major recent military interventions in Iraq and Libya. The section then turns to the activities of regional organizations.

1. U.N. Use of Force and Peacekeeping Efforts

Chapter VII of the U.N. Charter has several articles dealing with U.N. action with respect to threats to the peace and acts of aggression. Among the key ones are Articles 39-42.

Chapter VII. Action with Respect to Threats to the Peace, Breaches of the Peace, and Acts of Aggression

Article 39

The Security Council shall determine the existence of any threat to the peace, breach of the peace, or act of aggression and shall make recommendations, or decide what measures shall be taken in accordance with Articles 41 and 42, to maintain or restore international peace and security.

Article 40

In order to prevent an aggravation of the situation, the Security Council may, before making the recommendations or deciding upon the measures provided for in Article 39, call upon the parties concerned to comply with such provisional measures as it deems necessary or desirable. Such provisional measures shall be without prejudice to the rights, claims, or position of the parties concerned. The Security Council shall duly take account of failure to comply with such provisional measures.

Article 41

The Security Council may decide what measures not involving the use of armed force are to be employed to give effect to its decisions, and it may call upon the Members of the United Nations to apply such measures. These may include complete or partial interruption of economic relations and of rail, sea, air, postal, telegraphic, radio, and other means of communication, and the severance of diplomatic relations.

Article 42

Should the Security Council consider that measures provided for in Article 41 would be inadequate or have proved to be inadequate, it may take such action by air, sea, or land forces as may be necessary to maintain or restore international peace and security. Such action may include demonstrations, blockade, and other operations by air, sea, or land forces of Members of the United Nations.

Under Article 25 of the Charter, Security Council decisions taken under Chapter VII are binding on all Members, which are obliged "to accept and carry out decisions of the Security Council. . . ."

Chapter VII also includes Article 43, which envisioned that the United Nations itself would have the military forces to implement Security Council decisions to use force. Article 43 provides that all Members shall "undertake to make available to the Security Council, on its call and in accordance with a special agreement or agreements, armed forces, assistance, and facilities . . . necessary for the purpose of maintaining international peace and security." The special agreements were to "govern the numbers and types of forces, their degree of readiness and general location. . . ."

For a variety of reasons, including each Member's concerns about maintaining control over its military forces and the start of the Cold War soon after 1945, the U.N. has entered into no such special agreements. However, as Professor Thomas Franck notes, "the adaptive capacity of the Charter has functioned dramatically and controversially to fill the vacuum created by Article 43's non-implementation." Professor Franck then goes on to explain how.

Thomas M. Franck, Recourse to Force

24-40 (2002)

Faced with its failure to establish a police militia under Article 43, the Security Council has adapted by using, or authorizing states to use, *ad hoc* forces put together for the purpose of responding to a specific crisis. . . .

The Korean War is the first example of the Security Council's authorizing *ad hoc* collective measures in the absence of Article 43 forces. On June 25, 1950, Secretary-General Trygve Lie reported the previous night's attack by North Korea on the South. Qualifying the situation as a threat to international peace, he called on the Security Council as the "competent organ" to act at once by determining that the attack was a breach of the peace, calling for a cessation of hostilities, embargoing all "assistance to the North Korean authorities," and calling "upon all Members to render every assistance to the United Nations in the execution of this resolution." This was precisely the response voted by the Council. Its resolution determined that there had been a "breach of the peace" and thereby invoked Article 39, the prerequisite for collective measures under the Charter's Chapter VII.

. . . Resolution 83 of June 27 (passed with only Yugoslavia opposed and with the Soviet Union absent*) recommended . . . "that the Members of the United Nations furnish such assistance to the Republic of Korea as may be necessary to repel the armed attack and to restore international peace and security in the area." On July 7, with the Soviets still absent . . . , the Council recommended that all members providing military assistance make such forces available to a unified military command headed by the US, authorized that command to use the United Nations flag, and requested the US to report "as appropriate" to the Security Council.

Since the Charter makes no provision for a UN military response except with Article 43 forces, the Council's authorization of action in its name by *ad hoc* national contingents — what has since become known as a "coalition of the willing" — represented a creative adaption of the text. The practice of Security Council authorization of action by such coalitions of the willing subsequently became a firmly established part of the UN collective security system. In this first experience, the UN force was constituted by ground forces volunteered by ten states, naval units from eight nations, and air units from five. . . .**

*[The Soviet Union was absent because it was boycotting the Council over another issue at the time.–Eds.]

**[The international force was under the initial command of General Douglas MacArthur, numbered in the tens of thousands, and engaged in major battles.–Eds.]

In 1960, the Security Council authorized another coalition of the willing to respond to an appeal by the Government of the Republic of the Congo to restore order and facilitate the removal of Belgian troops from that newly-independent state. . . . Six years later, the Council authorized the British navy to enforce UN sanctions against the break-away white-supremacist regime of Ian Smith in the self-governing Crown Colony of Rhodesia.

Forty years after the Korean episode, the Security Council — still lacking an Article 43-based military capability of its own — once again authorized a massive coalition of the willing: this time to undertake operation "Desert Storm" after Iraq's invasion of Kuwait. . . . [The Iraq situation is discussed in more detail below.]

The drafters of the Charter . . . did not envisage such Council-mandated use of force in the absence of an Article 43-based military capability. There is no reason, however, why the Council's responses to aggression cannot be understood as a creative use of Article 42. . . . Textually, Article 42 can stand on its own feet and it now may be said to do so as a result of Council practice. . . .

Article 39 . . . empowers the Council to "take measures" under Article 42 without reference to Article 43, thereby creating room for the Council to order — or, more probably, to call for — states' participation in collective security measures. . . .

If the Council were to *order* states to use force, Article 25 would require all members to "agree and carry out" that decision. To date, however, all the resolutions authorizing *ad hoc* military forces have merely "called on" or "authorized" states to use force. . . . There have been several subsequent occasions on which the Security Council has authorized the use of force by states in coalitions of the willing: national military contingents assembled *ad hoc* for a particular task. The Council has also authorized a single state or a regional organization to lead a specified military operation. . . . Thus, on November 30, 1992, the Secretary-General informed the Council that "the situation in Somalia has deteriorated beyond the point at which it is susceptible to peace-keeping treatment." . . . He concluded that "the Security Council now has no alternative but to decide to adopt more forceful measures to secure the humanitarian operations. . . . It would therefore be necessary for the Security Council to make a determination under Article 39 of the Charter that a threat to the peace exists. . . ." Promptly, the Security Council made the requisite finding under Chapter VII and authorized the US, and any others "willing," to "use all necessary means" through an *ad hoc* Unified Task Force (UNITAF) to achieve the specified objectives. . . .

It is notable that the Council, in authorizing military intervention in Somalia, followed precisely the requisites of Article 42. . . .

These were not trivial operations. UNITAF engaged 37,000 (primarily American) forces. Its multinational successor, UNOSOM II, deploying 30,000 military personnel, was placed by the Council under the control of the UN Secretary-General and charged with enforcement powers and the task of creating peace, democracy and unity in that riven land. All the more significant is it to note that both operations — engaging the United Nations in an essentially humanitarian intervention with ad hoc forces and doing so even in the absence either of a clearly international crisis or the consent of Somalia — should have received the unopposed consent of the members of the Security Council. Although few members of the Council thought it prudent to spell out general principles of

Charter-interpretation underpinning this use of collective force—and, indeed, in Resolution 794 states took care to note the "unique character" of the crisis to which they were responding—the actions of the Council cannot but be seen as precedent-setting.

Another example of the expansion of the practice of deploying coalitions of the willing is the Council's—again, expressly "exceptional"—authorization, in 1994, of a multinational force under "unified command and control" to "use all necessary means" to facilitate the ouster from Haiti of the military leadership that had overthrown its democratically elected government. On this occasion the resolution was passed by 13-0 with Brazil and China abstaining. . . . Yet another instance is the mandate given by the Security Council to another *ad hoc* force, UNPROFOR, in the former Yugoslavia and the gradual extension of that military mandate to include the defense of Bosnian "safe areas." When those safe areas and the UN personnel in them came under attack, the Security Council authorized air strikes by NATO against Serb heavy weapons. . . . Despite *pro forma* protest from the Russian Federation, the ensuing "bombs of August" constituted the first effective military partnership between a regional military organization and the United Nations' own *ad hoc* multinational force, one that ultimately led to the defeat of Serb forces and, in turn, to the Dayton peace negotiations. . . .

There are other, even more recent examples of coalitions of the willing or individual states being authorized by the Security Council to use force as necessary, usually but not always under Chapter VII. Thus, the Security Council in 1994 authorized France to use "all necessary means" for security and humanitarian ends during the civil turmoil in Rwanda and in 1997 authorized Italy, with others, to deploy forces to prevent civil war in Albania and created INTERFET under Australian leadership to establish security in East Timor. In an effort to contain the civil war in Sierra Leone the Council, in 1999, created UNAMSIL, a force of 11,000 with authority, under Chapter VII, to use force "to afford protection to civilians under imminent threat of physical violence" as well as to "assist . . . the Sierra Leone law enforcement authorities in the discharge of their responsibilities."

It may thus be concluded that the failure to implement Article 43 has not seriously hampered the United Nations in carrying out its mission to provide collective security. On the contrary, *ad hoc* coalitions of the willing, in various logistical configurations, or designated surrogates . . . have been deployed with mandates, including interventions in essentially domestic conflicts for primarily humanitarian purposes. . . . It was the intention of the founders at San Francisco to create a living institution, equipped with dynamic political, administrative, and juridical organs, competent to interpret their own powers under a flexible constituent instrument in response to new challenges. The United Nations has fulfilled that mandate.

The Role of the General Assembly: Original Intent

Another issue left largely uncontemplated and wholly unresolved at Dumbarton Oaks and at San Francisco was this: what would happen if a palpable threat to the peace were to arise but the Security Council (either for lack of a majority or by exercise of the veto) were unable to act? . . . [T]his soon became the principal challenge to the effectiveness of the Charter system.

At Dumbarton Oaks some consideration had been given to allotting a secondary role to the General Assembly for the maintenance of international peace and security, but this was rejected. . . .

. . . Nevertheless, its power, set out in Article 11(2) of the Charter, does permit the Assembly to make recommendations as to "questions relating to the maintenance of international peace and security" as long as it refrains from doing so while [, in the words of Article 12(1),] "the Security Council is exercising in respect of any dispute or situation the functions assigned to it in the . . . Charter." . . .

This makes all the more remarkable the evolutionary growth of Assembly jurisdiction in matters requiring collective action, including the deployment of military forces. This adaption has occurred through two developments: the adoption of the "Uniting for Peace Resolution" and the invention of "Chapter 6 ½."

Adapting General Assembly Powers: "Uniting for Peace"

After being absent from the Security Council in June 1950 at the inception of North Korea's aggression, the Soviet Union resumed its participation in August. This presaged renewed deadlock in that organ. Accordingly, in October, at the beginning of the General Assembly's annual meeting, the US introduced an agenda item entitled "United Action for Peace." . . .

. . . [The General Assembly] endorsed the "Uniting for Peace" resolution by a resounding vote of 52-5 with only the Soviet bloc in opposition, and 2 abstentions (India and Argentina). The resolution:

> 1. *Resolves* that if the Security Council, because of lack of unanimity of the permanent members, fails to exercise its primary responsibility for the maintenance of international peace and security in any case where there appears to be a threat to the peace, breach of the peace, or act of aggression, the General Assembly shall consider the matter immediately with a view to making appropriate recommendations to Members for collective measures, including in the case of a breach of the peace or act of aggression the use of armed force when necessary, to maintain or restore international peace and security. . . .

. . . Canadian Secretary of State for External Affairs, Lester B. Pearson conceded that "some honest doubts have been expressed about [the resolution's] constitutionality and . . . the sponsors . . . respect them. Nevertheless . . . [w]e believe that the General Assembly has the power to make recommendations on the subjects dealt with [in the Charter], although it would not have the power to make decisions which would automatically impose commitments or enforce obligations on the Members of the United Nations." . . .

The resolution had its first full-scale test in 1956, during the Suez crisis. Israel having invaded the Sinai, and with Britain and France bombing Suez Canal cities in anticipation of an expeditionary landing, the US, on October 30, convened the Security Council demanding that it determine that there had been a breach of the peace and order Israeli forces back to the armistice lines established by the Council's cease-fire order of 11 August 1949.

. . . The US then introduced a draft resolution calling for withdrawal of Israeli forces and insisting that Britain and France not intervene. It received 7 votes in favor, with 2 opposed and 2 abstentions. The two negative votes having been cast by Britain and France, the resolution was vetoed.

Immediately, Yugoslavia . . . offered a resolution which, "taking into account" that the Council had been prevented "from exercising its primary responsibility for the maintenance of international peace and security" called for an emergency session of the General Assembly. . . .

The Assembly quickly adopted a resolution that "urged" a cease-fire. As fighting continued, Canada [successfully] submitted a resolution . . . urgently requesting the Secretary-General to propose a plan for an international emergency force (UNEF) to secure and supervise a cease-fire. Such a proposal . . . was adopted by 57-0 with 19 abstentions. [The Assembly] appointed a Chief of Staff . . . and authorized recruitment of a military force "from member states other than the permanent members of the Security Council." The same day the Secretary-General received Israel's unconditional agreement to a cease-fire, followed one day later by French and British acquiescence.

In his second and final report to the Assembly on the establishment of the new force, the Secretary-General emphasized that it had been authorized by, and would operate under, the "Uniting for Peace" resolution. He noted that it was being deployed with the consent of the countries concerned and would be stationed on Egyptian territory with that country's agreement as "required under generally recognized international law." . . .

. . . The moment, clearly, had been seized. The Organization, adapting to the circumstances of Cold War stasis in the Security Council, had found a new way to authorize, recruit, and deploy the military force necessary to allow it to fulfill its mission.

Less than four years later, the Assembly once again stepped forward to authorize UN military action in the face of Security Council deadlock. The force deployed in the Congo (ONUC) by the Security Council in July 1960 had become mired in a dispute between the West and the Soviet Union. . . . On September 17, the US invoked "Uniting for Peace" to convene another emergency session of the General Assembly, which, by a large majority, voted new instructions for the Secretary-General to "assist the Central Government of the Congo in the restoration and maintenance of law and order throughout the territory of the Republic of the Congo and to safeguard its unity, territorial integrity and political independence in the interests of international peace and security." This became an important extension of ONUC's mandate, leading to military operations against the secessionist regime of Katanga province. Only a year later was the Council again able to assume operational control over ONUC.

Large expenses were incurred by the United Nations to maintain ONUC's 25,000 military and support personnel. France and Russia, however, refused to pay their share, arguing that ONUC operations authorized by the Assembly were *ultra vires* the Charter. To test the legality of that proposition, the Assembly asked the International Court for an advisory opinion as to whether these expenditures constituted "expenses of the organization" that, under Article 17(2) of the Charter, must "be borne by the Members as apportioned . . ." Since Paris and Moscow were also refusing to pay their share of the cost of UNEF's Sinai operation, the

Court was also asked to consider the legality of that earlier Assembly-authorized deployment.

In responding, the Court had to decide on the legality of the General Assembly's role in military operations — UNEF and ONUC — under "Uniting for Peace." The judges, by a majority of 9 to 5, confirmed the *vires* of both.

Article 24 of the Charter states:

> In order to ensure prompt and effective action by the United Nations, its members confer on the Security Council primary responsibility for the maintenance of international peace and security. . . .

The Court reasoned that, while the text was clear in giving the Council "primary" responsibility, that term itself implied a "secondary" responsibility which the Assembly could exercise when the Council was stymied by a veto. In the majority's view, the Assembly has the right "by means of recommendations . . . [to] organize peacekeeping operations" although only "at the request or with the consent, of the States concerned."

In this opinion, the International Court both endorsed and shaped the "Uniting for Peace" Resolution, deeming it a lawful means by which the Assembly could exercise at least some of the Organization's responsibility for maintaining international peace and security when the Security Council was unable to do so. . . .

Inventing "Chapter 6 ½"

"Uniting for Peace" established a new procedure expanding General Assembly jurisdiction over peacekeeping operations. Concurrently, the United Nations began also to expand the kinds of such operations and their missions. Thus, the large UNEF military deployment in 1956 was a new venture both in scale and kind. "Blue helmets," lightly armed but in persuasive numbers, were deployed to observe a truce and to interpose themselves between hostile parties. They were not to engage in combat but, if attacked or hindered, were authorized to defend themselves and their mission. Thirty-eight peacekeeping operations based on this innovative precedent were deployed during the United Nations' first fifty years.

Most of these operations, unlike UNEF, have been authorized by the Security Council, but the resolutions creating them usually do not invoke the Council's unique Chapter VII enforcement powers. Yet, neither do they quite fit the parameters of Chapter VI, which deals only with "negotiation, enquiry, mediation, conciliation, arbitration, judicial settlement, resort to regional agencies or arrangements . . ." (Article 33). Hence, the blue helmets are commonly said to be authorized by "Chapter 6 ½." This is yet another illustration of the Charter's adaption in practice.

. . . The space occupied by the fictive Chapter 6 ½ is fluid, being defined by practice rather than Charter text. A Chapter 6 ½ operation may begin by the parties' acquiescence in deployment of a peacekeeping force. Over time, however, the operation may incur the hostility of one or several of the parties, requiring either its withdrawal (as in the instance of UNEF in the Sinai) or its difficult and risky transformation into a peace enforcement operation (as with ONUC in the Congo and UNPROFOR in the former Yugoslavia). This phenomenon of "mission-creep" . . . illustrates the ambiguity which may arise in conducting UN "blue helmet" military operations which, although initially not authorized or armed to engage in Chapter VII-based enforcement actions, are assigned new tasks that may involve them in combat operations. Nevertheless, the concept has proven to be of immense utility. . . .

The number of U.N. peacemaking, peacekeeping, and peacebuilding activities increased exponentially during the 1990s and reached what had been a high water mark in the 1993–1995 period, when over 70,000 civilian and military personnel were serving in 17 peacekeeping missions worldwide (including over 34,000 troops in the former Yugoslavia). By 1999, the number of U.N. peacekeepers had fallen to under 20,000, but U.N. missions deployed to address conflicts in Africa, Lebanon, East Timor, and Haiti beginning in 2003 created a new peacekeeping surge. U.N peacekeeping deployment reached a historic peak in 2010 of more than 123,000.

Current peacekeeping operations*

- United Nations Truce Supervision Organization (UNTSO, established 1948), in the Middle East (strength: military 149; civilian 216);
- United Nations Military Observer Group in India and Pakistan (UNMOGIP, 1949) (military 44; civilian 72);
- United Nations Peacekeeping Force in Cyprus (UNFICYP, 1964) (military 854; civilian police 68; civilian 150);
- United Nations Disengagement Observer Force (UNDOF, 1974), in the Syrian Golan Heights (military 1,045; civilian 144);
- United Nations Interim Force in Lebanon (UNIFIL, 1978) (military 11,961; civilian 987);
- United Nations Mission for the Referendum in Western Sahara (MINURSO, 1991) (military 236; police 6; civilian 283);
- United Nations Interim Administration Mission in Kosovo (UNMIK, 1999) (military 8; police 8; civilian 404);
- United Nations Mission in Liberia (UNMIL, 2003) (military 7,755; police 1,316; civilian 1,637);
- United Nations Operation in Côte d'Ivoire (UNOCI, 2004) (military 7,764; police 1,316; civilian 1,384);
- United Nations Stabilization Mission in Haiti (MINUSTAH, 2004) (military 8,744; police 3,240; civilian 1,942);
- United Nations Mission in the Sudan (UNMIS, 2005) (military 9,780; police 636; civilian 4,207);
- United Nations Integrated Mission in Timor-Leste (UNMIT, 2006) (military 35; police 1,482; civilian 1,428);

*As of December 31, 2010. Source: United Nations Department of Peacekeeping Operations Fact Sheet (2010).

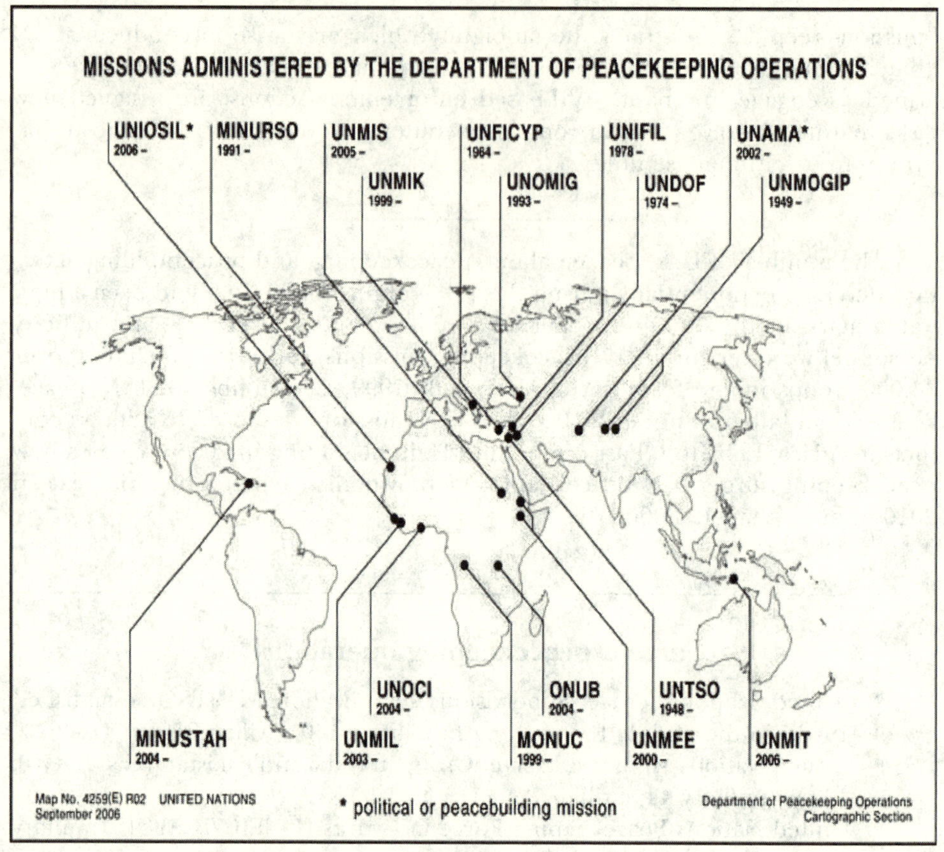

- African Union/United Nations Hybrid Operation in Darfur (UNAMID, 2007) (military 17,467; police 4,977; civilian 4,271);
- United Nations Mission in the Central African Republic and Chad (MINURCAT, 2007) (military 3; civilian 1,062);
- United Nations Organization Stabilization Mission in the Democratic Republic of the Congo (MONUSCO, 2010) (military 17,843; police 1,262; civilian 4,329).

As of December 2010, the United Nations had over 98,000 military and police personnel and some 22,000 civilians serving in 15 peacekeeping missions worldwide in the Congo, Western Sahara, East Timor, India-Pakistan, Cyprus, Kosovo, Golan Heights, Lebanon, Liberia, Côte d'Ivoire, Haiti, Burundi, Sudan, the Central African Republic-Chad, and the Middle East. The approved budget for these efforts for 2010–2011 was about $7.26 billion. U.N. officials expressed concerns about the financial, logistical, and administrative pressures of carrying out these missions and the shortage of military capabilities to execute a highly diverse set of peacekeeping missions. In addition, they noted that U.N. peacekeeping missions are increasingly engaged in post-conflict peacebuilding activities, requiring personnel with expertise in areas like rule of law promotion, demobilization and reintegration of former combatants, and making structural reforms in the security sector.

U.N. Intervention in "Internal" Matters. There has been a marked expansion of U.N.-authorized military intervention in events occurring within individual states. Professor Franck referred to several such deployments in the excerpt above, and he expands on this development below.

Thomas M. Franck, Recourse to Force

40-44 (2002)

Of particular significance is the gradual expansion of UN military intervention to meet threats to peace arising not out of aggression by one state against another but from events occurring within one nation. . . .

. . . [I]t is clear from the drafting history of the Charter's Articles 39, 42, 43, and 51 that the representatives at San Francisco had not intended to authorize a role for the United Nations in civil wars. Rather, Charter Articles 2(4) and 2(7) appear to forbid such intervention. In practice, however, the [1960 deployment of the ONUC military force to vanquish the Katanga separatists in the] Congo was but the first of several UN military involvements in precisely those sorts of conflict: in Yemen, Iraq, the former Yugoslavia, Somalia, Haiti, and Sierra Leone. It is worth emphasizing in this connection that the Charter's prohibition on UN intervention in matters "essentially . . . domestic" is not, textually, suspended even when a government asks for help in suppressing a domestic insurgency. Indeed, a literal reading of Article 2(7) precludes a positive response to such a request. The practice, however, has been much more flexible, treating an "invitation" from the government of a state as suspending the obligation not to intervene: or, alternatively, construing civil conflict, at least when it exceeds certain levels of virulence, as no longer "primarily . . . domestic."

The Charter also makes no provision for UN intervention in cases of gross violations of human rights, destruction of democracy, the disintegration of effective governance, or mass starvation and environmental degradation. The literal Charter text would appear to preclude any international action unless such "domestic" crises begin to threaten international peace. That threshold, however, has been gradually lowered in the practice of the United Nations' principal organs. In 1999, UN Secretary-General Kofi Annan stated that gross violations of human rights and denials of democratic fundamentals can no longer be regarded as purely "domestic" matters. He boldly called on the United Nations to "forge unity behind the principle that massive and systematic violations of human rights — wherever they may take place — should not be allowed to stand." . . .

The Secretary-General's observation . . . is based solidly on practice. Both the General Assembly and the Security Council have invoked Chapter VII measures, in 1966 against the white minority regime in Rhodesia and in 1977 against its equivalent in South Africa, in an effort to end those governments' gross racism. Chapter VII was also invoked in 1994 and military enforcement measures were authorized to reverse the military coup against the democratically elected government of Haiti. In 1998, Chapter VII was again used to threaten the Federal Republic of Yugoslavia with collective measures if it continued to repress its Kosovar minority. On September 28, 2001, the Security Council invoked Chapter VII to impose mandatory sanctions on terrorist groups, thereby extending the Council's enforcement powers to reach non-state actors.

It is increasingly apparent that, in practice, both the Security Council and the General Assembly now regard themselves as entitled to act against oppressive and racist regimes, and, in situations of anarchy, to restore civil society, order, and legitimate governance where these have unraveled. In some instances the United Nations has deployed military force (Congo, Somalia, Haiti, East Timor) or police (Namibia, Cambodia, Mozambique, Haiti) to neutralize or disarm factions or reintegrate them into a cohesive national army and otherwise to help recreate a civil society and establish democratic governance. . . .

The gradual attrition, in UN practice, of states' monopoly over matters of "domestic jurisdiction" has occurred in tandem with an expansion of activities and conditions seen to constitute "threats to the peace." Aggravated instances of racism, colonial repression, massive violations of human rights, tactical starvation, genocide, the overthrow by military juntas of democratically elected governments, and the "harbouring of terrorists" have all begun to be regarded as potentially constituting "threats to the peace" even if they are not instances of "aggression" in the traditional international legal sense.

This expansion of global jurisdiction has not happened at once and, like much legal reform, tends to occur in the guise of "legal fictions." . . . [T]he US Government defend[ed] ONUC's use of force to subdue Katanga secessionists in the Congolese civil war, by reference to the "potential involvement of outside powers" which threatened to turn "an internal matter" into "a clear threat to international peace and security." In 1977, the Security Council, invoking Chapter VII, found that the racist policies of the Government of South Africa "are fraught with danger to international peace and security," thereby opening the way for its first exercise of enforcement powers against a member. Later, the Secretary-General persuaded the Security Council to find a threat to the peace in the Somali civil war because of its "repercussions . . . on the entire region." . . . In determining in 1994 that the rule of the Haitian military junta constituted a threat to peace and security in the region and authorizing military intervention by a coalition of the willing, the Council referred to "the desperate plight of Haitian refugees" as evidence of a threat to the peace. This has rightly been called "unprecedented in authorizing the use of force to remove one regime and install another." . . . In reaction to the destruction of the New York World Trade Center, "international terrorism" was classified by the Council "as a threat to international peace and security" and subjected to Chapter VII mandatory sanctions.

These somewhat artificial "international" dimensions of what, in 1945, would have been seen as lamentable but primarily domestic tragedies or criminal matters subject to domestic police enforcement have not been advanced fraudulently or cynically. Rather, the meaning of "threat to the peace, breach of the peace and act of aggression" is gradually being redefined experientially and situationally. For the present, those doing this redefining understandably seek to contain it within familiar, or at least non-threatening, parameters. For example, an intervention to respond to the "inducing of massive flows of refugees" is as yet more acceptable to many governments than intervention to stop a government's slaughter of its own ethnic or political minorities, its subordination of women, or its failure to control calamitous domestic starvation and civil war.

. . . Nevertheless, the more remarkable fact is that the global system is responding, tentatively and flexibly, through *ad hoc* actions rather than by systematic implementation, to new facts and threats that are redefining the threshold of what is seen to constitute a threat to peace, requiring a powerful collective response.

Notes and Questions

1. In what ways does the Security Council's power to authorize the use of force differ from the rights that states possess on their own? One key distinction is that

> in contrast to the right of self-defense, the prior commission of an armed attack is not a prerequisite to the exercise of force under Security Council authority. Rather, the Security Council may authorize measures, including the use of force, merely in the face of "threats" to international peace and security, including threats that may not yet be imminent. The Security Council, moreover, has largely unfettered power to determine what events and developments constitute such a threat. [Weiner, The Use of Force and Contemporary Security Threats, supra, at 425.]

Does the ability of the Security Council to counter threats that have not yet ripened into armed attacks undermine the justification for recognizing a right on the part of states to anticipatory self-defense? Why might Security Council's legal authority not adequately address states' security needs?

2. What role, if any, should the U.N. General Assembly have in responding to breaches of and threats to international peace and security? Under what circumstances, if any, could the General Assembly authorize the use of force under the Uniting for Peace resolution? Could it ever provide states with a basis for using force beyond their existing Article 51 rights? Could it, for example, authorize states to forcibly stop humanitarian abuses perpetrated by a government against its own citizens?

3. As Professor Franck notes, Egypt consented to the deployment on its territory of the United Nations Emergency Force (UNEF) established by the General Assembly in 1956. In 1967, amid escalating tensions between Israel and Egypt, Egypt requested that UNEF forces withdraw from Egyptian territory. U.N. Secretary-General U Thant removed the force on the grounds that Egypt's consent to its presence had been withdrawn. Could the Uniting for Peace resolution have provided a basis for the continued deployment of UNEF even after Egypt withdrew its consent?

4. Many observers and sometimes the U.N. itself draw a clear distinction between U.N. peacekeeping and U.N. peace enforcement actions, although different elements are cited as the features that distinguish the two. Some note that peacekeeping is based on the consent of the opposing parties and involves the deployment of peacekeepers to implement an agreement approved by those parties, whereas consent is not required in the case of peace enforcement because the Security Council authorizes Member States to take all necessary measures to achieve a stated objective. A related distinction is the legal basis for the action; peacekeeping missions are authorized under Chapter VI of the Charter, while peace enforcement actions find their authority in Chapter VII. Some suggest that U.N. forces must remain impartial as between the parties in peacekeeping, but not in peace enforcement. Finally, some emphasize that peace enforcement missions may use force to carry out their missions, but that peacekeepers ordinarily may not.

As Professor Franck observes above, though, what begins as a peacekeeping force (or, as he also calls it, a Chapter 6 ½ operation) can sometimes "incur the hostility of one or several of the parties, requiring either its withdrawal . . . or its difficult and risky transformation into a peace enforcement operation. . . ." The distinction between peacekeeping and peace enforcement has accordingly been blurred in recent years. According to a U.N. panel appointed by the Secretary General to examine contemporary security challenges:

> There *is* a distinction between operations in which the robust use of force is integral to the mission from the outset (e.g., responses to cross-border invasions or an explosion of violence, in which the recent practice has been to mandate multinational forces) and operations in which there is a reasonable expectation that force may not be needed at all. . . .
>
> But both kinds of operation need the authorization of the Security Council . . . , and in peacekeeping cases as much as in peace-enforcement cases it is now the usual practice for a Chapter VII mandate to be given. . . . This is on the basis that even the most benign environment can turn sour—when spoilers emerge to undermine a peace agreement and put civilians at risk—and that it is desirable for there to be complete certainty about the mission's capacity to respond with force, if necessary. On the other hand, the difference between Chapter VI and VII mandates can be exaggerated: there is little doubt that peacekeeping missions operating under Chapter VI (and thus operating without enforcement powers) have the right to use force in self-defence—and this right is widely understood to extend to "defence of the mission."[United Nations High-level Panel on Threats, Challenges and Change, A More Secure World: Our Shared Responsibility, ¶¶212-213, U.N. Doc. A/59/565 (Dec. 2, 2004).]

5. To strengthen the U.N.'s peacekeeping efforts, there have been proposals for the creation of standing U.N. armies and rapid deployment forces that could be quickly sent to crisis areas around the world. These steps have generally been rejected by many nations, including the United States. What is your reaction to the proposal for the creation of a small, highly trained, and mobile U.N. force that is all-volunteer and recruited globally? Why do you think similar proposals have not received much support from major countries in the past? Would joint training exercises by designation national forces stand a better chance for success?

6. Is the U.N. Security Council's increasing willingness to authorize military intervention under Chapter VII to address crises *within* states a positive development? When should such intervention be allowed? When the government is committing genocide? Repressing a particular group or a large segment of the population? When there is a civil war or civil strife is rampant? Is it preferable for the Security Council—as opposed to a state or group of states acting without Security Council approval under the doctrine of humanitarian intervention—to act in such cases?

7. In recent years, a growing number of commentators have argued that the Security Council has not only a right, but a responsibility, to intervene in humanitarian catastrophes occurring within states. The Canadian Government in 2000 established the International Commission on Intervention and State Sovereignty, a commission of prominent former foreign policy leaders, politicians, and scholars. The Commission in 2001 produced an influential report called "The Responsibility to Protect," which argued that there is growing support for the

notion that the international community in general, and the Security Council in particular, has a "responsibility to protect" civilians "suffering serious harm as a result of internal war, insurgency, repression, or state failure" when their own government is either perpetrating the abuses or unable to stop them. International Commission on Intervention and State Sovereignty, The Responsibility to Protect xi, 15-16, 52 (2001).

At the 2005 United Nations "World Summit" of leaders from counties around the world, the U.N. General Assembly adopted a resolution reflecting their commitment to address major international problems. The resolution contained an endorsement of the "responsibility to protect" concept:

> The international community, through the United Nations, also has the responsibility to use appropriate diplomatic, humanitarian and other peaceful means, in accordance with Chapters VI and VIII of the Charter, to help to protect populations from genocide, war crimes, ethnic cleansing, and crimes against humanity. In this context, we are prepared to take collective action, in a timely and decisive manner, through the Security Council, in accordance with the Charter, including Chapter VII, on a case-by-case basis and in cooperation with relevant regional organizations as appropriate, should peaceful means be inadequate and national authorities are manifestly failing to protect their populations from genocide, war crimes, ethnic cleansing and crimes against humanity. We stress the need for the General Assembly to continue consideration of the responsibility to protect populations from genocide, war crimes, ethnic cleansing and crimes against humanity and its implications, bearing in mind the principles of the Charter and international law. We also intend to commit ourselves, as necessary and appropriate, to helping States build capacity to protect their populations from genocide, war crimes, ethnic cleansing and crimes against humanity and to assisting those which are under stress before crises and conflicts break out. [World Summit Outcome, G.A. Res. 60/1, ¶139, A/RES/60/1 (Oct. 24, 2005).]

What are the rationales that are used in support of collective intervention into internal matters? "Threats to peace"? "Consent"? Are these rationales presently clear in the U.N. Charter? In other international documents, such as the Convention on the Prevention and Punishment of the Crime Against Genocide? What weight should be given to Article 2(7) of the U.N. Charter, which provides that "[n]othing contained in the present Charter shall authorize the United Nations to intervene in matters which are essentially within the domestic jurisdiction of any state?" If there is a responsibility to protect, on whom does it fall? The United Nations? Or U.N. member states? If the U.N. decides to establish a peacekeeping mission in a state where atrocities are taking place, does that mean individual member states have a responsibility to provide the required military forces? Isn't that a decision each country would want to take on a case-by-case basis?

Also, what does the language in the World Summit Outcome suggest about the attitudes of countries toward military humanitarian intervention in the absence of a Chapter VII resolution by the Security Council?

8. Although the Security Council has been increasingly willing to intervene in internal humanitarian crises by determining that they present threats to international peace and security, the trend has faced setbacks. In January 2007, China and Russia vetoed a U.S.-drafted resolution that would have, among other things, called on the Government of Myanmar to halt attacks against civilians, to

stop widespread human rights violations in the country, and to unconditionally release all political prisoners in the country. In explaining China's vote against the proposed resolution, the Chinese representative indicated that the situation in Myanmar was "mainly the internal affair of a sovereign State." Both the Chinese and Russian representatives stated that conditions in Myanmar did not pose a threat to international or regional peace and security. U.N. SCOR, 62nd Sess., 5619th mtg. at 3, 6, U.N. Doc. S/PV.5619 (Jan. 12, 2007). Similarly, in 2008 both Russia and China vetoed a draft Security Council resolution that would have imposed an arms embargo against Zimbabwe in response to that government's campaign of violence against the political opposition. In explaining his country's vote, Russia's representative stated:

> [W]e have of late seen an increasingly obvious attempt to take the Council beyond its Charter prerogatives and beyond the maintenance of international peace and security. We believe such practices to be illegitimate and dangerous and apt to lead to a realignment of the entire United Nations system. The Russian Federation intends to continue to counter such trends, so that all States without exception will firmly comply with the Charter of the Organization.
>
> We are firmly convinced that the problems of Zimbabwe cannot be resolved by artificially elevating them to the level of a threat to international peace and security. The Council's application in this instance of enforcement measures under Chapter VII of the United Nations Charter is unjustified and excessive. Moreover, the draft resolution represents nothing but an attempt by the Council to interfere in the internal affairs of States, contrary to the Charter. [U.N. SCOR, 63rd Sess., 5633rd mtg. at 9, U.N. Doc. S/PV.5933 (July 11, 2008).]

Does the Security Council apply principled criteria in deciding when an internal humanitarian crisis poses a threat to international peace and security?

9. Should there be some international codification of the expanded rationales or criteria for collective intervention? How could this be done? An amendment to the U.N. Charter? A new treaty among major powers? Formal U.N. General Assembly resolutions adopted by consensus? Can one realistically expect that the international community will accept codification in a reasonable period of time?

10. *U.N. Peacebuilding Commission.* In December 2005, the General Assembly established a new Peacebuilding Commission to help coordinate international efforts to rebuild and stabilize countries emerging from conflict. The Commission's mandate contemplates that the 31 countries on the Commission, including ten states selected from the among leading financial and military contributors to U.N. missions, will marshal resources at the disposal of the international community to propose integrated strategies for post-conflict recovery, focusing attention on reconstruction, institution-building, and sustainable development. The Commission's goal is to establish a link between immediate post-conflict efforts and long-term recovery and development efforts. Through the end of 2010, the Commission concentrated its efforts on four countries: Sierra Leone and Burundi (beginning in 2006), Guinea-Bissau (2007), and the Central African Republic (2008). With respect to efforts in Sierra Leone and Burundi, a 2010 internal U.N. review of the Peacebuilding Commission's first years of operation found that "[d]espite initial difficulties, both . . . are now seen as generally positive experiences, resulting in some concrete benefits." The review observed that "Guinea-Bissau and the Central

African Republic were further back on the road to peace when they came on the [Commission's] agenda and have more serious capacity and resource issues." More generally, the U.N. review concluded that "despite committed and dedicated efforts, the hopes that accompanied the [Peacebuilding Commission's] founding resolutions have yet to be realized." U.N. Review of the United Nations Peacebuilding Architecture, U.N. Doc. A/64/868–S/2010/393 (July 21, 2010).

2. *U.N. and U.S. Response to Iraq*

Now that you have read about the U.N.'s power to authorize the use of force as a collective security matter, it may be useful to see how these principles apply—and how their application can be contested—in contemporary contexts. In this section we consider the international response to Iraq's 1990 invasion of Kuwait and the U.S.-led invasion of Iraq in 2003.

a. The First Gulf War

In August 1990, an Iraqi force of over 100,000 troops invaded and occupied neighboring Kuwait. Iraq claimed that Kuwait was historically part of its territory. The Iraqis systematically set about to loot Kuwait and to brutalize its people.

The international response to Iraq's invasion was generally hostile, and the reactions swift. The day of the Iraqi invasion, the Security Council passed Resolution 660, which determined that "there exists a breach of international peace and security." It "condemn[ed]" the invasion and demanded that Iraq "withdraw immediately and unconditionally all its forces." The vote was 14-0, with Yemen abstaining. (See the Documentary Supplement for Security Council Resolution 660 and other key resolutions cited in this section.)

In the following days and weeks, the Security Council enacted a series of additional resolutions to induce compliance with Resolution 660. For instance, in Resolution 661, the Council imposed a comprehensive trade and financial boycott against Iraq and occupied Kuwait; it declared Iraq's purported annexation of Kuwait null and void in Resolution 662. In the meantime, the United States and other countries opposed to Iraq's invasion rapidly built up their military forces in the region.

In November 1990, the Security Council adopted Resolution 678 by a vote of 12-2, with Cuba and Yemen opposed and permanent member China abstaining.

U.N. Security Council Resolution 678

(Nov. 29, 1990)

The Security Council . . .

Mindful of its duties and responsibilities under the Charter of the United Nations for the maintenance and preservation of international peace and security,

Determined to secure full compliance with its decisions,

Acting under Chapter VII of the Charter,

1. *Demands* that Iraq comply fully with Resolution 660 (1990) and all subsequent relevant resolutions and decides, while maintaining all its decisions, to allow Iraq one final opportunity, as a pause of good will, to do so;

2. *Authorizes* member states cooperating with the Government of Kuwait, unless Iraq on or before 15 January 1991 fully implements, as set forth in paragraph 1 above, the above-mentioned resolutions, to use all necessary means to uphold and implement the Security Council Resolution 660 and all subsequent relevant Resolutions and to restore international peace and security in the area. . . .

Saddam Hussein ignored the ultimatum to withdraw from Kuwait by January 15, and on January 16 allied warplanes bombed targets in Iraq and occupied Kuwait, thus beginning the first Persian Gulf War. By that time, there were 425,000 U.S. troops stationed in the region, joined by an additional 265,000 troops from 27 other countries. After six weeks of air strikes, an allied ground offensive was unleashed on February 26, 1991. The allied forces swiftly drove the depleted Iraqi forces from Kuwait and began to penetrate deep into Iraq. Although their forces were encountering diminished resistance, the allied countries suspended their offensive at midnight on February 28, exactly 100 hours after ground operations had commenced.

At the conclusion of the first Gulf War, the U.N. Security Council adopted Resolution 687, which imposed new obligations on Iraq and which would have broad future implications. (The resolution is in the Documentary Supplement.) A U.S. Department of State publication briefly explains the general provisions of the resolutions as follows:

> On April 3, 1991, at the end of the Gulf War, the U.N. Security Council adopted its famous "cease-fire resolution," numbered 687, which established a cease-fire on the basis of Iraq's acceptance of conditions deemed essential to the restoration of peace and stability in the area. This resolution required Iraq to give up its weapons of mass destruction, return Kuwaiti property, account for detainees, and renounce terrorism, as well as accept the U.N. demarcation of the Iraq-Kuwait border. It also set up UNIKOM—a U.N. peace-keeping force on the border. [Also established by the resolution were the U.N. Special Commission (UNSCOM), designed to dismantle Iraq's weapons of mass destruction and to provide long-term monitoring of Iraq's weapons systems; the Iraq-Kuwait Boundary Demarcation Commission, created to mark and restore the Iraq-Kuwait boundary to the position agreed to by the two countries in 1963; and the U.N. Compensation Commission (UNCC), which would provide reimbursement to those individuals who suffered damages as a result of the war.] [Ronald Neumann, Overview of U.S. Policy Toward Iraq: Address at the Meridian International Center, Dep't State Dispatch, Feb. 7, 1994, at 66.]

In Resolution 687, the Security Council "affirmed" the 13 resolutions it had adopted following Iraq's invasion of Kuwait, "except as expressly changed below to achieve the goals of the present resolution, including a formal cease-fire." After imposing the requirements summarized above on Iraq, the resolution stated:

> The Security Council . . .
>
> 33. *Declares* that, upon official notification by Iraq to the Secretary-General and to the Security Council of its acceptance of the above provisions, a formal cease-fire is effective between Iraq and Kuwait and the Member States cooperating with Kuwait in accordance with Resolution 678 (1990);

34. *Decides* to remain seized of the matter and to take such further steps as may be required for the implementation of the present resolution and to secure peace and security in the region.

Among the most important provisions of U.N. Security Council Resolution 687 were those regarding Iraq's weapons systems. The resolution required full disclosure by Iraq of its weapons of mass destruction (WMD) and ballistic missile programs. It authorized the U.N. to dismantle these weapons systems and establish a monitoring regime to ensure that Iraq could not reacquire banned weapons. To implement these provisions, the U.N. Special Commission (UNSCOM) was established by the Security Council to eliminate and verify the destruction of Iraq's biological, chemical, and ballistic missile programs. The International Atomic Energy Agency (IAEA) assumed responsibility for dismantling Iraq's nuclear program.

Although UNSCOM and IAEA inspection and monitoring activities severely curtailed Iraq's WMD programs, Iraq continued to pursue a policy of concealment and delay. Confrontations between the United Nations and Iraq continued through the decade. A particularly serious situation arose in 1998, when Iraq announced that it was suspending all cooperation with UNSCOM, preventing even the monitoring that had still been going on. UNSCOM inspectors and other U.N. personnel began to evacuate Iraq. On November 5, 1998, the U.N. Security Council unanimously adopted Resolution 1205, which formally condemned Iraq for halting cooperation with the weapons inspections and emphasized that the sanctions against Iraq could not be lifted unless Iraq reversed its decision "immediately and unconditionally" and fulfilled its obligations under Resolution 687. (Resolution 1205 is in the Documentary Supplement.) The U.N. inspectors returned to Iraq, but within days, they met new resistance from Iraq over the production of certain documents and then over visits to certain sites.

The language of Resolution 1205 does not specifically authorize military action. Although most Council members apparently contended that any military strike would require further specific authorization, the United States and Britain said that further Council permission was not needed. On December 17, U.S. and British forces launched an attack on Iraq aimed at degrading Iraq's ability to develop weapons of mass destruction. Over a three-day period, U.S. and British forces struck nearly 100 targets with 415 cruise missiles and hundreds of bombs. Nevertheless, for the next several years, Saddam Hussein remained defiant, and U.N. weapons inspections were not resumed.

Notes and Questions

1. Why was there a near-unanimous condemnation of Iraq's invasion of Kuwait? Was it in part the fear of countries, particularly the industrialized ones, that Iraq was gaining too much control over the world's oil supplies, especially given the fear that Iraq might continue its military campaign and seek to conquer Saudi Arabia ? Was it some sense of fair play that a relatively large country such as Iraq should not invade a smaller country?

Could international law be part of the reason? Was Iraq's invasion of Kuwait defensible under international law? Review the U.N. Charter's Articles 2(4) and

51. Other international treaties and declarations enshrine the territorial integrity and political independence of a state. Is this an example of where international law norms contributed to the intensity of the world's reaction to the Iraqi invasion?

2. Between the Security Council's authorization of collective measures at the time of the Korean War and its response to Iraq's 1990 invasion of Kuwait, resolutions authorizing coercive measures to give effect to the decisions of the Council were rare. U.N. economic sanctions had been explicitly imposed under Article 41 of the U.N. Charter in two situations—against Rhodesia and South Africa. White Rhodesians had made a "unilateral declaration of independence" from Great Britain in 1965, and initial British efforts to resolve the dispute failed. In December 1966, the Security Council passed Resolution 232, calling for selective mandatory sanctions. That was followed by Resolution 253 in 1968, which called for comprehensive sanctions.

In the case of South Africa, the Security Council in 1977 called for an embargo on shipments of arms, munitions, and military equipment to or from that country. S.C. Res. 418. For its part, the United States had already taken the required actions pursuant to its arms export laws. Indeed, U.S. sanctions against South Africa were more thoroughgoing than those mandated by the Security Council resolutions. The U.N. and U.S. sanctions against South Africa helped pressure the government of F.W. de Klerk to concede power in 1994 to Nelson Mandela.

Since 1990, the U.N. Security Council has also imposed economic sanctions of varying comprehensiveness in many conflicts.

3. Resolution 678's authorization to use "all necessary means" was understood to authorize the use of force after January 15, 1991. This was only the second time the Security Council had authorized the use of force. The first situation was the response 40 years before to the invasion of Korea. Why did the Council not specifically refer to "force" or "military action" in Resolution 678? Does that create any ambiguity about the nature or the scope of the authorization to use force?

4. Assume that Iraq refused to withdraw from Kuwait and the Security Council had been unable to pass a resolution authorizing any offensive military action against Iraq. Could the United States (possibly with the British) have then decided under Article 51 to conduct a major offensive against Iraq in an effort to dislodge Iraqi forces from Kuwait? Does it matter if the Emir of Kuwait requests the U.S. action? What if Saudi Arabia requested the U.S. action in cooperation with its forces in order to ensure that Iraq did not invade Saudi Arabia?

5. Iraq's refusal in late 1997 and early 1998 to permit the UNSCOM inspectors full access was a violation of its obligations regarding weapons of mass destruction under Resolution 687. Were the U.S.-British strikes in 1998 legally justified in response to Iraq's breach? Was the authority to use force against Iraq granted before the first Persian Gulf war in Resolution 678 still in effect? Recall that Resolution 687 provided only for a cease fire, which was contingent upon Iraq's acceptance of its obligations under that resolution, including its WMD-related disarmament obligations.

6. Resolution 687 was not the only resolution adopted in the immediate aftermath of the first Gulf War with broad long-term significance. Shortly after Resolution 687 was passed, a surge of repression in Iraq against rebel Kurdish groups in northern Iraq and Shi'ite groups in southern Iraq led to the passage of Resolution

688. The resolution condemned and demanded a halt to Iraq's repression of its own population. Significantly, the Council characterized the "massive flow of refugees towards and across international frontiers" and "cross border incursions" resulting from Iraq's repression as a threat to international peace and security. In addition, the resolution demanded that Iraq allow access to its territory by international humanitarian organizations. Professor Stromseth discusses the significance and implications of Resolution 688.

> The Security Council debate preceding passage of resolution 688 was both a response to urgent human needs and a wide-ranging philosophical discussion of the purpose and limits of the Security Council. The participants understood that the resolution would establish a precedent that would shape perceptions of the proper role of the Security Council in future crises growing out of internal conflict. Under article 39 of the UN Charter, the Security Council has broad authority to take action in response to threats to the peace. But at the heart of the debate over resolution 688 was the meaning and contemporary significance of article 2(7), which provides that nothing in the Charter authorizes the UN "to intervene in matters which are essentially within the domestic jurisdiction of any state." . . .
>
> The ten states that supported resolution 688 relied on three types of arguments. The predominant argument was fully consistent with a traditional state-centric view: namely, that the massive flow of refugees *across international borders* that Iraq's actions caused was a threat to international peace and security in the region. . . .
>
> A second, more human rights-oriented argument was advanced by several members of the Security Council, most notably France and Britain. These states contended that Iraq's violation of its citizens' human rights was itself a matter of international concern and thus not within Iraq's "domestic" jurisdiction. . . .
>
> The third type of argument made in support of Security Council action to protect the Kurds and Shi'ites was that the UN had a special responsibility to respond to developments growing out of its own decision to authorize the use of force to expel Iraq from Kuwait. . . . [Jane Stromseth, Iraq's Repression of Its Civilian Population: Collective Responses and Continuing Challenges, in Enforcing Restraint: Collective Intervention in Internal Conflicts 77, 86-88 (Lori Fisler Damrosch ed., 1993).]

Following the adoption of Resolution 688, the U.S. air force began dropping food, blankets, and clothing to Kurdish refugees. Later, U.S., British, and French military forces entered northern Iraq to establish a safe haven for Iraqi Kurds, arguing that Resolution 688 provided a legal basis for the operation.

To protect the Kurds and Shi'ites in the northern and southern regions, the United States, the United Kingdom, and France established "no-fly zones" within which Iraqi fixed wing aircraft could not operate. Iraq challenged the no-fly zones as illegal and unprecedented intrusions on its sovereignty. The Iraqi government's refusal to respect these no-fly zones led to U.S. bombing strikes against Iraq in January and June 1993.

Since 1990, the Security Council has on numerous occasions intervened in humanitarian and security crises within a country. When Resolution 688 was adopted, however, the notion that the Security Council could compel Iraq to grant access to its territory by humanitarian organizations was novel. Is this an illustration of the Security Council exercising a responsibility to protect? Could the Council (assuming it was not vetoed) pass a similar resolution against, say, Turkey or Kenya if that state was repressing an ethnic minority in its territory?

7. In general, up until the end of 1998, how effective was the U.N. response to the Iraqi invasion of Kuwait? To the longer-term problems on human rights and nonproliferation that Saddam Hussein and Iraq presented? Did the Security Council seem more effective in certain activities than in others?

8. From the standpoint of the United States through 1998, what were the advantages of working through the U.N. Security Council in reacting to the Iraqi invasion of Kuwait? In dealing with Iraq and Saddam Hussein on human rights and nonproliferation? What were the disadvantages?

b. The Second Gulf War

From the end of 1998 into 2002, Saddam Hussein remained hostile to U.N. sanctions, and he refused to readmit the U.N. weapons inspectors. In November 2002, following repeated confrontations with Iraq, the U.N. Security Council unanimously passed Resolution 1441. The preambular paragraphs of the Resolution (which is in the Documentary Supplement) recalled that the Resolution 687 had "imposed obligations on Iraq as a necessary step for its stated objective of restoring international peace and security in the area" and recalled that Resolution 687 had "declared that a ceasefire would be based on acceptance by Iraq of the provisions of that resolution." In its operative provisions, Resolution 1441 declared that Iraq was in "material breach of its obligations under relevant [past] resolutions," but decided to afford Iraq a "final opportunity" to comply with its disarmament obligations imposed by the previous resolutions. The Resolution ordered Iraq to submit a comprehensive declaration of its WMD programs; it also established a rigorous inspection regime and demanded that Iraq provide "immediate, unimpeded, unconditional, and unrestricted access to any and all" places and persons that the U.N. inspectors wished to investigate. The Resolution including the following concluding provisions:

U.N. Security Council Resolution 1441

(Nov. 8, 2002)

The Security Council, . . .

Acting under Chapter VII of the Charter of the United Nations, . . .

12. *Decides* to convene immediately upon receipt of a report in accordance with paragraphs 4 [concerning the possibility of false statements or omissions in Iraq's declaration regarding its WMD programmes] or 11 [regarding the possibility of interference by Iraq with WMD inspection activities] above, in order to consider the situation and the need for full compliance with all of the relevant Council resolutions in order to secure international peace and security;

13. *Recalls*, in that context, that the Council has repeatedly warned Iraq that it will face serious consequences as a result of its continued violations of its obligations;

14. *Decides* to remain seized of the matter.

In December 2002, pursuant to U.N. Resolution 1441, Iraq submitted a voluminous report. U.S. officials condemned the Iraqi report as incomplete and false. The chief U.N. weapons inspectors were more mixed in their comments on the report, saying essentially that the report contained much information, but that there were important gaps and questions. U.N. weapons inspectors arrived in Iraq in November and began to carry out inspections, which continued at an accelerating pace into March 2003.

In his January 2003 State of the Union address, President Bush sharply criticized Iraq for failing to fulfill its disarmament obligations and for its abhorrent human rights practices and support for international terrorism. He explained that although the United States would "consult" with other members of the Security Council, there should be "no misunderstanding" that if "Saddam Hussein does not fully disarm, for the safety of our people and for the peace of the world, we will lead a coalition to disarm him."

The governments of many other countries were not persuaded in early 2003 of the need to invade Iraq. Led by France and Germany, a coalition emerged that wanted, at a minimum, to allow the inspectors more time. Russia and China also appeared to be leaning against supporting a new U.N. resolution that could be interpreted as authorizing the use of force against Iraq. By mid-March, the U.S. and U.K. governments apparently concluded that that they did not have the nine votes for such a resolution and also faced a certain French veto.

In a March 16 television address, President Bush recounted Iraq's failure to disarm and its support for terrorism. In view of these threats, he asserted, the United States "has the sovereign authority to use force in assuring its own national security." He cited specifically U.N Resolutions 678 and 687, saying "both [were] still in effect," as well as Resolution 1441. He observed that today "no nation can possibly claim that Iraq has disarmed." Noting opposition from "some permanent members of the Security Council" to a new resolution, he concluded: "The United Nations Security Council has not lived up to its responsibilities, so we will rise to ours."

On March 20, 2003, the United States and the United Kingdom commenced military operations against Iraq. Although some Iraqi forces offered sharp resistance, the Iraqi opposition began to crumble sooner than many people expected, and U.S. forces quickly reached and entered Baghdad. Although President Bush announced in May that "[m]ajor combat operations in Iraq have ended," a violent insurgency erupted that lasted many years, and U.S. forces fought actively to support the new Iraqi government. Combat operations by U.S. forces ended only in September 2010, and as of February 2011 just under 50,000 U.S. troops remained in Iraq in a non-combat role providing support and training for the Iraqi military.

The following excerpt from an essay by the State Department Legal Adviser at the time of the 2003 invasion of Iraq and his colleague from the Legal Adviser's Office describe the Bush Administration's legal justification for U.S. actions.

William H. Taft IV & Todd F. Buchwald, Preemption, Iraq, and International Law

97 Am. J. Int'l L. 557, 558-560, 562-563 (2003)

[I]n November 1990, the [Security] Council adopted Resolution 678, which authorized the use of "all necessary means" to uphold and implement Resolution 660 . . . and to restore international peace and security in the area. The resolution provided Iraq with "one final opportunity" to comply with the Council's earlier decisions and authorized the use of force "unless Iraq on or before 15 January 1991 fully implements" the Council's resolutions. . . .

Iraq refused to comply with the resolutions by the January 15 deadline, and coalition forces commenced military operations the next day. Significantly, the Security Council did not make a further determination prior to January 15 as to whether or not Iraq had taken advantage of the "one final opportunity" it had been given two months earlier. Member states made that judgments themselves and relied on the Security Council's November decision as authority to use force.

On April 3, 1991, the Council adopted Resolution 687. That resolution did not return the situation to the status quo ante, the situation that might have existed if Iraq had never invaded Kuwait or if the Council had never acted. Rather, Resolution 687 declared that, upon official Iraqi acceptance of its provisions, a formal cease-fire would take effect, and it imposed several conditions on Iraq, including extensive obligations related to the regime's possession of weapons of mass destruction (WMD). . . .

As a legal matter, a material breach of the conditions that had been essential to the establishment of the cease-fire left the responsibility to member states to enforce those conditions, operating consistently with Resolution 678 to use all necessary means to restore international peace and security in the area. On numerous occasions in response to Iraqi violations of WMD obligations, the Council, through either a formal resolution or a statement by its president, determined that Iraq's actions constituted material breaches, understanding that such a determination authorized resort to force. Indeed, when coalition forces . . . used force following such a presidential statement in January 1993, then Secretary-General Boutros-Ghali stated that the

> raid was carried out in accordance with a mandate from the Security Council under resolution 678 (1991), and the motive for the raid was Iraq's violation of that resolution, which concerns the cease-fire. As Secretary-General of the United Nations, I can tell you that the action taken was in accordance with the resolutions of the Security Council and the Charter of the United Nations.

It was on this basis that the United States . . . concluded that the [U.S.-led use of force against Iraq in 1998,] following repeated efforts by the Iraqi regime to deny access to weapons inspectors, conformed with the Council's resolutions. . . . [Although there was debate about whether the Council had determined that Iraq was in material breach, or whether that was a matter member states could themselves determine,] all agreed that a Council determination that Iraq had committed a material breach would authorize individual member states to use force to secure compliance with the Council's resolutions.

This was well understood in the negotiations leading to the adoption of Resolution 1441. . . .

. . . [N]othing in Resolution 1441 required the Council to adopt any further resolution, or other form of approval, to establish the occurrence of the material breach that was the predicate for coalition forces to resort to force. . . . Paragraph 12 contemplated that the Council would "consider" the matter, but specifically stopped short of suggesting a requirement for a further decision. . . .

The similarities in this regard between Resolution 1441 and Resolution 678 are striking. Using the same terminology that it later adopted in Resolution 1441, the

Council in Resolution 678 decided to allow Iraq a "final opportunity" to comply with the obligations that the Council had established in previous resolutions. The Council then authorized member states to use force "unless Iraq on or before 15 January 1991 fully implemented" those resolutions. It was clear then that coalition members were not required to return for a further Council decision that Iraq had failed to comply; nor did they do so before commencing military operations. The language of Resolution 1441 tracked the language of Resolution 678, and the resolution operated in the same way to authorize coalition forces to bring Iraq into compliance with its obligations.

Consider Professor Franck's assessment of the Bush Administration's justification for the Iraq invasion.

Thomas M. Franck, What Happens Now? The United Nations After Iraq

97 Am. J. Int'l L. 607, 612-613 (2003)

The obligations imposed [on Iraq] by Resolution 687 are certainly onerous. . . . Baghdad had to agree to the verified destruction of its weapons of mass destruction and any industrial capacity to produce them. . . . Monitoring of compliance, both by a special commission to be created by the Secretary-General and by inspectors of the International Atomic Energy Agency, became mandatory. . . . What if Iraq failed to carry out these commitments to the Council and the United Nations? Clearly, this determination was to be made by the collective security process of the [U.N.] Organization. To ensure such follow-up, the Council, in [paragraph 34 of] Resolution 687, was "to remain seized of the matter and to take such further steps as may be required for the implementation of the present resolution and to secure peace and security in the area." *It* would take further steps, *not* individual member states acting without further authorization.

Neither the text nor the debates on the adoption of Resolution 687 reveal the slightest indication that the Council intended to empower any of its members, by themselves, to determine that Iraq was in material breach. Much less can the resolution be read to authorize any state to decide unilaterally to resume military action against Iraq, save in the event of an armed attack. . . . For the Council to have made a prospective grant of unilateral discretion to states to deploy armed force, in the absence of an actual (or imminent) armed attack, would have been an unprecedented derogation from the strictures of Article 2(4). At the least, to be plausible, such a derogation would have had to be explicit. Moreover, such a delegation of unlimited discretion to individual states cannot be assumed because it could not have been implemented alongside the Council's institution of an extensive system of inspections under *its* authority and control.

. . . [These objections cannot be overcome by an assertion] that a "material breach of resolution 687 revives the authority to use force under resolution 678." As we have noted, the authority to use force under Resolution 678 extended exclusively to the liberation of Kuwait and to restoring peace and security in the region.

In March 2003, the peace and security of the region did not require recourse to force, and the Council plainly did not think otherwise. What the Council thought is crucial. Resolution 687 would not have explicitly reserved sole discretion to the Council "to take such further steps as may be required for [its] implementation" if the Council had simultaneously intended to delegate that function to the sole discretion of member states.

Notes and Questions

1. Look carefully at the language of Resolution 1441, especially the closing paragraphs. Does the text of the resolution authorize the use of force if Iraq does not fully comply with the renewed weapons inspections? Why might the language on possible consequences be intentionally vague? If there is clear-cut Iraqi violation (such as hiding weapons of mass destruction), what is the next step under the resolution?

2. Consider the interrelation of Resolutions 678, 687, and 1441. Did those resolutions provide legal grounds for the U.S. and other coalition forces to mount a major attack on Iraq and force a change in the government? Or was another resolution required?

3. Despite emphatic assertions by U.S. officials before the March 2003 invasion that Iraq was in breach of its disarmament obligations under Resolution 687, the United States did not find WMD stockpiles in Iraq. How important was it to the validity of the U.S. legal position whether or not it actually found in Iraq any weapons of mass destruction that were prohibited under the earlier U.N. resolutions?

4. Did the U.S. and British governments weaken their position that the existing U.N. resolutions gave the coalition sufficient authority to attack when the United States and Britain sought another resolution in March 2003, only to drop that effort when it appeared they did not have a nine-vote majority?

5. Given U.S. concerns about what it believed were efforts by Iraq to "possess and conceal" weapons of mass destruction, and the danger that terrorists "with the help of Iraq" might one day use these weapons of mass destruction against the United States or other countries, could the United States have justified the use of force under Article 51 of the Charter? What about the language in Article 51 affirming the right of self-defense "if an armed attack occurs"? Would use of force against Iraq in 2003 satisfy the traditional standards for anticipatory self-defense? How far in advance of a potential armed attack could force be used preemptively under the concept of preemptive self-defense articulated by the Bush Administration in the 2002 U.S. National Security Strategy? (See Section B.5.b above.) Does the subsequent failure to find weapons of mass destruction in Iraq demonstrate the dangers of allowing states to use force on the basis of perceived dangers that have not yet materialized as immediate threats?

One senior Bush Administrations lawyer said privately that the U.S. government had purposely not adopted anticipatory self-defense or the possibility of preemptive actions as one of its justifications for the 2003 invasion of Iraq. Rather, the Bush Administration had intended to rely on the breach of the U.N. resolutions, while "reserving" the anticipatory self-defense and preemptive strike justifications. What do you think explains this approach?

6. From 1999 on, how effective was the U.N.'s handling of the situation in Iraq generally? How effective was it on issues involving human rights and nonproliferation in Iraq?

7. From the standpoint of the United States, what were the advantages and disadvantages of working through the U.N. Security Council after 1999 in reacting to Saddam Hussein on nonproliferation? On human rights? Is there anything that you think the United States should have done differently? If so, would these other steps be consistent with international law as you know it?

8. Given the events leading up the regime change in Iraq in 2003 (including the inability of the coalition led by the United States to obtain a U.N. resolution in March, but its decision to proceed anyway), what is the future role of the U.N. Security Council in cases of countries that might be harboring terrorists? Developing weapons of mass destruction? Brutally repressing large segments of their population? Does the fact that the United States did not find weapons of mass destruction and that the invasion of Iraq led to a long and costly military engagement by the United States strengthen the case for greater international consensus for major military operations of this type?

Collective Security in Afghanistan. The U.S. exercise of self-defense in Afghanistan in response to the attacks of September 11 is addressed in Section B above. But as noted in the case study in Chapter 1.E, the military response to events in Afghanistan has also involved a major collective security response on the part of NATO, the North Atlantic Treaty Organization. In the 2001 Bonn Agreement that established the transitional government in Afghanistan, the parties agreed to request the deployment of Security Council-authorized peacekeeping force to assist with maintaining security in Afghanistan. The Security Council, acting under Chapter VII, authorized the establishment of an International Security Assistance Force (ISAF) "to assist the Afghan Interim Authority in the maintenance of security in Kabul and its surrounding areas, so that the Afghan Interim Authority as well as the personnel of the United Nations can operate in a secure environment." In subsequent Security Council resolutions, ISAF's mandate has been renewed, and its authority has been expanded to enable operations throughout Afghanistan. Since 2003, ISAF has operated under NATO command.

ISAF represents a substantial "coalition of the willing" of the type described by Professor Franck. As of February 2011, there were over 130,000 troops participating in ISAF, including 90,000 from the United States. ISAF is a peacekeeping force operating pursuant to the legal authority of Security Council, but it is comprised of forces provided by a group of states for purposes of a particular mission, and it does not operate under the command of the United Nations.

3. *The Protection of Civilians and the Libya Intervention*

The U.N. authorization to use force against Iraq following its 1990 invasion of Kuwait is an illustration of the Security Council functioning as the U.N.'s founding states originally contemplated the organization would act — to counter international aggression by one state against other. As noted above, however, the past decades have witnessed an expansion of the willingness of the United Nations to authorize coercive responses to events taking place within a single country. In 1994, the Security Council authorized the use of "all necessary means" to "facilitate the departure from Haiti" of the de facto military regime that had overthrown the democratically elected government of Jean-Bertrand Aristide and had launched a campaign of "systematic violations of civil liberties." U.N. Security Council Resolution 940 (1994). (Members of a U.S. invasion force were airborne en route to Haiti when the leaders of the de facto regime agreed to step down.)

In 2011, the Security Council authorized a highly significant collective security response to an internal humanitarian crisis in Libya. In February 2011, many Libyans — inspired by events in Tunisia and Egypt earlier that year that led to the ouster of longstanding authoritarian leaders in those countries — began protests against the Qaddafi government. As more Libyans joined the movement, the opposition by late February gained control of a significant part of the country, particularly the eastern region around Benghazi. The government responded with a brutal military campaign in which many civilians were killed. The Security Council reacted on February 26 by adopting Resolution 1970 which, among other things, "[d]eplor[ed] the gross and systematic violation of human rights, including the repression of peaceful demonstrators," and "[d]emand[ed] an immediate end to the violence and call[ed] for steps to fulfil the legitimate demands of the population." The resolution imposed a series of sanctions, including an arms embargo on Libya, as well as a travel ban and asset freeze on Colonel Qaddafi and certain members of his inner circle. The resolution also referred the situation in Libya to the International Criminal Court.

In early March, the Libyan opposition announced the establishment of a Transitional National Council, which became the political leadership of the uprising. On March 10, France recognized the Council as the legitimate government of Libya, but other states had not done so by the end of March. In the meantime, the Libyan government's military forces had by early March regained the initiative, and — despite the Security Council's demand for a cessation of violence — began recapturing territory that had fallen under opposition control. In a national address, President Obama later characterized the brutality of the government's campaign:

> In the face of the world's condemnation, Qaddafi chose to escalate his attacks, launching a military campaign against the Libyan people. Innocent people were targeted for killing. Hospitals and ambulances were attacked. Journalists were arrested, sexually assaulted, and killed. Supplies of food and fuel were choked off. Water for hundreds of thousands of people . . . was shut off. Cities and towns were shelled, mosques were destroyed, and apartment buildings reduced to rubble. Military jets and helicopter gunships were unleashed upon people who had no means to defend themselves against assaults from the air. [President Barack Obama, Address to the Nation on the Situation in Libya, 2011 Daily Comp. Pres. Docs. No. 206 (March 28, 2011).]

By mid-March, opposition forces had been pushed back to their stronghold in Benghazi, Libya's second-largest city. In particularly chilling comments, Qaddafi announced on Libyan radio to the residents of Benghazi, "We are coming tonight. . . . We will find you in your closets." He stated that his forces would show "no mercy or compassion" for those who fought against them.

Even before Qaddafi's forces had reached Benghazi, the deteriorating humanitarian situation in Libya led to calls for outside states to intervene to halt the regime's attacks against civilians. Some voiced support for a "no-fly zone" to prevent Libyan aircraft from bombing opposition targets and transporting troops and supplies. On March 12, the League of Arab States, a regional organization of the type discussed below in subsection 4 of this section, met to review the situation in Libya and noted "the crimes and violations being perpetrated by the Libyan authorities against the Libyan people, in particular the use of military aircraft, mortars and heavy weaponry against the civilians." The Arab League adopted a resolution in which it

> call[ed] on the Security Council to bear its responsibilities towards the deteriorating situation in Libya, and to take the necessary measures to impose immediately a no-fly zone on Libyan military aviation, and to establish safe areas in places exposed to shelling as a precautionary measure that allows the protection of the Libyan people and foreign nationals residing in Libya, while respecting the sovereignty and territorial integrity of neighboring States. [Outcome of the Council of the League of Arab States meeting at the Ministerial level in its extraordinary session on the implications of the current events in Libya and the Arab position, Cairo (March 12, 2011).]

In response to the resolution of the Arab League, and fearful of a humanitarian catastrophe at Benghazi, the Security Council on March 17 adopted Resolution 1973, which deplored the Libyan government's failure to comply with the demands of Resolution 1970 and expressed "grave concern at the deteriorating situation, the escalation of violence, and the heavy civilian casualties." (Both Resolutions 1970 and 1973 are in the Documentary Supplement.) Acting under Chapter VII, the Council "demand[ed] the immediate establishment of a cease-fire and a complete end to violence and all attacks against, and abuses of, civilians." In language that seemed to invoke the concept of the "responsibility to protect" embraced by heads of state during the 2005 United Nations "World Summit," the Council in Resolution 1973 authorized U.N. member states

> to take all necessary measures . . . to protect civilians and civilian populated areas under threat of attack in [Libya], including Benghazi, while excluding a foreign occupation force of any form on any part of Libyan territory. [U.N. Security Council Resolution 973, ¶4, U.N. Doc S/RES/1973 (March 17, 2011).]

The resolution also established a ban on all flights in Libyan airspace "in order to help protect civilians" and authorized member states "to take all necessary measures to enforce compliance with the ban on flights." The resolution was adopted by a narrow margin. Ten states voted affirmatively, one more than the required minimum of nine. Although there were no negative votes, Russia, China, Brazil, India, and Germany abstained.

On March 19, French aircraft, and then U.S. and British forces, launched wide-ranging missile and air attacks against Libyan targets, including air defense systems and military forces that were poised to attack the opposition in Benghazi. Although the United States commanded most of the initial stages of the operation, by late March NATO took command of the campaign to enforce the no-fly zone, the arms embargo, and to protect Libyan civilians.

In response to the U.N.-authorized attacks, Libyan government forces withdrew from Benghazi, and opposition forces launched a swift new westward offensive in the direction of Tripoli, Libya's capital. By the end of March, however, government forces had halted and had begun to repel the opposition forces. The military situation was highly unstable.

In a letter submitted to Congress on March 21, shortly after military operations began, President Obama stated:

> The international community made clear that all attacks against civilians had to stop. . . .
>
> . . . Qadhafi's continued attacks and threats against civilians and civilian populated areas are of grave concern to neighboring Arab nations and, as expressly stated in U.N. Security Council Resolution 1973, constitute a threat to the region and to international peace and security. His illegitimate use of force not only is causing the deaths of substantial numbers of civilians among his own people, but also is forcing many others to flee to neighboring countries, thereby destabilizing the peace and security of the region. Left unaddressed, the growing instability in Libya could ignite wider instability in the Middle East, with dangerous consequences to the national security interests of the United States. Qadhafi's defiance of the Arab League, as well as the broader international community moreover, represents a lawless challenge to the authority of the Security Council and its efforts to preserve stability in the region. Qadhafi has forfeited his responsibility to protect his own citizens and created a serious need for immediate humanitarian assistance and protection, with any delay only putting more civilians at risk. [President Barack Obama, Letter to Congressional Leaders Reporting on the Commencement of Military Operations Against Libya, 2011 Daily Comp. Pres. Docs. No. 193 (March 21, 2011).]

A week later, in a public address explaining the justifications for American participation in the use of force against Libya, President Obama noted that Qaddafi's forces were "bearing down on the city of Benghazi, home to nearly 700,000 men, women and children who sought their freedom from fear." He continued:

> At this point, the United States and the world faced a choice. Qaddafi declared he would show no mercy to his own people. . . . We knew that if we . . . waited one more day, Benghazi, a city nearly the size of Charlotte, could suffer a massacre that would have reverberated across the region and stained the conscience of the world.
>
> It was not in our national interest to let that happen. I refused to let that happen. . . . [President Barack Obama, Address to the Nation on the Situation in Libya, supra, at 2.]

Notes and Questions

1. During the Libyan government's initial offensive against the opposition forces, Libyan military forces surrounded towns that had embraced the opposition cause and launched attacks that caused heavy civilian casualties. When those Libyan forces were attacked by U.N.-authorized strikes, they withdrew. When opposition forces sought to advance, however, they encountered resistance from Libyan government forces. Some in the opposition also called for airstrikes to support their efforts to advance against government forces. Are airstrikes in support of opposition fighters—most of whom were ordinary citizens who had taken up arms—consistent with the Resolution 1973's authorization for states to take all necessary measures "to protect civilians and civilian populated areas under threat of attack"?

2. In Resolution 1973, the Security Council authorized force to protect civilians and to enforce a no-fly zone. Does the resolution authorize states to use force to overthrow Colonel Qaddafi's regime? What if states concluded that airstrikes on Qaddafi's forces would not suffice to prevent him from attacking the opposition? Would Resolution 1973 then authorize them to use force to attack and remove the regime in order to "protect civilians"? Who would be empowered to interpret what the Council had authorized?

More generally, how far should the Security Council be willing to go in authorizing force in furtherance of the responsibility to protect civilians? Does that entail merely halting violence against civilians, or can it include overthrowing repressive regimes? How would a decision to pursue regime change comport with Article 2(7) of the Charter, which prohibits the United Nations from intervening in "matters which are essentially within the domestic jurisdiction" of a state?

3. A few days after the U.N.-authorized military strikes began, President Obama stated that "it is U.S. policy that Qaddafi needs to go." He indicated that the United States was utilizing various non-military means, including sanctions and a freeze of Libyan assets, to advance that policy. He explicitly noted that U.S. military action in Libya was not directed at bringing about regime change in Libya: "But when it comes to our military action, we are doing so in support of U.N. Security Resolution 1973, that specifically talks about humanitarian efforts. And we are going to make sure that we stick to that mandate." Some in the Libyan opposition—and some prominent political leaders in the United States—disagreed with this approach and urged the states using force in Libya forces to direct their efforts to deposing the Qaddafi regime.

4. Does the decision by the Security Council to authorize military measures in large part to protect civilians during an internal conflict strengthen or weaken the case for the existence of a right for states to use force on humanitarian intervention grounds on their own, without a Security Council resolution? See Section B.5.g.

5. As of late March, the Libyan opposition was desperately seeking weapons from outside sources to counter the superior firepower of Libyan government forces. Recall that Resolution 1970 decided that member states "shall immediately take the necessary measures to prevent the direct or indirect supply, sale or transfer to the Libyan Arab Jamahiriya . . . of arms and related materiel of all types." The term "Libyan Arab Jamahiriya" is generally understood to be the name of the country of Libya, not the Libyan government. Would supplying arms to the opposition violate Resolution 1970? If the opposition claims that it needs weapons to protect civilians from the Qaddafi regime's forces, could outside states argue that providing such weapons is authorized by the "all necessary measures . . . to protect civilians" language in Resolution 1973?

6. Although Resolution 1973 authorized states to take "all necessary measures" to protect civilians, it explicitly "exclud[ed] a foreign occupation force of any form on any part of Libyan territory." There were press reports in late March that small numbers of American and British intelligence and special forces operatives were on the ground in Libya to help in targeting Libyan military assets (and to obtain intelligence about the leadership of the opposition forces). If true, would that violate the exclusion in Resolution 1973? Could outside countries deploy ground troops to assist the opposition in their fight against the Qaddafi regime's forces, provided that they did not take control of Libya and occupy it?

7. The events in Libya in early 2011 took place within the context of a broader series of uprisings against authoritarian Arab governments, referred to by some as

the "Arab Spring." Governments in a number of countries, including Bahrain, Yemen, and Syria, used force—in some cases on a very large scale—against opposition movements. Although the United States pressed the governments of Yemen and Bahrain, countries where it has significant strategic interests, to engage opponents politically to address their grievances, there was no discussion in policy-making circles of using force against those governments to stop violence against the opposition. Although the scale of the Qaddafi regime's violence against its citizens was much greater, the events in the Arab world in early 2011 highlight important questions about collective security efforts to protect civilians. How severe must abuses be before the international community responds? Should states balance other policy considerations, including their strategic relationship with governments perpetrating abuses, against the goal of protecting civilians?

4. Regional Peacekeeping Efforts

Regional peacekeeping and peace enforcement efforts have occurred sporadically in the Western Hemisphere, Africa, and Europe. There have been several such efforts in the Western Hemisphere in the past century and an African regional group became active beginning in the 1990s. The NATO bombing campaign against the Federal Republic of Yugoslavia over the repression of Albanians in Kosovo discussed in Section B.5.g is sometimes seen as a regional "enforcement" action by a regional organization with potentially significant precedential value.

The principal regional security organization in the Western Hemisphere has been the Organization of American States (OAS), working through the Rio Treaty. Its effectiveness, however, has declined in the past decade after its major successes with the quarantine of Cuba in 1962 and sending peacekeeping forces to the Dominican Republic in 1965. (See Chapter 5.C regarding the OAS. The Cuba operation is analyzed below.)

Some commentators suggested in the early 1990s that regional groups might have less of a peacekeeping role to play in the future. It was the United Nations that created in 1989 a peacekeeping force for Central America, the first U.N. peacekeeping operation in the Western Hemisphere, then sent a U.N. observer mission to monitor Nicaraguan elections, and then authorized the creation of a U.S.-led multinational force for Haiti in 1994. However, other events indicate a possible growing trend in the opposite direction. In the 1990s, a West African regional group began peacekeeping operations in Liberia and Sierra Leone. Moreover, the NATO air strikes against the Federal Republic of Yugoslavia over Kosovo in 1999 were undertaken by NATO forces without explicit Security Council authorization. Although U.N. resolutions and, eventually, U.N. peacekeepers played a role in the aftermath, the primary actor in the Kosovo intervention was NATO, possibly indicating an increased role for regional organizations.

Today, it seems that both the United Nations and regional groups will remain active in peacekeeping. Since 1999, as noted above, the scale of U.N. peacekeeping operations has expanded dramatically. In Sudan, the United Nations and the African Union, a regional organization, have established a joint peacekeeping operation in an effort to halt the violence in Sudan's Darfur region.

The Cuban Quarantine. The Cuban missile crisis of 1962 involved a dramatic, direct, and potentially deadly confrontation between the United States and the Soviet Union. Both countries' military forces went on alert, and the possibility of nuclear warfare was not insignificant. The crisis also involved a regional organization, though some questions have been raised about whether the U.N. Charter was complied with regarding the linkage between the OAS action and the U.N. Security Council. Professor Henkin provides a succinct description and analysis of the crisis.

Louis Henkin, How Nations Behave: Law and Foreign Policy

280-281, 290-291, 294-295 (2d ed. 1979)

On October 22, 1962, President Kennedy addressed the people of the United States by television in an atmosphere of crisis. He announced that the United States had clear evidence that the Soviet Union was in the process of installing in Cuba "large, long-range, and clearly offensive weapons of sudden mass destruction." These weapons constituted "an explicit threat to the peace and security of all the Americas," and their introduction was "a deliberately provocative and unjustified change in the status quo which cannot be accepted by this country." The President announced that the United States would impose a defensive maritime quarantine to prevent the further introduction into Cuba of offensive missiles, and to induce the Soviet Union to withdraw the missiles already there.

On the same day, the United States placed the Cuban situation before the United Nations Security Council and asked for an urgent meeting of the Council. The Council met on the following day, October 23, and discussed the crisis and the proposed quarantine but took no action. On that day, the Organization of American States, acting under the Rio Treaty of 1947, adopted a resolution recommending that the members

> take all measures, individually and collectively, including the use of armed force, which they may deem necessary to ensure that the Government of Cuba cannot continue to receive from the Sino-Soviet powers military material and related supplies which may threaten the peace and security of the Continent and to prevent the missiles in Cuba with offensive capability from ever becoming an active threat to the peace and security of the Continent.

In the evening of October 23, after the action of the OAS, President Kennedy proclaimed the quarantine to take effect on the following day. Under the quarantine all vessels, of whatever nationality, in defined zones would be intercepted but would be allowed to continue to Cuba if they were not carrying prohibited materials.

Pursuant to the quarantine, vessels of the Soviet Union and of other nations were trailed, boarded, inspected. Soviet submarines were located, tracked, surfaced, and photographed. Other vessels apparently destined for Cuba changed course and proceeded elsewhere. No vessels were forcefully seized or diverted, and military force was not actually used.

The outcome is well known. The Soviet Union agreed to discontinue bringing missiles into Cuba; it agreed to discontinue building its missile bases in Cuba and to dismantle and remove missiles that had already been installed. The United States agreed to end the quarantine and gave assurances against an invasion of Cuba. . . .

The Legal Justifications . . .

Principally, U.S. lawyers based their case on the authorization from the Organization of American States. The OAS is a regional organization contemplated by Chapter VIII of the United Nations Charter; indeed, it was the inter-American system which the framers of the Charter had principally in mind. As the later embodiment of the inter-American system, the OAS can take collective action, or can authorize action by its members, in defense of the hemisphere. Just as the United Nations Charter was interpreted as permitting the General Assembly to act in support of international peace and security when the Security Council proved ineffective, so, argued the lawyers for the United States, the Charter should be interpreted to allow a similar role to such regional organizations when the organs of the United Nations cannot be effective.

It is true that Article 53 of the Charter provides that "no enforcement action shall be taken under regional arrangements or by regional agencies without the authorization of the Security Council." But the resolution of October 23, it was argued, was not "enforcement action"; it was only a recommendation. Also, the authorization required from the Security Council need not be prior authorization nor need it be expressed. The Security Council was informed of the OAS resolution and of the proposed action of the United States thereunder, and, in the words of the Deputy Legal Adviser of the State Department, "did not see fit to take action in derogation of the quarantine. Although a resolution condemning the quarantine was laid before the Council by the Soviet Union, the Council subsequently, by general consent, refrained from acting upon it." . . .

The Justifications Which the United States Avoided

What the United States did not say about Cuba . . . may have been more significant than what the United States did and said. . . .

. . . Although the President and others invoked the needs of American defense and security in political justifications, no responsible spokesman mentioned Article 51, even as possible alternative legal support for the quarantine. Repeatedly, the Legal Adviser and the Deputy Legal Adviser stressed that the United States "did not rest its case" on that ground. Report has it that reference to Article 51 was several times proposed for insertion in statements by the President and others, and every time alert and insistent lawyers succeeded in eliminating it.

The temptation must have been great. Pressed to justify the action of the United States, the lawyers relied on the authorization of the OAS, although some may have found that authorization flimsy and the argument under it strained. They eschewed Article 51, although, as some would interpret it, that article would have handsomely justified the quarantine, as well as bombing and perhaps even invasion of Cuba, without need of OAS authorization. But spokesmen for the United States apparently recognized the dangers which the argument entailed.

Notes and Questions

1. Under Article 53 of the U.N. Charter, was the quarantine an "enforcement action," which should have required the authorization of the U.N. Security Council? Did the Security Council provide authorization by its inaction? If you believe that the quarantine was an enforcement action requiring affirmative authorization by the Security Council, doesn't that view seriously weaken the possible role of regional organizations, given that the Security Council might be deadlocked because of a veto by a permanent power? Shouldn't strong regional organizations be encouraged?

2. Why do you think that U.S. officials avoided invoking the Article 51 justification of self-defense in the Cuban missile crisis? What is the explicit condition in the Article for resort to self-defense? Was it met here?

In his excellent book about the crisis, the Legal Adviser to the Department of State at the time, Professor Abram Chayes, gives his perspective on why he thought self-defense should not have been invoked:

> Intra-office discussions at the time emphasized that it would set a bad precedent if the United States were to rely on a self-defence theory. . . . [T]he normative atmosphere in which states act, though tenuous and impalpable perhaps, is affected by the earlier actions of others and their accompanying statements of what they take the governing law to be. An official United States position endorsing a latitudinarian construction of "armed attack" could not help but weaken those normative checks. To this extent there was something in the idea that a claim of self-defence would set a dangerous precedent.
>
> In retrospect, however, I think the central difficulty with the Article 51 argument was that it seemed to trivialize the whole effort at legal justification. No doubt the phrase "armed attack" must be construed broadly enough to permit some anticipatory response. But it is a very different matter to expand it to include threatening deployments or demonstrations that do not have imminent attack as their purpose or probable outcome. To accept that reading is to make the occasion for forceful response essentially a question for unilateral national decision that would not only be formally unreviewable, but not subject to intelligent criticism, either. There is simply no standard against which this decision could be judged. Whenever a nation believed that interests, which in the heat and pressure of a crisis it is prepared to characterize as vital, were threatened, its use of force in response would become permissible. . . .
>
> In this sense, I believe an Article 51 defence would have signalled that the United States did not take the legal issues involved very seriously, that in its view the situation was to be governed by national discretion not international law. [Abram Chayes, The Cuban Missile Crisis 63-66 (1974).]

Is the danger Professor Chayes identifies still a threat in today's world? Why did such concerns not preclude the Bush Administration from adopting a National Security Strategy, discussed above in Section B.5.b, that articulated a right of preventive or preemptive attacks? Would the embrace of a strategy of preemption by the United States weaken the restraints on other states' use of force?

3. *Interventions in Liberia and Sierra Leone.* In August 1990, the Economic Community of West African States (ECOWAS) — a regional organization originally founded to promote economic integration — began peacekeeping operations in Liberia in response to a civil war. The 15,000-strong peacekeeping force, called the Economic Community of West African States Monitoring Group (ECOMOG),

was arguably acting outside the terms of its 1981 self-defense pact, but with the refusal of the United Nations and United States to get involved, regional action seemed necessary.

The ECOMOG fought rebel forces and bombed rebel strongholds as necessary to enforce the ceasefire before eventually withdrawing. The members of ECOWAS justified their intervention by citing the need to stop the slaughter of civilians, to protect foreign nationals, and to eliminate the threat posed by anarchy to peace in the region. ECOMOG also intervened in Sierra Leone to conduct peacekeeping, or perhaps more precisely peace enforcement, activities.

Although the Security Council did not provide advance authorization for ECOMOG action in Liberia or Sierra Leone, in both cases it seemed to provide approval or endorsement of the interventions after the fact. In Security Council Resolution 1116 (1997), the Council "not[ed] with appreciation the active efforts of ECOWAS to restore peace, security, and stability to Liberia" and commended the African countries that were contributing to ECOMOG. The Council was more explicit after ECOMOG forces deployed to Sierra Leone. In Security Council Resolution 1132 (1997), the Council expressly acted under Chapter VII of the Charter to authorize ECOWAS to ensure implementation of a resolution that demanded, among other things, that the military junta governing the country relinquish power.

Is it consistent with the Charter for a regional peacekeeping organization to intervene in another country without Security Council authorization, in the hopes that it might later obtain Security Council approval? What would the legal status of such an intervention be if the Security Council does not subsequently approve or ratify it?

4. *Joint peacekeeping in Sudan.* Sudan, which became independent in 1956, has been plagued by civil war for most of its existence. Although a "Comprehensive Peace Agreement" concluded in 2005 brought an end to a long-running civil war between the government and rebel movements in the southern part of the country, fighting continued in a distinct conflict in Sudan's Darfur province. The United Nations authorized the deployment of a peacekeeping force in 2005 to support implementation of the Comprehensive Peace Agreement, but its mandate did not include attempting to stop the fighting in Darfur.

Initial peacekeeping efforts in Darfur were instead led by the African Union (AU). The African Union Mission in Sudan (AMIS) had, by late 2006, grown to a force of 7,000. The force was criticized as too small and too poorly equipped to stop the fighting. Despite the presence of the African Union troops and the conclusion in May 2006 of a Darfur Peace Agreement, fighting in the region intensified during the second half of 2006.

Faced with the deteriorating humanitarian conditions, the Security Council in 2006 adopted Resolution 1706, which authorized an expansion of the mandate of UNMIS — the U.N. Mission in Sudan that had been created to support implementation of the Comprehensive Peace Agreement — to permit it to operate in Darfur. Despite the fact that the Council expressly determined that the situation in Sudan constitutes a threat to international peace and security, however, the Resolution nevertheless "invites the consent of the Government [of Sudan] for this deployment." Sudan strenuously objected to the deployment of a peacekeeping mission undertaken solely by the United Nations, and UNMIS did not deploy to Darfur. Sudan ultimately agreed to the establishment of an innovative "hybrid" AU-UN peacekeeping mission of nearly 20,000 military personnel. The African Union/United Nations Hybrid Operation in Darfur, or UNAMID, was established in Security Council Resolution 1769 (2007); as of February 2011, there were over 17,000 peacekeeping troops on the ground in Darfur.

Why did the deployment of an expanded UNMIS peacekeeping force into Darfur initially authorized under Security Council Resolution 1706 (2006) require Sudan's consent? Doesn't the Security Council have the authority, under Chapter VII, to require Sudan to accept the deployment of peacekeepers? In Resolution 688, discussed in Section C.2 above, the Security Council required Iraq to permit humanitarian relief groups to enter its territory to respond to the humanitarian crisis produced by Saddam's suppression of his own population. Could the Security Council demand that Sudan allow U.N. peacekeepers into Darfur? What are the differences between the two cases?

5. Events in the Ivory Coast in 2010–2011 represented another cooperative effort by the United Nations and regional organizations, this time to respond to the political crisis occasioned by the refusal of President Laurent Gbagbo to step down after international election monitors and other observers determined that he clearly lost a November 2010 election to his rival, Alassane Ouattara. As discussed in Chapter 5.A.5, the U.N., the AU, and ECOWAS took a variety of military and economic measures.

6. In 2002, the African Union (AU) came into existence to replace the former Organization of African Unity and to deepen regional integration. The treaty establishing the AU, the Constitutive Act of the African Union, lists the following as one of the principles in accordance with which the AU shall function:

> the right of the Union to intervene in a Member State pursuant to a decision of the Assembly [of heads of state and government] in respect of grave circumstances, namely: war crimes, genocide and crimes against humanity. [Constitutive Act of the African Union, art. 4(h), Jul. 11, 2000, 2158 U.N.T.S. 3.]

The Charter permits the Assembly to adopt decisions, in the absence of consensus, by a two-thirds majority. Assuming the AU wanted to intervene militarily in a state to stop grave atrocities over the objection of the government of the state in question, what would be the legal basis for intervening? Does this reflect a right of humanitarian intervention (discussed in Section B.5.g) or the responsibility to protect (discussed in Section C.1)? Or the right of a regional organization to carry out collective security operations? Would such intervention amount to an "enforcement action" that requires the approval of the Security Council? Could the intervention be justified on a theory of consent of the territorial state, assuming it is a party to the Constitutive Act of the African Union?

D. REGULATION OF THE CONDUCT OF WAR: INTERNATIONAL HUMANITARIAN LAW

The preceding sections of this chapter have centered on the law governing when states may resort to force against one another, or *jus ad bellum.* Another important body of international law rules, referred to as the law of war, "international humanitarian law," or the "law of armed conflict," regulates the actual conduct of war. International humanitarian law, or *jus in bello*, sets limits on the permissible means of waging war, establishes basic humanitarian protections for the participants in and victims of warfare, and governs the role of "occupying powers" in war. Although questions about the application of international humanitarian law can arise in any armed conflict, a great deal of attention has been paid, in the wake of the attacks of September 11 and the U.S. response, to questions about whether and how international humanitarian law applies to the conflict in Afghanistan and, more generally, to the fight against terrorist actors.

1. *Development of International Humanitarian Law*

A starting point for analyzing current challenges about the role of international humanitarian law is understanding how the laws of war apply generally. The following excerpt by Frits Kalshoven, published by the International Committee of the Red Cross (ICRC), which supervises compliance with the 1949 Geneva Conventions for the protection of victims of war, explains the history of the Conventions.

Frits Kalshoven, Constraints on the Waging of War

1, 7-8, 10-11, 40, 71 (1987)

... [T]he cruelty of war and the suffering, death and destruction it causes ... raise an obvious question: is the behavior of belligerent parties subject to any limitations? The answer to this question is not hard to give: such limits do exist, even though they may not be unequivocal in all cases. To the extent they belong to the realm of law (rather than to that of morality alone) they constitute the body of "international humanitarian law applicable in armed conflict." ...

The tendency to start the treaty-making process with respect to rules of warfare dates back to the 1860s ... [Since then,] two distinct (though never entirely separate) trends in the law of armed conflict [have developed], each characterized by its particular perspective: one, the so-called law of Geneva, more particularly concerned with the condition of war victims who have fallen into enemy hands ..., and the other, ... the law of The Hague, relating to ... proper and permissible means and methods of war. ...

[Many steps had to be taken] before the "law of Geneva" acquired its present scope and relative completeness. Further steps served either to expand the circle of protected persons, or to improve the rules in the light of acquired experience. ...

The tragic events, successively, of the Spanish Civil War and the Second World War provided the incentive for yet another major revision and further development of the law of Geneva. To this end a diplomatic conference met in 1949 in Geneva. ... The three Conventions in force [that had been adopted 1929] ... were substituted by new Conventions, giving improved versions of many existing rules. ... To give just one example, the armed resistance in several European countries under German occupation during the Second World War led to the express recognition that members of organized resistance movements which fulfill a number of (severe) conditions would qualify as prisoners of war.

Then the law of Geneva was enriched by an entirely novel convention on the protection of civilian persons in time of war. This [Fourth] Convention serves to protect two categories of civilians in particular: enemy civilians in the territory of a belligerent party, and the inhabitants of occupied territory. . . . With this latest addition the law of Geneva had come to comprise four Conventions, dealing with the wounded and sick on land; the wounded, sick and shipwrecked at sea; prisoners of war; and protected civilians. . . .

The law of Geneva serves to provide protection for all those who, as a consequence of an armed conflict, have fallen into the hands of the adversary. The protection envisaged here is, hence, not protection against the violence of war itself, but against the arbitrary power which one belligerent party acquires in the course of the war over persons belonging to the other party. . . .

[Two Protocols Additional to the Geneva Conventions of 1949 were adopted in 1977.]* One (Protocol I) is applicable in international armed conflicts, and the other (Protocol II) in non-international armed conflicts. . . .

[I]t is worth noting that a good part of the provisions in the Protocols, and notably in Protocol I, is simply a codification of pre-existing rules of customary international law. . . .

As Professor Kalshoven notes, the 1949 Geneva Conventions represent major codifications of "Geneva law" concerning the humane treatment of victims of war. The first two Geneva Conventions provide for protection of wounded and sick soldiers and sailors. The Conventions' detailed rules require that the wounded and sick be collected and cared for by the party to the conflict which has them in its power. Medical personnel and medical establishments, transports, and equipment must be spared.

The Third Geneva Convention governs the status and treatment of prisoners of war (POWs). The Convention sets forth a variety of rights for POWs. For example, Article 17 provides that POWs, when interrogated, are required to give only their name, rank, and a few other pieces of information. Article 71 gives POWs the right to send and receive letters and cards. Article 87 states that, "Prisoners of war may not be sentenced by the military authorities and courts of the Detaining Power to any penalties except those provided for in respect of members of the armed forces of the said Power who have committed the same acts." In effect, this means that POWs cannot be tried for merely having participated in the military conflict. In addition, Article 118 provides that POWs "shall be released and repatriated without delay after the cessation of active hostilities."

The Fourth Geneva Convention governs the treatment of civilians who have fallen into the hands of the enemy. It mandates respect for fundamental rights of such persons and prohibits ill-treatment, including measures "of such a character as to cause the physical suffering or extermination" of protected persons. Fourth Geneva Convention, Art. 32. The Convention also regulates the "internment or placing in assigned residence" of enemy aliens in the territory of a warring party;

*[In addition to the two 1977 Protocols to the Geneva Conventions, a Third Protocol concluded in 2005 adopted the Red Crystal, along with the Red Cross and the Red Crescent, as a third distinctive symbol for those exercising humanitarian functions under the Geneva Conventions.–EDS.]

internment "may be ordered only if the security of the Detaining Power makes it absolutely necessary"; conditions of internment are carefully regulated by the Convention.

The "law of The Hague" traces its name to two major international peace conferences held in The Hague in 1899 and 1907, during which the parties made substantial progress in codifying "the laws and customs of war." The 1907 Conference produced the Hague "Regulations Respecting the Laws and Customs of War on Land,"* which established the general principle that the "right of belligerents to adopt means of injuring the enemy is not unlimited." 1907 Hague Regulations, Art. 22. Among the other rules contained in the 1907 Hague Regulations were prohibitions on using poisoned weapons, killing treacherously, employing arms "calculated to cause unnecessary suffering," destroying enemy property "unless such destruction or seizure be imperatively demanded by the necessities of war," declaring that no quarter will be given, and attacking undefended towns and villages. The 1907 Hague Regulations also elaborate on the rules that apply when one country's military occupies another country. Numerous treaties concluded since 1907 have produced many more substantive restraints on the methods and weapons that may be used in war; some of these are discussed below.

2. *The Scope of Application of International Humanitarian Law*

Wartime is an exceptional state in which a great deal of violence and the disregard of important human rights are legally accepted. Soldiers in wartime have what is known as the "combatant's privilege," which means they may lawfully kill their adversaries and destroy enemy military property. In addition, states may detain enemy soldiers without trial simply by virtue of their membership in the opposing force. At the same time, combatants in war are entitled to certain protections. As such, knowing when international humanitarian law is triggered is an important, but sometimes difficult, question that parties engaged in violent conflict must address.

a. International Armed Conflict

The four 1949 Geneva Conventions each contain an identical Article 2 ("Common Article 2") which defines the scope of application of the Conventions.

Common Article 2

In addition to the provisions which shall be implemented in peacetime, the present Convention shall apply to all cases of declared war or of any other armed

*The fourth convention produced at the 1907 Hague conference was the Convention Respecting the Laws and Customs of War on Land, Oct. 18, 1907, 36 Stat. 2277, T.S. 539. That Convention included an annex entitled "Regulations Respecting the Laws and Customs of War on Land." The Convention itself obligated member states to "issue instructions to their armed land forces which shall be in conformity with the [annexed] Regulations." References in this Chapter to the "1907 Hague Regulations" are to the provisions included in the Annex to the fourth 1907 Hague Convention.

conflict which may arise between two or more of the High Contracting Parties, even if the state of war is not recognized by one of them.

The following excerpt discusses the scope of the application of the Geneva Conventions in international armed conflict.

Steven R. Ratner, Jason S. Abrams & James L. Bischoff, Accountability for Human Rights Atrocities in International Law

85-87 (3d ed. 2009)

[P]rior to the Geneva Conventions, legal protections applied only in the event of war, which had a clear definition in both treaties and custom. The Geneva Conventions, however, apply in the case of . . . 'declared war or of any other armed conflict . . . even if the state of war is not recognized by one of them'. . . . The term 'armed conflict' is quite broad compared to the term 'declared war.' Neither party need recognize a state of war or sever diplomatic relations; only *de facto* hostilities are required. These provisions of the Convention do not regard hostilities between a state and a non-state actor, such as those between the United States and suspected Al Qaeda members, as an international armed conflict per se. . . . *

The precise level of hostilities required to trigger the Conventions is subject to some debate. . . . [A]ccording to the ICRC's official commentary, they encompass '[a]ny difference arising between two States and leading to the intervention of members of the armed forces,' regardless of the length of the conflict or the casualties on either side. . . . The traditional references to armed forces suggest a reluctance by states to consider many types of covert action as triggering the Conventions.

[There is a] lack of any 'exact, objective criterion' defining 'armed conflict.' The applicability of the Conventions will turn upon the perspectives of the belligerents and states observing the situation. States, courts, and commentators agree that it involves the use of armed forces, as opposed to police, and involves the use of force, although that may not involve the actual firing of weapons. Border skirmishes would seem to qualify to invoke the Conventions; even if only sporadic, they ought to trigger the Conventions at least during the period when they are in progress. However, they render a determination as to the termination of armed conflict difficult.

A related important issue concerns the extent to which the Geneva Conventions are triggered in the absence of a classic state-to-state armed conflict, but when one state intervenes in the civil war of another.** . . .

*[As discussed below, such conflicts are governed by Common Article 3 of the Geneva Conventions.–EDS.]

**[As discussed in Section B.5.c above, the traditional view is that an armed conflict becomes "international" only if an outside state intervenes on the side of the nonstate force; the government is permitted to seek outside assistance in using force against a domestic insurgency.–EDS.]

Notes and Questions

1. The 1949 Geneva Conventions are among the most widely adhered to treaties in the world. As of February 2011, 194 entities (including the Holy See) were parties to the four Conventions. (Excerpts of the Third and Fourth Geneva Conventions are in the Documentary Supplement.)

2. What was the legal character of U.S. involvement in Afghanistan after September 11? Recall that a civil war was already underway in Afghanistan in 2001 when the United States attacked Al Qaeda and the Taliban in October 2001. Assuming that the Taliban regime was the de facto government of Afghanistan, did U.S. involvement give rise to an international armed conflict? Could there have been an international armed conflict if the United States had not used force directly, but had merely supported the Northern Alliance, which was fighting against the Taliban? Was there an international armed conflict in Afghanistan after 2002, when the United States and other countries played a major role in assisting the newly-installed government of Afghanistan in fighting against the Taliban after it became an insurgency movement?

b. Common Article 3 and Armed Conflict "Not of an International Character"

The 1949 Geneva Conventions address principally armed conflict between two states that are parties to the Conventions. Each of the 1949 Conventions, however, also contains the identical Article 3, known as "Common Article 3," which applies in an "armed conflict not of an international character occurring in the territory of one" of the parties to the Conventions. Common Article 3 in part provides:

> In the case of armed conflict not of an international character occurring in the territory of one of the High Contracting Parties, each Party to the conflict shall be bound to apply, as a minimum, the follow provisions:
>
> (1) Persons taking no active part in the hostilities, including members of armed forces who have laid down their arms and those placed *hors de combat* by sickness, wounds, detention, or any other cause, shall in all circumstances be treated humanely, without any adverse distinction founded on race, colour, region or faith, sex, birth or wealth, or any other similar criteria.
>
> To this end, the following acts are and shall remain prohibited at any time and in any place whatsoever with respect to the above-mentioned persons:
>
> (a) violence to life and person, in particular murder of all kinds, mutilation, cruel treatment and torture;
>
> (b) taking of hostages;
>
> (c) outrages upon personal dignity, in particular, humiliating and degrading treatment;
>
> (d) the passing of sentences and the carrying out of executions without previous judgment pronounced by regularly constituted court, affording all the judicial guarantees which are recognized as indispensable by civilized peoples.
>
> (2) The wounded and sick shall be collected and cared for.

Common Article 3 is sometimes referred to as a "convention in miniature" that extends certain minimal guarantees to non-international armed conflicts; in the words of the authoritative commentary on the Geneva Conventions, Common Article 3 "at least ensures the application of the rules of humanity which are recognized as essential by civilized nations." Jean S. Pictet, Commentary, I Geneva Convention 48 (1952).

Notes and Questions

1. Given the breadth of the term "armed conflict," what is the outer limit of hostilities to which the Geneva Conventions would apply? In 1997, the Inter-American Commission on Human Rights determined that an attack by 42 armed civilians on the La Tablada military barracks in Argentina during peacetime constituted an internal armed conflict to which common Article 3 of the Geneva Conventions applied. Abella v. Argentina, Case No. 11.137, Inter-Am. C.H.R. 1997, ¶161 (Apr. 13, 1998) (*La Tablada* Case).

2. The Commentary to the 1949 Geneva Conventions recounts that the threshold for application of Common Article 3 was of great concern during the negotiations that led to the adoption of the conventions. States sought to distinguish "any form of anarchy, rebellion, or even plain banditry" from armed conflict to which Common Article 3 would apply. Although the parties did not ultimately adopt a definition of the phrase "armed conflict not of an international character," a number of conditions for application of the Convention were proposed during debates, including:

> (1) That the Party in revolt against the *de jure* Government possesses an organized military force, an authority responsible for its acts, acting within a determinate territory and having the means of respecting and ensuring respect for the Convention.
>
> (2) That the legal Government is obliged to have recourse to the regular military forces against insurgents organized as military and in possession of a part of the national territory.
>
> (3) (a) That the *de jure* Government has recognized the insurgents as belligerents; or
>
> (b) that it has claimed for itself the rights of a belligerent; or
>
> (c) that it has accorded the insurgents recognition as belligerents for the purposes only of the present Convention; or
>
> (d) that the dispute has been admitted to the agenda of the Security Council or the General Assembly of the United Nations as being a threat to international peace, a breach of the peace, or an act of aggression.
>
> (4) (a) That the insurgents have an organization purporting to have the characteristics of a State.
>
> (b) That the insurgent civil authority exercises *de facto* authority over persons within a determinate territory.
>
> (c) That the armed forces act under the direction of the organized civil authority and are prepared to observe the ordinary laws of war.
>
> (d) That the insurgent civil authority agrees to be bound by the provisions of the Convention.
>
> The above criteria are useful as a means of distinguishing a genuine armed conflict from a mere act of banditry or an unorganized and short-lived insurrection. [Pictet, Commentary, I Geneva Convention, supra, at 49-50.]

3. Although Common Article 3 by its own terms applies to armed conflicts "not of an international character occurring in the territory of one of the High Contracting Parties," the International Court of Justice in the *Nicaragua* case and the International Criminal Tribunal for the former Yugoslavia in the *Tadic* case have held that the substantive rules of Common Article 3 represent customary international law "providing a minimum set of rights not only during internal conflict, but also during an international armed conflict." Jordan J. Paust, The U.S. as Occupying Power over Portions of Iraq and Relevant Responsibilities under the Law of War, ASIL Insight (Apr. 2003).

4. Does armed conflict between the United States and Al Qaeda or other terrorist groups qualify as "armed conflict not of an international character" within the meaning of Common Article 3? The authoritative commentary to the Geneva Protocols states that "the conflicts referred to in Article 3 are armed conflicts . . . which are in many respects similar to an international war, but take place *within the confines of a single country*." Jean S. Pictet, Commentary, III Geneva Convention 37 (1960) (emphasis added). In *Hamdan v. Rumsfeld*, however, the Supreme Court held that a member of Al Qaeda captured in Afghanistan was covered by Common Article 3. (The case is discussed in Chapter 3.B.) The *Hamdan* Court held:

> The Court of Appeals thought, and the Government asserts, that Common Article 3 does not apply to Hamdan because the conflict with al Qaeda, being "international in scope," does not qualify as a "conflict not of an international character." That reasoning is erroneous. The term "conflict not of an international character" is used here in contradistinction to a conflict between nations. . . . Common Article 3 . . . affords some minimal protection, falling short of full protection under the Conventions, to individuals associated with neither a signatory nor even a nonsignatory "Power" who are involved in a conflict "in the territory of" a signatory. The latter kind of conflict is distinguishable from the conflict described in Common Article 2 chiefly because it does not involve a clash between nations (whether signatories or not). In context, then, the phrase "not of an international character" bears its literal meaning. . . .
>
> Although the official commentaries accompanying Common Article 3 indicate that an important purpose of the provision was to furnish minimal protection to rebels involved in one kind of "conflict not of an international character," i.e., a civil war, the commentaries also make clear "that the scope of the Article must be as wide as possible." In fact, limiting language that would have rendered Common Article 3 applicable "especially [to] cases of civil war, colonial conflicts, or wars of religion," was omitted from the final version of the Article, which coupled broader scope of application with a narrower range of rights than did earlier proposed iterations. [Hamdan v. Rumsfeld, 548 U.S. 557, 630-631 (2006).]

Should international humanitarian law apply to transnational armed conflict between the United States and nonstate groups such as terrorists? If so, should it apply only to entities as well organized as Al Qaeda was in 2001, or to any terrorist cell, or even to violence against individual terrorist actors?

5. Protocol II to the 1949 Geneva Conventions, adopted in 1977, provides additional rules in the cases of non-international armed conflicts. Although Protocol II elaborates on the substantive protections of Common Article 3, it appears to be triggered in more limited circumstances than Common Article 3, i.e., the

Protocol is triggered only for conflicts characterized by violence of greater intensity than would be required to trigger application of Common Article 3. Protocol II applies to armed conflicts "which take place in the territory of a High Contracting Party between its armed forces and dissident armed forces or other organized armed groups which, under responsible command, exercise such control over a part of its territory as to enable them to carry out sustained and concerted military operations and to implement this Protocol." Protocol II, Art. 1(1).

The United States signed Protocol II, and the Reagan Administration submitted it to the Senate for advice and consent to ratification, but the Senate has not acted on it.

c. Wars of National Liberation

Protocol I to the 1977 Geneva Conventions, adopted in 1977, further elaborates international humanitarian law in international armed conflicts. Protocol I generally applies in situations defined in Common Article 2 of the 1949 Geneva Conventions. However, the Protocol also extends its coverage to "armed conflicts in which peoples are fighting against colonial domination and alien occupation and against racist regimes in the exercise of their right of self-determination." During the negations, particular problems arose regarding the application to such conflicts — typically carried out by insurgent groups rather than regular armed forces — of the traditional requirements reflected in the 1949 Geneva Conventions that combatants engaged in military operations distinguish themselves from civilians. Article 44(3) of Protocol I provides:

> In order to promote the protection of the civilian population from the effects of hostilities, combatants are obliged to distinguish themselves from the civilian population while they are engaged in an attack or in a military operation preparatory to an attack. Recognizing, however, that there are situations in armed conflicts where, owing to the nature of the hostilities an armed combatant cannot so distinguish himself, he shall retain his status as a combatant, provided that, in such situations, he carries his arms openly:
>
> (a) during each military engagement, and
>
> (b) during such time as he is visible to the adversary while he is engaged in a military deployment preceding the launching of an attack in which he is to participate.

In the words of Professor Kalshoven, the approach taken in Protocol I reflects

> a compromise between, on the one hand, those who demanded that irregular fighters be accorded the status of combatants and yet be exempted from any obligation to distinguish themselves from civilians, and, on the other hand, those who were strongly opposed to making any exceptions in favour of irregular fighters in difficult situations. [Kalshoven, Constraints on Waging War, supra, at 77.]

The United States signed Protocol I in 1977, but the treaty has not been submitted to the Senate for ratification. The Reagan Administration announced U.S. opposition to Protocol I, largely because of the provisions related to combatants in wars of national liberation. In his letter transmitting Protocol II to the Senate for ratification, President Reagan noted that Protocol I would grant combatant status to irregular forces even if they do not satisfy the traditional "requirements to distinguish themselves from the civilian population and otherwise comply with the laws of war," which would "endanger civilians among whom terrorists and other irregulars attempt to conceal themselves." President Ronald Reagan, Message to the Senate Transmitting a Protocol to the 1949 Geneva Conventions (Jan. 29, 1987), 1 Pub. Papers 88, 89 (1987).

Although they are not as widely adhered to as the 1949 Geneva Conventions, the 1977 Protocols have nevertheless secured very broad acceptance. As of February 2011, there were 170 parties to Protocol I and 165 parties to Protocol II.

3. *Substantive International Humanitarian Law Rules*

International humanitarian law is a complex field of law. In this subsection, we highlight a few of the basic principles on which many of the more detailed treaty and customary international law rules are based.

Humane treatment. As noted above, the 1949 Geneva Conventions provide protection for victims of war who find themselves in the hands of the adversary. The Conventions contain extensive and detailed provisions for the treatment of the various classes of war victims they protect. Professor Kalshoven explains the general principles on which the Geneva Conventions are based:

> The core system of protection provided in the Geneva Conventions of 1949 may be described as the principle that protected persons must be respected and protected in all circumstances and must be treated humanely, without any distinction founded on sex, race, nationality, religion, political opinions, or any other similar criteria.
>
> "Respect" and "protection" are complementary notions. "Respect", as the passive element, indicates an obligation not to harm, not to expose to suffering, not to kill a protected person; "protection", as the active element, signifies a duty to ward off dangers and prevent harm. The third element involved in the principle, that of "humane" treatment, related to the mental attitude which should govern all aspects of the treatment of protected persons; this attitude should aim to ensure to these persons an existence worthy of human beings, in spite of—and with full recognition of—the harsh circumstances of their present situation. . . .
>
> Starting from these fundamental notions the some four hundred, in part highly detailed Articles of the Conventions provide an elaborate system of rules for the protection of the various categories of protected persons. [Kalshoven, Constraints on the Waging of War, supra, at 42-43.]

Permissible Means and Methods of War. The general principles in the 1907 Hague Regulations discussed above regarding the conduct of warfare represented an early effort to establish the principle that there are limits on the means parties may use during warfare; these principles are today widely regarded as rules of customary international law. The years after 1907 Peace Conference witnessed additional efforts to limit what were viewed as particularly cruel means of waging war. Among the most significant of these was the conclusion in 1925 of the first treaty prohibiting the use of chemical or biological weapons, the Geneva Protocol for the

Prohibition of the Use in War of Asphyxiating, Poisonous, or Other Gases, and of Bacteriological Methods of Warfare, 26 U.S.T. 571, 94 L.N.T.S. 65. The conclusion in 1954 of a convention for the protection of cultural property in times of armed conflict marked another significant development.

The 1977 Protocol I to the 1949 Geneva Conventions reaffirms the "basic rules" governing the means and methods of waging war.

Article 35. Basic Rules

1. In any armed conflict, the right of the Parties to the conflict to choose methods or means of warfare is not unlimited.

2. It is prohibited to employ weapons, projectiles and material and methods of warfare of a nature to cause superfluous injury or unnecessary suffering.

3. It is prohibited to employ methods or means of warfare which are intended, or may be expected, to cause widespread, long-term and severe damage to the natural environment.

Protection of civilians and targeting rules. Of particular significance in the evolution of the law of war has been the emergence and widespread acceptance of rules specifically aimed at the protection of civilians. Although the Fourth Geneva Convention is dedicated to the protection of civilians, as Professor Kalshoven explains, "it is not designed to protect the civilian population . . . against the dangers of warfare. . . . [I]ts protection starts when civilians find themselves in the power of the adversary." Kalshoven, Constraints on the Waging of War, supra, at 42. Protocol I, in contrast, contains rules that embody the principles of *distinction* and *proportionality*, the key principles meant to protect civilian populations in the course of combat itself.

Article 48 of Protocol I sets forth the basic principle of distinction.

Article 48. Basic Rule

In order to ensure respect for and protection of the civilian population and civilian objects, the Parties to the conflict shall at all times distinguish between the civilian population and combatants and between civilian objects and military objectives and accordingly shall direct their operations only against military objectives.

A treatise written by two members of the Legal Division of the ICRC after a detailed study of state practice concludes that the principle of distinction binds not only parties to Protocol I, but is an accepted principle of customary international law. Jean-Marie Henckaerts & Louise Doswald-Beck, 1 Customary International Humanitarian Law 3 (2005).

The principle of proportionality grows from the realization that the frequent proximity of military targets to civilian objects exposes civilians to grave danger, even when they are not directly targeted. The customary international law principle of proportionality accordingly imposes restrictions on attacks against even military targets if the attacks would produce excessive injury to civilians.

> Launching an attack which may be expected to cause incidental loss of civilian life, injury to civilians, damage to civilian objects, or a combination thereof, which would be excessive in relation to the concrete and direct military advantage anticipated, is prohibited. [Henckaerts & Doswald-Beck, Customary International Humanitarian Law, supra, at 46.]

Responsibilities of Occupying Powers. The 1907 Hague Regulations contained an early codification of the law governing the military occupation by one country of another. Article 43 of the Regulations emphasizes the duty of the occupying power to "take all the measures in [its] power to restore, and ensure, as far as possible, public order and safety, while respecting, unless absolutely prevented, the laws in force in the country." The lives and property of persons in occupied territory must be respected.

The Fourth 1949 Geneva Convention further elaborates rules that apply in the case of military occupation. It emphasizes the responsibilities of the occupying power in ensuring that the humanitarian needs of the population of the occupied territory are met. A number of provisions concern the transfer of persons in or out of occupied territory. Article 49 prohibits "[i]ndividual or mass forcible transfers, as well as deportations of protected persons from occupied territory to the territory of the Occupying Power or to that of any other country, . . . regardless of their motive." The same article prohibits an occupying power from "transfer[ing] parts of its own civilian population into the territory it occupies." The Fourth Convention envisages that occupation is an interim form of de facto administration that will leave the laws and governing structure of the occupied territory largely unaltered. Article 54 stipulates that an occupier "may not alter the status of public officials or judges in the occupied territories." In addition, Article 64 provides:

> The penal laws of the occupied territory shall remain in force, with the exception that they may be repealed or suspended by the Occupying Power in cases where they constitute a threat to its security or an obstacle to the application of the present Convention. Subject to the latter consideration and to the necessity for ensuring the effective administration of justice, the tribunals of the occupied territory shall continue to function in respect of all offences covered by the said laws.
>
> The Occupying Power may, however, subject the population of the occupied territory to provisions which are essential to enable the Occupying Power to fulfill its obligations under the present Convention, to maintain the orderly government of the territory, and to ensure the security of the Occupying Power, of the members and property of the occupying forces or administration, and likewise of the establishments and lines of communication used by them.

Notes and Questions

1. What qualifies as a "military objective" in applying the principle of distinction? Article 52(2) of Protocol I provides that "military objectives are limited to those objects which by their nature, location, purpose or use make an effective contribution to military action and whose total or partial destruction, capture or neutralization, in the circumstances ruling at the time, offers a definite military advantage." Does this definition provide much practical help? Would bombing

highways, railroads, or bridges on which both military supply vehicles and ordinary civilian traffic travel violate the principle of distinction? Is it permissible to attack factories involved in the production of munitions? To attack the electric grid in the capital city of the enemy country?

2. Protocol I makes it illegal for states to use civilians to attempt to shield military objectives from attack. Imagine that a state violates this provision by deploying its anti-aircraft batteries in the middle of densely populated urban areas. Will that state's adversary be prohibited by the principle of proportionality from attacking those batteries? Does respecting the principle of proportionality make sense in such circumstances?

3. Apart from the contentious issue of application to wars of national liberation, Professor Kalshoven suggests in the excerpt in subsection 1 of this Section that most of the substantive rules in Protocol I merely codify customary international law. The United States largely agrees with this position. Michael J. Matheson, The United States Position on the Relation of Customary International Law to the 1977 Protocols Additional to the 1949 Geneva Conventions, 2 Am. U. J. Int'l L. & Pol'y 419 (1987).

4. Through the efforts of the international Conference on Disarmament (CD), established by the U.N. General Assembly as a multilateral disarmament negotiating forum, a framework treaty and a number of protocols have been concluded that prohibit or limit the use of excessively injurious or indiscriminate conventional weapons. The five protocols adopted in the framework of this Convention on Conventional Weapons govern: (1) weapons that produce nondetectable fragments; (2) mines and booby-traps, and related devices; (3) incendiary weapons; (4) blinding lasers; and (5) "explosive remnants of war."

5. One commentator has observed that the assumption that "lies at the heart of the provisions on military occupation in the laws of war" is that because "the occupant's role [is] temporary, any alteration of the existing order in occupied territory should be minimal." Adam Roberts, Transformative Military Occupation: Applying the Laws of War and Human Rights, 100 Am. J. Int'l L. 580, 582 (2006). If so, is it legitimate for an occupying power to attempt to make fundamental changes in the economic, social, and political system as the United States and United Kingdom did in Iraq following the 2003 invasion? Is it a prudent idea to attempt to do so? Does it matter whether the purpose of the changes is to advance democracy and the respect for human rights? What is the legal basis for such changes if the occupier's authority arises from its military presence and strength, rather than a domestic constitutional basis or the consent of the population of the occupied state?

4. *Problems of Application: The Law of Armed Conflict and the Fight Against Terrorists*

The legal status and treatment of those against whom the United States has fought in Afghanistan and elsewhere after September 11, 2001, has generated considerable controversy. Sharp differences have arisen regarding the question of who may be targeted with lethal military force and whether persons detained are entitled to treatment as prisoners of war under the Third Geneva Convention.

Professor Gary Solis, a former Marine judge advocate, addresses in general terms the legal status of various participants in armed conflict.

Gary D. Solis, The Law of Armed Conflict: International Humanitarian Law in War

186-188, 190-191, 202, 205-206 (2010)

[A] foundational question . . . [is] the individual status of those on the battlefield. . . . Individual status determines the rights and protections afforded to a fighter, if captured, as well as the prohibitions that may apply to his/her conduct. . . .

Combatants fall into two categories: members of the armed forces of a party to a conflict. . . . and others who take a direct part in hostilities. The defining distinction of the lawful combatant's status is that upon capture he or she is entitled to the protections of a [prisoner of war, or] POW. . . .

Article 43.2 of 1977 Additional Protocol I defines combatants in common Article 2 [international] conflicts: "Members of the armed forces of a Party to a conflict . . . are combatants, that is to say, they have the right to participate directly in hostilities."

"Combatants may be attacked at any time until they surrender or are otherwise hors de combat, and not only when actually threatening the enemy." A combatant remains a combatant when he/she is not actually fighting. . . .

In a common Article 2 international conflict, captured combatants are entitled to POW status, with its Geneva Convention III rights and protections. . . .

What about common Article 3 non-international conflicts? The traditional view is that, just as there are no POWs in non-international armed conflicts, there are no "combatants," lawful or otherwise, in common Article 3 conflicts. There may be combat in the literal sense, but in terms of [the law of armed conflict] there are fighters, rebels, insurgents, or guerrillas who engage in armed conflict, and there are government forces, and perhaps armed forces allied to the government forces. There are no combatants as that term is used in customary law of war, however. Upon capture such fighters are simply prisoners of the detaining government; they are criminals to be prosecuted for their unlawful acts, either by a military court or under the domestic law of the capturing state. . . .

. . . [As for civilians, under the law of armed conflict, they may not be made the object of military attacks] "unless and for such time as they take direct part in hostilities." Publicists, practitioners, and scholars have debated the meaning of "for such time" and "direct part" since the publication of the [1977 Additional Protocol I.]

Direct participation in hostilities is a concept that applies only to civilians, and the hostilities may be either international or non-international. In an international armed conflict, civilians are "persons who are [not] members of the armed forces of a party to the conflict. . . ."

Continuous combat function is a new term to [the law of armed conflict]. . . . The term and its definition were necessitated by the reinvigoration of terrorism, combined with twenty-first century weaponry. . . .

Although the term "continuous combat function" is not found in the Conventions, the phrase "armed forces" in Geneva Convention common Article 3(1), by clear implication, includes the armed forces of nonstate parties — organized armed groups. The armed forces of the nonstate party . . . "refers exclusively to the armed or military wing of [the] non-state party; its armed forces in a functional sense." Membership in organized armed groups is not evidenced by uniform or ID card, but by function.

> [M]embership must depend on whether the continuous combatant function assumed by the individual corresponds to that exercised by the group as a whole, namely the conduct of hostilities on behalf of a non-State party to the conflict. . . . [T]he decisive criterion for individual membership in an organized group is whether a person assumed a continuous function for the group involving his or her direct participation in hostilities . . . [The notion of] "continuous combat function" . . . requires lasting integration into an organized armed group acting as the armed forces of a non-State party to an armed conflict. . . .

Thus, a civilian's unorganized or occasional hostile act does not constitute membership in an organized armed group or represent a continuous combat function. . . .

. . . [This] clarifies [, however,] that an al Qaeda leader does not regain civilian protection from direct attack merely because he temporarily stores his weapon to visit his family in government-controlled territory. A Taliban fighter who plants improvised antipersonnel mines remains a lawful target when he puts down his tools and walks home for lunch with his family. A senior terrorist insurgent may be targeted when he is asleep. An insurgent commander remains a lawful target whenever he may located and whatever he may be doing.

How do these categories apply to the U.S.-led conflict in Afghanistan? As noted above, the United States determined in February 2002 that the Geneva Conventions applied to the armed conflict in Afghanistan. The administration nevertheless concluded that because Al Qaeda is not a state party to the Geneva Conventions, its members could not be considered POWs under Article 4 of the Third Geneva Convention.

Article 4 of the Convention provides:

> A. Prisoners of war, in the sense of the present Convention, are persons belonging to one of the following categories, who have fallen into the power of the enemy:
>
> 1. Members of the armed forces of a Party to the conflict as well as member of militias or volunteer corps forming part of such armed forces.
>
> 2. Members of other militias and members of other volunteer corps, including those of organized resistance movements, belonging to a Party to the conflict and operating in or outside their own territory, even if this territory is occupied, provided that such militias or volunteers corps, including such organized resistance movements, fulfill the following conditions:
>
> (a) That of being commanded by a person responsible for his subordinates;
>
> (b) That of having a fixed distinctive sign recognizable at a distance;
>
> (c) That of carrying arms openly;
>
> (d) That of conducting their operations in accordance with the laws and customs of war.
>
> 3. Members of regular armed forces who profess allegiance to a government or an authority not recognized by the Detaining Power. . . .

According to a Bush Administration spokesman, neither the Taliban nor Al Qaeda fighters in Afghanistan fell within this definition:

> Under Article 4 of the Geneva Convention . . . Taliban detainees are not entitled to POW status. . . . The Taliban have not effectively distinguished themselves from the civilian population of Afghanistan. Moreover, they have not conducted their operations in accordance with the laws and customs of war. Instead, they have knowingly adopted and provided support to the unlawful terrorist objectives of the al Qaeda.
>
> Al Qaeda is an international terrorist group and cannot be considered a state party to the Geneva Convention. Its members, therefore, are not covered by the Geneva Convention, and are not entitled to POW status under the treaty. [The White House, Statement by the Press Secretary on the Geneva Convention (Feb. 7, 2002).]

Notes and Questions

1. Article 4(A)(1) of the Third Geneva Convention states that "[m]embers of the armed forces of a Party to the conflict" qualify as prisoners of war (POWs). Irregular forces can qualify for POW status under Article 4(A)(2) of that Convention if they meet four conditions. Does the absence of these conditions in the text of Article 4(A)(1) mean that "members of the armed forces" will qualify as POWs even if they do not, for example, wear a fixed distinctive sign? Or does it mean that compliance with the four requirements is inherent in the concept of membership in regular armed forces?

2. Should Taliban fighters captured on the battlefield when the United States was engaged in an international armed conflict with Afghanistan be treated as POWs? What about a member of Al Qaeda captured while fighting against U.S.-led forces? What evidence would you require to help you decide? Would you treat the Taliban fighter differently from the Al Qaeda member, and if so, why?

3. Article 5 of the Third Geneva Convention further provides: "Should any doubt arise as to whether persons, having committed a belligerent act and having fallen into the hands of the enemy, belong to any of the categories enumerated in Article 4, such persons shall enjoy the protection of the present Convention until such time as their status has been determined by a competent tribunal." Is the categorical determination by the Bush Administration that none of the Taliban and Al Qaeda fighters in Afghanistan fell within the terms of Article 4 of the Convention consistent with that requirement? Given the debate surrounding the status of detained Taliban and Al Qaeda members under international law, should the United States have provided them with a competent tribunal to determine their POW status instead of categorically denying them POW status?

4. As noted in Section B.5.f above, some commentators suggest that after the installation of the Karzai-led Interim Government in December 2001, the United States was no longer engaged in an international armed conflict in Afghanistan, but a non-international armed conflict against Al Qaeda terrorists and Taliban insurgents. See, e.g., Allen S. Weiner, Law, Just War, and the International Fight Against Terrorism: Is It War?, in Intervention, Terrorism, and Torture: Contemporary Challenges to Just War Theory 137, 147 (Steven P. Lee ed. 2007). Should Taliban or Al

Qaeda fighters captured in Afghanistan after the new Karzai government assumed authority in Afghanistan be treated as POWs? If those detainees have violated the laws of Afghanistan, would the government of Afghanistan have authority to hold and prosecute them under domestic law? If the conflict in Afghanistan is now a non-international armed conflict, what is the legal basis for the United States to detain them?

In Iraq, the international armed conflict triggered by the 2003 U.S.-led invasion underwent a similar transformation when governing authority was transferred from the Coalition Provisional Authority to Iraqi institutions in 2004. The International Committee for the Red Cross (ICRC) took the view that this changed the legal character of the conflict in Iraq, which ceased to be an international armed conflict. As a result, the ICRC stated that persons who had been detained by U.S.-led forces prior to the transfer of governing authority "should either be released, charged and tried or placed in another legal framework that regulates their continued internment." International Committee of the Red Cross, Iraq Post 28 June 2004: Protecting Persons Deprived of Freedom Remains a Priority (Aug. 5, 2004), available at http://www.icrc.org/eng/resources/documents/misc/63kkj8.htm.

5. The Obama Administration, in a brief submitted in March 2009 in litigation regarding the detention of persons at the Guantanamo Bay, Cuba, asserted:

> The President has the authority to detain persons that the President determines planned, authorized, committed, or aided the terrorist attacks that occurred on September 11, 2001, and persons who harbored those responsible for those attacks. The President also has the authority to detain persons who were part of, or substantially supported, Taliban or al-Qaida forces or associated forces that are engaged in hostilities against the United States or its coalition partners, including any person who has committed a belligerent act, or has directly supported hostilities, in aid of such enemy armed forces. [Respondents' Memorandum Regarding the Government's Detention Authority Relative to Detainees Held At Guantanamo Bay, In re Guantanamo Bay Litigation, No. 08-0442 (D.D.C. 2009), at 2.]

The Memorandum states that the government was basing its detention powers on authority conferred by the AUMF, which was in turn "necessarily informed by principles of the laws of war." Consider the different ways of thinking about the armed conflict against the Taliban discussed in Section B.5.f above. What does the Obama Administration's position on detention say about its legal understanding of the nature of the armed conflict?

6. The Military Commissions Act of 2009, which applies to detainees held at the U.S. Naval Station at Guantanamo, Cuba, provides a regime for prosecution before military commissions of "alien unprivileged enemy belligerent[s]." 10 U.S.C. §948c. Professor Solis describes this concept and its relationship to traditional status categories under the law of armed conflict:

> The terms "unlawful combatant" and "unprivileged belligerent," which describe the same individuals, do not appear in the Geneva Conventions, the Additional Protocols, or any other [law of armed conflict] treaty, convention, or protocol. Nevertheless, "unlawful combatant," a term frequently employed by the United States, is a *de facto* individual status.

> . . . [These terms] are germane only to common Article 2 international armed conflict. . . .
>
> "Unlawful combatant" has been described . . . "as describing all persons taking a direct part in hostilities without being entitled to do so and who therefore cannot be classified as prisoners of war on falling into the power of the enemy." . . .
>
> Recall that there are only two categories of individual on the battlefield: combatants and civilians. Unlawful combatants/unprivileged belligerents are *not* a third battlefield category. . . . [U]nlawful combatants are a subset of "civilian." . . .
>
> Being an unlawful combatant/unprivileged belligerent is not a war crime in itself. Rather, the price of being an unlawful combatant is that he forfeits the immunity of a lawful combatant — the combatant's privilege, and potential POW status — and he may be charged for the [international humanitarian law] violations he committed. . . . Judicial proceedings may be conducted before either military or domestic courts. . . .
>
> Unlawful combatants should not be confused with "unlawful enemy combatants," a purported battlefield status in the war on terrorism. . . .
>
> [With respect to this latter concept,] [t]he Military Commissions Act of 2006 contains a surprisingly broad definition of "unlawful enemy combatant." It includes one "who has purposefully and materially supported hostilities against the United States or its co-belligerents and who is not a lawful enemy combatant."* Under this definition an individual who supports hostilities against an ally of the United States, who has never been in a battlefield or place of hostile activity, may be an unlawful enemy combatant. This "dramatically expands of scope of combatancy." [Solis, The Law of Armed Conflict, supra, at 206-208, 211, 227-228.]

If an Al Qaeda member captured in combat in Afghanistan did not qualify as a POW but was an unlawful or unprivileged belligerent, could he be prosecuted under Afghan or U.S. laws for killing or attempting to kill a U.S. or Afghan soldier? Does it depend on whether the conflict is international or non-international in scope? How does the definition under the Military Commissions Act expand the scope of combatancy? If the scope of combatancy were not expanded, what options would the United States have for dealing with a person who had never been in a battlefield and who materially supported hostilities against the United States?

7. The 2010 speech by State Department Legal Adviser Harold Koh quoted in Section B.5.f above affirms that the United States "is in an armed conflict with al-Qaeda, as well as the Taliban and associated forces, in response to the horrific 9/11 attacks." Would there be negative ramifications from applying laws of war to Al Qaeda's terrorist acts? Professor Michael Scharf argues that one problem with applying the laws of war to terrorism

> is that, under this approach, terrorists can rely on the "combatant's privilege" under which combatants are immune from prosecution for common crimes. For example, killing a combatant is justified homicide, not murder. This means that terrorist attacks on military, police, or other government personnel would not be prosecutable or extraditable offenses. . . . [G]overnment installations are a lawful target of war. Thus terrorist attacks on military, police, or government buildings would not be regarded as

*[The 2009 Military Commissions Act employs the term "unprivileged enemy belligerent" in place of the term "unlawful enemy combatant" used in the 2006 Military Commissions Act. However, the definition of "unprivileged enemy belligerent" in the 2009 Act similarly includes someone (other than a privileged belligerent) who "has purposefully and materially supported hostilities against the United States or its coalition partners." 10U.S.C. §948a(7)(B).–Eds.]

> criminal. And the collateral damage doctrine would apply, such that injury or deaths to civilians would not be regarded as criminal so long as the target was a government installation, and reasonable steps were taken to minimize the risk to innocent civilians. [Michael P. Scharf, Defining Terrorism as the Peace Time Equivalent of War Crimes: A Case of Too Much Convergence Between International Humanitarian Law and International Criminal Law, 7 ILSA J. Int'l & Comp. L. 391, 396 (2001).]

8. At what point, if ever, must enemy combatants detained in the armed conflict against international terrorists be released? Article 118 of the Third Geneva Convention, as noted above, requires that POWs "shall be released and repatriated without delay after the cessation of active hostilities." When will hostilities in Afghanistan cease? In Hamdi v. Rumsfeld, discussed in Chapter 3, the Court in 2004 held that because "the record establishes that United States troops are still involved in active combat in Afghanistan," the United States retained authority to detain enemy combatants captured in Afghanistan. 542 U.S. at 521. Professor John Yoo extends the Court's reasoning; he argues that "[i]f American troops remain engaged in combat in Afghanistan in 2040, the laws of war do not require the United States to release Hamdi or any other Taliban prisoners." John Yoo, Courts at War, 91 Cornell L. Rev. 573, 583 (2006). Do you agree? Does it matter if the legal character of the armed conflict in Afghanistan has changed, as is discussed in Note 4 above? If so, is the United States still a party to an international armed conflict under which it is justified to detain enemy combatants?

5. *International Humanitarian Law and Human Rights Law*

The legal complexities of using force against terrorist groups highlight questions about the interaction between international humanitarian law and international human rights law. It is widely accepted that human rights principles have an important role to play, not only during peacetime, but also with respect to the treatment of detainees and other noncombatants in wartime, as well.

> It is well recognized that the international human rights commitments of states apply at all times, whether in times of peace or situations of armed conflict, to all persons subject to a state's authority and control. The [ICJ] has stated . . . that "the protection of the International Covenant on Civil and Political Rights does not cease in times of war, except by operation of Article 4 of the Covenant whereby certain provisions may be derogated from in a time of national emergency." International humanitarian law, on the other hand, generally does not apply in peacetime and its fundamental purpose is to place restraints on the conduct of warfare in order to diminish the effects of hostilities. . . . Consequently, in situations of armed conflict, both international human rights law and international humanitarian law apply concurrently, and a state that is a party to the conflict must afford the fundamental protections under these regimes of law to persons falling within its power. . . . [Robert K. Goldman & Brian D. Tittemore, Unprivileged Combatants and the Hostilities in Afghanistan: Their Status and Rights Under International Humanitarian and Human Rights Law 33, 39-40 (ASIL publication, 2002).]

Even if human rights principles apply in times of armed conflict, however, the precise boundaries between particular rules of international humanitarian law and international human rights law remain unclear. In its Advisory Opinion on the Legal Consequences of the Construction of a Wall in the Occupied Palestinian Territory, the International Court of Justice affirmed that "the protection offered by human rights conventions does not cease in case of armed conflict . . ." 2004 I.C.J. 136, 178 (July 9). Notwithstanding this general observation, however, the Court noted:

> As regards the relationship between international humanitarian law and human rights law, there are thus three possible situations: some rights may be exclusively matters of international humanitarian law; others may be exclusively matters of human rights law; yet others may be matters of both these branches of international law. [Id.]

One commentator who studied the ICJ's Advisory Opinion on the Legality of the Threat or Use of Nuclear Weapons, 1996 I.C.J. 226 (July 8), an earlier opinion in which the Court also examined the relationship between international human rights and international humanitarian law, finds that the Court's conclusions in that case

> underline the important point that [human rights] rules developed for peacetime circumstances cannot be applied in an unqualified manner to the conduct of armed conflict. Rather, they must be integrated in a sensible way into the structure of the law of armed conflict, which recognizes that intentional destruction of life and property is a necessary aspect of the conduct of hostilities, and that collateral damage and injury—even to noncombatants, civilian property, and the natural environment—are an inevitable (though regrettable) consequence. [Michael J. Matheson, The Opinions of the International Court of Justice on the Threat or Use of Nuclear Weapons, 91 Am. J. Int'l L. 417, 423 (1997).]

Not all observers agree with the notion that international human rights and international humanitarian law principles should be "assimilated" in times of armed conflict. They argue that even though both bodies of law seek to regulate and restrain state violence, there are fundamental differences that that militate against attempting to apply human rights norms along with the law of armed conflict during times of war:

> The [law of armed conflict, or] LOAC and [international human rights law, or] IHRL differ essentially in the nature of the considerations that they recognize as counterweights to the interest in restricting state violence. As a general matter, the LOAC represents an effort to achieve a realistic and sustainable balance between the countervailing imperatives of "military necessity" and the humanitarian imperatives of avoiding or mitigating the hardships, suffering, and death caused by armed conflict. By contrast, IHRL seeks to equilibrate the state's need to provide security against crime, maintain public order, and administer legal justice to the individual's interests in life, liberty, and property . . .
>
> . . . The conditions of armed conflict—especially, of course, when the life of the nation is at stake—permit and indeed require the state to practice violence on a scale, of a lethality, and with an intentionality that make it wholly different from the violence that the state may inflict when performing its common policing functions. The failure to acknowledge this fact condemns to futility the project of assimilating the LOAC into IHRL. [Robert J. Delahunty & John C. Yoo, What is the Role of International Human Rights Law in the War on Terror?, 59 DePaul L. Rev. 803, 846 (2010).]

Notes and Questions

1. As noted in Chapter 3, the Supreme Court in *Hamdan* concluded that the conflict with Al Qaeda constituted a non-international armed conflict within the meaning of Common Article 3 of the Geneva Conventions. The international humanitarian law rules in Common Article 3, however, are more limited those that apply during international armed conflict. One commentator observes that although international humanitarian law rules are to "an ever greater degree . . . making their way into common Article 3 conflicts," it is still the case that "[g]enerally speaking . . . the domestic law of the state involved, along with common Article 3 [itself], and human rights law, apply in non-international armed conflicts." Solis, The Law of Armed Conflict, supra, at 154. What are the implications for the relationship between international humanitarian law and international human rights law? Does international humanitarian law provide a basis for detention of opposing fighters in a non-international armed conflict, or should that be governed by domestic law and international human rights?

2. Does international humanitarian law provide adequate protection for persons detained as combatants in Afghanistan or elsewhere as combatants in an armed conflict against Al Qaeda, the Taliban, and associated forces? Can such persons be detained indefinitely, even if they are not convicted of committing any crimes? As of December 2010, there were 174 Taliban and Al Qaeda detainees still being held at Guantanamo Bay. Only approximately 25 have had charges filed against them, and only 5 have been convicted of any offenses. Does such lengthy detention without trial violate international law? Should human rights principles be applied in such cases to supplement the protections of international humanitarian law?

3. What protections would a detained Al Qaeda member have who had no relationship to the hostilities in Afghanistan? Could detained Al Qaeda members who have no relationship to the hostilities in Afghanistan be detained indefinitely without a hearing under law of armed conflict principles? Or are such persons covered by international human rights norms, including a prohibition on detention without charge?

4. The implications of the legal status of terrorist actors go beyond questions of detention. Could Al Qaeda members who have no relationship to the hostilities in Afghanistan be targeted for killing by the United States? In early 2010, press accounts indicated that the United States had authorized the targeted killing of Anwar al-Awlaki, a U.S. citizen linked to Al Qaeda who was accused of involvement in the 2009 fatal shootings of 13 people by a U.S. soldier at Fort Hood, Texas, and a foiled plot to detonate a bomb aboard a flight bound for Detroit on Christmas day 2009. Al-Awlaki was reported to be in Yemen at the time. (A lawsuit brought by al-Awlaki's father in federal court seeking to enjoin the intentional killing of his son was dismissed on standing and nonjusticiability grounds in December 2010.) Would such a killing be lawful? If an international conflict exists between the United States and Al Qaeda, is there any region outside the scope of the armed conflict?

5. Is domestic criminal law the most appropriate way to deal with Al Qaeda members and other terrorists? According to press accounts, between 2001 and 2010, U.S. federal courts have issued more than 200 terrorism convictions and sentences. At the same time, prosecutions in federal court present challenges. In the first

criminal prosecution in federal court of a person who had been detained at Guantanamo as an enemy combatant, Ahmed Khalfan Ghailani was charged with playing a key logistical role in the 1998 bombing of the U.S. Embassy in Tanzania. In November 2010, he was acquitted of all but one of the more than 280 charges of conspiracy and murder brought against him. He was convicted of a single count of conspiracy to destroy government buildings and property. Highlighting concerns about the impact of the due process protections that apply in criminal cases, the trial judge barred the testimony of an important prosecution witness because the government had learned about him in an interrogation during which Ghailani was allegedly tortured. Benjamin Weiser, Detainee Acquitted on Most Counts in '98 Bombings, N.Y. Times, Nov. 18, 2010, at A1. Prior to his trial in New York, Mr. Ghailani had been detained as an enemy combatant.

E. U.S. DOMESTIC LAW REGARDING THE USE OF FORCE

There are a host of U.S. treaties, laws, and regulations that affect the use of force. After the introduction, this section considers briefly one — the War Powers Resolution — which attempts to impose some limits on the President's authority to deploy U.S. armed forces abroad in certain situations.

To begin, though, we should note some of the other, often noncontroversial, laws in order to provide a sense of the complex system that exists. First, there are laws that limit the export and sales of weapons abroad. Such activities are covered by the Arms Export Control Act, the Atomic Energy Act of 1948 (as amended by the Nuclear Non-Proliferation Act of 1978), and the Export Administration Act (EAA) (though it lapsed in 2001 because of congressional deadlocks, and the President has since then resorted to the International Emergency Economic Powers Act to maintain the EAA's regulations). These laws effectively authorize the President to stop any and all arms exports unless he approves them. (As with other exports, the President often gives general approval for most sales to friendly countries, but requires specific approval by the Executive Branch for exports to certain countries or for sales of sensitive items.) Depending on the situation, Congress requires that the President must report to it in advance or within a certain period of time after approving certain arms sales, such as arms exports to countries that support terrorism or major arms sales to the Middle East.

Second, there are laws and executive orders limiting covert actions abroad by the U.S. government. "Covert action" can be roughly defined as an activity by an intelligence agency that is other than for the collection of intelligence. As a result, covert activities can range from secretly contributing to the election campaign of a political party in a foreign country, to bribing a foreign cabinet officer to influence his or her country's policies, to attempting to blow up a terrorist base clandestinely. Although covert actions are usually conducted by the Central Intelligence Agency and not the Department of Defense, they sometimes involve the use of force. An existing executive order, however, provides that "[n]o person employed by or acting on behalf of the United States Government shall engage in, or conspire to engage in, assassination." (Exec. Order No. 12,333 (1981), reprinted in 50 U.S.C.A. §401.) One important set of laws are those requiring the President to notify certain committees or members of Congress of covert actions.

There is also a wide panoply of laws and international agreements that regulate the type, number, and location of U.S. military forces in peacetime. Congress regularly passes legislation setting ceilings on the number of military personnel, with some limits regarding the foreign deployment of these forces. Some of these limits on forces are based on international agreements entered into with Russia or with several countries—for example, limits on nuclear arms and biological weapons. Some of these agreements will be considered in Section F below on nonproliferation.

There are also treaties, laws, and regulations limiting the actual conduct of U.S. forces when hostilities occur. Most publicized is the War Powers Resolution of 1973 (discussed below), which governs the roles of the President and the Congress in determining when the United States may resort to the use of force. In addition, the military services have their own rules regarding the conduct of war, which are often based on the international humanitarian law treaties and customary international law discussed in the preceding section.

The War Powers Resolution

The U.S. Constitution gives both Congress and the President important powers in foreign affairs and, more specifically, in the use of military force. Article I, Section 8, gives Congress numerous war-related powers, including the power to "declare War, grant Letters of Marque and Reprisal, and make Rules concerning Captures on Land and Water." Congress also is given important general powers, such as the power of the purse.

On the other hand, Article II of the Constitution makes the President the "Commander in Chief" and gives him the authority to make treaties, provided two-thirds of the Senate present concur. The Constitution also empowers him to nominate and appoint Ambassadors, with the advice and consent of a Senate majority. Article II also states that "[t]he executive Power" is vested in the President. The result is a less-than-clear allocation of powers between the President and Congress on many foreign policy matters, including the use of the military.

Since the adoption of the Constitution, the relative roles that the President and Congress have played in foreign affairs have evolved and varied over time, with a trend generally toward an increased role for the President.

By the early 1970s, the President's growing predominance in foreign policy began to trouble many people in Congress and elsewhere. American foreign policy had usually been "achieved by a zealous patriotic rallying behind the Presidential colors" during the 30 years after World War II. (Thomas M. Franck & Edward Weisband, Foreign Policy by Congress 3 (1979).)

The Watergate mess and growing opposition to the war in Vietnam contributed to the Presidency coming under heavy fire. During 1972 to 1977, there was a renaissance of congressional influence in the making of U.S. foreign policy. The War Powers Resolution of 1973, discussed below, was one of the first major achievements during this period. Also, congressional oversight was increased over foreign assistance (on such issues as human rights), arms sales, the making of executive agreements, and the conduct of CIA operations. Included in this congressional activity was the passage of the National Emergencies Act of 1976 and the International

Emergency Economic Powers Act (IEEPA) in 1977. (See Chapter 3.B.3 regarding emergency powers.)

The War Powers Resolution is one of the most misunderstood and maligned statutes that Congress has passed in recent decades. Briefly, the War Powers Resolution provides that the President "in every possible instance shall consult with Congress before introducing United States Armed Forces into hostilities, or into situations where imminent involvement in hostilities is clearly indicated by the circumstances." War Powers Resolution §3, 50 U.S.C.A. §1542. Moreover, in the absence of a declaration of war, in cases where the U.S. forces are introduced in specified circumstances (e.g., hostilities or imminent involvement in hostilities), the President shall report to Congress within 48 hours and regularly thereafter. Id. §4(a), 50 U.S.C.A. §1543(a). Within 60 calendar days after the 48-hour report is required to be submitted, the President should terminate any use of the U.S. armed forces in the situation requiring the report unless Congress has declared war, has enacted a specific authorization for this use, has extended the 60-day period by law, or is physically unable to meet because of an armed attack on the United States. The President can extend the initial 60-day period for another 30 days if he certifies to Congress that unavoidable military necessity requires the continued use of these forces in the course of removing them from the situation. Id. §5(b), 50 U.S.C.A. §1544(b).

The Resolution includes an early consultation and reporting requirement. However, as some observers have put it, the Resolution gives the President a "free" or unrestricted 60- or 90-day war before he needs any congressional approval. Moreover, once U.S. troops are engaged in combat or imminent danger thereof, how likely is it that Congress will not give the President the authority to continue the fight?

The statute is short. (The text is in the Documentary Supplement.) Except for the addition of section 1546a and minor procedural changes (none of which is of central importance), the law has not been amended since 1973.

The Resolution was passed over the veto of President Nixon who challenged, among other matters, the constitutionality of some of its provisions. No President since Nixon has supported the law's constitutionality, but many constitutional law scholars believe that its major provisions are constitutional, and no U.S. court has ruled otherwise. At least as important is the experience under the statute.

In practice, particularly in recent years, the Resolution has meant that the congressional leadership is consulted before U.S. forces are sent into hostilities, though such consultation often occurred even before the Resolution's enactment. In several cases, however, where the U.S. military was sent into hostilities or exposed to the imminent threat of hostilities, Presidents have not reported as required under section 4(a) or they have failed to specify that the report is a section 4(a) report, thus avoiding the start of the 60-day clock. Moreover, even when they do report, Presidents do not say that it is "pursuant to" the Resolution, but only "consistent with" it.

In some of the most recent situations where the Resolution might be applicable, Presidents have sought approval from Congress for major uses of force through joint resolutions requiring a majority vote of both the House and Senate and the signature of the President. (By their wording, these resolutions are not declarations of war. The last U.S. declaration of war was after the Japanese attack on Pearl Harbor in 1941.) This alternative approach is probably to avoid disputes over the Resolution, as well as to marshal broad-based support before sending U.S. forces into dangerous and potentially disastrous situations. President George H.W. Bush, for example, obtained such a resolution in 1991 before Operation Desert Storm.

Congress also passed resolutions authorizing the major uses of force launched against Afghanistan in 2001 and against Iraq in 2003. (Both resolutions are in the Documentary Supplement.) In each case, Congress expressly declared that the resolution, passed before military action commenced, constituted specific statutory authorization within the meaning of the War Powers Resolution. President Clinton, however, did not seek such a resolution before the U.S. and NATO forces began bombing the Federal Republic of Yugoslavia over the Kosovo crisis in 1999.

Thomas M. Franck, Rethinking War Powers: By Law or by "Thaumaturgic Invocation"?*

83 Am. J. Int'l L. 766, 770 (1989)

The case for reform does not rest solely on the merit of the constitutional balance among the branches which the Act tried, but failed, to ensure. One undesired and undesirable side effect of the War Powers Resolution, as it has evolved in practice, is that it has enveloped foreign policy in a miasma of legalities. It has transformed argument about the political wisdom of being involved in military encounters — in the Gulf of Tonkin, or the Persian Gulf, or the Gulf of Sidra — into an arcane debate about the legality and constitutionality of various foreign policy initiatives. This change in emphasis impoverishes the marketplace of ideas and shrinks the dimensions of public comprehension and participation. It simply leaves most Americans bewildered and disaffected.

The purpose of the Resolution was to encourage serious dialogue on war/peace issues between the branches of government, and between the Government and the public. In any reform of the War Powers Resolution, that objective must be restored as its centerpiece. This does not mean that the legal and constitutional separation of powers issues do not matter. They most certainly do. But the effect of the Resolution on the public life of our nation should be to resolve the constitutional issues with sufficient simplicity, clarity and certainty to permit concentration on the policy debate about the wisdom or folly of any particular engagement of the armed forces. Only if the law can make clear what is legal can the political process concentrate on what is wise.

Notes and Questions

1. Does the War Powers Resolution require congressional approval in advance for the President to send U.S. military forces into combat abroad? Could the President invade Iraq or Iran without advance approval?

2. What does the Resolution tell the President to do in advance? In every case? How much consultation is required? (The relevant provisions are in section 3 of the

*["Thaumaturgy" is the "supposed working of miracles; magic." Webster's New World Dictionary (3d ed. 1986).–Eds.]

War Powers Resolution, codified at 50 U.S.C.A. §1542.) What if some congressional leaders tell the President that his plans are a dumb and dangerous idea? Can the President still proceed? What might be the benefits of consultation?

3. The Resolution requires the President to report to Congress within 48 hours in "the absence of a declaration of war, in any case in which United States Armed Forces are introduced" into any of three situations. Compare the three situations. Which appears to be the most dangerous?

4. When does the Resolution require Congress to take action within 60 days (or 90 days in some cases)? In all three situations under section 4 (§1543)? (A time limit on actions, such as the 60-day one here, is sometimes referred to as a "sunset" provision.)

5. Where a report was required under section 4(a)(1) (§1543(a)(1)) and the President has sent it to Congress, can the U.S. combat forces remain in a situation for 60 (or possibly 90 days) without any action by Congress? Does the Resolution give the President a "free" 60- or 90-day war without requiring any congressional authorization? What exactly does the Resolution prevent the President from doing?

6. The "Authorization for Use of Military Force" resolution adopted on September 18, just one week after the September 11 attacks, provided that:

> the President is authorized to use all necessary and appropriate force against those nations, organizations, or persons he determines planned, authorized, committed, or aided the terrorist attacks that occurred on September 11, 2001, or harbored such organizations or persons, in order to prevent future acts of international terrorism against the United States by such nations, organizations or persons. [Pub. L. 107-40 (2001).]

A participant in the negotiations that produced the resolution recounts that White House negotiators originally proposed language that would have authorized the President to use force not only against the "nations, organizations, or persons" involved in the September 11 attacks, but also to use force "to deter and preempt any future acts of terrorism or aggression against the United States." Congressional reaction to the White House proposal "was immediately negative."

> [H]ad this authority become law, it would have authorized the President to use force not only against the perpetrators of the September 11 attacks, but also against (at least arguably) anyone who might be considering future acts of terrorism, as well as against any nation that was planning "aggression" against the United States. Given the breadth of activities potentially encompassed by the term "aggression," the President might never again have to seek congressional authorization for the use of force to combat terrorism. [David Abramowitz, The President, the Congress, and Use of Force: Legal and Political Considerations in Authorizing Use of Force Against International Terrorism, 43 Harv. Int'l L.J. 71, 73 (2002).]

7. What if the President does not file a report under section 4 even though U.S. armed forces have been deployed in, say, the Persian Gulf and firefights have quickly occurred between U.S. naval units and Iranian naval units. Does the 60-day period still begin to run? Who determines that the period has begun to run, and from what date? Is this clear in the Resolution?

8. Is it likely that a U.S. court will rule that the 60- (or 90-) day period has begun to run? Why not? What circumstances might be required?

9. So far, no court has upheld a challenge under the War Powers Resolution. Rather, these challenges have all been dismissed under limiting doctrines such as standing, ripeness, equitable discretion, and the political question doctrine. For example, see Doe v. Bush, 323 F.3d 133 (1st Cir. 2003) (dismissing challenge to planned invasion of Iraq on ripeness grounds); Campbell v. Clinton, 203 F.3d 19 (D.D.C. 2000) (lack of standing in suit over U.S. bombing campaign over Kosovo); Ange v. Bush, 752 F. Supp. 509 (D.D.C. 1990) (dismissing challenge to first Gulf War on political question, equitable discretion, and ripeness grounds).

10. Section 5(c) (§1544(c)) provides that Congress can direct the President by a concurrent resolution to remove U.S. armed forces from situations where they are engaged in hostilities abroad. (A concurrent resolution can be passed by a majority vote of the House and Senate, and it does not need the signature of the President.) When the War Powers Resolution was passed, this concurrent resolution provision had been viewed as an important limit on the President's power, in addition to the 60-day limit in certain situations. However, it is likely that this "legislative veto" provision is now void under the Supreme Court's ruling in Immigration and Naturalization Service v. Chadha, 462 U.S. 919 (1983), and other cases.

11. Congress can also seek to compel the removal of U.S. forces from combat by prohibiting the expenditure of funds necessary for them to carry out their activities. After the 1973 cease-fire agreement between the United States and North Vietnam, Congress enacted legislation providing that no congressionally appropriated funds could be expended "to finance directly or indirectly combat activities by United States military forces in or over or from off the shores of North Vietnam, South Vietnam, Laos or Cambodia." Pub. L. 93-52, §108 (1973). Congress also imposed financial restrictions on military operations in Somalia after 18 U.S. servicemen were killed in October 1993 during the "Battle of Mogadishu" between U.S. troops and forces loyal to Somali warlord Mohamed Farrah Aidid. Legislation adopted shortly thereafter imposed limits on the purposes for which funds could be used by U.S. Armed Forces in Somalia after March 31, 1994. Pub. L. 103-139, §8151(b)(2)(B). In addition, a defense appropriations bill enacted in September 1994 provided that none of the funds provided for under that act could be used for a "continuous presence" of U.S. military personnel in Somalia, except for the protection of U.S. personnel.

12. A distinguished commission of experts chaired by former Secretaries of State James A. Baker III and Warren Christopher in 2008 conducted a study of the War Powers Resolution and unanimously recommended replacing it with a new War Powers Consultation Act. The report suggested that there is "broad consensus . . . that the War Powers Resolution of 1973 does not provide a solution because it is at least in part unconstitutional and in any event has not worked as intended." The report suggested that there is nevertheless consensus about the importance of, and broad public support for, "getting the President and Congress to consult meaningfully and deliberate before committing the nation to war." National War Powers Commission Report, Miller Center of Public Affairs 6-7 (2008). The report described how the proposed new War Powers Consultation Act would operate:

> The stated purpose of the Act is to codify the norm of consultation and "describe a constructive and practical way in which the judgment of both the President and

> Congress can be brought to bear when deciding whether the United States should engage in significant armed conflict."
>
> The Act requires such consultation before Congress declares or authorizes war or the country engages in combat operations lasting, or expected to last, more than one week ("significant armed conflict"). There is an "exigent circumstances" carve-out that allows for consultation within three days after the beginning of combat operations. In cases of lesser conflicts — *e.g.*, limited actions to defend U.S. embassies abroad, reprisals against terrorist groups, and covert operations — such advance consultation is not required, but is strongly encouraged.
>
> Under the Act, once Congress has been consulted regarding a significant armed conflict, it too has obligations. Unless it declares war or otherwise expressly authorizes the conflict, it must hold a vote on a concurrent resolution within 30 days calling for its approval. If the concurrent resolution is approved, there can be little question that both the President and Congress have endorsed the new armed conflict. In an effort to avoid or mitigate the divisiveness that commonly occurs in the time it takes to execute the military campaign, the Act imposes an ongoing duty on the President and Congress regularly to consult for the duration of the conflict that has been approved.
>
> If, instead, the concurrent resolution of approval is defeated in either House, any member of Congress may propose a joint resolution of disapproval . . . If such a resolution of disapproval is passed, Congress has several options. If both Houses of Congress ratify the joint resolution of disapproval and the President signs it or Congress overrides his veto, the joint resolution of disapproval will have the force of law. If Congress cannot muster the votes to overcome a veto, it may take lesser measures. Relying on its inherent rule making powers, Congress may make internal rules providing, for example, that any bill appropriating new funds for all or part of the armed conflict would be out of order. [Id. at 8-9.]

Do you think the War Powers Consultation Act would be an improvement over the War Powers Resolution? Would it address Professor Franck's criticism that the existing War Powers Resolution privileges a "miasma of legalities" over a serious "policy debate about the wisdom or folly of any particular engagement of the armed forces"?

F. COMBATING THE PROLIFERATION OF WEAPONS OF MASS DESTRUCTION

The world has witnessed a long and mixed history of efforts designed to limit and even eliminate weapons. These endeavors have become even more important in the post-September 11 world. Some of the past emphasis has shifted from bilateral agreements between the United States and Russia or other countries to multilateral arrangements designed to include large numbers of states. The frequent goal is to combat the proliferation of weapons of mass destruction — nuclear, chemical, and biological weapons — and their delivery systems (WMD).

1. A Brief History and the Present Threat

Attempts at arms control are in part an outgrowth of earlier efforts to develop rules of war. A number of treaties have sought to prohibit the use of particularly inhumane weapons in war. Other efforts at arms control have attempted to regulate not only the use of weapons, but their possession as well. For example, the Washington Treaty of 1922 and the London Naval Treaty of 1930 included limitations on the number and type of naval ships that the participating countries were allowed, many of the limitations expressed in terms of ratios among the major countries. The London Treaty led to the destruction of several large naval ships that were under construction, including U.S. ships. Observance of these treaties was mixed. For example, Japan denounced them in 1934 and embarked on a major shipbuilding program, and the treaties became a dead letter by the eve of World War II.

A particularly worrying threat now to U.S. and international security comes from the possible use of weapons of mass destruction. Although the threat of nuclear attack from the former Soviet Union has diminished with the end of the Cold War, nuclear, chemical, and biological weapons are increasingly available to hostile states, terrorist groups, and even criminal organizations. The potential acquisition of WMD materials and technologies is more likely now than at any other time in history.

First, following the dissolution of the former Soviet Union and the resulting economic and political turmoil in the successor states, there have been more opportunities for groups or individuals to traffic in nuclear weapons, components, and technology (sometimes referred to as the "loose nukes" problem). Second, more and more countries have developed their own nuclear and other WMD programs in recent years — for example, India, Pakistan, North Korea, and Iran. Some of these countries face continuing friction with their neighbors, notably India and Pakistan over Kashmir, that could lead to pressure to use weapons of mass destruction.

Third, the increasing diffusion of modern technology through the growth of the world trade and the information revolution make it harder to detect illicit diversions of materials and technologies relevant to building WMD programs. For example, many of the technologies and components associated with chemical and biological weapons programs also have legitimate commercial applications unrelated to creating WMD, with some items being called "dual use" because they have the potential for both peaceful and dangerous uses. The 1995 chemical weapons attack by the Aum Shinrikyo cult in Japan demonstrated that the use of WMD was no longer restricted to sovereign states in the battlefield and revealed the ease of manufacturing chemical agents from legally supplied, commercial dual-use technology. The sect manufactured sarin gas and released it on the Tokyo subway, killing 12 people and injuring over 5,000.

Further, information gathered after the September 11, 2001, terrorist attacks against the United States indicate that Al Qaeda has pursued a long-term strategy of attempting to develop weapons of mass destruction, including biological weapons and an improvised nuclear device, capable of causing major attacks against civilians. And, as discussed below, North Korea's withdrawal from the Nuclear Nonproliferation Treaty in January 2003, its development of nuclear weapons, and its apparently unbridled willingness to obtain much-needed funds from exports of dangerous goods, underscore the growing threats posed by weapons of mass destruction. Iran's nuclear program, which many countries believe is aimed at producing nuclear weapons, presents a great threat to regional stability in the Middle East, particularly given Iran's ongoing development of missile delivery systems.

2. *Chemical and Biological Weapons*

The anthrax attacks in the United States in October 2001, the earlier Japanese cult attacks in Tokyo in 1995, and the horrific use of chemical weapons by Saddam Hussein against Iranians and against his own Kurdish population during the 1980s highlight the need for limiting, if not eliminating, chemical and biological weapons. For both types of weapons, there are treaties as well as a cooperative international export control regime.

Three main multilateral treaties exist for banning the use of chemical and biological weapons. The Geneva Protocol of 1925 was the first important multilateral agreement regarding chemical and biological weapons. It explicitly bans the use in international armed conflicts of "asphyxiating, poisonous or other gases" and "bacteriological methods of warfare." However, it does not ban the possession of these chemical weapons, nor does it contain limits on their production or deployment. Several parties to the Protocol, including the United Kingdom and France, have reserved the right to retaliate in kind if chemical or biological weapons are first used against them, thus rendering the Protocol essentially only a no-first-use agreement for these states.

The second multilateral agreement in effect is the Biological and Toxins* Weapons Convention (BWC) of 1972. Unlike the Geneva Protocol, this agreement applies solely to biological weapons, which in general are those produced by use of living organisms. Parties to the Biological Weapons Convention have agreed not to develop, produce, stockpile, or acquire biological agents or toxins "of types and in quantities that have no justification for prophylactic, protective, and other peaceful purposes." All such existing weapons were to be destroyed within nine months of the Convention's entry into force. The Convention contains no inspection or verification provisions. Instead, the parties are to "consult and cooperate" in solving any problems that arise. As of February 2011, there were 163 parties to the BWC.

The third and most recent multilateral agreement in the area of biological and chemical weapons is the Chemical Weapons Convention (CWC). The Convention came into force in 1997. The CWC forbids all parties from developing, producing, stockpiling, or using chemical weapons, and requires all member nations to destroy any existing chemical weapons by April 2007, ten years after the Convention entered into force. All declared chemical weapons productions facilities have been inactivated. Both the United States and Russia indicated, however, that were unable to complete the destruction of their existing chemical weapons stockpiles by April 2007 and sought extensions. Although Russia's leaders appeared committed to abolishing the weapons, bureaucratic resistance and shortage of funds meant that the Russian program for destroying chemical weapons was moving slowly. By December 2009, Russia had destroyed slightly less than half of its stockpile of 40,000 metric tons of chemical agents. Russia has depended heavily on international financial assistance to carry out chemical weapons destruction. In the United States, environmental and other regulatory hurdles have slowed destruction activities, as well; as of January 2010, 80 percent of the U.S. chemical weapons stockpile of 28,000 tons had been destroyed.

*Toxins are substances that, in rough terms, fall between biologicals and chemicals because they act like chemicals but are ordinarily produced by biological or microbic processes.

Like the BWC, the CWC parties must adopt measures to ensure that toxic chemicals and their precursors are only used for purposes not prohibited by the Convention. However, unlike the BWC, the CWC has detailed provisions for verifying compliance, including the creation of an international organization, the Organization for the Prohibition of Chemical Weapons (OPCW). Verification procedures include both routine visits from international teams of inspectors and "challenge inspections," which may be requested by a member nation if it believes another state is not complying with the terms of the Convention. Since 1997, the OPCW has conduct 4,167 inspections at 195 chemical weapon-related and 1,103 industrial sites on the territory of 81 countries.

As of February 2011, there were 188 parties to the CWC, but this did not include some countries that probably have active programs or stockpiled chemical weapons such as Egypt, Israel, North Korea, and Syria.

Notes and Questions

1. Although the parties to the BWC have sought to enhance transparency through voluntary data exchanges, the Convention's gap on inspection and verification remains a matter of concern. Efforts to create a verification protocol modeled loosely on that of the Chemical Weapons Convention collapsed in 2001 when the United States announced its opposition to the protocol. The United States claimed that the draft protocol, which would have provided for inspections of facilities engaged in treaty-related activities, would not have prevented states from pursuing covert biological weapons programs and could have resulted in compromise of commercial trade secrets of U.S. firms. Similar objections could have been raised about the inspection and verification regime in the Chemical Weapons Convention, which the United States ratified in 1997. But in the case of efforts to regulate chemical weapons, the U.S. chemical industry was supportive of ratification of the CWC. Can you identify any other factors that might explain why the United States has taken a different stance towards the biological weapons inspection regime? Might it reflect the different U.S. Administrations that made the decisions?

2. The BWC precludes states from producing or retaining biological agents or toxins "of types and in quantities that have no justification for prophylactic, protective, and other peaceful purposes." Could a state defend its development of new biological weapons on the basis of a need to develop defenses to such weapons that other states might be developing? Is it possible to distinguish between offensive and defensive biological weapons research activities?

3. Nuclear Arms Control

The capability of nuclear weapons to wipe out whole societies has consistently stimulated efforts to reduce the risk of nuclear war. Since the end of the cold war and the breakup of the Soviet Union, negotiators have endeavored to reduce the number of existing weapons, ensure responsible control over the remaining weapons, and prevent the production of new weapons. Other efforts have focused on preventing additional states from acquiring nuclear weapons capability (nuclear proliferation).

What follows is a description of some of the most important nuclear arms agreements—the test ban treaties, U.S-Soviet/Russian agreements, and the Nonproliferation Treaty. This is followed by a section on the North Korean and Iranian nuclear proliferation crises.

a. The Test Ban Treaties

The first nuclear weapons test was in 1945 at Alamogordo, New Mexico. After the end of World War II, the United States resumed its testing and the Soviet Union conducted its first weapons test in 1949. Both countries continued to make major improvements in their weapons and continued testing. There were fitful efforts to reach a test ban moratorium and then an actual moratorium in the late 1950s, but the moratorium had failed by 1961. By this time both Great Britain and France had arrived on the scene as nuclear powers, and France's first nuclear tests in 1960 and 1961 were one of the reasons that the Soviet Union gave to resume testing in 1961.

With the encouragement of President Kennedy, relatively rapid negotiations among the United States, Great Britain, and the Soviet Union led to the Limited Test Ban Treaty (LTBT) in the summer of 1963. The LTBT banned all nuclear explosions except for underground tests. The three original signatories plus over 120 other states are now parties to the LTBT.

France refused to sign the Treaty but did stop atmospheric testing in 1974. China also refused to sign, conducting its first atmospheric test in 1964, although it has since stopped atmospheric testing. India and Pakistan are parties to the LTBT. They conducted testing of their nuclear explosive devices underground.

Although the LTBT ended the severe environmental problems that arose as a result of atmospheric testing, underground testing continued at a significant pace after 1963. Two additional treaties concluded by the United States and Soviet Union, the Threshold Test Ban Treaty (TTBT) of 1974 and the Peaceful Nuclear Explosion Treaty (PNET) of 1976, together serve to reduce the size of underground nuclear tests, placing a limit of 150 kilotons on such tests. (The bomb that the United States dropped with devastating effects on Hiroshima in 1945 was approximately 13-15 kilotons, so the TTBT would allow tests up to ten times the size of that bomb. Nevertheless, the 150-kiloton limit is still much smaller than some of the weapons of 1,000 kilotons and more in the U.S. and Russian arsenals.)

Active negotiations for a comprehensive test ban treaty (CTBT), which included strong support from the United States, began at the United Nations Conference on Disarmament (CD) in Geneva in January 1994. In September 1996, the CTBT was drafted and opened for signature. Also in 1996, a preparatory commission for the CTBT Organization was established to set up a verification regime, including the International Monitoring System, International Data Center, and capabilities for conducting on-site inspections. By October 2010, 153 countries had ratified the treaty. However, the treaty will not enter into force until all 44 "nuclear-capable" states specified in Annex 2 to the instrument have ratified it. As of February 2011, 35 of these states have ratified the treaty, but several Annex 2 countries, including China, Egypt, India, Iran, Israel, Pakistan, North Korea, and the United States have yet to ratify the treaty. President Clinton submitted the CTBT to the U.S. Senate for its advice and consent, but the Senate dealt a severe blow to the near-term prospects for U.S. ratification when it refused by a 48-51 negative vote to provide its advice and consent in October 1999. No progress on U.S. ratification has been made since then.

Even though the CTBT has not entered into force, the five recognized nuclear weapons states under the Nuclear Nonproliferation Treaty (discussed below) have adhered to a voluntary moratorium on nuclear testing since 1996, when China detonated a nuclear device. India and Pakistan announced their own voluntary moratoria on nuclear testing in 1998, after each had tested nuclear devices. Since 2002, however, the U.S. Government has expended funds on a "test readiness program" to reduce the amount of time after a decision to test a nuclear device that would be required to actually carry out the test. Nevertheless, the United States has continued to adhere to the testing moratorium.

Notes and Questions

1. Recall the obligation under Article 18 of the Vienna Convention on the Law of Treaties, discussed in Chapter 2.A.1, for a state that has signed, but not yet ratified, a treaty to refrain from acts that would defeat the object and purpose of the treaty. Would a decision by the United States, which has signed but not ratified the Comprehensive Test Ban Treaty, to test a nuclear device defeat the object and purpose of the treaty?

2. In its current form, the CTBT requires all 44 "nuclear-capable" parties to ratify the agreement before it can enter into force. Does that make sense? Should the parties consider revising the agreement so that it can enter into force even if a few nuclear-capable states, such as the United States, decline to become parties to it? Would that increase or decrease the pressure on states with nuclear weapons programs, such as North Korea, India, Pakistan, and possibly Iran, to ratify the treaty? Or would doing so put nuclear-capable states that have ratified the treaty at an unfair strategic disadvantage because they would become bound by a binding obligation not to conduct nuclear tests that would not restrict those outside the treaty?

b. U.S.-Soviet/Russian Nuclear Arms Control

Since the 1972 summit between President Nixon and General Secretary Leonid Brezhnev, where the SALT I agreements were signed, the bilateral efforts to limit the large nuclear arsenals of the United States and the Soviet Union/Russia have been the centerpiece of many of these two countries' summit meetings and they have been a critical part of efforts to limit nuclear weapons generally. Even with the series of agreements that these two countries have reached, the American and Russian nuclear weapons inventories still far exceed those of any other country, though China's nuclear inventory is apparently growing.

The United States and the Soviet Union began Strategic Arms Limitations Talks (SALT) in 1969. They ultimately produced two agreements. First, there was the Anti-Ballistic Missile (ABM) Treaty that prevented both countries from deploying nationwide defenses against ballistic missiles, limiting each country to two fixed locations with 100 missile interceptors per location. (A protocol in 1974 halved the allowed number of locations and missiles.) The treaty is no longer in force after President George W. Bush gave the required six-month notice in December 2001 to withdraw from the treaty (as discussed in Chapter 2.A.6).

Second, there was an "Interim Agreement," more commonly known as SALT I, that essentially capped each side's land-based intercontinental ballistic missiles (ICBMs) and submarine-launched ballistic missiles (SLBMs) at their then-existing levels. The term of the Interim Agreement was five years, although the two countries continued to observe its limits for several years after that. In 1979, President Carter and General Secretary Brezhnev signed the SALT II treaty, which would have limited each side to 2,400 strategic nuclear delivery vehicles, but following the 1980 Soviet invasion of Afghanistan President Carter requested the Senate to delay consideration of ratification of the treaty, and the treaty never entered into force. President Carter announced the United States would respect the provisions of the Treaty as long as the Soviet Union reciprocated, which prompted a similar commitment by Premier Brezhnev. These limits were respected until 1986, when President Reagan determined the Soviets were not complying with their commitments. In 1991, the United States and Soviet Union signed and eventually ratified the Strategic Arms Reduction Treaty (START I), which required the parties to reduce their combined delivery vehicles (ICBMs, SLBMs, and strategic bombers) to a limit of 1,600, and their nuclear warheads to a limit of 6,000. The treaty provided for an intrusive verification regime, including on-site inspections, to ensure compliance. START I expired in 2009. START II, which was signed in 1993 and would have provided for further reductions in delivery vehicles and warheads, never entered into force.

In 2002, the United States and Russia concluded the Strategic Offensive Reduction Treaty (SORT), which provided that the United States and Russia would reduce their strategic arsenals to 1,700-2,200 warheads each. The treaty essentially codified reciprocal unilateral decisions each side had made about downsizing its nuclear forces; unlike past strategic arms agreements, which were highly detailed and technically complex, SORT contained only five articles and totaled fewer than 500 words. SORT differed from past treaties in other key respects, as well: it did not specify which warheads were to be reduced, or how; it did not stipulate obligations for the destruction of warheads or delivery vehicles to be "reduced"; and it contained no verification provisions for assessing compliance. See Arms Control Association, The Strategic Offensive Reductions Treaty (SORT) At a Glance Fact (Sept. 2006), at http://www.armscontrol.org/factsheets/sort-glance.

President Obama made the resumption of strategic arms negotiations with Russia a priority, and only 15 months into the Obama Administration, the United States and Russia signed the New Strategic Arms Reduction Treaty (New START). New START replaced START I, which, as noted above, expired in December 2009. It also superseded the SORT Treaty, which terminated upon entry into force of New START. The following excerpt provides details about New START.

Arms Control Association, New START at a Glance

Fact Sheet (2010) [updated to reflect the treaty's ratification]

. . . New START [is] the first verifiable U.S.-Russian nuclear arms control treaty to take effect since 1994. . . .

[LIMITS]

Nuclear warhead limit: Seven years after entry into force, New START limits accountable deployed strategic nuclear warheads and bombs to 1,550, down approximately 30 percent from the 2,200 limit set by SORT and down 74 percent from the START-accountable limit of 6,000. Each heavy bomber is counted as one warhead (see below).

Missile, bomber and launcher limits: Deployed Intercontinental Ballistic Missiles (ICBMs), Submarine-Launched Ballistic Missiles (SLBMs), and heavy bombers assigned to nuclear missions are limited to 700. Deployed and non-deployed ICBM launchers, SLBM launchers, and bombers are limited to 800. This . . . is approximately a 50 percent reduction from the 1,600 launcher-limit set under START (SORT did not cover launchers). The 800 ceiling is intended to limit the ability for "break out" of the treaty by preventing either side from retaining large numbers of non-deployed launchers and bombers. . . .

COUNTING RULES . . .

Warheads: For deployed ICBMs and SLBMs, the number of warheads counted is the actual number of re-entry vehicles (RVs) on each missile (an RV protects the warhead as it re-enters the atmosphere from space; it can carry only one warhead). START I did not directly count RVs, but instead counted missiles and bombers that were "associated with" a certain number of warheads. . . .

Delivery vehicles and launchers: Each deployed ICBM, SLBM, and nuclear-capable bomber is counted as one delivery vehicle against the 700 limit. Each deployed and non-deployed missile launcher or bomber is counted as one launcher against the 800 limit. Non-deployed missiles are monitored but not limited in number.

MONITORING AND VERIFICATION . . .

New START's verification regime includes relevant parts of START I as well as new provisions to cover items not previously monitored. For example, the new treaty contains detailed definitions of items limited by the treaty; provisions on the use of National Technical Means (NTM)*; an extensive database on the numbers, types and locations of treaty-limited items and notifications about those items; and inspections to confirm this information. Even so, the verification system has been simplified to make it cheaper and easier to operate than START and to reflect new strategic realities. New START monitoring has also been designed to reflect updated treaty limitations. . . .

Verification of treaty limits and conversion or elimination of delivery systems is carried out by NTM and 18 annual short-notice, on-site inspections. The treaty allows ten on-site inspections of deployed warheads and deployed and non-deployed delivery systems at ICBM bases, submarine bases and air bases ("Type One" inspections). It also allows eight on-site inspections at facilities that may hold only non-deployed delivery systems ("Type Two" inspections).

---

*["National Technical Means" refers to satellite and other intelligence-gathering methods.–EDS.]

After a contentious debate, the U.S. Senate voted to give advice and consent to ratification of the New START treaty in December 2010. The treaty entered into force on February 5, 2011.

Notes and Questions

1. As noted above, the United States and USSR negotiated a number of agreements that never entered into force. Nevertheless, in the case of one such agreement, SALT II, both the Soviet and U.S. governments adhered to its limits. Arms control accordingly can be achieved through formal treaties and other agreements or through reciprocal political commitments of varying degrees of formality. Also, there are occasional unilateral measures, such as a moratorium on nuclear testing or unilaterally giving up nuclear weapons (as South Africa apparently did). What are the relative advantages and disadvantages of formal agreements, informal understandings, and unilateral measures?

2. Might concerns over compliance and verification affect your answer to the questions in the preceding Note? Some of the more recent arms control agreements — for example, the 1987 Intermediate Nuclear Forces Agreement (under which the U.S. and the Soviet Union agreed to verifiably destroy all ground-launched nuclear missiles with ranges between 500 and 5,500 kilometers), START I, and the CWC — have much more extensive verification provisions than earlier treaties, such as SALT I. On the other hand, the 2002 Strategic Offensive Reduction Treaty (SORT) had only limited verification provisions. Since there are ways to design detailed verification requirements, should a country prefer seeking those over more limited verification? Of course, verification applies reciprocally to all parties.

3. Why might a state be more reluctant to bind itself in an agreement on arms control issues as compared to, say, an economic, environmental, or law of the sea agreement? Is an arms control agreement likely to involve more politically sensitive issues for a country than those other agreements? If so, what are the implications of this in terms of the ease with which a country might enter into an arms control/ nonproliferation agreement or accept, for instance, a long-term nonbinding arrangement?

4. Formal methods for resolving disputes about compliance in the area of arms control are much less developed than in many other areas, such as international trade. Why do you think that is the case? Could it be related to the fundamental national security interests that are involved and each country's concern that it does not want to limit its flexibility?

c. The Nuclear Nonproliferation Treaty

The dangers of the proliferation of nuclear weapons have been a threat ever since the atomic bomb was first developed. Progressively, more and more countries have acquired nuclear weapons or the technical capability to undertake a nuclear weapons program. As of February 2011, there were eight declared nuclear weapon states — the United States, Russia, Great Britain, France, China, India, Pakistan, and North Korea, which first detonated a nuclear device in October 2006. Israel is also widely believed to have nuclear weapons. South Africa had nuclear weapons but dismantled them. Many other nations are technically capable of undertaking a nuclear weapons program, including Germany, Japan, and Iran.

An important objective is slowing the spread of these weapons. The key treaty in this regard is the Nuclear Nonproliferation Treaty (NPT) of 1968. As of February 2011, there are 189 parties to the Treaty.* The NPT essentially involved a bargain at the time: The non-nuclear-weapon states agreed to renounce the development and acquisition of nuclear weapons in exchange for pledges from the nuclear-weapons states to share peaceful nuclear technology, such as for producing energy, and to take steps toward nuclear disarmament. Some states, however, that possess (or are presumed to possess) nuclear weapons — India, Israel, and Pakistan — are not NPT members. Moreover, as discussed below, North Korea announced in January 2003 that it was withdrawing from the Treaty.

Arms Control Association, The Nuclear Nonproliferation Treaty at a Glance

Fact Sheet (January 2005), http://www.armscontrol.org/factsheets/nptfact

[The treaty's] 189 states-parties are classified in two categories: nuclear-weapon states (NWS) — consisting of the United States, Russia, China, France, and the United Kingdom — and non-nuclear-weapon states (NNWS). Under the treaty, the five NWS commit to pursue general and complete disarmament, while the NNWS agree to forgo developing or acquiring nuclear weapons.

With its near-universal membership, the NPT has the widest adherence of any arms control agreement, with only India, Israel, and Pakistan remaining outside the treaty. In order to accede to the treaty, these states must do so as NNWS, since the treaty restricts NWS status to nations that "manufactured and exploded a nuclear weapon or other nuclear explosive device prior to 1 January 1967." For India, Israel, and Pakistan, all known to possess or suspected of having nuclear weapons, joining the treaty as NNWS would require that they dismantle their nuclear weapons and place their nuclear materials under international safeguards. South Africa followed this path to accession in 1991.

Select Treaty Articles

Under Articles I and II of the treaty, the NWS agree not to help NNWS develop or acquire nuclear weapons, and the NNWS permanently forswear the pursuit of such weapons. To verify these commitments and ensure that nuclear materials are not being diverted for weapons purposes, Article III tasks the International Atomic Energy Agency with the inspection of the non-nuclear-weapon states' nuclear facilities. In addition, Article III establishes safeguards for the transfer of fissionable materials between NWS and NNWS.

*This number includes North Korea. As discussed below, in 2003 North Korea announced its withdrawal from the NPT. In 2006, the U.N. Security Council in Resolution 1718 demanded that North Korea "immediately retract its announcement of withdrawal" from the NPT.

Article IV acknowledges the "inalienable right" of NNWS to research, develop, and use nuclear energy for non-weapons purposes. It also supports the "fullest possible exchange" of such nuclear-related information and technology between NWS and NNWS. . . .

Article VI commits the NWS to "pursue negotiations in good faith on effective measures relating to cessation of the nuclear arms race at an early date and to nuclear disarmament, and on a treaty on general and complete disarmament under strict and effective international control." . . .

. . . Article X establishes the terms by which a state may withdraw from the treaty, requiring three month's advance notice should "extraordinary events" jeopardize its supreme national interests.

. . . [The treaty provides for] a decision after 25 years on whether the treaty should be extended. The 1995 review conference extended the treaty indefinitely and enhanced the review process by mandating that the five-year review conferences review past implementation and address ways to strengthen the treaty.

Jan Lodal, a former senior official in the Pentagon and on the National Security Council staff, thoughtfully analyzes below the NPT's significance and offers suggestions on how the NPT regime can be strengthened.

Jan Lodal, The Price of Dominance

87-91 (2001)

The Nuclear Nonproliferation Treaty has been the backbone of America's nuclear nonproliferation strategy. . . . The NPT not only prohibits the acquisition of nuclear weapons by nonnuclear signatories of the treaty, but it also prohibits the transfer of nuclear weapons technology by nuclear weapons states to nonnuclear weapons states. Since the end of the Cold War, all states except India, Israel, and Pakistan and the five declared nuclear powers have renounced plans to develop nuclear weapons and have joined the NPT. Brazil, Argentina, Taiwan, South Korea, and South Africa all had nuclear weapons programs during the Cold War but have now renounced them. South Africa had built an operational arsenal of, according to its own statements, seven nuclear weapons. It has announced that these weapons have been destroyed, although no outside third party has verified [this]. . . .

The NPT was the first significant multilateral arms control agreement that included built-in enforcement provisions. . . . [T]he International Atomic Energy Agency (IAEA) . . . is responsible for monitoring nuclear facilities of nonnuclear states party to the treaty. This monitoring is designed to ensure that no "peaceful" nuclear activities are used covertly to develop nuclear weapons. . . .

It is important to understand the NPT for what it is worth, acknowledging what it can and cannot accomplish. The NPT will not lead to the elimination of nuclear weapons, despite the provisions of Article VI calling for nuclear abolition (nor will it lead to general and complete disarmament, also called for by Article VI). The NPT has not been able to stop all proliferation — India, Israel, and Pakistan refused to join so they could develop their own nuclear weapons. The NPT's enforcement arm, the IAEA, cannot prevent a determined covert program. North Korea and Iraq joined the NPT, but both countries successfully carried out covert nuclear weapons programs under the nose of the IAEA. The NPT has also motivated considerable foot-dragging by nonnuclear states. These states have used the Article VI call for nuclear disarmament to criticize the nuclear states and to justify their covert nuclear programs. India, Pakistan, and Iran have been the most voluble of those states in this regard. . . .

But the NPT has one crucial achievement—it has established an accepted international norm against transferring nuclear weapons technology from nuclear weapons states to a nonnuclear state. After the Cold War, the NPT became the mechanism by which states that had equivocated about nuclear weapons could make a legally binding commitment to forgo them. When Iraq and North Korea were caught cheating, the NPT became the rallying point for an international consensus to insist on compliance. When China and Russia were caught orchestrating (or at least condoning) prohibited exports of nuclear technology to rogue states, the NPT allowed the United States and its allies to raise the diplomatic stakes substantially and insist that the leakage be stopped. The NPT should remain the centerpiece of U.S. nonproliferation diplomacy, despite its weaknesses and contradictions. It should be strengthened, not undercut.

In strengthening the NPT regime, India and Pakistan present special problems. Pakistan will remain nuclear as long as India is nuclear, and India will remain nuclear as long as China is nuclear—which might be forever. India first detonated a "peaceful nuclear explosion" (i.e., a nuclear bomb) in 1974, so it has been a de facto nuclear power for a quarter of a century. But its decision to declare and test its nuclear weapons, highly popular with India's voters, eliminates the option of ambiguity concerning its intentions. Nuclear testing did the same for Pakistan.

Having two declared nuclear powers that are highly unlikely to roll back their nuclear programs leaves the NPT in a state of limbo. It is supposed to regulate the spread of nuclear weapons throughout the world, which is clearly impossible with two nuclear powers outside the treaty. It is not clear what rules govern them—are they bound by the export controls and commitment to work against further proliferation imposed by the NPT or not? . . .

The NPT would be stronger with both India and Pakistan admitted as nuclear weapons states. . . . A new "line in the sand" would be drawn at seven versus five nuclear powers. . . . The issue of who would be permitted by the international community to have nuclear weapons would be settled. Any state that refused to join the consensus could be treated as a rogue state and isolated. . . .

Israel has not and probably will not acknowledge its nuclear weapons program. Very strong historical and ideological reasons will prohibit Israel's giving up its program until there is a secure peace in the Middle East. When peace comes, there will be no further reason to keep it; Israel's conventional military dominance will be adequate for its security. In the interim, the ambiguity will remain the only option.

Perhaps the most important step related to the NPT would be to strengthen the capabilities of the IAEA. . . . [I]mprovements in intelligence cooperation . . . would help considerably. The recent challenge-inspection procedures, put in place in response to failures in Iraq and North Korea, must be implemented vigorously. Finally, the parties to the NPT must take a more realistic view of the limits of the

IAEA. The IAEA can only indict; it can never give a state a clean bill of health. It will remain up to the member states to find hidden proliferation and to organize the international community to take action against the offending state.

The IAEA announced in 2002 a stronger global safeguards system. The new approach, called "integrated safeguards," provides the IAEA with more flexibility in deciding where to focus its efforts and limited resources. Inspectors were being given wider authority and advanced verification tools. As Mohamed El Baradei, then the IAEA Director General, said in briefing the IAEA's Board of Directors in March 2002, "The discoveries in Iraq [of secret programs as a result of the far-ranging inspections mandated by the U.N. Security Council after the 1991 Gulf War], as well as later revelations involving the Democratic People's Republic of Korea, shattered assumptions about the world's nuclear nonproliferation regime."

Notes and Questions

1. In addition to the nonproliferation treaties, there are a number of nonproliferation "regimes" designed to prevent the spread of goods and technologies that can be used to produce weapons of mass destruction. The regimes are cooperative arrangements through which countries that export sensitive goods and technologies, including dual use items that can be used for both military and nonmilitary purposes, can exchange information and harmonize their export control systems. These regimes do not, however, impose binding legal obligations on their participants. The Australia Group (AG) is multilateral regime comprised of 39 countries that coordinates controls on chemical and biological weapons-related goods.

In the nuclear area, the Nuclear Nonproliferation Treaty and the IAEA are supplemented by the Nuclear Nonproliferation Treaty Exporters (Zangger) Committee. Its 37 members seek to harmonize implementation of the NPT's requirements in applying IAEA safeguards to nuclear exports. In addition, the Nuclear Suppliers Group (NSG), a voluntary multilateral nonproliferation regime, serves as a forum for its 46 participating states to coordinate efforts to prevent the proliferation of nuclear weapons.

The Missile Technology Control Regime (MCTR) was created in 1987 to limit the proliferation of missiles capable of delivering WMD and related equipment and technology. The MCTR Guidelines and Annex include a list of controlled items whose transfer is restricted. This regime has 34 participating countries.

2. Under the NPT, states are allowed to operate nuclear enrichment and reprocessing facilities as long as they place them under IAEA safeguards. A significant problem is that the technology used to enrich uranium to the levels used to fuel power plants is essentially same as the technology required to produce highly enriched uranium for nuclear weapons, and reprocessing technology can also be used to produce fissile materials for nuclear weapons. This means that a state can approach the nuclear weapons threshold as an NPT party and then withdraw from the treaty in accordance with Article X and move rapidly to develop nuclear weapons. This is sometimes described as the NPT's "loophole" or the "breakout scenario."

To address the breakout scenario, former IAEA Director General Mohamed ElBaradei called for the "internationalization" of the nuclear fuel cycle. Under this approach, enrichment and reprocessing of nuclear fuel — the stages at which the danger of weaponization is greatest — would be carried out by multilateral organizations or groups, not by individual states. The multilateral groups would guarantee nuclear fuel to any interested state. The IAEA took a first step in this direction in December 2010, when its Board of Governors authorized the IAEA Director General to establish a reserve of low enriched uranium (LEU), or an IAEA LEU bank. According to the IAEA, this LEU bank, which would be owned and managed by the IAEA,

> would help to assure a supply of LEU for power generation. Should an IAEA Member State's LEU supply be disrupted, and the supply cannot be restored by the commercial market, State-to-State arrangements, or by any other such means, it may call upon the IAEA LEU bank to secure LEU supplies, without distorting the commercial market. This initiative does not diminish in any way States' rights to establish or expand their own nuclear fuel production. [Factsheet: IAEA Low Enriched Uranium Reserve (2010), at http://www.iaea.org/Publications/Factsheets/English/iaea_leureserve.html.]

As noted, the IAEU fuel bank is not intended to preclude states from developing their own domestic nuclear fuel cycles. Will this address the danger that states might divert technology and fuel for nuclear power plants to weapons programs? Can internationalizing the nuclear fuel cycle be effective in preventing proliferation if states are not required to forgo domestic nuclear fuel production capability as a condition of participating in a nuclear fuel bank? What would be the obstacles to internationalizing the nuclear fuel cycle in this way? Should the idea nevertheless be pursued?

3. As noted above, Article VI commits the nuclear weapons states to "pursue negotiations in good faith on effective measures relating to cessation of the nuclear arms race at an early date and to nuclear disarmament, and on a treaty on general and complete disarmament under strict and effective international control." In the excerpt above, Mr. Lodal argues that some states have used the failure of the nuclear weapons states to make greater progress towards nuclear disarmament "to criticize the nuclear states and to justify their covert nuclear programs." Consider the efforts made by the United States and Russia discussed above to negotiate substantial reductions in their nuclear arsenals. Have they complied with their Article VI disarmament obligations? Does the retention by the nuclear weapons states of thousands of nuclear warheads contribute to nuclear proliferation? Does the failure of the nuclear weapons states to disarm undermine their demands that other states not acquire nuclear weapons? Or is the impetus for states to acquire nuclear weapons more likely to be driven by other considerations, such as regional security conditions?

4. In July 2005, the United States and India announced a Joint Statement under which the United States agreed to take steps to lift its longstanding moratorium on trade with India in nuclear-related technologies, including on equipment for enriching uranium or reprocessing plutonium and fuel for nuclear reactors. India, in return, committed to maintain strict controls on the exports of sensitive nuclear technology to non-nuclear weapons states and to grant IAEA inspectors access to

its civilian nuclear facilities to ensure they have safeguards in place to prevent diversion of nuclear technology to nuclear weapons purposes. In 2008, India concluded a safeguards agreement with the IAEA, and the Nuclear Suppliers Group (NSG) granted India a waiver permitting it to receive civilian nuclear technology and fuel from NSG member states. Later that year, the United States enacted the United States-India Nuclear Cooperation Approval and Non-proliferation Enhancement Act, which permits India to purchase nuclear fuel and technology from the United States. Proponents of the arrangement view it as a pragmatic way to bring India within the nonproliferation framework. Opponents argue that the arrangement undermines the NPT by rewarding India for developing nuclear weapons, that it fails to guard against further proliferation by exempting India's military nuclear weapons program from inspection, and that it will encourage other states, such as China, to support nuclear programs in countries that have refused to join the NPT regime, such as Pakistan, or that might withdraw from the treaty in the future.

Given that India is unlikely to abandon its nuclear weapons program and join the NPT as non-nuclear weapons state, is the U.S.-India nuclear arrangement a good way to advance the goals of the nonproliferation regime? Or does it improperly reward a state that has refused to accept the basic goal of stopping the spread of nuclear weapons beyond the five original nuclear weapons states? Would it be better to amend to the NPT to allow India to join as a nuclear weapons state than to attempt to bring India within the NPT's safeguards regime through a bilateral arrangement? If so, should such a treaty amendment also permit Pakistan to join the NPT as a nuclear weapons state, even though it has not yet agreed to maintain controls on the exports of sensitive nuclear technology to non-nuclear weapons states and to accept IAEA inspections? Given that any amendments to the NPT would require the unanimous agreement of all NPT parties, do you think a treaty amendment is a feasible option?

d. The North Korean and Iranian Proliferation Crises

Although efforts to stop the nonproliferation of nuclear weapons have had some success, as noted above, the number of nuclear-weapons states has grown over the years, and more states appear on the verge of developing these weapons. In recent years, concerns about nuclear weapons programs in North Korea and Iran have given rise to heightened international tensions and have called into question the viability of the nuclear nonproliferation system.

North Korea. The first North Korean nuclear crisis arose in 1994 when, as recounted by Professor Ashton B. Carter, then a U.S. Assistant Secretary of Defense, "North Korea was planning to take fuel rods out of its research reactor at Yongbyon and extract the six or so bombs' worth of weapons-grade plutonium they contained." The United States actively explored possible military options, but pushed for a diplomatic solution. See Ashton B. Carter, Prepared Testimony before Senate Committee on Foreign Relations, February 4, 2003. The United States and North Korea negotiated and signed an "Agreed Framework" in October 1994; under this document, North Korea committed to freezing operations at Yongbyon, subject to verification through IAEA on-site inspections. In return, through a multinational consortium, the Korean Peninsula Energy Development

Organization (KEDO), the United States agreed to help build two nuclear power reactors of a type (light-water) whose byproducts cannot easily be used in the development of nuclear weapons. Moreover, the consortium would supply North Korea with 500,000 metric tons of heating oil each year while the reactors were under construction.

The 1994 Agreed Framework did not provide for regular verification in North Korea outside of Yongbyon. In 2002, North Korea apparently admitted to a visiting senior U.S. official that it had a hidden uranium enrichment facility elsewhere and implied that North Korea would use it for building nuclear weapons. In reaction to North Korea's admission of its enrichment program, the U.S.-led consortium that was implementing the Framework Agreement announced in November that it was suspending fuel oil deliveries to North Korea. Then, in December 2002, North Korea announced that it was restarting the small reactor at Yongbyon, allegedly to produce electricity. North Korea removed seals and monitoring equipment from the nuclear facilities and ordered IAEA inspectors, who were responsible for monitoring the freeze, out of the country.

On January 10, 2003, North Korea announced its withdrawal from the Nuclear Nonproliferation Treaty (NPT), saying it was effective immediately, and stated that this withdrawal freed it from its Safeguards Agreement with the International Atomic Energy Agency (IAEA).

Instead of engaging in direct talks with North Korea, as it had in 1994, to address the nuclear crisis, the United States pursued negotiations in the framework of the so-called six-party talks, in which North and South Korea, Russia, China, Japan, and the United States have participated. These talks produced what was viewed as a significant breakthrough in September 2005, when the parties agreed to the terms of a Chinese-drafted Joint Statement in which North Korea "committed to abandoning all nuclear weapons and existing nuclear programs and returning at an early date" to the NPT. For its part, the United States: (1) affirmed that it has "no intention to attack or invade [North Korea] with nuclear or conventional weapons"; (2) undertook to normalize relations with North Korea; and (3) "agreed to discuss, at an appropriate time, the subject of the provision of light water reactor to [North Korea]."

The sense of progress achieved at the September 2005 session was shattered by North Korea's test of a nuclear device in October 2006. Days later, the Security Council, acting under its Chapter VII powers, adopted Resolution 1718, which condemned North Korea's nuclear test and decided unequivocally that North Korea must "abandon all nuclear weapons and existing nuclear programmes in a complete, verifiable and irreversible manner," subject to verification by the IAEA. The resolution imposed a series of binding sanctions, including an embargo on heavy conventional weapons to North Korea, the freezing of North Korean assets related to WMD programs, a travel ban on persons involved in North Korea's WMD programs, and a requirement for states to cooperate to prevent trafficking in WMD, including through inspections of cargo to and from North Korea.

Efforts to address the North Korean nuclear crisis continued through the six-party talks process, but these efforts were, in the words of one observer, "mired in distrust and accusations" and "led to alternate cycles of dialogue and confrontation." Siegfried S. Hecker, Lessons Learned from the North Korean Nuclear Crises, Daedalus, Winter 2010, at 44, 50. In 2007, North Korea committed to shutting down its research reactor at Yongbyon in exchange for food aid and other assistance, as well as pledges by the United States and Japan to begin talks aimed at normalizing their bilateral relations with North Korea. Although North Korea took steps to disable the reactor, it later announced, amid rising tensions with the United States, that it would begin to restore the facility.

In 2009, North Korea conducted a second nuclear weapons test. In response, the Security Council adopted Resolution 1874, which "condemn[ed]" North Korea's test "in the strongest terms" and adopted new sanctions, including a ban on all weapons exports from North Korea and the import of all but small arms. The resolution also called upon states "to inspect vessels, with the consent of the flag State, on the high seas, if they have information that provides reasonable grounds to believe that the cargo of such vessels contains items" subject to sanctions.

In November 2010, North Korea permitted a visiting delegation to observe a new uranium enrichment facility at Yongbyon, which could provide North Korea with an additional way of obtaining fuel for nuclear weapons. This development highlighted the challenges of addressing the North Korean nuclear challenge.

In the excerpts that follow, former Secretary of Defense Perry, former Chairman of the Joint Chiefs of Staff Shalikashvili, and Professor Carter highlight the security risks presented by North Korea's nuclear program. Then, Professor Siegfried Hecker, a member of the delegation that observed North Korea's uranium enrichment facilities in November 2010, addresses the prospects for persuading North Korea to abandon its nuclear weapons program.

William J. Perry, Ashton B. Carter, & John M. Shalikashvili, A Scary Thought; Loose Nukes in North Korea

Wall Street Journal, February 6, 2003, at 18

News reports indicate that North Korea has begun to move fuel rods containing six bombs' worth of plutonium from its nuclear facility at Yongbyon. . . . For eight years, since 1994, that plutonium has been stored at Yongbyon where it could be seen by on-site inspectors and, if necessary, entombed by an air strike of precision bombs. Now it is being trucked away, perhaps to one of North Korea's many caves, where it will be difficult to find or destroy.

This development undermines global nonproliferation efforts that have been successful for decades, and represents an imminent danger to the security of the region. Even more, in an age of terrorism it poses the additional specter of putting nuclear weapons into the hands of parties even more threatening than the North Korean government. North Korea has few cash-generating exports other than ballistic missiles. Now nuclear weapons or fissile material could take their place in its shopping catalogue. Or North Korea's government might collapse, losing control of the nukes in the process. While hijacked airlines and anthrax-dusted letters are a dangerous threat to civilized society, it would change the way Americans were forced to live if it became an ever-present possibility that a city could disappear in a mushroom cloud. . . .

Even if their nukes remain in the hands of the current government, a nuclear North Korea could prompt a domino effect of proliferation in East Asia. South

Korea once had a nuclear weapons program that it stopped because it was persuaded its security could be assured without them. Will some in South Korea start to reconsider? Similar questions might be asked in Japan and Taiwan—questions no government wants asked. . . .

Siegfried S. Hecker, Lessons Learned from the North Korean Nuclear Crises

Daedalus, Winter 2010, at 44, 52-53

North Korea is unlikely to give up its nuclear arsenal anytime soon because it has become crucial to how the regime assures its security. Nuclear weapons also play a supportive role domestically and provide diplomatic leverage. Pyongyang views its security concerns as existential. . . . In spite of having received numerous security guarantees that promised to respect its sovereignty along with assurances not to invade the country, Pyongyang still feels threatened today. It will require much more than another security guarantee to make Pyongyang feel secure.

Even if North Korea's security fears are assuaged, domestic factors favor keeping the bomb. The external threat is used to justify the need for the bomb and the sacrifices North Korea's people are asked to make. That threat also helps keep its people submissive and isolated from the international community. It also helps the regime continue to control all information and to blind its people to progress in the rest of the world, especially south of the [Demilitarized Zone]. . . .

Military might is the only source of Pyongyang's diplomatic power today. Nuclear weapons have become central to the projection of its military might, in spite of the fact that its nuclear arsenal has little war-fighting utility. Pyongyang views nuclear weapons as diplomatic equalizers with its much more prosperous and powerful, but non-nuclear rivals, South Korea and Japan. Without nuclear weapons, North Korea would get scant attention from the international community.

Many believe that the bomb is only a bargaining chip and that North Korea is willing to sell it for the right price. However, for reasons stated above, there is no price high enough for Pyongyang to sell. It is also not about to give up its nuclear weapons first as a condition of normalization. Pyongyang may agree to denuclearize in principle, but it will drag out implementation as it did during the six-party process.

It is also unlikely that North Korea can be forced to give up the bomb. Realistically, military options are off the table unless North Korea initiates a conflict. Additionally, sanctions are ineffective without China's support, but China will not support sanctions that bring Pyongyang to its knees. Beijing fears U.S. intervention in North Korea more than it does nuclear weapons in its neighbor's hands. It wants peace and stability on the Korean peninsula.

As undesirable as it may sound, the best hope is a long-term strategy to contain the nuclear threat while tackling the North Korean problem comprehensively, but in discrete steps. Both Beijing and Seoul favor taking the long view. Time is not on Pyongyang's side. The greatest threat to the regime is not from the outside, but from within. It can't hold back its people forever from the tide of change surrounding its borders. In the meantime, it is important to avoid a clash between Pyongyang and

Seoul or Tokyo. And it is essential to stop Pyongyang from doing additional damage around the world through nuclear cooperation and exports. Beijing is likely willing to restrain North Korea from expanding its nuclear program and, most importantly, to stop it from exporting its nuclear materials or technologies. That is how our joint efforts should be directed to reduce this dangerous threat.

Iran. The United States and other countries increasingly believe that Iran is also actively pursuing a nuclear weapons program, although it has not progressed as far as North Korea. Iran denies that it is pursuing nuclear weapons and claims merely to be developing a peaceful nuclear energy program. The following excerpt describes the efforts taken by the Permanent Members of the Security Council to address the Iranian nuclear threat.

Paul K. Kerr, Iran's Nuclear Program: Status

Congressional Research Service Report 4-7 (Dec. 29, 2009)

The recent public controversy over Iran's nuclear program began in August 2002, when the National Council of Resistance on Iran (NCRI), an Iranian exile group, revealed information during a press conference (some of which later proved to be accurate) that Iran had built nuclear-related facilities at Natanz and Arak that it had not revealed to the IAEA. . . .

States-parties to the nuclear Nonproliferation Treaty (NPT) are obligated to conclude a safeguards agreement with the IAEA. In the case of non-nuclear-weapon states-parties to the treaty (of which Iran is one), such agreements allow the agency to monitor nuclear facilities and materials to ensure that they are not diverted for military purposes. However, the agency's inspections and monitoring authority is limited to facilities that have been declared by the states-parties. Additional protocols to IAEA safeguards agreements augment the agency's ability to investigate clandestine nuclear facilities and activities by increasing the agency's authority to inspect certain facilities and demand additional information from states-parties. . . . Prior to the NCRI's revelations, [Iran had not concluded an additional protocol]. . . .

. . . [In 2003,] Iran concluded an agreement with France, Germany, and the United Kingdom, collectively known as the "E3," to suspend its enrichment activities, sign and implement an additional protocol to its 1974 IAEA safeguards agreement,* and comply fully with the IAEA's investigation. As a result, the IAEA board decided to refrain from referring the matter to the UN Security Council.

Ultimately, the IAEA's investigation, as well as information Tehran provided after the October 2003 agreement, revealed that Iran had engaged in a variety of clandestine nuclear-related activities, some of which violated Iran's safeguards agreement. These included plutonium separation experiments, uranium enrichment and conversion experiments, and importing various uranium compounds.

After October 2003, Iran continued some of its enrichment-related activities, but Tehran and the E3 agreed in November 2004 to a more detailed suspension agreement. However, Iran resumed uranium conversion in August 2005 under the

*[Iran signed the additional protocol but has not, as of December 2010, ratified it.–Eds.]

leadership of President Mahmoud Ahmadinejad, who had been elected two months earlier. Iran announced in January 2006 that it would resume research and development on its centrifuges at Natanz. In response, the IAEA board adopted a resolution [on] February 4, 2006, that referred the matter to the Security Council. Two days later, Tehran announced that it would stop implementing its additional protocol.

In June 2006, China, France, Germany, Russia, the United Kingdom, and the United States, collectively known as the "P5+1" [i.e., the permanent five members of the Security Council plus Germany], presented a proposal to Iran that offered a variety of incentives in return for Tehran taking several steps to assuage international concerns about its enrichment and heavy-water programs. The proposal called on the government to address the IAEA's "outstanding concerns . . . through full cooperation" with the agency's ongoing investigation of Tehran's nuclear programs, "suspend all enrichment-related and reprocessing activities," and resume implementing its additional protocol.

European Union High Representative for Common Foreign and Security Policy Javier Solana presented a revised version of the 2006 offer to Iran in June 2008. . . . Iran provided a follow-up response the next month, but the six countries deemed it unsatisfactory. Tehran has told the IAEA that it would implement its additional protocol "if the nuclear file is returned from the Security Council" to the agency. It is, however, unclear how the council could meet this condition. Iran's Minister for Foreign Affairs Manouchehr Mottaki told reporters [on] October 7, 2009, that Iran is not discussing ratification of the protocol.

The 2006 offer's requirements have also been included in several UN Security Council resolutions. . . . However, a November 2009 report from ElBaradei to the Security Council and the IAEA board indicated that Tehran has continued to defy the council's demands by continuing work on both its uranium enrichment program and heavy-water reactor program. Iranian officials maintain that Iran will not suspend its enrichment program. . . .

After an October 1 meeting in Geneva with the P5+1 and Solana, Iranian officials . . . agreed in principle to a proposal that would provide fuel enriched to 19.75% uranium-235 for Iran's . . . Tehran Research Reactor, which produces medical isotopes and operates under IAEA safeguards. . . .

According to the proposal, Iran would transfer approximately 1,200 kilograms of its low-enriched uranium hexafluoride to Russia [for enrichment]. . . . [As of October 30, 2009, Iran had produced 1,763 kilograms of low-enriched uranium hexafluoride.] Russia would then transfer the low-enriched uranium hexafluoride to France for fabrication into fuel assemblies. Finally, France would transfer the assemblies to Russia for shipment to Iran. . . .

. . . Tehran has agreed to "accept the essential elements" of the fuel supply proposal "but has also sought modifications to the formula," according to a November 10 [,2009,] Iranian television report. However, Foreign Minister Mottaki stated November 18 that Iran would not agree to ship its LEU to another country for further enrichment. . . .

. . . [In November 2009, the P5+1] issued a joint statement expressing disappointment with Tehran's failure to agree to another meeting or respond positively to the Tehran Research Reactor proposal. . . .

Representatives of the P5+1 states met with Iran again December 2010 and January 2011, but the negotiations produced no agreements or even substantive engagement on concrete proposals.

In the face of Iran's refusal to suspend enrichment and reprocessing activities, the Security Council has adopted a series of resolutions imposing an expanding set of sanctions against Iran. In December 2006, the Council adopted Resolution 1737, which decided that Iran must suspend all nuclear enrichment-related and reprocessing activities. The resolution imposed a series of sanctions specifically targeting trade in equipment and financing related to Iran's nuclear program. Iran's President Mahmoud Ahmadinejad responded in January 2007 by reiterating the claim that Iran has an inalienable right to develop nuclear power; he asserted that Resolution 1737 would "not affect Iran's economy and politics." In Resolution 1747, adopted in March 2007, the Security Council reaffirmed its demand that Iran suspend enrichment activities and expanded sanctions on persons and entities connected to Iran's nuclear and missile programs. Resolution 1803, adopted in March 2008, expanded sanctions and imposed a travel ban on persons linked to Iran's nuclear program. In June 2010, the Council in Resolution 1929 adopted a fourth round of international sanctions that bars Iran from acquiring an interest in any commercial activity in another State involving uranium mining, production, or use of nuclear materials and technology.

In addition to the sanctions adopted by the Security Council, both the United States and the European Union have imposed additional, more severe sanctions on Iran. Although the United States has few economic ties with Iran, the European Union is Iran's largest trading partner, meaning sanctions adopted by the EU in July 2010 could have a significant impact on Iran.

Notes and Questions

1. U.N. Security Council Resolution 1718 requires North Korea to "abandon all nuclear weapons and existing nuclear programmes in a complete, verifiable and irreversible manner." What is the legal basis for this demand? After North Korea withdrew from the NPT, is it not entitled to pursue nuclear weapons? Could the Security Council demand that other states that are not parties to the NPT, such as India, Pakistan, and Israel, abandon their nuclear weapons?

2. Resolution 1718 also demands that North Korea "immediately retract its announcement of withdrawal" from the NPT. Does the Security Council have the authority to make such a demand? How can this decision be reconciled with the view that a state's decision to become a party to a treaty, or to remain a member of a treaty that allows for withdrawal, is a matter of consent? Is there a distinction between demanding that a country become or remain a party to a treaty such as the NPT, as opposed to demanding that it not engage in certain behavior, such as developing nuclear weapons?

3. Similarly, the Security Council "call[ed] upon" Iran to act strictly in accordance with additional IAEA protocol it signed with the IAEA in 2003 and "to ratify [the protocol] promptly."

4. As noted above, Article IV of the NPT acknowledges the "inalienable right" of non-nuclear weapons states to research, develop, and use nuclear energy for non-weapons purposes. Iranian leaders have asserted that Iran will not abandon this

"inalienable right" to nuclear power. How can the security concerns of states about Iran's nuclear program be addressed in light of this right?

5. How should the United States and other countries deal with states that appear to be pursuing nuclear weapons programs? Will sanctions, either bilateral or multilateral, be effective in preventing such programs? Should the Security Council impose economic sanctions, or even authorize the use of military force, against such countries? If the Security Council is unwilling to authorize the use of force, should states like Israel or the United States use force unilaterally? Would they have a legal basis for using force?

6. There are reliable reports that some country or countries, possibly Israel or the United States, have undertaken covert actions against the Iranian nuclear program. This includes the possible assassination in Iran of at least one leading Iranian nuclear scientist. Also, it appears that a sophisticated computer virus, labeled Stuxnet, was introduced into the workings of Iranian centrifuges in 2010. This cyberweapon caused large numbers of the centrifuges to spin out of control and be damaged while sending signals to their operators that everything was operating normally. In January 2011, the retiring chief of Israel's Mossad intelligence agency and U.S. officials gave the virus, as well as economic sanctions, credit for delaying by several years Iran's efforts to make a nuclear bomb. William J. Broad, John Markoff & David Sanger, Israel Tests Called Crucial in Iran Nuclear Setback, N.Y. Times, Jan. 16, 2011, at A1. Do you think that a country's use of a computer virus, such as Stuxnet, against another country's major programs is permissible under international law? See the discussion of cyberattacks in Section B.3 above.

7. To date, the United States and other countries have sought sanctions against North Korea and Iran in connection with their nuclear programs, but have simultaneously held out the promise of improved relations if those countries address international demands regarding those programs. Does this seem like wise diplomacy? Or does offering to normalize relations with North Korea and provide it with assistance, or promising to expand diplomatic and economic relations with Iran, create incentives for other states to pursue nuclear weapons programs in the hopes that they can secure significant concessions from Western states for later abandoning those programs?

4. U.N. Security Council Resolution 1540

The potential use of the weapons of mass destruction by terrorists is perhaps today's the greatest security threat. The Security Council took action to address this threat in 2004, when it adopted Resolution 1540. In Resolution 1540, the Council affirmed that the proliferation of WMD constitutes a threat to international peace and security and expressed grave concern about "the threat of terrorism and the risk that non-State actors . . . may acquire, develop, traffic in or use nuclear, chemical and biological weapons and their means of delivery." Acting under Chapter VII, the Security Council decided that all United Nations member states must "adopt and enforce appropriate effective laws which prohibit any non-State actor" from acquiring or using WMD. Resolution 1540 also requires U.N. member states to submit reports on steps they have taken to fulfill the resolution's substantive requirements to a specially-constituted committee.

In imposing legal obligations on all U.N. member states to address the general threat of the risk of acquisition of WMD by terrorists, the Security Council has departed from its traditional practice of adopting legally binding measures only in response to particular security crises in a single country or region. The Security Council, in essence, has endeavored to enact a form of general international legislation. Through the creation of the 1540 Committee, the Security Council has in addition created a modest administrative apparatus to promote enforcement of that legislation. At the time Resolution 1540 was adopted, some states expressed concern about this approach to creating new international legal obligations. India's representative to the U.N., for instance, expressed concern

> over the increasing tendency of the Council in recent years to assume new and wider powers of legislation on behalf of the international community, with its resolutions binding on all States. . . . We are concerned that the exercise of legislative functions by the Council, combined with recourse to Chapter VII mandates, could disrupt the balance of power between the General Assembly and the Security Council, as enshrined in the Charter. [U.N. SCOR, 59th Sess., 4950th mtg. at 23, U.N. Doc. S/PV.4950 (Apr. 22, 2004) (statement of representative of India).]

Notes and Questions

1. The adoption of Resolution 1540 was the second time the Council enacted universal legal obligations to address a general threat to international peace and security. It first did so in 2001 in Resolution 1373, which imposed obligations on all states to, among other things, refrain from providing any support to terrorist groups, to enact legislation prohibiting the financing of terrorist acts, and to criminalize and prosecute participation by individuals in terrorist acts. See Chapter 1.E.

2. What are the advantages of attempting to change or create international law on matters of general interest through Security Council action, rather than through the traditional method of concluding multilateral treaties? What are the disadvantages? Are states likely to comply with legal rules they oppose, especially if they are adopted by a body like the Security Council, with its limited membership? Or does the obligation of all U.N. member states under Article 25 of the U.N. Charter to "accept and carry out the decisions of the Security Council" address this concern? See Stefan Talmon, The Security Council as World Legislature, 99 Am. J. Int'l L. 175 (2005).

12

International Criminal Law

International criminal activity, like legitimate behavior, often transcends national boundaries. Criminal enterprises engaged in activities ranging from the illegal movement of goods and persons to sophisticated financial fraud schemes often conduct operations in more than one state. Fugitives hoping to evade criminal accountability in one state may seek refuge by slipping across international borders. As a result, transnational crime has long been a subject of concern in the conduct of international relations and the development of international law. As we saw in Chapter 7, international law allows states to assert jurisdiction, including criminal jurisdiction, over persons and activities outside their territory that produce substantial harmful consequences in their countries. In addition, states have developed international arrangements, including treaties, to cooperate in the investigation and prosecution of crimes with a transnational component. One of the most well-known features of international cooperation in transnational criminal matters is extradition, by which persons residing in one state may be compulsorily transferred to another state to stand trial for crimes that violate the law of the state to which they are surrendered.

But international criminal law encompasses more than the allocation of jurisdictional claims among states and cooperation regarding the exercise of domestic criminal jurisdiction by states. International law also imposes criminal liability directly on individuals for conduct that threatens interests or values important to the international community as a whole and that states, through either treaties or customary international law, have made international crimes. This is not a new phenomenon; piracy was defined as an international crime centuries ago. Nevertheless, the emergence of a new and growing class of international crimes is largely a feature of the post-World War II era. During the same period that international law conferred rights directly on individuals as subjects of international law through the growth of the international human rights movement, it has also imposed duties on individuals through the expansion of international criminal law. Today, investigations of and prosecutions for the commission of international crimes, either before national courts or international tribunals, are an increasingly common feature of the international landscape.

This chapter will begin with a brief section on international cooperative responses to *transnational* crime. This area largely involves international cooperation regarding activities that are defined and prosecuted as crimes under domestic law, but that nevertheless have an international element. Next, we will examine acts that constitute *international* crimes, that is, breaches of international legal rules that give rise to individual criminal liability for individuals, as opposed to the responsibility of a state. We will consider basic questions of individual criminal responsibility under international law and then review the substantive crimes themselves. In the last section, we will explore the various institutional arrangements for prosecution of international crimes, including international criminal courts like the International Criminal Court, hybrid or mixed national-international tribunals, and domestic courts.

A. TRANSNATIONAL CRIMES AND INTERNATIONAL LEGAL COOPERATION

Globalization has brought with it a significant expansion of transnational crime. According to Professor Mueller, the concept of "transnational crime" refers to "certain criminal phenomena transcending international borders, transgressing the laws of several states or having an impact on another country." Examples of categories of transnational crime include money laundering, illicit drug trafficking, terrorist activities, trafficking in persons, and illicit traffic in arms, among others. Gerhard O.W. Mueller, Transnational Crime: Definitions and Concepts, Transnational Organized Crime, Autumn/Winter 1998, at 13, 13-14.

Countries have developed a number of cooperative responses to transnational criminal activity. A common challenge in this regard is that the country where the crimes are planned may not be the same country where the crime will be completed or where the harms associated with the crime will be felt most strongly. Criminal groups engaged in illegal arms trade, for instance, may buy weapons in Country A and ship them through Country B en route to Country C, where they will be used by insurgents in a civil war. In this case, Country C is the one that suffers most directly from the harms of the illegal arms trade. As noted in Chapter 7.B, however, section 432 of the Restatement posits that a "state's law enforcement officers may exercise their functions in the territory of another state only with the consent of the other state." This means Country C's authorities would not be permitted under international law to conduct investigations in, or prosecute persons present in, the territory of the other two states without the consent of the state concerned. On the other hand, Countries A and B may not have incentive to investigate and prosecute those engaged in the arms trade.

Mutual legal assistance. One common response to the problem of transnational crimes is the negotiation of mutual legal assistance treaties, or "MLATs," which create procedures through which states "regularize and improve the effectiveness of cooperation" between their domestic law enforcement agencies. Sean D. Murphy, Mutual Legal Assistance Treaties with the European Union, Germany, and Japan, 98 Am. J. Int'l L. 596, 596 (2004). Under the standard bilateral MLAT treaties concluded by the United States:

> . . . Both parties are obligated to assist in the investigation, prosecution, and suppression of offenses in all forms of proceedings (criminal, civil, or administrative). Among other things, the treaties address the ability of one government to summon witnesses located in the other government's territory, to compel the production of documents and other real evidence, to issue search warrants, and to serve process. [Id.]

States cooperate on transnational criminal matters not only through bilateral arrangements, but also through multilateral institutions as well. The International Criminal Police Organization, known as "Interpol," is an international organization with 188 member countries that facilitates cross-border police cooperation and supports authorities whose mission is to prevent or combat transnational crime. Interpol's three core functions include: (1) operating a global police communications system that provides police around the world with a platform through which they can share information about criminals and criminality; (2) maintaining databases with information on criminals such as names, fingerprints, and DNA profiles, and with information on stolen property such as passports, vehicles, and works of art; and (3) supporting law enforcement officials with emergency support and operational activities, especially in priority crime areas of fugitives, public safety and terrorism, drugs and organized crime, trafficking in human beings, and financial and high-tech crime.

Extradition. Another important form of transnational legal cooperation in criminal matters deals with efforts by a country to gain custody of persons who have been convicted of a crime or are wanted for trial who are located in a foreign country. The most common means for gaining custody of such persons is through extradition treaties. Only treaties create an obligation to extradite under international law, although some nations will voluntarily extradite suspects as a matter of comity. Some states will not extradite their own nationals to another country; the United States is generally amenable to extraditing its own nationals as long as the extradition treaty with the requesting nation allows for such extradition. See Charlton v. Kelly, 229 U.S. 447, 467 (1913).

The procedures a country uses to meet its extradition obligations under a treaty are generally established by its domestic laws. Extradition treaties typically establish a legally binding obligation to extradite fugitives, define the crimes covered by the extradition obligation, specify exceptions, and set forth the procedures and requisite evidence to activate the extradition obligation. In the United States, the procedures for extradition are governed by the relevant treaty, as supplemented by a statute. See 18 U.S.C. §§3184-3195.

A common requirement that must be met before a fugitive will be transferred under an extradition treaty is "dual (or double) criminality": the offense charged must be a crime both in the requesting and requested state. When considering an extradition request, however, the magistrates to whom the request is presented do not determine the guilt or innocence of the fugitive, only whether the standard of proof of criminality established by an extradition treaty is met. There are a number of different formulations for this standard; however, most have been defined as the equivalent of probable cause in domestic criminal cases.

In the United States, if the magistrate determines that extradition is appropriate, he certifies his decision to the Secretary of State, along with a record of the proceedings. The Secretary of State makes the final determination on extradition.

While no statute specifically limits the Secretary's discretion, she is bound by the relevant treaty. In other words, if she decides not to extradite, her decision must be based on a treaty exception.

If the person is extradited to the United States, the specialty doctrine requires that he "shall be tried only for the offence with which he is charged in the extradition proceedings and for which he was delivered up, and that if not tried for that, or after trial and acquittal, he shall have a reasonable time to leave the country before he is arrested upon the charge of any other crime committed previous to his extradition." United States v. Rauscher, 119 U.S. 407, 424 (1886). Many other states also apply this requirement in processing extradition requests.

A sometimes controversial exception to the obligation to extradite concerns "political offenses." Part of the difficulty arises from the fact that the exempted political offenses have generally not been defined or enumerated in extradition treaties. The exception is usually provided for in the general language. For example, Article V of the extradition treaty between the United States and Italy provides: "Extradition shall not be granted when the offense for which extradition is requested is a political offense, or if the person whose surrender is sought proves that the request for surrender has been made in order to try or punish him or her for a political offense."

Difficulties regarding this exception arose prominently in connection with U.K. extradition requests for Provisional Irish Republican Army (IRA) terrorists who fled to the United States, where the IRA had many supporters. For instance, in In re Doherty, 599 F. Supp. 270 (S.D.N.Y. 1984), Doherty had been convicted of a number of crimes in England, including the murder of a British Army officer and membership in the IRA. In addition, Doherty was wanted for crimes committed during his escape from prison. In considering Britain's extradition request, the district court stated that "[n]ot every act committed for a political purpose or during a political disturbance may or should properly be regarded as a political offense." Acts that are "violative of international law" or that "would be properly punishable . . . in the context of a declared war or in the heat of open military conflict," the court suggested, would not qualify as political offenses. However, observing that Doherty was not charged with "detonat[ing] [a bomb] in a department store, public tavern, or a resort hotel, causing indiscriminate personal injury, death, and property damage," the court concluded that Doherty's alleged crimes qualified as political offenses within the meaning of the then-applicable 1972 U.S.-U.K. extradition treaty. Id at 274-275.

The U.S. judiciary's refusal to allow extradition in *Doherty* and similar cases induced the British government to ask that a supplementary treaty be negotiated, which narrowed the political offense exception, so that violent offenders such as Doherty could not escape extradition. A U.S.-U.K. Supplementary Extradition Treaty was signed in 1985 and ratified in 1986. It explicitly provided that a number of offenses involving killing, seriously injuring a person, using explosives, or using firearms were not to be regarded as an "offense of a political character." In 1992, the U.S. Supreme Court agreed that Doherty could be deported to the United Kingdom, and he was.

In 2003, the United States and U.K. signed a new extradition treaty to replace the 1972 Treaty and the 1985 Supplementary Treaty; it further narrowed the political offense exception. (The 2003 Treaty, which entered into force in 2007, is excerpted in the Documentary Supplement.)

Irregular rendition. Extradition is the formal judicial means by which persons residing in one state are transferred to stand trial for crimes committed in another state. There are also transboundary transfers of suspects outside the formal extradition process. These are sometimes called "irregular renditions." An example occurred in United States v. Alvarez-Machain, 504 U.S. 655 (1992), where a suspect was kidnapped in Mexico by Mexican nationals who brought him to the United States to stand trial; they had been promised and then were given a reward by the U.S. Drug Enforcement Agency. (See Chapter 7.B.) Although the rendition in *Alvarez-Machain* was carried out without Mexico's knowledge or consent, this is not always the case. Law enforcement officials from different countries might cooperate to apprehend suspected criminals in one territory and expel them to another to face trial "without resort to formal extradition procedures," as U.S. and Mexican law enforcement officials have done in the past. María Celia Toro, The Internationalization of Police: The DEA in Mexico, 86 J. Am. Hist. 623, 629 (1999).

Irregular rendition has been used in some cases in connection with efforts to apprehend terrorists abroad and to bring them to the United States for trial. In his written testimony before the National Commission on Terrorist Attacks upon the United States ("the 9-11 Commission"), George Tenet, the former Director of Central Intelligence, stated that between 1986 and 2001, the Central Intelligence Agency could claim the successful rendition of "many dozens of terrorists." In August 2009, FBI agents seized a Lebanese citizen in Afghanistan and transferred him to the United States to face bribery charges, suggesting that, at least to some extent, "[t]he Obama Administration has continued [the] practice" of irregular rendition. Michael John Garcia, Congressional Research Service, Renditions: Constraints Imposed by Laws on Torture 3 (Sept. 8, 2009).

Notes and Questions

1. Does the political offense exception in extradition treaties serve a meaningful purpose in today's environment, when many serious transnational crimes, including terrorism-related offense, have political underpinnings? Would a rule simply prohibiting extradition where the subject of the request will be persecuted on the basis of race, religion, ethnicity, or nationality make more sense? Should judges decide whether not to extradite persons under the political offense doctrine, or is this a decision better vested in the Secretary of State?

2. Under the "rule of judicial noninquiry," courts have traditionally not refused extradition on the grounds that the means by which a state has secured evidence to request extradition, or the treatment defendants will face in the requesting state, fail to meet the due process standards that would apply in a trial in the requested state. More recently, U.S. courts — although they remain reluctant to refuse extradition based on a fugitive's anticipated treatment in the requesting country — have increasingly allowed fugitives to make a record regarding concerns of mistreatment. This approach "gives the [requesting] government an opportunity to contradict the relator's assertions and to make its own record in an open manner. On the basis of such a record, the Secretary of State can make a more enlightened and transparent decision." M. Cherif Bassiouni, International Extradition: United States Law and Practice 615 (5th ed. 2007). Particular issues regarding the rule of judicial noninquiry arise where the subject of an extradition request claims he or she would

be subject to torture in the state seeking extradition. Under Article 3 of the Convention Against Torture and Other Forms of Cruel, Inhuman or Degrading Treatment or Punishment, a state party may not "extradite a person to another State where there are substantial grounds for believing that he would be in danger of being subjected to torture."

Should courts be more assertive and decide that they will not only inquire, but sometimes deny an extradition request, based on the treatment the subject of the request will face in the requesting country? Should they do so on grounds of public policy? Or to ensure compliance with other international legal obligations, including the Torture Convention or other human rights treaties? Is it preferable for courts or the Secretary of State to decide whether a person will face mistreatment if he or she is extradited? Is there a danger that the Secretary of State will be reluctant to conclude that a person will face mistreatment in another country, particularly if it is an ally?

3. Considerable controversy continues to arise over irregular renditions that have purportedly taken place without the approval of the country on whose territory suspects or fugitives are apprehended by another state's law enforcement officials. In November 2009, for example, 23 U.S. citizens, most believed to be affiliated with the Central Intelligence Agency, were convicted in absentia by an Italian court for violating Italian law by abducting a radical Egyptian cleric, Hassan Mustafa Osama Nasr, in Milan in 2003, and transferring him to Egypt for interrogation. Nasr was freed in February 2007 from jail in Egypt, where he claims to have been tortured after the Milan kidnapping. The court's judgment represents the first criminal case involving the U.S. practice' of "extraordinary rendition," discussed in Chapter 8.B.8.

When, if ever, do you think irregular renditions without the consent of the host government are appropriate? Does it depend on whether there is an extradition treaty in place between the countries involved, and whether it would be possible for the requesting state to gain custody of the fugitive through procedures under that treaty? Would the United States consider it acceptable for foreign countries to abduct persons in the United States through irregular renditions? If the United States would object to the irregular rendition of an American from U.S. territory, on what basis would it defend such practices by U.S. authorities?

Even if the authorities of the host countries consent to an irregular rendition, does arresting and transferring a fugitive without judicial involvement violate the rights of the fugitive? What assurance is provided in the case of an irregular rendition that sufficient evidence exists to support the arrest? Or does the CIA's the reported successes in arresting "dozens of terrorists" justify the practice?

B. SUBSTANTIVE INTERNATIONAL CRIMINAL LAW

The preceding section addressed international cooperation in investigating, prosecuting, and suppressing acts deemed to be crimes under the *domestic* law of states that have a transnational scope. Some conduct by individuals, however, may also be deemed a crime under *international* law. International crimes, which are generally grave acts that implicate the interests or values of the international community as a whole, impose liability directly on individuals. Although the idea of holding individuals criminally accountable for violations of international law rules has distant foundations in the international criminalization of piracy and violations by soldiers of the laws of war, our discussion begins with the Nuremberg Charter and international tribunals right after World War II. We begin by exploring the basic principles of individual criminal responsibility under international law articulated in the Nuremberg trials, and then examine in greater detail several specific problems of individual criminal accountability, including the relationship between criminal liability and principles of immunity under international law, the doctrine of command responsibility, and vicarious responsibility for crimes. The section then discusses some of the major substantive categories of international crimes.

1. *Nuremberg and Individual Criminal Responsibility*

Even before World War II ended, the United States, Great Britain, the Soviet Union, and France were considering how to deal after the war not only with the aggression of Nazi Germany and Japan, but also with the increasingly obvious atrocities that had occurred in the concentration camps and elsewhere. In 1945, the parties concluded the Charter of the International Military Tribunal (discussed in Chapter 11.B.1) that defined certain crimes — crimes against peace, war crimes, and crimes against humanity. The Charter specified that an individual could be responsible for these crimes. It also provided that "[l]eaders, organizers, instigators and accomplices participating in the formulation or execution of a common plan or conspiracy to commit any of the foregoing crimes are responsible for all acts performed by any persons in execution of such plan." Article 6.

The International Military Tribunal (IMT) tried 24 top Nazi leaders who survived the war. Before the Tribunal, the defendants challenged the notion that they could be held criminally responsible as individuals for violations of international law. They also argued that their prosecution, particularly for the crime of "planning, preparation, initiation or waging of a war of aggression," violated the *nullum crimen sine lege, nulla poena sine lege* principle ("no crime without law, no punishment without law"), that is, the notion that persons may not be convicted for acts not considered to be crimes at the time they were committed. The IMT's judgment addressed these issues.

Judgment of the International Military Tribunal

Sept. 30-Oct. 1, 1946
1 Trial of the Major War Criminals Before the International Military Tribunal: Nuremberg 171, 219-223 (1947)

The Charter makes the planning or waging of a war of aggression or a war in violation of international treaties a crime; and it is therefore not strictly necessary to consider whether and to what extent aggressive war was a crime before the execution of the London Agreement [that created the Tribunal]. But in view of the great importance of the questions of law involved, the Tribunal has heard full argument from the Prosecution and the Defense, and will express its view on the matter.

It was urged on behalf of the defendants that a fundamental principle of all law—international and domestic—is that there can be no punishment of crime without a pre-existing law. "*Nullum crimen sine lege, nulla poena sine lege.*" It was submitted that *ex post facto* punishment is abhorrent to the law of all civilized nations, that no sovereign power had made aggressive war a crime at the time the alleged criminal acts were committed, that no statute had defined aggressive war, that no penalty had been fixed for its commission, and no court had been created to try and punish offenders.

In the first place, it is to be observed that the maxim *nullum crimen sine lege* is not a limitation of sovereignty, but is in general a principle of justice. To assert that it is unjust to punish those who in defiance of treaties and assurances have attacked neighboring states without warning is obviously untrue, for in such circumstances the attacker must know that he is doing wrong, and so far from it being unjust to punish him, it would be unjust if his wrong were allowed to go unpunished. Occupying the positions they did in the Government of Germany, the defendants, or at least some of them must have known of the treaties signed by Germany, outlawing recourse to war for the settlement of international disputes; they must have known that they were acting in defiance of all international law when in complete deliberation they carried out their designs of invasion and aggression. On this view of the case alone, it would appear that the maxim has no application to the present facts.

This view is strongly reinforced by a consideration of the state of international law in 1939, so far as aggressive war is concerned. The General Treaty for the Renunciation of War of 27 August 1928, more generally known as the Pact of Paris or the Kellogg-Briand Pact,* was binding on 63 nations, including Germany, Italy and Japan at the outbreak of war in 1939. . . .

The question is, what was the legal effect of this Pact? The nations who signed the Pact or adhered to it unconditionally condemned recourse to war for the future as an instrument of policy, and expressly renounced it. After the signing of the Pact, any nation resorting to war as an instrument of national policy breaks the Pact. In the opinion of the Tribunal, the solemn renunciation of war as an instrument of national policy necessarily involves the proposition that such a war is illegal in international law; and that those who plan and wage such a war, with its inevitable and terrible consequences, are committing a crime in so doing. War for the solution of international controversies undertaken as an instrument of national policy certainly includes a war of aggression, and such a war is therefore outlawed by the Pact. . . .

But it is argued [by the defendants] that the Pact does not expressly enact that such wars are crimes, or set up court to try those who make such wars. To that extent the same is true with regard to the laws of war contained in the Hague Convention. The Hague Convention of 1907** prohibited resort to certain methods of waging war. These included the inhuman treatment of prisoners, the employment of poisoned weapons, the improper use of flags of truce, and similar matters. Many of these prohibitions had been enforced long before the date of the Convention; but since 1907 they have certainly been crimes, punishable as offenses against the laws of

*[Discussed in Chapter 11.A.2.—Eds.]
**[Discussed in Chapter 11.D.1.—Eds.]

war; yet the Hague Convention nowhere designates such practices as criminal, nor is any sentence prescribed, nor any mention made of a court to try and punish offenders. For many years past, however, military tribunals have tried and punished individuals guilty of violating the rules of land warfare laid down by this Convention. In the opinion of the Tribunal, those who wage aggressive war are doing that which is equally illegal, and of much greater moment than a breach of one of the rules of the Hague Convention. In interpreting the words of the Pact, it must be remembered that international law is not the product of an international legislature, and that such international agreements as the Pact of Paris have to deal with the general principles of law, and not with administrative matters of procedure. The law of war is to be found not only in treaties, but in the customs and practices of states which gradually obtained universal recognition, and from general principles of justice applied by jurists and practised by military courts. This law is not static, but by continual adaptation follows the needs of a changing world. Indeed, in many cases treaties do no more than express and define for more accurate reference the principles of law already existing. . . .

At the meeting of the Assembly of the League of Nations on 24 September 1927, all the delegations then present (including the German, the Italian and the Japanese), unanimously adopted a declaration concerning wars of aggression. The preamble to the declaration stated:

> The Assembly:
> Recognizing the solidarity which unites the community of nations;
> Being inspired by a firm desire for the maintenance of general peace;
> Being convinced that a war of aggression can never serve as a means of settling international disputes, and is in consequence an international crime. . . .

The unanimous resolution of 18 February 1928, of 21 American Republics at the Sixth (Havana) Pan-American Conference, declared that "war of aggression constitutes an international crime against the human species."

All these expressions of opinion, and others that could be cited, so solemnly made, reinforce the construction which the Tribunal placed upon the Pact of Paris, that resort to a war of aggression is not merely illegal, but is criminal. The prohibition of aggressive war demanded by the conscience of the world, finds its expression in the series of pacts and treaties to which the Tribunal has just referred.

It is also important to remember that Article 227 of the Treaty of Versailles provided for the constitution of a special Tribunal, composed of representatives of five of the Allied and Associated Powers which had been belligerents in the first World War opposed to Germany, to try the former German Emperor "for a supreme offence against international morality and the sanctity of treaties." . . . In Article 228 of the Treaty, the German Government expressly recognized the right of the Allied Powers "to bring before military tribunals persons accused of having committed acts in violation of the laws and customs of war."

It was submitted [by the defendants] that international law is concerned with the actions of sovereign States, and provides no punishment for individuals; and further, that where the act in question is an act of state, those who carry it out are not personally responsible, but are protected by the doctrine of the sovereignty of the State. In the opinion of the Tribunal, both these submissions must be rejected.

That international law imposes duties and liabilities upon individuals as well as upon States has long been recognized. In the recent case of Ex Parte Quirin (1942 317 US 1), before the Supreme Court of the United States, persons were charged during the war with landing in the United States for purposes of spying and sabotage. The late Chief Justice Stone, speaking for the Court, said:

> From the very beginning of its history this Court has applied the law of war as including that part of the law of nations which prescribes for the conduct of war, the status, rights and duties of enemy nations as well as enemy individuals.

He went on to give a list of cases tried by the Courts, where individual offenders were charged with offenses against the laws of nations, and particularly the laws of war. . . . Crimes against international law are committed by men, not by abstract entities, and only by punishing individuals who commit such crimes can the provisions of international law be enforced. . . .

The principle of international law, which under certain circumstances, protects the representatives of a state, cannot be applied to acts which are condemned as criminal by international law. The authors of these acts cannot shelter themselves behind their official position in order to be freed from punishment in appropriate proceedings. Article 7 of the Charter expressly declares:

> The official position of defendants, whether as heads of State, or responsible officials in government departments, shall not be considered as freeing them from responsibility, or mitigating punishment.

On the other hand the very essence of the Charter is that individuals have international duties which transcend the national obligations of obedience imposed by the individual State. He who violates the laws of war cannot obtain immunity while acting in pursuance of the authority of the state if the state in authorizing action moves outside its competence under international law.

Notes and Questions

1. Do you agree with the Nuremberg Tribunal's rejection of the defendants' arguments that they were charged with some crimes (e.g., waging a war of aggression) that were not recognized as such until after the acts occurred? What were the Tribunal's principal precedents for responding to the *ex post facto* defense? Did these precedents establish criminal liability? One commentator has written that the IMT's reliance on the Kellogg-Briand Pact and the 1907 Hague Regulations on "the question of whether crimes against peace were already punishable" under international law did not provide a "convincing justification"; the 1907 Hague Regulations "did not penalize the violation of the law of war" and the Kellogg-Briand Pact "did not contain any sanction — not even a declaration to the effect that war as such was a crime." Hans-Heinrich Jescheck, The General Principles of International Criminal Law Set Out in Nuremberg, as Mirrored in the ICC Statute, 2 J. Int'l Crim. Just. 38, 41 (2004). Is it enough to satisfy the *nullem crimen* principle if the actor, in the words of the Tribunal, "must know that what he is doing is wrong?" Or must the actor also know that his conduct will give rise to individual criminal responsibility under international law?

2. Subsequent trials of other Nazi war criminals were conducted under the authority of Control Council Law No. 10. (The Control Council was a governing body composed of the four states that occupied Germany after the war.) These trials were conducted not by an international tribunal, but by tribunals constituted by each of the victorious powers in their zone of occupation. In one Control Council Law No. 10 case, the tribunal addressed the *nullum crimen* principle by stressing that the absence of a "codified statute[]" designating behavior as an international crime did not necessarily mean that the behavior was being criminalized on an *ex post facto* basis. "International law is not a body of authoritative codes or statutes; it is the gradual expression, case by case, of the moral judgments of the civilized world." United States v. Altstoetter ("Justice Case"), in 3 Trials of War Criminals Before the Nuremberg Military Tribunals under Control Council Law No. 10, at 954, 975 (1951) (quoting Henry L. Stimson).

3. Does the possibility of criminalizing conduct on the basis of customary international law norms create special problems regarding application of the *nullum crimen* principal in the realm of international criminal law? There is no definitive statement of customary international law, and there may be disagreement about its content, as well as about the degree of practice and the evidence of *opinio juris* necessary to establish a customary rule. Does the "gradual expression, case by case, of the moral judgments of the civilized world" provide clear notice to potential defendants of what conduct is criminalized by international law?

4. Does the Nuremberg Judgment provide a clear basis for knowing which violations of international law rules give rise to *individual* international criminal responsibility? The Tribunal indicated that violations of international law are committed by individuals, not abstract state entities. The Judgment also notes that international law can only be enforced if the individuals who violate the rules are punished. But don't these arguments apply as well to *any* violation of an international law rule that gives rise to state responsibility? Should any violation of international law by a state give rise to individual criminal liability? How can international crimes be distinguished from "ordinary" violations of international law for which only the state is responsible?

5. Shortly after the IMT issued its judgment against the top Nazi leaders, the U.N. General Assembly in Resolution 95 (1956) unanimously affirmed the principles of international law that were recognized in the Nuremberg Charter and Tribunal.

6. The Nuremberg Tribunal convicted 19 German defendants, sentencing 12 to death and the rest to imprisonment. Beyond this, there were thousands of war crimes trials held after the Second World War, including trials authorized by Control Council Law No. 10 and trials before military and civilian courts of the victorious parties, as well as in German courts. The following is an estimate of the number of war crimes trials held by major Allied nations as of 1963:

Country	*Number of sentences*	*Death sentences*
USA	1,814	450
UK	1,085	240
USSR	c. 10,000	?
West Germany	12,846	?

War Crimes, War Criminals, and War Crimes Trials 5 (Norman E. Tutorow ed., 1986). Moreover, "[i]In addition to war crimes trials conducted by foreign tribunals, there were thousands of denazification proceedings in Germany." Id. at 7. In the American zone of occupation, for instance, "over 930,000 defendants were eventually tried by denazification tribunals." Id. at 8.

7. The Allied nations also established an International Military Tribunal for the Far East. This tribunal was a result of the Potsdam Declaration of July 26, 1945, signed by China, Great Britain, and the United States, and later adhered to by the Soviet Union. The government of Japan accepted the provisions of the Potsdam Declaration on September 2, 1945, when it signed the Instrument of Surrender to the Allied Powers. Trials were conducted throughout the Far East. The most famous of these was the trial in Tokyo from 1946-1948, which resulted in the conviction of 25 major figures from the Japanese government, including General Tojo. For a complete account of the proceedings of this Tribunal, see R. John Pritchard & Sonia Magbanua Zaide, The Tokyo War Crimes Trial (1981).

2. *Additional Individual Responsibility Issues*

Although the Nuremberg Tribunal affirmed the principle that individuals can be held criminally responsible under international law, issues have arisen about the scope of that responsibility. One recurrent issue concerns the criminal responsibility of subordinates who commit crimes ordered by their superiors. During the Nuremberg trials, for example:

> It was . . . submitted on behalf of most of these defendants that in doing what they did they were acting under the orders of Hitler, and therefore cannot be held responsible for the acts committed by them in carrying out these orders. The Charter specifically provides in Article 8:
>
> > The fact that the Defendant acted pursuant to order of his Government or of a superior shall not free him from responsibility, but may be considered in mitigation of punishment.
>
> The provisions of this Article are in conformity with the law of all nations. That a soldier was ordered to kill or torture in violation of the international law of war has never been recognized as a defense to such acts of brutality, though, as the Charter here provides, the order may be urged in mitigation of the punishment. The true test, which is found in varying degrees in the criminal law of most nations, is not the existence of the order, but whether moral choice was in fact possible. [Judgment of the International Military Tribunal, in 1 Trial of the Major War Criminals Before the International Military, supra, at 171, 223-224.]

The issue of following orders also arose more recently before the International Criminal Tribunal for the Former Yugoslavia in the case of Drazen Erdemović, who admitted participating in the summary execution of hundreds of Bosnian Muslims civilians during the Bosnia Serb takeover of Srebrenica. As noted in Chapter 2.D, he argued that he should be excused for serving any sentence for these acts because he would have been killed had he refused to carry out his orders. The Appeals Chamber rejected Erdemović's duress defense. Two judges, in a concurring opinion, emphasized that although duress did not provide a defense to criminal responsibility, it "could in appropriate cases be taken into account in mitigation of sentence." Prosecutor v. Erdemović, Case No. IT-96-22-A, Appeals Judgement, at ¶86 (Oct. 7, 1997) (Joint Separate Opinion of Judges McDonald and Vohrah).

Some other important issues regarding individual responsibility include the relationship between international criminal responsibility and immunity principles under international law, the responsibility of commanders for the acts of subordinates, and the liability of persons who assist or participate with others in committing crimes.

a. Immunity

Article 7 of the Charter of the International Military Tribunal, as noted above, stipulated that the "official position of defendants, whether as Heads of State, or responsible officials in Government Departments, shall not be considered as freeing them from responsibility, or mitigating punishment" for violations of international criminal law. This principle is also reflected in the statutes of the international ad hoc tribunals for the former Yugoslavia and Rwanda and the International Criminal Court (ICC), discussed in Section C below.

The relationship between international criminal liability and immunity is particularly complicated outside the context of international criminal tribunals, namely, when the domestic courts of one country seek to prosecute senior officials of another country. In April 2000, a Belgian investigating magistrate issued an arrest warrant against the then-Minister of Foreign Affairs of the Democratic Republic of the Congo (DRC), Abdulaye Yerodia Ndombasi, seeking his extradition to Belgium for prosecution for violations of international criminal law. The DRC initiated a case in the International Court of Justice (ICJ), claiming that the arrest warrant violated the "absolute inviolability and immunity from criminal process of incumbent foreign ministers." Arrest Warrant of 11 April 2000 (Democratic Republic of the Congo v. Belgium), 2002 I.C.J. 3, 8 (Feb. 14).

The ICJ concluded that, under customary international law, foreign ministers, while in office, generally enjoy full immunity from criminal jurisdiction and inviolability. The Court then addressed Belgium's argument that such immunity did not apply with respect to the commission of war crimes or crimes against humanity under international law.

Arrest Warrant of 11 April 2000 (Democratic Republic of the Congo v. Belgium)

Int'l Court of Justice
2002 I.C.J. 3, 24-26 (Feb. 14)

58. The Court has carefully examined State practice, including national legislation and those few decisions of national higher courts, such as the House of Lords or the French Court of Cassation. It has been unable to deduce from this practice that there exists under customary international law any form of exception to the rule according immunity from criminal jurisdiction and inviolability to incumbent Ministers for Foreign Affairs, where they are suspected of having committed war crimes or crimes against humanity.

The Court has also examined the rules concerning the immunity or criminal responsibility of persons having an official capacity contained in the legal instruments creating international criminal tribunals, and which are specifically applicable to the latter (see Charter of the International Military Tribunal of Nuremberg, Art. 7; Charter of the International Military Tribunal of Tokyo, Art. 6; Statute of the International Criminal Tribunal for the former Yugoslavia, Art. 7, para. 2; Statute of the International Criminal Tribunal for Rwanda, Art. 6, para. 2; Statute of the International Criminal Court, Art. 27). It finds that these rules likewise do not enable it to conclude that any such an exception exists in customary international law in regard to national courts.

. . . [N]one of the decisions of the Nuremberg and Tokyo international military tribunals, or of the International Criminal Tribunal for the former Yugoslavia, cited by Belgium deal with the question of the immunities of incumbent Ministers for Foreign Affairs before national courts where they are accused of having committed war crimes or crimes against humanity. . . .

In view of the foregoing, the Court accordingly cannot accept Belgium's argument in this regard.

59. . . . [A]lthough various international conventions on the prevention and punishment of certain serious crimes impose on States obligations of prosecution or extradition, thereby requiring them to extend their criminal jurisdiction, such extension of jurisdiction in no way affects immunities under customary international law, including those of Ministers for Foreign Affairs. These remain opposable before the courts of a foreign State, even where those courts exercise such a jurisdiction under these conventions.

60. The Court emphasizes, however, that the immunity from jurisdiction enjoyed by incumbent Ministers for Foreign Affairs does not mean that they enjoy impunity in respect of any crimes they might have committed, irrespective of their gravity. Immunity from criminal jurisdiction and individual criminal responsibility are quite separate concepts. While jurisdictional immunity is procedural in nature, criminal responsibility is a question of substantive law. Jurisdictional immunity may well bar prosecution for a certain period or for certain offences; it cannot exonerate the person to whom it applies from all criminal responsibility.

61. Accordingly, the immunities enjoyed under international law by an incumbent or former Minister for Foreign Affairs do not represent a bar to criminal prosecution in certain circumstances.

First, such persons enjoy no criminal immunity under international law in their own countries, and may thus be tried by those countries' courts in accordance with the relevant rules of domestic law.

Secondly, they will cease to enjoy immunity from foreign jurisdiction if the State which they represent or have represented decides to waive that immunity.

Thirdly, after a person ceases to hold the office of Minister for Foreign Affairs, he or she will no longer enjoy all of the immunities accorded by international law in other States. Provided that it has jurisdiction under international law, a court of one State may try a former Minister for Foreign Affairs of another State in respect of acts committed prior or subsequent to his or her period of office, as well as in respect of acts committed during that period of office in a private capacity.

Fourthly, an incumbent or former Minister for Foreign Affairs may be subject to criminal proceedings before certain international criminal courts, where they have jurisdiction. Examples include the . . . International Criminal Court created by the 1998 Rome Convention. The latter's Statute expressly provides, in Article 27, paragraph 2, that "[i]mmunities or special procedural rules which may attach to the official capacity of a person, whether under national or international law, shall not bar the Court from exercising its jurisdiction over such a person."

The relationship between international criminal law and international law immunities arose in the case of Augusto Pinochet, the former dictator who served as President of Chile until 2000 after overthrowing the democratically elected regime of Salvador Allende in 1973. Pinochet was indicted by judicial authorities in Spain for a number of crimes, including torture, committed during his reign. During a visit by Pinochet to the United Kingdom, Spanish authorities sought his extradition. As noted in Chapter 6.A, the Law Lords of British House of Lords (the predecessor to the U.K. Supreme Court) concluded that although a head of state possesses absolute immunity from the jurisdiction of foreign courts while in office, immunity for a former head of state is more limited, and applies only to official acts, that is, "acts done in performance of . . . [his public] functions whilst in office." Regina v. Bow Street Metropolitan Stipendiary Magistrate and Others, Ex parte Pinochet Ugarte, [2000] 1 A.C. 147, 201-202 (H.L. 1999) (opinion of Lord Browne Wilkinson). Even though the Convention Against Torture and Other Cruel, Inhuman or Degrading Treatment or Punishment does not contain an express provision stating that persons charged with torture may not claim immunities under international law, the House of Lords also concluded that, after Chile became a party to the Torture Convention, torture could not be deemed an official or public act for which Pinochet could claim immunity.

> [I]f, as alleged, Senator Pinochet organised and authorised torture . . . , he was not acting in any capacity which gives rise to [official acts] immunity . . . because such actions were contrary to international law, Chile had agreed to outlaw such conduct and Chile had agreed with the other parties to the Torture Convention that all signatory states should have jurisdiction to try official torture (as defined in the Convention) even if such torture were committed in Chile. [Id. at 205.]

Notes and Questions

1. Do you agree with the ICJ's conclusion that persons with immunity under international law cannot be tried before other countries' domestic courts for the commission of international crimes? Doesn't the fact that the international community has defined an act as an international crime reflect a judgment that perpetrators should be held accountable, regardless of their position? Or should the immunities of heads of state, foreign ministers, and diplomats be presumed to be valid unless they are expressly overridden by a treaty or Security Council resolution, as happened in the case of the International Military Tribunal, the International Criminal Tribunals for the Former Yugoslavia and Rwanda, and the International Criminal Court?

2. In the *Pinochet* case, the House of Lords concluded that because Chile was obligated to outlaw torture, torture could not be deemed an official act for which Chile could claim immunity on behalf of former President Pinochet. Does this imply

that any act carried out by a government official that violates international law is not subject to immunity? Since a head of state presumably will not be held criminally responsible for lawful official acts, does the House of Lords' interpretation in the *Pinochet* case defeat the purpose of the head of state immunity doctrine?

3. Is the House of Lords' decision that Pinochet could not claim official acts immunity for torture consistent with the ICJ's decision in the *Arrest Warrant* case? It is important to keep in mind the distinction between personal immunity, which applies to heads of state, foreign ministers, and certain other officials while they are in office, and functional immunity, which continues to apply even after such persons have left office. Personal immunity is absolute, but functional immunity has traditionally been understood to apply only to "official acts." Antonio Cassese, When May Senior State Officials Be Tried for International Crimes? Some Comments on the *Congo v. Belgium* Case, 13 Euro. J. Int'l L. 853, 863 (2002). The ICJ in the *Arrest Warrant* case suggested that a former foreign minister would "no longer enjoy" immunity only for acts he had committed in a "private capacity." Do you think the acts of torture Pinochet allegedly committed were carried out in his private capacity? If not, doesn't that make them "official" acts for which Pinochet should have been immune from suit? Or is there a category of acts that should not benefit from immunity even though they are not "private" acts?

4. Although the House of Lords concluded that Pinochet could be extradited to Spain, at Chile's request, doctors examined Pinochet and found him unfit to stand trial in Spain. He returned to Chile, where courts ruled he could face trial in domestic courts for human rights abuses committed during his tenure. He died in December 2006 without having faced trial in the cases pending against him.

5. Issues of immunity of foreign officials from suit in U.S. courts were considered by the Supreme Court in Samantar v. Yousuf, 130 S.Ct. 2278 (2010), which is discussed in Chapter 6.A.

b. Command Responsibility

The trial of the Nazi leadership before the International Military Tribunal at Nuremberg was based on the notion that it is not only the individuals who directly perpetrate atrocities in violation of international criminal law who may be held accountable. Article 6 of the Charter of the Tribunal provided that "[l]eaders, organizers, instigators and accomplices participating in the formulation or execution of a common plan or conspiracy to commit . . . crimes [within the jurisdiction of the Tribunal] are responsible for all acts performed by any persons in the execution of such plan." The statutes of subsequent international criminal tribunals similarly incorporate the idea that a person who, in the words of the ICC Statute, "[o]rders, solicits or induces the commission" of a crime within the Court's jurisdiction bears responsibility just as the person who commits the offense does. Statute of the International Criminal Court, art. 25(3)(b).

International criminal law in some circumstances also imposes legal liability on political and military leaders even where they have not specifically ordered the commission of crimes. Following the Second World War, Japanese General Tomoyuki Yamashita, who had been the commanding general in charge of Japanese forces in the Philippines, was tried before a U.S. military tribunal in Manila for war crimes committed by troops under his command. The Supreme Court, considering his conviction on a petition of habeas corpus, addressed the doctrine referred to as "superior authority" or "command responsibility" for acts of subordinates.

In re Yamashita

U.S. Supreme Court
327 U.S. 1, 13-16, 28, 34-35 (1946)

STONE, C.J., delivered the opinion of the Court. . . .

The charge, so far as now relevant, is that petitioner, between October 9, 1944 and September 2, 1945, in the Philippine Islands, "while commander of armed forces of Japan at war with the United States of America and its allies, unlawfully disregarded and failed to discharge his duty as commander to control the operations of the members of his command, permitting them to commit brutal atrocities and other high crimes against people of the United States and of its allies and dependencies, particularly the Philippines; and he . . . thereby violated the laws of war." . . .

. . . [I]t is urged that the charge does not allege that petitioner has either committed or directed the commission of such acts, and consequently that no violation is charged as against him. But this overlooks the fact that the gist of the charge is an unlawful breach of duty by petitioner as an army commander to control the operations of the members of his command by "permitting them to commit" the extensive and widespread atrocities specified. The question then is whether the law of war imposes on an army commander a duty to take such appropriate measures as are within his power to control the troops under his command for the prevention of the specified acts which are violations of the law of war and which are likely to attend the occupation of hostile territory by an uncontrolled soldiery, and whether he may be charged with personal responsibility for his failure to take such measures when violations result. . . .

It is evident that the conduct of military operations by troops whose excesses are unrestrained by the orders or efforts of their commander would almost certainly result in violations which it is the purpose of the law of war to prevent. Its purpose to protect civilian populations and prisoners of war from brutality would largely be defeated if the commander of an invading army could with impunity neglect to take reasonable measures for their protection. Hence the law of war presupposes that its violation is to be avoided through the control of the operations of war by commanders who are to some extent responsible for their subordinates.

This is recognized by the Annex to the Fourth Hague Convention of 1907, respecting the laws and customs of war on land. Article I lays down as a condition which an armed force must fulfill in order to be accorded the rights of lawful belligerents, that it must be "commanded by a person responsible for his subordinates." . . . [The Court also relied on Article 19 of the Tenth Hague Convention of 1907, Article 26 of the 1929 Geneva Red Cross Convention, and Article 43 of the 1907 Hague Regulations.] These provisions plainly imposed on petitioner . . . an affirmative duty to take such measures as were within his power and appropriate in the circumstances to protect prisoners of war and the civilian population. . . .

Justice Murphy, dissenting.

. . . [Petitioner] was not charged with personally participating in the acts of atrocity or with ordering or condoning their commission. Not even knowledge of these crimes was attributed to him. It was simply alleged that he unlawfully disregarded and failed to discharge his duty as commander to control the operations of the members of his command, permitting them to commit the acts of atrocity. The recorded annals of warfare and the established principles of international law afford not the slightest precedent for such a charge. This indictment in effect permitted the military commission to make the crime whatever it willed, dependent upon its biased view as to petitioner's duties and his disregard thereof, a practice reminiscent of that pursued in certain less respected nations in recent years. . . .

. . . [R]ead against the background of military events in the Philippines subsequent to October 9, 1944, these charges amount to this: "We, the victorious American forces, have done everything possible to destroy and disorganize your lines of communication, your effective control of your personnel, your ability to wage war. In those respects we have succeeded. We have defeated and crushed your forces. And now we charge and condemn you for having been inefficient in maintaining control of your troops during the period when we were so effectively besieging and eliminating your forces and blocking your ability to maintain effective control. Many terrible atrocities were committed by your disorganized troops. Because these atrocities were so widespread we will not bother to charge or prove that you committed, ordered or condoned any of them. We will assume that they must have resulted from your inefficiency and negligence as a commander. In short, we charge you with the crime of inefficiency in controlling your troops. We will judge the discharge of your duties by the disorganization which we ourselves created in large part. Our standards of judgment are whatever we wish to make them."

Nothing in all history or in international law, at least as far as I am aware, justifies such a charge against a fallen commander of a defeated force. To use the very inefficiency and disorganization created by the victorious forces as the primary basis for condemning officers of the defeated armies bears no resemblance to justice or to military reality.

Notes and Questions

1. General Yamashita's conviction was upheld, and he was hanged in February 1946.

2. In the domestic U.S. context, criminal liability for serious offenses usually requires that a defendant act with a mental state of knowledge or intent, or at least recklessness. What standard did the Supreme Court apply in the *Yamashita* case? Do you agree with Justice Murphy that Yamashita was, in effect, convicted on the basis of "inefficiency and negligence?" When should commanders be held responsible for the acts of subordinates?

3. The principle of command responsibility has been incorporated in the statutes of recent international criminal tribunals. See, for example, Article 7 of the Statute of the International Criminal Tribunal for the Former Yugoslavia, Article 6 of the Statute of the International Criminal Tribunal for Rwanda, and Article 28 of the Statute of the International Criminal Court. (The Statute of the International Criminal Court is included in the Documentary Supplement.)

4. Both military and civilian leaders may be held responsible for crimes committed by subordinates on the theory of command responsibility. To be found liable on this basis, however, it must be established that the leader exercised de facto or de jure control over the subordinates, especially in cases involving civilian leaders. In a case before the International Criminal Tribunal for the Former Yugoslavia (ICTY) brought against a Dario Kordić, a local Bosnian Croatian political leader involved in planning war crimes, a Trial Chamber of the Tribunal ruled:

> Although [criminal] liability may attach to civilians as well as military personnel [on a command responsibility basis] . . . , great care must be taken in assessing the evidence to determine command responsibility in respect of civilians, lest an injustice is done. . . . [S]ubstantial influence (such as Kordić had), by itself, is not indicative of a sufficient degree of control for liability [on command responsibility grounds]. . . . [Prosecutor v. Kordić, Case No. IT-95-14/2-T, Judgement, at ¶¶840 (Feb. 26, 2001).]

The Tribunal concluded that Kordić lacked "effective control," defined as "a material ability to prevent or punish criminal conduct, however that control is exercised." Id.

Does the *Kordić* case establish different standards for "command responsibility" liability for military and civilian leaders? Does the difference reflect an assumption that military leaders exercise effective authority and control over subordinates who commit war crimes? Is it reasonable to establish liability on the basis of such an assumption, or should a prosecutor in any given case have to prove that a military commander in fact exercised effective authority and control?

5. The Statute of the International Criminal Court includes two separate provisions addressing the criminal liability of "military commanders" and other "superior and subordinate relationships." Examine the differences between the requirements in paragraphs (a) and (b) of Article 28 of the Statute, which is in the Document Supplement. Does the ICC Statute impose a lower standard on civilian leaders? Is that appropriate?

6. Slobodan Milošević, the former President of the Federal Republic of Yugoslavia, was on trial before the ICTY when he died in March 2006. He had been indicted for, among other things, crimes committed during the war in Bosnia aimed at forcibly removing non-Serbs, principally Bosnian Muslims and Bosnian Croats, from large areas of Bosnia. The Bosnia indictment highlights the difference between the direct responsibility of a leader for ordering the commission of crimes and responsibility on a command responsibility or "superior authority" basis. The indictment charged Milošević both with having "planned, instigated, ordered or otherwise aided and abetted" the underlying crimes, as well as failing to "take the necessary and reasonable measures to prevent such acts or to punish" the acts of subordinates over whom he held a position of superior authority. See Prosecutor v. Milošević, Case No. IT-02-54-T, Amended Indictment, at ¶¶26-27 (Apr. 21, 2004). Why did the Prosecutor of the ICTY charge Milošević on a command responsibility basis if she believed he directly planned, ordered, or instigated the crimes with which he was charged? What evidence would a prosecutor need to prove a leader directly planned or ordered an offense? Is it easier to win a conviction on a command responsibility basis? If so, do you support a doctrine that has the effect of easing the evidentiary burden on the prosecution?

c. Vicarious Responsibility

We have so far considered three bases for individual criminal responsibility under international law: directly committing an offense, ordering or instigating an offense, and incurring liability as a superior for the acts of subordinates. Individuals may also be responsible for international crimes on a vicarious or derivative liability basis if they are complicit in or assist the commission of international crimes. The case of Anto Furundžija before the ICTY involved a soldier who was charged with aiding and abetting the perpetration of outrages upon personal dignity, including rape, although he did not personally rape the victim.

Prosecutor v. Furundžija

Int'l Crim. Tribunal for the Former Yugoslavia
Case No. IT-95-17/1-T, Judgment, at ¶¶191, 232-235, 243, 245-246, 249, 274
(Dec. 10, 1998)

[Furundžija was present when another soldier in his unit raped "Witness A," a victim who testified at the trial. Furundžija did not personally rape "Witness A," but he was present in the room when the other soldier did, and he interrogated the victim while she was raped and subjected to other sexual assaults.]

191. . . . [The Trial Chamber] must establish both whether the accused's alleged presence in the locations where Witness A was assaulted would be sufficient to constitute the *actus reus* of aiding and abetting, and also the relevant mens rea required to accompany this action for responsibility to ensue. . . .

232. On the issue of [the *actus reus* of] the nature of assistance rendered, the [World War II-era] cases suggest that the assistance given by an accomplice need not be tangible and can consist of moral support in certain circumstances. While any spectator can be said to be encouraging a spectacle — an audience being a necessary element of a spectacle — the spectator in these cases was only found to be complicit if his status was such that his presence had a significant legitimising or encouraging effect on the principals. . . .

233. On the effect of the assistance given to the principal, none of the cases . . . suggests that the acts of the accomplice need bear a causal relationship to, or be a *conditio sine qua non* for, those of the principal. . . .

235. In sum, the Trial Chamber holds that the *actus reus* of aiding and abetting in international criminal law requires practical assistance, encouragement, or moral support which has a substantial effect on the perpetration of the crime. . . .

243. [With regard to *mens rea*] . . . , it is not necessary for an aider and abettor to meet all the requirements of mens rea for a principal perpetrator. In particular, it is not necessary that he shares and identifies with the principal's criminal will and purpose, provided that his own conduct was with knowledge. . . .

245. The above analysis leads the Trial Chamber to the conclusion that it is not necessary for the accomplice to share the *mens rea* of the perpetrator, in the sense of positive intention to commit the crime. Instead, the clear requirement in the vast majority of the cases is for the accomplice to have knowledge that his actions will assist the perpetrator in the commission of the crime. . . .

246. Moreover, it is not necessary that the aider and abettor should know the precise crime that was intended and which in the event was committed. If he is aware

that one of a number of crimes will probably be committed, and one of those crimes is in fact committed, he has intended to facilitate the commission of that crime, and is guilty as an aider and abettor. . . .

249. In sum, the Trial Chamber holds the legal ingredients of aiding and abetting in international criminal law to be the following: the *actus reus* consists of practical assistance, encouragement, or moral support which has a substantial effect on the perpetration of the crime. The *mens rea* required is the knowledge that these acts assist the commission of the offence. . . .

274. On the evidence on record, the Trial Chamber is satisfied that the Prosecution has proved its case against the accused beyond reasonable doubt. . . . [T]he Trial Chamber holds that the presence of the accused and his continued interrogation aided and abetted the crimes committed by [the other soldier in his unit]. He is individually responsible for outrages upon personal dignity including rape, a violation of the laws or customs of war. . . .

Notes and Questions

1. Rebel groups participating in a number of recent or ongoing civil wars, including in Sierra Leone and the Democratic Republic of the Congo, have funded their military campaigns by selling raw materials like diamonds and other minerals in territory under their control. If such a rebel group commits international crimes, would a person who knows about the crimes and who buys raw materials from the rebels be guilty of aiding and abetting?

2. Is the conduct of someone who aids and abets a crime as morally blameworthy as that of the perpetrator? Is it sufficiently grave to justify making it criminal under international law?

3. An additional form of international criminal liability is known as "joint criminal enterprise," or JCE. Under this form of liability, "an individual may be held responsible for all crimes committed pursuant to the existence of a common plan or design which involves the commission of [an international] crime . . . if the defendant participates with others in the common design." Allison Marston Danner & Jenny S. Martinez, Guilty Associations: Joint Criminal Enterprise, Command Responsibility, and the Development of International Criminal Law, 93 Cal. L. Rev. 75 (2005). Commentators have identified three different forms of JCE liability that have been applied by various courts and tribunals. In the first, individual members of a group may be held liable for acts agreed upon when making a common criminal plan or design, where all participants shared the intent to commit the crimes in question. "All are responsible, whatever their role and position in carrying out the common criminal plan." Amicus Curiae Brief of Professor Antonio Cassese and Members of the Journal of International Criminal Justice on Joint Criminal Enterprise Doctrine before the Extraordinary Chambers in the Court of Cambodia, reprinted in 20 Crim. L. Forum 289, 296 (2009). Under a second variant, JCE liability "applies to persons carrying out a task within a criminal design implemented in an institutional framework such as an internment or a concentration camp," even if there is no proof of a plan or agreement among the participants. Id. In the third variant, an individual who enters into a common criminal plan can be held criminally liable for foreseeable crimes committed in the course of the criminal enterprise, even if that person "did not have the intent to

commit the 'incidental' offence." Id. at 297. Some commentators have expressed concern about the potentially expansive application of JCE liability, noting that an individual could be convicted for a crime "even though the crime was committed by someone else and he did not intend to commit such a crime." Danner & Martinez, supra, at 135. Such a result, they argue, "raises the specter of guilt by association." Id. at 137. Do you agree? Or do you believe that in those mass atrocity situations where governmental orchestration of crimes is systemic, criminal liability should be based on the defendant's connection to that criminal system?

3. *International Crimes*

The preceding section exposed you to principles of individual criminal liability under international criminal law. This section examines some acts that constitute international crimes. We begin with Professor Cassese, a former president of the International Criminal Tribunal for the Former Yugoslavia, who provides an overview of the rationale for treating certain offenses as international crimes.

Antonio Cassese, International Criminal Law

11-12 (2d ed. 2008)

International crimes are breaches of international rules entailing the personal criminal liability of the individuals concerned (as opposed to the responsibility of the state of which the individuals may act as organs).

. . . [I]nternational crimes result from the cumulative presence of the following elements:

1. They consist of violations of international *customary* rules (as well as treaty provisions, where such provisions exist and either codify or spell out customary law or have contributed to its formation).

2. Such rules are intended to protect *values* considered important by the whole international community and consequently binding all states and individuals. The values at issue are not propounded by scholars or thought up by starry-eyed philosophers. Rather, they are laid down in a string of international instruments, which however, do not necessarily spell them out in so many words.

3. There exists a universal interest in repressing these crimes. Subject to certain conditions, under international law their alleged authors may in principle be prosecuted and punished *by any state*, regardless of any territorial or nationality link with the perpetrator or the victim. . . .

Under this definition international crimes include war crimes, crimes against humanity, genocide, torture (as distinct from torture as one of the categories of war crimes or crimes against humanity), aggression, and some extreme forms of international terrorism.

a. Genocide

Article 1 of the 1948 Genocide Convention states: "The Contracting Parties confirm that genocide, whether committed in time of peace or in time of war, is a crime under international law which they undertake to prevent and to punish." As of May 2011, there were 141 parties to the Convention (which is included in the Documentary Supplement). The prohibition on genocide is also generally viewed as part of customary international law binding even on states that are not parties to the Convention. See William A. Schabas, Genocide in International Law: The Crimes of Crimes 648 (2d ed. 2009).

The Genocide Convention defines the offense and establishes criminal liability and the duty of states to prosecute crimes of genocide as follows:

Convention on the Prevention and Punishment of the Crime of Genocide (Dec. 9, 1948)

Article 2

In the present Convention, genocide means any of the following acts committed with intent to destroy, in whole or in part, a national, ethnical, racial or religious group, as such:

(a) Killing members of the group;
(b) Causing serious bodily or mental harm to members of the group;
(c) Deliberately inflicting on the group conditions of life calculated to bring about its physical destruction in whole or in part;
(d) Imposing measures intended to prevent births within the group;
(e) Forcibly transferring children of the group to another group.

Article 3

The following acts shall be punishable:

(a) Genocide;
(b) Conspiracy to commit genocide;
(c) Direct and public incitement to commit genocide;
(d) Attempt to commit genocide;
(e) Complicity in genocide.

The Convention provides that persons who commit acts prohibited by Article 3 "shall be punished," regardless of their official position. (Article 4.) Parties to the Genocide Convention must enact legislation to "provide effective penalties" for persons guilty of genocide (Article 5); Article 6 provides that persons charged with genocide "shall be tried" by the courts of the state where the offense was committed or "by such international penal tribunal as may have jurisdiction with respect to those [states] which shall have accepted its jurisdiction."

The single worst atrocity committed during the conflict in the former Yugoslavia beginning in 1991 was the 1995 massacre by Bosnian Serb forces of between 7,000 and 10,000 Bosnian Muslim men in the town of Srebrenica. Radislav Krstić was a general in the Bosnian Serb Army (VRS), which carried out the massacres. Krstić was charged with genocide for his role in the killings and tried before the International Criminal Tribunal for the Former Yugoslavia. An important issue in the case was whether the killing of Bosnian Muslim men of Srebrenica satisfied the requirement of the Genocide Convention that the offender act with "intent to destroy, in whole or in part, a national, ethnical, racial or religious group, as such." The Tribunal also had to assess whether Krstić personally acted with the requisite intent to be guilty of genocide.

Prosecutor v. Krstić

Int'l Crim. Tribunal for the Former Yugoslavia
IT-98-33-A, Appeals Judgement, at ¶¶6, 8, 12, 15-16, 28, 35, 79, 83, 121, 129, 134, 137, 140 (Apr. 19, 2004)

6. Article 4 of the Tribunal's Statute, like the Genocide Convention, covers certain acts done with "intent to destroy, in whole or in part, a national, ethnical, racial or religious group, as such." The Indictment in this case alleged . . . that Radislav Krstić "intend[ed] to destroy a part of the Bosnian Muslim people as a national, ethnical, or religious group." . . . The Trial Chamber determined that the Bosnian Muslims were a specific, distinct national group. . . .

8. It is well established that where a conviction for genocide relies on the intent to destroy a protected group "in part," the part must be a substantial part of that group. The aim of the Genocide Convention is to prevent the intentional destruction of entire human groups, and the part targeted must be significant enough to have an impact on the group as a whole. . . .

12. The intent requirement of genocide . . . is therefore satisfied where evidence shows that the alleged perpetrator intended to destroy at least a substantial part of the protected group. The determination of when the targeted part is substantial enough to meet this requirement may involve a number of considerations. The numeric size of the targeted part of the group is the necessary and important starting point, though not in all cases the ending point of the inquiry. The number of individuals targeted should be evaluated not only in absolute terms, but also in relation to the overall size of the entire group. In addition to the numeric size of the targeted portion, its prominence within the group can be a useful consideration. If a specific part of the group is emblematic of the overall group, or is essential to its survival, that may support a finding that the part qualifies as substantial within the meaning of [the Genocide Convention]. . . .

15. In this case, having identified the protected group as the national group of Bosnian Muslims, the Trial Chamber concluded that the part the VRS Main Staff and Radislav Krstić targeted was the Bosnian Muslims of Srebrenica, or the Bosnian Muslims of Eastern Bosnia. . . . Although this population constituted only a small percentage of the overall Muslim population of Bosnia and Herzegovina at the time, the importance of the Muslim community of Srebrenica is not captured solely by its size. . . . Srebrenica (and the surrounding . . . region) were of immense strategic importance to the Bosnian Serb leadership. . . . The capture and ethnic purification of Srebrenica would . . . severely undermine the military efforts of the Bosnian Muslim state to ensure its viability . . . Control over the Srebrenica region was consequently essential to . . . the continued survival of

the Bosnian Muslim people. Because most of the Muslim inhabitants of the region had, by 1995, sought refuge within the Srebrenica enclave, the elimination of that enclave would have accomplished the goal of purifying the entire region of its Muslim population.

16. In addition, Srebrenica was important due to its prominence in the eyes of both the Bosnian Muslims and the international community. The town of Srebrenica was the most visible of the "safe areas" established by the UN Security Council in Bosnia. . . . In its resolution declaring Srebrenica a safe area, the Security Council announced that it "should be free from armed attack or any other hostile act." . . . The elimination of the Muslim population of Srebrenica . . . would serve as a potent example to all Bosnian Muslims of their vulnerability and defenselessness in the face of Serb military forces. The fate of the Bosnian Muslims of Srebrenica would be emblematic of that of all Bosnian Muslims. . . .

28. [The Trial Chamber concluded that the killing of the Bosnian Muslim men of military age was evidence of an intent to destroy *all* the Bosnian Muslims of Srebrenica. In reaching this conclusion, the] Trial Chamber was also entitled to consider the long-term impact that the elimination of seven to eight thousand men from Srebrenica would have on the survival of that community. . . . As the Trial Chamber found, the massacred men amounted to about one fifth of the overall Srebrenica community. The Trial Chamber found that, given the patriarchal character of the Bosnian Muslim society in Srebrenica, the destruction of such a sizeable number of men would "inevitably result in the physical disappearance of the Bosnian Muslim population at Srebrenica." Evidence introduced at trial supported this finding, by showing that, with the majority of the men killed officially listed as missing, their spouses are unable to remarry and, consequently, to have new children. The physical destruction of the men therefore had severe procreative implications for the Srebrenica Muslim community, potentially consigning the community to extinction. . . .

35. In this case, the factual circumstances, as found by the Trial Chamber, permit the inference that the killing of the Bosnian Muslim men was done with genocidal intent. . . .

79. It remains for the Appeals Chamber to determine whether the Trial Chamber erred in finding that Radislav Krstić [himself] shared the genocidal intent . . . to commit genocide against the Bosnian Muslims of Srebrenica. . . .

83. . . . [In finding that Krstić possessed genocidal intent,] the Trial Chamber relied upon evidence establishing his knowledge of the intention on the part of [the top VRS military commander] General Mladić and other members of the VRS Main Staff to execute the Bosnian Muslims of Srebrenica, his knowledge of the use of personnel and resources of the Drina Corps to carry out that intention given his . . . position [as commander of the Corps], and upon evidence that Radislav Krstić supervised the participation of his subordinates in carrying out those executions. . . .

121. . . . [Krstić's contacts with other VRS officers who were the "main participants" in the execution of Muslim men] establish, at most, that Krstić was aware that those executions were taking place. Radislav Krstić's knowledge of those executions is insufficient to support an inference that he shared the intent to commit genocide. . . .

129. . . . [The evidence that personnel and resources of the units commanded by Krstić were used in the executions established] his knowledge of the executions and his knowledge of the use of personnel and resources under his command to assist in those executions. . . .

134. . . . [A]ll that the evidence can establish is that Krstić was aware of the intent to commit genocide on the part of some members of the VRS Main Staff, and with that knowledge, he did nothing to prevent the use of Drina Corps personnel and resources to facilitate those killings. This knowledge on his part alone cannot support an inference of genocidal intent. Genocide is one of the worst crimes known to humankind, and its gravity is reflected in the stringent requirement of specific intent. Convictions for genocide can be entered only where that intent has been unequivocally established. There was a demonstrable failure by the Trial Chamber to supply adequate proof that Radislav Krstić possessed the genocidal intent. Krstić, therefore, is not guilty of genocide as a principal perpetrator. . . .

137. . . . Radislav Krstić had knowledge of the genocidal intent of some of the Members of the VRS Main Staff. Radislav Krstić was aware that the Main Staff had insufficient resources of its own to carry out the executions and that, without the use of Drina Corps resources, the Main Staff would not have been able to implement its genocidal plan. Krstić knew that by allowing Drina Corps resources to be used he was making a substantial contribution to the execution of the Bosnian Muslim prisoners. Although the evidence suggests that Radislav Krstić was not a supporter of that plan, as Commander of the Drina Corps he permitted the Main Staff to call upon Drina Corps resources and to employ those resources. The criminal liability of Krstić is therefore more properly expressed as that of an aider and abettor to genocide, and not as that of a perpetrator. . . .

140. . . . [A]n individual who aids and abets a specific intent offense [such as genocide] may be held responsible if he assists the commission of the crime knowing the intent behind the crime. . . . The conviction for aiding and abetting genocide upon proof that the defendant knew about the principal perpetrator's genocidal intent is permitted by the Statute and case-law of the Tribunal.

Notes and Questions

1. The Appeals Chamber set aside Krstić's conviction as a participant in a joint criminal enterprise to commit genocide, and instead found him guilty of aiding and abetting genocide. The Appeals Chamber reduced Krstić's initial sentence of 46 years' imprisonment to 35 years' imprisonment. Consider the discussion of joint criminal enterprise liability in Note 3 in Section B.2.c above. Based on its findings about Krstić's actions and mental state, why would he not be guilty of genocide under that mode of criminal liability?

2. The Appeals Chamber acknowledged that the Bosnian Muslim population of the Srebrenica region "constituted only a small percentage of the overall Muslim population of Bosnia" when the killings occurred. Under the circumstances, are you persuaded that the intent to destroy the Bosnian Muslim population in Srebrenica reflected an intention to destroy the Bosnian Muslim population in "substantial part" within the meaning of the Genocide Convention? Was it correct to consider the strategic importance of Srebrenica to the viability of the Bosnian Muslim state?

Even if the attacks on Srebrenica had the effect of "purifying" Eastern Bosnia of its Muslim population, would that result in the destruction of a "substantial part" of the Bosnian Muslim people?

3. How substantial a part of a national, ethnic, or other group must a perpetrator intend to destroy to be guilty of genocide? Should this be assessed only in numerical terms, or do you agree with the ICTY Appeals Chamber that destruction of an "emblematic" part of a group may constitute genocide?

4. If Krstić knew that the VRS was engaging in genocide, cooperated with other members of the VRS participating in the commission of genocide, and allowed resources under his command to be used to carry out genocide, why is he not guilty of genocide? What further evidence would be required to show he had the specific intent to commit genocide?

5. The fact that an offense is recognized as a crime under international law does not necessarily mean that all states have a duty to prosecute persons who have committed such a crime. There must ordinarily be a separate legal basis for a duty to prosecute such crimes. Article 6 of the Genocide Convention imposes an obligation to prosecute acts of genocide in certain cases. What is the scope of that obligation? If a Rwandan accused of genocide is found in the United States, does the United States have a duty under the Genocide Convention to prosecute him?

6. In 1993, during the midst of the wars in the former Yugoslavia, Bosnia brought a claim in the International Court of Justice alleging that the country then known as the Federal Republic of Yugoslavia (FRY) was committing genocide in Bosnia. In its 2007 judgment in the case, the Court concluded that although widespread killings of Bosnian Muslims were perpetrated during the conflict, it was not "conclusively established" that most of those killings "were committed with the specific intent (*dolus specialis*) on the part of the perpetrators to destroy, in whole or in part, the group." Application of the Convention on the Prevention and Punishment of the Crime of Genocide (Bosnia and Herzegovina v. Serbia and Montenegro), at ¶277 (Feb. 26, 2007), reprinted in 46 I.L.M. 188 (2007). Relying substantially on the ICTY's *Krstić* judgment, however, the ICJ concluded that the massacres at Srebrenica "were committed with the specific intent to destroy in part the group of the Muslims of Bosnia and Herzegovina as such; and accordingly that these were acts of genocide, committed by members of the VRS [the Bosnian Serb Army]." Id. at ¶297.

Even with respect to the genocide perpetrated by the Bosnian Serb forces at Srebrenica, the ICJ did not find Serbia responsible. Applying the standard of "effective control" articulated in its *Nicaragua* judgment for attributing the conduct of non-state actors to a state (see Chapter 8.A.2), the Court ruled:

> [I]t has not been established that those massacres were committed on the instructions, or under the direction of organs of the Respondent State, nor that the Respondent exercised effective control over the operations in the course of which those massacres, which . . . constituted the crime of genocide, were perpetrated.
>
> The Applicant has not proved that instructions were issued by the federal authorities in Belgrade, or by any other organ of the FRY, to commit the massacres. . . . All indications are to the contrary: that the decision to kill the adult male population of the Muslim community in Srebrenica was taken by some members of the VRS Main Staff, but without instructions from or effective control by the FRY. [Id. at ¶413.]

The ICJ found that although the FRY was not directly responsible for the genocide at Srebrenica, "it did nothing to prevent the Srebrenica massacres," which constituted a violation of the duty to prevent genocide under Article 1 of the Convention. The Court took note in this regard of the FRY's "known influence" over the VRS. To establish a state's breach of its obligation of prevention, "it does not need to be proven that the State concerned definitely had the power to prevent the genocide; it is sufficient that it had the means to do so and that it manifestly refrained from using them." Id. at ¶438. The duty to prevent genocide, the Court held, obligates states "to employ all means reasonably available to them, so as to prevent genocide so far as possible." Id. at ¶430.

What is the precise scope of the obligation for a state to employ "all means reasonably available" to prevent genocide? Would it require states that are members of the Security Council to vote to authorize coercive measures, including the use of force, to halt on ongoing genocide? Would it obligate a state with advanced military capabilities to use force unilaterally to stop genocide occurring in another country?

7. In the genocide prosecution of Jean Paul Akayesu before the International Criminal Tribunal for Rwanda (ICTR), the Trial Chamber heard evidence of the commission of widespread acts of rape and sexual violence against Tutsi women. The Chamber found that such acts constituted genocide:

> With regard . . . to the acts . . . [of] rape and sexual violence, the Chamber wishes to underscore the fact that in its opinion, they constitute genocide in the same way as any other act as long as they were committed with the specific intent to destroy, in whole or in part, a particular group, targeted as such. Indeed, rape and sexual violence certainly constitute infliction of serious bodily and mental harm on the victims and are even, according to the Chamber, one of the worst ways [to] inflict harm on the victim as he or she suffers both bodily and mental harm. In light of all the evidence before it, the Chamber is satisfied that the acts of rape and sexual violence described above, were committed solely against Tutsi women, many of whom were subjected to the worst public humiliation, mutilated, and raped several times, often in public . . . , and often by more than one assailant. These rapes resulted in physical and psychological destruction of Tutsi women, their families and their communities. Sexual violence was an integral part of the process of destruction, specifically targeting Tutsi women and specifically contributing to their destruction and to the destruction of the Tutsi group as a whole. [Prosecutor v. Akayesu, Case No. ICTR-96-4-T, Judgment, at ¶731 (Sept. 2, 1998).]

8. In 1975, a Communist group known as the Khmer Rouge came to power in Cambodia. The Khmer Rouge launched a radical campaign to transform Cambodian society. The government abolished banking, finance, and currency, outlawed religions, confiscated private property, and relocated people from urban areas to collective farms where forced labor was widespread. The regime also engaged in widespread oppression of political opponents and other suspected groups, including intellectuals. It is estimated that between 1 and 2 million Cambodians were killed or starved to death during the Khmer Rouge's 1975-1979 reign.

Do the acts of the Khmer Rouge, which do not appear to have targeted groups primarily on the basis of their religion, nationality, ethnicity, or race, amount to genocide? Some have argued that the mass killing of members of the "national group" to which the perpetrators themselves belong reflects an intent to destroy a substantial portion of that group, and thus constitutes genocide. See, e.g., Hurst Hannum, International Law and Cambodian Genocide: The Sounds of Silence, 11 Hum. Rts. Q. 82, 88-94, 103-107 (1989). Others counter that

> [t]he argument that the Khmer Rouge committed genocide with respect to the Khmer national group appears to be relatively weak in light of the facts. Most of the literature suggests that the Khmer Rouge did not target their non-minority victims as members of the Khmer nation "as such." Rather, it indicates either that the regime targeted them as economic, social, or political elements whom the Khmer Rouge sought to eradicate but whom the Convention does not protect. . . . Adoption of the alternative legal interpretation, though morally appealing, would, as a practical matter, enlarge the deliberately limited scope of the Convention's list of protected groups, insofar as almost any political, social, or economic element of a population can be viewed as a part of a larger national group. [Steven R. Ratner, Jason S. Abrams & James L. Bischoff, Accountability for Human Rights Atrocities in International Law: Beyond the Nuremberg Legacy 322 (3rd ed. 2009).]

The question of the legal character of the Cambodian atrocities has arisen before a special court known as the Extraordinary Chambers in the Courts of Cambodia, which was established in 2006 to prosecute those who were most responsible for the crimes committed under the Khmer Rouge regime. (This "hybrid" court is discussed in Section C.3 below.) Although the Court's statute grants it jurisdiction over the crime of genocide as defined in the Genocide Convention, in the court's first case against the director of a notorious Khmer Rouge detention and torture center, the prosecution did not bring genocide charges. This may reflect the prosecution's judgment that the killing by the Khmer Rouge of large numbers of persons on the basis of their perceived political views and social status did not satisfy the legal definition of genocide. The indictment in the court's second case against four senior Khmer Rouge leaders, which was scheduled to begin in mid-2011, does include genocide charges. Those charges focus on crimes committed against members of Vietnamese and Cham national or ethnic groups — not crimes committed against the Khmer population itself.

9. The United States signed the Genocide Convention in 1948, but did not become a party until 1988. The United States appended a number of Reservations, Declarations, and Understandings (RUDs) at the time of ratification, including an understanding that "the term 'intent to destroy, in whole or in part, a national, ethnical, racial, or religious group as such' appearing in article II means the specific intent to destroy, in whole or in substantial part, a national, ethnical, racial or religious group as such by the acts specified in article II." (The U.S. RUDs are in the Documentary Supplement.) As required by Article 5 of the Convention, the United States enacted legislation to "provide effective penalties for persons guilty of genocide." The U.S. implementing legislation, codified at 18 U.S.C. §1091, applies only if "the offense is committed within the United States" or if "the alleged offender is a national of the United States."

b. Crimes Against Humanity

Unlike the crime of genocide, which is defined in a treaty, crimes against humanity are a category of international crimes that arose initially under customary international law. They have since been reflected in the statutes and treaties establishing various international criminal tribunals. The International Military Tribunal (IMT) at Nuremberg was vested with jurisdiction over crimes against humanity, although the phrase was used as early as 1915 to describe Turkish massacres of Armenians during World War I. Article 6(c) of the Charter of the IMT defined the offense as follows:

> *Crimes against humanity:* namely, murder, extermination, enslavement, deportation, and other inhuman acts committed against any civilian population, before or during the war, or persecutions on political, racial or religious grounds in execution of or in connection with any crime within the jurisdiction of the Tribunal, whether or not in violation of the domestic law of the country where perpetrated.

The following case before the ICTY discusses some of the key features of the concept of "crimes against humanity."

Prosecutor v. Kunarac *et al.*, Case No. IT-96-23 & 23/1

Int'l Crim. Tribunal for the Former Yugoslavia IT-96-23 & 23/1-A, Appeals Judgement, at ¶¶85-86, 90-91, 93-96, 98, 100, 102-103 (June 12, 2002)

[From April 1992 to February 1993, during the armed conflict in Bosnia, non-Serb civilians in the area of Foča were killed, raped, or otherwise mistreated by Bosnian Serb forces. Kunarac participated in this campaign, which sought to "cleanse" the area of its non-Serb inhabitants. The targets of the campaign included Muslim women who were detained in various centers, where they were subjected to many acts of physical violence, including multiple rapes. A Trial Chamber found Kunarac guilty of, among other things, crimes against humanity on the counts of enslavement, rape, and torture. He and his co-accused appealed claiming, among other things, that there was no "attack" directed against non-Serb civilians in Foča, that the non-Serb civilians of Foča did not constitute a "population," that any attack was neither widespread nor systematic, and that they had no knowledge of an attack or of the policy behind it.]

... Legal Requirements of an "Attack"

85. In order to amount to a crime against humanity, the acts of an accused must be part of a widespread or systematic attack "directed against any civilian population". This phrase has been interpreted by the Trial Chamber, and the Appeals Chamber agrees, as encompassing five elements:

(i) There must be an attack.
(ii) The acts of the perpetrator must be part of the attack.
(iii) The attack must be directed against any civilian population.
(iv) The attack must be widespread or systematic.
(v) The perpetrator must know that his acts constitute part of a pattern of widespread or systematic crimes directed against a civilian population and know that his acts fit into such a pattern.

86. The concepts of "attack" and "armed conflict" are not identical. . . . Under customary international law, the attack could precede, outlast, or continue during the armed conflict, but it need not be a part of it. Also, the attack in the context of a crime against humanity is not limited to the use of armed force; it encompasses any mistreatment of the civilian population. . . .

. . . The Attack Must Be Directed Against Any Civilian Population

90. . . . [T]he use of the word "population" does not mean that the entire population of the geographical entity in which the attack is taking place must have been subjected to that attack. It is sufficient to show that enough individuals were targeted in the course of the attack, or that they were targeted in such a way as to satisfy the Chamber that the attack was in fact directed against a civilian "population", rather than against a limited and randomly selected number of individuals.

91. . . . [T]he expression "directed against" is an expression which "specifies that in the context of a crime against humanity the civilian population is the primary object of the attack". In order to determine whether the attack may be said to have been so directed, the Trial Chamber will consider, *inter alia*, the means and method used in the course of the attack, the status of the victims, their number, the discriminatory nature of the attack, the nature of the crimes committed in its course, the resistance to the assailants at the time and the extent to which the attacking force may be said to have complied or attempted to comply with the precautionary requirements of the laws of war. . . .

. . . The Attack Must Be Widespread *or* Systematic

93. The requirement that the attack be "widespread" or "systematic" comes in the alternative. Once it is convinced that either requirement is met, the Trial Chamber is not obliged to consider whether the alternative qualifier is also satisfied. . . .

94. . . . [T]he phrase "widespread" refers to the large-scale nature of the attack and the number of victims, while the phrase "systematic" refers to "the organised nature of the acts of violence and the improbability of their random occurrence". The Trial Chamber correctly noted that "patterns of crimes — that is the non-accidental repetition of similar criminal conduct on a regular basis — are a common expression of such systematic occurrence".

95. . . . [T]he assessment of what constitutes a "widespread" or "systematic" attack is essentially a relative exercise in that it depends upon the civilian population which, allegedly, was being attacked. A Trial Chamber must therefore "first identify the population which is the object of the attack and, in light of the means, methods, resources and result of the attack upon the population, ascertain whether the attack was indeed widespread or systematic". The consequences of the attack upon the targeted population, the number of victims, the nature of the acts, the possible participation of officials or authorities or any identifiable patterns of crimes, could be taken into account to determine whether the attack satisfies either or both requirements of a "widespread" or "systematic" attack vis-à-vis this civilian population.

96. As correctly stated by the Trial Chamber, "only the attack, not the individual acts of the accused, must be widespread or systematic". In addition, the acts of the

accused need only be a part of this attack and, all other conditions being met, a single or relatively limited number of acts on his or her part would qualify as a crime against humanity, unless those acts may be said to be isolated or random. . . .

... THE REQUIREMENT OF A POLICY OR PLAN AND NEXUS WITH THE ATTACK

98. Contrary to the Appellants' submissions, neither the attack nor the acts of the accused needs to be supported by any form of "policy" or "plan". There was nothing in the Statute [of the ICTY] or in customary international law at the time of the alleged acts which required proof of the existence of a plan or policy to commit these crimes. As indicated above, proof that the attack was directed against a civilian population and that it was widespread or systematic, are legal elements of the crime. But to prove these elements, it is not necessary to show that they were the result of the existence of a policy or plan. . . .

100. The acts of the accused must be part of the "attack" against the civilian population, but they need not be committed in the midst of that attack. A crime which is committed before or after the main attack against the civilian population or away from it could still, if sufficiently connected, be part of that attack. The crime must not, however, be an isolated act. A crime would be regarded as an "isolated act" when it is so far removed from that attack that, having considered the context and circumstances in which it was committed, it cannot reasonably be said to have been part of the attack. . . .

... *MENS REA* FOR CRIMES AGAINST HUMANITY

102. Concerning the required *mens rea* for crimes against humanity, the Trial Chamber correctly held that the accused must have had the intent to commit the underlying offence or offences with which he is charged, and that he must have known "that there is an attack on the civilian population and that his acts comprise part of that attack, or at least [that he took] the risk that his acts were part of the attack." This requirement, as pointed out by the Trial Chamber, does not entail knowledge of the details of the attack.

103. For criminal liability pursuant to Article 5 of the Statute, "the motives of the accused for taking part in the attack are irrelevant and a crime against humanity may be committed for purely personal reasons." Furthermore, the accused need not share the purpose or goal behind the attack. It is also irrelevant whether the accused intended his acts to be directed against the targeted population or merely against his victim. It is the attack, not the acts of the accused, which must be directed against the target population and the accused need only know that his acts are part thereof. At most, evidence that he committed the acts for purely personal reasons could be indicative of a rebuttable assumption that he was not aware that his acts were part of that attack.

Notes and Questions

1. Under the definition of crimes against humanity used by the Nuremberg Tribunal, what is the difference between genocide and crimes against humanity? What are the differences in terms of the qualifying acts and the required mental

state? Was General Krstić guilty of crimes against humanity? Is genocide more morally blameworthy than crimes against humanity?

2. In the Statute of the International Criminal Court, the list of acts that constitute a crime against humanity "when committed as part of a widespread or systematic attack directed against any civilian population" is considerably more extensive than those specified in the Charter of the Nuremberg Tribunal. Acts that can constitute crimes against humanity before the ICC include torture; rape, sexual slavery, enforced prostitution, forced pregnancy, and enforced sterilization; persecution against a group on political, racial, national, ethnic, cultural, religious, gender, or other prohibited grounds; enforced disappearance of persons; and apartheid. See Article 7 of the Statute of the ICC in the Documentary Supplement.

3. There is some disagreement under international law about whether the existence of a state of armed conflict is a requirement for crimes against humanity. The Statute of the ICTY, which the Tribunal applied in the *Kunarac* case above, limits crimes against humanity to certain crimes "when committed in armed conflict." The most recent definition of crimes against humanity agreed upon by states in the Statute of the ICC, in contrast, does not require a connection to armed conflict.

4. How do we determine whether an attack is against a "civilian population," as opposed to particular civilians? Would targeted killings of a small number of political or symbolic leaders of a minority ethnic group amount to a crime against humanity? Would it depend on whether those killings were meant to intimidate the entire group? Would an order to destroy a city for purportedly military reasons alone, without regard to the identity of the inhabitants, be a crime against humanity? Would such an attack be directed "against a civilian population?" What factors would you look to in making a determination?

5. Is there a duty for states to prosecute crimes against humanity? What would be the source of such an obligation? Given that the crimes initially arose under customary international law, would you require evidence that states consistently prosecute persons who commit crimes against humanity, and do so out of a sense of international legal obligation, to establish such a duty? Or could the fact that crimes against humanity are now included within the jurisdiction of the ICTY, the ICTR, and the ICC provide the basis for a duty to prosecute?

Some international law scholars suggest that customary international law has created a duty to prosecute perpetrators of crimes against humanity. See, e.g., M. Cherif Bassiouni, Crimes Against Humanity in International Law 219 (2d ed. 1999) ("'Crimes against humanity' is a category of international crimes and as such, a general duty exists to try or extradite"). Others, however, reject the idea that customary international law imposes any such duty, given "the litany of contrary state practice." Michael Scharf, The Letter of the Law: The Scope of the International Legal Obligation to Prosecute Human Rights Crimes, 59 Law & Contemp. Probs. 41, 58 (1996).

6. Who can commit crimes against humanity? Although the offense was traditionally seen as requiring governmental action, more recent approaches have broadened the definition to reach attacks against civilian populations perpetrated by nonstate actors. Article 7(2)(a) of the Statute of the ICC, for example, defines crimes against humanity as an attack against any civilian population, "pursuant to or in furtherance of a State *or organizational policy* to commit such attack"

(emphasis added). Can *any* non-state actor commit a crime against humanity? Would a killing of a large number of civilians by a small terrorist cell constitute a crime against humanity? Were the terrorist attacks of September 11, 2001, crimes against humanity? Or should liability for such offenses be limited to larger organized groups, for example, groups that would be recognized as parties to an armed conflict under the international humanitarian law? (See Chapter 11.D.2 above.)

c. War Crimes

In Chapter 11.D we reviewed a number of the important international law rules regulating the means and methods of waging war and providing for the humane treatment of victims of war, or *jus in bello.* As noted in the judgment of the International Military Tribunal at Nuremberg, military tribunals established by warring parties had long "tried and punished individuals guilty of violating the rules of land warfare laid down" by instruments such as the 1907 Hague Regulations (discussed in Chapter 11.D.1). The Nuremberg Tribunal had jurisdiction over war crimes, and the Nazi leaders were charged under that heading with such offenses as the murder and ill-treatment of civilian populations in occupied territory, including torture and the performance of medical experiments on living human subjects; deportation of civilians for slave labor; the murder and ill-treatment of prisoners of war, including torture and subjecting prisoners to inhumane labor conditions; and the wanton destruction of cities, towns, and villages not justified by military necessity.

After World War II, the adoption of the 1949 Geneva Conventions not only expanded the protections of victims of war, but — unlike earlier treaties on the law of war — specifically provided for individual criminal responsibility for certain treaty violations. As explained in Chapter 11, each of the four 1949 Geneva Conventions applies to a particular category of victims of war in the context of international armed conflict. The first two Geneva Conventions provide for protection of wounded and sick soldiers and sailors. The Third Geneva Convention governs the status and treatment of prisoners of war (POWs), and the Fourth Convention applies to civilians who have fallen into the hands of the enemy. Each Convention contains detailed provisions concerning the treatment of those covered by the treaty.

Each of the Conventions additionally designates the most severe forms of mistreatment of persons protected by the Conventions as "grave breaches." Article 50 of the First Geneva Convention, for instance, provides:

First Geneva Convention for the Amelioration of the Condition of the Wounded and Sick in Armed Forces in the Field (Aug. 12, 1949)

Article 50

Grave breaches . . . [of the Convention] shall be those involving any of the following acts, if committed against persons or property protected by the Convention: wilful killing, torture or inhuman treatment, including biological experiments, wilfully causing great suffering or serious injury to body or health, and extensive destruction and appropriation of property, not justified by military necessity and carried out unlawfully and wantonly.

The Convention imposes on all parties the following obligations to make grave breaches of the Conventions crimes under their domestic law and to ensure that persons who commit grave breaches are criminally punished:

Article 49

The High Contracting Parties undertake to enact any legislation necessary to provide effective penal sanctions for persons committing, or ordering to be committed, any of the grave breaches of the present Convention defined in . . . Article [50].

Each High Contracting Party shall be under the obligation to search for persons alleged to have committed, or to have ordered to be committed, such grave breaches, and shall bring such persons, regardless of their nationality, before its own courts. It may also, if it prefers, and in accordance with the provisions of its own legislation, hand such persons over for trial to another High Contracting Party concerned, provided such High Contracting Party has made out a prima facie case. . . .

Each of three other 1949 Conventions contains comparable provisions for the repression of abuses, although the precise definition of "grave breaches" varies in some of the conventions. See the Second Geneva Convention for the Amelioration of the Condition of Wounded, Sick and Shipwrecked Members of Armed Forces at Sea, arts. 50-51; Third Geneva Convention Relative to the Treatment of Prisoners of War, arts. 129-130; Fourth Geneva Convention Relative to the Protection of Civilian Persons in Time of War, arts. 146-147.

Each Convention also provides that "No High Contracting Party shall be allowed to absolve itself or any other High Contracting Party of any liability incurred by itself or by another High Contracting Party in respect of [grave] breaches." See First Geneva Convention, art. 51; Second Geneva Convention, art. 52; Third Geneva Convention, art. 131; Fourth Geneva Convention, art. 148.

The 1977 Protocol I to the 1949 Geneva Conventions expands the protections applicable in times of international armed conflict. In addition, as noted in Chapter 11.D.3, the Protocol goes beyond setting down protections for victims of war who find themselves in hands of the enemy. It incorporates a number of the fundamental rules governing the means and methods of waging war, including the principle of distinction (which requires parties to an armed conflict to distinguish between civilians and military objects and to limit their attacks to military targets) and the principle of proportionality (which forbids attacks against even military targets that will cause harm to civilians that is excessive in comparison to the military advantage to be gained). The Protocol includes expanded "grave breach" provisions corresponding to the broader protections of the treaty. Although the United States is not a party to Protocol I, it views many of the substantive rules regarding the conduct of war in the Protocol as customary international law. Nevertheless, the

United States has not enacted legislation making grave breaches of Protocol I, as such, crimes under either the Uniform Code of Military Justice or federal criminal law.

Protocol Additional to the Geneva Conventions of 12 August 1949, and Relating to the Protection of Victims of International Armed Conflicts (Protocol I) (June 8, 1977)

Article 85

1. The provisions of the [1949 Geneva] Conventions relating to the repression of breaches and grave breaches, supplemented by this Section, shall apply to the repression of breaches and grave breaches of this Protocol. . . .

3. . . . [T]he following acts shall be regarded as grave breaches of this Protocol, when committed wilfully, in violation of the relevant provisions of this Protocol, and causing death or serious injury to body or health:

(a) making the civilian population or individual civilians the object of attack;

(b) launching an indiscriminate attack affecting the civilian population or civilian objects in the knowledge that such attack will cause excessive loss of life, injury to civilians or damage to civilian objects . . . ;

(c) launching an attack against works or installations containing dangerous forces in the knowledge that such attack will cause excessive loss of life, injury to civilians or damage to civilian objects . . . ;

(d) making non-defended localities and demilitarized zones the object of attack;

(e) making a person the object of attack in the knowledge that he is *hors de combat;* . . .

4. In addition to the grave breaches defined in the preceding paragraphs and in the Conventions, the following shall be regarded as grave breaches of this Protocol, when committed wilfully and in violation of the Conventions or the Protocol:

(a) the transfer by the Occupying Power of parts of its own civilian population into the territory it occupies, or the deportation or transfer of all or parts of the population of the occupied territory within or outside this territory, in violation of Article 49 of the Fourth Convention;

(b) unjustifiable delay in the repatriation of prisoners of war or civilians;

(c) practices of apartheid and other inhuman and degrading practices involving outrages upon personal dignity, based on racial discrimination; . . .

(d) depriving a person protected by the Conventions . . . of the rights of fair and regular trial.

5. Without prejudice to the application of the Conventions and of this Protocol, grave breaches of these instruments shall be regarded as war crimes.

Notes and Questions

1. In what kinds of conflicts does the grave breach regime of the Geneva Conventions apply? Recall that Common Article 3 to the 1949 Geneva Conventions, discussed in Chapter 11.D.2.b, provides for certain basic protections of victims of war in "armed conflict not of an international character occurring in the territory of

one of the" parties to the Conventions. Is a "person taking no active part in the hostilities" in a non-international armed conflict a person protected by the Geneva Conventions? Would the intentional killing of such a person in violation of Common Article 3 constitute a "grave breach" of the Conventions? The Appeals Chamber of the ICTY took up this question in the first trial conducted before the Tribunal, Prosecutor v. Tadić. The Tribunal concluded that

> the notion of "protected persons or property" must perforce cover . . . persons or objects protected only to the extent that they are caught up in an international armed conflict. By contrast, those provisions do not include persons or property coming within the purview of common Article 3 of the four Geneva Conventions. . . . [Prosecutor v. Tadić, Case No. IT-94-1-A, Decision on Defence Motion for Interlocutory Appeal on Jurisdiction, at ¶81 (Oct. 2, 1995).]

The Second 1977 Additional Protocol to the Geneva Conventions (Protocol II), which concerns the protection of victims of non-international armed conflicts, contains no grave breach provisions or other obligations to prosecute those who commit violations of the treaty. Does this reinforce the conclusion of the Appeals Chamber in the *Tadić* case that states do "not want to give other States jurisdiction over serious violations of international humanitarian law committed in their internal armed conflicts — at least not the mandatory universal jurisdiction involved in the grave breaches system"? Id. at ¶80. Since international human rights norms increasingly regulate relations between a government and its own citizens, is the failure to extend the grave breaches regime to persons involved in internal armed conflict anachronistic?

2. Although the 1949 Geneva Conventions and the 1977 Protocols, under the widely held view reflected in the *Tadić* decision, did not treat intentional killings of civilians and other violations of international humanitarian law war that occur during non-international armed conflict as grave breaches giving rise to international criminal liability, state views have changed considerably since then. The Statute of the International Criminal Court grants the Court jurisdiction over an extensive list of international humanitarian law violations that occur during non-international armed conflict. These include not only violations of Common Article 3, but also such acts as intentionally directing attacks against the civilian population; attacking humanitarian assistance or peacekeeping mission personnel; committing rape, sexual slavery, enforced prostitution, forced pregnancy, and other prohibited forms of sexual violence; and conscripting child soldiers, among others. See Articles 8(c) and 8(e) of the ICC Statute in the Documentary Supplement. Why do you think a growing number of states are prepared to subject atrocities committed in internal conflicts to international prosecution?

3. Although many of the cases brought before international criminal tribunals to date have involved the mistreatment of victims of war who find themselves in hands of the enemy, such as detainees or civilians in areas controlled by the opposing military, international criminal prosecutions have also been brought for violations of the rules governing the means and methods of waging war. In two separate cases, Trial Chambers of the International Criminal Tribunal for the Former Yugoslavia convicted Generals Stanislav Galić and Dragomir Milošević, for their actions as commanders of Bosnian Serb Army forces that continuously engaged in shelling

and sniper fire during the 1992-1996 siege of Sarajevo, which resulted in the killing and serious injury of many civilians. They were each convicted of violations of the laws and customs of war in connection with impermissible attacks against the civilian population. See Prosecutor v. Galić, Case No. IT-98-29-T (Dec. 5, 2003); Prosecutor v. Milošević, Case No. IT-98-29/1-T (Dec. 12, 2007).

4. The Geneva Conventions obligate states parties to "search for persons alleged to have committed" grave breaches and to either bring them before domestic courts or, alternatively, to "hand such persons over for trial to another" party. This "try or extradite" principle, also known as the *aut dedere aut judicare* principle, has been incorporated into a number of other international conventions designating acts as crimes, including the Torture Convention and many of the conventions criminalizing specific acts of terrorism, discussed below. These conventions generally impose obligations on states in whose territory an offender is found to either try or extradite the offender, regardless of where the offense was committed.

5. In 1996, the U.S. Congress first adopted the "War Crimes Act," which made certain violations of the laws of war federal crimes. The statute applies to any "war crime" where "the person committing such war crime or the victim of such war crime is a member of the Armed Forces of the United States or a national of the United States." 18 U.S.C. §2441(b). The statute defines a war crime as, among other things, any conduct:

> (1) defined as a grave breach in any of the international conventions signed at Geneva 12 August 1949, or any protocol to such convention to which the United States is a party;
>
> (2) prohibited by Article 23, 25, 27, or 28 of the Annex to the Hague Convention IV, Respecting the Laws and Customs of War on Land, signed 18 October 1907;
>
> (3) which constitutes a grave breach of common Article 3 (as defined in subsection (d)) when committed in the context of and in association with an armed conflict not of an international character . . . [18 U.S.C. §2441(c).]

Is this provision fully consistent with the try-or-extradite obligations of the United States under the Geneva Conventions?

d. Aggression

Article 6(a) of the Charter of the International Military Tribunal at Nuremberg vested the Tribunal with criminal jurisdiction over the "crimes against peace," defined as "planning, preparation, initiation or waging of a war of aggression, or a war in violation of international treaties, agreements or assurances, or participation in a common plan or conspiracy for the accomplishment of any of the foregoing." As the discussion of the use of force in Chapter 11 demonstrates, however, there is considerable disagreement about the circumstances under which states may use force in accordance with the U.N. Charter. It took many years for the General Assembly to reach agreement on the definition of aggression contained in General Assembly Resolution 3314 of 1974; the United States has traditionally taken the view that this can only be determined based on the factual circumstances prevailing at the time. The United States has also generally taken the view that determinations of whether an act of aggression has occurred should be made by a political body such as the Security Council, not an international court.

The crime of aggression is included in the Statute of the International Criminal Court. During the original negotiations of the ICC's Statute, the parties were unable to agree on a definition of aggression and so deferred the Court's power to exercise jurisdiction over the crime until a definition was adopted. As noted in Chapter 11.B.3, in June 2010 the parties to the ICC Statute adopted a proposed amendment to the Statute that defines the "crime of aggression" as:

> the planning, preparation, initiation or execution, by a person in a position effectively to exercise control over or to direct the political or military action of a State, of an act of aggression which, by its character, gravity and scale, constitutes a manifest violation of the Charter of the United Nations. [International Criminal Court Review Conference, ICC Rev. Conf., Res. RC/Res.6 (June 11, 2010) (proposed Article 8 *bis*).]

The term "act of aggression" is in turn drawn from the General Assembly's definition of aggression in Resolution 3314.

Reflecting continuing caution about asserting jurisdiction over international criminal prosecutions of aggression, the amendment provides that the ICC will not be able to exercise jurisdiction over the crime until the ICC parties take another decision on the matter, which under the terms of the amendment cannot be done before January 2017.

Notes and Questions

1. What would make a violation of the U.N. Charter's prohibitions on the use of force "manifest"? Would the forcible seizure by one state of a small bit of territory of another, with relatively little combat between the military forces of the two countries, constitute a manifest violation? What about a situation like the 2003 U.S.-led invasion of Iraq, where an extensive military deployment led to the overthrow of the incumbent regime, but where the legality of the invasion was sharply contested? What about a military intervention to stop widespread humanitarian abuses in another state undertaken without Security Council authorization, like the 1999 NATO use of force against the Federal Republic of Yugoslavia to stop atrocities in Kosovo?

2. The proposed definition of aggression does not permit the ICC to exercise jurisdiction over the crime when it is committed by a national of a state that is not a party to the ICC Statute. With respect to other crimes falling within its jurisdiction, the Court can in certain circumstances exercise jurisdiction over nationals of non-parties, which has given rise to strenuous U.S. objections. The ICC and U.S. attitudes toward it are discussed further in Section C below.

e. Torture

The 1984 Convention against Torture and Other Cruel, Inhuman or Degrading Treatment or Punishment, discussed in Chapter 8.B.4, is not only an international human rights instrument; it also makes torture a crime under international law. The Torture Convention (which is included in the Documentary Supplement) defines "torture" as follows:

Article 1

For the purposes of this Convention, the term "torture" means any act by which severe pain or suffering, whether physical or mental, is intentionally inflicted on a person for such purposes as obtaining from him or a third person information or a confession, punishing him for an act he or a third person has committed or is suspected of having committed, or intimidating or coercing him or a third person, or for any reason based on discrimination of any kind, when such pain or suffering is inflicted by or at the instigation of or with the consent or acquiescence of a public official or other person acting in an official capacity. It does not include pain or suffering arising only from, inherent in or incidental to lawful sanctions. . . .

Each party to the Torture Convention is required to ensure that torture is an offense under its domestic law (Article 4) and to take measures "to establish its jurisdiction" over acts of torture committed in territory "under its jurisdiction" or by one of its nationals. The Convention also provides that each party may establish jurisdiction over cases in which its national is a victim of the offense if the state "considers it appropriate." (Article 5.) Article 7 obligates each party to try or extradite any person alleged to have committed torture who is "found" in its territory; if the state does not extradite the alleged offender, it must establish its jurisdiction over him or her even if the crime did not occur on its territory and was not perpetrated by or against one of its nationals.

Notes and Questions

1. The United States became a party to the Torture Convention in 1994. If a Chilean national accused of committing torture in Chile against Chilean nationals during the years the Pinochet regime was in power traveled to the United States, would the United States be obligated to prosecute him for torture? Why is torture, even if it is a purely "domestic" matter, a matter of such concern to the entire international community that it should be treated as an international crime? How does this compare to the failure to extend the grave breach provisions of the Geneva Conventions to internal armed conflicts?

2. As part of the process of ratifying the Torture Convention, the United States enacted a criminal statute that specifically criminalizes acts of torture committed outside U.S. territory. 18 U.S.C. §2340A makes it an offense for any person "outside the United States" to commit or attempt to commit torture. The statute further provides that:

> There is jurisdiction over the activity prohibited in subsection (a) if—
>
> (1) the alleged offender is a national of the United States; or
>
> (2) the alleged offender is present in the United States, irrespective of the nationality of the victim or alleged offender. [18 U.S.C. §2340A(b).]

f. Terrorism-Related Offenses

The United Nations Security Council, in paragraph 2(e) of Resolution 1373 (2001), imposed obligations on all U.N. member states pursuant to Chapter VII of the Charter to:

> Ensure that any person who participates in the financing, planning, preparation or perpetration of terrorist acts or in supporting terrorist acts is brought to justice and ensure that, in addition to any other measures against them, such terrorist acts are established as serious criminal offences in domestic laws and regulations and that the punishment duly reflects the seriousness of such terrorist acts . .

As noted in Chapter 11, however, the definition of "terrorism" is highly controversial, and neither Resolution 1373 nor other U.N. instruments contain a comprehensive definition of the term. Because of the dangers posed by international terrorism, however, the international community has been able to achieve a high degree of consensus on the criminalization of particular forms of terrorist acts, such as hijacking, aircraft sabotage, the taking of hostages, and the killing of diplomats and other internationally protected persons, and has negotiated a series of treaties criminalizing these acts. These conventions typically define the offense that is the subject of the treaty, obligate all member states to make the offense a crime under their domestic law, and impose a try-or-extradite obligation on all states with respect to persons found in their territory alleged to have committed the offense.

The 1998 International Convention for the Suppression of Terrorist Bombings illustrates how these terrorist conventions operate.

International Convention for the Suppression of Terrorist Bombings (Jan. 12, 1998)

Article 2

1. Any person commits an offence within the meaning of this Convention if that person unlawfully and intentionally delivers, places, discharges or detonates an explosive or other lethal device in, into or against a place of public use, a State or government facility, a public transportation system or an infrastructure facility:

(a) With the intent to cause death or serious bodily injury; or

(b) With the intent to cause extensive destruction of such a place, facility or system, where such destruction results in or is likely to result in major economic loss. . . .

Article 5

Each State Party shall adopt such measures as may be necessary, including, where appropriate, domestic legislation, to ensure that criminal acts within the scope of this Convention, in particular where they are intended or calculated to provoke a state of terror in the general public or in a group of persons or particular persons, are under no circumstances justifiable by considerations of a political, philosophical, ideological, racial, ethnic, religious or other similar nature and are punished by penalties consistent with their grave nature.

Article 6

1. Each State Party shall take such measures as may be necessary to establish its jurisdiction over the offences set forth in article 2 when:

(a) The offence is committed in the territory of that State; or

(b) The offence is committed on board a vessel flying the flag of that State or an aircraft which is registered under the laws of that State at the time the offence is committed; or

(c) The offence is committed by a national of that State.

2. A State Party may also establish its jurisdiction over any such offence when:

(a) The offence is committed against a national of that State; or

(b) The offence is committed against a State or government facility of that State abroad, including an embassy or other diplomatic or consular premises of that State; or

(c) The offence is committed by a stateless person who has his or her habitual residence in the territory of that State; or

(d) The offence is committed in an attempt to compel that State to do or abstain from doing any act; or

(e) The offence is committed on board an aircraft which is operated by the Government of that State. . . .

4. Each State Party shall likewise take such measures as may be necessary to establish its jurisdiction over the offences set forth in article 2 in cases where the alleged offender is present in its territory and it does not extradite that person to any of the States Parties which have established their jurisdiction in accordance with paragraph 1 or 2 of the present article. . . .

Article 8

1. The State Party in the territory of which the alleged offender is present shall, in cases to which article 6 applies, if it does not extradite that person, be obliged, without exception whatsoever and whether or not the offence was committed in its territory, to submit the case without undue delay to its competent authorities for the purpose of prosecution, through proceedings in accordance with the laws of that State. Those authorities shall take their decision in the same manner as in the case of any other offence of a grave nature under the law of that State. . . .

Notes and Questions

1. The Terrorist Bombing Convention applies only if there is an international aspect to the bombing. Article 3 provides that the Convention does not apply:

> where the offence is committed within a single State, the alleged offender and the victims are nationals of that State, the alleged offender is found in the territory of that State and no other State has a basis under article 6, paragraph 1 or paragraph 2, of this Convention to exercise jurisdiction . . .

2. One of the longstanding difficulties in reaching an agreed definition of "terrorism" is the question of whether the term should reach only conduct of non-state actors, or whether state action can also be deemed terrorism. The Terrorist

Bombing Convention excludes acts that might fall within the definition of the offense when committed by armed forces during armed conflict. That exclusion is justified on the grounds that the bombing of civilian targets by official armed forces is "governed by other rules of international law," namely, the laws of war, and thus need not be criminalized under the Terrorist Bombings Convention. See art. 19(2).

Is this a satisfactory resolution of concerns about acts by government officials that terrorize civilians? Would it apply to a covert bombing organized by a government's intelligence services of the kind perpetrated in 1986 by Libyan operatives at a disco in Berlin frequented by U.S. military personnel? (A Libyan diplomat and three others were convicted of crimes related to the bombing by a German court in 1996.)

3. How should terrorism be defined? Should it be limited to acts by non-state actors? Should it be limited to attacks against civilians? How is terrorism distinguished from an "ordinary" crime? Does it depend on the political motivation of the perpetrator? Would a bombing by an insurgent group fighting for independence be an act of terrorism, or would it be part of the conduct of armed conflict? Does it depend on the target of the bombing?

Under 22 U.S.C. §2656f, which requires the State Department to prepare and submit to Congress annual country reports on terrorism, "terrorism" is defined as "premeditated, politically motivated violence perpetrated against noncombatant targets by subnational groups or clandestine agents." 22 U.S.C. §2656f(d)(2). "International terrorism" is defined as "terrorism involving citizens or the territory of more than one country." 22 U.S.C. §2656f(d)(1)

4. The following list shows the 13 major multilateral conventions on terrorism and indicates the number of parties to each, as of May 2011. The United States is a party to all of these conventions except the International Convention for the Suppression of Acts of Nuclear Terrorism, which it has signed but not yet ratified.

1. Convention on Offences and Certain Other Acts Committed on Board Aircraft (the "Tokyo Convention") (1963): 185 parties
2. Convention for the Suppression of Unlawful Seizure of Aircraft (the "Hague Convention") (1970): 185 parties
3. Convention for the Suppression of Unlawful Acts against the Safety of Civil Aviation (the "Montreal Convention") (1971): 188 parties
4. Convention on the Prevention and Punishment of Crimes against Internationally Protected Persons, including Diplomatic Agents (1973): 173 parties
5. International Convention against the Taking of Hostages (1979): 168 parties
6. Convention on the Physical Protection of Nuclear Material (1980): 144 parties
7. Protocol for the Suppression of Unlawful Acts of Violence at Airports Serving International Civil Aviation, supplementary to the Convention for the Suppression of Unlawful Acts against the Safety of Civil Aviation (1988): 171 parties
8. Convention for the Suppression of Unlawful Acts against the Safety of Maritime Navigation (1988): 157 parties
9. Protocol for the Suppression of Unlawful Acts against the Safety of Fixed Platforms Located on the Continental Shelf (1988): 146 parties

10. Convention on the Marking of Plastic Explosives for the Purpose of Detection (1991): 145 parties
11. International Convention for the Suppression of Terrorist Bombings (1997): 164 parties
12. International Convention for the Suppression of the Financing of Terrorism (1999): 173 parties
13. International Convention for the Suppression of Acts of Nuclear Terrorism (2005): 77 parties

5. A common feature of the major multilateral counterterrorism conventions is a requirement that states must either try or extradite persons found in their territory who are alleged to have committed offenses defined in the treaties, without regard to where the offense took place. In United States v. Yunis, 924 F.2d 1086 (D.C. Cir. 1991), the Court of Appeals affirmed the conviction in U.S. courts of a Lebanese national who was prosecuted for commandeering a Royal Jordanian Airlines aircraft from Beirut to Tunisia. Yunis was charged with offenses enacted by Congress to implement two of the multilateral counterterrorism conventions noted above, the 1970 Convention for the Suppression of Unlawful Seizure of Aircraft (the "Hague Convention") and the 1979 International Convention against the Taking of Hostages. Lebanon was a party to the Hague Convention but not the Hostage Taking Convention. The only U.S. connection to the offense was the presence of several American nationals on the plane.

Consider the principles of jurisdiction in Chapter 7. Would the United States have an international law basis for exercising prescriptive jurisdiction over Yunis's acts if it were not a party to the Hague Convention and the Hostage Taking Convention? What if there had been no Americans on the hijacked plane? Where the extraterritorial assertion of jurisdiction is based on treaty obligations pursuant to a counterterrorism convention, is it permissible for a state to exercise jurisdiction over nationals of non-parties to the convention?

The *Yunis* court noted that aircraft hijacking "may well be one of the few crimes so clearly condemned under the law of nations that states may assert universal jurisdiction to bring offenders to justice," but made no such finding with respect to hostage taking. Id. at 1092. For conduct that is not generally recognized as being subject to universal jurisdiction, how many parties must there be to a treaty defining that conduct as an offense before it becomes a matter of universal jurisdiction? Imagine that 25 countries become parties to a treaty that makes it an offense for any person "to depict or defame sacred religious figures," and that further obligates parties to the treaty either to try or extradite persons found in their territory who have committed that offense. Imagine further that a cartoonist, who is a national of Country A, which is not a party to the treaty, draws a cartoon depicting Jesus, Moses, and Mohammed. He later visits Country B, which is a party to the treaty. Would it be permissible under international law for a Country B to assert jurisdiction over and prosecute the cartoonist? Is this scenario distinguishable from the U.S. prosecution of Yunis for hostage taking in Lebanon, even though Lebanon at the time was not a party to the Hostage Taking Convention?

C. INSTITUTIONAL ARRANGEMENTS FOR THE PROSECUTION OF INTERNATIONAL CRIMES

The preceding sections explored the principles and scope of individual criminal liability under international law and some of the most important substantive international crimes. This section considers the different kinds of courts or tribunals before which international crimes may be tried. Prosecutions for international crimes may take place before either national courts or international tribunals. We begin with a discussion of prosecutions before domestic courts, and then turn to international tribunals and "hybrid" courts comprised of national and international components. We conclude with a brief discussion of alternatives to criminal prosecution.

1. *Prosecution of International Crimes before Domestic Courts*

The tradition of trying international offenses before domestic courts is a venerable one. Article 1, section 8, of the U.S. Constitution grants Congress the "power to define and punish . . . Offenses against the law of Nations." The judgment of the International Military Tribunal at Nuremberg noted the longstanding practice of prosecuting violations of the laws or customs of war before military commissions. U.S. military personnel generally are subject to the Uniform Code of Military Justice, which incorporates international war crimes as offenses and provides a comprehensive criminal justice system. See Evolving Military Justice (Eugene R. Fidell & Dwight H. Sullivan eds., 2002). The Supreme Court in Hamdan v. Rumsfeld, 548 U.S. 557, 592 (2006), relying on the Second World War-era prosecution of German saboteurs captured in the United States in Ex parte Quirin, 317 U.S. 1, 28 (1942), noted that Congress can provide for military tribunals "to try offenders or offenses against the law of war." Following the ruling in *Hamdan*, Congress in the Military Commissions Act of 2006, as amended by the Military Commissions Act of 2009, codified at 10 U.S.C. §§948a et seq., has authorized the establishment of military commissions to try alien unprivileged enemy belligerents (including members of Al Qaeda) for, among other things, "violations of the law of war." 10 U.S.C. §948b(a).

Offenses that constitute violations of international law can also be prosecuted in civilian national courts as violations of "ordinary" domestic offenses, such as murder or assault. They may also be prosecuted under statutes that specifically make international crimes an offense under domestic law, such as 18 U.S.C. §1091, which makes genocide a crime under U.S. law, or the "War Crimes Act," 18 U.S.C. §2441, which makes it a violation of U.S. law for certain categories of persons to commit "war crimes," which are defined as certain acts prohibited under a number of international law of war treaties. The statutes are noted above in Section B.3.a and B.3.c, respectively.

In other cases, special civilian courts may be established to try international crimes. The need for such courts is sometimes justified by the special nature and complexity of war crimes trials. Bosnia, for example, has created a Special War Crimes Chamber in its court system to try such offenses. As we have seen, states may exercise domestic criminal jurisdiction over persons who commit international crimes consistent with international law prescriptive jurisdiction principles where the crimes are committed on their territory, by their nationals, or against their nationals. In addition, as the *Pinochet* case shows, under treaties that impose "try-or-extradite" obligations on states to prosecute offenses defined in the treaty, states may exercise jurisdiction over offenders found in their territory, even if none of those jurisdictional principles applies. Finally, the most severe international crimes, including genocide, crimes against humanity, grave breaches of the Geneva Conventions, torture, and certain terrorism-related offenses are generally seen as "offenses recognized by the community of nations as of universal concern" that are subject to universal jurisdiction. The principle of universal jurisdiction, under which a state may exercise jurisdiction regardless of where the offense occurred, is predicated on the notion that "certain offenses may be punished by any state because the offenders are 'common enemies of all mankind and all nations have an equal interest in their apprehension and punishment.'" In re Demjanjuk, 612 F. Supp. 544, 556 (N.D. Ohio 1985).

Notes and Questions

1. A prominent example of a national court exercising territorial jurisdiction over international crimes is the Supreme Iraqi Criminal Tribunal, a body established under Iraqi national law to try Iraqi nationals or residents accused of genocide, crimes against humanity, war crimes, or other serious crimes committed between 1968 and 2003. The Tribunal, originally known as the Iraqi Special Tribunal, was initially established pursuant to an order issued by the U.S.-led Coalition Provisional Authority during the occupation of Iraq. Iraqi authorities enacted a new statute in 2005 and renamed the court the Supreme Iraqi Criminal Tribunal.

The Tribunal's most prominent case was the prosecution of ousted Iraqi dictator Saddam Hussein and several co-defendants for crimes against humanity in connection with the massacre of Shiites in the village of Dujail in 1982. Saddam was convicted and hanged in 2006. Other prominent prosecutions involved Ali Hassan al-Majid (known as "Chemical Ali"), who was convicted of genocide for acts committed during the Anfal campaign against Iraqi Kurds in 1988 (during which Iraqi forces used chemical weapons) and the 1991 uprising of Iraq Shiites following the first Gulf war. One detailed review of the Anfal trial concludes that "the evidence presented [at trial] was quite solid and the Trial Chamber Judgment was generally well-reasoned." Jennifer Trahan, Justice for Iraq: The Work of the Iraqi High Tribunal: Remarks Regarding The Iraqi High Tribunal's "Anfal" Trial, 15 ILSA J. Int'l & Comp. L. 587, 588 (2009). At the same time, the review concluded, there were a number of fair trial problems that plagued the trial, including governmental interference regarding the composition of the trial chamber, difficulty for the accused to produce defense witnesses, passivity on the part of assigned defense counsel, and a failure on the part of the trial chamber to give reasoned responses to defense motions. Id. at 598-600.

2. One commentator has observed that the principal benefit of the exercise of universal jurisdiction by states "is the provision of an alternate means of bringing to justice serious criminals when the State where the crimes occurred is unable or unwilling to prosecute." In many cases, "prosecution under the universality principle may be the preferred way to avoid impunity for serious international

criminals." William W. Burke-White, A Community of Courts: Toward a System of International Criminal Law Enforcement, 24 Mich. J. Int'l L. 1, 20 (2002).

Not all observers are as sanguine. Consider the following comment:

> . . . [A] universal jurisdiction prosecution may cause more harm than the original crime it purports to address. Universal jurisdiction courts and prosecutors possess neither the competence nor the incentive to fully consider these harms. They are . . . completely unaccountable to the citizens of the nation whose fate they are ruling upon. It doesn't matter that they act with benevolent intent. What matters is that they may do something that harms people to whom they have no real connection and whose interests they are poorly positioned to assess. Because relevant constituencies cannot hold courts exercising universal jurisdiction accountable for the negative consequences of their rulings, the courts themselves will invariably be less disciplined and prudent than would otherwise be the case.
>
> The inability of universal jurisdiction courts to consider the consequences of their actions in affected countries is a particular threat to amnesties, reconciliations, truth commissions, and similar programs that can successfully facilitate transitional justice. . . . [These programs can be] best viewed as prudential arrangements that sacrifice some benefits—such as punishment of the guilty and restoration of the respect and integrity of victims—for the sake of other values, including the minimization of human suffering, closure, a stable peace, and the like. In recent years, amnesties have been an important component in several peaceful settlements of bloody civil conflicts, including ones in Chile, Haiti, Sierra Leone, and South Africa.
>
> . . . [A] rejection of amnesty and an insistence on criminal prosecutions "can prolong . . . conflict, resulting in more deaths, destruction, and human suffering." . . .
>
> Because universal jurisdiction prosecutions take place outside affected communities, universal jurisdiction courts and prosecutors lack the incentive, or the institutional capacity, to consider such tradeoffs. [Jack Goldsmith & Stephen D. Krasner, The Limits of Idealism, Daedalus, Winter 2003, at 47, 51-52.]

Do you agree that it is up to the citizens of each state whether to pursue prosecution of those who have committed international crimes, or would that allow perpetrators of abuses to insulate themselves from accountability? In the Pinochet example, does it matter that Chile was party to a treaty under which it had agreed to prosecute persons who committed torture? What role can and do legislatures and courts play in providing limits on the scope of universal jurisdiction?

3. In 2004, a U.S. human rights organization called the Center for Constitutional Rights (CCR) filed a complaint with federal German prosecutors requesting Germany to open a criminal investigation against then-Secretary of Defense Donald Rumsfeld, former Director of Central Intelligence George Tenet, and other senior U.S. officials for alleged war crimes committed by U.S. forces against detainees at the Abu Ghraib prison in Iraq. CCR based the request on a 2002 German law known as the "Code of Crimes against International Law," which provides for "universal jurisdiction" for war crimes, genocide, and crimes against humanity. The German prosecutor applied the principle of "subsidiarity," under which "uninvolved third countries" should exercise jurisdiction over crimes subject to universal jurisdiction only if "criminal prosecution by primarily competent states, or an international court, is not ensured or cannot be ensured." In November 2006, CCR filed a new request in Germany, arguing that only low-ranking military personnel had been

prosecuted in connection with the Abu Ghraib abuses, and that "no investigations are under way against higher-ranking officers, not to mention the highest civilian and military authorities, for either torture or fatalities" there. CCR, Criminal Complaint Against United States Secretary of Defense Donald Rumsfeld, et al., available at CCR's Web site at http://ccrjustice.org/. The German Federal Prosecutor declined to initiate criminal proceedings, noting that Germany had "no direct connection with the acts complained of" and that it would be futile to proceed with a case that would require investigations in the United States. Prosecutor General at the Federal Supreme Court Karlsruhe, Memorandum re: Criminal Complaint against Donald Rumsfeld et al., 3 ARP 156/06-2 (April 5, 2007), available at http://ccrjustice.org/.

4. The prospect of prosecutions by foreign courts is a matter of growing concern to leaders alleged to have committed international crimes when they travel. Former Secretary of Defense Donald Rumsfeld was reported to have fled from an event during a visit to France in October 2007 after human rights organizations filed a complaint accusing him of responsibility for torture of detainees at Abu Ghraib. Alternet, Rumsfeld Flees France, Fearing Arrest (Oct. 27, 2007), at http://www.alternet.org/story/66425/. Israeli officials reportedly cancelled a trip to Britain in late 2010 because of fear of arrest in connection with allegations of war crimes against Palestinians that pro-Palestinian activists threatened to file. Isabel Kershner, Israel: Officials Cancel Trip to Britain, N.Y. Times, Nov. 4, 2010, at A14. In February 2011, former President George W. Bush cancelled a trip to Switzerland, in part due to reports that international human rights groups were urging Swiss authorities to open a criminal investigation while he was in the country regarding his alleged responsibility for torture. James Risen, Protest Threats in Geneva Derail Bush's Planned Visit, N.Y. Times, Feb. 6, 2011, at A21.

Despite the growing importance of national courts in trying international crimes, we will in the remainder of this section focus on international tribunals and "hybrid" courts comprised of national and international components. We have already discussed the International Military Tribunal at Nuremberg and the International Military Tribunal for the Far East at Tokyo, the most prominent of 20th century international criminal tribunals.* We turn now to more modern international criminal tribunals.

2. *The Tribunals for the Former Yugoslavia and Rwanda*

Although the creation of a standing international criminal tribunal was contemplated as early as 1948, at the time of the negotiating of the Genocide Convention, the project to establish such a court received little attention over the following decades. The mass atrocities in the former Yugoslavia and Rwanda during the early 1990s changed that. The events prompted the Security Council to create

* The Second World War-era tribunals were not, however, the first international war crimes tribunals of the twentieth century. Tribunals were also established at Leipzig and Constantinople after the First World War to try German and Turkish perpetrators of atrocities during that conflict. These Tribunals proved largely to be failures. See generally Gary Jonathan Bass, Stay the Hand of Vengeance (2000).

two separate "ad hoc" tribunals to deal with the serious international humanitarian law violations arising out of these two situations.

The International Criminal Tribunal for the Former Yugoslavia. The vicious civil war that erupted in the former Socialist Federal Republic of Yugoslavia in 1991 was replete with torture, incarceration, forced deportation, systematic rape, willful killing, and indiscriminate shelling of civilians. Appalled by these atrocities and encouraged by the U.S. Ambassador to the United Nations, Madeleine K. Albright, the U.N. Security Council decided in Resolution 808 (Feb. 22, 1993) to establish "an international tribunal . . . for the prosecution of serious violations of international humanitarian law" committed in the former Yugoslavia. Three months later, in Resolution 827 (in the Documentary Supplement), the Security Council adopted the Statute of the International Criminal Tribunal for the Former Yugoslavia (ICTY). It was the first international war crimes tribunal since the tribunals right after World War II.

The Security Council relied on Chapter VII of the U.N. Charter as a legal basis for establishing the Tribunal. Violations of international humanitarian law were found to be a threat to international peace and security. The Statute gave the Tribunal subject matter jurisdiction over genocide, grave breaches of the Geneva Conventions, war crimes, and crimes against humanity. Resolution 827 and the Statute required every state to comply with requests for assistance or orders issued by Trial Chambers of the Tribunal, including orders for the arrest and surrender of indicted individuals. By virtue of Article 25 of the Charter, the resolution imposed binding obligations on all U.N. member states. In the face of a state's refusal to comply with an order of a Trial Chamber, the Tribunal's Rules of Procedure and Evidence empower the Tribunal's President to report the matter to the Security Council. ICTY Rules of Procedure and Evidence, IT/32/Rev.45, Rule 7 *bis* (as amended through Dec. 8, 2010). The Council retains discretion to decide what measures, if any, to take in response to such noncompliance.

In November 1993, the 11 judges of the Tribunal, elected by the U.N. General Assembly, took oaths enabling them to indict, try, and sentence suspects. The Tribunal, which is based in The Hague in the Netherlands, initially consisted of two trial chambers of three judges each and a single five-judge appellate chamber. The limited number of trial chambers created significant delays in trying cases, however, and the number of judges has expanded. As of May 2011, the ICTY had a total of 27 judges, including 16 permanent judges augmented by 11 "ad litem" judges designated to sit on a particular case.

Particularly in its early years, the Tribunal's work was stymied by the lack of cooperation by some of the states of the former Yugoslavia and their refusal to surrender key suspects. According to the former President of the ICTY, as of spring 1998, "the Tribunal had issued some 205 arrest warrants and only six had been executed by the states." Gabrielle Kirk McDonald, Problems, Obstacles, and Achievements of the ICTY, 2 J. Int'l Crim. Just. 558, 563 (2004). The fact that the vast majority of those indicted by the ICTY were at large raised doubts about the ICTY's effectiveness.

Beginning in late 1997, though, the tide began to turn. The Tribunal started to use sealed indictments, which diminished the chances that persons would go into hiding after being indicted, and the NATO-led military Stabilization Force (SFOR) in Bosnia began to arrest ICTY fugitives. The United States and other countries brought economic and diplomatic pressure to bear on the countries of the former Yugoslavia, and governments in those states that had been sympathetic to the regimes responsible for the atrocities began to give way to regimes interested in improving relations with Europe and the United States. By the time of the ICTY's Fifth Annual Report to the General Assembly and Security Council in August 1998, the increase in activity at the Tribunal led to it to declare that the year had been "characterized by the unprecedented growth and development of the institution, which has now, without any doubt, become a fully-fledged international criminal institution." The Tribunal registered a major breakthrough in 2001, when Serbia turned over its former president, Slobodan Milošević, whom the ICTY had indicted for a wide range of war crimes. His well-publicized trial began in February 2002, but Milošević died in his prison cell in The Hague in March 2006, before the conclusion of his trial. The Tribunal continued to obtain custody over and proceed to trial against senior civilian and political leaders, including the notorious wartime president of the self-proclaimed Bosnian Serb Republic, Radovan Karadžić, who was arrested by Serbian authorities in Belgrade in July 2008, and Ratko Mladić, the general in charge of Bosnian Serb forces during the killings at Srebrenica in 1995, who was arrested in Serbia in May 2011.

Through May 2011, 161 accused individuals have been indicted by the ICTY. Of these, 64 have received their final sentence, 13 have been found not guilty. Proceedings are underway in the cases of another 35 accused persons. Cases of 13 ICTY indictees were transferred to national courts in the former Yugoslavia as part of the Tribunal's "completion strategy," discussed below. Although the Tribunal was criticized in its early years for trying only low-ranking perpetrators, or "small fish," the Tribunal has managed to obtain custody of virtually all of the senior military and political leaders of interest to it in the former Yugoslavia. In contrast to its early days, when the great majority of indictees were beyond the ICTY's reach, by May 2011 only one indictee was at large.

The International Criminal Tribunal for Rwanda. In November 1994, the U.N. Security Council created the International Criminal Tribunal for Rwanda to prosecute genocide, crimes against humanity, and war crimes in Rwanda in response to the widespread killings and other crimes had occurred there. To simplify getting the arrangement underway, the new tribunal initially had the same prosecutor and appeals judges as the ICTY. In 2003, the Security Council decided to give the ICTR its own Chief Prosecutor, but the two tribunals still share a common Appeals Chamber. As of May 2011, the Tribunal had 6 permanent and 11 "ad litem" judges, in addition to the judges who serve on the joint ICTY-ICTR Appeals Chamber.

Although progress at the ICTR was initially slow, and the tribunal was plagued by management problems, it has also had successes. As of May 2011, the Tribunal has issued trial judgments involving 55 defendants, including many senior figures such as a prime minister, other government ministers, and others holding leadership positions. In one notable case against three leading media figures, a Trial Chamber recognized guarantees under international law of the right to freedom of expression, but stated that it was "critical to distinguish between the discussion of ethnic consciousness and the promotion of ethnic hatred." Prosecutor v. Nahimana, Case No. ICTR-99-52-T, Judgment, at ¶93 (Dec. 3, 2003). The Trial Chamber convicted the defendants of genocide, incitement to genocide, conspiracy, and crimes against humanity. Cases of two ICTR indictees were transferred to

France as part of the Tribunal's "completion strategy," discussed below. Trials involving another 20 defendants were underway as of May 2011. Nearly 17 years after the establishment of the Tribunal, however, ten ICTR indictees remain at large.

The Complete Strategy. The Tribunals for the former Yugoslavia and Rwanda have been criticized for the slow pace at which they have dispensed justice and for their high cost. Since their inception, the total cost of operating the two tribunals has exceeded $3.5 billion. The cumulative budgets of the ICTY through 2011 alone have totaled nearly $1.9 billion.

In response to these criticisms, the Tribunals — at the urging of U.N. member states — developed "completion strategies" setting out how they will finish their work. The Tribunals formulated plans under which they will pursue prosecutions of only "the highest-ranking political, military, paramilitary and civilian leaders" and will refer the cases of some indicted persons to national courts. Daryl A. Mundis, The Judicial Effects of the "Completion Strategies" on the Ad Hoc International Tribunals, 99 Am. J. Int'l L. 142, 143 (2005) (quoting then-ICTY President Jorda). In Resolution 1503 (2003), the Security Council "call[ed] on the ICTY and the ICTR to take all possible measures to complete investigations by the end of 2004, to complete all trial activities at first instance by the end of 2008, and to complete all work in 2010." Although these deadlines have been extended, the Tribunals are no longer issuing new indictments. As part of the completion strategy, the ICTY has, as of May 2011, transferred 13 indictees to Bosnia, Croatia, and Serbia for trials before domestic courts. The ICTR Prosecutor has sought to transfer the cases of five indictees to courts in Rwanda, but ICTR Trial Chambers denied those requests because they "were not satisfied that the accused would receive a fair trial." Erik Møse, The ICTR's Completion Strategy: Challenges and Possible Solutions, 6 J. Int'l Crim. Justice 667, 674 (2008). Two ICTR indictees were transferred to France for prosecution before national courts there.

In December 2010, the Security Council adopted Resolution 1966, which calls upon the ICTY and ICTR to complete all their remaining work by December 31, 2014. Recognizing that additional tasks — including appeals from cases decided by trial chambers of the two tribunals and prosecutions of fugitives who may be arrested in the future — may arise, the Council established a new body, called the "International Residual Mechanism for Criminal Tribunals," to finish the remaining tasks of two tribunals. The Mechanism will have two branches, one for each tribunal, and will begin functioning in July 2012 for the ICTR and in July 2013 for the ICTY. The Mechanism will have the power, among other things, to try fugitives who may be arrested less than a year before the relevant branch begins functioning. It will also be empowered to transfer cases of persons indicted by the Tribunals who "are not among the most senior leaders" to national courts and also to hear appeals of persons whose notices of appeal are filed after the commencement of the relevant branch of the Mechanism. The Mechanism will not be able to issue new indictments. Resolution 1966 contemplates that the Mechanism be a "small, temporary and efficient structure, whose functions and size will diminish over time, with a small number of staff commensurate with its reduced functions."

Assessment. The Tribunals for the former Yugoslavia and Rwanda have contributed in important ways to the development of international criminal justice. The decisions of the tribunals have led to a substantial expansion of the body of international criminal law and have elaborated principles of international criminal procedure. In addition, one commentator argues that in the case of the ICTY, it has had a positive impact on victims of atrocities:

> . . . [T]he ICTY has mattered greatly to many Bosniaks — who endured the largest number of crimes charged by the ICTY Prosecutor — even as the Tribunal has disappointed their expectations. While many of the Tribunal's sentences have struck Bosniaks as derisorily short, some judgments have provided a sense of justice not readily captured or commonly reflected in assessments of the Tribunal. For example, many Sarajevans were gratified by a November 2006 Appeals Chamber judgment imposing a sentence of life imprisonment on a defendant, Stanislav Galić, for his role in the siege of Sarajevo; in their view, the judgment honored their suffering and helped restore a moral balance that had been frightfully put awry.
>
> Many Bosniaks felt a similar sense of vindication by the ICTY's determination in an earlier case that the July 1995 massacre by Serbian forces of Muslim men in Srebrenica was a genocide. As one Bosniak told us (and as many said in similar terms), the ICTY's "finding that what happened at Srebrenica was genocide is the most important achievement and without the ICTY this would not be possible." [Diane F. Orentlicher, Shrinking the Space for Denial: The Impact of the ICTY in Serbia 14 (2008.)]

Not all commentators have been as positive in evaluating the records of the Tribunal for the former Yugoslavia. One review of attitudes toward the ICTY in the former Yugoslavia found that public perceptions were generally negative in all countries. In Serbia, the Tribunal was seen as biased against Serbs; in Croatia, statements by public figures about the Tribunal were "hostile and increasingly derogatory, contemptuous, and disparaging" toward the ICTY; and even in Bosnia, where most of the Muslim majority supports the Tribunal, the public is "disappointed by the small number of accused, the lengthy trials, and prison sentences they see as too lenient." Mirko Klarin, The Impact of the ICTY Trials on Public Opinion in the Former Yugoslavia, 7 J. Int'l Crim. Justice 89, 89, 90 (2009).

Another commentator, based on interviews with victims of atrocities committed during the wars in the former Yugoslavia, has concluded that it "would be erroneous to claim that in [Bosnia-Herzegovina] today reconciliation has been achieved."

> . . . [W]hen asked whether the ICTY has contributed to reconciliation in [Bosnia-Herzegovina] and whether it can do so, 90% of interviewees answered no, offering a variety of different reasons. The Bosnian Serb and Bosnian Croat interviewees insisted that a tribunal that is biased cannot aid reconciliation. In the words of a Bosnian Serb man in Prijedor, internally displaced from the central Bosnian town of Travnik, "The Hague Tribunal cannot help reconciliation because it is only judging Serbs!" The Bosnian Muslim interviewees also dismissed the notion that the ICTY can aid reconciliation. According to a female widow in Trnopolje, "The Hague Tribunal cannot assist reconciliation because the Serbs do not accept its judgements." Others maintained that reconciliation cannot be achieved via a court. To cite a male interviewee in Goražde, "Reconciliation is a natural process. It cannot be imposed by our politicians or by international bodies like the Hague Tribunal. There just needs to be communication between people. Where there is communication, there can be reconciliation."
>
> Still others argued that there can be no reconciliation without justice. Epitomizing this view, a female interviewee in Kozarac and a survivor of the Trnopolje camp contended that, "There can be no reconciliation when war criminals are given low sentences and when so many of them are still free." The most common response given,

however, was that the Tribunal has not and cannot contribute to reconciliation in [Bosnia-Herzegovina] because it is too far away. To quote a female interviewee in Srebrenica who lost her two sons, "No reconciliation can come from a court than has so little relevance to our daily lives." [Janine Natalya Clark, Judging the ICTY: Has it Achieved its Objectives?, 9 Southeast European & Black Sea Studies 123, 135-136 (2009).]

Notes and Questions

1. In the years before the establishment of the ICTY, most proponents of international criminal tribunals assumed that such an institution would be established by treaty, as was later the case with the International Criminal Court (ICC). Why were the ICTY and ICTR created by Security Council resolution? Do you believe it was appropriate for the Security Council to establish the ICTY and ICTR in this manner? Look again at Article 41 of the U.N. Charter. Is the establishment of an international criminal tribunal the kind of "measure" the Charter contemplates the Security Council may employ to give effect to its decisions? Even if the Security Council was legally empowered to establish the ICTY, do you think creating the Tribunal in this way affected its legitimacy or effectiveness? Would participation by a broader group of states have been helpful? Why or why not?

2. The ICTY was established while the armed conflict in the former Yugoslavia was still ongoing. One commentator has written that "[t]he establishment of the Tribunal was widely perceived to be no more than a fig-leaf to cover the failure of the international community to act to prevent or halt the atrocities taking place in the former Yugoslavia." Rachel Kerr, The International Criminal Tribunal for the Former Yugoslavia: An Exercise in Law, Politics, and Diplomacy 209 (2004). Similar claims have been made about the ICTR. Arguing that the Security Council had "turned a blind eye to genocide" in Rwanda and that U.N. peacekeeping forces "had been morally responsible for some of the murders," Geoffrey Robertson, who would later serve at the President of the Special Court for Sierra Leone, has written that the ICTR was created because the Uinted Nations "needed a figleaf for its failure." Geoffrey Robertson, Crimes Against Humanity: The Struggle for Global Justice 73 (1999).

3. Although progress has often seemed to be slow, why does it appear that the criminal tribunals for the former Yugoslavia and Rwanda have had at least some success? Might it help that their jurisdiction is limited? Does it help that they were both authorized by the U.N. Security Council, including the United States and the other four permanent members with vetoes?

4. As noted above, the international community's support for the ICTY during its early years was more limited than the advocates of the Tribunal would have liked. On those occasions when the ICTY's president reported noncompliance by states to which orders had been directed, "the Security Council failed to adopt concrete measures in response to these reports." McDonald, Problems, Obstacles, and Achievements of the ICTY, supra, at 571. NATO peacekeepers for the first several years after their deployment to Bosnia in 1995 did not arrest ICTY indictees. In the words of one commentator, only later, when "the interests of justice and the interests of States in restoring and maintaining peace coincided," did the Tribunal receive the cooperation necessary to enable it to begin effectively to discharge its mandate. Kerr, The International Criminal Tribunal for the Former Yugoslavia, supra, at 212.

Why do you think the Security Council did not respond more actively to reports of noncompliance with orders of the ICTY? How does the apparent dependence of the tribunals for the former Yugoslavia and Rwanda on the politically variable willingness of states to support them hamper the effectiveness of these courts? Can this problem be surmounted? How?

5. Although the Security Council in Resolution 808 stated that establishing an international criminal tribunal would advance the aim of putting an end to serious violations of international humanitarian law taking place in the former Yugoslavia, the fighting continued until 1995, two years after the ICTY was established. In that time, many additional crimes were committed, including the 1995 massacre of Bosnian Muslims at Srebrenica, the worst single atrocity of the conflict. What does this suggest about the Tribunal's capacity to deter crimes? Would the Tribunal have had more success in deterring crime if states had supported it more actively in its early years? As a more general matter, is the existence of an international criminal tribunal likely to deter the commission of international crimes?

6. As noted above, public attitudes in the former Yugoslavia toward the ICTY are generally not favorable, and the extent to which the Tribunals have provided the victims of atrocities with a sense of justice, contributed to political reconciliation, or promoted peace in the affected societies remains unclear. How would one evaluate what impact the ICTY and the ICTR have had in contributing to reconciliation in Rwanda and the former Yugoslavia? Even if it may not be easy to assess their records in promoting peace and reconciliation, do you think the Tribunals have made other contributions? Do you think such contributions have justified the costs of the Tribunals?

7. For more information on the former Yugoslavia and Rwanda tribunals, see Victor Peskin, International Justice in Rwanda and the Balkans: Virtual Trials and the Struggle for State Cooperation (2008); and William A. Schabas, The UN International Criminal Tribunals: The Former Yugoslavia, Rwanda and Sierra Leone (2006). The ICTY's Web site is http://www.icty.org/. The ICTR's Web site is http://www.unictr.org/.

3. *Hybrid ("Mixed") Tribunals*

Before the establishment of the ICC as a standing international criminal court, the costs and political challenges of establishing international tribunals such as the ICTR and ICTY as U.N. organizations generated a search for new approaches to providing for prosecutions of international crimes, particularly in countries emerging from mass atrocity situations that may not have highly developed domestic judiciaries. The following excerpt discusses the role of "hybrid" courts, in which there is some degree of joint participation by elements from the international system and the domestic courts of the country where the crimes occurred.

Laura A. Dickinson, The Promise of Hybrid Courts

97 Am. J. Int'l L. 295, 295, 306-307 (2003)

. . . [A] newly emerging . . . form of accountability and reconciliation . . . [is the use of] hybrid domestic-international courts. Such courts are "hybrid" because both the institutional apparatus and the applicable law consist of a blend of the international and the domestic. Foreign judges sit alongside their domestic counterparts to try cases prosecuted and defended by teams of local lawyers working with those from other countries. The judges apply domestic law that has been reformed to accord with international standards. This hybrid model has developed in a range of settings, generally postconflict situations where no politically viable full-fledged international tribunal exists, as in East Timor or Sierra Leone, or where an international tribunal exists but cannot cope with the sheer number of cases, as in Kosovo. Most recently, an agreement to create a hybrid court in Cambodia has been reached. . . .

. . . [I]n both Kosovo and East Timor the appointment of foreign judges to domestic courts to sit alongside local judges and the appointment of foreign prosecutors to team up with local prosecutors helped to create a framework for consultation that may have enhanced the general perception of the institution's legitimacy. By working together and sharing responsibilities, international and local officials necessarily consulted with each other.

The appointment of international judges to the local courts in these highly sensitive cases may also have helped to enhance the perception of the independence of the judiciary and therefore its legitimacy within a broad cross-section of the local population. In Kosovo this was most apparent, as the previous attempts at domestic justice had failed to win any support among Serbs. . . .

The sharing of responsibilities among local and international officials is not a complete cure for legitimacy problems, of course. . . . When international actors wield more power than local officials—when the majority of judges on a given panel is international, for example, or when the local prosecutors merely serve as deputies to international prosecutors—some may charge that the international actors control the process and that such control smacks of imperialism. In East Timor, some local actors involved in the criminal justice process criticized the hybrid court on these grounds. On the other hand, too little international control may lead to concerns about the independence and impartiality of overly locally controlled processes. . . . Nonetheless, the shared arrangement does offer more promise of working out these difficulties than a purely international or a purely domestic process.

The hybrid process offers advantages in the arena of capacity-building as well. The side-by-side working arrangements allow for on-the-job training that is likely to be more effective than abstract classroom discussions of formal legal rules and principles. And the teamwork can allow for sharing of experiences and knowledge in both directions. International actors have the opportunity to gain greater sensitivity to local issues, local culture, and local approaches to justice at the same time that local actors can learn from international actors. . . .

Sierra Leone. The Special Court for Sierra Leone is an independent institution established by an agreement between the United Nations and Sierra Leone. It was created in 2002 with a focus on prosecuting the individuals who organized and oversaw the atrocities that occurred starting in 1996 during Sierra Leone's civil war. These atrocities include hacking off the limbs and ears of victims, the mass use of rape as a weapon of terror, and the kidnapping of young children to be forced into combat. The Court derives its legal basis from U.N. Security Council Resolution 1513 (2000), which called for the establishment of the Special Court for Sierra Leone, and domestic Sierra Leonean legislation. Unlike the tribunals for the former Yugoslavia and Rwanda, the Sierra Leone court ordinarily sits in the country and has eight judges (five appointed by the United Nations and three by Sierra Leone). The Statute of the Special Court also limits prosecution to those who "bear greatest responsibility" for the atrocities. Direct contributions from individual U.N. members fund the Special Court, rather than the general U.N. budget.

The Special Court for Sierra Leone has indicted 13 individuals for war crimes, crimes against humanity, and other serious violations of international humanitarian law. Indictments against three persons were withdrawn in due to the deaths of the accused, and one indictee is at large. Three trials against eight of the accused have been completed, resulting in convictions and lengthy prison sentences of all accused.

In March 2003, the Special Court issued an indictment for former Liberian President Charles Taylor, who was charged with war crimes and crimes against humanity for his provision of "financial support, military training, personnel, arms, ammunition, and other support and encouragement to Sierra Leone's rebel forces" in order to "obtain access to the mineral wealth . . . particularly the diamond wealth of Sierra Leone, and to destablilize the State." Indictment, Prosecutor v. Charles Ghankay Taylor, Case No. SCSL-03-01, ¶20 (Mar. 3, 2003). Shortly after the indictment was released, Taylor, in exile from Liberia, sought refuge in Nigeria and remained there for three years, while the international community pressured the Nigerian Government to turn the former leader over to the Special Court. Taylor was finally surrendered to the Court in March 2006, but because of security concerns about holding his trial in Sierra Leone, the case was transferred to The Hague, where the Special Court has conducted the trial. The presentation of evidence, which began in January 2007, concluded in March 2011; no judgment had been issued by April 2011.

Cambodia. Many years after the widespread killings in Cambodia that took place during the 1975-1979 reign of the Khmer Rouge, the United Nations and Cambodia concluded an agreement to establish a special court, known as the Extraordinary Chambers in the Courts of Cambodia (ECCC), to try those responsible for the atrocities. Cambodia enacted a domestic statute to establish the Court in accordance with the terms of the agreement with the United Nations

The court has jurisdiction to try senior Khmer Rouge leaders who were "most responsible" for the crimes, including serious violations of international humanitarian law, that were committed during the period from 17 April 1975 to 6 January 1979. Both Cambodian judges and judges nominated by the United Nations sit on the Court. Cambodian judges comprise a majority in both the Trial Chamber (made up of three Cambodian and two international judges) and in the Appeals Chamber (made up of four Cambodian and three international judges), but under a "supermajority" formula built into the court's statute, "[n]o judicial decision of any consequence can be made without the consent of at least one international judge." Patricia M. Wald, Iraq, Cambodia, and International Justice, 21 Am. U. Int'l L. Rev. 541, 552 (2006). The Court, which employs the civil law system, has both Cambodian and international co-prosecutors and co-investigative judges. The ECCC launched its first case in February 2009 against Kaing Guek Eav, known as "Duch," who was charged in connection with his role in supervising the notorious S-21 Security Office (also known as Tuol Sleng), which he supervised from 1975 to 1979. Of the 14,000 people believed to have been imprisoned at the S-21, only 12 survived. The rest were tortured to death or executed. In July 2010, a Trial Chamber of the ECCC convicted Duch of crimes against humanity and grave breaches of the Geneva Conventions. He was sentenced to a term of 35 years' imprisonment.

The ECCC co-Prosecutors have also issued a second indictment (running more than 750 pages in length) against four of the most senior surviving Khmer Rouge leaders, including Nuon Chea, who was second in command to Khmer Rouge leader Pol Pot and was known as "Brother Number Two." The four are charged with crimes against humanity, grave breaches of the Geneva Conventions, and genocide (with respect to killings of members of the Vietnamese and Cham minority groups). The trial is expected to begin in mid-2011.

Lebanon. Following the 2005 bombing attack that killed Lebanese Prime Minister Rafiq Hariri, an attack in which some believed Syrian officials were complicit, Lebanon sought U.N. support for the creation of a tribunal with an international character to try those allegedly responsible for the assassination. Lebanon and the United Nations negotiated an agreement to establish the Special Tribunal for Lebanon. Because of an impasse within the Lebanese government, Lebanon never concluded the domestic ratification process. As a result, in Resolution 1757 (2007), the Security Council, acting under Chapter VII of the U.N. Charter, decided that the terms of the unratified agreement "shall enter into force on 10 June 2007."

The mandate of the Special Tribunal, which is based in The Hague, is to prosecute persons responsible for the attack that killed former Prime Minister Hariri and killed or injured others. The substantive law applied by the Special Tribunal is provisions of the Lebanese Criminal Code relating to terrorism and other crimes against life and personal integrity. The Special Tribunal has a mixed composition of Lebanese and international judges; two international judges serve along with one Lebanese judge on the three-judge Trial Chamber, and three international judges serve with two Lebanese judges on the Appeals Chamber. The Prosecutor is international and is appointed by the U.N. Secretary-General. The Tribunal is funded through a mix of voluntary contributions by U.N. member states and funding from Lebanon.

The Tribunal began operation in March 2009. Rumors that the Tribunal will issue indictments against members of Lebanon's Hezbollah faction contributed to a political crisis leading to the January 2011 collapse of the Lebanese government headed by Saad Hariri, the son of the Prime Minister slain in 2005. Although there were reports that the Tribunal's prosecutor had filed a confidential indictment for confirmation by a pretrial judge, no indictment had been issued by April 2011.

Notes and Questions

1. What are the advantages of holding trials before domestic courts? Before international criminal courts? Before mixed tribunals? Do trials before international or hybrid tribunals increase the legitimacy of the process? Or is the function of trying

war criminals, particularly for offenses that occurred within a single country, a matter that is best addressed by that country's institutions?

2. What should be the basis for deciding to make the prosecution of a terrorist crime like the assassination of Lebanese Prime Minister Rafiq Hariri the subject of an internationalized hybrid court? Is it odd for the international community to address a single episode like this, rather than a broader situation in which many atrocities were committed, as in the case of the hybrid tribunals for Sierra Leone and Cambodia? What factors might explain this? According to one commentator:

> Hope that the STL might become a significant precedent for international justice region-wide dissipated as the probe became enmeshed in, and contaminated by, a vicious local and regional tug of war. From inception, the international investigation was promoted by an assortment of Lebanese and non-Lebanese players pursuing a variety of goals. Some sought revenge and accountability, others to deter future political assassinations and bolster Lebanon's sovereignty. A few (notably France and the U.S.) saw an opportunity to promote a lasting political realignment in Beirut by strengthening a pro-Western alliance, dramatically lessen Syria's and its allies' influence there or even—a goal nurtured more in Washington than in Paris—destabilise the Syrian regime. There was, too, hope of a breakthrough in the Arab world for international justice principles and an end to the culture of impunity. The result was a remarkably wide consensus among actors who converged on a narrowly defined judicial process, resting on the assumption that Syria was guilty, and that its guilt could and would be established beyond doubt. [International Crisis Group, Trial by Fire: The Politics of the Special Tribunal for Lebanon, at i (Dec. 2, 2010.]

What should be the criteria for deciding when to pursue criminal justice through international mechanisms? Are the geopolitical considerations described above appropriate considerations? If not, what criteria should we use?

3. The Web site of the Special Court for Sierra Leone is http://www.sc-sl.org. The Web site of the Extraordinary Chambers in the Courts of Cambodia is http://www.eccc.gov.kh/. The website of the Special Tribunal for Lebanon is http://www.stl-tsl.org/action/home.

4. *The International Criminal Court*

In March 2003, the 18 judges of the International Criminal Court (ICC) were sworn in and the ICC began business in The Hague, the Netherlands, where the International Court of Justice is also located. The ICC was established by the so-called Rome Treaty, which was finalized at a U.N. Conference in Rome in 1998, attended by delegates from 130 countries. The Rome Treaty, containing the ICC Statute, came into force on July 1, 2002, after the required 60 ratifications were deposited. (Excerpts of the ICC Statute are in the Documentary Supplement.)

Although the United States was a strong supporter of the ad hoc war crimes tribunals for the former Yugoslavia and Rwanda (discussed above in subsection 2 of this Section), it did not join the 120 countries that approved the treaty. Instead, during the Rome Conference, the United States lobbied to amend the proposed treaty in order to reduce the power of the ICC. After its lobbying efforts failed, the United States voted with Iraq, Libya, Qatar, Yemen, China, and Israel to reject the establishment of the ICC. As of May 2011, 115 states were party to the Statute of the ICC.

The ICC has jurisdiction over only "the most serious crimes of concern to the international community as a whole," including genocide, crimes against humanity, war crimes, and aggression. As noted in Section B.3.d above, however, the Court will only be able to exercise jurisdiction over the crime of aggression after the amendment defining the crime of aggression that was negotiated by ICC state parties in June 2010 is approved and then is affirmed in another decision on the matter, which, under the terms of the proposed amendment, cannot be done before January 2017.

Articles 12 and 13 of the Rome Statute establish the circumstances under which the Court may exercise jurisdiction.

Rome Statute of the International Criminal Court (July 12, 1998)

Article 12

Preconditions to the exercise of jurisdiction

1. A State which becomes a Party to this Statute thereby accepts the jurisdiction of the Court with respect to the crimes [within its jurisdiction].

2. In the case of [a referral by a State or the initiation of a case by the Prosecutor under] article 13, paragraph (a) or (c), the Court may exercise its jurisdiction if one or more of the following States are Parties to this Statute or have [separately] accepted the jurisdiction of the Court. . . .

(a) The State on the territory of which the conduct in question occurred . . . ;

(b) The State of which the person accused of the crime is a national. . . .

Article 13

Exercise of jurisdiction

The Court may exercise its jurisdiction with respect to a crime [within its jurisdiction] in accordance with the provisions of this Statute if:

(a) A situation in which one or more of such crimes appears to have been committed is referred to the Prosecutor by a State Party . . . ;

(b) A situation in which one or more of such crimes appears to have been committed is referred to the Prosecutor by the Security Council acting under Chapter VII of the Charter of the United Nations; or

(c) The Prosecutor has initiated an investigation in respect of such a crime . . . .

Even if a crime over which the ICC has jurisdiction is committed by a national of or on the territory of a state party, the Court will not necessarily act. Under the principle of "complementarity," a case is not "admissible" before the Court if the domestic judicial system of a state has taken or is taking steps to investigate or prosecute the perpetrator. If such an investigation or prosecution is underway, a case may not proceed before the ICC, unless the state is "unwilling or genuinely unable" to carry out the investigation or prosecution. Similarly, if a state with jurisdiction has conducted an investigation and decided not to prosecute the person concerned, the case is inadmissible before the ICC, unless the decision "resulted from the unwillingness or inability of the State genuinely to prosecute."

Despite these provisions on complementary, many states were, in Professor Leila Nadya Sadat's words, "concerned that the independent prosecutor could become an 'independent counsel for the universe,' unaccountable to anyone and liable to file complaints against States on the basis of political prejudices rather than legal concerns." Leila Nadya Sadat, The International Criminal Court and the Transformation of International Law: Justice for the New Millennium 94 (2002). As a check, Article 15 of the Rome statute provides that the prosecutor may commence an investigation "only if both he or she and the Pre-Trial Chamber (composed of three judges) have determined that a 'reasonable basis' exists to initiate the investigation." Id. at 95. In addition, the Rome Statute includes formal procedural mechanisms that allow both accused persons and concerned states to challenge a determination that a case is admissible under the principle of complementarity. See Articles 18 and 19 of the Rome Statute. The excerpt from Professor Gary Solis, which appears below after the statement from Marc Grossman, elaborates on these mechanisms.

U.S. Views Towards the International Criminal Court. President Clinton signed the Rome Treaty as one of the last acts of his administration on December 31, 2000, although he noted "our concerns about significant flaws in the treaty." He pointed out, however, that under the terms of the Rome Treaty, the United States would only be able to work to change the treaty from within if it signed the treaty before January 1, 2001.

Under the subsequent Bush Administration, the United States in May 2002 sent a letter to the U.N. Secretary-General indicating that "the United States does not intend to become a party to the treaty. Accordingly, the United States has no legal obligations arising from its signature on December 31, 2000." Besides substantive objections to some of the treaty provisions (discussed below), the administration was apparently concerned that if it had remained a signatory to the treaty, the United States might be "obliged to refrain from acts which would defeat the object and purpose of the treaty." (See the discussion of Article 18 of the Vienna Convention on Treaties in Chapter 2.A.1.c.) Congress then passed the American Servicemembers' Protection Act of 2002, which barred the U.S. government from cooperating with the ICC. (Section 2004.) The law also, controversially, authorized the President to use "all means necessary and appropriate to bring about the release" of Americans held by or for the ICC. (Section 2008.)

A senior Bush Administration official, Under Secretary of State Marc Grossman, identified some of the administration's principal objections to the Rome Treaty:

> . . . [W]e believe the ICC is an institution of unchecked power. In the United States, our system of government is founded on the principle that, in the words of John Adams, "power must never be trusted without a check." . . .
>
> But in the rush to create a powerful and independent court in Rome, there was a refusal to constrain the Court's powers in any meaningful way. . . . The treaty created a self-initiating prosecutor, answerable to no state or institution other than the Court itself. . . .
>
> . . . [T]he treaty threatens the sovereignty of the United States. The Court, as constituted today, claims the authority to detain and try American citizens, even though

> our democratically elected representatives have not agreed to be bound by the treaty. While sovereign nations have the authority to try non-citizens who have committed crimes against their citizens or in their territory, the United States has never recognized the right of an international organization to do so absent consent or a UN Security Council mandate. . . .
>
> . . . [W]e believe that by putting U.S. officials, and our men and women in uniform, at risk of politicized prosecutions, the ICC will complicate U.S. military cooperation with many friends and allies who will now have a treaty obligation to hand over U.S. nationals to the Court—even over U.S. objections.
>
> The United States has a unique role and responsibility to help preserve international peace and security. At any given time, U.S. forces are located in close to 100 nations around the world conducting peacekeeping and humanitarian operations and fighting inhumanity.
>
> We must ensure that our soldiers and government officials are not exposed to the prospect of politicized prosecutions and investigations. Our President is committed to a robust American engagement in the world to defend freedom and defeat terror; we cannot permit the ICC to disrupt that vital mission. . . . [Marc Grossman, American Foreign Policy and the International Criminal Court, Prepared Remarks to the Center for Strategic and International Studies, Washington, D.C. (May 6, 2002).]

Many observers, including states that are parties to the ICC and human rights groups, took issue with the Bush Administration's objections to the Court. They argue that the Bush Administration's complaints misrepresent the facts, and that the Court has a number of safeguards in place to prevent the problems that the United States claimed to exist. One critic is Dr. Gary Solis, a retired Marine lieutenant colonel and a law professor.

Gary D. Solis, The ICC and Mad Prosecutors

Remarks delivered at Georgetown University (March 27, 2003)

Why is America opposed to the ICC? Every army, including ours, commits law of war violations, but few armies so strongly condemned them, or so religiously prosecute them. Witness our Vietnam-era court-martial convictions of 95 soldiers and 27 Marines for law of war related crimes. . . .

Concern for our warfighters? . . . American servicemen and women are already well-covered by prosecutorial options in the Uniform Code of Military Justice. But echoes of the 1999 Pinochet case continue to resonate in the Pentagon's "E" Ring. . . .

What are we afraid of? Thanks to complementarity, a provision that we sponsored and insisted upon, the ICC is a court of last resort. Complementarity holds that the ICC may only exercise jurisdiction if a good-faith prosecution is not carried out by the accused's state. . . .

Some are shocked that the ICC suggests exercising jurisdiction over nationals of states that are not parties to the ICC Statute. This overlooks, for example, the 1970 Convention for Suppression of Unlawful Seizure of Aircraft, the 1971 Montreal Convention on Civil Aviation Safety, the 1988 Convention and Protocol on Maritime Navigation, and the 1979 Hostages Convention. These four, and several others—including the 1949 Geneva Conventions—all reach citizens of non-parties, a concept America embraced in prosecuting U.S. v. Yunis* when we tried a Lebanese national who hijacked a Jordanian plane carrying American passengers [for, among other offenses, hostage taking]. Lebanon is not a party to the [Hostage Taking] Convention, and did not consent (or object) to jurisdiction. Nor is that the only case in which we have convicted a foreign national non-party, contrary to the accused's state's wishes.[8] Yet we complain of the possibility that the same shoe might be fit to us.

Familiar American trial rights are present in the ICC Statute: the presumption of innocence[9]; the guarantee against double jeopardy[10]; the right against self-incrimination[11]; right to remain silent[12]; to be informed of charges[13]; to have counsel, either of choice or appointed[14]; a public trial[15]; the prosecutorial burden of proof[16]; to present and challenge evidence[17]; to cross-examine witnesses[18]; proof of guilt beyond a reasonable doubt[19]; and the right of appeal.[20] There is even provision for the protection of national security information.[21]

It is true that there is no right to a jury trial—just as there is no such right in American courts-martial under our Uniform Code of Military Justice. . . .

. . . Under the ICC Statute [the Chief Prosecutor] may initiate an investigation—but only with the authorization of a three-judge Pre-Trial Chamber.[22] That finding of jurisdiction, if confirmed, may be appealed to another Trial Chamber panel.[23] Even with both panels' authorizations, any prosecution may be delayed for a year by the UN Security Council, the year's delay being renewable.[24] Finally, the Prosecutor may be removed by simple majority vote. If this is a U.S. railroad job, it isn't the fast track. . . .

Finally, the ICC is a fledgling international body bearing the high hopes of many democratic nations. The Court's success, even its continued long-term existence, depends upon the good will of, and acceptance by, the international community. Is the ICC likely to facilitate its own marginalization through biased indictments and politically-motivated prosecutions? . . .

To address the risk that other countries might themselves be faced with a demand to transfer U.S. officials present on their territory to the ICC, the Bush

*[The Yunis case is discussed above in Section B.3.f.—Eds.]

8. See also, U.S. v. Marino-Garcia, 679 F.2d 1373 (11th Cir. 1982), a case involving the Law of the Sea Convention.

9. Art. 66.1.

10. Art. 20.

11. Art. 55.1.

12. Arts. 55.2 and 67.1.

13. Arts. 55.2, 61.3, 64.8, and 67.1.

14. Arts. 55.2 and 67.1.

15. Arts. 64.7 and 67.1.

16. Art. 67.1.

17. Art. 61.6.

18. Art. 67.1.

19. Art. 66.3.

20. Art. 81.

21. Art. 72.

22. Art. 15.

23. Art. 19.

24. Art. 16.

Administration began insisting, as a condition of foreign aid, that other countries sign bilateral agreements promising not to transfer to the ICC any U.S. personnel on their territory indicted by the Court. These so-called Article 98 Agreements, named after the article in the ICC Statute that the United States claims authorizes their use, have been signed by over 100 countries, including some that are parties to the ICC. Other ICC member states, including Canada and Germany, have refused to sign such agreements, and the European Union has encouraged its member states to refuse U.S. requests. The initiative to negotiate Article 98 agreements seems to have come to an end; no such agreements have been concluded since 2007.

In contrast to the Bush Administration, the Obama Administration has moved cautiously toward a closer relationship with the ICC. The Obama Administration's first National Security Strategy Document noted that the Court's effort to pursue criminal accountability was, at least in some cases, consistent with U.S. interests:

> Although the United States is not at present a party to the Rome Statute of the International Criminal Court (ICC), and will always protect U.S. personnel, we are engaging with State Parties to the Rome Statute on issues of concern and are supporting the ICC's prosecution of those cases that advance U.S. interests and values, consistent with the requirements of U.S. law. [The National Security Strategy 48 (2010).]

In June 2010, a U.S. delegation participated actively as observers at the Review Conference of ICC parties. Reflecting on the U.S. role at that conference, State Department Legal Adviser Harold Koh stated, "After 12 years, I think we have reset the default on the U.S. relationship with the court from hostility to positive engagement." During the same briefing, the Obama Administration's U.S. Ambassador-at-Large for War Crimes Issues stated that "it's clear that joining the court is not on the table . . . at this time." Nevertheless, he noted:

> I think what we're looking at here is how this court develops. . . .
>
> . . . [O]ver time, there's a possibility that we may gain confidence in this institution and that would enable us to move forward. And who knows what the future may hold? But at this time, we recognize that this institution is the international court where justice will be delivered if it can't be delivered at the national or the regional level, that the United Nations is not going to step up and establish a Rwanda or Yugoslavia court and spend a hundred million or more a year on a court, as they have with those, when 111 countries are dues-paying members to this one.
>
> And so this is where accountability is to be delivered. It's also recognized, as we've seen with Darfur, that the UN Security Council, of which we're a permanent member, has the ability to send cases to it . . . [I]t's a tool in the international toolbox . . . for achieving accountability instead of establishing a separate, one-off institution. [Stephen J. Rapp, Special Briefing: U.S. Engagement with the International Criminal Court and the Outcome of the Recently Concluded Review Conference, Washington, DC (June 15, 2010).]

Jurisdiction over Nationals of Nonparties. One of the principal objections the United States has raised against the ICC is that it is empowered to exercise jurisdiction over U.S. nationals even though the United States has not become a party to the Rome Treaty. Under its Statute, the ICC can exercise jurisdiction over a U.S. national only if he or she commits a crime within the court's jurisdiction on the territory of a state that is a party to the Treaty. Moreover, as noted above, the United States is party to a number of conventions, such as the 1949 Geneva Conventions and various counterterrorism treaties, that obligate states either to try or extradite persons found in their territory who have committed offenses defined by the treaty. How much of a departure from existing international law principles does the ICC represent? If an American commits an international crime on the territory of another state, is there a difference between that state exercising jurisdiction over the case and the state transferring the accused to the ICC for trial?

In the following excerpt, Professor Morris argues that trials before the ICC would differ significantly from prosecution before national courts exercising territorial jurisdiction.

Madeline Morris, High Crimes and Misconceptions: The ICC and Non-Party States

64 Law & Contemp. Probs. 13, 14-15, 27, 29-30, 33, 43, 45 (2001)

. . . Even while individuals, and not states, will be named in ICC indictments, there will be cases in which those individuals are indicted for official acts taken pursuant to state policy and under state authority. . . . In these sorts of ICC cases, notwithstanding the presence of individual defendants in the dock, the cases will represent bona fide legal disputes between states. . . .

. . . ICC jurisdiction over non-party nationals would appear to be exorbitant jurisdiction under international law. . . . The right of a state to be free from the exercise of exorbitant jurisdiction over its nationals cannot be abrogated by a treaty to which it is not a party. . . .

[One theory to defend the ICC's assertion of jurisdiction over nationals of nationals of non-parties is] a theory of delegated territorial jurisdiction. The notion here is that, when a non-party national is prosecuted before the ICC for crimes committed on the territory of a state that consents to ICC jurisdiction, the ICC exercises territorial jurisdiction that is delegated to the Court by the territorial state. . . .

Here, the question arises whether, as a matter of customary international law, territorial jurisdiction may be delegated to an international court without the consent of the defendant's state of nationality. . . . [T]he consequences of delegated territorial jurisdiction [exercised by an international tribunal] are quite different from those of territorial jurisdiction exercised by the territorial state, particularly for interstate-dispute type cases. . . .

. . . [The] reasons [why a state might object to the delegation of another state's territorial jurisdiction to an international court] . . . arise from the fact that the consequences for states of the compulsory jurisdiction of an international court are fundamentally different from the consequences of the jurisdiction of the national courts. . . .

[In another part of the article, Professor Morris discusses the reasons states might object to the delegation of jurisdiction.]

. . . A state might reject compulsory third-party adjudication before the ICC in order to retain the discretion to address interstate-dispute type cases through bilateral relations, even while recognizing the possibility that those bilateral relations might in some cases entail the prosecution of that state's national in another state's courts. . . .

States value the advantages that diplomatic methods of dispute settlement often afford. . . . States may, therefore, perceive a number of drawbacks associated with compulsory adjudication before the ICC.

First, compromise outcomes of various sorts may be desirable in interstate-dispute type cases, especially in circumstances where the law or the facts are ambiguous. But compromise outcomes are unlikely to emerge from adjudicated rather than negotiated resolutions.

Second, states would have reason to be more concerned about the political impact of adjudications before an international court than before an individual states' courts. An even-remotely successful international court will have significant prestige and authority. The political repercussions of such a court's determining that a state's acts or policies were unlawful would be substantial indeed, and categorically different from the repercussion of the same verdict rendered by a national court. If a guilty verdict were passed by a national court in an official-acts case, the matter would remain a disagreement among equals, one state maintaining that an unlawful act had been committed, the other disputing its occurrence or defending its lawfulness. By contrast, were the ICC to pronounce an official act to constitute a crime, the decision would bear an authoritative weight and resulting political impact of a categorically different nature. The special political impact of ICC decisions will itself create heightened risks for states. . . .

A third matter that may be of substantial concern to states is the role of an international criminal court in shaping the law. Because the decisions of an international court will tend to be more authoritative than would those of any individual state's courts, an international court would have the power to create international law in a manner disproportionate to that of any state. This may be more law-making power than some states are comfortable granting to one international institution, especially in sensitive areas involving military activities and international security. . . .

. . . States may have legitimate concerns about the compulsory jurisdiction of . . . [the ICC]; they may not see fit to have an international tribunal in effect legislate international law in areas where the law is relatively undeveloped. States might have sound reasons for preferring to retain more direct control, diffused among many states, over the shaping of international law in this critical field rather than to relegate a substantial proportion of that control to a single international entity. . . .

Activity at the ICC. As of May 2011, the ICC's Chief Prosecutor has commenced investigations in six situations. In three of these situations—Uganda, the Democratic Republic of the Congo (DRC), and the Central African Republic—ICC state parties referred events occurring in their own territories to the ICC under Article 14 of the Rome Statute as "auto-referrals." Situations involving Sudan and Libya were referred to the ICC by the Security Council in accordance with Article 13(b) of the Statute pursuant to Resolutions 1593 (2005) and 1970 (2011), respectively. In March 2010, a pre-trial Chamber of the ICC approved the Prosecutor's request to open an investigation into crimes committed in Kenya in during the post-election violence in that country in 2007-2008. This is the first case in which the Prosecutor has initiated an investigation under his *proprio motu* authority under Article 15 of the

State. In April 2011, a Pre-Trial Chamber found reasonable grounds to believe that four Kenyans identified by the prosecutor were criminally responsible for the crimes against humanity committed in Kenya; hearings to consider confirmation of the charges were set for September 2011. The Prosecutor thereafter sought to initiate another investigation *proprio motu* in connection with the severe violence in Côte d'Ivoire that arose after President Laurent Gbagbo's refused to step down from power after he lost an election in November 2010 to challenger Alassane Ouattara. As of May 2011, the Prosecutor was awaiting authorization from a pre-trial Chamber of the ICC to open that investigation.

In the DRC situation, the ICC has issued indictments against five individuals. As of May 2011, trials were underway in two cases involving three defendants. The ICC's first trial against Thomas Lubanga Dyilo, which began in 2009, related to forced conscription of child soldiers to fight in the DRC. A second trial against two other defendants alleging multiple charges of crimes against humanity and war crimes for, among other things, directing attacks against civilians and rape began in November 2009. A fourth indictee was in ICC custody awaiting trial, and the fifth indictee was at large. The ICC's first trial against Lubanga has been beset by procedural difficulties. On two occasions, the Trial Chamber has ordered that proceedings in the case be stayed and that Lubanga be released due to noncompliance by the prosecution with various disclosure orders issued by the Trial Chamber, but those rulings have been reversed by the Appeals Chamber. The case was still before the Trial Chamber as of May 2011.

In the Uganda case, a Pre-Trial Chamber in 2005 issued arrest warrants for Joseph Kony, the leader of the Lord's Resistance Army, and four others in connection with armed conflict in Northern Uganda. One of the indictees has since died, and the other four remain at large.

One of the ICC's most prominent cases arises out of the situation in Darfur. The prosecutor has indicted six individuals, including Omar Hassan Ahmad Al-Bashir, the sitting President of Sudan, who has been charged with multiple counts of war crimes, crimes against humanity, and genocide. Despite the Security Council's demand under Chapter VII that Sudan "shall cooperate fully with and provide any necessary assistance to the Court and the Prosecutor," Al-Bashir and two other senior Sudanese indicted by the ICC remained at large as of May 2011; as early as May 2010, the ICC had made a formal finding that Sudan was not cooperating with the ICC. Of grave concern to the Court was the fact that Al-Bashir has made visits to at least three ICC state parties — Kenya, Chad, and Djibouti — that did not detain the Sudanese president despite the outstanding ICC arrest warrants against him. In a second Sudan case, two defendants were in custody in April 2011 awaiting the start of their trial following the confirmation of the charges against them by a Pre-Trial Chamber. In another Sudan case, however, an ICC Pre-Trial Chamber refused to confirm the charges against the accused on the grounds that the evidence produced by the prosecution was insufficient to establish his criminal responsibility.

Another high-profile situation under investigation by the ICC arises out of the internal conflict that began in Libya in 2011. In February 2011, many Libyans — inspired by events in Tunisia and Egypt that led to the ouster of those countries' longstanding rulers — began protests against the Qaddafi government. The Libyan opposition by late February had gained control of a significant part of the country. The government responded with a brutal military campaign involving the killing of many civilians. In response, the Security Council adopted Resolution 1970, which, among other things, "[d]eplor[ed] the gross and systematic violation of human rights, including the repression of peaceful demonstrators, express[ed] deep concern at the deaths of civilians, and reject[ed] unequivocally the incitement to hostility and violence against the civilian population made from the highest level of the Libyan government." The resolution imposed a series of sanctions against Libya. In addition, as in the Sudan case, the Council acted under Chapter VII of the U.N. Charter and "refer[red] the situation in [Libya] since 15 February 2011 to the Prosecutor of the International Criminal Court." The resolution also imposed an obligation on Libya, which is not party to the Rome Statute of the ICC, to "cooperate fully with and provide any necessary assistance to the Court and the Prosecutor." The United States voted in favor of the resolution, which was approved unanimously.

The Prosecutor moved swiftly in the Libya matter; in May 2011, he requested a pre-trial Chamber to issue arrest warrants against Libyan leader Muammar Qaddafi, his son Saif Al Islam Qaddafi, and the head of Libyan intelligence services for crimes against humanity committed in Libya after February 2011. The Prosecutor's request was based on his determination that there were "reasonable grounds" to believe that the three individuals had committed the crimes described in the application.

Notes and Questions

1. Is there a need for an International Criminal Court with broad geographic jurisdiction? What are the alternatives? Ad hoc international tribunals such as those for Yugoslavia and Rwanda? Or a hybrid tribunal, such as the Sierra Leone tribunal discussed earlier? National courts?

2. The Bush Administration suggested that U.S. officials (present or former) or American men and women in uniform might be subject to ICC jurisdiction in certain situations and was concerned about "politicized prosecutions." Do you agree? If the ICC prosecutor decided to initiate a case against a U.S. service person in a foreign country that was a party to the ICC, what are the safeguards against that situation arising? Would the Court have jurisdiction if the U.S. government investigated and acted upon the case itself? Even if the United States did not act or there were questions about the U.S. investigation, would the ICC Pre-Trial Chamber have a say about whether the ICC prosecutor could move forward? Could the Security Council have a say in the process?

3. Should the U.S. Executive Branch seek the advice and consent of the Senate to the Rome Treaty? If so, why? If not, what are the principal reasons not to? Should the U.S. government resume efforts to try to obtain rules and interpretations from the ICC that would allow the United States to join? Or should the United States simply remain a non-party? If the United States should resume efforts to join the Court, what seem to be the most important protections to seek?

4. Another U.S. concern about the ICC is that investigations and prosecutions could impede international efforts to resolve ongoing conflicts and that the Court accordingly usurps the functions of the Security Council. Recall that the international tribunals for the former Yugoslavia and Rwanda were established

only after the Security Council decided that such tribunals would contribute to efforts to establish peace and security.

Under Article 16 of the ICC Statute, "[n]o investigation or prosecution may be commenced or proceeded with . . . for a period of 12 months after the Security Council, in a resolution adopted under Chapter VII of the Charter of the United Nations, has requested the Court to that effect; that request may be renewed by the Council under the same conditions." Does that address U.S. concerns? What would happen if the United States opposed an investigation or prosecution but other Security Council members supported it? What should be the relationship between the Security Council and the ICC?

The issue is particularly problematic in the context of prosecutions for aggression. The proposed amendment defining aggression adopted by ICC parties in 2010 adopts a complicated scheme to try to accommodate the interests of the two institutions. The amendment contemplates that when the prosecutor concludes that "there is a reasonable basis to proceed with an investigation in respect of a crime of aggression," he or she "shall first ascertain whether the Security Council has made a determination of an act of aggression committed by the State concerned." Where the Security Council has made such a determination, the Prosecutor may proceed with the investigation in respect of a crime of aggression. However, "if no such determination is made within six months after the date of notification, the Prosecutor may proceed with the investigation in respect of a crime of aggression, provided that the Pre-Trial Division has authorized the commencement of the investigation in respect of a crime of aggression . . . ." The Security Council retains authority under Article 16 to issue a resolution postponing any investigation or prosecution for a year. International Criminal Court Review Conference, ICC Rev. Conf., Res. RC/Res.6 (June 11, 2010) (proposed Article 15 *bis*). Does this provision strike the appropriate balance between the ICC and the Council?

5. Despite the Bush Administration's opposition to the ICC, the United States abstained during the 2005 vote for Security Council Resolution 1593 that referred "the situation in Darfur since 1 July 2002" to the ICC. The State Department's Under Secretary of State for Political Affairs explained that although this was a "difficult decision" for the United States in view of its longstanding position,

> the Secretary [of State nevertheless] felt very strongly, as did many others in the Administration, that we had to join the international community in a serious effort to see that justice was done in Sudan and that it was very important that the international community speak with one voice on this issue of justice to see if it's possible that together we can make sure that those guilty of war crimes and atrocities are brought to justice, they're held accountable and that they are tried before a competent international court and, if they are convicted by that court, serve long sentences. . . . [Nicholas Burns, Remarks to the Press on Sudan, Washington, DC (April 1, 2005).]

Can the United States plausibly support prosecutions before the ICC in situations like Sudan and the DRC if it is unwilling to become a party to the treaty establishing the Court?

6. Do you agree with Professor Morris that the ICC is likely to "legislate" international law? Is it not likely to simply apply the statute approved by states? If the United States has already accepted the principle (by joining various treaties)

that U.S. nationals who commit certain crimes may be prosecuted in any state where they may be found, do you agree that the delegation by states with jurisdiction of the authority to prosecute to an international court changes the legal nature of the exercise of jurisdiction? Isn't this precisely what happened with the post-World War II Nuremberg and Tokyo Tribunals discussed in Section B.1? And why would the Court's ability to exercise jurisdiction over the nationals of nonparty states for crimes committed on the territory of a party enhance concerns about its role in developing international criminal law? Could the same argument be made for any international tribunal, such as the International Court of Justice or the World Trade Organization Dispute Settlement body, interpreting and applying the rules of international law?

7. In addition to the sources above, much has been written on the International Criminal Court. See, for example, William A. Schabas, The International Criminal Court: A Commentary on the Rome Statute (2010); and The Emerging Practice of the International Criminal Court (Carsten Stahn & Göran Sluiter, eds. 2009). For a careful study of what U.S. policy toward the ICC should be, see the Report of an Independent Task Force Convened by the American Society of International Law, U.S. Policy Toward the International Criminal Court: Furthering Positive Engagement (2009). For a critical assessment of the performance of Luis Moreno Ocampo, the ICC's first Chief Prosecutor, see David Kaye, Who's Afraid of the International Criminal Court?, For. Aff., May/June 2011, at 118. The Web site of the ICC is http://www.icc-cpi.int/.

5. *Alternatives to Criminal Prosecution*

Societies emerging from widespread human rights abuses, including international crimes, sometimes opt to give a wide amnesty to all perpetrators of crimes, particularly for crimes seen as having a political dimension or connection to the conflict in which crimes occurred. The following excerpt examines the rationales for and legality of such amnesties.

Leila Nadya Sadat, Universal Jurisdiction, National Amnesties, and Truth Commissions: Reconciling the Irreconcilable

Universal Jurisdiction: National Courts and the Prosecution of Serious Crimes Under International Law 193, 196-197, 202-204 (Stephen Macedo ed., 2004)

NATIONAL AMNESTIES

Amnesty is essentially an act of oblivion. . . . [It] . . . "connotes that the offender's crime has been overlooked because that course of action benefits the public welfare more than punishment would." Unlike pardons, which imply forgiveness of the offender and are generally particularized in nature, amnesties typically apply to groups of offenders, and neither eradicate the offense nor the moral guilt that might be associated therewith. They are thus practical, if somewhat unsatisfactory solutions to the problem of mass atrocities: justice is traded for peace, or at least a temporary truce, in the hopes that the atrocities will stop and the society will be able to move on.

Domestically, two principal justifications have been advanced for offering blanket amnesties for human rights violations committed by a regime in power against its citizens. First, dictators and military leaders have often demanded impunity as a condition of relinquishing power. In response, societies eager to end a conflict and fearful of repercussions from attempts to pursue accountability may shy away from criminal trials or other proceedings to hold responsible those accused of committing human rights violations in the former regime. . . . Second, even if a new regime is committed to prosecuting past international crimes, it may face considerable obstacles in doing so. Rwanda is a case in point. As a result of the genocide, over 80 percent of Rwanda's justice system personnel, including judges and magistrates, simply and tragically disappeared. Moreover, the judicial system faced serious shortages or resources, basic facilities, and equipment. . . . In such a case it is unclear whether imposing individual criminal responsibility is a viable strategy, an all-too-common scenario in cases involving mass atrocities. . . .

The Validity of Amnesties in International Law

As regards the validity of amnesties for war crimes, most commentators appear to make a distinction between international and noninternational armed conflict. With respect to international armed conflict, . . . the expectation [after the Second World War] that war criminals would be punished . . . [was] codified in the four Geneva Conventions of 1949 . . . and expanded upon in the 1977 Protocol Additional to the Geneva Conventions of 12 August 1948 . . . (Protocol 1), which extends the grave breaches regime substantially. It is generally agreed that these conventions are now a source of customary international law. Thus, while it is certainly possible that only the substantive provisions of the conventions and not their procedural provisions have risen to the level of custom, most commentators have accepted that, at least with respect to war crimes committed in international armed conflict that fall within the grave breaches regime, a fair (but not watertight) case can be made not only for the existence of a customary international law duty to prosecute or extradite the offender but also, as a corollary, for a rule prohibiting blanket amnesties.

As regards noninternational armed conflicts, at least some take the view that general amnesties are not only permitted but are encouraged by existing law. This view relies upon Article 6(5) of Protocol 2 relating to the Protection of Victims of Noninternational Armed Conflict, which provides: "At the end of hostilities, the authorities in power shall endeavor to grant the broadest possible amnesty to persons who have participated in the armed conflict, or those deprived of their liberty for reasons related to the armed conflict, whether they are interned or detained." . . .

. . . [A] lower South African court held that this provision permitted the South African Truth and Reconciliation Commission to grant amnesties in regard to human rights violations committed under the apartheid regime. . . .

With respect to crimes against humanity and genocide, some commentators have strenuously argued for the existence of a duty to investigate and punish human rights violations committed under a prior regime. Certainly, the Genocide Convention and the Torture Convention suggest that a duty is assumed by states parties to those conventions to pursue and punish (or extradite, in the case of the Torture Convention) those who violate the conventions' terms. However, even those treaties are unclear as to the precise modalities of such punishment. They would thus appear to leave a certain degree of discretion to national legal systems in their implementation.

As to a generalized customary international law rule requiring punishment, the evidence of state practice seems weak. . . . Many countries have granted amnesties to the perpetrators of atrocities under a prior regime, and while some lower national courts have overturned them, they have generally been sustained by higher courts. . . .

Truth commissions have emerged as yet another mechanism for pursuing accountability for atrocities, including international crimes, in societies emerging from war or widespread human rights abuses. A truth commission is an official investigative or quasi-judicial body established to investigate the atrocities. Typically, truth commissions issue reports describing the causes and history of the atrocities, and some specifically identify individuals who have perpetrated crimes.

Professor Martha Minow, who has written thoughtfully on this topic, suggests that truth commissions can be more effective than trials in producing "a coherent . . . narrative about the entire nation's trauma, and the multiple sources and expressions of its violence." Martha Minow, Between Vengeance and Forgiveness 58 (1998). She also notes that providing information via a non-adversarial truth commission process is better than testifying in a criminal trial in helping victims to overcome trauma. Minow reaches the following conclusions about truth commissions:

> If the affirmative case for truth commissions rests on the goal of healing, then the working hypothesis is that testimony of the victims and perpetrators, offered publicly to a truth commission, affords opportunities for individuals and the nation as a whole to heal. With the aim of producing a fair and thorough account of the atrocities, a truth commission proceeds on the assumption that it helps individuals to tell their stories and to have them acknowledged officially. Also assumed here is the premise that a final report can create a framework for the nation to deal with is past. Echoing the assumption of psychotherapy, religious confession, and journalistic muckraking, truth commissions presume that telling and hearing truth is healing. . . .
>
> It remains an open question whether through taking testimony and publishing reports, a truth commission can also help to reconcile groups that have been warring or otherwise engaged in deep animosities. Even a minimal form of reconciliation would require capacities for constructive cooperation between those most victimized and those who committed, ordered, or countenanced their victimization. Crucial here would be demonstrable evenhandedness and honest acknowledgement of injuries and wrongs committed by the competing sides without losing hold the distinction between those who abused government power and those who resisted abuses. [Id. at 61, 79.]

Notes and Questions

1. Is it permissible for a country to extend amnesty to persons who have committed genocide, grave breaches of the Geneva Conventions, or torture? Consider

the obligations to punish or extradite persons embodied in the conventions making those acts international crimes. If a state did provide for such an amnesty, would it preclude other states from indicting or prosecuting offenders if they travel outside their country? Consider the example of General Pinochet, discussed above in Section B.2.a., who was indicted by a Spanish investigating magistrate even though he had been granted amnesty in Chile.

Is the situation different with crimes against humanity, where the obligation to try or extradite is less clear? See Section B.3.b above. What about violations of Common Article 3 of the Geneva Conventions committed during a civil war within a single state?

2. Separately from the question of whether it is legally permissible to grant amnesty for international crimes, do you think amnesties should be given at the end of conflicts involving widespread atrocities? What if agreeing to amnesty is the only way to put an end to a conflict, and to bring the abuses to a halt? Do you believe a society can achieve political reconciliation if perpetrators of abuses are not punished? Or does the criminal justice process merely highlight tensions between perpetrator and victim groups?

3. Under the procedures of the Truth and Reconciliation Commission (TRC) established by South Africa, a person who committed serious crimes could receive amnesty only if he or she appeared before the TRC and fully and credibly acknowledged his or her conduct. Do you feel differently about amnesty issued under these circumstances than you would about a blanket amnesty?

4. Consider the complementarity regime in Article 17 of the ICC Statute of the International Criminal Court. Have cases in which a person is granted amnesty by South Africa's TRC been "investigated or prosecuted" by South Africa in a way that would make them inadmissible before the ICC under the principle of complementarity?

5. Other mechanisms to promote accountability for atrocities and international crimes include civil redress against perpetrators in domestic courts, such as cases under the Alien Tort Statute (discussed in Chapter 3.C); "lustration," which generally involves making perpetrators of offenses ineligible to hold public positions; the development of memorials to recount atrocities; and immigration sanctions such as denying refugee status or immigration admission to offenders.

6. For additional readings on transitional justice, see Transitional Justice: Global Mechanisms and Local Realities after Genocide and Mass Violence (Alexander Laban Hinton, ed. 2010); and Jack Snyder & Leslie Vinjamuri, Trials and Errors: Principles and Pragmatism in Strategies of International Justice, 28 International Security 5 (Winter 2003/2004). For an insightful analysis of the difficulties not only of addressing atrocities, but of creating the rule of law in post-conflict societies, see Jane Stromseth, David Wippman & Rosa Brooks, Can Might Make Rights?: Building the Rule of Law after Military Interventions (2006).

Table of Cases

Principal cases appear in italics. Cases cited in excerpted materials are not listed here.

Index